W9-BKI-688

Collins *gem*

Collins
Russian
Dictionary

HarperCollins Publishers
Westerhill Road
Bishopbriggs
Glasgow
G64 2QT
Great Britain

Third Edition 2003

Reprint 10 9 8 7 6 5 4 3 2 1

© William Collins Sons & Co.
Ltd 1958
© HarperCollins Publishers
1996, 2003

ISBN 978-0-00-722416-6

Collins Gem® and Bank of
English® are registered
trademarks of HarperCollins
Publishers Limited

www.collins.co.uk

A catalogue record for this
book is available from the
British Library

HarperCollins Publishers,
10 East 53rd Street,
New York, NY 10022

COLLINS GEM RUSSIAN
DICTIONARY.
Third US Edition 2005

ISBN-13 978-0-00-714304-7
ISBN-10 0-00-714304-4

www.harpercollins.com

Typeset by
Morton Word Processing Ltd,
Scarborough

Printed in Italy by
Legoprint S.p.A.

Acknowledgements
We would like to thank those
authors and publishers who
kindly gave permission for
copyright material to be used
in the Collins Word Web. We
would also like to thank Times
Newspapers Ltd for providing
valuable data.

СОДЕРЖАНИЕ

CONTENTS

Торговые знаки

Слова, которые по нашему мнению, являются торговыми знаками, получили соответствующее обозначение. Наличие или отсутствие обозначения не влияет на юридический статус того или иного торгового знака.

Trademarks

Words which we have reason to believe constitute trademarks have been designated as such. However, neither the presence or the absence of such designation should be regarded as affecting the legal status of any trademark.

Авторский коллектив/Contributors
Albina Ozieva • Olga Stott

Заведующий редакцией/Editorial Management
Jeremy Butterfield • Michela Clari

Ведущий редактор/Managing Editor
Maree Airlie

Редакторы/Editorial Staff
Isobel Gordon • Andrew Knox • Pat Cook

Компьютерное обслуживание/Computing
Thomas Widmann • André Gautier • Robert McMillan

Редактор серии/Series Editor
Lorna Sinclair Knight

ВВЕДЕНИЕ

Мы рады, что вы выбрали словарь, подготовленный издательством Коллинз. Мы надеемся, что он окажется вам полезен, где бы вы им ни пользовались – дома, на отдыхе или на работе.

В настоящем введении излагаются некоторые советы по эффективному использованию данного издания: его обширного словника и сведений, содержащихся в каждой словарной статье. Данная информация поможет вам не только читать и понимать современный английский, но также овладеть устной речью.

INTRODUCTION

We are delighted that you have decided to use the Collins Russian Dictionary and hope that you will enjoy and benefit from using it at home, on holiday or at work.

This introduction gives you a few tips on how to get the most out of your dictionary – not simply from its comprehensive wordlist but also from the information provided in each entry. This will help you to read and understand modern Russian, as well as communicate and express yourself in the language.

О ПОЛЬЗОВАНИИ СЛОВАРЁМ

Заглавные слова

Заглавными называются слова, начинающие словарную статью. Они напечатаны жирным шрифтом и расположены в алфавитном порядке. При многих из них приводятся словосочетания и сращения. Они напечатаны жирным шрифтом меньшего размера.

Перевод

Перевод заглавных слов напечатан обычным шрифтом. Варианты перевода, разделённые запятой синонимичны. Различные значения многозначного слова разделены точкой с запятой.

Переводы для значений производных слов часто разделены только точкой с запятой и перед ними даётся одна помета типа (*см прил*). Это означает, что последующее разделение значений рассматриваемого слова и его переводов даётся при слове, от которого это слово образовано. Например, **careful/carefully**.

В случаях, когда точный перевод невозможен, даётся приблизительный эквивалент. Он обозначается знаком ≈. Если же таковой отсутствует, то приводится толкование.

Пометы

Пометы служат для разделения значений многозначного слова. Их цель – помочь читателю выбрать перевод, наиболее подходящий в том или ином контексте. Пометы напечатаны курсивом и заключены в круглые скобки.

При заглавных словах даны необходимые стилистические пометы. Нецензурные слова помечены восклицательным знаком (!).

Произношение

В англо-русской части словаря все заглавные слова снабжены транскрипцией. Транскрипция не даётся для производных слов, о произношении которых можно судить, исходя из произношения исходного слова, например, **enjoy/enjoyment**. Список фонетических знаков приводится на страницах xv–xvi.

В русско-английской части словаря все русские слова снабжены знаком ударения. Омографы (слова, имеющие одинаковое написание, но различное ударение и значение) приводятся как отдельные заглавные слова в том порядке, в котором в них проставлено ударение, например, первым даётся слово за́мок, затем – замо́к. Более подробную информацию о принципах русского произношения читатель может найти в разделе на страницах xiv–xv.

Служебные слова
В словаре уделяется особое внимание русским и английским словам, которые обладают сложной грамматической структурой. Таковыми являются в первую очередь служебные слова, вспомогательные глаголы, местоимения, частицы итп. Они обозначены пометой **KEYWORD**.

Английские фразовые глаголы
Фразовыми глаголами называются устойчивые сочетания глагола с элементами **in, up** итп, типа **blow up, cut down** итп. Они приводятся при базовых глаголах, таких как **blow, cut**, и расположены в алфавитном порядке.

Культурные реалии
Описание культурных реалий даётся в соответствующих словарных статьях и оттеняется серым светом.

Употребление *or/или*, косой черты и скобок
Между взаимозаменяемыми вариантами перевода фраз в англо-русской части употребляется союз "*or*", в русско-английской – "*или*". Косая черта (/) означает, что приведённые варианты перевода не являются взаимозаменяемыми. В круглые скобки заключаются возможные, но необязательные в данном выражении слова.

Употребление тильды (~)
Тильда в англо-русской части заменяет заглавное слово в словосочетаниях. Например, если заглавным является слово "order", то фраза "out of order" будет представлена следующим образом: out of ~. В русско-английской части тильда заменяет: 1) целое заглавное слово: например, в статье "**до́бр|ый**" фраза "**до́брый день**" показана следующим образом: ~ день, 2) тильда заменяет часть заглавного слова, предшествующую вертикальной черте: например, в статье "**до́бр|ый**" фраза "**до́брое у́тро**" показана следующим образом: ~ое у́тро.

USING THE DICTIONARY

Headwords

The **headword** is the word you look up in a dictionary. They are listed in alphabetical order, and printed in bold type. Each headword may contain phrases, which are in smaller bold type. The two headwords appearing at the top of each page indicate the first and last word dealt with on that page.

Where appropriate, words related to headwords are grouped in the same entry (eg. **enjoy, enjoyment**) in smaller bold type than the headword.

Translations

The translations of the headword are printed in ordinary roman type. Translations separated by a comma are interchangeable, those separated by a semi-colon are not interchangeable. Where the indicator refers to a different part of speech eg. (*see adj*), the translations mirror the splits shown at the other part of speech eg. **careful/carefully**.

Where it is not possible to give an exact translation equivalent, an approximate (cultural) equivalent is given preceded by ≈. If this also isn't possible, then a gloss is given to explain the source item.

Indicators

Indicators are pieces of information given in italic type and in brackets.

They offer contexts in which the headword might appear or provide synonyms, guiding you to the most appropriate translation.

Colloquial and informal language in the dictionary is marked at the headword. Rude or offensive translations are also marked with (!).

Pronunciation

On the English-Russian side of the dictionary you will find the phonetic spelling of the word in square brackets after the headword, unless the word is grouped under another headword and the pronunciation can be easily derived eg. **enjoy/ enjoyment**. A list of the symbols used is given on pages xv–xvi.

For Russian-English, stress is given on all Russian words as a guide to pronunciation. Words which are spelt in the same way, but have different stress positions are treated as separate entries, the order following the order of the stress eg. **за́мок** comes before **замо́к**. The section on pages xiv–xv explains Russian phonetics in more detail.

Keywords

In the dictionary special status is given to "key" Russian and English words. These words can be grammatically complex, often having many different usages, and are labelled **KEYWORD**.

Cultural boxes

On both sides of the dictionary cultural information is shown in a shaded grey box.

"You" in phrases

The Russian formal form is used to translate "you/your" and imperative phrases, unless the phrase is very colloquial and the informal form would be more natural.

Use of или/или, oblique and brackets

"*or*" on the English-Russian side, and "*или*" on the Russian-English side are used between interchangeable parts of a translation or phrase, whereas the oblique (/) is used between non-interchangeable alternatives. Round brackets are used to show optional parts of the translation or phrase.

Use of the swung dash (~)

The swung dash (~) is used on the English-Russian side to stand for the headword in phrases eg. at "order" the phrase "out of order" is shown as "out of ~". On the Russian-English side the swung dash can either stand for the full headword eg. at "добрый" the phrase "добрый день" is shown as "~ день", or it can stand for the part of the word before the hairline eg. at "добрый" the phrase "доброе утро" appears as "~ое утро".

American variants

American spelling variants are generally shown at the British headword eg. **colour/color** and may also be shown as a separate entry. Variant forms are generally shown as separate headwords eg. **trousers/pants**, unless the British and American forms are alphabetically adjacent, when the American form is only shown separately if phonetics are required eg. **cut-price/cut-rate**.

Russian reflexive verbs

Russian reflexive verbs eg. мыться, краситься are listed under the basic verb eg. мыть, красить.

STYLE AND LAYOUT OF THE DICTIONARY
RUSSIAN-ENGLISH

Inflectional and grammatical information

Inflectional information is shown in the dictionary in brackets straight after the headword and before the part of speech eg. **стол** (-á) *м.*

Grammatical information is shown after the part of speech and refers to the whole entry eg. **завид|овать** (**-ую**); *pf* **позавидовать**) *несов: – +dat.* Note that transitive verbs are labelled *перех*, and intransitive verbs have no label other than aspect. Where grammatical information eg. *no pf* is given in the middle of the entry, it then governs all the following senses.

Use of the hairline (|)

The hairline is used in headwords to show where the inflection adds on eg. **книг|а** (**-и**).

Stress

Stress changes are shown where they occur, the last form given being indicative of the rest of the pattern eg. **игр|á** (**-ы́**; *nom pl* **-ы**). In this example the stress is on the last syllable in the singular moving to the first syllable in the plural.

Nouns, numerals and pronouns

In order to help you determine the declension and stress pattern of nouns, numerals and pronouns, we have shown the genitive in each case.

This is given as the first piece of information after the headword and is not labelled eg. **стол** (**-á**).

Where the headword has further irregularities in declension these are shown at the headword and labelled eg. **я́блок|о** (**-а**; *nom pl* **-и**).

Verbs

The majority of verbs are dealt with in aspectual pairs, and the translation is shown at the base form of the pair. The other aspect is generally shown separately and cross-referred to the base form. To help you see how a verb conjugates, inflections are shown immediately after the headword.

In phrases both aspects are shown if both work in the context.

The past tense is shown at the headword if it is irregularly formed.

Inflections given as separate entries

Some irregular inflected forms are also shown at their alphabetical position and cross-referred to the base headword.

Spelling rules

The following spelling rules apply to Russian:
– after ж, ч, ш, щ, г, к and х, ы is replaced by и, я by а and ю by у.
– after ж, ч, ш, щ and ц, е replaces an unstressed o.

Gender

The gender of Russian noun translations is only shown for:
- nouns ending in -ь
- neuter nouns ending in -я
- masculine nouns ending in -a
- nouns with a common gender
- indeclinable nouns
- substantivized adjectives
- plural noun translations if a singular form exists.

Feminine forms

The feminine forms of masculine nouns are shown as follows:
- the feminine ending adds on to the masculine form, eg. учи́тель(ница)
- the feminine ending substitutes part of the masculine form, the last common letter of both forms being shown before the feminine ending (unless it is a substantivized adjective), eg. актёр(три́са).
- the feminine form is given in full, eg. чех (че́шка).

Adjectives

Russian translations of adjectives are always given in the masculine, unless the adjective relates only to a feminine noun eg. бере́менная.

Verbs

Imperfective and perfective aspects are shown in translation where they both apply to a verb. to do де́лать (сде́лать pf). If only one aspect is shown, it means that only one aspect works for this sense. The same applies to translations of infinitive phrases eg. to buy sth покупа́ть (купи́ть pf) что-н.

Where the English phrase contains the construction "to do" standing for any verb, it has been translated by +infin/+impf infin/+pf infin, depending on which aspects of the Russian verb work in the context.

Where the English phrase contains the past tense of a verb in the 1st person singular, the Russian translation gives only the masculine form eg. I was glad я был рад

Prepositions

Unless bracketed, prepositions and cases which follow verbs, adjectives etc are obligatory as part of the translation eg. to inundate with зава́ливать (завали́ть pf) +instr

Where they are separated by or they are interchangeable.

An oblique (/) is used to separate prepositions when the preposition depends on the following noun not the preceding verb eg. идти́ в/на.

RUSSIAN ABBREVIATIONS

aviation	*АВИА*	авиация
automobiles	*АВТ*	автомобильное дело
administration	*АДМИН*	администрация
anatomy	*АНАТ*	анатомия
architecture	*АРХТ*	архитектура
impersonal	*безл*	безличный
biology	*БИО*	биология
botany	*БОТ*	ботаника
parenthesis	*вводн сл*	вводное слово
military	*ВОЕН*	военный термин
reflexive	*возв*	возвратный глагол
geography	*ГЕО*	география
geometry	*ГЕОМ*	геометрия
verb	*глаг*	глагол
offensive	*груб!*	грубо
singular	*ед*	единственное число
feminine	*ж*	женский род
zoology	*ЗООЛ*	зоология
history	*ИСТ*	история
et cetera	*итп*	и тому подобное
predicate	*как сказ*	как сказуемое
commercial	*КОММ*	коммерция
computing	*КОМП*	компьютер
somebody	*кто-н*	кто-нибудь
culinary	*КУЛИН*	кулинария
linguistics	*ЛИНГ*	лингвистика
masculine	*м*	мужской род
mathematics	*МАТ*	математика
medicine	*МЕД*	медицина
exclamation	*межд*	междометие
pronoun	*мест*	местоимение
plural	*мн*	множественное число
nautical	*МОР*	морской термин
music	*МУЗ*	музыка
adverb	*нареч*	наречие
invariable	*неизм*	неизменяемое
intransitive	*неперех*	непереходный глагол
indeclinable	*нескл*	несклоняемое
imperfective	*несов*	несовершенный вид
figurative	*перен*	в переносном значении
transitive	*перех*	переходный
subject	*подлеж*	подлежащее
politics	*ПОЛИТ*	политика
superlative	*превос*	превосходная степень

xii

preposition	**предл**	предлог
pejorative	**пренебр**	пренебрежительное
adjective	**прил**	прилагательное
possessive	**притяж**	притяжательный
school	**ПРОСВЕЩ**	просвещение
psychology	**ПСИХОЛ**	психология
informal	**разг**	разговорное
religion	**РЕЛ**	религия
agriculture	**С.-Х.**	сельское хозяйство
see	**см**	смотри
collective	**собир**	собирательное
perfective	**сов**	совершенный вид
abbreviation	**сокр**	сокращение
neuter	**ср**	средний род
comparative	**сравн**	сравнительная степень
construction	**СТРОИТ**	строительство
noun	**сущ**	имя существительное
television	**ТЕЛ**	телевидение
technology	**ТЕХ**	техника
printing	**ТИПОГ**	типографский термин
diminutive	**уменьш**	уменьшительное
physics	**ФИЗ**	физика
photography	**ФОТО**	фотография
chemistry	**ХИМ**	химия
particle	**част**	частица
somebody's	**чей-н**	чей-нибудь
numeral	**чис**	числительное
something	**что-н**	что-нибудь
economics	**ЭКОН**	экономика
electricity	**ЭЛЕК**	электроника
law	**ЮР**	юридический термин
registered trademark	**®**	зарегистрированный торговый знак
introduces a cultural equivalent	**≈**	вводит культурный эквивалент

АНГЛИЙСКИЕ СОКРАЩЕНИЯ

сокращение	**abbr**	abbreviation
винительный падеж	**acc**	accusative
прилагательное	**adj**	adjective
администрация	**ADMIN**	administration
наречие	**adv**	adverb
сельское хозяйство	**AGR**	agriculture
анатомия	**ANAT**	anatomy
архитектура	**ARCHIT**	architecture

автомобильное дело	*AUT*	automobiles
вспомогательный глагол	*aux vb*	auxiliary verb
авиация	*AVIAT*	aviation
биология	*BIO*	biology
ботаника	*BOT*	botany
британский английский	*BRIT*	British English
химия	*CHEM*	chemistry
коммерция	*COMM*	commerce
компьютер	*COMPUT*	computing
союз	*conj*	conjunction
строительство	*CONSTR*	construction
сращение	*cpd*	compound
кулинария	*CULIN*	culinary
дательный падеж	*dat*	dative
склоняется	*decl*	declines
определённый артикль	*def art*	definite article
уменьшительное	*dimin*	diminutive
экономика	*ECON*	economics
электроника	*ELEC*	electricity
особенно	*esp*	especially
и тому подобное	*etc*	et cetera
междометие	*excl*	exclamation
женский род	*f*	feminine
в переносном значении	*fig*	figurative
родительный падеж	*gen*	genitive
география	*GEO*	geography
геометрия	*GEOM*	geometry
безличный	*impers*	impersonal
несовершенный вид	*impf*	imperfective verb
несклоняемое	*ind*	indeclinable
неопределённый артикль	*indef art*	indefinite article
разговорное	*inf*	informal
грубо	*inf!*	offensive
инфинитив	*infin*	infinitive
творительный падеж	*instr*	instrumental
неизменяемое	*inv*	invariable
неправильный	*irreg*	irregular
лингвистика	*LING*	linguistics
местный падеж	*loc*	locative
мужской род	*m*	masculine
субстантивированное	*m/f/nt adj*	adjectival noun
прилагательное		
математика	*MATH*	mathematics
медицина	*MED*	medicine
военный термин	*MIL*	military
музыка	*MUS*	music

существительное	**n**	noun
морской термин	**NAUT**	nautical
именительный падеж	**nom**	nominative
существительное во множественном числе	**npl**	plural noun
средний род	**nt**	neuter
числительное	**num**	numeral
себя	**o.s.**	oneself
разделительный	**part**	partitive
пренебрежительный	**pej**	pejorative
совершенный вид	**pf**	perfective verb
фотография	**PHOT**	photography
физика	**PHYS**	physics
физиология	**PHYSIOL**	physiology
множественное число	**pl**	plural
политика	**POL**	politics
страдательное причастие	**pp**	past participle
предлог	**prep**	preposition
местоимение	**pron**	pronoun
предложный падеж	**prp**	prepositional
психология	**PSYCH**	psychiatry
прошедшее время	**pt**	past tense
религия	**REL**	religion
кто-нибудь	**sb**	somebody
просвещение	**SCOL**	school
единственное число	**sg**	singular
что-нибудь	**sth**	something
подлежащее	**subj**	subject
превосходная степень	**superl**	superlative
техника	**TECH**	technology
телесвязь	**TEL**	telecommunications
театр	**THEAT**	theatre
телевидение	**TV**	television
типографский термин	**TYP**	printing
американский английский	**US**	American English
обычно	**usu**	usually
глагол	**vb**	verb
непереходный глагол	**vi**	intransitive verb
звательный падеж	**voc**	vocative case
фразовый глагол	**vt fus**	inseparable verb
переходный глагол	**vt**	transitive verb
зоология	**ZOOL**	zoology
зарегистрированный торговый знак	**®**	registered trademark
вводит культурный эквивалент	**≈**	introduces a cultural equivalent

RUSSIAN PRONUNCIATION

Vowels and diphthongs

Letter	Symbol	Russian Example	English Example/Explanation
А,а	[a]	да́ть	after
Е,е	[ɛ]	сел	get
Ё,ё	[jo]	ёлка, моё	yawn
И,и	[i]	их, ни́ва	sheet
Й,й	[j]	йод, мой	yield
О́,о	[o]	кот	dot
О,о	[ʌ]	нога́	cup
У,у	[u]	ум	shoot
Ы,ы	[ɨ]	сын	pronounced like "ee", but with the tongue arched further back in the mouth
Э,э	[æ]	э́то	cat
Ю,ю	[ju]	юг	you, youth
Я,я	[ja]	я́сно	yak

Consonants

Letter	Symbol	Russian Example	English Example/Explanation
Б,б	[b]	банк	but
В,в	[v]	вот	vat
Г,г	[g]	год	got
Д,д	[d]	дом	dog
Ж,ж	[ʒ]	жена́	measure
З,з	[z]	за́втра	doze
К,к	[k]	кот	cat
Л,л	[l]	ло́дка	lot
М,м	[m]	мать	mat
Н,н	[n]	нас	no
П,п	[p]	пасть	put
Р,р	[r]	рот	pronounced like rolled Scots "r"
С,с	[s]	сад	sat
Т,т	[t]	ток	top
Ф,ф	[f]	фо́рма	fat
Х,х	[x]	ход	pronounced like Scots "ch" in "loch"
Ц,ц	[ts]	цель	bits
Ч,ч	[tʃ]	ча́сто	chip
Ш,ш	[ʃ]	шу́тка	shoot
Щ,щ	[ʃʃ]	щит	fresh sheets

Russian vowels are inherently short. Russian stressed vowels tend to be slightly longer than unstressed vowels. In unstressed positions all vowels are "reduced". Unstressed "o" sounds like "a" eg. **города** [gərʌˈda], except in some loanwords and acronyms eg. **ра́дио** [ˈraɟio], **госба́нк** [gosˈbank]. Unstressed "e" is pronounced like "bit" eg. **село́** [şiˈlo]. The same is true of "**я**" before stressed syllables eg. **пяти́** [pi'ţi], and of "**a**" when it follows "**ч**" or "**щ**" eg. **щади́ть**[ʃʃi`ɖiţ].

The letter "**ё**" is used only in grammar books, dictionaries etc. to avoid ambiguity eg. **нёбо** and **не́бо**.

АНГЛИЙСКОЕ ПРОИЗНОШЕНИЕ

Гласные и Дифтонги

Знак	Английский Пример	Русское Соответствие/Описание
[ɑ:]	f**a**ther	м**а́**ма
[ʌ]	b**u**t, c**o**me	**а**льянс
[æ]	m**a**n, c**a**t	**э́**тот
[ə]	f**a**ther, **a**go	р**а́**на
[ə:]	b**i**rd, h**ea**rd	ф**ё**дор
[ɛ]	g**e**t, b**e**d	г**е**н
[ɪ]	**i**t, b**i**g	к**и**т
[i·]	t**ea**, **sea**	**и́**ва
[ɔ]	h**o**t, w**a**sh	х**о**д
[ɔ:]	s**aw**, **a**ll	**о́**чень
[u]	p**u**t, b**oo**k	б**у**к
[u:]	t**oo**, y**ou**	**у́**лица
[aɪ]	fl**y**, h**igh**	л**ай**
[au]	h**ow**, h**ou**se	**а́у**т
[ɛə]	th**ere**, b**ear**	*произно́сится как сочета́ние "э" и кра́ткого "а"*
[eɪ]	d**ay**, ob**ey**	**эй**
[ɪə]	h**ere**, h**ear**	*произно́сится как сочета́ние "и" и кра́ткого "а"*
[əu]	g**o**, n**o**te	**о́у**
[ɔɪ]	b**oy**, **oi**l	**бой**

| [uə] | p**oor**, s**ure** | *произно́сится как сочета́ние "у" и кра́ткого "а"* |
| [juə] | p**ure** | *произно́сится как сочета́ние "ю" и кра́ткого "а"* |

Согла́сные

[b]	**b**ut	**б**ал
[d]	**d**ot	**д**ом
[g]	**g**o, **g**et, bi**g**	**г**ол, ми**г**
[dʒ]	**g**in, **j**udge	**дж**и́нсы, и́ми**дж**
[ŋ]	si**ng**	*произно́сится как ру́сское "н", но не ко́нчиком языка́, а за́дней ча́стью его́ спи́нки*
[h]	**h**ouse, **h**e	**х**а́ос, **х**и́мия
[j]	**y**oung, **y**es	**й**од, **й**е́мен
[k]	**c**ome, mo**ck**	**к**а́мень, ро**к**
[r]	**r**ed, t**r**ead	**р**от, т**р**ава́
[s]	**s**and, ye**s**	**с**ад, ри**с**
[z]	ro**s**e, **z**ebra	ро́**з**а, **з**е́бра
[ʃ]	**sh**e, ma**ch**ine	**ш**и́на, ма**ш**и́на
[tʃ]	**ch**in, ri**ch**	**ч**ин, кули́**ч**
[v]	**v**alley	**в**альс
[w]	**w**ater, **wh**ich	**у**о́тергейт, уи**к**-э́нд
[ʒ]	vi**s**ion	ва́**ж**ный
[θ]	**th**ink, my**th**	*произно́сится как ру́сское "с", но ко́нчик языка́ нахо́дится ме́жду зуба́ми*
[ð]	**th**is, **th**e	*произно́сится как ру́сское "з", но ко́нчик языка́ нахо́дится ме́жду зуба́ми*
[f]	**f**ace	**ф**акт
[l]	**l**ake, **l**ick	**л**ай, **л**ом
[m]	**m**ust	**м**ат
[n]	**n**ut	**н**ет
[p]	**p**at, **p**ond	**п**ар, **п**от
[t]	**t**ake, ha**t**	э́**т**от, не**т**
[x]	lo**ch**	**х**од

А, а

а союз **1** but; **он согласи́лся, а я отказа́лась** he agreed, but I refused

2 (*выражает присоединение*) and

3 (*во фразах*): **а (не) то** or (else); **а вот** but

♦ *част* (*обозначает отклик*): **иди́ сюда́! - а, что тако́е!** come here! - yes, what is it?; **а как же** (*разг*) of course, certainly

♦ *част* (*выражает ужас, боль*) oh; **а ну** (*разг*) go on; **а ну́ его́!** (*разг*) stuff him!

абажу́р (**-а**) *м* lampshade
абза́ц (**-а**) *м* paragraph
абитурие́нт (**-а**) *м* entrant to university, college etc
абонеме́нт (**-а**) *м* season ticket
абоне́нт (**-а**) *м* subscriber
або́рт (**-а**) *м* abortion
абрико́с (**-а**) (*плод*) apricot
абсолю́тный *прил* absolute
абстра́ктный *прил* abstract
абсу́рдный *прил* absurd
аванга́рд (**-а**) *м* vanguard; (*ИСКУССТВО*) avant-garde
ава́нс (**-а**) *м* (*КОММ*) advance
авантю́ра (**-ы**) *ж* adventure
авари́йный *прил* emergency; (*дом*) unsafe; **~ сигна́л** alarm signal
ава́рия (**-и**) *ж* accident; (*повреждение*) breakdown
а́вгуст (**-а**) *м* August
а́виа *нескл* (*авиапочта*) air mail
авиакомпа́ния (**-и**) *ж* airline

авиано́сец (**-ца**) *м* aircraft carrier
авиа́ция (**-и**) *ж* aviation
Австра́лия (**-и**) *ж* Australia
А́встрия (**-и**) *ж* Austria
автоба́за (**-ы**) *ж* depot
автобиогра́фия (**-и**) *ж* autobiography
авто́бус (**-а**) *м* bus
автовокза́л (**-а**) *м* bus station
авто́граф (**-а**) *м* autograph
автозаво́д (**-а**) *м* car (*BRIT*) или automobile (*US*) plant
автозапра́вочная (**-ой**) *ж* (*также*: **~ ста́нция**) filling station
автомагистра́ль (**-и**) *ж* motorway (*BRIT*), expressway (*US*)
автома́т (**-а**) *м* automatic machine; (*ВОЕН*) sub-machine-gun
автомаши́на (**-ы**) *ж* (motor)car, automobile (*US*)
автомеха́ник (**-а**) *м* car mechanic
автомоби́ль (**-я**) *м* (motor)car, automobile (*US*); **легково́й ~** (passenger) car
автоно́мный *прил* autonomous
автоотве́тчик (**-а**) *м* answering machine
а́втор (**-а**) *м* author
авторите́т (**-а**) *м* authority
авторите́тный *прил* authoritative
а́вторский *прил* author's; **~ое пра́во** copyright; **~ое свиде́тельство** patent
авторуч́ка (**-ки**; *gen pl* **-ек**) *ж* fountain pen
автостра́да (**-ы**) *ж* motorway (*BRIT*), expressway (*US*)
аге́нт (**-а**) *м* agent
аге́нтство (**-а**) *ср* agency
агити́ровать (**-ую**) *несов*: **~ (за** +*acc*) to campaign (for)
аго́ния (**-и**) *ж* death throes *мн*
агра́рный *прил* agrarian
агрега́т (**-а**) *м* machine
агре́ссия (**-и**) *ж* aggression

агроно́м (-а) м agronomist

ад (-а) м hell

адапти́р|оваться (-уюсь) (не)сов возв to adapt

адвока́т (-а) м counsel; (в суде́) barrister (BRIT), ≈ attorney (US)

адеква́тный прил adequate

администра́тор (-а) м administrator; (в гости́нице) manager

администра́ци|я (-и) ж administration; (гости́ницы) management

а́дрес (-а; nom pl -а́) м address

а́дресный прил: ~ **стол** residents' registration office

адрес|ова́ть (-у́ю) (не)сов перех: ~ **что-н кому́-н** to address sth to sb

ажу́рный прил lace

аза́рт (-а) м ardour (BRIT), ardor (US)

аза́ртн|ый прил ardent; ~**ая игра́** gambling

а́збук|а (-и) ж alphabet; (буква́рь) first reading book

Азербайджа́н (-а) м Azerbaijan

Ази|я (-и) ж Asia

азо́т (-а) м nitrogen

а́ист (-а) м stork

ай межд (выража́ет боль) ow, ouch

а́йсберг (-а) м iceberg

акаде́мик (-а) м academician

акаде́ми|я (-и) ж academy

акваре́л|ь (-и) ж watercolours мн (BRIT), watercolors мн (US); (карти́на) watercolo(u)r

аква́риум (-а) м aquarium, fish tank

аккомпани́р|овать (-ую) несов: ~ +dat to accompany

акко́рд (-а) м chord

аккредити́в (-а) м letter of credit

аккумуля́тор (-а) м accumulator

аккура́тный прил (посеще́ние) regular; (рабо́тник) meticulous; (рабо́та) accurate; (костю́м) neat

акселера́тор (-а) м accelerator

акт (-а) м act; (докуме́нт) formal document

актёр (-а) м actor

акти́в (-а) м assets мн

акти́вный прил active

актри́с|а (-ы) ж actress

актуа́льный прил topical; (зада́ча) urgent

аку́л|а (-ы) ж shark

акушёр (-а) м obstetrician

акушёр|ка (-ки; gen pl -ок) ж midwife

акце́нт (-а) м accent

акци́з (-а) м excise (tax)

акционе́р (-а) м shareholder

акционе́рный прил joint-stock

а́кци|я (-и) ж (КОММ) share; (де́йствие) action

а́лгебр|а (-ы) ж algebra

а́либи ср нескл alibi

алиме́нт|ы (-ов) мн alimony ед, maintenance ед

алкого́лик (-а) м alcoholic

алкого́л|ь (-я) м alcohol

аллерге́н (-а) м allergen

аллерги́|я (-и) ж allergy

алле́|я (-и) ж alley

алло́ межд hello

алма́з (-а) м diamond

алта́р|ь (-я́) м chancel

алфави́т (-а) м alphabet

а́лый прил scarlet

альбо́м (-а) м album

альмана́х (-а) м anthology

альпини́зм (-а) м mountaineering

альт (-а) м (инструме́нт) viola

альтернати́в|а (-ы) ж alternative

алья́нс (-а) м alliance

алюми́ни|й (-я) м aluminium (BRIT), aluminum (US)

амбулато́ри|я (-и) ж doctor's

surgery (BRIT) или office (US)

Аме́рик|а (-и) ж America

америка́нск|ий прил American

амети́ст (-а) м amethyst

ами́нь част (РЕЛ) amen

амнисти́р|овать (-ую) (не)сов перех to grant (или amnesty to

амни́сти|я (-и) ж amnesty

амора́льный прил immoral

амортиза́тор (-а) м (ТЕХ) shock absorber

амортиза́ци|я (-и) ж (ТЕХ) shock absorption; (ЭКОН) depreciation

а́мпул|а (-ы) ж ampoule (BRIT), ampule (US)

ампути́р|овать (-ую) (не)сов перех to amputate

АН ж сокр (= Акаде́мия нау́к) Academy of Sciences

ана́лиз (-а) м analysis

анализи́р|овать (-ую; pf про~) несов перех to analyse (BRIT), analyze (US)

анали́тик (-а) м analyst

аналоги́чный прил analogous

анало́ги|я (-и) ж analogy; **по~ и** (с +instr) in a similar way (to)

анана́с (-а) м pineapple

ана́рхи|я (-и) ж anarchy

анато́ми|я (-и) ж anatomy

анаш|а́ (-и́) ж hashish

анга́р (-а) м hangar

а́нгел (-а) м (также разг) angel

анги́н|а (-ы) ж tonsillitis

англи́йский прил English; **~ язы́к** English

англича́н|ин (-ина; nom pl -е, gen pl -) м Englishman

А́нгли|я (-и) ж England

анекдо́т (-а) м joke

анеми́|я (-и) ж anaemia (BRIT), anemia (US)

анестезио́лог (-а) м anaesthetist (BRIT), anesthiologist (US)

анестези́|я (-и) ж anaesthesia

(BRIT), anesthesia (US)

анке́т|а (-ы) ж (опро́сный лист) questionnaire; (бланк для сведе́ний) form; (сбор све́дений) survey

аннота́ци|я (-и) ж précis

аннули́р|овать (-ую) (не)сов перех (брак, догово́р) to annul

анони́мный прил anonymous

анса́мбл|ь (-я) м ensemble; (танцева́льный) company; (эстра́дный) group

Антаркти́д|а (-ы) ж Antarctica

Анта́рктик|а (-и) ж the Antarctic

анте́нн|а (-ы) ж aerial (BRIT), antenna (US); **~ косми́ческой свя́зи** satellite dish

антибио́тик (-а) м antibiotic

антивое́нный прил antiwar

антиква́рный прил antique

антисанита́рный прил unhygienic, insanitary

антисемити́зм (-а) м anti-Semitism

антифаши́стский прил antifascist

анти́чный прил classical; **~ мир** the Ancient World

антра́кт (-а) м interval

аню́тины прил: **~ гла́зки** pansy ед

А/О ср сокр (= акционе́рное о́бщество) joint-stock company

апа́ти|я (-и) ж apathy

апелли́р|овать (-ую) (не)сов (ЮР) to appeal

апелля́ци|я (-и) ж (также ЮР) appeal

апельси́н (-а) м orange

аплоди́р|овать (-ую) несов: **~** +dat to applaud

аплодисме́нт|ы (-ов) мн applause ед

апо́стол (-а) м apostle

аппара́т (-а) м apparatus; (ФИЗИОЛОГИЯ) system; (штат) staff

аппарату́р|а (-ы) ж собир equipment

аппендици́т (-а) м appendicitis

аппети́т (-а) м appetite; **прия́тного ~а!** bon appétit!

апре́л|ь (-я) м April

апте́к|а (-и) ж pharmacy

апте́кар|ь (-я) м pharmacist

ара́б (-а) м Arab

ара́бский прил (страны) Arab; **~ язы́к** Arabic

ара́хис (-а) м peanut

арби́тр (-а) м (в спорах) arbitrator; (в футболе) referee

арбитра́ж (-а) м arbitration

арбу́з (-а) м watermelon

аргуме́нт (-а) м argument

аргументи́р|овать (-ую) (не)сов перех to argue

аре́н|а (-ы) ж arena; (цирка) ring

аре́нд|а (-ы) ж (наём) lease

аре́ндн|ый прил lease; **~ая пла́та** rent

аренд|ова́ть (-у́ю) (не)сов перех to lease

аре́ст (-а) м (преступника) arrest

аресто́ванн|ый (-ого) м person held in custody

арест|ова́ть (-у́ю; impf **аресто́вывать)** сов перех (преступника) to arrest

аристокра́ти|я (-и) ж aristocracy

арифме́тик|а (-и) ж arithmetic

а́ри|я (-и) ж aria

а́р|ка (-ки; gen pl **-ок)** ж arch

А́рктик|а (-и) ж the Arctic

армату́р|а (-ы) ж the steel framework

арме́йский прил army

Арме́ни|я (-и) ж Armenia

а́рми|я (-и) ж army

армяни́н (-а; nom pl **армя́не,** gen pl **армя́н)** м Armenian

армя́н|ка (-ки; gen pl **-ок)** ж Armenian

арома́т (-а) м (цветов) fragrance;

(кофе итп) aroma

арсена́л (-а) м (склад) arsenal

арте́ри|я (-и) ж (также перен) artery

арти́кл|ь (-я) м (линг) article

артилле́ри|я (-и) ж artillery

арти́ст (-а) м actor

арти́ст|ка (-ки; gen pl **-ок)** ж actress

артри́т (-а) м arthritis

а́рф|а (-ы) ж harp

арха́нгел (-а) м archangel

архео́лог (-а) м archaeologist (BRIT), archeologist (US)

архи́в (-а) м archive

архиепи́скоп (-а) м archbishop

архипела́г (-а) м archipelago

архите́ктор (-а) м architect

архитекту́р|а (-ы) ж architecture

асбе́ст (-а) м asbestos

аспе́кт (-а) м aspect

аспира́нт (-а) м postgraduate (doing PhD)

аспиранту́р|а (-ы) ж postgraduate studies мн (leading to PhD)

аспири́н (-а) м aspirin

ассамбле́|я (-и) ж assembly

ассигн|ова́ть (-у́ю) (не)сов перех to allocate

ассими́ли́р|оваться (-уюсь) (не)сов возв to become assimilated

ассисте́нт (-а) м assistant; (в вузе) assistant lecturer

ассортиме́нт (-а) м range

ассоциа́ци|я (-и) ж association

ассоции́р|овать (-ую) (не)сов перех to associate

а́стм|а (-ы) ж asthma

а́стр|а (-ы) ж aster

астроло́ги|я (-и) ж astrology

астроно́м (-а) м astronomer

астрономи́ческий прил (также перен) astronomic(al)

асфа́льт (-а) м asphalt

асфальти́р|овать (-ую; pf за~) (не)сов перех to asphalt

ата́к|а (-и) ж attack

атак|ова́ть (-у́ю) (не)сов перех to attack

атама́н (-а) м ataman (Cossack leader)

атеи́ст (-а) м atheist

ателье́ ср нескл studio; (мод) tailor's shop; **телевизио́нное ~** television repair shop; **~ прока́та** rental shop

атланти́ческий прил: **Атланти́ческий океа́н** the Atlantic (Ocean)

а́тлас (-а) м atlas

атле́тик|а (-и) ж: **лёгкая ~** track and field events: **тяжёлая ~** weight lifting

атмосфе́р|а (-ы) ж atmosphere

а́том (-а) м atom

атрофи́р|оваться (3sg -уется) (не)сов возв to atrophy

АТС ж сокр (= автомати́ческая телефо́нная ста́нция) automatic telephone exchange

атташе́ м нескл attaché

аттеста́т (-а) м certificate; **~ зре́лости** ≈ GCSE

аттеста́т зре́лости - Certificate of Secondary Education. This is obtained by school-leavers after sitting their final exams. This document records all the marks the pupils have attained during their exams and enables them to apply to a higher education institution. See also note at **проходно́й балл**.

аттест|ова́ть (-у́ю) (не)сов перех to assess

аттракцио́н (-а) м (в ци́рке)

attraction; (в па́рке) amusement

ауди́т (-а) м audit

аудито́ри|я (-и) ж lecture hall ♦ собир (слу́шатели) audience

аукцио́н (-а) м auction

а́ут (-а) м (в те́ннисе) out; (в футбо́ле): **мяч в а́уте** the ball is out of play

афери́ст (-а) м swindler

афи́ш|а (-и) ж poster

А́фрик|а (-и) ж Africa

ах межд: **~!** oh!, ah!; **~ да!** (разг) ah yes!

ацето́н (-а) м acetone

аэро́бик|а (-и) ж aerobics

аэро́бус (-а) м airbus

аэровокза́л (-а) м air terminal (esp BRIT)

аэродро́м (-а) м aerodrome

аэрозо́л|ь (-я) м aerosol, spray

аэропо́рт (-а; loc sg -у́) м airport

АЭС ж сокр (= а́томная электроста́нция) atomic power station

Б, б

б част см. **бы**

ба́б|а (-ы) ж (разг) woman

ба́б|а-яг|а́ (-ы, -и) ж Baba Yaga (old witch in Russian folk-tales)

ба́б|ий прил womanish; **~ье ле́то** Indian summer

ба́б|ка (-ки; gen pl -ок) ж grandmother

ба́бочк|а (-ки; gen pl -ек) ж butterfly; (га́лстук) bow tie

ба́буш|ка (-ки; gen pl -ек) ж grandmother, grandma

бага́ж (-а́) м luggage (BRIT), baggage (US)

бага́жник (-а) м (в автомоби́ле) boot (BRIT), trunk (US); (на *велосипеде)* carrier

багро́вый *прил* crimson

бадминто́н (-а) *м* badminton

ба́з|**а** (-ы) *ж* basis; *(ВОЕН, АРХИТ)* base; *(для туристов)* centre *(BRIT)*, center *(US)*; *(товаров)* warehouse

база́р (-а) *м* market; *(книжный) fair*; *(перен: разг)* racket

бази́р|**овать** (-ую) *несов перех*: ~ **что-н на** +*prp* to base sth on; ~**ся** *несов возв*: ~**ся** (**на** +*prp*) to be based (on)

байда́р|**ка** (-ки; *gen pl* -**ок**) *ж* canoe

Байка́л (-а) *м* Lake Baikal

бак (-а) *м* tank

бакале́|**я** (-и) *ж* grocery section; *(товары)* groceries *мн*

ба́кен (-а) *м* buoy

бакенба́рд|**ы** (-) *мн* sideburns *мн*

баклажа́н (-а; *gen pl* - *или* -**ов**) *м* aubergine *(BRIT)*, eggplant *(US)*

бакс (-а) *м (разг)* dollar

бакте́ри|**я** (-и) *ж* bacterium

бал (-а; *loc sg* -**у́**, *nom pl* -**ы́**) *м* ball

балала́|**йка** (-йки; *gen pl* -**ек**) *ж* balalaika

бала́нс (-а) *м* balance

баланси́р|**овать** (-ую) *несов*: ~ (**на** +*prp*) to balance (on)

балери́н|**а** (-ы) *ж* ballerina

бале́т (-а) *м* ballet

ба́лк|**а** (-и; *gen pl* -**ок**) *ж* beam

балка́нский *прил* Balkan

Балка́н|**ы** (-) *мн* the Balkans

балко́н (-а) *м (АРХИТ)* balcony; *(ТЕАТР)* circle *(BRIT)*, balcony *(US)*

балл (-а) *м* mark; *(СПОРТ)* point

балла́д|**а** (-ы) *ж* ballad

баллисти́ческий *прил* ballistic

балло́н (-а) *м (газовый)* cylinder; *(для жидкости)* jar

баллоти́р|**овать** (-ую) *несов перех* to vote for; ~**ся** *несов*

возв: ~**ся в** +*acc или* **на пост** +*gen* to stand *(BRIT) или* run *(US)* for

бал|**ова́ть** (-**у́ю**; *pf* **из**~) *несов перех* to spoil; ~**ся** *несов возв (ребёнок)* to be naughty

балти́йск|**ий** *прил*: **Балти́йское мо́ре** the Baltic (Sea)

бальза́м (-а) *м* balsam

ба́льн|**ый** *прил*: ~**ое пла́тье** ball gown

ба́мпер (-а) *м* bumper

бана́льный *прил* banal, trite

бана́н (-а) *м* banana

ба́нд|**а** (-ы) *ж* gang

бандеро́л|**ь** (-и) *ж* package

банди́т (-а) *м* bandit

банк (-а) *м* bank

ба́н|**ка** (-ки; *gen pl* -**ок**) *ж* jar; *(жестяная)* tin *(BRIT)*, can *(US)*

банке́т (-а) *м* banquet

банки́р (-а) *м* banker

банкно́т (-а; *gen pl* -) *м* banknote

ба́нковский *прил* bank

банкома́т (-а) *м* cash machine

банкро́т (-а) *м* bankrupt

банкро́тств|**о** (-а) *ср* bankruptcy

бант (-а) *м* bow

ба́н|**я** (-и; *gen pl* -**ь**) *ж* bathhouse

бапти́ст (-а) *м* Baptist

бар (-а) *м* bar

бараба́н (-а) *м* drum

бараба́н|**ить** (-ю, -ишь) *несов* to drum

бараба́нн|**ый** *прил*: ~**ая перепо́нка** eardrum

бара́к (-а) *м* barracks *мн*

бара́н (-а) *м* sheep

бара́ний *прил (котлета)* lamb; *(тулуп)* sheepskin

бара́нин|**а** (-ы) *ж* mutton; *(молодая)* lamb

барахл|**о́** (-**а́**) *ср собир* junk

барахо́л|**ка** (-ки; *gen pl* -**ок**) *ж* flea market

барда́к (-а́) м (груб!: беспоря́док) hell broke loose (!)

барелье́ф (-а) м bas-relief

ба́рж|а (-и) ж barge

барито́н (-а) м baritone

ба́рмен (-а) м barman bartender (US)

баро́метр (-а) м barometer

баррика́д|а (-ы) ж barricade

барсу́к (-а́) м badger

ба́ртер (-а) м barter

ба́рхат (-а) м velvet

барье́р (-а) м (в бе́ге) hurdle; (на ска́чках) fence; (перен) barrier

бас (-а; nom pl -ы́) м bass

баскетбо́л (-а) м basketball

ба́сн|я (-ни; gen pl -ен) ж fable

бассе́йн (-а) м (swimming) pool; (реки, о́зера итп) basin

бастова́ть (-у́ю) несов to be on strike

батальо́н (-а) м battalion

батаре́|йка (-йки; gen pl -ек) ж (ЭЛЕК) battery

батаре́|я (-и) ж (отопи́тельная радиа́тор; ВОЕН, ЭЛЕК) battery

бати́ст (-а) м cambric, lawn

бато́н (-а) м (white) loaf (long or oval)

ба́тюш|ка (-ки; gen pl -ек) м father

бахром|а́ (-ы́) ж fringe (BRIT), bangs мн (US)

ба́ш|ня (-ни; gen pl -ен) ж tower

баю́ка|ть (-ю) несов перех to lull to sleep

бая́н (-а) м bayan (kind of concertina)

бди́тельный прил vigilant

бег (-а) м run, running; **на ~у́** hurriedly; *см. также* **бега́**

бег|а́ (-о́в) мн the races мн

бе́га|ть (-ю) несов to run

бегемо́т (-а) м hippopotamus, hippo (inf)

беги́(те) несов см. **бежа́ть**

бегле́ц (-а́) м fugitive

бе́глый прил escaped; (речь, чте́ние) fluent; (обзо́р) brief

бегов|о́й прил (ло́шадь) race; **~а́я доро́жка** running track

бего́м нареч quickly; (перен: разг) in a rush

бе́гств|о (-а) ср flight; (из пле́на) escape

бегу́ итп несов см. **бежа́ть**

бегу́н (-а́) м runner

бегу́н|ья (-ьи; gen pl -ий) ж runner

бед|а́ (-ы́; nom pl -ы) ж tragedy; (несча́стье) misfortune, trouble; **про́сто** ~ it's just awful; **не** ~! (разг) (it's) nothing!, not to worry!

бедне́|ть (-ю; pf о~) несов to become poor

бе́дност|ь (-и) ж poverty

бе́дный прил poor

бедня́г|а (-и) м/ж (разг) poor thing

бедня́к (-а́) м poor man

бедр|о́ (-а́; nom pl бёдра, gen pl бёдер) ср thigh; (таз) hip

бе́дственный прил disastrous

бе́дстви|е (-я) ср disaster

бе́дств|овать (-ую) несов to live in poverty

бе|жа́ть (см. Table 20) несов to run; (вре́мя) to fly

бе́жевый прил beige

бе́жен|ец (-ца) м refugee

без предл: +gen without; ~ **пяти́/десяти́ мину́т шесть** five to/ten to six

безала́берный прил (разг) sloppy

безалкого́льный прил nonalcoholic, alcohol-free; ~ **напи́ток** soft drink

безапелляцио́нный прил peremptory

безбиле́тник (-а) *м* fare dodger
безбо́жный *прил* (*разг*) shameless
безболе́зненный *прил* painless
безбре́жный *прил* boundless
безве́тренный *прил* calm
безвку́сный *прил* tasteless
безвла́сти|**е** (-я) *ср* anarchy
безвозвра́т|**ный** *прил* irretrievable; ~**ая ссу́да** nonrepayable loan
безво́льный *прил* weak-willed
безвы́ходный *прил* hopeless
безгра́мотный *прил* illiterate; (*работник*) incompetent
безграни́чный *прил* boundless
безда́рный *прил* (*человек*) talentless; (*произведение*) mediocre
безде́йств|**овать** (-**ую**) *несов* to stand idle; (*человек*) to take no action
безде́льник (-а) *м* (*разг*) loafer
безде́льнича|**ть** (-**ю**) *несов* (*разг*) to loaf *или* lounge about
безде́тный *прил* childless
бе́здн|**а** (-**ы**) *ж* abyss; **у меня́ ~ дел** (*разг*) I've got heaps of things to do
бездо́мный *прил* (*человек*) homeless; (*собака*) stray
бездо́нный *прил* bottomless
безду́мный *прил* thoughtless
безду́шный *прил* heartless
безе́ *ср нескл* meringue
безжа́лостный *прил* ruthless
безжи́зненный *прил* lifeless
беззабо́тный *прил* carefree
беззако́ни|**е** (-я) *ср* lawlessness
беззасте́нчивый *прил* shameless
беззащи́тный *прил* defenceless (*BRIT*), defenseless (*US*)
беззву́чный *прил* inaudible
беззу́бый *прил* toothless
безли́чный *прил* impersonal

безлю́дный *прил* deserted
безме́рный *прил* boundless
безмо́лвный *прил* silent
безмяте́жный *прил* tranquil
безнадёжный *прил* hopeless
безнака́занный *прил* unpunished
безнали́чный *прил* noncash; ~ **расчёт** clearing settlement
безнра́вственный *прил* immoral
безо *предл см.* **без**
безоби́дный *прил* harmless
безо́блачный *прил* cloudless; (*перен: жизнь*) carefree
безобра́зи|**е** (-я) *ср* ugliness; (*поступок*) outrage; ~ **!** it's outrageous!, it's a disgrace!
безобра́зный *прил* ugly; (*поступок*) outrageous, disgraceful
безогово́рочный *прил* unconditional
безопа́сность (-**и**) *ж* safety; (*международная*) security
безопа́сный *прил* safe
безору́жный *прил* unarmed
безотве́тный *прил* (*любовь*) unrequited; (*существо*) meek
безотве́тственный *прил* irresponsible
безотка́зный *прил* reliable
безотлага́тельный *прил* urgent
безотноси́тельно *нареч:* ~ **к** +*dat* irrespective of
безоши́бочный *прил* correct
безрабо́тиц|**а** (-**ы**) *ж* unemployment
безрабо́тн|**ый** *прил* unemployed
♦ (**-ого**) *м* unemployed person
безра́достный *прил* joyless
безразли́чно *нареч* indifferently
♦ *как сказ:* **мне** ~ it doesn't matter *или* makes no difference to me; ~ **кто/что** no matter who/what
безразли́чный *прил* indifferent
безразме́рн|**ый** *прил:* ~**ые**

носки́ one-size socks

безрезульта́тный *прил* fruitless

безрука́в|**ка (-ки;** *gen pl* **-ок)** *ж* (*кофта*) sleeveless top; (*куртка*) sleeveless jacket

безукори́зненный *прил* irreproachable; (*работа*) flawless

безу́ми|**е (-я)** *ср* madness; **до ~я** madly

безу́мно *нареч* (*любить*) madly; (*устать*) terribly

безу́мный *прил* mad; (*о чувстве*) wild

безупре́чный *прил* irreproachable; (*работа*) flawless

безусло́вно *нареч* (*доверять*) unconditionally ♦ *част* (*несомненно*) without a doubt; (*конечно*) naturally

безуспе́шный *прил* unsuccessful

безуча́стный *прил* indifferent

безъя́дерный *прил* nuclear-free

безымя́нный *прил* (*герой, автор*) anonymous; **~ па́лец** ring finger

бой(сл) *носов см.* **би́ть(ся)**

Белару́с|**ь (-и)** *ж* Belarus

белору́с (-а) *м* Belorussian

беле́|**ть (-ю;** *pf* **по~) не***сов* (*лицо*) to go *или* turn white; (*no pf*; *цветы*) to show white

бели́л|**а (-)** *мн* emulsion *ед*

бел|**и́ть (-ю́, -ишь;** *pf* **по~) не***сов перех* to whitewash

бе́личий *прил* squirrel's; (*шуба*) squirrel (fur)

бе́л|**ка (-ки;** *gen pl* **-ок)** *ж* squirrel

белко́вый *прил* proteinous

бел|**о́к (-ка́)** *м* protein; (*яйца*) (egg) white; (*АНАТ*) white (of the eye)

белокро́ви|**е (-я)** *ср* (*МЕД*) leukaemia (*BRIT*), leukemia (*US*)

белоку́рый *прил* (*человек*) fair(-haired); (*волосы*) fair

белосне́жный *прил* snow-white

бе́лый *прил* white; **~ медве́дь** polar bear

Бе́льги|**я (-и)** *ж* Belgium

бель|**ё (-я́)** *ср собир* linen; **ни́жнее ~** underwear

бельэта́ж (-а) *м* (*ТЕАТР*) dress circle

бемо́л|**ь (-я)** *м* (*МУЗ*) flat

бензи́н (-а) *м* petrol (*BRIT*), gas (*US*)

бензоба́к (-а) *м* petrol (*BRIT*) *или* gas (*US*) tank

бензоколо́н|**ка (-ки;** *gen pl* **-ок)** *ж* petrol (*BRIT*) *или* gas (*US*) pump

Бенилю́кс (-а) *м* Benelux

бенуа́р (-а) *м* (*ТЕАТР*) boxes *мн*

бе́рег (-а; *loc sg* **-у́,** *nom pl* **-а́)** *м* (*моря, озера*) shore; (*реки*) bank

бережли́вый *прил* thrifty

бе́режный *прил* caring

берёз|**а (-ы)** *ж* birch (tree)

берём *несов см.* **брать**

бере́мене|**ть (-ю;** *pf* **за~) не***сов* to get pregnant

бере́менн|**ая** *прил* pregnant ♦ **(-ой)** *ж* pregnant woman

бере́менность (-и) *ж* pregnancy

бере́т (-а) *м* beret

берёт *etc несов см.* **брать**

бер|**е́чь (-егу́, -ежёшь** *etc*, **-егу́т;** *pt* **-ёг, -егла́) не***сов перех* (*здоровье, детей*) to look after, take care of; (*деньги*) to be careful with; (*время*) to make good use of; **~ся (** *pf* **по~ся)** *несов возв*: **~ся** **+gen** to watch out for; **~еги́тесь!** watch out!

Берли́н (-а) *м* Berlin

беру́(сь) *etc несов см.* **брать(ся)**

бесе́д|**а (-ы)** *ж* conversation; (*популярный доклад*) talk

бесе́д|**ка (-ки;** *gen pl* **-ок)** *ж* pavilion

бесе́д|**овать (-ую)** *несов*: **~ (с**

+instr) to talk (to)

бе́|си́ть (-шу́, -сишь) *несов*
перех (*разг*) to infuriate; ~ся *несов возв*
(*разг*) to run wild; (*pf* вз~ся;
раздража́ться) to become furious

бескомпроми́ссный *прил*
uncompromising

бесконе́чност|ь (-и) *ж* infinity;
до ~и (*очень до́лго*) endlessly;
(*очень си́льно*) infinitely

бесконе́чный *прил* endless;
(*любовь, не́нависть*) undying

бесконтро́льный *прил*
uncontrolled

бескоры́стный *прил* unselfish

бескро́вный *прил* bloodless

бесперспекти́вный *прил*
(*рабо́та*) without prospects

беспе́чный *прил* carefree

беспла́тный *прил* free

беспло́дный *прил* (*же́нщина*)
infertile; (*по́чва*) barren, infertile;
(*попы́тки, диску́ссии*) fruitless

бесповоро́тный *прил* irrevocable

бесподо́бный *прил* (*разг*)
fantastic

беспоко́|ить (-ю, -ишь; *pf* по~)
несов перех (*меша́ть*) to disturb,
trouble; (*pf* о~; *трево́жить*) to
worry; ~ся *несов возв*
(*утружда́ть себя*) to trouble o.s.
(*трево́житься*); ~ся о +*prp* или за
+*acc* to worry about

беспоко́йный *прил* anxious;
(*ребёнок*) restless; (*вре́мя*)
troubled

беспоко́йств|о (-а) *ср* anxiety;
(*хло́поты*) trouble; прости́те за
~! sorry to trouble you!

бесполе́зный *прил* useless

беспо́мощный *прил* helpless

беспоря́д|ок (-ка) *м* disorder; в
~ке (*ко́мната, дела́*) in a mess;

см. также беспоря́дки

беспоря́дочный *прил* disorderly;
(*расска́з*) confused

беспоса́дочный *прил* nonstop

беспо́чвенный *прил* groundless

беспо́шлинный *прил* duty-free

беспоща́дный *прил* merciless

бесправный *прил* without (civil)
rights

беспреде́л (-а) *м* lawlessness

беспреде́льный *прил* boundless;
(*о чу́встве*) immeasurable

беспреко́сло́вный *прил*
unquestioning

беспрепя́тственный *прил*
unimpeded

беспрецеде́нтный *прил*
unprecedented

беспри́быльный *прил*
unprofitable

беспризо́рный *прил* homeless

беспринци́пный *прил*
unscrupulous

беспристра́стный *прил*
unbias(s)ed

беспричи́нный *прил* unfounded

беспроце́нтный *прил* interest-
free

бессвя́зный *прил* incoherent

бессерде́чный *прил* heartless

бесси́льный *прил* feeble, weak;
(*гнев*) impotent; (*президе́нт*)
powerless

бессме́ртный *прил* immortal

бессмы́сленный *прил*
meaningless, senseless;
(*бесполе́зный*) pointless; (*взгляд*)
inane

бессо́вестный *прил* (*нече́стный*)
unscrupulous; (*на́глый*) shameless

бессодержа́тельный *прил*
(*речь*) empty

бессозна́тельн|ый *прил*
(*де́йствия*) instinctive; быть (*impf*)
в ~ом состоя́нии to be

unconscious

бессо́нниц|а (-ы) ж insomnia

бессо́нный прил (ночь) sleepless

беспо́рный прил indisputable

бесстра́шный прил fearless

бессты́дный прил shameless

беста́ктный прил tactless

бестолко́вый прил (глупый) stupid

бестсе́ллер (-а) м best seller

бесхозя́йственный прил (руководитель) inefficient

бесцве́тный прил colourless (BRIT), colorless (US)

бесце́льный прил futile

бесце́нный прил priceless

бесце́нок м: **за** ~ dirt cheap, for next to nothing

бесчелове́чный прил inhuman

бесче́|стить (-щу, -стишь; pf о~**)** несов перех (девушку) to violate

бесчи́сленный прил countless

бесчу́вственный прил (жестокий) unfeeling; (без сознания) senseless

бето́н (-а) м concrete

бетони́р|овать (-ую; pf за~**)** несов перех to concrete

бефстро́ганов м нескл boeuf или beef stroganoff

бе́шенств|о (-а) ср (МЕД) rabies; (раздражение) rage

бе́шеный прил (взгляд) furious; (характер, ураган) violent; (разг: цены) crazy

биатло́н (-а) м biathlon

Би-би-си́ ж сокр (= Брита́нская радиовеща́тельная корпора́ция) BBC

библе́йский прил biblical

библиогра́фи|я (-и) ж bibliography

библиоте́к|а (-и) ж library

библиоте́кар|ь (-я) м librarian

библиоте́чный прил library

Би́бли|я (-и) ж the Bible

бигуди́ ср/мн нескл curlers мн

бидо́н (-а) м (для молока) churn

бижуте́ри|я (-и) ж costume jewellery

би́знес (-а) м business

бизнесме́н (-а) м businessman

бики́ни ср нескл bikini

биле́т (-а) м ticket; (чле́нский) (membership) card; **обра́тный** ~ return (BRIT) или roundtrip (US) ticket; **входно́й** ~ entrance ticket (for standing room)

биллио́н (-а) м billion (one thousand million)

билья́рд (-а) м (игра) billiards

бино́кл|ь (-я) м binoculars мн

бинт (-а́) м bandage

бинт|ова́ть (-у́ю; pf за~**)** несов перех to bandage

биогра́фи|я (-и) ж biography

био́лог (-а) м biologist

биоло́ги|я (-и) ж biology

биосфе́р|а (-ы) ж biosphere

би́рж|а (-и) ж (КОММ) exchange; **фо́ндовая** ~ stock exchange или market

биржеви́к (-а́) м stockbroker

биржево́й прил (сделка) stock-exchange; ~ **бро́кер** stockbroker

би́рк|а (-и; gen pl **-ок)** ж tag

бирюза́ (-ы́) ж turquoise

бис межд: **Бис!** encore!

би́сер (-а) м собир glass beads мн

бискви́т (-а) м sponge (cake)

бит (-а) м (КОМП) byte

би́тв|а (-ы) ж battle

битко́м нареч: ~ **(наби́т)** (разг) jam-packed

бить (бью, бьёшь; imper **бей(те)**; pf **поби́ть)** несов перех to beat; (стёкла) to break ♦ (pf **проби́ть)** неперех (часы) to strike; ~ (impf) **в** +acc (в дверь) to bang at; (дождь, ветер) to beat against; (орудие) to hit; **его́ бьёт озно́б** he's got a fit of the shivers; **би́ться** несов возв (сердце) to beat; (стекло) to be breakable; (сражаться) to fight; **би́ться** (impf) **о** +acc (сердце) to beat; **би́ться** (impf) **над** +instr (над зада́чей) to struggle with

бифште́кс (-а) м steak

бла́г|а (-) мн rewards мн; **всех благ!** all the best!

бла́г|о (-а) ср benefit; см. также **бла́га**

благови́дный прил plausible

благодар|и́ть (-ю́, -и́шь; pf по~) несов перех to thank

благода́рность (-и) ж gratitude; thanks мн

благода́р|ный прил grateful; (тема) rewarding; **я Вам о́чень ~ен** I am very grateful to you

благодаря́ предл: ~ +dat thanks to ♦ союз: ~ **тому́, что** owing to the fact that

благ|о́й прил: ~**и́е наме́рения** good intentions мн

благополу́чи|е (-я) ср (в семье) welfare; (материальное) prosperity

благополу́чный прил successful; ~**ая семья́** good family

благоприя́тный прил favourable (BRIT), favorable (US)

благоразу́мный прил prudent

благоро́дный прил noble

благослов|и́ть (-лю́, -и́шь; impf **благословля́ть**) сов перех to bless

благосостоя́ни|е (-я) ср well-being, prosperity

благотвори́тел|ь (-я) м benefactor

благотвори́тельность (-и) ж charity

благотвори́тельн|ый прил

charitable; ~**ая организа́ция** charity (organization); ~ **конце́рт** charity concert

благоустро́енный прил (дом) with all modern conveniences

блаже́нный прил blissful; (РЕЛ) Blessed

блаже́нств|о (-а) ср bliss

бланк (-а) м form; (организации) headed notepaper

блат (-а) м (разг) connections мн; **по бла́ту** (разг) through (one's) connections

бледне́|ть (-ю; pf по~) несов to (grow) pale

бле́дный прил pale; (перен) dull

блеск (-а) м (огней) brilliance, brightness; (металла) shine; **с бле́ском** to perform brilliantly

блесн|у́ть (-у́, -ёшь) сов to flash; (на экза́мене) to do brilliantly

бле|сти́ (-щу́ <щу́шь или, блещешь) несов (звёзды, металл) to shine; (сделать) to sparkle

блестя́щий прил (звезда) bright; (металл) shining; (глаза) sparkling; (перен) brilliant

бле́|ять (-ю) несов to bleat

ближа́йший прил (город, дом) the nearest; (год) the next; (планы) immediate; (друг, участие) closest; ~ **ро́дственник** next of kin

бли́же сравн прил от **бли́зкий** ♦ сравн нареч от **бли́зко**

ближневосто́чный прил Middle-Eastern

бли́жний прил (город) neighbouring; **бли́жнее зарубе́жье** former Soviet republics; **Бли́жний Восто́к** Middle East

бли́зк|ие (-их) мн relatives мн

бли́зкий прил close; (конец) imminent; ~ **кому́-н** (интересы,

те́ма close to sb's heart; **~ по** +dat (*по содержа́нию, по це́ли*) similar *или* close in

бли́зко *нареч* near *или* close by ♦ *как сказ* not far off; **~ от** +gen near, close to

близне́ц (-**а́**) *м* (*обы́чно мн*) twin; **бра́тья/сёстры-близнецы́** twin brothers/sisters; *см. также* **Близнецы́**

Близнецы́ (-**о́в**) *мн* Gemini *ед*

близору́кий *прил* short-sighted (*BRIT*), nearsighted (*US*)

бли́зость (-**и**) *ж* proximity; (*интере́сов, мне́ний*) closeness

блин (-**а́**) *м* pancake

блок (-**а**) *м* bloc; (*ТЕХ*) unit

блока́да (-**ы**) *ж* (*ВОЕН*) siege; (*экономи́ческая*) blockade

блоки́р|овать (-**ую**) (*не*)*сов перех* to block; (*го́род*) to blockade

блокно́т (-**а**) *м* notebook, jotter

блонди́н (-**а**) *м*: **он ~ ~** he is blond

блонди́н|ка (-**ки**; *gen pl* -**ок**) *ж* blonde

блох|а́ (-**и́**; *nom pl* -**и**) *ж* flea

блужда́|ть (-**ю**) *несов* to wander *или* roam (around)

блу́з|ка (-**ки**; *gen pl* -**ок**) *ж* blouse

блю́д|о (-**а**) *ср* dish

блю|сти́ (-**ду́**, -**дёшь**; *pt* -**л**, -**ла́**, -**ло́**; *pf* **со~**) *несов перех* (*интере́сы*) to guard; (*чистоту́*) to maintain

боб (-**а**) *м* (*обы́чно мн*) bean

бобр (-**а́**) *м* beaver

Бог (-**а**; *voc* **Бо́же**) *м* God; **не дай ~!** God forbid!; **ра́ди Бо́га!** for God's sake!; **сла́ва Бо́гу** (*к сча́стью*) thank God

богате́|ть (-**ю**; *pf* **раз~**) *несов* to become rich

бога́тств|а (-) *мн* (*приро́дные*) resources *мн*

бога́тств|о (-**а**) *ср* wealth, riches *мн*; *см. также* **бога́тства**

бога́тый *прил* rich; **~ урожа́й** bumper harvest

богаты́р|ь (-**я́**) *м* warrior hero of Russian folk epics; (*перен*) Hercules

бога́ч (-**а́**) *м* rich man

боги́н|я (-**и**) *ж* goddess

Богоро́диц|а (-**ы**) *ж* the Virgin Mary

богосло́ви|е (-**я**) *ср* theology

богослуже́ни|е (-**я**) *ср* service

боготвор|и́ть (-**ю́**, -**и́шь**) *несов перех* to worship

бо́дрый *прил* energetic; (*настрое́ние, му́зыка*) cheerful

боеви́к (-**а́**) *м* militant; (*фильм*) action movie

боево́й *прил* military; (*настрое́ние, дух*) fighting

боеголо́в|ка (-**ки**; *gen pl* -**ок**) *ж* warhead

боеприпа́с|ы (-**ов**) *мн* ammunition *ед*

бо|е́ц (-**йца́**) *м* (*солда́т*) soldier

Бо́же *сущ см.* **Бог** ♦ *межд*: **(ты мой)!** good Lord *или* God!; **~!** кака́я красота́!** God, it's beautiful!; **~ упаси́** (*разг*) God forbid

бо́жеский *прил* (*РЕЛ*) divine; (*разг: це́ны, усло́вия*) half-decent

боже́ственный *прил* divine

Бо́ж|ий *прил* God's; **ка́ждый бо́жий день** (*разг*) every single day; **бо́жья коро́вка** ladybird

бо|й (-**я**; *loc sg* -**ю́**, *nom pl* -**и́**, *gen pl* -**ёв**) *м* battle; (*боксёров*) fight; (*бараба́нов*) beating; (*часо́в*) striking

бо́йкий *прил* (*речь, отве́т*) quick; (*продаве́ц*) smart; (*ме́сто*) busy

бойко́т (-**а**) *м* boycott

бойкоти́р|овать (-**ую**) (*не*)*сов перех* to boycott

бо́|йня (-йни; *gen pl* -ен) ж slaughterhouse, abattoir; (*на войне*) carnage

бок (-а; *loc sg* -ý, *nom pl* -á) м side

бока́л (-а) м (wine)glass, goblet

бо́ком *нареч* sideways

бокс (-а) м (СПОРТ) boxing; (МЕД) isolation ward

боксёр (-а) м boxer

болва́н (-а) м (*разг*) blockhead

Болга́ри|я (-и) ♦ ж Bulgaria

бо́лее *нареч* more; ~ **или ме́нее** more or less; ~ **того́** what's more; **тем** ~ **и** all the more so

боле́зненный *прил* sickly; (*укол*) painful; (*перен: подозрительность*) unhealthy; (*самолюбие*) unnatural

боле́зн|ь (-и) ж illness; (*заразная*) disease

боле́льщик (-а) м fan

бол|е́ть (-е́ю) *несов* ~ (+*instr*) to be ill (with); (СПОРТ): ~ **за** +*acc* to be a fan of; (*3sg* -и́т; *руки итп*) to ache

болеутоля́ющий *прил*: ~ее **сре́дство** painkiller

боло́н|ка (-ки; *gen pl* -ок) ж lapdog

боло́нь|я (-и) ж (*ткань*) lightweight waterproof material

боло́т|о (-а) *ср* marsh, bog

болт (-а) м bolt

болта́|ть (-ю) *несов перех* (*разг: вздор*) to talk ♦ *неперех* (*разговаривать*) to chat; (: *много*) to chatter; (*impf* **нога́ми**) to dangle one's legs

болтовн|я́ (-и́) ж (*разг*) waffle

болту́н (-а́) м chatterbox

болту́ш|ка (-ки; *gen pl* -ек) ж см. **болту́н**

бол|ь (-и) ж pain; **зубна́я** ~ toothache; **головна́я** ~ headache

больни́ц|а (-ы) ж hospital

больни́чный *прил* hospital; ~ **лист** medical certificate

бо́льно *нареч* (*удариться, упасть*) badly, painfully; (*обидеть*) deeply; ~**!** that hurts!; **мне** ~ I am in pain

больн|о́й *прил* (*рука итп*) sore; (*воображение*) morbid; (*нездоров*) ill, sick ♦ (-о́го) м (*болеющий*) sick person; (*пациент*) patient; ~ **вопро́с** a sore point

бо́льше *сравн прил от* **большо́й** ♦ *сравн нареч от* **мно́го** ♦ *нареч*: ~ +*gen* (*часа, килограмма итп*) more than; (*не хотеть, не жить*) anymore; **не бу́ду** (*разг*) I won't do it again; ~ **так не де́лай** don't do that again

большинств|о́ (-а́) *ср* majority

большо́й *прил* big, large; (*радость*) great; (*дети*) grown-up; **бо́льшей ча́стью, по бо́льшей ча́сти** for the most part; ~**ая бу́ква** capital letter

боля́ч|ка (-ки; *gen pl* -ек) ж sore

бо́мб|а (-ы) ж bomb

бомбардиро́в|ка (-ки; *gen pl* -ок) ж bombing

бомбардиро́вщик (-а) м bomber

бомб|и́ть (-лю́, -и́шь) *несов перех* to bomb

бомбоубе́жищ|е (-а) *ср* bomb shelter

бомж (-а́) м homeless person

бордо́вый *прил* dark red, wine

бордю́р (-а) м (*тротуара*) kerb (BRIT), curb (US); (*салфетки*) border

бор|е́ц (-ца́) м (*за свободу итп*) fighter; (СПОРТ) wrestler

борм|ота́ть (-очу́, -о́чешь) *несов перех* to mutter

борода́ (*acc sg* -оду, *gen sg* -оды́, *nom pl* -оды, *gen pl* -о́д, *dat pl*

-**ода́м**) ж beard

борода́в|ка (-**ки**; gen pl -**ок**) ж wart

бор|о́ться (-**ю́сь, -ешься**) несов возв (СПОРТ) to wrestle; ~ (impf) (с +instr) to fight (with или against)

борт (-**а**; acc sg за́-, loc sg за́-, instr sg за бо́ртом или за ~о́м, loc sg -у́, nom pl -а́) м side; на -у́ или ~ on board, aboard; **челове́к за ~о́м!** man overboard!

бортпроводни́к (-а́) м steward (on plane)

бортпроводни́ц|а (-**ы**) ж air hostess, stewardess (on plane)

борщ (-а́) м borsch (beetroot-based soup)

борьб|а́ (-**ы́**) ж (за мир) fight, struggle; (СПОРТ) wrestling

босико́м нареч barefoot

босо́й прил barefoot

босоно́ж|ка (-**ки**; gen pl -**ек**) ж (обычно мн) sandal; (: с закры́тым носом) slingback

бота́ник|а (-**и**) ж botany

боти́н|ок (-**ка**; gen pl обычно мн) ankle boot

бо́цман (-**а**) м boatswain, bosun

бо́ч|ка (-**ки**; gen pl -**ек**) ж barrel

бо|я́ться (-**ю́сь, -и́шься**) несов возв: ~ (+gen) to be afraid (of); ~ (impf) +infin to be afraid of doing или to do

бра́во межд bravo

бразды́ мн: ~ **правле́ния** the reins мн of power

брак (-**а**) м (супружество) marriage; (продукция) rejects мн; (дефект) flaw

брако́ванный прил reject

брак|ова́ть (-**у́ю**; pf за-) несов перех to reject

браконье́р (-**а**) м poacher

браконье́рств|о (-**а**) ср poaching

бракосочета́ни|е (-**я**) ср marriage ceremony

бран|и́ть (-**ю́, -и́шь**) несов to scold

брасле́т (-**а**) м (на часа́х) bracelet; (украшение) bangle

брасс (-**а**) м breaststroke

брат (-**а**; nom pl -**ья**, gen pl -**ьев**) м brother; **двою́родный** ~ cousin

бра́тск|ий прил brotherly, fraternal; **~ая моги́ла** communal grave

бра́тств|о (-**а**) ср brotherhood

бра|ть (**беру́, берёшь**; pt -**л**, -**ла́, -ло**; pf **взять**) несов перех to take; (билет) to get; (работника) to take on; (барьер) to clear; (разг: арестовать) to nick; **бра́ться** (pf **взя́ться**) несов возв: **бра́ться за** +acc (хватать рукой) to take hold of; (за работу) to get down to; (за книгу) to begin (за решение проблемы) to take on; **бра́ться (взя́ться) за ум** to see sense

бра́тья etc сущ см. **брат**

бра́чный прил (контракт) marriage; (союз) conjugal

бревн|о́ (-**а́**; nom pl **брёвна**, gen pl **брёвен**) ср log; (СПОРТ) the beam

бред (-**а**; loc sg -**у́**) м delirium; (вздор) nonsense

бре́|дить (-**жу, -дишь**) несов to be delirious; ~ (impf) **кем-н/чем-н** to be mad about sb/sth

брезгли́вый прил (человек) fastidious; (взгляд) disgusted

брезг|овать (-**ую**; pf **по**-) несов: ~ +instr to be fastidious about

брезе́нт (-**а**) м tarpaulin

бре́м|я (-**ени**; как **вре́мя**; см. Table 4) ср burden

бр|ести́ (-**еду́, -едёшь**; pt -**ёл**, -**ела́, -ело́**) несов to trudge

брига́д|а (-**ы**) ж (ВОЕН) brigade,

(work) team

бригади́р (-а) м team leader

бриллиа́нт (-а) м (cut) diamond

брита́н|ец (-ца) м Briton; **~цы** the British

Брита́ни|я (-и) ж Britain

брита́нский прил British

бри́тв|а (-ы) ж razor; **безопа́сная ~** safety razor

бритоголо́в|ый (-ого) м skinhead

бри|ть (-е́ю, -е́ешь; pf по~и́ть) несов перех (человека) to shave; (бо́роду) to shave off; **~ться** (pf по~и́ться) несов возв to shave

бри́финг (-а) м briefing

бро́в|ь (-и; gen pl -е́й) ж eyebrow

бро|ди́ть (-жу́, -дишь) несов to wander

бродя́г|а (-и) м/ж tramp

броже́ни|е (-я) ср fermentation; (перен: в обществе) ferment

бро́кер (-а) м broker

бронежиле́т (-а) м bullet-proof jacket

бронетранспортёр (-а) м armoured (BRIT) или armored (US) personnel carrier

бро́нз|а (-ы) ж bronze

брони́р|овать (-ую; pf за~) (не)сов перех to reserve

бронх (-а) м bronchial tube

бронхи́т (-а) м bronchitis

бро́н|я (-и) ж reservation

брон|я́ (-и́) ж armour (BRIT) или armor (US) plating

броса́|ть (-ю) несов от **бро́сить**; **~ся** несов от **броси́ться** ♦ возв: **~ся снежка́ми/камня́ми** to throw snowballs/stones at each other

бро́|сить (-шу, -сишь; impf **броса́ть**) сов перех (ка́мень, мяч итп) to throw; (я́корь, се́ти) to cast; (семью́, друга) to abandon; (войска́) to dispatch;

(спорт) to give up; **меня́ ~сило в жар** I broke out in a sweat;

бро́сить (~ pf) +infin to give up doing; **~ся** (impf **броса́ться**) сов возв: **~ на** +acc (на врага́) to throw o.s. at; **броса́ться** (~ся pf) в **ата́ку** to rush to the attack

бро́сов|ый прил (разг: вещь) trashy; **~ая цена́** giveaway price

бро́шк|а (-ки; gen pl -ек) ж brooch

брош|ь (-и) см. **бро́шка**

брошю́р|а (-ы) ж (книжка) booklet

брус (-а; nom pl -ья, gen pl -ьев) м beam; см. та́кже **бру́сья**

брусни́к|а (-и) ж cowberry

брус|о́к (-ка́) м (для то́чки) whetstone; (мыла) bar

бру́сь|я (-ев) мн parallel bars мн

бру́тто прил неизм gross

бры́з|гать (-жу, -жешь) несов to splash; (-гаю; опры́скивать) **~ на** +acc to spray

бры́зг|и (-) мн splashes мн; (ме́лкие) spray ед

бры́нз|а (-ы) ж feta cheese

брю́кв|а (-ы) ж swede

брю́к|и (-) мн trousers мн, pants мн (US)

брюне́т (-а) м: **он ~** he has dark hair

брюне́т|ка (-ки; gen pl -ок) ж brunette

Брюссе́л|ь (-я) м Brussels

брюшн|о́й прил abdominal; **~ тиф** typhoid (fever)

БТР сокр = **бронетранспортёр**

бу́блик (-а) м bagel

бу́бн|ы (-ён; dat pl -нам) мн (КА́РТЫ) diamonds мн

буг|о́р (-ра́) м mound; (на ко́же) lump

Будапе́шт (-а) м Budapest

будди́ст (-а) м Buddhist

бу́дем *несов см.* **быть**

бу́дет *несов см.* **быть** ♦ *част* that's enough; **~ тебе́!** that's enough from you!

бу́дешь *etc несов см.* **быть**

буди́льник (-а) *м* alarm clock

буди́ть (-жу́, -дишь; *pf* **раз~)** *несов перех* to wake (up), awaken

бу́дка (-ки; *gen pl* **-ок)** *ж* (*сторожа*) hut; (*для собаки*) kennel; **телефо́нная ~** phone box

бу́дни (-ей) *мн* working *или* week days *мн*; (*перен: повседневность*) routine *ед*

бу́дто *союз* (*якобы*) supposedly; (*словно*): **(как) (бы)** as if; **он уверя́ет, ~ сам её ви́дел** he claims to have seen her himself

бу́ду *etc несов см.* **быть**

бу́дущее (-его) *ср* the future; **в ~ем** in the future

бу́дущий *прил* (*следующий*) next; (*предстоящий*) future; **~ее вре́мя** future tense

бу́дь(те) *несов см.* **быть** ♦ *союз*: **будь то** be it

бужени́на (-ы) *ж* cold cooked and seasoned pork

буй (-я; *nom pl* **-й)** *м* buoy

бу́йвол (-а) *м* buffalo

бу́йный *прил* wild; (*растительность*) luxuriant, lush

бук (-а) *м* beech

бу́ква (-ы) *ж* letter

буква́льный *прил* literal

буква́рь (-я́) *м* first reading book

буке́т (-а) *м* bouquet

букинисти́ческий *прил*: **~ магази́н** second-hand bookshop

букле́т (-а) *м* booklet

букси́р (-а) *м* tug; (*трос*) towrope

була́вка (-ки; *gen pl* **-ок)** *ж* pin

бу́лка (-ки; *gen pl* **-ок)** *ж* roll; (*белый хлеб*) loaf

бу́лочка (-ки; *gen pl* **-ек)** *ж* small

roll

бу́лочная (-ой) *ж* baker, baker's

булы́жник (-а) *м* cobblestone

булы́жный *прил*: **~ая мостова́я** cobbled street

бульва́р (-а) *м* boulevard

бульва́рный *прил* boulevard; **~ая пре́сса** gutter press

бульдо́г (-а) *м* bulldog

бульдо́зер (-а) *м* bulldozer

бульо́н (-а; *part gen* **-у)** *м* stock

бум (-а) *м* boom

бума́га (-и) *ж* paper; **це́нные ~и** securities

бума́жка (-ки; *gen pl* **-ек)** *ж* piece of paper

бума́жник (-а) *м* wallet, pocketbook (*US*)

бума́жный *прил* paper

бу́нкер (-а) *м* bunker

бунт (-а) *м* (*мятеж*) riot; (*: на корабле*) mutiny

бунтова́ть (-у́ю) *несов* (*см сущ*) to riot; to mutiny

бура́вить (-лю, -ишь; *pf* **пробура́вить)** *несов перех* to drill

бура́н (-а) *м* blizzard, snowstorm

буре́ние (-я) *ср* boring, drilling

буржуази́я (-и) *ж* bourgeoisie; **ме́лкая ~** petty bourgeoisie

буржуа́зный *прил* bourgeois

бури́ть (-ю́, -и́шь; *pf* **про~)** *несов перех* to bore, drill

бурли́ть (-ю́, -и́шь) *несов* (*ручей*) to bubble; (*толпа*) to seethe

бу́рный *прил* (*погода, океан*) stormy; (*чувство*) wild; (*рост*) rapid

бурово́й *прил* boring, drilling; **~ая вы́шка** derrick; **~ая сква́жина** bore(hole)

бу́рый *прил* brown

бу́ря (-и) *ж* storm

бу́с|ы (-) мн beads мн

бутафо́рия (-и) ж (ТЕАТР) props мн; (перен) sham

бутербро́д (-а) м sandwich

буто́н (-а) м bud

бу́тс|а (-ы) ж football boot

буты́л|ка (-ки; gen pl -ок) ж bottle

буты́лочный прил bottle; (цвет) bottle-green

бу́фер (-а; nom pl -а́) м buffer

буфе́т (-а) м snack bar; (шкаф) sideboard

буфе́тчик (-а) м barman

буха́н|ка (-ки; gen pl -ок) ж loaf

Бухаре́ст (-а) м Bucharest

бухга́лтер (-а) м accountant, book-keeper

бухгалте́ри|я (-и) ж accountancy, book-keeping; (отдел) accounts office

бухга́лтерск|ий прил book-keeping, accountancy; **~ие кни́ги** books; **~ учёт** book-keeping, accountancy

бу́хт|а (-ы) ж bay

буш|ева́ть (-у́ю) несов (пожар, ураган) to rage

KEYWORD

бы част 1 (выражает возможность): купи́л бы, е́сли бы бы́ли де́ньги I would buy it if I had the money; я бы давно́ уже́ купи́л э́ту кни́гу, е́сли бы у меня́ бы́ли де́ньги I would have bought this book long ago if I had the money

2 (выражает пожелание): я бы хоте́л поговори́ть с тобо́й I would like to speak to you

3 (выражает совет): ты бы написа́л ей you should write to her

4 (выражает опасение): не захвати́л бы нас дождь I hope

we don't get caught in the rain; **отдохну́ть/погуля́ть бы** it would be nice to have a rest/go for a walk

---

быва́ло част expresses repeated action in the past; **~ сиди́м и разгова́риваем** we used to или would sit and talk

быва́|ть (-ю) несов (посеща́ть) to be; (случа́ться) to happen, take place; **он ~ет у нас ча́сто** he often comes to see us; **как ни в чём не ~ло** (разг) as if nothing had happened

бы́вший прил former

бык (-а́) м bull; (рабочий) ox

был etc несов см. быть

были́н|а (-ы) ж heroic poem

быль (-и) ж true story

бы́стро нареч quickly

быстрот|а́ (-ы́) ж speed; (ума, рук) quickness

бы́стрый прил (машина итп) fast; (руки, взгляд, речь) quick

быт (-а; loc sg -у́) м life; (повседневность) everyday life; **слу́жба бы́та** consumer services

бытов|о́й прил everyday; **~о́е обслу́живание населе́ния** consumer services; **~а́я те́хника** household electrical appliances

---

KEYWORD

быть (см. Table 21) несов 1 (omitted in present tense) to be; **кни́га на столе́** the book is on the table; **за́втра я бу́ду в шко́ле** I will be at school tomorrow; **дом был на краю́ го́рода** the house was или stood on the edge of the town; **на ней краси́вое пла́тье** she is wearing a beautiful dress; **вчера́ был дождь** it rained yesterday

2 (часть составного сказ) to be; **я хочу́ быть учи́телем** I want to

be a teacher; **я был рад ви́деть
тебя́** I was happy to see you; **так и
быть!** so be it!; **как быть?** what is
to be done?; **э́того не мо́жет
быть** that's impossible; **кто/како́й
бы то ни́ был** whoever/whatever it
might be; **бу́дьте добры́!** excuse
me!; **бу́дьте добры́, позови́те
его́!** would you be so good или
kind as to call him?; **бу́дьте
здоро́вы!** take care!
*3 (образует будущее время;
+impf vb)*: **ве́чером я бу́ду писа́ть
пи́сьма** I'll be writing letters this
evening; **я бу́ду люби́ть тебя́
всегда́** I'll love you forever

бью(сь) *etc несов см.* **бить(ся)**

бюдже́т (-а) *м* budget; **дохо́дный
~ revenue; **расхо́дный ~
expenditure

бюдже́тник (-а) *м* person working in
a state-funded institution

бюдже́тн|ый *прил* budgetary;
(организация) state-funded

бюллете́н|ь (-я) *м* bulletin; *(на
вы́борах)* ballot paper; *(справка)*
medical certificate

бюро́ *ср нескл* office; **~ нахо́док**
lost property office

бюрокра́т (-а) *м* bureaucrat
бюрокра́ти|я (-и) *ж* bureaucracy
бюст (-а) *м* bust
бюстга́льтер (-а) *м* bra

В, в

В *сокр (= вольт)* v.

KEYWORD

в *предл; +acc* 1 *(о месте
направления: in(to))* **я положи́л
кни́гу в портфе́ль** I put the book

in(to) my briefcase; **я сел в
маши́ну** I got in(to) the car
2 *(уе́хать, пойти́)* to; **он уе́хал в
Москву́** he went to Moscow
3 *(об изменении состояния)*:
погружа́ться в рабо́ту to be
absorbed in one's work
4 *(об объекте физического
действия)*: **он постуча́л в дверь**
he knocked on the door; **он
посмотре́л мне в глаза́** he looked
me in the eyes; **мать поцелова́ла
меня́ в щёку** mother kissed me on
the cheek
5 *(о времени совершения
чего-н)*: **он пришёл в
понеде́льник** he came on
Monday; **я ви́дел его́ в про́шлом
году́** I saw him last year; **я
встре́тил его́ в два часа́** I met
him at two o'clock; **э́то случи́лось
в ма́рте/в двадца́том ве́ке** it
happened in March/in the
twentieth century
6 *(о размере, количестве)*: **ве́сом
в 3 то́нны** 3 tons или tonnes in
weight; *(+prp)*: **дра́ма в трёх частя́х**
a drama in three acts; **в пяти́ ме́трах
от доро́ги** five metres *(BRIT)* или
meters *(US)* from the road
7 *(о соотношении величин)*: **в
два ра́за бо́льше/длинне́е** twice
as big/long; **во мно́го раз
лу́чше/умне́е** much better/cleverer
8 *(обозначает форму, вид)*:
брю́ки в кле́тку checked trousers;
лека́рство в табле́тках medicine
in tablet form
9 *(+prp; о месте)* in; **ко́шка сиди́т в
корзи́не** the cat is sitting in the
basket; **я живу́ в дере́вне** I live in
the country; **сын у́чится в шко́ле**
my son is at school
10 *(о чём-н облегающем,
покрыва́ющем)*: **ру́ки в кра́ске**

са́же hands covered in paint/soot; **това́р в упако́вке** packaged goods

11 (об одежде) in; **мужчи́на в очка́х/в ша́пке** a man in или wearing glasses/a hat

12 (о состоянии): **быть в у́жасе/ негодова́нии** to be terrified/ indignant

в. сокр (= век) с; (= восто́к) E

ваго́н (-а) м (пассажирский) carriage (BRIT), coach (BRIT), car (US); (товарный) wagon (BRIT), truck; **спа́льный ~** couchette car; **мя́гкий ~** sleeping car; **~рестора́н** dining (BRIT) или club (US) car

ва́жный прил important

ва́з|**а** (-ы) ж vase

вазели́н (-а) м Vaseline ®

вака́нси|**я** (-и) ж vacancy

вака́нтн|**ый** прил vacant; **~ая до́лжность** vacancy

ва́куум (-а) м vacuum

вакци́н|**а** (-ы) ж vaccine

вакцини́р|**овать** (-ую) (не)сов перех to vaccinate

вал (-а; loc sg -ý, nom pl -ы́) м (насыпь) bank; (ТЕХ, стержень) shaft; (ТЕХ) weld; (картофель) to boil; (волна) breaker

ва́лен|**ок** (-ка) м felt boot

валериа́нк|**а** (-и) ж valerian drops

вале́т (-а) м (КАРТЫ) jack

ва́лик (-а) м (в механизме) cylinder; (для краски) roller; (подушка) bolster

вал|**и́ть** (-ю́, -ишь; pf с~ или по~) несов перех (заставлять падать) to knock over; (рубить) to fell; (pf с~; разг: бросать) to dump ♦ неперех (дым, пар) to pour out; **~** (с~ pf) вину́ на +асс (разг) to point the finger at; **~ся** (pf с~ся или по~ся) несов возв

(па́дать) to fall; **~ся** (impf) **с ног** (разг) to be dead on one's feet

валово́й прил (доход) gross

валу́н (-а́) м boulder

вальс (-а) м waltz

валю́т|**а** (-ы) ж currency ♦ собир foreign currency

валю́тный прил currency; **~ курс** rate of exchange

валя́|**ть** (-ю) несов перех (катать) to roll; (pf с~; скатывать) to shape; **~ся** несов возв (кататься) to roll about; (разг: человек, бумаги итп) to lie about

вам etc мест см. **вы**

вампи́р (-а) м vampire

вани́ль (-и) ж vanilla

ва́нн|**а** (-ы) ж bath

ва́нн|**ая** (-ой) ж bathroom

ва́рвар (-а) м barbarian

ва́рварство (-а) ср barbarism; (жестокость) barbarity

ва́реж|**ка** (-ки; gen pl -ек) ж mitten

ва́реный прил boiled

варе́нь|**е** (-я) ср jam

вариа́нт (-а) м variant

вар|**и́ть** (-ю́, -ишь; pf с~) несов перех (обед) to cook; (суп, кофе) to make; (картофель) to boil; (ТЕХ) to weld; **~ся** (pf с~ся) несов возв (обед) to be cooking

Варша́в|**а** (-ы) ж Warsaw

варьете́ ср нескл variety show

варьи́р|**овать** (-ую) несов (не)перех to vary

вас мест см. **вы**

ва́т|**а** (-ы) ж cotton wool (BRIT), (absorbent) cotton (US)

ва́тман (-а) м heavy paper for drawing etc

ва́тный прил cotton-wool (BRIT), absorbent cotton (US)

ватру́ш|**ка** (-ки; gen pl -ек) ж curd tart

ватт (-а) *м* watt

ва́учер (-а) *м* voucher

ва́ф|**ля** (-**ли**; *gen pl* -**ель**) *ж* wafer

ва́хт|**а** (-ы) *ж* watch; **стоя́ть** (*impf*) **на ~е** to keep watch

вахтёр (-а) *м* caretaker, janitor (*esp US, SCOTTISH*)

ваш (-**его**; *f* -**а**, *nt* -**е**, *pl* -**и**; *как* **наш**; см. Table 9) *притяж мест* your; **э́то ва́ше** this is yours

Вашингто́н (-а) *м* (ГЕО) Washington

вбе|жа́ть (*как* **бежа́ть**; см. Table 20; *impf* **вбега́ть**) *сов*: ~ (**в** +*acc*) to run in(to)

вбить (**вобью́, вобьёшь**; *impf* **вбива́ть**) *сов перех*: ~ (**в** +*acc*) to drive *или* hammer in(to)

вблизи́ *нареч* nearby ♦ *предл*: ~ +*gen или* **от** +*gen* near to

вбок *нареч* sideways

вбро́|**сить** (-**шу**, -**сишь**; *impf* **вбра́сывать**) *сов перех* to throw in

ввали́ться (-**юсь**, -**ишься**; *impf* **вва́ливаться**) *сов возв* (*щёки, глаза*) to become sunken

введе́ни|**е** (-**я**) *ср* introduction

ввезти́ (-**у́**, -**ёшь**; *pt* **ввёз**, -**ла́**, -**ло́**; *impf* **ввози́ть**) *сов перех* to take in; (*в страну*) to import

вверх *нареч* up ♦ *предл*: ~ **по** +*dat* up; ~ **по тече́нию** upstream; **в до́ме всё** ~ **дном** (*разг*) everything in the house is topsy-turvy; ~ **нога́ми** (*разг*) upside down

вверху́ *нареч* up ♦ *предл*: ~ +*gen* at the top of

вве|сти́ (-**ду́**, -**дёшь**; *pt* -**ёл**, -**ела́**, *impf* **вводи́ть**) *сов перех* to take in; (*лекарство*) to inject; (*в компьютер*) to enter; (*закон*) to introduce; (*сделать*

действующим): ~ **что-н в** +*acc* to put sth into

ввиду́ *предл*: ~ +*gen* in view of ♦ *союз*: ~ **того́, что** in view of the fact that

ввод (-а) *м* bringing in; (*данных*) input, feeding in

вво|ди́ть (-**жу́**, -**дишь**) *несов от* **ввести́**

вво́дн|ый *прил* introductory; ~**ое сло́во** parenthesis

ввоз (-а) *м* (*процесс*) importation; (*импорт*) imports *мн*

вво|зи́ть (-**жу́**, -**зишь**) *несов от* **ввезти́**

ввозн|о́й *прил* imported; ~**ые по́шлины** import duty

ВВП *м сокр* (= *валово́й вну́тренний проду́кт*) GDP

вглубь *нареч* (down) into the depths ♦ *предл*: ~ +*gen* (*вниз*) into the depths of; (*внутрь*) into the heart of

вда|ва́ться (-**ю́сь**) *несов от* **вда́ться**

вдав|и́ть (-**лю́**, -**ишь**; *impf* **вда́вливать**) *сов перех*: ~ (**в** +*acc*) to press in(to)

вдалеке́ *нареч* in the distance; ~ **от** +*gen* a long way from

вдали́ *нареч* = **вдалеке́**

вдаль *нареч* into the distance

вда́ться (*как* **дать**; см. Table 16; *impf* **вдава́ться**) *сов возв*: ~ **в** +*acc* to jut out into (*перен*): **в рассужде́ния** to get caught up in; **вдава́ться** (~ *pf*) **в подро́бности** to go into details

вдво́е *нареч* (*сложить*) in two; ~ **сильне́е** twice as strong

вдвоём *нареч*: **они́ живу́т** ~ the two of them live together

вдвойне́ *нареч* double (the amount)

вде́|ть (-**ну**, -**нешь**; *impf*

вдева́ть *сов перех* to put in

вдоба́вок *нареч (разг)* in addition ♦ *предл*: ~ к +*dat* in addition to

вдов|**а́** (-ы́; *nom pl* -ы) *ж* widow

вдове́ц (-ца́) *м* widower

вдо́воль *нареч* to one's heart's content

вдоль *нареч (сломаться)* lengthways *предл*: ~ +*gen* along

вдох (-а) *м* inhalation; **де́лать** (**сде́лать** *pf*) ~ to breathe in

вдохнове́ни|**е** (-я) *ср* inspiration

вдохнов|**и́ть** (-лю́, -и́шь; *impf* **вдохновля́ть**) *сов перех* to inspire

вдохн|**у́ть** (-у́; *impf* **вдыха́ть**) *сов перех (воздух)* to breathe in; *(дым, лекарство)* to inhale

вдре́безги *нареч* to smithereens

вдруг *нареч* suddenly; (*а если*) what if

вду́ма|**ться** (-юсь; *impf* **вду́мываться**) *сов возв*: ~ в +*acc* to think over

вдыха́|**ть** (-ю) *несов от* **вдохну́ть**

вегетариа́н|**ец** (-ца) *м* vegetarian

вегетариа́нский *прил* vegetarian

ве́да|**ть** (-ю) *несов*: ~ +*instr (управлять)* to be in charge of

ве́дени|**е** (-я) *ср* authority

веде́ни|**е** (-я) *ср* conducting; *(войны)* waging; ~ **хозя́йства** housekeeping

ведёт(ся) *etc несов см.* **вести́(сь)**

ве́дом *ср о/без* ~ **а кого́-н** *(согласие)* with/without sb's consent; *(уведомление)* with/without sb's knowledge

ве́домост|**ь** (-и; *gen pl* -е́й) *ж* register; **расчётная** *или* **платёжная** ~ payroll

ве́домств|**о** (-а) *ср* department

ведр|**о́** (-а́; *nom pl* **вёдра**, *gen pl* **вёдер**) *ср* bucket, pail

веду́щ|**ий** *прил* leading ♦ (-его) *м* presenter

ведь *нареч (в вопросе)*: ~ **ты хо́чешь пое́хать?** you do want to go, don't you?; ~ **она́ не спра́вится одна́!** she can't surely manage alone! ♦ *союз (о причине)* seeing as; **пое́шь,** ~ **ты го́лоден** you should eat, seeing as you're hungry

ве́дьм|**а** (-ы) *ж* witch

ве́ер (-а; *nom pl* -а́) *м* fan

ве́жливый *прил* polite

везде́ *нареч* everywhere; ~ **и всю́ду** everywhere you go

вездехо́д (-а) *м* ≈ Landrover ®

везе́ни|**е** (-я) *ср* luck

вез|**ти́** (-у́, -ёшь) *несов перех* to transport, take; *(сани)* to pull; *(тачку)* to push ♦ (*pf* **по**~) *безл*: ~ +*dat (разг)* to be lucky

век (-а; *nom pl* -а́) *м* century; *(период)* age; **на** -а́, **во ве́ки** -о́в forever

ве́к|**о** (-а) *ср* eyelid

веково́й *прил* ancient

ве́ксель (-я; *nom pl* -я́) *м* promissory note

вел|**е́ть** (-ю́, -и́шь) *(не)сов*: ~ +*dat* to order

велика́н (-а) *м* giant

вели́к|**ий** *прил* great ♦ *как сказ* **сапоги́ мне велики́** the boots are too big for me; ~**ие держа́вы** the Great Powers

Великобрита́ни|**я** (-и) *ж* Great Britain

великоду́шный *прил* magnanimous, big-hearted

великору́сский *прил* Great Russian

великоле́пный *прил* magnificent

вели́чественный *прил* majestic

величин|**а́** (-ы) *ж* size; *(МАТ)* quantity

велого́н|ка (-ки; gen pl **-ок)** ж
cycle race

велосипе́д (-а) м bicycle

вельве́т (-а) м corduroy

Ве́н|а (-ы) ж Vienna

ве́н|а (-ы) ж vein

Ве́нгри|я (-и) ж Hungary

венери́ческий прил venereal

ве́ник (-а) м broom

вен|о́к (-ка́) м wreath

вентиля́тор (-а) м (ventilator) fan

венча́|ть (-ю; pf **об-** или **по-)**
несов перех to marry (in church); **~**
(impf) **на ца́рство кого́-н** to crown
sb; **~ся** (pf **об-ся)** несов возв to
be married (in church)

ве́р|а (-ы) ж faith; (в Бо́га) belief

вера́нд|а (-ы) ж verandah

ве́рб|а (-ы) ж pussy willow

верблю́д (-а) м camel

ве́рбн|ый прил: **Ве́рбное
воскресе́нье** ≈ Palm Sunday

верб|ова́ть (-у́ю; pf **за-)** несов
перех to recruit

верёв|ка (-ки; gen pl **-ок)** ж
(толстая) rope; (тонкая) string

ве́р|ить (-ю, -ишь; pf **по-)**
несов: **~** +dat to believe;
(доверять) to trust; **~ (по-** pf) **в
кого́-н/что-н** to believe in sb/sth; **~
(по-** pf) **на́ сло́во кому́-н** to take
sb at his итп word; **~ся** несов
безл: **не -́ится, что э́то пра́вда**
it's hard to believe it's true

вермише́л|ь (-и) ж vermicelli

ве́рмут (-а) м vermouth

верне́е вводн сл or rather; **~
всего́** most likely

ве́рно нареч (преданно) faithfully;
(правильно) correctly ♦ как сказ
that's right

верн|у́ть (-у́, -ёшь) сов перех to
return; (долг) to pay
back; (здоровье, надежду) to
restore; **~ся** сов возв: **~ся (к** +dat)

to return (to)

ве́рный прил (друг) faithful;
(надёжный) sure; (правильный)
correct; **~ сло́ву** true to one's word

ве́ровани|е (-я) ср (обычно мн)
faith

вероиспове́дани|е (-я) ср faith

вероло́мный прил (друг)
treacherous; (нападение) deceitful

вероя́тно как сказ it is probable
♦ вводн сл probably

вероя́тн|ый прил probable; **~ее
всего́** most likely или probably

ве́рси|я (-и) ж version

верста́к (-а́) м (TEX) (work)bench

вер|те́ть (-чу́, -тишь) несов
перех (руль) to turn; **~** (impf) **в
рука́х что-н** to fiddle with sth; **~ся**
несов возв (колесо) to spin;
(человек) to fidget

вертика́льный прил vertical

вертолёт (-а) м helicopter

ве́рующ|ий (-его) м believer

верф|ь (-и) ж shipyard

верх (-а; loc sg **-у́,** nom pl **-и́)** м
(дома, стола; обуви) upper; **~
соверше́нства/глу́пости** the
height of perfection/stupidity; см.
также **верхи́**

верх|и́ (-о́в) мн: **в -а́х** at the top;
встре́ча/перегово́ры в -а́х
summit meeting/talks

ве́рхн|ий прил top; **~яя оде́жда**
outer clothing или garments;
Ве́рхняя пала́та Upper Chamber

верхо́вный прил supreme;
Верхо́вный Суд High Court
(BRIT), Supreme Court (US)

верхов|о́й прил: **~а́я езда́** horse
(BRIT) или horseback (US) riding

верхо́м нареч astride

верху́ш|ка (-ки; gen pl **-ек)** ж
(дерева, насыпи) top; (перен:
правящая) elite

верши́н|а (-ы) ж top; (горы)

summit

вес (-а; *nom pl* -а́) *м* weight; (*перен: влияние*) authority

веселе́|ть (-ю; *pf* по~) *несов* to cheer up

весел|и́ть (-ю́, -и́шь; *pf* раз~) *несов перех* to amuse; ~ся *несов возв* to have fun

ве́село *нареч* cheerfully ♦ *как сказ:* **здесь** ~ it's fun here; **мне** ~ I'm having fun

весёлый *прил* cheerful

весе́ль|е (-я) *ср* merriment

весе́нний *прил* spring

ве́с|ить (-шу, -сишь) *несов* to weigh

ве́ский *прил* (*аргумент*) potent

весл|о́ (-а́; *nom pl* вёсла, *gen pl* вёсел) *ср* оаг

весн|а́ (-ы́; *nom pl* вёсны, *gen pl* вёсен) *ж* spring

весно́й *нареч* in (the) spring

весну́шк|а (-и; *gen pl* -ек) *ж* freckle

весо́мый *прил* (*вклад*) substantial

вес|ти́ (-ду́, -дёшь; *pt* вёл, -ла́, -ло́) *несов перех* to take; (*машину*) to drive; (*корабль*) to navigate; (*отряд*) to lead; (*заседание*) to chair; (*работу*) to conduct; (*хозяйство*) to run; (*записи*) to keep ♦ (*pf* привести́) *неперех:* **вести́к** ~ *+dat* to lead to; **вести́** (*impf*) **себя́** to behave; **вести́сь** *несов возв* (*расследование*) to be carried out; (*переговоры*) to go on

вестибю́л|ь (-я) *м* lobby

вест|ь (-и) *ж* news; **пропада́ть** (**пропа́сть** *pf*) **бе́з ~и** (*ВОЕН*) to go missing; **без** ~ **и** *или* **пропа́вший** (*ВОЕН*) missing feared dead; **Бог** ~ **кто**/**что** (*разг*) God knows who/ what

вес|ы́ (-о́в) *мн* scales *мн*;

(*созвездие*): **Весы́** Libra

весь (всего́; *f* вся, *nt* всё, *pl* все; *см. Table 13*) *мест* all; **всего́ хоро́шего** *или* **до́брого!** all the best!

ве́тв|ь (-и; *gen pl* -ей) *ж* branch

ве́т|ер (-ра) *м* wind

ветера́н (-а) *м* veteran

ветерина́р (-а) *м* vet (*BRIT*), veterinarian (*US*)

ве́т|ка (-ки; *gen pl* -ок) *ж* branch

ве́то *ср нескл* veto

ве́треный *прил* windy

ветрово́й *прил:* ~ **о́е стекло́** windscreen (*BRIT*), windshield (*US*)

ветря́н|ка (-ки) *ж* (*МЕД*) chickenpox

ветряно́й *прил* wind-powered; ~**я́я о́спа** chickenpox

ве́тхий *прил* (*дом*) dilapidated; (*одежда*) shabby; **Ве́тхий Заве́т** the Old Testament

ветчин|а́ (-ины́; *nom pl* -и́ны) *ж* ham

ве́х|а (-и) *ж* landmark

ве́чер (-а; *nom pl* -а́) *м* evening; (*праздник*) party

вече́рний *прил* evening

вече́рнее отделе́ние - People who do not want to give up their job may opt to do a degree by taking courses in the evening. This course runs over 4 days a week with over 20 contact hours a week and is very much like the day-time course. Because of the reduced hours the entire degree takes 6 years to complete. See also notes at **зао́чный** and **о́чный**.

ве́чером *нареч* in the evening

ве́чно *нареч* eternally; (*разг: жаловаться*) perpetually

ве́чность (-и) *ж* eternity

ве́чный *прил* eternal, everlasting

ве́шалка (-ки; *gen pl* -ок) *ж*
(*планка*) rack; (*стойка*) hatstand;
(*плечики*) coat hanger;
(*гардероб*) cloakroom; (*петля*)
loop

ве́ша|ть (-ю; *pf* **пове́сить**) *несов
перех* to hang; (*pf* **с~**; *товар*) to
weigh; ~**ся** (*pf* **пове́ситься**)
несов возв to hang o.s.

веща́|ть (3sg -**ет**) *несов* to
broadcast

веще́ственный *прил* material

вещество́ (-**а́**) *ср* substance

вещь (-и; *gen pl* -**е́й**) *ж* thing;
(*книга, фильм*) piece

ве́|ять (-ю, -ешь) *несов* (*ветер*)
to blow lightly

взаи́мный *прил* mutual

взаимоде́йстви|е (-я) *ср* (*связь*)
interaction

взаимоотноше́ни|е (-я) *ср*
(inter)relationship

взаимопо́мощь (-и) *ж* mutual
assistance *или* aid

взаимопонима́ни|е (-я) *ср*
mutual understanding

взаимосвя́зь (-и) *ж*
interconnection

взаймы́ *нареч*: дава́ть/брать
де́ньги ~ to lend/borrow money

взаме́н *нареч* in exchange for
♦ *предл*: ~ +*gen* (*вместо*) instead
of; (*в обмен*) in exchange for

взаперти́ *нареч* under lock and
key

взбить (**взобью́, взобьёшь**;
imper **взбе́й(те)**, *impf* **взбива́ть**)
сов перех (*яйца*) to beat;
(*сливки*) to whip; (*волосы*) to fluff
up; (*подушки*) to plump up

взва́л|ить (-ю, -ишь; *impf*
взва́ливать) *сов перех*: ~ **что-н**
на +*acc* to haul sth up onto

взве́|сить (-шу, -сишь; *impf*
взве́шивать) *сов перех* (*товар*)
to weigh; (*факты*) to weigh up

взве|сти́ (-ду́, -дёшь; *pt* **взвёл**,
-ла́; *impf* **взводи́ть**) *сов перех*: ~
куро́к to cock a gun

взве́шенный *прил* considered

взве́шива|ть (-ю) *несов от*
взве́сить

взвин|ти́ть (-чу́, -ти́шь; *impf*
взви́нчивать; *сов перех* (*разг*:
цены) to jack up

взвод (-а) *м* platoon; **на взво́де**
(*куро́к*) cocked

взво|ди́ть (-жу́, -дишь) *несов
от* **взвести́**

взволно́ванный *прил* agitated;
(*радостный*) excited

взволн|ова́ть(ся) (-у́ю(сь)) *сов
от* **волнова́ть(ся)**

взв|ыть (-о́ю, -о́ешь) *сов* to
howl; (*сирена*) to wail

взгляд (-а) *м* glance;
(*выражение*) look; (*перен*:
мнение) view; **на мой/твой** ~ in
my/your view

взгля́н|уть (-у́, -ешь) *сов*: ~ **на**
+*acc* to look at

вздор (-а) *м* (*разг*) rubbish

вздо́рный *прил* (*нелепый*)
absurd

вздох (-а) *м* sigh; (*ужаса*) gasp

вздохн|у́ть (-у́, -ёшь) *сов* to sigh

вздра́гива|ть (-ю) *сов* to shudder

вздума|ть (-ю) *сов* (*разг*): **не**
-**йте лгать!** don't even think of
lying!

вздыха́|ть (-ю) *несов* to sigh

взима́|ть (-ю) *несов перех*
(*налоги*) to collect

взлёт (-а) *м* (*самолёта*) takeoff

взле|те́ть (-чу́, -ти́шь; *impf*
взлета́ть) *сов* (*птица*) to soar;
(*самолёт*) to take off; **взлета́ть** (~

взлётный прил: ~ая полоса́
runway, airstrip

взлома́|ть (-ю; impf взла́мывать)
сов перех to break open, force;
(КОМП) to hack into

взло́мщик (-а) м burglar

взмахн|у́ть (-у́, -ёшь; impf
взма́хивать) сов: ~ +instr (руко́й)
to wave; (крыло́м) to flap

взмо́рь|е (-я) ср seashore

взнос (-а) м payment; (в фонд)
contribution; (чле́нский) fee

взойти́ (как **идти́**; impf
всходи́ть или восходи́ть) сов to rise; (семена́) to come up;
(на трон) to ascend

взорв|а́ть (-у́, -ёшь; impf
взрыва́ть) сов перех (бо́мбу) to
detonate; (дом, мост) to blow up;
~ся (impf взрыва́ться) сов возв
(бо́мба) to explode; (мост, дом)
to be blown up

взреве́|ть (-у́, -ёшь) сов to roar

взросле́|ть (-ю; pf по~) несов to
grow up; (духо́вно) to mature

взро́сл|ый прил (челове́к)
grown-up; (фильм) adult ♦ (-ого)
м adult

взрыв (-а) м explosion; (до́ма)
blowing up; ~ +gen (возмуще́ния)
outburst of

взрыва́|ть(ся) (-ю(сь)) несов от
взорва́ть(ся)

взрывоопа́сный прил explosive

взрывча́т|ка (-ки; gen pl -ок) ж
explosive (substance)

взы́ск|ать (-щу́, -щешь; impf
взы́скивать) сов перех (долг)
to recover; (штраф) to exact
♦ неперех: ~ с кого́-н to call sb to
account

взя́т|ка (-ки; gen pl -ок) ж bribe

взя́точник (-а) м bribe-taker

взя́|ть (возьму́, возьмёшь) сов

от **брать** ♦ перех: возьми́ (да)
и откажу́сь (разг) I could refuse just
like that; с чего́ или отку́да ты
~л? (разг) whatever gave you that
idea?; ~ся́ться сов от **бра́ться**

вид (-а; part sgen -у, loc sg -ý) м
(вне́шность) appearance;
(предме́та, иску́сства) form;
(пано́рама) view; (расте́ний,
живо́тных) species; (спо́рта) type;
(линг) aspect; в ви́де +gen in the
form of; на ~у́ у +gen in full view
of; под ви́дом +gen in the guise of;
~ на о́зеро/го́ры view of the
lake/hills; име́ть (impf) в ~ý to
mean; (учи́тывать) to bear in
mind; (де́лать) (сде́лать pf) ~ to
pretend; упуска́ть (упусти́ть pf) ~
из ви́ду что-н (факт) to lose sight of
sth; теря́ть (потеря́ть pf)
кого́-н из ви́ду to lose sight of sb;
~ на жи́тельство residence
permit

вида́|ть (pt -л, -ла, -ло; pf по~)
несов перех (разг) to see;
(испыта́ть) to know; ~ся (pf
по~ся) несов возв (разг) to see
each other

ви́део ср нескл video

видеоза́пис|ь (-и) ж video
recording

видеоигр|а́ (-ы́; nom pl -ы) ж
video game

видеока́мер|а (-ы) ж camcorder,
videocamera

видеокассе́т|а (-ы) ж video
cassette

видеомагнитофо́н (-а) м video
(recorder)

ви́|деть (-жу, -дишь) несов to
see ♦ (pf у~) перех to see;
(испыта́ть) to know; ~дите ли
you see; ~ся (pf у~ся) несов возв
to see each other

ви́димо вводн сл apparently

ви́димо-неви́димо нареч (разг): наро́ду в го́роде ~ there are masses of people in the city

ви́димость (-и) ж visibility; (подобие) appearance; по всей ~и apparently

видне́ться (3sg -ется) несов возв to be visible

ви́дно как сказ one can see; (понятно) clearly ♦ вводн сл probably; тебе́ видне́е you know best; там ~ бу́дет we'll see

ви́дный прил (заметный) visible; (известный) prominent

ви́жу(сь) несов см. ви́деть(ся)

ви́з|**а** (-ы) ж visa

визажи́ст (-а) м make-up artist

визг (-а) м (собаки) yelp; (ребёнка) squeal; (металла) screech

визж|**а́ть** (-у́, -и́шь) несов (см сущ) to yelp; to squeal

визи́т (-а) м visit

визи́т|**ка** (-ки; gen pl -ок) ж business card

визи́тный прил: ~ая ка́рточка (business) card

викторин|**а** (-ы) ж quiz game

ви́л|**ка** (-ки; gen pl -ок) ж fork; (штепсельная) ~ plug

ви́лл|**а** (-ы) ж villa

ви́л|**ы** (-) мн pitchfork ед

виля́|**ть** (-ю) несов: ~ +instr (хвостом) to wag; (бёдрами) to wiggle

вин|**а́** (-ы́) м blame; (чувство) guilt

винегре́т (-а) м beetroot salad

вини́тельный прил: ~ паде́ж accusative (case)

вин|**и́ть** (-ю́, -и́шь) несов перех: ~ кого́-н в +prp to blame sb for; (упрекать: за лень) ~ кого́-н за +acc to accuse sb of

вин|**о́** (-а́; nom pl -а) ср wine

винова́тый прил (взгляд итп) guilty; ~ (в +prp) (в неудаче) responsible или to blame (for); винова́т! sorry!, excuse me!

вино́вность (-и) ж guilt

вино́вный прил guilty ♦ (-ого) м guilty party

виногра́д (-а) м (растение) (grape)vine; (ягоды) grapes мн

виногра́дник (-а) м vineyard

винт (-а́) м screw

винто́в|**ка** (-ки; gen pl -ок) ж rifle

виолонче́ль (-и) ж cello

вира́ж (-а́; gen pl -е́й) м (поворот) turn

виртуа́льный прил virtual

виртуо́з (-а) м virtuoso

виртуо́зный прил masterly; ~ое исполне́ние a virtuoso performance

ви́рус (-а) м virus

ви́селиц|**а** (-ы) ж gallows

ви|**се́ть** (-шу́, -сишь) несов to hang; (КОМП) to freeze

ви́ски ср нескл whisky (BRIT), whiskey (US, IRELAND)

висо́к (-ка́) м (АНАТ) temple

високо́сный прил: ~ год leap year

витами́н (-а) м vitamin

вита́|**ть** (-ю) несов to hang in the air

вито́й прил twisted

вит|**о́к** (-ка́) м (спирали) twist

витра́ж (-а́) м stained-glass window

витри́н|**а** (-ы) ж (в магазине) shop window; (в музее) display case

ви|**ть** (вью, вьёшь; imper вей(те); pf c~) несов перех (венок) to weave; (гнездо) to build; **ви́ться** несов возв (растения) to trail; (волосы) to curl

вихрь (-я) м whirlwind

ви́це-президе́нт (-а) *м* vice president

ВИЧ *м сокр* (= **ви́рус иммунодефици́та челове́ка**) HIV; **~-инфици́рованный** HIV-positive

ви́шня (-ни; *gen pl* -ен) *ж* cherry

вка́лывать (-ю) *несов от* **вколо́ть**

вкати́ть (-чу́, -тишь; *impf* **вка́тывать**) *сов перех* (что-н на колёсах) to wheel in; (что-н кру́глое) to roll in

вклад (-а) *м* (в нау́ку) contribution; (в ба́нке) deposit

вкла́дчик (-а) *м* investor

вкла́дывать (-ю) *несов от* **вложи́ть**

включа́ть (-ю) *несов от* **включи́ть**; *перех*: ~ (в себя́) to include; ~**ся** *несов от* **включи́ться**

включа́я *предл*: ~ +*acc* including

включи́тельно *нареч* inclusive

включи́ть (-у́, -и́шь; *impf* **включа́ть**) *сов перех* to turn *или* switch on; **включа́ть** (~ *pf*) кого́-н/ что-н во что-н to include sb/sth in sth; ~**ся** (*impf* **включа́ться**) *сов возв* to come on; (в *спор*) ~**ся** в +*acc* to join in

вколо́ть (-ю́, -ешь; *impf* **вка́лывать**) *сов перех* to stick in

вкра́тце *нареч* briefly

вкривь *нареч*: ~ и вкось (*разг*) all over the place

вкрути́ть (-чу́, -тишь; *impf* **вкру́чивать**) *сов перех* to screw in

вкруту́ю *нареч*: яйцо́ ~ hard-boiled egg

вкус (-а) *м* taste; она́ оде́та со вку́сом she is tastefully dressed

вку́сно *нареч* ♦ *как сказ*: о́чень ~ it's delicious; она́ ~ гото́вит she is a good cook

вку́сный *прил* tasty; (*обед*) delicious

вла́га (-и) *ж* moisture

владе́лец (-ьца) *м* owner

владе́ние (-я) *ср* ownership; (*поме́щика*) estate

владе́ть (-ю) *несов*: ~ +*instr* (*облада́ть*) to own, possess; (*языко́м*) to be proficient in; (*ору́жием*) to handle proficiently; ~ (*impf*) собо́й to control o.s.; ~ (*impf*) рука́ми/нога́ми to have the use of one's arms/legs

вла́жность (-и) *ж* humidity

вла́жный *прил* damp; (*глаза́, ко́жа*) moist

вла́ствовать (-ую) *несов*: ~ над +*instr* to rule; (*перен*) to hold sway over

вла́сти (-е́й) *мн* authorities *мн*

вла́стный *прил* (*челове́к*) imperious; (*структу́ра*) holding power; он не ~ен +*infin* ... it's not within his power to ...

власть (-и; *gen pl* -е́й) *ж* power; (*роди́тельская*) authority; *см. также* **вла́сти**

вле́во *нареч* (to the) left

влезть (-у, -ешь; *pt* -, -ла, -ло; *impf* **влеза́ть**) *сов*: ~ на +*acc* to climb (up); (*на кры́шу*) to climb onto; (*в дом*) to break in

влете́ть (-чу́, -ти́шь; *impf* **влета́ть**) *сов*: ~ в +*acc* to fly into

влече́ние (-я) *ср*: ~ (к +*dat*) attraction to

влечь (-ку́, -чёшь *etc*, -ку́т; *pt* влёк, -кла́, *pf* **повле́чь**) *несов перех*: ~ за собо́й to lead to; его́ ~чёт нау́ка he is drawn to science

влива́ние (-я) *ср* (*де́нег*) injection

влить (волью́, вольёшь; *pt* -л, -ла́, -ло, *imper* вле́й(те); *impf* **влива́ть**) *сов перех* to pour in;

(де́ньги) to inject

влия́ни|е (-я) *ср* influence

влия́тельный *прил* influential

влия́|ть (-ю) *несов*: ~ **на** +*acc* to influence; (*на органи́зм*) to affect

вложи́ть (-у́, -ишь) *impf* **вкла́дывать** *сов перех* to insert; (*сре́дства*) to invest

влюби́|ться (-лю́сь, -ишься), *impf* **влюбля́ться** *сов возв*: ~ **в** +*acc* to fall in love with

влюблённ|ый *прил* in love; (*взгляд*) loving ♦ (**-ого**) *м*: ~**ые** lovers

вме́сте *нареч* together; ~ **с тем** at the same time

вмести́тельный *прил* spacious

вме|сти́ть (-щу́, -сти́шь), *impf* **вмеща́ть** *сов перех* (*о за́ле*) to hold; (*о гости́нице*) to accommodate; ~**ся** (*impf* **вмеща́ться**) *несов возв* to fit in

вме́сто *предл*: ~ +*gen* (*взаме́н*) instead of ♦ *союз*: ~ **того́ что́бы** instead of, rather than

вмеша́тельств|о (-а) *ср* (*экон*) intervention

вмеша́|ть (-ю) *impf* **вме́шивать** *сов перех* (*доба́вить*) to mix in; (*перен*): ~ **кого́-н в** +*acc* to get sb mixed up in; ~**ся** (*impf* **вме́шиваться**) *сов возв* to interfere; (*в перегово́ры итп*) to intervene

вмеща́|ть(ся) (-ю(сь)) *несов от* **вмести́ть(ся)**

вмиг *нареч* instantly

вмя́тин|а (-ы) *ж* dent

внаём *нареч*: **отдава́ть** ~ to let, rent out

внача́ле *нареч* at first

вне *предл*: ~ +*gen* outside; ~ **о́череди** out of turn; **он был** ~ **себя́** he was beside himself

внебра́чный *прил* extramarital;

(*ребёнок*) illegitimate

внедоро́жник (-а) *м* 4-wheel drive

внедре́ни|е (-я) *ср* introduction

внеза́пный *прил* sudden

внеочередно́й *прил* unscheduled

внес|ти́ (-у́, -ёшь, *pt* **внёс, -ла́, -ло́,** *impf* **вноси́ть** *сов перех* (*ве́щи*) to carry and bring in; (*су́мму*) to pay; (*законопрое́кт*) to bring in; (*попра́вку*) to insert

вне́школьный *прил* extracurricular

вне́шн|ий *прил* (*стена́*) exterior; (*споко́йствие*) outward; (*свя́зи*) external; ~ **мир** outside world; ~ **вид** appearance; ~**яя поли́тика/ торго́вля** foreign policy/trade

вне́шност|ь (-и) *ж* appearance

внешта́тный *прил* freelance

вниз *нареч*: ~ (**по** +*dat*) down; ~ **по тече́нию** downstream

внизу́ *нареч* below; (*в зда́нии*) downstairs ♦ *предл*: ~ **страни́цы** at the foot *или* bottom of the page

вни́к|нуть (-ну, *pt* **-, -ла,** *impf* **вника́ть** *сов*: ~ **во что-н** to understand sth well; (*изуча́ть*) to scrutinize sth

внима́ни|е (-я) *ср* attention

внима́тельный *прил* attentive; (*рабо́та*) careful; (*сын*) caring

вничью́ *нареч* (*спорт*): **оыгра́ть** ~ to draw

вновь *нареч* again

вно|си́ть (-шу́, -сишь) *несов от* **внести́**

внук (-а; *nom pl* **-ки** *или* **-ча́та**) *м* grandson; *см. также* **вну́ки**

вну́к|и (-ов) *мн* grandchildren *мн*

вну́тренн|ий *прил* interior; (*побужде́ние, го́лос*) inner; (*поли́тика, ры́нок*) domestic; (*ра́на*) internal; **Министе́рство** ~**их дел** ≈ the Home Office

(BRIT), ≈ the Department of the Interior (US)

внутри́ нареч inside ♦ предл: ~ +gen (дома) inside; (организации) within

внутри́ нареч inside ♦ предл: ~ +gen inside

вну́чка (-ки; gen pl -ек) ж granddaughter

внуша́ть (-ю) несов от внуши́ть

внуши́тельный прил imposing; (сумма, успех) impressive

внуши́ть (-у́, -и́шь; impf внуша́ть) сов перех: ~ что-н кому́-н (чувство) to inspire sb with sth; (идею) to instil (BRIT) или instill (US) sth in sb

вня́тный прил articulate, audible

во предл см. в

вовле́чь (-еку́, -ечёшь etc -еку́т; pt -ёк, -екла́; impf вовлека́ть) сов перех: ~ кого́-н в +acc to draw sb into

во́время нареч on time

во́все нареч (разг) completely; ~нет not at all

во-вторы́х вводн сл secondly, in the second place

вода́ (acc sg -у, gen sg -ы́, nom pl -ы) ж water; см. также во́ды

води́тель (-я) м driver

води́тельский прил: ~ие права́ driving licence (BRIT), driver's license (US)

води́ть (-жу́, -дишь) несов перех (ребёнка) to take; (машину, поезд) to drive; (самолёт) to fly; (корабль) to sail; ~ся несов возв (рыба итп) to be (found)

во́дка (-и) ж vodka

во́дный прил water

водоём (-а) м reservoir

водола́з (-а) м diver

Водоле́й (-я) м Aquarius

водонепроница́емый прил waterproof

водоочистно́й прил water-purifying

водопа́д (-а) м waterfall

водопрово́д (-а) м water supply system; у них в до́ме есть ~ their house has running water

водопрово́дный прил (труба, кран) water; (система) plumbing

водопрово́дчик (-а) м plumber

водоро́д (-а) м hydrogen

во́доросль (-и) ж (разг: в реке) waterweed; (в море) seaweed

водосто́чный прил: ~ая труба́ drainpipe; ~ая кана́ва gutter

водохрани́лище (-а) ср reservoir

во́ды (-) мн (государственные) waters мн; (минеральные) spa ед

водяни́стый прил watery

водяно́й прил water; ~ знак watermark

воева́ть (-ю́ю) несов (страна) to be at war; (человек) to fight

военача́льник (-а) м (military) commander

военкома́т (-а) м сокр (= вое́нный комиссариа́т) office for military registration and enlistment

вое́нно-возду́шный прил: ~ые си́лы (the) air force

вое́нно-морско́й прил: ~ флот (the) navy

военнообя́занный (-ого) м person eligible for compulsory military service

военноплённый (-ого) м prisoner of war

вое́нно-промы́шленный прил: ~ ко́мплекс military-industrial complex

военнослу́жащий (-его) м serviceman

вое́нн|ый *прил* military; (*врач*) army ♦ (**-ого**) *м* serviceman **-ое положе́ние** martial law

вожде́ни|е (-я) *ср* (*машины*) driving; (*судна*) steering

вождь (-я́) *м* (*племени*) chief, chieftain; (*партии*) leader

вожж|а́ (-и́; *nom pl* **-и,** *gen pl* **-е́й)** *ж* rein

возбу|ди́ть (-жу́, -у́дишь; *impf* **возбужда́ть)** *сов перех* (*вызвать*) to arouse; (*взволновать*) to excite; возбужда́ть ~ *pf* де́ло *или* проце́сс про́тив +*gen* to bring a case *или* proceedings against; **-ся** *сов возв* (*человек*) to become excited

возбужде́ни|е (-я) *ср* (*волнение*) agitation; (: *радостное*) excitement

возбуждённый *прил* (*см прил*) agitated; excited

возве|сти́ (-ду́, -дёшь; *pt* **возвёл, -ла́;** *impf* **возводи́ть)** *сов перех* to erect

возвра́т (-а) *м* return; (*долга*) repayment; **без ~а** irrevocably

возвра|ти́ть (-щу́, -ти́шь; *impf* **возвраща́ть)** *сов перех* to return; (*долг*) to repay; (*здоровье, счастье*) to restore; **-ся** (*impf* **возвраща́ться**) *сов возв* **~ся (к** +*dat*) to return *или* come back (to)

возвраще́ни|е (-я) *ср* return

возвы́шенный *прил* (*идея, цель*) lofty; (*натура, музыка*) sublime

возгла́в|ить (-лю, -ишь; *impf* **возглавля́ть)** *сов перех* to head

во́зглас (-а) *м* exclamation

возда́|ть (как дать; см. Table 16; *impf* **воздава́ть)** *сов перех* **~ кому́-н по заслу́гам** (*в награду*) to reward sb for their services; (*в*

наказание) to give sb what they deserve; **воздава́ть (~ *pf*) до́лжное кому́-н** to give sb their due

воздви́г|нуть (-ну; *pt* **-, -ла;** *impf* **воздвига́ть)** *сов перех* to erect

возде́йстви|е (-я) *ср* effect; (*идеологическое*) influence

возде́йств|овать (-ую) (*не)сов*: **~ на** +*acc* to have an effect on

возде́ла|ть (-ю; *impf* **возде́лывать)** *сов перех* (*поле*) to cultivate

воздержа́вш|ийся (-егося) *м* (*полит*) abstainer

возд|ержа́ться (-ержу́сь, -е́ржишься; *impf* **возде́рживаться)** *сов возв*: **~ от** +*gen* to refrain from; (*от голосова́ния*) to abstain from

во́здух (-а) *м* air; **на (откры́том) ~е** outside, outdoors

возду́шный *прил* air; (*десант*) airborne; **возду́шный флот** civil aviation; (*воен*) air force

воззва́ни|е (-я) *ср* appeal

во|зи́ть (-жу́, -зишь) *несов перех* to take; (*см несов возв* to potter about; **-ся** (*impf*) *возв* (*разг*: *с рабо́той итп*) to dawdle over; (*с детьми итп*) to spend a lot of time with

во́зле *нареч* nearby ♦ *предл*: **~** +*gen* near

возлож|и́ть (-у́, -ишь; *impf* **возлага́ть)** *сов перех* (*венок*) to lay; (*зада́чу*) to entrust

возлю́бленн|ый (-ого) *м* beloved

возме́зди|е (-я) *ср* retribution

возме|сти́ть (-щу́, -сти́шь; *impf* **возмеща́ть)** *сов перех* (*убытки*) to compensate for; (*затра́ты*) to refund, reimburse

возмо́жно *как сказ* it is possible

♦ *вводн сл* (*может быть*) possibly
возмо́жност|и (-ей) *мн* (*творческие*) potential *ед*; **фина́нсовые ~** financial resources

возмо́жность (-и) *ж* opportunity; (*вероятность*) possibility; **по (ме́ре) ~** as far as possible; *см. также* **возмо́жности**

возмо́жный *прил* possible

возмужа́|ть (-ю) *сов от* **мужа́ть**

возмути́тельный *прил* appalling

возмути́ть (-щу́, -ти́шь; *impf* **возмуща́ть)** *сов перех* to appal (*BRIT*), appall (*US*); **~ся** *impf* **возмуща́ться)** *сов возв* to be appalled

возмуще́ни|е (-я) *ср* indignation

вознагради́ть (-жу́, -ди́шь; *impf* **вознагражда́ть)** *сов перех* to reward

возникнове́ни|е (-я) *ср* emergence

возни́к|нуть (-ну; *pt* **-, -ла;** *impf* **возника́ть)** *сов* to arise

возн|я́ (-и́) *ж* (*при игре*) frolicking; **~** *c +instr* (*хлопоты*) bother with

возобнови́ть (-лю́, -и́шь; *impf* **возобновля́ть)** *сов перех* (*работу*) to resume; (*контракт*) to renew; **~ся** *impf* **возобновля́ться)** *сов возв* to resume

возраже́ни|е (-я) *ср* objection

возраз|и́ть (-жу́, -зи́шь; *impf* **возража́ть)** *сов*: **~** (*+dat*) to object (to)

во́зраст (-а) *м* age; **он был уже́ в ~е** he was getting on in years

возр|асти́ (3sg -асте́т, *pt* **-ос, -осла́;** *impf* **возраста́ть)** *сов* to grow

возро|ди́ть (-жу́, -ди́шь; *impf* **возрожда́ть)** *сов перех* to revive; **~ся** (*impf* **возрожда́ться)** *сов возв* to revive

возрожде́ни|е (-я) *ср* revival; (*нации, веры*) rebirth; **Возрожде́ние** Renaissance

возьму́(сь) *etc сов см.* **взять(ся)**

во́ин (-а) *м* warrior

во́инский *прил* military; **~ая обя́занность** conscription

вои́нственный *прил* belligerent; (*депутат*) militant

во́й (-я) *м* howl

во́йлок (-а) *м* felt

войн|а́ (-ы́; *nom pl* **-ы)** *ж* war

во́йск|о (-а; *nom pl* **-а́)** *ср* (the) forces *мн*

войти́ (как идти́; *см.* **Table 18;** *impf* **входи́ть)** *сов*: **~ (в** *+acc*) to enter, go in(to); (*в комитет*) to become a member (of); (*уместиться*) to fit in(to)

вока́льный *прил* vocal; (*конкурс*) singing

вокза́л (-а) *м* station

вокру́г *нареч* around, round
♦ *предл*: **~ +gen** (*кругом*) around, round; (*по поводу*) about, over; **ходи́ть (**impf**) да о́коло** (*разг*) to beat about the bush

вол (-а) *м* ox bullock

вола́н (-а) *м* (*на одежде*) flounce; (*СПОРТ*) shuttlecock

волды́р|ь (-я́) *м* blister

волево́й *прил* strong-willed

волейбо́л (-а) *м* volleyball

волк (-а; *gen pl* **-о́в)** *м* wolf

волн|а́ (-ы́; *nom pl* **во́лны)** *ж* wave

волне́ни|е (-я) *ср* (*радостное*) excitement; (*нервное*) agitation; (*обычно мн.* **волне́ния** *в массах*) unrest *ед*

волни́стый *прил* (*волосы*) wavy

волн|ова́ть (-у́ю; *pf* **вз~)** *несов перех* to be concerned about; (*подлеж:музыка*) to excite; **~ся** (*pf* **вз~ся**) *несов возв* (*море*) to be rough; (*человек*) to worry

волокно́ (-окна́; *nom pl* **-о́кна**,

gen pl **-о́кон** ср fibre (BRIT), fiber (US)

во́лос (-а; gen pl **воло́с**, dat pl **-а́м**) м hair только ед

волосо́к (-ка́) м hair; **быть** (impf) или **находи́ться** (impf) **на** ~ или **на** ~**ке́ от** +gen to be within a hair's-breadth of

волочи́ть (-у́, -и́шь) несов перех to drag

во́лчий прил wolf

волше́бник (-а) м wizard

волше́бница (-ы) ж (good or white) witch

волше́бный прил magic; (музыка) magical

во́льно нареч freely; ~! (ВОЕН) at ease!

во́льный прил (свободный) free ♦ как сказ: ~**ен** +infin he is free to do

вольт (-а; gen pl -) м volt

во́ля (-и) ж will; (стремление): ~ **к побе́де** the will to win

вон нареч (разг: прочь) out; (: там) (over) there; ~ **отсю́да**! get out of here!; ~ **(оно́) что** so that's it!

вонь (-и) ж (разг) pong

воня́ть (-ю) несов (разг) to pong

вообрази́ть (-жу́, -зи́шь) сов перех от **воображать**

вообража́ть (-ю) несов перех to imagine

вообще́ нареч (в общем) on the whole; (совсем) absolutely; (+noun: без частностей) in general; ~ **говоря́** generally speaking

воодушеви́ть (-лю́, -и́шь) impf **воодушевля́ть** сов перех to inspire; ~**ся** сов возв: ~**ся** +instr to be inspired by

воодушевле́ни|**е** (-я) ср inspiration

вооружа́|**ть(ся)** (-ю(сь)) несов см. **вооружи́ть(ся)**

вооруже́ни|**е** (-я) ср (процесс) arming; (оружие) arms мн

вооружённый прил armed; ~**ые си́лы** (the) armed forces

вооружи́ть (-у́, -и́шь) impf **вооружа́ть** сов перех to arm; (перен) to equip; ~**ся** (impf) **вооружа́ться** сов возв to arm o.s.

во-пе́рвых нареч firstly, first of all

воплоти́ть (-щу́, -ти́шь) impf **воплоща́ть** сов перех to embody; **воплоти́ть** (~ pf) **в жизнь** to realize; ~**ся** (impf) **воплоща́ться** сов возв: ~**ся в** +prp to be embodied in; **воплоти́ться** (~**ся** pf) **в жизнь** to be realized

воплоще́ни|**е** (-я) ср embodiment

вопл|**ь** (-я) м scream

вопреки́ предл: ~ +dat contrary to

вопро́с (-а) м question; (проблема) issue; **задава́ть** (**зада́ть** pf) ~ to ask a question

вопроси́тельный прил (взгляд) questioning; (ЛИНГ) interrogative; ~ **знак** question mark

вор (-а; gen pl -о́в) м thief

ворва́ться (-у́сь, -ёшься; impf **врыва́ться**) сов возв to burst in

воробе́й (-ья́) м sparrow

воров|**а́ть** (-у́ю) несов перех to steal

воровств|**о́** (-а́) ср theft

воро́н (-а) м raven

воро́н|**а** (-ы) ж crow

воро́нка (-ки; gen pl -ок) ж (для переливания) funnel; (после взрыва) crater

во́рот (-а) м neck (of clothes)

воро́т|**а** (-) мн gates мн; (СПОРТ) goal ед

воротни́к (-а) м collar

воро́чать (-ю) несов перех to shift ♦ неперех: ~ +instr (разг:

деньгами) to have control of; **~ся**
несов возв to toss and turn

ворс (-а) *м* (*на тка́ни*) nap

ворч|**а́ть** (-у́, -и́шь) *несов*
(*зверь*) to growl; (*челове́к*) to
grumble

ворчли́вый *прил* querulous

восемна́дцатый *чис* eighteenth

восемна́дцать (-и; *как* **пять**;
см. Table 26) *чис* eighteen

во́с|**емь** (-ьми́; *как* **пять**; *см.
Table 26*) *чис* eight

во́с|**емьдесят** (-ьми́десяти; *как*
пятьдеся́т; *см. Table 26*) *чис*
eighty

вос|**емьсо́т** (-ьмисо́т; *как*
пятьсо́т; *см. Table 28*) *чис* eight
hundred

воск (-а) *м* wax

воскли́кн|**уть** (-у; *impf*
восклица́ть) *сов* to exclaim

восклица́ние (-я) *ср* exclamation

восклица́тельный *прил*
exclamatory; **~ знак** exclamation
mark (BRIT) *или* point (US)

восково́й *прил* wax

воскреса́|**ть** (-ю) *несов от*
воскре́снуть

воскресе́ни|**е** (-я) *ср* resurrection

воскресе́нь|**е** (-я) *ср* Sunday

воскре|**си́ть** (-шу́, -си́шь; *impf*
воскреша́ть) *сов перех* to
resurrect; (*перен*) to revive

воскре́с|**нуть** (-ну; *pt* -, -ла; *impf*
воскреса́ть) *сов* to be
resurrected; (*перен*) to be revived

воскре́сный *прил* Sunday

воспале́ни|**е** (-я) *ср* inflammation;
~ лёгких pneumonia

воспал|**и́ться** (*3sg* -и́тся; *impf*
воспаля́ться) *сов возв* to
become inflamed

воспита́ни|**е** (-я) *ср* upbringing;
(*граждан*) education; (*че́стности*)
fostering

воспи́танный *прил* well-brought-
up

воспита́тел|**ь** (-я) *м* teacher; (*в
ла́гере*) instructor

воспита́|**ть** (-ю; *impf*
воспи́тывать) *сов перех* to bring up;
(*ребёнка*) to bring up;
(*трудолю́бие*) to foster

воспо́льз|**оваться** (-уюсь) *сов
от* **по́льзоваться**

воспомина́ни|**е** (-я) *ср*
recollection; *см. также*
воспомина́ния

воспомина́ни|**я** (-й) *мн* memoirs
мн, reminiscences *мн*

воспрепя́тств|**овать** (-ую) *сов
от* **препя́тствовать**

воспреща́|**ться** (*3sg* -ется) *несов
возв* to be forbidden

восприи́мчивый *прил* receptive

воспри|**ня́ть** (-иму́, -и́мешь;
impf **воспринима́ть**) *сов перех*
(*смысл*) to comprehend

воспроизвед|**ести́** (-у́, -ёшь;
pt -ёл, -ела́, -ело́; *impf*
воспроизводи́ть) *сов перех* to
reproduce

воспроти́в|**иться** (-люсь,
-ишься) *сов от* **проти́виться**

восста|**ва́ть** (-ю́, -ёшь) *несов от*
восста́ть

восста́ни|**е** (-я) *ср* uprising

восстан|**ови́ть** (-овлю́, -о́вишь;
impf **восстана́вливать**) *сов
перех* to restore

восста́|**ть** (-ну, -нешь; *impf*
восстава́ть) *сов*: **~ (про́тив** +*gen*)
to rise up (against)

восто́к (-а) *м* east; **Восто́к** the
East, the Orient

восто́рг (-а) *м* rapture

восто́рженный *прил*
(*покло́нник*) ecstatic; (*похвала́*)
rapturous

восторжеств|**ова́ть** (-у́ю) *сов*

от торжествова́ть

восто́чный прил eastern; ~ ве́тер
east wind

востре́бовани|е (-я) ср (багажа́)
claim; письмо́ до ~я a letter sent
poste restante (BRIT) или general
delivery (US)

восхити́тельный прил delightful

восхи|ти́ть (-щу́, -ти́шь; impf
восхища́ть) сов перех: меня́
~ща́ет он/его́ хра́брость I admire
him/his courage; ~ся (impf
восхища́ться) сов возв: ~ся
+instr to admire

восхище́ни|е (-я) ср admiration

восхо́д (-а) м: ~ со́лнца sunrise; ~
луны́ moonrise

восхо|ди́ть (-жу́, -́дишь)
несов от взойти́

восьмёр|ка (-ки; gen pl **-ок)** ж
(разг: цифра) eight

восьмидеся́тый чис eightieth

восьмиуго́льник (-а) м octa-
gon

восьмичасово́й прил eight-hour;
(по́езд) eight-o'clock

восьмо́й чис eighth

KEYWORD

вот част **1** (о бли́зком предме́те):
вот моя́ ма́ма here is my mother;
вот мои́ де́ти here are my children
2 (выража́ет указа́ние) this;
в чём де́ло this is what it's about;
вот где ну́жно иска́ть this is
where we need to look
3 (при эмфа́тике): **вот ты и
сде́лай э́то** YOU do this; **вот
негодя́й!** what a rascal!
4 (во фра́зах): **вот-во́т** (разг: вот
и́менно) that's it; **он вот-во́т
ля́жет спать** he is just about to go
to bed; (разг) not likely!;
вот (оно́) как или **что!** is that so
или right?; **вот тебе́ и на** или **те**

раз! (разг) well I never!

воткн|у́ть (-у́, -ёшь; impf
втыка́ть) сов перех to stick in

во́тум (-а) м: ~ дове́рия/
недове́рия vote of confidence/no
confidence

вошёл etc сов см. войти́

вошь (instr sg **во́шью,** nom pl
вши) ж louse

впада́|ть (-ю) несов от впасть
♦ неперех: ~ в +acc to flow into

впа́дин|а (-ы) ж (в земле́) gully

впа|сть (-ду́, -дёшь; impf
впада́ть) сов (щёки, глаза́) to
become sunken; **впада́ть (~ pf) в**
+prp (в исте́рику) to go into

впервы́е нареч for the first time

вперёд нареч (идти́, е́хать)
forward; (заплати́ть) in advance

впереди́ нареч in front; ♦ предл: ~ +gen
in front of

впечатле́ни|е (-я) ср impression

впечатли́тельный прил
impressionable

впечатля́|ть (-ю) несов to be
impressive

впи|са́ть (-шу́, -шешь; impf
впи́сывать) сов перех to insert

впита́|ть (-ю; impf **впи́тывать)**
сов перех to absorb; ~ся сов
возв to be absorbed

вплавь нареч by swimming

вплотну́ю нареч close (by)
♦ предл: ~ к +dat (к го́роду) right up
close to; (к стене́) right up against

вплоть нареч: ~ до +gen (зимы́)
right up till; (включа́я) right up to

вполго́лоса нареч softly

впо́ру как сказ: пла́тье/шля́па
мне ~ the dress/hat fits me nicely

впосле́дствии нареч
subsequently

впра́ве как сказ: ~ +infin (знать,

требовать) to have a right to do

впра́во *нареч* to the right

впредь *нареч* in future ♦ *предл:* ~
до +*gen* pending

впро́голодь *нареч:* жить ~ to live
from hand to mouth

впро́чем *союз* however, though
♦ *вводн сл* but then again

впусти́ть (-щу́, -стишь; *impf*
впуска́ть) *сов перех* to let in

враг (-а́) *м* enemy

вражда́ (-ы́) *ж* enmity, hostility

вражде́бный *прил* hostile

вражд|ова́ть (-у́ю) *несов:* ~ (с
+*instr*) to be on hostile terms (with)

вразре́з *нареч:* ~ с +*instr* in
contravention of

вразуми́тельный *прил*
comprehensible

вран|ьё (-я́) *ср* (*разг*) lies *мн*

врасплóх *нареч* unawares

врата́р|ь (-я́) *м* goalkeeper

вр|ать (-у́, -ёшь; *pf* совра́ть)
несов (*разг: человек*) to fib

врач (-а́) *м* doctor

враче́бный *прил* medical

враща́|ть (-ю) *несов перех*
(*колесо*) to turn; **~ся** *несов возв*
to revolve, rotate

враще́ни|е (-я) *ср* rotation

вред (-а́) *м* damage ♦ *предл:* во ~
+*dat* to the
detriment of

вреди́тел|ь (-я) *м* (*насекомое*)
pest

вре|ди́ть (-жу́, -ди́шь; *pf* на~)
несов: ~ +*dat* to harm;
(*здоровью*) to damage; (*врагу*) to
inflict damage on

вре́дно *нареч:* ~ влия́ть на +*асс*
to have a harmful effect on ♦ *как
сказ:* кури́ть ~ smoking is bad for
you

вре́дный *прил* harmful; (*разг:
человек*) nasty

вре́|заться (-жусь, -жешься;
impf вреза́ться) *сов возв:* ~ в +*gen*
(*верёвка*) to cut into; (*машина*) to
plough (*BRIT*) или plow (*US*) into;
(*в память*) to engrave itself in

времена́ми *нареч* at times

вре́менный *прил* temporary

вре́м|я (-ени; *см. Table 4*) *ср* time;
(*линг*) tense ♦ *предл:* во ~ +*gen*
during ♦ *союз:* в то ~ как или
когда́ while; (а) в то же ~ (but) at
the same time; ~ от ~ени from
time to time; в после́днее ~
recently; в своё ~ (*когда
необходимо*) in due course; в
своё ~ она́ была́ краса́вицей she
was a real beauty in her day; на ~
for a while; со ~енем with или in
time; тем ~енем meanwhile;
ско́лько ~ени? what time is it?;
хорошо́ проводи́ть (провести́ *pf*)
~ to have a good time; ~ го́да
season

вро́вень *нареч:* ~ с +*instr* level with

вро́де *предл:* ~ +*gen* like ♦ *част*
sort of

врождённый *прил* innate;
(*болезнь*) congenital

врозь *нареч* (*жить*) apart

вруч|и́ть (-у́, -и́шь; *impf*
вруча́ть) *сов перех:* ~ что-н
кому́-н to hand sth (over) to sb

вручну́ю *нареч* (*разг*) by hand

врыва́|ться (-юсь) *несов от*
ворва́ться

вряд *част:* ~ли hardly; ~ли она́
придёт she's unlikely to come

вса́дник (-а) *м* rider, horseman

все *мест см.* весь

KEYWORD

всё (всего́) *мест см.* весь
♦ *ср* (*как сущ: без исключения*)
everything; вот и всё, э́то всё
that's all; ча́ще всего́ most often;

лу́чше всего́ написа́ть ей письмо́ it would be best to write to her; меня́ э́то волну́ет ме́ньше всего́ that is the least of my worries; мне всё равно́ it's all the same to me; Вы хоти́те чай и́ли ко́фе? - всё равно́ do you want tea or coffee? - I don't mind; я всё равно́ пойду́ туда́ I'll go there all the same

♦ *нареч* 1 (*разг*: всё вре́мя) all the time

2 (*то́лько*) all; э́то всё он винова́т it's all his fault

3 (*о нараста́нии при́знака*): шум всё уси́ливается the noise is getting louder and louder

4 (*о постоя́нстве при́знака*): всё так же still the same; всё там же still there; всё же all the same; всё ещё still

всевозмо́жный *прил* all sorts of

всегда́ *нареч* always

всего́ *мест см.* весь; всё ♦ *нареч* in all ♦ *част* only; ~ лишь (*разг*) only; ~на́всего (*разг*) only, mere

вселе́нн|ая (-ой) *ж* the whole world; Вселе́нная universe

восли́|ть (-ю, -и́шь) *impf* вселя́ть (*перех*) (*жильцо́в*) to install; ~ся (*impf* вселя́ться *сов возв*) (*жильцы́*) to move in

всем *мест см.* весь; всё; всём

всеме́рный *прил* all possible

всеми́рн|ый *прил* worldwide; (*конгре́сс*) world; ~ая паути́на (*комп*) World-Wide Web

всемогу́щий *прил* omnipotent

всенаро́дный *прил* national

всено́щн|ая (-ой) *ж* vespers

всео́бщ|ий *прил* universal; ~ая забасто́вка general strike

всеобъе́млющий *прил* comprehensive

всеросси́йский *прил* all-Russia

всерьёз *нареч* in earnest; ты э́то говори́шь ~? are you serious?

всесторо́нний *прил* comprehensive

всё-таки *част* still, all the same ♦ *союз*: а ~ all the same, nevertheless

всеуслы́шание *ср*: во ~ publicly

вска́кива|ть (-ю) *несов от* вскочи́ть

вскачь *нареч* at a gallop

вски́н|уть (-у; *impf* вски́дывать) *сов перех* (*мешо́к, ружьё*) to shoulder; (*го́лову*) to jerk up

вскип|е́ть (-лю́, -и́шь; *impf* кипе́ть) *сов* to boil; (*перен*) to flare up

вско́льзь *нареч* in passing

вско́ре *нареч* soon ♦ *предл*: ~ по́сле +*gen* soon или shortly after

вскоч|и́ть (-у́, -ишь; *impf* вска́кивать) *сов*: ~ в/на +*acc* to leap up onto

вскри́кн|уть (-у; *impf* вскри́кивать) *сов* to cry out

вскр|ы́ть (-о́ю, -о́ешь; *impf* вскрыва́ть) *сов перех* (*сейф*) to open; (*недоста́тки*) to reveal; (*нары́в*) to lance; (*труп*) to carry out a postmortem on; **вскры́ться** *сов возв* (*недоста́тки*) to come to light, be revealed

вслед *нареч* (*бежа́ть*) behind ♦ *предл*: ~ (*за* +*instr*) after; ~ +*dat* (*дру́гу, по́езду*) after

всле́дствие *предл*: ~ +*gen* as a result of, because of ♦ *союз*: ~ того́ что because; ~ чего́ as a result of which

вслух *нареч* aloud

всмя́тку *нареч*: яйцо́ ~ soft-boiled egg

всплеск (-а) *м* (*волны́*) splash

всплесн|у́ть (-у́, -ёшь; *impf* **всплёскивать**) *сов* (*рыба*) to splash; ~ (*pf*) **рука́ми** to throw up one's hands

всплы́|ть (-ву́, -вёшь; *impf* **всплыва́ть**) *сов* to surface

вспо́мн|ить (-ю, -ишь; *impf* **вспомина́ть**) *сов перех* to remember ♦ *неперех*: ~ **о** +*prp* to remember about

вспомога́тельный *прил* supplementary; (*судно, отряд*) auxiliary; ~ **глаго́л** auxiliary verb

вспорхн|у́ть (-у́, -ёшь) *сов* to fly off

вспоте́|ть (-ю) *сов от* **поте́ть**

вспугн|у́ть (-у́, -ёшь; *impf* **вспу́гивать**) *сов перех* to scare away *или* off

вспу́хн|уть (-у) *сов от* **пу́хнуть**

вспы́льчивый *прил* short-tempered

вспы́хн|уть (-у; *impf* **вспы́хивать**) *сов* (*зажечься*) to burst into flames; (*конфликт*) to flare up; (*покрасне́ть*) to blush

вспы́ш|ка (-ки; *gen pl* -ек) *ж* flash; (*гне́ва*) outburst; (*боле́зни*) outbreak

встава́|ть (-ю́; *imper* -ва́й(те)) *несов от* **встать**

встáв|ить (-лю, -ишь; *impf* **вставля́ть**) *сов перех* to insert, put in

встáв|ка (-ки; *gen pl* -ок) *ж* insertion

вставн|о́й *прил* (*рамы*) removable; ~**ы́е зу́бы** dentures, false teeth

вста|ть (-ну, -нешь; *impf* **встава́ть**) *сов* (*на ноги*) to stand up; (*с посте́ли*) to get up; (*со́лнце*) to rise; (*вопро́с*) to arise

встрево́ж|ить(ся) (-у(сь), -ишь(ся)) *несов от*

трево́жить(ся)

встре́|тить (-чу, -тишь; *impf* **встреча́ть**) *сов перех* to meet; (*факт*) to come across; (*оппози́цию*) to encounter; (*пра́здник итп*) to celebrate; ~**ся** (*impf* **встреча́ться**) *сов возв*: ~**ся с** +*instr* to meet; **мне ~тились интере́сные фа́кты** I came across some interesting facts

встре́ч|а (-и) *ж* meeting

встреча́|ть(ся) (-ю(сь)) *несов от* **встре́тить(ся)**

встре́чный *прил* (*маши́на*) oncoming; (*ме́ра*) counter; ~ **ве́тер** head wind

встряхн|у́ть (-у́, -ёшь; *impf* **встря́хивать**) *сов перех* to shake (out)

вступи́тельный *прил* (*речь, статья́*) introductory; ~ **экза́мен** entrance exam

---

вступи́тельные экза́мены - entrance exams. All higher education institutions in Russia require the applicants to sit entrance exams, both written and oral. Normally the candidates sit four exams, the subjects depend on what the applicants want to specialize in. An essay on Russian literature is a requirement for all departments.

вступ|и́ть (-лю́, -ишь; *impf* **вступа́ть**) *сов*: ~ **в** +*acc* to enter; (*в па́ртию*) to join; (*в перегово́ры*) to enter into; ~**ся** (*impf* **вступа́ться**) *сов возв*: ~**ся за** +*acc* to stand up for

вступле́ние (-я) *ср* entry; (*в па́ртию*) joining; (*в кни́ге*) introduction

всхли́пыва|ть (-ю) *несов* to sob

всхо|ди́ть (-жу́, -дишь) *несов от* **взойти́**

всхо́д|ы (-ов) *мн* shoots *мн*

всю́ду *нареч* everywhere

вс|я (-ей) *мест см.* **весь**

вся́к|ий *мест* (*каждый*) every; (*разнообразный*) all kinds of; (*любой*) any ♦ (-ого) *м* (*любой*) anyone; (*каждый*) everyone

вся́ческий *мест* all possible; (*товары*) all kinds of

вся́чин|а (-ы) *ж* (*разг*): **вся́кая ~** all sorts of things

Вт *сокр* (= **ватт**) W

вта́щ|ить (-у́, -ишь) *impf* **вта́скивать** *сов перех*: **~ (в** +*acc*) to drag in(to)

втере́ть (вотру́, вотрёшь; *pt* **втёр, втёрла**; *impf* **втира́ть**) *сов перех*: **~ (в** +*acc*) to rub in(to)

втисн|уть (-у; *impf* **вти́скивать**) *сов перех*: **~ (в** +*acc*) to cram in(to)

вто́рг|нуться (-усь; *impf* **вторга́ться**) *сов возв*: **~ в** +*acc* to invade

втори́чный *прил* (*повторный*) second; (*фактор*) secondary

вто́рник (-а) *м* Tuesday

втор|о́е (-о́го) *ср* main course

втор|о́й *прил* second; **сейча́с ~ час** it's after one; **сейча́с полови́на ~о́го** it's half past one

второпя́х *нареч* in a hurry

второстепе́нный *прил* secondary

в-тре́тьих *ввод сл* thirdly, in the third place

втро́е *нареч* (*больше*) three times; (*увеличить*) threefold

втро́ём *нареч* in a group of three

втро́йне *нареч* three times as much

втыка́|ть (-ю) *несов от* **воткну́ть**

втян|у́ть (-у́; *impf* **втя́гивать** *сов*

вта́гивать (**~** *pf*) **кого́-н** в +*acc* (*в де́ло*) to involve sb in

вуа́л|ь (-и) *ж* veil

вуз (-а) *м сокр* (= **вы́сшее уче́бное заведе́ние**) higher education establishment

вулка́н (-а) *м* volcano

вульга́рный *прил* vulgar

вход (-а) *м* (*движение*) entry; (*место*) entrance; (*ТЕХ*) inlet; (*КОМП*) input

вхо|ди́ть (-жу́, -дишь) *несов от* **войти́**

входно́й *прил* (*дверь*) entrance; (*КОМП*) input

вцеп|и́ться (-лю́сь, -ишься) *сов возв*: **~ в** +*acc* to seize

вчера́ *нареч, м нескл* yesterday

вчера́шний *прил* yesterday's

вче́тверо *нареч* four times

вчетвер|о́м *нареч* in a group of four

вши *etc сущ см.* **вошь**

вширь *нареч* in breadth

въезд (-а) *м* (*движение*) entry; (*место*) entrance

въездно́й *прил* entry

въе́|хать (*как* **е́хать**; *см. Table 19*; *impf* **въезжа́ть**) *сов* to enter; (*в новый дом*) to move in; (*наверх: на маши́не*) to drive up; (*: на коне́, велосипе́де*) to ride up

Вы (**Вас**; *см. Table 6b*) *мест* you (*formal*)

вы (**вас**; *см. Table 6b*) *мест* you (*plural*)

вы́бе|жать (*как* **бежа́ть**; *см. Table 20*; *impf* **выбега́ть**) *сов* to run out

выбива́|ть(ся) (-ю(сь)) *несов от* **вы́бить(ся)**

выбира́|ть (-ю) *несов от* **вы́брать**

вы́б|ить (-ью, -ьешь) *impf*

выбива́ть сов перех to knock out; (противника) to oust; (ковёр) to beat; (надпись) to carve; выбива́ть (~ pf) чек (кассир) to ring up the total; ~ся (impf выбива́ться) сов возв: ~ся из +gen (освободиться) to get out of

вы́бор (-а) м choice

вы́борный прил (кампания) election; (пост, орган) elective

выборочный прил selective; ~ая прове́рка spot check

вы́бор|ы (-ов) мн election ед

выбра́сыва|ть(ся) (-ю(сь)) несов от выбросить(ся)

выб|ра́ть (-еру, -ерешь; impf выбира́ть) сов перех to choose; (голосованием) to elect

вы́брос (-а) м (газа) emission; (отходов) discharge; (нефти) spillage

вы́бро|сить (-шу, -сишь; impf выбра́сывать) сов перех to throw out; (отходы) to discharge; (газы) to emit; ~ся (impf выбра́сываться) сов возв to throw oneself out; выбра́сываться (~ся pf) с парашю́том to bale out

вы́|ть (как быть; см. Table 21; impf выбыва́ть) сов: ~ из +gen to leave

выведе́ни|е (-я) ср (формулы) deduction; (породы) breeding; (вредителей) extermination

вы́вез|ти (-у, -ешь; impf вывози́ть) сов перех to take; (товар: из страны) to take out

вы́верн|уть (-у; impf вывёртывать) сов перех (винт) to unscrew; (карманы, рукава) to turn inside out; ~ся (impf вывёртываться) сов возв (винт) to come unscrewed

вы́ве|сить (-шу, -сишь; impf вывешивать) сов перех (флаг)

to put up; (бельё) to hang out

вы́вес|ка (-ки; gen pl -ок) ж sign

вы́ве|сти (-ду, -дешь; impf выводи́ть) сов перех to take out; (войска: из города) to pull out, withdraw; (формулу) to deduce; (птенцов) to hatch; (породу) to breed; (уничтожить) to exterminate; (исключить) to ~ кого́-н из +gen (из партии) to expel sb from; выводи́ть (~ pf) кого́-н из терпе́ния to exasperate sb; выводи́ть (~ pf) кого́-н из себя́ to drive sb mad; ~ся (impf выводи́ться) сов возв (цыплята) to hatch (out); (исчезнуть) to be eradicated

вывешива|ть (-ю) несов от вы́весить

вы́вих (-а) м dislocation

вы́вихн|уть (-у) сов перех to dislocate

вы́вод (-а) м (войск) withdrawal; (умозаключение) conclusion

выво|ди́ть(ся) (-жу(сь), -дишь(ся)) несов от вы́вести(сь)

вы́воз (-а) м removal; (товаров) export

выво|зи́ть (-жу́, -́зишь) несов от вы́везти

вывора́чива|ть(ся) (-ю(сь)) несов от вы́вернуть(ся)

выгиба́|ть (-ю) несов от вы́гнуть

вы́гля|деть (-жу, -дишь) несов to look

выгля́|дывать (-ю) несов от вы́глянуть

вы́гля|нуть (-у; impf выгля́дывать) сов to look out

вы́г|нать (-оню, -онишь; impf выгоня́ть) сов перех to throw out; (стадо) to drive out

вы́гн|уть (-у; impf выгиба́ть) сов перех to bend; (спину) to arch

вы́говор (-а) м (произношение)

accent; (*наказание*) reprimand

вы́говор|ить (-ю, -ишь; *impf*
выгова́ривать) *сов перех*
(*произнести*) to pronounce

вы́год|а (-ы) *ж* advantage, benefit;
(*прибыль*) profit

вы́годно *нареч* (*продать*) at a
profit ♦ *как сказ* it is profitable;
мне э́то ~ this is to my advantage;
(*прибыльно*) this is profitable for
me

вы́годный *прил* (*сделка*)
profitable; (*условия*) advantageous

выгоня́|ть (-ю) *несов от*
вы́гнать

вы́гор|еть (3sg -ит; *impf*
выгора́ть) *сов* (*сгореть*) to burn
down; (*выцвести*) to fade

вы́грес|ти (-бу, -бешь; *pt* -б,
-бла, -бло; *impf* **выгреба́ть**) *сов
перех* to rake out

вы́гру|зить (-жу, -зишь; *impf*
выгружа́ть) *сов перех* to
unload; **~ся** (*impf* **выгружа́ться**)
сов возв to unload

выда|ва́ть(ся) (-ю́(сь)) *несов от*
вы́дать(ся)

вы́дав|ить (-лю, -ишь; *impf*
выда́вливать) *сов перех*
(*лимон*) to squeeze

вы́да|ть (как **дать**; см. Table 16;
impf **выдава́ть**) *сов перех* to give
out; (*патент*) to issue;
(*продукцию*) to produce; (*тайну*)
to give away; **выдава́ть (~ *pf*)
кого́-н/что́-л за** +*acc* to pass sb/sth
off as; **выдава́ть (~ *pf*) де́вушку
за́муж** to marry a girl off; **~ся** (*impf*
выдава́ться) *сов возв* (*берег*) to
jut out

вы́дач|а (-и) *ж* (*справки*) issue;
(*продукции*) output;
(*заложников*) release

выдаю́щийся *прил* outstanding

выдвига́|ть(ся) (-ю(сь)) *несов*

от вы́двинуть(ся)

выдвиже́ни|е (-я) *ср*
(*кандидата*) nomination

вы́дви|нуть (-у; *impf* **выдвига́ть**)
сов перех to put forward; (*ящик*)
to pull out; (*обвинение*) to level;
~ся (*impf* **вы́двига́ться**) *сов возв*
to slide out; (*работник*) to advance

выделе́ни|е (-я) *ср* (*средств*)
allocation; (*физиология*) secretion

вы́дел|ить (-ю, -ишь; *impf*
выделя́ть) *сов перех* to assign,
allocate; (*отличить*) to pick out;
(*газы*) to emit; **~ся** (*impf*
выделя́ться) *сов возв* (*пот*) to
be secreted; (*газ*) to be emitted;
выделя́ться (~ся *pf*) чем-н to
stand out by virtue of sth

выдёргива|ть (-ю) *несов от*
вы́дернуть

вы́держанный *прил* (*человек*)
self-possessed; (*вино, сыр*) mature

вы́держ|ать (-у, -ишь; *impf*
выде́рживать) *сов перех*
(*давление*) to withstand; (*боль*)
to bear; (*экзамен*) to get through
♦ *неперех* (*человек*) to hold out;
(*мост*) to hold; **не ~** (*pf*) (*человек*)
to give in

вы́держ|ка (-ки; *gen pl* -ек) *ж*
(*самообладание*) self-control;
(*отрывок*) excerpt; (*ФОТО*)
exposure

вы́дер|нуть (-у; *impf*
выдёргивать) *сов перех* to pull
out

вы́дох (-а) *м* exhalation; **де́лать
(сде́лать *pf*) ~** to breathe out

вы́дохн|уть (-у; *impf* **выдыха́ть**)
сов перех to exhale, breathe out

вы́дум|ать (-ю; *impf*
выду́мывать) *сов перех*
(*историю*) to make up, invent;
(*игру*) to invent

вы́дум|ка (-ки; *gen pl* -ок) *ж*

invention

выдыха́ни|е (**-я**) *ср* exhalation

выдыха́|ть (**-ю**) *несов от* **выдохнуть**

вы́езд (**-а**) *м* (*отъезд*) departure; (*место*) way out; **игра́ на ~е** (*СПОРТ*) away game

выездно́й *прил* (*документ*) exit; ~ **спекта́кль** guest performance; ~ **матч** away match

вы́е|хать (*как* **е́хать**; *см* Table 19; *impf* **выезжа́ть**) *сов* (*уехать*) to leave; (*машина*) to drive out

вы́ж|ать (**-му, -мешь**; *impf* **выжима́ть**) *сов перех* (*лимон*) to squeeze; (*бельё*) to wring (out)

вы́ж|ечь (**-гу, -жешь** *итп* **-гут**; **-ег, -гла**; *impf* **выжига́ть**) *сов перех* to burn; (*подлеж: солнце*) to scorch

выжива́ни|е (**-я**) *ср* survival

выжива́|ть (**-ю**) *несов от* **вы́жить**

выжига́|ть (**-ю**) *несов от* **вы́жечь**

выжима́|ть (**-ю**) *несов от* **вы́жать**

вы́жи|ть (**-ву, -вешь**; *impf* **выжива́ть**) *сов* to survive ♦ *перех* (*разг*) to drive out

выз|ва́ть (**-ову, овешь**; *impf* **вызыва́ть**) *сов перех* to call; (*гнев, критику*) to provoke; (*восторг*) to arouse; (*пожар*) to cause; **вызыва́ть (~ *pf*) кого́-н на что́-н** to challenge sb to sth; **~ся** (*impf* **вызыва́ться**) *сов возв*: **~ся** +*infin* to volunteer to do

вы́здорове|ть (**-ю, -ешь**; *impf* **выздора́вливать**) *сов* to recover

вы́зов (**-а**) *м* call; (*в суд*) summons; ~ +*dat* (*обществу, родителям итп*) challenge; **броса́ть (бро́сить *pf*) ~ кому́-н/чему́-н** to challenge sb/sth

вы́зубр|ить (**-ю, -ишь**) *сов от* **зубри́ть**

вызыва́|ть(ся) (**-ю(сь)**) *несов от* **вы́звать(ся)**

вызыва́ющий *прил* challenging

вы́игра|ть (**-ю**; *impf* **выи́грывать**) *сов перех* to win

вы́игрыш (**-а**) *м* (*матча*) winning; (*денежный*) winnings *мн*; (*выгода*) advantage

вы́игрышный *прил* (*выгодный*) advantageous; ~ **вклад** ≈ premium bonds

вы́|йти (*как* **идти́**; *см* Table 18; *impf* **выходи́ть**) *сов* to leave; (*из игры*) to drop out; (*из автобуса*) to get off; (*книга*) to come out; (*случиться*) to ensue; (*оказаться*): ~ +*instr* to come out; **выходи́ть (~ *pf*) за́муж за** +*acc* to marry (*of woman*); **выходи́ть (~ *pf*) из больни́цы** to leave hospital

выка́лыва|ть (**-ю**) *несов от* **вы́колоть**

выка́пыва|ть (**-ю**) *несов от* **вы́копать**

выка́рмлива|ть (**-ю**) *несов от* **вы́кормить**

выка́ча|ть (**-ю**; *impf* **выка́чивать**) *сов перех* to pump out

вы́кидыш (**-а**) *м* miscarriage

вы́кин|уть (**-у**; *impf* **выки́дывать**) *сов перех* to throw out; (*слово*) to omit

выкипе́|ть (*3sg* -**ит**; *impf* **выкипа́ть**) *сов* to boil away

выкла́дыва|ть (**-ю**) *несов от* **вы́ложить**

выключа́тел|ь (**-я**) *м* switch

вы́ключ|ить (**-у, -ишь**; *impf* **выключа́ть**) *сов перех* to turn off; **~ся** (*impf* **выключа́ться**) *сов возв* (*мотор*) to go off; (*свет*) to go out

вы́к|овать (**-ую**) *impf*

вы́ко́вывать) *сов перех* (металл) to forge

вы́кол|**оть** (-**ю**, -**ешь**; *impf* **выка́лывать**) *сов перех* to poke out

вы́копа|**ть** (-**ю**) *сов от* копа́ть ♦ (*impf* **выка́пывать**) *перех* (*яму*) to dig; (*овощи*) to dig up

вы́корм|**ить** (-**лю**, -**ишь**; *impf* **выка́рмливать**) *сов перех* to rear

вы́крик (-**а**) *м* shout

вы́крикн|**уть** (-**у**; *impf* **выкри́кивать**) *сов перех* to shout *или* cry out

вы́кро́йка (-**йки**; *gen pl* -**ек**) *ж* pattern

вы́кру|**тить** (-**чу**, -**тишь**; *impf* **выкру́чивать**) *сов перех* to unscrew; **~ся** *сов возв* to come unscrewed

вы́куп (-**а**) *м* (заложника) ransoming; (вещей) redemption; (плата) ransom

вы́купа|**ть(ся)** (-**ю(сь)**) *сов от* купа́ть(ся)

вы́куп|**ить** (-**лю**, -**ишь**; *impf* **выкупа́ть**) *сов перех* (заложника) to ransom; (вещи) to redeem

выла́влива|**ть** (-**ю**) *несов от* вы́ловить

выла́мыва|**ть** (-**ю**) *несов от* вы́ломать

вы́лез|**ти** (-**у**, -**ешь**; *pt* -, -**ла**; *impf* **вылеза́ть**) *сов* to fall out; **вылеза́ть** (**~** *pf*) **из** +*gen* to climb out of

вы́леп|**ить** (-**лю**, -**ишь**) *сов от* лепи́ть

вы́лет (-**а**) *м* departure

вы́ле|**теть** (-**чу**, -**тишь**; *impf* **вылета́ть**) *сов* to fly out; **его́ и́мя** **~тело у меня́ из головы́** his name has slipped my mind

вы́леч|**ить** (-**у**, -**ишь**; *impf* **выле́чивать**) *сов перех* to cure; **~ся** *несов возв* to be cured

вы́л|**ить** (-**ью**, -**ьешь**; *impf* **вылива́ть**) *сов перех* to pour out; (*impf* лить; *деталь, статую*) to cast; **~ся** *сов возв* to pour out; **вылива́ться** (**~ся** *pf*) **в** +*acc* to turn into

вы́лов|**ить** (-**лю**, -**ишь**; *impf* **выла́вливать**) *сов перех* to catch

вы́лож|**ить** (-**у**, -**ишь**; *impf* **выкла́дывать**) *сов перех* to lay out; **выкла́дывать** (**~** *pf*) **что-н чем-н** (*плиткой*) to face sth with sth

вы́лома|**ть** (-**ю**; *impf* **выла́мывать**) *сов перех* to break open

вы́луп|**иться** (*3sg* -**ится**; *impf* **вылупливаться**) *сов возв* (*птенцы*) to hatch (out)

выма́чива|**ть** (-**ю**) *несов от* вы́мочить

вы́мер|**еть** (*3sg* -**рет**; *impf* **вымира́ть**) *сов* (*динозавры*) to become extinct; (*город*) to be dead

вы́ме|**сти** (-**ту**, -**тешь**; *pt* -**л**, -**ла**; *impf* **вымета́ть**) *сов перех* to sweep out

вы́ме|**стить** (-**щу**, -**стишь**; *impf* **вымеща́ть**) *сов перех*: **~ что-н на ком-н** to take sth out on sb

вымета́|**ть** (-**ю**) *несов от* вы́мести

вымира́|**ть** (*3sg* -**ет**) *несов от* вы́мереть

вымога́тельств|**о** (-**а**) *ср* extortion

вымога́|**ть** (-**ю**) *несов перех* to extort

вы́мокн|**уть** (-**ну**, -**нешь**; *pt* -, -**ла**) *сов* to get soaked through

вы́моч|ить (-у, -ишь; *impf*
вымáчивать) *сов перех* to soak

вы́мпел (-а) *м* (*на корабле*)
pennant; (*награда*) trophy (*in the
form of a pennant*)

вы́мыс|ел (-ла) *м* fantasy; (*ложь*)
fabrication

вы́м|ыть (-ою, -оешь) *сов от*
мыть

вы́мышленный *прил* fictitious

вы́м|я (-ени; *как* **врéмя**; *см. Table
4*) *ср* udder

вынáшива|ть (-ю) *несов перех*
to nurture

вы́нес|ти (-у, -ешь; *pt* -, -ла; *impf*
выноси́ть) *сов перех* to carry
или take out; (*приговор*) to pass,
pronounce; (*знания*) to gain; (*боль,
оскорблéние*) to bear

вынима́|ть (-ю) *несов от*
вы́нуть

вын|оси́ть (-ошу́, -óсишь)
несов от **вы́нести ♦** *перех*: я
егó не ~ошу́ I can't bear *или*
stand him

выно́сливый *прил* resilient

вы́ну|дить (-жу, -дишь; *impf*
вынуждáть) *сов перех*: ~
кого́-н/что́-н к чему́-н to force
sb/sth into sth

вы́нужденн|ый *прил* forced; **~ая
поса́дка** emergency landing

вы́н|уть (-у) *сов от* **вынима́ть**
сов перех to take out

вы́нырн|уть (-у) *сов* (*из воды*)
to surface; (*разг: из-за угла*) to
pop up

выпада́|ть (-ю) *несов от*
вы́пасть

выпадéни|е (-я) *ср* (*осадков*) fall;
(*зубов, волос*) falling out

вы́па|сть (-ду, -дешь; *impf*
выпада́ть) *сов* to fall out;
(*осадки*) to fall; (*задача итп*): ~

+*dat* to fall to; **мне** ~**л случáй/**~**ло
счáстье встрéтить его́** I chanced
to/had the luck to meet him

вы́пивк|а (-и) *ж* booze

вы́пи|сать (-шу, -шешь; *impf*
выпи́сывать) *сов перех* to copy
или write out; (*пропуск, счёт,
рецéпт*) to make out; (*газéту*) to
subscribe to; (*пациéнта*) to
discharge; **~ся** to be
discharged

вы́писыва|ться *несов возв* (*из
больни́цы*) to be discharged; (*с
áдреса*) to change one's residence
permit

вы́пис|ка (-ки; *gen pl* -ок) *ж*
(*цитáта*) extract

вы́п|ить (-ью, -ьешь; *imper*
-**ей(те)**) *сов от* **пить**

вы́плав|ить (-лю, -ишь; *impf*
выплавля́ть) *сов перех* to smelt

вы́плат|а (-ы) *ж* payment

вы́пла|тить (-чу, -тишь; *impf*
выпла́чивать) *сов перех* to pay;
(*долг*) to pay off

вы́плесн|уть (-у) *сов перех* to
pour out

вы́плы|ть (-ву, -вешь; *impf*
выплыва́ть) *сов* to swim out

вы́полз|ти (-у; *pt* -, -ла, -ло;
impf **выполза́ть**) *сов* to crawl out

выполни́мый *прил* feasible

вы́полн|ить (-ю, -ишь; *impf*
выполня́ть) *сов перех*
(*задáние, закáз*) to carry out;
(*план, услóвие*) to fulfil (*BRIT*),
fulfill (*US*)

вы́потрош|ить (-у, -ишь) *сов от*
потроши́ть

выпра́шива|ть (-ю) *несов перех*
to beg for

вы́про|сить (-шу, -сишь) *сов
перех*: **он ~сил у отца́ маши́ну**
he persuaded his father to give him
the car

вы́прыгн|уть (-у; *impf*
выпры́гивать) *сов* to jump out
выпрям|и́ть (-лю, -ишь; *impf*
выпрямля́ть) *сов перех* to
straighten (out); **~ся** (*impf*
выпрямля́ться) *несов возв* to
straighten (up)
вы́пуклый *прил* (лоб итп)
bulging; (линза) convex
вы́пуск (-а) *м* (продукции)
output; (газа) emission, release;
(книги) publication; (денег,
акций) issue; (учащиеся) school-
leavers *мн* (BRIT), graduates *мн* (US)
выпуска́|ть (-ю) *несов от*
вы́пустить
выпускни́к (-а́) *м* (вуза)
graduate; **~ шко́лы** school-leaver
(BRIT), graduate (US)
выпускно́й *прил* (класс) final-
year; (ТЕХ): **~ кла́пан** exhaust
valve; (вечер) graduation; **~**
экза́мен final exam, finals *мн*

> **выпускны́е экза́мены** - final
> exams. These exams are set by
> pupils at the end of their
> secondary education. Pupils have
> no choice as to the subjects they
> study and the exams they
> subsequently take. They have to
> study all the subjects in the
> curriculum. All exams, except an
> essay on Russian literature and an
> exam in maths, are oral.

вы́пу|стить (-щу, -стишь; *impf*
выпуска́ть) *сов перех* to let out;
(дым) to exhale; (заключённого)
to release; (специалистов) to turn
out; (продукцию) to produce;
(книгу) to publish; (заём, марки)
to issue; (акции) to put into
circulation; (исключить):
параграф to omit

вы́пью *etc сов см.* **вы́пить**
вы́работа|ть (-ю; *impf*
выраба́тывать) *сов перех* to
produce; (план) to work out;
(привычку) to develop
выра́внива|ть (-ю) *несов от*
вы́ровнять
выража́|ть(ся) (-ю(сь)) *несов от*
вы́разить(ся)
выраже́ни|е (-я) *ср* expression
вырази́тельный *прил* expressive
вы́ра|зить (-жу, -зишь; *impf*
выража́ть) *сов перех* to express;
~ся (*impf* **выража́ться**) *сов возв*
(чувство) to manifest *или* express
itself; (человек) to express o.s.
выр|асти́ (-асту, -астешь; *pt*
-ос, -осла, -осли) *сов от* расти́
♦ (*impf* **выраста́ть**) *неперех*
(появиться) to rise up; **выраста́ть**
(**~** *pf*) **в** +*acc* (grow to)
become
вы́ра|стить (-щу, -стишь) *сов*
от расти́ть
выра́щивани|е (-я) *ср*
(растений) cultivation;
(животных) rearing
выра́щива|ть (-ю; *pf* **вы́растить**)
несов перех = расти́ть
вырв|а́ть (-у, -ешь; *impf*
вырыва́ть) *сов перех* to pull out;
(отнять): **~ что-н у кого́-н** to
snatch sth from sb ♦ (*impf* **рвать**)
безл (разг): **её -́ало** she threw
up; **ему́ -́али зуб** he had his tooth
taken out; **~ся** (*impf* **вырыва́ться**)
сов возв (из тюрьмы) to escape;
(перен: в театр) to manage to get
away; (пламя) to shoot out
вы́рез (-а) *м*: **пла́тье с больши́м**
~ом a low-cut dress
вы́ре|зать (-жу, -жешь; *impf*
выреза́ть) *сов перех* to cut out;
(опухоль, гнойник) to remove;
(из дерева, из кости итп) to

carve; (*на камне, на металле итп*) to engrave; (*убить*) to slaughter

вы́рез|ка (**-ки**; *gen pl* **-ок**) *ж* (*газетная*) cutting, clipping; (*мясная*) fillet

вы́ровня|ть (**-ю**) *сов от* **ровня́ть ♦** (*impf* **выра́внивать**) *перех* to level

вы́род|иться (*3sg* **-ится**; *impf* **вырожда́ться**) *сов возв* to degenerate

вырожде́ни|е (**-я**) *ср* degeneration

вы́рон|ить (**-ю**, **-ишь**) *сов перех* to drop

вы́рос *etc см.* **вы́расти**

вы́руб|ить (**-лю**, **-ишь**; *impf* **выруба́ть**) *сов перех* (*деревья*) to cut down; (*свет*) to cut off

выруга́|ть(ся) (**-ю(сь)**) *сов от* **руга́ть(ся)**

вы́руч|ить (**-у**, **-ишь**; *impf* **выруча́ть**) *сов перех* to help out; (*деньги*) to make

вы́руч|а (**-и**) *ж* rescue; (*деньги*) takings *мн*

вырыва́|ть(ся) (**-ю(сь)**) *несов от* **вы́рвать(ся)**

вы́р|ыть (**-ою**, **-оешь**) *сов от* **рыть ♦** (*impf* **вырыва́ть**) *перех* to dig up; (*яму*) to dig

вы́са|дить (**-жу**, **-дишь**; *impf* **выса́живать**) *сов перех* (*растение*) to plant out; (*пассажира: дать выйти*) to drop off; (*: силой*) to throw out; (*войска*) to land; **~ся** (*impf* **выса́живаться**) *сов возв*: **~ся** (*из* +*gen*) to get off; (*войска*) to land

выса́сыва|ть (**-ю**) *несов от* **вы́сосать**

высвобо|ди́ть (**-жу́**, **-ди́шь**; *impf* **высвобожда́ть**) *сов перех*

(*ногу, руку*) to free; (*время*) to set aside

вы́сел|ить (**-ю**, **-ишь**; *impf* **выселя́ть**) *сов перех* to evict

вы́си|деть (**-жу**, **-дишь**; *impf* **выси́живать**) *сов перех* to hatch; (*перен: лекцию*) to sit out

вы́с|иться (*3sg* **-ится**) *несов возв* to tower

вы́ска|зать (**-жу**, **-жешь**; *impf* **выска́зывать**) *сов перех* to express; **~ся** (*impf* **выска́зываться**) *сов возв* to speak one's mind; **выска́зываться** (**~ся** *pf*) **про́тив** +*gen*/**за** +*acc* to speak out against/in favour of

выска́зывани|е (**-я**) *ср* statement

выска́кива|ть (**-ю**) *несов от* **вы́скочить**

выскользн|у́ть (**-у**; *impf* **выска́льзывать**) *сов* to slip out

вы́скоч|ить (**-у**, **-ишь**; *impf* **выска́кивать**) *сов* to jump out; **его́ и́мя ~ло у меня́ из головы́** (*разг*) his name has slipped my mind

вы́|слать (**-шлю**, **-шлешь**; *impf* **высыла́ть**) *сов перех* to send off; (*изгнать*) to deport

вы́сле|дить (**-жу**, **-дишь**; *impf* **высле́живать**) *сов перех* to track down

вы́слуг|а (**-и**) *ж*: **за ~у лет** for long service

вы́слуша|ть (**-ю**; *impf* **выслу́шивать**) *сов перех* to hear out

вы́сме|ять (**-ю**; *impf* **высме́ивать**) *сов перех* to ridicule

вы́сморка|ть(ся) (**-ю(сь)**) *сов от* **сморка́ть(ся)**

высо́выва|ть(ся) (**-ю(сь)**) *несов от* **вы́сунуть(ся)**

высо́кий *прил* high; (*человек*)

tall; (*честь*) great; (*гость*)
distinguished

высоко́ *нареч* high (up) ♦ *как
сказ* it's high (up)

высокого́рный *прил* alpine

высокоме́рный *прил* haughty

высокопа́рный *прил* (*речи*)
high-flown, pompous

высокопоста́вленный *прил*
high-ranking

вы́сос|ать (-у, -ешь; *impf*
выса́сывать) *сов перех* to suck
out; (*насосом*) to pump out

высот|а́ (-ы́, *nom pl* -ы) *ж*
height; (*ГЕО*) altitude; (*звука*) pitch

высо́тный *прил* (*здание*) high-
rise

высох|нуть (-ну; *pt* -, -ла, -ло)
сов от **со́хнуть**

высо́честв|о (-а) *ср*: Ва́ше *итп*
Высо́чество Your *etc* Highness

вы́сп|аться (-люсь, -ишься; *impf*
высыпа́ться) *сов возв* to sleep
well

вы́став|ить (-лю, -ишь; *impf*
выставля́ть) *сов перех*
(*поставить наружу*) to put out;
(*грудь*) to stick out;
(*кандидатуру*) to put forward;
(*товар*) to display; (*охрану*) to
post; (*разг*: *выгнать*) to chuck out

вы́став|ка (-ки; *gen pl* -ок) *ж*
exhibition

выставля́|ть (-ю) *несов от*
вы́ставить

вы́стира|ть (-ю) *сов от* **стира́ть**

вы́стрел (-а) *м* shot

вы́стрел|ить (-ю, -ишь) *сов* to
fire

вы́стро|ить(ся) (-ю(сь),
-ишь(ся)) *сов от* **стро́ить(ся)**

вы́ступ (-а) *м* ledge

выступа́|ть (-ю) *несов от*
вы́ступить ♦ *неперех* (*берег*) to
jut out; (*скулы*) to protrude

выступ|а́ть (-лю, -ишь; *impf*
выступа́ть) *сов* (*против, в
защиту*) to come out; (*из толпы*)
to step out; (*актёр*) to perform;
(*пот, сыпь*) to break out; (*в
поход, на поиски*) to set off *или*
out

выступле́ни|е (-я) *ср* (*актёра*)
performance; (*в печати*) article;
(*речь*) speech

вы́сун|уть (-у; *impf* **высо́вывать**)
сов перех to stick out; **~ся** (*impf*
высо́вываться) *сов возв* (*из
окна́*) to lean out; (*рука, нога*) to
stick out

вы́суш|ить(ся) (-у(сь),
-ишь(ся)) *сов от* **суши́ть(ся)**

вы́счита|ть (-ю; *impf*
высчи́тывать) *сов перех* to
calculate

вы́сш|ий *прил* (*орган власти*)
highest, supreme; в **~ей сте́пени**
extremely; **~ая ме́ра наказа́ния**
capital punishment; **~ее
образова́ние** higher education;
~ее уче́бное заведе́ние = вуз

высыла́|ть (-ю) *несов от*
вы́слать

вы́сып|ать (-лю, -лешь; *impf*
высыпа́ть) *сов перех* to pour
out; (*разг*: *высыпа́ться*) *сов
возв* to pour out

выта́лкива|ть (-ю) *несов от*
вы́толкнуть

вы́тащ|ить (-у, -ишь) *сов от*
тащи́ть ♦ (*impf* **выта́скивать**)
перех (*мебель*) to drag out

вытека́|ть (*3sg* -ет) *несов от*
вы́течь ♦ *неперех* (*вывод*) to
follow; (*река*) to flow out

вы́тер|еть (-ру, -решь; *impf*
вытира́ть) *сов перех* to wipe up;
(*посуду*) to dry (up); (*руки,
глаза*) to wipe; **~ся** (*impf*
вытира́ться) *сов возв* (*человек*)

to dry o.s.

вы́тесн|ить (-ю, -ишь; *impf* **вытесня́ть**) *сов перех* (*удалить*) to oust; (*заменить собой*) to supplant

вы́те|чь (*3sg* -чет, *3pl* -кут, *pt* -к, -кла; *impf* **вытека́ть**) *сов* to flow out

вытира́|ть(ся) (-ю(сь)) *несов от* **вы́тереть(ся)**

вы́толкн|уть (-у; *impf* **выта́лкивать**) *сов перех* to push out

вы́трав|ить (-лю, -ишь; *impf* **вытравля́ть**) *сов перех* (*пятно*) to remove; (*крыс*) to exterminate; (*рисунок*) to etch

вытрезви́тел|ь (-я) *м* overnight police cell for drunks

вы́трях|нуть (-у; *impf* **вытря́хивать**) *сов перех* to shake out

вы|ть (**во́ю, во́ешь**) *несов* (*зверь, ветер*) to howl; (*сирена*) to wail

вы́тян|уть (-у; *impf* **вытя́гивать**) *сов перех* to pull out; (*дым*) to extract; (*руки*) to stretch; **~ся** (*impf* **вытя́гиваться**) *сов возв* (*на диване, вдоль берега*) to stretch out; (*встать смирно*) to stand at attention

вы́у|дить (-жу, -дишь; *impf* **выу́живать**) *сов перех* (*рыбу*) to catch; (*разг*: *сведения*) to wheedle out

вы́уч|ить(ся) (-у(сь), -ишь(ся)) *сов от* **учи́ть(ся)**

выха́жив|ать (-ю) *несов от* **выходить**

выхва́т|ить (-чу, -тишь; *impf* **выхва́тывать**) *сов перех* to snatch

выхлопн|о́й *прил* exhaust; **~ы́е га́зы** exhaust fumes

вы́ход (-а) *м* (*войск*) withdrawal; (*из кризиса*) way out; (*на сцену*) appearance; (*в море*) sailing; (*книги*) publication; (*на экран*) showing; (*место*) exit

выхо|ди́ть (-жу, -дишь; *impf* **выха́живать**) *сов перех* (*больного*) to nurse (back to health)

вых|оди́ть (-ожу́, -о́дишь) *несов от* **вы́йти** ♦ *неперех*: ~ **на** +*acc* (*юг, север*) to face; **окно́ ~о́дит в парк** the window looks out onto the park

вы́ход|ка (-ки) *ж* prank

выходн|о́й *прил* exit; (*платье*) best ♦ (-о́го) *м* day off (work); **сего́дня ~ день** today is a holiday; **~ы́е** weekend *ед*

вы́цве|сти (*3sg* -тет; *impf* **выцвета́ть**) *сов* to fade

вы́черкн|уть (-у; *impf* **вычёркивать**) *сов перех* to cross или score out

вы́че|сть (-ту, -тешь; *impf* **вычита́ть**) *сов перех* (*мат*) to subtract; (*долг, налог*) to deduct

вы́чет (-а) *м* deduction ♦ *предл*: **за ~ом** +*gen* minus

вычисле́ни|е (-я) *ср* calculation

вычисли́тельн|ый *прил* (*операция*) computing; **~ая маши́на** computer; **~ая те́хника** computers *мн*; **~ центр** computer centre (*BRIT*) или center (*US*)

вы́числ|ить (-ю, -ишь; *impf* **вычисля́ть**) *сов перех* to calculate

вычита́ни|е (-я) *ср* subtraction

вычита́|ть (-ю) *несов от* **вы́честь**

вы́ше *сравн прил от* **высо́кий** ♦ *сравн нареч от* **высоко́** ♦ *нареч* higher; (*в те́ксте*) above ♦ *предл*: ~ +*gen* above

вышел *сов см.* **вы́йти**

вышестоя́щий *прил* higher

вышива́ть (-ю) *несов от* **вы́шить**

вы́шив|ка (-ки; *gen pl* -ок) *ж* embroidery

вы́ш|ить (-ью, -ьешь; *impf* **вышива́ть**) *сов перех* to embroider

вы́ш|ка (-ки; *gen pl* -ек) *ж* (*строение*) tower; (*СПОРТ*) diving board; **бурова́я** *или* **нефтяна́я ~** derrick

вышла *etc сов см.* **вы́йти**

вы́яв|ить (-лю, -ишь; *impf* **выявля́ть**) *сов перех* (*талант*) to discover; (*недостатки*) to expose; **~ся** (*impf* **выявля́ться**) *сов возв* to come to light, be revealed

вы́ясн|ить (-ю, -ишь; *impf* **выясня́ть**) *сов перех* to find out; **~ся** (*impf* **выясня́ться**) *сов возв* to become clear

Вьетна́м (-а) *м* Vietnam

вью́г|а (-и) *ж* snowstorm, blizzard

вя́жущий *прил* (*вкус*) acerbic; (*материал*) binding

вяз (-а) *м* elm

вяза́ни|е (-я) *ср* knitting

вя́заный *прил* knitted

вя|за́ть (-жу́, -жешь; *pf* **с~**) *несов перех* to tie up; (*свитер*) to knit

вя́зкий *прил* (*тягучий*) viscous; (*топкий*) boggy

вя́з|нуть (-ну; *pt* -, -ла, -ло; *pf* **за~** *или* **у~**) *несов*: **~ (в** +*prp*) to get stuck in

вя́лый *прил* (*листья, цветы*) wilted, withered; (*человек, речь*) sluggish

вя́н|уть (-у; *pf* **за~** *или* **у~**) *несов* (*цветы*) to wilt, wither; (*красота*) to fade

Г, г

г *сокр* (= **грамм**) g, gm

г. *сокр* = **год**; **го́род**

Гаа́га (-и) *ж* The Hague

габари́т (-а) *м* (*ТЕХ*) dimension

Гава́йи *м нескл* Hawaii

га́ван|ь (-и) *ж* harbour (*BRIT*), harbor (*US*)

гада́|ть (-ю) *несов* (*предполагать*) to guess; **~ (по~** *pf*) **кому́-н** to tell sb's fortune

га́дост|ь (-и) *ж* filth

гадю́к|а (-и) *ж* viper, adder

га́ечный *прил*: **~ ключ** spanner

газ (-а) *м* gas; *см. также* **га́зы**

газе́т|а (-ы) *ж* newspaper

газиро́ванн|ый *прил*: **~ая вода́** carbonated water

га́зов|ый *прил* gas; **~ая плита́** gas cooker

газо́н (-а) *м* lawn

газопрово́д (-а) *м* gas pipeline

га́з|ы (-ов) *мн* (*МЕД*) wind *ед*

ГАИ *ж сокр* (= **Госуда́рственная автомоби́льная инспе́кция**) state motor vehicle inspectorate

га́йк|а (-и; *gen pl* -ек) *ж* nut

галантере́|я (-и) *ж* haberdashery (*BRIT*), notions store (*US*)

галере́|я (-и) *ж* gallery

га́л|ка (-ки; *gen pl* -ок) *ж* jackdaw

галло́н (-а) *м* gallon

галлюцина́ци|я (-и) *ж* hallucination

га́лоч|ка (-ки; *gen pl* -ек) *ж* (*в тексте*) tick, check (*US*)

га́лстук (-а) *м* tie, necktie (*US*)

га́льк|а (-и) *ж собир* pebbles *мн*

га́мбургер (-а) *м* hamburger

га́мм|а (-ы) *ж* (*МУЗ*) scale

гангре́н|а (-ы) *ж* gangrene

га́нгстер (-а) м gangster

гандбо́л (-а) м handball

ганте́ль (-и) ж dumbbell

гара́ж (-á) м garage

гара́нт (-а) м guarantor

гаранти́йный прил guarantee

гаранти́р|овать (-ую) (не)сов перех to guarantee

гара́нти|я (-и) ж guarantee

гардеро́б (-а) м wardrobe; (в общественном здании) cloakroom

гармони́р|овать (-ую) несов: ~ с +instr (о угля) cinders мн

гармони́ст (-а) м concertina player

гармо́ни|я (-и) ж harmony

гармо́шк|а (-ки; gen pl -ек) ж (разг) ≈ squeeze-box

гарнизо́н (-а) м garrison

гарни́р (-а) м side dish

гарниту́р (-а) м (мебель) suite

гар|ь (-и) ж (угля) cinders мн

га́|сить (-шý, -сишь; pf по~) несов перех (свет) to put out; (пожар) to extinguish

га́с|нуть (-ну; pt - или -нул, -ла; pf по~ или у~) (огни) to go out

гастри́т (-а) м gastritis

гастро́ли (-ей) мн performances of touring company; **е́здить/е́хать** (поéхать pf) на ~ to go on tour

гастроли́р|овать (-ую) несов to be on tour

гастроно́м (-а) м food store

гастроно́ми|я (-и) ж delicatessen

гаши́ш (-а) м cannabis

гва́рди|я (-и) ж (ВОЕН) Guards мн

гвозди́к|а (-и) ж (цветок) carnation; (пряность) cloves мн

гвозд|ь (-я́) м nail

гг сокр = го́ды, господа́

где нареч where; (разг: где-

нибудь) somewhere, anywhere ♦ союз where; ~ Вы живёте? where do you live?

где-ли́бо нареч = **где-нибудь**

где-нибудь нареч somewhere; (в вопросе) anywhere

где-то нареч somewhere

гекта́р (-а) м hectare

геморро́й (-я) м piles мн

ген (-а) м gene

генера́л (-а) м (ВОЕН) general

генера́льный прил general; (главный) main; **~ая убо́рка** spring-clean; **~ая репети́ция** dress rehearsal

генера́тор (-а) м generator

гене́тик|а (-и) ж genetics

генети́ческ|ий прил genetic; **~и модифици́рованный** genetically modified

гениа́льный прил great

ге́ни|й (-я) м genius

ге́нный прил (терапия) gene

геноци́д (-а) м genocide

геогра́фи|я (-и) ж geography

гео́лог (-а) м geologist

геоме́три|я (-и) ж geometry

гера́н|ь (-и) ж geranium

герб (-á) м coat of arms; **госуда́рственный ~** national emblem

ге́рбов|ый прил: **~ая бума́га** stamped paper

геркуле́с (-а) м (КУЛИН) porridge oats мн

Герма́ни|я (-и) ж Germany

герма́нский прил German

гермети́чный прил hermetic

герои́зм (-а) м heroism

герои́н|я (-и) ж heroine

герои́ческий прил heroic

геро́й (-я) м hero

г-жа́ м сокр = **госпожа́**

ги́бел|ь (-и) ж (человека) death; (армии) destruction; (самолёта) наде́жды) loss; (карье́ры) ruin

ги́бкий прил flexible

ги́б|нуть (-ну; pt -, -ла; pf по~)
несов to perish; (перен) to come
to nothing

гибри́д (-а) м hybrid

гига́нт (-а) м giant

гига́нтский прил gigantic

гигие́н|а (-ы) ж hygiene

гигиени́чный прил hygienic

гид (-а) м guide

гидравли́ческий прил hydraulic

гидрометцентр (-а) м сокр (=
Гидрометеорологи́ческий
центр) meteorological office

гидроэлектроста́нци|я (-и) ж
hydroelectric power station

гимн (-а) м: **госуда́рственный** ~
national anthem

гимна́зи|я (-и) ж ≈ grammar
school

> **гимна́зия** ~ grammar school. This
> institution of secondary education
> strives for higher academic
> standards than comprehensive
> schools. Pupils can study subjects
> which are not offered by
> mainstream education, e.g. classics
> and two modern languages.

гимна́ст (-а) м gymnast

гимна́стик|а (-и) ж exercises мн;
(спорти́вная) ~ gymnastics;
худо́жественная ~ modern
rhythmic gymnastics

гинеко́лог (-а) м gynaecologist
(BRIT), gynecologist (US)

гипертони́|я (-и) ж high blood
pressure

гипно́з (-а) м hypnosis

гипнотизи́р|овать (-ую; pf за~)
несов перех to hypnotize

гипо́тез|а (-ы) ж hypothesis

гипотони́|я (-и) ж low blood

pressure

гиппопота́м (-а) м hippopotamus,
hippo (inf)

гипс (-а) м (ИСКУССТВО) plaster of
Paris; (МЕД) plaster

гирля́нд|а (-ы) ж garland

ги́р|я (-и) ж (весо́в) weight;
(СПОРТ) dumbbell

гита́р|а (-ы) ж guitar

глав|а́ (-ы́; nom pl -ы) ж (кни́ги)
chapter; (зда́ния) dome ♦ (-ы́;
nom pl -ы) м/ж (делега́ции)
head; **во ~е́ с** +instr
headed by; **во ~е́** +gen at the head
of

глава́р|ь (-я́) м (ба́нды) leader

главнокома́ндующ|ий (-его) м
commander in chief

гла́вн|ый прил main; (ста́рший
по положе́нию) senior, head; **~ым
о́бразом** chiefly, mainly

глаго́л (-а) м verb

гла́дильн|ый прил: **~ая доска́**
ironing board

гла́|дить (-жу, -дишь; pf по~)
несов перех to iron; (во́лосы) to
stroke

гла́дкий прил (ро́вный) smooth

глаз (-а; loc sg -у́, nom pl -а́, gen pl
-) м eye; **с гла́зу на́** ~ tête à tête;
на ~ roughly

глазно́й прил eye

глазу́нь|я (-и) ж fried egg

гла́нд|а (-ы) ж (обы́чно мн) tonsil

гла́сность|ь (-и) ж openness

гла́сн|ый (-ого) м vowel;
(откры́тый) open, public

гли́н|а (-ы) ж clay

гли́няный прил clay

глоба́льный прил universal

гло́бус (-а) м globe

глота́|ть (-ю; pf проглоти́ть)
несов перех to swallow

глот|о́к (-ка́) м gulp, swallow;
(воды́, ча́я) drop

гло́х|нуть (-ну; pt -, -ла; pf по~)

несов to grow deaf; (мотор) to stall

глу́бже сравн прил от **глубо́кий**
♦ сравн нареч от **глубоко́**

глуб|ина́ (-**и́ны**; nom pl -**и́ны**) ж depth; (леса) heart; (перен): в ~ине́ души́ in one's heart of hearts

глубо́кий прил deep; (провинция) remote; (мысль) profound

глубоко́ нареч deeply ♦ как сказ: здесь ~ it's deep here

глубокоуважа́емый прил dear

глупе́|ть (-**ю**; pf по~) несов to grow stupid

глу́по как сказ it's stupid или silly

глу́пость (-**и**) ж stupidity, silliness; (поступок) stupid или silly thing; (слова) nonsense

глу́пый прил stupid, silly

глухо́й прил deaf; (звук) muffled

глухонем|о́й прил deaf-and-dumb ♦ (-**о́го**) м deaf-mute

глуши́тель (-**я**) м (TEX) silencer; (ABT) silencer (BRIT), muffler (US)

глуш|и́ть (-**у́**, -**и́шь**; pf за~) несов перех (звуки) to muffle; (мотор) to turn off

глушь (-**и**; instr sg -**ью**, loc sg -**и́**) ж wilderness

глы́б|а (-**ы**) ж (ледяна́я) block

глюко́з|а (-**ы**) ж glucose

гля́нцевый прил glossy

гля|де́ть (-**жу́**, -**ди́шь**; pf по~) несов to look

гна|ть (гоню́, го́нишь; pt -**л**, -**ла́**) несов перех (стадо) to drive; (человека) to throw out; (машину) to drive fast; **гна́ться** несов возв: **гна́ться за** +instr to pursue

гнев (-**а**) м wrath

гнезд|о́ (-**а́**; nom pl **гнёзда**, gen pl **гнёзд**) ср (птиц) nest

гне|сти́ (-**ту́**, -**тёшь**) несов перех to gnaw

гнёт (-**а**) м (бедности итп) yoke

гнету́щий прил depressing

гнило́й прил rotten

гнил|ь (-**и**) ж rotten stuff

гни|ть (-**ю**, -**ёшь**; pf с~) несов to rot

гно|и́ть (-**ю**, -**и́шь**; pf с~) несов перех to let rot; ~**ся** несов возв (рана) to fester

гно|й (-**я**) м pus

ГНС сокр (= Госуда́рственная нало́говая слу́жба) ≈ Inland Revenue

гн|уть (-**у**, -**ёшь**; pf согну́ть) несов перех to bend; **гну́ться** несов возв (ветка) to bend

говор|и́ть (-**ю́**, -**и́шь**; pf сказа́ть) несов перех to say; (правду) to tell ♦ неперех; no pf to speak, talk; (обсуждать): ~ о +prp to talk about; (общаться): ~ с +instr to talk to или with

говя́дин|а (-**ы**) ж beef

год (-**а**; loc sg -**у́**, nom pl -**ы**, gen pl -**о́в/лет**) м year; прошло́ 3 го́да/5 лет 3/5 years passed; из го́да в год year in year out; кру́глый ~ all year round

го|ди́ться (-**жу́сь**, -**ди́шься**) несов возв: ~ +dat to suit; ~ (impf) для +gen to be suitable for

го́д|ный прил: ~ к +dat или для +gen fit или suitable for; биле́т ~ен до ... the ticket is valid until ...

годовщи́н|а (-**ы**) ж anniversary

гол (-**а**; nom pl -**ы**) м goal

Голла́нди|я (-**и**) ж Holland

голла́ндский прил Dutch; ~ язы́к Dutch

гол|ова́ (-**овы́**; acc sg -**ову**, dat sg -**ове́**, nom pl -**овы**, gen pl -**о́в**, dat pl -**ова́м**) ж head

головно́й прил (офис) main; (боль) head

головокруже́ни|е (-я) *ср* giddiness

го́лод (-а) *м* hunger; *(недоедание)* starvation; *(бедствие)* famine

голода́ни|е (-я) *ср (воздержание)* fasting; **кислоро́дное ~** oxygen deficiency

голода́|ть (-ю) *несов* to starve; *(воздерживаться от пищи)* to fast

голо́дный *прил* hungry; *(год, время)* hunger-stricken

голодо́в|ка (-ки; gen pl -ок) *ж* hunger strike

гололёд (-а) *м* black ice

го́лос (-а; part gen -у, nom pl -á) *м* voice; *(ПОЛИТ)* vote; **во весь ~** at the top of one's voice

голосова́ни|е (-я) *ср* ballot

голос|ова́ть (-у́ю; pf про~) *несов* to vote; *(разг: на дороге)* to hitch (a lift)

голуб|о́й *прил* light blue ♦ **(-о́го)** *м (разг)* gay

го́луб|ь (-я; gen pl -е́й) *м* pigeon; dove

го́лый *прил (человек)* naked

гольф (-а) *м* golf; *(обычно мн: чулки)* knee sock

гомеопа́т (-а) *м* homoeopath *(BRIT)*, homeopath *(US)*

го́мик (-а) *м (разг)* homo(sexual)

гомосексуали́ст (-а) *м* homosexual

гоне́ни|е (-я) *ср* persecution

го́н|ка (-ки; gen pl -ок) *ж (разг: спешка)* rush; *(соревнования)* race; **~ вооруже́ний** arms race

гонора́р (-а) *м* fee; **а́вторский ~** royalty

го́ночный *прил* racing

го́нщик (-а) *м* racing *(BRIT)* или race car *(US)* driver; *(велосипедист)* racing cyclist

гоня́|ть (-ю, -ешь) *несов перех (ученика)* to grill ♦ *неперех* to race; **~ся** *несов возв:* **~ся за** +*instr (преследовать)* to chase (after); *(перен)* to pursue

гор. *сокр* = **го́род**

гор|а́ (acc sg -у, gen sg -ы́, nom pl -ы, dat pl -а́м) *ж* mountain; *(небольшая)* hill

гора́здо *нареч* much

горб (-á; loc sg -ý) *м* hump

горба́тый *прил* hunchbacked

горб|ить (-лю, -ишь; pf с~) *несов перех:* **~ спи́ну** to stoop; **~ся (pf с~ся)** *несов возв* to stoop

горбу́ш|ка (-ки; gen pl -ек) *ж* crust

гор|ди́ться (-жу́сь, -ди́шься) *несов перех:* **~** +*instr* to be proud of

го́рдость (-и) *ж* pride

го́рдый *прил* proud

го́р|е (-я) *ср (скорбь)* grief; *(несчастье)* misfortune

гор|ева́ть (-ю́ю) *несов* to grieve

горе́лый *прил* burnt

гор|е́ть (-ю́, -и́шь; pf с~) *несов* to burn; *(no pf; дом)* to be on fire; *(больной)* to be burning hot; *(глаза)* to shine

го́реч|ь (-и) *ж* bitter taste; *(потери)* bitterness

горизо́нт (-а) *м* horizon

горизонта́л|ь (-и) *ж* horizontal; *(на карте)* contour

горизонта́льный *прил* horizontal

гори́лл|а (-ы) *ж* gorilla

гори́стый *прил* mountainous

го́р|ка (-ки; gen pl -ок) *ж* hill; *(кучка)* small pile

го́рл|о (-а) *ср* throat

го́рлыш|ко (-ка; nom pl -ки, gen pl -ек) *ср (бутылки)* neck

гормо́н (-а) *м* hormone

гормона́льный *прил* hormonal

го́рный *прил* mountain; *(лыжи)*

downhill; (промышленность) mining

го́род (-а; nom pl -а́) м (большой) city; (небольшой) town

горожа́н|ин (-ина; nom pl -е, gen pl -) м city dweller

гороско́п (-а) м horoscope

горо́х (-а) м собир peas мн

горо́ш|ек (-ка) м собир peas мн; (на платье итп) polka dots мн; ткань в ~ spotted material

горо́шин|а (-ы) ж pea

горст|ь (-и; gen pl -ей) ж handful

горч|и́ть (3sg -и́т) несов to taste bitter

горчи́ц|а (-ы) ж mustard

горчи́чник (-а) м mustard plaster

горш|о́к (-ка́) м pot

го́рький прил bitter

го́рько нареч (плакать) bitterly
♦ как сказ: **во рту** ~ I have a bitter taste in my mouth

горю́ч|ее (-его) ср fuel

горю́чий прил flammable

горя́ч|ий прил hot; (перен: любовь) passionate; (: спор) heated; (: желание) burning; (: человек) hot-tempered; **~ая ли́ния** hot line

горячо́ нареч (спорить, любить) passionately ♦ как сказ it's hot

гос. сокр = **госуда́рственный**

Госба́нк (-а) м сокр (= госуда́рственный банк) state bank

госбезопа́сност|ь (-и) ж сокр (= госуда́рственная безопа́сность) national security

госбюдже́т (-а) м сокр (= госуда́рственный бюдже́т) state budget

госпитализи́р|овать (-ую) (не)сов перех to hospitalize

го́спитал|ь (-я) м army hospital

господа́ итп сущ см. **господи́н**

♦ мн (при фамилии, при звании) Messrs

го́спод|и межд: **Го́споди!** good Lord!

господ|и́н (-ина; nom pl -а́, gen pl -) м gentleman; (хозяин) master; (при обращении) sir; (при фамилии) Mr

госпо́дств|о (-а) ср supremacy

госпо́дств|овать (-ую) несов to rule; (мнение) to prevail

Госпо́д|ь (Го́спода; voc Го́споди) м (также: ~ **Бог**) the Lord; **не дай Го́споди!** God forbid!; **сла́ва тебе́ Го́споди!** Glory be to God!; (разг) thank God!

госпож|а́ (-и́) ж lady; (хозяйка) mistress; (при обращении, при звании) Madam; (при фамилии: замужняя) Mrs; (: незамужняя) Miss; (: замужняя или незамужняя) Ms

госстра́х (-а) м сокр (= госуда́рственное страхова́ние) ≈ national insurance

гостеприи́мный прил hospitable

гости́н|ая (-ой) ж living или sitting room, lounge (BRIT)

гости́ниц|а (-ы) ж hotel

го|сти́ть (-щу́, -сти́шь) несов to stay

гост|ь (-я; gen pl -е́й) м guest; **идти́ (пойти́ pf) в го́сти к кому́-н** to go to see sb; **быть (impf) в ~я́х у кого́-н** to be at sb's house

госуда́рственный прил state

госуда́рств|о (-а) ср state

гото́в|ить (-лю, -ишь; pf при-) несов перех to get ready; (уроки) to prepare; (обед) to prepare, make; (pf под~; специалиста) to train ♦ неперех to cook; **~ся** (pf при~ся) несов to get ready; **~ся** (к отъезду) to get ready for; **~ся** (под~ся pf) **к** +dat (к экзамену) to prepare for

готóвност|ь (-и) ж: ~ *или* +infin readiness *или* willingness to do

готóво *как сказ* that's it

готóв|ый *прил* (изделие) ready-made; **я/обéд готóв!** I am/dinner is ready; **~ к** +dat/ +infin prepared for/ to do

гр. *сокр* (= граждани́н) Mr (= гражда́нка) Mrs

граб|éж (-ежá) м robbery; (дома) burglary

граби́тел|ь (-я) м robber

граби́тельск|ий *прил* (война) predatory; **~ое нападéние** (на дом) burglary; (на банк) robbery

граб|и́ть (-лю, -ишь; *pf* **о~)** *несов перех* (человека) to rob; (дом) to burgle; (pf **раз~)** to pillage

грáбл|и (-ель *или* **-лей)** мн rake ед

грáви|й (-я) м gravel

гравир|овáть (-ую; *pf* **вы~)** *несов перех* to engrave

гравюр|а (-ы) ж (оттиск) engraving; (офорт) etching

град (-а) м (также перен) hail

грáдус (-а) м degree

грáдусник (-а) м thermometer

граждани́н (-а; *nom pl* **грáждане,** *gen pl* **грáждан)** м citizen

граждáн|ка (-ки; *gen pl* **-ок)** ж citizen

граждáнск|ий *прил* civil; (долг) civic; (платье) civilian

граждáнств|о (-а) *ср* citizenship

грамм (-а) м gram(me)

граммáтик|а (-и) ж grammar

граммати́ческ|ий *прил* grammatical; (упражнение) grammar

грáмот|а (-ы) ж (документ) certificate

грáмотный *прил* (человек)

literate; (текст) correctly written; (специалист, план) competent

грампласти́нк|а (-и) ж record

гранáт|а (-ы) ж grenade

грандиóзный *прил* grand

гранёный *прил* (стакан) cut-glass

грани́ц|а (-ы) ж (государства) border; (участка) boundary; (обычно мн: перен) limit; **éхать (поéхать** *pf*) **за ~у** to go abroad; **жить (impf) за ~ей** to live abroad; **из-за ~ы** from abroad

грани́ч|ить (-у, -ишь) *несов*: ~ **с** +instr to border on (перен) to verge on

грант (-а) м grant

гран|ь (-и) ж (ГЕОМ) face; (алмаза) facet; **на грáни** +gen on the brink *или* verge of

граф|á (-ы́) ж column

грáфик (-а) м (МАТ) graph; (план) schedule, timetable

графи́н (-а) м (для вина) decanter; (открытый) carafe

графи́ческий *прил* graphic

грáци|я (-и) ж grace

гребён|ка (-ки; *gen pl* **-ок)** ж comb

гребеш|óк (-кá) м comb

грéбл|я (-и) ж rowing

грéйпфрут (-а) м grapefruit

грек (-а) м Greek (man)

грéл|ка (-ки; *gen pl* **-ок)** ж hot-water bottle

грем|éть (-лю, -и́шь; *pf* **про~)** *несов* (поезд) to thunder by; (гром) to rumble; ~ **(про~** *pf*) +instr (ведром) to clatter

грéн|ка (-ки; *gen pl* **-ок)** ж toast

грес|ти́ (-бу́, -бёшь; *pt* **грёб, -блá)** *несов* (веслом) to row; (веслом, руками) to paddle ♦ *перех* (листья) to rake

грет|ь (-ю) *несов перех* (подлеж: солнце) to heat, warm; (: шуба) to keep warm; (*воду*) to heat (up); (*руки*) to warm; **грéться** *несов возв* (*человек*) to warm o.s.; (*вода*) to warm *или* heat up

грех (**-á**) *м* sin

Грéци|**я** (**-и**) *ж* Greece

грéцкий *прил*: ~ **орéх** walnut

грéческий *прил* Greek; ~ **язык** Greek

грéчк|**а** (**-и**) *ж* buckwheat

грéчневый *прил* buckwheat

греш|**úть** (**-ý, -úшь**; *pf* **со**~) *несов* to sin

гриб (**-á**) *м* (*съедобный*) (edible) mushroom; **несъедóбный** ~ toadstool

грибнóй *прил* (*суп*) mushroom

гриб|**óк** (**-кá**) *м* (*на коже*) fungal infection; (*на дереве*) fungus

грим (**-а**) *м* stage make-up, greasepaint

гримáс|**а** (**-ы**) *ж* grimace

гримир|**овáть** (**-ýю**; *pf* **за**~) *несов перех*: ~ **когó-н** to make sb up

грипп (**-а**) *м* flu

гриф (**-а**) *м* (*МУЗ*) fingerboard

грúфел|**ь** (**-я**) *м* (pencil)lead

гроб (**-а**; *loc sg* **-ý**, *nom pl* **-ы**) *м* coffin

гр|**озá** (**-озы**; *nom pl* **-óзы**) *ж* thunderstorm

грозд|**ь** (**-и**; *gen pl* **-éй**) *ж* (*винограда*) bunch; (*сирени*) cluster

гро|**зúть** (**-жý, -зúшь**) *несов* (*опасность*) to loom; ~ (*impf*) +*instr* (*катастрофой*) to threaten to become; ~ (*impf*) +*dat* **комý-н чем-н** to threaten sb with sth

грóзный *прил* threatening; (*противник, оружие*) formidable

грозов|**óй** *прил*: ~**áя тýча** storm cloud

гром (**-а**; *gen pl* **-óв**) *м* thunder

громáдный *прил* enormous, huge

гром|**úть** (**-лю́, -úшь**) *несов перех* to destroy

грóмкий *прил* (*голос*) loud; (*скандал*) big

грóмко *нареч* loudly

громóздкий *прил* cumbersome

грóмче *сравн прил от* **грóмкий** ◆ *сравн нареч от* **грóмко**

грóхот (**-а**) *м* racket

грох|**отáть** (**-очý, -óчешь**; *pf* **про**~) *несов* to rumble

груб|**éть** (**-ю**; *pf* **о**~) *несов* (*человек*) to become rude; (*pf* **за**~) (*кожа*) to become rough

груб|**úть** (**-лю́, -úшь**; *pf* **на**~) *несов*: ~ +*dat* to be rude to

грубиáн (**-а**) *м* rude person

грýбо *нареч* (*отвечать*) rudely; (*подсчитать*) roughly; ~ **говоря** roughly speaking

грýбость (**-и**) *ж* rudeness

грýбый *прил* (*человек*) rude; (*ткань, пища*) coarse; (*кожа, подсчёт*) rough; (*ошибка, шутка*) crude; (*нарушение правил*) gross

грýд|**а** (**-ы**) *ж* pile, heap

грудúнк|**а** (**-и**) *ж* (*говядина*) brisket; (*копчёная свинина*) bacon

груднóй *прил* (*молоко*) breast; (*кашель*) chest; ~ **ребёнок** baby

гр|**удь** (**-удú**; *instr sg* **-ýдью**, *nom pl* **-ýди**) *ж* (*АНАТ*) chest; (: *женщины*) breasts *мн*; **кормúть** (*impf*) **~ýдью** to breast-feed

гружёный *прил* loaded

груз (**-а**) *м* (*тяжесть*) weight; (*товар*) cargo

грузúн (**-а**) *м* Georgian

гру|**зúть** (**-ужý, -ýзишь**; *pf* **за**~ *или* **на**~) *несов перех* (*корабль итп*) to load (up); ~ (**по**~ *pf*) (*в/на* +*acc*) (*товар*) to load (onto)

Грýзи|**я** (**-и**) *ж* Georgia

грузови́к (-а́) м lorry (BRIT), truck (US)

грузов|о́й прил (судно, самолёт) cargo; **~ая маши́на** goods vehicle; **~о́е такси́** removal (BRIT) или moving (US) van

грузоподъёмность|ь (и) ж freight или cargo capacity

гру́зчик (-а) м porter; (в магазине) stockroom worker

грунт (-а) м soil; (краска) primer

гру́пп|а (-ы) ж group; **~ кро́ви** blood group

группиров|а́ть (-у́ю; pf **с~**) несов перех (отдел) to set up; (данные, цифры) to group, classify

гру|сти́ть (-щу́, -сти́шь) несов to feel melancholy или very sad; (impf **по** +dat или **о** +prp to pine for, miss

гру́стно нареч sadly ♦ как сказ: **мне ~** I feel sad

гру́стный прил sad

гру́ш|а (-и) ж pear

грыз|ть (-у́, -ёшь; pt -, -ла) несов перех (яблоки) to nibble (at); (pf **разгры́зть**; кость) to gnaw (on)

гряд|а́ (-ки; gen pl -ок) ж row

гря́зно как сказ безл: **до́ма/на у́лице ~** the street/house is filthy

гря́зный прил dirty

грязь (-и; loc sg -и́) ж dirt; (на дороге) mud; (перен) dirt

губ|а́ (-ы́; nom pl -ы, dat pl -а́м) ж lip

губе́рни|я (-и) ж gubernia (administrative region)

губерна́тор (-а) м governor

губи́ть (-лю́, -ишь; pf **по~**) несов перех to kill; (здоровье) to ruin

гу́б|ка (-ки; gen pl -ок) ж sponge

губн|о́й прил: **~а́я пома́да** lipstick; **~а́я гармо́шка** harmonica

гу|де́ть (-жу́, -ди́шь) несов (шмель, провода) to hum; (ветер) to moan

гуд|о́к (-ка́) м (автомобиля) horn; (парохода, завода) siren; (звук) hoot

гул (-а) м (голосов) drone

гу́лкий прил (шаги) resounding; (свод) echoing

гуля́|ть (-ю; pf **по~**) несов to stroll; (быть на улице) to be out; (на свадьбе) to have fun, enjoy o.s.; **идти́ (пойти́** pf) **~** to go for a walk

гуманита́рный прил (помощь) humanitarian; (образование) arts

гума́нный прил humane

гу́сеница (-ы) ж caterpillar; (трактора) caterpillar track

гуси́н|ый прил (яйцо) goose; **~ая ко́жа** goose flesh, goose pimples (BRIT) или bumps (US)

густе́|ть (3sg -ет; pf **по~**) несов (туман) to become denser; (pf **за~**; каша) to thicken

густо́й прил (лес) dense; (брови) bushy; (облака, суп, волосы) thick; (цвет, бас) rich

густонаселённый прил densely populated

гусь (-я; gen pl -е́й) м goose, gander

гуся́тниц|а (-ы) ж casserole (dish)

гу́щ|а (-и; gen pl (кофейная) grounds мн; (заросли) thicket; **в ~е собы́тий** at the centre of events

ГЭС ж сокр = **гидроэлектроста́нция**

Д, д

KEYWORD

да *част* 1 (*выражает согласие*)
yes

2 (*не так ли*): **ты придёшь, да?**
you're coming, aren't you?; **ты
меня́ лю́бишь, да?** you love me,
don't you?

3 (*пусть: в лозунгах, в
призывах*); **да здра́вствует
демокра́тия!** long live democracy!

4 (*во фразах*): **вот э́то да!** (*разг*)
cool!; **ну да!** (*разг*) sure!;
(*выражает недоверие*) I'll bet!;
да ну́! (*разг*) no way!

♦ *союз* (*и*) and; **у неё то́лько
одно́ пла́тье, да и то ста́рое** she
only has one dress and even that's
old

дава́й(те) *несов см.* **дава́ть**
♦ *част* let's; ~ **пить чай** let's have
some tea; **дава́й-дава́й!** (*разг*)
come on!, get on with it!

дава́ть (-ю; *imper* ~**вай(те))**
несов от **дать**

дави́ть (-лю́, -ишь) *несов перех*
(*подлеж: обувь*) to pinch; (*pf* **за~;**
калечить) to crush, trample;
(*подлеж: машина*) to run over; (*pf*
раз~; *насекомых*) to squash; (*impf*)
на +*acc* (*налегать*) to press
или weigh down on; ~**ся** *несов
возв:* ~**ся (по~ся** *pf)* +*instr*
(*костью*) to choke on

да́вк|а (-и; *gen pl* **-ок)** *ж* crush

давле́ни|е (-я) *ср* pressure

да́вн|ий *прил:* **с ~их пор** for a
long time

давно́ *нареч* (*случиться*) a long

time ago; (*долго*) for a long time;
~ **бы так!** about time too!

давны́м-давно́ *нареч* (*разг*) ages
ago

дади́м *etc сов см.* **дать**

да́же *част* even

дай(те) *etc сов см.* **дать**

дал *etc сов см.* **дать**

да́лее *нареч* further; **и так ~** and
so on

далёкий *прил* distant, far-off

далеко́ *нареч* (*о расстоянии*) far
away ♦ *как сказ* it's a long way
away; ~ **за** +*acc* long after; ~ **не** by
no means

дало́ *etc сов см.* **дать**

дальне́йш|ий *прил* further; **в ~ем**
in the future

да́льний *прил* distant; (*поезд*)
long-distance; **Да́льний Восто́к**
the Far East

дальнови́дный *прил* far-sighted

дальнозо́ркий *прил* long-sighted
(*BRIT*), far-sighted (*US*)

да́льше *сравн прил от* **далёкий**
♦ *сравн нареч от* **далеко́**

дам *сов см.* **дать**

да́м|а (-ы) *ж* lady; (*КАРТЫ*) queen

да́мский *прил* (*одежда*) ladies'

Да́ни|я (-и) *ж* Denmark

да́нн|ые (-ых) *мн* (*сведения*)
data *ед*; (*способности*) talent *ед*

да́нный *прил* this, the given

дань (-и) *ж* tribute

дар (-а; *nom pl* **-ы́)** *м* gift

дари́ть (-ю́, -ишь; *pf* **по~)** *несов
перех* to give

да́ром *нареч* (*бесплатно*) free, for
nothing; (*бесполезно*) in vain

даст *сов см.* **дать**

да́т|а (-ы) *ж* date

да́тельный *прил:* ~ **паде́ж** the
dative (case)

дати́р|овать (-ую) (*не)сов перех*
to date

дать (см. Table 16; impf **давáть**) сов to give; (позволить): **комý-н** +infin to allow sb to do, let sb do; **я тебé дам!** (угроза) I'll show you!

дáч|а (-и) ж (дом) dacha (holiday cottage in the country); (показаний) provision

дашь сов см. **дать**

дв|а (-ух; см. Table 23; f ~**е**, nt ~) м чис two ♦ м нескл (ПРОСВЕЩ) ≈ poor (school mark)

двадцатилéтний прил (период) twenty-year; (человек) twenty-year-old

двадцáтый чис twentieth

двáдцать (-и; как **пять**; см. Table 26) чис twenty

двáжды нареч twice; ~ **три** - **шесть** two times three is six

две ж чис см. **два**

двенáдцатый чис twelfth

двенáдцат|ь (-и; как **пять**; см. Table 26) чис twelve

двер|ь (-и; loc sg -**и**, gen pl -**éй**) ж door

двéсти (-ухсóт; см. Table 28) чис two hundred

двúгател|ь (-я) м engine, motor

двúга|ть (-ю; pf **двúнуть**) несов перех to move; (no pf; механизм) to drive; ~**ся** (pf **двúнуться**) несов возв to move; (отправляться): ~**ся в/на** +acc to set off или start out **движéни|е** (-я) ср movement; (дорожное) traffic; (души) impulse; **прáвила дорóжного** или **ýличного ~** ≈ the Highway Code

двúн|уть(ся) (-у(сь)) сов от **двúга|ть(ся)**

дво|é (-**úх**; см. Table 30a) м чис two

двоебóрь|е (-я) ср biathlon

двоетóчи|е (-я) ср (ЛИНГ) colon

дво|́йка (-́йки; gen pl -ек) ж (цифра, карта) two; (ПРОСВЕЩ) ≈ fail, ≈ E (school mark)

двойнóй прил double

двой|ня (-**йни**; gen pl -**ен**) ж twins мн

двóйственный прил (позиция) ambiguous

двор (-á) м yard; (королевский) court

двор|éц (-цá) м palace

двóрник (-а) м (работник) road sweeper; (АВТ) windscreen (BRIT) или windshield (US) wiper

дворня́ж|ка (-ки; gen pl -ек) ж mongrel

дворя́нств|о (-а) ср nobility

двою́родн|ый прил: ~ **брат** (first) cousin (male); ~**ая сестрá** (first) cousin (female)

двузнáчный прил (число) two-digit; (слово) with two senses

двукрáтн|ый прил: ~ **чемпиóн** two-times champion; **в ~ом размéре** twofold

двум etc чис см. **два**

двумстáм etc чис см. **двéсти**

двусмы́сленный прил ambiguous

двуспáльн|ый прил: ~**ая кровáть** double bed

двусторóнний прил (движение) two-way; (соглашение) bilateral

двух чис см. **два**

двухлéтний прил (период) two-year; (ребёнок) two-year-old

двухмéстный прил (номер) double; (купе, каюта) two-berth

двухсóт чис см. **двéсти**

двухсóтый чис two hundredth

двухстá etc чис см. **двéсти**

двуязы́чный прил bilingual

дебатúр|овать (-ую) несов перех to debate

дебáт|ы (-ов) мн debate ед

дебет (-а) *м* debit

дебил (-а) *м* mentally handicapped person; (*разг: глупый*) idiot

дебильный *прил* mentally handicapped

дебют (-а) *м* debut; (*в шахматах*) opening

дева (-ы) *ж*: **старая** ~ spinster; (*созвездие*): **Дева** Virgo

девальвация (-и) *ж* devaluation

деваться (-юсь) *несов от* деться

девиз (-а) *м* motto

девичий *прил*: ~**ья фамилия** maiden name

девочка (-ки; *gen pl* -ек) *ж* (*ребёнок*) little girl

девушка (-ки; *gen pl* -ек) *ж* girl

девяносто (-а; *как* сто; *см. Table 27*) *чис* ninety

девяностый *чис* ninetieth

девятисотый *чис* nine-hundredth

девятка (-ки; *gen pl* -ок) *ж* nine

девятнадцатый *чис* nineteenth

девятнадцать (-и; *как* пять; *см. Table 26*) *чис* nineteen

девятый *чис* ninth

девять (-и; *как* пять; *см. Table 26*) *чис* nine

девятьсот (-исот; *как* пятьсот; *см. Table 28*) *чис* nine hundred

дёготь (-тя) *м* tar

деградировать (-ую) (*не*)*сов* to degenerate

дед (-а) *м* grandfather; **Дед Мороз** ≈ Father Christmas, ≈ Santa (Claus)

дедовщина (-ы) *ж* mental and physical harassment in the army by older conscripts

дедушка (-ки; *gen pl* -ек) *м* grandpa

деепричастие (-я) *ср* gerund

дежурить (-ю, -ишь) *несов* to be on duty

дежурный *прил*: ~ **врач** doctor on duty ♦ (*-ого*) *м* person on duty

дезинфицировать (-ую) (*не*)*сов перех* to disinfect

дезинформировать (-ую) (*не*)*сов перех* to misinform

дезодорант (-а) *м* antiperspirant, deodorant

действенный *прил* effective

действие (-я) *ср* (*механизма*) functioning; (*романа итп*) action; (*часть пьесы*) act; (*лекарства*) effect; *см. также* **действия**

действительно *нареч, вводн сл* really

действительность (-и) *ж* reality

действительный *прил* real, actual; (*документ*) valid

действия (-й) *мн* (*поступки*) actions *мн*

действовать (-ую) *несов* (*человек*) to act; (*механизмы, закон*) to operate; (*pf* по~; *влиять*): ~ **на** +*acc* to have an effect on

действующий *прил*: ~**ие лица** (*персонажи*) characters *мн*; ~**ая армия** standing army; ~ **вулкан** active volcano

декабрь (-я) *м* December

декан (-а) *м* dean

деканат (-а) *м* faculty office

декларация (-и) *ж* declaration; **таможенная** ~ customs declaration

декольте *ср нескл, прил неизм* décolleté

декоративный *прил* ornamental; (*искусство*) decorative

декорация (-и) *ж* (*ТЕАТР*) set

декрет (-а) *м* (*приказ*) decree; (*разг: отпуск*) maternity leave

декретный *прил*: ~ **отпуск** maternity leave

делать (-ю; *pf* с~) *сов перех* to make; (*упражнения, опыты итп*) to do; ~ **не́чего** there is nothing to be done; ~ **ся** (pf **с~ся**) несов возв; ~ся +instr to become

делега́т (-а) м delegate

делега́ция (-и) ж delegation

деле́ни|е (-я) ср division; (на линейке и в термометре) point

деле́ц (-ьца́) м dealer

деликате́с (-а) м delicacy

дел|и́ть (-ю́, -ишь; pf **по~** или **раз~**) несов перех (также МАТ) to divide; ~ (**раз~** pf) что-н на +acc to divide sth by; ~ (**раз~** pf) что-н с +instr to share sth with; ~ся (pf **раз~ся**) несов возв: ~ся (на +acc) (отряд) to split up (into); ~ся (**по~ся** pf) чем-н с ком-н to share sth with sb

де́л|о (-а; nom pl -á) ср matter; (надобность, также КОММ) business; (положение) situation; (поступок) act; (ЮР) case; (АДМИН) file; **э́то моё** ~ that's my business; **э́то не твоё** ~ it's none of your business; **как дела́?** how are things?; **в чём** ~? what's wrong?; **в том, что ...** the thing is that ...; **на (са́мом)** ~е in (actual) fact; **на** ~е in practice; **то и** ~ every now and then

делово́й прил business; (дельный) efficient; (вид, тон) businesslike

де́льный прил (человек) efficient; (предложение) sensible

дельфи́н (-а) м dolphin

демаго́ги|я (-и) ж demagogy

демисезо́нн|ый прил: ~ое **пальто́** coat for spring and autumn wear

демобилиз|ова́ться (-у́юсь) (не)сов возв to be demobilized

демокра́т (-а) м democrat

демократи́ческий прил democratic

демокра́ти|я (-и) ж democracy

де́мон (-а) м demon

демонстра́нт (-а) м demonstrator

демонстра́ци|я (-и) ж demonstration; (фильма) showing

демонстри́р|овать (-ую) (не)сов (ПОЛИТ) to demonstrate ♦ несов перех to show

демонти́р|овать (-ую) (не)сов to dismantle

де́нежный прил monetary; (рынок) money; ~ **знак** banknote

день (дня) м day; **на днях** (скоро) in the next few days; (недавно) the other day; ~ **рожде́ния** birthday

де́ньг|и (-ег; dat pl -ьга́м) мн money ед

депо́ ср нескл depot

депорти́р|овать (-ую) (не)сов перех to deport

депре́сси|я (-и) ж depression

депута́т (-а) м deputy (POL)

дёрга|ть (-ю) несов перех to tug или pull (at) ♦ неперех: ~ +instr (плечом, головой) to jerk; ~**ся** несов возв (машина, лошадь) to jerk; (лицо, губы) to twitch

дереве́нский прил country, village; (пейзаж) rural

дере́в|ня (-ни; gen pl -е́нь, dat -ня́м) ж (селение) village; (местность) the country

де́рев|о (-ева; nom pl -е́вья, gen pl -е́вьев) ср tree; (древесина) wood

деревя́нный прил wooden

держа́в|а (-ы) ж power

держа́тель (-я) м holder

держа́|ть (-у́, -ишь) сов перех to keep; (в руках, во рту, в зубах) to hold; ~ (impf) себя́ в рука́х to keep one's head; ~ся несов возв to stay; (на колоннах, на сваях) to be supported; (иметь *оса́нку*) to stand; (*вести́ себя́*) to behave; **~ся** (*impf*) +*gen* (*берега́, стены итп*) to keep to

де́рзкий *прил* (*гру́бый*) impertinent; (*сме́лый*) audacious

дёрн (**-а**) *м* turf

дёрн|уть (**-у**) *несов перех* to tug (at) ♦ *неперех*: **~** +*instr* (*плечо́м, голово́й*) to jerk; **~ся** *несов возв* (*маши́на*) to start with a jerk; (*гу́бы*) to twitch

деса́нт (**-а**) *м* landing troops *мн*

деса́нтник (**-а**) *м* paratrooper

десе́рт (**-а**) *м* dessert

десн|а́ (**-ы́**; *nom pl* **дёсны**, *gen pl* **дёсен**) *ж* (*АНАТ*) gum

десятибо́рь|е (**-я**) *ср* decathlon

десятиле́ти|е (**-я**) *ср* (*срок*) decade

деся́тичный *прил* decimal

деся́тк|и (**-ов**) *мн*: **~** люде́й/книг scores *мн* of people/books

деся́т|ок (**-ка**) *м* ten

деся́тый *прил* tenth

де́сят|ь (**-и́**; *как* **пять**; *см. Table 26*) *чис* ten

дета́л|ь (**-и**) *ж* detail; (*механи́зма*) component, part

дета́льный *прил* detailed

детдо́м (**-а**; *nom pl* **-а́**) *м* *сокр* = **де́тский дом**

детекти́в (**-а**) *м* (*фильм*) detective film; (*кни́га*) detective novel

детёныш (**-а**) *м* cub

дет|и (**-е́й**; *dat pl* **-я́м**, *instr pl* **-ьми́**, *prp pl* **-я́х**, *nom sg* **ребёнок**) *мн* children *мн*

де́тский *прил* (*го́ды, боле́знь*) childhood's; (*кни́га, игра́*) children's; (*рассужде́ние*) childish; **~ая площа́дка** playground; **~ дом** children's home; **~ сад** kindergarten

---

де́тский сад - kindergarten or nursery. Children go to kindergarten from around the ages of three and stay there until they are six or seven. The kindergartens provide full-time childcare and pre-primary education five days a week.

де́тств|о (**-а**) *ср* childhood

де|ть (**-ну, -нешь**; *impf* **-ва́ть**) *сов перех* (*разг*) to put; (*вре́мя, де́ньги*) to do with; **~ться** **дева́ться** *сов возв* (*разг*) to get to

дефе́кт (**-а**) *м* defect

дефи́с (**-а**) *м* hyphen

дефици́т (**-а**) *м* deficit; (*нехва́тка*): **~** +*gen или в* +*prp* shortage of

дефици́тный *прил* in short supply

деформи́р|овать (**-ую**) (*не*)*сов перех* to deform

дециме́тр (**-а**) *м* decimetre (*BRIT*), decimeter (*US*)

дешеве́|ть (*3sg* **-ет**; *pf* **по~**) *несов* to go down in price

дешёвый *прил* cheap

де́ятел|ь (**-я**) *м*: **госуда́рственный ~** statesman; **полити́ческий ~** politician

де́ятельн|ость (**-и**) *ж* work; (*се́рдца, мо́зга*) activity

де́ятельный *прил* active

джаз (**-а**) *м* jazz

джем (**-а**) *м* jam

джи́нс|ы (**-ов**) *мн* jeans *мн*

джу́нгл|и (**-ей**) *мн* jungle *ед*

дзю́до *ср нескл* judo

диа́гноз (**-а**) *м* diagnosis

диагности́р|овать (**-ую**) (*не*)*сов перех* to diagnose

диагона́л|ь (**-и**) *ж* diagonal

диагра́мм|а (**-ы**) *ж* diagram

диале́кт (**-а**) *м* dialect

диало́г (**-а**) *м* dialogue

диа́метр (-а) м diameter

диапазо́н (-а) м range; (*часто́т*) waveband

диапозити́в (-а) м (*ФОТО*) slide

диафра́гма (-ы) ж diaphragm

дива́н (-а) м sofa

дива́н-крова́ть (-и) ж sofa bed

диверса́нт (-а) м saboteur

диве́рсия (-и) ж sabotage

дивиде́нд (-а) м dividend

диви́зия (-и) ж division

ди́во (-а) ср wonder; **на ~** wonderfully

дие́з (-а) м (*МУЗ*) sharp

дие́та (-ы) ж diet

диза́йн (-а) м design

диза́йнер (-а) м designer

дизентери́я (-и) ж dysentery

дика́рь (-я́) м savage

ди́кий *прил* wild; (*посту́пок*) absurd; (*нра́вы*) barbaric

ди́кость (-и) ж (*см прил*) wildness; absurdity; barbarity

дикта́нт (-а) м dictation

дикта́тор (-а) м dictator

диктату́ра (-ы) ж dictatorship

дикт|ова́ть (-у́ю; *pf* **про~**) *несов перех* to dictate

ди́ктор (-а) м newsreader, newscaster; (*на вокза́ле*) announcer

ди́лер (-а) м: ~ (**по** +*prp*) dealer (in)

дина́мик (-а) м (loud)speaker

дина́мика (-и) ж dynamics мн

динами́чный *прил* dynamic

дина́стия (-и) ж dynasty

диноза́вр (-а) м dinosaur

дипло́м (-а) м (*университе́та*) degree certificate; (*учи́лища*) diploma; (*рабо́та*) dissertation (*for undergraduate degree*)

диплома́т (-а) м diplomat; (*разг: портфе́ль*) briefcase

дир. *сокр* (= **дире́ктор**) dir.

директи́ва (-ы) ж directive

дире́ктор (-а; *nom pl* -á) м director; ~ **шко́лы** headmaster

дире́кция (-и) ж (*заво́да*) management; (*шко́лы*) senior management

дирижёр (-а) м (*МУЗ*) conductor

дирижи́р|овать (-ую) *несов*: ~ +*instr* to conduct

диск (-а) м (*та́кже КОМП*) disc, disk (*esp US*); (*СПОРТ*) discus; (*МУЗ*) record; **ги́бкий/жёсткий ~** floppy/hard disk

дисквалифици́р|овать (-ую) (*не*)*сов перех* (*врача́, юри́ста*) to strike off; (*спортсме́на*) to disqualify

диске́та (-ы) ж diskette

дисково́д (-а) м (*КОМП*) disc drive

дискоте́ка (-и) ж discotheque; (*пласти́нки*) record collection

дискримина́ция (-и) ж discrimination

диску́ссия (-и) ж discussion

диспансе́р (-а) м specialized health centre

диспе́тчер (-а) м controller

диссерта́ция (-и) ж ≈ PhD thesis

диссиде́нт (-а) м dissident

дистанцио́нный *прил*: ~**ое управле́ние** remote control

диста́нция (-и) ж distance

дистрибью́тор (-а) м distributor

дисципли́на (-ы) ж discipline

дисциплини́рованный *прил* disciplined

дифтери́т (-а) м diphtheria

дичь (-и) ж *собир* game

длина́ (-ы́) ж length; **в ~у́** lengthways

дли́нный *прил* long; (*разг: челове́к*) tall

дли́тельный *прил* lengthy

дли́ться (*3sg* -ится, *pf* **про~**) *несов возв* (*уро́к, бесе́да*) to last

для предл; +gen for; (в отношении): ~ **меня это очень важно** this is very important to me; ~ **того чтобы** in order to; **крем для лица** face cream; **альбом ~ рисования** sketch pad

дневни́к (-á) м diary; (ПРОСВЕЩ) register

дневн|о́й прил daily; ~**о́е вре́мя** daytime

днём сущ см. **день ♦** нареч: ~ in the daytime; (после обеда) in the afternoon

дни etc сущ см. **день**

дн|о (-а) ср (ямы) bottom; (моря, реки) bottom, bed

KEYWORD

до предл; +gen 1 (о пределе движения) as far as, to; **мы дое́хали до реки́** we went as far as или to the river; **я проводи́л его́ до ста́нции** I saw him off at the station

2 (о расстоянии) to; **до го́рода 3 киломе́тра** it is 3 kilometres (BRIT) или kilometers (US) to the town

3 (о временно́м преде́ле) till, until; **я отложи́л заседа́ние до утра́** I postponed the meeting till или until morning; **до свида́ния!** goodbye!

4 (перед) before; **мы зако́нчили до переры́ва** we finished before the break

5 (о пределе состояния): **мне бы́ло оби́дно до слёз** I was so hurt I cried

6 (полностью): **я отда́л ей всё до копе́йки** I gave her everything down to my last kopeck; **он вы́пил буты́лку до дна́** he drank the bottle dry

7 (направление действия): **ребёнок дотро́нулся до**

игру́шки the child touched the toy

доба́в|ить (-лю, -ишь; impf **добавля́ть**) сов перех to add

добавле́ни|е (-я) ср addition

добежа́ть (как **бежа́ть**; см. Table 20; impf **добега́ть**) сов: ~ **до** +gen to run to или as far as

доб|и́ться (-ью́сь, -ье́шься; impf **добива́ться**) сов возв: ~ +gen to achieve

доб|ра́ться (-еру́сь, -ерёшься; impf **добира́ться**) сов возв: ~ **до** +gen to get to, reach

добре́|ть (-ю; pf **по~**) несов to become kinder

добр|о́ (-á) ср good; (разг: имущество) belongings мн, property; ~ **пожа́ловать (в Москву́)!** welcome (to Moscow)!; **э́то не к ~у** this is a bad omen

доброво́л|ец (-ьца) м volunteer

доброво́льный прил voluntary

добр0 ду́шный прил good-natured

доброжела́тельный прил benevolent

доброка́чественный прил quality; (опухоль) benign

добросо́вестный прил conscientious

доброт|а́ (-ы́) ж kindness

до́бр|ый прил kind; (совет, имя) good; (**бу́дьте добры́!** excuse me!; **бу́дьте добры́, позвони́те нам за́втра!** would you be so good as to phone us tomorrow?; **всего́ ~ого!** all the best!; ~**ого здоро́вья!** take care!; ~ **день/ве́чер!** good afternoon/evening!; ~**ое у́тро!** good morning!

добы́ть (как **быть**; см. Table 21; impf **добыва́ть**) сов перех to get; (нефть) to extract; (руду) to mine

добы́ч|а (-и) ж (нефти)

extraction; (*руды*) mining, extraction; (*то, что добыто*) output; (*на охоте*) catch

довез|ти́ (-у́) *pt* **довёз, -ла́**; *impf* **довози́ть** *сов перех*: ~ кого́-н **до** +*gen* to take sb *или* as far as

дове́ренность (-и) *ж* power of attorney

дове́ренн|ый (-ого) *м* (*также*: ~ое лицо́) proxy

дове́ри|е (-я) *ср* confidence, trust; **телефо́н** *или* **Слу́жба** ~ help line

дове́р|ить (-ю, -ишь) *impf* **доверя́ть** *сов перех*: ~ что-н кому́-н to entrust sb with sth

дове́рчивый *прил* trusting

дове|сти́ (-ду́, -дёшь; *pt* **довёл, -ла́**, *impf* **доводи́ть**) *сов перех*: ~ кого́-н/что-н **до** +*gen* to take sb/ sth to *или* as far as; **доводи́ть** (~ *pf*) что-н **до конца́** to see sth through to the end; **доводи́ть** (~ *pf*) что-н **до све́дения** кого́-н to inform sb of sth

дов|оди́ться (-ожу́сь, -о́дишься) *несов*: ~ +*dat* to be related to

довое́нный *прил* prewar

дов|ози́ть (-ожу́, -о́зишь) *несов от* **довезти́**

дово́льно *нареч* (*сильный*) quite
♦ *как сказ* (that is) enough

дово́льный *прил* satisfied, contented

догада́|ться (-юсь) *impf* **дога́дываться** *сов возв* to guess

дога́д|ка (-ки; *gen pl* -ок) *ж* guess

до́гм|а (-ы) *ж* dogma

дог|на́ть (-оню́, -о́нишь) *impf* **догоня́ть** *сов перех* to catch up with

догово́р (-а) *м* (*ПОЛИТ*) treaty; (*КОММ*) agreement

договорённость (-и) *ж*

agreement

договор|и́ть (-ю́, -и́шь; *impf* **догова́ривать**) *сов (не)перех* to finish

договор|и́ться (-ю́сь, -и́шься) *impf* **догова́риваться**) *сов возв*: ~ **с кем-н о чём-н** (*о встрече*) to arrange sth with sb; (*о цене*) to agree sth with sb

договорно́й *прил* (*цена*) agreed; (*обязательство*) contractual

догола́ *нареч*: **разде́ться** ~ to strip bare *или* naked

догор|е́ть (-ю́, -и́шь) *impf* **догора́ть**) *сов* to burn out

доде́ла|ть (-ю; *impf* **доде́лывать**) *сов перех* to finish

доду́ма|ться (-юсь, *impf* **доду́мываться**) *сов возв*: ~ **до** +*gen* to hit on; **как ты мог до тако́го** ~? what on earth gave you that idea?

доеда́|ть (-ю) *несов от* **дое́сть**

дое́ду *etc сов см.* **дое́хать**

доезжа́|ть (-ю) *несов от* **дое́хать**

дое́м *сов см.* **дое́сть**

дое́сть (*как* **есть**; *см. Table 15*) *impf* **доеда́ть** *сов перех* to eat up

дое́хать (*как* **е́хать**; *см. Table 19*) *impf* **доезжа́ть** *сов*: ~ **до** +*gen* to reach

дожд|а́ться (-у́сь, -ёшься; *imper* -и́(те)сь) *сов возв*: ~ кого́-н/ чего́-н to wait until sb/sth comes

дождли́вый *прил* rainy

дождь (-я́) *м* rain; ~ **идёт** it's raining; ~ **пошёл** it has started to rain

дожида́|ться (-юсь) *несов возв*: ~ +*gen* to wait for

дожи́|ть (-ву́, -вёшь; *impf* **дожива́ть**) *сов непepex*: ~ **до**

+gen to live to

дóз|а (-ы) ж dose

дозвон|и́ться (-ю́сь, -и́шься;
impf **дозва́ниваться**) сов возв to
get through

доигра́|ть (-ю; impf **дои́грывать**)
сов перех to finish playing

доистори́ческий прил prehistoric

до|и́ть (-ю́, -ишь; pf **по~**) несов
перех to milk

дойти́ (как **идти́**; см. Table 18; impf
доходи́ть) сов: ~ до +gen to
reach

док (-а) м dock

доказа́тельств|о (-а) ср proof,
evidence

доказа́|ть (-жу́, -жешь; impf
дока́зывать) сов перех
(правду, виновность) to prove

докла́д (-а) м (на съезде итп)
paper; (начальнику) report

докла́дчик (-а) м speaker

докла́дыва|ть (-ю) несов от
доложи́ть

дóктор (-а; nom pl -á) м doctor; ~
нау́к Doctor of Sciences
(postdoctoral research degree in Russia)

дóкторский прил (МЕД) doctor's;
(ПРОСВЕЩ) postdoctoral

доктри́н|а (-ы) ж doctrine

докуме́нт (-а) м document

документа́льный прил
documentary; ~ фильм
documentary

документа́ци|я (-и) ж собир
documentation

долг (-а; loc sg -ý, nom pl -и́) м
debt; **дава́ть (дать pf)/брать
(взять pf)** что-н в ~ to lend/
borrow sth; **быть** (impf) **в ~ý
пéред кем-н** или **у когó-н** to be
indebted to sb

дóлгий прил long

дóлго нареч for a long time; **как ~
...?** how long ...?

долгов|óй прил: ~а́я распи́ска
IOU

долгожда́нный прил long-
awaited

долгоигра́ющ|ий прил: ~ая
пласти́нка LP

долгосрóчный прил long-term

долгот|а́ (-ы́) ж length; (ГЕО)
longitude

дóлж|ен (-на́, -нó, -ны́) часть
сказуемого; +infin 1 (обязан): **я
дóлжен уйти́** I must go; **я
дóлжен бýду уйти́** I will have to
go; **онá должна́ была́ уйти́** she
had to go

2 (выража́ет предположе́ние):
он дóлжен скóро прийти́ he
should arrive soon

3 (о долге): **ты дóлжен мне 5
рубле́й** you owe me 5 roubles

4: должнó быть (вероятно)
probably; **должнó быть, онá
óчень уста́ла** she must have been
very tired

должни́к (-á) м debtor

должностн|óй прил official; ~óе
лицó official

дóлжност|ь (-и; gen pl -е́й) ж post

дóлжный прил required

доли́н|а (-ы) ж valley

дóллар (-а) м dollar

дол|ожи́ть (-ожу́, -óжишь; impf
докла́дывать) сов перех to
report

долот|ó (-отá; nom pl -óта) ср
chisel

дóльше сравн прил от **дóлгий**
♦ сравн нареч от **дóлго**

дóль|ка (-ьки; gen pl -ек) ж
segment

дóл|я (-и; gen pl -éй) ж share;
(пирога) portion; (судьба) fate; ~

секу́нды a fraction of a second

дом (-а; *nom pl* -а́) *м* house; (*своё жильё*) home; (*семья*) household;

дом моде́лей fashion house;

дом о́тдыха ≈ holiday centre (*BRIT*) *или* center (*US*)

до́ма *нареч* at home

дома́шн|ий *прил* (*адрес*) home; (*еда*) home-made; (*животное*) domestic; **~яя хозя́йка** housewife; **~ее зада́ние** homework

домини́р|овать (-ую) *несов* to dominate

домино́ *ср нескл* (*игра*) dominoes; (*фишка, костюм*) domino

домкра́т (-а) *м* (*ТЕХ*) jack

домовладе́л|ец (-ьца) *м* home owner

домовладе́ни|е (-я) *ср* (*дом*) house with grounds attached

домово́дств|о (-а) *ср* home economics

домо́й *нареч* home

домоуправле́ни|е (-я) *ср* ≈ housing department

домохозя́|йка (-йки; *gen pl* -ек) *ж* = **дома́шняя хозя́йка**

домрабо́тниц|а (-ы) *ж*: ~ = **дома́шняя рабо́тница** domestic help (*BRIT*), maid (*US*)

до́мысел (-ла) *м* conjecture

донесе́ни|е (-я) *ср* report

донес|ти́ (-у́, -ёшь; *pt* донёс, -ла́; *impf* доноси́ть) *сов перех* to carry ♦ *неперех*: ~ **на** +*acc* to inform on; ~ (*pf*) **о** +*prp* to report on; **~сь** (*impf* **доноси́ться** *возв*): **~сь до** +*gen* to reach

до́низу *нареч* to the bottom; **све́рху** ~ from top to bottom

до́нор (-а) *м* (*МЕД*) donor

доно́с (-а) *м*: ~ (**на** +*acc*) denunciation (of)

несов от донести́

доно́счик (-а) *м* informer

допива́|ть (-ю) *несов от* **допи́ть**

до́пинг (-а) *м* drugs *мн*

допис|а́ть (-шу́, -шешь; *impf* **допи́сывать**) *сов перех* to finish (writing)

допи́ть (допью́, допьёшь; *imper* допе́й(те); *impf* допива́ть) *сов перех* to drink up

доплат|а (-ы) *ж* surcharge; ~ **за бага́ж** excess baggage (charge)

доплы́|ть (-ву́, -вёшь; *impf* **доплыва́ть**) *сов*: ~ **до** (*на корабле́*) to sail to; (*вплавь*) to swim to

дополне́ни|е (-я) *ср* supplement; (*линг*) object; **в** ~ (**к** +*dat*) in addition (to)

дополни́тельный *прил* additional

допо́лн|ить (-ю, -ишь; *impf* **дополня́ть**) *сов перех* to supplement

допра́шива|ть (-ю) *несов от* **допроси́ть**

допро́с (-а) *м* interrogation

допро|си́ть (-шу́, -сишь; *impf* **допра́шивать**) *сов перех* to interrogate, question

до́пуск (-а) *м* (*в здание*) admittance; (*к документам*) access

допуска́|ть (-ю; *pf* **допусти́ть**) *несов перех* to admit, allow in; (*предположить*) to assume

допу́стим *вводн сл* let us assume

допуще́ни|е (-я) *ср* assumption

дораст|и́ (-у́, -ёшь; *pt* доро́с, доросла́, доросло́; *impf* **дораста́ть**) *сов*: ~ **до** +*gen* to grow to

доро́г|а (-и) *ж* road, way; **по** ~**е** on the way

до́рого *нареч* (*купить, продать*) at a high price ♦ *как сказ* it's

дорого́й 68 досье́

дорого́й прил expensive; (цена́) high; (друг, мать) dear; (воспомина́ния, пода́рок) cherished ♦ (-óго) м dear, darling

дорожа́ть (3sg -ет; pf по~) несов to go up или rise in price

доро́же сравн прил от дорого́й ♦ сравн нареч от до́рого

дорожи́ть (-у́, -и́шь) несов: ~ +instr to value

доро́жка (-ки; gen pl -ек) ж pathway; (для пла́вания) lane; (для бе́га, на магнитофо́не) track; (ковёр) runner

доро́жный прил road; (костю́м, расхо́ды) travelling (BRIT), traveling (US); (су́мка) travel

доса́д|а (-ы) ж annoyance; кака́я ~ what a pity!

доса́дный прил annoying; (печа́льный) upsetting

доск|а́ (-и́; nom pl -и, gen pl -о́к) ж board; (деревя́нная) plank; (мра́морная) slab; (чугу́нная) plate; ~ объявле́ний notice (BRIT) или bulletin (US) board

доскона́льный прил thorough

досло́во нареч word for word

досло́вный прил literal, word-for-word

дослу́ша|ть (-ю; impf дослу́шивать) сов перех to listen to

досмо́тр (-а) м: тамо́женный ~ customs examination

досм|отре́ть (-отрю́, -о́тришь; impf досма́тривать) сов перехto watch the end of; (бага́ж) to check

досро́чно нареч ahead of time

досро́чный прил early

доста|ва́ть(ся) (-ю́(сь)) несов от доста́ть(ся)

достав|и́ть (-лю, -ишь; impf доставля́ть) сов перех (груз) to deliver; (пассажи́ров) to carry, transport; (удово́льствие, возмо́жность) to give

доста́в|ка (-ки; gen pl -ок) ж delivery

доста́т|ок (-ка) м prosperity

доста́точно нареч: ~ хорошо́/подро́бно good/detailed enough ♦ как сказ that's enough

доста́|ть (-ну, -нешь; imper ~нь(те); impf достава́ть) сов перех to take; (раздобы́ть) to get ♦ неперех: ~ до +gen to reach; ~ся (impf достава́ться) сов возв (при разде́ле): мне ~лся дом I got the house

достига́|ть (-ю) несов от дости́чь

достиже́ни|е (-я) ср achievement; (преде́ла, во́зраста) reaching

дости́|чь (-гну, -гнешь; pt -г, -гла; impf достига́ть) сов +gen to reach; (результа́та, це́ли) to achieve; (положе́ния) to attain

достове́рный прил reliable

досто́инств|о (-а) ср (кни́ги, пла́на) merit; (уваже́ние к себе́) dignity; (КОММ) value

досто́йный прил (награ́да, ка́ра) fitting; (челове́к) worthy

достопримеча́тельност|ь (-и) ж sight; (музе́я) showpiece; осма́тривать (осмотре́ть pf) ~и to go sightseeing

достоя́ни|е (-я) ср property; станови́ться (стать pf) ~м обще́ственности to become public knowledge

до́ступ (-а) м access

досту́пный прил (ме́сто) accessible; (це́ны) affordable; (объясне́ние) comprehensible

досу́г (-а) м leisure (time); на ~е in one's spare или free time

досье́ ср нескл dossier, file

дота́ци|я (-и) ж subsidy

дотла́ нареч: **сгоре́ть** ~ to burn down (to the ground)

дотро́н|уться (-усь, -ешься; impf **дотра́гиваться**) сов возв: ~ до +gen to touch

дот|яну́ть (-яну́, -я́нешь; impf **дотя́гивать**) сов перех: ~ что-н до +gen to extend sth as far as; ~ся (impf **дотя́гиваться**) сов возв: ~ся до +gen to reach

до́хлый прил dead

до́х|нуть (-ну; pt -, -ла; pf по~) несов (животное) to die

дохо́д (-а) м income, revenue; (человека) income

доходи́ть несов от **дойти́**

дохо́дный прил profitable; (выгодный) revenue-producing; **дохо́дная статья́** credit side (of accounts)

дохо́дчивый прил clear, easy to understand

доце́нт (-а) м ≈ reader (BRIT), ≈ associate professor (US)

до́ч|ка (-ки; gen pl -ек) ж daughter

дочь (-ери; см. Table 2) ж daughter

дошёл сов см. **дойти́**

дошко́льник (-а) м preschool child

дошла́ итп сов см. **дойти́**

доя́р|ка (-ки; gen pl -ок) ж milkmaid

ДПР ж сокр = **Демократи́ческая Па́ртия Росси́и** **ЛДПР**

драгоце́нность (-и) ж jewel

драгоце́нный прил precious

дразн|и́ть (-ю́, -ишь) несов перех to tease

дра́к|а (-и) ж fight

драко́н (-а) м dragon

дра́м|а (-ы) ж drama

драматизи́р|овать (-ую) (не)сов перех to dramatize

драмати́ческий прил dramatic; (актёр) stage

драма́тург (-а) м playwright

драматурги́|я (-и) ж drama ◆ собир plays мн

драпир|ова́ть (-у́ю; pf за~) несов перех: ~ что-н (чем-н) to drape sth (with sth)

драть (деру́, дерёшь; pf разодра́ть) несов перех (бума́гу, оде́жду) to tear или rip up; (pf задра́ть; подлеж: волк) to tear to pieces; (pf содра́ть; кору́, обо́и) to strip; **дра́ться** (pf подра́ться) несов возв: **подра́ться** (с +instr) to fight (with)

дре́безг м: **в** ~ **и** to smithereens

дребезж|а́ть (3sg -и́т) несов to jingle; (стекла́) to rattle

древеси́н|а (-ы) ж close grain timber

древе́сный прил wood; ~ **у́голь** charcoal

дре́вний прил ancient

дрейф|ова́ть (-у́ю) несов to drift

дрель (-и) ж drill

дрем|а́ть (-лю́, -лешь) несов to doze

дрессир|ова́ть (-у́ю; pf вы~) несов перех to train

дроб|и́ть (-лю́, -ишь; pf раз~) несов перех to crush; (си́лы) to split

дробь (-и; gen pl -е́й) ж fraction; (бараба́на) beat

дров|а́ (-; dat pl -а́м) мн firewood ед

дро́г|нуть (-ну) сов (стекла́, ру́ки) to shake; (го́лос, лицо́) to quiver

дрож|а́ть (-у́, -и́шь) несов to shake, tremble; (лицо́) to quiver; ~ (impf) **за** +acc или **над** +instr (разг) to fuss over

дро́жж|и (-е́й) мн yeast ед

дрозд (-а́) м thrush; **чёрный** ~

blackbird

друг | **г** (-га; *nom pl* -зья́, *gen pl* -зе́й) *м* friend; ~ **а** each other, one another; ~ **дру́гу** (говори́ть) to each other *или* one another; ~ **за дру́гом** one after another; ~ **о дру́ге** (говори́ть) about each other *или* one another

друг | **о́й** *прил* (ино́й) another; (второ́й) the other; (не тако́й, как э́тот) different ♦ (-о́го) *м* (кто-то ино́й) another (person); (второ́й) the other (one); **в ~ раз** another time; **и тот и ~** both

дру́жб | **а** (-ы) *ж* friendship

дружелю́бный *прил* friendly, amicable

дру́жеский *прил* friendly

дру́жественный *прил* friendly

дружи́ть (-у́, -ишь) *несов*: ~ **с** +*instr* to be friends with

дру́жный *прил* close-knit; (смех) general; (уси́лия) concerted

друж | **о́к** (-ка́) *м* (друг) friend, pal (inf)

друзья́ *etc см* **друг**

дря́блый *прил* sagging; (те́ло) flabby

дрян | **ь** (-и) *ж* (разг) rubbish (BRIT), trash (US)

дуб (-а; *nom pl* -ы́) *м* (БОТ) oak (tree); (древеси́на) oak

дуби́н | **ка** (-ки; *gen pl* -ок) *ж* cudgel; (рези́новая) ~ truncheon

дублён | **ка** (-ки; *gen pl* -ок) *ж* sheepskin coat

дублёр (-а) *м* backup; (КИНО) double

дублика́т (-а) *м* duplicate

дубли́р | **овать** (-ую) *несов перех* to duplicate; (КИНО) to dub; (КОМП) to back up

дуг | **а́** (-и́; *nom pl* -и) *ж* (ГЕОМ) arc

ду́л | **о** (-а) *ср* muzzle; (ствол) barrel

ду́м | **а** (-ы) *ж* (размышле́ние) thought; **Ду́ма** (ПОЛИТ) the Duma (lower house of Russian parliament)

ду́ма | **ть** (-ю) *несов*: ~ (о чём-н) to think (about sth); ~ (*impf*) **над чем-н** to think sth over; **я ~ю, что да**/**нет** I think/don't think so

ду́м | **ец** (-ца) *м* (разг) member of the Duma

ду́мск | **ой** *прил*: ~ **ое заседа́ние** meeting of the Duma

ду́н | **уть** (-у) *сов см* **дуть**

дуп | **ло́** (-ла́; *nom pl* -ла, *gen pl* -ел) *ср* (де́рева) hollow

дур | **а** (-ы) *ж* (разг) fool

дура́к (-а́) *м* (разг) fool

дура́цкий *прил* (разг) foolish; (шля́па) silly

дура́ч | **ить** (-у, -ишь; *pf* **о**~) *несов перех* (разг) to con; ~ **ся** *несов возв* (разг) to play the fool

дур | **и́ть** (-ю́, -и́шь; *pf* **об**~) *несов перех* to fool

ду́рно *нареч* badly

дуро́ч | **ка** (-ки; *gen pl* -ек) *ж* (разг) silly girl

дуршла́г (-а) *м* colander

ду́ | **ть** (-ю, -ешь) *несов* to blow ♦ (*pf* **вы**~) *перех* (ТЕХ) to blow; **здесь ду́ет** it's draughty (BRIT) *или* drafty (US) in here

дух (-а; *part gen* -у) *м* spirit; **быть** (*impf*) **в ду́хе**/**не в ду́хе** to be in high/low spirits

духи́ (-о́в) *мн* perfume *ед*, scent *ед*

духове́нств | **о** (-а) *ср собир* clergy; (правосла́вное) priesthood

духо́вка (-и) *ж* oven

духо́вный *прил* spiritual; (религио́зный) sacred, church

духов | **о́й** *прил* (МУЗ) wind; ~ **ые инструме́нты** brass section (in orchestra); ~ **орке́стр** brass band

духот | **а́** (-ы́) *ж* stuffiness; (жара́)

closeness

душ (-а) *м* shower

душ|**а** (*acc sg* -**у**, *gen sg* -**й**, *nom pl* -**и**) *ж* soul; **на душу (населе́ния)** per head (of the population); **он в ней ~й не ча́ет** she's the apple of his eye; **говори́ть** (*impf*)/**бесе́довать** (*impf*) **по ~м** to have a heart-to-heart talk/chat; **в глубине́ ~й** in one's heart of hearts

душевнобольн|**о́й** (-**о́го**) *м* mentally-ill person

душе́вн|**ый** *прил* (*силы, подъём*) inner; (*разговор*) sincere; (*челове́к*) kindly; **~ое потрясе́ние** shock

душераздира́|**ющий** *прил* (*крик*) bloodcurdling; (*плач*) heart-rending

души́стый *прил* (*цветок*) fragrant; (*мыло*) perfumed, scented

душ|**и́ть** (-**у́**, -**ишь**; *pf* **за~** *или* **у~**) *несов перех* to strangle; (*свобо́ду, прогре́сс*) to stifle; (*pf* **на~**; *плато́к*) to perfume, scent

ду́шно *как сказ* it's stuffy *или* close

дуэ́т (-а) *м* (*произведе́ние*) duet; (*исполни́тели*) duo

дыбо́м *нареч*: **встава́ть ~** (*во́лосы, шерсть*) to stand on end

дыбы́ *мн*: **станови́ться на ~** (*ло́шадь*) to rear up

дым (-а) *м* smoke

дым|**и́ть** (-**лю́**, -**и́шь**; *pf* **на~**) *несов* (*печь, дрова́*) to smoulder (*BRIT*), smolder (*US*); **~ся** *несов возв* (*труба́*) to be smoking

ды́мка (-**и**) *ж* haze

дымохо́д (-а) *м* flue

ды́мчатый *прил* (*стекла́*) tinted

ды́н|**я** (-**и**) *ж* melon

дыр|**а́** (-**ы́**; *nom pl* -**ы**) *ж* hole

ды́р|**ка** (-**ки**; *gen pl* -**ок**) *ж* hole

дыроко́л (-а) *м* punch

дыха́ни|**е** (-**я**) *ср* breathing, respiration

дыш|**а́ть** (-**у́**, -**ишь**) *несов* to breathe; **~** (*impf*) +*instr* (*не́навистью*) to exude; (*любо́вью*) to radiate

дья́вол (-а) *м* devil

дья́кон (-а) *м* deacon

дю́жин|**а** (-**ы**) *ж* dozen

дю́н|**а** (-**ы**; *обычно мн*) *ж* dune

дя́д|**я** (-**и**) *м* uncle; (*разг*) bloke

дя́т|**ел** (-**ла**) *м* woodpecker

Е, е

Ева́нгели|**е** (-**я**) *ср* the Gospels *мн*; (*одна из книг*) gospel

евре́|**й** (-**я**) *м* Jew

евре́йский *прил* (*наро́д, обы́чаи*) Jewish; **~ язык** Hebrew

е́вро *м нескл* euro

Евро́п|**а** (-**ы**) *ж* Europe

европе́|**ец** (-**йца**) *м* European

европе́йский *прил* European; **Европе́йский Сове́т** Council of Europe; **Европе́йское Соо́бщество** European Community

его́ *мест см.* **он**; **оно́** ♦ *притяж мест* (*о мужчи́не*) his; (*о предме́те*) its

ед|**а́** (-**ы**) *ж* (*пища*) food; (*проце́сс*) за **~о́й**, **во вре́мя ~ы́** at mealtimes

едва́ *нареч* (*с трудо́м: нашёл, доста́л, дое́хал итп*) only just; (*то́лько, немно́го*) barely, hardly; (*то́лько что*) just ♦ *союз* (*как то́лько*) as soon as; **~ ли** hardly

е́дем *etc сов см.* **е́хать**

еди́м *несов см.* **есть**

едини́ц|**а** (-**ы**) *ж* (*ци́фра*) one; (*измере́ния, часть це́лого*) unit;

де́нежная ~ monetary unit
единобо́рств|о (-а) *ср* single combat
единовре́менн|ый *прил*: **~ая су́мма** lump sum
единогла́сный *прил* unanimous
единоду́шный *прил* unanimous
еди́нственн|ый *прил* (the) only; **~ое число́** (*линг*) singular
еди́ный *прил* (*цельный*) united; (*общий*) common; **все до ~ого** to a man; **~ (проездно́й) биле́т** travel card (*for use on all forms of transport*)

> **еди́ный проездно́й биле́т** - travel card. This is a cheap and convenient way of city travel. It covers all types of transport including the underground.

еди́те *несов см.* **есть**
е́ду *etc несов см.* **е́хать**
едя́т *несов см.* **есть**
её *мест см.* **она́** ♦ *притяж мест* (*о женщине итп*) her; (*о предмете итп*) its
ёж (-а́) *м* hedgehog
ежего́дный *прил* annual
ежедне́вник (-а) *м* diary
ежедне́вный *прил* daily
ежеме́сячный *прил* monthly
еженеде́льный *прил* weekly
езд|а́ (-ы́) *ж* journey
е́з|дить (-жу, -дишь) *несов* to go; **~** (*impf*) **на** +*prp* (*на лошади, на велосипеде*) to ride; (*на поезде, на автобусе итп*) to travel *или* go by
ей *мест см.* **она́**
ел *etc несов см.* **есть**
е́ле *нареч* (*с трудом*) only just; (*едва*) barely, hardly; **~~** with great difficulty
ёл|ка (-ки; *gen pl* **-ок)** *ж* fir (tree);

(*праздник*) New Year party for children; (*рожде́ственская или* **нового́дняя) ~** ≈ Christmas tree
ело́вый *прил* fir
ёлочн|ый *прил*: **~ые игру́шки** Christmas-tree decorations *мн*
ел|ь (-и) *ж* fir (tree)
ем *несов см.* **есть**
ёмкост|ь (-и) *ж* (*объём*) capacity; (*вместилище сосуд*) container
ему́ *мест см.* **он; оно́**
ерунд|а́ (-ы́) *ж* rubbish, nonsense
ЕС *сокр* (**= Европе́йский Сою́з**) EU

> KEYWORD

е́сли *союз* **1** (*в том случае когда*) if; **е́сли она́ придёт, дай ей э́то письмо́** if she comes, give her this letter; **е́сли ..., то ... (е́сли)** if ..., then ...; **е́сли он опозда́ет, то иди́ оди́н** if he is late, (then) go alone
2 (*об условном действии*): **е́сли бы(, то** *или* **тогда́)** if; **е́сли бы я мог, (то) помо́г бы тебе́** if I could, I would help you
3 (*выражает сильное желание*): **(ах** *или* **о) е́сли бы!** if only; **ах е́сли бы он пришёл!** oh, if only he would come!; **е́сли уж на то пошло́** if it comes to it; **что е́сли...?** (*а вдруг*) what if...?

ест *несов см.* **есть**
есте́ственно *нареч* naturally
♦ *вводн сл* (*конечно*) of course
есте́ственный *прил* natural
есть *несов* (*один предмет*) there is; (*много предметов*) there are; **у меня́ ~ друг** I have a friend
есть (*см.* Table 15; *pf* **пое́сть** *или* **съ~**) *несов перех* (*питаться*) to eat; (*pf* **съ~**; *металл*) to corrode;
мне хо́чется ~ I'm hungry

е́хать (*см. Table 19*) *несов* to go; (*поезд, автомобиль: приближаться*) to come; (*: двигаться*) to go; (*разг: скользить*) to slide; **~** (*impf*) **на** +*prp* (*на лошади, на велосипеде*) to ride; **~** (*impf*) +*instr* или **на** +*prp* (*на поезде, на автобусе*) to travel или ride

ехи́дный *прил* spiteful

ешь *несов см.* **есть**

ещё *нареч* (*дополнительно*) more; **хочу́ ~ ко́фе** I want more coffee

ЕЭС *ср сокр* (= Европе́йское экономи́ческое соо́бщество) EEC

е́ю *мест см.* **она́**

Ж, ж

ж *союз, част см.* **же**

жа́б|а (**-ы**) *ж* (*ЗООЛ*) toad

жа́бр|а (**-ы**) *ж* (*ЗООЛ*) gill

жа́воронок (**-ка**) *м* (*ЗООЛ*) lark

жа́дничать (**-ю**; *pf* **по~**) *несов* (*разг*) to be mingy

жа́дность (**-и**) *ж*: **~ (к** +*dat*) (*к вещам, к деньгам*) greed (for)

жа́дный *прил* greedy

жа́жд|а (**-ы**) *ж* thirst

жаке́т (**-а**) *м* (woman's) jacket

жале́|ть (**-ю**; *pf* **по~**) *несов перех* to feel sorry for; (*: скупиться*) to grudge ♦ *неперех*: **~ о** +*prp* to regret; **не ~я сил** sparing no effort

жа́л|ить (**-ю, -ишь**; *pf* **у~**) *несов перех* (*подлеж: оса*) to sting; (*: змея*) to bite

жа́лкий *прил* (*вид*) pitiful, pathetic

жа́лко *как сказ* = **жаль**

жа́л|о (**-а**) *ср* (*пчелы*) sting; (*змеи*) bite

жа́лоб|а (**-ы**) *ж* complaint

жа́лобный *прил* plaintive

жа́лован|е (**-я**) *ср* salary

жа́л|оваться (**-уюсь**; *pf* **по~**) *несов возв*: **~ на** +*acc* to complain about; (*ябедничать*) to tell on

жа́лость (**-и**) *ж*: **~ к** +*dat* sympathy for; **кака́я ~!** what a shame!

KEYWORD

жаль *как сказ* 1 (*+acc; о сострада́нии*): **(мне) жаль дру́га** I am sorry for my friend

2 (*+acc или +gen*, *о сожале́нии, о доса́де*): **(мне) жаль вре́мени/де́нег** I grudge the time/money

3 (*+infin*): **жаль уезжа́ть** it's a pity или shame to leave

---

жанр (**-а**) *м* genre

жар (**-а**) *м* heat; (*МЕД*) fever

жар|а́ (**-ы**) *ж* heat

жарго́н (**-а**) *м* slang; (*профессиона́льный*) jargon

жа́реный *прил* (*на сковороде*) fried; (*в духовке*) roast

жа́р|ить (**-ю, -ишь**; *pf* **за~**) *несов перех* (*на сковороде*) to fry; (*в духовке*) to roast; **~ся** (*pf* **за~ся**) *несов возв* to fry

жа́ркий *прил* hot; (*спор*) heated

жа́рко *нареч* (*спорить*) heatedly ♦ *как сказ* it's hot; **мне ~** I'm hot

жасми́н (**-а**) *м* jasmine

жа́тв|а (**-ы**) *ж* harvest

жать (**жму, жмёшь**) *несов перех* (*руку*) to shake; (*лимон, сок*) to squeeze; **сапоги́ мне жмут** my boots are pinching (my feet)

жать (**жну, жнёшь**; *pf* **с~**) *несов перех* to harvest

жва́чк|а (**-ки**; *gen pl* **-ек**) *ж* (*разг: резинка*) chewing gum

ж.д. *сокр* (= желе́зная доро́га)

R., г., RR (US)

жд|ать (-у, -ёшь; pt -ал, -ала,
-ало) несов (не)перех: ~ +acc
или +gen (письмо, гостей) to
expect; (поезда) to wait for

KEYWORD

же союз 1 (при
противопоставлении) but; **я не
люблю математику, литературу
же обожаю** I don't like
mathematics, but I love literature
2 (вводит дополнительные
сведения) and; **успех зависит от
наличия ресурсов, ресурсов же
мало** success depends on the
presence of resources, and the
resources are insufficient

♦ част 1 (ведь): **выпей ещё чаю,
хочешь же!** have more tea, you
want some, don't you?
2 (именно): **приду сейчас же** I'll
come right now
3 (выражает сходство): **такой
же** the same; **в этом же году** this
very year

ж|евать (-ую) несов перех to
chew

желани|е (-я) ср (просьба)
request; ~ +gen/ +infin desire for/to
do

желательный прил desirable

жела|ть (-ю; pf по~) несов ~
+gen to desire; ~ (по~ pf) +infin to
wish или want to do; ~ (по~ pf)
кому-н счастья/всего хорошего
to wish sb happiness/all the best

желающий (-его) м: **~ие
поехать/поработать** those
interested in going/working

желе ср нескл jelly (BRIT), jello
(US)

жел|еза (-езы; nom pl -езы, gen pl
-ёз, dat pl -езам) ж gland

железнодорожный прил

(вокзал) railway (BRIT), railroad
(US); (транспорт) rail

железный прил iron; **~ая
дорога** railway (BRIT), railroad (US)

желез|о (-а) ср iron

железобетон (-а) м reinforced
concrete

жёлоб (-а; nom pl -а) м gutter

желте|ть (-ю; pf по~) несов to
turn yellow

желт|ок (-ка) м yolk

желтух|а (-и) ж jaundice

жёлтый прил yellow

желуд|ок (-ка) м (АНАТ) stomach;
(сок) gastric

жёлудь (-я) м acorn

жёлчный прил: ~ **пузырь** gall
bladder

жёлчь (-и) ж (также перен) bile

жемчуг (-а; nom pl -а) м pearls мн

жемчужин|а (-ы) ж pearl

жен|а (-ы; nom pl жёны, gen pl
жён) ж wife

женатый прил married (of man);
он ~ на +prp he is married to; **они
~ы** they are married

Женев|а (-ы) ж Geneva

жен|ить (-ю, -ишь; pf (не)сов
перех (сына, внука): ~ **кого-н
(на +prp)** to marry sb (off) (to); ~
(не)сов возв: ~ся **на +prp** to marry
(of man); (pf по~ся; разг) to get
hitched

жених (-а) м (до свадьбы) fiancé;
(на свадьбе) (bride)groom

женский прил women's; (логика,
органы) female; ~ **пол** the female
sex; ~ **род** feminine gender

женственный прил feminine

женщин|а (-ы) ж woman

жердь (-и; gen pl -ей) ж pole

жереб|ёнок (-ёнка; nom pl -ята,
gen pl -ят) м foal

жеребьёвк|а (-ки; gen pl -ок) ж

casting *или* drawing of lots

жéртв|**а** (-ы) ж victim; *(РЕЛ)*
sacrifice; **человéческие** ~ы
casualties

жéртвовать (-ую; *pf* по~) *несов*
♦ +*instr (жизнью)* to sacrifice
♦ *перех (деньги)* to donate

жест (-а) м gesture

жестикулировать (-ую) *несов*
to gesticulate

жёсткий *прил (кровать,
человек)* hard; *(мясо)* tough;
(волосы) coarse; *(услóвия)* strict;
~ **вагóн** railway carriage with hard
seats; ~ **диск** hard disk

жестóкий *прил* cruel; *(морóз)*
severe

жестóкост|**ь** (-и) ж cruelty

жест|**ь** (-и) ж tin-plated sheet metal

жетóн (-а) м tag; *(в метрó)* token

жечь (жгу, жжёшь *etc*, жгут; *pt*
жёг, жгла, *pf* с~) *несов перех* to
burn

жжéни|**е** (-я) *ср* burning sensation

живóй *прил* alive; *(организм)*
living; *(животнóе)* live; *(человéк:
энергичный)* lively

живопи́сный *прил* picturesque

жи́вопис|**ь** (-и) ж painting

живóт (-á) м stomach; *(разг)*
tummy

животновóдств|**о** (-а) *ср* animal
husbandry

живóтн|**ое** (-ого) *ср* animal

живóтный *прил* animal

живу́ *etc несов см.* **жить**

жи́дкий *прил* liquid

жи́дкост|**ь** (-и) ж liquid

жи́жа (-и) ж slurry

жи́зненный *прил (вопрос,
интерéсы)* vital; *(необходимость)*
basic; ~ **у́ровень** standard of living;
~ **о́пыт** experience

жизнерáдостный *прил* cheerful

жизнеспосóбный *прил* viable

жизн|**ь** (-и) ж life

жил *etc несов см.* **жить**

жилéт (-а) м waistcoat *(BRIT)*, vest
(US)

жил|**éц** (-ьцá) м *(дóма)* tenant

жили́щный *прил* housing

жил|**óй** *прил (дом, здáние)*
residential; ~**áя плóщадь**
accommodation

жиль|**ё** (-я) *ср* accommodation

жир (-а; *nom pl* -ы́) м fat;
(растительный) oil

жирáф (-а) м giraffe

жи́рный *прил (пища)* fatty;
(человéк) fat; *(вóлосы)* greasy

жи́тел|**ь** (-я) м resident

жи́тельств|**о** (-а) *ср* residence

жить (-ву́, -вёшь; *pt* -л, -лá,
-ло) *несов* to live; ~л-был there
once was, once upon a time there
was

жму́р|**ить** (-ю, -ишь; *pf* за~)
несов: ~ **глазá** to screw up one's
eyes; ~**ся** *(pf* за~**ся)** *несов возв* to
squint

жокéй (-я) м jockey

жонглёр (-а) м juggler

жонглировать (-ую) *несов*: ~
+*instr* to juggle *(with)*

жрéби|**й** (-я) м: **бросáть** ~ to cast
lots

ЖСК м *сокр* (= **жилищно-
строи́тельный кооперати́в**) ≈
housing cooperative

жужж|**áть** (-у́, -и́шь) *несов* to
buzz

жук (-á) м beetle

жу́лик (-а) м swindler; *(в игре́)*
cheat

жу́льничеств|**о** (-а) *ср*
underhandedness; *(в игре́)*
cheating

журнáл (-а) м magazine;
(клáссный) register

журнали́ст (-а) м journalist

журнали́стик|а (-и) ж journalism

журча́ть (-у́, -и́шь) несов (ручей, вода) to babble, murmur

жу́ткий прил terrible

жЭК (-а) м сокр (= жили́щно-эксплуатацио́нная конто́ра) ≈ housing office

жюри́ ср нескл panel of judges

З, з

з сокр (= за́пад) W; (= за́падный) W

> **KEYWORD**

за предл; +acc **1** out (of); **выходи́ть (вы́йти** pf**) за дверь** to go out (of) the door

2 (позади) behind; **пря́таться (спря́таться** pf**) за де́рево** to hide behind a tree

3 (около: сесть, встать) at; **сади́ться (сесть** pf**) за стол** to sit down at the table

4 (свыше какого-н предела) over; **ему́ за со́рок** he is over forty

5 (при указании на расстояние, на время): **за пять киломе́тров отсю́да** five kilometres (BRIT) или kilometers (US) from here; **за три часа́ до нача́ла спекта́кля** three hours before the beginning of the show

6 (при указании объекта действия): **держа́ться за** +acc to hold onto; **ухвати́ться (** pf**) за** +acc to take hold of; **брать (взять** pf**) кого́-н за́ руку** to take sb by the hand; **бра́ться (взя́ться** pf**) за рабо́ту** to start work

7 (об объекте чувств) for; **ра́доваться (** impf**) за сы́на** to be happy for one's son;

беспоко́иться (impf**) за му́жа** to worry about one's husband

8 (о цели) for; **сража́ться (** impf**) за побе́ду** to fight for victory

9 (в пользу) for, in favour (BRIT) или favor (US) of; **голосова́ть (проголосова́ть** pf**) за предложе́ние** to vote for или in favour of a proposal

10 (по причине, в обмен) for; **благодарю́ Вас за по́мощь** thank you for your help; **плати́ть (** impf**) за что-н** to pay for sth

11 (вместо кого-н) for; **рабо́тать (** impf**) за дру́га** to fill in for a friend

♦ предл; +instr **1** (по другую сторону) on the other side of; **жить (** impf**) за реко́й** to live on the other side of the river

2 (вне) outside; **жить (** impf**) за́ го́родом** to live outside the town; **за грани́цей** abroad

3 (позади) behind; **стоя́ть (** impf**) за две́рью** to stand behind the door

4 (около: стоять, сидеть) at; **сиде́ть (** impf**) за столо́м** to sit at the table

5 (о смене событий) after; **год за го́дом** year after year

6 (во время чего-н) over; **за за́втраком** over breakfast

7 (о объекте внимания): **смотре́ть** или **уха́живать за** +instr to look after

8 (с целью получить, достать что-н) for; **я посла́л его́ за газе́той** I sent him out for a paper

9 (по причине) owing to

♦ как сказ (согласен) in favour; **кто за?** who is in favour?

♦ ср нескл pro; **взве́сить (** pf**) все за и про́тив** to weigh up all the pros and cons

заба́вный прил amusing

забасто́в|ка (-ки; gen pl **-ок) ж** strike

забасто́вщик (-а) м striker

забе́г (-а) м (СПОРТ) race (in running); (: отбо́рочный) heat

забежа́ть (как **бежа́ть;** см. Table 20; impf **забега́ть)** сов: **~ в** (+асс) (в дом, в дере́вню) to run in(to); (разг: на недо́лго) to drop in(to); **забега́ть** (**~** pf) **вперёд** to run ahead

забира́|ть(ся) (-ю(сь)) несов от **забра́ть(ся)**

заб|и́ть (-ью́, -ьёшь сов (часы́) to begin to strike; (вода́) to begin to flow ♦ impf **забива́ть** перех (гвоздь, сва́ю) to drive in; (СПОРТ, гол) to score; (наполни́ть) to overfill; (засори́ть) to clog (up); (скот, зве́ря) to slaughter; **~ся** возв (се́рдце) to start beating; (impf **забива́ться;** спря́таться) to hide (away)

забле|сте́ть (-щу́, -сти́шь сов (слёзы) to glisten; (глаза́) to light up; (мета́лл) to gleam

забл|уди́ться (-ужу́сь, -у́дишься) сов возв to get lost

заблужда́|ться (-юсь) несов возв to be mistaken

заблужде́ни|е (-я) ср misconception

заболева́ни|е (-я) ср illness

заболе́|ть (-ю; impf заболева́ть) сов (нога́, го́рло) to begin to hurt; **заболева́ть** (**~** pf) **+instr** (гри́ппом) to fall ill with

забо́р (-а) м fence

забо́т|а (-ы) ж (беспоко́йство) worry; (ухо́д) care; (обычно мн: хло́поты) trouble ед

забо́|титься (-чусь, -тишься; pf **по~)** несов возв: **~ о +prp** to take care of

забо́тливый прил caring

забра́сыва|ть (-ю) несов от **заброса́ть, забро́сить**

заб|ра́ть (-еру́, -ерёшь; impf **забира́ть)** сов перех to take; **~ся** (impf **забира́ться)** сов возв (влезть): **~ся на** +асс to climb up; (прони́кнуть): **~ся в** +асс to get into

заброса́|ть (-ю; impf **забра́сывать)** сов перех: **~ +instr** (кана́ву, я́му) to fill with; (цвета́ми) to shower with

забро́|сить (-шу, -сишь; impf **забра́сывать)** сов перех (мяч, ка́мень) to fling; (деса́нт) to drop; (учёбу) to neglect

забро́шенный прил (дом) derelict; (сад, ребёнок) neglected

забры́зга|ть (-ю; impf **забры́згивать)** сов перех to splash

забы́ть (как **быть;** см. Table 21; impf **забыва́ть)** сов перех to forget

зав. сокр = **заве́дующий**

зава́л (-а) м obstruction

зав|али́ть (-алю́, -а́лишь; impf **зава́ливать)** сов перех (вход) to block off; (разг: экза́мен) to mess up; **зава́ливать** (**~** pf) **+instr** (доро́гу: сне́гом) to cover with; (я́му: землёй) to fill with; **~ся** (impf **зава́ливаться)** сов возв (забо́р) to collapse; (разг: на экза́мене) to come a cropper

зав|ари́ть (-арю́, -а́ришь; impf **зава́ривать)** сов перех (чай, ко́фе) to brew; (ТЕХ) to weld

зава́рк|а (-и) ж (де́йствие: ча́я) brewing; (зава́ренный чай) brew

заварно́й прил: **~ крем** custard

заведе́ни|е (-я) ср establishment

заве́д|овать (-ую) несов: **~ +instr** to be in charge of

заве́дующ|ий (-его) м manager; (лабораторией, кафедрой) head; ~ хозя́йством (в шко́ле) bursar; (на заво́де) person in charge of supplies

заве́р|ить (-ю, -ишь; impf заверя́ть) сов перех (ко́пию, по́дпись) to witness; заверя́ть (~ pf) кого́-н в чём-н to assure sb of sth

заверн|у́ть (-у́, -ёшь; impf завора́чивать) сов перех (рука́в) to roll up; (га́йку) to tighten up; (нале́во, напра́во, за у́гол) to turn; завора́чивать (~ pf) (в +acc) (посы́лку, кни́гу, ребёнка) to wrap (in); ~ся (impf завора́чиваться) сов возв: ~ся в +acc (в полоте́нце, в плед) to wrap o.s. up in

заверша́|ть (-ю) несов от заверши́ть

заверша́ющий прил final

заверше́ни|е (-я) ср completion; (разгово́ра, ле́кции) conclusion

заверш|и́ть (-у́, -и́шь; impf заверша́ть) сов перех to complete; (разгово́р) to end

заверя́|ть (-ю) несов от заве́рить

зав|ести́ (-еду́, -едёшь; pt -ёл, -ела́, -ело́; impf заводи́ть) сов перех to take; (приобрести́) to get; (установи́ть) to introduce; (перепи́ску, разгово́р) to initiate; (часы́) to wind up; (маши́ну) to start; ~сь (impf заводи́ться) сов возв (появи́ться) to appear; (мото́р, часы́) to start working

заве́т (-а) м (наставле́ние) precept; (РЕЛ): Ве́тхий/Но́вый Заве́т the Old/New Testament

завеща́ни|е (-я) ср (докуме́нт) will, testament

завеща́|ть (-ю) (не)сов перех: ~

что-н кому́-н (насле́дство) to bequeath sth to sb

завива́|ть(ся) (-ю(сь)) несов от зави́ть(ся)

зави́вк|а (-и) ж (воло́с) curling; (причёска) curly hair

зави́дно как сказ: ему́ ~ he feels envious

зави́д|овать (-ую; pf по~) несов: ~ +dat to envy, be jealous of

завин|ти́ть (-чу́, -ти́шь; impf зави́нчивать) сов перех to tighten (up)

зави́|сеть (-шу, -сишь) несов: ~ от +gen to depend on

зави́симост|ь (-и) ж (отноше́ние) correlation; ~ (от +gen) dependence (on); в ~и от +gen depending on

зави́стливый прил envious, jealous

за́вист|ь (-и) ж envy, jealousy

зави́т|о́к (-ка́) м (ло́кон) curl

зави́|ть (-ью, -ьёшь; impf завива́ть) сов перех (во́лосы) to curl; ~ся (impf зави́ться) сов возв (во́лосы) to curl; (сде́лать зави́вку) to curl one's hair

заво́д (-а) м factory; (в часа́х, у игру́шки) clockwork

заво́д|ить(ся) (-ожу́(сь), -о́дишь(ся)) несов от завести́(сь)

заводно́й прил (механи́зм) clockwork; (ру́чка) winding

завоева́ни|е (-я) ср (страны́) conquest; (успе́х) achievement

завоева́тел|ь (-я) м conqueror

завоева́тельный прил aggressive

заво|ева́ть (-юю; impf завоёвывать) сов перех to conquer

завора́чива|ть(ся) (-ю(сь)) несов от заверну́ть(ся)

за́втра нареч, ср нескл tomorrow;

до ~! see you tomorrow!

за́втрак (-а) м breakfast

за́втрака|ть (-ю; impf по~) несов to have breakfast

за́втрашний прил tomorrow's; **~ день** tomorrow

завуч (-а) м сокр ≈ deputy head

завхо́з (-а) м сокр = **заве́дующий хозя́йством**

зав|**яза́ть** (-яжу́, -я́жешь; impf **завя́зывать**) сов перех (верёвку) to tie; (руку, посылку) to bind; (разговор) to start (up); (дружбу) to form; **~ся** (impf **завя́зываться**) сов возв (шнурки) to be tied; (разговор) to start (up); (дружба) to form

загада́ть (-ю; impf **зага́дывать**) сов перех (загадку) to set; (желание) to make

зага́д|**ка** (-ки; gen pl -ок) ж riddle; (перен) puzzle

зага́дочный прил puzzling

зага́р (-а) м (sun)tan

загиба́ть(ся) (-ю(сь)) несов от **загну́ть(ся)**

загла́ви|**е** (-я) ср title

загла́вн|**ый** прил: **~ая бу́ква** capital letter, **~ая роль** title role

загла́|**дить** (-жу, -дишь; impf **загла́живать**) сов перех (складки) to iron

заглохн|**у́ть** (-у) сов от **гло́хнуть**

заглуш|**и́ть** (-у́, -и́шь) сов от **глуши́ть**

загл|**яну́ть** (-яну́, -я́нешь; impf **загля́дывать**) сов (в окно, в комнату) to peep; (в книгу, в словарь) to glance; (разг: посетить) to pop in

заг|**на́ть** (-оню́, -о́нишь; pt -на́л, -нала́, -на́ло; impf **загоня́ть**) сов (коров, детей) to drive

загн|**и́ть** (-ию́, -иёшь)

загнива́ть сов to rot

загно|**и́ться** (-ю́сь, -и́шься) возв (рана) to fester; (глаз) to become inflamed

загн|**у́ть** (-у́, -ёшь; impf **загиба́ть**) сов перех to bend; (край) to fold; **~ся** (impf **загиба́ться**) сов возв (гвоздь) to bend; (край) to fold

за́говор (-а) м conspiracy

заговор|**и́ть** (-ю́, -и́шь) сов (начать говорить) to begin to speak

заголо́в|**ок** (-ка) м headline

заго́н (-а) м (для коров) enclosure; (для овец) pen

загоня́ть (-ю) несов от **загна́ть**

загора́жива|**ть** (-ю) несов от **загороди́ть**

загора́ть(ся) (-ю(сь)) несов от **загоре́ть(ся)**

загоре́лый прил tanned

загор|**е́ть** (-ю́, -и́шь; impf **загора́ть**) сов to go brown, get a tan; **~ся** (impf **загора́ться**) сов возв (дрова, костёр) to light; (здание итп) to catch fire; (лампочка, глаза) to light up

за́город (-а) м (разг) the country

загор|**оди́ть** (-ожу́, -о́дишь; impf **загора́живать**) сов перех to block off; (свет) to block out

за́городный прил (экскурсия) out-of-town; (дом) country

загото́в|**ить** (-лю, -ишь; impf **загота́вливать**) сов перех to lay in; (документы итп) to prepare

заграждёни|**е** (-я) ср barrier

заграни́ца (-ы) ж (разг) foreign countries мн

заграни́чный прил foreign, overseas; **~ па́спорт** passport (for travel abroad)

загрем|**е́ть** (-лю́, -и́шь) сов (гром) to crash

загро́бн|ый прил; ~ый мир the next world; ~ая жизнь the afterlife

загр|узи́ть (-ужу́, -у́зишь) сов от **грузи́ть** ♦ (impf **загружа́ть**) перех (машину) to load up; (КОМП) to boot up

загрязне́ни|е (-я) ср pollution; ~ окружа́ющей среды (environmental) pollution

загрязн|и́ть (-ю́, -и́шь), impf **загрязня́ть** сов перех to pollute; ~ся (impf **загрязня́ться**) сов возв to become polluted

ЗАГС (-а) м сокр (= за́пись а́ктов гражда́нского состоя́ния) ≈ registry office

зад (-а; nom pl -ы́, gen pl -о́в) (челове́ка) behind; (живо́тного) rump; (маши́ны) rear

зада|ва́ть(ся) (-ю́(сь), -ёшь(ся)) несов от **зада́ть(ся)**

зад|ави́ть (-авлю́, -а́вишь) сов от **дави́ть** ♦ перех to crush; ~ави́ла маши́на he was run over by a car

зада́ни|е (-я) ср task; (уче́бное) exercise; (ВОЕН) mission; дома́шнее ~ homework

зада́т|ок (-ка) м deposit

зада́|ть (как дать; см. Table 16; impf **задава́ть**) сов перех to set; **задава́ть** (~ pf) кому́-н вопро́с to ask sb a question; ~ся (impf **задава́ться**) сов возв; ~ся це́лью +infin to set o.s. the task of doing

зада́ч|а (-и) ж task; (МАТ) problem

задви́га|ть (-ю) сов; ~ +instr to begin to move; ~ся сов возв to begin to move

задви́жк|а (-и) ж bolt

задви́н|уть (-у) сов перех (ящик, занаве́ски) to close

задева́|ть (-ю) несов от **заде́ть**

заде́ла|ть (-ю; impf **заде́лывать**) сов перех to seal up

задёргива|ть (-ю) несов от **задёрнуть**

заде|ржа́ть (-ержу́, -е́ржишь; impf **заде́рживать**) сов перех to delay, hold up; (престу́пника) to detain; я не хочу́ Вас **заде́рживать** I don't want to hold you back; ~ся (impf **заде́рживаться**) сов возв to be delayed или held up; (ждать) to pause

задёрж|ка (-ки; gen pl -ек) ж delay, hold-up

задёрн|уть (-у; impf **задёргивать**) сов перех (што́ры) to pull shut

заде́|ть (-ну, -нешь; impf **задева́ть**) сов перех (перен: самолю́бие) to wound; **задева́ть** (~ pf) за +acc (за сто́л) to brush against; (кость) to graze against

задира́|ть(ся) (-ю) несов от **задра́ть(ся)**

за́дн|ий прил back; помеча́ть (поме́тить pf) ~им число́м to backdate; опла́чивать (оплати́ть pf) ~им число́м to make a back payment; ~ие но́ги hind legs

задо́лго нареч; ~ до +gen long before

задо́лженност|ь (-и) ж debts мн

за́дом нареч backwards (BRIT), backward (US); ~ наперёд back to front

задохн|у́ться (-у́сь, -ёшься; impf **задыха́ться**) сов возв (в дыму́) to suffocate; (от бе́га) to be out of breath; (от зло́сти) to choke

зад|ра́ть (-еру́, -ерёшь; impf **задира́ть**) сов перех (пла́тье) to hitch или hike up; ~ся (impf **задира́ться**) сов возв (пла́тье итп) to ruck up

задр|ема́ть (-емлю́, -е́млешь)
сов to doze off

задрож|а́ть (-у́, -и́шь) *сов*
(человек, голос) to begin to
tremble; *(здание)* to begin to
shake

заду́ма|ть (-ю) *impf* **заду́мывать)**
сов перех (план) to think up;
(карту, число) to think of;
заду́мывать (~ pf) *+infin (уехать*
итп) to think of doing; **~ся** *(impf*
заду́мываться) *сов возв* to be
deep in thought

заду́мчивый *прил* pensive,
thoughtful

заду́мыва|ть(ся) (-ю(сь)) *несов*
от **заду́мать(ся)**

зад|уши́ть (-ушу́, -у́шишь) *сов*
от **души́ть**

задыха́|ться (-юсь) *несов от*
задохну́ться

заеда́|ть (-ю) *несов от* **зае́сть**

зае́зд (-а) *м (СПОРТ)* race *(in horse-
racing, motor-racing)*

заезжа́|ть (-ю) *несов от* **зае́хать**

заём (за́йма) *м* loan

заёмщик (-а) *м* borrower

зае́|сть (как есть; см. Table 15;
impf **заеда́ть)** *сов перех (подлеж: комары)* to eat ♦ *безл*
(разг: ружьё) to jam; **пласти́нку**
~ло *(разг)* the record is stuck

зае́хать (как е́хать; см. Table 19;
impf **заезжа́ть) (~ pf) ~ за кем-н** to
go to fetch sb; **заезжа́ть (~ pf)** в
+асс (в канаву, во двор) to drive
into; *(в Москву, в магазин итп)* to
stop off at

зажа́|ть (-му́, -мёшь) *impf*
зажима́ть) *сов перех* to squeeze;
(рот, уши) to cover

заж|е́чь (-гу́, -жёшь итп, -гу́т; *pt*
-ёг, -гла́) *сов перех (спичку)* **сов**
перех *(спичку)* *(свет)* to
turn on; **~ся** *(impf* **зажига́ться)**

сов возв *(спичка)* to light; *(свет)*
to go on

зажива́|ть (-ю) *несов от* **зажи́ть**

зажига́л|ка (-ки; *gen pl* **-ок)** *ж*
(cigarette) lighter

зажига́ни|е (-я) *ср (АВТ)* ignition

зажига́|ть(ся) (-ю(сь)) *несов от*
заже́чь(ся)

зажима́|ть (-ю) *несов от* **зажа́ть**

заж|и́ть (-иву́, -ивёшь) *сов; impf*
зажива́ть *(рана)* to heal
(up)

заземле́ни|е (-я) *ср (ЭЛЕК,*
устройство) earth *(BRIT)*, ground
(US)

заземл|и́ть (-ю́, -и́шь; *impf*
заземля́ть) *сов перех* to earth
(BRIT), ground *(US)*

зазу́брин|а (-ы) *ж* serration

заигра́|ть (-ю) *сов (не)перех* to
begin to play ♦ *неперех (музыка)* to
begin

заи́грыва|ть (-ю) *несов*: **~ с** *+instr*
(разг: любезничать) to flirt with;
(заискивать) to woo

заика́|ться (-юсь) *несов возв* to
have a stutter; **(заикну́ться** *pf) ~ o*
+prp (упомянуть) to mention

займств|овать (-ую; *несов* **по~)**
(не)сов перех to borrow; *(опыт)*
to take on board

заинтересо́ванный *прил*
interested; **я заинтересо́ван в**
э́том де́ле I have an interest in the
matter

заинтерес|ова́ть (-у́ю) *сов*
перех to interest; **~ся** *сов возв*:
~ся *+instr* to become interested in

заи́скива|ть (-ю) *несов*: **~ пе́ред**
+instr to ingratiate o.s. with

зайти́ (как идти́; см. Table 18; *impf*
заходи́ть) (~ pf) (солнце, луна) to
go down; *(спор, разговор)* to
start up; *(посетить)*: **~ в/на** *+асс/к*
+dat to call in (at); *(попасть)*: **~ в/**

на +acc to stray into; **заходи́ть** (~ pf) **за кем-н** to go to fetch sb; **заходи́ть** (~ pf) **спра́ва/сле́ва** to come in from the right/left

закавка́зский прил Transcaucasian

зака́з (-а) м (см глаг) ordering; booking; commissioning; (заказанный предмет) order; **по ~y** to order

зак|аза́ть (-ажу́, -а́жешь; impf **зака́зывать**) сов перех to order; to book; (портрет) to commission

заказн|о́й прил: ~**ое уби́йство** contract killing; ~**ое письмо́** registered letter

зака́зчик (-а) м customer

закалённый прил resistant

закал|и́ть (-ю́, -и́шь; impf **закаля́ть**) сов перех (сталь) to temper; (ребёнка, организм) to toughen up; ~**ся** (impf **закаля́ться**) сов возв to toughen

зака́лк|а (-и) ж (см глаг) tempering; toughening up

зака́лыва|ть (-ю) несов от **заколо́ть**

зака́нчива|ть(ся) (-ю) несов от **зако́нчить(ся)**

зака́па|ть (-ю; impf **зака́пывать**) сов перех (запачкать) to splatter; (лекарство) to apply

зака́пыва|ть (-ю) несов от **зака́пать**, **закопа́ть**

закида́|ть (-ю; impf **заки́дывать**) сов = **заброса́ть**

заки́н|уть (-у; impf **заки́дывать**) сов перех to throw

закип|е́ть (3sg -и́т; impf **закипа́ть**) сов to start to boil; (перен: работа) to intensify

заки́с|нуть (-ну; pt -, -ла; impf **закиса́ть**) сов to turn sour

за́кис|ь (-и) ж oxide

закла́дк|а (-и) ж (в книге) bookmark

закладн|а́я (-о́й) ж mortgage deed

закла́дыва|ть (-ю) несов от **заложи́ть**

закле́|ить (-ю, -ишь; impf **закле́ивать**) сов перех to seal (up)

заклина́ни|е (-я) ср plea; (магические слова) incantation

заклина́|ть (-ю) несов перех (духов, змея) to charm; (перен: умолять) to plead with

заклин|и́ть (-ю, -и́шь; impf **закли́нивать**) сов перех to jam

заключа́|ть (-ю) несов от **заключи́ть**; ~**ся** несов возв: ~**ся в** +prp (состоять в) to lie in; (содержаться в) to be contained in; **пробле́ма** ~**ется в том, что ...** the problem is that ...

заключе́ни|е (-я) ср conclusion; (в тюрьме) imprisonment, confinement

заключённ|ый (-ого) м prisoner

заключи́тельный прил concluding, final

заключ|и́ть (-у́, -и́шь; impf -а́ть) сов перех (договор, сделку) to conclude

заколдо́ванный прил enchanted; ~ **круг** vicious circle

зако́лк|а (-и) ж (для волос) hairpin

зак|оло́ть (-олю́, -о́лешь) сов от **коло́ть** ♦ (impf **зака́лывать**) *перех (волосы)* to pin up

зако́н (-а) *м* law; **объявля́ть (объяви́ть** *pf)* кого́-л вне ~а to outlaw sb

зако́нность (-и) *ж (документа)* legality; *(в стране)* law and order

зако́нный *прил* legitimate, lawful; *(право)* legal

законода́тельный *прил* legislative

законода́тельств|**о** (-а) *ср* legislation

закономе́рный *прил* predictable; *(понятный)* legal

законопрое́кт (-а) *м (полит)* bill

зако́нченный *прил* complete

зако́нч|**ить** (-у, -ишь; *impf* **зака́нчивать)** *сов перех* to finish; *(impf* **зака́нчиваться)** *сов возв* to finish, end

закопа́ть (-ю; *impf* **зака́пывать)** *сов перех* to bury; *(яму)* to fill in

закопти́ть (-чу́, -ти́шь) *сов от* **копти́ть**; **~ся** *сов возв* to be covered in smoke

закреп|**и́ть** (-лю́, -и́шь; *impf* **закрепля́ть)** *сов перех* to fasten; *(победу, пози́цию)* to consolidate; *(фо́то)* to fix

закрича́ть (-у́, -и́шь) *сов* to start shouting

закругл|**и́ть** (-ю́, -и́шь; *impf* **закругля́ть)** *сов перех (край, бесе́ду)* to round off

закру|**ти́ть** (-чу́, -у́тишь; *impf* **закру́чивать)** *сов перех (волосы)* to twist; *(га́йку)* to screw in

закрыва́|ть(ся) (-ю(сь)) *несов от* **закры́ть(ся)**

закры́ти|**е** (-я) *ср* closing (time)

закры́тый *прил* closed, shut; *(терра́са, маши́на)* enclosed; *(стадио́н)* indoor; *(собра́ние)* closed, private; *(ра́на)* internal; **в**

~ом помеще́нии indoors

закры́|**ть** (-о́ю, -о́ешь; *impf* **закрыва́ть)** *сов перех* to close, shut; *(заслони́ть, накры́ть)* to cover (up); *(прохо́д, грани́цу)* to close (off); *(во́ду, газ итп)* to shut off; **~ся** *(impf* **закрыва́ться)** *сов возв* to close, shut; *(магази́н)* to close *или* shut down; *(запере́ться: в до́ме итп)* to shut o.s. up

заку́р|**ить** (-ю́, -у́ришь; *impf* **заку́ривать)** *сов перех* to light (up)

заку|**си́ть** (-шу́, -у́сишь; *impf* **заку́сывать)** *сов (пое́сть)* to have a bite to eat

заку́ск|**а** (-и) *ж* snack; *(обычно мн: для во́дки)* zakuska nibbles *мн*; *(в нача́ле обе́да)* hors d'oeuvre

заку́сочн|**ая** (-ой) *ж* snack bar

заку́та|**ть(ся)** (-ю(сь)) *сов от* **ку́тать(ся)**

зал (-а) *м* hall; *(в библиоте́ке)* room; **~ ожида́ния** waiting room

заледене́лый *прил* covered in ice; *(руки)* icy

заледене́|ть (-ю) *сов (доро́га)* to ice over; *(перен: руки)* to freeze

зале́з|**ть** (-у, -ешь; *impf* **залеза́ть)** *сов*: **~ на** +*acc (на кры́шу)* to climb onto; *(на де́рево)* to climb (up); *(разг)*: **~ в** +*acc (в кварти́ру)* to break into; *(в долги́)* to run up

зале|**те́ть** (-чу́, -ти́шь; *impf* **залета́ть)** *сов*: **~ в** +*acc* to fly in(to)

залеч|**и́ть** (-ечу́, -е́чишь; *impf* **зале́чивать)** *сов перех* to heal

зали́в (-а) *м* bay; *(дли́нный)* gulf

зал|**и́ть** (-ью́, -ьёшь; *impf* **залива́ть)** *сов перех* to flood; *(костёр)* to extinguish; **залива́ть (~** *pf)* **бензи́н в маши́ну** to fill a

car with petrol; **~ся** (*impf*
залива́ться) *сов возв* (*вода*) to
seep; **залива́ться** (**~ся** *pf*)
слеза́ми/сме́хом to burst into
tears/out laughing

зало́г (**-а**) *м* (*действие: вещей*)
pawning; (*: квартиры*)
mortgaging; (*заложенная вещь*)
security; (*линг*) voice

зал|ожи́ть (**-ожу́, -о́жишь;** *impf*
закла́дывать) *сов перех*
(*покрыть*) to clutter up;
(*отметить*) to mark; (*кольцо,
шубу*) to pawn; (*дом*) to
mortgage; (*заполнить*) to block
up; **у меня́ ~ожи́ло нос/го́рло**
(*разг*) my nose/throat is all bunged
up

зало́жник (**-а**) *м* hostage
залп (**-а**) *м* salvo volley
за́лпом *нареч* all in one go
зам. *м сокр* (= **замести́тель**)
dep.

зама́з|ать (**-жу, -жешь;** *impf*
зама́зывать) *сов перех* (*щели*)
to fill with putty; (*запачкать*) to
smear

зама́зк|а (**-и**) *ж* putty

зам|ани́ть (**-аню́, -а́нишь;** *impf*
зама́нивать) *сов перех* to lure,
entice

зама́нчивый *прил* tempting

замахн|у́ться (**-у́сь, -ёшься;**
impf **зама́хиваться**) *сов возв:* **~
на** +*асс* (*на ребёнка*) to raise one's
hand to; (*перен*) to set one's sights
on

зама́чива|ть (**-ю**) *несов от*
замочи́ть

замедл|ить (**-ю, -ишь;** *impf*
замедля́ть) *сов перех* to slow
down; **~ся** (*impf* **замедля́ться**)
сов возв to slow down

заме́н|а (**-ы**) *ж* replacement;
(*спорт*) substitution

зам|ени́ть (**-еню́, -е́нишь;** *impf*
заменя́ть) *сов перех* to replace

зам|ере́ть (**-ру́, -рёшь;** *pt* **-ер,
-ерла́;** *impf* **замира́ть**) *сов*
(*человек*) to stand dead; (*перен:
сердце*) to stand still; (*: рабо́та,
страна*) to come to a standstill;
(*звук*) to die away

замёрз|нуть (**-ну;** *pt* **-, -ла;** *impf*
замерза́ть) *сов* to freeze; (*окно́*)
to ice up; **я** ~ I'm freezing

заме|си́ть (**-ешу́, -е́сишь;** *impf*
заме́шивать) *сов перех* to
knead

замести́тел|ь (**-я**) *м* (*директора*)
deputy

заме|сти́ть (**-щу́, -сти́шь;** *impf*
замеща́ть) *сов от* **замести́ть**

заме́|тить (**-чу, -тишь;** *impf*
замеча́ть) *сов перех* to notice;
(*сказа́ть*) to remark

заме́т|ка (**-ки;** *gen pl* **-ок**) *ж* note;
(*в газе́те*) short piece *или* article

заме́тно *нареч* it's obvious ♦ *как
сказ (видно)* it's obvious

заме́тный *прил* noticeable;
(*ли́чность*) prominent

замеча́ни|е (**-я**) *ср* comment,
remark; (*вы́говор*) reprimand

замеча́тельно *нареч* (*краси́в,
умён*) extremely; (*де́лать что-н*)
wonderfully, brilliantly ♦ *как сказ:*
~! that's wonderful *или* brilliant!

замеча́тельный *прил* wonderful,
brilliant

замеча́|ть (**-ю**) *несов от*
заме́тить

замеша́тельств|о (**-а**) *ср*
confusion

заме́шива|ть (**-ю**) *несов от*
замеси́ть

замеща́|ть (**-ю**) *несов перех*
(*вре́менно*) to stand in for; (*pf*
замести́ть; *заменя́ть:
рабо́тника итп*) to replace;

(: *игрока*) to substitute; (*вакансию*) to fill

замеще́ни|е (-я) *ср* (*работника*) replacement; (*игрока*) substitution

зами́н|ка (-ки; *gen pl* **-ок)** *ж* hitch

замира́|ть (-ю) *несов от* **замере́ть**

за́мкнутый *прил* (*жизнь*) cloistered; (*человек*) reclusive

замкн|у́ть (-у́, -ёшь; *impf* **замыка́ть)** *сов перех* to close; **~ся** (*impf* **замыка́ться)** *сов возв* to close; (*перен: обособиться*) to shut o.s. off

за́м|ок (-ка) *м* castle

зам|о́к (-ка́) *м* lock; (*также:* **вися́чий ~**) padlock

замо́лк|нуть (-ну; *pt* **-, -ла)** *impf* **замолка́ть** *сов* to fall silent

замолч|а́ть (-у́, -и́шь) *сов* (*человек*) to go quiet; **~и́!** be quiet!, shut up!

замора́живани|е (-я) *ср* (*продуктов*) refrigeration; **~ цен/ зарпла́ты** price/wage freeze

заморо́|зить (-жу, -зишь; *impf* **замора́живать)** *сов перех* to freeze

за́морозк|и (-ов) *мн* frosts *мн*

замо́ч|ить (-у́, -о́чишь; *impf* **зама́чивать)** *сов перех* to soak

за́муж *нареч*: **выходи́ть ~** (*за* +*acc*) to get married (to), marry

за́мужем *нареч* married

заму́жеств|о (-а) *ср* marriage

заму́жняя *прил* married

замуч|ить (-у, -ишь) *сов от* **му́чить ♦** *перех*: **~** (*pf*) *кого-н* до **сме́рти** to torture sb to death; **~ся** *сов от* **му́читься**

за́мш|а (-и) *ж* suede

замыка́ни|е (-я) *ср* (*также:* **коро́ткое ~**) short circuit

замыка́|ть(ся) (-ю(сь)) *несов от* **замкну́ть(ся)**

за́мыс|ел (-ла) *м* scheme

замы́сли|ть (-ю, -ишь; *impf* **замышля́ть)** *сов перех* to think up

за́навес (-а) *м* (ТЕАТР) curtain

занаве́|сить (-шу, -сишь; *impf* **занаве́шивать)** *сов перех* to hang a curtain over

занаве́с|ка (-ки; *gen pl* **-ок)** *ж* curtain

зан|ести́ (-есу́, -есёшь; *pt* **-ёс, -есла́;** *impf* **заноси́ть)** *сов перех* (*принести*) to bring; (*записать*) to take down; (*доставить*): **доро́гу ~есло́ сне́гом** the road is covered (over) with snow

занима́тельный *прил* engaging

занима́|ть (-ю) *несов от* **заня́ть**; **~ся** *несов возв* (*на рояле и т.п.*) to practise (*BRIT*), practice (*US*); **~ся** (*impf*) +*instr* (*учиться*) to study; (*уборкой*) to do; **~ся** (*impf*) **спо́ртом/му́зыкой** to play sports/ music; **чем ты сейча́с ~ешься?** what are you doing at the moment?

за́ново *нареч* again

зано́з|а (-ы) *ж* splinter

зано́с (-а) *м* (*обычно мн*) drift

зан|оси́ть (-ошу́, -о́сишь) *несов от* **занести́**

зано́счивый *прил* arrogant

за́нят *прил* busy; **он был о́чень ~** he was very busy; **телефо́н ~** the phone *или* line is engaged

заня́ти|е (-я) *ср* occupation; (*в школе*) lesson, class; (*времяпрепровождение*) pastime

за́нятост|ь (-и) *ж* employment

заня́ть (займу́, займёшь; *impf* **занима́ть)** *сов перех* to occupy; (*позицию*) to take up; (*деньги*) to borrow; (*время*) to take; **~** (*pf*) **пе́рвое/второ́е ме́сто** to take first/second place; **~ся** *сов возв*:

~**ся** +*instr* (*языком, спортом*) to take up; (*бизнесом*) to go into; ~**ся** (*pf*) **собо́й/детьми́** to devote time to o.s./one's children

заодно́ *нареч* (*вместе*) as one

зао́чный *прил* part-time

> **зао́чное отделе́ние** - Part-time study is one of the ways of obtaining a degree, and is for people who do not want to give up their job. Most students work independently with regular postal communication with their tutors. Two exam sessions a year are preceded by a month of intensive lectures and tutorials which prepare students for the exams. See also notes at **о́чный** and **вече́рний**.

за́пад (-а) *м* west; **За́пад** (*полит*) the West

западноевропе́йский *прил* West European

за́падный *прил* western; (*ветер*) westerly

западн|я́ (-и́) *ж* trap

запа́с (-а) *м* store; (*руды*) deposit; (*воен*) the reserves *мн*

запаса́|ть(ся) (-ю(сь)) *несов от* запасти́(сь)

запасн|о́й *прил* spare ♦ (-о́го) *м* (*спорт: также*: ~ **игро́к**) substitute; ~**áя часть** spare part

зап|асти́ (-асу́, -асёшь; *impf* запаса́ть) *сов перех* to lay in; ~**сь** (*impf* запаса́ться) *сов возв*: ~**сь** +*instr* to stock up (on)

за́пах (-а) *м* smell

запая́|ть (-ю) *сов перех* to solder

зап|ере́ть (-ру́, -рёшь; *impf* запира́ть) *сов перех* (*дверь*) to lock; (*дом, человека*) to lock up; ~**ся** (*impf* запира́ться) *сов возв* (*дверь*) to lock; (*человек*) to lock

o.s. up

зап|е́ть (-ою́, -оёшь) *сов* (не)*перех* to start singing

запеча́та|ть (-ю; *impf* запеча́тывать) *сов перех* to seal up

запира́|ть(ся) (-ю(сь)) *несов от* запере́ть(ся)

зап|иса́ть (-ишу́, -и́шешь; *impf* запи́сывать) *сов перех* to write down; (*концерт, пластинку*) to record; (*на курсы*) to enrol; ~**ся** (*impf* запи́сываться) *сов возв* (*на курсы*) to enrol (o.s.); (*на плёнку*) to make a recording; ~**ся** (*pf*) (**на приём**) **к врачу́** to make a doctor's appointment

запи́ск|а (-и) *ж* note; (*служебная*) memo

записн|о́й *прил*: ~**áя кни́жка** notebook

запи́сыва|ть(ся) (-ю(сь)) *несов от* записа́ть(ся)

за́пис|ь (-и) *ж* record; (*в дневнике*) entry; (*муз*) recording; (*на курсы*) enrolment (*brit*), enrollment (*us*); (*на приём к врачу́*) appointment

запла́ка|ть (-чу, -чешь) *сов* to start crying *или* to cry

запла́т|а (-ы) *ж* patch

заплат|и́ть (-ачу́, -а́тишь) *сов от* плати́ть

запл|ести́ (-ету́, -етёшь; *pt* -ёл, -ела́, -ело́, *impf* заплета́ть) *сов перех* (*волосы*) to plait

заплы́в (-а) *м* (*спорт*) race (*in swimming*); (: *отборочный*) heat

заплы|́ть (-ву́, -вёшь; *impf* заплыва́ть) *сов* (*человек*) to swim off; (*глаза*) to become swollen

запове́дник (-а) *м* (*природный*) nature reserve

за́повед|ь (-и) *ж* commandment

заподо́зр|ить (-ю, -ишь) *сов*
перех to suspect

запо́лн|ить (-ю, -ишь); *impf*
заполня́ть (*сов перех*) to fill;
(*анкету, бланк*) to fill in *или* out;
~ся (*impf* **заполня́ться**) *сов возв*
to fill up

заполя́рный *прил* polar

запо́мн|ить (-ю, -ишь; *impf*
запомина́ть) *сов перех* to
remember

запо́нк|а (-и) *ж* cuff link

запо́р (-а) *м* (*МЕД*) constipation;
(*замо́к*) lock

запоте́|ть (-ю) *сов* to steam up

запра́в|ить (-лю, -ишь); *impf*
заправля́ть *сов перех*
(*руба́шку*) to tuck in; (*сала́т*) to
dress; **запра́вить** (~ *pf*) **маши́ну**
to fill up the car; **~ся** (*impf*
заправля́ться) *сов возв* (*разг.*
горю́чим) to tank up

запра́в|ка (-ки; *gen pl* -ок) *ж*
(*маши́ны, самолёта итп*)
refuelling; (*кули́н*) dressing; (*разг.*
ста́нция) filling station

запра́вочн|ый *прил*: **~ая**
ста́нция filling station

запре́т (-а) *м*: ~ (**на что-н**/ +infin)
ban (on sth/on doing)

запре|ти́ть (-щу́, -ти́шь; *impf*
запреща́ть) *сов перех* to ban;
запреща́ть (~ *pf*) **кому́-н** +infin to
forbid sb to do

запре́тный *прил* forbidden

запреща́|ние (-я) *ср* banning;
суде́бное ~ injunction

запрещённый *прил* banned

запро́с (-а) *м* inquiry; (*обычно*
мн: тре́бования) expectation

запря|га́ть (-га́ю, -жа́ешь) *итп,*
-**ягу́т**; *pt* -**яг,** -**ягла́**) *impf*
запряга́ть (*сов перех* (*ло́шадь*)
to harness

запуга́|ть (-ю; *impf* **запу́гивать**)

запу́гивать (-а) *сов* (*станка́*) starting;
(*раке́ты*) launch

запус|ти́ть (-ущу́, -у́стишь;
impf **запуска́ть** *сов перех* (*бро́сить*)
to hurl; (*стано́к*) to start (up);
(*раке́ту*) to launch; (*хозя́йство,*
боле́знь) to neglect ♦ *неперех*: ~
чем-н в кого́-н to hurl sth at sb;
запуска́ть (~ *pf*) **что-н в**
произво́дство to launch
(production of) sth

запу́танный *прил* (*ни́тки,*
во́лосы) tangled; (*де́ло, вопро́с*)
confused

запу́та|ть(ся) (-ю(сь)) *сов от* **пу́тать(ся)**;
~ся *сов от* **пу́таться** ♦ (*impf*
запу́тываться) *возв* (*челове́к*)
to get caught up; (*де́ло, вопро́с*)
to become confused

запу́щенный *прил* neglected

запча́ст|ь (-и) *ж сокр* =
запасна́я часть

запя́сть|е (-ья; *gen pl* -ий) *ср* wrist

запя́т|ая (-о́й) *ж* comma

зарабо́та|ть (-ю; *impf*
зараба́тывать) *сов перех* to
earn ♦ *неперех*; (*no impf*; *нача́ть*
рабо́тать) to start up

за́работн|ый *прил*: **~ая пла́та**
pay, wages *мн*

за́работ|ок (-ка) *м* earnings *мн*

заража́|ть(ся) (-ю(сь)) *несов от*
зарази́ть(ся)

зараже́ни|е (-я) *ср* infection;
(*ме́стности*) contamination

зара́з|а (-ы) *ж* infection

зара|зи́ть (-жу́, -зи́шь); *impf*
заража́ть *сов перех* to infect;
(*ме́стность*) to contaminate; **~ся**
(*impf* **заража́ться**) *сов возв*: **~ся**
+instr (*гри́ппом итп*) to catch

зара́зный *прил* infectious

зара́нее *нареч* in advance

зар|асти́ (-асту́, -астёшь; *pt* -о́с,

-осла́; *impf* зараста́ть) *сов*
(зажить: *рана*) to close up;
зараста́ть (~ *pf* +*instr* травой) to
be overgrown with

заре́|зать (-жу, -жешь) *сов от*
ре́зать ♦ *перех* (*человека*) to
stab to death

зарекомендова́ть (-у́ю) *сов*: ~
себя́ +*instr* to prove oneself to be

зароди́ться (3sg -и́тся; *impf*
зарожда́ться) *сов возв*
(*явление*) to emerge; (*перен*:
чувство) to arise

заро́ды|ш (-а) *м* (БИО) embryo;
(*растения, также перен*) germ

зарожде́ни|е (-я) *ср* emergence;
(*идеи, чувства*) conception

за́росл|ь (-и) *ж* (*обычно мн*)
thicket

зарпла́т|а (-ы) *ж сокр* (=
за́работная пла́та) pay

зарубе́жный *прил* foreign

зарубе́жь|е (-я) *ср* overseas;
ближнее ~ former Soviet republics

зар|ы́ть (-о́ю, -о́ешь; *impf*
зарыва́ть) *сов перех* to bury;
~ся (*impf* зарыва́ться) *сов возв*:
~ся в +*acc* to bury o.s. in

зар|я́ (-и́; *nom pl* зо́ри, *gen pl*
зорь, *dat pl* зо́рям) *ж* dawn;
(*вечерняя*) sundown; **ни свет ни**
~ at the crack of dawn

заря́|д (-а) *м* (ВОЕН, ЭЛЕК) charge;
(*перен*: бодрости) boost

заря|ди́ть (-жу́, -дишь; *impf*
заряжа́ть) *сов перех* (*оружие*);
(*батарейку*) to charge; ~ся (*impf*
заряжа́ться) *сов возв* to
recharge

заря́дк|а (-и) *ж* (СПОРТ) exercises
мн; (*батареи*) charging

заса́д|а (-ы) *ж* ambush; (*отряд*)
ambush party

заса́сыва|ть (3sg -ет) *несов от*
засоса́ть

засверка́|ть (-ю) *сов* to flash

засв|ети́ть (-ечу́, -е́тишь; *impf*
засве́чивать) *сов перех* (*ФОТО*)
to expose

засева́|ть (-ю) *несов от* засе́ять

заседа́ни|е (-я) *ср* meeting;
(*парламента, суда*) session

заседа́тел|ь (-я) *м*: прися́жный ~
member of the jury

заседа́|ть (-ю) *несов* (на
совещании) to meet; (*в
парламенте, в суде*) to sit;
(*парламент, суд*) to be in session

засека́|ть (-ю) *несов от* засе́чь

засел|и́ть (-ю́, -ишь; *impf*
заселя́ть) *сов перех* (*земли*) to
settle; (*дом*) to move into

засе́|чь (-еку́, -ечёшь *etc*, -еку́т;
pt -ёк, -екла́, -екло́; *impf*
засека́ть) *сов перех* (*место*) to
locate; **засе́чь** (~ *pf*) **вре́мя** to
record the time

засе́|ять (-ю; *impf* засева́ть) *сов
перех* to sow

засло́н (-а) *м* shield

заслон|и́ть (-ю́, -ишь; *impf*
заслоня́ть) *сов перех* to shield

заслу́г|а (-и) *ж* (*обычно мн*)
service; **награди́ть** (*pf*) кого́-н по
~м to fully reward sb; **его́
наказа́ли по** ~м he got what he
deserved

заслу́женный *прил* well-
deserved; (*врач, учёный итп*)
renowned

заслу́ж|ить (-ужу́, -у́жишь; *impf*
заслу́живать) *сов перех* to earn

заслу́ша|ть (-ю; *impf*
заслу́шивать) *сов перех* to
listen to

засме|я́ться (-ю́сь, -ёшься) *сов
возв* to start laughing

засн|у́ть (-у́, -ёшь; *impf*
засыпа́ть) *сов* to go to sleep, fall
asleep

засо́в (-а) *м* bolt

засо́вывать (-ю) *несов от* **засу́нуть**

засоре́ни|е (-я) *ср* (*рек*) pollution; (*туале́та*) blockage

засор|и́ть (-ю́, -и́шь; *impf* **засоря́ть**) *сов перех* (*туале́т*) to clog up, block; **~ся** (*impf* **засоря́ться**) *сов возв* (*туале́т*) to become clogged up *или* blocked

засос|а́ть (-у́, -ёшь; *impf* **заса́сывать**) *сов перех* to suck in

засо́хн|уть (-у; *impf* **засыха́ть**) *сов* (*грязь*) to dry up; (*расте́ние*) to wither

заста́в|а (-ы) *ж* (*также*: **пограни́чная ~**) frontier post

застава́ть (-ю́, -ёшь) *несов от* **заста́ть**

заста́в|ить (-лю, -ишь; *impf* **заставля́ть**) *сов перех* (*заня́ть*) to clutter up; **заставля́ть** (~ *pf*) **кого́-н** +*infin* to force sb to do, make sb do

заста́|ть (-ну, -нешь; *impf* **застава́ть**) *сов перех* to catch, find

застегн|у́ть (-у́, -ёшь; *impf* **застёгивать**) *сов перех* to do up; **~ся** (*impf* **застёгиваться**) *сов возв* (*на пу́говицы*) to button o.s. up; (*на мо́лнию*) to zip o.s. up

застёж|ка (-ки; *gen pl* -ек) *ж* fastener

застекл|и́ть (-ю́, -и́шь; *impf* **застекля́ть**) *сов перех* to glaze

застел|и́ть (-ю́, -и́шь; *impf* **застила́ть**) *сов перех* (*крова́ть*) to make up

засте́нчивый *прил* shy

застига́|ть (-ю) *несов от* **засти́чь**

застила́|ть (-ю) *несов от* **застели́ть**

засти́|чь (-гну, -гнешь; *pt* -г,

-гла, -гло; *impf* **застига́ть**) *сов перех* to catch

засто́|й (-я) *м* (*в дела́х*) standstill; (*в жи́зни*) stagnation

засто́йный *прил* stagnant

застра́ива|ть (-ю) *несов от* **застро́ить**

застрах|ова́ть(ся) (-у́ю(сь)) *от* **страхова́ть(ся)**

застрева́|ть (-ю) *несов от* **застря́ть**

застре́л|ить (-ю́, -е́лишь; *impf* **застре́ливать**) *сов перех* to gun down; **~ся** *сов возв* to shoot o.s.

застро́|ить (-ю, -ишь; *impf* **застра́ивать**) *сов перех* to develop

застря́|ть (-ну, -нешь; *impf* **застрева́ть**) *сов* to get stuck

заступ|и́ться (-уплю́сь, -у́пишься; *impf* **заступа́ться**) *сов возв*: **~ за кого́-н** to stand up for

засты́|ть (-ну, -нешь; *impf* **застыва́ть**) *сов* to freeze; (*цеме́нт*) to set

засу́н|уть (-у; *impf* **засо́вывать**) *сов перех*: **~ что-н в** +*acc* to thrust sth into

за́сух|а (-и) *ж* drought

засу́ш|ить (-у́, -у́шишь; *impf* **засу́шивать**) *сов перех* to dry up

засу́шливый *прил* dry

засчита́|ть (-ю; *impf* **засчи́тывать**) *сов перех* (*гол*) to allow (to stand)

засып|а́ть (-лю, -лешь; *impf* **засыпа́ть**) *сов перех* (*я́му*) to fill (up); (*покры́ть*) to cover; **засыпа́ть** (~ *pf*) **кого́-н вопро́сами** to bombard sb with questions; **засыпа́ть** (~ *pf*) **кого́-н пода́рками** to shower sb with gifts

засыпа́|ть (-ю) *несов от* **засну́ть**

засыха́|ть (-ю) *несов от*

затаи́ть 90 затяну́ть

засо́хнуть

зата|и́ть (-ю́, -и́шь; *impf*
зата́ивать) *сов перех*
(*неприязнь*) to harbour (*BRIT*),
harbor (*US*); ~ **ся** *сов возв* to hide

зата́пливать (-ю) *несов от*
затопи́ть

затащ|и́ть (-а́щу, -а́щишь; *impf*
зата́скивать) *сов перех* to drag

затверде́|ть (*3sg* -ет; *impf*
затвердева́ть) *сов* to harden;
(*раствор*) to solidify

затво́р (-а) *м* shutter

затева́|ть (-ю) *несов от* **зате́ять**

затека́|ть (-ю) *несов от* **зате́чь**

зате́м *нареч* (*потом*) then; (*для
того*) for that reason; ~ **что́бы** in
order to

затемн|и́ть (-ю́, -и́шь; *impf*
затемня́ть) *сов перех* to darken

зате́|чь (*3sg* -чёт, *pt* -ёк, -екла́,
-екло́; *impf* **затека́ть**) *сов*
(*опухнуть*) to swell up; (*онеметь*)
to go numb; **затека́ть** (~ *pf*) **за**
+*acc* **в** +*acc* (*вода*) to seep behind/
into

зате́|я (-и) *ж* (*замысел*) idea,
scheme

зате́|ять (-ю; *impf* **затева́ть**) *сов
перех* (*разговор, игру*) to start
(up)

зати́х|нуть (-ну; *pt* -, -ла; *impf*
затиха́ть) *сов* to quieten (*BRIT*)
или quiet (*US*) down; (*буря*) to die
down

зати́шь|е (-я) *ср* lull

заткн|у́ть (-у́, -ёшь; *impf*
затыка́ть) *сов перех* to plug; ~
(*pf*) **что́-н за** +*acc*/**в** +*acc* to stuff sth
behind/into; ~ **кого́-н** *или* **рот кому́-н** (*разг*)
to shut sb up; ~**ся** (*impf* **затыка́ться**)
сов возв (*разг*: *замолчать*) to
shut up; ~**и́сь!** (*разг*: *пренебр*)

shut it!

затме́ни|е (-я) *ср* eclipse

зато́ *союз* (*также*: **но** ~) but then
(again)

зат|ону́ть (-ону́, -о́нешь) *сов* to
sink

зат|опи́ть (-оплю́, -о́пишь; *impf*
зата́пливать (*печь*)
to light; (*impf* **затопля́ть**;
деревню) to flood; (*судно*) to sink

зато́р (-а) *м* congestion; (*на
улице*) traffic jam

затра́гива|ть (-ю) *несов от*
затро́нуть

затра́т|а (-ы) *ж* expenditure

затра́|тить (-чу, -тишь; *impf*
затра́чивать) *сов перех* to
expend

затро́н|уть (-у; *impf*
затра́гивать) *сов перех* (*перен:
тему*) to touch on; (: *человека*) to
affect

затрудне́ни|е (-я) *ср* difficulty

затрудни́тельный *прил* difficult,
awkward

затрудн|и́ть (-ю́, -и́шь; *impf*
затрудня́ть) *сов перех*: ~ **что́-н**
to make sth difficult; **е́сли Вас не
~и́т** if it isn't too much trouble; ~**ся**
(*impf* **затрудня́ться**) *сов возв*:
~**ся** +*infin*/**с чем-н** to have difficulty
doing/with sth

зат|упи́ть(ся) (-уплю́, -у́пишь)
сов от **тупи́ть(ся)**

зат|уши́ть (-ушу́, -у́шишь) *сов
от* **туши́ть**

затыка́|ть(ся) (-ю(сь)) *несов от*
заткну́ть(ся)

заты́л|ок (-ка) *м* the back of the
head

затян|у́ть (-у́, -я́нешь; *impf*
зата́гивать) *сов перех* (*шнурки,
гайку*) to tighten; (*дело*) to drag
out; (*вовлечь*): ~ **кого́-н в** +*acc* to
drag sb into; ~**ся** (*impf*

зата́гиваться) *сов возв* (*петля, узел*) to tighten; (*рана*) to close up; (*дело*) to overrun; (*при куре́нии*) to inhale

заура́дный *прил* mediocre

зау́трен|я (-и) *ж* (*РЕЛ*) dawn mass

за|учи́ть (-учу́, -у́чишь; *impf* **-у́чивать)** *сов перех* to learn, memorize

захва́т (-а) *м* seizure, capture; (*СПОРТ*) hold; (*ТЕХ*) clamp

захв|ати́ть (-ачу́, -а́тишь; *impf* **захва́тывать)** *сов перех* to seize, capture; (*взять с собой*) to take; (*подлеж: музыка*) to captivate; (*болезнь, пожар*) to catch (in time); **дух ~а́тывает** it takes your breath away; **у меня́ дух ~а́тило от волне́ния** I was breathless with excitement

захва́тнический *прил* aggressive

захва́тчик (-а) *м* invader

захва́тывающий *прил* gripping; (*вид*) breathtaking

захлебн|у́ться (-у́сь, -ёшься; *impf* **захлёбываться)** *сов возв* to choke

захлопа|ть (-ю) *сов:* ~ (**в ладо́ши**) (*зри́тели*) to start clapping

захлопн|у́ть (-у; *impf* **захло́пывать)** *сов перех* to slam (shut); ~**ся** (*impf* **захло́пываться**) *сов возв* to slam shut

захо́д (-а) *м* (*также:* ~ **со́лнца**) sundown; (*в порт*) call; (*попы́тка*) go; **с пе́рвого/второ́го ~а** at the first/second go

зах|оди́ть (-ожу́, -о́дишь) *несов от* **зайти́**

захор|они́ть (-оню́, -о́нишь) *сов перех* to bury

зах|оте́ть (как хоте́ть; *см. Table 14*) *сов* to want; ~**ся** *сов безл:* **мне ~оте́лось есть/пить** I

started to feel hungry/thirsty

зац|епи́ть (-еплю́, -е́пишь; *impf* **зацепля́ть)** *сов перех* (*поддеть*) to hook up; (*разг: заде́ть*) to catch against; ~**ся** *сов возв:* ~**ся за** +*acc* (*заде́ть за*) to catch или get caught on; (*ухвати́ться за*) to grab hold of

зача́ти|е (-я) *ср* conception

зача́т|ок (-ка; *nom pl* **-ки**) *м* (*иде́и итп*) beginning, germ *ед*

заче́м *нареч* why

заче́м-то *нареч* for some reason

зачеркн|у́ть (-у́, -ёшь; *impf* **зачёркивать)** *сов перех* to cross out

зачерпн|у́ть (-у́, -ёшь; *impf* **заче́рпывать)** *сов перех* to scoop up

зач|еса́ть (-ешу́, -е́шешь; *impf* **зачёсывать)** *сов перех* to comb

зачёт (-а) *м* (*ПРОСВЕЩ*) test; **сдава́ть** (*impf*)/**сдать** (*pf*) ~ **по фи́зике** to sit (*BRIT*) или take/pass a physics test

зачётн|ый *прил:* ~**ая рабо́та** assessed essay (*BRIT*), term paper (*US*); ~**ая кни́жка** student's record book

> **зачётная кни́жка** - student's record book. This is a special booklet into which all exam marks attained by the students are entered. It is the students' responsibility to look after their own record books.

зачи́нщик (-а) *м* instigator

зачи́сл|ить (-ю, -ишь; *impf* **зачисля́ть)** *сов перех* (*в институ́т*) to enrol; (*на рабо́ту*) to take on; (*на счёт*) to enter

зачита́|ть (-ю; *impf* **зачи́тывать)** *сов перех* to read out

зашёл *сов см.* **зайти́**

заши́|ть (**-ью, -ьёшь**) *impf* **зашива́ть** *сов перех* (*дырку*) to mend; *impf* (*шов, рану*) to stitch

зашла́ *etc сов см.* **зайти́**

заштопа́|ть (**-ю**) *сов от* **што́пать**

защёлк|а (**-и**) *ж* (*на двери*) latch

защёлкн|уть (**-у**) *impf* **защёлкивать** *сов перех* to snap

защи́т|а (**-ы**) *ж* (*также* ЮР, СПОРТ) defence (BRIT), defense (US); (*от комаров, от пыли*) protection; (*диплома*) (public) viva

защити́|ть (**-щу́, -ти́шь**) *impf* **защища́ть** *сов перех* to defend; (*от солнца, от комаров итп*) to protect; **~ся** (*impf* **защища́ться**) *сов возв* to defend o.s.; (*студент*) to defend one's thesis

защи́тник (**-а**) *м* (*также* СПОРТ) defender; (ЮР) defence counsel (BRIT), defense attorney (US); **ле́вый/пра́вый ~** (*футбол*) left/right back

защи́тный *прил* protective; **~ цвет** khaki

защища́|ть (**-ю**) *несов от* **защити́ть** ♦ *перех* (ЮР) to defend; **~ся** *несов от* **защити́ться**

заяв|и́ть (**-лю́, -я́вишь**) *impf* **заявля́ть** *сов перех* (*протест*) to make ♦ *неперех*: **~ о** +*prp* to announce; **заявля́ть** (**~** *pf*) **на кого́-н в мили́цию** to report sb to the police

заяв|ка (**-ки**; *gen pl* **-ок**) *ж*: **~** (*на* +*acc*) application (for)

заявле́ни|е (**-я**) *ср* (*правительства*) statement; (*просьба*): **~ (о** +*prp*) application (for)

заявля́|ть (**-ю**) *несов от* **заяви́ть**

за́яц (**-йца**) *м* (ЗООЛ) hare

зва́ни|е (**-я**) *ср* (*воинское*) rank;

(*учёное, почётное*) title

зва|ть (**зову́, зовёшь**) *pf* **позва́ть** *несов перех* to call; (*приглашать*) to ask; (*no pf*; *называть*): **~ кого́-н** to call sb sth; **как Вас зову́т?** what is your name?; **меня́/его́ зову́т Алекса́ндр** my/his name is Alexander; **~** (**позва́ть** *pf*) **кого́-н в го́сти/в кино́** to ask sb over/to the cinema

звезд|а́ (**-ы́**; *nom pl* **звёзды**) *ж* star

звен|е́ть (**-ю́, -и́шь**) *несов* (*звонок*) to ring; (*голос*) to ring out; (*стаканы*) to clink

звен|о́ (**-а́**; *nom pl* **-ья**, *gen pl* **-ьев**) *ср* (*цепи*) link; (*конструкции*) section

звери́ный *прил* (wild) animal

зве́рский *прил* (*поступок*) brutal

зве́рств|о (**-а**) *ср* (*жестокость*) brutality; (*поступок*) atrocity

зве́рств|овать (**-ую**) *несов* to commit atrocities

зверь (**-я**; *gen pl* **-е́й**) *м* (wild) animal, beast

звон (**-а**) *м* clinking; (*колокола*) chime

звон|и́ть (**-ю́, -и́шь**; *pf* **по~**) *несов* to ring; (ТЕЛ): **~ кому́** to ring *или* phone *или* call (US) sb

зво́нкий *прил* sonorous

звон|о́к (**-ка́**; *nom pl* **-ки́**) *м* bell; (*звук*) ring; (*по телефону*) (telephone) call

звук (**-а**) *м* sound

звуков|о́й *прил* sound, audio; **~а́я доро́жка** track (*on audio tape*); **~а́я аппарату́ра** hi-fi equipment

звукоза́пис|ь (**-и**) *ж* sound recording

звуч|а́ть (*3sg* **-и́т**) *несов* (*гитара*) to sound; (*гнев*) to be heard

зда́ни|е (**-я**) *ср* building

здесь *нареч* here

здоро́ва|ться (**-юсь**; *pf* **по~**)

несов возв: ~ **с** +*instr* to say hello to

здоро́во *нареч* (*разг: отлично*) really well ♦ *как сказ* (*разг*) it's great

здоро́в|ый *прил* healthy; (*перен: идея*) sound; (*разг: большой*) hefty; **бу́дьте ~ы!** (*при прощании*) take care!; (*при чихании*) bless you!

здоро́вь|е (-я) *ср* health; **как Ва́ше ~?** how are you keeping?; **за Ва́ше ~!** (to) your good health!; **на ~!** enjoy it!

здравомы́слящий *прил* sensible

здравоохране́ни|е (-я) *ср* health care; **министе́рство ~я** ≈ Department of Health

здра́вств|овать (-ую) *несов* to thrive; **~уйте** hello; **да ~ует...!** long live ...!

здра́вый *прил* sound

зе́бр|а (-ы) *ж* zebra; (*переход*) zebra crossing (*BRIT*), crosswalk (*US*)

зева́|ть (-ю) *несов* to yawn ♦ *перех* (*разг*) to miss out

зевн|у́ть (-у́, -ёшь) *сов* to yawn

зелене́|ть (-ю) *pf* **по~** *несов* to go *или* turn green

зелё́ный *прил* green

зе́лен|ь (-и) *ж* (*цвет*) green ♦ *собир* (*растительность*) greenery; (*овощи и травы*) greens *мн*

земе́льный *прил* land; ~ **наде́л** *или* **уча́сток** plot of land

землевладе́л|ец (-ьца) *м* landowner

землевладе́ни|е (-я) *ср* landownership

земледе́ли|е (-я) *ср* arable farming

земледе́льческий *прил* (*район*) agricultural; (*машины*) farming

землетрясе́ни|е (-я) *ср*

earthquake

земл|я́ (-и́; *acc sg* **-лю,** *nom pl* **-ли,** *gen pl* **-е́ль)** *ж* land; (*поверхность*) ground; (*почва*) earth, soil; (*планета*) **Земля́** Earth

земля́к (-а́) *м* compatriot

земляни́к|а (-и) *ж* (*растение*) wild strawberry (plant) ♦ *собир* (*ягоды*) wild strawberries *мн*

земно́й *прил* (*поверхность, кора*) earth's; (*перен: желания*) earthly; ~ **шар** the globe

зени́т (-а) *м* zenith

зени́тный *прил* (*ВОЕН*) anti-aircraft

зе́рк|ало (-ала; *nom pl* **-ала́,** *gen pl* **-а́л,** *dat pl* **-ала́м)** *ср* mirror

зерка́льный *прил* glassy

зерн|о́ (-а́; *nom pl* **зёрна,** *gen pl* **зёрен)** *ср* (*пшеницы*) grain; (*кофе*) bean; (*мака*) seed ♦ *собир* (*семенное, на хлеб*) grain

зернохрани́лищ|е (-а) *ср* granary

зигза́г (-а) *м* zigzag

зим|а́ (-ы́; *acc sg* **-у,** *dat sg* **-е́,** *nom pl* **-ы)** *ж* winter

зи́мний *прил* (*день*) winter's; (*погода*) wintry; (*лес, одежда*) winter

зим|ова́ть (-у́ю; *pf* **про~)** *несов* (*человек*) to spend the winter; (*птицы*) to winter

зимо́в|ка (-ки; *gen pl* **-ок)** *ж* wintering place; (*для птиц*) wintering ground

зимо́й *нареч* in the winter

зл|ить (-ю, -ишь; *pf* **разозли́ть)** *несов перех* to annoy; **зли́ться** (*pf* **разозли́ться)** *несов возв* to get angry

зл|о (-а; *gen pl* **зол)** *ср* evil; (*неприятность*) harm ♦ *нареч* (*посмотреть, сказать*) spitefully; **со ~а** out of spite; **меня́ ~ берёт**

(*разг*) it makes me angry; **у меня́ на неё ~а не хвата́ет** (*разг*) she annoys me no end

зло́б|а (-ы) *ж* malice; **на ~у дня** on a topical issue

зло́бный *прил* mean; (*улыбка*) evil; (*голос*) nasty

злободне́вный *прил* topical

злове́щий *прил* sinister

злоде́|й (-я) *м* villain

злоде́йский *прил* wicked

злой *прил* evil; (*собака*) vicious; (*глаза, лицо*) mean; (*карикатура*) scathing; **я зол на тебя́** I'm angry with you

злока́чественный *прил* malignant

злора́дный *прил* gloating

злостный *прил* malicious

злость (-и) *ж* malice

злоупотреб|и́ть (-лю́, -и́шь; *impf* **злоупотребля́ть**) *сов*: ~ +*instr* to abuse; (*доверием*) to breach

злоупотребле́ни|е (-я) *ср* (*обычно мн*: *преступление*) malpractice *ед*; ~ **нарко́тиками** drug abuse; ~ **дове́рием** breach of confidence

змеи́ный *прил* (*кожа*) snake; ~ **яд** venom

зме|й (-я; *gen pl* -ев) *м* serpent; (*также*: **возду́шный** ~) kite

зме|я́ (-и́; *nom pl* -и́и, *gen pl* -е́й) *ж* snake

знак (-а) *м* sign, symbol; (*комп*) character; **в** ~ +*gen* as a token of; **под зна́ком** +*gen* in an atmosphere of; (*астрологический*) sign; **зна́ки зодиа́ка** signs of the Zodiac

знако́м|ить (-лю, -ишь; *pf* **по~**) *несов перех*: ~ **кого́-н** +*instr* to introduce sb to; ~**ся** (*pf* **по~ся**) *несов возв*: ~**ся с** +*instr* to

(*с человеком*) to meet; (*pf* **о~ся**) to study

знако́мств|о (-а) *ср* acquaintance

знако́м|ый *прил*: ~ (**с** +*instr*) familiar (with) ♦ (-**ого**) *м* acquaintance

знамена́тел|ь (-я) *м* denominator

знамена́тельный *прил* momentous

знамени́тый *прил* famous

зна́м|я (-ени; *как* **вре́мя**; *см.* Table 4) *ср* banner

зна́ни|е (-я) *ср* knowledge *ед*; **со ~м де́ла** expertly

зна́тный *прил* (*род, человек*) noble

знато́к (-á) *м* (*литературы*) expert; (*вин*) connoisseur

зна|ть (-ю) *несов перех* to know; **как зна́ешь** as you wish; **ну, зна́ешь!** well I never!

значе́ни|е (-я) *ср* (*слова, взгляда*) meaning; (*победы*) importance

зна́чит *вводн сл* (*разг*) so ♦ *союз* (*следовательно*) that means

значи́тельный *прил* significant; (*вид, взгляд*) meaningful

зна́ч|ить (-у, -ишь) *несов* (*не*)*перех* to mean; ~**ся** *несов возв* (*состоять*) to appear

значо́к (-ка́) *м* badge; (*пометка*) mark

зна́ющий *прил* knowledgeable

зноб|и́ть (*3sg* -и́т) *несов безл*: **его́ ~и́т** he's shivery

зно|й (-я) *м* intense heat

зно́йный *прил* scorching

зов (-а) *м* call

зов|у́ *итп несов см.* **звать**

зоди́ак (-а) *м* zodiac

зол|а́ (-ы́) *ж* cinders *мн*

золо́в|ка (-ки; *gen pl* -ок) *ж* sister-in-law, husband's sister

золоти́стый *прил* golden

золоти́ть (-чу́, -ти́шь; pf по~) несов перех to gild

зо́лот|**о** (-а) ср gold

золото́й прил golden; (перен: человек, время) wonderful

Зо́лушк|**а** (-и) ж Cinderella

зо́н|**а** (-ы) ж zone; (лесная) area; (для заключённых) prison camp

зона́льный прил (граница, деление) zone; (местный) regional

зонд (-а) м probe

зонт (-а́) м (от дождя) umbrella; (от солнца) parasol

зо́нтик (-а) м = **зонт**

зооло́ги|**я** (-и) ж zoology

зоомагази́н (-а) м pet shop

зоопа́рк (-а) м zoo

зрач|**о́к** (-ка́) м (АНАТ) pupil

зре́лищ|**е** (-а) ср sight; (представление) show

зре́лый прил mature; (плод) ripe

зре́ни|**е** (-я) ср (eye)sight

зре́|**ть** (-ю; pf созре́ть) несов to mature; (плод) to ripen

зри́мый прил visible

зри́тел|**ь** (-я) м (в театре, в кино) member of the audience; (на стадионе) spectator; (наблюдатель) onlooker

зри́тельный прил (память) visual; ~ зал auditorium

зря нареч (разг: без пользы) for nothing, in vain; ~ **тра́тить** (**потра́тить** pf) **де́ньги/вре́мя** to waste money/time; ~ **ты ему́ э́то сказа́л** you shouldn't have told him about it

зуб (-а; nom pl -ы, gen pl -о́в) м tooth; (nom pl -ья, gen pl -ьев, пилы) tooth; (грабель, вилки) prong

зубно́й прил dental; ~ **а́я щётка** toothbrush; ~ **врач** dentist

зубр|**и́ть** (-ю́, -и́шь; impf

вы́зубрить) несов перех (разг) to swot

зуд (-а) м itch

зы́бкий прил shaky

зыб|**ь** (-и) ж ripple

зят|**ь** (-я) м (муж до́чери) son-in-law; (муж сестры́) brother-in-law

И, и

и союз 1 and; **я и мой друг** my friend and I; **и вот показа́лся лес** and then a forest came into sight

2 (тоже): **и он пошёл в теа́тр** he went to the theatre too; **и он не пришёл** he didn't come either

3 (даже): even; **и сам он не рад** even he himself is not pleased

4 (именно): **о том и речь!** that's just it!

5 (во фразах): **ну и нагле́ц же ты!** what a cheek you have!; **туда́ и сюда́** here and there; **и ... и ...** both ... and ...

и́в|**а** (-ы) ж willow

игл|**а́** (-ы́; nom pl -ы) ж needle; (ежа́) spine; (прои́грывателя) needle, stylus

иглока́лывани|**е** (-я) ср acupuncture

иго́лк|**а** (-ки; gen pl -ок) ж = **игла́**

иго́рный прил: ~ **дом** gaming club

игр|**а́** (-ы́; nom pl -ы) ж game; (на скри́пке итп) playing; (актёра) performance; ~ **слов** play on words

игра́льный прил: ~**ые ка́рты** playing cards

игра́|**ть** (-ю) несов to play ♦ (pf **сыгра́ть**) перех to play; (пье́су) to perform; **~ (сыгра́ть** *pf*) **в** +*acc* (*СПОРТ*) to play

игри́стый *прил* sparkling

игрово́й *прил*: **~ ко́мната** playroom; **~ автома́т** fruit machine

игро́к (-á) *м* player

игру́шечный *прил* toy

игру́ш|ка (- *ен pl* **-ек)** *ж* toy; **ёлочные ~ки** Christmas tree decorations

идеализи́р|овать (-ую) *(не)сов перех* to idealize

идеа́льный *прил* ideal

иде́йный *прил* ideological

идём *несов см.* **идти́**

идеологи́ческий *прил* ideological

идеоло́ги|я (-и) *ж* ideology

идёшь *etc несов см.* **идти́**

иде́|я (-и) *ж* idea; **по ~е** (*разг*) supposedly

идио́м|а (-ы) *ж* idiom

идио́т (-а) *м* idiot

идти́ (*см. Table 18*) *несов* to go; (*пешко́м*) to walk; (*годы*) to go by; (*фильм*) to be on; (*часы́*) to work; (*подходить: одежда*): **~ к** +*dat* to go with; **иди́ сюда́!** come here!; **иду́!** (I'm) coming!; **идёт по́езд/авто́бус** the train/bus is coming; **идёт дождь/снег** it's raining/snowing; **дела́ иду́т хорошо́/пло́хо** things are going well/badly; **Вам идёт э́та шля́па** the hat suits you; **(пойти́** *pf*) **пешко́м** to walk, go on foot

ие́н|а (-ы) *ж* yen

KEYWORD

из *предл*; +*gen* **1** (*о направлении*) out of; **он вы́шел из ко́мнаты** he went out of the room

2 (*об источнике*) from; **све́дения из кни́ги** information from a book;

я из Москвы́ I am from Moscow

3 (*при выделении части из це́лого*) of; **вот оди́н из приме́ров** here is one of the examples

4 (*о материале*) made of; **э́тот стол сде́лан из сосны́** this table is made of pine; **ва́за из стекла́** a glass vase; **варе́нье из я́блок** apple jam

5 (*о причине*) out of; **из осторо́жности/за́висти** out of wariness/envy; **из эконо́мии** in order to save money

6 (*во фразах*): **из го́да в год** year in, year out; **я бежа́л изо всех сил** I ran at full speed

изба́ (-ы́; *nom pl* **-ы)** *ж* hut

изба́в|ить (-лю, -ишь; *impf* **избавля́ть)** *сов перех*: **~ кого́-н от** +*gen* (*от проблем*) to free sb from; (*от врагов*) to deliver sb from; **~ся** (*impf* **избавля́ться**) *сов возв*: **~ся от** +*gen* to get rid of; (*от страха*) to get over

изба́лованный *прил* spoilt

избега́|ть (-ю) *несов от* **избежа́ть ► несов**: **~ чего́-н** +*infin* to avoid sth/doing

избежа́|ть (как бежа́ть; *см. Table 20; impf* **избега́ть)** *сов*: **~** +*gen* to avoid

избива́|ть (-ю) *несов от* **изби́ть**

избира́тел|ь (-я) *м* voter

избира́тельный *прил* (*система*) electoral; **~ая кампа́ния** election campaign; **~ уча́сток** polling station; **~ бюллете́нь** ballot paper

избира́|ть (-ю) *несов от* **избра́ть**

изби́|ть (-обью́, -обьёшь; *impf* **избива́ть)** *сов перех* to beat up

и́збранный *прил* (*рассказы*) selected; (*люди, круг*) select

избр|а́ть (-еру́, -ерёшь; *pt* -ра́л, -рала́, -ра́ло; *impf* избира́ть) *сов перех* (профессию) to choose; (президента) to elect

избы́т|ок (-ка) *м* (излишек) surplus; (обилие) excess

избы́точный *прил* (вес) excess

изверже́ни|е (-я) *ср* eruption

изве́сти|е (-я) *ср* news; см. также **изве́стия**

изве|сти́ть (-щу́, -сти́шь; *impf* извеща́ть) *сов перех*: ~ кого́-н о +*prp* to inform sb of

изве́сти|я (-й) *мн* (издание) bulletin *ед*

известк|а́ (-и́) *ж* slaked lime

изве́стно *как сказ*: ~, что ... it is well known that ...; мне э́то ~ I know about it; наско́лько мне ~ as far as I know; как ~ as well known

изве́стност|ь (-и) *ж* fame; ста́вить (поста́вить *pf*) кого́-н в ~ to inform sb

изве́стный *прил* famous, well-known; (*разг*: лентяй) notorious; (условия) certain

и́звест|ь (-и) *ж* lime

извеща́|ть (-ю) *несов от* **извести́ть**

извеще́ни|е (-я) *ср* notification

извива́|ться (-юсь) *несов возв* (змея) to slither; (человек) to writhe

изви́листый *прил* winding

извине́ни|е (-я) *ср* apology; (оправдание) excuse

извини́тельный *прил* (тон, улыбка) apologetic

извин|и́ть (-ю́, -и́шь; *impf* извиня́ть) *сов перех* (простить): ~ что-н (кому́-н) to excuse (sb for) sth; ~и́те! excuse me!; ~и́те, Вы не ска́жете, где вокза́л? excuse me, could you tell me where the

station is?; ~ся (*impf* извиня́ться) *сов возв*: ~ся (за +*асс*) to apologize (for)

извл|е́чь (-еку́, -ечёшь *итп*, -еку́т; *pt* -ёк, -екла́, -екло́; *impf* извлека́ть) *сов перех* (осколок) to remove; (*перен*) to derive

извраще́ни|е (-я) *ср* distortion; полово́е ~ sexual perversion

изги́б (-а) *м* bend

изгиба́|ть(ся) (-ю(сь)) *несов от* **изогну́ть(ся)**

изгна́ни|е (-я) *ср* (ссылка) exile

изг|на́ть (-оню́, -о́нишь; *pt* -на́л, -нала́, -на́ло; *impf* изгоня́ть) *сов перех* to drive out; (сослать) to exile

и́згород|ь (-и) *ж* fence; живая ~ hedge

изгото́в|ить (-лю, -ишь; *impf* изготовля́ть) *сов перех* to manufacture

изда|ва́ть (-ю́, -ёшь) *несов от* **изда́ть**

издалека́ *нареч* from a long way off

и́здали *нареч* = **издалека́**

изда́ни|е (-я) *ср* publication; (изданная вещь) edition

изда́тел|ь (-я) *м* publisher

изда́тельств|о (-а) *ср* publisher, publishing house

изда́ть (*как* дать; см. Table 16; *impf* издава́ть) *сов перех* (книгу) to publish; (закон) to issue; (стон) to let out

издева́тельств|о (-а) *ср* mockery; (жестокое) abuse

издева́|ться (-юсь) *несов возв*: ~ над +*instr* (над подчинёнными) to make a mockery of; (над чьей-н одеждой) to mock, ridicule

изде́ли|е (-я) *ср* (товар) product, article

изде́рж|ки (-ек) *мн* expenses *мн*

суде́бные ~ legal costs

изжо́га (-и) *ж* heartburn

из-за *предл:* ~ +*gen (занаве́ски)* from behind; *(угла́)* from around; *(по вине́)* because of; ~ **того́ что** because

излага́ть (-ю) *несов от* **изложи́ть**

излече́ние (-я) *ср (выздоровле́ние)* recovery

излеч|**и́ться** (-у́сь, -е́чишься; *impf* **изле́чиваться**) *сов возв:* ~ **от** +*gen* to be cured of

изли́ш|**ек** (-ка) *м (остаток)* remainder; ~ +*gen (веса́)* excess of

изли́шний *прил* unnecessary

изложе́ние (-я) *ср* presentation

изл|**ожи́ть** (-ожу́, -о́жишь; *impf* **излага́ть**) *сов перех (события́)* to recount; *(про́сьбу)* to state

излуч|**а́ть** (-ю) *несов перех* to radiate

излуче́ние (-я) *ср* radiation

изме́н|**а** (-ы) *ж (ро́дине)* treason; *(друго́му)* betrayal; **супру́жеская** ~ adultery

измене́ние (-я) *ср* change; *(попра́вка)* alteration

изме́н|**ить** (-ю́, -ишь; *impf* **изменя́ть**) *сов перех* to change ♦ *неперех:* ~ +*dat (роди́не, дру́гу)* to betray; *(супру́гу)* to be unfaithful to; *(па́мять)* to fail; **~ся** (*impf* **изменя́ться**) *сов возв* to change

изме́нник (-а) *м* traitor

измере́ние (-я) *ср* measurement; *(величина́)* dimension

измери́тельный *прил* measuring

изме́р|**ить** (-ю, -ишь) *сов от* **ме́рить** ♦ (*impf* **измеря́ть**) *перех* to measure

изму́ченный *прил (челове́к)* worn-out; *(лицо́)* haggard

изму́ч|**ить** (-у, -ишь) *сов от*

му́чить

измышле́ние (-я) *ср* fabrication

изм|**я́ть** (-ону́, -онёшь) *сов от* **мять**

изна́нк|**а** (-и) *ж (оде́жды)* inside; *(тка́ни)* wrong side

изнаси́лование (-я) *ср* rape

изнаси́л|**овать** (-ую) *сов от* **наси́ловать**

изна́шива|**ть(ся)** (-ю(сь)) *несов от* **износи́ть(ся)**

изнемога́|**ние** (-я) *ср* exhaustion

изнемога́ть (-ю) *несов от* **изнемо́чь**

изнеможе́ние (-я) *ср* exhaustion

изнем|**о́чь** (-огу́, -о́жешь *итп*, -о́гут; *pt* -о́г, -огла́, -огло́; *impf* **изнемога́ть**) *сов* to be exhausted

изно́с (-а) *м (механи́змов)* wear

изн|**оси́ть** (-ошу́, -о́сишь; *impf* **изна́шивать**) *сов перех* to wear out; **~ся** (*impf* **изна́шиваться**) *сов возв* to wear out

изнури́тельный *прил* exhausting

изнур|**и́ть** (-ю́, -и́шь; *impf* **изнуря́ть**) *сов перех* to exhaust

изнутри́ *нареч* from inside

изо *предл* = **из**

изоби́лие (-я) *ср* abundance

изобража́ть (-ю) *несов от* **изобрази́ть**

изображе́ние (-я) *ср* image; *(де́йствие: собы́тий)* depiction, portrayal

изобрази́тельный *прил* descriptive; ~**ое иску́сство** fine art

изобра|**зи́ть** (-жу́, -зи́шь; *impf* **изобража́ть**) *сов перех* to depict, portray

изобр|**ести́** (-ету́, -етёшь; *pt* -ёл, -ела́; *impf* **изобрета́ть**) *сов перех* to invent

изобрета́тель (-я) *м* inventor

изобрета́тельный *прил*

inventive

изобрете́ни|е (-я) *ср* invention

изогн|у́ть (-у́, -ёшь; *impf* **изгиба́ть**) *сов перех* to bend; **~ся** (*impf* **изгиба́ться**) *сов возв* to bend

изоли́рованный *прил* (*провод*) insulated; (*комната*) separate

изоли́р|овать (-ую) (*не*)*сов перех* to isolate; (*вход*) to cut off; (*ТЕХ, ЭЛЕК*) to insulate

изоля́тор (-а) *м* (*ТЕХ, ЭЛЕК*) insulator; (*в больнице*) isolation unit

изоля́ци|я (-и) *ж* (*см глаг*) isolation; cutting off; insulation

изощрённый *прил* sophisticated

из-под *предл*: ~ +*gen* from under(neath); (*около*) from outside; **ба́нка ~ варе́нья** jam jar

Изра́иль (-я) *м* Israel

израильтя́н|ин (-ина; *nom pl* **-е**) *м* Israeli

изра́ильский *прил* Israeli

и́зредка *нареч* now and then

изувеч|ить (-у, -ишь; *impf* **изуве́чивать**) *сов перех* to maim

изуми́тельный *прил* marvellous (*BRIT*), marvelous (*US*), wonderful

изум|и́ть (-лю́, -и́шь; *impf* **изумля́ть**) *сов перех* to amaze, astound; **~ся** (*impf* **изумля́ться**) *сов возв* to be amazed *или* astounded

изумле́ни|е (-я) *ср* amazement

изумру́д (-а) *м* emerald

изуча́|ть (-ю) *несов от* **изучи́ть** ♦ *перех* (*процесс*) to study

изуче́ни|е (-я) *ср* study

изуч|и́ть (-у́, -у́чишь; *impf* **изуча́ть**) *сов перех* (*язык, предмет*) to learn; (*понять*) to get to know; (*исследовать*) to study

изъяв|и́ть (-лю́, -и́вишь; *impf* **изъявля́ть**) *сов перех* to indicate

изъя́н (-а) *м* defect

изъя́ть (**изыму́, изы́мешь**; *impf* **изыма́ть**) *сов перех* to withdraw

изы́сканный *прил* refined, sophisticated

изю́м (-а) *м собир* raisins *мн*

изя́щный *прил* elegant

ика́|ть (-ю) *несов* to hiccup

ико́н|а (-ы) *ж* (*РЕЛ*) icon

икр|а́ (-ы́) *ж* (*чёрная, красная*) caviar(е); (*nom pl* **-ы**) (*АНАТ*) calf

ИЛ (-а) *м сокр* = **самолёт констру́кции С.В. Илью́шина**

ил (-а) *м* silt

и́ли *союз* or; ~ ... ~ ... either ... or ...

иллюмина́тор (-а) *м* (*корабля*) porthole; (*самолёта*) window

иллюстра́ци|я (-и) *ж* illustration

иллюстри́р|овать (-ую) *pf* *или* **про**~) *несов перех* to illustrate

им *мест см.* **он**; **оно́**; **они́**

им. *сокр* = **и́мени**

и́мени *etc сущ см.* **и́мя**

име́ни|е (-я) *ср* estate

имени́нник (-а) *м person celebrating his name day or birthday*

имени́тельный *прил* (*ЛИНГ*): ~ **паде́ж** the nominative (case)

и́менно *част* exactly, precisely ♦ *союз* (*перед перечислением*): **а ~** namely; **вот ~**! exactly!, precisely!

име́|ть (-ю) *несов перех* to have; **~** (*impf*) **ме́сто** (*событие*) to take place; **~** (*impf*) **де́ло с** +*instr* to deal with; **~** (*impf*) **в виду́** to bear in mind; (*подразумевать*) to mean; **~ся** *несов возв* (*сведения*) to be available

и́ми *мест см.* **они́**

иммигра́нт (-а) *м* immigrant

иммиграцио́нный *прил* immigration

иммигра́ци|я (-и) *ж* immigration

иммигри́р|овать (-ую) *(не)сов*
to immigrate

иммуните́т (-а) *м (МЕД, перен):* ~
(к +*dat*) immunity (to)

импера́тор (-а) *м* emperor

импе́ри|я (-и) *ж* empire

и́мпорт (-а) *м (ввоз)* importation

импорти́р|овать (-ую) *(не)сов*
перех to import

и́мпортный *прил* imported

импровизи́р|овать (-ую) *(не)сов;
pf* ~ *или* **сымпровизи́ровать)**
(не)сов перех to improvise

и́мпульс (-а) *м* impulse

иму́ществ|о (-а) *ср* property;
(принадлежность) belongings *мн*

и́м|я (-ени; *как* **вре́мя;** *см.* Table
4) *ср (также перен)* name;
(также: **ли́чное** ~) first *или*
Christian name; **во** ~ +*gen (ради)*
in the name of; **на** ~ +*gen*
(письмо) addressed to; **от** ~**ени**
+*gen* on behalf of

ина́че *нареч (по-другому)*
differently ♦ *союз* otherwise, or else

инвали́д (-а) *м* disabled person

инвали́дный *прил:* ~**ая коля́ска**
wheelchair; ~ **дом** home for the
disabled

инвали́дность (-и) *ж* disability;
получа́ть (получи́ть *pf)* ~**ь** to be
registered as disabled

инвалю́т|а (-ы) *ж сокр (=
иностра́нная валю́та)* foreign
currency

инвести́р|овать (-ую) *(не)перех
(ЭКОН)* to invest

инвести́ци|я (-и) *ж* investment

инде́|ец (-йца) *м* Native American,
North American Indian

инде́йк|а (-и; gen pl -ек) *ж*
turkey

и́ндекс (-а) *м (цен, книг)* index;
(также: **почто́вый** ~) post *(BRIT)*
или zip *(US)* code

индивидуа́льный *прил*
individual

инди́|ец (-йца) *м* Indian

инди́йский *прил* Indian;
Инди́йский океа́н the Indian
Ocean

И́нди|я (-и) *ж* India

индустриа́льный *прил* industrial

индустри́|я (-и) *ж* industry

и́не|й (-я) *м* hoarfrost

ине́рци|я (-и) *ж* inertia

инжене́р (-а) *м* engineer

инициа́л|ы (-ов) *мн* initials *мн*

инициати́в|а (-ы) *ж* initiative

инициати́вный *прил*
enterprising; ~**ая гру́ппа** ≈
pressure group

инициа́тор (-а) *м* initiator

инкасса́тор (-а) *м* security guard
(employed to collect and deliver money)

инкуба́тор (-а) *м* incubator

иногда́ *нареч* sometimes

иногоро́дн|ий *прил* from another
town ♦ *(-его)* *м* person from another
town

ин|о́й *прил* different ♦ *мест
(некоторые)* some (people); ~**ыми
слова́ми** in other words; **не что**
~**о́е, как ..., не кто** ~, **как ...** none
other than ...

инома́рк|а (-и; gen pl -ок) *ж*
foreign car

**инопланетя́н|ин (-ина; nom pl
-е)** *м* alien

иноро́дный *прил* alien; ~**ое
те́ло** *(МЕД)* foreign body

иностра́н|ец (-ца) *м* foreigner

иностра́нный *прил* foreign;
Министе́рство ~**ых дел** Ministry
of Foreign Affairs; ≈ Foreign Office
(BRIT), ≈ State Department *(US)*

инспекти́р|овать (-ую; pf про-)
несов перех to inspect

инспе́ктор (-а) *м* inspector

инспе́кци|я (-и) *ж* inspection

инста́нци|я (-и) ж authority

инсти́нкт (-а) м instinct

институ́т (-а) м institute

инструкти́р|овать (-ую) pf **про~)** (не)сов перех to instruct

инстру́кци|я (-и) ж instructions мн; (также: **~ по эксплуата́ции)** instructions (for use)

инструме́нт (-а) м instrument

инсули́н (-а) м insulin

инсу́льт (-а) м (МЕД) stroke

инсцени́р|овать (-ую) (не)сов перех (роман) to adapt

интегра́ци|я (-и) ж integration

интелле́кт (-а) м intellect

интеллектуа́л (-а) м intellectual

интеллектуа́льный прил intellectual

интеллиге́нт (-а) м member of the intelligentsia

интеллиге́нтный прил cultured and educated

интеллиге́нци|я (-и) ж собир the intelligentsia

интенси́вный прил intensive; (окраска) intense

интерва́л (-а) м interval

интервью́ ср нескл interview

интервьюи́р|овать (-ую) pf **про~)** (не)сов перех to interview

интере́с (-а) м: **~ (к** +dat) interest (in)

интере́сно нареч: **он о́чень ~ расска́зывает** he is very interesting to listen to ♦ как сказ: **~(, что ...)** it's interesting (that ...); **мне э́то о́чень ~** I find it very interesting; **~, где он э́то нашёл** I wonder where he found that

интере́сный прил interesting; (внешность, женщина) attractive

интерес|ова́ть (-у́ю) несов перех to interest; **~ся** несов возв: **~ся** +instr to be interested in; (осведомля́ться) to inquire after;

он ~ова́лся, когда́ ты прие́зжаешь he was asking when you would be arriving

интерна́т (-а) м boarding school

интернациона́льный прил international

Интерне́т (-а) м Internet

интерпрета́ци|я (-и) ж interpretation

интерье́р (-а) м (здания) interior

инти́мный прил intimate

интона́ци|я (-и) ж intonation; (недово́льная итп) note

интри́г|а (-и) ж (политическая) intrigue; (любовная) affair

интриг|ова́ть (-у́ю) pf **за~)** несов перех to intrigue

интуити́вный прил intuitive

интуи́ци|я (-и) ж intuition

Интури́ст (-а) м сокр (= Гла́вное управле́ние по иностра́нному тури́зму) Russian tourist agency dealing with foreign tourism

интури́ст (-а) м сокр = **иностра́нный тури́ст**

инфа́ркт (-а) м (также: **~ миока́рда)** heart attack

инфекцио́нный прил infectious

инфе́кци|я (-и) ж infection

инфинити́в (-а) м infinitive

инфля́ци|я (-и) ж (ЭКОН) inflation

информацио́нн|ый прил information; **~ая програ́мма** news programme (BRIT) или program (US)

информа́ци|я (-и) ж information

информи́р|овать (-ую) pf **или про~)** несов перех to inform

инфраструкту́р|а (-ы) ж infrastructure

инциде́нт (-а) м incident

инъе́кци|я (-и) ж injection

иня́з (-а) м сокр (= факульте́т иностра́нных языко́в) modern languages department

и.о. *сокр* (= исполня́ющий обя́занности) acting

Иорда́ни|я (-и) *ж* Jordan

ипоте́к|а (-и) *ж* (*комм*) mortgage

ипоте́чн|ый *прил* mortgage; **~ая ссу́да** mortgage; **~ банк** ≈ building society

ипподро́м (-а) *м* racecourse (*BRIT*), racetrack (*US*)

Ира́к (-а) *м* Iraq

Ира́н (-а) *м* Iran

и́рис (-а) *м* (*бот*) iris

ирла́нд|ец (-ца) *м* Irishman

Ирла́нди|я (-и) *ж* Ireland

ирла́нд|ка (-ки; gen pl -ок) *ж* Irishwoman

иронизи́р|овать (-ую) *несов*: **~ (над +instr)** to be ironic (about)

иро́ни|я (-и) *ж* irony

иск (-а) *м* lawsuit; **предъявля́ть (предъяви́ть** *pf*) **~ кому́-н** to take legal action against sb

искажа́|ть(ся) (-ю(сь)) *несов от* **искази́ть(ся)**

искаже́ни|е (-я) *ср* distortion

иска|зи́ть (-жу́, -зи́шь; *impf* **искажа́ть)** *сов перех* (*факты*) to distort; (*лицо*) to contort; **~ся** (*impf* **искажа́ться)** *сов возв* to be distorted; (*голос*) to contort

иска́|ть (ищу́, и́щешь) *несов перех* to look или search for

исключе́ни|е (-я) *ср* (*из списка*) exclusion; (*из институ́та*) expulsion; (*отклоне́ние*) exception; **за~м** +gen with the exception of; **де́лать (сде́лать** *pf*) **что-н в ви́де ~я** to make an exception of sth

исключи́тельно *нареч* (*особенно*) exceptionally; (*то́лько*) exclusively

исключи́тельный *прил* exceptional

исключ|и́ть (-у́, -и́шь; *impf* **исключа́ть)** *сов перех* to exclude;

(*из институ́та*) to expel; (*оши́бку*) to exclude the possibility of; **~ено́** that is out of the question

иско́нный *прил* (*населе́ние, язы́к*) native, original; (*пра́во*) intrinsic

ископа́ем|ое (-ого) *ср* fossil; (*также*: **поле́зное ~**) mineral

искорен|и́ть (-ю́, -и́шь; *impf* **искореня́ть)** *сов перех* to eradicate

и́скр|а (-ы) *ж* spark

и́скренне *нареч* sincerely; **~ Ваш** Yours sincerely

и́скренний *прил* sincere

и́скренность (-и) *ж* sincerity

искрив|и́ть (-лю́, -и́шь; *impf* **искривля́ть)** *сов перех* to bend

искупа́|ть(ся) (-ю(сь)) *сов от* **купа́ть(ся)**

иск|упи́ть (-уплю́, -у́пишь; *impf* **искупа́ть)** *сов перех* to atone for

иску́сный *прил* (*рабо́тник*) skilful (*BRIT*), skillful (*US*); (*рабо́та*) fine

иску́сственный *прил* artificial; (*ткань*) synthetic; (*мех*) fake

иску́сств|о (-а) *ср* art

искуша́|ть (-ю) *несов перех* to tempt

искуше́ни|е (-я) *ср* temptation

исла́м (-а) *м* Islam

исла́мский *прил* Islamic

Исла́нди|я (-и) *ж* Iceland

испа́н|ец (-ца) *м* Spaniard

Испа́ни|я (-и) *ж* Spain

испаре́ни|е (-я) *ср* (*де́йствие: воды́*) evaporation; (*обы́чно мн: проду́кт*) vapour *ед* (*BRIT*), vapor *ед* (*US*)

испар|и́ться (3sg -и́тся, *сов возв* (*impf* **испаря́ться**) to evaporate

испа́чка|ть(ся) (-ю(сь)) *сов от* **па́чкать(ся)**

испове́дани|е (-я) *ср* denomination

испове́дник (-а) м (РЕЛ) confessor

испове́довать (-ую) несов перех (религию, идею) to profess ♦ (не)сов перех (РЕЛ): ~ кого́-н to hear sb's confession; **~ся** (не)сов возв: ~ся кому́-н или у кого́-н to confess to sb

и́споведь (-и) ж confession

исполко́м (-а) м сокр (= исполни́тельный комите́т) executive committee

исполне́ни|е (-я) ср (приказа) execution; (обещания) fulfilment (BRIT), fulfillment (US); (роли) performance

исполни́тель (-я) м ~ performer; судебный ~ bailiff

исполни́тельный прил (власть) executive; (работник) efficient

испо́лн|ить (-ю, -ишь; impf **исполня́ть**) сов перех (приказ) to carry out; (обещание) to fulfil (BRIT), fulfill (US); (роль) to perform; **~ся** (impf **исполня́ться**) сов возв (желание) to be fulfilled; **ему́ ~илось 10 лет** he is 10

испо́льзование (-я) ср use

испо́льз|овать (-ую) (не)сов перех to use

испра́в|ить (-лю, -ишь; impf **исправля́ть**) сов перех (повреждение) to repair; (ошибку) to correct; (характер) to improve; **~ся** (impf **исправля́ться**) сов возв (человек) to change (for the better)

исправле́ни|е (-я) ср (повреждения) repairing; (преступника) reforming; (текста) correction

испра́вный прил (механизм) in good working order

испу́г (-а) м fright; **в ~е, с ~у** in или with fright

испу́ганный прил frightened

испуга́|ть(ся) (-ю(сь)) сов от **пуга́ть(ся)**

испыта́ни|е (-я) ср (машины) testing

испыта́тельный прил: ~ срок trial period, probation

испыта́|ть (-ю; impf **испы́тывать**) сов перех (механизм) to test; (нужду, радость) to experience

иссле́довани|е (-я) ср (см глаг) research; examination; (научный труд) study

иссле́дователь (-я) м researcher

иссле́довательск|ий прил: ~ая рабо́та research; ~ институ́т research institute

иссле́д|овать (-ую) (не)сов перех to research; (больного) to examine

исся́к|нуть (3sg -нет, pt -, -ла; impf **иссяка́ть**) сов (запасы) to run dry; (перен: терпение) to run out

истека́|ть (-ю) несов от **исте́чь**

исте́рик|а (-и) ж hysterics мн

истери́чный прил hysterical

истёц (-ца́) м plaintiff

ист|е́чь (3sg -ечёт, pt -ёк, -екла́, -екло́; impf **истека́ть**) сов (срок) to expire; (время) to run out

и́стинный прил true

исто́к (-а) м (реки) source

исто́рик (-а) м historian

истори́ческий прил historical; (важный) historic; ~ факульте́т history department

исто́ри|я (-и) ж (наука) history; (рассказ) story

исто́чник (-а) м (водный) spring; (сил) source

истоще́ни|е (-я) ср exhaustion

истощённый прил (человек) malnourished; (вид) drained

истра́|тить (-чу, -тишь) *сов от* **тра́тить**

истреби́тель (-я) *м (самолёт)* fighter (plane); *(лётчик)* fighter pilot

истребля́|ть (-лю, -йшь; *impf* **истребля́ть)** *сов перех* to destroy; *(крыс)* to exterminate

исхо́д (-а) *м* outcome

исх|оди́ть (-ожу, -о́дишь) *несов*: ~ **из** +*gen* (сведения) to originate from; *(основываться)* to be based on; **~одя́ из** +*gen* **или от** +*gen* on the basis of

исхо́дный *прил* primary

исходя́щий *прил* outgoing; ~ **но́мер** *(АДМИН)* reference number

исче́з|нуть (-ну, -нешь; *pt* **-,** **-ла,** *impf* **исчеза́ть)** *сов* to disappear

исче́рп|ать (-ю; *impf* **исче́рпывать)** *сов перех* to exhaust

исче́рпывающий *прил* exhaustive

исчисля́|ться (3pl -ются) *несов возв*: ~ +*instr* to amount to

ита́к *союз* thus, hence

Ита́ли|я (-и) *ж* Italy

италья́н|ец (-ца) *м* Italian

италья́нский *прил* Italian; ~ **язы́к** Italian

и т.д. *сокр* (= **и так да́лее**) etc.

ито́г (-а) *м (работы)* result; *(общая сумма)* total; **в ~е** *(при подсчёте)* in total; **в (коне́чном) ~е** in the end; **подводи́ть (подвести́** *pf*) ~и to sum up

итого́ *нареч* in total, altogether

ито́говый *прил (сумма)* total

и т.п. *сокр* (= **и тому́ подо́бное**) etc.

иудаи́зм (-а) *м* Judaism

их *мест см.* **они́** ♦ *притяж мест* their

и́хн|ий *притяж мест (разг)* their;

по ~ему (in) their way

ищу́ *итп несов см.* **иска́ть**

ию́л|ь (-я) *м* July

ию́н|ь (-я) *м* June

Й, й

йо́г|а (-и) *ж* yoga

йо́гурт (-а) *м* yoghurt

йод (-а) *м* iodine

К, к

к *предл*; +*dat* **1** *(о направлении)* towards; **я пошёл к до́му** I went towards the house; **звать (позва́ть** *pf*) **кого́-н к телефо́ну** to call sb to the phone; **мы пое́хали к друзья́м** we went to see friends; **поста́вь ле́стницу к стене́** put the ladder against the wall

2 *(о добавлении, включении)* to; **э́та ба́бочка отно́сится к о́чень ре́дкому ви́ду** this butterfly belongs to a very rare species

3 *(об отношении)* of; **любо́вь к му́зыке** love of music; **он привы́к к хоро́шей еде́** he is used to good food; **к моему́ удивле́нию** to my surprise

4 *(назначение)* with; **припра́вы к мя́су** seasonings for meat

каба́н (-а́) *м (дикий)* wild boar

кабачо́к (-ка́) *м* marrow *(BRIT)*, squash *(US)*

ка́бел|ь (-я) *м* cable

каби́н|а (-ы) *ж (телефо́нная)* booth; *(грузовика)* cab;

(самолёта) cockpit; (лифта) cage

кабине́т (-а) м (в доме) study; (на работе) office; (школьный) classroom; (врача) surgery (BRIT), office (US); (ПОЛИТ: также: ~ мини́стров) cabinet

каблу́к (-а́) м heel

кавале́ри|**я** (-и) ж cavalry

Кавка́з (-а) м Caucasus

кавка́з|**ец** (-ца) м Caucasian

кавы́ч|**ки** (-ек; dat pl -кам) мн inverted commas мн, quotation marks мн

кадр (-а) м (ФОТО, КИНО) shot

ка́др|**ы** (-ов) мн (работники) personnel ед, staff ед

ка́ждый прил each, every

коз|**а́к** (-ака́; nom pl -аки́) м Cossack

каза́рм|**а** (-ы) ж barracks мн

ка|**за́ться** (-жу́сь, -жешься; pf по-) несов возв: ~ +instr to look, seem; (мне) **ка́жется, что ...** it seems (to me) that ...

каза́чий прил Cossack

кази́но ср нескл casino

казн|**а́** (-ы́) ж treasury

казн|**и́ть** (-ю́, -и́шь) (не)сов перех to execute

казн|**ь** (-и) ж execution

каи́м|**а́** (-ы́; nom pl -ы́, gen pl -ём) м hem

KEYWORD

как местоименное нареч 1 (вопросительное) how; **как Вы себя́ чу́вствуете?** how do you feel?; **как дела́?** how are things?; **как тебя́ зову́т?** what's your name?

2 (относительное): **я сде́лал, как ты проси́л** I did as you asked; **я не зна́ю, как э́то могло́ случи́ться** I don't know how that could have happened

3 (насколько): **как бы́стро/давно́** how quickly/long ago

4 (до какой степени): **как краси́во** how beautiful!; **как жаль!** what a pity или shame!

5 (выражает возмущение) what
♦ союз 1 (подобно) as; **мя́гкий, как ва́та** as soft as cotton wool; **как мо́жно скоре́е/гро́мче** as soon/loud as possible; **он оде́т, как бродя́га** he is dressed like a tramp

2 (в качестве) as

3 (о временных отношениях: о будущем, об одновременности) when; (: о прошлом) since; **как зако́нчишь, позвони́ мне** phone (BRIT) или call (US) me when you finish; **прошло́ два го́да, как она́ исче́зла** two years have passed since she disappeared

4: **как бу́дто, как бы** as if; **он согласи́лся как бы не́хотя** he agreed as if unwillingly; **как же** of course; **как говоря́т** или **говори́тся** as it were; **как ни** however; **как ника́к** after all; **как раз во́время/то, что на́до** just in time/what we need; **э́то пла́тье/пальто́ мне как раз** this dress/coat is just my size; **как ..., так и ...** both ... and ...; **как то́лько** as soon as

---

кака́о ср нескл сосоа

ка́к-либо нареч = **ка́к-нибудь**

ка́к-нибудь нареч (так или иначе) somehow; (когда-нибудь) sometime

как-ника́к нареч after all

KEYWORD

как|**о́й** (-а́я, -о́е, -и́е) мест 1 (вопросительное) what; **како́й тебе́ нра́вится цвет?** what colour do you like?

2 (относительное) which; **скажи**, **какая книга интереснее** tell me which book is more interesting

3 (выражает оценку) what; **какой подлец!** what a rascal!

4 (разг: неопределённое) any; **нет ли каких вопросов?** are there any questions?

5 (во фразах): **ни в какую** not for anything; **каким образом** in what way

какой-либо мест = **какой-нибудь**

как|ой-нибудь мест (тот или иной) any; (приблизительно) some; **он ищет ~ работы** he's looking for any kind of work

как|ой-то мест: **Вам ~ое-то письмо** there's a letter for you; (напоминающий): **она ~ая-то странная сегодня** she is acting kind of oddly today

как-то мест (каким-то образом) somehow; (в некоторой степени) somewhat; (разг): ~ **раз** once

кактус (-а) м cactus

калек|а (-и) м/ж cripple

календар|ь (-я́) м calendar

калеч|ить (-у, -ишь; pf **по~** или **ис~**) несов перех to cripple; (мина) to maim

калибр (-а) м calibre (BRIT), caliber (US)

кали|й (-я) м potassium

кали́т|ка (-ки; gen pl -ок) ж gate

калори|я (-и) ж calorie

калькуля́тор (-а) м calculator

ка́льци|й (-я) м calcium

ка́мбал|а (-ы) ж flatfish

камене́|ть (-ю) несов от **окамене́ть**

ка́менный прил stone

ка́менщик (-а) м bricklayer

ка́м|ень (-ня; gen pl -не́й) м stone

ка́мер|а (-ы) ж (тюремная) cell; (также: **теле~, кино~**) camera; ~ **хране́ния** (на вокзале) left-luggage office (BRIT), checkroom (US); (в музее) cloakroom

ка́мерный прил: ~**ая му́зыка** chamber music

ками́н (-а) м fireplace

кампа́ни|я (-и) ж campaign

камы́ш (-á) м rushes мн

кана́в|а (-ы) ж ditch

Кана́д|а (-ы) ж Canada

кана́л (-а) м canal; (связь тел, перен) channel

канализацио́нн|ый прил: ~**ая труба́** sewer pipe

канализа́ци|я (-и) ж sewerage

кана́т (-а) м cable

кана́тн|ый прил: ~**ая доро́га** cable car

кандида́т (-а) м candidate; (ПРОСВЕЩ): ~ **нау́к** ≈ Doctor

кандидату́р|а (-ы) ж candidacy; **выставля́ть (вы́ставить** pf) **чью-н** ~**y** to nominate sb

кани́кул|ы (-) мн holidays мн (BRIT), vacation ед (US)

кани́стр|а (-ы) ж jerry can

кано́э ср нескл canoe

кану́н (-а) м eve; **в** ~ +gen on the eve of

канцеля́ри|я (-и) ж office

канцеля́рский прил office

ка́па|ть (-ю) несов (вода) to drip ♦ (pf **на~**) перех: ~ (**ми́кстуру**) to pour sth out drop by drop

капе́лл|а (-ы) ж (муз) choir

ка́пельниц|а (-ы) ж (мед) drip

капита́л (-а) м (комм) capital

капитали́зм (-а) м capitalism

капиталисти́ческий прил capitalist

капиталовложе́ни|я (-й) мн

capital investment ед
капита́льный прил (ЭКОН, КОММ) capital; (сооруже́ние, труд) main; (ремо́нт, поку́пка) major
капита́н (-а) м captain
капитули́р|овать (-ую) (не)сов to capitulate
капка́н (-а) м trap
ка́п|ля (-ли; gen pl -ель) ж (также перен) drop
капо́т (-а) м (АВТ) bonnet (BRIT), hood (US)
капри́з (-а) ж caprice, whim
капри́знича|ть (-ю) несов to behave capriciously
капри́зный прил (челове́к) capricious
капро́н (-а) м synthetic thread
ка́псул|а (-ы) ж capsule
капу́ст|а (-ы) ж cabbage; цветна́я ~ cauliflower
капюшо́н (-а) м hood
кара́бка|ться (-юсь; pf вс~) несов возв: ~ на +асс (челове́к) to clamber up
кара́кулевый прил astrakhan
караме́л|ь (-и) ж собир (леденцы́) caramels мн
каранда́ш (-á; gen pl -е́й) м pencil
каранти́н (-а) м quarantine
кара́|ть (-ю; pf по~) несов перех to punish
карау́л (-а) м guard
карау́л|ить (-ю, -ишь) несов перех to guard
карбюра́тор (-а) м carburettor (BRIT), carburetor (US)
кардина́льный прил cardinal, of cardinal importance
кардио́лог (-а) м cardiologist, heart specialist
кардиоло́ги|я (-и) ж cardiology
ка́рий прил (глаза́) brown
карикату́р|а (-ы) ж caricature
карка́с (-а) м framework (of

building)
ка́рка|ть (-ю) несов to caw
ка́рлик (-а) м dwarf
карма́н (-а) м pocket
карма́нный прил (де́ньги, часы́) pocket; ~ нож pocketknife; ~ые расхо́ды petty expenses
карнава́л (-а) м carnival
карни́з (-а) м (для штор) curtain rail
карп (-а) м carp
ка́рт|а (-ы) ж (ГЕО) map; (также: игра́льная ~) (playing) card; магни́тная ~ (swipe)card
карти́н|а (-ы) ж picture
карти́н|ка (-ки; gen pl -ок) ж (иллюстра́ция) picture (in book etc)
карто́н (-а) м (бума́га) cardboard
картоте́к|а (-и) ж card index
картофе́лин|а (-ы) ж potato
карто́фел|ь (-я) м (плод) potato; potatoes мн
карто́фельный прил potato
ка́рточ|ка (-ки; gen pl -ек) ж card; (также: фо́то~) photo
карто́ш|ка (-ки; gen pl -ек) ж (разг) = карто́фелина, карто́фель
ка́ртридж (-а) м (КОМП) cartridge
карусе́л|ь (-и) ж merry-go-round (BRIT), carousel (US)
карье́р|а (-ы) ж career
каса́|ться (-юсь; pf косну́ться) несов возв: ~ +gen (дотра́гиваться) to touch; (затра́гивать) to touch on; (име́ть отноше́ние) to concern; э́то тебя́ не ~ется it doesn't concern you; что ~ется Вас, то ... as far as you are concerned ...
ка́ск|а (-и; gen pl -ок) ж helmet
каспи́йск|ий прил: Каспи́йское мо́ре Caspian Sea
ка́сс|а (-ы) ж (ТЕА́ТР, КИНО́) box office; (железнодоро́жная) ticket

office; (*в магазине*) cash desk
кассе́т|а (**-ы**) *ж* (*магни́тофонная*) cassette; (*ФОТО*) cartridge
касси́р (**-а**) *м* cashier
кастрю́л|я (**-и**) *ж* saucepan
катало́г (**-а**) *м* catalogue (*BRIT*), catalog (*US*)
ката́р (**-а**) *м* catarrh
катастро́ф|а (**-ы**) *ж* disaster
катастрофи́ческий *прил* catastrophic, disastrous
ката́|ть (**-ю**) *несов перех* (*что-н кру́глое*) to roll; (*что-н на колёсах*) to wheel; ~ **кого́-н на маши́не** to take sb for a drive; **~ся** *несов возв* (*кататься на маши́не/велосипе́де*) to go for a drive/cycle; **~ся** (*impf*) **на конька́х/ло́шади** to go skating/horse (*BRIT*) *или* horseback (*US*) riding
категори́чный *прил* categorical
катего́ри|я (**-и**) *ж* category
ка́тер (**-а**) *м* boat
ка|ти́ть (**-чу́, -тишь**) *несов перех* (*что-н кру́глое*) to roll; (*что-н на колёсах*) to wheel; **~ся** *несов возв* to roll; (*капли*) to run
като́к (**-ка́**) *м* ice *или* skating rink; (*ТЕХ: также*: **асфа́льтовый ~**) steamroller
като́лик (**-а**) *м* Catholic
католи́ческий *прил* Catholic
кату́шка (**-ки**; *gen pl* **-ек**) *ж* spool
кафе́ *ср нескл* café
ка́федр|а (**-ы**) *ж* (*ПРОСВЕЩ*) department; (*РЕЛ*) pulpit; **заве́дующий ~ой** chair
ка́фел|ь (**-я**) *м собир* tiles *мн*
ка́фельный *прил* (*пол*) tiled; **~ая пли́тка** (ceramic) tile
кафете́ри|й (**-я**) *м* cafeteria
кача́|ть (**-ю**) *несов перех* (*колыбель*) to rock; (*нефть*) to pump; **~** (*impf*) **голово́й** to shake one's head; **~ся** *несов возв* to

swing; (*на волна́х*) to rock, roll
каче́л|и (**-ей**) *мн* swing *ед*
ка́чественный *прил* qualitative; (*товар, изде́лие*) high-quality
ка́честв|о (**-а**) *ср* quality ♦ *предл*: **в ~е** +*gen* as; **в ~е приме́ра** by way of example
ка́ш|а (**-и**) *ж* ≈ porridge
ка́шел|ь (**-ля**) *м* cough
ка́шл|я|ть (**-ю**) *несов* to cough
кашта́н (**-а**) *м* chestnut
каю́т|а (**-ы**) *ж* (*МОР*) cabin
ка́|яться (**-юсь, -ешься**; *pf* **по-**) *несов возв*: **~ (в чём-н пе́ред кем-н**) to confess (sth to sb); (*pf* **рас-**; *гре́шник*) to repent
кв. *сокр* = **квадра́тный**) sq.; (= **кварти́ра**) Apt.
квадра́т (**-а**) *м* square
квадра́тный *прил* square
ква́к|ать (*3sg* **-ет**) *несов* to croak
квалифика́ци|я (**-и**) *ж* qualification; (*специа́льность*) profession
квалифици́рованный *прил* (*рабо́тник*) qualified; (*труд*) skilled
кварта́л (**-а**) *м* quarter
кварте́т (**-а**) *м* quartet
кварти́р|а (**-ы**) *ж* flat (*BRIT*), apartment (*US*); (*снима́емое жильё*) lodgings *мн*
квартира́нт (**-а**) *м* lodger
квартпла́т|а (**-ы**) *ж* (= **кварти́рная пла́та**) rent (*for a flat*)
квас (**-а**) *м* kvass (*malted drink*)
ква́шен|ый *прил*: **~ая капу́ста** sauerkraut, pickled cabbage
квита́нци|я (**-и**) *ж* receipt
кг *сокр* (= **килогра́мм**) kg
КГБ *м сокр* (*ИСТ*) (= **Комите́т госуда́рственной безопа́сности**) KGB
ке́д|ы (**-**) *м* pumps *мн*
кекс (**-а**) *м* (fruit)cake
кем *мест см.* **кто**

ке́мпинг (-а) *м* camping site, campsite

ке́п|**ка** (-ки; *gen pl* -ок) *ж* cap

кера́мик|**а** (-и) *ж собир* ceramics *мн*

керами́ческий *прил* ceramic

кефи́р (-а) *м* kefir (yoghurt drink)

кива́|**ть** (-ю) *несов* = +*dat* to nod to

кивн|**у́ть** (-у́, -ёшь) *сов* = (+*dat*) to nod (to)

кида́|**ть** (-ю) *несов от* **ки́нуть**; ~**ся** *несов от* **ки́нуться** ♦ *возв:* ~**ся камня́ми** to throw stones at each other

ки́ллер (-а) *м* hitman

килогра́мм (-а) *м* kilogram(me)

киломе́тр (-а) *м* kilometre (*BRIT*), kilometer (*US*)

кинематогра́фи|**я** (-и) *ж* cinematography

кино́ *ср нескл* cinema; (*разг: фильм*) film, movie (*US*); **идти́ (пойти́** *pf*) **в ~** (*разг*) to go to the pictures (*BRIT*) *или* movies (*US*)

киноактёр (-а) *м* (film) actor

киноактри́с|**а** (-ы) *ж* (film) actress

кинокарти́н|**а** (-ы) *ж* film

кинотеа́тр (-а) *м* cinema

кинофи́льм (-а) *м* film

ки́н|**уть** (-у; *impf* **кида́ть**) *сов перех* (*камень*) to throw; (*взгляд*) to cast; (*друзей*) to desert; (*разг: обмануть*) to cheat; ~**ся** (*impf* **кида́ться**) *сов возв:* ~**ся на** +*acc* (*на врага*) to attack; (*на еду*) to fall upon

кио́ск (-а) *м* kiosk

ки́п|**а** (-ы) *ж* bundle

кипе́ни|**е** (-я) *ср* boiling

кип|**е́ть** (-лю́, -и́шь; *pf* вс~) *несов* (*вода*) to boil; (*страсти*) to run high

кипя|**ти́ть** (-чу́, -ти́шь; *pf* вс~) *несов перех* to boil; ~**ся** *несов*

возв (*овощи*) to boil

кипят|**о́к** (-ка́) *м* boiling water

кипячёный *прил* boiled

кирпи́ч (-а́) *м* brick

кислоро́д (-а) *м* oxygen

кисл|**ота́** (-оты́; *nom pl* -о́ты) *ж*

ки́с|**лый** *прил* sour; ~**ая капу́ста** sauerkraut

ки́с|**нуть** (-ну; *pt* -, -ла; *pf* про~ *или* с~) *несов* to go off

кисть (-и) *ж* (*АNAT*) hand; (*гроздь: рябины*) cluster; (: *винограда*) bunch; (*на скатерти итп*) tassel; (*художника, маляра*) (paint)brush

кит (-а́) *м* whale

кита́|**ец** (-йца) *м* Chinese

Кита́|**й** (-я) *м* China

кита́йский *прил* Chinese; ~ **язы́к** Chinese

кише́чник (-а) *м* intestines *мн*

киш|**ка́** (-ки́; *gen pl* -о́к, *dat pl* -ка́м) *ж* gut, intestine

клавиату́р|**а** (-ы) *ж* keyboard

кла́виш|**а** (-и) *ж* key

клад (-а) *м* treasure

кла́дбищ|**е** (-а) *ср* cemetery

кладо́в|**ка** (-ки; *gen pl* -ок) *ж* (*разг*) cubby-hole

кладу́ *etc несов см.* **класть**

кладь (-и) *ж*: **ручна́я ~** hand luggage

клал *etc несов см.* **класть**

кла́ня|**ться** (-юсь; *pf* **поклони́ться**) *несов возв:* ~ +*dat* to bow to

кла́пан (-а) *м* valve

класс (-а) *м* class; (*комната*) classroom

кла́ссик|**а** (-и) *ж* classics *мн*

классифици́р|**овать** (-ую) (*не*)*сов перех* to classify

класси́ческий *прил* (*пример, работа*) classic; (*музыка,* *литерату́ра*) classical

кла́ссный *прил* (ПРОСВЕЩ) class;
(*разг: хоро́ший*) cool

кла|**сть** (-ду́, -дёшь; *pt* -л, -ла́; *pf*
положи́ть) *несов перех* to put;
(*pf* **сложи́ть**; *фунда́мент*) to lay

клева́ть (-ю́ю) *несов перех*
(*подлеж: пти́ца*) to peck ♦
непере́х (*ры́ба*) to bite

клевета́ (-ы́) *ж* (*устная*) slander;
(*письменная*) libel

клеве|**та́ть** (-ещу́, -е́щешь; *pf*
на~) *несов*: ~ **на** +*acc* (*см сущ*)
to slander; to libel

клеёнка (-ки; *gen pl* -ок) *ж*
oilcloth

кле́|ить (-ю, -ишь; *pf* с~) *несов
перех* to glue; ~ся *несов возв* to
stick

клей (-я) *м* glue

кле́йкий *прил* sticky; ~ая ле́нта
sticky tape

клейм|**о́** (-а́; *nom pl* -а) *ср* stamp;
(*на ско́те, на осуждённом*)
brand; ~ **позо́ра** stigma

клён (-а) *м* maple (tree)

кле́т|**ка** (-ки; *gen pl* -ок) *ж* (*для
птиц, живо́тных*) cage; (*на
тка́ни*) check; (*на бума́ге*) square;
(БИО) cell; **ткань в** ~**ку** checked
material

кле́тчатый *прил* (*ткань итп*)
chequered (BRIT), checked

клёш *прил неизм*: **брю́ки** ~ flares;
ю́бка ~ flared skirt

клешн|**я́** (-и́; *gen pl* -е́й) *ж* claw,
pincer

кле́щ|**и** (-е́й) *мн* tongs *мн*

клие́нт (-а) *м* client

клиенту́р|**а** (-ы) *ж собир* clientèle

кли́зм|**а** (-ы) *ж* enema

кли́макс (-а) *м* (БИО) menopause

кли́мат (-а) *м* (*также перен*)
climate

клин (-а; *nom pl* -ья, *gen pl* -ьев) *м*
wedge

кли́ник|**а** (-и) *ж* clinic

кли́пс|**ы** (-ов) *мн* clip-on earrings
мн

кли́ринговый *прил* (КОММ)
clearing

кли́ч|**ка** (-ки; *gen pl* -ек) *ж* (*кошки
итп*) name; (*челове́ка*) nickname

клише́ *ср нескл* (*перен*) cliché

кло|**к** (-ка́; *nom pl* -чья, *gen pl*
-чьев) *м* (*во́лос*) tuft; (*ва́ты*) wad

клони́ровать (-ую) (*не*)*сов
перех* to clone

клон|**и́ть** (-ю́, -ишь) *несов*: его́
~**и́ло ко сну** he was drifting off to
sleep; **к чему́ ты кло́нишь?** what
are you getting at *или* driving at?

кло́ун (-а) *м* clown

клоч|**о́к** (-ка́) *м уменьш от* **клок**;
(*земли́*) plot; (*бума́ги*) scrap

клуб (-а) *м* club; (*nom pl* -ы́;
обы́чно мн: дыма, пыли) cloud

клуб|**и́ться** (3sg -и́тся) *несов
возв* to swirl

клубни́к|**а** (-и) *ж собир* (*я́годы*)
strawberries *мн*

клуб|**о́к** (-ка́) *м* (*ше́рсти*) ball

клу́мб|**а** (-ы) *ж* flowerbed

клык (-а́) *м* (*живо́тного*) fang

клюв (-а) *м* beak

клю́кв|**а** (-ы) *ж собир* (*я́годы*)
cranberries *мн*

клю́н|**уть** (-у) *сов перех* to peck

ключ (-а́) *м* (*также перен*) key;
(*родни́к*) spring; (МУЗ): **басо́вый/
скрипи́чный** ~ bass/treble clef;
га́ечный ~ spanner

ключево́й *прил* (*гла́вный*) key

клю́ш|**ка** (-ки; *gen pl* -ек) *ж*
(ХОККЕЙ) hockey stick; (ГОЛФ)
club

кля́|сться (-ну́сь, -нёшься; *pt*
-лся, -ла́сь; *pf* по~) *несов возв*
to swear; ~ (**по**~ *pf*) **в чём-н** to
swear sth

кля́тв|а (-ы) ж oath

км. *сокр* (= **киломе́тр**) km

кни́г|а (-и) ж book

кни́ж|ка (-ки; *gen pl* -ек) ж *уменьш от* **кни́га**; (*разг*) book; **трудова́я ~** employment record book; **че́ковая ~** chequebook (*BRIT*), checkbook (*US*)

кни́жный *прил*: **~ магази́н** bookshop

кни́зу *нареч* downwards

кно́п|ка (-ки; *gen pl* -ок) ж (*звонка*) button; (*канцелярская*) drawing pin (*BRIT*), thumbtack (*US*); (*застёжка*) press stud, popper (*BRIT*)

КНР ж *сокр* (= **Кита́йская Наро́дная Респу́блика**) PRC

княз|ь (-я; *gen pl* -ья́, *gen pl* -е́й) м prince (*in Russia*)

ко *предл см.* **к**

кобы́л|а (-ы) ж mare

кова́рный *прил* devious

ков|ёр (-ра́) м carpet

ко́врик (-а) м rug; (*дверной*) mat; (*КОМП*) mouse mat

ковш (-а́) м ladle

ковыря́|ть (-ю) *несов перех* to dig in; **~** (*impf*) **в зуба́х/носу́** to pick one's teeth/nose

когда́ *нареч* when; **~ как** it depends

когда́-либо *нареч* = **когда́-нибудь**

когда́-нибудь *нареч* (*в вопросе*) ever; (*в утверждении*) some *или* one day; **Вы ~ там бы́ли?** have you ever been there?; **я ~ туда́ пое́ду** I'll go there some *или* one day

когда́-то *нареч* once

кого́ *мест от* **кто**

ко́г|оть (-тя; *gen pl* -те́й) м claw

код (-а) м code

ко́декс (-а) м code

коди́р|овать (-ую; *pf* **за~**) *несов перех* to encode, code

ко́е-где *нареч* here and there

ко́е-как *нареч* (*небрежно*) any old how; (*с трудом*) somehow

ко́е-како́й (**ко́е-како́го**) *мест* some

ко́е-кто (**ко́е-кого́**) *мест* (*некоторые*) some (*people*)

ко́е-что (**ко́е-чего́**) *мест* (*нечто*) something; (*немногое*) a little

ко́ж|а (-и) ж skin; (*материал*) leather

ко́жаный *прил* leather

ко́жный *прил*: **~ые боле́зни** skin diseases

кожур|а́ (-ы́) ж (*апельсина итп*) peel

коз|а́ (-ы́; *nom pl* -ы) ж (*nanny*) goat

козёл (-ла́) м (*billy*) goat

Козеро́г (-а) м (*созвездие*) Capricorn

ко́й|ка (-йки; *gen pl* -ек) ж (*в казарме*) bunk; (*в больнице*) bed

кокаи́н (-а) м cocaine

коке́тливый *прил* flirtatious

коке́тнича|ю (-ю) *несов* to flirt

коклю́ш (-а) м whooping cough

кокте́йл|ь (-я) м cocktail

кол (-а́; *nom pl* -ья) м stake

колбас|а́ (-ы́) ж sausage

колго́т|ки (-ок) *мн* tights *мн* (*BRIT*), pantihose *мн* (*US*)

колд|ова́ть (-у́ю) *несов* to practise (*BRIT*) *или* practice (*US*) witchcraft

колду́н (-а́) м sorcerer, wizard

колеба́ни|е (-я) ср (*маятника*) swing; (*почвы, здания*) vibration; (*перен: цен*) fluctuation

коле́ба|ть (-́блю, -́блешь) *несов перех* to rock, swing; (*pf* **по~**; *авторитет*) to shake; **~ся** *несов возв* (*ФИЗ*) to oscillate;

(пламя итп) to flicker; (цены) to
fluctuate; (сомневаться) to waver
коле́н|**о** (-а; nom pl -и, gen pl -ей)
cp knee
коле́с|**о** (-еса́; nom pl -ёса) cp
wheel
коле|**я́** (-и́) ж (на доро́ге) rut;
(железнодоро́жная) track
коли́честв|**о** (-а) cp quantity
ко́лкост|**ь** (-и) ж (насме́шка)
biting remark
колле́г|**а** (-и) м/ж colleague
колле́ги|**я** (-и) ж: адвока́тская ~
≈ the Bar; редакцио́нная ~
editorial board
колле́дж (-а) м college
коллекти́в (-а) м collective
коллекти́вный прил collective
коллекциони́р|**овать** (-ую)
несов перех to collect
колле́кци|**я** (-и) ж collection
коло́д|**а** (-ы) ж (бревно́) block;
(карт) pack, deck
коло́д|**ец** (-ца) м well; (в ша́хте)
shaft
ко́локол (-а; nom pl -а́) м bell
колоко́льчик (-а) м bell; (бот)
bluebell
колониа́льный прил colonial
коло́ни|**я** (-и) ж colony;
исправи́тельно-трудова́я ~ penal
colony
коло́н|**ка** (-ки; gen pl -ок) ж
column; (га́зовая) water heater;
(для воды, для бензина) pump
коло́нн|**а** (-ы) ж (архит) column
колори́т (-а) м (перен: эпохи)
colour (BRIT), color (US)
колори́тный прил colourful
(BRIT), colorful (US)
ко́ло|**с** (-са; nom pl -о́сья, gen pl
-о́сьев) м ear (of corn, wheat)
колосса́льный прил colossal
кол|**оти́ть** (-очу́, -о́тишь) несов:
~ по столу́/в дверь to thump the

table/on the door; ~ся несов возв
(сердце) to thump
кол|**о́ть** (-ю́, -ешь; pf рас-)
несов перех (дрова) to chop
(up); (орехи) to crack; (pf за-;
штыко́м итп) to spear; (pf у-;
иго́лкой итп) to prick; (разг: делать
укол): ~ кого́-н to give sb an
injection; (pf y-; разг) to inject sb with sth; у меня́
ко́лет в боку́ I've got a stitch; ~ся
несов возв (ёж, шипо́вник) to be
prickly; (наркома́н) to be on drugs
колыбе́льн|**ая** (-ой) ж (также: ~
пе́сня) lullaby
кольцев|**о́й** прил round, circular;
~**а́я доро́га** ring road; ~**а́я
ли́ния** (в метро) circle line
кол|**ьцо́** (-ьца́; nom pl -ьца, gen
pl -е́ц) cp ring; (в маршруте) circle
колю́чий прил (куст) prickly; ~**ая
про́волока** barbed wire
колю́ч|**ка** (-ки; gen pl -ек) ж thorn
коля́с|**ка** (-ки; gen pl -ок) ж:
(де́тская) ~ pram (BRIT), baby
carriage (US); инвали́дная ~
wheelchair
ком мест см. кто ♦ (-а; nom pl
-ья, gen pl -ьев) м lump
кома́нд|**а** (-ы) ж command;
(су́дна) crew; (СПОРТ) team
команди́р (-а) м commander,
commanding officer
командиро́в|**ка** (-ки; gen pl -ок)
ж (коро́ткая) business trip;
(дли́тельная) secondment (BRIT),
posting
кома́ндовани|**е** (-я) cp: ~ (+instr)
(су́дном, во́йском) command (of)
♦ собир command
кома́нд|**овать** (-ую; pf с~) несов
to give orders; ~ (impf) +instr
(а́рмией) to command; (му́жем)
to order around
кома́ндующий (-его) м

commanding officer, commander

комáр (-á) *м* mosquito

комбáйн (-а) *м (С.-Х.)* combine (harvester); **кýхонный ~** food processor

комбинáт (-а) *м* plant

комбинáци|я (-и) *ж* combination; *(женское бельё)* slip

комбинезóн (-а) *м* overalls *мн*; *(детский)* dungarees *мн*

комбинúр|овать (-ую; *pf* с~) *несов перех* to combine

комедúйный *прил* comic; *(актёр)* comedy

комéди|я (-и) *ж* comedy

комéт|а (-ы) *ж* comet

кóмик (-а) *м* comedian, comic

комиссиóнный *прил*: ~ **магазúн** second-hand shop which sells goods on a commission basis

комúсси|я (-и) *ж* commission

комитéт (-а) *м* committee

кóмка|ть (-ю; *pf* с~) *несов перех* to crumple

коммéнтари|й (-я) *м* commentary

коммéнтатор (-а) *м* commentator

комментúр|овать (-ую) *(не)сов перех (текст)* to comment on; *(матч)* to commentate on

коммерсáнт (-а) *м* businessman

коммéрческий *прил* commercial; **~ магазúн** privately-run shop

коммунáльн|ый *прил* communal; **~ые платежú** bills; **~ые услýги** utilities

---

коммунáльные услýги - The communal services include water supply, hot water and heating, public radio, rubbish collection and street sweeping, and building maintenance. All these are paid for on a standing charge basis.

Electricity and telephone are metered and hence paid for separately.

коммунúзм (-а) *м* communism

коммуникáци|я (-и) *ж* communication

коммунúст (-а) *м* communist

кóмнат|а (-ы) *ж* room

кóмнатн|ый *прил* indoor; **~ая температýра** room temperature; **~ое растéние** house plant

компáкт-дúск (-а) *м* compact disc

компáктный *прил* compact

компáни|я (-и) *ж (КОММ)* company; *(друзья́)* group of friends

компаньóн (-а) *м (КОММ)* partner

компáрти|я (-и) *ж сокр (= коммунистúческая пáртия)* Communist Party

кóмпас (-а) *м* compass

компенсáци|я (-и) *ж* compensation

компенсúр|овать (-ую) *(не)сов перех*: ~ *(кому́-н)* to compensate (sb) for

компетéнтный *прил (человек)* competent; *(органы)* appropriate

кóмплекс (-а) *м* complex; *(мер)* range

кóмплексный *прил* integrated

комплéкт (-а) *м* set

комплект|овáть (-ýю; *pf* у~) *несов перех* to build up

комплимéнт (-а) *м* compliment

композúтор (-а) *м* composer

компонéнт (-а) *м* component

компостúр|овать (-ую; *pf* за~) *сов перех* to punch *или* clip *(ticket)*

компóт (-а) *м* compote

компрéсс (-а) *м (МЕД)* compress

компрометúр|овать (-ую; *pf* с~)

несов перех to compromise

компроми́сс (-а) *м* compromise

компью́тер (-а) *м* computer

компью́терщик (-а) *м (разг)*
computer specialist

кому́ *мест см.* **кто**

комфо́рт (-а) *м* comfort

комфорта́бельный *прил*
comfortable

конве́йер (-а) *м* conveyor (belt)

конве́рси|я (-и) *ж* conversion

конве́рт (-а) *м* envelope

конверти́ровать (-ую) *(не)сов*
перех (деньги) to convert

конверти́руемый *прил*
convertible

конво́й (-я) *м* escort

конгре́сс (-а) *м (съезд)* congress

конди́терск|ая (-ой) *ж*
confectioner's

конди́терский *прил*
confectionery; ~ **магази́н**
confectioner's

кондиционе́р (-а) *м* air
conditioner

кон|ёк (-ька́) *м (обычно мн,*
СПОРТ) skate; **ката́ться** *(impf)* **на**
~ька́х to skate; *см. также* **коньки́**

кон|е́ц (-ца́) *м* end; **без ~ца́**
endlessly; **в ~це́ ~цо́в** in the end;
биле́т в оди́н ~ single (BRIT) *или*
one-way ticket; **под ~** towards the
end

коне́чно *вводн сл* of course,
certainly

коне́чност|ь (-и) *ж (АНАТ)* limb

коне́чный *прил (цель, итог)*
final; *(станция)* last

конкре́тно *нареч (говорить)*
specifically; *(именно)* actually

конкре́тный *прил (реальный)*
concrete; *(факт)* actual

конкуре́нт (-а) *м* competitor

конкурентоспосо́бный *прил*
competitive

конкуре́нци|я (-и) *ж* competition

конкури́ровать (-ую) *несов:* ~
с +*instr* to compete with

ко́нкурс (-а) *м* competition

консе́нсус (-а) *м* consensus

консервати́вный *прил*
conservative

консерва́тор (-а) *м* conservative

консервато́ри|я (-и) *ж (МУЗ)*
conservatoire (BRIT), conservatory
(US)

консерви́ровать (-ую) *(не)сов*
перех to preserve; *(в жестяных*
банках) to can

консе́рвн|ый *прил:* **~ая ба́нка**
can

консе́рв|ы (-ов) *мн* canned food
ед

конспе́кт (-а) *м* notes *мн*

конспекти́ровать (-ую) *pf* **за~**)
несов перех to take notes on

конспира́ци|я (-и) *ж* conspiracy

конститу́ци|я (-и) *ж* constitution

констру́и́ровать (-ую) *pf* **с~**)
несов перех to construct

констру́ктор (-а) *м* designer;
(детская игра) construction set

констру́кторск|ий *прил:* **~ое**
бюро́ design studio

констру́кци|я (-и) *ж* construction

ко́нсул (-а) *м* consul

ко́нсульств|о (-а) *ср* consulate

консульта́нт (-а) *м* consultant

консульта́ци|я (-и) *ж (у врача, у*
юриста) consultation;
(учреждение) consultancy;
же́нская ~ gynaecological and
antenatal (BRIT) *или* gynecological
and prenatal (US) clinic

консульти́ровать (-ую) *pf*
про~) *несов перех* to give
professional advice to; **~ся** *(impf*
про~ся) *несов возв:* **~ся с**
кем-н to consult sb

конта́кт (-а) *м* contact

конта́ктный *прил (линзы)*
contact; ~ **телефо́н** contact
number

контéйнер (-а) *м* container

контéкст (-а) *м* context

контингéнт (-а) *м* contingent

континéнт (-а) *м* continent

конто́ра (-ы) *ж* office

конто́рский *прил* office

контраба́нд|а (-ы) *ж* smuggling;
(товары) contraband

контрабанди́ст (-а) *м* smuggler

контрабáс (-а) *м* double bass

контра́кт (-а) *м* contract

контра́ктный *прил* contractual

контра́ст (-а) *м* contrast

контрацепти́в (-а) *м*
contraceptive

контролёр (-а) *м (в поезде)*
(ticket) inspector; *(театральный)*
≈ usher; *(сберкассы)* cashier

контроли́р|овать (-ую) *несов*
перех to control

контро́л|ь (-я) *м (наблюдение)*
monitoring; *(проверка)* testing,
checking; *(в транспорте)* ticket
inspection; *(в магазине)* checkout

контро́льн|ая (-ой) *ж (также*: ~
рабо́та) class test

контро́льн|ый *прил*: ~**ая
коми́ссия** inspection team; ~**ые
ци́фры** control figures

контрразвéдк|а (-и) *ж*
counterespionage

ко́нтур (-а) *м* contour

конур|а́ (-ы́) *ж (собачья)* kennel

ко́нус (-а) *м* cone

конферансьé *ср нескл* compère

конферéнц-за́л (-а) *м* conference
room

конферéнци|я (-и) *ж* conference

конфéт|а (-ы) *ж* sweet

конфиденциа́льный *прил*
confidential

конфиск|ова́ть (-у́ю) *(не)сов*

перех to confiscate

конфли́кт (-а) *м (военный)*
conflict; *(в семье, на работе)*
tension

конфликт|ова́ть (-у́ю) *несов*: ~
с +*instr (разг)* to be at loggerheads
with

конфо́рк|а (-ки; *gen pl* -**ок**) *ж* ring
(on cooker)

конфронта́ци|я (-и) *ж*
confrontation

концентра́ци|я (-и) *ж*
concentration

концентри́р|овать (-ую; *pf* **с~**)
несов перех to concentrate; ~**ся**
(pf **с~ся**) *несов возв (капитал)* to
be concentrated; *(ученик)* to
concentrate

концéпци|я (-и) *ж* concept

концéрн (-а) *м (ЭКОН)* concern

концéрт (-а) *м* concert

концла́гер|ь (-я; *nom pl* -**я́**) (=
концентрацио́нный ла́герь)
concentration camp

конча́|ть(ся) (-ю(сь)) *несов от*
ко́нчить(ся)

ко́нчик (-а) *м* tip *(of finger etc)*

ко́нч|ить (-у, -ишь; *impf*
конча́ть) *сов перех* to end;
(университет, книгу, работу) to
finish; ~**ся** *(impf* **конча́ться)** *сов*
возв (разговор, книга) to end,
finish; *(запасы)* to run out; *(лес*
итп) to end

кон|ь (-я́; *nom pl* -**и**, *gen pl* -**éй**) *м*
(лошадь) horse; *(ШАХМАТЫ)*
knight

конькú (-óв) *мн* skates *мн*

конья́к (-á) *м* brandy, cognac

конъюнкту́р|а (-ы) *ж (КОММ)*
situation; ~ **ры́нка** market
conditions

кооперати́в (-а) *м* cooperative;
(разг: квартира) flat in housing
cooperative; **жили́щный** ~

cooperative (form of house or flat ownership)

кооперати́вный прил cooperative; ~ **магази́н** или **ларёк** со-ор

коопера́тор (-а) м member of private enterprise

коопера́ци|я (-и) ж cooperative enterprise

координа́т|а (-ы) ж (ГЕОМ, обычно мн) coordinate; (разг: адрес) number (and address)

координи́р|овать (-ую) (не)сов перех to coordinate

копа́|ть (-ю) несов перех (землю) to dig; (pf **вы́копать**; коло́дец) to sink; (о́вощи) to dig up; **~ся** несов возв (в чужи́х веща́х) to snoop about; (разг: возиться) to dawdle

копе́|йка (-йки; gen pl **-ек)** ж kopeck

копира́йт (-а) м copyright

копирова́льн|ый прил: **~ая маши́на** photocopying machine, photocopier; **~ая бума́га** carbon paper

копи́р|овать (-ую; pf **с~)** несов перех to copy

коп|и́ть (-лю́, -ишь; pf **на~** или **с~)** несов перех to save; (pf **на~ся** или **с~ся)** несов возв to accumulate

ко́пи|я (-и) ж copy; (перен: о челове́ке) spitting image

ко́пот|ь (-и) ж layer of soot

копт|и́ть (-чу́, -ти́шь) несов (ла́мпа) to give off soot ♦ (pf **за~)** перех (мя́со, ры́бу) to smoke

копчёный прил smoked

копы́т|о (-а) ср hoof

коп|ьё (-ья́; nom pl **-ья**, gen pl **-ий)** ср spear; (СПОРТ) javelin

кор|а́ (-ы́) ж (де́рева) bark; **земна́я ~** the earth's crust

кораблекруше́ни|е (-я) ср shipwreck

кораблестрое́ни|е (-я) ср shipbuilding

кора́бл|ь (-я́) м ship

кора́лл (-а) м coral

кордебале́т (-а) м corps de ballet

коренн|о́й прил (населе́ние) indigenous; (вопро́с, рефо́рмы) fundamental; **~ым о́бразом** fundamentally; **~ зуб** molar

ко́р|ень (-ня; gen pl **-не́й)** м root; **в ~не** fundamentally

кореш|о́к (-ка́) м (переплёта) spine

Коре́|я (-и) ж Korea

корзи́н|а (-ы) ж basket

коридо́р (-а) м corridor

кори́ц|а (-ы) ж cinnamon

кори́чневый прил brown

ко́р|ка (-ки; gen pl **-ок)** ж (апельси́нная) peel

корм (-а; nom pl **-á)** м (для скота́) fodder, feed; (ди́ких живо́тных) food

корм|а́ (-ы́) ж stern

корми́л|ец (-ьца) м breadwinner

корм|и́ть (-лю́, -ишь; pf **на~)** несов перех: **~ кого́-н чем-н** to feed sb sth; (pf **про~**; содержа́ть) to feed, keep; **~** (impf) **гру́дью** to breast-feed; **~ся** (pf **про~ся)** несов возв (живо́тное) to feed; (челове́к): **~ся** +instr to survive

коро́б|ка (-ки; gen pl **-ок)** ж box; **~ скоросте́й** gearbox

коро́в|а (-ы) ж cow

короле́в|а (-ы) ж queen

короле́вский прил royal

короле́вств|о (-а) ср kingdom

коро́л|ь (-я́) м king

коро́н|а (-ы) ж crown

коро́н|ка (-ки; gen pl **-ок)** ж (на зубе́) crown

корон|ова́ть (-у́ю) (не)сов перех

to crown

коро́тк|ий *прил* short; **~ие во́лны** short wave; **~ое замыка́ние** short circuit

ко́ротко *нареч* briefly; (*стричься*) short ♦ *как сказ*: **э́то пла́тье мне ~** this dress is too short for me

коро́че *сравн нареч*: **~ говоря́** to put it briefly, in short

корпора́ци|я (-и) *ж* corporation

ко́рпус (-а; *nom pl* **-ы́)** *м* body; (*самолёта*) fuselage; (*nom pl* **-а́;** *судна, зда́ния*) frame; (*зда́ние*) block; (*дипломати́ческий*) corps

корректи́в (-а) *м* amendment

корректи́р|овать (-ую; *pf* **от~)** *несов перех* (*оши́бку*) to correct

корреспонде́нт (-а) *м* correspondent

корреспонде́нци|я (-и) *ж* correspondence

корро́зи|я (-и) *ж* corrosion

коррумпи́рованный *прил* corrupt

корру́пци|я (-и) *ж* corruption

корт (-а) *м* (tennis) court

ко́рточк|и (-ек) *мн*: **присе́сть на ~** to squat down; **сиде́ть** (*impf*) **на ~ках** to squat

корчева́|ть (-у́ю) *несов перех* to uproot; (*перен*) to root out

ко́рч|иться (-усь, -ишься; *pf* **с~)** *несов возв* (*от бо́ли*) to double up

кор|ь (-и) *ж* measles *мн*

коря́вый *прил* (*де́рево*) gnarled

кос|а́ (-ы́; *acc sg* **-у,** *dat sg* **-е́,** *nom pl* **-ы)** *ж* (*во́лосы*) plait; (*ору́дие*) scythe

ко́свенный *прил* indirect; (*дополне́ние, паде́ж*) oblique

коси́л|ка (-ки; *gen pl* **-ок)** *ж* mower (*machine*)

ко|си́ть (-шу́, -сишь; *pf* **с~)** *несов перех* (*газо́н, се́но*) to

mow; (*глаза́*) to slant

косме́тик|а (-и) *ж* make-up ♦ *собир* cosmetics *мн*

косме́тиче́ский *прил* cosmetic; **~ кабине́т** beauty salon

космети́ч|ка (-ки; *gen pl* **-ек)** *ж* (*специали́стка*) beautician; (*су́мочка*) make-up bag

косми́ческий *прил* space; **~ое простра́нство** (outer) space

космона́вт (-а) *м* cosmonaut; (*в США итп*) astronaut

ко́смос (-а) *м* the cosmos

косн|у́ться (-у́сь, -ёшься) *сов от* **каса́ться**

косогла́зый *прил* cross-eyed

косо́й *прил* (*глаза́*) squinty; (*дождь, лучи́*) slanting

кост|ёр (-ра́) *м* campfire

костля́вый *прил* bony

ко́стный *прил* (*АНАТ*): **~ мозг** (bone) marrow

ко́сточ|ка (-ки; *gen pl* **-ек)** *ж* (*абрико́совая, вишнёвая*) stone; (*виногра́да*) seed; (*лимо́на*) pip

косты́л|ь (-я́) *м* (*инвали́да*) crutch

кост|ь (-и; *gen pl* **-е́й)** *ж* bone

костю́м (-а) *м* outfit; (*на сце́не*) costume; (*пиджа́к и брю́ки/ю́бка*) suit

костя́ш|ка (-ки; *gen pl* **-ек)** *ж* (*па́льцев*) knuckle

косы́н|ка (-ки; *gen pl* **-ок)** *ж* (triangular) scarf

кося́к (-а́) *м* (*две́ри*) jamb; (*рыб*) school, shoal

кот (-а́) *м* tomcat

кот|ёл (-ла́) *м* (*парово́й*) boiler

котел|о́к (-ка́) *м* (*кастрю́ля*) billy(can); (*шля́па*) bowler (hat) (*BRIT*), derby (*US*)

коте́льн|ая (-ой) *ж* boilerhouse

кот|ёнок (-ёнка; *nom pl* **-я́та,** *gen pl* **-я́т)** *м* kitten

ко́тик (-а) м (тюлень) fur seal

коти́р|оваться (-уюсь) несов возв (КОММ): ~ (в +acc) to be quoted (at); (также перен) to be highly valued

котле́т|а (-ы) ж rissole; (также: **отбивна́я** ~) chop

кото́р|ый (-ая, -ое, -ые) мест 1 (вопросительное) what which; **кото́рый час?** what time is it? 2 (относительное: о предмете) which; (: о человеке) who; **же́нщина, кото́рую я люблю́** the woman I love 3 (не первый): **кото́рый день/ год мы не ви́делись** we haven't seen each other for many days/ years

ко́фе м нескл coffee; ~ **в зёрнах** coffee beans

кофева́р|ка (-ки; gen pl -ок) ж percolator

кофе́йник (-а) м coffeepot

кофе́йный прил coffee

кофемо́л|ка (-ки; gen pl -ок) ж coffee grinder

ко́фт|а (-ы) ж blouse; (шерстяная) cardigan

коча́н (-а) м: ~ **капу́сты** cabbage

кочене́|ть (-ю; pf о~) несов (руки) to go stiff; (человек) to get stiff

коша́чий прил (мех, лапа) cat's

кошел|ёк (-ька́) м purse

ко́ш|ка (-ки; gen pl -ек) ж cat

кошма́р (-а) м nightmare

кошма́рный прил nightmarish

коэффицие́нт (-а) м coefficient

краб (-а) м crab

краево́й прил regional

кра́ж|а (-и) ж theft; ~ **со взло́мом** burglary

кра|й (-я; loc sg -ю́, nom pl -я́, gen pl -ёв) м edge; (чашки, коробки) rim; (местность) land; (полит) krai (regional administrative unit)

кра́йне нареч extremely

кра́йн|ий прил extreme; (дом) last; (пункт маршрута) last, final; **в ~ем слу́чае** as a last resort; **по ~ей ме́ре** at least; **Кра́йний Се́вер** the Arctic; ~ **срок** (final) deadline

кран (-а) м tap, faucet (US); (СТРОИТ) crane

крапи́в|а (-ы) ж nettle

краси́вый прил beautiful; (мужчина) handsome; (решение, фраза) fine

краси́тель (-я) м dye

кра́|сить (-шу, -сишь; pf по~) несов перех to paint; (волосы) to dye; (pf на~; губы итп) to make up; ~**ся** (pf на~ся) несов возв to wear make-up

кра́с|ка (-ки; gen pl -ок) ж paint; (обычно мн: нежные, весенние итп) colour (BRIT), color (US)

красне́|ть (-ю; pf по~) несов to turn red; (от стыда) to blush, flush; (от гнева) to go red

красноречи́вый прил (оратор, письмо) eloquent; (взгляд, жест) expressive; (факты) revealing

кра́сн|ый прил red; ~**ая ры́ба** salmon; ~**ая строка́** new paragraph

красот|а́ (-ы́; nom pl -о́ты) ж beauty

кра́сочный прил colourful (BRIT), colorful (US)

кра|сть (-ду́, -дёшь; pf укра́сть) несов перех to steal; **кра́сться** несов возв (человек) to creep, steal

кра́тер (-а) м crater

кра́тк|ий прил short; (беседа)

brief, short; ~ое прилага́тельное short-term adjective

кратковре́менный *прил* short; ~ дождь shower

краткосро́чный *прил* short; (*заём, ссуда*) short-term

кра́тный *прил* divisible

крах (-а) *м* collapse

крахма́л (-а) *м* starch

крахма́л|ить (-ю, -ишь; *pf* на~) *несов перех* to starch

кра́шеный *прил* (*мех, ткань*) dyed; (*стол, дверь*) painted

креве́т|ка (-ки; *gen pl* -ок) *ж* shrimp

креди́т (-а) *м* credit

креди́т|ный *прил* credit; ~ая ка́рточка credit card; ~ счёт credit account

кредито́р (-а) *м* creditor

кредитоспосо́бный *прил* solvent

кре́до *ср нескл* credo

кре́йсер (-а) *м* (ВОЕН) battleship

крем (-а) *м* cream; сапо́жный ~ shoe polish

кремато́ри|й (-я) *м* crematorium

кремир|ова́ть (-ую) (*не)сов перех* to cremate

кремл|ь (-я́) *м* citadel; Кремль the Kremlin

кре́мовый *прил* cream

креп|и́ть (-лю́, -и́шь) *несов перех* to fix

кре́пкий *прил* strong

кре́пко *нареч* strongly; (*спать, люби́ть*) deeply; (*завяза́ть*) tightly

крепле́ни|е (-я) *ср* reinforcement; (*обычно pl*: *лыжные*) binding

кре́п|нуть (-ну; *pt* -, -ла; *pf* о~) *несов* to get stronger; (*уве́ренность*) to grow

кре́пост|ь (-и) *ж* (ВОЕН) fortress

кре́сл|о (-а; *gen pl* -ел) *ср* armchair; (*в теа́тре*) seat

крест (-а́) *м* cross

кре|сти́ть (-щу́, -стишь; *pf* о~) *несов перех* to christen, baptize; ~ (*пере~ pf*) кого́-н to make the sign of the cross over sb; ~ся (*не)сов возв* to be christened *или* baptized; (*pf* пере~ся; крести́ть себя́) to cross o.s.

кре́стный *прил*: ~ая мать godmother; ~ оте́ц godfather

крестья́н|ин (-ина; *nom pl* -е, *gen pl* -) *м* peasant

крестья́нский *прил* peasant

креще́ни|е (-я) *ср* christening, baptism; (*праздник*): Креще́ние ≈ the Epiphany

крив|и́ть (-лю́, -и́шь; *pf* с~ *или* по~) *несов перех* to curve; (*лицо, губы*) to twist

кривля́|ться (-юсь) *несов возв* (*гримасничать*) to squirm

криво́й *прил* (*линия, палка, улыбка*) crooked; (*ноги*) bandy

кри́зис (-а) *м* crisis

крик (-а; *part gen* -у) *м* cry

крикли́вый *прил* loud; (*голос*) yapping

кри́к|нуть (-у) *сов* to shout

кримина́л (-а) *м* crime

криминали́ст (-а) *м* specialist in crime detection

кримина́льный *прил* (*случай*) criminal; (*исто́рия, хро́ника*) crime

криминоге́нный *прил* (*райо́н*) crime-ridden; (*ситуа́ция*) conducive to crime

криста́лл (-а) *м* crystal

крите́ри|й (-я) *м* criterion

кри́тик (-а) *м* critic

кри́тик|а (-и) *ж* criticism

критик|ова́ть (-у́ю) *несов перех* to criticize

крити́ческий *прил* critical

крич|а́ть (-у́, -и́шь) *несов*

(*человек: от боли, от гнева*) to cry (out); (: *говорить громко*) to shout; ~ (*impf*) **на** +*асс* (*бранить*) to shout at

крова́вый *прил* bloodied; (*рана, битва*) bloody

крова́т|**ь** (-**и**) *ж* bed

кро́вл|**я** (-**и**; *gen pl* -**ель**) *ж* roof

кро́вн|**ый** *прил* (*родство*) blood; **~ые интере́сы** vested interest *ед*; **~ враг** deadly enemy

кровожа́дный *прил* bloodthirsty

кровообраще́ни|**е** (-**я**) *ср* (*МЕД*) circulation

кровопроли́тный *прил* bloody

кровотече́ни|**е** (-**я**) *ср* bleeding

кровоточ|**и́ть** (*3sg* -**и́т**) *несов* to bleed

кров|**ь** (-**и**; *loc sg* -**и́**) *ж* blood

кро|**и́ть** (-**ю́**, -**и́шь**) *несов перех* to cut out

крокоди́л (-**а**) *м* crocodile

кро́лик (-**а**) *м* rabbit; (*мех*) rabbit fur

кро́личий *прил* rabbit

кро́ме *предл*: ~ +*gen* (*за исключением*) except; (*сверх чего-н*) as well as; ~ **того́** besides

кро́н|**а** (-**ы**) *ж* (*дерева*) crown

кронште́йн (-**а**) *м* (*балкона*) support; (*полки*) bracket

кропотли́вый *прил* painstaking

кросс (-**а**) *м* (*бег*) cross-country; (*гонки*) cross-country race

кроссво́рд (-**а**) *м* crossword

кроссо́вк|**а** (-**и**; *gen pl* -**ок**) *ж* (*обычно мн*) trainer

кро́хотный *прил* tiny

кро́шечный *прил* (*разг*) teeny-weeny, tiny

крош|**и́ть** (-**у́**, -**и́шь**) *несов перех* (*хлеб*) to crumble; **~ся** *несов возв* (*хлеб, мел*) to crumble

кро́ш|**ка** (-**ки**; *gen pl* -**ек**) *ж*

(*кусочек*) crumb; (*ребёнок*) little one

круг (-**а**; *nom pl* -**и́**) *м* circle; (*СПОРТ*) lap; (*loc sg* -**у́**; *перен: знакомых*) circle; (: *обязанностей, интересов*) range

круг|**о́м** (-**о́м**) *мн* (*литературные, политические*) circles *мн*

круглосу́точный *прил* (*работа*) round-the-clock; (*магазин*) twenty-four-hour

кру́глый *прил* round; (*дурак*) total; **~ год** all year (round); **~ые су́тки** twenty-four hours

круговоро́т (-**а**) *м* cycle

кругозо́р (-**а**) *м*: **он челове́к широ́кого ~a** he is knowledgeable

круго́м *нареч* around

кругосве́тный *прил* round-the-world

кружевно́й *прил* lace

кру́жев|**о** (-**а**; *gen pl* -**а**) *ср* lace

круж|**и́ть** (-**у́**, -**и́шь**) *несов перех* to spin ♦ *неперех* (*птица*) to circle; **~ся** *несов возв* (*в танце*) to spin (around); **у меня́ голова́ кру́жится** my head's spinning

кру́ж|**ка** (-**ки**; *gen pl* -**ек**) *ж* mug

круж|**о́к** (-**ка́**) *м* circle; (*организация*) club

круи́з (-**а**) *м* cruise

круп|**а́** (-**ы́**; *nom pl* -**ы**) *ж* grain

кру́пно *нареч* (*нарезать*) coarsely; **писа́ть** (**написа́ть** *pf*) ~ to write in big letters

кру́пный *прил* (*размеры, фирма*) large; (*песок, соль*) coarse; (*учёный, дело*) prominent; (*событие, успех*) major; **~ план** close-up

кру|**ти́ть** (-**чу́**, -**тишь**) *несов перех* (*руль*) to turn; (*pf* **с~**; *руки*) to twist; **~ся** *несов возв* (*вертеться*) to turn around; (: *колесо*) to spin; (: *дети*) to fidget

кру́то *нареч (подниматься)* steeply; *(повернуть)* sharply ♦ *как сказ (разг: хорошо)* it's cool

круто́й *прил* steep; *(перемены)* sharp; *(разг: хороший)* cool

круше́ни|е (-я) *ср (поезда)* crash; *(перен: надежд, планов)* shattering

крыжо́вник (-а) *м собир (ягоды)* gooseberries *мн*

крыл|о́ (-а́; *nom pl* -ья, *gen pl* -ьев) *ср* wing

крыльц|о́ (-а́) *ср* porch

Крым (-а; *loc sg* -ý) *м* Crimea

кры́с|а (-ы) *ж* rat

кры́тый *прил* covered

кр|ы́ть (-о́ю, -о́ешь; *pf* **покры́ть**) *несов перех* to cover

кры́ш|а (-и) *ж* roof; *(разг: перен)* protection

кры́шк|а (-и; *gen pl* -ек) *ж (ящика, чайника)* lid

крюк (-а́; *nom pl* -чья, *gen pl* -чьев) *м* hook

крючо́к (-ка́) *м* hook; ~ **для вяза́ния** crochet hook

кря́ка|ть (-ю) *несов (утка)* to quack

кряхте́ть (-чу́, -ти́шь) *несов* to groan

ксероко́пи|я (-и) *ж* photocopy, Xerox ®

ксе́рокс (-а) *м* photocopier; *(копия)* photocopy, Xerox ®

кста́ти *вводн сл (между прочим)* incidentally, by the way; *(случайно)* by any chance ♦ *нареч (сказать, прийти)* at the right time

KEYWORD

кто (кого́; *см. Table 7*) *мест* **1** *(вопросительное, относительное)* who; **кто там?** who is there?

2 *(разг: кто-нибудь)* anyone; **е́сли кто позвони́т, позови́ меня́** if anyone phones, please call me **3: ма́ло ли кто** many (people); **ма́ло кто** few (people); **ма́ло кто пошёл в кино́** only a few of us went to the cinema; **кто из вас ...** which of you ...; **кто (его́) зна́ет!** who knows!

кто́-либо (кого́-либо; *как кто*; *см. Table 7*) *мест* = **кто́-нибудь**

кто́-нибудь (кого́-нибудь; *как кто*; *см. Table 7*) *мест (в вопросе)* anybody, anyone; *(в утверждении)* somebody, someone

кто́-то (кого́-то; *как кто*; *см. Table 7*) *мест* somebody, someone

куб (-а) *м (ГЕОМ, МАТ)* cube

ку́бик (-а) *м (игрушка)* building brick *или* block

ку́б|ок (-ка) *м (СПОРТ)* cup

кубоме́тр (-а) *м* cubic metre *(BRIT)* или meter *(US)*

кувши́н (-а) *м* jug *(BRIT)*, pitcher *(US)*

кувырка́|ться (-юсь) *несов возв* to somersault

куда́ *нареч (вопросительное, относительное)* where; ~ **ты положи́л мою́ ру́чку?** where did you put my pen?; **скажи́,** ~ **ты идёшь** tell me where you are going

куда́-либо *нареч* = **куда́-нибудь**

куда́-нибудь *нареч (в вопросе)* anywhere; *(в утверждении)* somewhere

куда́-то *нареч* somewhere

ку́др|и (-ей) *мн* curls *мн*

кудря́вый *прил (волосы)* curly; *(человек)* curly-haired

кузне́чик (-а) *м* grasshopper

ку́зов (-а; *nom pl* -а́) *м (АВТ)* back *(of van, lorry etc)*

кукаре́ка|ть (-ю) *несов* to crow

кукаре́ку *межд* cock-a-doodle-doo

ку́кл|а (-ы; *gen pl* -ол) *ж* (*также* *перен*) doll; (*в театре*) puppet

ку́кольный *прил*: ~ теа́тр puppet theatre (*BRIT*) *или* theater (*US*)

кукуру́з|а (-ы) *ж* (*БОТ*) maize; (*КУЛИН*) (sweet)corn

куку́шк|а (-и; *gen pl* -ек) *ж* cuckoo

кула́к (-а́) *м* fist

кул|ёк (-ька́) *м* paper bag

кулина́р (-а) *м* master chef

кулинари́|я (-и) *ж* (*КУЛИН*) cookery; (*магазин*) ≈ delicatessen

кули́с|а (-ы) *ж* (*ТЕАТР*) wing

куло́н (-а) *м* (*украшение*) pendant

кулуа́р|ы (-ов) *мн* (*ПОЛИТ*) lobby *ед*

кульмина́ци|я (-и) *ж* (*перен*) high point, climax

культ (-а) *м* cult

культу́р|а (-ы) *ж* culture

культу́рный *прил* cultural; (*растение*) cultivated

куми́р (-а) *м* (*также перен*) idol

купа́льник (-а) *м* swimming *или* bathing costume (*BRIT*), bathing suit (*US*)

купа́льный *прил*: ~ костю́м swimming *или* bathing costume (*BRIT*), bathing suit (*US*)

купа́|ть (-ю; *pf* вы́купать *или* ис~) *несов перех* to bath; ~ся (*pf* вы́купаться *или* ис~ся) *несов возв* to bathe; (*плавать*) to swim; (*в ванне*) to have a bath

купе́ *ср нескл* compartment (*in railway carriage*)

купе́йный *прил*: ~ ваго́н Pullman (car)

купи́рованный *прил* = **купе́йный**

куп|и́ть (-лю́, -ишь) *impf*

покупа́ть) *сов перех* to buy

купле́т (-а) *м* couplet

куплю́ *сов см.* **купи́ть**

ку́пол (-а; *nom pl* -а́) *м* cupola

купо́н (-а) *м* (*ценных бумаг*) ticket; **пода́рочный ~** gift voucher

купю́р|а (-ы) *ж* (*ЭКОН*) denomination; (*сокращение*) cut

куре́ни|е (-я) *ср* smoking

кури́льщик (-а) *м* smoker

кури́ный *прил* (*бульон*) chicken

кур|и́ть (-ю́, -ишь) *несов* (не)*перех* to smoke

ку́риц|а (-ицы; *nom pl* -ы) *ж* hen, chicken; (*мясо*) chicken

кур|о́к (-ка́) *м* hammer (*on gun*)

куро́рт (-а) *м* (*holiday*) resort

курс (-а) *м* course; (*ПОЛИТ*) policy; (*КОММ*) exchange rate; (*ПРОСВЕЩ*) year (*of university studies*); **быть** (*impf*) **в ку́рсе** (**де́ла**) to be well-informed; **входи́ть** (*impf*) **в че́го-н** to bring o.s. up to date on sth; **вводи́ть** (**ввести́** *pf*) **кого́-н в ~** (**чего́-н**) to put sb in the picture (*about* sth)

курса́нт (-а) *м* (*ВОЕН*) cadet

курси́в (-а) *м* italics *мн*

курси́р|овать (-ую) *несов*: ~ **ме́жду** +*instr* ... **и** +*instr* ... (*самолёт, автобус*) to shuttle between ... and ...; (*судно*) to sail between ... and ...

курсово́|й *прил*: ~**а́я рабо́та** project; ~**а́я ра́зница** (*КОММ*) difference in exchange rates

курсо́р (-а) *м* cursor

ку́рт|ка (-ки; *gen pl* -ок) *ж* jacket

курча́вый *прил* (*волосы*) curly; (*человек*) curly-haired

ку́р|ы *мн от* **ку́рица**

курье́р (-а) *м* messenger

куря́тин|а (-ы) *ж* chicken

куса́|ть (-ю) *несов перех* to bite; ~**ся** *несов возв* (*животные*) to bite

кусо́к (-ка́) м piece; ~ са́хара
sugar lump; ~ мы́ла bar of soap

куст (-а́) м (БОТ) bush

куста́рник (-а) м shrubbery

ку́та|ть (-ю; pf за~) несов перех
(плечи) to cover up; (ребёнка) to
bundle up; ~ся (pf за~ся) несов
возв: ~ся в +acc to wrap o.s. up in

ку́хн|я (-ни; gen pl -онь) ж
(помещение) kitchen; ру́сская ~
Russian cuisine

ку́хонный прил kitchen

ку́ч|а (-и) ж (песка, листьев) pile,
heap; (разг): +gen (денег,
проблем) loads of

ку́ша|ть (-ю; pf по~ или с~)
несов перех to eat

куше́т|ка (-ки; gen pl -ок) ж couch

кюве́т (-а) м ditch

Л, л

лабири́нт (-а) м maze; (перен)
labyrinth

лабора́нт (-а) м lab(oratory)
technician

лаборато́ри|я (-и) ж laboratory

ла́в|ка (-ки; gen pl -ок) ж (скамья)
bench; (магазин) shop

лавро́вый прил: ~ лист bay leaf

ла́гер|ь (-я) м camp

ладо́н|ь (-и) ж palm

ла́дно част (разг) О.К., all right

ла́зер (-а) м laser

ла́з|ить (-жу, -зишь) несов to
climb; (под стол) to crawl

ла́|й (-я) м barking

ла́йнер (-а) м liner

лак (-а) м (для ногтей, для пола)
varnish; ~ для воло́с hairspray

лакир|ова́ть (-у́ю; pf от~) несов

перех (изделие) to lacquer

лакони́чный прил (речь) laconic

ла́мп|а (-ы) ж lamp; (ТЕХ) tube; ~
дневно́го све́та fluorescent light

ла́мпоч|ка (-ки; gen pl -ек) ж
lamp; (для освещения) light bulb

ла́ндыш (-а) м lily of the valley

ла́п|а (-ы) ж (зверя) paw; (птицы)
foot

лапто́п (-а) м laptop

ларёк (-ька́) м stall

ласк|а́ть (-ю) несов перех
(ребёнка, девушку) to caress;
(собаку) to pet

ла́сковый прил affectionate

ла́стик (-а) м (разг) rubber (BRIT),
eraser

ла́сточ|ка (-ки; gen pl -ек) ж
swallow

Ла́тви|я (-и) ж Latvia

лату́н|ь (-и) ж brass

латы́н|ь (-и) ж Latin

лауреа́т (-а) м winner (of award)

ла́цкан (-а) м lapel

ла́|ять (-ю; pf про~) несов to bark

лга́ть (лгу, лжёшь итп, лгут; pf
солга́ть) несов to lie

лгун (-а́) м liar

ЛДПР ж сокр = Либера́льно-
демократи́ческая Па́ртия Росси́и

ле́бед|ь (-я; gen pl -е́й) м swan

лев (льва) м lion; (созвездие):
Лев Leo

левосторо́нний прил on the left

левш|а́ (-и́; gen pl -е́й) м/ж left-
handed person

ле́вый прил left; (ПОЛИТ) left-wing

лёг итп сов см. лечь

леге́нд|а (-ы) ж legend

лёгк|ий прил (груз) light;
(задача) easy; (боль, насморк)
slight; (характер, человек) easy-
going; ~ая атле́тика athletics
(BRIT), track (US)

легко́ нареч easily ♦ как сказ: это

легкó it's easy

легкоатлéт (-а) м athlete (in track and field events)

легковóй прил: **~áя маши́на, ~óй автомоби́ль** car, automobile (US)

лёгк|ое (-ого) ср (обычно мн) lung

легкомы́сленный прил frivolous, flippant; (поступок) thoughtless

легкомы́сли|е (-я) ср frivolity

лёгкост|ь (-и) ж (задания) simplicity, easiness

лéгче сравн прил от **лёгкий ♦** сравн нареч от **легкó ♦** как сказ: **больнóму сегóдня лéгче** the patient is feeling better today

лёд (льда́; loc sg **льду)** м ice

ледене́ц (-цá) м fruit drop

ледяной прил (покров) ice; (вода, взгляд) icy

леж|áть (-ý, -и́шь) несов (человек, животное) to lie; (предмет, вещи) to lie; ♦ (impf) в **больни́це** to be in hospital

лез etc несов см. **лезть**

лéзви|е (-я) ср blade

лез|ть (-у, -ешь; pt **-, -ла)** несов (выпадать: волосы) to fall out; (проникать): **~ в** +acc to climb in; **~** (impf) **на** +acc to climb (up)

лéйк|а (-и; gen pl **-ек)** ж watering can

лейкопла́стыр|ь (-я) м sticking plaster (BRIT), adhesive tape (US)

лейтена́нт (-а) м lieutenant

лéктор (-а) м lecturer

лéкци|я (-и) ж lecture

лён (льна) м (БОТ) flax; (ткань) linen

лени́вый прил lazy

лени́|ться (-ю́сь, -ишься; pf

по~) несов возв to be lazy

лéнт|а (-ы) ж ribbon; (ТЕХ) tape

лентя́|й (-я) м lazybones

лен|ь (-и) ж laziness ♦ как сказ: **ему́ ~ учи́ться/рабóтать** he can't be bothered studying/working

лепестóк (-кá) м petal

леп|и́ть (-лю́, -ишь; pf **вы́лепить)** несов перех to model; (pf **с~;** соты, гнёзда) to build

лес (-а; loc sg **-ý,** nom pl **-á)** м (большой) forest; (небольшой) wood ♦ собир (материал) timber (BRIT), lumber (US)

лесби́нк|а (-и; gen pl **-ок)** ж lesbian

лéск|а (-и) ж fishing line

леснóй прил forest

лéстниц|а (-ы) ж staircase; (ступени) stairs мн; (переносная) ladder; (стремянка) stepladder

лéстничн|ый прил: **~ая клéтка** stairwell

лéстный прил flattering

лест|ь (-и) ж flattery

лет etc сущ см. **год;** (возраст): **скóлько Вам лет?** how old are you?; **ему́ 16 лет** he is 16 (years old)

лет|áть (-ю) несов to fly

ле|тéть (-чý, -ти́шь) несов to fly

лéтний прил summer

лётн|ый прил: **~ое пóле** airfield

лéт|о (-а) ср summer

лéтом нареч in summer

лету́ч|ий прил: **~ая мышь** bat

лётчик (-а) м pilot

лéчащ|ий прил: **~ врач** ≈ consultant-in-charge (BRIT), ≈ attending physician (US)

лечéбниц|а (-ы) ж clinic

лечéбный прил (учреждение) medical; (трава) medicinal

лечéни|е (-я) ср (больных) treatment; (от простуды) cure

лечи́ть (**-у́, -ишь**) несов перех to treat; (**больно́го**) to treat sb for; **+gen** to treat sb for; **~ся** несов возв to undergo treatment

лечу́ несов см. **лете́ть**

ле́чь (**ля́гу, ля́жешь** итп, **ля́гут**; pt **лёг, -гла́**, impf **ложи́ться**) сов to lie down; (перен): **~ на** +acc (зада́ча) to fall on; **ложи́ться** (**~** pf) **в больни́цу** to go into hospital

лжец (**-а́**) м liar

лжи сущ см. **ложь**

лжи́вый прил (челове́к) deceitful

ли част (в вопро́се): **зна́ешь ~ ты, что ...** do you know that ... (в ко́свенном вопро́се): **спроси́, смо́жет ~ он нам помо́чь** ask if he can help us; (в раздели́тельном вопро́се): **она́ краси́вая, не так ~?** she's beautiful, isn't she?

либера́льный прил liberal

ли́бо союз (или) or

ли́вень (**-ня**) м downpour

ли́га (**-и**) ж (полит, спорт) league

ли́дер (**-а**) м leader

лиди́ровать (**-ую**) несов to lead, be in the lead

лиза́ть (**-жу́, -жешь**) несов перех (таре́лку, моро́женое) to lick

лизну́ть (**-у́, -ёшь**) сов перех to lick

ликвиди́ровать (**-ую**) (не)сов перех (фи́рму) to liquidate; (ору́жие) to destroy

ликви́дный прил (комм) liquid; (фи́рма) solvent

ликёр (**-а**) м liqueur

ли́лия (**-и**) ж lily

ли́ловый прил purple

лими́т (**-а**) м (на бензи́н) quota; (цен) limit

лимити́ровать (**-ую**) (не)сов

перех to limit; (це́ны) to cap

лимо́н (**-а**) м lemon

лимона́д (**-а**) м lemonade

лимо́нный прил lemon; **~ая кислота́** citric acid

лине́йка (**-йки**; gen pl **-ек**) ж (ли́ния) line; (инструме́нт) ruler; **тетра́дь в ~йку** lined notebook

ли́нза (**-ы**) ж lens

ли́ния (**-и**) ж line; **по ~и** +gen in the line of; **железнодоро́жная ~** railway (BRIT) или railroad (US) track

лино́леум (**-а**) м linoleum

линя́ть (3sg **-ет**; pf **по~**) несов (colour); (pf **об~**; живо́тные) to moult (BRIT), molt (US)

ли́пкий прил sticky

ли́пнуть (**-ну; -нул, -ла**; pf **при~**) несов (грязь, те́сто) to stick

липу́чка (**-ки**; gen pl **-ек**) ж (разг: застёжка) Velcro ® fastening

ли́рика (**-и**) ж lyric poetry

лири́ческий прил lyrical

лиса́ (**-ы́**; nom pl **-ы**) ж fox

лист (**-а́**; nom pl **-ья** м (расте́ния) leaf; (nom pl **-ы́**; бума́ги, желе́за) sheet

листа́ть (**-ю**) несов перех (страни́цы) to turn

листва́ (**-ы́**) ж собир foliage, leaves мн

листо́вка (**-ки**; gen pl **-ок**) ж leaflet

листо́к (**-ка́**) м (бума́ги) sheet

ли́стья итп сущ см. **лист**

Литва́ (**-ы́**) ж Lithuania

литерату́ра (**-ы**) ж literature; (та́кже: **худо́жественная ~**) fiction

литерату́рный прил literary

литр (**-а**) м litre (BRIT), liter (US)

ли́тровый прил (буты́лка итп) (one-)litre (BRIT), (one-)liter (US)

литурги́я (**-и**) ж liturgy

ли|ть (лью, льёшь; *pt* -л, -ла́) *несов перех* (*воду*) to pour; (*слёзы*) to shed; (*тех, детали, изделия*) to cast, mould (*BRIT*), mold (*US*) ♦ *неперех* (*вода, дождь*) to pour; **ли́ться** *несов возв* (*вода*) to pour out

лифт (-а) *м* lift

ли́фчик (-а) *м* bra

лихора́дк|а (-и) *ж* fever; (*на губах*) cold sore

лицев|о́й *прил*: ~**ая сторона́ мате́рии** the right side of the material

лице́|й (-я) *м* lycée, ≈ grammar school

лицеме́р (-а) *м* hypocrite

лицеме́рный *прил* hypocritical

лице́нзи|я (-и) *ж* licence (*BRIT*), license (*US*)

лиц|о́ (-а́; *nom pl* -ца) *ср* face; (*перен: индивидуальности*) image; (*ткани итп*) right side; (*линг*) person; **от** ~**ца́** +*gen* in the name of, on behalf of

ли́чно *нареч* (*знать*) personally; (*встретить*) in person

ли́чность (-и) *ж* individual

ли́чный *прил* personal; (*частный*) private

лиша́|ть(ся) (-ю) *несов от* **лиши́ть(ся)**

лише́ни|е (-я) *ср* (*прав*) deprivation; ~ **свобо́ды** imprisonment

лиш|и́ть (-у́, -и́шь; *impf* **лиша́ть**) *сов перех*: ~ **кого́-н/что-н** +*gen* (*отнять: прав, привилегий*) to deprive sb/sth of; (*покоя, счастья*) to rob sb/sth of

ли́шний *прил* (*вес*) extra; (*деньги, билет*) spare; ~ **раз** once again *или* more

лишь *част* (*только*) only ♦ *союз* (*как только*) as soon as; ~ **бы она́ согласи́лась!** if only she would

agree!

лоб (лба; *loc sg* лбу) *м* forehead

ло́бби *ср нескл* lobby

лобов|о́й *прил* frontal; ~**ое стекло́** windscreen (*BRIT*), windshield (*US*)

лов|и́ть (-лю́, -ишь; *pf* **пойма́ть**) *несов перех* to catch; (*момент*) to seize; ~ (*impf*) **ры́бу** to fish

ло́вкий *прил* (*человек*) agile; (*движение*) nimble; (*удар*) swift

ло́вл|я (-и) *ж* (*действие*) catching; **ры́бная** ~ fishing

лову́шк|а (-ки; *gen pl* -ек) *ж* trap

ло́гик|а (-и) *ж* logic

логи́чный *прил* logical

лого́тип (-а) *м* logo

ло́д|ка (-ки; *gen pl* -ок) *ж* boat

лоды́жк|а (-ки; *gen pl* -ек) *ж* ankle

ло́дыр|ь (-я) *м* (*разг*) idler

ло́ж|а (-и) *ж* (*в театре, в зале*) box

лож|и́ться (-у́сь, -и́шься) *несов от* **лечь**

ло́ж|ка (-ки; *gen pl* -ек) *ж* spoon

ло́жный *прил* false; (*вывод*) wrong

ложь (лжи; *instr sg* ло́жью) *ж* lie

лоз|а́ (-ы́; *nom pl* -ы) *ж* vine

ло́зунг (-а) *м* (*призыв*) slogan; (*плакат*) banner

ло́кон (-а) *м* ringlet

ло́к|оть (-тя; *gen pl* -те́й, *dat pl* -тя́м) *м* elbow

лом (-а) *м* crowbar ♦ *собир* (*для переработки*) scraps мн

лома́|ть (-ю) *несов перех* to break; (*традиции*) to challenge; (*планы*) to frustrate; (*механизм*) to break; ~ (*impf*) **го́лову над чем-то** to rack one's brains over sth; ~**ся** (*pf* **по-**) *несов возв* to break

ло́мтик (-а) *м* slice

Ло́ндон (-а) *м* London

ло́пас|ть (-и; *gen pl* -**е́й**) ж blade

лопа́т|а (-ы) ж spade

лопа́т|ка (-ки; *gen pl* -**ок**) ж
уменьш от **лопа́та**; (*АНАТ*)
shoulder blade

ло́пн|уть (-у; *pf* **ло́паться**) *сов*
(шар) to burst; (стекло) to shatter;
(*разг*: банк) to go bust

лоску́т (-**а́**) м (материи) scrap

лосо́с|ь (-я) м salmon

лос|ь (-я; *gen pl* -**е́й**) м elk, moose

лосьо́н (-а) м lotion

лотере́|я (-и) ж lottery

лото́ ср нескл lotto

лот|о́к (-**а́**) м (прилавок) stall

лохма́тый прил (животное)
shaggy; (человек) dishevelled

лохмо́т|ья (-**ев**) мн rags мн

ло́шад|ь (-и; *gen pl* -**е́й**) ж horse

луг (-а; *loc sg* -**у́**, *nom pl* -**а́**) м
meadow

лу́ж|а (-и) ж (на дороге) puddle;
(на полу, на столе) pool

лук (-а) м собир (плоды) onions
мн ♦ м (оружие) bow; **зелёный ~**
spring onion (*BRIT*), scallion

лу́кович|а (-ы) ж bulb

лун|а́ (-**ы́**) ж moon

лу́н|ка (-ки; *gen pl* -**ок**) ж hole

лу́нный прил: **~ свет** moonlight

лу́п|а (-ы) ж magnifying glass

луч (-**а́**) м (фонаря) beam

лучев|о́й прил: **~а́я боле́знь**
radiation disease

лу́чше сравн прил от **хоро́ший**
♦ сравн нареч от **хорошо́** ♦ как
сказ: **так ~** that's better ♦ част: **~
не опра́вдывайся** don't try and
justify yourself ♦ вводн сл: **~
(всего́), позвони́ ве́чером** it
would be better if you phone in the
evening; **больно́му ~** the patient is
feeling better; **нам ~, чем им** we're
better off than them; **как
нельзя́ ~** couldn't be better

лу́чш|ий прил (самый хоро́ший)
best; **в ~ем слу́чае мы зако́нчим
за́втра** the best-case scenario is
that we'll finish tomorrow; **э́то
(всё) к ~ему** it's (all) for the best

лы́ж|а (-и) ж (обычно мн) ski; см.
также **лы́жи**

лы́ж|и (-) мн (спорт) skiing ед;
во́дные ~ water-skis; (спорт)
water-skiing; **го́рные ~** downhill
skis; (спорт) downhill skiing

лы́жник (-а) м skier

лы́жный прил (крепления, мазь
итп) ski; (соревнования) skiing

лыжн|я́ (-**и́**) ж ski track

лысе́|ть (-ю; *pf* **об~** или **по~**)
несов to go bald

лы́син|а (-ы) ж bald patch

лы́сый прил bald

ль част = **ли**

льго́т|а (-ы) ж benefit;
(предприятиям итп) special term;
нало́говые ~ы tax relief

льго́тный прил (тариф)
concessionary; (условия)
privileged; (заём) special-rate; **~
биле́т** concessionary ticket

льди́н|а (-ы) ж ice floe

льняно́й прил (полотенце) linen

льс|ти́ть (-**щу**, -**сти́шь**; *pf*
по~сти́ть) несов: **~** +dat
(хвалить) to flatter; (самолюбию)
to gratify

любе́зност|ь (-и) ж (одолжение)
favour (*BRIT*), favor (*US*)

любе́зный прил polite; **бу́дьте
~!** excuse me, please!; **бу́дьте
~ы, принеси́те нам ко́фе!** would
you be so kind as to bring us some
coffee?

люб|и́мец (-**ца**) м favourite (*BRIT*),
favorite (*US*)

люби́мый прил (женщина, брат)
beloved; (писатель, занятие итп)
favourite (*BRIT*), favorite (*US*)

люби́тел|ь (-я) *м*
(*непрофессионал*) amateur;
~му́зыки/спо́рта music-/sports-
lover

люби́тельский *прил* amateur

люби́ть (-лю́, -ишь) *несов*
перех to love; (*музыку, спорт*
итп) to like

люб|ова́ться (-у́юсь, -у́ешься)
несов возв: **~ +instr** to admire

любо́вник (-а) *м* lover

любо́вный *прил* (*дела*) lover's;
(*песня, письмо*) love;
(*отношение, подход*) loving

люб|о́вь (-ви́; *instr sg* **-о́вью)** *ж*
love; (*привязанность*): **~ к +dat** (к
родине, к матери итп) love for; (к
чтению, к искусству итп) love of

любозна́тельный *прил*
inquisitive

люб|о́й *мест* (*всякий*) any
♦ **(-о́го)** *м* (*любой человек*)
anyone

любопы́тный *прил* (*случай*)
interesting; (*человек*) curious

любопы́тств|о (-а) *ср* curiosity

лю́бящий *прил* loving

лю́д|и (-е́й; *dat pl* **-ям,** *instr pl*
-ьми́, *prp pl* **-ях)** *мн* people *мн*;
(*кадры*) staff *ед*; **молоды́е**
~ young men; (*молодёжь*) young
people; *см. также* **челове́к**

лю́дный *прил* (*улица итп*) busy

людое́д (-а) *м* (*человек*) cannibal

людско́й *прил* human

люк (-а) *м* (*танка*) hatch; (*на*
доро́ге) manhole

люкс (-а) *м* (*о вагоне*) first-class
carriage; (*в гостинице*) first-class cabin
♦ *прил неизм* first-class

лю́стр|а (-ы) *ж* chandelier

ляга́|ть (-ю) *несов перех*
(*подлеж: лошадь, корова*) to
kick; **~ся** *несов возв* (*лошадь,*
корова) to kick

ля́гу *итп сов см.* **лечь**

лягу́шк|а (-и; *gen pl* **-ек)** *ж* frog

ля́жешь *итп сов см.* **лечь**

ля́ж|ка (-ки; *gen pl* **-ек)** *ж* thigh

ля́м|ка (-ки; *gen pl* **-ок)** *ж* strap

М, м

М *сокр* = **метро́**

м *сокр* (= **метр**) m

мавзоле́|й (-я) *м* mausoleum

магази́н (-а) *м* shop

маги́стр (-а) *м* master's degree

магистра́л|ь (-и) *ж* main line

маги́ческий *прил* magic

магни́т (-а) *м* magnet

магнитофо́н (-а) *м* tape recorder

ма́|зать (-жу, -жешь; *pf* **на~** *или*
по~) *несов перех* to spread; (*pf*
из~; *разг: пачкать*) to get dirty;
~ся (*pf* **из~ся)** *несов возв* (*разг:*
пачкаться) to get dirty; **~ся**
(**на~ся** *pf*) **кре́мом** to apply cream

маз|о́к (-ка́) *м* (*МЕД*) smear

маз|ь (-и) *ж* (*МЕД*) ointment; (*ТЕХ*)
grease

ма|й (-я) *м* May

---

1 Ма́я - International Day of
Workers' solidarity. Although, as
the name suggests, this holiday is
highly political, for most people it
is an opportunity to celebrate the
spring and to enjoy a short
holiday.

ма́|йка (-йки; *gen pl* **-ек)** *ж* vest
(*BRIT*), sleeveless undershirt (*US*)

майоне́з (-а) *м* mayonnaise

майо́р (-а) *м* (*ВОЕН*) major

мак (-а) *м* poppy

макаро́н|ы (-) *мн* pasta *ед*

мака́|ть (-ю) *несов перех* to dip

маке́т (-а) м model

ма́клер (-а) м (КОММ) broker

макну́ть (-у́, -ёшь) сов перех to dip

максима́льный прил maximum

ма́ксимум (-а) м maximum

макулату́р|а (-ы) ж собир wastepaper (for recycling)

малахи́т (-а) м malachite

мале́йший прил (ошибка) the slightest

ма́ленький прил small, little

мали́н|а (-ы) ж (кустарник) raspberry cane или bush; (ягоды) raspberries мн

KEYWORD

ма́ло чис: **ма́ло** +gen (друзей, книг) only a few, (работы, денег) not much, little; **нам да́ли ма́ло книг** they only gave us a few books; **у меня́ ма́ло де́нег** I don't have much money; **ма́ло ра́дости** little joy

♦ нареч not much; **она́ ма́ло измени́лась** she hasn't changed much

♦ как сказ: **мне э́того ма́ло** this is not enough for me; **ма́ло ли что** so what?; **ма́ло ли кто/где/когда́** it doesn't matter who/where/when; **ма́ло того́** (and) what's more; **ма́ло того́ что** not only

---

маловероя́тный прил improbable

малоду́шный прил cowardly

малокро́ви|е (-я) ср (sickle-cell) anaemia (BRIT) или anemia (US)

малоле́тний прил young

малообеспе́ченный прил disadvantaged

малоразви́тый прил underdeveloped

малочи́сленный прил small

ма́л|ый прил small, little; (доход, скорость) low ♦ как сказ: **пла́тье/пальто́ мне ма́ло** the dress/coat is too small for me; **са́мое ~ое** at the very least

малы́ш (-а́) м little boy

малы́ш|ка (-ки; gen pl -ек) ж little girl

ма́льчик (-а) м boy

малю́т|ка (-ки; gen pl -ок) м/ж baby

маля́р (-а́) м painter (and decorator)

маляри́|я (-и) ж malaria

ма́м|а (-ы) ж mummy (BRIT), mommy (US)

мама́ш|а (-и) ж mummy (BRIT), mommy (US)

мандари́н (-а) м tangerine

манда́т (-а) м mandate

мане́вр (-а) м manoevre (BRIT), maneuver (US)

мане́ж (-а) м (для верховой езды) manège; (цирка) ring; (для младенцев) playpen; (также: **легкоатлети́ческий ~**) indoor stadium

манеке́н (-а) м (портного) dummy; (в витрине) dummy, mannequin

манеке́нщиц|а (-ы) ж model

мане́р|а (-ы) ж manner; (художника) style

манже́т (-а) м cuff

маникю́р (-а) м manicure

манипули́р|овать (-ую) несов ~ +instr to manipulate

мани́|ть (-ю́, -ишь; pf по~) несов перех to beckon; (no pf: привлекать) to draw

манифе́ст (-а) м manifesto

манифеста́ци|я (-и) ж rally

ма́ни|я (-и) ж mania

ма́нный прил: ~**ая ка́ша**, ~**ая крупа́** semolina

маньяк (-а) м maniac

маразм (-а) м (МЕД) dementia; (перен: разг) idiocy; **старческий** ~ senile dementia

марафон (-а) м marathon

марафон|ец (-ца) м marathon runner

марган|ец (-ца) м manganese

маргарин (-а) м margarine

маргарит|ка (-ки; gen pl -ок) ж daisy

марин|овать (-ую; pf за~) несов перех (овощи) to pickle; (мясо, рыбу) to marinate, marinade

марионет|ка (-ки; gen pl -ок) ж puppet

мар|ка (-ки; gen pl -ок) ж (почтовая) stamp; (сорт) brand; (качество) grade; (модель) make; (деньги) mark; **торговая** ~ trademark

маркетинг (-а) м marketing

марксизм (-а) м Marxism

марл|я (-и) ж gauze

мармелад (-а) м fruit jellies мн

мародёр (-а) м looter

марочный прил (изделие) branded; (вино) vintage

Марс (-а) м Mars

март (-а) м March

марш (-а) м march

маршал (-а) м marshal

маршир|овать (-ую; pf про~) несов to march

маршрут (-а) м route

маршрутн|ый прил: ~ое такси fixed-route taxi

мас|ка (-ки; gen pl -ок) ж mask; (косметическая) face pack

маскарад (-а) м masked ball

маскир|овать (-ую; pf за~) несов перех to camouflage; **~ся** (pf за~ся) несов возв to camouflage o.s.

масленица (-ы) ж ≈ Shrovetide

маслён|ка (-ки; gen pl -ок) ж butter dish; (ТЕХ) oilcan

масленый прил (в масле) buttery

маслин|а (-ы) ж (дерево) olive (tree); (плод) olive

мас|ло (-ла; nom pl -ла, gen pl -ел) ср oil; (сливочное) butter

масляный прил oil; (пятно) oily

масон (-а) м (Free)mason

масс|а (-ы) ж (также физ) mass; (древесная) pulp; (много) loads мн

массаж (-а) м massage

массажист (-а) м masseur

массив (-а) м (водный) expanse; (земельный) tract; **горный** ~ massif; **жилой** или **жилищный** ~ housing estate (BRIT) или project (US)

массивный прил massive

массов|ый прил mass; **товары** ~**ого спроса** consumer goods

мастер (-а; nom pl -а) м master; (в цеху) foreman

мастерск|ая (-ой) ж workshop; (художника) studio

мастерств|о (-а) ср skill

масти|ка (-и) ж floor polish

мастит (-а) м mastitis

маст|ь (-и; gen pl -ей) ж (лошади) colour (BRIT), color (US); (КАРТЫ) suit

масштаб (-а) м scale

масштабный прил scale;

(*большой*) large-scale

мат (**-а**) *м* (ШАХМАТЫ) checkmate; (*половик, также* СПОРТ) mat; (*ругательства*) bad language

матема́тик (**-а**) *м* mathematician

матема́тик|**а** (**-и**) *ж* mathematics

ма́тери *etc сущ см.* **мать**

материа́л (**-а**) *м* material; (*обычно мн: следствия*) document

материа́льный *прил* material; (*финансовый*) financial

мате́рик (**-а́**) *м* continent; (*суша*) mainland

матери́нский *прил* maternal

матери́нств|**о** (**-а**) *ср* motherhood

мате́ри|**я** (**-и**) *ж* matter; (*разг: ткань*) cloth

матёрый *прил* (*зверь*) full-grown, mature; (*преступник*) hardened

ма́тер|**ь** (**-и**) *ж*: **Ма́терь Бо́жья** Mother of God

ма́терью *etc сущ см.* **мать**

ма́т|**ка** (**-ки**; *gen pl* **-ок**) *ж* uterus, womb; (ЗООЛ: *также*: **пчели́ная** ~) queen bee

ма́товый *прил* (*без блеска*) mat(t); **~ое стекло́** frosted glass

матра́с (**-а**) *м* mattress

матрёш|**ка** (**-ки**; *gen pl* **-ек**) *ж* Russian doll (*containing range of smaller dolls*)

ма́тричный *прил*: ~ **при́нтер** (КОМП) dot-matrix printer

матро́с (**-а**) *м* sailor

ма́туш|**ка** (**-ки**; *gen pl* **-ек**) *ж* (*мать*) mother

матч (**-а**) *м* match

мат|**ь** (**-ери**; *см.* Table 1) *ж* mother; **~-одино́чка** single mother

мафио́зный *прил* mafia

ма́фи|**я** (**-и**) *ж* the Mafia

мах (**-а**) *м* (*крыла*) flap; (*рукой*) swing; **одни́м ~ом** in a stroke; **с ма́ху** straight away

маха́ть (**-шу́, -шешь**) *несов*: ~ +*instr* to wave; (*крыльями*) to flap; ~ (*impf*) **кому́-н руко́й** to wave to sb

махина́тор (**-а**) *м* machinator

махина́ци|**я** (**-и**) *ж* machination

махн|**у́ть** (**-у́, -ёшь**) *сов* to wave

махо́рк|**а** (**-и**) *ж* coarse tobacco

махро́вый *прил* (*халат*) towelling; (*перен: отъявленный*) out-and-out; **~ая ткань** terry towelling

ма́чех|**а** (**-и**) *ж* stepmother

ма́чт|**а** (**-ы**) *ж* mast

маши́н|**а** (**-ы**) *ж* machine; (*автомобиль*) car

маши́нальный *прил* mechanical

машини́ст (**-а**) *м* driver, operator

машини́ст|**ка** (**-ки**; *gen pl* **-ок**) *ж* typist

маши́н|**ка** (**-ки**; *gen pl* **-ок**) *ж* machine; **пи́шущая** ~ typewriter

маши́нный *прил* machine; **~ое отделе́ние** engine room

машинопи́сный *прил* (*текст*) typewritten; **~ое бюро́** typing pool

машинострое́ни|**е** (**-я**) *ср* mechanical engineering

мая́к (**-а́**) *м* lighthouse

ма́ятник (**-а**) *м* (*часов*) pendulum

МВД *ср сокр* (= **Министе́рство вну́тренних дел**) ≈ the Home Office (BRIT), ≈ the Department of the Interior (US)

МВФ *м сокр* (= **Междунаро́дный валю́тный фонд**) IMF

мгл|**а** (**-ы**) *ж* haze; (*вечерняя*) gloom

мгнове́ни|**е** (**-я**) *ср* moment

мгнове́нный *прил* instant; (*злость*) momentary

МГУ *м сокр* (= **Моско́вский госуда́рственный университе́т**) Moscow State University

ме́бель (-и) ж собир furniture

мёд (-а) м honey

меда́ль (-и) ж medal

медальо́н (-а) м medallion

медве́диц|а (-ы) ж she-bear;
Больша́я Медве́дица the Great
Bear

медве́дь (-я) м bear

медвеж|**о́нок** (-**о́нка**; nom pl
-**а́та**, gen pl -**а́т**) м bear cub

ме́дик (-а) м medic

медикаме́нт (-а) м medicine

медици́н|а (-ы) ж medicine

ме́дленный прил slow

медли́тельный прил slow

ме́дл|**ить** (-ю, -ишь) несов to
delay; ~ (impf) **с реше́нием** to be
slow in deciding

ме́дный прил copper; (МУЗ) brass

медо́вый прил honey; ~ **ме́сяц**
honeymoon

медпу́нкт (-а) м сокр (=
медици́нский пункт) ≈ first-aid
centre (BRIT) или center (US)

медсестр|а́ (-ы́) ж сокр (=
медици́нская сестра́) nurse

меду́з|а (-ы) ж jellyfish

медь (-и) ж copper

междоме́ти|е (-я) ср interjection

ме́жду предл: ~ +instr between; ~
+gen (в окруже́нии) amongst; ~
про́чим (попутно) in passing;
(кста́ти) by the way; ~ **тем**
meanwhile; ~ **тем как** while; **они́
договори́лись** ~ **собо́й** they
agreed between them

междугоро́дный прил intercity

междунаро́дный прил
international

мел (-а) м chalk

меле́|**ть** (3sg -ет, pf **об**~) несов to
become shallower

ме́лкий прил small; (песо́к,
дождь) fine; (интере́сы) petty

мело́ди|я (-и) ж tune, melody

ме́лочный прил petty

ме́лоч|**ь** (-и; gen pl -**е́й**) ж
(пустяк) triviality; (подро́бность)
detail ♦ ж собир little things мн;
(де́ньги) small change

мель (-и; loc sg -и́) ж shallows мн;
сади́ться (**сесть** pf) **на** ~ (МОР) to
run aground

мелька́|**ть** (-ю) несов to flash past

мелькн|**у́ть** (-у́, -ёшь) сов to
flash

ме́льком нареч in passing

ме́льниц|а (-ы) ж mill

мельхио́р (-а) м nickel silver

ме́льче сравн прил от **ме́лкий**

мельч|**и́ть** (-у́, -и́шь, pf из~ или
раз~) несов перех (ножо́м) to
cut up into small pieces; (в сту́пке)
to crush

мемора́ндум (-а) м
memorandum

мемориа́л (-а) м memorial

мемуа́р|ы (-ов) мн memoirs мн

ме́неджер (-а) м manager

ме́неджмент (-а) м management

ме́нее сравн нареч от **ма́ло**
♦ нареч (опа́сный) less; (го́да)
less than; **тем не** ~ nevertheless

менинги́т (-а) м meningitis

менструа́ци|я (-и) ж
menstruation

ме́ньше сравн прил от **ма́лый**,
ма́ленький ♦ сравн нареч от
ма́ло less than; ~ **всего́**
least of all

ме́ньш|**ий** сравн прил от
ма́лый, **ма́ленький** ♦ прил: **по**
~**ей ме́ре** at least; **са́мое** ~**ее** no
less than

меньшинств|**о́** (-**а́**) ср собир
minority

меню́ ср нескл menu

меня́ мест см. **я**

мен|**я́ть** (-ю; pf **по**~) несов перех
to change; ~ (**по**~ pf) **что-н** +acc

to exchange sth for; **~ся** (pf **по~**) несов возв to change

ме́р|а (**-ы**) ж measure; (предел) limit; **в по́лной ~е** fully; **по ~е** +gen with; **по ~е того́ как** as

мерза́в|ец (**-ца**) м scoundrel

ме́рзкий прил disgusting; (погода, настроение) foul

мерзлот|а́ (**-ы́**) ж: **ве́чная ~** permafrost

мёрзлый прил (земля) frozen

мёрз|нуть (**-ну**; pt **-**, **-ла**, pf **за~**) несов to freeze

ме́р|ить (**-ю**, **-ишь**; pf **с~** или **из~**) несов перех to measure; (pf **по~**; примерять) to try on

ме́р|ка (**-ки**; gen pl **-ок**) ж measurements мн; (перен: критерий) standard

мерк|нуть (3sg **-нет**, pf **по~**) несов (также перен) to fade

ме́рный прил measured

мероприя́ти|е (**-я**) ср measure; (событие) event

мертве́|ть (**-ю**; pf **о~**) несов (от холода) to go numb; (pf **по~**; от страха, от горя) to be numb

мертве́ц (**-á**) м dead person

мёртвый прил dead

мерца́|ть (3sg **-ет**) несов to glimmer, flicker; (звёзды) to twinkle

ме|си́ть (**-шу́**, **-сишь**; pf **с~**) несов перех (тесто) to knead

ме́сс|а (**-ы**) ж (РЕЛ) Mass

ме|сти́ (**-ту́**, **-тёшь**; pt **мёл**, **-ла́**, pf **под~**) несов перех (пол) to sweep; (мусор) to sweep up

ме́стность (**-и**) ж area

ме́стный прил local

ме́ст|о (**-а**; nom pl **-á**) ср place; (действия) scene; (в театре, в поезде итп) seat; (багажа) item

местожи́тельств|о (**-а**) ср place of residence

местоиме́ни|е (**-я**) ср pronoun

местонахожде́ни|е (**-я**) ср location

месторожде́ни|е (**-я**) ср (угля, нефти) field

мест|ь (**-и**) ж revenge, vengeance

ме́сяц (**-а**; nom pl **-ы**) м month; (часть луны) crescent moon; (диск луны) moon

ме́сячный прил monthly

мета́лл (**-а**) м metal

металло́м (**-а**) м scrap metal

металлу́рги|я (**-и**) ж metallurgy

ме|та́ть (**-чу́**, **-чешь**) несов перех (гранату, диск итп) to throw; (pf **на~**; шов) to tack (BRIT), baste; **~ся** несов возв (в постели) to toss and turn; (по комнате) to rush about

мете́л|ь (**-и**) ж snowstorm, blizzard

метеоро́лог (**-а**) м meteorologist

метеосво́д|ка (**-ки**; gen pl **-ок**) ж сокр (= метеорологи́ческая сво́дка) weather forecast или report

метеоста́нци|я (**-и**) ж сокр (= метеорологи́ческая ста́нция) weather station

ме́|тить (**-чу**, **-тишь**; pf **по~**) несов перех to mark ♦ неперех: **~ в** +acc (в цель) to aim at; (pf **на~**) несов возв: **~ся в** +acc to aim at

ме́т|ка (**-ки**; gen pl **-ок**) ж mark

ме́ткий прил (точный) accurate; (замечание) apt

метл|á (**-ы́**) ж broom

метн|у́ть (**-у́**, **-ёшь**) сов перех to throw; **~ся** сов возв to rush

ме́тод (**-а**) м method

метр (**-а**) м metre (BRIT), meter (US); (линейка) measure

метрдоте́л|ь (**-я**) м head waiter

ме́трик|а (**-и**) ж birth certificate

метри́ческий прил metric

метро́ *ср нескл* metro, tube (BRIT),
subway (US)

мех (-а; *nom pl* -á) *м* fur

мех|а́ (-о́в) *мн* (кузнечный)
bellows *мн*

механи́зм (-а) *м* mechanism

меха́ник (-а) *м* mechanic

механи́ческий *прил* mechanical;
(цех) machine

мехово́й *прил* fur

мецена́т (-а) *м* patron

меч (-а́) *м* sword

мече́т|ь (-и) *ж* mosque

мечт|а́ (-ы; *gen pl* -а́ний) *ж* dream

мечта́ни|е (-я) *ср* daydream

мечта́|ть (-ю) *несов*: ~ (о +prp) to
dream (of)

меша́|ть (-ю); *pf* по~ *несов
перех* (суп, чай) to stir; (pf с~;
напитки, краски) to mix ♦ (pf
по~) *неперех* ♦ +dat (быть
помехой) to disturb, bother;
(реформам) to hinder; ~ (по~ pf)
кому́-н +infin (препятствовать) to
make it difficult for sb to do; ~ся
(pf с~ся) *несов возв* (путаться)
to get mixed up

меш|о́к (-ка́) *м* sack

меща|ни́н (-ани́на; *nom pl* -а́не,
gen pl -а́н) *м* petty bourgeois

меща́нский *прил*
petty-bourgeois; (вкусы) philistine

миг (-а) *м* moment

мига́|ть (-ю) *несов* to wink;
(огни) to twinkle

мигн|у́ть (-у́, -ёшь) *сов* to wink

ми́гом *нареч* (разг) in a jiffy

мигра́ци|я (-и) *ж* migration

МИД (-а) *м сокр* (=
Министе́рство иностра́нных
дел) ≈ the Foreign Office (BRIT), ≈
the State Department (US)

ми́довский *прил* (разг) Foreign
Office

ми́зерный *прил* meagre (BRIT),

meager (US)

мизи́н|ец (-ца) *м* (на руке) little
finger; (на ноге) little toe

микроавто́бус (-а) *м* minibus

микро́б (-а) *м* microbe

микрорайо́н (-а) *м* ≈ catchment
area

> **микрорайо́н** - These are modern
> housing estates with densely built
> blocks of flats and are a feature of
> all big Russian cities. They have
> their own infrastructure of schools,
> health centres, cinemas, and
> shops.

микроско́п (-а) *м* microscope

микрофи́льм (-а) *м* microfilm

микрофо́н (-а) *м* microphone

ми́ксер (-а) *м* mixer

миксту́р|а (-ы) *ж* mixture

милитари́ст (-а) *м* militarist

милиционе́р (-а) *м* policeman (in
Russia)

мили́ци|я (-и) *ж, собир* police (in
Russia)

миллиа́рд (-а) *м* billion

миллигра́мм (-а) *м* milligram(me)

миллиме́тр (-а) *м* millimetre
(BRIT), millimeter (US)

миллио́н (-а) *м* million

миллионе́р (-а) *м* millionaire

ми́л|овать (-ую); *pf* по~ *несов
перех* to have mercy on;
(преступника) to pardon

милови́дный *прил* pleasing

милосе́рди|е (-я) *ср* compassion

милосе́рдный *прил*
compassionate

ми́лостын|я (-и) *ж* alms *мн*

ми́лост|ь (-и) *ж* (доброта) kind-
heartedness; ~и про́сим! welcome!

ми́лый *прил* (симпатичный)
pleasant, nice; (дорогой) dear

ми́л|я (-и) *ж* mile

ми́мик|а (-и) *ж* expression

ми́мо *нареч* past ♦ *предл:* ~ +*gen* past

мимолётный *прил* fleeting

мимохо́дом *нареч* on the way; (*упомяну́ть*) in passing

ми́н|а (-ы) *ж* (*ВОЕН*) mine

минда́лин|а (-ы) *ж* (*МЕД*) tonsil

минда́л|ь (-я́) *м* almond

минера́л (-а) *м* mineral

минздра́в (-а) *м сокр* (= **министе́рство здравоохране́ния**) Ministry of Health

миниатю́р|а (-ы) *ж* miniature; (*ТЕАТР*) short play

миниатю́рный *прил* miniature

минима́льный *прил* minimum

ми́нимум (-а) *м* minimum ♦ *нареч* at least, minimum; **прожи́точный ~** minimum living wage

мини́р|овать (-ую); *pf* **за~)** (*не*)*сов перех* (*ВОЕН*) to mine

министе́рств|о (-а) *ср* ministry

мини́стр (-а) *м* (*ПОЛИТ*) minister

ми́нный *прил* mine; **~ое по́ле** minefield

мин|ова́ть (-у́ю) (*не*)*сов перех* to pass

мину́вший *прил* past

ми́нус (-а) *м* minus

мину́т|а (-ы) *ж* minute

мину́тный *прил* (*стрелка*) minute; (*дело*) brief

ми́н|уть (*3sg* **-ет**) *сов* (*испо́лниться*): **ей/ему́ -уло 16 лет** she/he has turned 16 '

минфи́н (-а) *м сокр* (*разг.* = **Министе́рство фина́нсов**) Ministry of Finance

мир (-а; *nom pl* **-ы́)** *м* world; (*Вселе́нная*) universe; (*loc sg* **-у́;** *рел*) (secular) world; (*состоя́ние без войны́*) peace

мир|и́ть (-ю́, -и́шь; *pf* **по~** *или* **при~**) *несов перех* to reconcile; **~ся** (*pf* **по~ся**) *несов возв:* **~ся с** +*instr* to make up *или* be reconciled with; (*pf* **при~ся; с недоста́тками**) to reconcile o.s to, come to terms with

ми́рн|ый *прил* peaceful; **~ое вре́мя** peacetime; **~ое населе́ние** civilian population; **~ые перегово́ры** peace talks *или* negotiations

мировоззре́ни|е (-я) *ср* philosophy of life

мирово́й *прил* world

миролюби́вый *прил* peaceable

миротво́р|ец (-ца) *м* peacemaker, peacekeeper

миротво́рческ|ий *прил* peacemaking; **~ие войска́** peacekeeping force

мирско́й *прил* secular, lay

ми́сси|я (-и) *ж* mission

ми́стер (-а) *м* Mr

ми́стик|а (-и) *ж* mysticism

ми́тинг (-а) *м* rally

митрополи́т (-а) *м* metropolitan

миф (-а) *м* myth

мише́н|ь (-и) *ж* target

младе́н|ец (-ца) *м* infant, baby

мла́дш|ий *сравн прил от* **молодо́й**

мла́дший *прил* younger; (*сотру́дник, класс*) junior

млекопита́ющ|ее (-его) *ср* mammal

мле́чный *прил:* **Мле́чный Путь** the Milky Way

мм *сокр* (= **миллиме́тр**) mm

мне *мест см.* **я**

мне́ни|е (-я) *ср* opinion

мни́мый *прил* imaginary; (*ло́жный*) fake

мни́тельный *прил* suspicious

мно́г|ие *прил* many ♦ (**-их**) *мн*

(мно́го люде́й) many (people)

мно́го чис: ~ +gen (книг, друзе́й) many, a lot of; (рабо́ты) much, a lot of ♦ нареч (разгова́ривать, пить итп) a lot; (+comparative: гора́здо) much; ~ книг тебе́ да́ли? did they give you many или a lot of books?; ~ рабо́ты тебе́ да́ли? did they give you much или a lot of work?

многоде́тный прил with a lot of children

мно́гое (-ого) ср a great deal

многозначи́тельный прил significant

многозна́чный прил (число́) multi-digit; (сло́во) polysemous

многокра́тный прил repeated

многоле́тний прил (пла́ны) long-term; (труд) of many years; (расте́ния) perennial

многолю́дный прил crowded

многонациона́льный прил multinational

многообеща́ющий прил promising

многообра́зие (-я) ср variety

многообра́зный прил varied

многосло́вный прил verbose

многосторо́нний прил (перегово́ры) multilateral; (ли́чность) many-sided; (интере́сы) diverse

многото́чие (-я) ср (линг) ellipsis

многоуважа́емый прил (в обраще́нии) Dear

многочи́сленный прил numerous

многоэта́жный прил multistorey (BRIT), multistory (US)

мно́жественный прил: ~ое число́ (линг) the plural (number)

мно́жеств|о (-а) ср: ~ +gen a great number of

множи́тельн|ый прил: ~ая

те́хника photocopying equipment

мно́ж|ить (-у, -ишь; pf y~) несов перех to multiply

мной мест см. я

мобилиз|ова́ть (-у́ю) (не)сов перех to mobilize

моби́льник (-а) м (разг) mobile

моби́льн|ый прил mobile; ~ телефо́н mobile phone

мог итп несов см. мочь

моги́л|а (-ы) ж grave

могу́ etc несов см. мочь

могу́чий прил mighty

могу́ществ|о (-а) ср power, might

мо́д|а (-ы) ж fashion; см. также мо́ды

модели́р|овать (-ую) (не)сов перех (оде́жду) to design; (pf с~; проце́сс, поведе́ние) to simulate

моде́л|ь (-и) ж model

модель́ёр (-а) м fashion designer

моде́м (-а) м (комп) modem

модернизи́р|овать (-ую) (не)сов перех to modernize

мо́дный прил fashionable

мо́д|ы (-) мн fashions мн; журна́л мод fashion magazine

мо́жет несов см. мочь ♦ вводн сл (та́кже: ~ быть) maybe

мо́жно как сказ (возмо́жно): ~ +infin it is possible to do; (войти́)? may I (come in)?; как ~ лу́чше as well as possible

мозаи́к|а (-и) ж (узо́р) mosaic

мозг (-а; loc sg -у́, nom sg -и́) м brain; спинно́й ~ spinal cord

мозгово́й прил cerebral; ~ центр (перен) nerve centre (BRIT) или center (US)

мозо́л|ь (-и) ж callus

мой (моего́; см. Table 8; f моя́, притяж мест nt моё, pl мои́) my; по-мо́ему my way; (по моему́ мне́нию) in my opinion

МОК (-а) м сокр (= Междунаро́дный олимпи́йский комите́т) IOC

мо́к|нуть (-ну; pt -, -ла) несов to get wet; (лежа́ть в воде́) to be soaking

мо́крый прил wet

мол (-а; loc sg -ý) м breakwater, mole ♦ част (разг): он, ~, ничего́ **не зна́ет** he says he knows nothing

молв|á (-ы) ж rumour (BRIT), rumor (US)

моле́б|ен (-на) м (РЕЛ) service

моле́кул|а (-ы) ж molecule

моли́тв|а (-ы) ж prayer

моли́твенник (-а) м prayer book

мол|и́ться (-ю́сь, -и́шься; pf по~) несов возв: ~ +dat to pray to

мо́лни|я (-и) ж lightning; (застёжка) zip (fastener) (BRIT), zipper (US)

молодёжный прил youth; (мода, газета) for young people

молодёж|ь (-и) ж собир young people мн

молоде́|ть (-ю; pf по~) несов to become younger

молод|е́ц (-ца́) м strong fellow; ~! (разг) well done!; она́/он ~! (разг) she/he has done well!

молодожён (-а) м (обычно мн) newlywed

молодо́й прил young; (карто́фель, листва́) new

мо́лодост|ь (-и) ж youth

моложа́вый прил (челове́к) young-looking; (вид, лицо́) youthful

моло́же сравн прил от **молодо́й**

молок|о́ (-а́) ср milk

мо́лот (-а) м hammer

молот|о́к (-ка́) м hammer

мо́лотый прил (ко́фе, пе́рец) ground

моло́|ть (**мелю́, ме́лешь**; pf **с~**

или **по~**) несов перех to grind

моло́чник (-а) м (посу́да) milk jug

моло́чный прил (проду́кты, скот) dairy; (кокте́йль) milk

мо́лча нареч silently; (согласи́ться) tacitly

молчали́вый прил silent; (согла́сие) tacit

молча́ни|е (-я) ср silence

молч|а́ть (-ý, -и́шь) несов to be silent; ~ (impf) о +prp to keep silent или quiet about

мол|ь (-и) ж moth

мольбе́рт (-а) м easel

моме́нт (-а) м moment; (докла́да) point; теку́щий ~ the current situation

момента́льный прил instant

монасты́р|ь (-я́) м (мужско́й) monastery; (же́нский) convent

мона́х (-а) м monk

мона́хин|я (-и; gen pl -ь) ж nun

моне́т|а (-ы) ж coin

моне́тный прил: ~ двор mint

монито́р (-а) м monitor

монографи|я (-и) ж monograph

монопо́ли|я (-и) ж monopoly

моното́нный прил monotonous

монта́ж (-а́) м (сооруже́ния) erection; (механи́зма) assembly; (ка́дров) editing

монтёр (-а) м fitter; (ЭЛЕК) electrician

монти́р|овать (-ую; pf с~) несов перех (обору́дование) to assemble; (фильм) to edit

монуме́нт (-а) м monument

мора́л|ь (-и) ж morals мн, ethics мн; (ба́сни, ска́зки) moral

мора́льный прил moral

морато́ри|й (-я) м moratorium

морг (-а) м morgue

морга́|ть (-ю) несов to blink; (подми́гивать): ~ +dat to wink (at)

моргн|у́ть (-у́, -ёшь) *сов* to blink; (*подмигнуть*): ~ (+*dat*) to wink (at)

мо́рд|а (-ы) *ж (животного)* muzzle; (*разг: человека*) mug

мо́р|е (-я; *nom pl* **-я́,** *gen pl* **-е́й)** *ср* sea

морехо́дный *прил* naval

морж (-а́) *м* walrus

мор|и́ть (-ю́, -и́шь; *pf* **по~)** *несов перех (насекомых)* to exterminate

морко́в|ь (-и) *ж* carrots *мн*

моро́жен|ое (-ого) *ср* ice cream

моро́женый *прил* frozen

моро́з (-а) *м* frost

моро́зильник (-а) *м* freezer

морози́льн|ый *прил:* ~**ая ка́мера** deepfreeze

моро́|зить (-жу, -зишь) *несов перех* to freeze

моро́зный *прил* frosty

морос|и́ть (3sg **-и́т)** *несов* to drizzle

моро́ч|ить (-у, -ишь; *pf* **за~)** *несов перех:* ~ **го́лову кому́-н** (*разг*) to pull sb's leg

морск|о́й *прил* sea; (*био*) marine; (*курорт*) seaside; ~**о́е пра́во** maritime law; ~**а́я боле́знь** seasickness; ~**а́я сви́нка** guinea pig

морщи́н|а (-ы) *ж (на лице)* wrinkle

морщи́нистый *прил* wrinkled

мо́рщ|ить (-у, -ишь; *pf* **на~)** *несов перех (брови)* to knit; (*лицо*) to screw up; ~**ся** (*pf* **с~ся**) *несов возв:* ~**ся от** (+*gen от старости*) to become wrinkled from; (*от боли*) to wince in

моря́к (-а́) *м* sailor

Москв|а́ (-ы́) *ж* Moscow

москви́ч (-а́) *м* Muscovite

мост (-а́; *loc sg* **-у́)** *м* bridge

мо́стик (-а) *м* bridge; **капита́нский** ~ bridge (*NAUT*)

мо|сти́ть (-щу́, -сти́шь; *pf* **вы́мостить)** *несов перех* to pave

мостов|а́я (-о́й) *ж* road

мота́|ть (-ю; *pf* **на~)** *несов перех (нитки)* to wind ♦ (*pf* **по~**) *неперех:* ~ (+*instr головой*) to shake; ~**ся** *несов возв* to swing

моте́л|ь (-я) *м* motel

моти́в (-а) *м (преступления)* motive; (*мелодия*) motif

мотиви́р|овать (-ую) (*не*)*сов перех* to justify

мот|о́к (-ка́) *м* skein

мото́р (-а) *м* motor; (*автомобиля, лодки*) engine

моторо́ллер (-а) *м* (motor) scooter

мотоци́кл (-а) *м* motorcycle

мотыл|ёк (-ька́) *м* moth

мох (мха; *loc sg* **мху,** *nom pl* **мхи)** *м* moss

мохе́р (-а) *м* mohair

мохна́тый *прил (животное)* shaggy

моч|а́ (-и́) *ж* urine

моча́л|ка (-ки; *gen pl* **-ок)** *ж* sponge

мочево́й *прил:* ~ **пузы́рь** bladder

моч|и́ть (-у́, -ишь; *pf* **за~)** *несов перех* to wet; (*pf* **за~;** *белье*) to soak

мо|чь (-гу́, -жешь *etc,* **-гут;** *pt* **-г, -гла́, -гло́;** *pf* **с~)** *несов:* ~ +*infin* can do, to be able to do; ~ **гу́ игра́ть на гита́ре/говори́ть по-англи́йски** I can play the guitar/speak English; **он мо́жет прийти́** he can come, he is able to come; **я сде́лаю всё, что** ~**гу́** I will do all I can; **за́втра мо́жешь не приходи́ть** you don't have to come tomorrow; **он мо́жет**

обидеться he may well be offended; **не ~гу поня́ть э́того** I can't understand this; **мо́жет быть** maybe; **не мо́жет быть!** it's impossible!

моше́нник (-а) *м* swindler

моше́ннича|ть (-ю); *pf* с~) *несов* to swindle

мо́ш|ка (-ки; *gen pl* -ек) *ж* midge

мо́щност|ь (-и) *ж* power

мо́щный *прил* powerful

мощь (-и) *ж* might, power

мо́|я́ (-е́й) *притяж мест см.* мой

мрак (-а) *м* darkness

мра́мор (-а) *м* marble

мрачне́|ть (-ю; *pf* по~) *несов* to grow dark; *(лицо)* to darken

мра́чный *прил* gloomy

мсти́тел|ь (-я) *м* avenger

мсти́тельный *прил* vindictive

мстить (мщу, мстишь; *pf* отомсти́ть) *несов*: ~ кому́-н to take revenge on sb

МТС *ж сокр* (= междунаро́дная телефо́нная ста́нция) ≈ intercity telephone exchange

му́дрост|ь (-и) *ж* wisdom

му́дрый *прил* wise

муж (-а; *nom pl* -ья́, *gen pl* -е́й) *м* husband

мужа́|ть (-ю; *pf* воз~) *несов* to mature; **~ся** *несов возв* to take heart, have courage

му́жественный *прил (поступок)* courageous

му́жеств|о (-а) *ср* courage

мужи́к (-а́) *м (разг: мужчина)* geezer, guy

мужско́й *прил* men's; *(характер)* masculine; *(органы, клетка)* male; **~ род** masculine gender

мужчи́н|а (-ы) *м* man

музе́|й (-я) *м* museum

му́зык|а (-и) *ж* music

музыка́л|ьный *прил* musical; **~ая**

шко́ла music school

музыка́нт (-а) *м* musician

му́к|а (-и) *ж* torment

мук|а́ (-и́) *ж* flour

му́льтик (-а) *м (разг)* cartoon

мультимеди́йный *прил (КОМП)* multimedia

мультиплика́тор (-а) *м* animator

мультипликацио́нный *прил*: **~ фильм** cartoon, animation film

мунди́р (-а) *м* uniform; **карто́фель в ~е** jacket potatoes

муниципалите́т (-а) *м* municipality, city council

мураве́|й (-ья́) *м* ant

мура́ш|ки (-ек) *мн*: **у меня́ ~ по спине́ бе́гают** shivers are running down my spine

мурлы́|кать (-чу, -чешь) *несов* to purr

муска́т (-а) *м (орех)* nutmeg

му́скул (-а) *м* muscle

мускули́стый *прил* muscular

му́сор (-а) *м* rubbish (BRIT), garbage (US)

му́сорн|ый *прил* rubbish (BRIT), garbage (US); **~ое ведро́** dustbin (BRIT), trash can (US)

мусоропрово́|д (-а) *м* refuse *или* garbage (US) chute

мусульма́нин (-а) *м* Muslim

мута́нт (-а) *м* mutant

мута́ци|я (-и) *ж* mutation

мути́|ть (-чу́, -тишь; *pf* вз~ *или* за~) *несов перех (жидкость)* to cloud; **~ся** *(pf* за~*ся) несов возв (вода, раствор)* to become cloudy

мутне́|ть *(3sg* -ет; *pf* по~) *несов (жидкость)* to become cloudy; *(взор)* to grow dull

му́тный *прил (жидкость)* cloudy; *(стекло)* dull

му́х|а (-и) *ж* fly

мухомо́р (-а) *м (БОТ)* fly agaric

муче́ни|е (-я) *ср* torment, torture

мученик (-а) *м* martyr

мучитель (-я) *м* tormentor

мучительный *прил* agonizing

мучить (-у, -ишь; *pf* **за~** *или* **из~**) *несов перех* to torment; **~ся** (*pf* **за~ся**) *несов возв*: **~ся** +*instr* (*сомнениями*) to be tormented by; **~ся** (*impf*) **над** +*instr* to agonize over

мчать (-у, -ишь) *несов* (*машину*) to speed along; (*лошадь*) to race along; **мчаться** *несов возв* (*поезд*) to speed along; (*лошадь*) to race along

мщени|е (-я) *ср* vengeance, revenge

мы (*нас*; *см*. Table 6b) *мест* we; **~ с тобой/женой** you/my wife and I

мыл|ить (-ю, -ишь; *pf* **на~**) *несов перех* to soap; **~ся** (*pf* **на~ся**) *несов возв* to soap o.s.

мыл|о (-а) *ср* soap

мыльниц|а (-ы) *ж* soap dish

мыльный *прил* (*пена*) soap; **~ая опера** soap (opera)

мыс (-а; *loc sg* **-ý**, *nom pl* **-ы**) *м* point

мысленный *прил* mental

мыслитель (-я) *м* thinker

мысл|ить (-ю, -ишь) *несов* to think ♦ *перех* to imagine

мысл|ь (-и) *ж* thought; (*идея*) idea; **задняя ~** ulterior motive; **образ мыслей** way of thinking

мыть (**мою, моешь**; *pf* **вы~** *или* **помыть**) *несов перех* to wash; **мыться** (*pf* **вы~ся** *или* **помыться**) *несов возв* to wash o.s.

мыч|ать (-ý, -ишь; *pf* **про~**) *несов* (*корова*) to moo

мышеловк|а (-и; *gen pl* **-ок**) *ж* mousetrap

мышечный *прил* muscular

мышк|а (-и; *gen pl* **-ек**) *ж* mouse;

под ~кой under one's arm

мышлени|е (-я) *ср* (*способность*) reason; (*процесс*) thinking

мышц|а (-ы) *ж* muscle

мыш|ь (-и) *ж* (*ЗООЛ, КОМП*) mouse

мэр (-а) *м* mayor

мэри|я (-и) *ж* city hall

мягкий *прил* soft; (*движения*) smooth; (*характер, климат*) mild; (*наказание*) lenient; **~ вагон** railway carriage with soft seats; **~ знак** soft sign (*Russian letter*)

мягко *нареч* softly; (*упрекать*) mildly; **~ говоря** to put it mildly

мякот|ь (-и) *ж* flesh; (*мясо*) fillet

мямл|ить (-ю, -ишь; *pf* **про~**) *несов перех* to mumble

мясник (-а) *м* butcher

мясной *прил* (*котлета*) meat; **~ магазин** the butcher's

мяс|о (-а) *ср* meat

мясорубк|а (-и; *gen pl* **-ок**) *ж* mincer (*BRIT*), grinder (*US*); (*перен*) carnage

мят|а (-ы) *ж* mint

мятеж (-á) *м* revolt

мятный *прил* mint

мятый *прил* (*одежда*) creased

мять (**мну, мнёшь**; *pf* **измять** *или* **с~**) *несов перех* (*одежду*) to crease; (*бумагу*) to crumple; **мяться** *несов возв* (*разг*: *человек*) to shilly-shally; (*pf* **помяться** *или* **смяться**; *одежда*) to get creased

мяука|ть (-ю; *pf* **про~**) *несов* to miaow, mew

мяч (-á) *м* ball; **футбольный ~** football

Н, н

KEYWORD

на предл; +acc **1** (направление на поверхность) on; **положи́ таре́лку на стол** put the plate on the table

2 (направление в какое-нибудь место) to; **сесть** (pf) **на по́езд** to get on(to) the train

3 (об объекте воздействия): **обрати́ внима́ние на э́того челове́ка** pay attention to this man; **нажми́ на педа́ль/кно́пку** press the pedal/button; **я люблю́ смотре́ть на дете́й/на звёзды** I love watching the children/the stars

4 (о времени, сроке) for; **он уе́хал на ме́сяц** he has gone away for a month

5 (о цели, о назначении) for; **де́ньги на кни́ги** money for books

6 (о мере) into; **дели́ть** (impf) **что-н на ча́сти** to divide sth into parts

7 (при сравнении): **я получа́ю на сто рубле́й ме́ньше** I get one hundred roubles less

8 (об изменении состояния) into; **на́до перевести́ текст на англи́йский** the text must be translated into English

♦ предл; +prp **1** (нахождение на поверхности) on; **кни́га на по́лке** the book is on the shelf; **на де́вочке ша́пка/шу́ба** the girl has a hat/fur coat on

2 (о пребывании где-нибудь) in; **на Украи́не/Кавка́зе** in the Ukraine/Caucasus; **на у́лице** in the street; **быть** (impf) **на рабо́те/**

заседа́нии to be at work/at a meeting

3 (о времени осуществления чего-л): **встре́тимся на сле́дующей неде́ле** let's meet next week

4 (об объекте воздействия) on; **сосредото́читься** (pf)/**останови́ться** (pf) **на чём-н** to concentrate/dwell on sth

5 (о средстве осуществления чего-л): **е́здить на по́езде/ велосипе́де** to travel by train/ bicycle; **игра́ть** (impf) **на роя́ле/ скри́пке** to play the piano/violin; **ката́ться** (impf) **на лы́жах/конька́х** to go skiing/skating; **говори́ть** (impf) **на ру́сском/англи́йском языке́** to speak (in) English/Russian

6 (о составной части предмета): **ка́ша на воде́** porridge made with water

на (на́те) част (разг) here (you are)

набежа́ть (как **бежа́ть**; см. Table 20; impf **набега́ть**; сов (разг: тучи) to gather; (наскочить): ~ **+acc** to run into; (о волны: на берег) to lap against

набело нареч: **переписа́ть что-н** ~ to write sth out neatly

на́бережн|ая (-ой) ж embankment

набива́|ть(ся) (-ю(сь)) несов от **наби́ть(ся)**

наби́вк|а (-и) ж stuffing

набира́|ть (-ю) несов от **набра́ть**

наби́ть (-ью, -ьёшь; impf **набива́ть)** сов перех: ~ (**+instr**) to stuff (with); **набива́ть (~ pf) це́ну** (разг) to talk up the price; **~ся** (impf **набива́ться)** сов возв (разг): **~ся в +acc** to be crammed into

наблюда́тел|ь (-я) *м* observer

наблюда́тельный *прил* (человек) observant; **~ пункт** observation point

наблюда́|ть (-ю) *несов перех* to observe ♦ *неперех:* **~ за** +*instr* to monitor

набо́к *нареч* to one side

набо́р (-а) *м* (совокупность) set; (типог) typesetting

набо́рщик (-а) *м* typesetter

набра́сыва|ть (-ю) *несов от* **наброса́ть, набро́сить; ~ся** *несов от* **набро́ситься**

набра́|ть (-еру́, -ерёшь; *pt* **-ра́л, -рала́, -ра́ло,** *impf* **набира́ть)** *сов перех:* **~** +*gen* (цветы) to pick; (воду) to take; (студентов) to take on; (скорость, высоту, баллы) to gain; (код) to dial; (текст) to typeset

наброса́|ть (-ю; *impf* **набра́сывать)** *сов перех* (план, текст) to sketch out ♦ *(не)перех:* **~** +*acc или* +*gen* (вещей, окурков) to throw about

набро́|сить (-шу, -сишь; *impf* **набра́сывать)** *сов перех* (пальто, платок) to throw on; **~ся** *(impf* **набра́сываться)** *сов возв:* **~ся на** +*acc* (на жертву) to fall upon

набро́с|ок (-ка) *м* (рисунок) sketch; (статьи) draft

набу́х|нуть (3sg -нет, *pt* **-, -ла,** *impf* **набуха́ть)** *сов* to swell up

навал|и́ть (-алю́, -а́лишь; *impf* **нава́ливать)** *сов (не)перех:* **~** +*acc или* +*gen* (мусору) to pile up; **~ся** *(impf* **нава́ливаться)** *сов возв:* **~ся на** +*acc* (на дверь итп) to lean into

нава́лом *как сказ:* **~** +*gen* (разг) loads of; **у него́ де́нег ~** he has

loads of money

наведе́ни|е (-я) *ср* (порядка) establishment; (справок) making

навек(и) *нареч* (навсегда) forever

наве́рно(е) *вводн сл* probably

наверняка́ *вводн сл* (конечно) certainly ♦ *нареч* (несомненно) definitely, for sure

наверста́|ть (-ю; *impf* **навёрстывать)** *сов перех* (типог) to typeset; **навёрстывать (~ pf) упу́щенное** *или* **поте́рянное вре́мя** to make up for lost time

наве́рх *нареч* up; (на ве́рхний этаж) upstairs; (на пове́рхность) to the top

наверху́ *нареч* at the top; (на верхнем этаже) upstairs

наве́с (-а) *м* canopy

нав|ести́ (-еду́, -едёшь; *pt* **-ёл, -ела́, -ело́,** *impf* **наводи́ть)** *сов перех* (ужас, грусть итп) to cause; (бинокль) to focus; (орудие) to aim; (порядок) to establish; **наводи́ть (~ pf) кого́-н на** +*acc* (на место, на след) to lead sb to; **наводи́ть (~ pf) спра́вки** to make inquiries

наве́|стить (-щу́, -сти́шь; *impf* **навеща́ть)** *сов перех* to visit

навзни́чь *нареч* on one's back

навига́ци|я (-и) *ж* navigation

нави́с|нуть (-ну; *pt* **-, -ла;** *impf* **нависа́ть)** *сов:* **~ на** +*acc* (волосы: на лоб) to hang down over

нав|оди́ть (-ожу́, -о́дишь) *несов от* **навести́**

наводне́ни|е (-я) *ср* flood

наво́з (-а) *м* manure

наво́лочк|а (-ки; *gen pl* **-ек)** *ж* pillowcase

навреди́|ть (-жу́, -ди́шь) *сов от* **вреди́ть**

навсегда́ *нареч* forever; раз и ~ once and for all

навстре́чу *предл*: ~ +*dat* towards ♦ идти́ ~ кому́-н (*перен*) to give sb a hand

на́вык (-а) *м* skill

навы́нос *нареч* to take away (*BRIT*), to go (*US*)

на́выпуск *нареч* outside, over

навяза́ть (-яжу́, -я́жешь; *impf* навя́зывать) *сов перех*: ~ что-н кому́-н to impose sth on sb; ~ся (*impf* навя́зываться) *сов возв* to impose o.s.

навя́зчивый *прил* persistent

нагиба́ть(ся) (-ю(сь)) *несов от* нагну́ть(ся)

нагле́ть (-ю; *pf* об~) *несов* to get cheeky

нагле́ц (-а́) *м* impudent upstart

наглу́хо *нареч* tight, securely

на́глый *прил* cheeky, impertinent

нагля́дный *прил* (*пример, случай*) clear; (*метод обучения*) visual

нагна́ть (-ну́, -нишь; *impf* нагоня́ть) *сов перех* (*беглеца*) to catch up with; (*упущенное*) to make up for; нагоня́ть (~ *pf*) страх на кого́-н to strike fear into sb

нагнета́ть (-ю) *несов перех* (*воздух*) to pump; (*перен*: *напряжение*) to heighten

нагну́ть (-у́, -ёшь; *impf* нагиба́ть) *сов перех* (*ветку*) to pull down; (*голову*) to bend; ~ся (*impf* нагиба́ться) *сов возв* to bend down

наговори́ть (-ю́, -и́шь) *сов* (*разг*: наклеветать): ~ на +*acc* to slander; (~ *pf*) чепухи́ to talk a lot of nonsense; ~ся *сов возв* to talk one's fill

наго́й *прил* (*человек*) naked, nude

на́голо *нареч*: остри́чься ~ to shave one's head

нагоня́ть (-ю) *несов от* нагна́ть

нагото́ве *нареч* at the ready

награ́да (-ы) *ж* reward, prize; (*ВОЕН*) decoration

награди́ть (-жу́, -ди́шь; *impf* награжда́ть) *сов перех*: ~ кого́-н чем-н (*орденом*) to award sth to sb; (*перен*: *талантом*) to endow sb with sth

нагрева́тельный *прил*: ~ прибо́р heating appliance

нагре́ть (-ю; *impf* нагрева́ть) *сов перех* to heat, warm; ~ся (*impf* нагрева́ться) *сов возв* to warm up

нагроможде́ние (-я) *ср* pile

нагруби́ть (-лю́, -и́шь) *сов от* груби́ть

нагру́дник (-а) *м* bib

нагру́дный *прил*: ~ карма́н breast pocket

нагрузи́ть (-ужу́, -у́зишь) *сов от* грузи́ть ♦ (*impf* нагружа́ть) *перех* to load up

нагру́зка (-и) *ж* load

над *предл*: ~ +*instr* above; рабо́тать (*impf*) ~ +*instr* to work on; ду́мать (*impf*) ~ +*instr* to think about; смея́ться (*impf*) ~ +*instr* to laugh at; сиде́ть (*impf*) ~ кни́гой to sit over a book

надави́ть (-авлю́, -а́вишь; *impf* нада́вливать) *сов*: ~ на +*acc* (*на дверь итп*) to lean against; (*на кнопку*) to press

надба́вка (-и) *ж* (*к зарплате*) rise; (*к цене*) mark-up

надви́нуть (-у; *impf* надвига́ть) *сов перех*: ~ что-н (на +*acc*) to pull sth down (over); ~ся (*impf* надвига́ться) *сов возв* (*опасность, старость*) to approach

на́двое *нареч* in half
надгро́би|е (-я) *ср* gravestone
надева́ть (-ю) *несов от* наде́ть
наде́жд|а (-ы) *ж* hope
надёжный *прил* reliable; (*механизм*) secure
наде́ла|ть (-ю) *сов (не)перех*: ~ +*acc или* +*gen* (*ошибок*) to make lots of; **что ты ~л?** what have you done?
надел|и́ть (-ю́, -и́шь; *impf* **наделя́ть) *сов перех*: ~ **кого́-н чем-н** (*землёй*) to grant sb sth
наде́|ть (-ну, -нешь; *impf* **надева́ть)** *сов перех* to put on
наде́|яться (-юсь, -ешься; *несов возв*: ~ +*infin* to hope to do; ~ (**по~** *pf*) **на** +*acc* (*на друга*) to rely on; (*на улучшение*) to hope for
надзе́мный *прил* overground
надзира́тел|ь (-я) *м* guard
надзо́р (-а) *м* control; (*орган*) monitoring body
надл|оми́ть (-омлю́, -о́мишь; *impf* **надла́мывать)** *сов перех* to break; (*здоровье, психику*) to damage
надме́нный *прил* haughty

KEYWORD

на́до *как сказ* 1 (*следует*): **на́до ему́ помо́чь** it is necessary to help him; **на́до, что́бы он пришёл во́время** he must come on time; **на́до всегда́ говори́ть пра́вду** one must always speak the truth; **мне/ему́ на́до зако́нчить рабо́ту** I/he must finish the job; **помо́чь тебе́? - не на́до!** can I help you? - there's no need!; **не на́до!** (*не делай это*) don't!
2 (*о потребности*): **на́до мно́го лет** it takes many years; **им на́до 5 рубле́й** they need 5 roubles; **что тебе́ на́до?** what do you want?;

так ему́/ей и на́до (*разг*) it serves him/her right; **на́до же!** (*разг*) of all things!

на́до *предл см.* над
надоедли́вый *прил* tiresome
надо́е|сть (как есть; *см.* Table 15; *impf* **надоеда́ть)** *сов*: ~ **кому́-н** (+*instr*) (*разговорами, упрёками*) to bore sb (with); **мне ~ло ждать** I'm tired of waiting; **он мне ~л** I've had enough of him
надо́лго *нареч* for a long time
надорв|а́ться (-у́, -ёшь; *impf* **надрыва́ться)** *сов* (*силы*) to tax; (*здоровье*) to put a strain on; ~**ся** (*impf* **надрыва́ться)** *сов возв* to do o.s. an injury; (*перен*) to overexhaust o.s.
надп|иса́ть (-ишу́, -и́шешь; *impf* **надпи́сывать)** *сов перех* to inscribe; (*конверт*) to address
надруга́|ться (-юсь) (*не*)*сов возв*: ~ **над** +*instr* (*над могилой, над женщиной*) to violate; (*над чувствами*) to abuse
надсмо́трщик (-а) *м* (*тюремный*) warden
наду́|ть (-ю, -ешь; *impf* **надува́ть)** *сов перех* (*мяч, колесо*) to inflate, blow up; (*разг: обмануть*) to con; ~**ся** (*impf* **надува́ться)** *сов возв* (*матрас, мяч*) to inflate; (*парус*) to billow; (*вены*) to swell; (*перен: от важности*) to swell up; (: *разг: обидеться*) to sulk
наеда́|ться (-юсь) *несов от* **нае́сться**
наедине́ *нареч* ~ (**с** +*instr*) alone (with); **они́ оста́лись** ~ they were left on their own
нае́здник (-а) *м* rider
наезжа́|ть (-ю) *несов от*

нае́хать

на|ём (-йма) м hiring; (квартиры) renting

наёмник (-а) м mercenary; (работник) casual worker

наёмный прил (труд, работник) hired; **~ убийца** hitman

нае́|сться (как есть; см. Table 15; impf **наеда́ться**) сов возв: ~ +gen (сладкого) to eat a lot of; **я ~лся** I'm full

нае́хать (как е́хать; см. Table 19; impf **наезжа́ть**) сов (разг: гости) to arrive in droves; **наезжа́ть (~ pf) на** +acc to drive into

нажа́|ть (-му, -мёшь; impf **нажима́ть)** сов (перен): ~ **на** +acc (на кнопку) to press

нажда́чный прил: **~ая бума́га** emery paper

нажи́м (-а) м pressure

нажима́|ть (-ю) несов от **нажа́ть**

нажи́|ть (-ву́, -вёшь; impf **нажива́ть)** сов перех (состояние) to acquire; **~ся** (impf **нажива́ться)** сов возв: **~ся (на** +prp) to profiteer (from)

наза́д нареч back; (нагнуться, катиться итп) backwards; (тому) ~ ago; **де́сять лет/неде́лю (тому)** ~ ten years/one week ago

назва́ни|е (-я) ср name; **торго́вое** ~ trade name

назва́|ть (-ову́, -овёшь; impf **называ́ть)** сов перех (дать имя) to call; (назначить) to name

назе́мный прил surface; **~ые войска́** ground troops

на́земь нареч to the ground

назло́ нареч out of spite; ~ **кому-н** to spite sb; **как ~** to make things worse

назначе́ни|е (-я) ср (цены итп) setting; (на работу) appointment;

(функция) function; **пункт или ме́сто** ~ destination

назна́ч|ить (-у, -ишь; impf **назнача́ть)** сов перех (на работу) to appoint; (цену) to set; (встречу) to arrange; (лекарство) to prescribe

назо́йливый прил persistent

назре́|ть (3sg -ет; impf **назрева́ть)** сов (вопрос) to become unavoidable

называ́емый прил: **так называ́емый** so-called

называ́|ть (-ю) несов от **назва́ть; ~ся** несов возв (носить название) to be called

наибо́лее нареч: ~ **интере́сный/ краси́вый** the most interesting/ beautiful

наибо́льший прил the greatest

наи́вный прил naive

наизна́нку нареч inside out

наизу́сть нареч: **знать/вы́учить** ~ to know/learn by heart

наиме́нее нареч: ~ **уда́чный/ спосо́бный** the least successful/ capable

наименова́ни|е (-я) ср name; (книги) title, name

наиме́ньший прил (длина, вес) the smallest; (усилие) the least

на|йти́ (-йду́, -йдёшь; pt **-шёл, -шла́, -шло́;** impf **находи́ть)** сов перех to find; **на меня́ ~шёл смех** I couldn't help laughing; **~сь** (impf **находи́ться)** сов возв (потерянное) to turn up; (добровольцы) to come forward; (не растеряться) to regain control

наказа́ни|е (-я) ср punishment

нак|аза́ть (-ажу́, -а́жешь; impf **нака́зывать)** сов перех to punish

нака́л (-а) м (борьбы) heat

накали́|ть (-ю́, -ишь; impf **накали́ть)** сов перех to heat up;

(перен: обстановку) to hot up;
~**ся** (impf **накаля́ться**) сов возв
to heat; (перен: обстановка) to
hot up

накану́не нареч the day before,
the previous day ♦ предл: ~ +gen
on the eve of

нака́плива|ть(ся) (-ю(сь)) несов
от **накопи́ть(ся)**

нак|ати́ть (-ачу́, -а́тишь; impf
нака́тывать) сов перех: ~ (на +acc)
(волну) to roll up (onto)

накача́|ть (-ю) impf **нака́чивать**)
сов перех (камеру) to pump up

наки́д|ка (-ки; gen pl -ок) ж
(одежда) wrap; (покрывало)
bedspread, throw

наки́н|уть (-у; impf **наки́дывать**)
сов перех (платок) to throw on;
~**ся** (impf **наки́дываться**) сов
возв: ~**ся на** +acc (на человека)
to hurl o.s. at; (разг: на еду, на
книгу) to get stuck into

наки́п|ь (-и) ж (на бульоне)
scum; (в чайнике) fur (BRIT), scale
(US)

накладн|а́я (-о́й) ж (КОММ) bill of
lading (BRIT), waybill (US);
грузова́я (BRIT), overhead (US);
note

накладн|о́й прил: ~ые расхо́ды
overheads мн (BRIT), overhead (US)

накла́дыва|ть (-ю) несов от
наложи́ть

накле́|ить (-ю, -ишь; impf
накле́ивать) сов перех to stick on

накле́|йка (-йки; gen pl -ек) ж
label

накло́н (-а) м incline, slope

наклон|и́ть (-оню́, -о́нишь; impf
наклоня́ть) сов перех to tilt; ~**ся**
(impf **наклоня́ться**) сов возв to
bend down

накло́нность|ь (-и) ж: ~ к +dat (к
музыке итп) aptitude for;
дурны́е/хоро́шие ~и bad/good

habits

накова́льня (-ьни; gen pl -ен) ж
anvil

нак|оло́ть (-олю́, -о́лешь; impf
нака́лывать) сов перех (руку)
to prick; (прикрепить): ~ (на +acc)
(на шляпу, на дверь) to pin
on(to)

наконе́ц нареч at last, finally
♦ вводн сл at last all; ~**то!** at long
last!

наконе́чник (-а) м tip, end

накоп|и́ть (-лю́, -ишь) сов от
копи́ть ♦ (impf **нака́пливать**)
перех (силы, информацию) to
store up; (средства) to
accumulate; ~**ся** сов от **копи́ться**
♦ (impf **нака́пливаться**) возв
(силы) to build up; (средства) to
accumulate

нак|орми́ть (-ормлю́,
нако́рмишь) сов от **корми́ть**

на́крест нареч (также: **крест-~**)
crosswise

накрича́|ть (-у́, -и́шь) сов: ~ на
+acc to shout at

накру|ти́ть (-чу́, -у́тишь; impf
накру́чивать) сов перех: ~ (на
+acc) (гайку) to screw on(to);
(канат) to wind (round)

накр|ы́ть (-о́ю, -о́ешь; impf
накрыва́ть) сов перех to cover;
накрыва́ть (~ pf) (на) **стол** to lay
the table; ~**ся** (impf **накрыва́ться**)
сов возв: ~**ся** (+instr) (одея́лом)
to cover o.s. up (with)

налага́|ть (-ю) несов от
наложи́ть

нала́|дить (-жу, -дишь; impf
нала́живать) сов перех
(механизм) to repair; to fix;
(сотрудничество) to initiate;
(хозяйство) to sort out; ~**ся** (impf
нала́живаться) сов возв
(работа) to go well; (отношения

здоровье) to improve

нале́во *нареч* (to the) left; (*разг*: продать) on the side

налегке́ *нареч* (ехать) without luggage

налёт (-а) *м* raid; (пыли, плесени) thin coating *или* layer

налете́ть (-чу́, -ти́шь; *impf* **налета́ть**) *сов* (буря) to spring up; **налета́ть** (~ *pf*) **на** +*acc* (натолкну́ться) to fly against; (напа́сть) to swoop down on

нали́ть (-ью́, -ьёшь; *impf* **налива́ть**) *сов перех* to pour (out)

налицо́ *как сказ*: **фа́кты** ~ the facts are obvious; **доказа́тельство** ~ there is proof

нали́чие (-я) *ср* presence

нали́чность (-и) *ж* cash

нали́чные (-ых) *мн* cash *ед*

нали́чн|ый *прил*: **~ые де́ньги** cash; ~ **расчёт** cash payment; ~ **счёт** cash account

нало́г (-а) *м* tax; ~ **на ввоз** +*gen* import duty on

нало́гов|ый *прил* tax; **~ая декла́рация** tax return

налоговик (-а) *м* taxman

налогоплате́льщик (-а) *м* taxpayer

нало́женн|ый *прил*: ~**ым платежо́м** cash on delivery

нал|ожи́ть (-ожу́, -о́жишь; *impf* **накла́дывать**) *сов перех* to put *или* place on; (компресс, бинт, лак) to apply; (*impf* **налага́ть**) (штраф) to impose

нам *мест см.* **мы**

нама́|зать (-жу, -жешь) *сов от* **ма́зать**

нама́тыва|ть (-ю) *несов от* **намота́ть**

намёк (-а) *м* hint

намека́|ть (-ю; *pf* **намекну́ть**) *несов*: ~ **на** +*acc* to hint at

намерева́|ться (-юсь) *несов возв*: ~ +*infin* to intend to do

наме́рен *как сказ*: **он** ~ **уе́хать** he intends to leave

наме́рени|е (-я) *ср* intention

наме́ренный *прил* deliberate

намета́|ть (-ю) *сов от* **мета́ть**

наме́|тить (-чу, -тишь; *impf* **намеча́ть**) *сов перех* to plan; (план) to project; **~ся** *сов* (*impf* **намеча́ться**) *возв* to begin to show; (событие) to be coming up

на́ми *мест см.* **мы**

намно́го *нареч* much, far; ~ **ху́же/интере́снее** much worse/ more interesting

намо́кн|уть (-у; *impf* **намока́ть**) *сов* to get wet

намо́рдник (-а) *м* muzzle

намо́рщ|ить (-у, -ишь) *сов от* **мо́рщить**

намота́|ть (-ю) *сов от* **мота́ть**

намо́ч|ить (-очу́, -о́чишь) *сов от* **мочи́ть**

нан|ести́ (-есу́, -есёшь; *pt* -ёс, -есла́, -есло́; *impf* **наноси́ть**) *сов перех* (мазь, кра́ску) to apply; (рисунок) to draw; (на ка́рту) to plot; (удар) to deliver; (урон) to inflict; (~ *pf*) **кому́-н визи́т** to pay sb a visit

нани́зыва|ть (-ю) *несов перех* to string

на|ня́ть (-йму, -ймёшь; *impf* **нанима́ть**) *сов перех* (работника) to hire; (лодку, маши́ну) to hire, rent; **~ся** (*impf* **нанима́ться**) *сов возв* to get a job

наоборо́т *нареч* (де́лать) the wrong way (round) ♦ *вводн сл*, *част* on the contrary

наобу́м *нареч* without thinking

наотре́з *нареч* flatly, point-blank

напада́|ть (-ю) *несов от*

напа́сть см напада́ть

напада́ющ|ий (-его) м (СПОРТ) forward

нападе́ни|е (-я) ср attack; (СПОРТ) forwards мн

напа́д|ки (-ок) мн attacks мн

нап|а́сть (-аду́, -адёшь) impf **напада́ть** сов: ~ **на** +acc to attack; (обнаружить) to strike; (тоска, страх) to grip, seize

напе́в (-а) м tune, melody

напева́|ть (-ю) несов от **напе́ть ♦ перех (песенку)** to hum

наперебо́й нареч vying with each other

наперегонки́ нареч (разг) racing each other

наперёд нареч (знать, угадать) beforehand; **за́дом** ~ back to front

напереко́р предл: ~ +dat in defiance of

напёрст|ок (-ка) м thimble

нап|е́ть (-ою́, -оёшь) impf **напева́ть** сов перех (мотив, песню) to sing

напи́льник (-а) м file

напира́|ть (-ю) несов: ~ **на** +acc (теснить) to push against

написа́ни|е (-я) ср writing; (слова) spelling

нап|иса́ть (-ишу́, -и́шешь) сов от **писа́ть**

напи́т|ок (-ка) м drink

нап|и́ться (-ью́сь, -ьёшься) impf **напива́ться** сов возв: ~ **(+gen)** to have a good drink (of); (разг: опьянеть) to get drunk

напл|ева́ть (-юю́) сов от **плева́ть**

наплы́в (-а) м (туристов) influx; (: заявлений, чувств) flood

наплы́|ть (-ву́, -вёшь) сов (перен:

воспоминания) to come flooding back; **наплыва́ть (~ pf) на** (на мель, на камень) to run against

напова́л нареч (убить) outright

наподо́бие предл: ~ +gen resembling

нап|о́ить (-ою́, -о́ишь) сов от **пои́ть**

напока́з нареч for show

напо́лн|ить (-ю, -ишь) impf **наполня́ть** сов перех: ~ +instr to fill with; (~ся impf наполня́ться) сов возв: ~**ся** +instr to fill with

наполови́ну нареч by half; (наполнить) half

напомина́|ть (-ю) несов от **напо́мнить ♦** (иметь сходство) to resemble

напо́мн|ить (-ю, -ишь) impf **напомина́ть** сов (не)перех: **кому́-н** +acc **или о** +prp to remind sb of

напо́р (-а) м pressure

напосле́док нареч finally

напра́в|ить (-лю, -ишь) impf **направля́ть** сов перех to direct; (к врачу́) to refer; (посла́ние) to send; (~ся impf направля́ться) сов возв: ~**ся в** +acc/к +dat итп to make for

направле́ни|е (-я) ср direction; (де́ятельности, та́кже ВОЕН) line; (поли́тики) orientation; (докуме́нт: в больни́цу) referral; (: на рабо́ту, на учёбу) directive; **по** ~**ю к** +dat towards

напра́во нареч (идти́) (to the) right

напра́сно нареч in vain

напра́сный прил (труд) vain; (трево́га) unfounded

напра́шива|ться (-юсь) несов от **напроси́ться**

наприме́р вводн сл for example или instance

напрока́т *нареч*: взять ~ to hire; отдава́ть (отда́ть *pf*) ~ to hire out

напроло́м *нареч* without a break

напропалу́ю *нареч* stopping at nothing

напр|оси́ться (-ошу́сь, -о́сишься; *impf* **напра́шиваться**) *сов возв* (*разг*: *в гости*) to force o.s.; **напра́шиваться** (~ *pf*) **на** +*acc* (*на комплимент*) to invite

напро́тив *нареч* opposite ♦ *вводн сл* on the contrary ♦ *предл*: ~ +*gen* opposite

напряга́|ть(ся) (-ю(сь)) *несов от* **напря́чь(ся)**

напряже́ни|е (-я) *ср* tension; (*физ, механическое*) strain, stress; (: *электрическое*) voltage

напряжённый *прил* tense; (*отношения, встреча*) strained

напрями́к *нареч* (*идти*) straight

напр|я́чь (-ягу́, -яжёшь *итп*, **-ягу́т;** *pt* **-я́г, -ягла́;** *impf* **напряга́ть**) *сов перех* to strain; **~ся** (*impf* **напряга́ться**) *сов возв* (*мускулы*) to become tense; (*человек*) to strain

напыл|и́ть (-ю́, -и́шь) *сов от* **пыли́ть**

напы́щенный *прил* pompous

наравне́ *нареч*: ~ с +*instr* (*по одной линии*) on a level with; (*на равных правах*) on an equal footing with

нарас|ти́ (3sg -тёт; *impf* **-та́ть)** *сов* (*проценты*) to accumulate; (*волнение, сопротивление*) to grow

нарасхва́т *нареч* like hot cakes

нара́щива|ть (-ю) *несов перех* (*темпы, объём итп*) to increase

нарв|а́ть (-у́, -ёшь) *сов* (*не)перех*: ~ +*acc* или +*gen* (*цветов, ягод*) to pick; **~ся** (*impf* **нарыва́ться**) *сов возв* (*разг*):

~ся на +*acc* (*на хулигана*) to run up against; (*на неприятность*) to run into

наре́за|ть (-жу, -жешь) *сов перех* to cut

нареза́ть (-а́ю) *сов перех* to cut

наре́чи|е (-я) *ср* (*линг, часть речи*) adverb; (: *говоры*) dialect

нарис|ова́ть (-у́ю) *сов от* **рисова́ть**

наркоби́знес (-а) *м* drug trafficking

наркодиле́р|ец (-ьца) *м* drug dealer

нарко́з (-а) *м* (*МЕД*) narcosis, anaesthesia (*BRIT*), anesthesia (*US*)

наркологи́ческий *прил*: ~ диспансе́р drug-abuse clinic

наркома́н (-а) *м* drug addict или abuser

наркома́ни|я (-и) *ж* (*МЕД*) drug addiction или abuse

нарко́тик (-а) *м* drug

наркоти́ческий *прил* (*средства*) drug

наро́д (-а; *part gen* **-у)** *м* people *мн*

наро́дность (-и) *ж* nation

наро́дный *прил* national; (*фронт*) popular; (*искусство*) folk

наро́читый *прил* deliberate

наро́чно *нареч* purposely, on purpose; **как ~** (*разг*) to make things worse

нар|уби́ть (-ублю́, -у́бишь; *impf* **наруба́ть)** *сов* (*не)перех*: ~ +*acc* или +*gen* to chop

нару́жность (-и) *ж* appearance

нару́жный *прил* (*дверь, стена*) exterior; (*спокойствие*) outward

нару́жу *нареч* out

нару́чник (-а) *м* (*обычно мн*) handcuff

нару́чный *прил*: **~ые часы́** (wrist)watch *ед*

наруша́|ть(ся) (-ю(сь)) *несов от* **нару́шить(ся)**

наруши́тель (-я) *м* (*закона*)

infringer, transgressor; (*ЮР, порядка*) offender; ~ **грани́цы** *person who illegally crosses a border*; ~ **дисципли́ны** troublemaker

нару́ш|**ить** (-у, -ишь; *impf* **наруша́ть**) *сов перех* (*покой*) to disturb; (*связь*) to break; (*правила, договор*) to violate; (*дисциплину*) to breach;
наруша́ть (~ *pf*) **грани́цу** to illegally cross a border; ~**ся** (*impf* **наруша́ться**) *сов возв* to be broken *или* disturbed

нарци́сс (-а) *м* daffodil, narcissus

нары́в (-а) *м* (*МЕД*) abscess, boil

нарыва́ть (3sg -ет) *несов* (*рана*) to fester

наря́д (-а) *м* (*одежда*) attire; (*красивый*) outfit; (*КОММ*) order; (*распоряжение*) directive

наря́д|**ить** (-жу́, -ядишь; *impf* **наряжа́ть**) *сов перех* (*одеть*) to dress; **наряжа́ть** (~ *pf*) **ёлку** ≈ to decorate (*BRIT*) *или* trim (*US*) the Christmas tree; ~**ся** (*impf* **наряжа́ться**) *сов возв*: ~**ся** (**в** +*acc*) to dress o.s. (in)

наря́дный *прил* (*человек*) well-dressed; (*комната, улица*) nicely decorated; (*шляпа, платье*) fancy

наряду́ *нареч*: ~ **с** +*instr* along with; (*наравне*) on an equal footing with

наряжа́ть(ся) (-ю(сь)) *несов от* **наряди́ть(ся)**

нас *мест см.* **мы**

насеко́мое (-ого) *ср* insect

населе́ни|**е** (-я) *ср* population

населённый *прил* (*район*) populated; ~ **пункт** locality

насел|**и́ть** (-ю́, -и́шь; *impf* **населя́ть**) *сов перех* (*регион*) to settle

населя́|**ть** (-ю) *несов от* **насели́ть** ♦ *перех* (*проживать*) to inhabit

насе́ч|**ка** (-ки; *gen pl* -ек) *ж* notch

наси́ли|**е** (-я) *ср* violence

наси́л|**овать** (-ую; *pf* **из**~) *несов перех* (*женщину*) to rape

наси́льно *нареч* forcibly

наси́льственный *прил* violent

наска́кива|**ть** (-ю) *несов от* **наскочи́ть**

наскво́зь *нареч* through

наско́лько *нареч* so much

наск|**очи́ть** (-очу́, -о́чишь; *impf* **наска́кивать**) *сов*: ~ **на** +*acc* to run into

наску́ч|**ить** (-у, -ишь) *сов*: ~ **кому́-н** to bore sb

насла|**ди́ться** (-жу́сь, -ди́шься; *impf* **наслажда́ться**) *сов возв*: ~ +*instr* to relish

наслажде́ни|**е** (-я) *ср* enjoyment, relish

насле́ди|**е** (-я) *ср* (*культурное*) heritage; (*идеологическое*) legacy

насле́дник (-а) *м* heir; (*перен: преемник*) inheritor

насле́д|**овать** (-ую) *(не)сов перех* to inherit; (*престол*) to succeed to

насле́дственный *прил* inherited; (*черты, болезнь*) hereditary

насле́дств|**о** (-а) *ср* (*имущество*) inheritance; (*культурное*) heritage; (*идеологическое*) legacy

наслы́шан *как сказ*: **я** ~ **об э́том** I have heard a lot about it

насма́рку *нареч* (*разг*): **идти́** ~ to be wasted

на́смерть *нареч* (*сражаться*) to the death; (*ранить*) fatally

насмеха́|**ться** (-юсь) *несов возв*: ~ **над** +*instr* to taunt

насме|**и́ть** (-ю́, -и́шь) *сов от* **смеши́ть**

насме́ш|**ка** (-ки; *gen pl* -ек) *ж* jibe

насме́шливый *прил* mocking

насмея́|ться (-ю́сь) *сов возв*: ~ **над** +*instr* to offend

на́сморк (-а) *m* runny nose

насовсе́м *нареч* (*разг*) for good

насор|и́ть (-ю́, -и́шь) *сов от* **сори́ть**

насо́с (-а) *m* pump

на́спех *нареч* hurriedly

настава́|ть (*3sg* -ёт) *несов от* **наста́ть**

наста́вник (-а) *m* mentor

наставля́|ть (-ю) *несов от* **настоя́ть**

наста́|ть (-нет, *impf* **наставля́ть**) *сов* to come; (*ночь*) to fall

на́стежь *нареч* (*открыть*) wide

насти́|чь (-гну, -гнешь, *pt* -г, -гла; *impf* **настига́ть**) *сов перех* to catch up with

насто́|йка (-йки; *gen pl* -ек) *ж* (*экстракт*) tincture; (*алкоголь*) liqueur

насто́йчивый *прил* persistent; (*просьба*) insistent

насто́лько *нареч* so

насто́льный *прил* (*лампа, часы*) table; (*календарь*) desk

насторо́же *как сказ*: **он всегда́ ~** he is always on the alert

насторож|и́ть (-у́, -и́шь; *impf* **настора́живать**) *сов перех* to alert; **~ся** (*impf* **настора́живаться**) *сов возв* to become more alert

настоя́ни|е (-я) *ср*: **по ~ю кого́-н** on sb's insistence

настоя́тельный *прил* (*просьба*) persistent; (*задача*) urgent

насто́|я́ть (-ю́, -и́шь; *impf* **настоя́ть**) *сов*: **~ на** +*prp* to insist on ♦ *перех* (*травы*) to infuse

настоя́щий *прил* real; (*момент*) present; **по~ему** (*как надо*) properly; (*пре́данный*) really; **~ее**

вре́мя (*линг*) the present tense

настра́ива|ть(ся) (-ю(сь)) *несов от* **настро́ить(ся)**

настрое́ни|е (-я) *ср* mood; (*антивое́нное*) feeling; **не в ~и** in a bad mood

настро́|ить (-ю, -ишь; *impf* **настра́ивать**) *сов перех* (*пиани́но или гита́ру*) to tune; (*механи́зм*) to adjust; **настра́ивать** (~ *pf*) **кого́-н на** +*acc* to put sb in the right frame of mind for; **настра́ивать** (~ *pf*) **кого́-н про́тив** +*gen* to incite sb against; **~ся** (*impf* **настра́иваться**) *сов возв*: **~ся** (*pf*) +*infin* to be disposed to do

настро́|й (-я) *m* mood

настро́йщик (-а) *м*: **~ роя́ля** piano tuner

наступа́|ть (-ю) *несов от* **наступи́ть** ♦ *неперех* (*ВОЕН*) to go on the offensive

наступ|и́ть (-уплю́, -у́пишь; *impf* **наступа́ть**) *сов* to come; (*ночь*) to fall; **наступа́ть** (~ *pf*) **на** +*acc* (*на ка́мень или пол*) to step on

наступле́ни|е (-я) *ср* (*ВОЕН*) offensive; (*весны, ста́рости*) beginning; (*темноты́*) fall

на́сухо *нареч*: **вы́тереть что-н ~** to dry sth thoroughly

насу́щный *прил* vital

насчёт *предл*: ~ +*gen* regarding

насчита́|ть (-ю; *impf* **насчи́тывать**) *сов перех* to count

насчи́тыва|ть (-ю) *несов от* **насчита́ть** ♦ *неперех* to have

насып|а́ть (-лю, -лешь; *impf* **насыпа́ть**) *сов перех* to pour

на́сып|ь (-и) *ж* embankment

насы́|тить (-щу, -тишь; *impf* **насыща́ть**) *сов перех* (*накорми́ть*) to satiate; (*водо́й,* *ра́достью*) to fill; (*рынок*) to saturate; ~ся (*impf* **насыща́ться**) (*pf* **наесться**) to eat one's fill; (*рынок*) to be saturated

ната́лкива|ть(ся) (-ю(сь)) *несов от* **натолкну́ть(ся)**

натвор|и́ть (-ю́, -и́шь) *сов (не)перех*: ~ +*acc или* +*gen* (*разг*) to get up to

нат|ере́ть (-ру́, -рёшь; *pt* -ёр, -ёрла; *impf* **натира́ть**) *сов перех* (*ботинки, полы*) to polish; (*ногу*) to chafe; (*морковь, сыр итп*) to grate

на́тиск (-а) *м* pressure

наткн|у́ться (-у́сь, -ёшься; *impf* **натыка́ться**) *сов возв*: ~ на +*acc* to bump into

НАТО *ср сокр* NATO

натолкн|у́ть (-у́, -ёшь; *impf* **ната́лкивать**) *сов перех*: ~ кого́-н на +*acc* (*на иде́ю*) to lead sb to; ~ся (*impf* **ната́лкиваться**) *сов возв*: ~ся на +*acc* to bump into

натоща́к *нареч* on an empty stomach

на́три|й (-я) *м* sodium

нату́р|а (-ы) *ж* (*хара́ктер*) nature; (*нату́рщик*) model (*ART*); ~ой, в ~е (*ЭКОН*) in kind

натура́льный *прил* natural; (*мех, ко́жа*) real

нату́рщик (-а) *м* model (*ART*)

натыка́|ться (-юсь) *несов от* **наткну́ться**

натюрмо́рт (-а) *м* still life

натя́гива|ть(ся) (-ю) *несов от* **натяну́ть(ся)**

натя́нутый *прил* strained

нат|яну́ть (-яну́, -я́нешь; *impf* **натя́гивать**) *сов перех* to pull tight; (*перчатки*) to pull on; ~ся (*impf* **натя́гиваться**) *сов возв* to tighten

науга́д *нареч* at random

нау́к|а (-и) *ж* science; **есте́ственные ~и** science; **гуманита́рные ~и** arts

нау́тро *нареч* next morning

нау|чи́ть(ся) (-чу́(сь), -́чишь(ся)) *сов от* **учи́ть(ся)**

нау́чно-популя́рный *прил* science

нау́чно-техни́ческий *прил* scientific

нау́чный *прил* scientific

нау́шник (-а) *м* (*обычно мн*; *также*: **магнитофо́нные ~и**) headphones *мн*

наха́л (-а) *м* (*разг*) cheeky beggar

наха́льный *прил* cheeky

нахлын|у́ть (*3sg* -ет) *сов* to surge

нахму́р|ить(ся) (-ю(сь), -ишь(ся)) *несов от* **хму́рить(ся)**

нах|оди́ть (-ожу́, -о́дишь) *несов от* **найти́**; ~ся *несов от* **найти́сь** ♦ *возв* (*дом, го́род*) to be situated; (*челове́к*) to be

нахо́д|ка (-ки; *gen pl* -ок) *ж* (*поте́рянного*) discovery; **он ~ для нас** he is a real find for us; **Бюро́ ~ок** lost property office (*BRIT*), lost and found (*US*)

нахо́дчивый *прил* resourceful

наце́л|ить (-ю, -ишь; *impf* **наце́ливать) *сов перех*: ~ кого́-н на +*acc* to push sb towards; ~ся *сов от* **це́литься**

наце́н|ка (-ки; *gen pl* -ок) *ж* (*на това́р*) surcharge

наци́зм (-а) *м* Nazism

национализи́р|овать (-ую) (*не)сов перех* to nationalize

национали́зм (-а) *м* nationalism

национали́ст (-а) *м* nationalist

национа́льност|ь (-и) *ж* nationality; (*на́ция*) nation

национа́льный *прил* national

наци́ст (-а) *м* Nazi

на́ци|я (-и) ж nation;
**Организа́ция Объединённых
На́ций** United Nations
Organization

начади́ть (-жу́, -ди́шь) сов от
чадить

нача́л|о (-а) ср beginning, start;
быть (impf) **под ~м кого́-н** или **у
кого́-н** to be under sb

нача́льник (-а) м
(руководитель) boss; (цеха) floor
manager; (управления) head

нача́льн|ый прил (период) initial;
(глава книги) first; **~ая шко́ла**
(ПРОСВЕЩ) primary (BRIT) или
elementary (US) school; **~ые
кла́ссы** (ПРОСВЕЩ) the first three
classes of school

нача́льные кла́ссы - Children
start school at the age of six or
seven. There are no separate
primary schools in Russia. The first
three classes of the 10-year
education system are referred to
as **нача́льные кла́ссы**. The
main emphasis is on reading,
writing and arithmetic. Other
subjects taught include drawing,
PE and singing.

нача́льств|о (-а) ср (власть)
authority ♦ собир (руководители)
management

нач|а́ть (-ну́, -нёшь) impf
начина́ть) сов перех to begin, start

начеку́ нареч **быть ~** to be on
one's guard

на́черно нареч rough

нач|ерти́ть (-ерчу́, -е́ртишь)
сов от черти́ть

начёс (-а) м (на ткани) пар; (вид
причёски) bouffant

начина́ни|е (-я) ср initiative

начина́|ть (-ю) несов от нача́ть

начина́ющ|ий прил (писатель)
novice ♦ (-его) м beginner

начина́я предл: **~ +**instr (включая)
including; **~ с +**gen from; (при
отсчёте) starting from; **~ от +**gen
(включая) including

начин|и́ть (-ю́, -и́шь, impf
начиня́ть) сов перех (пирог) to
fill

начи́н|ка (-ки; gen pl **-ок)** ж filling

начну́ итп сов см. нача́ть

наш (-его; см. Table 9; f **-а,**
притяж мест nt **-е,** pl **-и)** our; **чей
э́то дом? - ~** whose is this house? -
ours; **чьи э́то кни́ги? - на́ши**
whose are these books? - ours; **по-
на́шему** our way; (по нашему
мнению) in our opinion

нашаты́рный прил: **~ спирт**
(МЕД) liquid ammonia

наше́стви|е (-я) ср invasion

нащу́па|ть (-ю; impf
нащу́пывать) сов перех to find

наяву́ нареч in reality; **как ~**
distinctly

НДС м сокр (= нало́г на
доба́вленную сто́имость) VAT

не част не; **я не написа́л э́то
письмо́** I didn't write this letter; **я
~ рабо́таю** I don't work; **~
пла́чь/опозда́й** don't cry/be
late; **~ могу́ ~ согласи́ться/~
возрази́ть** I can't help agreeing/
objecting; **~ мне на́до помо́чь, а
ему́** I am not the one who needs
help, he is; **~ до +**gen no time for;
мне ~ до тебя́ I have no time for
you; **~ без того́** (разг) that's about
it; **~ то** (разг: в противном
случае) or else

небе́сный прил (тела) celestial;
(перен) heavenly; **~ цвет** sky blue

неблагода́рный прил ungrateful;
(работа) thankless

не́бо (-а; *nom pl* **небеса́**, *gen pl* **небе́с**) *ср* sky; (РЕЛ) Heaven

не́бо (-а) *ср* (АНАТ) palate

небольшо́й *прил* small

небоскло́н (-а) *м* sky above the horizon

небоскрёб (-а) *м* skyscraper

небре́жный *прил* careless

небыва́лый *прил* unprecedented

нева́жно *нареч* (*делать что-н*) not very well ♦ *как сказ* it's not important

нева́жный *прил* unimportant; (*не очень хоро́ший*) poor

неве́дени|**е** (-я) *ср* ignorance; **он пребыва́ет в по́лном ~и** he doesn't know anything (about it)

неве́жа (-и) *м/ж* boor

неве́жд|**а** (-ы) *м/ж* ignoramus

неве́жественный *прил* ignorant

неве́жеств|**о** (-а) *ср* ignorance

невезе́ни|**е** (-я) *ср* bad luck

неве́рный *прил* (*оши́бочный*) incorrect; (*муж*) unfaithful

невероя́тный *прил* improbable; (*чрезвыча́йный*) incredible

неве́рующ|**ий** (-его) *м* unbeliever

неве́ст|**а** (-ы) *ж* (*по́сле помо́лвки*) fiancée; (*на сва́дьбе*) bride

неве́ст|**ка** (-ки; *gen pl* -ок) *ж* (*жена́ сы́на*) daughter-in-law; (*жена́ бра́та*) sister-in-law

невзго́д|**а** (-ы) *ж* adversity *ед*

невзира́я *предл*: **~ на** +*acc* in spite of

невзлюби́ть (-юблю́, -ю́бишь) *сов перех* to take a dislike to

невзнача́й *нареч* (*разг*) by accident

невзра́чный *прил* dowdy

неви́данный *прил* unprecedented

невиди́м|**ка** (-ки; *gen pl* -ок) *ж* (*шпи́лька*) hairpin

неви́димый *прил* invisible

неви́нный *прил* innocent

невино́вный *прил* innocent

невменя́емый *прил* deranged

невмеша́тельств|**о** (-а) *ср* nonintervention; (ЭКОН) laissez faire

невнима́тельный *прил* (*учени́к*) inattentive; (*муж*) inconsiderate

невня́тный *прил* muffled

нево́д (-а) *м* fishing net

невозмо́жно *нареч* (*большо́й, тру́дный*) impossibly ♦ *как сказ*: it is impossible to do; (*э́то*) ~ that's impossible

невозмо́жный *прил* impossible

невозмути́мый *прил* (*челове́к*) unflappable; (*тон*) unruffled

нево́льный *прил* (*улы́бка, свиде́тель*) involuntary; (*ложь*) unintentional

нево́л|**я** (-и) *ж* captivity

невооружённ|**ый** *прил* unarmed; **~ым гла́зом** (*без прибо́ров*) with the naked eye; **э́то ви́дно ~ым гла́зом** (*перен*) it's plain for all to see

невоспи́танный *прил* ill-bred

невпопа́д *нареч* (*разг*) out of turn

невраст|**е́ник** (-а) *м* neurotic

неврастени́|**я** (-и) *ж* (МЕД) nervous tension

невреди́мый *прил* (*челове́к*) unharmed

невро́з (-а) *м* neurosis

невропато́лог (-а) *м* neurologist

невыноси́мый *прил* unbearable, intolerable

негати́в (-а) *м* (ФОТО) negative

негати́вный *прил* negative

не́где *как сказ*: ~ **отдохну́ть** *итп* there is nowhere to rest *итп*; **мне** ~ **жить** I have nowhere to live

негла́сный *прил* secret

него́ *мест от* он, оно́

него́дность (-и) *ж*: приходи́ть (прийти́ *pf*) в ~ (*оборудование*) to become defunct

него́дный *прил* unusable; (*скверный*) good-for-nothing

негодова́ние (-я) *ср* indignation

негодова́ть (-у́ю) *несов* to be indignant

негодя́|й (-я) *м* scoundrel

негра́мотный *прил* illiterate; (*работа*) incompetent

негритя́нский *прил* black

неда́вний *прил* recent; до ~его вре́мени until recently

неда́вно *нареч* recently

недалёк|ий *прил* (*перен: человек, ум*) limited; в ~ом бу́дущем in the near future

недалеко́ *нареч* (*жить, быть*) nearby; (*идти, ехать*) not far ♦ *как сказ*: ~ (до +*gen*) it isn't far (to); ~ от +*gen* not far from

неда́ром *нареч* (*не напрасно*) not in vain; (*не без цели*) for a reason

недви́жимость (-и) *ж* property

недви́жим|ый *прил*: ~ое иму́щество = **недви́жимость**

неде́льный *прил* (*срок*) one-week; (*запас, заработок*) a или one week's

неде́л|я (-и) *ж* week; че́рез ~ю in a week('s time); на про́шлой/э́той/сле́дующей ~е last/this/next week

недове́ри|е (-я) *ср* mistrust, distrust

недове́рчивый *прил* mistrustful, distrustful

недово́льный *прил* discontented, dissatisfied

недово́льств|о (-а) *ср*: ~ (+*instr*) dissatisfaction (with)

недогова́ри|ть (-ю, -и́шь) *impf*

недогова́ривать) *сов перех* to leave unsaid; to say что-то

недогова́ривает there is something that he's not saying

недоеда́|ть (-ю) *несов* to eat badly

недолюбли́ва|ть (-ю) *несов перех* to dislike

недомога́ни|е (-я) *ср*: чу́вствовать (*impf*) ~ to feel unwell

недомога́|ть (-ю) *несов* to feel unwell

недоно́шенный *прил*: ~ ребёнок premature baby

недооцени́|ть (-еню́, -е́нишь; *impf* недооце́нивать) *сов перех* to underestimate

недопусти́мый *прил* unacceptable

недора́звитый *прил* underdeveloped

недоразуме́ни|е (-я) *ср* misunderstanding

недосмо́тр (-а) *м* oversight

недоста|ва́ть (3sg -ёт) *несов безл*: мне ~ёт сме́лости I lack courage; мне ~ёт де́нег I need money

недоста́т|ок (-ка; *nom pl* -ки *м*): ~ +*gen* shortage или lack of; (*в работе*) shortcoming in

недоста́точно *нареч* insufficiently ♦ *как сказ*: у нас ~ еды́/де́нег we don't have enough food/money; я ~ зна́ю об э́том I don't know enough about it

недоста́точный *прил* insufficient

недоста́ч|а (-и) *ж* (*мало*) lack; (*при прове́рке*) shortfall

недостаю́щий *прил* missing

недосто́йный *прил*: ~ (+*gen*) unworthy (of)

недоумева́|ть (-ю) *несов* to be perplexed или bewildered

недоуме́ни|е (-я) *ср* perplexity,

bewilderment

недоучка (-ки; *gen pl* -ек) *м/ж* (*разг*) drop-out

недочёт (-а) *м* (*в подсчётах*) shortfall; (*в работе*) deficiency

недр|**а** (-) *мн* depths *мн*; в ~х земли in the bowels of the earth

неё *мест см.* **она**

нежданный *прил* unexpected

нежиться (-усь, -ишься) *несов возв* to laze about

нежность|ь (-и) *ж* tenderness

нежный *прил* tender, gentle; (*кожа, пух*) soft; (*запах*) subtle

незабудка (-ки; *gen pl* -ок) *ж* forget-me-not

незабываемый *прил* unforgettable

независимо *нареч* independently; ~ от +*gen* regardless of

независимость|ь (-и) *ж* independence

независимый *прил* independent

незадолго *нареч*: ~ до +*gen или* перед +*instr* shortly before

незаметно *нареч* (*изменяться*) imperceptibly ♦ *как сказ* it isn't noticeable; **он ~ подошёл** he approached unnoticed

незаметный *прил* barely noticeable; (*перен: человек*) unremarkable

незанятый *прил* free; (*дом*) unoccupied; **~ая часть населения** the non-working population

незаурядный *прил* exceptional

незачем *как сказ* (*разг*): ~ ходить/это делать there's no reason to go/do it

нездоровиться (3sg -ится) *несов безл*: **мне нездоровится** I feel unwell, I don't feel well

незнакомец|ец (-ца) *м* stranger

незначительный *прил* (*сумма*) insignificant; (*факт*) trivial

неизбежный *прил* inevitable

неизвестный *прил* unknown ♦ (-ого) *м* stranger

неизгладимый *прил* indelible

неизлечимый *прил* (*болезнь*) incurable; (*больной*) terminally ill

неизменный *прил* unchanging

неимени|е (-я) *ср*: за ~м +*gen* for want of

неимоверный *прил* extreme

неимущий *прил* deprived

неиссякаемый *прил* inexhaustible

неистовый *прил* intense

неистощимый *прил* inexhaustible

ней *мест см.* **она**

нейлон (-а) *м* nylon

нейрохирург (-а) *м* neurosurgeon

нейтралитет (-а) *м* neutrality

нейтральный *прил* neutral

некем *мест см.* **некого**

некий (-ого; *f* -ая, *nt* -ое, *pl* -ие) *мест* a certain

некогда *как сказ* (*читать*) there is no time; **ей ~** she is busy; **ей ~** +*infin* ... she has no time to ...

некого (*как кто; см. Table 7*) *мест*: ~ спросить/позвать there is nobody to ask/call

некому *мест см.* **некого**

некоторый (-ого; *f* -ая *nt* -ое, *pl* -ые) *мест* some

некролог (-а) *м* obituary

некстати *нареч* at the wrong time ♦ *как сказ*: это ~ this is untimely

некто *мест* a certain person

некуда *как сказ* (*идти*) there is nowhere; дальше *или* хуже/ лучше ~ (*разг*) it can't get any worse/better

нелегитимный *прил* illegitimate

нелепый *прил* stupid

нелётный *прил*: ~ая погода poor weather for flying

нельзя *как сказ* (*невозможно*) it

is impossible; (*не разреша́ется*) it is forbidden; **~ ли?** would it be possible?; **как ~ лу́чше** as well as could be expected

нём *мест см.* **он**; **оно́**

неме́дленно *нареч* immediately

неме́дленный *прил* immediate

неме́|ть (**-ю**), *pf* **о~**) *несов* (*от ужаса, от восто́рга*) to be struck dumb; (*нога, рука́*) to go numb

не́м|ец (**-ца**) *м* German

неме́цкий *прил* German; **~ язы́к** German

немину́емый *прил* unavoidable

нём|а (**-ки**; *gen pl* **-ок**) *ж см.* **не́мец**

немно́г|ие (**-их**) *мн* few

немно́го *нареч* (*отдохну́ть, ста́рше*) a little, a bit; **~ +gen** a few; (*де́нег*) a bit

немно́жко *нареч* (*разг*) = **немно́го**

нем|о́й *прил* (*челове́к*) dumb; (*перен: вопро́с*) implied ♦ (**-о́го**) *м* mute; **~ фильм** silent film

нéмощный *прил* sick, ailing

нему́ *мест см.* **он**, **оно́**

немы́слимый *прил* unthinkable

ненави́|деть (**-жу, -дишь**) *несов перех* to hate

ненави́стный *прил* hated

не́нависть (**-и**) *ж* hatred

нена́силие (**-я**) *ср* non-violence

нена́стный *прил* wet and dismal

нена́сть|е (**-я**) *ср* awful weather

ненасы́тный *прил* insatiable

ненорма́льн|ый *прил* abnormal; (*разг: сумасше́дший*) mad ♦ (**-ого**) *м* (*разг*) crackpot

необита́емый *прил* (*ме́сто*) uninhabited; **~ о́стров** desert island

необозри́мый *прил* vast

необосно́ванный *прил* unfounded

необходи́мо *как сказ* it is

necessary; **мне ~ с Ва́ми поговори́ть** I really need to talk to you

необходи́мость (**-и**) *ж* necessity

необходи́мый *прил* necessary

необъя́тный *прил* vast

необыкнове́нный *прил* exceptional

необыкнове́нный *прил* = **необыкнове́нный**

необы́чный *прил* unusual

неожи́данность (**-и**) *ж* surprise

неожи́данный *прил* unexpected

неопределённый *прил* indefinite; (*отве́т, жест*) vague

неоспори́мый *прил* (*преиму́щество*) unquestionable; (*аргуме́нт*) incontrovertible

неотврати́мый *прил* inevitable

неотдели́мый *прил*: **~ (от +gen)** inseparable (from)

не́откуда *как сказ*: **мне ~ де́нег взять** I can't get money from anywhere

неотло́жн|ый *прил* urgent; **~ая медици́нская по́мощь** emergency medical service

неотрази́мый *прил* irresistible; (*впечатле́ние*) powerful

неотъе́млемый *прил* (*пра́во*) inalienable; (*часть*) integral

неофаши́зм (**-а**) *м* Neo-fascism

неофаши́ст (**-а**) *м* Neo-fascist

неохо́т|а (**-ы**) *ж* (*разг: нежела́ние*) reluctance ♦ *как сказ*: **мне ~ спо́рить** I don't feel like arguing

неоцени́мый *прил* invaluable

непереходный *прил*: **~ глаго́л** (*линг*) intransitive verb

неповтори́мый *прил* unique

непого́д|а (**-ы**) *ж* bad weather

неподви́жный *прил* motionless; (*взгляд*) fixed

неподде́льный *прил* genuine

неподку́пный *прил* (человек)
incorruptible

непоколеби́мый *прил*
unshakable

непола́д|ки (-ок) *мн* fault *ед*

неполноце́нност|ь (-и) *ж*
inadequacy; **ко́мплекс ~и**
inferiority complex

неполноце́нный *прил*
inadequate, insufficient

непоня́тно *нареч*
incomprehensibly ♦ *как сказ* it is
incomprehensible; **мне э́то ~ I**
cannot understand this

непоня́тный *прил*
incomprehensible

неисправи́мый *прил* (ошибка)
irreparable

непосре́дственный *прил*
(начальник) immediate;
(результат, участник) direct

непостижи́мый *прил* (загадка,
сила) incomprehensible

непоча́тый *прил:* **~ край** no end,
a great deal

непра́вд|а (-ы) *ж* lie, untruth
♦ *как сказ* it's not true; **э́то ~!** this
is a lie!

непра́вильно *нареч* (решить)
incorrectly, wrongly ♦ *как сказ:*
э́то ~ it's wrong

непра́вильный *прил* wrong;
(форма, глагол) irregular

непредви́денный *прил*
unforeseen

непредска́зуемый *прил*
unpredictable

непрекло́нный *прил* firm

непреме́нный *прил* necessary

непреры́вный *прил* continuous

непривы́чно *как сказ:* **мне ~**
+*infin* I'm not used to doing

неприе́млемый *прил*
unacceptable

неприкоснове́нност|ь (-и) *ж*

inviolability; **дипломати́ческая ~**
diplomatic immunity

неприли́чный *прил* indecent

неприме́тный *прил* (человек,
жизнь) unremarkable

непримири́мый *прил*
irreconcilable

непринуждённый *прил* informal

непристо́йный *прил* obscene

непристу́пный *прил* (крепость)
impregnable

неприя́зн|ь (-и) *ж* hostility

неприя́тно *как сказ:* **~** +*infin* it's
unpleasant to do; **мне ~ говори́ть
об э́том** I don't enjoy talking about
it

неприя́тност|ь (-и) *ж* (обычно
мн: на работе, в семье) trouble
ед

неприя́тный *прил* unpleasant

непроизво́льный *прил*
involuntary

непромока́емый *прил*
waterproof

нера́венств|о (-а) *ср* inequality

неравнопра́ви|е (-я) *ср*
inequality (of rights)

нера́вный *прил* unequal

неразбери́х|а (-и) *ж* (разг)
muddle

неразреши́мый *прил* insoluble

неразры́вный *прил* indissoluble

неразу́мный *прил* unreasonable

нерв (-а) *м* (АНАТ) nerve; **не́рвы**
(вся система) nervous system

не́рвнича|ть (-ю) *несов* to fret

не́рвный *прил* nervous

нерво́зный *прил* (человек)
nervous, highly (*BRIT*) или high (*US*)
strung

нереши́тельный *прил* indecisive

нержаве́ющ|ий *прил* rustproof;
~ая ста́ль stainless steel

неро́вный *прил* (поверхность)
uneven; (характер) unbalanced

неря́шливый *прил* (человек, одежда) scruffy; (работа) careless

нёс *несов см.* **нести́**

несбы́точный *прил* unrealizable

несваре́ни|е (-я) *ср:* ~ желу́дка indigestion

несгиба́емый *прил* staunch

несгора́емый *прил* fireproof

несклоня́емый *прил (линг)* indeclinable

не́скольк|о (-их) *чис:* ~ +*gen* a few ♦ *нареч* (обидеться) somewhat

нескро́мный *прил* (человек) immodest; (вопрос) indelicate; (жест, предложение) indecent

неслы́ханный *прил* unheard of

неслы́шно *нареч* (сделать) quietly ♦ *как сказ:* **мне** ~ I can't hear

неслы́шный *прил* inaudible

несмотря́ *предл:* ~ **на** +*acc* in spite of, despite; ~ **на то что ...** in spite of *или* despite the fact that ...; ~ **ни на что** no matter what

несовершенноле́тний (-его) *прил* minor ♦ *прил:* ~ **ребёнок** minor

несоверше́нный *прил* flawed; ~ **вид** *(линг)* imperfective (aspect)

несовмести́мый *прил* incompatible

несогласо́ванный *прил* (действия) uncoordinated

несомне́нно *нареч* (правильный, хороший итп) indisputably ♦ *вводн сл* without a doubt ♦ *как сказ:* **это** ~ this is indisputable; ~, **что он придёт** there is no doubt that he will come

несомне́нный *прил* indisputable

несостоя́тельный *прил (КОММ)* insolvent; (начальник) incompetent

несправедли́вость (-и) *ж* injustice

несправедли́вый *прил* (человек, суд, упрёк) unfair, unjust

непроста́ *нареч (разг)* for a reason

нес|ти́ (-у́, -ёшь; *pt* **нёс, -ла́)** *несов от* **носи́ть** ♦ *перех* to carry; (влечь: неприятности) to bring; (*pf* **по~**; службу) to carry out; (*pf* **с~**; яйцо) to lay; **~сь** *несов возв* (человек, машина) to race; (*pf* **с~сь**; курица) to lay eggs

несча́стный *прил* unhappy; (разг: жалкий) wretched; ~ **слу́чай** accident

несча́сть|е (-я) *ср* misfortune; **к ~ю** unfortunately

несъедо́бный *прил* inedible

<u>KEYWORD</u>

нет *част* **1** (при отрицании, несогласии) no; **ты согла́сен?** - **нет** do you agree? - no; **тебе́ не нра́вится мой суп?** - **нет, нра́вится** don't you like my soup? - yes, I do

2 (для привлечения внимания): **нет, ты то́лько посмотри́ на неё!** would you just look at him!

3 (выражает недоверие): **нет, ты действи́тельно не се́рдишься?** so you are really not angry?

♦ *как сказ:* **нет** +*gen* (не имеется: об одном предмете) there is no; (: о нескольких предметах) there are no; **нет вре́мени** there is no time; **нет биле́тов** *или* биле́тов **нет** there are no tickets; **у меня́ нет де́нег** I have no money; **его́ нет в го́роде** he is not in town

♦ *союз* (во фразах): **нет - так нет** it can't be helped; **чего́ то́лько нет!** what don't they have!; **нет что́бы извини́ться** (*разг*) instead of saying sorry

нетерпе́ни|е (-я) *ср* impatience; **~м ждать** (*impf*)/**слу́шать** (*impf*) to wait/listen impatiently; **с ~м жду Ва́шего отве́та** I look forward to hearing from you

нетерпи́мый *прил* intolerable; (*непримири́мый*): **~ к** +*dat* (*ко лжи*) intolerant of

нетре́зв|ый *прил* drunk; **в ~ом состоя́нии** drunk

нетрудово́й *прил*: **~ дохо́д** unearned income

нетрудоспосо́бност|ь (-и) *ж* disability; **посо́бие по ~и** disability living allowance

нетрудоспосо́бный *прил* unable to work through disability

не́тто *прил неизм* (*о ве́се*) net

неуда́ч|а (-и) *ж* bad luck; (*в дела́х*) failure

неуда́чный *прил* (*попы́тка*) unsuccessful; (*фильм, стихи́*) bad

неудо́бно *нареч* (*располо́женно, сиде́ть*) uncomfortably ♦ *как сказ* it's awkward; **мне ~** I am uncomfortable; **~ задава́ть лю́дям таки́е вопро́сы** it's awkward to ask people such questions; **(мне) ~ сказа́ть ему́ об э́том** I feel uncomfortable telling him that

неудо́бный *прил* uncomfortable

неудовлетвори́тельный *прил* unsatisfactory

неудово́льстви|е (-я) *ср* dissatisfaction

неуже́ли *част* really

неузнава́емост|ь (-и) *ж*: **до ~и** beyond (all) recognition

неузнава́емый *прил* unrecognizable

неукло́нный *прил* steady

неуклю́жий *прил* clumsy

неулови́мый *прил* imperceptible; (*челове́к*) elusive

неуме́стный *прил* inappropriate

неумоли́мый *прил* relentless; (*зако́н*) stringent

неурожа́йный *прил*: **~ год** year with a poor harvest

неуро́чный *прил* (*вре́мя*) unearthly

неуря́диц|а (-ы) *ж* (*разг: обы́чно мн: ссо́ры*) squabble

неуста́нный *прил* indefatigable

неутоли́мый *прил* insatiable; (*жа́жда*) unquenchable

неутоми́мый *прил* untiring

неформа́льный *прил* (*организа́ция*) non-formal

нефри́т (-а) *м* (*МЕД*) nephritis; (*ГЕО*) jade

нефтедобыва́ющий *прил* (*промы́шленность*) oil

нефтедобы́ч|а (-и) *ж* drilling for oil

нефтеперерабо́тк|а (-и) *ж* oil processing

нефтепрово́д (-а) *м* oil pipeline

нефт|ь (-и) *ж* oil, petroleum

нефтя́ник (-а) *м* worker in the oil industry

нефтяно́й *прил* oil

нехва́тк|а (-и) *ж*: **~** +*gen* shortage of

нехорошо́ *нареч* badly ♦ *как сказ* it's bad; **мне ~** I'm not well

не́хотя *нареч* unwillingly

неча́янный *прил* unintentional; (*неожи́данный*) chance

не́чего *как сказ*: **~ рассказа́ть** there is nothing to tell; **не сле́дует** there's no need to do; **не́ за что!** (*в отве́т на благода́рность*) not at all!, you're welcome! (*US*); **де́лать ~** there's

nothing else to be done
нечётный *прил (число)* odd
нечто *мест* something
неясно *нареч*: он ~ объяснил положение he didn't explain the situation clearly ♦ *как сказ* it's not clear; мне ~, почему он отказался I'm not clear *или* it's not clear to me why he refused
неясный *прил (очертания, звук)* indistinct; *(мысль, вопрос)* vague

---

KEYWORD

ни *част* 1 *(усиливает отрицание)* not a; ни один not one, not a single; она не произнесла ни слова she didn't say a word; она ни разу не пришла she didn't come once; у меня не осталось ни рубля I don't have a single rouble left
2: кто/что/как ни who-/what-/however; сколько ни however much; что ни говори whatever you say; как ни старайся however hard you try
♦ *союз (при перечислении)*: ни ..., ни ... neither ... nor ...; ни за что no way

нигде *нареч* nowhere; его ~ не было he was nowhere to be found; ~ нет моей книги I can't find my book anywhere, my book is nowhere to be found; я ~ не мог поесть I couldn't find anywhere to get something to eat
ниже *сравн прил от* **низкий**
♦ *сравн нареч от* **низко** ♦ *нареч (далее)* later on ♦ *предл*: ~ +gen below
нижн|ий *прил (ступенька, ящик)* bottom; ~ этаж ground (*BRIT*) *или* first (*US*) floor; ~ее бельё underwear; ~яя юбка underskirt

низ (-а) *м (стола, юбки)* bottom
низкий *прил (также перен)* low
низко *нареч* low
низкопробный *прил (золото)* low-grade; *(книга)* trashy
низовой *прил* grass-roots
низший *сравн прил от* **низкий**; *(звание)* junior
НИИ *м сокр* (= научно-исследовательский институт) scientific research institute
никак *нареч (никаким образом)* no way; ~ не могу запомнить это слово I can't remember this word at all; дверь ~ не открывалась this door just wouldn't open
никак|ой *мест*: нет ~ого сомнения there is no doubt at all; ~ие деньги не помогли no amount of money would have helped
никел|ь (-я) *м (хим)* nickel
никогда *нареч* never; как ~ as never before
никого *мест см.* **никто**
ник|ой *нареч*: ~оим образом at all; ни в коем случае under no circumstances
ни|кто (-кого; *как кто*; *см. Table 7*) *мест* nobody
никуда *нареч*: я ~ не поеду I'm not going anywhere; ~ я не поеду I'm going nowhere; это ~ не годится that just won't do
ниоткуда *нареч* from nowhere; ~ нет помощи I get no help from anywhere
нисколько *нареч* not at all; *(не лучше)* no; *(не рад)* at all
нит|ка (-ки; *gen pl* -ок) *ж (для шитья)* thread *ед*; (: для вязания) yarn *ед*
нит|ь (-и) *ж* = **нитка**
них *мест см.* **они**

ничего́ мест см. **ничто́** ♦ нареч fairly well; всё идёт не так, как надо, но всё в порядке all right that ...; извини́те, я Вас побеспоко́ю – ~! sorry to disturb you - it's all right!; как живёшь? – ~ how are you? - all right; ~ себе́ (сносно) fairly well; ~ себе́! (удивление) well, I never!

ниче́й (-ьего́; f -ья́, nt -ьё, pl -ьи́) (как чей; см. Table 5) мест nobody's

ниче́йн|ый прил: ~ результа́т/ ~ая па́ртия draw

ничко́м нареч face down

ничт|о́ (-его́; как что; см. Table 7) мест, ср nothing; **ничего́ подо́бного не ви́дел** I've never seen anything like it; **ничего́ подо́бного!** (разг: совсем не так) nothing like it!; **ни за что́** (ни в коем случае) no way!; **ни за что́ не соглаша́йся** whatever you do, don't agree; **я здесь ни при чём** it has nothing to do with me; **ничего́ не поде́лаешь** there's nothing to be done

ничто́жный прил paltry

ничу́ть нареч (нисколько) not at all; (не лучше, не больше) no; (не испугался, не огорчился) at all

ничь|я́ (-е́й) ж (СПОРТ) draw; **сыгра́ть** (pf) в ~ю́ to draw (BRIT), tie (US)

ни́щенск|ий прил (зарплата) meagre (BRIT), meager (US); ~ая жизнь life of begging

нищет|а́ (-ы́) ж poverty

ни́щ|ий прил poverty-stricken ♦ (-его) м beggar

но союз but ♦ межд: ~! gee up!

нова́тор (-а) м innovator

нове́лл|а (-ы) ж novella

но́венький прил (разг) new

новизн|а́ (-ы́) ж novelty

нови́нк|а (-и; gen pl -ок) ж new product

новичо́к (-ка́) м newcomer; (в классе) new pupil

новобра́н|ец (-ца) м new recruit

новобра́чн|ый (-ого) м newlywed

нового́дн|ий прил New Year; ~яя ёлка ≈ Christmas tree

новорождённый прил newborn ♦ (-ого) м newborn boy

новосёл (-а) м (дома) new owner

новосе́ль|е (-я; gen pl -ий) ср house-warming (party)

но́вост|ь (-и; gen pl -е́й) ж news

но́вшеств|о (-а) ср (явление) novelty; (метод) innovation

но́в|ый прил new; ~ая исто́рия modern history; **Но́вый Заве́т** the New Testament; **Но́вая Зела́ндия** New Zealand

ног|а́ (-и́; acc sg -у, nom pl -и, gen pl -, dat sg -а́м) ж (ступня) foot; (выше ступни) leg; **вверх ~ми** upside down

но́гот|ь (-тя; gen pl -те́й) м nail

нож (-а́) м knife

но́ж|ка (-ки; gen pl -ек) ж уменьш от **нога́**; (стула, стола итп) leg; (циркуля) arm

но́жниц|ы (-) мн scissors мн

ножно́й прил foot

ножо́в|ка (-ки; gen pl -ок) ж hacksaw

ноздр|я́ (-и́; nom pl -и, gen pl -е́й) ж (обычно мн) nostril

нол|ь (-я́) м (МАТ) zero, nought; (о температуре) zero; (перен: человек) nothing; ~ це́лых пять деся́тых, 0.5 zero или nought point five, 0.5; **в де́сять ~~** at exactly ten o'clock

номенклату́р|а (-ы) ж (товаров) list ♦ собир (работники) nomenklatura

но́мер (-а; nom pl -á) м number; (журнала) issue; (в гости́нице) room; ~ маши́ны registration (number)

номерно́й прил ~ знак (автомоби́ля) (car) number (BRIT) или license (US) plate

номеро́к (-ка́) ж (для пальто́) ≈ ticket

нор|а́ (-ы́; nom pl -ы) ж (зайца) burrow; (лисы́) den; (барсука́) set; (пере́) hole

Норве́ги|я (-и) ж Norway

но́рк|а (-и; gen pl -ок) ж mink

но́рм|а (-ы) ж standard; (вы́работки) rate

нормализова́ть (-у́ю) (не)сов перех to normalize; ~ся (не)сов возв to stabilize

норма́льно нареч normally ♦ как сказ: э́то вполне́ ~ this is quite normal; как дела́? - не пло́хо how are things? - not bad; у нас всё ~ everything's fine with us

норма́льный прил normal

нос (-а; loc sg -у́, nom pl -ы́) м nose; (корабля́) bow; (пти́цы) beak, bill; (боти́нка) toe

носи́л|ки (-ок) мн stretcher ед

носи́льщик (-а) м porter

носи́тель (-я) м (инфе́кции) carrier; ~ языка́ native speaker

носи́ть (-шу́, -сишь; несов перех to carry; (пла́тье, очки́) to wear; (усы́, причёску) to sport; (фами́лию му́жа) to use; ~ся несов возв (челове́к) to rush; (слу́хи) to spread; (оде́жда) to wear; (разг: увлека́ться): ~ся с +instr (с иде́ей) to be preoccupied with; (с челове́ком) to make a fuss of

носово́й прил (звук) nasal; ~а́я часть bow; ~ плато́к handkerchief

носо́к (-ка́; gen pl -о́к) м (обы́чно мн: чуло́к) sock; (gen pl -ко́в; боти́нка, чулка́, ноги́) toe

носоро́г (-а) м rhinoceros, rhino

ностальги́|я (-и) ж nostalgia

но́т|а (-ы) ж note; см. та́кже но́ты

нотариа́льн|ый прил (услу́ги) notarial; ~ая конто́ра notarial office

нота́риус (-а) м notary (public)

но́т|ы (-) мн (МУЗ) sheet music

ноутбу́к (-а) м (КОМП) notebook

ночева́ть (-у́ю; pf пере~) несов to spend the night

ночёв|ка (-ки; gen pl -ок) ж: останови́ться на ~ку to spend the night

ночле́г (-а) м (ме́сто) somewhere to spend the night; остана́вливаться (останови́ться pf) на ~ to spend the night

ночно́й прил (час, хо́лод) night; ~áя руба́шка nightshirt

ночь (-и; loc sg -и́, nom pl -и, gen pl -е́й) ж night; на ~ before bed; споко́йной но́чи! good night!

но́чью нареч at night

но́шеный прил second-hand

ношу́(сь) несов см. носи́ть(ся)

ноя́бр|ь (-я́) м November

нрав (-а) м (челове́ка) temperament; см. та́кже нра́вы

нра́в|иться (-люсь, -ишься; pf по~) несов возв: мне/им ~ится э́тот фильм I/they like this film; мне ~ится чита́ть/гуля́ть I like to read или reading/to go for a walk

нра́вственный прил moral

нра́в|ы (-ов) мн morals

н.с. сокр = но́вого сти́ля) NS, New Style

НТР ж сокр = нау́чно-техни́ческая револю́ция

ну межд 1 (выражает побуждение к действию): ну, начина́й! come on, get started!

2 (выражает восхищение) what; ну и си́ла! what strength!

3 (выражает иронию) well (well)

♦ част 1 (неужели): (да) ну?! not really?!

2 (усиливает выразительность): ну коне́чно! why of course!; я тебе́ покажу́! why, I'll show you!

3 (допустим): ты говори́шь по-англи́йски? - ну, говорю́ do you speak English? - what if I do?

4 (во фразах): ну и ну! (разг) well well!; ну-ка! (разг) come on!; ну тебя́/его́! (разг) forget it!

ну́дный прил tedious

нужд|**а́** (-ы́; nom pl -ы) ж (no pl; бедность) poverty; (потребность): ~ (в +prp) need (for)

нужда́|**ться** (-юсь) несов возв (бедствовать) to be needy; ~ (impf) в +prp to need, be in need of

ну́жно как сказ (необходимо): ~, что́бы им помогли́, ~ им помо́чь it is necessary to help them; мне ~ идти́ I have to go, I must go; мне ~ 10 рубле́й I need 10 roubles; о́чень ~! (разг) my foot!

ну́жный прил necessary

нулев|**о́й** прил: ~**а́я температу́ра** temperature of zero; ~**а́я отме́тка** (mark of) zero

нул|**ь** (-я́) м (мат) zero, nought; (о температуре) zero; (перен: человек) nonentity; **начина́ть; начина́ть** рf **с** ~**а́** to start from scratch

нумер|**ова́ть** (-у́ю; pf про~) несов перех to number

ну́три|**я** (-и) ж (зоол) coypu

ны́не нареч today

ны́нешний прил the present

нырн|**у́ть** (-у́, -ёшь) сов to dive

ныря́|**ть** (-ю) несов to dive

ны́|**ть** (**но́ю, но́ешь**) несов (рана) to ache; (жаловаться) to moan

Нью-Йо́рк (-а) м New York

н.э. сокр (= на́шей э́ры) AD

нюх (-а) м (собаки) nose

ню́ха|**ть** (-ю; pf по~) несов перех (цветы, воздух) to smell

ня́неч|**ка** (-ки; gen pl -ек) ж (разг) = ня́ня

ня́нч|**ить** (-у, -ишь) несов перех; ~**ся** несов возв: ~**ся с** +instr (с младенцем) to mind

ня́н|**ька** (-ьки; gen pl -ек) ж (разг: ребёнка) nanny

ня́н|**я** (-и; gen pl -ь) ж nanny; (работающая на дому) child minder; (в больнице) auxiliary nurse; (в детском саду) cleaner; **приходя́щая ~** babysitter

О, о

о межд oh ♦ предл: ~ +prp about; ~ +асс (опереться, ударитьс́я) against; (споткнуться) over

об предл = **о**

о́б|**а** (-о́их; см. Table 25; f -е, nt ~) м чис both

обанкро́|**титься** (-чусь, -тишься) сов возв to go bankrupt

обая́ни|**е** (-я) ср charm

обая́тельный прил charming

обва́л (-а) м (снежный) avalanche; (здания, экономики) collapse

обвали́ться (3sg -ится) impf

обва́ливаться) сов возв to collapse

обв|ести́ (-еду́, -едёшь; pt -ёл, -ела́; impf **обводи́ть)** сов перех (букву, чертёж) to go over; **обводи́ть** (~ pf) **вокру́г** +gen to lead или take round

обвине́ни|е (-я) ср: ~ (в +prp) accusation (of); (ЮР) charge (of) ♦ собир (обвиняющая сторона) the prosecution

обвини́тел|ь (-я) м accuser; (ЮР) prosecutor

обвини́тельный прил (речь) accusatory; ~ пригово́р (ЮР) verdict of guilty; ~ акт (ЮР) indictment

обвин|и́ть (-ю́, -и́шь; impf **обвиня́ть)** сов перех: ~ кого́-н (в +prp) to accuse sb (of); (ЮР) to charge sb (with)

обвиня́ем|ый (-ого) м the accused, the defendant

обвиня́|ть (-ю) несов от обвини́ть ♦ перех (ЮР) to prosecute

об|ви́ть (-овью́, -овьёшь; impf **обвива́ть)** сов перех (подлеж: плющ) to twine around; **обвива́ть** (~ pf) **кого́-н/что-н чем-н** to wind sth round sb/sth

обв|яза́ть (-яжу́, -я́жешь; impf **обвя́зывать)** сов перех: ~ кого́-н/что-н чем-н to tie sth round sb/sth; ~ся (impf **обвя́зываться)** сов возв: ~ся чем-н to tie sth round o.s.

обгоня́|ть (-ю) несов от обогна́ть

обгор|е́ть (-ю́, -и́шь; impf -а́ть) сов (дом) to be burnt; (на со́лнце) to get sunburnt

обгры́з|ть (-у́, -ёшь; impf

обгрыза́ть) сов перех to gnaw

обдира́ть (-ю) несов от ободра́ть

обду́манный прил considered

обду́ма|ть (-ю; impf **обду́мывать)** сов перех to consider, think over

об|е (-е́их) ж чис см. о́ба

обега́|ть (-ю) несов от обежа́ть

обе́д (-а) м lunch, dinner; (время) lunch или dinner time; по́сле ~a after lunch или dinner; (по́сле 12 часо́в дня) in the afternoon

обе́да|ть (-ю; pf по~) несов to have lunch или dinner

обе́денный прил (стол, сервиз) dinner; (время) lunch, dinner

обедне́|ть (-ю) сов от бедне́ть

обе́дн|я (-и; gen pl -ей) ж Mass

обежа́ть (как бежа́ть; см. Table 20; impf обега́ть) сов: ~ вокру́г +gen to run round

обезбо́ливающ|ее (-его) ср painkiller

обезбо́л|ить (-ю, -ишь; impf **обезбо́ливать)** сов перех to anaesthetize (BRIT), anesthetize (US)

обезвре́|дить (-жу, -дишь; impf **обезвре́живать)** сов перех ещ вуагыуж (престу́пника) to disarm

обездо́ленный прил deprived

обезору́ж|ить (-у, -ишь; impf **обезору́живать)** сов перех to disarm

обезу́ме|ть (-ю) сов: ~ от +gen to go out of one's mind with

обезья́н|а (-ы) ж (с хвосто́м) monkey; (без хвоста́) ape; (перен: разг) copycat

обе́их чис см. о́бе

оберега́|ть (-ю) несов перех (челове́ка) to protect

оберн|у́ть (-у́, -ёшь; impf **обёртывать** или **обора́чивать)** сов перех to wrap (up); ~ся (impf

обора́чиваться *сов возв* (повернуться назад) to turn (round); **обора́чиваться** (**~ся** *pf*) +*instr* (неприятностями) to turn out to be

обёрт|ка (**-ки**; *gen pl* **-ок**) *ж* (конфетная) wrapper

обёрточн|ый *прил*: **~ая бума́га** wrapping paper

обёртыва|ть (**-ю**) *несов от* **оберну́ть**

обеспе́чени|е (**-я**) *ср* (мира, договора) guarantee; **~** +*instr* (сырьём) provision of; **материа́льное ~** financial security

обеспе́ченность (**-и**) *ж* (material) comfort; **фина́нсовая ~** financial security

обеспе́ченн|ый *прил* well-off, well-to-do

обеспе́ч|ить (**-у, -ишь**; *impf* **обеспе́чивать**) *сов перех* (семью) to provide for; (мир, успех) to guarantee; **обеспе́чивать** (**~** *pf*) **кого́-н/что-н чем-н** to provide *или* supply sb/sth with sth

обесси́ле|ть (**-ю**; *impf* **обесси́ливать**) *сов* to become *или* grow weak

обесцве́|тить (**-чу, -тишь**; *impf* **обесцве́чивать**) *несов перех* to bleach

обесце́н|ить (**-ю, -ишь**; *impf* **обесце́нивать**) *сов перех* to devalue; **~ся** (*impf* **обесце́ниваться**) *сов возв* to be devalued; (вещи) to depreciate

обеща́ни|е (**-я**) *ср* promise

обеща́|ть (**-ю**; *pf* **~** *или* **по~**) *несов (не)перех* to promise

обжа́ловани|е (**-я**) *ср* appeal

обжа́л|овать (**-ую**) *сов перех* to appeal against

об|же́чь (**-ожгу́, -ожжёшь** *etc*,

-ожгу́т; *pt* **-жёг, -ожгла́, -ожгло́**; *impf* **обжига́ть**) *сов перех* to burn; (кирпич итп) to fire; (подлеж: крапива) to sting; **~ся** (*impf* **обжига́ться**) *сов возв* to burn o.s.

обзо́р (**-а**) *м* view; (новостей) review

обзо́рный *прил* general

обива́|ть (**-ю**) *несов от* **оби́ть**

оби́вк|а (**-и**) *ж* upholstery

оби́|да (**-ы**) *ж* insult; (горечь) grievance; **кака́я ~!** what a pity!; **быть** (*impf*) **в ~е на кого́-н** to be in a huff with sb

оби́|деть (**-жу, -дишь**; *impf* **обижа́ть**) *сов перех* to hurt, offend; **~ся** (*impf* **обижа́ться**) *сов возв*: **~ся (на** +*acc*) to be hurt *или* offended (by)

оби́дно *как сказ (см прил)* it's offensive; it's upsetting; **мне ~ слы́шать э́то** it hurts me to hear this

оби́дный *прил* offensive; (разг: досадный) upsetting

оби́дчивый *прил* touchy

обижа́|ть(ся) (**-ю(сь)**) *несов от* **оби́деть(ся)**

оби́женный *прил* aggrieved

оби́ли|е (**-я**) *ср* abundance

оби́льный *прил* abundant

обита́|ть (**-ю**) *несов* to live

об|и́ть (**-обью, -обьёшь** *etc*; *impf* **обива́ть**; *imper* **обе́й(те)**) *сов перех*: **~ (**+*instr*) to cover (with)

обихо́д (**-а**) *м*: **быть в ~е** to be in use

обкле́|ить (**-ю, -ишь**; *impf* **обкле́ивать**) *сов перех* (плакатами) to cover; (обоями) to (wall)paper

обкра́дыва|ть (**-ю**) *несов от* **обокра́сть**

обл. *сокр* = **о́бласть**

обла́в|а (**-ы**) *ж* (на

преступников) roundup

облага́|ть (-ю) *несов от* обложи́ть

облада́|ть (-ю) *несов*: ~ +*instr* to possess

о́блак|о (-а; *nom pl* -á, *gen pl* -о́в) *ср* cloud

областно́й *прил* ≈ regional

о́бласт|ь (-и; *gen pl* -éй) *ж* region; (АДМИН) ≈ region, oblast; (науки, искусства) field

о́блачный *прил* cloudy

облега́|ть (-ю) *несов от* обле́чь
♦ *перех* to fit

облега́ющий *прил* close-fitting

облегче́ни|е (-я) *ср* (жизни) improvement; (успокоение) relief

облегч|и́ть (-у́, -и́шь; *impf* облегча́ть) *сов перех* (вес) to lighten; (жизнь) to make easier; (боль) to relieve

обле́з|ть (-у, -ешь; *impf* облеза́ть) *сов* (разг) to grow mangy; (краска, обои) to peel (off)

облека́|ть (-ю) *несов от* обле́чь
♦ *перех* to fly round
♦ *неперех* (листья) to fall off

обл|е́чь (-еку́, -ечёшь итп, -еку́т; *pt* -ёк, -екла́) *impf* облека́ть) *сов перех*: ~ кого́-н/ что́-н чем-н (властью, доверием) to vest sb/sth with sth; (*impf* облега́ть, *3sg* -я́жет, *pt* -я́г, -егла́, -егло́; платье) to envelop

облива́|ть (-ю) *несов от* обли́ть; ~ся *несов от* обли́ться ♦ *возв*: ~ся слеза́ми to be in floods of tears

облига́ци|я (-и) *ж* (КОММ) bond

обл|иза́ть (-ижу́, -и́жешь; *impf* обли́зывать) *сов перех* to lick

о́блик (-а) *м* appearance

обл|и́ть (-олью́, -ольёшь; *impf*

облива́|ть; *сов перех*: ~ кого́-н/ что-н чем-н (намеренно) to pour sth over sb/sth; (случайно) to spill sth over sb/sth; ~ся (*impf*

облива́ться) *сов возв*: ~ся чем-н (водо́й) to sluice o.s. with sth

обл|ожи́ть (-ожу́, -о́жишь; *impf* облага́ть) *сов перех*: ~ нало́гом to tax

обло́ж|ка (-ки; *gen pl* -ек) *ж* (книги, тетради) cover

облок|оти́ться (-очу́сь, -о́тишься) *сов возв*: ~ на +*acc* to lean one's elbows on

обло́м|ок (-ка) *м* fragment

облуче́ни|е (-я) *ср* irradiation

облуч|и́ть (-у́, -и́шь; *impf*

облуча́ть) *сов перех* to irradiate; ~ся (*impf* облуча́ться) *сов возв* to be irradiated

облысе́|ть (-ю) *сов от* лысе́ть

обмакн|у́ть (-у́, -ёшь; *impf*

обма́кивать) *сов перех*: ~ что-н в +*acc* to dip sth into

обма́н (-а) *м* deception

обма́нный *прил*: ~ым путём fraudulently

обм|ану́ть (-ану́, -а́нешь; *impf*

обма́нывать) *сов перех* to deceive; (поступить нечестно) to cheat

обма́нчивый *прил* deceptive

обма́ныва|ть (-ю) *несов от* обману́ть

обма́тыва|ть (-ю) *несов от* обмота́ть

обме́н (-а) *м* exchange; (документов) renewal; (также: ~ веще́ств: БИО) metabolism; (также: ~ жилпло́щадью) exchange (of flats etc)

обме́нный *прил* exchange

обмен|я́ть (-ю; *impf*

обме́нивать) *сов перех* (вещи, билеты) to change; ~ся (*impf*

обме́ниваться *сов возв*: ~**ся**
+*instr* to exchange

обморо́|**зить** (-жу, -зишь; *impf*
обмора́живать) *сов перех*: ~
но́гу to get frostbite in one's foot

обморок (-а) *м гл*; **па́дать
(упа́сть** *pf*) в ~ to faint

обмота́|**ть** (-ю) *impf*
обма́тывать) *сов перех*: ~
кого́-н/что́-н чем-н to wrap sth
round sb/sth

обм|**ы́ть** (-о́ю, -о́ешь; *impf*
обмыва́ть) *сов перех* (*ра́ну*) to
bathe; (*разг: собы́тие*) to
celebrate (*by drinking*)

обнагле́ть (-ю) *сов от* **нагле́ть**

обнадёж|**ить** (-у, -ишь; *impf*
обнадёживать) *сов перех* to
reassure

обнажённый *прил* bare

обнаж|**и́ть** (-у́, -и́шь; *impf*
обнажа́ть) *сов перех* (*руки, но́ги*) to bare; (*ветки*) to
strip bare; ~**ся** (*impf* **обнажа́ться**)
сов возв to be exposed; (*челове́к*)
to strip

обнаро́довать (-ую) *сов перех*
(*фа́кты, статью́*) to make public;
(*зако́н, указ*) to promulgate

обнару́ж|**ить** (-у, -ишь; *impf*
обнару́живать) *сов перех*
(*найти́*) to find; (*прояви́ть*) to
show; ~**ся**
(*impf* **обнару́живаться**)
сов возв
(*найти́сь*) to be found; (*ста́ть
я́вным*) to become evident

обн|**ести́** (-есу́, -есёшь; *pt* -ёс,
-есла́, -есло́; *impf* **обноси́ть**) *сов
перех*: ~ **что-н/кого́-н вокру́г**
+*gen* to carry sth/sb round;
(*огороди́ть*): ~ **что-н чем-н** to
surround sth with sth

обнима́ть(ся) (-ю(сь)) *несов от*
обня́ть(ся)

обни́мк|**а** *ж*: в ~**у** (*разг*) with their

arms around each other

обнов|**и́ть** (-лю́, -и́шь; *impf*
обновля́ть) *сов перех*
(*обору́дование, гардеро́б*) to
replenish; (*репертуа́р*) to refresh;
~**ся** (*impf* **обновля́ться**) *сов возв*
(*репертуа́р*) to be refreshed;
(*органи́зм*) to be regenerated

обн|**я́ть** (-иму́, -и́мешь; *pt* -ял,
-яла́, -яло; *impf* **обнима́ть**) *сов
перех* to embrace; ~**ся** (*impf*
обнима́ться) *сов возв* to
embrace (each other)

обо *предл см.* **о**

обобщ|**и́ть** (-у́, -и́шь; *impf* ~**а́ть**)
сов перех (*фа́кты*) to generalize
from; (*статью́*) to summarize

обога|**ти́ть** (-щу́, -ти́шь; *impf*
обогаща́ть) *сов перех* to enrich;
~**ся** (*impf* **обогаща́ться**) *сов возв*
(*челове́к, страна́*) to be enriched

об|**огна́ть** (-гоню́, -го́нишь; *impf*
обгоня́ть) *сов перех* to overtake;
(*перен*) to outstrip

обогре́ть (-ю; *impf* **обогрева́ть**)
сов перех (*помеще́ние*) to heat;
(*челове́ка*) to warm

о́б|**од** (-ода; *nom pl* -о́дья, *gen pl*
-о́дьев) *м* (*ра́кетки*) frame

обо́дранный *прил* (*оде́жда*)
shabby; (*руки*) scratched

об|**одра́ть** (-деру́, -дерёшь; *impf*
обдира́ть) *сов перех* (*ко́ру,
шку́ру*) to strip; (*ру́ки*) to scratch

ободр|**и́ть** (-ю́, -и́шь; *impf*
ободря́ть) *сов перех* to
encourage

обо́з (-а) *м* convoy

обознача́|**ть** (-ю) *несов от*
обозна́чить ♦ *перех* to signify

обозна́ч|**ить** (-у, -ишь; *impf*
обознача́ть) *сов перех*
(*грани́цу*) to mark; (*сло́во*) to
mean

обозрева́тель (-я) *м* (*собы́тий*)

observer; (*на радио итп*) editor

обозре́ни|е (-я) *ср* review

обо́|и (-ев) *мн* wallpaper *ед*

обо́их *чис см.* о́ба

обойти́ (*как идти́; см. Table 18*; *impf* обходи́ть) *сов перех* to go round; (*закон*) to get round; (*обогнать*) to pass; ~сь (*impf* обходи́ться (*уладиться*) to turn out well; (*стоить*): ~сь в +*acc* to cost; обходи́ться (~сь *pf*) с кем-н/чем-н to treat sb/sth; обходи́ться (~сь *pf*) без +*gen* (*разг*) to get by without

обокра́сть (-краду́, -крадёшь; *impf* обкра́дывать) *сов перех* to rob

оболо́ч|ка (-ки; *gen pl* -ек) *ж* (*плода*) pericarp; (*Земли́*) crust

обоня́ни|е (-я) *ср* sense of smell

обора́чива|ться(ся) (-юсь(ся)) *несов от* оберну́ть(ся)

оборв|а́ть (-у́, -ёшь; *pt* -а́л, -ала́, -а́ло, *impf* обрыва́ть) *сов перех* (*верёвку*) to break; (*ягоды, цветы*) to pick; (*перен: разговор, дружбу*) to break off; (: *разг: говоря́щего*) to cut short; ~ся (*impf* обрыва́ться) *сов возв* (*верёвка*) to break; (*перен: жизнь, разговор*) to be cut short

обо́р|ка (-ки; *gen pl* -ок) *ж* frill

оборо́н|а (-ы) *ж* defence (*BRIT*), defense (*US*)

оборо́нный *прил* defence (*BRIT*), defense (*US*)

обороня́|ть (-ю) *несов перех* to defend; ~ся *несов возв* (*защищаться*) to defend o.s.

оборо́т (-а) *м* (*полный круг*) revolution; (*КОММ*) turnover; (*обратная сторона*) back; (*перен: поворот событий*) turn; (*ЛИНГ*) turn of phrase; (*употребление*)

circulation

обору́довани|е (-я) *ср* equipment

обору́д|овать (-ую) (*не*)*сов перех* to equip

обосн|ова́ть (-у́ю; *impf* обосно́вывать) *сов перех* (*теорию, вывод*) to substantiate; ~ся (*impf* обосно́вываться) *сов возв* (*расположиться*) to settle

обосо́бленный *прил* (*дом*) detached; (*жизнь*) solitary

обостри́|ть (-ю́, -и́шь; *impf* обостря́ть) *сов перех* to sharpen; (*желания, конфликт*) to intensify; ~ся (*impf* обостря́ться) *сов возв* (*см перех*) to sharpen; to intensify

обошёл(ся) *etc сов см.* обойти́(сь)

обою́дный *прил* mutual

обраба́т|ывать (-ю; *impf* обраба́тывать) *сов перех* (*камень*) to cut; (*кожу*) to cure; (*деталь*) to turn; (*текст*) to polish up; (*землю*) to till; (*перен: разг: человека*) to work on

обра́д|овать(ся) (-ую(сь)) *сов от* ра́довать(ся)

о́браз (-а) *м* image; (*ЛИТЕРАТУРА*) figure; (*жизни итп*) way; (*икона*) icon; каки́м ~ом? in what way?; таки́м ~ом in this way; (*следовательно*) consequently; гла́вным ~ом mainly; не́которым ~ом to some extent

образе́ц (-ца́) *м* sample; (*скромности, мужества*) model

образова́ни|е (-я) *ср* formation; (*получение знаний*) education

образо́ванный *прил* educated

образ|ова́ть (-у́ю; *impf* ~) (*не*)*сов перех* to form; ~ся (*impf* ~ся) (*не*)*сов возв* to form; (*группа, комиссия*) to be formed

образцо́вый прил exemplary

обрати́мый прил reversible; (валюта) convertible

обрати́ть (-щу́, -ти́шь; impf **обраща́ть**) сов перех (взгляд, мысли) to turn; **обраща́ть** (~ pf) кого́-н/что́-н в +acc to turn sb/sth into; **обраща́ть** (~ pf) внима́ние на +acc to pay attention to; ~**ся** (impf **обраща́ться**) сов возв (взгляд) to turn; (превратиться): ~**ся в** +acc to turn into; **обраща́ться** (~**ся** pf) к +dat (к врачу итп) to consult; (к проблеме) to address; **обраща́ться** (~**ся** pf) **в суд** to go to court

обра́тно нареч back; туда́ и ~ there and back; биле́т туда́ и ~ return (BRIT) или round-trip (US) ticket

обра́тн|ый прил reverse; (дорога, путь) return; **на** ~**ом пути́** on the way back; **в** ~**ую сто́рону** in the opposite direction; ~**ая сторона́** reverse (side); ~ **а́дрес** return address

обраща́|ть (-ю) несов от **обрати́ть**; ~**ся** несов от **обрати́ться** ♦ возв (деньги, товар) to circulate; ~**ся** (impf) **с** +instr (с машиной) to handle; (с человеком) to treat

обраще́ни|е (-я) ср address; (ЭКОН) circulation; ~ **к** +dat (к народу итп) address to; ~ **с** +instr (с прибором) handling of

обремен|и́ть (-ю́, -и́шь; impf **обременя́ть**) сов перех: ~**кого́-н чем-н** to load sb down with sth

о́бруч (-а) м hoop

обруча́льный прил: ~**ое кольцо́** wedding ring

обруш|и́ть (-у, -ишь; impf **обру́шивать**) сов перех (стену, крышу) to bring down; ~**ся** (impf **обру́шиваться**) сов возв (крыша, здание) to collapse; **обру́шиваться** (~**ся** pf) **на** +acc (на голову) to crash down onto; (на врага) to fall upon

обры́в (-а) м (ГЕО) precipice

обрыва́|ть(ся) (-ю(сь)) несов от **оборва́ть(ся)**

обры́в|ок (-ка) м (бумаги) scrap; (воспоминаний) fragment

обры́вочный прил fragmentary

обры́зга|ть (-ю; impf **обры́згивать**) сов перех: ~ **кого́-н/что-н** +instr (водой) to splash sb/sth with; (грязью) to splatter sb/sth with; ~**ся** (impf **обры́згиваться**) сов возв: ~**ся** +instr (см перех) to get splashed with; to get splattered with

обря́д (-а) м ritual

обсле́д|овать (-ую) (не)сов перех to inspect; (больного) to examine

обслу́живани|е (-я) ср service

обслу́ж|и́ть (-у́жу́, -у́жишь; impf **обслу́живать**) сов перех (клиентов) to serve; (подлеж: поликлиника) to see to

обста́в|ить (-лю, -ишь; impf **обставля́ть**) сов перех (квартиру) to furnish

обстано́в|ка (-ки; gen pl -ок) ж situation; (квартиры) furnishings мн

обстоя́тельств|о (-а) ср circumstance; **смотря́ по** ~**ам** depending on the circumstances; (как ответ на вопрос) it depends

обсу|ди́ть (-у́жу́, -у́дишь; impf **обсужда́ть**) сов перех to discuss

обсужде́ни|е (-я) ср discussion

обува́|ть(ся) (-ю(сь)) несов от **обу́ть(ся)**

обувно́й прил shoe

о́бувь (-и) ж footwear

обусло́в|**ить** (-лю, -ишь; impf **обусла́вливать**) сов перех (явиться причиной) to lead to

обу́|**ть** (-ю; impf **обува́ть**) сов перех (ребёнка) to put shoes on; **~ся** (impf **обува́ться**) сов возв to put on one's shoes or boots

обуче́ни|**е** (-я) ср: **~** +dat (преподавание) teaching of

обхва́т|**ить** (-ачу́, -а́тишь; impf **обхва́тывать**) сов перех: **~ что-н (рука́ми)** to put one's arms round sth

обхо́д (-а) м (путь) way round; (в больни́це) round; **в** +gen (о́зера, зако́на) bypassing

обх|**оди́ть(ся)** (-ожу́(сь), -о́дишь(ся)) несов от **обойти́(сь)**

обходно́й прил (путь) detour

обши́рный прил extensive

обща́|**ться** (-юсь) несов возв: **~ с** +instr to mix with; (с одни́м челове́ком) to see; (вести́ разгово́р) to communicate with

общегосуда́рственный прил state

общедосту́пный прил (спо́соб) available to everyone; (це́ны) affordable; (ле́кция) accessible

о́бщ|**ее** (-его) ср similarity; **в ~ем** (разг) on the whole; **у них мно́го ~его** they have a lot in common

общежи́ти|**е** (-я) ср (рабо́чее) hostel; (студе́нческое) hall of residence (BRIT), dormitory hall (US)

общеизве́стный прил well-known

обще́ни|**е** (-я) ср communication

общеобразова́тельный прил comprehensive

общепри́знанный прил universally recognized

общепри́нятый прил generally accepted

обще́ственност|**ь** (-и) ж собир community

обще́ственн|**ый** прил social; (не ча́стный) public; (организа́ция) civic; **~ое мне́ние** public opinion

о́бществ|**о** (-а) ср society

о́бщий прил general; (труд) communal; (дом) shared; (друзья́) mutual; (интере́сы) common; (коли́чество) total; (карти́на, описа́ние) general; **в ~ей сло́жности** altogether

общи́тельный прил sociable

о́бщность|**ь** (-и) ж (иде́й) similarity; (социа́льная) community

объедине́ни|**е** (-я) ср (сил) uniting; (производственное) association

объединённый прил joint

объедин|**и́ть** (-ю́, -и́шь; impf **объединя́ть**) сов перех to join, unite; (ресу́рсы) to pool; (компа́нии) to amalgamate; (impf **объединя́ться**) сов возв to unite

объе́зд (-а) м detour; (с це́лью осмо́тра) tour

объезжа́|**ть** (-ю) несов от **объе́хать**

объе́кт (-а) м subject; (СТРОИТ, ВОЕН) site

объекти́в (-а) м lens

объекти́вный прил objective

объём (-а) м volume

объёмный прил voluminous

объе́|**хать** (как е́хать; см. Table 19; impf **объезжа́ть**) сов перех (я́му) to go around; (друзе́й, стра́ны) to visit

объяв|**и́ть** (-лю́, -я́вишь; impf **объявля́ть**) сов перех to announce; (войну́) to declare ♦

непереx: ~ **о** +*prp* to announce
объявле́ни|**е (-я)** *ср*
announcement; *(войны́)*
declaration; *(рекла́ма)*
advertisement; *(извеще́ние)* notice
объясне́ни|**е (-я)** *ср* explanation
объясн|**и́ть (-ю́, -и́шь)**, *impf*
объясня́ть *сов переx* to explain;
~**ся** *(impf* **объясня́ться)** *сов*
возв: ~**ся (c** +*instr)* to clear things
up (with)
объясня́|**ться (-юсь)** *несов от*
объясни́ться ♦ *возв (на*
англи́йском языке́) to
communicate; ~ *(impf)* +*instr*
(тру́дностями) to be explained by
обы́денный *прил* mundane
обыкнове́нный *прил* ordinary
обы́ск (-а) *м* search
об|**ыска́ть (-ыщу́, -ы́щешь)**, *impf*
обы́скивать *сов переx* to
search
обы́ча|**й (-я)** *м* custom
обы́чно *нареч* usually
обы́чный *прил* usual;
(заура́дный) ordinary
обя́занност|**и (-ей)** *мн* duties *мн*,
responsibilities *мн*; **исполня́ть**
(impf) +*gen* to act as
обя́занност|**ь (-и)** *ж* duty; *см.*
также **обя́занности**
обя́занный *прил:* ~ +*infin*
(сде́лать что-л) obliged to do
обяза́тельно *нареч* definitely; **не**
~ not necessarily
обяза́тельный *прил (пра́вило)*
binding; *(исполне́ние, обуче́ние)*
compulsory, obligatory; *(рабо́тник)*
reliable
обяза́тельств|**о (-а)** *ср*
commitment; *(обы́чно мн, КОММ)*
liability
ова́л (-а) *м* oval
овдове́|**ть (-ю)** *сов (же́нщина)* to
become a widow, be widowed

(мужчи́на) to become a widower,
be widowed
Ов|**ён (-на́)** *м (созве́здие)* Aries
ов|**ёс (-са́)** *м собир* oats *мн*
ове́чий *прил (шерсть, сыр)*
sheep's
ОВИ́Р (-а) *м сокр = отде́л ви́з и*
регистра́ций
овладе́|**ть (-ю, -ешь)**, *impf*
овладева́ть *сов:* ~ +*instr*
(го́родом, внима́нием) to
capture; *(языко́м, профе́ссией)* to
master
о́вощ (-а) *м* vegetable
овощно́й *прил (суп, блю́до)*
vegetable; *(магази́н)*
greengrocer's *(BRIT)*, fruit and
vegetable shop
овра́г (-а) *м* ditch
овся́нк|**а (-и)** *ж собир (ка́ша)*
porridge *(BRIT)*, oatmeal *(US)*
овся́ный *прил* oat
ов|**ца́ (-цы́;** *nom pl* **-цы,** *gen pl* **-е́ц)**
ж sheep; *(са́мка)* ewe
овча́р|**ка (-ки;** *gen pl* **-ок)** *ж*
sheepdog
овчи́н|**а (-ы)** *ж* sheepskin
оглавле́ни|**е (-я)** *ср* (table of)
contents
огло́хн|**уть (-у)** *сов от* **гло́хнуть**
огл|**уши́ть (-ушу́, -у́шишь)**, *impf*
оглуша́ть *сов переx:* ~ **кого́-н**
чем-л to deafen sb with sth
огля|**де́ть (-жу́, -ди́шь)** *сов переx* to look
round; ~**ся** *(impf* **огля́дываться)**
сов возв to look around
огл|**яну́ться (-яну́сь, -я́нешься)**,
impf **огля́дываться** *сов возв* to
look back; **(я) не успе́л** ~, **как ...**
before I knew it ...
о́гненный *прил* fiery
огнеопа́сный *прил* (in)flammable
огнестре́льн|**ый** *прил:* ~**ое**
ору́жие firearms *мн*; ~**ая ра́на**

bullet wound

огнетуши́тел|ь (-я) *м* fire-extinguisher

ого́н|ь (-ня́) *м* fire; *(фонарей, в окне)* light

огоро́д (-а) *м* vegetable *или* kitchen garden

огорче́ни|е (-я) *ср* distress; **к моему́ ~ю** to my dismay

огорч|и́ть (-у́, -и́шь; *impf* **огорча́ть)** *сов перех* to distress; **~ся** *(impf* **огорча́ться)** *сов возв* to be distressed *или* upset

ограб|и́ть (-лю, -ишь) *сов от* **гра́бить**

ограбле́ни|е (-я) *ср* robbery

огра́д|а (-ы) *ж (забор)* fence; *(решётка)* railings *мн*

огра|ди́ть (-жу́, -ди́шь; *impf* **огражда́ть)** *сов перех (сберечь)* to shelter, protect

огражде́ни|е (-я) *ср* = **огра́да**

ограниче́ни|е (-я) *ср* limitation; *(правило)* restriction

ограни́ченный *прил* limited; *(человек)* narrow-minded

ограни́ч|ить (-у, -ишь; *impf* **ограни́чивать)** *сов перех* to limit, restrict; **~ся** *(impf* **ограни́чиваться)** *сов возв:* **~ся +instr** *(удовлетвориться)* to content o.s. with; *(свестись)* to become limited to

огро́мный *прил* enormous

огры́з|ок (-ка) *м (яблока)* half-eaten bit; *(карандаша)* stub

огуре́|ц (-ца́) *м* cucumber

одалжива|ть (-ю) *несов от* **одолжи́ть**

одарённый *прил* gifted

одева́|ть(ся) (-ю(сь)) *несов от* **оде́ть(ся)**

оде́жд|а (-ы) *ж* clothes *мн*

одеколо́н (-а) *м* eau de Cologne

оде́ну(сь) *etc сов см.* **оде́ть(ся)**

од|ержа́ть (-ержу́, -е́ржишь; *impf* **оде́рживать)** *сов перех:* **~ побе́ду** to be victorious

оде́тый *прил* dressed

оде́|ть (-ну, -нешь; *impf* **одева́ть)** *сов перех* to dress; **~ся** *(impf* **одева́ться)** *сов возв* to get dressed; *(тепло, краси́во)* to dress

одея́л|о (-а) *ср (шерстяное)* blanket; *(стёганое)* quilt

KEYWORD

од|и́н (-ного́; *см. Table 22;* f **одна́,** nt **одно́,** pl **одни́)** *м чис* one; **одна́ кни́га** one book; **одни́ брю́ки** one pair of trousers

♦ *прил* alone; *(единственный, единый)* one; *(одинаковый, тот же самый)* the same; **он идёт в кино́ оди́н** he goes to the cinema alone; **есть то́лько оди́н вы́ход** there is only one way out; **у них одни́ взгля́ды** they hold similar views

♦ *мест* **1** *(какой-то)* **оди́н мой знако́мый** a friend of mine; **одни́ неприя́тности** nothing but problems

2 *(во фразах):* **оди́н из +gen pl** one of; **оди́н и тот же** the same; **одно́ и то же** the same thing; **оди́н раз** once; **оди́н на оди́н** one to one; **все до одного́** all to a man; **ни оди́н** not one; **оди́н за други́м** one after the other; **по одному́** one by one; **оди́н-еди́нственный** only one

---

одина́ковый *прил* similar

оди́ннадцатый *чис* eleventh

оди́ннадцат|ь (-и; *как* **пять;** *см. Table 26)* *чис* eleven

одино́кий *прил (жизнь, человек)* lonely; *(не семейный)* single

одино́честв|о (-а) *ср* loneliness

одино́чный *прил* single

одн|**а́** (**-о́й**) *ж сущ см.* **оди́н**

одна́жды *нареч* once

одна́ко *союз, вводн сл* however; **~!** well, I never!

одни́ (**-х**) *мн чис см.* **оди́н**

одн|**о́** (**-ого́**) *ср чис см.* **оди́н**

одного́ *etc чис см.* **оди́н**; **одно́**

одновре́менно *нареч* **~ (с** +*instr*) at the same time (as)

одноме́стный *прил* (*купе, номер*) single; (*каюта*) single-berth

однозна́чный *прил* (*тождественный*) synonymous; (*с одним значением: слово*) monosemous; (*: выражение, ответ*) unambiguous; (*МАТ*) single-figure; **~ое число́** single-digit number

однообра́зный *прил* monotonous

одноразовый *прил* disposable

однород|**ный** *прил* (*явления*) similar; (*масса*) homogeneous

односторо́нний *прил* unilateral; (*движение*) one-way

одноцве́тный *прил* plain

одноэта́жный *прил* single-storey (*BRIT*), single-story (*US*), one-storey (*BRIT*), one-story (*US*)

одобре́ни|**е** (**-я**) *ср* approval

одобри́тельный *прил* (*отзыв*) favourable (*BRIT*), favorable (*US*); (*восклицание*) approving

одобр|**ить** (**-ю, -ишь;** *impf* **одобря́ть**) *сов перех* to approve

одолже́ни|**е** (**-я**) *ср* favour (*BRIT*), favor (*US*)

одолж|**и́ть** (**-у́, -и́шь;** *impf* **ода́лживать**) *сов перех:* **~ что-н кому́-н** to lend sth to sb; **ода́лживать** (**~** *pf*) **что-н у кого́-н** (*разг*) to borrow sth from sb

одува́нчик (**-а**) *м* dandelion

ожере́ль|**е** (**-ья;** *gen pl* **-ий**) *ср* necklace

ожесточе́ни|**е** (**-я**) *ср* resentment

ожесточённый *прил* (*человек*) resentful, embittered; (*спор*) fierce

ожива́|**ть** (**-ю**) *несов от* **ожи́ть**

ожив|**и́ть** (**-лю́, -и́шь;** *impf* **оживля́ть**) *сов перех* to revive; (*глаза, лицо*) to light up; **~ся** (*impf* **оживля́ться**) *сов возв* to liven up; (*лицо*) to brighten

оживлённый *прил* lively; (*беседа, спор*) animated

ожида́ни|**е** (**-я**) *ср* anticipation; (*обычно мн: надежды*) expectation

ожида́|**ть** (**-ю**) *несов перех* (*ждать*) to expect; (*надеяться*): **~** +*gen* to expect; **э́того мо́жно бы́ло** ~ that was to be expected; **~ся** *несов возв* to be expected

ож|**и́ть** (**-иву́, -ивёшь;** *impf* **оживать**) *сов* to come to life

ожо́г (**-а**) *м* burn

озабо́ченный *прил* worried

озагла́в|**ить** (**-лю, -ишь**) *сов перех* to entitle

озада́ч|**ить** (**-у, -ишь;** *impf* **озада́чивать**) *сов перех* to puzzle, perplex

оздорови́тельн|**ый** *прил* health-improving

о́з|**еро** (**-ера;** *nom pl* **-ёра**) *ср* lake

озира́|**ться** (**-юсь**) *несов возв:* **~ (по сторона́м)** to glance about или around

означа́|**ть** (**-ю**) *несов перех* to mean, signify

озно́б (**-а**) *м* shivering

озо́н (**-а**) *м* ozone

озо́нов|**ый** *прил:* **~ слой** ozone layer; **~ая дыра́** hole in the ozone layer

ой *межд:* **~!** (*выражает испуг*) argh!; (*выражает боль*) ouch!, ow!

ок|аза́ть (-ажу́, -а́жешь; *impf* **ока́зывать**) *сов перех*: ~ **по́мощь кому́-н** to provide help for sb; **ока́зывать** (~ *pf*) **влия́ние/давле́ние на** +*acc* to exert influence/pressure on; **ока́зывать** (~ *pf*) **внима́ние кому́-н** to pay attention to sb; **ока́зывать** (~ *pf*) **сопротивле́ние (кому́-н)** to offer resistance (to sb); **ока́зывать** (~ *pf*) **услу́гу кому́-н** to do sb a service; **~ся** (*impf* **ока́зываться**) *сов возв* to appear; **(очути́ться: на о́строве** *итп*) to end up; **ока́зываться** (**~ся** *pf*) +*instr* (**во́ром, шпио́ном**) to turn out to be; **ока́заться** (~ся *pf*) +*instr* (**скандалом**) to result in

окамене́|ть (*impf* **камене́ть**) *сов* (*перен: лицо́*) to freeze; (: *се́рдце*) to turn to stone

ока́нчива|ть (-ю) *несов от* **око́нчить**; **~ся** *несов от* **око́нчиться** ♦ *возв*: **~ся на гла́сную/согла́сную** to end in a vowel/consonant

океа́н (-а) *м* ocean

оки́н|уть (-у; *impf* **оки́дывать**) *сов перех*: ~ **кого́-н/что́-н взгля́дом** to glance over at sb/sth

о́кис|ь (-и) *ж* oxide

оккупи́р|овать (-ую) (*не)сов перех* to occupy

окла́д (-а) *м* (*зарпла́та*) salary

оклев|ета́ть (-ещу́, -е́щешь) *сов перех* to slander

окле́|ить (-ю, -ишь; *impf* **окле́ивать**) *сов перех*: ~ **что́-н чем-н** to cover sth with sth

окн|о́ (-а́; *nom pl* **-на**, *gen pl* **-он**) *ср* window

о́коло *нареч* nearby ♦ *предл*: ~ +*gen* (*ря́дом с*) near; (*приблизи́тельно*) about, around

околозе́мный *прил* around the earth

око́нн|ый *прил*: **-ая ра́ма** window frame; **~ое стекло́** windowpane

оконча́ни|е (-я) *ср* end; (*линг*) ending

оконча́тельно *нареч* (*отве́тить*) definitely; (*победи́ть*) completely; (*отредакти́ровать*) finally

оконча́тельный *прил* final; (*побе́да, сверже́ние*) complete

око́нч|ить (-у, -ишь; *impf* **ока́нчивать**) *сов перех* to finish; (*вуз*) to graduate from; **~ся** (*impf* **ока́нчиваться**) *сов возв* to finish; **~ся** (*pf*) +*instr* (*сканда́лом*) to result in

око́п (-а) *м* trench

око́рок (-а; *nom pl* **-а́**) *м* gammon

околене́|ть (-ю) *сов от* **околене́ть**

окра́ин|а (-ы) *ж* (*го́рода*) outskirts *мн*; (*страны́*) remote parts *мн*

окра́с|ка (-ки; *gen pl* **-ок**) *ж* (*стены́*) painting; (*живо́тного*) colouring (*BRIT*), coloring (*US*)

окре́пн|уть (-у) *сов от* **кре́пнуть**

окре́стность (-и) *ж* (*обычно мн*) environs *мн*

окре́стный *прил* (*дере́вни*) neighbouring (*BRIT*), neighboring (*US*)

о́крик (-а) *м* shout

окри́кн|уть (-у; *impf* **окри́кивать**) *сов перех*: ~ **кого́-н** to shout to sb

о́круг (-а) *м* (*администрати́вный*) district; (*избира́тельный*) ward; (*национа́льный*) territory; (*го́рода*) borough

округл|и́ть (-ю́, -и́шь; *impf* **округля́ть**) *сов перех* (*фо́рму*) to round off; (*ци́фру*) to round up/down

окружа́|ть (-ю) *несов от*

окружи́ть ♦ *перех* to surround

окружа́ющ|ее (-его) *ср* environment

окружа́ющ|ие (-их) *мн (также:* **~ лю́ди)** the people around one

окружа́ющий *прил* surrounding

окруже́ни|е (-я) *ср (компания)* circles *мн;* (ВОЕН) encirclement; **в ~и** *+gen (среди)* surrounded by

окруж|и́ть (-у́, -и́шь); *impf* **окружа́ть** *сов перех* to surround

окружн|о́й *прил* regional; **~а́я доро́га** bypass

окру́жность (-и) *ж* circle

октя́бр|ь (-я́) *м* October

окули́ст (-а) *м* ophthalmologist

окун|у́ть (-у́, -ёшь); *impf* **-а́ть)** *сов перех* to dip

окупа́емость (-и) *ж* viability

ок|упи́ть (-уплю́, -у́пишь); *impf* **окупа́ть)** *сов перех (расходы)* to cover; *(поездку, проект)* to cover the cost of

окур|о́к (-ка; *nom pl* **-ки)** *м* stub, butt

ола́д|ья (-ьи; *gen pl* **-ий)** *ж* ≈ drop scone, ≈ (Scotch) pancake

оле́н|ий *прил* deer's; **~ьи рога́** antlers

оле́н|ь (-я) *м* deer

оли́вк|а (-и) *ж* olive

олимпиа́д|а (-ы) *ж (СПОРТ)* the Olympics *мн; (по физике итп)* Olympiad

олимпи́йский *прил* Olympic; **~ие и́гры** the Olympic Games

о́лов|о (-а) *ср (ХИМ)* tin

омерзи́тельный *прил* disgusting

омле́т (-а) *м* omelette

ОМО́Н *м сокр (= отря́д мили́ции осо́бого назначе́ния)* special police force

омо́ним (-а) *м* homonym

омо́нов|ец (-ца) *м* member of the special police force

омрач|и́ть (-у́, -и́шь); *impf* **омрача́ть)** *сов перех (лицо)* to cloud; **~ся** *(impf* **омрача́ться)** *сов возв* to darken

он (его́; *см. Table 6a) мест (челове́к)* he; *(живо́тное, предме́т)* it

она́ (её; *см. Table 6a) мест (челове́к)* she; *(живо́тное, предме́т)* it

они́ (их; *см. Table 6b) мест* they

онкологи́ческ|ий *прил* oncological; **~ая кли́ника** cancer clinic

онла́йновый *прил (КОМП)* on-line

оно́ (его́; *см. Table 6a) мест* it

и ви́дно! *(разг)* sure! (used ironically); **вот ~ что** *или* **как!** *(разг)* so that's what it is!

ООН *ж сокр (= Организа́ция Объединённых На́ций)* UN(O)

опа́здыва|ть (-ю) *несов от* **опозда́ть**

опаса́|ться (-юсь) *несов возв:* **~ +gen** to be afraid of; **~ (impf) за +acc** to be worried about

опасе́ни|е (-я) *ср* apprehension

опа́сность (-и) *ж* danger

опа́сный *прил* dangerous

опе́к|а (-и) *ж (госуда́рства)* guardianship; *(ма́тери, отца́)* custody; *(забо́та)* care

опека́|ть (-ю) *несов перех* to take care of; *(сироту́)* to be guardian to

о́пер|а (-ы) *ж* opera

операти́вн|ый *прил (ме́ры)* efficient; *(хирурги́ческий)* surgical; **~ая гру́ппа** ≈ task force; **~ое запомина́ющее устро́йство** RAM

опера́тор (-а) *м* operator

операцио́нный *прил* surgical; **~ стол** operating table

опера́ци|я (-и) *ж* operation

опере|ди́ть (-жу́, -ди́шь; *impf* опережа́ть) *сов перех* to outstrip

опере́тт|а (-ы) *ж* operetta

опер|е́ться (обопру́сь, обопрёшься; *pt* опёрся, -ла́сь; *impf* опира́ться) *сов*: ~ на +*acc* to lean on

опери́р|овать (-ую) *pf* ~ или про~) *несов перех* (больного) to operate on ♦ *неперех* (*no pf*; *ВОЕН*) to operate; ~ (*impf*) +*instr* (акциями) to deal in; (*перен*: цифрами, фактами) to use

о́перный *прил* operatic; (*певец*) opera

опеча́т|ать (-ю; *impf* опеча́тывать) *сов перех* to seal

опеча́т|ка (-ки; *gen pl* -ок) *ж* misprint

опи́л|ки (-ок) *мн* (*древесные*) sawdust *ед*; (*металлические*) filings *мн*

опира́|ться (-юсь) *несов от* опере́ться

описа́ни|е (-я) *ср* description

оп|иса́ть (-ишу́, -и́шешь; *impf* опи́сывать) *сов перех* to describe

опла́т|а (-ы) *ж* payment

опл|ати́ть (-ачу́, -а́тишь; *impf* опла́чивать) *сов перех* (работу, труд) to pay for; (счёт) to pay

оплодотвор|и́ть (-ю́, -и́шь; *impf* оплодотворя́ть) *сов перех* to fertilize

опло́т (-а) *м* stronghold, bastion

опове|сти́ть (-щу́, -сти́шь; *impf* оповеща́ть) *сов перех* to notify

опозда́ни|е (-я) *ср* lateness; (*поезда, самолёта*) late arrival

опозда́|ть (-ю; *impf* опа́здывать) *сов*: ~ (в/на +*acc*) (в школу, на работу *итп*) to be late (for)

опознава́|тельный *прил* (знак) identifying

опозна́|ть (-ю; *impf* опознава́ть) *сов перех* to identify

опозо́р|ить(ся) (-ю(сь)) *сов от* позо́рить(ся)

опо́мн|иться (-юсь, -ишься) *сов возв* (прийти в сознание) to come round; (одуматься) to come to one's senses

опо́р|а (-ы) *ж* support

опо́рный *прил* supporting; ~ прыжо́к vault; ~ пункт base

оппозицио́нный *прил* opposition

оппози́ци|я (-и) *ж* opposition

оппоне́нт (-а) *м* (в споре) opponent; (диссертации) external examiner

опра́в|а (-ы) *ж* frame

оправда́ни|е (-я) *ср* justification; (*ЮР*) acquittal; (извинение) excuse

опра́вданный *прил* justified

оправда́|ть (-ю; *impf* опра́вдывать) *сов перех* to justify; (надежды) to live up to; (*ЮР*) to acquit; ~ся *сов возв* to justify o.s.; (расходы) to be justified

опра́в|ить (-лю, -ишь; *impf* оправля́ть) *сов перех* (платье, постель) to straighten; (линзы) to frame; ~ся (*impf* оправля́ться) *сов возв*: ~ся от +*gen* to recover from

опра́шива|ть (-ю) *несов от* опроси́ть

определе́ни|е (-я) *ср* determination; (*ЛИНГ*) attribute

определённый *прил* (установленный) definite; (некоторый) certain

определ|и́ть (-ю́, -и́шь; *impf* определя́ть) *сов перех* to determine; (понятие) to define

оприхо́д|овать (-ую) *сов от* прихо́довать

опрове́ргн|уть (-у; *impf*
опроверга́ть) *сов перех* to
refute

опроки́н|уть (-у; *impf*
опроки́дывать) *сов перех*
(*стакан*) to knock over; **~ся** (*impf*
опроки́дываться) *сов возв*
(*стакан, стул, человек*) to fall
over; (*лодка*) to capsize

опроме́тчивый *прил* precipitate

опро́с (-а) *м* (*свидетелей*)
questioning; (*населения*) survey; **~**
обще́ственного мне́ния
opinion poll

опр|оси́ть (-ошу́, -о́сишь; *impf*
опра́шивать) *сов перех*
(*свидетелей*) to question;
(*население*) to survey

опро́сный *прил*: **~ лист**
questionnaire

опротесто́в|ать (-у́ю) *сов перех*
(*ЮР*) to appeal against

опря́тный *прил* neat, tidy

опт (-а) *м* (*КОММ, крупная*
партия) wholesale

оптима́льный *прил* optimum

оптими́зм (-а) *м* optimism

оптимисти́чный *прил* optimistic

опти́ческий *прил* optical

опто́в|ый *прил* wholesale; **~ые**
заку́пки (*КОММ*) bulk buying

о́птом *нареч*: **купи́ть/прода́ть ~**
to buy/sell wholesale

опуска́|ть(ся) (-ю(сь)) *несов от*
опусти́ть(ся)

опусте́|ть (*3sg* **-ет)** *сов от*
пусте́ть

оп|усти́ть (-ущу́, -у́стишь; *impf*
опуска́ть) *сов перех* to lower;
(*пропустить*) to miss out;
опусти́ть что-н в +*acc* (*в ящик*) to
drop *или* put in(to); **~ся** (*impf*
опуска́ться) *сов возв* (*человек:*
на диван, на землю) to sink
(down); (*солнце*) to sink; (*мост,*

шлагба́ум) to be lowered; (*перен:*
человек) to let o.s. go

опустош|и́ть (-у́, -и́шь; *impf*
опустоша́ть) *сов перех*
(*страну*) to devastate

опу́хн|уть (-у) *сов от* **пу́хнуть**
♦ *impf* **опуха́ть)** *неперех* to swell
(up)

о́пухол|ь (-и) *ж* (*рана*) swelling;
(*внутренняя*) tumour (*BRIT*),
tumor (*US*)

опу́хший *прил* swollen

о́пыт (-а) *м* experience;
(*эксперимент*) experiment

о́пытный *прил* (*рабочий*)
experienced; (*лаборатория*)
experimental

опьяне́|ть (-ю) *сов от* **пьяне́ть**

опя́ть *нареч* again; **~ же** (*разг*) at
that

ора́нжевый *прил* orange

ора́тор (-а) *м* orator;
(*выступающий*) speaker

ор|а́ть (-у́, -ёшь) *несов* (*разг*) to
yell; (*ребёнок*) to bawl, howl

орби́т|а (-ы) *ж* orbit

о́рган (-а) *м* (*также АНАТ*) organ;
(*власти*) body; (*орудие*): **о́рган**
+*gen* (*пропаганды*) vehicle for;
ме́стные ~ы вла́сти local
authorities (*BRIT*) *или* government
(*US*); **полово́е ~ы** genitals

орга́н (-а) *м* (*МУЗ*) organ

организа́тор (-а) *м* organizer

организа́ци|я (-и) *ж* organization;
(*устройство*) system

органи́зм (-а) *м* organism

организо́ванный *прил* organized

организ|ова́ть (-у́ю) (*не)сов*
перех (*создать*) to organize

органи́ческий *прил* organic

оргкомите́т (-а) *м сокр* (=
организацио́нный комите́т)
organizational committee

оргте́хник|а (-и) *ж* office

automation equipment

о́рден (-а; nom pl -á) м order

о́рдер (-а) м (ЮР) warrant; (на кварти́ру) authorization

орёл (орла́; nom pl орлы́) м eagle

оре́х (-а) м nut

оригина́л (-а) м original

оригина́льный прил original

ориенти́р (-а) м landmark

орке́стр (-а) м orchestra

орна́мент (-а) м (decorative) pattern

оробе́ть (-ю) сов от **робе́ть**

ороси́тельный прил irrigation

ороше́ни|е (-я) ср irrigation

ортодокса́льный прил orthodox

ортопе́д (-а) м orthopaedic (BRIT) или orthopedic (US) surgeon

ортопеди́ческий прил orthopaedic (BRIT), orthopedic (US)

ору́ди|е (-я) ср tool; (ВОЕН) gun (used of artillery)

ору́жи|е (-я) ж weapon

орфогра́фи|я (-и) ж spelling

ОС ж нескл сокр (КОМП: = операцио́нная систе́ма) operating system

ос|а́ (-ы́; nom pl о́сы) ж wasp

оса́д|а (-ы) ж siege

оса́д|ок (-ка) м sediment; см. также **оса́дки**

оса́д|ки (-ков) мн precipitation ед

осва́ива|ть(ся) (-ю(сь)) несов от **осво́ить(ся)**

осве́дом|ить (-лю, -ишь; impf осведомля́ть) сов перех to inform; ~**ся** (impf осведомля́ться) сов возв: ~ся о +prep to inquire about

освеж|и́ть (-у́, -и́шь; impf освежа́ть) сов перех (знания) to refresh; ~**ся** (impf освежа́ться) сов возв (во́здух) to freshen; (челове́к) to freshen up

освети́тельный прил: ~ прибо́р

light

осве|ти́ть (-щу́, -ти́шь; impf освеща́ть) сов перех to light up; (пробле́му) to cover; ~**ся** (impf освеща́ться) сов возв to be lit up

освеще́ни|е (-я) ср lighting; (пробле́мы, дела́) coverage

освобо|ди́ть (-жу́, -ди́шь; impf освобожда́ть) сов перех (из тюрьмы́) to release; (го́род) to liberate; (вре́мя) to vacate; (вре́мя) to free up; ~ (pf) кого́-н от до́лжности to dismiss sb; (impf освобожда́ться) сов возв (из тюрьмы́) to be released; (дом) to be vacated

освобожде́ни|е (-я) ср release; (го́рода) liberation; ~ от до́лжности dismissal

осво́|ить (-ю, -ишь; impf осва́ивать) сов перех (те́хнику, язы́к) to master; (зе́мли) to cultivate; (impf осва́иваться) сов возв (на но́вой рабо́те) to find one's feet

освя|ти́ть (-щу́, -ти́шь; impf освяща́ть) сов перех (РЕЛ) to bless

оседа́|ть (-ю) несов от **осе́сть**

осёл (-ла́) м donkey

осе́нний прил autumn, fall (US)

осе́н|ь (-и) ж autumn, fall (US)

о́сенью нареч in autumn или the fall (US)

осе́|сть (-я́ду, -я́дешь; impf оседа́ть) сов (пыль, оса́док) to settle

осётр (-етра́) м sturgeon (ZOOL)

осетри́н|а (-ы) ж sturgeon (CULIN)

оси́н|а (-ы) ж aspen

оси́ный прил: ~ое гнездо́ (перен) hornet's nest

оскверн|и́ть (-ю́, -и́шь; impf оскверня́ть) сов перех to defile оско́л|ок (-ка) м (стекла) piece; (снаряда) shrapnel ед

оскорби́тельный прил offensive

оскорб|и́ть (-лю́, -и́шь; impf оскорбля́ть) сов перех to insult; ~ся (impf оскорбля́ться) сов возв to be offended, take offence или offense (US)

оскорбле́ни|е (-я) ср insult

осла́б|ить (-лю, -ишь; impf ослабля́ть) сов перех to weaken; (дисциплину) to relax

ослепи́тельный прил dazzling

ослеп|и́ть (-лю́, -и́шь; impf ослепля́ть) сов перех to blind; (подлеж: красота) to dazzle

ослеп|ну́ть (-ну; pt -, -ла) сов от слепну́ть

осложне́ни|е (-я) ср complication

осложн|и́ть (-ю́, -и́шь; impf осложня́ть) сов перех to complicate; ~ся (impf осложня́ться) сов возв to become complicated

осма́трива|ть(ся) (-ю(сь)) несов от осмотре́ть(ся)

осме́ле|ть (-ю) сов от смеле́ть

осме́л|иться (-юсь, -ишься; impf осме́ливаться) сов возв to dare

осмо́тр (-а) м inspection; (больного) examination; (музея) visit

осм|отре́ть (-отрю́, -о́тришь; impf осма́тривать сов перех (см сущ) to inspect; to examine; to visit; ~ся (impf осма́триваться) сов возв (по сторонам) to look around; (перен: на новом месте) to settle in

осмотри́тельный прил cautious

осна|сти́ть (-щу́, -сти́шь; impf оснаща́ть) сов перех to equip

оснаще́ни|е (-я) ср equipment

осно́в|а (-ы) ж basis;

(сооружения) foundations мн; на ~e +gen on the basis of; см. также осно́вы

основа́ни|е (-я) ср base; (теории) basis; (поступка) grounds мн; без вся́ких ~й without any reason; до ~ completely; на ~и +gen on the grounds of; на како́м ~и? on what grounds?

основа́тель (-я) м founder

основа́тельный прил (анализ) thorough

основа́|ть (pt -л, -ла, -ло; impf осно́вывать) сов перех to found; осно́вывать (~ pf) что-н +prp to base sth on или upon; ~ся (impf осно́вываться) сов возв (компания) to be founded

основн|о́й прил main; (закон) fundamental; в ~о́м on the whole

осно́выва|ть(ся) (-ю(сь)) несов от основа́ть(ся)

осно́в|ы (-) мн (физики) basics мн

осо́бенно нареч particularly; (хорошо) especially, particularly

осо́бенный прил special, particular

особня́к (-а́) м mansion

осо́б|ый прил (вид, случай) special, particular; (помещение) separate

осозна́|ть (-ю; impf осознава́ть) сов перех to realize

о́сп|а (-ы) ж smallpox

оспа́рива|ть (-ю) несов от оспо́рить ♦ (первенство) to contend или compete for

оспо́р|ить (-ю, -ишь; impf оспа́ривать) сов перех to question

оста|ва́ться (-ю́сь, -ёшься) несов от оста́ться

оста́в|ить (-лю, -ишь; impf оставля́ть) сов перех to leave; (сохранить) to keep;

(*прекратить*) to stop; (*перен: надежды*) to give up; **~ы!** stop it!

остально́е (**-ого**) *ср* the rest *мн*; **в ~ом** in other respects

остально́й *прил* (*часть*) the remaining

остальны́е (**-ых**) *мн* the others *мн*

остан|ови́ть (**-овлю́, -о́вишь**; *impf* **остана́вливать**) *сов перех* to stop; **~ся** (*impf* **остана́вливаться**) *сов возв* to stop; (*в гостинице, у друзей*) to stay; (*на вопросе*) to dwell on; (*на решении*) to come to; (*взгляд*) to rest on

остано́вк|а (**-и**) *ж* stop; (*мотора*) stopping; (*в работе*) pause

оста́т|ок (**-ка**) *м* (*пищи, дня*) remainder, the rest; **~ки** (*дома*) remains; (*еды*) leftovers

оста́|ться (**-нусь**; *impf* **остава́ться**) *сов возв* (*не уйти*) to stay; (*сохраниться*) to remain; (*оказаться*) to be left

остекл|и́ть (**-ю́, -и́шь**) *сов от* **стекли́ть**

осторо́жно *нареч* (*взять*) carefully; (*ходить, говорить*) cautiously; **~!** look out!

осторо́жность (**-и**) *ж* care; (*поступка, поведения*) caution

осторо́жный *прил* careful

остри|ё (**-я́**) *ср* point; (*ножа*) edge

остр|и́ть (**-ю́, -и́шь**; *pf* **с~**) *несов* to make witty remarks

о́стров (**-а**; *nom pl* **-а́**) *м* island

остросюже́тный *прил* (*пьеса*) gripping; (*фильм, рома́н*) thriller

остро́т|а (**-ы**) *ж* witticism

острот|а́ (**-ы́**) *ж* (*зрения*) sharpness; (*ситуации*) acuteness

остроу́мный *прил* witty

о́стрый *прил* (*нож, память, вкус*)

sharp; (*борода, нос*) pointed; (*зрение, слух*) keen; (*шутка, слово*) witty; (*еда*) spicy; (*желание*) burning; (*боль, болезнь*) acute; (*ситуация*) critical

ост|уди́ть (**-ужу́, -у́дишь**; *impf* **остужа́ть**) *сов перех* to cool

осты́|ть (**-ну, -нешь**) *сов от* **сты́ть ♦** (*impf* **остыва́ть**) *неперех* to cool down

ос|уди́ть (**-ужу́, -у́дишь**; *impf* **осужда́ть**) *сов перех* to condemn; (*приговорить*) to convict

осужде́ни|е (**-я**) *ср* (*см глаг*) condemnation; conviction

осужде́нный (**-ого**) *м* convict

ос|уши́ть (**-ушу́, -у́шишь**; *impf* **осуша́ть**) *сов перех* to drain

осуществ|и́ть (**-лю́, -и́шь**; *impf* **осуществля́ть**) *сов перех* (*мечту, идею*) to realize; (*план*) to implement; **~ся** (*impf* **осуществля́ться**) *сов возв* (*мечты, идея*) to be realized

осчастли́в|ить (**-лю, -ишь**) *сов перех* to make happy

осып|а́ть (**-лю, -лешь**; *impf* **осыпа́ть**; *pf* **осыпа́ть** (~ *pf*) кого́-н/что-н чем-н to scatter sth over sth/sth; (*перен: подарками*) to shower sb/sth with sth; **~ся** (*impf* **осыпа́ться**) *сов возв* (*насыпь*) to subside; (*листья*) to fall

ос|ь (**-и**; *loc sg* **-и́**) *ж* (*механизма*) axle; (*ГЕОМ*) axis

осьмино́г (**-а**) *м* octopus

KEYWORD

от *предл*; *+gen* 1 from; **он отошёл от стола́** he moved away from the table; **он узна́л об э́том от дру́га** he found out about it from a friend

2 (указывает на причину):
бумáга размóкла от дождя the
paper got wet with rain; **от злóсти**
with anger; **от рáдости** for joy; **от
удивлéния** in surprise; **от
разочарoвáния/стрáха** out of
disappointment/fear

3 (указывает на что-н, против
чего направлено действие) for;
лекáрство от кáшля medicine for
a cough, cough medicine

4 (о части целого): **рýчка/ключ
от двéри** door handle/key; **я
потерял пýговицу от пальтó** I
lost the button off my coat

5 (в датах): **письмó от пéрвого
февраля** или dated the
first of February

6 (о временнóй
послéдовательности): **год от
гóда** from year to year; **врéмя от
врéмени** from time to time

отáплива|ть (-ю) несов перех to
heat; **~ся** несов возв to be heated

отбежá|ть (как бежáть; см. Table
20; impf **отбегáть**) сов to run off

отбе|лить (-елю, -éлишь; impf
отбéливать) сов перех to bleach

отбивн|áя (-óй) ж tenderized
steak; (также: **~ котлéта**) chop

отбирá|ть (-ю) несов перех to
отобрáть

от|би́ть (-обью, -обьёшь; impf
отбивáть) сов перех (отколóть)
to break off; (мяч, удар) to fend
off; (атаку) to repulse; (мясо) to
tenderize; **~ся** (impf **отбивáться**)
сов возв: **~ся** (pf) **от** +gen (от
нападáющих) to defend o.s.
(against); (отстáть) to fall behind

отблагодар|и́ть (-ю, -и́шь) сов
перех to show one's gratitude to

отбóр (-а) м selection

отбóрный прил selected

отбóрочный прил (СПОРТ)
qualifying

отбрóсить (-шу, -сишь; impf
отбрáсывать) сов перех to
throw aside; (сомнéния) to cast
aside; (тень) to cast

отбрóсы (-ов) мн
(произвóдства) waste ед;
(пищевые) scraps мн

от|быть (как быть; см. Table 21;
impf **отбывáть**) сов: **~** (из +gen/в
+acc) to depart (from/for) ♦ (pt
-был, -былá, -было) перех ♦
наказáние to serve a sentence

отвáжный прил brave

отвáр (-а) м (мяснóй) broth

отвар|и́ть (-арю, -áришь; impf
отвáривать) сов перех to boil

отв|езти (-езý, -езёшь; pt **-ёз,
-езлá**, impf **отвозить**) сов перех
(увезти) to take away; **отвозить**
(~ pf) **когó-н/что-н в гóрод/на
дáчу** to take sb/sth off to town/the
dacha

отвéргн|уть (-у; impf **отвергáть**)
сов перех to reject

отверн|у́ть (-ý, -ёшь; impf
отвёртывать) сов перех (гáйку)
to unscrew; (impf **отворáчивать**;
лицо, гóлову) to turn away; **~ся**
(impf **отворáчиваться**) сов возв
(человéк) to turn away

отвéрсти|е (-я) ср opening

отвёртк|а (-и; gen pl **-ок**) ж
screwdriver

отв|ести (-едý, -едёшь; impf
отводить) сов перех
(человéка: домóй, к врачý) to
take (off); (: от окнá) to take away;
(глазá) to avert; (кандидатýру) to
reject; (учáсток) to allot;
(срéдства) to allocate

отвéт (-а) м (на вопрóс) answer;
(реáкция) response; (на письмó,
на приглашéние) reply; **в ~** (на

+acc) in response (to); **быть** (impf) в ~**е за** +acc to be answerable for

ответвле́ни|**е** (-я) ср branch

отве́|тить (-чу, -тишь; impf **отвеча́ть**) сов: ~ (**на** +acc) to answer, reply (to); ~ pf (**за** +acc (за преступле́ние) to answer for

отве́тственность (-и) ж (за посту́пки) responsibility; (зада́ния) importance; **нести́** (**понести́** pf) ~ to be responsible for; **привлека́ть** (**привле́чь** pf) кого́-н к ~и to call sb to account

отве́тственный прил: ~ (**за** +acc) responsible (for); (ва́жный) important; ~ **рабо́тник** executive

отвеча́|ть (-ю) несов от **отве́тить** ⊳ неперех: ~ +dat (тре́бованиям) to meet; (описа́нию) to answer; ~ (impf) за кого́-н/что-н to be responsible for sb/sth

отвле́|чь (-еку́, -ечёшь итп, -еку́т; pt -ёк, -екла́) impf **отвлека́ть** сов перех: ~ (**от** +gen) (от дел) to distract (from); (проти́вника) to divert (from); ~**ся** (impf **отвлека́ться**) сов возв: ~**ся** (**от** +gen) to be distracted (from); (от те́мы) to digress (from)

отв|оди́ть (-ожу́, -о́дишь) несов от **отвести́**

отво|ева́ть (-ю́ю) impf **отвоёвывать** сов перех to win back

отво|зи́ть (-ожу́, -о́зишь) несов от **отвезти́**

отвора́чива|ть(ся) (-ю(сь)) несов от **отверну́ть(ся)**

отврати́тельный прил disgusting

отвраще́ни|**е** (-я) ср disgust

отвы́к|нуть (-ну; pt -, -ла; impf **отвыка́ть**) сов: ~ **от** +gen (от люде́й, от рабо́ты) to become

unaccustomed to; (**от** нарко́тиков) to give up

отв|яза́ть (-яжу́, -я́жешь; impf **отвя́зывать**) сов перех (верёвку) to untie; ~**ся** (impf **отвя́зываться**) сов возв (разг): ~**ся от** +gen (отдела́ться) to get rid of

отгада́|ть (-ю; impf **отга́дывать** сов перех to guess

отгов|ори́ть (-ю́, -и́шь; impf **отгова́ривать**) сов перех: ~ кого́-н от чего́-н/+infin to dissuade sb from sth/from doing

отгово́р|ка (-ки; gen pl -ок) ж excuse

отгоня́|ть (-ю) несов от **отогна́ть**

отгу́л (как дать; см. Table 16)

отда|ва́ть (-ю, -ёшь) несов от **отда́ть**

отдалённый прил distant; (ме́сто, схо́дство) remote

отда́|ть (как дать; см. Table 16; impf **отдава́ть**) сов перех (возврати́ть) to return; (дать) to give; (ребёнка в шко́лу) to send; **отдава́ть** (~ pf) кого́-н **под суд** to prosecute sb; **отдава́ть** (~ pf) кому́-н честь to salute sb; **отдава́ть** (~ pf) себе́ отчёт в +prep to realize

отде́л (-а) м (учрежде́ния) department; (газе́ты) section; (исто́рии, нау́ки) branch; ~ **ка́дров** personnel department

отде́л|ать (-аю; impf **отде́лывать** сов перех (кварти́ру) to do up; **отде́лывать** (~ pf) что-н чем-н (пальто́: ме́хом) to trim sth with sth; ~**ся** (impf **отде́лываться**) сов возв: ~**ся от** +gen (разг) to get rid of; ~**ся** (pf) +instr (разг: испу́гом) to get away with

отделе́ни|**е** (-я) ср section;

(*учрежде́ния*) department; (*филиа́л*) branch; (*конце́рта*) part; ~ **свя́зи** post office; ~ **мили́ции** police station

отде́л|и́ть (-ю́, -ишь) *impf* **отделя́ть** *сов перех* to separate; ~**ся** (*impf* **отделя́ться**) *сов возв:* ~**ся (от** +*gen*) to separate (from)

отде́л|ка (-ки; *gen pl* -ок) *ж* decoration; (*на пла́тье*) trimmings *мн*

отде́лыва|ть(ся) (-ю(сь)) *несов от* **отде́лать(ся)**

отде́льный *прил* separate

отдохн|у́ть (-у́, -ёшь; *impf* **отдыха́ть**) *сов* to (have a) rest; (*на мо́ре*) to have a holiday, take a vacation (*US*)

о́тдых (-а) *м* rest; (*отпуск*) holiday, vacation (*US*); **на** ~**е** (*в о́тпуске*) on holiday; **дом** ~**а** holiday centre (*BRIT*) *или* center (*US*)

отдыха́|ть (-ю) *несов от* **отдохну́ть**

отдыха́ющ|ий (-его) *м* holidaymaker (*BRIT*), vacationer (*US*)

отёк (-а) *м* swelling

отека́|ть (-ю) *несов от* **отёчь**

оте́л|ь (-я) *м* hotel

от|е́ц (-ца́) *м* father

оте́чественн|ый *прил* domestic (*промышленность*); **Оте́чественная Война́** patriotic war (*fought in defence of one's country*)

оте́чество (-а) *ср* fatherland

от|е́чь (-еку́, -ечёшь *итп*, -еку́т; *pt* -ёк, -екла́, -екло́, **отека́ть**) *сов* to swell up

о́тзвук (-а) *м* echo

о́тзыв (-а) *м* (*реце́нзия*) review

отзыва́|ть(ся) (-ю(сь)) *несов от* **отозва́ть(ся)**

отзы́вчивый *прил* ready to help

отка́з (-а) *м* refusal; (*от реше́ния*)

rejection; (*механи́зма*) failure;

закру́чивать (закрути́ть *pf*) **что-н до** ~**а** to turn sth full on; **набива́ть (наби́ть** *pf*) **до** ~**а** to cram

отк|аза́ть (-ажу́, -а́жешь) *impf* **отка́зывать** *сов* (*мото́р, не́рвы*) to fail; **отка́зывать** (~ *pf*) **кому́-н в чём-н** to refuse sb sth; (*в по́мощи*) to deny sb sth; ~**ся** (*impf* **отка́зываться**) *сов возв:* ~**ся (от** +*gen*) to refuse; (*от о́тдыха, от мы́сли*) to give up; **отка́зываться (~ся** *pf*) **от свои́х слов** to retract one's words

отка́лыва|ть(ся) (-ю(сь)) *несов от* **отколо́ть(ся)**

откача́|ть (-ю; *impf* **отка́чивать**) *сов перех* to pump (out)

отки́н|уть (-у; *impf* **отки́дывать**) *сов перех* to throw; (*верх, сиде́нье*) to open; (*во́лосы, го́лову*) to toss back; ~**ся** (*impf* **отки́дываться**) *сов возв:* ~**ся на** +*acc* to lean back against

откла́дыва|ть (-ю) *несов от* **отложи́ть**

откл|они́ть (-оню́, -о́нишь; *impf* **отклоня́ть**) *сов перех* (*перен: про́сьбу, предложе́ние*) to reject; ~**ся** (*impf* **отклоня́ться**) *сов возв* (*стре́лка*) to deflect; (*перен: в сто́рону, от уда́ра*) to dodge; (*в ку́рса, на се́вер*) to be deflected; **отклоня́ться (~ся** *pf*) **от те́мы** to digress

отключ|и́ть (-у́, -и́шь; *impf* **отключа́ть**) *сов перех* to switch off; (*телефо́н*) to cut off; ~**ся** (*impf* **отключа́ться**) *сов возв* to switch off

отк|оло́ть (-олю́, -о́лешь; *impf* **отка́лывать**) *сов перех* (*кусо́к*) to break off; (*бант, була́вку*) to unpin; ~**ся** (*impf* **отка́лываться**) *сов возв* to break off

откорректи́р|овать (-ую) *сов*
от **корректи́ровать**

открове́нно *нареч* frankly

открове́нный *прил* frank;
(обман) blatant

откро́ю(сь) *etc сов см.*
откры́ть(ся)

откру|ти́ть (-учу́, -у́тишь) *impf*
откру́чивать) *сов перех to*
unscrew

открыва́л|ка (-ки; *gen pl* **-ок)** *ж*
(разг: для консервов) tin-opener;
(для бутылок) bottle-opener

открыва́|ть(ся) (-ю(сь)) *несов*
от **откры́ть(ся)**

откры́ти|е (-я) *ср* discovery;
(сезона, выставки) opening

откры́т|ка (-ки; *gen pl* **-ок)** *ж*
postcard

откры́тый *прил* open; *(голова)*
bare; *(взгляд, человек)* frank

откр|ы́ть (-о́ю, -о́ешь; *impf*
открыва́ть) *сов перех to* open;
(намерения, правду итп) to
reveal; *(воду, кран)* to turn on;
(возможность, путь) to open up;
(закон) to discover; **~ся** *(impf*
открыва́ться) *сов возв to* open;
(возможность, путь) to open up

отку́да *нареч* where from ♦ *союз*
from where, whence; **Вы ~ ?** where
are you from?; **~ Вы прие́хали?**
where have you come from?; **~ ты**
э́то зна́ешь? how do you know
about that?

отку́да-нибудь *нареч* from
somewhere (or other)

отку́да-то *нареч* from somewhere

отк|уси́ть (-ушу́, -у́сишь; *impf*
отку́сывать) *сов перех to* bite
off

отлага́тельств|о (-а) *ср* delay

отла́мыва|ть(ся) (-ю) *несов от*
отломи́ть(ся)

отле|те́ть (-чу́, -ти́шь; *impf*

отлета́ть) *сов to* fly off; *(мяч) to*
fly back

отли́в (-а) *м (в мо́ре)* ebb;
(отте́нок) sheen

отли́ч|ить (-у) *несов от*
отличи́ть; ~ся *возв (быть*
други́м) to be different (from)

отли́чи|е (-я) *ср* distinction; **в ~ от**
+gen unlike

отличи́тельный *прил (черта́)*
distinguishing

отлич|и́ть (-у́, -и́шь; *impf*
отлича́ть) *сов перех*
(награди́ть) to honour *(BRIT)*,
honor *(US)*; **отлича́ть (~ *pf*)**
кого́-л/что-н **от** +gen to tell sb/sth
from

отли́чник (-а) *м* 'A'grade pupil

отли́чно *нареч* extremely well
♦ *как сказ* it's excellent *или* great
♦ *ср нескл (ПРОСВЕЩ)* excellent
или outstanding *(school mark)*; **он ~**
зна́ет, что он винова́т he knows
perfectly well that he's wrong;
учи́ться *(impf)* **на ~** to get top
marks

отли́чный *прил* excellent; *(иной)*:
~ от *+gen* distinct from

отл|ожи́ть (-ожу́, -о́жишь; *impf*
откла́дывать) *сов перех*
(де́ньги) to put aside; *(собра́ние) to*
postpone

отл|оми́ть (-омлю́, -о́мишь;
impf **отла́мывать)** *сов перех to*
break off; **~ся** *(impf*
отла́мываться) *сов возв to*
break off

отмах|ну́ться (-у́сь, -ёшься;
impf **отма́хиваться)** *сов возв:* **~**
от *+gen (от му́хи) to* brush away
или wave aside; *(от предложе́ния) to* brush *или*
wave aside

отме́н|а (-ы) *ж (см глаг)* repeal;
reversal; abolition; cancellation

отме|ни́ть (-еню́, -е́нишь; *impf* **отменя́ть**) *сов перех* (*закон*) to repeal; (*решение, приговор*) to reverse; (*налог*) to abolish; (*лекцию*) to cancel

отме́|тить (-чу, -тишь; *impf* **отмеча́ть**) *сов перех* (*на карте, в книге*) to mark; (*указать*) to note; (*юбилей*) to celebrate; **~ся** (*impf* **отмеча́ться**) *сов возв* to register

отме́т|ка (-ки; *gen pl* -ок) *ж* mark; (*в документе*) note

отме́тка - mark. The Russian scale of marking is from 1 to 5, with 5 being the highest mark. + can be added to marks 3, 4 and 5.

отмеча́|ть(ся) (-ю(сь)) *несов от* **отме́тить(ся)**

отморо́|зить (-жу, -зишь; *impf* **отмора́живать**) *сов перех*: ~ ру́ки/но́ги to get frostbite in one's hands/feet

отмы́|ть (-о́ю, -о́ешь; *impf* **отмыва́ть**) *сов перех*: ~ что-н to get sth clean; (*грязь*) to wash sth out; (*деньги*) to launder sth

отн|ести́ (-есу́, -есёшь; *pt* -ёс, -есла́; *impf* **относи́ть**) *сов перех* (*отнести (от)*); (*подлеж: течение*) to carry off; (*причислить к*): ~ что-н к (*к периоду, к году*) to date sth back to; (*к число группе*) to categorize sth as; (*к категории*) to put sth into; **относи́ть(ся)** *сов возв*: **~сь к** +*dat* (*к человеку*) to treat; (*к предложению, к событию*) to take

отня́ть (-ю́) *несов от* **отня́ть**

относи́тельно *нареч* relatively ♦ *предл*: ~ +*gen* (*в отношении*)

regarding, with regard to

относи́тельный *прил* relative

отн|оси́ть (-ошу́, -о́сишь) *несов от* **отнести́**; **~ся** *несов от* **отнести́сь** ♦ *возв*: **~ся к** +*dat* to relate to; (*к классу*) to belong to; (*к году*) to date from; **он к ней хорошо́ ~о́сится** he likes her; **как ты ~о́сишься к нему́?** what do you think about him?; **э́то к нам не ~о́сится** it has nothing to do with us

отноше́ни|е (-я) *ср* (*МАТ*) ratio; ~ (**к** +*dat*) attitude (to); (*связь*) relation (to); **в ~и** +*gen* with regard to; **по ~ю к** +*dat* towards; **в э́том ~и** in this respect *или* regard; **в не́котором ~и** in certain respects; **име́ть** (*impf*) ~ **к** +*dat* to be connected with; **не име́ть** (*impf*) ~я **к** +*dat* to have nothing to do with

отню́дь *нареч*: ~ **не** by no means, far from; ~ **нет** absolutely not

отн|я́ть (-иму́, -и́мешь; *impf* **отнима́ть**) *сов перех* to take away; (*силы, время*) to take up

ото *предл см.* **от**

от|обра́ть (-беру́, -берёшь; *impf* **отбира́ть**) *сов перех* (*отнять*) to take away; (*выбрать*) to select

отовсю́ду *нареч* from all around

от|огна́ть (-гоню́, -го́нишь; *impf* **отгоня́ть**) *сов перех* to chase away

отодви́н|уть (-у; *impf* **отодвига́ть**) *сов перех* (*шкаф*) to move; (*засов*) to slide back; (*срок, экзамен*) to put back; **~ся** (*impf* **отодвига́ться**) *сов возв* (*человек*) to move

от|озва́ть (-зову́, -зовёшь; *impf* **отзыва́ть**) *сов перех* to call back; (*посла, документы*) to recall; **отзыва́ть** (~ *pf*) **кого́-н в сто́рону**

to take sb aside; **~ся** (impf **отзыва́ться**) сов возв: **~ся (на** +acc) to respond (to); **хорошо́/ пло́хо ~ся** (pf) **о** +prp to speak well/badly of

отойти́ (как **идти́**; см. Table 18); impf **отходи́ть**) сов (поезд, автобус) to leave; (пятно) to come out; (отлучиться) to go off; **отходи́ть** (~ pf) **от** +gen to move away from; (перен: от друзей, от взглядов) to distance o.s. from; (от темы) to depart from

отомсти́ть (-щу́, -сти́шь) сов **от** мстить

отопи́тельный прил (прибор) heating; **~ сезо́н** the cold season

отопи́тельный сезо́н . The heating comes on around the middle of October and goes off around the middle of May. The central heating is controlled centrally and individual home owners do not have any say over it.

отопле́ни|е (-я) ср heating

оторва́|ть (-у́, -ёшь; impf **отрыва́ть**) сов перех to tear off; **отрыва́ть** (~ pf) (**от** +gen) to tear away (from); **~ся** (impf **отрыва́ться**) сов возв (пуговица) to come off; **оторва́ться** (**~ся** pf) (**от** +gen) (от работы) to tear o.s. away (from); (убежать) to break away (from); (от семьи) to lose touch (with); **отрыва́ться** (**~ся** pf) **от земли́** (самолёт) to take off

отпева́ни|е (-я) ср funeral service

отпева́|ть (-ю) несов от **отпе́ть**

от|пере́ть (-опру́, -опрёшь; pt **-пер**, **-перла́**, **-перло**) impf **отпира́ть** сов перех to unlock

отпе́|ть (-ою́, -оёшь; impf **отпева́ть**) сов перех (РЕЛ) to conduct a funeral service for

отпеча́та|ть (-ю; impf **отпеча́тывать**) сов перех to print; **~ся** (impf **отпеча́тываться**) сов возв to leave a print; (перен: в памяти) to imprint itself

отпеча́т|ок (-ка) м imprint; **~ки па́льцев** fingerprints

отпира́|ть (-ю) несов от **отпере́ть**

отпл|ати́ть (-ачу́, -а́тишь; impf **отпла́чивать**) сов: **~** +dat (наградить) to repay; (отомстить) to pay back

отплы́|ть (-ву́, -вёшь; impf **отплыва́ть**) сов (человек) to swim off; (корабль) to set sail

отполз|ти́ (-у́, -ёшь; impf **отполза́ть**) сов to crawl away

отпо́р (-а) м: дать **~** +dat (врагу) to repel, repulse

отправи́тел|ь (-я) м sender

отпра́в|ить (-лю, -ишь; impf **отправля́ть**) сов перех to send; **~ся** (impf **отправля́ться**) сов возв (человек) to set off

отпра́в|ка (-ки; gen pl -ок) ж (письма) posting; (груза) dispatch

отправле́ни|е (-я) ср (письма) dispatch; (почтовое) item

отправн|о́й прил: **~ пункт** point of departure; **~а́я то́чка** (перен) starting point

отпр|оси́ться (-ошу́сь, -о́сишься; impf **отпра́шиваться**) сов перех to ask permission to leave

о́тпуск (-а) м holiday (BRIT), vacation (US); **быть** (impf) **в ~е** to be on holiday

отп|усти́ть (-ущу́, -у́стишь; impf **отпуска́ть**) сов перех to let out;

(из рук) to let go of; *(товар)* to sell; *(деньги)* to release; *(бороду)* to grow

отрабо́та|ть (-ю); *impf* **отраба́тывать** *сов перех (какое-то время)* to work; *(освоить)* to perfect, polish
♦ *неперех (кончить работать)* to finish work

отр|ави́ть (-авлю́, -а́вишь; *impf* **отравля́ть**) *сов перех* to poison; *(перен: праздник)* to spoil; **~ся** *сов, (impf* **отравля́ться)** *возв* to poison o.s.; *(едо́й)* to get food-poisoning

отравле́ни|е (-я) *ср* poisoning

отраже́ни|е (-я) *ср (см глаг)* reflection; deflection

отра|зи́ть (-жу́, -зи́шь; *impf* **отража́ть)** *сов перех* to reflect; *(удар)* to deflect; **~ся** *(impf* **отража́ться** *(~ся рl)* *возв:* **~ся** *в +prp* to be reflected in; **отража́ться** *(~ся рl) в зе́ркале)* to be reflected in; **отража́ться** *(~ся рl) +prp (на здоро́вье)* to have an effect on

о́трасл|ь (-и) *ж* branch *(of industry)*

отр|асти́ (*3sg* **-асте́т**, *pt* **-о́с, -осла́**, *impf* **отраста́ть**) *сов* to grow

отра|сти́ть (-щу́, -сти́шь; *impf* **отра́щивать**) *сов перех* to grow

отре́з (-а) *м* piece of fabric

отре́|зать (-жу, -жешь; *impf* **отреза́ть**) *сов перех* to cut off

отре́з|ок (-ка) *м (ткани)* piece; *(пути)* section; *(времени)* period

отр|е́чься (**-еку́сь, -ече́шься** *etc*, **-еку́тся, -е́кся, -екла́сь**, *impf* **отрека́ться)** *сов возв:* **~ от** *+gen* to renounce; **отрека́ться** *(~ рl)* **от престо́ла** to abdicate

отрица́ни|е (-я) *ср* denial; *(линг)* negation

отрица́тельный *прил* negative

отрица́|ть (-ю) *несов перех* to deny; *(моду итп)* to reject

отро́ст|ок (-ка) *м (побег)* shoot

отр|уби́ть (-ублю́, -у́бишь; *impf* **отруба́ть)** *сов перех* to chop off

отруга́|ть (-ю) *сов от* **руга́ть**

отры́в (-а) *м:* **~ от** *+gen (от семьи́)* separation from; **ли́ния ~а** a perforated line; **быть** *(impf)* **в ~е от** *+gen* to be cut off from

отрыва́|ть(ся) (-ю(сь)) *несов от* **оторва́ть(ся)**

отры́в|ок (-ка) *м* excerpt

отры́вочный *прил* fragmented

отря́д (-а) *м* party, group; *(ВОЕН)* detachment

отряхн|у́ть (-у́, -ёшь; *impf* **отря́хивать)** *сов перех (снег, пыль)* to shake off; *(пальто́)* to shake down

отсе́к (-а) *м* compartment

отс|е́чь (-еку́, -ече́шь *etc*, **-еку́т**, *pt* **-ёк, -екла́**; *impf* **отсека́ть)** *сов перех* to cut off

отск|очи́ть (-очу́, -о́чишь; *impf* **отска́кивать)** *сов (в сто́рону, наза́д)* to jump; *(разг: пуговица, кно́пка)* to come off; **отска́кивать** *(~ рl)* **от** *+gen (мяч)* to bounce off; *(челове́к)* to jump off

отсоедин|и́ть (-ю́, -и́шь; *impf* **отсоединя́ть)** *сов перех* to disconnect

отсро́ч|ить (-у, -ишь; *impf* **отсро́чивать)** *сов перех* to defer

отста|ва́ть (-ю́, -ёшь) *несов от* **отста́ть**

отста́в|ка (-ки; *gen pl* **-ок**) *ж* retirement; *(кабине́та)* resignation; **подава́ть (пода́ть** *рl)* **в ~ку** to offer one's resignation

отста́ива|ть(ся) (-ю) *несов от* **отстоя́ть(ся)**

отста́лый *прил* backward

отста́|ть (-ну, -нешь; *impf*

отстава́ть сов (перен: в учёбе, в работе) to fall behind; (часы) to be slow; **отстава́ть** (~ pf) (от +gen) (от группы) to fall behind; (от поезда, от автобуса) to be left behind; ~нь от меня́! stop pestering me!

отстегн|у́ть (-у́, -ёшь; impf **отстёгивать**) сов перех to unfasten

отсто|я́ть (-ю́, -и́шь; impf **отста́ивать** сов перех (город, своё мнение) to defend; (раствор) to allow to stand; (два часа итп) to wait; ~ся (impf **отста́иваться**) сов возв to settle

отстран|и́ть (-ю́, -и́шь; impf **отстраня́ть**) сов перех (отодвинуть) to push away; (уволить): ~ от +gen to remove, dismiss; ~ся (impf **отстраня́ться**) сов возв: ~ся от +gen (от должности) to relinquish; (отодвинуться) to draw back

отступ|и́ть (-уплю́, -у́пишь; impf **отступа́ть**) сов (назад) to step back; (воен) to retreat; (перен: перед трудностями) to give up

отступле́ни|е (-я) ср retreat; (от темы) digression

отсу́тстви|е (-я) ср (человека) absence; (денег, вкуса) lack

отсу́тствующ|ий прил (взгляд, вид) absent ♦ (-его) м absentee

отсчёт (-а) м (минут) calculation; то́чка ~а point of reference

отсчита́|ть (-ю; impf **отсчи́тывать** (деньги) to count out

отсю́да нареч from here

отта́ива|ть (-ю) несов от **отта́ять**

отта́лкива|ть(ся) несов от **оттолкну́ть(ся)**

отт|ащи́ть (-ащу́, -а́щишь; impf **отта́скивать**) сов перех to drag

отта́|ять (-ю; impf **отта́ивать** сов (земля) to thaw; (мясо) to thaw out

отте́н|ок (-ка) м shade

о́ттепел|ь (-и) ж thaw

о́ттиск (-а) м (ступни) impression; (рисунка) print

оттого́ нареч for this reason; ~ что because

оттолкн|у́ть (-у́, -ёшь; impf **отта́лкивать** сов перех to push away; ~ся (impf **отта́лкиваться** сов возв: ~ся от чего-н (от берега) to push o.s. away или back from sth (перен: от данных) to take sth as one's starting point

отту́да нареч from there

отт|яну́ть (-яну́, -я́нешь; impf **отта́гивать** сов перех to pull back; (карман) to stretch; (разг: выполнение) to delay; **оття́гивать** (~ pf) **вре́мя** to play for time

от|учи́ть (-учу́, -у́чишь; impf **отуча́ть** сов перех: ~ кого-н +gen (от курения) to wean sb off; **отуча́ть** (~ pf) кого-н +infin (врать) to teach sb not to do; ~ся (impf **отуча́ться** сов возв: ~ся +infin to get out of the habit of doing

отхлын|у́ть (3sg -ет) сов (волны) to roll back

отхо́д (-а) м departure; (воен) withdrawal; см. также **отхо́ды**

отх|оди́ть (-ожу́, -о́дишь) несов от **отойти́**

отхо́д|ы (-ов) мн waste ед

отца́ итп сущ см. **оте́ц**

отцо́вский прил father's; (чувства, права) paternal

отча́ива|ться (-юсь) *несов от*
отча́яться

отча́л|ить (-ю, -ишь; *impf*
отча́ливать) *сов* to set sail

отча́сти *нареч* partially

отча́яни|е (-я) *ср* despair

отча́янно *нареч* (*пытаться*)
desperately; (*спорить*) fiercely

отча́янный *прил* desperate;
(*смелый*) daring

отча́я|ться (-юсь; *impf*
отча́иваться) *сов возв*: ~ (+*infin*)
to despair (of doing)

отчего́ *нареч* (*почему*) why
♦ *союз* (*вследствие чего*) which
is why

отчего́-нибудь *нареч* for any
reason

отчего́-то *нареч* for some reason

о́тчеств|о (-а) *ср* patronymic

о́тчество - patronymic. The full
name of a Russian person must
include his or her patronymic.
Besides being the formal way of
addressing people, the use of the
patronymic also shows your
respect for that person.
Patronymics are not as officious as
they sound to some foreign ears.
In fact, quite often the patronymic
replaces the first name and is used
as an affectionate way of
addressing people you know well.

отчёт (-а) *м* account;
фина́нсовый ~ financial report;
(*выписка*) statement; отдава́ть
(отда́ть *pf*) себе́ ~ в чём-н to
realize sth

отчётливый *прил* distinct;
(*объяснение*) clear

отчётность (-и) *ж* accountability
♦ *собир* (*документы*) records

отчётный *прил* (*собрание*)

review; (*период, год*) accounting;
~ докла́д report

отчи́зн|а (-ы) *ж* mother country

о́тчим (-а) *м* stepfather

отчисле́ни|е (-я) *ср* (*работника*)
dismissal; (*студента*) expulsion;
(*обычно мн*: на строительство)
allocation *ед*; (: *денежные*:
удержание) deduction;
(: *выделение*) assignment

отчи́сл|ить (-ю, -ишь; *impf*
отчисля́ть) *сов перех*
(*работника*) to dismiss;
(*студента*) to expel; (*деньги*:
удержать) to deduct;
(: *выделить*) to assign

отчита́|ть (-ю; *impf* отчи́тывать)
сов перех (*ребёнка*) to tell off;
~ся (*impf* отчи́тываться) *сов
возв* to report

отчужде́ни|е (-я) *ср*
estrangement

отше́льник (-а) *м* hermit

отъе́зд (-а) *м* departure; быть
(*impf*) в ~е to be away

отъе́хать (*как* е́хать; *см. Table
19, impf* отъезжа́ть) *сов* to travel;
отъезжа́ть (~ *pf*) от +*gen* to move
away from

отъя́вленный *прил* utter

отыгра́|ть (-ю; *impf* оты́грывать)
сов перех to win back; ~ся (*impf*
оты́грываться) *сов возв* (*в
карты, в шахматы*) to win again;
(*перен*) to get one's own back

оты́ск|ать (-ищу́, -и́щешь; *impf*
оты́скивать) *сов перех* to hunt
out; (*КОМП*) to retrieve

о́фис (-а) *м* office

офице́р (-а) *м* (*ВОЕН*) officer;
(*разг*: ШАХМАТЫ) bishop

официа́льн|ый *прил* official; ~ое
лицо́ official

официа́нт (-а) *м* waiter

оформи́тел|ь (-я) *м*: ~

спекта́кля set designer: ~ **витри́н** window dresser

офо́рм|ить (-**лю, -ишь**; *impf* **оформля́ть**) *сов перех* (*документы, договор*) to draw up; (*книгу*) to design the layout of; (*витрину*) to dress; (*спектакль*) to design the sets for; **оформля́ть** (~ *pf*) **кого́-н на рабо́ту** +*instr* to take sb on (as); **~ся** (*impf* **оформля́ться**) *сов возв* (*взгляды*) to form; **оформля́ться** (**~ся** *pf*) **на рабо́ту** (+*instr*) to be taken on (as)

оформле́ни|е (-**я**) *ср* design; (*документов, договора*) drawing up; (*музыкальное*) ~ music

оформля́|ть(ся) (-**ю(сь)**) *несов от* **офо́рмить(ся)**

оффшо́рный *прил* (*КОММ*) offshore

охва|ти́ть (-**чу́, -́тишь**; *impf* **охва́тывать**) *сов перех* (*подлеж: пламя, чувства*) to engulf; (*население*) to cover; **охва́тывать** (~ *pf*) **что-н чем-н** (*руками, лентой*) to put sth round sth

охладе́|ть (-**ю**; *impf* **охладева́ть**) *сов* (*отношения*) to cool; **охладева́ть** (~ *pf*) **к** +*dat* (*к мужу*) to grow cool towards

охла|ди́ть (-**жу́, -ди́шь**; *impf* **охлажда́ть**) *сов перех* (*воду, чувства*) to cool; **~ся** (*impf* **охлажда́ться**) *сов возв* (*печка, вода*) to cool down

охо́т|а (-**ы**) *ж* hunt; (*разг: желание*) desire

охо́|титься (-**чусь, -тишься**) *несов возв*: **~ на** +*acc* to hunt (*to kill*); ~ (*impf*) **за** +*instr* to hunt (*to catch*); (*перен: разг*) to hunt for

охо́тник (-**а**) *м* hunter

охо́тничий *прил* hunting

охо́тно *нареч* willingly

охра́н|а (-**ы**) *ж* (*защита*) security; (*группа людей*) bodyguard; (*растений, животных*) protection; (*здоровья*) care; ~ **труда́** health and safety regulations

охра́нник (-**а**) *м* guard

охраня́|ть (-**ю**) *несов перех* to guard; (*природу*) to protect

оце|ни́ть (-**ню́, -́нишь**; *impf* **оце́нивать**) *сов перех* (*вещь*) to value; (*знания*) to assess; (*признать достоинства*) to appreciate

оце́н|ка (-**ки**; *gen pl* -**ок**) *ж* (*вещи*) valuation; (*работника, поступка*) assessment; (*отметка*) mark

оцеп|и́ть (-**лю́, -́пишь**; *impf* **оцепля́ть**) *сов перех* to cordon off

оча́г (-**á**) *м* hearth; (*перен: заболевания*) source

очарова́ни|е (-**я**) *ср* charm

очарова́тельный *прил* charming

очар|ова́ть (-**у́ю**; *impf* **очаро́вывать**) *сов перех* to charm

очеви́д|ец (-**ца**) *м* eyewitness

очеви́дно *нареч, част* obviously ♦ *как сказ*: ~, **что он винова́т** it's obvious that he is guilty ♦ *вводн сл*: ~, **он не придёт** apparently he's not coming

очеви́дный *прил* (*факт*) plain; (*желание*) obvious

о́чень *нареч* (+*adv*, +*adj*) very; (+*vb*) very much

очередно́й *прил* next; (*ближайший: задача*) immediate; (: *номер газеты*) latest; (*повторяющийся*) another

о́черед|ь (-**и**) *ж* (*порядок*) order; (*место в порядке*) turn; (*группа людей*) queue (*BRIT*), line (*US*); (*в строительстве*) section; **в пе́рвую** ~ in the first instance; **в поря́дке**

~и when one's turn comes; **в свою́ ~** in turn; **по ~и** in turn

о́черк (-а) *м* (*литературный*) essay; (*газетный*) sketch

очерта́ни|е (-я) *ср* outline *ед*

оче́чник (-а) *м* spectacle case

очисти́тельный *прил* purification

очи́|стить (-щу, -стишь; *impf* **очища́ть**) *сов перех* to clean; (*газ, воду*) to purify; (*город, кварти́ру*) to clear; **~ся** (*impf* **очища́ться**) *сов возв* (*газ, вода*) to be purified

очи́стк|а (-и) *ж* purification

очистн|о́й *прил*: **~ы́е сооруже́ния** purification plant *ед*

очища́|ть(ся) (-ю) *несов от* **очи́стить(ся)**

очи́щенный *прил* (*хим*) purified; (*я́блоко, карто́шка*) peeled

очк|и́ (-о́в) *мн* (*для чте́ния*) glasses *мн*, spectacles *мн*; (*для пла́вания*) goggles *мн*; **защи́тные ~и́** safety specs

очк|о́ (-а́) *ср* (*СПОРТ*) point; (*КА́РТЫ*) pip

очн|у́ться (-у́сь, -ёшься) *сов возв* (*по́сле сна*) to wake up; (*по́сле обмо́рока*) to come round

о́чный *прил* (*обуче́ние, институ́т итп*) with direct contact between students and teachers; **~ая ста́вка** (*ЮР*) confrontation

о́чное отделе́ние - This is one of the ways of obtaining a degree. It is a full time course with over 30 contact hours a week and two exam sessions. See also notes at **зао́чный** and **вече́рний**.

оч|ути́ться (*2sg* **-у́тишься**) *сов возв* to end up

оше́йник (-а) *м* collar

ош|иби́ться (-ибу́сь, -ибёшься; *pt* **-и́бся, -и́блась**) *impf* **ошиба́ться** *сов возв* to make a mistake; **ошиба́ться** (**~** *pf*) **в ком-н** to misjudge sb

оши́б|ка (-ки; *gen pl* **-ок**) *ж* mistake, error; **по ~ке** by mistake

ошибо́чный *прил* (*мне́ние*) mistaken, erroneous; (*сужде́ние, вы́вод*) wrong

ощу́па|ть (-ю; *impf* **ощу́пывать**) *сов перех* to feel

о́щуп|ь (-и) *ж*: **на ~** by touch; **пробира́ться** (*impf*) **на ~** to grope one's way through

ощу|ти́ть (-щу́, -ти́шь; *impf* **ощуща́ть**) *сов перех* (*жела́ние, боль*) to feel

ощуще́ни|е (-я) *ср* sense; (*ра́дости, бо́ли*) feeling

П, п

павильо́н (-а) *м* pavilion

павли́н (-а) *м* peacock

па́губный *прил* (*после́дствия*) ruinous; (*влия́ние*) pernicious

па́да|ть (-ю; *pf* **упа́сть** *или* **пасть**) *несов* to fall; (*настрое́ние*) to sink; (*дисципли́на, нра́вы*) to decline

паде́ж (-а́) *м* (*ЛИНГ*) case

паде́ни|е (-я) *ср* fall; (*нра́вов, дисципли́ны*) decline

па|й (-я; *nom pl* **-и́**) *м* (*ЭКОН*) share; **на ~я́х** jointly

па́йщик (-а) *м* shareholder

паке́т (-а) *м* package; (*мешо́к*) (paper *или* plastic) bag

пак|ова́ть (-у́ю; *pf* **за~** *или* **у~**) *несов перех* to pack

пала́т|а (-ы) *ж* (*в больни́це*) ward; (*ПОЛИТ*) chamber, house

пала́т|ка (-ки; *gen pl* -ок) *ж* tent

па́л|ец (-ьца) *м* (*руки*) finger; (*ноги*) toe; **большо́й ~** (*руки*) thumb; (*ноги*) big toe

пали́тр|а (-ы) *ж* palette

па́л|ка (-ки; *gen pl* -ок) *ж* stick

пало́мничество (-а) *ср* pilgrimage

па́лоч|ка (-ки; *gen pl* -ек) *ж* (*МУЗ*): **дирижёрская ~** (conductor's) baton; **волше́бная ~** magic wand

па́луб|а (-ы) *ж* (*МОР*) deck

па́льм|а (-ы) *ж* palm (tree)

пальто́ *ср нескл* overcoat

па́мятник (-а) *м* monument; (*на моги́ле*) tombstone

па́мятный *прил* (*день*) memorable; (*пода́рок*) commemorative

па́мят|ь (-и) *ж* memory; (*воспомина́ние*) memories *мн*

пана́м|а (-ы) *ж* Panama (hat)

пане́л|ь (-и) *ж* (*СТРОИТ*) panel

па́ник|а (-и) *ж* panic

паник|ова́ть (-у́ю) *несов* (*разг*) to panic

панихи́д|а (-ы) *ж* (*РЕЛ*) funeral service; **гражда́нская ~** civil funeral

пани́ческий *прил* panic-stricken

панора́м|а (-ы) *ж* panorama

пансиона́т (-а) *м* boarding house

па́п|а (-ы) *м* dad; (*также*: **Ри́мский ~**) the Pope

папиро́с|а (-ы) *ж* *type of cigarette*

папиро́сный *прил*: **~ая бума́га** (*то́нкая бума́га*) tissue paper

па́п|ка (-ки; *gen pl* -ок) *ж* folder (*BRIT*), file (*US*)

пар (-а; *nom pl* -ы́) *м* steam; *см. также* пары́

па́р|а (-ы) *ж* (*ту́фель итп*) pair; (*супру́жеская*) couple

пара́граф (-а) *м* paragraph

пара́д (-а) *м* parade

пара́дн|ое (-ого) *ср* entrance

пара́дный *прил* (*вход, ле́стница*) front, main

парадо́кс (-а) *м* paradox

парадокса́льный *прил* paradoxical

парази́т (-а) *м* parasite

парализ|ова́ть (-у́ю) (*не*)*сов перех* to paralyze

парали́ч (-а́) *м* paralysis

паралле́л|ь (-и) *ж* parallel

пара́метр (-а) *м* parameter

парашю́т (-а) *м* parachute

па́рен|ь (-я) *м* (*разг*) guy

пари́ *ср нескл* bet

Пари́ж (-а) *м* Paris

пари́к (-а́) *м* wig

парикма́хер (-а) *м* hairdresser

парикма́херск|ая (-ой) *ж* hairdresser's (*BRIT*), beauty salon (*US*)

па́р|иться (-юсь, -ишься) *несов возв* (*в ба́не*) to have a sauna

пар|и́ть (-ю́, -и́шь) *несов* to glide

парк (-а) *м* park

парке́т (-а) *м* parquet

парк|ова́ть (-у́ю) *несов перех* to park

парла́мент (-а) *м* parliament

парла́ментский *прил* parliamentary

парни́к (-а́) *м* greenhouse

парнико́вый *прил*: **~ эффе́кт** greenhouse effect

парово́з (-а) *м* steam engine

парово́й *прил* steam; **~ое отопле́ние** central heating

паро́ди|я (-и) *ж*: **~ (на** +*acc*) parody of

паро́л|ь (-я) *м* password

паро́м (-а) *м* ferry

парохо́д (-а) *м* steamer, steamship

па́рт|а (-ы) *ж* desk (*in schools*)

парте́р (-а) *м* the stalls *мн*

партиза́н (-а; *gen pl* -) *м* partisan

guerrilla

парти́йный *прил* party

па́рти|я (-и) *ж* (ПОЛИТ) party;
(МУЗ) part; (груза) consignment;
(изделий: в производстве)
batch; (СПОРТ): ~ **в ша́хматы/
волейбо́л** a game of chess/
volleyball

партнёр (-а) *м* partner

партнёрств|о (-а) *ср* partnership

па́рус (-а; *nom pl* **-а́)** *м* sail

парфюме́ри|я (-и) *ж собир*
perfume and cosmetic goods

пар|ы́ (-о́в) *мн* vapour *ед* (BRIT),
vapor *ед* (US)

пас (-а) *м* (СПОРТ) pass

па́смурный *прил* overcast, dull

па́спорт (-а; *nom pl* **-а́)** *м* passport;
(автомобиля, станка) registration
document

па́спорт - passport. Russian
citizens are required by law to
have a passport at the age of 16.
The passport serves as an essential
identification document and has
to be produced on various
occasions ranging from applying
for a job to collecting a parcel
from the post office. Those who
travel abroad have to get a
separate passport for foreign
travel.

пассажи́р (-а) *м* passenger

пасси́вный *прил* passive

па́ст|а (-ы) *ж* paste; (тома́тная)
purée; **зубна́я ~** toothpaste

пас|ти́ (-у́, -ёшь; *pt* **-, -ла́)** *несов
перех* (скот) to graze; **~сь** *несов
возв* to graze

пас|ти́ла́ (-и́лы; *nom pl* **-и́лы)** *ж*
≈ marshmallow

пасту́х (-а́) *м* (коров) herdsman;
(овец) shepherd

па|сть (-ду́, -дёшь; *pt* **-л, -ла,
-ло)** *сов от* **па́дать** ♦ **(-сти)** *ж*
(зверя) mouth

Па́сх|а (-и) *ж* (в иудаизме)
Passover; (в христианстве)
≈ Easter

пате́нт (-а) *м* patent

пате́нт|овать (-у́ю; *pf* **за~)** *несов
перех* to patent

патоло́ги|я (-и) *ж* pathology

патриа́рх (-а) *м* patriarch

патрио́т (-а) *м* patriot

патриоти́зм (-а) *м* patriotism

патро́н (-а) *м* (ВОЕН) cartridge;
(лампы) socket

патрули́р|овать (-ую) *несов
(не)перех* to patrol

патру́л|ь (-я́) *м* patrol

па́уз|а (-ы) *ж* (также МУЗ) pause

пау́к (-а́) *м* spider

паути́н|а (-ы) *ж* spider's web,
spiderweb (US); (в помещении)
cobweb; (перен) web

пах (-а; *loc sg* **-у́)** *м* groin

па|ха́ть (-шу́, -шешь; *pf* **вс~)**
несов перех to plough (BRIT),
plow (US)

па́х|нуть (-ну; *pt* **-, -ла)** *несов:* ~
(+instr) to smell (of)

пацие́нт (-а) *м* patient

па́чк|а (-ки; *gen pl* **-ек)** *ж* (бума́г)
bundle; (чая, сигаре́т итп) packet

па́чка|ть (-ю; *pf* **за~** *или* **ис~)**
несов перех: ~ **что-н** to get sth
dirty; **~ся** (*pf* **за~ся** *или* **ис~ся)**
несов возв to get dirty

паште́т (-а) *м* pâté

пая́|ть (-ю) *несов перех* to solder

певи́ц|а (-ы) *ж см.* **певе́ц**

певе́ц (-ца́) *м* singer

педаго́г (-а) *м* teacher

педагоги́ческий *прил*
(коллекти́в) teaching; ~ **институ́т**
teacher-training (BRIT) *или*
teachers' (US) college; ~ **сове́т** staff

meeting

педа́ль (-и) ж pedal

педиа́тр (-а) м paediatrician (BRIT), pediatrician (US)

пей несов см. **пить**

пе́йджер (-а) м pager

пейза́ж (-а) м landscape

пе́йте несов см. **пить**

пека́рня (-ни; gen pl -ен) ж bakery

пелена́ть (-ю; pf за~) несов перех to swaddle

пелёнка (-ки; gen pl -ок) ж swaddling clothes мн

пельме́нь (-я; nom pl -и) м (обычно мн) ≈ ravioli ед

пе́на (-ы) ж (мыльная) suds мн; (морская) foam; (бульонная) froth

пена́л (-а) м pencil case

пе́ние (-я) ср singing

пе́ниться (3sg -ится; pf вс~) несов возв to foam, froth

пеницилли́н (-а) м penicillin

пе́нка (-и) ж (на молоке) skin

пенсионе́р (-а) м pensioner

пенсио́нный прил (фонд) pension

пе́нсия (-и) ж pension; выходи́ть (вы́йти pf) на ~ю to retire

пень (пня) м (tree) stump

пе́пел (-ла) м ash

пе́пельница (-ы) ж ashtray

пе́рвенство (-а) ср championship; (место) first place

перви́чный прил (самый ранний) initial; (низовой) grass-root

первобы́тный прил primeval

пе́рвое (-ого) ср first course

первокла́ссник (-а) м pupil in first year at school

первонача́льный прил (исходный) original, initial

первосо́ртный прил top-quality,

top-grade

первостепе́нный прил (задача, значение) paramount

пе́рвый чис first; (по времени) first, earliest; ~ эта́ж (BRIT) или first (US) floor; ~ое вре́мя at first; в ~ую о́чередь in the first place или instance; ~ час дня/ но́чи after midday/midnight; това́р ~ого со́рта top grade product (on a scale of 1-3); ~ая по́мощь first aid

перебежа́ть (как бежа́ть; см. Table 20; impf **перебега́ть**) сов: ~ (че́рез +acc) to run across

перебива́ть (-ю) несов от **переби́ть**

перебира́ть(ся) (-ю(сь)) несов от **перебра́ть(ся)**

переби́ть (-ью, -ьёшь; impf **перебива́ть**) сов перех to interrupt; (разбить) to break

перебо́й (-я) м (двигателя) misfire; (задержка) interruption

переболе́ть (-ю) сов: ~ +instr to recover from

перебо́ро́ть (-орю́, -о́решь) сов перех to overcome

перебра́сывать (-ю) несов от **перебро́сить**

перебра́ть (-еру́, -ерёшь; impf **перебира́ть**) сов перех (бумаги) to sort out; (крупу, ягоды) to sort; (события) to go over или through (in one's mind); ~ся (impf **перебира́ться**) сов возв (через реку) to manage to get across

перебро́сить (-шу, -сишь; impf **перебра́сывать**) сов перех (мяч) to throw; (войска) to transfer

перева́л (-а) м (в горах) pass

перева́лочный прил: ~ пункт/ ла́герь transit area/camp

перев|арить (-арю́, -а́ришь;
impf **перева́ривать**) *сов перех* to
overcook (*by boiling*); (*пищу,
информацию*) to digest; **~ся** (*impf*
перева́риваться) *сов возв* to be
overcooked *или* overdone; (*пища*)
to be digested

перев|езти́ (-езу́, -езёшь; *pt* -ёз,
-езла́; *impf* **перевози́ть**) *сов
перех* to take *или* transport across

переверн|у́ть (-у́, -ёшь; *impf*
перевора́чивать) *сов перех* to
turn over; (*изменить*) to change
(completely); (*no impf*; *комнату*) to
turn upside down; **~ся** (*impf*
перевора́чиваться) *сов возв* to
turn over; (*человек*) to turn over; (*лодка,
машина*) to overturn

переве́с (-а) *м* (*преимущество*)
advantage

перев|ести́ (-еду́, -едёшь; *pt*
-ёл, -ела́; *impf* **переводи́ть**) *сов
перех* (*помочь перейти*) to take
across; (*часы*) to reset;
(*учреждение, сотрудника*) to
transfer, move; (*текст*) to translate;
(: *устно*) to interpret; (*переслать:
деньги*) to transfer; (*доллары,
метры итп*) to convert; **~сь** (*impf*
переводи́ться) *сов возв* to
move

перево́д (-а) *м* transfer; (*стрелки
часов*) resetting; (*текст*)
translation; (*деньги*) remittance

перев|оди́ть(ся) (-ожу́(сь),
-о́дишь(ся)) *несов от*
перевести́(сь)

перево́дчик (-а) *м* translator;
(*устный*) interpreter

перев|ози́ть (-ожу́, -о́зишь)
несов от **перевезти́**

перево́з|ка (-ки; *gen pl* -ок) *ж*
conveyance, transportation (*US*)

перевора́чива|ть(ся) (-ю(сь))
несов от **переверну́ть(ся)**

переворо́т (-а) *м* (*полит*) coup
(d'état); (*в судьбе*) turning point

перевоспита́|ть (-ю) *impf*
перевоспи́тывать *сов перех* to
re-educate

перев|яза́ть (-яжу́, -я́жешь;
impf **перевя́зывать**) *сов перех*
(*руку, раненого*) to bandage;
(*рану*) to dress, bandage;
(*коробку*) to tie up

перевя́з|ка (-ки; *gen pl* -ок) *ж*
bandaging

перег|на́ть (-оню́, -о́нишь; *pt*
-на́л, -нала́, -на́ло, *impf*
перегоня́ть) *сов перех*
(*обогнать*) to overtake; (*нефть*) to
refine; (*спирт*) to distil (*BRIT*), distill
(*US*)

перегова́рива|ться (-юсь)
несов возв: **~** (с +*instr*) to
exchange remarks (with)

переговóрный *прил*: **~ пункт**
telephone office (*for long-distance
calls*)

перегово́р|ы (-ов) *мн*
negotiations *мн*, talks *мн*; (*no
телефону*) call *ед*

перегоня́|ть (-ю) *несов от*
перегна́ть

перегор|е́ть (3sg -и́т; *impf* **~а́ть**)
сов (*лампочка*) to fuse;
(*двигатель*) to burn out

перегор|оди́ть (-жу́, -ди́шь;
impf **перегора́живать**) *сов
перех* (*комнату*) to partition (off);
(*дорогу*) to block

перегр|узи́ть (-ужу́, -у́зишь;
impf **перегружа́ть**) *сов перех* to
overload

перегру́з|ка (-ки; *gen pl* -ок) *ж*
overload; (*обычно мн: нервные*)
strain *ед*

─────────
KEYWORD
─────────

пе́ред *предл*; +*instr* **1** (*o

положе́нии, в прису́тствии) in front of

2 (ра́ньше чего́-н) before

3 (об объе́кте возде́йствия): **пе́ред тру́дностями** in the face of difficulties; **извиня́ться (извини́ться** pf) **пе́ред кем-н** to apologize to sb; **отчи́тываться (отчита́ться** pf) **пе́ред** +instr to report to

4 (по сравне́нию) compared to

5 (как сою́з): **пе́ред тем как** before; **пе́ред тем как зако́нчить** before finishing

передава́|ть (-ю; imper **~ва́й(те))** несо́в от **переда́ть**

передаду́т etc сов см. **переда́ть**

переда́тчик (-а) м transmitter

переда́|ть (как дать; см. Table 16; impf **передава́ть;** сов перех: ~ что-н (кому́-н) (письмо́, пода́рок) to pass или hand sth (over) (to sb); (изве́стие, интере́с) to pass sth on (to sb); **~йте ему́ (мой) приве́т** give him my regards; **~йте ей, что я не приду́** tell her I am not coming; **передава́ть (~** pf) что-н по телеви́дению/ра́дио to televise/broadcast sth

переда́ч|а (-и) ж (де́нег, письма́) handing over; (ма́тча) transmission; (ТЕЛ, РА́ДИО) programme (BRIT), program (US); **програ́мма** = television and radio guide

переда́шь сов см. **переда́ть**

передвига́|ть(ся) (-ю(сь)) несо́в от **передви́нуть(ся)**

передвиже́ни|е (-я) ср movement; **сре́дства ~я** means of transport

передви́н|уть (-у; impf **передвига́ть)** сов перех to move; **~ся** (impf **передвига́ться)**

сов возв to move

переде́ла|ть (-ю; impf **переде́лывать)** сов перех (рабо́ту) to redo; (хара́ктер) to change

пере́дний прил front

пере́дн|яя (-ей) ж (entrance) hall

пе́редо предл = **пе́ред**

передов|а́я (-о́й) ж (та́кже: ~ статья́) editorial; (та́кже: ~ пози́ция: ВОЕН) vanguard

передов|о́й прил (техноло́гия) advanced; (писа́тель, взгля́ды) progressive

передразни́ть (-азню́, -а́знишь; impf **передра́знивать)** сов перех to mimic

переды́шк|а (-ки; gen pl **-ек)** ж respite

перее́зд (-а) м (в но́вый дом) move

перее́хать (как е́хать; см. Table 19; impf **переезжа́ть)** сов (пересели́ться) to move; **переезжа́ть (~** pf) **(че́рез** +acc) to cross

пережива́ни|е (-я) ср feeling

пережива́|ть (-ю) несо́в от **пережи́ть** ♦ непере́х: ~ **(за** +acc) (разг) to worry (about)

пережи́|ть (-ву́, -вёшь; impf **пережива́ть)** сов перех (вы́терпеть) to suffer

перезвон|и́ть (-ю́, -и́шь; impf **перезва́нивать)** сов to phone (BRIT) или call (US) back

переизбра́ть (-еру́, -ерёшь; pt **-ра́л, -рала́;** impf **переизбира́ть)** сов перех to re-elect

переизда́|ть (как дать; см. Table 16; impf **переиздава́ть)** сов перех to republish

пере|йти́ (как идти́; см. Table 18; impf **переходи́ть)** сов (не)перех: ~ **(че́рез** +acc) to cross ♦ непере́х

~ в/на +acc (поменять место) to
go (over) to; (на другую работу)
to move to; **переходить** (~ pf) к
+dat (к сыну итп) to pass to; (к
делу, к обсуждению) to turn to;
переходить (~ pf) на +acc to
switch to

переки́н|**уть** (-у; impf
переки́дывать) сов перех to
throw

перекла́дин|**а** (-ы) ж crossbeam;
(СПОРТ) (horizontal или high) bar

перекла́дыва|**ть** (-ю) несов от
переложи́ть

переключа́тел|**ь** (-я) m switch

переключ|**и́ть** (-у́, -и́шь; impf
переключа́ть) сов перех to
switch; ~**ся** (impf
переключа́ться) сов возв: ~**ся**
(на +acc) (внимание) to shift (to)

перекопа́|**ть** (-ю) сов перех
(огород) to dig up; (разг: шкаф)
to rummage through

перекр|**ести́ть** (-ещу́, -е́стишь)
сов от **крести́ть**; ~**ся** сов от
крести́ться (impf
перекре́щиваться) возв
(дороги, интересы) to cross

перекрёст|**ок** (-ка) m crossroads

перекр|**ы́ть** (-о́ю, -о́ешь; impf
перекрыва́ть) сов перех (реку)
to dam; (воду, газ) to cut off

перекуп|**и́ть** (-уплю́, -у́пишь;
impf **перекупа́ть**) сов перех to
buy

перекупщик (-а) m dealer

перекус|**и́ть** (-ушу́, -у́сишь) сов
(разг) to have a snack

переле́з|**ть** (-у, -ешь; pt -, -ла;
impf **перелеза́ть**) сов (не)перех:
~ (+acc) (забор, канаву) to
climb (over)

перелёт (-а) m flight; (птиц)
migration

переле|**те́ть** (-чу́, -ти́шь; impf

перелета́ть сов (не)перех: ~
(че́рез +acc) to fly over

перелётный прил (птицы)
migratory

перелива́ни|**е** (-я) ср: ~ кро́ви
blood transfusion

перелива́|ть (-ю) несов от
перели́ть

перелиста́|**ть** (-ю; impf
перели́стывать сов перех
(просмотреть) to leaf through

перел|**и́ть** (-ью́, -ьёшь; impf
перелива́ть) сов перех to pour
(from one container to another);
перелива́ть (~ pf) кровь кому́-н
to give sb a blood transfusion

перел|**ожи́ть** (-ожу́, -о́жишь;
impf **перекла́дывать** сов перех
to move; **перекла́дывать** (~ pf)
что-н на кого́-н (задачу) to pass
sth onto sb

перело́м (-а) m (МЕД) fracture;
(перен) turning point

перело́мный прил critical

перема́тыва|**ть** (-ю) несов от
перемота́ть

переме́н|**а** (-ы) ж change; (в
шко́ле) break (BRIT), recess (US)

переме́нный прил (успех,
ветер) variable; ~ **ток** alternating
current

переме|**сти́ть** (-щу́, -сти́шь; impf
перемеща́ть сов перех
(предмет) to move; (людей) to
transfer; ~**ся** (impf
перемеща́ться сов возв to
move

переме|**ша́ть** (-ю; impf
переме́шивать сов перех
(кашу) to stir; (угли, дрова) to
poke; (вещи, бумаги) to mix up

переме|**сти́ть(ся** (-щу(сь)) несов
от **перемести́ть(ся**

перемеще́ни|**е** (-я) ср transfer

переми́ри|**е** (-я) ср truce

перемота́|ть (-ю; *impf*
перема́тывать) *сов перех*
(*нитку*) to wind; (*плёнку*) to
rewind

перенапряга́|ть (-ю) *несов от*
перенапря́чь

перенапряже́ни|е (-я) *ср*
overexertion

перенапря́|чь (-гу́, -жёшь *итп*,
-гу́т; *pt* -г, -гла́; *impf*
перенапряга́ть) *сов перех* to
overstrain

перенаселённый *прил*
overpopulated

перен|ести́ (-есу́, -есёшь; *pt*
-ёс, -есла́, -есло́; *impf*
переноси́ть) *сов перех*: ~ что-н
че́рез +*acc* to carry sth over *или*
across; (*поменять место*) to
move; (*встречу, заседание*) to
reschedule; (*болезнь*) to suffer
from; (*голод, холод итп*) to
endure

перенима́|ть (-ю) *несов от*
переня́ть

перено́с (-а) *м* (*предмета*)
transfer; (*встречи*) rescheduling;
(*линг*) hyphen

перен|оси́ть (-ошу́, -о́сишь)
несов от **перенести́** ♦ *перех*: не
~ **антибио́тиков/самолёта** to
react badly to antibiotics/flying

перено́сиц|а (-ы) *ж* bridge of the
nose

переносно́й *прил* portable

перено́сный *прил* (*значение*)
figurative

перено́счик (-а) *м* (*МЕД*) carrier

переноч|ева́ть (-у́ю) *сов от*
ночева́ть

пере|ня́ть (-йму́, -ймёшь; *pt*
-ня́л, -няла́; *impf* **перенима́ть**)
сов перех (*опыт, идеи*) to
assimilate; (*обычаи, привычки*) to
adopt

переоде́|ть (-ну, -нешь; *impf*
переодева́ть) *сов перех*
(*одежду*) to change (out of);
переоде́ться (~ *pf*) **кого́-н** to
change sb *или* sb's clothes; **-ся**
(*impf* **переодева́ться**) *сов возв*
to change, get changed

переоце́н|ить (-ю́, -ишь;
impf **переоце́нивать**) *сов перех*
to overestimate

перепа́д (-а) *м*: ~ +*gen* fluctuation
in

перепеча́та|ть (-ю) *сов перех*
(*напечатанное*) to reprint;
(*рукопись*) to type

переп|иса́ть (-ишу́, -и́шешь;
impf **переписывать**) *сов перех*
(*написать заново*) to rewrite;
(*скопировать*) to copy

перепи́с|ка (-ки; *gen pl* -ок) *ж*
(*см глаг*) rewriting; copying;
(*деловая, личная*) correspondence

перепи́сыва|ть (-ю) *несов от*
переписа́ть; **-ся** *несов возв*:
-ся (**с** +*instr*) to correspond (with)

пе́репис|ь (-и) *ж* (*населения*)
census; (*имущества*) inventory

перепла|ти́ть (-чу́, -а́тишь;
impf **перепла́чивать**) *сов* to
overpay

переплет|сти́ (-ету́, -етёшь; *pt*
-ёл, -ела́; *impf* **переплета́ть**) *сов
перех* (*книгу*) to bind

переплёт (-а) *м* (*обложка*)
binding; **око́нный** ~ window sash

переплы|ть (-ву́, -вёшь; *pt* -л,
-ла́; *impf* **переплыва́ть**) *сов*
(*не*)*перех*: ~ (**че́рез** +*acc*)
(*вплавь*) to swim (across); (*на
лодке, на корабле*) to sail (across)

переполз|ти́ (-у́, -ёшь; *pt* -л, -ла́,
-ло́; *impf* **переполза́ть**) *сов
(не)перех*: ~ (**че́рез** +*acc*) to crawl
across

перепо́лн|ить (-ю, -ишь; *impf*

переполня́ть *сов перех (сосуд, контейнер)* to overfill; *(вагон, автобус итп)* to overcrowd; **~ся** *(impf* **переполня́ться)** *сов возв (сосуд)* to be overfilled

переполо́х (-а) *м* hullabaloo

перепо́н|ка (-ки; *gen pl* -ок) *ж* membrane

переправа (-ы) *ж* crossing

переправ|ить (-лю, -ишь; *impf* **переправля́ть**) *сов перех*: ~ кого-н/что-н че́рез +*acc* to take across; **~ся** *(impf* **переправля́ться)** *сов возв*: **~ся че́рез** +*acc* to cross

перепрода́ть (как **дать**; см. **Table 16**; *impf* **перепродава́ть)** *сов перех* to resell

перепры́гн|уть (-у; *impf* **перепры́гивать)** *сов (не)перех*: ~ (че́рез +*acc*) to jump (over)

перепуга́ть (-ю) *сов перех*: ~ кого-н to scare the life out of sb

перепу́та|ть (-ю) *сов от* **пу́тать**

перерабо́та|ть (-ю; *impf* **перераба́тывать)** *сов перех (сырьё, нефть)* to process; *(идеи, статью, теорию)* to rework

перер|асти́ (-асту́, -астёшь; *pt* -о́с, -осла́; *impf* **перераста́ть)** *сов перех* to outgrow ♦ *неперех*: ~ **в** +*acc (превратиться)* to turn into

перере́|зать (-жу, -жешь; *impf* **перереза́ть)** *сов перех (провод)* to cut in two; *(путь)* to cut off

переры́в (-а) *м* break; **де́ла|ть (сде́лать** *pf)* ~ to take a break

перес|ади́ть (-ажу́, -а́дишь; *impf* **переса́живать)** *сов перех* to move; *(дерево, цветок, сердце)* to transplant; *(кость, кожу)* to graft

переса́д|ка (-ки; *gen pl* -ок) *ж (на*

поезд итп) change; *(МЕД, сердца)* transplant; *(: кожи)* graft

переса́жива|ть (-ю) *несов от* **пересади́ть**; **~ся** *несов от* **пересе́сть**

пересека́|ть(ся) (-ю(сь)) *несов от* **пересе́чь(ся)**

пересел|и́ть (-ю́, -и́шь; *impf* **переселя́ть)** *сов перех (на новые зе́мли)* to settle; *(в новую кварти́ру)* to move; **~ся** *(impf* **переселя́ться)** *сов возв (в новый дом)* to move

перес|е́сть (-я́ду, -я́дешь; *impf* **переса́живаться)** *сов (на друго́е ме́сто)* to move; **переса́живаться** (~ *pf)* **на друго́й по́езд/самолёт** to change trains/planes

пересече́ни|е (-я) *ср (действие)* crossing; *(ме́сто)* intersection

перес|е́чь (-еку́, -ечёшь *etc*, -еку́т; *pt* -ёк, -екла́; *impf* **пересека́ть)** *сов перех* to cross; **~ся** *(impf* **пересека́ться)** *сов возв* to intersect; *(интере́сы)* to cross

переска́з (-а) *м* retelling

переск|аза́ть (-ажу́, -а́жешь; *impf* **переска́зывать)** *сов перех* to tell

пере|сла́ть (-шлю́, -шлёшь; *impf* **пересыла́ть)** *сов перех (отосла́ть)* to send; *(по друго́му а́дресу)* to forward

пересм|отре́ть (-отрю́, -о́тришь; *impf* **пересма́тривать)** *сов перех (реше́ние, вопро́с)* to reconsider

пересн|я́ть (-иму́, -и́мешь; *pt* -я́л, -яла́, *impf* **переснима́ть)** *сов перех (докуме́нт)* to make a copy of

пересол|и́ть (-ю́, -о́лишь; *impf* **переса́ливать)** *сов перех*: ~ что-н to put too much salt in sth

пересо́х|нуть (3sg -нет, pt -, -ла; impf **пересыха́ть**) сов (почва, бельё) to dry out; (река) to dry up

переспро́с|ить (-ошу́, -о́сишь; impf **переспра́шивать**) сов перех to ask again

переста|ва́ть (-ю́) несов от **переста́ть**

переста́в|ить (-лю, -ишь; impf **переставля́ть**) сов перех to move; (изменить порядок) to rearrange

перестара́|ться (-юсь) сов возв to overdo it

переста́|ть (-ну, -нешь; impf **переставать**) сов to stop; **переста́ть** (~ pf) +infin to stop doing

перестра́ива|ть (-ю) несов от **перестро́ить**

перестре́л|ка (-ки; gen pl -ок) ж exchange of fire

перестро́|ить (-ю, -ишь; impf **перестра́ивать**) сов перех (дом) to rebuild; (экономику) to reorganize

перестро́|йка (-йки; gen pl -ек) ж (дома) rebuilding; (экономики) reorganization; (ист) perestroika

пересту|пи́ть (-плю́, -у́пишь; impf **переступа́ть**) сов перех (закон) to overstep ♦ (не)перех: ~ **(че́рез** +acc) (порог, предмет) to step over

пересчёт (-а) м count; (повторный) re-count

пересчита́|ть (-ю; impf **пересчи́тывать**) сов перех to count; (повторно) to re-count, count again; (в других единицах) to convert

пересыла́|ть (-ю) несов от **пересла́ть**

пересы́па|ть (-лю, -лешь; impf **пересыпа́ть**) сов перех

(насыпать) to pour

пересыха́|ть (3sg -ет) несов от **пересо́хнуть**

перет|ащи́ть (-ащу́, -а́щишь; impf **перета́скивать**) сов перех (предмет) to drag over

перетру|ди́ться (-жу́сь, -у́дишься; impf **перетружда́ться**) сов возв (разг) to be overworked

перет|яну́ть (-яну́, -я́нешь; impf **перетя́гивать**) сов перех (передвинуть) to pull, tow; (быть тяжелее) to outweigh

переубе|ди́ть (-жу́, -ди́шь; impf **переубежда́ть**) сов перех: ~ **кого́-н** to make sb change his итп mind

переу́л|ок (-ка) м lane, alley

переутом|и́ться (-лю́сь, -и́шься; impf **переутомля́ться**) сов возв to tire o.s. out

переутомле́ни|е (-я) ср exhaustion

переучёт (-а) м stocktaking

переу|чи́ть (-чу́, -у́чишь; impf **переу́чивать**) сов перех to retrain; **~ся** (impf **переу́чиваться**) сов возв to undergo retraining

перехитр|и́ть (-ю́, -и́шь) сов перех to outwit

перехо́д (-а) м crossing; (к друго́й системе) transition; (подземный, в здании) passage

переход|и́ть (-ожу́, -о́дишь) несов от **перейти́**

перехо́дный прил (промежуточный) transitional; ~ **глаго́л** transitive verb

пе́р|ец (-ца) м pepper

пере́ч|ень (-ня) м list

перечеркн|у́ть (-у́, -ёшь; impf **перечёркивать**) сов перех to cross out

перечи́сл|ить (-ю, -ишь; impf

перечисля́ть) *сов перех* (упомяну́ть) to list; (КОММ) to transfer

перечита́ть (-ю; *impf* **перечи́тывать**) *сов перех* (кни́гу) to reread, read again

перешагну́ть (-у́, -ёшь; *impf* **переша́гивать**) *сов (не)перех*: ~ (че́рез +*acc*) to step over

перешёл *итп сов см.* **перейти́**

переши́ть (-ью́, -ьёшь; *impf* **перешива́ть**) *сов перех* (пла́тье) to alter; (пу́говицу) to move (*by sewing on somewhere else*)

переэкзамено́вка (-ки; *gen pl* -ок) *ж*

пери́ла (-) *мн* railing *ед*; (ле́стницы) ban(n)isters *мн*

пери́метр (-а) *м* perimeter

пери́од (-а) *м* period; **пе́рвый/ второ́й ~ игры́** (СПОРТ) first/ second half (*of the game*)

периоди́ческий *прил* periodical

перифери́я (-и) *ж* the provinces *мн*

перламу́тр (-а) *м* mother-of-pearl

перло́вый *прил* barley

пер|о́ (-а́; *nom pl* -ья, *gen pl* -ьев) *ср* (пти́цы) feather; (*для письма́*) nib

перочи́нный *прил*: ~ **нож** penknife

перпендикуля́рный *прил* perpendicular

перро́н (-а) *м* platform (RAIL)

пе́рсик (-а) *м* peach

персона́ж (-а) *м* character

персона́л (-а) *м* (АДМИН) personnel, staff

персона́льный *прил* personal; ~ **компью́тер** PC

перспекти́ва (-ы) *ж* (ГЕОМ) perspective; (*вид*) view; (*обычно мн: пла́ны*) prospects; **в ~е** (*в бу́дущем*) in store

перспекти́вный *прил* (*изображе́ние*) in perspective; (*плани́рование*) long-term; (*учени́к*) promising

пе́рст|ень (-ня) *м* ring

перча́т|ка (-ки; *gen pl* -ок) *ж* glove

пе́рч|ить (-у, -ишь; *pf* на~) *сов перех* to pepper

перши́ть (*3sg* -и́т) *несов безл* (*разг*): **у меня́ ~и́т в го́рле** I've got a frog in my throat

пе́рья *etc сущ см.* **перо́**

пёс (пса) *м* dog

песе́ц (-ца́) *м* arctic fox

пе́сн|я (-ни; *gen pl* -ен) *ж* song

песо́к (-ка́; *part gen* -ку́) *м* sand

песо́чный *прил* (*пече́нье*) short

пессимисти́чный *прил* pessimistic

пёстрый *прил* (*ткань*) multi-coloured (BRIT), multi-colored (US)

песча́ный *прил* sandy

пе́т|ля (-ли; *gen pl* -ель) *ж* loop; (*в вяза́нии*) stitch; (*две́ри, кры́шки*) hinge; (*для пу́говицы*) buttonhole

петру́шка (-и) *ж* parsley

пету́х (-а́) *м* cock, rooster (US)

петь (пою́, поёшь; *imper* **пой(те)**; *pf* с~) *несов перех* to sing

пехо́т|а (-ы) *ж* infantry

печа́л|ь (-и) *ж* (*грусть*) sadness, sorrow

печа́льный *прил* sad; (*оши́бка, судьба́*) unhappy

печа́т|ать (-ю; *pf* на~) *несов перех* (*та́кже* ФОТО) to print; (*публикова́ть*) to publish; (*на компью́тере*) to type

печа́тный *прил* (*стано́к*) printing; ~**ые бу́квы** block letters

печа́т|ь (-и) *ж* stamp; (*на дверя́х, на се́йфе*) seal; (*изда́тельское де́ло*) printing; (*след: страда́ний*) mark ♦ собир (пресса) press

печён|ка (**-ки**; gen pl **-ок**) ж liver

печёный прил baked

печен|ь (**-и**) ж (АНАТ) liver

печень|е (**-я**) ср biscuit (BRIT), cookie (US)

печ|ка (**-ки**; gen pl **-ек**) ж stove

печ|ь (**-и**; loc sg **-и́**, gen pl **-éй**) ж stove; (ТЕХ) furnace ♦ (**-ку́**, **-чёшь** etc, **-ку́т**; pt пёк, **-кла́**, pf испéчь) несов перех to bake;

микроволновая ~ microwave oven; **пéчься** (pf испéчься) несов возв to bake

пешехо́д (**-а**) м pedestrian

пешехо́дный прил pedestrian

пéш|ка (**-ки**; gen pl **-ек**) ж pawn

пешко́м нареч on foot

пещер|а (**-ы**) ж cave

пиани́но ср нескл (upright) piano

пиани́ст (**-а**) м pianist

пивн|а́я (**-о́й**) ж ≈ bar, ≈ pub (BRIT)

пивно́й прил (бар, бочка) beer

пи́в|о (**-а**) ср beer

пиджа́к (**-а́**) м jacket

пижа́м|а (**-ы**) ж pyjamas мн

пик (**-а**) м peak ♦ прил неизм (часы, период, время) peak; **часы́ ~** rush hour

пи́к|и (**-**) мн (в картах) spades мн

пи́ковый прил (в картах) of spades

пил|а́ (**-ы́**; nom pl **-ы**) ж saw

пил|и́ть (**-ю́**, **-ишь**) несов перех to saw; (перен: разг) to nag

пи́л|ка (**-ки**; gen pl **-ок**) ж nail file

пило́т (**-а**) м pilot

пило́тный прил (пробный) pilot, trial

пина́|ть (**-ю**) несов перех to kick

пингви́н (**-а**) м penguin

пин|о́к (**-ка́**) м kick

пионе́р (**-а**) м pioneer; (в СССР)

member of Communist Youth organization

пипе́т|ка (**-ки**; gen pl **-ок**) ж pipette

пир (**-а**; nom pl **-ы́**) м feast

пирами́д|а (**-ы**) ж pyramid

пира́т (**-а**) м pirate

пиро́г (**-а́**) м pie

пиро́жн|ое (**-ого**) ср cake

пирож|о́к (**-ка́**) м (с мясом) pie; (с вареньем) tart

писа́ни|е (**-я**) ср: Свяще́нное Писа́ние Holy Scripture

писа́тел|ь (**-я**) м writer

пи|са́ть (**-шу́**, **-шешь**; pf на~) несов перех to write; (картину) to paint ♦ неперех (no pf, ребёнок) to be able to write; (ручка) to write; **~ся** несов возв (слово) to be spelt или spelled

писк (**-а**) м squeak; (птицы) cheep

пискля́вый прил (голос) squeaky

пистоле́т (**-а**) м pistol

пи́сьменно нареч in writing

пи́сьменный прил (просьба, экзамен) written; (стол, прибор) writing; **в ~ой форме** in writing

пис|ьмо́ (**-ьма́**; nom pl **-ьма**, gen pl **-ем**) ср letter; (no pl; алфавитное) script

пита́ни|е (**-я**) ср (ребёнка) feeding; (ТЕХ) supply; (вегетарианское) diet; **обще́ственное ~** public catering

пита́тельный прил (вещества) nutritious; (крем) nourishing

пита́|ть (**-ю**) несов перех (перен: любовь) to feel; **~ся** несов возв: **~ся** +instr (человек, растение) to live on; (животное) to feed on

пито́мник (**-а**) м (БОТ) nursery

пи|ть (пью, пьёшь; pt **-л**, **-ла́**, imper **пе́й(те)**; pf вы~) несов перех to drink ♦ неперех: **~ за кого́-н/что-н** to drink to sb/sth

питьев|о́й *прил:* ~**а́я вода́** drinking water

пи́цц|а (-ы) *ж* pizza

пиццери́|я (-и) *ж* pizzeria

пи́чка|ть (-ю; *pf* **на**~) *несов перех* to stuff

пишу́ *etc несов см.* **писа́ть(ся)**

пи́щ|а (-и) *ж* food

пищ|а́ть (-у́, -и́шь) *несов* (*птицы*) to cheep; (*животные*) to squeak

пищеваре́ни|е (-я) *ср* digestion

пищев|о́й *прил* food; (*соль*) edible; ~**а́я со́да** baking soda

ПК *м сокр* = **персона́льный компью́тер**

пл. *сокр* (= **пло́щадь**) Sq.

пла́вани|е (-я) *ср* swimming; (*на судне*) sailing; (*рейс*) voyage

пла́вательный *прил:* ~ **бассе́йн** swimming pool

пла́ва|ть (-ю) *несов* to swim; (*корабль*) to sail; (*в воздухе*) to float

пла́в|ить (-лю, -ишь; *pf* **рас**~) *несов* to smelt; ~**ся** (*pf* **рас**~**ся**) *несов возв* to melt

пла́в|ки (-ок) *мн* swimming trunks *мн*

пла́вленый *прил:* ~ **сыр** processed cheese

плавни́к (-а́) *м* (*у рыб*) fin

пла́вный *прил* smooth

плаву́чий *прил* floating

плака́т (-а) *м* poster

пла́|кать (-чу, -чешь) *несов* to cry, weep; ~ (*impf*) **от** +*gen* (*от боли итп*) to cry from; (*от ра́дости*) to cry with; (*от го́ря*) to cry in

пла́м|я (-ени; *как* **вре́мя**; *см. Table 4*) *ср* flame

план (-а) *м* plan; (*чертёж*) plan, map; **пере́дний** ~ foreground; **за́дний** ~ background

планёр (-а) *м* glider

плане́т|а (-ы) *ж* planet

планета́ри|й (-я) *м* planetarium

плани́р|овать (-ую) *несов перех* to plan; (*pf* **за**~) to plan

планиро́вк|а (-и) *ж* layout

пла́нк|а (-ки; *gen pl* -ок) *ж* slat

пла́новый *прил* planned; (*отдел, комиссия*) planning

планоме́рный *прил* systematic

пласт (-а́) *м* (*также перен*) stratum; **лежа́ть** (*impf*) ~**о́м** to lie flat

пла́стик (-а) *м* = **пластма́сса**

пластили́н (-а) *м* plasticine

пласти́н|а (-ы) *ж* plate

пласти́нк|а (-ки; *gen pl* -ок) *ж* уменьш **от пласти́на**; (*муз*) record

пласти́ческий *прил* plastic

пласти́чный *прил* (*жесты, движения*) graceful; (*материалы, вещества*) plastic

пластма́сс|а (-ы) *ж сокр* (= **пласти́ческая ма́сса**) plastic

пла́стыр|ь (-я) *м* (*мед*) plaster

пла́т|а (-ы) *ж* (*за труд, за услуги итп*) pay; (*за кварти́ру*) payment; (*за прое́зд*) fee; (*перен: награ́да*) reward

платёж (-ежа́) *м* payment

платёжеспосо́бный *прил* (*комм*) solvent

платёжн|ый *прил* (*комм*): ~ **бланк** payslip; ~**ая ве́домость** payroll

пла́тин|а (-ы) *ж* platinum

пла|ти́ть (-чу́, -тишь; *pf* **за**~ *или* **у**~) *несов перех* to pay

пла́тный *прил* (*вход, стоянка*) chargeable; (*школа*) fee-paying; (*больница*) private

плат|о́к (-ка́) *м* (*головно́й*) headscarf; (*наплечный*) shawl;

(также: **носово́й ~**) handkerchief

платфо́рм|а (-ы) ж platform; (*станция*) halt; (*основание*) foundation

пла́ть|е (-я; *gen pl* -ев) *ср* dress ♦ *собир* (*одежда*) clothing, clothes мн

плафо́н (-а) *м* (*абажур*) shade (for ceiling light)

плацда́рм (-а) *м* (*ВОЕН*) bridgehead

плаце́нт|а (-ы) ж (*МЕД*) placenta

плацка́ртный *прил*: **~ ваго́н** railway car with open berths instead of compartments

плач (-а) *м* crying

пла́чу *etc vb см.* **пла́кать**

плачу́ *несов см.* **плати́ть**

плащ (-á) *м* raincoat

плева́ть (-ю́ю) *несов* to spit; (*pf* **на~**; *перен*): **~ на** +*acc* (*разг* (на правила, на мнение других) to not give a damn about; **~ся** *несов возв* to spit

плед (-а) *м* (tartan) rug

пле́йер (-а) *м* Walkman ®

пле́м|я (-ени; *как* **вре́мя**; *см. Table 4*) *ср* (также *перен*) tribe

племя́нник (-а) *м* nephew

племя́нниц|а (-ы) ж niece

плен (-а; *loc sg* -ý) *м* captivity; **брать** (**взять** *pf*) **кого́-н в ~** to take sb prisoner; **попада́ть** (**попа́сть** *pf*) **в ~** to be taken prisoner

плён|ка (-ки; *gen pl* -ок) ж film; (*кожица*) membrane; (*магнитофонная*) tape

пле́нн|ый (-ого) *м* prisoner

пле́нум (-а) *м* plenum

пле́сень (-и) ж mould (*BRIT*), mold (*US*)

плеск (-а) *м* splash

пле|ска́ться (-щу́сь, -щешься) *несов возв* to splash

пле́сневе|ть (3sg -ет; *pf* **за**~) *несов* to go mouldy (*BRIT*) или moldy (*US*)

пле|сти́ (-ету́, -етёшь; *pt* -ёл, -ела́; *pf* **с~**) *несов перех* (*сети*) to weave; (*венок, волосы*) to plait

плетёный *прил* wicker

плёт|ка (-ки; *gen pl* -ок) ж whip

пле́чик|и (-ов) *мн* (*вешалка*) coat hangers мн; (*подкладки*) shoulder pads мн

плеч|о́ (-á; *nom pl* -и) *ср* shoulder

пли́нтус (-а) *м* skirting board (*BRIT*), baseboard (*US*)

плиссе́ *прил неизм*: **ю́бка/пла́тье ~** pleated skirt/dress

плит|а́ (-ы́; *nom pl* -ы) ж (*каменная*) slab; (*металлическая*) plate; (*печь*) cooker, stove

плит|ка (-ки; *gen pl* -ок) ж (*керамическая*) tile; (*шоколада*) bar; (*электрическая*) hot plate; (*газовая*) camping stove

плове́|ц (-ца́) *м* swimmer

плод (-á) *м* (*БОТ*) fruit; (*БИО*) foetus (*BRIT*), fetus (*US*); **~** +*gen* (*перен: усилий*) fruits of

плод|и́ться (3sg -и́тся; *pf* **рас**~) *несов возв* to multiply

плодоро́дный *прил* fertile

плодотво́рный *прил* fruitful

пло́мб|а (-ы) ж (*в зубе*) filling; (*на дверях, на сейфе*) seal

пломби́р (-а) *м* rich creamy ice-cream

пломби́р|овать (-у́ю; *pf* **за**~) *несов перех* (*зуб*) to fill; (*pf* **о**~; *дверь, сейф*) to seal

пло́ский *прил* flat

плоскогу́бц|ы (-ев) *мн* pliers мн

пло́скост|ь (-и; *gen pl* -е́й) ж plane

плот (-á; *loc sg* -ý) *м* raft

плоти́н|а (-ы) ж dam

пло́тник (-а) *м* carpenter

плотный прил (туман) dense, thick; (толпа) dense; (бумага, кожа) thick; (обед) substantial

плохо нареч (учиться, работать) badly ♦ как сказ it's bad; мне ~ I feel bad; у меня ~ с деньгами I am short of money

плохой прил bad

площадка (-и; gen pl -ок) ж (детская) playground; (спортивная) ground; (строительная) site; (часть вагона) corridor; лестничная ~ landing; посадочная ~ landing pad

площадь (-и; gen pl -ей) ж (место) square; (пространство, также МАТ) area; (также: жилая ~) living space

плуг (-а; nom pl -и) м plough (BRIT), plow (US)

плыть (-ву, -вёшь; pt -л, -ла) несов to swim; (судно) to sail; (облако) to float

плюнуть (-у) сов to spit; плюнь! (разг) forget it!

плюс м нескл, союз plus

пляж (-а) м beach

пневмония (-и) ж pneumonia

ПО ср нескл сокр (= программное обеспечение) software; (КОММ: = производственное объединение) ≈ large industrial company

KEYWORD

по предл; +dat 1 (о месте действия, вдоль) along; лодка плывёт по реке the boat is sailing on the river; спускаться (спуститься pf) по лестнице to go down the stairs

2 (при глаголах движения) round; ходить (impf) по комнате/саду to walk round the room/garden; плыть (impf) по течению to go downstream

3 (об объекте воздействия; on): ударить (impf) по врагу to deal a blow to the enemy

4 (в соответствии с): действовать по закону/правилам to act in accordance with the law/the rules; по расписанию/плану according to schedule/plan

5 (об основании): судить по внешности to judge by appearances; жениться (impf/pf) по любви to marry for love

6 (вследствие) due to; по необходимости out of necessity

7 (посредством): говорить по телефону to speak on the phone; отправлять (отправить pf) что-н по почте to send sth by post; передавать (передать pf) что-н по радио/телевидению to broadcast/televise sth

8 (с целью, для): органы по борьбе с преступностью organizations in the fight against crime; я позвал тебя по делу I called on you on business

9 (о какой-н характеристике объекта) in; по профессии by profession; дед по матери maternal grandfather; товарищ по школе school friend

10 (о сфере деятельности) in

11 (о мере времени): по вечерам/утрам in the evenings/mornings; по воскресеньям/пятницам on Sundays/Fridays; я работаю по целым дням all day long; работа рассчитана по минутам the work is planned by the minute

12 (о единичности предметов)

ма́ма дала́ всем по я́блоку Mum gave them each an apple; **мы купи́ли по одно́й кни́ге** we bought a book each
♦ предл; +acc 1 (вплоть до) up to; **с пе́рвой по пя́тую главу́** from the first to (BRIT) and through (US) the fifth chapter; **я за́нят по го́рло** (разг: перен) I am up to my eyes in work; **он по́ у́ши в неё влюблён** he is head over heels in love with her
2 (при обозначении цены): **по два/три рубля́ за шту́ку** two/three roubles each
3 (при обозначении количества): **по два/три челове́ка** in twos/threes
♦ предл; (+prp; после) оп; **по прие́зде** on arrival

п/о сокр (= почто́вое отделе́ние) post office
по-англи́йски нареч in English
побе́г (-а) м (из тюрьмы́) escape; (БОТ) shoot, sprout
побегу́ etc сов см. **побежа́ть**
побе́д|**а** (-ы) ж victory
победи́тель (-я) м (в войне́) victor; (в состяза́нии) winner
побе|**ди́ть** (2sg -ди́шь, 3sg -ди́т; impf **побежда́ть**) сов перех to defeat ♦ неперех to win
победоно́сный прил victorious
побежа́ть (как бежа́ть; см. Table 20) (на человек, животное) to start running; (дни, годы) to start to fly by; (ручьи, слёзы) to begin to flow
побежда́|**ть** (-ю) несов от **победи́ть**
побеле́ть (-ю) сов от **беле́ть**
побели́ть (-ю, -ишь) сов от **бели́ть**
побе́лк|**а** (-и) ж whitewash

(де́йствие) whitewashing
побере́ж|**ье** (-ья; gen pl -ий) ср coast
побеспоко́ить (-ю, -ишь) сов от **беспоко́ить**
поб|**и́ть** (-ью, -ьёшь) сов от **бить** ♦ перех (повреди́ть) to destroy; (разби́ть) to break
побли́зости нареч nearby
♦ предл: ~ от +gen near (to), close to
побо́рник (-а) м champion (of cause)
побо|**ро́ть** (-орю́, -о́решь) сов перех (также перен) to overcome
побо́чный прил (продукт, реакция) secondary; ~ **эффе́кт** side effect
побу|**ди́ть** (-жу́, -ди́шь) сов перех: ~ **кого́-н к чему́** и/ +infin to prompt sb into sth/to do
побужде́ни|**е** (-я) ср (к де́йствию) motive
побыва́|**ть** (-ю) сов: ~ **в Африке/у роди́телей** to visit Africa/one's parents
побы́ть (как быть; см. Table 21) сов to stay
пова́л|**и́ть(ся)** (-алю́(сь), -а́лишь(ся)) сов от **вали́ть(ся)**
по́вар (-а; nom pl -а́) м cook
пова́ренн|**ый** прил: ~**ая кни́га** cookery (BRIT) или cook (US) book; ~**ая соль** table salt
поведе́ни|**е** (-я) ср behaviour (BRIT), behavior (US)
повез|**ти́** (-у́, -ёшь; pt -ёз, -езла́) сов от **везти́**
пове́ренн|**ый** (-ого) м: ~ **в дела́х** chargé d'affaires
пове́р|**ить** (-ю, -ишь) сов от **ве́рить**
поверн|**у́ть** (-у́, -ёшь; impf **повора́чивать**) сов (не)перех to turn; ~**ся** (impf **повора́чиваться**)

сов возв to turn

пове́рх *предл:* ~ +*gen* over

пове́рхностный *прил* surface; *(перен)* superficial

пове́рхность (-и) *ж* surface

пове́рье (-ья; *gen pl* **-ий)** *ср* (popular) belief

пове́сить(ся) (-шу(сь), -сишь(ся) *сов от* **ве́шать(ся)**

повествова́ние (-я) *ср* narrative

пов|ести́ (-еду́, -еде́шь; *pt* **-ёл, -ла́)** *сов перех (начать вести: ребёнка)* to take; *(: войска)* to lead; *(машину, поезд)* to drive; *(войну, следствие итп)* to begin ♦ *(impf* **поводи́ть)** *неперех:* ~ +*instr (бровью)* to raise; *(плечом)* to shrug; ~ *(pf)* **себя́** to start behaving

пове́ст|ка (-ки; *gen pl* **-ок)** *ж* summons; *(также:* ~ **дня)** agenda

по́вест|ь (-и) *ж* story

по-ви́димому *вводн сл* apparently

повидл|о (-а) *ср* jam *(BRIT),* jelly *(US)*

пови́нност|ь (-и) *ж:* **во́инская** ~ conscription

повин|ова́ться (-у́юсь) *сов возв:* ~ +*dat* to obey

повинове́ни|е (-я) *ср* obedience

пови́с|нуть (-ну; *pt* **-, -ла;** *impf* **повиса́ть)** *сов* to hang; *(тучи)* to hang motionless

повл|е́чь (-еку́, -ече́шь *итп,* **-еку́т;** *pt* **-ёк, -екла́, -екло́)** *сов от* **влечь**

по́вод (-ода; *loc sg* **-оду́,** *nom pl* **-о́дья,** *gen pl* **-ьев)** *м (лошади)* rein; *(nom pl* **-оды;** *причина)* reason ♦ *предл:* **по** ~у +*gen* regarding, concerning

пово|ди́ть (-ожу́, -о́дишь) *несов от* **повести́**

повод|о́к (-ка́) *м* lead, leash

пово́з|ка (-ки; *gen pl* **-ок)** *ж* cart

повора́чива|ть(ся) (-ю(сь)) *несов от* **повернуть(ся)**

поворо́т (-а) *м (действие)* turning; *(место)* bend; *(перен)* turning point

поворо́тный *прил (ТЕХ)* revolving; ~ **пункт** *или* **моме́нт** *(перен)* turning point

повре|ди́ть (-жу́, -ди́шь; *impf* **поврежда́ть)** *сов перех (поранить)* to injure; *(поломать)* to damage

поврежда́ть *сов перех (поранить)* to injure; *(поломать)* to damage

поврежде́ни|е (-я) *ср (см глаг)* injury; damage

повседне́вный *прил* everyday, routine; *(занятия, встречи)* daily

повсеме́стный *прил* widespread

повсю́ду *нареч* everywhere

по-ра́зному *нареч* in different ways

повторе́ни|е (-я) *ср* repetition; *(урока)* revision

повтор|и́ть (-ю́, -и́шь; *impf* **повторя́ть)** *сов перех* to repeat; ~**ся** *(impf* **повторя́ться)** *сов возв (ситуация)* to repeat itself; *(болезнь)* to recur

повто́рный *прил* repeated

повы́|сить (-шу, -сишь; *impf* **повыша́ть)** *сов перех* to increase; *(интерес)* to heighten; *(качество, культуру)* to improve; *(работника)* to promote; **повы́сить** *(~ pf)* **го́лос** to raise one's voice; ~**ся** *(impf* **повыша́ться)** *сов возв* to increase; *(интерес)* to heighten; *(качество, культура)* to improve

повы́шенный *прил (спрос)* increased; *(интерес)* heightened; ~**ое давле́ние** high blood pressure

повя|за́ть (-жу́, -жешь; *impf* **повя́зывать)** *сов перех* to tie

повя́з|ка (-ки; *gen pl* **-ок)** *ж*

bandage

пога́н|ка (**-ки**; *gen pl* **-ок**) *ж* toadstool

пог|аси́ть (**-ашу́, -а́сишь**) *сов от* **гаси́ть** ♦ (*impf* **погаша́ть**) *перех* (*заплати́ть*) to pay (off)

погас|ну́ть (**-ну**; *pt* **-, -ла**) *сов от* **га́снуть**

погаша́|ть (**-ю**) *несов от* **погаси́ть**

погиб|ну́ть (**-ну**; *pt* **-, -ла**) *сов от* **ги́бнуть**

поги́бш|ий (**-его**) *м* casualty (*dead*)

погло|ти́ть (**-щу́, -о́тишь**; *impf* **поглоща́ть**) *сов перех* to absorb; (*время*) to take up; (*фи́рму*) to take over

поглоще́ни|е (**-я**) *ср* absorption; (*КОММ*) takeover

пог|на́ться (**-оню́сь, -о́нишься**) *сов возв*: **~ за кем-н/чем-н** to set off in pursuit of sb/sth

поговор|ка (**-ки**; *gen pl* **-ок**) *ж* saying

пого́д|а (**-ы**) *ж* weather

пого́дный *прил* weather

поголо́вь|е (**-я**) *ср* (*скота́*) total number

пого́н (**-а**) *м* (*обычно мн*) (shoulder) stripe

пого́н|я (**-и**) *ж*: **~ за** +*instr* pursuit of

пограни́чник (**-а**) *м* frontier *или* border guard

пограни́чный *прил* border

по́греб (**-а**; *nom pl* **-á**) *м* cellar

погреба́льный *прил* funeral

погрему́ш|ка (**-ки**; *gen pl* **-ек**) *ж* rattle

погре́|ть (**-ю**) *сов перех* to warm up; **~ся** *сов возв* to warm up

погро́м (**-а**) *м* pogrom; (*разг*: *беспоря́док*) chaos

пог|рузи́ть (**-ужу́, -у́зишь**) *сов*

перех *от* **грузи́ть** ♦ (**-ужу́, -у́зишь**; *impf* **погружа́ть**) *перех*: **~ что-н в** +*acc* to immerse sth in; **~ся** (*impf* **погружа́ться**) *сов возв*: **~ся в** +*acc* (*челове́к*) to immerse o.s. in; (*предме́т*) to sink into

погру́з|ка (**-ки**; *gen pl* **-ок**) *ж* loading

погру́зочный *прил* loading

погря́зн|уть (**-у**; *impf* **погряза́ть**) *сов*: **~ в** +*prp* (*в долга́х, во лжи*) to sink into

---

KEYWORD

под *предл*; +*acc* **1** (*ни́же*) under; **идти́** (*impf*) **по́д го́ру** to go downhill

2 (*подде́рживая сни́зу*) by

3 (*ука́зывает на положе́ние, состоя́ние*) under; **отдава́ть** (**отда́ть** *pf*) **кого́-н под суд** to prosecute sb; **попада́ть** (**попа́сть** *pf*) **под дождь** to be caught in the rain

4 (*бли́зко к*): **под у́тро/ве́чер** towards morning/evening; **под ста́рость** approaching old age

5 (*ука́зывает на фу́нкцию*) as; **мы приспосо́били помеще́ние под магази́н** we fitted out the premises as a shop

6 (*в ви́де чего́-н*): **сте́ны под мра́мор** marble-effect walls

7 (*в обме́н на*) on; **брать** (**взять** *pf*) **что-н под зало́г/че́стное сло́во** to take sth on security/trust

8 (*в сопровожде́нии*): **под роя́ль/скри́пку** to the piano/violin; **мне э́то не под си́лу** that is beyond my powers

♦ *предл* (+*instr*) **1** (*ни́же чего́-н*) under

2 (*о́коло*) near; **под но́сом у кого́-н** under sb's nose; **под руко́й** to hand, at hand

3 (*об условиях существования объекта*); **быть** (*impf*) **под наблюде́нием/аре́стом** to be under observation/arrest; **под назва́нием, под и́менем** under the name of

4 (*вследствие*) under; **под влия́нием/тя́жестью чего-н** under the influence/weight of sth; **понима́ть** (*impf*)/**подразумева́ть** (*impf*) **под чем-н** to understand/ imply by sth

подава́|ть (**-ю**) *несов от* **пода́ть**

подав|и́ть (**-авлю́, -а́вишь**) *impf* **подавля́ть** *сов перех* to suppress; **~ся** *сов от* **дави́ться**

подавле́ни|е (**-я**) *ср* suppression

пода́вленн|ый (*настрое́ние, челове́к*) depressed

подавля́|ть (**-ю**) *несов от* **подави́ть**

подавля́ющий *прил* (*большинство́*) overwhelming

подар|и́ть (**-ю́, -ишь**) *сов от* **дари́ть**

пода́р|ок (**-ка**) *м* present, gift

пода́рочный *прил* gift

пода́|ть (*как* **дать**; *см. Table 16*; *impf* **подава́ть**) *сов перех* to give; (*еду*) to serve up; (*поезд, такси итп*) to bring; (*заявле́ние, жа́лобу итп*) to submit; (*СПОРТ, в те́ннисе*) to serve; (**~** *pf*) to pass; **подава́ть** (**~** *pf*) **го́лос за** +*acc* to cast a vote for; **подава́ть** (**~** *pf*) **в отста́вку** to hand in *или* submit one's resignation; **подава́ть** (**~** *pf*) **на кого́-н в суд** to take sb to court; **подава́ть** (**~** *pf*) **кому́-н ру́ку** (*при встре́че*) to give sb one's hand

пода́ч|а (**-и**) *ж* (*действие: заявле́ния*): submission; (*СПОРТ, в те́ннисе*) serve; (: *в футбо́ле*) pass

подбежа́ть (*как* **бежа́ть**; *см. Table 20*; *impf* **подбега́ть**) *сов* to run up

подбива́|ть (**-ю**) *несов от* **подби́ть**

подбира́|ть (**-ю**) *несов от* **подобра́ть**

под|би́ть (**-обью́, -обьёшь**) *impf* **подбива́ть** *сов перех* (*пти́цу, самолёт*) to shoot down; (*глаз, крыло́*) to injure

подбо́р (**-а**) *м* selection

подборо́д|ок (**-ка**) *м* chin

подбро́|сить (**-шу, -сишь**) *impf* **подбра́сывать** *сов перех* (*мяч, ка́мень*) to toss; (*нарко́тик*) to plant; (*разг: подвезти́*) to give a lift

подва́л (**-а**) *м* cellar; (*для жилья́*) basement

подва́льный *прил* (*помеще́ние*) basement

подведе́ни|е (**-я**) *ср*: **~ ито́гов** summing-up

подвез|ти́ (**-у́, -ёшь**; *pt* **-ёз, -езла́**; *impf* **подвози́ть**) *сов перех* (*маши́ну, това́р*) to take up; (*челове́ка*) to give a lift

подве́рг|нуть (**-ну**; *pt* **-, -ла**; *impf* **подверга́ть**) *сов перех*: **~ кого́-н/ что-н чему́-н** to subject sb/sth to sth; **подверга́ть** (**~** *pf*) **кого́-н ри́ску/опа́сности** to put sb at risk/in danger; **~ся** (*impf*) **подверга́ться**) *сов возв*: **~ся** +*dat* to be subjected to

подве́рженн|ый *прил*: **~** +*dat* (*дурно́му влия́нию*) subject to (*простуде*) susceptible to

подверн|у́ть (**-у́, -ёшь**; *impf* **подвора́чивать**) *сов перех* (*сде́лать коро́че*) to turn up; **подвора́чивать** (**~** *pf*) **но́гу** to turn *или* twist one's ankle; **~ся** (*impf* **подвора́чиваться**) *сов возв* (*разг: попасться*) to turn up

подве́|сить (**-шу, -сишь**; *impf* **подве́шивать**) *сов перех* to hang up

подв|ести́ (**-еду́, -едёшь**; *pt* **-ёл, -ела́**; *impf* **подводи́ть**) *сов перех* (*разочаровать*) to let down;

подводи́ть (**~** *pf*) **к** +*dat* (*человека*) to bring up to; (*машину*) to drive up to; (*поезд*) to bring into; (*корабль*) to sail up to; (*электричество*) to bring to; **подводи́ть** (**~** *pf*) **глаза́/гу́бы** to put eyeliner/lipstick on; **подводи́ть** (**~** *pf*) **ито́ги** to sum up

подве́шива|ть (**-ю**) *несов от* **подве́сить**

по́двиг (**-а**) *м* exploit

подви́га|ться (**-ю(сь)**) *несов от* **подви́нуть(ся)**

подви́жный *прил* agile

подви́н|уть (**-у**; *impf* **подвига́ть**) *сов перех* (*передвинуть*) to move; **~ся** (*impf* **подвига́ться**) *сов возв* (*человек*) to move

подвла́стный *прил*: ~ +*dat* (*закону*) subject to; (*президенту*) under the control of

подво|ди́ть (**-жу́, -óдишь**) *несов от* **подвести́**

подво́дный *прил* (*растение, работы*) underwater; **~ая ло́дка** submarine

подво|зи́ть (**-жу́, -óзишь**) *несов от* **подвезти́**

подвора́чива|ть(ся) (**-ю(сь)**) *несов от* **подверну́ть**

подгиба́|ть(ся) (**-ю(сь)**) *несов от* **подогну́ть(ся)**

подгля|де́ть (**-жу́, -ди́шь**; *impf* **подгля́дывать**) *сов перех* to peep through

подгор|е́ть (*3sg* **-и́т**; *impf* **подгора́ть**) *сов* to burn slightly

подготови́тельный *прил*

(*работа*) preparatory

подгото́в|ить (**-лю, -ишь**; *impf* **подгота́вливать**) *сов перех* to prepare; **~ся** (*impf* **подгота́вливаться**) *сов возв* to prepare (o.s.)

подгото́вк|а (**-и**) *ж* preparation; (*запас знаний*) training

подгу́зник (**-а**) *м* nappy (BRIT), diaper (US)

подда|ва́ться (**-ю́сь**) *несов от* **подда́ться** ♦ *возв*: **не ~ сравне́нию/описа́нию** to be beyond comparison/words

по́дданн|ый (**-ого**) *м* subject

по́дданств|о (**-а**) *ср* nationality

подда́|ться (*как* **дать**; *см.* Table 16; *impf* **поддава́ться**) *сов возв* (*дверь итп*) to give way; **поддава́ться** (**~** *pf*) +*dat* (*влиянию, соблазну*) to give in to

подде́ла|ть (**-ю**; *impf* **подде́лывать**) *сов перех* to forge

подде́лк|а (**-ки**; *gen pl* **-ок**) *ж* forgery

подде́льный *прил* forged

подде́рж|ать (**-ержу́, -е́ржишь**; *impf* **подде́рживать**) *сов перех* to support; (*падающего*) to hold on to; (*предложение итп*) to second; (*беседу*) to keep up

подде́ржива|ть (**-ю**) *несов от* **подде́ржа́ть** ♦ *перех* (*переписку*) to keep up; (*порядок, отношения*) to maintain

подде́ржк|а (**-и**) *ж* support

подде́ла|ть (**-ю**) *сов перех* (*разг*) to do; **что ~ешь** (*разг*) it can't be helped

под|ели́ть(ся) (**-елю́(сь), -е́лишь(ся)**) *сов от* **дели́ть(ся)**

поде́ржанный *прил* (*одежда, мебель итп*) second-hand

под|же́чь (**-ожгу́, -ожжёшь** *etc*,

-ожгу́т) *impf* **поджига́ть**) *сов перех* to set fire to

подзаты́льник (-а) *м* (*разг*) clip round the ear

подзе́мный *прил* underground

подзо́рный *прил*: ~ая труба́ telescope

подк|ати́ть (-ачу́, -а́тишь) *impf* **подка́тывать**) *перех* (*что-н кру́глое*) to roll; (*что-н на колёсах*) to wheel

подка́шива|ть(ся) (-ю(сь)) *несов от* **подкоси́ть(ся)**

подки́н|уть (-у) *сов* = **подбро́сить**

подки́дыва|ть (-ю) *сов* = **подброси́ть**

подкла́д|ка (-ки; *gen pl* -ок) *ж* lining

подкла́дыва|ть (-ю) *несов от* **подложи́ть**

подключ|и́ть (-у́, -и́шь; *impf* **подключа́ть**) *сов перех* (*телефо́н*) to connect; (*ла́мпу*) to plug in; (*специалиста*) to involve

подко́в|а (-ы) *ж* (*лошади итп*) shoe

подко́в|а́ть (-у́ю; *impf* **подко́вывать**) *сов перех* to shoe

подко|си́ть (-шу́, -о́сишь; *impf* **подка́шивать**) *сов перех* (*подлеж: несча́стье*) to devastate; ~**ся** (*impf* **подка́шиваться**) *сов возв*: **у него́ но́ги/коле́ни подкоси́лись** his legs/knees gave way

подкра́|сться (-ду́сь, -дёшься; *impf* **подкра́дываться**) *сов возв* to sneak *или* steal up

подкреп|и́ть (-лю́, -и́шь; *impf* **подкрепля́ть**) *сов перех* to support, back up

подкрепле́ни|е (-я) *ср* (*воен*) reinforcement

по́дкуп (-а) *м* bribery

подку|пи́ть (-плю́, -у́пишь; *impf* **подкупа́ть**) *сов перех* to bribe

подлежа́ть (3sg -и́т) *несов*: ~ +dat (*прове́рке, обложе́нию нало́гом*) to be subject to; **э́то не ~и́т сомне́нию** there can be no doubt about that

подлежа́щ|ее (-его) *ср* (*линг*) subject

подле́ц (-а́) *м* scoundrel

подли́в|ка (-ки; *gen pl* -ок) (*кулин*) sauce

по́длинник (-а) *м* original

по́длинный *прил* original; (*докуме́нт*) authentic; (*чу́вство*) genuine; (*сам посту́пок*) base thing

по́дло *нареч* (*поступи́ть*) meanly

подло́г (-а) *м* forgery

подл|ожи́ть (-ожу́, -о́жишь; *impf* **подкла́дывать**) *сов перех* (*бо́мбу*) to plant; (*доба́вить*) to put; (*дров, са́хара*) to add

подлоко́тник (-а) *м* arm(rest)

по́длость (-и) *ж* (*посту́пка*) baseness; (*сам посту́пок*) base thing

по́длый *прил* base

подмен|и́ть (-ю́, -и́шь; *impf* **подме́нивать**) *сов перех* to substitute; (*колле́гу*) to stand in for

подм|ести́ (-ету́, -етёшь; *pt* -ёл, -ела́) *сов от* **мести́** ♦ (*impf* **подмета́ть**) *перех* (*пол*) to sweep; (*му́сор*) to sweep up

подмётк|а (-и; *gen pl* -ок) *ж* (*у подо́швы*) sole

подмигн|у́ть (-у́, -ёшь; *impf* **подми́гивать**) *сов*: ~ **кому́-н** to wink at sb

подмы́шк|а (-и; *gen pl* -ек) *ж* armpit

поднес|ти́ (-у́, -ёшь; *impf* **подноси́ть**) *сов перех*: ~ **что-н к чему́-н** to bring sth up to sth

поднима́|ть(ся) (-ю(сь)) *несов*

от подня́ть(ся)
подно́жи|е (-я) *ср* (*горы*) foot
подно́ж|**ка** (-ки; *gen pl* -ек) *ж*
(*автобуса итп*) step; **поста́вить**
(*pf*) ~**ку кому́-н** to trip sb up
подно́с (-а) *м* tray
подн|**оси́ть** (-ошу́, -о́сишь)
несов от поднести́
подн|**я́ть** (-иму́, -и́мешь; *impf*
поднима́ть) *сов перех* to raise;
(*что-н лёгкое*) to pick up; (*что-н
тяжёлое*) to lift (up); (*флаг*) to
hoist; (*спящего*) to rouse;
(*панику, восстание*) to start;
(*экономику, дисциплину*) to
improve; (*архивы, документацию
итп*) to unearth; **поднима́ть** (~ *pf*)
крик *или* **шум** to make a fuss; ~**ся**
(*impf* **поднима́ться**) *сов возв* to
rise; (*на этаж, на сцену*) to go up;
(*с постели, со стула*) to get up;
(*паника, метель, драка*) to break
out; **поднима́ться** (~**ся** *pf*) **на́
го́ру** to climb a hill; ~**я́лся крик**
there was an uproar
подо *предл см.* **под**
подоба́ющий *прил* appropriate
подо́бно *предл*: ~ +*dat* like, similar
to
подо́бн|**ый** *прил*: ~ +*dat*
(*сходный*) like, similar to; **и
тому́** ~**ое** et cetera, and so on; **
ничего́** ~**ого** (*разг*) nothing of the
sort
под|**обра́ть** (-беру́, -берёшь;
impf **подбира́ть**) *сов перех* to
pick up; (*приподнять*) to gather
(up); (*выбрать*) to pick, select
подобре́|**ть** (-ю) *сов от* **добре́ть**
подогре́в|**уть** (-у, -ёшь; *impf*
подгиба́ть) *сов перех* (*рукава*)
to turn up; ~**ся** (*impf*
подгиба́ться) *сов возв* to curl
under
подогре́|**ть** (-ю; *impf*

подогрева́ть) *сов перех* to
warm up
пододви́н|**уть** (-у; *impf*
пододвига́ть) *сов перех* to
move closer
пододея́льник (-а) *м* ≈ duvet
cover
подожда́ть (-у́, -ёшь; *pt* -а́л,
-ала́) *сов перех* to wait for; ~ (*pf*)
с чем-н to put sth off
подозрева́|**ть** (-ю) *несов перех*
to suspect; ~ (*impf*) **кого́-н в чём-н**
to suspect sb of sth; ~ (*impf*) (**о
чём-н**) to have an idea (about sth)
подозре́ни|**е** (-я) *ср* suspicion
подозри́тельный *прил*
suspicious
подо|**йти́** (-ю́, -ишь) *сов от*
дойти́
подойти́ (*как* **идти́**; *см.* Table 18;
impf **подходи́ть**) *сов*: ~ **к** +*dat* to
approach; (*соответствовать*): ~ **к**
+*dat* (*юбка*) to go (well) with; **э́то
мне подхо́дит** this suits me
подоко́нник (-а) *м* windowsill
подо́л (-а) *м* hem
подо́лгу *нареч* for a long time
подо́пытный *прил*: ~ **кро́лик**
(*перен*) guinea pig
подорв|**а́ть** (-у́, -ёшь; *pt* -а́л,
-ала́; *impf* **подрыва́ть**) *сов перех*
to blow up; (*перен: авторитет*) to
undermine; (: *здоровье*) to destroy
подотчётный *прил* accountable;
~**ые де́ньги** expenses
подохо́дный *прил*: ~ **нало́г**
income tax
подо́шв|**а** (-ы) *ж* (*обуви*) sole
подошёл *etc сов см.* **подойти́**
под|**пере́ть** (-опру́, -опрёшь; *pt*
-пёр, -пёрла; *impf* **подпира́ть**)
сов перех: ~ **что-н чем-н** to prop
sth up with sth
подписа́ни|**е** (-я) *ср* signing
подп|**иса́ть** (-ишу́, -и́шешь) *impf*

подпи́с|ывать) *сов перех* to sign; **~ся** (*impf* **подпи́сываться**) *сов возв*: **~ся под** +*instr* to sign; **подпи́сываться** (**~ся** *pf*) **на** +*acc* (*на газету*) to subscribe to

подпи́с|ка (-ки; *gen pl* -ок) *ж* subscription; (*о невыезде*) signed statement

подпи́счик (-а) *м* subscriber

по́дпис|ь (-и) *ж* signature

подплы́|ть (-ву́, -вёшь; *pt* -л, -ла́; *impf* подплыва́ть) *сов* (*лодка*) to sail (up); (*пловец, рыба*) to swim (up)

подполко́вник (-а) *м* lieutenant colonel

подпо́льный *прил* underground

подпо́р|ка (-ки; *gen pl* -ок) *ж* prop, support

подпры́гн|уть (-у; *impf* подпры́гивать) *сов* to jump

подп|усти́ть (-ущу́, -у́стишь; *impf* подпуска́ть) *сов перех* to allow to approach

подрабо́та|ть (-ю) *сов* (не)*перех*: **~** +*acc или* +*gen* to earn extra

подра́внива|ть (-ю) *несов от* подровня́ть

подража́ни|е (-я) *ср* imitation

подража́|ть (-ю) *несов*: **~** +*dat* to imitate

подразделе́ни|е (-я) *ср* subdivision; (*воинское*) subunit

подразделя́|ться (*3sg* -ется) *несов возв* to be subdivided

подразумева́|ть (-ю) *несов перех* to imply; **~ся** *несов возв* to be implied

подр|асти́ (-асту́, -астёшь; *pt* -о́с, -осла́; *impf* подраста́ть) *сов* to grow

подр|а́ться (-еру́сь, -ерёшься) *сов от* дра́ться

подре́за|ть (-жу, -жешь; *impf*

подреза́ть) *сов перех* (*волосы*) to cut

подро́бность (-и) *ж* detail

подро́бный *прил* detailed

подровня́|ть (-ю; *impf* подра́внивать) *сов перех* to trim

подростко́вый *прил* teenage; **~ во́зраст** adolescence

подро́ст|ок (-ка) *м* teenager, adolescent

подру́г|а (-и) *ж* (girl)friend

по-друго́му *нареч* (*иначе*) differently

подр|ужи́ться (-ужу́сь, -у́жишься) *сов возв*: **~ с** +*instr* to make friends with

подру́чный *прил*: **~ материа́л** the material to hand

подрыва́|ть (-ю) *несов от* подорва́ть

подрывно́й *прил* subversive

подря́д *нареч* in succession ♦ (-а) *м* (*рабочий догово́р*) contract; **все/всё** ~ everyone/everything without exception

подря́дный *прил* contract

подря́дчик (-а) *м* contractor

подса́жива|ться (-юсь) *несов от* подсе́сть

подсве́чник (-а) *м* candlestick

подс|е́сть (-я́ду, -я́дешь; *impf* подса́живаться) *сов*: **~ к** +*dat* to sit down beside

подск|аза́ть (-ажу́, -а́жешь; *impf* подска́зывать) *сов перех* (*перен: идею*) to suggest; (*разг: адрес*) to give out; подска́зывать (**~** *pf*) что-н кому́-н to prompt sb with sth

подска́з|ка (-ки; *gen pl* -ок) *ж* prompt

подслу́ша|ть (-ю; *impf* подслу́шивать) *сов перех* to eavesdrop on

подсм|отре́ть (-отрю́, -о́тришь; *impf* **подсма́тривать**) *сов перех* (*увидеть*) to spy on

подсне́жник (-а) м snowdrop

подсо́бный *прил* subsidiary

подсо́выва|ть (-ю) *несов от* **подсу́нуть**

подсозна́ни|е (-я) *ср* the subconscious

подсозна́тельный *прил* subconscious

подсо́лнечн|ый *прил*: ~ое ма́сло sunflower oil

подсо́лнух (-а) м (*разг*) sunflower

подста́в|ить (-лю, -ишь; *impf* **подставля́ть**) *сов перех*: ~ под +*acc* to put under

подста́в|ка (-ки, *gen pl* -ок) ж stand

подставля́|ть (-ю) *несов от* **подста́вить**

подста́нци|я (-и) ж substation

подстере́|чь (-гу́, -жёшь *итп*, -гу́т; *impf* **подстерега́ть**) *сов перех* to lie in wait for

подстра́ива|ть (-ю) *несов от* **подстро́ить**

подстрел|и́ть (-елю́, -е́лишь; *impf* **подстре́ливать**) *сов перех* to wound

подстр|и́чь (-игу́, -ижёшь *итп*, -игу́т; *pt* -г, -ла; *impf* **подстрига́ть**) *сов перех* to trim; (*для укорачивания*) to cut; (~ся *impf* **подстрига́ться**) *сов возв* to have one's hair cut

подстро́|ить (-ю, -ишь; *impf* **подстра́ивать**) *сов перех* to fix

по́дступ (-а) м (*обычно мн*) approach

подступ|и́ть (-уплю́, -у́пишь; *impf* **подступа́ть**) *сов* (*слёзы*) to well up; (*рыдания*) to rise; **подступа́ть** (~ *pf*) к +*dat* (к го́роду, к те́ме) to approach

подсуди́м|ый (-ого) м (*ЮР*) the accused, the defendant

подсу́дный *прил* (*ЮР*) sub judice

подсу́н|уть (-у; *impf* **подсо́вывать**) *сов перех* to shove

подсчёт (-а) м counting; (*итог*) calculation

подсчита́|ть (-ю; *impf* **подсчи́тывать**) *сов перех* to count (up)

подталкива|ть (-ю) *несов от* **подтолкну́ть**

подтверд|и́ть (-жу́, -ди́шь; *impf* **подтвержда́ть**) *сов перех* to confirm; (*фактами*) to back up; ~ся (*impf* **подтвержда́ться**) *сов* to be confirmed

подтвержде́ни|е (-я) *ср* confirmation

подтолкн|у́ть (-у́, -ёшь; *impf* **подта́лкивать**) *сов перех* to nudge; (*побудить*) to urge on

подтя́гива|ть(ся) (-ю(сь)) *несов от* **подтяну́ть(ся)**

подтя́ж|ки (-ек) мн (*для брюк*) braces мн (*BRIT*), suspenders мн (*US*)

подтя́нутый *прил* smart

подт|яну́ть (-яну́, -я́нешь; *impf* **подтя́гивать**) (*тяжёлый предмет*) to haul up; (*гайку*) to tighten; (*войска*) to bring up; ~ся (*impf* **подтя́гиваться**) *сов возв* (*на брусьях*) to pull o.s. up; (*войска*) to move up

поду́ма|ть (-ю) *сов*: ~ (о +*prp*) to think (about); ~ (*pf*) над +*instr* или о +*prp* to think about; ~ (*pf*), что... to think that ...; кто бы мог ~! who would have thought it!

поду́|ть (-ю) *сов* to blow; (*ветер*) to begin to blow

под|уши́ть (-ушу́, -у́шишь) *сов*

перех to spray lightly with perfume

поду́ш|ка (**-ки**; *gen pl* **-ек**) *ж* (*для сидения*) cushion; (*под голову*) pillow

подхват|и́ть (**-ачу́, -а́тишь**; *impf* **подхва́тывать**) *сов перех* (*падающее*) to catch; (*подлеж: течение, толпа*) to carry away; (*идею, болезнь*) to pick up

подхо́д (**-а**) *м* approach

подхо|ди́ть (**-ожу́, -о́дишь**) *несов от* **подойти́**

подходя́щий *прил* (*дом*) suitable; (*момент, слова*) appropriate

подчеркн|у́ть (**-у́, -ёшь**; *impf* **подчёркивать**) *сов перех* (*в тексте*) to underline; (*в речи*) to emphasize

подчине́ни|е (**-я**) *ср* obedience

подчинённ|ый *прил* subordinate
♦ (**-ого**) *м* subordinate

подчин|и́ть (**-ю́, -и́шь**; *impf* **подчиня́ть**) *сов перех* (*страну*) to subjugate; **подчини́ть** (~ *pf*) **что-н кому́-н** to place sth under the control of sb; ~**ся** (*impf* **подчиня́ться**) *сов возв*: ~**ся** +*dat* to obey

подше́фный *прил*: ~ **де́тский дом** children's home under patronage

подшива́|ть (**-ю**) *несов от* **подши́ть**

подши́в|ка (**-ки**; *gen pl* **-ок**) *ж* (*газет, документов*) file

подши́пник (**-а**) *м* (*ТЕХ*) bearing

под|ши́ть (**-ошью́, -ошьёшь**; *imper* **-ше́й(те)**; *impf* **подшива́ть**) *сов перех* (*рукав*) to hem; (*подол*) to take up

подшу|ти́ть (**-чу́, -у́тишь**; *impf* **подшу́чивать**) *сов*: ~ **над** +*instr* to make fun of

подъе́ду *etc сов см.* **подъе́хать**

подъе́зд (**-а**) *м* (*к городу, к дому*) approach; (*в здании*) entrance

подъезжа́|ть (**-ю**) *несов от* **подъе́хать**

подъём (**-а**) *м* (*груза*) lifting; (*флага*) raising; (*на гору*) ascent; (*промышленный*) revival

подъёмник (**-а**) *м* lift (*BRIT*), elevator (*US*)

подъёмный *прил* lifting; ~ **кран** crane

подъе́хать (*как* **е́хать**; *см. Table 19*; *impf* **подъезжа́ть**) *сов* (*на автомобиле*) to drive up; (*на коне*) to ride up

поды́ша|ть (**-шу́, -шешь**) *сов* to breathe

пое́дешь *etc сов см.* **пое́хать**

пое́дим *итп сов см.* **пое́сть**

поеди́те *сов см.* **пое́сть**

пое́ду *etc сов см.* **пое́хать**

поедя́т *сов см.* **пое́сть**

по́езд (**-а**; *nom pl* **-а́**) *м* train

пое́зд|ка (**-ки**; *gen pl* **-ок**) *ж* trip

поезжа́й(те) *сов см.* **пое́хать**

пое́сть (*как* **есть**; *см. Table 15*) *сов* +*перех*: ~ **чего́-н** to eat a little bit of sth

пое́хать (*как* **е́хать**; *см. Table 19*) *сов* to set off

пое́шь *сов см.* **пое́сть**

пожале́|ть (**-ю**) *сов от* **жале́ть**

пожа́л|овать (**-ую**) *сов*: **добро́ ~** welcome; ~**ся** *сов от* **жа́ловаться**

пожа́луйста *част* please; (*в ответ на благодарность*) don't mention it (*BRIT*), you're welcome (*US*); ~, **помоги́те мне** please help me; **скажи́те, ~, где вокза́л!** could you please tell me where the station is; **мо́жно здесь сесть?** – ~! may I sit here? – please do!

пожа́р (**-а**) *м* fire

пожа́рник (**-а**) *м* (*разг*) fireman

пожа́рн|ый (-ого) м fireman
♦ прил: ~ая кома́нда fire brigade
(BRIT) или department (US); ~ая
маши́на fire engine

пож|а́ть (-му́, -мёшь; impf
пожима́ть) сов перех to
squeeze; **он ~а́л мне ру́ку** he
shook my hand; **пожима́ть** (~ pf)
плеча́ми to shrug one's shoulders

пожела́ни|е (-я) ср wish;
прими́те мой наилу́чшие ~я
please accept my best wishes

пожела́|ть (-ю) сов от **жела́ть**

пож|ени́ться (-еню́сь,
-е́нишься) сов возв to marry,
got married

пожертвова́ни|е (-я) ср donation

пожива́|ть (-ю) несов (разг)· **как
ты ~ешь?** how are you?

пожи́зненн|ый прил lifelong;
~ое заключе́ние life
imprisonment

пожил|о́й прил elderly

пожима́|ть (-ю) несов от
пожа́ть

пож|и́ть (-иву́, -ивёшь; pt -и́л,
-ила́) сов (пробы́ть) to live for a
while

по́з|а (-ы) ж posture; (перен:
поведе́ние) pose

позавчера́ нареч the day before
yesterday

позади́ нареч (сза́ди) behind; (в
про́шлом) in the past ♦ предл: ~
+gen behind

позаи́мствовать (-ую) сов от
заи́мствовать

позапро́шлый прил before last

позв|а́ть (-ову́, -овёшь) сов от
звать

позво́л|ить (-ю, -ишь; impf
позволя́ть) сов to permit ♦
перех: ~ что-н кому́-н to allow sb
sth; **позволя́ть** (~ pf) **себе́** что-н
(поку́пку) to be able to afford sth

позвон|и́ть (-ю́, -и́шь) сов от
звони́ть

позвоно́чник (-а) м spine, spinal
column

поздне́е сравн нареч от **по́здно**
♦ нареч later ♦ предл: ~ +gen
after; **(не)** ~ +gen (no) later than

по́здн|ий прил late; **са́мое ~ее**
(разг) at the latest

по́здно нареч late ♦ как сказ it's
late

поздоро́ва|ться (-юсь) сов от
здоро́ваться

поздрави́тельный прил
greetings

поздра́в|ить (-лю, -ишь; impf
поздравля́ть) сов перех: ~
кого́-н с +instr to congratulate sb
on; **поздравля́ть** (~ pf) **кого́-н с
днём рожде́ния** to wish sb a
happy birthday

поздравле́ни|е (-я) ср
congratulation; **(с днём
рожде́ния)** greetings мн

по́зже нареч = **поздне́е**

позити́вный прил positive

пози́ци|я (-и) ж position

познако́м|ить(ся) (-лю(сь),
-ишь(ся)) сов от **знако́мить(ся)**

позна́ни|я (-й) мн knowledge ед

позову́ итп сов см. **позва́ть**

позо́р (-а) м disgrace

позо́р|ить (-ю, -ишь; pf о~)
несов перех to disgrace; **~ся** (pf
о~ся) несов возв to disgrace o.s.

позо́рный прил disgraceful

пои́м|ка (-ки; gen pl -ок) ж
capture

поинтерес|ова́ться (-у́юсь) сов
возв: ~ +instr to take an interest in

по́иск (-а) м search; (нау́чный)
quest; см. также **по́иски**

поиск|а́ть (-ищу́, -и́щешь) сов
перех to have a look for

по́иск|и (-ов) мн: ~ +gen search

ед (for); **в ~ах** +gen in search of

по|**и́ть** (-ю́, -ишь; imper ~и́(те)) pf **на~**) несов перех **~ кого́-н чем-н** to give sb sth to drink

пойду́ etc сов см. **пойти́**

пойма́|**ть** (-ю) сов перех см **лови́ть**
♦ перех to catch

пойму́ etc сов см. **поня́ть**

пойти́ (как **идти́**; см. Table 18) сов to set off; (по пути реформ) to start off; (о механизмах, к цели) to start working; (о дождь, снег) to begin to fall; (дым, пар) to begin to rise; (кровь) to start flowing; (фильм итп) to start showing; (подойти): ~ +dat или к +dat (шляпа, поведение) to suit

---

KEYWORD

пока́ нареч 1 (некоторое время) for a while
2 (тем временем) in the meantime
♦ союз 1 (в то время как) while
2 (до того времени как): **пока́ не** until; **пока́!** so long!; **пока́ что** for the moment

покажу́(сь) etc сов см. **показа́ть(ся)**

пока́з (-а) м (фильма) showing; (опыта) demonstration

показа́ние (-я) ср (ЮР, обычно мн) evidence ед; (на счётчике итп) reading

показа́тель (-я) м indicator; (мат, экон) index

показа́тельный прил (пример) revealing

пока|**за́ть** (-жу́, -жешь; impf **пока́зывать**) сов перех to show
♦ неперех (на суде) to testify; **пока́зывать** (~ pf) **приме́р** to set an example; **~ся** сов от **каза́ться**
♦ (impf **пока́зываться**) возв to appear; **пока́зываться** (~ся pf) **врачу́** to see a doctor

поката́|**ть** (-ю) сов перех: ~ **кого́-н на маши́не** to take sb for a drive; **~ся** сов возв to go for a ride

пок|**ати́ть** (-ачу́, -а́тишь) сов перех (что-н круглое) to roll; (что-н на колёсах) to wheel; **~ся** сов возв to start rolling или to roll

покача́|**ть** (-ю) сов перех to rock
♦ неперех: ~ **голово́й** to shake one's head; **~ся** сов возв (на качелях) to swing

пока́чива|**ться** (-юсь) несов возв to rock

покая́ние (-я) ср repentance

поки́н|**уть** (-у; impf **покида́ть**) сов перех to abandon

поклада́: не ~ **рук** tirelessly

покло́н (-а) м (жест) bow; (приветствие) greeting

покл|**они́ться** (-оню́сь, -о́нишься) сов от **кла́няться**

покло́нник (-а) м admirer

поклоня́|**ться** (-юсь) несов возв: ~ +dat to worship

поко́|**иться** (3sg -ится) несов возв: ~ **на** +prp to rest on

поко́|**й** (-я) м peace; **оставля́ть** (**оста́вить** pf) **кого́-н в ~е** to leave sb in peace

поко́йный прил the late ♦ (-**ого**) м the deceased

поколе́ние (-я) ср generation

поко́нч|**ить** (-у, -ишь) сов: ~ +instr (с дела́ми) to be finished with; (с бе́дностью, с пробле́мой) to put an end to; ~ (pf) **с собо́й** to kill o.s., commit suicide

покор|**и́ть** (-ю́, -и́шь; impf **покоря́ть**) сов перех (страну́, наро́д) to conquer; **покоря́ть** (~ pf) **кого́-н** (заста́вить люби́ть) win sb's heart; **~ся** (impf **покоря́ться**) сов возв: **~ся** +dat to submit (to)

поко́рный прил submissive

покрови́тельств|о (-а) ср protection

покро́|й (-я) ср cut (of clothing)

покрыва́л|о (-а) ср bedspread

покры́ти|е (-я) ср covering

покры́|ть (-ю, -оешь) сов от **крыть ♦** (impf **покрыва́ть**) перех (звуки) to cover up; (расходы, расстояние) to cover; **~ся** (impf **покрыва́ться**) сов возв: **~ся** +instr (одея́лом) to cover o.s. with; (сне́гом итп) to be covered in

по́крыш|ка (-ки, gen pl -ек) ж (АВТ) tyre (BRIT), tire (US)

покупа́тель (-я) м buyer; (в магази́не) customer

покупа́тельский прил (спрос, интере́сы) consumer

покупа́|ть (-ю) несов от **купи́ть**

поку́п|ка (-ки, gen pl -ок) ж purchase; **де́лать (сде́лать** pf) **~ки** to go shopping

покуша́|ться (-юсь) несов возв: **~ на** +acc to attempt to take

покуше́ни|е (-я) ср: **~ (на** +acc) (на свобо́ду, на права́) infringement (of); (на жизнь) attempt (on)

пол (-а́; loc sg **-у́,** nom pl **-ы́)** м floor; (nom pl **-ы́,** gen pl **-о́в,** dat pl **-а́м)** sex

полага́|ть (-ю) несов (ду́мать) to suppose; **на́до ~** supposedly

пол|го́да (-уго́да) ср/мн half a year

по́лдень (полу́дня или **по́лдня)** м midday, noon; **2 часа́ по́сле полу́дня** 2 pm

по́л|е (-я; nom pl **-я́,** gen pl **-е́й)** ср activity; **~ де́ятельности** sphere of activity; **~ зре́ния** field of vision

полев|о́й прил (цвето́к) meadow; **~ команди́р** warlord; **~ые рабо́ты** work in the fields

поле́зн|ый прил useful; (пища) healthy; **~ые ископа́емые** minerals

поле́з|ть (-у, -ешь) сов: **~ на** +acc (на го́ру) to start climbing или to climb; **~** (pf) **в дра́ку, в спор** to get involved in; **~** (pf) **в карма́н** to put one's hand in(to) one's pocket

поле́мик|а (-и) ж polemic

поле́н|о (-а; nom pl **-ья,** gen pl **-ьев)** ср log

полёт (-а) м flight

полете́|ть (-чу, -ти́шь) сов (пти́ца, самолёт) to fly off; (вре́мя) to start to fly by

по́лза|ть (-ю) несов to crawl

ползти́ (-у́, -ёшь; pt **-,** -ла́) несов to crawl

ползунк|и́ (-о́в) мн rompers мн

полива́|ть (-ю) несов от **поли́ть**

поливитами́н|ы (-ов) мн multivitamins мн

полиго́н (-а) м (для уче́ний) shooting range; (для испыта́ния ору́жия) test(ing) site

поликли́ник|а (-и) ж health centre (BRIT) или center (US)

поликли́ника - health centre. These centres are staffed by a range of specialist doctors: surgeons, eye doctors, dermatologists etc. Patients can make an appointment with a number of doctors at any time.

полир|ова́ть (-у́ю; pf **от~)** несов перех to polish

по́лис (-а) м: **страхово́й ~** insurance policy

политехни́ческий прил:

институ́т polytechnic

поли́тик (-а) *м* politician

поли́тик|а (-и) *ж (курс)* policy; *(события, наука)* politics

полити́ческий *прил* political

пол|и́ть (-ью́, -ьёшь; *pt* **-и́л, -ила́,** *impf* **полива́ть)** *сов (дождь)* to start pouring *или* to pour down • *перех: ~ что-н чем-н (соусом)* to pour sth over sth; **полива́ть (~** *pf***) цветы́** to water the flowers

полице́йск|ий *прил* police
♦ **(-ого)** *м* policeman **~ уча́сток** police station

полици́я (-и) *ж* police

поли́чн|ое (-ого) *ср:* **пойма́ть кого́-н с ~ым** to catch sb at the scene of a crime; *(перен)* to catch sb red-handed *или* in the act

полиэтиле́н (-а) *м* polythene

полк (-а́; *loc sg* **-у́)** *м* regiment

по́л|ка (-ки; *gen pl* **-ок)** *ж (в поезде: для багажа)* luggage rack; **(:** *для лежания)* berth; **кни́жная ~** bookshelf

полко́вник (-а) *м* colonel

полне́|ть (-ю; *pf* **по~)** *несов* to put on weight

полномо́чи|е (-я) *ср* authority; *(обычно мн: право)* power

полномо́чный *прил* fully authorized

полнопра́вный *прил (гражданин)* fully-fledged; *(наследник)* rightful

по́лностью *нареч* fully, completely

полноце́нный *прил* proper

по́л|ночь (-уночи) *ж* midnight

по́лный *прил (зал; (победа, счастье итп)* complete, total; *(толстый)* stout; **~ +gen** *или* **+instr** full of; *(тревоги, любви итп)* filled with

полови́к (-а́) *м* mat

полови́н|а (-ы) *ж* half; **на ~ доро́ги** halfway; **сейча́с ~ пе́рвого/второ́го** it's (now) half past twelve/one

поло́вник (-а) *м* ladle

полово́дь|е (-я) *ср* high water

половой *прил (тряпка, мастика)* floor; *(БИО)* sexual

положе́ни|е (-я) *ср* situation; *(географическое)*, location, position; *(тела, головы итп)* position; *(социальное, семейное итп)* status; *(правила)* regulations *мн; (обычно мн: тезис)* point; **она́ в ~и** *(разг)* she's expecting; **~ дел** the state of affairs

поло́женный *прил* due

положи́тельный *прил* positive

пол|ожи́ть (-ожу́, -о́жишь) *сов от* **класть**

поло́м|ка (-ки; *gen pl* **-ок)** *ж* breakdown

поло́с|а́ (-ы́; *nom pl* **по́лосы,** *gen pl* **поло́с,** *dat pl* **по́лосам)** *ж (ткани, металла)* strip; *(на ткани, на рисунке итп)* stripe

полоса́тый *прил* striped, stripy

поло́с|ка (-ки; *gen pl* **-ок)** *ж (ткани, бумаги)* (thin) strip; *(на ткани)* (thin) stripe; **в ~ку** striped

пол|оска́ть (-ощу́, -о́щешь; *pf* **про~)** *несов перех (бельё, посуду)* to rinse; *(рот)* to rinse out

по́лост|ь (-и; *gen pl* **-е́й)** *ж (АНАТ)* cavity

полоте́нц|е (-а; *gen pl* **-ец)** *ср* towel

пол|отно́ (-отна́; *nom pl* **-о́тна,** *gen pl* **-о́тен)** *ср (ткань)* sheet; *(картина)* canvas

пол|о́ть (-ю́, -ешь; *pf* **про~)** *несов перех* to weed

полпути́ *м нескл* half *(of journey)*; **на ~** halfway

пол|тора́ (-у́тора; (f ~торы́)) м/ср чис one and a half

полуботи́н|ок (-ка) м ankle boot

полуго́ди|е (-я) ср (ПРОСВЕЩ) semester; (ЭКОН) half (of the year)

полузащи́т|а (-ы) ж midfield

полузащи́тни|к (-а) м midfielder

полукру́г (-а) м semicircle

полума́рак (-а) м semidarkness

полуо́стров (-а) м peninsular

полупальто́ ср нескл jacket, short coat

полупроводни́к (-а́) м (ЭЛЕК) semiconductor

полуфабрика́т (-а) м (КУЛИН) partially prepared food

полуфина́л (-а) м semifinal

получа́тель (-я) м recipient

получа́|ть(ся) (-ю(сь)) несов от **получи́ть(ся)**

получе́ни|е (-я) ср receipt; (урожая, результата) obtaining

пол|учи́ть (-учу́, -у́чишь; impf **получа́ть**) сов перех to receive, get; (урожай, насморк, удовольствие) to get; (известность) to gain ♦ неперех (разг: быть наказанным) to get it in the neck; **~ся** (impf **получа́ться**) сов возв to turn out; (удаться) to work; (фотография) to come out; **из него́ ~у́чится хоро́ший учи́тель** he'll make a good teacher; **у меня́ э́то не ~уча́ется** I can't do it

полу́ч|ка (-ки; gen pl -ек) ж (разг) pay

полуша́ри|е (-я) ср hemisphere

пол|часа́ (-у́часа) м half an hour

по́лый прил hollow

по́льз|а (-ы) ж benefit; **в ~у** +gen in favour (BRIT) или favor (US) of

по́льзовани|е (-я) ср: ~ (+instr) use (of)

по́льз|оваться (-уюсь; pf вос~)

несов возв: ~ +instr to use; (no pf; авторите́том, успе́хом итп) to enjoy

по́льский прил Polish; ~ язы́к Polish

По́льш|а (-и) ж Poland

пол|юби́ть (-юблю́, -ю́бишь; сов перех (человека) to come to love; ~ (pf) что-н/ +infin to develop a love for sth/doing

по́люс (-а; nom pl -á) м pole

пол|я́ (-е́й) мн (шля́пы) brim ед; (на страни́це) margin ед

поля́н|а (-ы) ж glade

поля́рный прил (ГЕО) polar; (разные) diametrically opposed

пома́д|а (-ы) ж (также: губна́я ~) lipstick

пом|аха́ть (-ашу́, -а́шешь) сов: ~ +instr to wave

помедл|и́ть (-ю, -ишь) сов: ~ с +instr/ +infin to linger over sth/doing

поменя́|ть(ся) (-ю(сь)) сов от **меня́ть(ся)**

поме́р|ить (-ю, -ишь) сов от **ме́рить**

поме|сти́ть (-щу́, -сти́шь; impf **помеща́ть**) сов перех to put; **~ся** (impf **помеща́ться**) сов возв (уместиться) to fit

помёт (-а) м dung; (пти́цы) droppings мн; (детёныши) litter

поме́т|а (-ы) ж note

поме́|тить (-чу, -тишь) сов от **ме́тить** ♦ (impf **помеча́ть**) перех to note

поме́т|ка (-ки; gen pl -ок) ж note

поме́х|а (-и) ж hindrance; (связь, обычно мн) interference ед

помеча́|ть (-ю) несов от **поме́тить**

помеша́|ть (-ю) сов от **меша́ть**

помеща́|ть(ся) (-ю(сь)) несов от **помести́ть(ся)**

помеще́ни|е (-я) ср room; (под

офис) premises *мн*; *жило́е ~* living space

помидо́р (-а) *м* tomato

поми́л|овать (-ую) *сов от* **ми́ловать**

поми́мо *предл*: ~ +*gen* besides; *(без участия)* bypassing; *~ того́/всего́ про́чего* apart from that/anything else

поми́н|ки (-ок) *мн* wake *ед*

помину́тный *прил* at one-minute intervals; *(очень частый)* constant

помир|и́ть(ся) (-ю́(сь), -и́шь(ся)) *сов от* **мири́ть(ся)**

по́мн|ить (-ю, -ишь) *несов (не)перех*: ~ (о +*prp или* про +*acc*) to remember

помог|а́ть (-а́ю) *несов от* **помо́чь**

по-мо́ему *нареч* my way ♦ *вводн сл* in my opinion

помо́|и (-ев) *мн* dishwater *ед*; *(отходы)* slops *мн*

помо́|йка (-йки; *gen pl* -ек) *ж (яма)* cesspit; *(для мусора)* rubbish *(BRIT) или* garbage *(US)* heap

помолч|а́ть (-у́, -и́шь) *сов* to pause

помо́рщ|иться (-усь, -ишься) *сов возв* to screw up one's face

помо́ст (-а) *м (для обозрения)* platform; *(для выступлений)* rostrum

помо́|чь (-гу́, -о́жешь *итп*, -о́гут; *pt* -о́г, -огла́; *impf* **помога́ть**) *сов*: ~ +*dat* to help; *(другой стране)* to help

помо́щник (-а) *м* helper; *(должностное)* assistant

по́мощь (-и) *ж* help, assistance

пом|ы́ть(ся) (-о́ю(сь), -о́ешь(ся)) *сов от* **мы́ть(ся)**

помя́тый *прил* rumpled; *(бок машины)* dented

понадоб|иться (-люсь, -ишься) *сов возв* to be needed

по-настоя́щему *нареч* properly

по-на́шему *нареч* our way

понеде́льник (-а) *м* Monday

понемно́гу *нареч* a little; *(постепенно)* little by little

пон|ести́ (-есу́, -есёшь; *pt* -ёс, -есла́) *сов от* **нести́**; **~сь** *сов возв (человек)* to tear off; *(лошадь)* to charge off; *(машина)* to speed off

по́ни *м нескл* pony

понижа́|ть(ся) (-ю(сь)) *несов от* **пони́зить(ся)**

пониже́ни|е (-я) *ср* reduction; *(в должности)* demotion

пони́|зить (-жу, -зишь; *impf* **понижа́ть**) *сов перех* to reduce; *(в должности)* to demote; *(голос)* to lower; **~ся** *(impf* **понижа́ться)** *сов возв* to be reduced

понима́|ть (-ю) *несов от* **поня́ть** ♦ *перех* to understand ♦ *неперех*: ~ **в** +*prp* to know about; **~ете** you see

поно́с (-а) *м* diarrhoea *(BRIT)*, diarrhea *(US)*

пон|оси́ть (-ошу́, -о́сишь) *сов перех* to carry for a while; *(одежду)* to wear

поно́шенный *прил (одежда)* worn

понра́в|иться (-люсь, -ишься) *сов от* **нра́виться**

по́нчик (-а) *м* doughnut *(BRIT)*, donut *(US)*

поня́ти|е (-я) *ср* notion; *(знание)* idea; **~я не име́ю** *(разг)* I've no idea

поня́тно *нареч* intelligibly ♦ *как сказ*: **мне ~** I understand; **~! I see!; **~?** got it?

поня́тный *прил* intelligible; *(ясный)* clear; *(оправданный)* understandable

по|ня́ть (-йму́, -ймёшь; *pt* **нял,**
-няла́; *impf* **понима́ть**) *сов*
перех to understand

поощре́ни|е (-я) *ср*
encouragement

поощр|и́ть (-ю́, -и́шь; *impf*
поощря́ть) *сов перех* to
encourage

поп (-а́) *м* (*разг*) priest

попада́ни|е (-я) *ср* hit

попада́|ть(ся) (-ю(сь)) *несов от*
попа́сть(ся)

попа́рно *нареч* in pairs

попа|сть (-ду́, -дёшь; *impf*
попада́ть) *сов*: ~ **в** +*acc* (*в цель*)
to hit; (*в вороmа*) to end up in; (*в
чужо́й го́род*) to find o.s. in; (*в
беду́*) to land in; **мне ~ло мне в
глаза́** the soap got in my eyes;
попа́сть (~ *pf*) **в ава́рию** to have
an accident; **попа́сть** (~ *pf*) **в
плен** to be taken prisoner;
попа́сть (~ *pf*) **под дождь** to be
caught in the rain; **ему́ ~ло** (*разг*)
he got a hiding; **(Вы) не туда́ ~ли**
you've got the wrong number; **~ся**
(*impf* **попада́ться**) *сов возв*
(*престу́пник*) to be caught; **мне
~ла́сь интере́сная кни́га** I came
across an interesting book;
попада́ться (*~ся pf*) **кому́-н на
глаза́** to catch sb's eye

попе́й(те) *сов см.* **попи́ть**

поперёк *нареч* crossways
♦ *предл*: ~ +*gen* across

попере́чный *прил* horizontal

поперхн|у́ться (-у́сь, -ёшься)
сов возв to choke

поперч|и́ть (-у, -ишь) *сов от*
пе́рчить

попе́чени|е (-я) *ср* (*о де́тях*)
care; (*о дела́х, о до́ме*) charge

попечи́тел|ь (-я) *м* guardian;
(*комм*) trustee

поп|и́ть (-ью́, -ьёшь; *pt* **-и́л,**
-ила́, *imper* **-е́й(те)**) *сов перех* to
have a drink of

попл|ы́ть (-ву́, -вёшь; *pt* **-л, -ла́**)
сов to start swimming; (*су́дно*) to
set sail

попола́м *нареч* in half; ~ **с** +*instr*
mixed with

пополне́ни|е (-я) *ср* (*запа́сов*)
replenishment; (*колле́кции*)
expansion; (*во́инское*)
reinforcement

попо́лн|ить (-ю, -ишь; *impf*
пополня́ть) *сов перех*: ~ **что-н**
+*instr* (*запа́сы*) to replenish sth
with; (*колле́кцию*) to expand sth
with; (*коллекти́в*) to reinforce sth
with; **~ся** (*impf* **пополня́ться**) *сов
возв* (*запа́сы*) to be replenished;
(*колле́кции*) to be expanded

поправи́мый *прил* rectifiable

попра́в|ить (-лю, -ишь; *impf*
поправля́ть) *сов перех* to
correct; (*га́лстук, пла́тье*) to
straighten; (*причёску*) to tidy;
(*здоро́вье, дела́*) to improve; **~ся**
(*impf* **поправля́ться**) *сов возв* to
improve; (*пополне́ть*) to put on
weight

попра́в|ка (-ки; *gen pl* **-ок**) *ж*
(*оши́бки*) correction; (*в реше́ние,
в зако́н*) amendment

по-пре́жнему *нареч* as before;
(*всё ещё*) still

попро́б|овать (-ую) *сов от*
про́бовать

попро|си́ть(ся) (-ошу́(сь),
-о́сишь(ся)) *сов от* **проси́ть(ся)**

попроща́|ться (-юсь) *сов возв*:
~ **с** +*instr* to say goodbye to

попуга́|й (-я) *м* parrot

популя́рность (-и) *ж* popularity

популя́рный *прил* popular;
(*поня́тный*) accessible

попу́тный *прил* (*замеча́ние*)

accompanying; (*машина*) passing; (*ветер*) favourable (*BRIT*), favorable (*US*)

попу́тчик (-а) м travelling (*BRIT*) или traveling (*US*) companion

попы́т|ка (-ки; gen pl **-ок)** ж attempt

попью́ итп сов см. **попи́ть**

попя́|титься (-чусь, -тишься) сов возв to take a few steps backwards (*BRIT*) или backward (*US*)

по́р|а (-ы) ж pore

пор|а́ (-ы́) acc sg **-у,** dat sg **-е́,** nom pl **-ы)** ж time ♦ *как сказ* it's time; **до каки́х ~?** until when?; **до тех ~ (ра́ньше)** up till now; **(всё ещё)** still; **до тех ~ until then; до тех ~, пока́** until; **с каки́х ~?** since when?

поравня́|ться (-юсь) сов возв: **~ с** +instr (*человек*) to draw level with; (*машина*) to come alongside

пораже́ни|е (-я) ср (*цели*) hitting; (*МЕД*) damage; (*проигрыш*) defeat; **наноси́ть (нанести́** pf) **кому́-н ~** to defeat sb; **терпе́ть (потерпе́ть** pf) **~** to be defeated

порази́тельный прил striking; (*о неприятном*) astonishing

пора́н|ить (-ю, -ишь) сов перех to hurt

порв|а́ть(ся) (-у́, -ёшь) сов от **рва́ть(ся)**

поре́з (-а) м cut

поре́|зать (-жу, -жешь) сов перех to cut; **~ся** сов возв to cut o.s.

порногра́фи|я (-и) ж pornography

по́ровну нареч equally

поро́г (-а) м (*также перен*) threshold

поро́д|а (-ы) ж (*животных*) breed

поро́дистый прил pedigree

поро́й нареч from time to time

поро́к (-а) м vice; (*МЕД*) abnormality

пороло́н (-а) м foam rubber

порос|ёнок (-ёнка; nom pl **-я́та,** gen pl **-я́т)** м piglet

по́рох (-а; part gen **-у)** м gunpowder

порош|о́к (-ка́) м powder

порт (-а; loc sg **-у́,** nom pl **-ы,** gen pl **-о́в)** м port

портати́вный прил portable

портве́йн (-а) м port (*wine*)

по́р|тить (-чу, -тишь; pf **ис~)** несов перех to damage; (*настроение, праздник, ребёнка*) to spoil; **~ся** (pf **ис~ся)** сов возв (*механизм*) to be damaged; (*здоровье, погода*) to deteriorate; (*настроение*) to be spoiled; (*молоко*) to go off; (*мясо, овощи*) to go bad

портни́х|а (-и) ж (*женская*) dressmaker; (*мужская*) tailor

портн|о́й (-о́го) м (*мужской*) tailor; (*женский*) dressmaker

портре́т (-а) м portrait

Португа́ли|я (-и) ж Portugal

португа́льский прил Portuguese; **~ язы́к** Portuguese

портфе́л|ь (-я) м briefcase; (*ПОЛИТ, КОММ*) portfolio

портье́р|а (-ы) ж curtain

поруга́|ться (-юсь) сов от **руга́ться** ♦ возв (*разг*): **~ся** +instr to fall out (with)

пору́к|а (-и) ж: **брать кого́-н на ~и** to take sb on probation; (*ЮР*) to stand bail for sb

по-ру́сски нареч (*говори́ть, писа́ть*) in Russian; **говори́ть** (*impf*)/**понима́ть** (*impf*) **~** to speak/ understand Russian

поруча́|ть (-ю) несов от **поручи́ть**

поруче́ни|е (-я) *ср (задание)* errand; (: *важное*) mission

по́руч|ень (-ня) *м* handrail

поручи́тельств|о (-а) *ср* guarantee

пор|учи́ть (-учу́, -у́чишь; *impf* **поруча́ть**) *сов*: ~ кому́-н что-н to entrust sb with sth; **поруча́ть** (~ *pf*) кому́-н +*infin* to instruct sb to do; **поруча́ть** (~ *pf*) кому́-н кого́-н/что-н (*отдать на попечение*) to leave sb/sth in sb's care; **~ся** *сов от* **руча́ться**

по́рци|я (-и) *ж* portion

по́рш|ень (-ня) *м* (*в двигателе*) piston; (*в насосе*) plunger

поры́в (-а) *м* (*ветра*) gust

поры́вистый *прил* (*ветер*) gusty

поря́дков|ый *прил* (*номер*) ordinal; **~ое числи́тельное** ordinal (number)

поря́д|ок (-ка) *м* order; (*правила*) procedure; **в ~ке** +*gen* (*в качестве*) as; **всё в ~ке** everything's OK; **~ дня** agenda

поря́дочный *прил* (*честный*) decent; (*значительный*) fair

пос|ади́ть (-ажу́, -а́дишь) *сов от* **сажа́ть**

поса́д|ка (-ки; *gen pl* -ок) *ж* (*овощей*) planting; (*пассажиров*) boarding; (*самолёта итп*) landing

поса́дочный *прил* (*талон*) boarding; (*площадка*) landing

по-сво́ему *нареч* his *итп* way; **он ~ прав** in his own way, he is right

посвя|ти́ть (-щу́, -ти́шь; *impf* **посвяща́ть**) *сов перех*: ~ что-н +*dat* to devote sth to; (*книгу*) to dedicate sth to

посе́в (-а) *м* sowing

посе́в|ы (-ов) *мн* crops *мн*

поселе́ни|е (-я) *ср* settlement

пос|ели́ть(ся) (-елю́(сь),

-е́лишь(ся) *сов от* **сели́ть(ся)**

посё́л|ок (-ка) *м* village; **да́чный ~** village made up of dachas

посереди́не *нареч* in the middle ♦ *предл*: ~ +*gen* in the middle of

посети́тел|ь (-я) *м* visitor

посе|ти́ть (-щу́, -ти́шь; *impf* **посеща́ть**) *сов перех* to visit

посеще́ни|е (-я) *ср* visit

посе́|ять (-ю, -ишь) *сов от* **се́ять**

посиде́ть (-жу́, -ди́шь) *сов* to sit for a while

поскольз|ну́ться (-у́сь, -ёшься) *сов возв* to slip

поско́льку *союз* as

посла́ни|е (-я) *ср* message

посла́нник (-а) *м* envoy

по|сла́ть (-шлю́, -шлёшь; *impf* **посыла́ть**) *сов перех* to send

по́сле *нареч* (*потом*) afterwards (*BRIT*), afterward (*US*) ♦ *предл*: ~ +*gen* after ♦ *союз*: ~ того́ как after

послевое́нный *прил* postwar

после́дн|ий *прил* last; (*новости*, *мода*) latest; **за** *или* **в ~ее вре́мя** recently

после́дователь (-я) *м* follower

после́довательност|ь (-и) *ж* sequence; (*политики*) consistency

после́довательный *прил* (*один за другим*) consecutive; (*логический*) consistent

после́д|овать (-ую) *сов от* **сле́довать**

после́дстви|е (-я) *ср* consequence

послеза́втра *нареч* the day after tomorrow

посло́виц|а (-ы) *ж* proverb, saying

послу́ша|ть (-ю) *сов от* **слу́шать** ♦ *перех*: ~ что-н to listen to sth for a while; **~ся** *сов от* **слу́шаться**

послу́шный *прил* obedient

посме́|ть (-ю) *сов от* сметь

посм|отре́ть (-отрю́, -о́тришь) *сов от* смотре́ть; ~о́трим (*разг*) we'll see; ~ся *сов от* смотре́ться

посо́би|е (-я) *ср* (*помощь*) benefit; (*ПРОСВЕЩ, уче́бник*) textbook; (*: нагля́дное*) visual aids *мн*; ~ по безрабо́тице unemployment benefit; ~ по инвали́дности disability living allowance

посо́л (-ла́) *м* ambassador

посо́л|ить (-ю́, -о́лишь) *сов от* соли́ть

посо́льств|о (-а) *ср* embassy

поспе́|ть (3sg -е́ет) *сов от* спеть

поспеш|и́ть (-у́, -и́шь) *сов от* спеши́ть

поспо́р|ить (-ю, -ишь) *сов от* спо́рить

посреди́ *нареч* in the middle ♦ *предл*: ~ +gen in the middle of

посреди́не *нареч* in the middle ♦ *предл*: ~ +gen in the middle of

посре́дник (-а) *м* intermediary; (*при конфли́кте*) mediator; торго́вый ~ middleman

посре́днический *прил* (*КОММ*) intermediary; (*услу́ги*) agent's

посре́дничеств|о (-а) *ср* mediation

посре́дственно *нареч* (*учи́ться, писа́ть*) averagely ♦ *ср нескл* (*ПРОСВЕЩ*) ≈ satisfactory (*school mark*)

посре́дственный *прил* mediocre

посре́дством *предл*: ~ +gen by means of; (*челове́ка*) through

поссо́р|ить(ся) (-ю(сь), -ишь(ся)) *сов от* ссо́рить(ся)

пост (-а́; *loc sg* -у́) *м* (*лю́ди*) guard; (*ме́сто*) lookout post; (*до́лжность*) post; (*РЕЛ*) fast

поста́в|ить (-лю, -ишь) *сов от* ста́вить ♦ (*impf* поставля́ть) *перех* (*това́р*) to supply

поста́в|ка (-ки; *gen pl* -ок) *ж* (*снабже́ние*) supply

поставщи́к (-а́) *м* supplier

постаме́нт (-а) *м* pedestal

постан|ови́ть (-овлю́, -о́вишь; *impf* постановля́ть) *сов*: ~ +infin to resolve to do

постано́в|ка (-ки; *gen pl* -ок) *ж* (*ТЕА́ТР*) production; ~ вопро́са/пробле́мы the formulation of the question/problem

постановле́ни|е (-я) *ср* (*реше́ние*) resolution; (*распоряже́ние*) decree

постано́вщик (-а) *м* producer

постара́|ться (-юсь) *сов от* стара́ться

пост|ели́ть (-елю́, -е́лишь) *сов от* стели́ть

посте́л|ь (-и) *ж* bed

посте́льный *прил*: ~ое бельё bedclothes *мн*

постепе́нно *нареч* gradually

постепе́нный *прил* gradual

постира́|ть (-ю) *сов от* стира́ть

пост|и́ться (-щу́сь, -сти́шься) *несов возв* (*РЕЛ*) to fast

по́стный *прил* (*суп*) vegetarian; ~ое ма́сло vegetable oil

посто́льку *союз*: ~ ... поско́льку insofar as ...

посторо́нн|ий *прил* (*чужо́й*) strange; (*по́мощь, влия́ние*) outside; (*вопро́с*) irrelevant ♦ (-его) *м* stranger, outsider; ~им вход воспрещён authorized entry only

постоя́нный *прил* (*рабо́та, а́дрес*) permanent; (*шум*) constant; ~ое запомина́ющее устро́йство ROM

посто|я́ть (-ю́, -и́шь) *сов от*

стоя́ть ~ *неперех (стоя́ть недо́лго)* to stand for a while
постри́|чь(ся) (-гу́(сь), -жёшь(ся) итп; pt **-г(ся), -гла(сь))** *сов от* **стри́чь(ся)**
постро́|ить (-ю, -ишь) *сов от* **стро́ить**
постро́йка (-йки; gen pl **-ек)** ж construction; *(зда́ние)* building
пост|упи́ть (-уплю́, -у́пишь; impf **поступа́ть)** *сов (челове́к)* to act; *(това́р, изве́стия)* to come in; *(жа́лоба)* to be received;
поступа́ть (~ pf) в/на +acc *(в университе́т, на рабо́ту)* to start
поступле́ни|е (-я) ср *(де́йствие: в университе́т, на рабо́ту)* starting; *(обы́чно мн: бюдже́тное)* revenue ед; *(в библиоте́ке)* acquisition
посту́п|ок (-ка) м deed
постуч|а́ть(ся) (-у́(сь), -и́шь(ся)) *сов от* **стуча́ть(ся)**
посу́д|а (-ы) ж собир crockery; **ку́хонная** ~ kitchenware; **стекля́нная** ~ glassware; **мыть (помы́ть** pf) ~у to wash the dishes, wash up
посчита́|ть (-ю) *сов от* **счита́ть**
посыла́|ть (-ю) *несов от* **посла́ть**
посы́лка (-ки; gen pl **-ок)** ж *(де́йствие: книг, де́нег)* sending; *(по́сланное)* parcel
посыпа́|ть (-ю, -лешь) перех to sprinkle; **~ся** *сов от* **сы́паться**
пот (-а; loc sg **-у́)** м sweat
по-тво́ему нареч your way
потенциа́л (-а) м potential
потенциа́льный прил potential
потенци́|ровать (-рую) несов перех to rub; ▸у warmer spell
пот|ере́ть (-ру́, -рёшь; pt **-ёр, -ёрла)** *сов перех (уши́б)* to rub;

(морко́вь) to grate
потерпе́вш|ий (-его) м *(ЮР)* victim
пот|ере́ть (-ерплю́, -е́рпишь) *сов от* **терпе́ть**
поте́р|я (-и) ж loss
потеря́|ть(ся) (-ю(сь)) *сов от* **теря́ть(ся)**
поте́|ть (-ю; impf вс~) несов to sweat
по́тный прил sweaty
пото́к (-а) м stream
потол|о́к (-ка́) м ceiling
пото́м нареч *(че́рез не́которое вре́мя)* later; *(по́сле)* then ▸ союз: **а/и** ~ and then, anyhow; **на** ~ for later
пото́мк|и (-ов) мн descendants мн
пото́мственный прил hereditary; *(пра́во)* inherited
пото́мств|о (-а) ср собир descendants мн; *(де́ти)* offspring мн
потому́ нареч: ~ **(и)** that's why; ~ **что** because
пото́п (-а) м flood
потороп|и́ть(ся) (-лю́(сь), -ишь(ся)) *сов от* **торопи́ть(ся)**
пото́чный прил *(произво́дство)* mass; **~ая ли́ния** production line
потра́|тить (-чу, -тишь) *сов от* **тра́тить**
потреби́тель (-я) м consumer
потреби́тельский прил *(спрос)* consumer
потреб|и́ть (-лю́, -и́шь) *сов от* **потребля́ть**
потребле́ни|е (-я) ср *(де́йствие)* consumption; **това́ры широ́кого ~я** consumer goods
потребля́|ть (-ю; pf **потреби́ть)** несов перех to consume
потре́бност|ь (-и) ж need
потре́б|овать(ся) (-ую(сь)) сов

от **требовать(ся)**

потрёпанный *прил* (книга, одежда) tattered; (вид, лицо) worn

потрох|а́ (-о́в) *мн* (птицы) giblets *мн*

потроши́|ть (-у́, -и́шь; *pf* **вы́потрошить)** *несов перех* (курицу, рыбу) to gut

потру|ди́ться (-жу́сь, -ди́шься) *сов возв* to work; ~ *(pf)* +infin to take the trouble to do

потряса́ющий *прил* (музыка, стихи) fantastic; (красота) stunning

потрясе́ни|е (-я) *ср* (нервное) breakdown; (социальное) upheaval; (впечатление) shock

потряс|ти́ (-у́, -ёшь; *pt* **-, -ла́)** *сов перех* to shake; (взволновать) to stun

поту́хн|уть (3sg -ет; *impf* **потуха́ть)** *сов* (лампа, свет) to go out

поту|ши́ть (-ушу́, -у́шишь) *сов от* **туши́ть**

пот|яну́ться (-яну́сь, -я́нешься; *impf* **потя́гиваться)** *сов возв* (в постели, в кресле) to stretch out

поу́жина|ть (-ю) *сов от* **у́жинать**

поумне́|ть (-ю) *сов от* **умне́ть**

поучи́тельный *прил* (пример) instructive; (тон) didactic

похвал|а́ (-ы́) *ж* praise

похва́ста|ться (-юсь) *сов от* **хва́статься**

похити́тел|ь (-я) *м* (см глаг) thief; abductor; kidnapper

похи́|тить (-щу, -тишь; *impf* **похища́ть)** *сов перех* (предмет) to steal; (человека) to abduct; (: для выкупа) to kidnap

похище́ни|е (-я) *ср* (см глаг) theft; abduction; kidnap(ping)

похло́па|ть (-ю) *сов перех* to pat

похме́ль|е (-я) *ср* hangover

похо́д (-а) *м* (военный) campaign; (туристический) hike (walking and camping expedition)

похо|ди́ть (-ожу́, -о́дишь) *несов*: ~ **на** +acc/на кого-н/что-н to resemble sb/sth ♦ *сов* to walk

похо́дк|а (-и) *ж* gait

похо́ж|ий *прил*: ~ **(на** +acc или с +instr) similar (to); **он ~ на бра́та, они́ с бра́том ~и** he looks like his brother; **они́ ~и** they look alike; ~ **на то, что ...** it looks as if ...; **на него́ (не) ~е** it's (not) like him

похоло́да|ни|е (-я) *ср* cold spell

похолода́|ть (3sg -ет) *сов от* **холода́ть**

похор|они́ть (-оню́, -о́нишь) *сов от* **хорони́ть**

похоро́нный *прил* funeral; ~ **бюро́** undertaker's

по́хор|оны (-о́н; *dat pl* **-она́м)** *мн* funeral *ед*

поцел|ова́ть(ся) (-у́ю(сь)) *сов от* **целова́ть(ся)**

поцелу́|й (-я) *м* kiss

почасово́й *прил* (оплата) hourly

поча́т|ок (-ка) *м* (кукуру́зы) cob

по́чв|а (-ы) *ж* soil; (перен) basis; **на ~е** +gen arising from

почём *нареч* (разг) how much?

почему́ *нареч* why; **вот** ~ that is why

почему́-либо *нареч* for some reason or other

почему́-нибудь *нареч* = **почему́-либо**

почему́-то *нареч* for some reason

по́черк (-а) *м* handwriting

почерне́|ть (-ю) *сов от* **черне́ть**

поче|са́ть(ся) (-шу́(сь), -шешь(ся)) *сов от* **чеса́ть(ся)**

почёт (-а) *м* honour (BRIT), honor (US)

почётный прил (гость) honoured (BRIT), honored (US); (член) honorary; (обязанность) honourable (BRIT), honorable (US); **~ карау́л** guard of honour (BRIT) или honor (US)

почи́нить (-иню́, -и́нишь) сов от **чини́ть**

почи́н|ка (-ки; gen pl -ок) ж repair

почи́стить (-щу, -стишь) сов от **чи́стить**

почита́тель (-я) м admirer

почита́|ть (-ю) сов перех (книгу) to read ♦ несов перех to admire

по́чк|а (-ки; gen pl -ек) ж (БОТ) bud; (АНАТ) kidney

по́чт|а (-ы) ж (учреждение) post office; (письма) post, mail

почтальо́н (-а) м postman (BRIT), mailman (US)

почта́мт (-а) м main post office

почте́ни|е (-я) ср respect, veneration

почти́ нареч almost, nearly; **~ что** (разг) almost

почти́тельный прил respectful

почти́ть (как чтить; см. Table 17) сов перех (память) to pay homage to

почто́вый прил postal; (марка) postage; **~ая откры́тка** postcard; **~ и́ндекс** postcode (BRIT), zip code (US); **~ перево́д** (деньги) postal order; **~ я́щик** postbox

почу́вств|овать (-ую) сов от **чу́вствовать**

пошатн|у́ть (-у́, -ёшь) сов перех (веру) to damage; (здоровье) to damage; **~ся** сов возв to sway; (авторитет) to be undermined

пошёл сов см. **пойти́**

поши́в (-а) м (действие) sewing; **индивидуа́льный ~** tailoring

пошла́ etc сов см. **пойти́**

по́шлин|а (-ы) ж duty

пошло́ сов см. **пойти́**

по́шлый прил vulgar; (анекдот) corny

пошлю́ итп сов см. **посла́ть**

пошут|и́ть (-учу́, -у́тишь) сов от **шути́ть**

пощад|а́ (-ы) ж mercy

пощад|и́ть (-жу́, -ди́шь) сов от **щади́ть**

пощёчин|а (-ы) ж slap across the face

поэ́зи|я (-и) ж poetry

поэ́м|а (-ы) ж poem

поэ́т (-а) м poet

поэте́сс|а (-ы) ж см. **поэ́т**

поэти́ческий прил poetic

поэ́тому нареч therefore

пою́ итп несов см. **петь**

по|яви́ться (-явлю́сь, -я́вишься; impf **появля́ться)** сов возв to appear; **у него́ ~яви́лись иде́и/сомне́ния** he has had an idea/begun to have doubts

появле́ни|е (-я) ср appearance

появл|я́ться (-я́юсь) несов от **появи́ться**

по́яс (-а; nom pl -а́) м (ремень) belt; (талия) waist; (ГЕО) zone

поясне́ни|е (-я) ср explanation; (к схеме) explanatory note

поясн|и́ть (-ю́, -и́шь; impf **поясня́ть)** сов перех to explain

поясни́ц|а (-ы) ж small of the back

пр. сокр = **прое́зд, проспе́кт**

прабабу́шк|а (-ки; gen pl -ек) ж great-grandmother

прав|а́ (-) мн (также: **води́тельские ~**) driving licence ед (BRIT), driver's license ед (US); **~ челове́ка** human rights

пра́вд|а (-ы) ж truth ♦ нареч really; ♦ вводн сл true; **как сказа́ть it's true;** **~у** или **по ~е говоря́** или **сказа́ть** to tell the truth

правди́вый *прил* truthful

правдоподо́бный *прил* plausible

пра́вил|о (-а) *ср* rule; э́то не в мои́х ~ах that's not my way; как ~ as a rule; по всем ~ам by the rules; ~а доро́жного движе́ния rules of the road, ≈ Highway Code

пра́вильно *нареч* correctly ♦ *как сказ* that's correct *или* right

пра́вильный *прил* correct; (*вывод, ответ*) right

прави́тель (-я) *м* ruler

прави́тельственный *прил* government

прави́тельств|о (-а) *ср* government

пра́в|ить (-лю, -ишь) *несов перех* (*исправлять*) to correct ♦ *неперех*: ~ +*instr* (*страной*) to rule, govern; (*машиной*) to drive

правле́ни|е (-я) *ср* government; (*орган*) board

пра́внук (-а) *м* great-grandson

пра́в|о (-а; *nom pl* **-á)** *ср* (*свобода*) right; (*нормы, наука*) law; име́ть (*impf*) ~ на что-н/ +*infin* to be entitled *или* have the right to sth/to do sth; на ра́вных права́х с +*instr* on equal terms with; *см. также* **права́**

правомо́чный *прил* (*орган*) competent; (*лицо*) authorized

правонаруше́ни|е (-я) *ср* offence

правонаруши́тель (-я) *м* offender

правописа́ни|е (-я) *ср* spelling

правопоря́д|ок (-ка) *м* law and order

правосла́ви|е (-я) *ср* orthodoxy

правосла́вный *прил* (*церковь, обряд*) orthodox ♦ (*-ого*) *м* member of the Orthodox Church

правосу́ди|е (-я) *ср* justice

правот|а́ (-ы́) *ж* correctness

пра́вый *прил* right; (*полит*) right-wing; **он прав** he is right

пра́вящий *прил* ruling

Пра́г|а (-и) *ж* Prague

праде́душ|ка (-ки; *gen pl* **-ек)** *м* great-grandfather

пра́зднеств|о (-а) *ср* festival

пра́здник (-а) *м* public holiday; (*религиозный*) festival; (*нерабочий день*) holiday; (*радость, торжество*) celebration; **с ~ом!** best wishes!

пра́здничный *прил* (*салют, обед*) celebratory; (*одежда, настроение*) festive; **~ день** holiday

пра́здн|овать (-ую) *несов перех* to celebrate

пра́ктик|а (-и) *ж* practice; (*часть учёбы*) practical experience *или* work; **на ~е** in practice

практика́нт (-а) *м* trainee (*on placement*)

практик|ова́ть (-у́ю) *несов перех* to practise (*BRIT*), practice (*US*); (*-ся несов возв* (*обучаться*): **~ся в чём-н** to practise sth

практи́чески *нареч* (*на деле*) in practice; (*по сути дела*) practically

практи́чный *прил* practical

прах (-а) *м* (*умершего*) ashes *мн*

пра́чечн|ая (-ой) *ж* laundry

пребыва́ни|е (-я) *ср* stay

пребыва́|ть (-ю) *несов* to be

превзойти́ (*как* идти́; *см.* Table 18; *impf* **превосходи́ть**) *сов перех* (*врага, соперника*) to beat; (*результаты, ожидания*) to surpass; (*доходы, скорость*) to exceed

превосхо|ди́ть (-жу́, -дишь) *несов от* **превзойти́**

превосхо́дно *нареч* superbly ♦ *как сказ* it's superb ♦ *част*: (*хорошо*) excellent!

превосхо́дн|ый *прил* superb; **~ая сте́пень** superlative degree

превосхо́дств|о (-а) *ср* superiority

преврати́ть (-щу́, -ти́шь; *impf* **превраща́ть)** *сов перех* во **что-н/кого́-н в** +*acc* to turn *или* transform sth/sb into; **~ся (***impf* **превраща́ться)** *сов возв:* **~ся (в** +*acc*) to turn (into)

превраще́ни|е (-я) *ср* transformation

превы́|сить (-шу, -сишь; *impf* **превыша́ть)** *сов перех* to exceed

прегра́д|а (-ы) *ж* barrier

прегра|ди́ть (-жу́, -ди́шь; *impf* **прегражда́ть)** *сов перех:* **~ кому́-н доро́гу/вход** to block *или* bar sb's way/entrance

преда|ва́ть (-ю́) *несов от* **преда́ть**

пре́данный *прил* devoted

преда́тел|ь (-я) *м* traitor

преда́тельств|о (-а) *ср* treachery

преда́ть (как дать; *см.* Table 16; *impf* **предава́ть)** *сов перех* to betray; **предава́ть (~ *pf*) что-н гла́сности** to make sth public

предвари́тельный *прил* preliminary; (*продажа*) advance

предвзя́тый *прил* prejudiced

предви́|деть (-жу, -дишь) *сов перех* to predict

предводи́тел|ь (-я) *м* leader

предвы́борный *прил* (*собрание*) pre-election; **~ая кампа́ния** election campaign

преде́л (-а) *м* (*обычно мн: города, страны*) boundary; (*перен: приличия*) bound; (: *терпения*) limit; (*подлости, совершенства*) height; (*мечтаний*) pinnacle; **на ~е** at breaking point; **в ~ах** +*gen*

(*закона, года*) within; (*приличия*) within the bounds of; **за ~ами** +*gen* (*страны, города*) outside

преде́льный *прил* maximum; (*восторг, важность*) utmost; **~ срок** deadline

предисло́ви|е (-я) *ср* foreword, preface

предлага́ть (-ю) *несов от* **предложи́ть**

предло́г (-а) *м* pretext; (*линг*) preposition; **под ~ом** +*gen* on the pretext of

предложе́ни|е (-я) *ср* suggestion, proposal; (*замужества*) proposal; (*комм*) offer; (*линг*) sentence; **де́лать (сде́лать** *pf***) кому́-н (де́вушке)** to propose to sb; (*комм*) to make sb an offer; **вноси́ть (внести́** *pf***) ~ (на собрании)** to propose a motion

предл|ожи́ть (-ожу́, -о́жишь; *impf* **предлага́ть)** *сов перех* to offer; (*план, кандидату́ру*) to propose ♦ *неперех* to suggest, propose

предло́жный *прил* (*линг*) prepositional

предме́т (-а) *м* object; (*обсуждения, изучения*) subject

преднаме́ренный *прил* (*преступление*) premeditated; (*обман итп*) deliberate

пре́д|ок (-ка) *м* ancestor

предоста́в|ить (-лю, -ишь) *сов перех:* **~ что-н кому́-н** to give sb sth ♦ *неперех:* **~ кому́-н** +*infin* (*выбирать, решать*) to let sb do

предостереже́ни|е (-я) *ср* warning

предостер|е́чь (-егу́, -ежёшь *etc*, **-егу́т;** *pt* **-ёг, -егла́;** *impf* **предостерега́ть)** *сов перех:* **~ кого́-н (от** +*gen*) to warn sb (against)

предосторо́жност|ь (-и) ж
caution; **ме́ры ~и** precautionary
measures, precautions

предотвра|ти́ть (-щу́, -ти́шь;
impf **предотвраща́ть**) *сов перех*
to prevent; *(войну, кризис)* to
avert

предохрани́тел|ь (-я) м safety
device; *(ЭЛЕК)* fuse (BRIT), fuze (US)

предохран|и́ть (-ю́, -и́шь; *impf*
предохраня́ть) *сов перех* to
protect

предполага́|ть (-ю) *несов от*
предположи́ть ♦ *перех*
(требовать) to presuppose
♦ *неперех* **+infin**
(намереваться) to intend to do

предположе́ни|е (-я) *ср*
(догадка) supposition

предположи́тельно *нареч*
supposedly

предположи́тельный *прил*
anticipated

предпол|ожи́ть (-ожу́,
-о́жишь; *impf* **предполага́ть**)
сов перех (допустить
возможность) to assume,
suppose; **~о́жим (возможно)** let's
assume *or* suppose

предпосле́дний *прил (номер,*
серия) penultimate; *(в очереди)*
last but one

предпосы́л|ка (-ки; *gen pl* **-ок)** ж
(условие) precondition,
prerequisite

предприи́мчивый *прил*
enterprising

предпринима́тел|ь (-я) м
entrepreneur, businessman

предпринима́тельств|о (-а) *ср*
enterprise

предпр|иня́ть (-иму́, -и́мешь;
pt **-и́нял, -иняла́,** *impf*
предпринима́ть) *сов перех* to
undertake

предприя́ти|е (-я) *ср* plant;
(КОММ) enterprise, business

предрассу́д|ок (-ка) м prejudice

председа́тел|ь (-я) м chairman

предсказа́ни|е (-я) *ср* prediction

предск|аза́ть (-ажу́, -а́жешь;
impf **предска́зывать**) *сов перех*
to predict; *(чью-н судьбу)* to
foretell

предсме́ртный *прил (агония)*
death; *(воля)* dying

представи́тел|ь (-я) м
representative

представи́тельный *прил*
representative

представи́тельств|о (-а) *ср*
(ПОЛИТ) representation;
дипломати́ческое ~ diplomatic
corps

предста́в|ить (-лю, -ишь; *impf*
представля́ть) *сов перех* to
present; **представля́ть (~ pf)**
кого́-н кому́-н *(познакомить)* to
introduce sb to sb; **представля́ть**
(~ pf) (себе́) *(вообразить)* to imagine; **~ся**
(impf
представля́ться) *несов возв* to
introduce o.s.; *(возможность)* to present
itself

представле́ни|е (-я) *ср*
presentation; *(ТЕАТР)* performance;
(знание) idea; **не име́ть** *(impf*
(никако́го) ~я о *+prp* to have no
idea about

представля́|ть (-ю) *несов от*
предста́вить ♦ *перех*
(организацию, страну) to
represent; **~ (impf) (себе́) что-н**
(понимать) to understand sth; **~ся**
несов от **предста́виться**

предсто|я́ть (3sg -и́т) *несов* to lie
ahead

предстоя́щий *прил (сезон)*
coming; *(встреча)* forthcoming

предубежде́ни|е (-я) *ср*

предупреди́ть

prejudice

предупре|ди́ть (-жу́, -ди́шь)
impf **предупрежда́ть** сов перех
to warn; (остановить) to prevent

предупрежде́ни|е (-я) ср
warning; (аварии, заболевания)
prevention

**предусм|отре́ть (-отрю́,
-о́тришь)**
предусма́тривать сов перех
(учесть) to foresee;
(приготовиться) to provide for

предусмотри́тельный прил
prudent

предчу́встви|е (-я) ср
premonition

предше́ствующий прил previous

предъяви́тел|ь (-я) м bearer

предъ|яви́ть (-явлю́, -я́вишь),
impf **предъявля́ть** сов перех
(паспорт, билет итп) to show;
(доказательства) to produce;
(требования, претензии) to
make; (иск) to bring;
**предъявля́ть (~ pf) права́ на
что-н** to lay claim to sth

предыду́щий прил previous

предысто́ри|я (-и) ж background

прее́мник (-а) м successor

пре́жде нареч (в прошлом)
formerly; (сначала) first ♦ предл:
~ +gen before; **~ всего́** first of all; **~
чем** before

преждевре́менный прил
premature

пре́жний прил former

презента́ци|я (-и) ж presentation

презервати́в (-а) м condom

президе́нт (-а) м president

прези́диум (-а) м presidium

презира́|ть (-ю) несов перех to
despise

презре́ни|е (-я) ср contempt

презри́тельный прил
contemptuous

преиму́ществ|о (-а) ср
advantage

прейскура́нт (-а) м price list

преклоне́ни|е (-я) ср: **~ (пе́ред
+instr)** admiration (for)

преклоня́|ться (-юсь) несов
возв: **~ пе́ред +instr** to admire

прекра́сно нареч (сделать)
brilliantly ♦ част: **~! excellent!; ты
~ зна́ешь, что ты не прав** you
know perfectly well that you are
wrong

прекра́сный прил beautiful;
(врач, результат) excellent

прекра|ти́ть (-щу́, -ти́шь), impf
прекраща́ть сов перех to stop
♦ неперех: **~ +infin** to stop doing;
~ся (impf **прекраща́ться**) сов
возв (дождь, занятия) to stop;
(отношения) to end

преле́стный прил charming

пре́лесть (-и) ж charm

прелю́ди|я (-и) ж prelude

пре́ми|я (-и) ж (работнику)
bonus; (победителя) prize;
(КОММ) premium

премье́р (-а) м premier

премье́р|а (-ы) ж премьера

премье́р-мини́стр (-а) м prime
minister, premier

пренебреже́ни|е (-я) ср
(законами итп) disregard;
(: обязанностями) neglect;
(высокомерие) contempt

пренебрежи́тельный прил
patronising

пренебр|е́чь (-егу́, -еже́шь etc,
-гу́т, pt **-ёг, -егла́)** impf
пренебрега́ть сов: **~ +instr**
(опасностью) to disregard;
(богатством, правилами) to
scorn; (советом, просьбой) to
ignore

пре́ни|я (-й) мн debate ед

преоблада́|ть (3sg -ет) несов: ~ (над +instr) to predominate (over)

преобразова́ни|е (-я) ср transformation

преобраз|ова́ть (-у́ю; impf преобразо́вывать) сов перех to transform

преодоле́|ть (-ю; impf преодолева́ть) сов перех to overcome; (барьер) to clear

препара́т (-а) м (МЕД: также: медици́нский ~) drug

препина́ни|е (-я) ср: зна́ки ~я punctuation marks мн

преподава́тел|ь (-я) м (школы, курсов) teacher; (вуза) lecturer

препода|ва́ть (-ю́, -ёшь) несов перех to teach

преподн|ести́ (-есу́, -есёшь; pt -ёс, -есла́; impf преподноси́ть) сов перех: ~ что-н кому́-н to present sb with sth

препя́тстви|е (-я) ср obstacle

препя́тств|овать (-ую; pf вос~) несов: ~ +dat to impede

прерв|а́ть (-у́, -ёшь; impf прерыва́ть) сов перех (разговор, работу итп) to cut short; (отношения) to break off; (говорящего) to interrupt; ~ся (impf прерыва́ться) сов возв (разговор, игра) to be cut short; (отношения) to be broken off

преры́вистый прил (звонок) intermittent; (линия) broken

прес|е́чь (-еку́, -ечёшь etc, -еку́т; pt -ёк, -екла́; impf пресека́ть) сов перех to suppress

пресле́довани|е (-я) ср pursuit; (сексуальное) harassment; (инакомыслия) persecution

пресле́д|овать (-ую) несов перех to pursue;

(инакомыслящих) to persecute; (насмешками) to harass

пресло́ву́тый прил notorious

пресмыка́ющ|ееся (-егося) ср reptile

пресново́дный прил freshwater

пре́сный прил (вода) fresh; (пища) bland

пресс (-а) (ТЕХ) press

пре́сс|а (-ы) ж собир the press

пресс-конфере́нци|я (-и) ж press conference

пресс-рели́з (-а) м press release

пресс-секрета́р|ь (-я́) м press secretary

пресс-центр (-а) м press office

престаре́лый прил aged; дом (для) ~ых old people's home

прести́ж (-а) м prestige

прести́жный прил prestigious

преступле́ни|е (-я) ср crime

престу́пник (-а) м criminal

престу́пност|ь (-и) ж (количество) crime

престу́пный прил criminal

претенде́нт (-а) м (на до́лжность) candidate; (СПОРТ) contender

претенд|ова́ть (-у́ю) несов: ~ +acc (стремиться) to aspire to; (заявлять права) to lay claim to

прете́нзи|я (-и) ж (обычно мн: на наследство) claim ед; (: на ум, на красоту итп) pretension; (жалоба) complaint

преткнове́ни|е (-я) ср: ка́мень ~я stumbling block

преувели́ч|ить (-у, -ишь; impf преувели́чивать) сов перех to exaggerate

преуме́ньш|ить (-у, -ишь; impf преуменьша́ть) сов перех to underestimate

преуспе́|ть (-ю; impf преуспева́ть) сов (в учёбе) to be successful; (в жизни) to prosper, thrive

прецеде́нт (-а) *м* precedent

при *предл*: ~ +*prp* (*возле*) by, near; (*о части*) at; (*в присутствии*) in front of; (*о времени*) under; (*о наличии чего-н у кого-н*) on; **он всегда́ с деньга́х** he always has money on him; **я здесь ни с чём** it has nothing to do with me

приба́в|ить (-лю, -ишь; *impf* **прибавля́ть**) *сов перех* to add; (*увеличить*) to increase; **-ся** (*impf* **прибавля́ться**) *сов возв* (*проблемы, работа итп*) to mount up ♦ *безл* (*воды в реке*) to rise

прибежа́ть (*как* **бежа́ть**; *см. Table 20*) *сов* to come running

приб|и́ть (-ью, -ьёшь; *imper* **-е́й(те)**; *impf* **прибива́ть**) *сов перех* (*гвоздями*) to nail

приближа́|ться(ся) (-ю(сь)) *несов от* **прибли́зить(ся)**

приближе́ни|е (-я) *ср* approach

приблизи́тельный *прил* approximate

прибли́з|ить (-жу, -зишь; *impf* **приближа́ть**) *сов перех* (*придвинуть*) to move nearer; (*ускорить*) to bring nearer; **-ся** (*impf* **приближа́ться**) *сов возв* to approach

прибо́|й (-я) *м* breakers *мн*

прибо́р (-а) *м* (*измерительный*) device; (*оптический*) instrument; (*нагревательный*) appliance; (*бритвенный*) set; **столо́вый ~** setting

прибре́жный *прил* (*у моря*) coastal; (*у реки*) riverside

прибыва́|ть (-ю) *несов от* **прибы́ть**

при́быль (-и) *ж* profit

при́быльный *прил* profitable

прибы́ти|е (-я) *ср* arrival

прибы́ть (*как* **быть**; *см. Table 21*; *impf* **прибыва́ть**) *сов* to arrive

приватиза́ци|я (-и) *ж* privatization

приватизи́р|овать (-ую) (*не*)*сов перех* to privatize

прив|езти́ (-езу́, -езёшь; *pt* **-ёз, -езла́**; *impf* **привози́ть**) *сов перех* to bring

прив|ести́ (-еду́, -едёшь; *pt* **-ёл, -ела́**) *сов от* **вести́** ♦ (*impf* **приводи́ть**) *перех* (*сопроводить*) to bring; (*подлеж*: *дорога: к дому*) to take; (*пример*) to give; **~** (*pf*) **в у́жас** to horrify; **приводи́ть** (**~** *pf*) **в восто́рг** to delight; **приводи́ть** (**~** *pf*) **в изумле́ние** to astonish; **приводи́ть** (**~** *pf*) **в исполне́ние** to put into effect; **приводи́ть** (**~** *pf*) **в поря́док** to put in order

приве́т (-а) *м* regards *мн*; (*разг*: *при встрече*) hi; (: *при расстава́нии*) bye; **передава́ть** (**переда́ть** *pf*) **кому́-н ~** to give sb one's regards

приве́тливый *прил* friendly

приве́тстви|е (-я) *ср* (*при встрече*) greeting; (*делегации*) welcome

приве́тств|овать (-ую; *pf* **по~**) *несов перех* to welcome

приви́в|ка (-ки; *gen pl* **-ок**) *ж* (*МЕД*) vaccination

привиде́ни|е (-я) *ср* ghost

привилегиро́ванный *прил* privileged

привиле́ги|я (-и) *ж* privilege

привин|ти́ть (-чу́, -ти́шь; *impf* **приви́нчивать**) *сов перех* to screw on

при́вкус (-а) *м* flavour (*BRIT*), flavor (*US*)

привлека́тельный *прил*

attractive

привлека́ть (-ю) *несов от* **привле́чь**

привлече́ни|е (-я) *ср* (*покупателей, внимания*) attraction; (*ресурсов*) use

привле́|чь (-еку́, -ечёшь *etc*, -еку́т; *pt* -ёк, -екла́; *impf* **привлека́ть**) *сов перех* to attract; (*ресурсы*) to use; **привлека́ть** (~ *pf*) **кого́-н к** +*dat* (*к работе, к участию*) to involve sb in; (*к суду́*) to take sb to; **привлека́ть** (~ *pf*) **кого́-н к отве́тственности** to call sb to account

прив|оди́ть (-ожу́, -о́дишь) *несов от* **привести́**

прив|ози́ть (-ожу́, -о́зишь) *несов от* **привезти́**

привы́к|нуть (-ну; *pt* -, -ла; *impf* **привыка́ть**) *сов*: ~ +*infin* to get into the habit of doing; **привыка́ть** (~ *pf*) **к** +*dat* (*к новому*) to get used to

привы́ч|ка (-ки; *gen pl* -ек) *ж* habit

привы́чный *прил* familiar

привя́занност|ь (-и) *ж* attachment

привя́з|ать (-яжу́, -я́жешь; *impf* **привя́зывать**) *сов перех*: ~ **что-н/кого́-н к** +*dat* to tie sth/sb to; **~ся** (*impf* **привя́зываться**) *сов возв*: **~ся к** +*dat* (*к сиденью*) to fasten o.s. to; (*полюбить*) to become attached to

пригласи́тельный *прил*: ~ **биле́т** invitation

пригла|си́ть (-шу́, -си́шь; *impf* **приглаша́ть**) *сов перех* to invite

приглаше́ни|е (-я) *ср* invitation

пригово́р (-а) (*ЮР*) sentence; (*перен*) condemnation; **выноси́ть** (**вы́нести** *pf*) ~ to pass sentence

пригово́р|ить (-ю́, -и́шь; *impf* **пригова́ривать**) *сов перех*: ~ **кого́-н к** +*dat* to sentence sb to

приго|ди́ться (-жу́сь, -ди́шься) *сов возв*: ~ +*dat* to be useful to

приго́дный *прил* suitable

пригор|е́ть (*3sg* -и́т; *impf* **пригора́ть**) *сов* to burn

при́город (-а) *м* suburb

при́городный *прил* suburban; (*поезд*) commuter

пригото́в|ить (-лю, -ишь) *сов от* **гото́вить ♦** (*impf* **приготовля́ть**) *перех* to prepare; (*посте́ль*) to make; **~ся** *сов от* **гото́виться ♦** *возв*: **~ся** (**к** +*dat*) (*к путеше́ствию*) to get ready (for); (*к уро́ку*) to prepare (o.s.) (for)

приготовле́ни|е (-я) *ср* preparation

пригро|зи́ть (-жу́, -зи́шь) *сов от* **грози́ть**

прида|ва́ть (-ю́, -ёшь) *несов от* **прида́ть**

прида́т|ок (-ка) *м* appendage

прида́ть (*как* **дать**; *см.* Table 16; *impf* **придава́ть**) *сов*: ~ **чего́-н кому́-н** (*уверенности в себе*) (*BRIT*) *или* instill (*US*) sth in sb **♦** *перех*: ~ **что-н чему́-н** (*вид, форму*) to give sth to sth; (*важность*) to attach sth to sth

прида́ч|а (-и) *ж*: **в ~у** in addition

придви́н|уть (-у; *impf* **придвига́ть**) *сов перех*: ~ **к** +*dat*) to move over *или* up (to)

приде́л|ать (-ю; *impf* **приде́лывать**) *сов перех*: ~ **что-н к** +*dat* to attach sth to

прид|ержа́ть (-ержу́, -е́ржишь; *impf* **приде́рживать**) *сов перех* (*дверь*) to hold (steady); (*лошадь*) to restrain

приде́рживаться (-юсь) *несов*

возв: ~ +*gen (взглядов)* to hold

придира́ться (-юсь) *несов см* **придра́ться**

приди́рчивый *прил (человек)* fussy; *(замечание, взгляд)* critical

придра́ться (-ерусь, -ерёшься) *сов возв:* ~ **к** +*dat* to find fault with

приду́ *etc сов см* **прийти́**

приду́ма|ть (-ю) *impf* **приду́мывать** *сов перех (отговорку, причину)* to think of *или* up; *(новый прибор и т.п.)* to devise; *(песню, стихотворение)* to make up

прие́ду *etc сов см* **прие́хать**

прие́зд (-а) *м* arrival

приезжа́|ть (-ю) *несов от* **прие́хать**

приезж|ий (-его) *м* visitor ♦ *прил* visiting

прие́м (-а) *м* reception; *(у врача)* surgery (BRIT), office (US); *(СПОРТ)* technique; *(наказания, воздействия)* means; **в два/три ~а** in two/three attempts; **запи́сываться (записа́ться pf) на ~ к** +*dat* to make an appointment with

прие́мн|ая (-ой) *ж (также:* ~ **ко́мната)** reception

прие́мник (-а) *м* receiver; *(радио)* radio

прие́мный *прил (часы)* reception; *(день)* visiting; *(экзамены)* entrance; *(комиссия)* selection; *(родители, дети)* adoptive

прие́хать (как е́хать; см Table 19, *impf* **приезжа́ть)** *сов* to arrive *или* come *(by transport)*

прижа́|ть (-му, -мёшь) *сов перех:* **что-н/кого́-н к** +*dat* to press sth *или* against; ~**ся** *(impf*

прижима́ться) *сов возв:* ~**ся к** +*dat* to press o.s. against; *(к груди)* to snuggle up to

приз (-а; *nom pl* **-ы́)** *м* prize

призва́ни|е (-я) *ср (к науке и т.п.)* vocation

приз|ва́ть (-ову́, -ове́шь; *pt* **-ва́л, -вала́)** *impf* **призыва́ть** *сов перех (к борьбе, к защите)* to call; **призыва́ть (~ pf) к ми́ру** to call for peace; **призыва́ть (~ pf) кого́-н к поря́дку** to call sb to order; **призыва́ть (~ pf) в а́рмию** to call up (to join the army)

приземл|и́ть (-ю́, -и́шь, *impf* **приземля́ть)** *сов перех* to land; ~**ся** *(impf* **приземля́ться)** *сов возв* to land

призёр (-а) *м* prizewinner

при́зм|а (-ы) *ж* prism

признава́ть(ся) (-ю́(сь), -ёшь(ся)) *несов от* **призна́ть(ся)**

при́знак (-а) *м (кризиса, успеха)* sign; *(отравления)* symptom

призна́ни|е (-я) *ср* recognition; *(согласие)* acknowledgement; *(в любви)* declaration; *(в преступлении)* confession

при́знанный *прил* recognized

призна́тельност|ь (-и) *ж* gratitude

призна́тельный *прил* grateful

призна́|ть (-ю; *impf* **признава́ть)** *сов перех* to recognize; *(счесть):* ~ **что-н/кого́-н** *+instr* to recognize sth/sb as; ~**ся** *(impf* **признава́ться)** *сов возв:* ~**ся кому́-н в чём-н** to confess sth to sb; **признава́ться (~ся pf) кому́-н в любви́** to make a declaration of love to sb

при́зрак (-а) *м* ghost

призы́в (-а) *м* call; *(в а́рмию)*

conscription, draft (US); (лозунг) slogan

призыва́|ть (-ю) несов от **призва́ть**

призывни́к (-а́) м conscript

прийти́ (как **идти́**; см. Table 18; impf **приходи́ть**) сов (идя, достичь) to come (on foot); (телеграмма, письмо) to arrive; (весна, час свободы) to come; (достигнуть): ~ **к** +dat (к власти, к демократии) to achieve; (к выводу) to come to; **приходи́ть** (~ pf) **в у́жас/недоуме́ние** to be horrified/bewildered; **приходи́ть** (~ pf) **в восто́рг** to go into raptures; **приходи́ть** (~ pf) **кому́-н в го́лову** или **на ум** to occur to sb; **приходи́ть** (~ pf) **в себя́** (после обморока) to come to или round; (успокоиться) to come to one's senses; **~сь** (impf **приходи́ться**) сов возв: **~сь** (impf +acc to fall on; **(нам) придётся согласи́ться** we'll have to agree

прика́з (-а) м order

приказа́ни|е (-я) ср = **прика́з**

прик|аза́ть (-ажу́, -а́жешь; impf **прика́зывать**) сов: **~ кому́-н** +infin to order sb to do

прика́лыва|ть (-ю) несов от **приколо́ть**

прика́сы|ться (-юсь) несов от **прикосну́ться**

прикла́д (-а) м (ружья) butt

прикладно́й прил applied

прикла́дыва|ть (-ю) несов от **приложи́ть**

прикле́|ить (-ю, -ишь) impf **прикле́ивать**) сов перех to glue, stick; **~ся** (impf **прикле́иваться**) сов возв to stick

приключе́ни|е (-я) ср adventure

прик|оло́ть (-олю́, -о́лешь; impf

прика́лывать) сов перех to fasten

прикосн|у́ться (-у́сь, -ёшься; impf **прикаса́ться**) сов возв: **~ +dat** to touch lightly

прикреп|и́ть (-лю́, -и́шь; impf **прикрепля́ть**) сов перех: **~ что-н/кого́-н к** +dat to attach sth/sb to

прикры́ти|е (-я) ср (махина́ций) cover-up; (ВОЕН) cover; **под ~м** +gen under the guise of

прикр|ы́ть (-о́ю, -о́ешь; impf **прикрыва́ть**) сов перех to cover; (закрыть) to close (over)

прик|ури́ть (-урю́, -у́ришь; impf **прику́ривать**) сов to get a light (from a lit cigarette)

прила́в|ок (-ка) м (в магазине) counter; (на рынке) stall

прилага́тельн|ое (-ого) ср (ЛИНГ: также: **и́мя ~**) adjective

прилага́|ть (-ю) несов от **приложи́ть**

прилега́|ть (3sg -ет) несов: **~ к** чему́-н (одежда) to fit sth tightly

приле́жный прил diligent

приле|те́ть (-чу́, -ти́шь; impf **прилета́ть**) сов to arrive (by air), fly in

прил|е́чь (-я́гу, -я́жешь etc, -я́гут; pt -ёг, -егла́) сов to lie down for a while

прили́в (-а) м (в море) tide

прилип|нуть (-ну; pt -, -ла; impf **прилипа́ть** или **ли́пнуть**) сов: **~ к** +dat to stick to

прили́чный прил (человек) decent; (сумма, результат) fair, decent

приложе́ни|е (-я) ср (знаний, энергии) application; (к журна́лу) supplement; (к документу) addendum

прил|ожи́ть (-ожу́, -о́жишь;

impf **прилага́ть** *сов перех*
(*присоедини́ть*) to attach; (*си́лу,
зна́ния*) to apply; **прикла́дывать**
(~ *pf*) **что-н к** +*dat* (*ру́ку: ко лбу*)
to put sth to; **ума́ не ~ожу́** (*разг*)
I don't have a clue

примене́ни|**е** (-**я**) *ср* (*ору́жия,
маши́н*) use; (*лека́рств*)
application; (*мер, ме́тода*)
adoption

прим|**ени́ть** (-**еню́, -е́нишь**; *impf*
применя́ть) *сов перех* (*ме́ры*)
to implement; (*си́лу*) to use,
apply; **применя́ть что-н**
(**к** +*dat*) (*ме́тод, тео́рию*) to
apply sth to

применя́|**ться** (*3sg* -**ется**) *несов*
(*испо́льзоваться*) to be used

приме́р (-**а**) *м* example

приме́р|**ка** (-**ки**; *gen pl* -**ок**) *ж*
trying on

приме́рно *нареч* in an exemplary
fashion; (*о́коло*) approximately

приме́рный *прил* (*образцо́вый*)
exemplary; (*ци́фры*) approximate

при́месь (-**и**) *ж* dash

приме́т|**а** (-**ы**) *ж* (*при́знак*) sign;
(*суеве́рная*) omen

примета́|**ть** (-**ю**; *impf*
примётывать) *сов перех* to
stitch on

примеча́ни|**е** (-**я**) *ср* note

примире́ни|**е** (-**я**) *ср*
reconciliation

примити́вный *прил* primitive

примо́рский *прил* seaside

принадлеж|**а́ть** (-**у́, -и́шь**)
несов: ~ +*dat* to belong to;
(*заслу́га*) to go to

принадле́жност|**ь** (-**и**) *ж*
characteristic; (*обы́чно мн:
компле́кт*) tackle *ед*;
(: *пи́сьменные*) accessories *мн*

прин|**ести́** (-**есу́, -есёшь**; *pt* -**ёс,
-есла́**; *impf* **приноси́ть**) *сов*

перех to bring; (*извине́ния,
благода́рность*) to express;
(*прися́гу*) to take; **приноси́ть** (~
pf) **по́льзу** +*dat* to be of use to;
приноси́ть (~ *pf*) **вред** +*dat* to
harm

принима́|**ть(ся)** (-**ю(сь)**) *несов
от* **приня́ть(ся)**

прин|**оси́ть** (-**ошу́, -о́сишь**)
несов от **принести́**

при́нтер (-**а**) *м* (*КОМП*) printer

прину|**ди́тельный** *прил* forced

прину|**ди́ть** (-**жу, -дишь**; *impf*
принужда́ть) *сов перех*:
кого́-н/что-н к чему́-н +*infin* to
force sb/sth into sth/to do

принц (-**а**) *м* prince

принце́сс|**а** (-**ы**) *ж* princess

при́нцип (-**а**) *м* principle

принципиа́льный *прил*
(*челове́к, поли́тика*)
uncompromising; (*согла́сие*) in
principle

при́нятый *прил* accepted

при|**ня́ть** (-**му́, -мешь**; *pt* -**нял,
-няла́**; *impf* **принима́ть**) *сов
перех* to take; (*пода́рок,
усло́вия*) to accept; (*пост*) to take
up; (*госте́й, телегра́мму*) to
receive; (*зако́н, резолю́цию*) to
pass; (*отноше́ние, вид*) to take
on; (*христиа́нство итп*) to adopt;
принима́ть (~ *pf*) **на/в** +*acc* (*в
университе́т, на рабо́ту*) to
accept for; **принима́ть** (~ *pf*)
что-н/кого́-н за +*acc* to mistake
sth/sb for; (*счесть*) to take sth/sb
as; (~**ся**) (*принима́ться*) *сов
возв*: ~**ся** +*infin* (*приступи́ть*) to
get down to doing; **принима́ться**
(~**ся** *pf*) **за** +*acc* (*приступи́ть*) to
get down to

приоб|**рести́** (-**рету́, -ретёшь**; *pt*
-**ёл, -ела́**; *impf* **приобрета́ть**)
сов перех to acquire, obtain;

приобрете́ние **приспособле́ние**

(друзе́й, враго́в) to make
приобрете́ни|е (-я) ср
acquisition; (КОММ) procurement
приорите́т (-а) м priority
**приостан|ови́ть (-овлю́,
-о́вишь;** impf
приостана́вливать) сов перех
to suspend
припо́лз|ок (-ка) м (МЕД) attack
припа́с|ы (-ов) мн supplies мн;
(ВОЕН) ammunition ед
припе́в (-а) м (песни) chorus,
refrain
прип|иса́ть (-ишу́, -и́шешь; impf
припи́сывать) сов перех to add;
приписа́ть (~ +dat) что-н кому́-н
to attribute sth to sb
припол|зти́ (-у́, -ёшь; impf **-а́ть)**
сов перех to crawl in
припо́мн|ить (-ю, -ишь; impf
припомина́ть) сов перех to
remember
припра́в|а (-ы) ж seasoning
приравня́|ть (-ю; impf
прира́внивать) сов перех: ~
кого́-н/что-н к +dat to equate sb/
sth with
приро́д|а (-ы) ж nature; (места́
вне го́рода) countryside
приро́дный прил natural
приро́ст (-а) м (населе́ния)
growth; (дохо́дов, урожа́я)
increase
прируч|и́ть (-у́, -и́шь; impf
прируча́ть) сов перех to tame
приса́жива|ться (-юсь) несов от
присе́сть
присво́|ить (-ю, -ишь; impf
присва́ивать) сов перех
(чужо́е) to appropriate; (дать): ~
что-н кому́-н (зва́ние) to confer
sth on sb
приседа́ни|е (-я) ср squatting
(physical exercise)
прис|е́сть (-я́ду, -я́дешь; impf

приседа́ть) сов to squat; (impf
приса́живаться; на стул) to sit
down (for a short while)
приск|ака́ть (-ачу́, -а́чешь; impf
приска́кивать) сов to gallop или
come galloping up
при|сла́ть (-шлю́, -шлёшь; impf
присыла́ть) сов перех to send
прислон|и́ть (-ю́, -и́шь; impf
прислоня́ть) сов перех: ~ что-н
к +dat to lean sth against; **~ся** (impf
прислоня́ться) сов возв: ~ся к
+ dat to lean against
прислу́жива|ть (-ю) несов: ~
+dat (официа́нту) to wait on
прислу́ша|ться (-юсь; impf
прислу́шиваться) сов возв: ~
+dat (к зву́ку) to listen to
присмо́тр (-а) м care
**присм|отре́ть (-отрю́,
-о́тришь;** impf **присма́тривать)**
сов: ~ за +instr to look after;
(найти́) to spot
присни́ться (3sg -и́тся) сов от
сни́ться
присоедине́ни|е (-я) ср
attachment; (провода́) connection;
(террито́рии) annexation
присоедин|и́ть (-ю́, -и́шь; impf
присоединя́ть) сов перех: ~
что-н к +dat to attach sth to;
(про́вод) to connect sth to;
(террито́рию) to annex sth to; **~ся**
(impf **присоединя́ться)** сов возв:
~ся к +dat to join (к мне́нию) to
support
приспособ|ить (-лю, -ишь; impf
приспоса́бливать) сов перех to
adapt; **~ся** (impf
приспоса́бливаться) сов возв
(де́лать что-н) to learn how; (к
усло́виям) to adapt (o.s.)
приспособле́ни|е (-я) ср (к
усло́виям итп) adaptation;
(механи́зм итп) appliance

приставá|ть (-ю, -ёшь) *несов от* **пристáть**

пристáв|ить (-лю, -ишь) *impf* **приставлять** *сов перех*: ~ **что-н к** +*dat* to put sth against

пристáв|ка (-ки; *gen pl* -ок) *ж* (*линг*) prefix; (*тех*) attachment

приставля́|ть (-ю) *несов от* **пристáвить**

при́стальный *прил* (взгляд, внимание) fixed; (интерес, наблюдение) intent

при́стан|ь (-и) *ж* pier

пристá|ть (-ну, -нешь; *impf* **приставáть**) *сов*: ~ **к** +*dat* (прилипнуть) to stick to; (присоединиться) to join; (*разг*: с вопросами) to pester; (причалить) to moor

пристегн|у́ть (-у́, -ёшь; *impf* **пристёгивать**) *сов перех* to fasten; ~**ся** (*impf* **пристёгиваться**) *сов возв* (в самолёте итп) to fasten one's seat belt

пристрáива|ть (-ю) *несов от* **пристрóить**

пристрел|и́ть (-ю́, -ишь; *impf* **пристрéливать**) *сов перех* (животное) to put down

пристрó|ить (-ю, -ишь; *impf* **пристрáивать**) *сов перех* (комнату) to build on

пристрóй|ка (-ки; *gen pl* -ек) *ж* extension

при́ступ (-а) *м* (атака, сердечный) attack; (смеха, гнева, кашля) fit

приступ|и́ть (-лю́, -у́пишь; *impf* **приступáть**) *сов*: ~ **к** +*dat* (начать) to commence

присуд|и́ть (-жу́, -у́дишь; *impf* **присуждáть**) *сов перех*: ~ **что-н кому-н** to award sth to sb; (учёную степень) to confer sth

on sb

присýтстви|е (-я) *ср* presence

присýтств|овать (-ую) *несов* to be present

присýтствующ|ие (-их) *мн* those present *мн*

присылá|ть (-ю) *несов от* **прислáть**

прися́г|а (-и) *ж* oath

прися́жн|ый (-ого) *м* (*ЮР*: *также*: ~ **заседáтель**) juror; **суд ~ых** jury

притá|щить (-щу́, -щишь; *impf* **притáскивать**) *сов перех* to drag

притвор|и́ться (-ю́сь, -и́шься; *impf* **притворя́ться**) *сов возв*: ~ +*instr* to pretend to be

прити́х|нуть (-ну, -нешь; *pt* -, -ла; *impf* **притихáть**) *сов* to grow quiet

прито́к (-а) *м* (река) tributary; ~ +*gen* (энергии, средств) supply of; (населения) influx of

притóм *союз* and what's more

притóн (-а) *м* den

притóрный *прил* sickly sweet

притуп|и́ться (*3sg* -у́пится; *impf* **притупля́ться**) *сов возв* (нож) to go blunt; (*перен*: внимание итп) to diminish; (: чувства) to fade; (: слух) to fail

притяже́ни|е (-я) *ср* gravitation

притяза́ни|е (-я) *ср*: ~ **на** +*acc* claim to

приурóч|ить (-у, -ишь) *сов перех*: ~ **что-н к** +*dat* to time sth to coincide with

приуч|и́ть (-у́, -у́чишь; *impf* **приучáть**) *сов перех*: ~ **кого-н к** +*dat*/+*infin* to train sb to/to do; ~**ся** (*impf* **приучáться**) *сов возв*: ~**ся к** +*dat*/+*infin* to train for/to do

прихват|и́ть (-ачу́, -áтишь) *сов*

перех (разг: взять) to take

прихо́д (-а) *м* arrival; *(комм)* receipts *мн*; *(рел)* parish; **~ и расхо́д** *(комм)* credit and debit

прих|оди́ть (-ожу́, -о́дишь) *несов см* **прийти́**; **~ся** *см* **прийти́сь** ♦ *возв* **~ся** кому́-н ро́дственником to be sb's relative

прихо́д|овать (-ую; *pf* **о~**) *несов перех (комм: су́мму)* to enter *(in receipt book)*

приходя́щ|ий *прил* nonresident; **~ая ня́ня** babysitter

прихожа́н|ин (-ина; *nom pl* -е) *м (рел)* parishioner

прихож|ая (-ей) *ж* entrance hall

прихожу́(сь) *несов см* **приходи́ть(ся)**

при́хот|ь (-и) *ж* whim

прице́л (-а) *м (ружья́, пу́шки)* sight

прице́л|иться (-юсь, -ишься; *impf* **прице́ливаться**) *сов возв* to take aim

прице́п (-а) *м* trailer

прицеп|и́ть (-лю́, -е́пишь; *impf* **прицепля́ть**) *сов перех (ваго́н)* to couple

прича́л (-а) *м* mooring; *(пассажи́рский)* quay; *(грузово́й, ремо́нтный)* dock

прича́л|ить (-ю, -ишь; *impf* **прича́ливать**) *сов (не)перех* to moor

прича́сти|е (-я) *ср (линг)* participle; *(рел)* communion

прича|сти́ть (-щу́, -сти́шь; *impf* **причаща́ть**) *сов перех (рел)* to give communion to; **~ся** *(impf* **причаща́ться**) *сов возв (рел)* to receive communion

прича́стный *прил (свя́занный)*: **~ к** +*dat* connected with

причаща́|ть(ся) (-ю(сь)) *несов от* **причасти́ть(ся)**

причём *союз* moreover

прич|еса́ть (-ешу́, -е́шешь; *impf* **причёсывать**) *сов перех (расчёской)* to comb; *(щёткой)* to brush; **причёсывать** ~ *pf* кого́-н to comb/brush sb's hair; **~ся** *(см перех)* to comb one's hair; to brush one's hair

причёс|ка (-ки; *gen pl* -ок) *ж* hairstyle

причи́н|а (-ы) *ж (то, что вызыва́ет)* cause; *(обоснова́ние)* reason; **по ~е** +*gen* on account of

причин|и́ть (-ю́, -и́шь; *impf* **причиня́ть**) *сов перех* to cause

причу́д|а (-ы) *ж* whim

прише́л(ся) *сов см* **прийти́(сь)**

приш|и́ть (-ью́, -ьёшь; *imper* **-е́й(те)**; *impf* **пришива́ть**) *сов перех* to sew on

пришла́ *etc сов см* **прийти́**

прищем|и́ть (-лю́, -и́шь; *impf* **прищемля́ть**) *сов перех* to catch

прищу́р|ить (-ю, -ишь; *impf* **прищу́ривать**) *сов перех (глаза́)* to screw up; **~ся** *(impf* **прищу́риваться**) *сов возв* to screw up one's eyes

прию́т (-а) *м* shelter; *(для сиро́т)* orphanage

прию|ти́ть (-чу́, -ти́шь) *сов перех* to shelter; **~ся** *сов возв* to take shelter

прия́тел|ь (-я) *м* friend

прия́тно *нареч (удивлён)* pleasantly ♦ *как сказ* it's nice *или* pleasant; **мне ~ э́то слы́шать** I'm glad to hear that; **о́чень ~ (при знако́мстве)** pleased to meet you

прия́тный *прил* pleasant

про *предл*: ~ +*acc* about

про́б|а (-ы) *ж (испыта́ние)* test; *(образе́ц)* sample; *(зо́лота)*

standard (of quality); (клеймо)
hallmark

пробе́г (-а) м (СПОРТ) race;
(: лыжный) run; (АВТ) mileage

пробежа́ть (как бежа́ть; см.
Table 20; impf **пробега́ть**) сов
перех (текст) to skim; (5
километров) to cover ♦ неперех
(время) to pass; (миновать
бегом): ~ **ми́мо** +gen to run past;
(появиться и исчезнуть): ~ **по**
+dat (шум, дрожь) to run through;
~ся сов возв to run

пробе́л (-а) м (также перен) gap

пробива́ть(ся) (-ю(сь) несов
от **проби́ть(ся)**

пробира́ться (-юсь несов от
пробра́ться

пробирка (-ки; gen pl -ок) ж
test-tube

проби́ть (-ью, -ьёшь сов от
бить ♦ (impf **пробива́ть**) перех
(дыру) to knock; (крышу, стену)
to make a hole in; **~ся** (impf
пробива́ться) сов возв
(прорваться) to fight one's way
through; (растения) to push
through или up

про́бка (-ки; gen pl -ок) ж cork;
(перен: на дороге) jam; (ЭЛЕК)
fuse (BRIT), fuze (US)

пробле́ма (-ы)** ж problem

проблемати́чный прил
problematic(al)

про́бный прил trial

про́бовать (-ую; pf по~) несов
перех (пирог, вино) to taste;
(пытаться) ♦ +infin to try to do

пробо́ина (-ы)** ж hole

пробо́р (-а) м parting (of hair)

**пробра́ться (-ерусь,
-ерёшься; impf **пробира́ться**)
сов возв (с трудом пройти) to
fight one's way through; (тихо
пройти) to steal past или through

пробужде́ние (-я)** ср (ото сна)
waking up; (сознания, чувств)
awakening

пробы́ть (как быть; см. Table 21)
сов (прожить) to stay, remain

прова́л (-а) м (в почве, в стене)
hole; (перен: неудача) flop;
(: памяти) failure

**провали́ть (-алю, -а́лишь; impf
прова́ливать) сов перех
(крышу, пол) to cause to collapse;
(разг: перен: дело, затею) to
botch up; (: студента) to fail; **~ся**
(impf **прова́ливаться**) сов возв
(человек) to fall; (крыша) to
collapse; (разг: перен: студент,
попытка) to fail; **как сквозь
зе́млю ~али́лся** he disappeared
into thin air

проведу́ etc сов см. **провести́**

**провезти́ (-езу, -езёшь; pt -ёз,
-езла́; impf **провози́ть**) сов
перех (незаконно) to smuggle;
(везя, доставить): ~ **по** +dat/
ми́мо +gen/**че́рез** +acc to take
along/past/across

**прове́рить (-ю, -ишь; impf
проверя́ть) сов перех to check;
(знание, двигатель) to test; **~ся**
(impf **проверя́ться**) сов возв (у
врача) to get a check-up

прове́рка (-ки; gen pl -ок) ж (см
глаг) check-up; test

**провести́ (-еду́, -едёшь; pt -ёл,
-ела́; impf **проводи́ть**) сов перех
(черту, границу) to draw;
(дорогу) to build; (план,
реформу) to implement; (урок,
репетицию) to hold; (операцию)
to carry out; (детство, день) to
spend; **проводи́ть (~ pf) ми́мо**
+gen/**че́рез** +acc (людей) to take
past/across

**прове́трить (-ю, -ишь; impf
прове́тривать) сов перех to air;

~ся (impf прове́триваться) сов
возв (комната, одежда) to have
an airing

провини́ться (-ю́сь, -и́шься)
сов возв: ~ (в +prp) to be guilty
(of)

провинциа́льный прил
provincial

прови́нция (-и) ж province

про́вод (-а; nom pl -а́) м cable

провод|и́ть (-ожу́, -о́дишь)
несов от **провести́ ♦** (impf
провожа́ть) сов перех to see off;
провожа́ть (~ pf) глаза́ми/
взгля́дом кого́-н to follow sb with
one's eyes/gaze

прово́д|ка (-ки; gen pl -ок) ж
(ЭЛЕК) wiring

проводни́к (-а́) м (в гора́х)
guide; (в поезде) steward (BRIT),
porter (US)

про́вод|ы (-ов) мн (прощание)
send-off ед

провожа́|ть (-ю) несов от
проводи́ть

провожу́ (не)сов см. проводи́ть

прово́з (-а) м (багажа) transport;
(незаконный) smuggling

провозгла|си́ть (-шу́, -си́шь;
impf **провозглаша́ть**) сов перех
to proclaim

провоз|и́ть (-ожу́, -о́зишь)
несов от провезти́

провокацио́нный прил
provocative

провока́ци|я (-и) ж provocation

про́волок|а (-и) ж wire

прово́рный прил agile

провоци́р|овать (-ую; pf с~)
несов перех to provoke

прогиба́|ть(ся) (-ю(сь)) несов от
прогну́ть(ся)

прогл|оти́ть (-очу́, -о́тишь; impf
прогла́тывать или глота́ть)
сов перех (также перен) to

swallow

прог|на́ть (-оню́, -о́нишь; pt
-на́л, -нала́, impf **прогоня́ть**)
сов перех (заставить уйти) to
turn out

прогно́з (-а) м forecast

прогн|у́ть (-у́, -ёшь) impf
прогиба́ть сов перех: ~ что-н
to cause sth to sag; ~ся (impf
прогиба́ться) сов возв to sag

прогоня́|ть (-ю) несов от
прогна́ть

програ́мм|а (-ы) ж programme
(BRIT), program (US); (полит)
manifesto; (также: веща́тельная
~) channel; (ПРОСВЕЩ) curriculum;
(КОМП) program

программи́р|овать (-ую; pf за~)
несов перех (КОМП) to program

программи́ст (-а) м (КОМП)
programmer

програ́ммный прил
programmed (BRIT), programed
(US); (экзамен, зачёт) set; ~ое
обеспе́чение (КОМП) software

прогре́сс (-а) м progress

прогресси́вный прил progressive

прогу́л (-а) м (на работе)
absence; (в школе) truancy

прогу́лива|ть (-ю) несов от
прогуля́ть

прогу́л|ка (-ки; gen pl -ок) ж
walk; (недалёкая поездка) trip

прогу́льщик (-а) м (об ученике)
truant

прогуля́|ть (-ю; impf
прогу́ливать) сов перех
(работу) to be absent on;
(уроки) to miss; (гулять) to walk

прода|ва́ть (-ю́) несов от
прода́ть

продаве́ц (-ца́) м seller; (в
магазине) (shop-)assistant

продавщи́ц|а (-ы) ж см.
продаве́ц

прода́ж|а (-и) ж (дома, товара) sale; (торговля) trade

прода́ть (как дать; см. Table 16; impf **продава́ть**) сов перех to sell; (перен: друга) to betray

продвига́|ть(ся) (-ю(сь)) несов от **продви́нуть(ся)**

продвиже́ни|е (-я) ср (войск) advance; (по службе) promotion

продви́н|уть (-у; impf **продвига́ть)** сов перех to move; (перен: работника) to promote; **~ся** (impf **продвига́ться)** сов возв to move; (перен: работник) to be promoted; (перен: работа) to progress

продева́|ть (-ю) несов от **проде́ть**

проде́ла|ть (-ю; impf **проде́лывать)** сов перех (отверстие) to make; (работу) to do

проде́|ть (-ну, -нешь; impf **продева́ть)** сов перех to thread

продлева́|ть (-ю) несов от **продли́ть**

продле́ни|е (-я) ср (см глаг) extension; prolongation

продл|и́ть (-ю́, -и́шь; impf **продлева́ть)** сов перех to extend; (жизнь) to prolong

продл|и́ться (3sg -и́тся) сов от **дли́ться**

продово́льственный прил food; **~ магази́н** grocer's (shop) (BRIT), grocery (US)

продово́льстви|е (-я) ср provisions мн

продолгова́тый прил elongated

продолжа́|ть (-ю; pf **продо́лжить)** несов перех to continue; **~** (**продо́лжить** pf) +infin to continue или carry on doing; **~ся** (pf **продо́лжиться)** несов возв to continue, carry on

продолже́ни|е (-я) ср (борьбы, лекции) continuation; (романа) sequel; **в ~** +gen for the duration of

продолжи́тельность (-и) ж duration; (сре́дняя) **~ жи́зни** (average) life expectancy

продолжи́тельный прил (болезнь, разговор) prolonged

продо́лж|ить(ся) (-у(сь), -ишь(ся)) сов от **продолжа́ть(ся)**

продо́льный прил longitudinal

проду́кт (-а) м product; см. также **проду́кты**

продукти́вность (-и) ж productivity

продукти́вный прил productive

проду́ктовый прил food

проду́кт|ы (-ов) мн (также: **~ пита́ния)** foodstuffs мн

проду́кци|я (-и) ж produce

проду́манный прил well thought-out

проду́ма|ть (-ю, impf **проду́мывать)** сов перех (действия) to think out

прое́зд (-а) м (в транспорте) journey; (место) passage

проездно́й прил (документ) travel; **~ биле́т** travel card

прое́здом нареч en route

проезжа́|ть (-ю) несов от **прое́хать**

прое́зж|ий прил (люди) passing through: **~ая часть (у́лицы)** road

прое́кт (-а) м project; (дома) design; (закона, договора) draft

проекти́р|овать (-ую; pf **с~)** несов перех (дом) to design; (дороги) to plan; (pf **за~;** наметить) to plan

прое́ктор (-а) м (ОПТИКА) projector

проём (-а) м (дверно́й) aperture

прое́хать (как е́хать; см. Table

19) сов перех (миновать) to pass; (пропустить) to miss ♦ (impf **проезжа́ть**) неперех: ~ **ми́мо** +gen/**по** +dat/**че́рез** +acc итп to drive past/along/across итп; ~**ся** сов возв (на маши́не) to go for a drive

прожёктор (-а) м floodlight

прож|е́чь (-гу́, -жёшь итп, -гу́т; pt -ёг, -гла́; impf **прожига́ть**) сов перех to burn a hole in

прожива́ни|е (-я) ср stay

прожива́|ть (-ю) несов от **прожи́ть** ♦ неперех to live

прожига́|ть (-ю) несов от **проже́чь**

прожи́|ть (-ву́, -вёшь) сов (пробы́ть живы́м) to live; (жить) to spend

про́з|а (-ы) ж prose

про́звищ|е (-а) ср nickname

прозева́|ть (-ю) сов от **зева́ть**

прозра́чный прил transparent; (ткань) see-through

проигра́|ть (-ю; impf **прои́грывать**) сов перех to lose; (игра́ть) to play

прои́грыватель (-я) м record player

про́игрыш (-а) м loss

произведе́ни|е (-я) ср work

произвес|ти́ (-еду́, -едёшь; pt -ёл, -ела́; impf **производи́ть**) сов перех (опера́цию) to carry out; (впечатле́ние, сумато́ху) to create

производи́тель (-я) м producer

производи́тельнос|ть (-и) ж productivity

производи́тельный прил (продукти́вный) productive

произво|ди́ть (-жу́, -о́дишь) несов от **произвести́** ♦ перех (изготовля́ть) to produce, manufacture

произво́дственн|ый прил (проце́сс, план) production; ~**ое объедине́ние** large industrial company; см. **ПО**

произво́дств|о (-а) ср (това́ров) production, manufacture; (о́трасль) industry; (заво́д, фа́брика) factory; **промы́шленное** ~ industrial output; (о́трасль) ~ industry

произво́л (-а) м despotism

произво́льный прил (свобо́дный) free; (спорт) freestyle; (вы́вод) arbitrary

произн|ести́ (-есу́, -есёшь; pt -ёс, -есла́; impf **произноси́ть**) сов перех (сло́во) to pronounce; (речь) to make

произн|оси́ть (-ошу́, -о́сишь) несов от **произнести́**

произноше́ни|е (-я) ср pronunciation

произойти́ (как **идти́**; см. Table 18; impf **происходи́ть**) сов to occur

происх|оди́ть (-ожу́, -о́дишь) несов от **произойти́** ♦ неперех: ~ **из/из** +gen to come from

происхожде́ни|е (-я) ср origin

происше́стви|е (-я) ср event; **доро́жное** ~ road accident

пройти́ (как **идти́**; см. Table 18; impf **проходи́ть**) сов перех to pass; (расстоя́ние) to cover; (слух) to spread; (доро́га, кана́л итп) to stretch; (дождь, снег) to fall; (опера́ция, перегово́ры итп) to go ♦ перех (пра́ктику, слу́жбу итп) to complete; (изучи́ть: те́му итп) to do; (про́йти (~ pf) в +acc (в институ́т итп) to get into; ~**сь** (impf **проха́живаться**) сов возв (по ко́мнате) to pace; (по па́рку) to stroll

прока́лыва|ть (-ю) несов от

проколо́ть

прока́т (-а) *м (телевизора)* hire; *(также: кино~)* film distribution; **брать (взять** *pf***) что-н на ~** to hire sth

прок|ати́ть (-ачу́, -а́тишь) *сов перех*: ~ **кого́-н** *(на машине итп)* to take sb for a ride; **~ся** *возв (на машине)* to go for a ride

проки́с|нуть (3sg **-нет**, *pt* -, **-ла**) *сов от* **ки́снуть**

прокла́д|ка (-ки; *gen pl* **-ок**) *ж (действие: труб)* laying out; *(: провода)* laying; *(защитная)* padding

прокла́дыва|ть (-ю) *несов от* **проложи́ть**

прокл|я́сть (-яну́, -яне́шь; *pt* **-я́л, -яла́, -я́ло,** *impf* **проклина́ть**) *сов перех* to curse

прокля́тый *прил* damned

проко́л (-а) *м (см глаг)* puncturing; lancing; piercing; *(отверстие: в шине)* puncture

прок|оло́ть (-олю́, -о́лешь; *impf* **прока́лывать**) *сов перех (шину)* to puncture; *(нарыв)* to lance; *(уши)* to pierce

прокра́|сться (-ду́сь, **-дёшься;** *impf* **прокра́дываться**) *сов возв*: ~ **в** +*acc*/**ми́мо** +*gen*/**че́рез** +*acc итп* to creep *(BRIT)* или sneak *(US)* in(to)/ past/through *итп*

прокрич|а́ть (-у́, **-и́шь**) *сов перех (выкрикнуть)* to shout out

прокру|ти́ть (-чу́, **-́тишь;** *impf* **прокру́чивать**) *сов перех (провернуть)* to turn; *(мясо)* to mince; *(разг: деньги)* to invest illegally

прокуро́р (-а) *м (города)* procurator; *(на суде)* counsel for the prosecution

прокла́га|ть (-ю) *несов от*

проложи́ть

прола́мыва|ть (-ю) *несов от* **проломи́ть**

прола|я́ть (-ю) *сов от* **ла́ять**

проле|жа́ть (-у́, **-и́шь**) *сов* to lie

проле́з|ть (-у, **-ешь;** *impf* **пролеза́ть**) *сов* to get through

проле|те́ть (-чу́, **-ти́шь;** *impf* **пролета́ть**) *сов* to fly; *(человек, поезд)* to fly past; *(лето, отпуск)* to fly by

проли́в (-а) *м* strait(s) *(мн)*

пролива́|ть(ся) (-ю(сь)) *несов от* **проли́ть(ся)**

проливно́й *прил*: ~ **дождь** downpour

прол|и́ть (-ью́, **-ьёшь;** *pt* **-и́л, -ила́,** *impf* **пролива́ть)** *сов перех* to spill; **~ся** *(impf* **пролива́ться)** *сов возв* to spill

прол|ожи́ть (-ожу́, **-о́жишь;** *impf* **прокла́дывать)** *сов перех* to lay

прол|оми́ть (-омлю́, **-о́мишь;** *impf* **прола́мывать)** *сов перех (лёд)* to break; *(череп)* to fracture

про́мах (-а) *м* miss; *(перен)* blunder

промахн|у́ться (-у́сь, **-ёшься;** *impf* **прома́хиваться)** *сов возв* to miss

прома́чива|ть (-ю) *несов от* **промочи́ть**

промедле́ни|е (-я) *ср* delay

промедл|ить (-ю, **-ишь)** *сов*: ~ +*instr* to delay

промежу́т|ок (-ка) *м* gap

промельк|ну́ть (-у́, **-ёшь)** *сов* to flash past; ~ *(pf)* **в** +*prp (в голове)* to flash through; *(перед глазами)* to flash past

промока́|ть (-ю) *несов от* **промокну́ть, промокну́ть**

♦ *неперех* to let water through

промока́ш|ка (-ки; *gen pl* **-ек)** *ж*

(*разг*) blotting paper

промо́кн|уть (-у; *impf* **промока́ть**) *сов* to get soaked

промокну́|ть (-у́, -ёшь; *impf* **промока́ть**) *сов перех* to blot

промолч|а́ть (-у́, -и́шь) *сов* to say nothing

пром|очи́ть (-очу́, -о́чишь; *impf* **прома́чивать**) *сов перех* to get wet

промтова́рный *прил*: ~ **магази́н** small department store

промтова́р|ы (-ов) *мн* = **промы́шленные това́ры**

промч|а́ться (-у́сь, -и́шься) *сов возв* (*поезд, жизнь*) to fly by; (*pf*) **ми́мо** +*gen*/**че́рез** +*acc* (*поезд, человек*) to fly past/through

промыва́ни|е (-я) *ср* (*желудка*) pumping; (*глаза, раны*) bathing

пром|ы́ть (-о́ю, -о́ешь; *impf* **промыва́ть**) *сов перех* (*желудок*) to pump; (*рану, глаз*) to bathe

промы́шленник (-а) *м* industrialist

промы́шленност|ь (-и) *ж* industry

промы́шленн|ый *прил* industrial; ~**ые това́ры** manufactured goods

прон|ести́ (-есу́, -есёшь; *pt* -ёс, -есла́; *impf* **проноси́ть**) *сов перех* to carry; (*секретно*) to sneak in; ~**сь** (*impf* **проноси́ться**) *сов возв* (*машина, пуля, бегун*) to shoot by; (*время*) to fly by; (*буря*) to whirl past

пронзи́тельный *прил* piercing

проник|ну́ть (-ну; *pt* -, -ла; *impf* **проника́ть**) *сов*: ~ **в** +*acc* to penetrate; (*залезть*) to break into; ~**ся** (*impf* **проника́ться**) *сов возв*: ~**ся** +*instr* to be filled with

проница́тельный *прил* (*человек, ум*) shrewd; (*взгляд*)

penetrating

прон|оси́ть(ся) (-ошу́(сь), -о́сишь(ся)) *несов от* **пронести́(сь)**

пропага́нд|а (-ы) *ж* propaganda; (*спорта*) promotion

пропаганди́р|овать (-ую) *несов перех* (*политику*) to spread propaganda about; (*знания, спорт*) to promote

пропада́|ть (-ю) *несов от* **пропа́сть**

пропа́ж|а (-и) *ж* (*денег, документов*) loss

про́паст|ь (-и) *ж* precipice

проп|а́сть (-аду́, -адёшь; *impf* **пропада́ть**) *сов* to disappear; (*деньги, письмо*) to go missing; (*аппетит, голос, слух*) to go; (*усилия, билет в театр*) to be wasted; **пропада́ть** (~ *pf*) **без вести** (*человек*) to go missing

пропе́ллер (-а) *м* (*АВИА*) propeller

проп|е́ть (-ою́, -оёшь) *сов от* **петь**

проп|иса́ть (-ишу́, -и́шешь; *impf* **пропи́сывать**) *сов перех* (*человека*) to register; (*лекарство*) to prescribe; ~**ся** *сов возв* to register

пропи́ск|а (-ки) *ж* registration

прописн|о́й *прил*: ~**а́я бу́ква** capital letter

пропи́сыва|ть (-ю) *несов от* **прописа́ть**

пропита́ни|е (-я) *ср* food
проплы́ть (-ыву́, -ывёшь; *impf* **проплыва́ть)** *сов* (человек) to swim; (: миновать) to swim past; (судно) to sail; (: миновать) to sail past
пропове́дник (-а) *м* (РЕЛ) preacher; (перен: теории) advocate
пропове́д|овать (-ую) *несов перех* (РЕЛ) to preach; (теорию) to advocate
про́поведь (-и) *ж* (РЕЛ) preaching
проползти́ (-у́, -ёшь; *pt* **-, -ла́)** *сов:* **~ по** +*dat/*в +*acc итп* (насекомое, человек) to crawl along/in(to) итп; (змея) to slither along/in(to) итп
прополоска́|ть (-ю) *сов от* **полоска́ть**
прополо́ть (-олю́, -о́лешь) *сов от* **поло́ть**
пропорциона́льный *прил* (фигура) well-proportioned; (развитие, распределение) proportional
пропо́рци|я (-и) *ж* proportion
про́пуск (-а) *м* (действие: в зал, через границу итп) admission; (в тексте, в изложении) gap; (неявка: на работу, в школу) absence; (*nom pl* **-а́**; документ) pass
пропуска́|ть (-ю) *несов от* **пропусти́ть** ♦ *перех* (свет итп) to let through; (воду, холод) to let in
пропу|сти́ть (-щу́, -у́стишь; *impf* **пропуска́ть)** *сов перех* to miss; (разрешить) to allow; **пропуска́ть (~** *pf*) **кого́-н вперёд** to let sb by
прораба́та|ть (-ю; *impf* **прораба́тывать)** *сов* to work

прор|асти́ (3sg **-астёт,** *pt* **-о́с, -осла́, -осло́;** *impf* **прораста́ть)** *сов* (семена) to germinate; (трава) to sprout
прорв|а́ть (-у́, -ёшь; *pt* **-а́л, -ала́,** *impf* **прорыва́ть)** *сов перех* (плотину) to burst; (оборону, фронт) to break through; **~ся** (*impf* **прорыва́ться)** *сов возв* (плотина, шарик) to burst; **прорыва́ться (~ся** *pf*) **в** +*acc* to burst in(to)
проре́|зать (-жу, -жешь; *impf* **проре́зывать)** *сов перех* to cut through; **~ся** *сов от* **ре́заться**
проре́ктор (-а) *м* vice-principal
проро́к (-а) *м* (РЕЛ, перен) prophet
проро́ч|ить (-у, -ишь; *pf* **на~)** *несов перех* to predict
прор|уби́ть (-ублю́, -у́бишь; *impf* **~уба́ть)** *сов перех* to make a hole in
про́руб|ь (-и) *ж* ice-hole
проры́в (-а) *м* (фронта) break-through; (плотины) bursting; (прорванное место) breach
прорыва́|ть(ся) (-ю(сь)) *несов от* **прорва́ть(ся)**
прор|ы́ть (-о́ю, -о́ешь; *impf* **прорыва́ть)** *сов перех* to dig
проса́чива|ться (3sg **-ется)** *несов от* **просочи́ться**
просверл|и́ть (-ю́, -и́шь; *impf* **просве́рливать** *и* **сверли́ть)** *сов перех* to bore, drill
просве́т (-а) *м* (в тучах) break; (перен: в кризисе) light at the end of the tunnel
просве|ти́ть (-щу́, -ети́шь; *impf* **просвеща́ть)** *сов перех* to enlighten
просвеще́ни|е (-я) *ср* (ясность) lucidity
просве́чива|ть (-ю) *несов от*

просвети́ть ♦ *неперех (солнце, луна)* to shine through; *(ткань)* to let light through

просвеща́|ть (-ю) *несов от* просвети́ть

просвеще́ни|е (-я) *ср* education

просви|сте́ть (-щу́, -сти́шь) *сов от* свисте́ть ♦ *неперех (пуля)* to whistle past

просе́|ять (-ю; *impf* ~ивать) *сов перех (муку, песок)* to sift

проси|де́ть (-жу́, -ди́шь; *impf* проси́живать) *сов (сиде́ть)* to sit; *(пробы́ть)* to stay

проси́тельный *прил* pleading

про|си́ть (-шу́, -сишь; *pf* по~) *несов перех* to ask; ~шу́ Вас! if you please!; (~ *pf* по~) *кого́-н* о чём-н/ +*infin* to ask sb for sth/to do; (~ *pf* по~) *кого́-н* за кого́-н to ask sb a favour (BRIT) или favor (US) on behalf of sb; ~ся (*pf* по~ся) *несов возв (о про́сьбе)* to ask permission

проск|ака́ть (-ачу́, -а́чешь) *сов*: ~ че́рез/сквозь +*acc (ло́шадь)* to gallop across/through

проскользн|у́ть (-у́, -ёшь; *impf* проска́льзывать) *сов (моне́та)* to slide in; *(челове́к)* to slip in; *(перен: сомне́ние)* to creep in

просла́в|ить (-лю, -ишь; *impf* прославля́ть) *сов перех (сде́лать изве́стным)* to make famous; *(impf* прославля́ть *или* сла́вить; *восхваля́ть)* to glorify; ~ся *(impf* прославля́ться) *сов возв* to become famous

просла́вленный *прил* renowned

просле|ди́ть (-жу́, -ди́шь; *impf* просле́живать) *сов перех (глаза́ми)* to follow; *(иссле́довать)* to trace ♦ *неперех*: ~ за +*instr* to follow; *(контроли́ровать)* to monitor

просмо́тр (-а) *м (фи́льма)*

viewing; *(докуме́нтов)* inspection

просм|отре́ть (-отрю́, -о́тришь; *impf* просма́тривать) *сов перех (ознако́миться: чита́я)* to look through; (: *смотря́)* to view; *(пропусти́ть)* to overlook

просн|у́ться (-у́сь, -ёшься; *impf* просыпа́ться) *сов возв* to wake up; *(перен: любо́вь, страх итп)* to be awakened

просо́ч|иться (3sg -и́тся; *impf* проса́чиваться) *сов возв (та́кже перен)* to filter through

просп|а́ть (-лю́, -и́шь; pt -а́л, -ала́, -а́ло *(спать)* to sleep; *(impf* просыпа́ть; *встать по́здно)* to oversleep, sleep in

проспе́кт (-а) *м (в го́роде)* avenue; *(изда́ние)* brochure

просро́ч|ить (-у, -ишь; *impf* просро́чивать) *сов перех (платёж)* to be late with; *(па́спорт, биле́т)* to let expire

проста́ива|ть (-ю) *несов от* простоя́ть

простира́|ться (-юсь; *pf* простере́ться) *несов возв* to extend

проститу́т|ка (-ки; gen pl -ок) *ж* prostitute

прости́|ть (прощу́, прости́шь; *impf* проща́ть) *сов перех* to forgive; проща́ть (~ *pf*) что-н кому́-н to excuse или forgive sb (for) sth; ~те, как пройти́ на ста́нцию? excuse me, how do I get to the station?; ~ся *(impf* проща́ться) *сов возв*: ~ся с +*instr* to say goodbye to

про́сто *нареч (де́лать)* easily; *(объясня́ть)* simply ♦ *част* just; всё э́то ~ недоразуме́ние all this is just a misunderstanding; ~ (так) for no particular reason

прост|о́й *прил* simple; *(оде́жда)*

plain; (*задача*) easy, simple; (*человек, манеры*) unaffected; (*обыкновенный*) ordinary ♦ (**-о́я**) *м* downtime; (*рабочих*) stoppage; **~ каранда́ш** lead pencil

прост|она́ть (**-ону́, -о́нешь**) *сов* (*не)перех* to groan

просто́р (**-а**) *м* expanse; (*свобода*) scope

просто́рный *прил* spacious

простот|а́ (**-ы́**) *ж* (*см прил*) simplicity; plainness; easiness; simplicity; unaffectedness

просто|я́ть (**-ю́, -и́шь**; *impf* **проста́ивать**) *сов* to stand; (*бездействуя*) to stand idle

простра́нств|о (**-а**) *ср* space; (*территория*) expanse

простр|ели́ть (**-елю́, -е́лишь**; *impf* **простре́ливать**) *сов перех* to shoot through

просту́д|а (**-ы**) *ж* (*МЕД*) cold

прост|уди́ть (**-ужу́, -у́дишь**; *impf* **простужа́ть**) *сов перех*: **~ кого́-н** to give sb a cold; **~ся** (*impf* **простужа́ться**) *сов возв* to catch a cold

простуженный *прил*: **ребёнок просту́жен** the child has got a cold

прост|упи́ть (*3sg* **-у́пит**; *impf* **проступа́ть**) *сов* (*пот, пятна*) to come through; (*очертания*) to appear

просту́п|ок (**-ка**) *м* misconduct

простын|я́ (**-и́**; *nom pl* **про́стыни**, *gen pl* **просты́нь**, *dat pl* **-я́м**) *ж* sheet

просу́н|уть (**-у, -ешь**; *impf* **просо́вывать**) *сов перех*: **~ в** +*acc* to push in

просчёт (**-а**) *м* (*счёт*) counting; (*ошибка*: *в подсчётах*) error; (*: в действиях*) miscalculation

просчи́т|ывать (**-аю**; *impf* **просчи́тывать**) *сов перех* (*считать*) to count; (*ошибиться*) to miscount; **~ся** (*impf* **просчи́тываться**) *сов возв* (*при счёте*) to miscount; (*в планах*) to miscalculate

просы́п|ать (**-лю, -лешь**; *impf* **просыпа́ть**) *сов перех* to spill; **~ся** (*impf* **просыпа́ться**) *сов возв* to spill

просыпа́|ть (**-ю**) *несов от* **проспа́ть, просы́пать; ~ся** *несов от* **просну́ться, проспа́ться**

про́сьб|а (**-ы**) *ж* request

прота́лкива|ть (**-ю**) *несов от* **протолкну́ть**

прота́щ|ить (**-ащу́, -а́щишь**; *impf* **прота́скивать**) *сов перех* to drag

проте́з (**-а**) *м* artificial или prosthetic limb; **зубно́й ~** denture

протека́|ть (*3sg* **-ет**) *несов от* **проте́чь** ♦ *неперех* (*вода*) to flow; (*болезнь, явление*) to progress

проте́кци|я (**-и**) *ж* patronage

прот|ере́ть (**-ру́, -рёшь**; *pt* **-ёр, -ёрла́**, *impf* **протира́ть**) *сов перех* (*износить*) to wear a hole in; (*очистить*) to wipe; **~ся** (*impf* **протира́ться**) *сов возв* (*износиться*) to wear through

проте́ст (**-а**) *м* protest; (*ЮР*) objection

протеста́нт (**-а**) *м* Protestant

протеста́нтский *прил* Protestant

протест|ова́ть (**-у́ю**) *несов*: **~ (про́тив** +*gen*) to protest (against)

проте́ч|ка (**-ки**; *gen pl* **-ек**) *ж* leak

прот|е́чь (*3sg* **-ечёт**, *pt* **-ёк, -екла́**; *impf* **протека́ть**) *сов* (*вода*) to seep; (*крыша*) to leak

про́тив *предл*: **~** +*gen* against; (*прямо перед*) opposite ♦ *как* *сказ:* **я ~ э́того** I am against this

про́тив|ень (-ня) *м* baking tray

проти́в|иться (-люсь, -ишься; *pf* **вос~)** *несов возв* **: ~ +dat** to oppose

проти́вник (-а) *м* opponent
♦ *собир (ВОЕН)* the enemy

проти́вно *нареч* offensively ♦ *как сказ безл* **it's disgusting**

проти́вный *прил (мнение)* opposite; *(неприятный)* disgusting

противовозду́шный *прил* anti-aircraft

противога́з (-а) *м* gas mask

противоде́йств|овать (-ую) *несов:* **~ +dat** to oppose

противозако́нный *прил* unlawful

противозача́точн|ый *прил* contraceptive; **~ое сре́дство** contraceptive

противопожа́рный *прил (меры)* fire-prevention; *(техника)* fire-fighting

противополо́жный *прил (берег)* opposite; *(мнение)* opposing

противопоста́в|ить (-лю, -ишь, *impf* **противопоставля́ть)** *сов перех:* **~ кого-н/что-н +dat** to contrast sb/sth with

противоречи́вый *прил* contradictory

противоре́чи|е (-я) *ср* contradiction; *(классовое)* conflict

противоре́ч|ить (-у, -ишь) *несов:* **~ +dat (человеку)** to contradict; *(логике, закону итп)* to defy

противосто|я́ть (-ю́, -и́шь) *несов:* **~ +dat (ветру)** to withstand; *(угово́рам)* to resist

противоя́ди|е (-я) *ср* antidote

протира́|ться (-ю(сь)) *несов от* **протере́ть(ся)**

проткн|у́ть (-у́, -ёшь; *impf* **протыка́ть)** *сов перех* to pierce

прото́к (-а) *м (рукав реки)* tributary; *(соединяющая реки)* channel

протоко́л (-а) *м (собрания)* minutes *мн*; *(допроса)* transcript; *(соглашение)* protocol

протолкн|у́ть (-у́, -ёшь; *impf* **прота́лкивать)** *сов перех* to push through

прото́чный *прил (вода)* running

протух|ну́ть (3sg -ет; *impf* **протуха́ть или ту́хнуть)** *сов* to go bad *или* off

протыка́|ть (-ю) *несов от* **проткну́ть**

протя́гива|ть(ся) (-ю(сь)) *несов от* **протяну́ть(ся)**

протяже́ни|е (-я) *ср:* **на ~и двух неде́ль/ме́сяцев** over a period of two weeks/months

протяжённость (-и) *ж* length

протяжённый *прил* prolonged

протян|у́ть (-у́, -ешь) *сов от* **тяну́ть** ♦ *(impf* **протя́гивать)** *перех (верёвку)* to stretch; *(провод)* to extend; *(руки, ноги)* to stretch (out); *(предмет)* to hold out; **~ся** *(impf* **протя́гиваться)** *сов возв (дорога)* to stretch; *(провод)* to extend; *(рука)* to stretch out

про|учи́ть (-учу́, -у́чишь; *impf* **проу́чивать)** *сов перех (разг: наказать)* to teach a lesson; **~ся** *сов возв* to study

проф. *сокр (= профе́ссор)* Prof.

профессиона́л (-а) *м* professional

профессиона́льный *прил* professional; *(болезнь, привычка, обучение)* occupational; *(обучение)* vocational; **~ сою́з** trade *(BRIT)* или labor *(US)* union

профе́сси|я (-и) *ж* profession

профе́ссор (-а; nom pl -á) м professor

профила́ктик|а (-и) ж prevention

профилакти́ческий прил (меры) prevent(at)ive; (прививка) prophylactic

про́фил|ь (-я) м profile

профсою́з (-а) м сокр = **профессиона́льный сою́з**

профсою́зный прил trade-union

прожива́|ться (-юсь) несов от **пройти́сь**

прохла́д|а (-ы) ж cool

прохлади́тельный прил: ~ **напи́ток** cool soft drink

прохла́дно нареч (встретить) coolly ♦ как сказ it's cool

прохла́дный прил cool

прохо́д (-а) м passage

прох|оди́ть (-ожу́, -о́дишь) несов от **пройти́**

проходн|а́я (-о́й) ж checkpoint (at entrance to factory etc)

проходно́й прил: ~ **балл** pass mark

проходно́й балл - pass mark. This is the score which the student has to achieve to be admitted into a higher education institution. The score is calculated using the marks attained during the four entrance exams and the average mark in the Certificate of Secondary Education. The score varies from year to year and depends on the number and standard of the applicants. The score required by popular departments can be as high as 25. See also notes at **аттеста́т зре́лости** and **вступи́тельные экза́мены.**

прохо́ж|ий (-его) м passer-by

процвета́|ть (-ю) несов (фирма,

бизнесме́н) to prosper; (театр, нау́ка) to flourish; (хорошо́ жить) to thrive

проц|еди́ть (-ежу́, -е́дишь) сов отцеди́ть ♦ (impf **проце́живать**) перех (бульо́н, сок) to strain

процеду́р|а (-ы) ж procedure; (МЕД, обычно мн) course ед of treatment

процеду́рный прил procedural; ~ **кабине́т** treatment room

проце́жива|ть (-ю) несов от **процеди́ть**

проце́нт (-а) м percentage; **в разме́ре 5 ~ов годовы́х** at a yearly rate of 5 percent; см. также **проце́нты**

проце́нтн|ый прил percentage; ~**ая ста́вка** interest rate

проце́нт|ы (-ов) мн (КОММ) interest ед; (пла́та) commission ед

проце́сс (-а) м process; (ЮР, поря́док) proceedings мн; (: также: **суде́бный ~**) trial; **воспали́тельный ~** inflammation; **в ~е** +gen in the course of

проце́ссор (-а) м (КОМП) processor

прочёл сов см. **проче́сть**

прочёсть (-ту́, -тёшь; pt -ёл, -ла́) сов от **чита́ть**

про́ч|ий прил other; **поми́мо всего́ ~его** apart from anything else

прочита́|ть (-ю) сов от **чита́ть**

прочла́ etc сов см. **проче́сть**

про́чно нареч (закрепи́ть) firmly

про́чный прил (материа́л итп) durable; (постро́йка) solid; (зна́ния) sound; (отноше́ния, семья́) stable; (мир, сча́стье) lasting

прочту́ etc сов см. **проче́сть**

прочь нареч (в сто́рону) away; **ру́ки ~!** hands off!

прошéдш|ий *прил* (*прошлый*) past; **~ее врéмя** past tense

прошёл(ся) *сов см.* **пройти(сь)**

прошéни|е (-я) *ср* plea; (*ходатайство*) petition

прошепта́ть (-епчу́, -е́пчешь) *сов перех* to whisper

прошла́ *итп см. см.* **пройти**

прошлого́дний *прил* last year's

про́шл|ое (-ого) *ср* the past

про́шл|ый *прил* last; (*прежний*) past; **в ~ раз** last time; **на ~ой неде́ле** last week; **в ~ом ме́сяце/году́** last month/year

прошу́(сь) *несов см.* **проси́ть(ся)**

проща́йте *част* goodbye, farewell

проща́льный *прил* parting; (*вечер*) farewell

проща́ни|е (-я) *ср* (*действие*) parting; **на ~** on parting

проща́ть(ся) (-ю(сь)) *несов от* **прости́ть(ся)**

про́ще *сравн нареч от* **про́сто** ♦ *сравн прил от* **просто́й**

проще́ни|е (-я) *ср* (*ребёнка, друга итп*) forgiveness; (*преступника*) pardon; **проси́ть (попроси́ть** *pf*) **~я** to say sorry; **прошу́ ~я!** (I'm) sorry!

проявител|ь (-я) *м* (*ФОТО*) developer

про|яви́ть (-явлю́, -я́вишь; *impf* **проявля́ть**) *сов перех* to display; (*ФОТО*) to develop; **~ся** (*impf* **проявля́ться**) *сов возв* (*талант, потенциал итп*) to reveal itself; (*ФОТО*) to be developed

проявле́ни|е (-я) *ср* display

проявля́ть(ся) (-ю(сь)) *несов от* **прояви́ть(ся)**

прояс|ни́ть (-ю́, -ни́шь; *impf* **проясня́ть**) *сов перех* (*обстановку*) to clarify; **~ся** (*impf* **проясня́ться**) *сов возв* (*погода,*

небо) to brighten *или* clear up; (*обстановка*) to be clarified; (*мысли*) to become lucid

пруд (-а́; *loc sg* -ý) *м* pond

пружи́н|а (-ы) *ж* (*ТЕХ*) spring

прут (-а́; *nom pl* -ья) *м* twig

прыга́л|ка (-ки; *gen pl* -ок) *ж* skipping-rope (*BRIT*), skip rope (*US*)

прыга|ть (-ю) *несов* to jump; (*мяч*) to bounce

прыг|ну́ть (-у) *сов* to jump; (*мяч*) to bounce

прыгу́н (-а́) *м* (*СПОРТ*) jumper

прыж|о́к (-ка́) *м* jump; (*в воду*) dive; **~ки́ в высоту́/длину́** high/long jump

прыщ (-а́) *м* spot

прядь (-и) *ж* lock (*of hair*)

пря́ж|а (-и) *ж* yarn

пря́ж|ка (-ки; *gen pl* -ек) *ж* (*на ремне*) buckle; (*на юбке*) clasp

пряма́я (-о́й) *ж* straight line

пря́мо *нареч* (*о направлении*) straight ahead; (*ровно*) upright; (*непосредственно*) directly ♦ *част* (*действительно*) really

прям|о́й *прил* straight; (*путь, слова, человек*) direct; (*ответ, политика*) open; (*вызов, обман*) obvious; (*улики*) hard; (*сообщение, обязанность итп*) direct; (*выгода, смысл*) real; (*значение слова*) literal; **~а́я трансля́ция** live broadcast; **~ое дополне́ние** direct object

прямоуго́льник (-а) *м* rectangle

пря́ник (-а) *м* gingerbread

пря́ность (-и) *ж* spice

пря́ный *прил* spicy

пря́|тать (-чу, -чешь; *pf* **с~**) *несов перех* to hide; **~ся** (*pf* **с~ся**) *сов возв* to hide; (*человек: от холода*) to shelter

пря́т|ки (-ок) *мн* hide-and-seek *ед*

(BRIT), hide-and-go-seek *ед* (US)

псало́м (**-ма́**) *м* psalm

псалты́р|ь (**-и**) *ж* Psalter

псевдони́м (**-а**) *м* pseudonym

псих (**-а**) *м* (*разг*) nut

психиа́тр (**-а**) *м* psychiatrist

психиатри́ческий *прил* psychiatric

психиатри́|я (**-и**) *ж* psychiatry

пси́хик|а (**-и**) *ж* psyche

психи́ческий *прил* (*заболевание*) mental

психо́з (**-а**) *м* (*МЕД*) psychosis

психо́лог (**-а**) *м* psychologist

психологи́ческий *прил* psychological

психоло́ги|я (**-и**) *ж* psychology

психотерапе́вт (**-а**) *м* psychotherapist

птен|е́ц (**-ца́**) *м* chick

пти́ц|а (**-ы**) *ж* bird *♦ собир*: (*дома́шняя*) ~ poultry

пти́чий *прил* (*корм, клетка*) bird

публик|а (**-и**) *ж собир* audience; (*общество*) public

публика́ци|я (**-и**) *ж* publication

публик|ова́ть (**-у́ю**; *pf* **о~**) *несов перех* to publish

публици́ст (**-а**) *м* social commentator

публици́стик|а (**-и**) *ж собир* sociopolitical journalism

публицисти́ческий *прил* sociopolitical

публи́чный *прил* public; ~ **дом** brothel

пу́гал|о (**-а**) *ср* scarecrow; (*перен*: *о человеке*) fright

пуга́|ть (**-ю**; *pf* **ис~** *или* **на~**) *несов перех* to frighten, scare; **~ся** (*pf* **ис~ся** *или* **на~ся**) *несов возв* to be frightened *или* scared

пу́говиц|а (**-ы**) *ж* button

пу́дел|ь (**-я**) *м* poodle

пу́динг (**-а**) *м* ≈ pudding

пу́др|а (**-ы**) *ж* powder; **са́харная ~** icing sugar

пу́дрениц|а (**-ы**) *ж* powder compact

пу́др|ить (**-ю, -ишь**; *pf* **на~**) *несов перех* to powder; **~ся** (*pf* **на~ся**) *несов возв* to powder one's face

пузыр|ёк (**-ька́**) *м уменьш от* **пузы́рь**; (*для лекарства, чернил*) vial

пузыр|и́ться (*3sg* **-и́тся**) *несов возв* (*жидкость*) to bubble; (*краска*) to blister

пузы́р|ь (**-я́**) *м* (*мы́льный*) bubble; (*на ко́же*) blister

пулемёт (**-а**) *м* machine gun

пуленепробива́емый *прил* bullet-proof

пуло́вер (**-а**) *м* pullover

пульвериза́тор (**-а**) *м* atomizer

пульс (**-а**) *м* (*МЕД, перен*) pulse

пульси́р|овать (*3sg* **-ует**) *несов* (*артерии*) to pulsate; (*кровь*) to pulse

пульт (**-а**) *м* panel

пу́л|я (**-и**) *ж* bullet

пункт (**-а**) *м* point; (*документа*) clause; (*медицинский*) centre (BRIT), center (US); (*наблюда́тельный, кома́ндный*) post; **населённый ~** small settlement

пункти́р (**-а**) *м* dotted line

пунктуа́льный *прил* (*человек*) punctual

пунктуа́ци|я (**-и**) *ж* punctuation

пуп|о́к (**-ка́**) *м* (*АНАТ*) navel

пург|а́ (**-и́**) *ж* snowstorm

пуск (**-а**) *м* (*завода итп*) launch

пуска́|ться (**-юсь**) *несов от* **пусти́ть(ся)**

пусте́|ть (*3sg* **-ет**; *pf* **о~**) *несов* to become empty; (*улицы*) to become deserted

пу|сти́ть (-щу́, -стишь; *impf*
пуска́ть) *сов перех* (руку,
человека) to let go of; (лошадь,
санки итп) to send off; (станок) to
start; (в вагон, в зал) to let in;
(пар, дым) to let out; (камень,
снаряд) to throw; (корни) to put
out; пуска́ть (~ *pf*) что-н на +*acc*/
под +*acc* (испо́льзовать) to use
sth as/for; пуска́ть (~ *pf*) кого́-н
куда́-нибудь to let sb go
somewhere; ~ся (*impf* пуска́ться)
сов возв: ~ся в +*acc* (в
объясне́ния) to go into;
пуска́ться (~ся *pf*) в ~ть to set off

пу́сто *нареч* ♦ *как сказ* (ничего
нет) it's empty; (никого́
нет) there's no one there

пусто́й *прил* empty

пуст|ота́ (-оты́; *nom pl* -о́ты) *ж*
emptiness; (*полое место*) cavity

пусты́нный *прил* desert;
(безлю́дный) deserted

пусты́н|я (-и; *gen pl* -ь) *ж* desert

пусты́р|ь (-я́) *м* wasteland

пусты́ш|ка (-ки; *gen pl* -ек) *ж*
(*разг*: соска) dummy (*BRIT*),
pacifier (*US*)

KEYWORD

пусть *част*; +*3sg/pl* **1** (*выражает
прика́з, угро́зу*): **пусть он
придёт у́тром** let him come in the
morning; **пусть она́ то́лько
попро́бует отказа́ться** let her just
try to refuse

2 (*выражает согла́сие*): **пусть
бу́дет так** so be it; **пусть бу́дет
по-тво́ему** have it your way

3 (*всё равно́*) OK, all right

пустя́к (-á) *м* trifle; (неце́нный
предме́т) trinket ♦ *как сказ*: э́то ~
it's nothing

пу́таниц|а (-ы) *ж* muddle

пу́таный *прил* muddled

пу́та|ть (-ю; *pf* за~ и́ли с~) *несов
перех* (нитки, во́лосы) to tangle;
(сбить с то́лку) to confuse; (*pf* за~
и́ли пере~) (бума́ги, фа́кты итп)
to mix up; (*pf* с~; *разг*): ~ кого́-н
в +*acc* to get sb mixed up in; **я его́
с ке́м-то ~ю** I'm confusing him
with somebody else; **он всегда́ ~л
на́ши имена́** he always got our
names mixed up; ~ся (*pf* за~ и́ли
с~ся и́ли с~ся) *несов возв* (*во́лосы*)
to get tangled; (в расска́зе, в
объясне́ниях) to get mixed up

путёв|ка (-ки; *gen pl* -ок) *ж*
holiday voucher; (*води́теля*)
manifest (*of cargo drivers*)

путеводи́тел|ь (-я) *м* guidebook

путём *предл*: ~ +*gen* by means of

путеше́ственник (-а) *м* traveller
(*BRIT*), traveler (*US*)

путеше́стви|е (-я) *ср* journey,
trip; (*морско́е*) voyage

путеше́ств|овать (-ую) *несов* to
travel

пу́тник (-а) *м* traveller (*BRIT*),
traveler (*US*)

путч (-а) *м* (*полит*) putsch

пут|ь (-и́; *см. Table 3*) *м* (*также
перен*) way; (*платфо́рма*)
platform; (*ре́льсы*) track;
(*путеше́ствие*) journey; во́дные
~и́ waterways; возду́шные ~и́ air
lanes; нам с Ва́ми не по ~и́ we're
not going the same way;
счастли́вого ~и́! have a good
trip!; ~и́ сообще́ния transport
network

пух (-а; *loc sg* -у́) *м* (*у живо́тных*)
fluff; (*у птиц, у челове́ка*) down;
ни пу́ха ни пера́! good luck

пу́хлый *прил* (*щёки, челове́к*)
chubby; (*портфе́ль*) bulging

пу́х|нуть (-ну; *pt* -, -ла; *pf* вс~
и́ли о~) *несов* to swell (up)

пухо́вый прил (*подушка*) feather; (*платок*) angora

пуч|о́к (**-ка́**) м bunch; (*света*) beam

пуши́стый прил (*мех, ковёр итп*) fluffy; (*волосы*) fuzzy; (*кот*) angora

пу́ш|ка (**-ки**; *gen pl* **-ек**) ж cannon; (*на танке*) artillery gun

пчел|а́ (**-ы́**; *nom pl* **пчёлы**) ж bee

пчели́ный прил (*мёд*) bee's

пчелово́д (**-а**) м bee-keeper

пшени́ц|а (**-ы**) ж wheat

пшени́чный прил wheat

пшённ|ый прил: **~ая ка́ша** millet porridge

пшен|о́ (**-а́**) ср millet

пыла́|ть (**-ю**) несов (*костёр*) to blaze; (*перен: лицо*) to burn

пылесо́с (**-а**) м vacuum cleaner, hoover ®

пылесо́с|ить (**-ишь**; *pf* **про~**) сов перех to vacuum, hoover ®

пыли́н|ка (**-ки**; *gen pl* **-ок**) ж speck of dust

пыл|и́ть (**-ю́, -и́шь**; *pf* **на~**) несов to raise dust; **~ся** (*pf* **за~ся**) несов возв to get dusty

пы́лкий прил ardent

пыл|ь (**-и**; *loc sg* **-и́**) ж dust; **вытира́ть** (**вы́тереть** *pf*) **~** to dust

пыльный прил dusty

пыльц|а́ (**-ы́**) ж pollen

пыта́|ть (**-ю**) несов перех to torture; **~ся** (*pf* **по~ся**) несов возв: **~+infin** to try to do

пы́т|ка (**-ки**; *gen pl* **-ок**) ж torture

пы́шный прил (*волосы*) bushy; (*обстановка, приём*) splendid

пьедеста́л (**-а**) м (*основание*) pedestal; (*для победителей*) rostrum

пье́с|а (**-ы**) ж (*ЛИТЕРАТУРА*) play; (*муз*) piece

пью *etc* несов см. **пить**

пью́щий (**-его**) м heavy drinker

пьяне́|ть (**-ю**; *pf* **о~**) несов to get drunk

пья́ниц|а (**-ы**) м/ж drunkard

пья́нств|о (**-а**) ср heavy drinking

пья́нств|овать (**-ую**) несов to drink heavily

пья́н|ый прил (*человек*) drunk; (*крики, песни итп*) drunken
♦ (**-ого**) м drunk

пюре́ ср нескл (*фруктовое*) purée; **карто́фельное ~** mashed potato

пят|а́ (**-ы́**) ж: **одна́ ~** one fifth

пятёр|ка (**-ки**; *gen pl* **-ок**) ж (*цифра, карта*) five; (*ПРОСВЕЩ*) ≈ A (*school mark*); (*группа из пяти*) group of five

пя́теро (**-ы́х**; *как* **че́тверо**; *см. Table 30b*) чис five

пятибо́рь|е (**-я**) ср pentathlon

пятидеся́ти чис см. **пятьдеся́т**

пятидесятиле́ти|е (**-я**) ср fifty years мн; (*годовщина*) fiftieth anniversary

пятидесятиле́тний прил (*период*) fifty-year; (*человек*) fifty-year-old

пятидеся́тый чис fiftieth

пя́|титься (**-чусь, -тишься**; *pf* **по~**) несов возв to move backwards

пятиуго́льник (**-а**) м pentagon

пятичасово́й прил (*рабочий день*) five hour; (*поезд*) five-o'clock

пятиэта́жный прил five-storey (*BRIT*), five-story (*US*)

пя́т|ка (**-ки**; *gen pl* **-ок**) ж heel

пятна́дцатый чис fifteenth

пятна́дцат|ь (**-и**; *как* **пять**; *см. Table 26*) чис fifteen

пятни́стый прил spotted

пя́тниц|а (**-ы**) ж Friday

пятн|о́ (**-а́**; *nom pl* **пя́тна**, *gen pl* **-ен**) ср (*также перен*) stain;

(*другого цвета*) spot

пя́тый *чис* fifth

пять (**-и́**; *см. Table 26*) *чис* five;
(*ПРОСВЕЩ*) ≈ A (school mark)

пятьдеся́т (**-и́десяти**; *см. Table 26*) *чис* fifty

пятьсо́т (**-исо́т**; *см. Table 28*) *чис* five hundred

Р, р

р. *сокр* (= *река́*) R., r.; (= *роди́лся*) b.; (= *рубль*) R., r.

раб (**-а́**) *м* slave

рабо́т|**а** (**-ы**) *ж* work; (*источник заработка*) job; **сме́нная ~** shiftwork

рабо́та|**ть** (**-ю**) *несов* to work; (*магазин*) to be open; ~ (*impf*) **на кого́-н/что-н** to work for sb/sth; **кем Вы ~ете?** what do you do for a living?

рабо́тник (**-а**) *м* worker; (*учреждения*) employee

работода́тел|**ь** (**-я**) *м* employer

работоспосо́бный *прил* (*человек*) able to work hard

рабо́ч|**ий** (**-его**) *прил* worker's; (*человек, одежда*) working ♦ (**-его**) *м* worker; **~ая си́ла** workforce; **~ день** working day (*BRIT*), workday (*US*)

ра́бский *прил* (*жизнь*) slave-like

ра́бств|**о** (**-а**) *ср* slavery

рабы́н|**я** (**-и**) *ж* slave

равви́н (**-а**) *м* rabbi

ра́венств|**о** (**-а**) *ср* equality; **знак ~а** (*МАТ*) equals sign

равни́н|**а** (**-ы**) *ж* plain

равно́ *нареч* equally ♦ *союз*: ~ (**как**) **и** as ♦ *как сказ*: **э́то всё ~** it doesn't make any difference; **мне всё ~** I don't mind;

я всё ~ приду́ I'll come anyway

равнове́си|**е** (**-я**) *ср* equilibrium; **~ сил** balance of power

равноду́шный *прил*: ~ (**к** +*dat*) indifferent (to)

равноме́рный *прил* even

равнопра́ви|**е** (**-я**) *ср* equality

равноси́льный *прил*: ~ +*dat* equal to; **э́то ~о отка́зу** this amounts to a refusal

равноце́нный *прил* of equal value *или* worth

ра́в|**ный** *прил* equal; **~ым о́бразом** equally

равня́|**ть** (**-ю**; *pf* с~) *несов перех*: ~ (**с** +*instr*) (*делать равным*) to make equal (with); **~ся** *несов возв*: ~**ся по** +*dat* to draw level with; (*считать себя равным*) **~ся с** +*instr* to compare o.s. with; (*быть равносильным*) **~ся** +*dat* to be equal to

рагу́ *ср нескл* ragout

рад *как сказ*: ~ (+*dat*) glad (of); ~ +*infin* glad *или* pleased to do; ~ **познако́миться с Ва́ми** pleased to meet you

ра́ди *предл*: ~ +*gen* for the sake of; ~ **Бо́га!** (*разг*) for God's sake!

радиа́ци|**я** (**-и**) *ж* radiation

радика́льный *прил* radical

радикули́т (**-а**) *м* lower back pain

ра́дио *ср нескл* radio

радиоакти́вный *прил* radioactive

радиовеща́ни|**е** (**-я**) *ср* (radio) broadcasting

радиопереда́ч|**а** (**-и**) *ж* radio programme (*BRIT*) *или* program (*US*)

радиоприёмник (**-а**) *м* radio (set)

радиослу́шател|**ь** (**-я**) *м* (radio) listener

радиоста́нци|**я** (**-и**) *ж* radio station

ра́диус (**-а**) *м* radius

ра́д|овать (-ую, pf об~) несов
перех: ~ кого́-н to make sb
happy, please sb; ~ся несов возв
(перен: душа) to rejoice; ~ся
(об~ся pf) +dat (успехам) to take
pleasure in; **он всегда́ ~уется
гостя́м** he is always happy to have
visitors

ра́достный прил joyful

ра́дост|ь (-и) ж joy; **с ~ю** gladly

ра́дуг|а (-и) ж rainbow

ра́дужн|ый прил (перен:
прия́тный) bright; **~ая оболо́чка**
(АНАТ) iris

раду́шный прил warm

раз (-а; nom pl -ы́, gen pl -) м time
♦ нескл (оди́н) one ♦ нареч
(разг: одна́жды) once ♦ сою́з
(разг: е́сли) if; **в тот/про́шлый ~**
that/last time; **на э́тот ~** this time;
ещё ~ (once) again; **и навсегда́**
once and for all; **ни ра́зу** not once;
(оди́н) ~ в день once a day; **~...
то ...** (разг) if ... then ...

разба́в|ить (-лю, -ишь), impf
разбавля́ть сов перех to dilute

разбе́г (-а) м (атлета) run-up

разбежа́|ться (как бежа́ть; см.
Table 20; impf **разбега́ться** сов
возв to run off, scatter; (перед
прыжко́м) to take a run-up; **у
меня́ глаза́ разбега́ются** (разг)
I'm spoilt for choice

разбива́|ть(ся) (-ю(сь)) несов от
разби́ть(ся)

разбира́|ть (-ю) несов от
разобра́ть; ~ся несов от
разобра́ться сов (разг:
понима́ть): ~ся в +prp to be an
expert in

разби́|ть (-обью, -обьёшь), imper
-бе́й(те), impf **разбива́ть** сов
перех to break; (маши́ну) to
smash up; (а́рмию) to crush;
(алле́ю) to lay; ~ся (impf

разбива́|ться сов возв to break,
smash; (в ава́рии) to be badly
hurt; (на гру́ппы, на уча́стки) to
break up

разбогате́|ть (-ю) сов от
богате́ть

разбо́|й (-я) м robbery

разбо́йник (-а) м robber

разбо́р (-а) м (статьи́, вопро́са)
analysis; **без ~а** indiscriminately

разбо́рк|а (-и) ж in-fighting

разбо́рный прил (ме́бель) flat-
pack

разбо́рчивый прил (челове́к,
вкус) discerning; (по́черк) legible

разбра́сыва|ть(ся) (-ю(сь)) несов от
разброса́ть; ~ся несов возв:
~ся +instr (деньга́ми) to waste;
(друзья́ми) to underrate

разброса́|ть (-ю); impf
разбра́сывать сов перех to
scatter

разбуди́ть (-ужу́, -у́дишь) сов
от **буди́ть**

разва́л (-а) м chaos

разва́лин|а (-ы) ж ruins мн

развал|и́ть (-алю́, -а́лишь) impf
разва́ливать сов перех to ruin;
~ся (impf **разва́ливаться**) сов
возв to collapse

разва́р|иться (3sg -ится) impf
разва́риваться сов возв to be
overcooked

ра́зве част really; **~ он
согласи́лся/не знал?** did he really
agree/not know?; **~ то́лько** или
что except that

разве́ва|ть (3sg -ется) несов
возв (флаг) to flutter

разведе́ни|е (-я) ср (живо́тных)
breeding; (расте́ний) cultivation

разведённый прил (в разво́де)
divorced

разве́д|ка (-ки; gen pl -ок) ж (ГЕО)
prospecting; (шпиона́ж)

intelligence; (ВОЕН) reconnaissance
разве́дчик (-а) м (ГЕО)
prospector; (шпион) intelligence
agent; (ВОЕН) scout
разве́зти́ (-езу́, -езёшь; pt -ёз,
-езла́, -езло́; impf **развози́ть**)
сов перех (товар) to take
разверну́ть (-у́, -ёшь; impf
развёртывать или
развора́чивать) сов перех
(бумагу) to unfold; (торговлю
итп) to launch; (корабль,
самолёт) to turn around;
(батальон) to deploy; **~ся** (impf
развёртываться или
развора́чиваться) сов возв
(кампания, работа) to get under
way; (автомобиль) to turn
around; (вид) to open up
развесели́ть (-ю́, -и́шь) сов от
весели́ть
разве́сить (-шу, -сишь; impf
разве́шивать) сов перех to
hang
разве́сти́ (-еду́, -едёшь; pt -ёл,
-ела́; impf **разводи́ть**) сов перех
(доставить) to take; (порошок) to
dissolve; (сок) to dilute;
(животных) to breed; (цветы,
сад) to grow; (мост) to raise; **~сь**
(impf **разводи́ться**) сов возв:
~сь (с +instr) to divorce, get
divorced from)
разветвле́ние (-я) ср (дороги)
fork
разве́ять (-ю; impf **разве́ивать**)
сов перех (облака) to disperse;
(сомнения, грусть) to dispel; **~ся**
(impf **разве́иваться**) сов возв
(облака) to disperse; (человек) to
relax
развива́ть(ся) (-ю(сь)) несов от
разви́ть(ся)
развива́ющийся прил: **~аяся
страна́** developing country

разви́лка (-ки; gen pl -ок) ж fork
(in road)
разви́тие (-я) ср development
разви́тый прил developed
разви́ть (-овью, -овьёшь; imper
-ве́й(те); impf **развива́ть**) сов
перех to develop; **~ся** (impf
развива́ться сов возв to
develop
развлека́тельный прил
entertaining
развлече́ние (-я) ср entertaining
развле́чь (-еку́, -ечёшь etc,
-еку́т; pt -ёк, -екла́; impf
развлека́ть) сов перех to
entertain; **~ся** (impf
развлека́ться) сов возв to have
fun
разво́д (-а) м (супругов) divorce
разво́ди́ть(ся) (-ожу́(сь),
-о́дишь(ся)) несов от
развести́(сь)
разводно́й прил: **~ мост**
drawbridge
развора́чива́ть(ся) (-ю(сь))
несов от **разверну́ть(ся)**
разворо́т (-а) м (машины) U-
turn; (в книге) double page
развра́т (-а) м promiscuity;
(низкие нравы) depravity
развраща́ть (-щу́, -ти́шь; impf
развраща́ть) сов перех to
pervert; (деньгами) to debauch,
corrupt; **~ся** (impf **развраща́ться**)
сов возв (см перех) to become
promiscuous; to become corrupted
развяза́ть (-яжу́, -я́жешь; impf
развя́зывать) сов перех
(шнурки) to untie; (: войну́) to
unleash; **~ся** (impf
развя́зываться) сов возв
(шнурки) to come untied
развя́зка (-ки; gen pl -ок) ж
(конец) finale; (АВТ) junction
разгада́ть (-ю; impf

разга́дывать *сов перех* (загадку) to solve; (замыслы, тайну) to guess

разга́р (-а) м: в ~е +gen (сезона) at the height of; (боя) in the heart of; (кани́кулы в по́лном) ~е the holidays are in full swing

разгиба́|ть(ся) (-ю(сь)) несов от **разогну́ть(ся)**

разгла́|дить (-жу, -дишь; *impf* **разгла́живать**) *сов перех* to smooth out

разгла|си́ть (-шу́, -си́шь; *impf* **разглаша́ть**) *сов перех* to divulge, disclose

разгова́рива|ть (-ю) *несов*: ~ (с +instr) to talk (to)

разгово́р (-а) м conversation

разгово́рник (-а) м phrase book

разгово́рный *прил* colloquial

разгово́рчивый *прил* talkative

разго́н (-а) м (демонстрации) breaking up; (автомоби́ля) acceleration

разгоня́|ть(ся) (-ю(сь)) несов от **разогна́ть(ся)**

разгор|е́ться (3sg -и́тся; *impf* **разгора́ться**) *сов возв* to flare up

разгоряч|и́ться (-у́сь, -и́шься) *сов возв* (от волне́ния) to get worked up; (от бе́га) to be hot

разграни́ч|ить (-у, -ишь; *impf* **разграни́чивать**) *сов перех* to demarcate

разгро́м (-а) м rout; (разг: беспоря́док) mayhem

разгром|и́ть (-лю́, -и́шь) *сов перех* (врага́) to crush; (кни́гу) to slam

разгру|зи́ть (-жу́, -у́зишь; *impf* **разгружа́ть**) *сов перех* to unload

разгры́з|ть (-у, -ёшь) *сов от* **грызть**

разгу́л (-а) м revelry; ~ +gen (реа́кции) rule of

раздава́|ть(ся) (-ю́, -ёшь(ся)) несов от **разда́ть(ся)**

разда́в|ить (-авлю́, -а́вишь) *сов от* **дави́ть**

разда́ть (как дать; см. Table 16; *impf* **раздава́ть**) *сов перех* to give out, distribute; ~ся (*impf* **раздава́ться**) *сов возв* (звук) to be heard

раздва́ива|ться (-юсь) несов от **раздво́иться**

раздви́н|уть (-у; *impf* **раздвига́ть**) *сов перех* to move apart

раздво|и́ться (-ю́сь, -и́шься; *impf* **раздва́иваться**) *сов возв* (доро́га, река́) to divide into two; (перен: мне́ние) to be divided

раздева́л|ка (-ки; gen pl -ок) ж changing room

раздева́|ть(ся) (-ю(сь)) несов от **разде́ть(ся)**

разде́л (-а) м (иму́щества) division; (часть) section

разде́ла|ть (-ю; *impf* **разде́лывать**) *сов перех* (тушу) to cut up; ~ся (*impf* **разде́лываться**) *сов возв* (разг): ~ся с +instr (с дела́ми) to finish; (с долга́ми) to settle

разде|ли́ть (-елю́, -е́лишь) *сов от* **дели́ть** ♦ (*impf* **разделя́ть**) *перех* (мне́ние) to share; ~ся *сов от* **дели́ться** ♦ (*impf* **разделя́ться**) *возв* (мне́ния, о́бщество) to become divided

разде́|ть (-ну, -нешь; *impf* **раздева́ть**) *сов перех* to undress; ~ся (*impf* **раздева́ться**) *сов возв* to get undressed

раздира́|ть (-ю) *несов перех* (ду́шу, о́бщество) to tear apart

раздраже́ни|е (-я) *ср* irritation

раздражённый *прил* irritated

раздражи́тельный *прил* irritable

раздраж|и́ть (-у́, -и́шь; *impf* **раздража́ть**) *сов перех* to irritate, annoy; (*нервы*) to agitate; **~ся** (*impf* **раздража́ться**) *сов возв* (*кожа, глаза*) to become irritated; (*человек*): **~ся** (+*instr*) to be irritated (by)

раздува́|ть(ся) (-ю(сь)) *несов от* **разду́ть(ся)**

разду́ма|ть (-ю; *impf* **разду́мывать**) *сов*: **~** +*infin* to decide not to do

разду́мыва|ть (-ю) *несов от* **разду́мать** ♦ *неперех*: **~ о** (+*prp*) (*долго думать*) to contemplate

разду́мь|е (-я) *ср* contemplation

разд|у́ть (-у́ю; *impf* **раздува́ть**) *сов перех* (*огонь*) to fan; **у неё ~у́ло щёку** her cheek has swollen up; **~ся** (*impf* **раздува́ться**) *сов возв* (*щека*) to swell up

раз|жа́ть (-ожму́, -ожмёшь; *impf* **разжима́ть**) *сов перех* (*пальцы, губы*) to relax; **~ся** (*impf* **разжима́ться**) *сов возв* to relax

разж|ева́ть (-у́ю; *impf* **разжёвывать**) *сов перех* to chew

раз|жечь (-ожгу́, -ожжёшь *итп*, -огжу́т; *pt* -жёг, -ожгла́; *impf* **разжига́ть**) *сов перех* to kindle

разлага́|ть(ся) (-ю) *несов от* **разложи́ть(ся)**

разла́д (-а) *м* (*в делах*) disorder; (*с женой*) discord

разла́мыва|ть (-ю) *несов от* **разлома́ть, разломи́ть**

разле|те́ться (-чу́сь, -ти́шься; *impf* **разлета́ться**) *сов возв* to fly off (*in different directions*)

разли́в (-а) *м* flooding

раз|ли́ть (-олью́, -ольёшь; *impf* **разлива́ть**) *сов перех* (*пролить*) to spill; **~ся** (*impf* **разлива́ться** *сов возв* (*пролиться*) to spill; (*река*) to overflow

различа́|ть (-ю) *несов от* **различи́ть**; **~ся** *несов возв*: **~ся по** (+*dat*) to differ in

разли́чи|е (-я) *ср* difference

различ|и́ть (-у́, -и́шь; *impf* **различа́ть**) *сов перех* (*увидеть, услышать*) to make out; (*отличить*): **~ (по** +*dat*) to distinguish (by)

разли́чный *прил* different

разложе́ни|е (-я) *ср* decomposition; (*общества итп*) disintegration

разл|ожи́ть (-ожу́, -о́жишь; *impf* **раскла́дывать**) *сов перех* (*карты*) to arrange; (*диван*) to open out; (*impf* **разлага́ть**; *хим, био*) to decompose; **~ся** (*impf* **разлага́ться** *сов возв* (*хим, био*) to decompose; (*общество*) to disintegrate

разл|оми́ть (-омлю́, -о́мишь; *impf* **разла́мывать**) *сов перех* (*на части*) to break up

разлу́к|а (-и) *ж* separation

разлуч|и́ть (-у́, -и́шь; *impf* **разлуча́ть**) *сов перех*: **~ кого-н с** +*instr* to separate sb from; (*impf* **разлуча́ться**) *сов возв*: **~ся (с** +*instr*) to be separated (from)

разл|юби́ть (-юблю́, -ю́бишь) *сов перех*: **~** +*infin* (*читать, гуля́ть итп*) to lose one's enthusiasm for doing; **он меня́ ~юби́л** he doesn't love me any more

разма́|зать (-жу, -жешь; *impf* **разма́зывать**) *сов перех* to smear

разма́тыва|ть (-ю) *несов от* **размота́ть**

разма́х (-а) *м* (*рук*) span; (*перен*:

деятельности) scope; (: проекта)
scale; ~ **крýльев** wingspan

размáхива|ть (-ю) несов: ~ +instr
to wave; (оружием) to brandish

размахн|ýться (-ýсь, -ёшься;
impf **размáхиваться)** сов возв to
bring one's arm back; (перен:
разг: в делах итп) to go to town

размéн (-а) м (денег, пленных)
exchange; ~ **квартúры** flat swap
(of one large flat for two smaller ones)

размéнн|ый прил: ~ **автомáт**
change machine; ~**ая монéта**
(small) change

разменя́|ть (-ю; impf
размéнивать) сов перех to change; (квартиру) to
exchange; ~**ся** (impf
размéниваться) сов возв
(перен: разг: обменять
жилплощадь) to do a flat swap (of
one large flat for two smaller ones)

размéр (-а) м size

размéренный прил measured

размес|тúть (-щý, -стúшь; impf
размещáть) сов перех (в отеле)
to place; (на столе) to arrange;
~**ся** (impf **размещáться)** сов
возв (по комнатам) to settle o.s.

размé|тить (-чу, -тишь; impf
размечáть) сов перех to mark
out

размешáть (-ю; impf
размéшивать) сов перех to stir

размещá|ть(ся) (-ю(сь)) несов
от **разместúть(ся)**

разминá|ть(ся) (-ю(сь)) несов
от **размя́ть(ся)**

разминúр|овать (-ую) (не)сов
перех: ~ **пóле** to clear a field of
mines

размúн|ка (-ки; gen pl **-ок)** ж
(спортсменов) warm-up

размин|ýться (-ýсь, -ёшься)
сов возв (не встретиться) to miss

each other; (дать пройти) to pass

размнóж|ить (-у, -ишь) impf
размножáть) сов перех to make
(multiple) copies of; ~**ся** (pf
размножáться) сов возв (БИО)
to reproduce

размóк|нуть (-ну; pt **-, -ла;** impf
размокáть) сов (хлеб, картон)
to go soggy; (почва) to become
sodden

размóлв|ка (-ки) ж quarrel

разморó|зить (-жу, -зишь) impf
разморáживать) сов перех to
defrost

разморáживаться) сов возв to
defrost

размотá|ть (-ю; impf
размáтывать) сов перех to
unwind

разм|ы́ть (3sg -óет; impf
размывáть) сов перех to wash
away

размышля́|ть (-ю) несов: ~ (о
+prp) to contemplate, reflect (on)

размягч|úть (ý, -úшь; impf
размягчáть) сов перех to soften

размя́к|нуть (-ну; pt **-, -ла;** impf
размякáть) сов to soften

раз|мя́ть (-омнý, -омнёшь; impf
разминáть) сов перех to loosen
up; ~**ся** (impf **разминáться)** сов
возв to warm up

разнáшива|ть(ся) (-ю) несов от
разносúть(ся)

разн|естú (-есý, -есёшь; pt **-ёс,
-еслá;** impf **разносúть)** сов
перех (письма) to deliver;
(тарелки) to put out; (тучи) to
disperse; (заразу, слухи) to
spread; (раскритиковать) to slam;
~**сь** (impf **разносúться)** сов возв
(слух, запах) to spread; (звук) to
resound

разнимá|ть (-ю) несов от
разня́ть

ра́зниц|а (-ы) ж difference; **кака́я ~?** what difference does it make?

разнови́дност|ь (-и) ж (био) variety; (людей) type, kind

разногла́си|е (-я) ср disagreement

разнообра́зи|е (-я) ср variety

разнообра́зный прил various

разноро́дный прил heterogeneous

разно́с (-а) м delivery; (разг: выговор) battering

разн|оси́ть (-ошу́, -о́сишь) несов от **разнести́** ♦ (impf (обувь) to break in; **~ся** несов от **разнести́сь** ♦ (impf

разна́шивать сов перех (обувь) to be broken in

разносторо́нний прил (деятельность) wide-ranging; (ум, личность) multifaceted

ра́зность (-и) ж difference

разноцве́тный прил multicoloured (BRIT), multicolored (US)

ра́зный прил different

разн|я́ть (-иму́, -и́мешь; impf **разнима́ть**) сов перех (руки) to unclench; (деру́щихся) to separate

разоб|ла́ть (-у́, -и́шь; impf **разоблача́ть**) сов перех to expose

раз|обра́ть (-беру́, -берёшь; impf **разбира́ть**) сов перех (бумаги) to sort out; (текст) to analyse (BRIT), analyze (US); (вкус, подпись итп) to make out; **разбира́ть** (~ pf) (на ча́сти) to take apart; **~ся** (impf **разбира́ться**) сов возв: **~ся в** +prp (в вопросе, в деле) to sort out

разобщённый прил divided

ра́зовый прил: **~ биле́т** single

(BRIT) или one-way ticket

раз|огна́ть (-гоню́, -го́нишь; impf **разгоня́ть**) сов перех (толпу) to break up; (тучи) to disperse; (машину) to increase the speed of; **~ся** (impf **разгоня́ться**) сов возв to build up speed, accelerate

разог|ну́ть (-у́, -ёшь; impf **разгиба́ть**) сов перех (проволоку) to straighten out; **~ся** (impf **разгиба́ться**) сов возв to straighten up

разогре́|ть (-ю; impf **разогрева́ть**) сов перех (чайник, суп) to heat; **~ся** (impf **разогрева́ться**) сов возв (суп) to heat up

разозл|и́ть(ся) (-ю́(сь), -и́шь(ся)) сов от **зли́ть(ся)**

разойти́сь сов как **идти́**; см. **расходи́ться** (impf **расходи́ться**) сов возв (гости) to leave; (толпа) to disperse; (тираж) to sell out; (не встретиться) to miss each other; (супруги) to split up; (шов, крепления) to come apart; (перен: мнения) to diverge; (разг: дать волю себе) to get going

ра́зом нареч (разг: все вместе) all at once; (: в оди́н приём) in one go

разомк|ну́ть (-у́, -ёшь; impf **размыка́ть**) сов перех (цепь) to unfasten; **~ся** (impf **размыка́ться**) сов возв to come unfastened

разорв|а́ть (-у́, -ёшь; impf **рвать** или **разрыва́ть**) сов от **рвать** ♦ (impf **разрыва́ть**) сов перех (нитки) to tear или rip up; (перен: связь) to sever; (: договор) to break; **~ся** сов от **рва́ться** ♦ (impf **разрыва́ться**) возв (одежда) to tear, rip; (верёвка, цепь) to break; (связь) to be severed; (снаряд) to explode

разоре́ни|е (-я) *ср* (человека)
impoverishment; (*компании*)
(financial) ruin

разор|и́ть (-ю́, -и́шь; *impf*
разоря́ть) *сов перех* (деревню,
гнездо) to plunder; (*население*)
to impoverish; (: *компанию*,
страну) to ruin; **~ся** (*impf*
разоря́ться) *сов возв* (человек)
to become impoverished;
(*компания*) to go bust *или*
bankrupt

разоруже́ни|е (-я) *ср* disarming;
(*полит*) disarmament

разоруж|и́ть (-у́, -и́шь; *impf*
разоружа́ть) *сов перех* to
disarm; **~ся** (*impf* **разоружа́ться**)
сов возв to disarm

разоря́|ть(ся) (-ю(сь)) *несов от*
разори́ть(ся)

разо|сла́ть (-шлю́, -шлёшь; *impf*
рассыла́ть) *сов перех* to send
out

разостла́ть (**расстелю́**,
рассте́лешь) *несов* =
расстели́ть

разочарова́ни|е (-я) *ср* disap-
pointment; (*потеря веры*): **~ в**
+*prp* (в идее) disenchantment with

разочаро́ванный *прил*
disappointed; **~ в** +*prp* (в идее)
disenchanted with

разочаро́в|ать (-ую; *impf*
разочаро́вывать) *сов перех* to
disappoint; **~ся** (*impf*
разочаро́вываться) *сов возв*:
~ся в +*prp* to become
disenchanted with

разрабо́та|ть (-ю; *impf*
разраба́тывать) *сов перех* to
develop

разрабо́т|ка (-ки) *ж*
development; **га́зовые ~ки** gas
fields *мн*; **нефтяны́е ~ки** oilfields
мн

разра|зи́ться (-жу́сь, -зи́шься;
impf **разража́ться**) *сов возв* to
break out

разр|асти́сь (*3sg* -асте́тся, *pt*
-о́сся, -осла́сь; *impf*
разраста́ться) *сов возв* (*лес*) to
spread

разре́з (-а) *м* (на юбке) slit;
(*ГЕОМ*) section

разре́|зать (-жу, -жешь) *сов от*
ре́зать

разреша́|ть (-ю) *несов от*
разреши́ть; **~ся** *несов от*
разреши́ться ♦ *неперех*
(*допускаться*) to be allowed *или*
permitted

разреше́ни|е (-я) *ср* (действие)
authorization; (*родителей*)
permission; (*проблемы*) resolution;
(*документ*) permit

разреш|и́ть (-у́, -и́шь; *impf*
разреша́ть) *сов перех* (*решить*)
to resolve; (*позволить*): **~ кому́-н**
+*infin* to allow *или* permit sb to do;
~йте? may I come in?; **~йте**
пройти́ may I pass; **~ся** (*impf*
разреша́ться) *сов возв* to be
resolved

разровня́|ть (-ю) *сов от*
ровня́ть

разр|уби́ть (-ублю́, -у́бишь;
impf **разруба́ть**) *сов перех* to
chop in two

разру́х|а (-и) *ж* devastation

разруши́тельный *прил*
(*война*) devastating; (*действие*)
destructive

разру́ш|ить (-у, -ишь; *impf*
разруша́ть) *сов перех* to
destroy; **~ся** (*impf* **разруша́ться**)
сов возв to be destroyed

разры́в (-а) *м* (отношений)
severance; (*снаряда*) explosion;
(*во времени, в цифрах*) gap

разрыва́|ть(ся) (-ю(сь)) *несов*

от разорва́ть(ся)

разря́д (-а) *м* (*тип*) category; (*квалифика́ция*) grade

разря|ди́ть (-жу́, -ди́шь; *impf* **разряжа́ть**) *сов перех* (*ружьё*) to discharge; **разряжа́ть** (~ *pf*) **обстано́вку** to diffuse the situation

разря́д|ка (-ки; *gen pl* -ок) *ж* escape; (*в те́ксте*) spacing; **разря́дка (междунаро́дной напряжённости)** détente

разряжа́|ть (-ю) *несов от* разряди́ть

разубе|ди́ть (-жу́, -ди́шь; *impf* **разубежда́ть**) *сов перех*: ~ **кого́-н** (**в** +*prp*) to dissuade sb (from)

разува́|ть(ся) (-ю(сь)) *несов от* разу́ть(ся)

ра́зум (-а) *м* reason

разуме́|ться (*3sg* -ется) *сов возв*: **под э́тим** ~**ется, что ...** by this is meant that ...; (*само́ собо́й*) ~**ется** that goes without saying ♦ *вводн сл*: **он,** ~**ется, не знал об э́том** naturally, he knew nothing about it

разу́мный *прил* (*существо́*) intelligent; (*посту́пок, реше́ние*) reasonable

разу́тый *прил* (*без о́буви*) barefoot

разу́|ть (-ю; *impf* **разува́ть**) *сов перех*: ~ **кого́-н** to take sb's shoes off; ~**ся** (*impf* **разува́ться**) *сов возв* to take one's shoes off

разучи́ть (-учу́, -у́чишь; *impf* **разу́чивать**) *сов перех* to learn; ~**ся** (*impf* **разу́чиваться**) *сов возв*: ~ +*infin* to forget how to do sth

разъеда́|ть (*3sg* -ет) *несов от* разъе́сть

разъеди|ни́ть (-ю́, -и́шь; *impf* **разъединя́ть**) *сов перех* (*провода́, телефо́н*) to disconnect

разъезжа́|ть (-ю) *несов* (*по дела́м*) to travel; (*ката́ться*) to ride about; ~**ся** *несов от* разъе́хаться

разъе́|сть (*как* есть; *см.* Table 15; *impf* **разъеда́ть**) *сов перех* to corrode

разъе́|хаться (*как* е́хать; *см.* Table 19; *impf* **разъезжа́ться**) *сов возв* (*го́сти*) to leave

разъярённый *прил* furious

разъясне́ни|е (-я) *ср* clarification

разъясн|и́ть (-ю́, -и́шь; *impf* **разъясня́ть**) *сов перех* to clarify

разыгра́|ть (-ю; *impf* **разы́грывать**) *сов перех* (*МУЗ, СПОРТ*) to play; (*сце́ну*) to act out; (*в лотере́ю*) to raffle; (*разг: подшути́ть*) to play a joke *или* trick on

разыска́|ть (-ищу́, -и́щешь; *impf* **разы́скивать**) *сов перех* to find

РАИС *ср сокр* (= **Росси́йское аге́нтство интеллектуа́льной со́бственности**) copyright protection agency

рай (-я; *loc sg* -ю́) *м* paradise

райо́н (-а) *м* (*страны́*) region; (*го́рода*) district

райо́нный *прил* district

ра́йский *прил* heavenly

рак (-а) *м* (*ЗООЛ, речно́й*) crayfish; (*: морско́й*) crab; (*МЕД*) cancer; (*созве́здие*): **Рак** Pac Cancer

раке́т|а (-ы) *ж* rocket; (*ВОЕН*) missile; (*су́дно*) hydrofoil

раке́т|ка (-ки; *gen pl* -ок) *ж* (*СПОРТ*) racket

ра́кови|на (-ы) *ж* (*ЗООЛ*) shell; (*для умыва́ния*) sink

ра́ковый *прил* (*ЗООЛ, КУЛИН*) crab; (*МЕД*) cancer

ра́м|а (-ы) *ж* frame; (*АВТ*) chassis

ра́м|ка (-ки; *gen pl* -ок) *ж* frame;

см. также ра́мки

ра́м|ки (-ок) мн: ~ +gen (рассказа, обязанностей) framework ед of; (закона) limits мн of; в ~ках +gen (закона, приличия) within the bounds of; (переговоров) within the framework of; за ~ками +gen beyond the framework of

РАН м сокр (= Росси́йская акаде́мия нау́к) Russian Academy of Sciences

ра́н|а (-ы) ж wound

ра́неный прил injured; (ВОЕН) wounded

ра́н|ец (-ца) м (школьный) satchel

ра́н|ить (-ю, -ишь) (не)сов перех to wound

ра́нний прил early

ра́но нареч early ♦ как сказ it's early; ~ и́ли по́здно sooner or later

ра́ньше сравн нареч от ра́но ♦ нареч (прежде) before ♦ предл: ~ +gen before; ~ вре́мени (радоваться итп) too soon

ра́порт (-а) м report

рапорт|ова́ть (-у́ю) (не)сов: ~ (кому́-н о чём-н) to report back (to sb on sth)

ра́с|а (-ы) ж race

раси́зм (-а) м racism

раси́ст (-а) м racist

раска́ива|ться (-юсь) несов от **раска́яться**

раскал|и́ть (-ю́, -и́шь; impf **раскаля́ть**) сов перех to bring to a high temperature; **раскали́ться** (impf **раскаля́ться**) сов возв to get very hot

раска́лыва|ть(ся) (-ю(сь)) несов от **расколо́ть(ся)**

раска́пыва|ть (-ю) несов от **раскопа́ть**

раска́т (-а) м (грома) peal

раската́|ть (-ю; impf **раска́тывать**) сов перех (ковёр) to unroll; (тесто) to roll out; (дорогу) to flatten (out)

раска́яни|е (-я) ср repentance

раска́|яться (-юсь; impf **раска́иваться**) сов возв: ~ (в +prp) to repent (of)

раскид|а́ть (-а́ю; impf **раски́дывать**) сов перех to scatter

раски́н|уть (-у; impf **раски́дывать**) сов перех (руки) to throw open; (сети) to spread out; (лагерь) to set up; **~ся** (impf **раски́дываться**) сов возв to stretch out

раскладно́й прил folding

раскладу́ш|ка (-ки; gen pl -ек) ж (разг) camp bed (BRIT), cot (US)

раскла́дыва|ть (-ю) несов от **разложи́ть**

раскле́|ить (-ю, -ишь; impf **раскле́ивать**) сов перех (заклеенное) to unstick; (плакаты) to paste up

раско́ванный прил relaxed

раско́л (-а) м (организации) split; (РЕЛ) schism

раскол|о́ть (-олю́, -о́лешь; impf **раска́лывать**) сов перех to split; (лёд, орех) to crack; **~ся** (impf **раска́лываться**) сов возв (полено, орех) to split open; (перен: организация) to be split

раскопа́|ть (-ю; impf **раска́пывать**) сов перех to dig up

раско́п|ки (-ок) мн (работы) excavations мн; (место) (archaeological) dig ед

раскра́|сить (-шу, -сишь; impf **раскра́шивать**) сов перех to colour (BRIT) или color (US) (in)

раскро́|ить (-ю́, -и́шь) сов

перех to cut

раскр|ути́ть (-учу́, -у́тишь; *impf* **раскру́чивать**) *сов перех* (*винт*) to unscrew; (*рекламировать*) to hype up; (*дело*) to set in motion

раскру́тк|а (-и; *gen pl* -ок) ж (*разг*) hyping up

раскр|ы́ть (-о́ю, -о́ешь; *impf* **раскрыва́ть**) *сов перех* to open; (*перен*: чью-нибудь тайну, план) to discover; (: свою тайну, план) to disclose; **~ся** (*impf* **раскрыва́ться**) *сов возв* to open

раск|упи́ть (-уплю́, -у́пишь; *impf* **раскупа́ть**) *сов перех* to buy up

ра́совый *прил* racial

распа́д (-а) *м* break-up; (*хим*) decomposition

распада́|ться (*3sg* -ется) *несов от* **распа́сться** ♦ *возв* (*состоять из частей*): **~ на** +*acc* to be divided into

распа́|сться (*3sg* -дётся; *impf* **распада́ться**) *сов возв* to break up; (*молекула*) to decompose

распахн|у́ть (-у́, -ёшь; *impf* **распа́хивать**) *сов перех* to throw open; **~ся** (*impf* **распа́хиваться**) *сов возв* to fly open

распашо́нк|а (-и; *gen pl* -ок) ж cotton baby top without buttons

распеча́т|ка (-и; *gen pl* -ок) ж (*доклада*) print-out

распеча́та|ть (-ю; *impf* **распеча́тывать**) *сов перех* (*письмо, пакет*) to open; (*размножить*) to print off

распил|и́ть (-илю́, -и́лишь; *impf* **распи́ливать**) *сов перех* to saw up

распина́|ть (-ю) *несов от* **распя́ть**

расписа́ни|е (-я) *ср* timetable, schedule

расп|иса́ть (-ишу́, -и́шешь; *impf*

распи́сывать) *сов перех* (*дела*) to arrange; (*стены, шкатулку*) to paint; (*разг*: женить) to marry (in registry office); **~ся** (*impf*

распи́сываться) *сов возв* (*поставить подпись*) to sign one's name; **распи|са́ться** (**~ся** *pf*) **с** +*instr* to marry (in registry office)

распи́ск|а (-и; *gen pl* -ок) ж (*о получении денег*) receipt; (*о невыезде*) warrant

распла́т|а (-ы) ж payment; (*перен*: за преступление) retribution

распла|ти́ться (-чу́сь, -ти́шься; *impf* **распла́чиваться**) *сов возв*: **~** +*instr* to pay; (*перен*: с предателем*) to revenge o.s. on

распл|еска́ть (-ещу́, -е́щешь; *impf* **расплёскивать**) *сов перех* to spill; **~ся** (*impf* **расплёскиваться**) *сов возв* to spill

распл|ы́вчатый *прил* (*рисунок, очертания*) blurred; (*перен*: ответ, намёк*) vague

распл|ы́ться (-ву́сь, -вёшься; *impf* **расплыва́ться**) *сов возв* (*краски*) to run; (*перен*: фигуры) to be blurred

распого́д|иться (*3sg* -ится) *сов возв* (*о погоде*) to clear up

распозна́|ть (-ю; *impf* **распознава́ть**) *сов перех* to identify

распола́га|ть (-ю) *несов от* **расположи́ть** ♦ *неперех*: **~** +*instr* (*временем*) to have available; **~ся** *несов от* **расположи́ться** ♦ *возв* (*находиться*) to be situated *или* located

расположе́ни|е (-я) *ср* (*место*: лагеря) location; (*комнат*) layout; (*симпатия*) disposition

располо́женный *прил*: ~ к +*dat* (к человеку) well-disposed towards; (к болезни) susceptible to

распол|ожи́ть (-ожу́, -о́жишь; *impf* **располага́ть**) *сов перех* (мебель, вещи итп) to arrange; (отряд) to station; **располага́ть** (~ *pf*) кого́-н к себе́ to win sb over; **~ся** (*impf* **располага́ться**) *сов возв* (человек) to settle down; (отряд) to position itself

распоряди́тел|ь (-я) *м* (КОММ) manager

распоряди́тельный *прил*: ~ дире́ктор managing director

распоря|ди́ться (-жу́сь, -ди́шься; *impf* **распоряжа́ться**) *сов возв* to give out instructions

распоря́д|ок (-ка) *м* routine

распоряжа́|ться (-юсь) *несов от* **распоряди́ться** *возв*: ~ (+*instr*) to be in charge (of)

распоряже́ни|е (-я) *ср* (управление) management; (указ) enactment; **ба́нковское** ~ banker's order; **в** ~ кого́-н/чего́-н at sb's/ sth's disposal

распра́в|ить (-лю, -ишь; *impf* **расправля́ть**) *сов перех* to straighten out; (крылья) to spread; **~ся** (*impf* **расправля́ться**) *сов возв* (см перех) to be straightened out; to spread

распределе́ни|е (-я) *ср* distribution; (после институ́та) work placement

распредел|и́ть (-ю́, -и́шь; *impf* **распределя́ть**) *сов перех* to distribute; **~ся** (*impf* **распределя́ться**) *сов возв*: **~ся (по** +*dat*) (по группа́м) to divide up (into)

распрода́ж|а (-и) *ж* sale

распрода́|ть (как **дать**; см. Table 16; *impf* **распродава́ть**) *сов*

перех to sell off; (биле́ты) to sell out of

распростране́ни|е (-я) *ср* spreading; (оружия) proliferation; (приказа) application

распространённый *прил* widespread

распростран|и́ть (-ю́, -и́шь; *impf* **распространя́ть**) *сов перех* to spread; (правило, приказ) to apply; (газе́ты) to distribute; (запах) to emit; **~ся** (*impf* **распространя́ться**) *сов возв* to spread; **~ся** (*pf*) **на** +*acc* to extend to; (приказ) to apply to

распрям|и́ть (-лю́, -и́шь; *impf* **распрямля́ть**) *сов перех* (проволоку) to straighten (out); (плечи) to straighten

распу|сти́ть (-щу́, -у́стишь; *impf* **распуска́ть**) *сов перех* (армию) to disband; (волосы) to let down; (парламент) to dissolve; (слухи) to spread; (перен: ребёнка итп) to spoil; **~ся** (*impf* **распуска́ться**) *сов возв* (цветы, почки) to open out; (дети, люди) to get out of hand

распу́та|ть (-ю; *impf* **распу́тывать**) *сов перех* (узел) to untangle; (перен: преступление, загадку) to unravel; **~ся** (*impf* **распу́тываться**) *сов возв* (см перех) to come untangled; to unravel itself

распу́хн|уть (-у; *impf* **распуха́ть**) *сов* to swell up

распу́щенный *прил* unruly; (безнравственный) dissolute

распыл|и́ть (-ю́, -и́шь; *impf* **распыля́ть**) *сов перех* to spray

распя́ти|е (-я) *ср* crucifixion

распя́|ть (-ну́, -нёшь; *impf* **распина́ть**) *сов перех* to crucify

рассад|а (-ы) ж собир (БОТ) seedlings мн

расс|адить (-ажу́, -а́дишь; impf **расса́живать**) сов перех (гостей, публику) to seat; (цветы) to thin out

рассве|сти́ (3sg -тёт, pt -ло́; impf **рассвета́ть**) сов безл: ~ло́ dawn was breaking

рассве́т (-а) м daybreak

рассе́ива|ть(ся) (-ю(сь)) несов от **рассе́ять(ся)**

рассека́|ть (-ю) несов от **рассе́чь**

расс|ели́ть (-елю́, -е́лишь; impf **расселя́ть**) сов перех (по комнатам) to accommodate

расс|ерди́ть(ся) (-ержу́(сь), -е́рдишь(ся)) сов от **серди́ть(ся)**

расс|е́сться (-я́дусь, -я́дешься; pt -е́лся, -е́лась) сов возв (по столам, в зале) to take one's seat

расс|е́чь (-еку́, -ечёшь etc, -еку́т; pt -ёк, -екла́; impf **рассека́ть**) сов перех (губу, лоб) to cut in two

рассе́янный прил absent-minded

рассе́|ять (-ю; impf **рассе́ивать**) сов перех (семена, людей) to scatter; (перен: сомнения) to dispel; **~ся** (impf **рассе́иваться**) сов возв (люди) to be scattered; (тучи, дым) to disperse

расска́з (-а) м story; (свидетеля) account

расск|аза́ть (-ажу́, -а́жешь; impf **расска́зывать**) сов перех to tell

расска́зчик (-а) м storyteller; (автор) narrator

рассла́б|ить (-лю, -ишь; impf **расслабля́ть**) сов перех to relax; **~ся** (impf **расслабля́ться**) сов возв to relax

рассле́д|овать (-ую) (не)сов перех to investigate

рассма́трива|ть (-ю) несов от **рассмотре́ть** ♦ перех: ~ что-н как to regard sth as

рассме|ши́ть (-у́, -ши́шь) сов от **смеши́ть**

рассме|я́ться (-ю́сь, -ёшься) сов возв to start laughing

рассм|отре́ть (-отрю́, -о́тришь; impf **рассма́тривать**) сов перех (изучить) to examine; (различить) to discern

рассо́л (-а) м brine

расспр|оси́ть (-ошу́, -о́сишь; impf **расспра́шивать**) сов перех: ~ о +prp to question (about)

рассро́ч|ка (-ки; gen pl -ек) ж installment (BRIT), instalment (US); в ~ку on hire purchase (BRIT), on the installment plan (US)

расстава́ни|е (-я) ср parting

расстава́|ться (-ю́сь, -ёшься) сов от **расста́ться**

расста́в|ить (-лю, -ишь; impf **расставля́ть**) сов перех to arrange

расстано́в|ка (-ки; gen pl -ок) ж (мебели, книг) arrangement

расста́|ться (-нусь, -нешься; impf **расстава́ться**) сов возв: ~ +instr to part with

расстег|ну́ть (-у́, -ёшь; impf **расстёгивать**) сов перех to undo; **~ся** (impf **расстёгиваться**) сов возв (человек) to unbutton o.s.; (рубашка, пуговица) to come undone

расст|ели́ть (-елю́, -е́лишь; impf **расстила́ть**) сов перех to spread out

расстоя́ни|е (-я) ср distance

расстра́ива|ть(ся) (-ю(сь)) несов от **расстро́ить(ся)**

расстре́л (-а) м: ~ +gen shooting или firing at; (казнь) execution (by *firing squad*

расстреля́|ть (-ю; *impf*
расстре́ливать) *сов перех*
(*демонстрацию*) to open fire on;
(*казнить*) to shoot

расстро́енный *прил* (*здоровье,
нервы*) weak; (*человек, вид*)
upset; (*рояль*) out of tune

расстро́|ить (-ю, -ишь; *impf*
расстра́ивать) *сов перех*
(*планы*) to disrupt; (*человека,
желудок*) to upset; (*здоровье*) to
damage; (*МУЗ*) to put out of tune;
~ся (*impf* **расстра́иваться**) *сов
возв* (*планы*) to fall through;
(*человек*) to get upset; (*нервы*) to
weaken; (*здоровье*) to be
damaged; (*МУЗ*) to go out of tune

расстро́йств|о (-а) *ср*
(*огорчение*) upset; (*речи*)
dysfunction; **~ желу́дка** stomach
upset

рассту́п|иться (3sg -упится; *impf*
расступа́ться) *сов возв* (*толпа*)
to make way

рассу́д|ить (-ужу́, -у́дишь) *сов*:
она́ ~уди́ла пра́вильно her
judgement was correct

рассу́д|ок (-ка) *м* reason

рассужда́|ть (-ю) *несов* to
reason; (*impf* и *prp* о *+prp*) to debate

рассужде́ни|е (-я) *ср*
judg(e)ment

рассчита́|ть (-ю; *impf*
рассчи́тывать) *сов перех* to
calculate; (*impf*
рассчи́тываться) *сов возв*: **~ся**
(*с +instr*) (*с продавцом*) to settle
up (with)

рассчи́тыва|ть (-ю) *несов от*
рассчита́ть ♦ *неперех*: **~ на** *+acc*
(*надеяться*) to count *или* rely on;
~ся *несов от* **рассчита́ться**

рассыла́|ть (-ю) *несов от*
разосла́ть

рассы́п|ать (-лю, -лешь; *impf*
рассыпа́ть) *сов перех* to spill;
~ся (*impf* **рассыпа́ться**) *сов возв*
(*сахар, бусы*) to spill; (*толпа*) to
scatter

раста́плива|ть (-ю) *несов от*
растопи́ть

раста́птыва|ть (-ю) *несов от*
растопта́ть

раста́|ять (-ю) *сов от* **та́ять**

раство́р (-а) *м* (*ХИМ*) solution;
(*строительный*) mortar

раствори́мый *прил* soluble; **~
ко́фе** instant coffee

раствори́тел|ь (-я) *м* solvent

раствор|и́ть (-ю́, -и́шь; *impf*
растворя́ть) *сов перех*
(*порошок*) to dissolve; (*окно,
дверь*) to open; **~ся** (*impf*
растворя́ться) *сов возв* (*см
перех*) to dissolve; to open

расте́ни|е (-я) *ср* plant

растениево́дств|о (-а) *ср*
horticulture

раст|ере́ть (разотру́,
разотрёшь; *pt* -ёр, -ёрла; *impf*
растира́ть) *сов перех* (*рану,
тело*) to massage

расте́рянный *прил* confused

растеря́|ться (-юсь) *сов возв*
(*человек*) to be at a loss, be
confused; (*письма*) to disappear

раст|е́чься (3sg -ечётся, *pt* -ёкся,
-екла́сь; *impf* **растека́ться**) *сов
возв* (*вода*) to spill

раст|и́ (-у́, -ёшь; *pt* рос, росла́,
росло́; *pf* вы́~и) *несов* to grow

растира́|ть (-ю) *несов от*
растере́ть

расти́тельн|ый *прил* (*БОТ*) plant;
~ое ма́сло vegetable oil

ра|сти́ть (-щу́, -сти́шь; *pf*
вы́растить) *несов перех* (*детей*)
to raise; (*цветы*) to grow

растоп|и́ть (-оплю́, -о́пишь;

impf **растапливать**) *сов перех* (печку) to light; (воск, жир, лёд) to melt; **~ся** *сов от* **топиться**

раст|оптать (-опчу, -опчешь; *impf* **растаптывать**) *сов перех* to trample on

расторг|нуть (-ну; *pt* -, -ла; *impf* **расторгать**) *сов перех* to annul

растрат|а (-ы) *ж* (времени, денег) waste; (хищение, embezzlement

растра|тить (-чу, -тишь; *impf* **растрачивать**) *сов перех* to waste; (расхитить) to embezzle

растрог|анный *прил* (человек) touched, moved; (голос) emotional

растрог|ать (-ю) *сов перех*: ~ кого-н (+*instr*) to touch *или* move sb (by); **~ся** *сов возв* to be touched *или* moved

раст|януть (-яну, -янешь; *impf* **растягивать**) *сов перех* to stretch; (связки) to strain; **~ся** (*impf* **растягиваться**) *сов возв* (человек, обоз) to stretch out; (связки) to be strained

расхажива|ть (-ю) *несов* to saunter

расхвата|ть (-ю; *impf* **расхватывать**) *сов перех* (разг) to snatch up

расхи|тить (-щу, -тишь; *impf* **расхищать**) *сов перех* to embezzle

расход (-а) *м* (энергии) consumption; (обычно мн: затраты) expense; (: комм, в бухгалтерии) expenditure *ед*

расх|одиться (-ожусь, -одишься) *несов от* **разойтись**

расходн|ый *прил*: ~ ордер (комм) expenses form; **~ые материалы** consumables

расход|овать (-ую; *pf* из~) *несов перех* (деньги) to spend;

(материалы) to use up

расхождени|е (-я) *ср* discrepancy; (во взглядах) divergence

расхо|теть (как **хотеть**; см. *Table* 14) *сов*: ~ +*infin* (спать, гулять *итп*) to no longer want to do; **~ся** *сов безл*: (мне) расхотелось спать I don't feel sleepy any more

расцве|сти (-ту, -тёшь; *pt* -ёл, -ела, -ело; *impf* **расцветать**) *сов* to blossom

расцвет (-а) *м* (науки) heyday; (таланта) blossoming; **он в ~е сил** he is in the prime of life

расцветк|а (-и; *gen pl* -ок) *ж* colour (*BRIT*) *или* color (*US*) scheme

расцениватъся (*3sg* -ется) *несов*: ~ как to be regarded as

расц|енить (-еню, -енишь; *impf* **расценивать**) *сов перех* to judge

расценк|а (-и; *gen pl* -ок) *ж* (работы) rate; (цена) tariff

расч|есать (-ешу, -ешешь; *impf* **расчёсывать**) *сов перех* (волосы) to comb; **расчёсывать** (~ *pf*) кого-н to comb sb's hair

расчёс|ка (-ки; *gen pl* -ок) *ж* comb

расчёт (-а) *м* (стоимости) calculation; (выгода) advantage; (бережливость) economy; **из ~а** +*gen* on the basis of; **брать (взять** *pf*) *или* **принимать (принять** *pf*) **что-н в ~** to take sth into account; **я с Вами в ~е** we are all even

расчётливый *прил* (экономный) thrifty; (политик) calculating

расчётный *прил*: ~ **день** payday; ~ **счёт** debit account

расчи|стить (-щу, -стишь; *impf* **расчищать**) *сов перех* to clear

расшата|ть (-ю; *impf* **расшатывать**) *сов перех* (стул) to make wobbly; (здоровье) to damage; **~ся** (impf (стул) to become wobbly; (здоровье) to be damaged

расшире́ни|е (-я) ср widening; (связей, дела) expansion; (знаний) broadening

расши́р|ить (-ю, -ишь; impf **расширя́ть)** сов перех to widen; (дело) to expand; **~ся** (impf **расширя́ться)** сов возв (см перех) to widen; to expand

расщеп|и́ть (-лю́, -и́шь; impf **расщепля́ть)** сов перех (также физ) to split; (хим) to decompose; **~ся** (impf **расщепля́ться)** сов возв to splinter; (физ) to split; (хим) to decompose

ратифика́ци|я (-и) ж ratification

ратифици́р|овать (-ую) (не)сов перех to ratify

ра́унд (-а) м (СПОРТ, ПОЛИТ) round

рафина́д (-а) м sugar cubes мн

рахи́т (-а) м (МЕД) rickets

рацио́н (-а) м ration

рационализи́р|овать (-ую) (не)сов перех to rationalize

рациона́льн|ый прил rational; **~ое пита́ние** well-balanced diet

ра́ци|я (-и) ж walkie-talkie; (ВОЕН) radio set

рва́ный прил torn; (ботинки) worn

рв|ать (-у, -ёшь; pf **по~а́ть** или **разорва́ть)** несов перех to tear, rip; (перен: дружбу) to break off; (pf **вы~;** предмет из рук) to snatch; (pf **сорва́ть;** цветы, траву) to pick ♦ (pf **вы~)** безл: **его́ ~ёт** he is vomiting или being sick; **рва́ться** или **порва́ться** или **разорва́ться)** несов возв to tear, rip; (обувь) to become worn; (pf **разорва́ться;** снаряд) to

explode; **рва́ться** (impf) **к вла́сти** to be hungry for power

рве́ни|е (-я) ср enthusiasm

рво́т|а (-ы) ж vomiting

реабилити́р|овать (-ую) (не)сов перех to rehabilitate

реаги́р|овать (-ую) несов: ~ (**на** +acc) (на свет) to react (to); (pf **от~** или **про~;** на критику, на слова) to react или respond (to)

реакти́вный прил: ~ **дви́гатель** jet engine; ~ **самолёт** jet (plane)

реа́ктор (-а) м reactor

реакцио́нный прил reactionary

реа́кци|я (-и) ж reaction

реализа́ци|я (-и) ж (см глаг) implementation; disposal

реали́зм (-а) м realism

реализ|ова́ть (-у́ю) (не)сов перех to implement; (товар) to sell

реали́ст (-а) м realist

реалисти́ческий прил realistic; (искусство) realist

реа́льность (-и) ж reality; (плана) feasibility

реа́льный прил real; (политика) realistic; (план) feasible

реанима́ци|я (-и) ж resuscitation; **отделе́ние ~** intensive care unit

ребёнок (-ка; nom pl **де́ти** или **ребя́та)** м child; (грудной) baby

ребр|о́ (-а́; nom pl **рёбра)** ср (АНАТ) rib; (кубика итп) edge

ребя́т|а (-) мн от **ребёнок;** (разг: парни) guys мн

рёв (-а) м roar

рева́нш (-а) м revenge

реве́н|ь (-я́) м rhubarb

реве́|ть (-у́, -ёшь; несов to roar

ревизио́нный прил: **~ая коми́ссия** audit commission

реви́зи|я (-и) ж (КОММ) audit; (теории) revision

ревиз|ова́ть (-у́ю) (не)сов перех

(КОММ) to audit

ревизо́р (-а) м (КОММ) auditor

ревмати́зм (-а) м rheumatism

ревни́вый прил jealous

ревн|ова́ть (-у́ю) несов перех: ~ (кого́-н) to be jealous (of sb)

ре́вностный прил ardent, zealous

ре́вность (-и) ж jealousy

революционе́р (-а) м revolutionary

револю́ци|я (-и) ж revolution

ре́гби ср нескл rugby

регби́ст (-а) м rugby player

регио́н (-а) м region

региона́льный прил regional

реги́стр (-а) м register; (на пишущей машинке): ве́рхний/ ни́жний ~ upper/lower case

регистра́тор (-а) м receptionist

регистрату́р|а (-ы) ж reception

регистри́р|овать (-ую; pf за~) несов перех to register; ~ся (pf за~ся) несов возв to register; (оформлять брак) to get married (at a registry office)

регла́мент (-а) м (порядок) order of business; (время) speaking time

регули́р|овать (-ую) несов перех to regulate; (pf от~; мотор) to adjust

регулиро́вщик (-а) м: ~ у́личного движе́ния traffic policeman

регуля́рный прил regular

редакти́р|овать (-ую; pf от~) несов перех to edit

реда́ктор (-а) м editor; (КОМП) spellchecker

редакцио́нный прил editorial; ~ая колле́гия editorial board; ~ая статья́ editorial

реда́кци|я (-и) ж (действие: текста) editing; (формулировка: статьи закона) wording; (учреждение) editorial offices мн;

(на радио) desk; (на телевидении) division; **под ~ей** +gen edited by

реде́|ть (3sg -ет; pf по~) несов to thin out

реди́с (-а) м radish

ре́дкий прил rare; (волосы) thin

ре́дко нареч rarely, seldom

редколле́гия (-и) ж сокр = **редакцио́нная колле́гия**

ре́дкость (-и) ж rarity; **на ~** unusually

режи́м (-а) ж regime; (больничный) routine; (КОМП) mode

режиссёр (-а) м director (of film, play etc); **~-постано́вщик** (stage) director

ре́|зать (-жу, -жешь; pf раз~) несов перех (металл, кожу) to cut; (хлеб) to slice; (pf за~; свинью) to slaughter; (no pf; фигурки итп) to carve; **~ся** (pf про~ся) несов возв (зубы, рога) to come through

ре́звый прил agile

резе́рв (-а) м reserve

резе́рвный прил reserve; (КОМП) backup

рез|е́ц (-ца́) м (инструмент) cutting tool; (АНАТ) incisor

резиде́нци|я (-и) ж residence

рези́н|а (-ы) ж rubber

рези́н|ка (-ки; gen pl -ок) ж (ластик) rubber (BRIT), eraser (esp US); (тесёмка) elastic

рези́новый прил rubber

ре́зкий прил sharp; (свет, голос) harsh; (запах) pungent

ре́зко нареч sharply

резн|я́ (-и́) ж slaughter

резолю́ци|я (-и) ж (съезда) resolution; (распоряжение) directive

резона́нс (-а) м (ФИЗ) resonance;

(перен, реакция) response

результа́т (-а) м result

результати́вный _прил_ productive

резьб|а́ (-ы́) ж carving; _(винта)_ thread

резюме́ _ср нескл_ resume, summary

рейд (-а) м raid; _(МОР)_ anchorage

рейс (-а) м _(самолёта)_ flight; _(автобуса)_ run; _(парохода)_ sailing

ре́йсовый _прил_ regular

ре́йтинг (-а) м popularity rating

рейту́з|ы (-) мн thermal pants мн

рек|а́ (-и́; _acc sg_ -у, _dat sg_ -е́, _nom pl_ -и) ж river

рекла́м|а (-ы) ж _(действие: торговля)_ advertising; _(средство)_ advert (BRIT), advertisement

реклами́р|овать (-ую) _(не)сов перех_ to advertise

рекла́мный _прил (отдел, колонка)_ advertising; _(статья, фильм)_ publicity; ~ **ро́лик** advertisement; _(фильма)_ trailer

реклама́те|ль (-я) м advertiser

рекоменда́тельный _прил_: ~ое **письмо́** letter of recommendation

рекоменд|ова́ть (-у́ю) _(не)сов перех_ to recommend

реконструи́р|овать (-ую) _(не)сов перех_ to rebuild; _(здание)_ to reconstruct

реко́рд (-а) м record

реко́рдный _прил_ record(-breaking)

рекордсме́н (-а) м recordholder

ре́ктор (-а) м ≈ principal

ректора́т (-а) м principal's office

религио́зный _прил_ religious

рели́ги|я (-и) ж religion

рельс (-а) м _(обычно мн)_ rail

реме́н|ь (-ня́) м belt; _(сумки)_ strap; **привязны́е** ~**ни** seat belt

ремесл|о́ (-а́; _nom pl_ **ремёсла**,

gen pl **ремёсел**) _ср_ trade

ремеш|о́к (-ка́) м strap

ремо́нт (-а) м repair; _(здания: крупный)_ refurbishment; (: _мелкий)_ redecoration; **теку́щий** ~ maintenance

ремонти́р|овать (-ую, _pf_ от~) _несов перех_ to repair; _(здание)_ to renovate

ремо́нтный _прил_: ~ые **рабо́ты** repairs мн; ~**ая мастерска́я** repair workshop

рента́бельный _прил_ profitable

рентге́н (-а) м _(МЕД)_ X-ray

рентгено́лог (-а) м radiologist

реорганиз|ова́ть (-у́ю) _(не)сов перех_ to reorganize

репертуа́р (-а) м repertoire

репети́р|овать (-ую, _pf_ от~) _несов (не)перех_ to rehearse

репети́тор (-а) м private tutor

репети́ци|я (-и) ж rehearsal

ре́плик|а (-и) ж remark

репорта́ж (-а) м report

репортёр (-а) м reporter

репре́сси|я (-и) ж repression _ед_

репроду́ктор (-а) м loudspeaker

репроду́кци|я (-и) ж reproduction _(of painting etc)_

репута́ци|я (-и) ж reputation

ресни́ц|а (-ы) ж _(обычно мн)_ eyelash

респонде́нт (-а) м respondent

респу́блик|а (-и) ж republic

рессо́р|а (-ы) ж spring

реставра́тор (-а) м restorer

реставра́ци|я (-и) ж restoration

реставри́р|овать (-ую; _pf_ ~ _или_ от~) _несов перех_ to restore

рестора́н (-а) м restaurant

ресу́рс (-а) м _(обычно мн)_ resource

рефера́т (-а) м synopsis

рефере́ндум (-а) м referendum

рефле́кс (-а) м reflex

рефо́рм|а (-ы) ж reform

рефо́рма|тор (-а) м reformer

рецензи́р|овать (-ую), pf **про~**) несов перех to review

реце́нзи|я (-и) ж: **реце́нзия** (на +acc) review (of)

реце́пт (-а) м (МЕД) prescription; (КУЛИН, перен) recipe

речево́й прил speech

речно́й прил river

реч|ь (-и) ж speech; (разговорная итп) language; **~ идёт о том, как/где/кто ...** the matter in question is how/where/who ...; **об э́том не мо́жет быть и ре́чи** there can be absolutely no question of this; **о чём ~!** (разг) sure!, of course!

реша́|ть(ся) (-ю(сь)) несов от **реши́ть(ся)**

реша́ющий прил decisive; (слово, матч) deciding

реше́ни|е (-я) ср decision; (проблемы) solution

решёт|ка (-ки; gen pl -ок) ж (садовая) trellis; (оконная) grille; **за ~кой** behind bars

реши́мост|ь (-и) ж resolve

реши́тельно нареч resolutely; (действовать) decisively

реши́тельный прил (человек, взгляд) resolute; (меры) drastic

реш|и́ть (-у́, -и́шь; impf **реша́ть**) сов перех to decide; (проблему) to solve; **~ся** (impf **реша́ться**) сов возв (вопрос, судьба) to be decided; **реша́ться** (**~ся** pf) +infin to resolve to do; **реша́ться** (**~ся** pf) **на** +acc to decide on

ре́шк|а (-и) ж (на монете) tails; **орёл или ~?** heads or tails?

ре́|ять (3sg -ет) сов (флаг) to fly

ржа́ве|ть (3sg -ет; pf **за~**) несов to rust

ржа́вчин|а (-ы) ж rust

ржа́вый прил rusty

ржано́й прил rye

рж|ать (-у, -ёшь) несов to neigh

ржи итп сущ см. **рожь**

РИА ср сокр (= Росси́йское информацио́нное аге́нтство) Russian News Agency

Рим (-а) м Rome

ринг (-а) м (boxing) ring

ри́н|уться (-усь) сов возв to charge

рис (-а) м rice

риск (-а) no pl м risk

риско́ванный прил risky

риск|ова́ть (-у́ю), pf **рискну́ть**) несов to take risks; **~** (**рискну́ть** pf) +instr (жизнью, работой) to risk

рисова́ни|е (-я) ср (карандашом) drawing; (красками) painting

рис|ова́ть (-у́ю; pf **на~**) несов перех (карандашом) to draw; (красками) to paint

ри́совый прил rice

рису́н|ок (-ка) м drawing; (на ткани) pattern

ритм (-а) м rhythm

ритми́ческий прил rhythmic(al)

ритуа́л (-а) м ritual

риф (-а) м reef

ри́фм|а (-ы) ж rhyme

р-н сокр = **райо́н**

робе́|ть (-ю; pf **о~**) несов to go shy

ро́бкий прил shy

ро́бот (-а) м robot

р|ов (-ва; loc sg -ву) м ditch

рове́сник (-а) м: **он мой ~** he is the same age as me

ро́вно нареч (писать) evenly; (чертить) straight; (через год) exactly; **~ в два часа́** at two o'clock sharp

ро́вный прил even; (линия) straight

ровня́|ть (-ю; *pf* с~ *или*
вы́ровнять) *несов перех*
(*строй*) to straighten; (*pf* раз~ *или*
с~; *дорожку*) to level

рог (-а; *nom pl* -а́) *м* (*также МУЗ*)
horn; (*оле́ний* ~ *antler*; у чёрта на
~а́х (*разг*) in the middle of
nowhere

рога́тый *прил* horned; **кру́пный ~
скот** cattle

род (-а; *loc sg* -ý, *nom pl* -ы́) *м* clan;
(*о семье*) clan, family; (*расте́ний,
живо́тных*) genus; (*вид*) type;
(*линг*) gender; **своего́ ро́да** a kind
of; **в не́котором ро́де** to some
extent; **что-то в э́том или тако́м
ро́де** something like that

род. *сокр* (= **роди́лся**) b.

роддо́м (-а) *м сокр* =
роди́льный дом

роди́льный *прил*: **~ дом**
maternity hospital

роди́м|ый *прил*: **~ое пятно́**
birthmark

ро́дин|а (-ы) *ж* homeland

ро́дин|ка (-ки; *gen pl* -ок) *ж*
birthmark

роди́тел|и (-ей) *мн* parents *мн*

роди́тельный *прил*: **~ паде́ж** the
genitive (case)

роди́тельск|ий *прил* parental;
~ое собра́ние parents' meeting

роди́|ть (-жу́, -ди́шь; *impf*
рожа́ть *или* **рожда́ть**) (*не*)*сов
перех* to give birth to; **~ся** (*impf*
рожда́ться) (*не*)*сов возв* to be
born

родни́к (-а́) *м* spring (*water*)

родно́й *прил* (*брат, мать итп*)
natural; (*го́род, страна́*) native; (*в
обраще́нии*) dear; **~ язы́к** mother
tongue; *см. также* **родны́е**

родны́е (-х) *мн* relatives *мн*

родово́й *прил* (*поня́тие,
при́знак*) generic; (*линг*) gender;

(*име́ние*) family; (*МЕД, су́дороги,
тра́вма*) birth

родосло́вн|ая (-ой) *ж* (*семьи́*)
ancestry; (*соба́ки*) pedigree

родосло́вн|ый *прил*: **~ое де́рево**
family tree

ро́дственник (-а) *м* relation,
relative

ро́дственный *прил* family;
(*языки́, нау́ки*) related

родство́ (-а́) *ср* relationship;
(*душ, иде́й*) affinity

ро́д|ы (-ов) *мн* labour *ед* (BRIT),
labor *ед* (US); **приня́ть** (*pf*)
(приня́ть *pf*) ~ to deliver a baby

рожа́|ть (-ю) *несов от* **роди́ть**

рожда́емость (-и) *ж* birth rate

рожда́|ть(ся) (-ю(сь)) *несов от*
роди́ть(ся)

рожде́ни|е (-я) *ср* birth; **день ~я**
birthday

рожде́ственский *прил* Christmas

Рождество́ (-а́) *ср* (РЕЛ) Nativity;
(*пра́здник*) Christmas; **С ~м!**
Happy *или* Merry Christmas!

рожени́ц|а (-ы) *ж* woman in labour;
(*то́лько что роди́вшая*) woman
who has given birth

рож|о́к (-ка́) *м* (МУЗ) horn; (*для
о́буви*) shoehorn

рожь (ржи) *ж* rye

ро́з|а (-ы) *ж* (*расте́ние*)
rose(bush); (*цвето́к*) rose

розе́т|ка (-ки; *gen pl* -ок) *ж* power
point

ро́зниц|а (-ы) *ж* retail goods *мн*;
продава́ть (прода́ть *pf*) **в ~у** to
retail

ро́зничный *прил* retail

ро́зов|ый *прил* rose; (*цвет*) pink;
(*мечты́*) rose

ро́зыгрыш (-а) *м* (*лотере́и*)
draw; (*шу́тка*) prank

ро́зыск (-а) *м* search; **Уголо́вный
~ Criminal Investigation**

Department (BRIT), Federal Bureau of Investigation (US)

ро́|й (-я; nom pl -и́) м (пчёл) swarm

рок (-а) м (судьба) fate; (также: ~-му́зыка) rock

роково́й прил fatal

ро́лик (-а) м (валик) roller; (колеса) caster; (фотоплёнки, бумаги) roll; (обычно мн: коньки на колесиках) roller skate

роль (-и; gen pl -е́й) ж role

ром (-а) м rum

рома́н (-а) м novel; (любовная связь) affair

романи́ст (-а) м novelist

рома́нс (-а) м (муз) romance

рома́нтик (-а) м (мечтатель) romantic; (писатель) romanticist

рома́шка (-ки; gen pl -ек) ж camomile

ромб (-а) м rhombus

роня́|ть (-ю; pf урони́ть) несов перех to drop; (авторитет) to lose

рос итп несов см. расти́

рос|а́ (-ы́; nom pl -ы) ж dew

роси́н|ка (-ки; gen pl -ок) ж dewdrop

роско́шный прил luxurious, glamorous

ро́скош|ь (-и) ж luxury

ро́спис|ь (-и) ж (узор: на шкатулке) design; (: на стенах) mural; (подпись) signature

ро́спуск (-а) м (армии) disbandment; (парламента) dissolution

росси́йск|ий прил Russian; **Росси́йская Федера́ция** the Russian Federation

Росси́|я (-и) ж Russia

россия́н|ин (-ина; nom pl -е, gen pl -) м Russian

рост (-а) м growth; (увеличение) increase; (размер: человека) height; (nom pl -а́; длина: пальто,

платья) length

ро́стбиф (-а) м roast beef

рост|о́к (-ка́) м (БОТ) shoot

рот (рта; loc sg рту́) м mouth

ро́т|а (-ы) ж (ВОЕН) company

ротаприн́т (-а) м offset duplicator

ро́щ|а (-и) ж grove

роя́л|ь (-я) м grand piano

РПЦ ж сокр (= Ру́сская правосла́вная це́рковь) Russian Orthodox Church

р/с сокр = расчётный счёт

рта etc сущ см. рот

рту́т|ь (-и) ж mercury

руб. сокр (= рубль) R., r.

руба́ш|ка (-ки; gen pl -ек) ж (мужская) shirt; ни́жняя ~ (женская) slip; ночна́я ~ nightshirt

рубе́ж (-а́) м (государства) border; (: водный, лесной) boundary; **он живёт за рубежо́м** he lives abroad

руби́н (-а) м ruby

руб|и́ть (-лю́, -ишь; pf с~) сов перех (дерево) to fell; (ветку) to chop off

рубл|ь (-я́) м rouble

ру́брик|а (-и) ж (раздел) column; (заголовок) heading

руга́тельн|ый прил: ~ое сло́во swearword

руга́тельств|о (-а) ср swearword

руга́|ть (-ю; pf вы́ругать или от~) несов перех to scold; ~ся несов возв (бранить): ~ся с +instr to scold; (перен: ругаться) to swear; ~ся (по~ся pf) с +instr (с мужем, с другом) to fall out with

руд|а́ (-ы́; nom pl -ы) ж ore

рудни́к (-а́) м mine

ружь|ё (-я́; nom pl -ья, gen pl -ей) ср rifle

ру́|ины (-н) мн ruins

рук|а́ (acc sg -у, gen sg -и́, dat sg -и́, gen pl -, dat pl -а́м) ж hand;

(*ве́рхняя коне́чность*) arm; **из пе́рвых ~** first hand; **под ~о́й, под ~ми** to hand, handy; **отсю́да до го́рода ~о́й пода́ть** it's a stone's throw from here to the town; **э́то ему́ на́ ~у** that suits him

рука́в (-а́) м (*оде́жды*) sleeve

рукави́ц|а (-ы) ж mitten

руководи́тел|ь (-я) м leader; (*ка́федры, предприя́тия*) head

руководи́ть (-жу́, -ди́шь) несов: **~** +*instr* to lead; (*учрежде́нием*) to be in charge of; (*страно́й*) to govern; (*аспира́нтами*) to supervise

руково́дств|о (-а) ср leadership; (*заво́дом, институ́том*) management; (*посо́бие*) manual; (*по эксплуата́ции, по ухо́ду*) instructions мн

руководя́щий прил (*рабо́тник*) managerial; (*о́рган*) governing

рукоде́ли|е (-я) ср needlework

рукопи́сный прил (*текст*) handwritten

ру́копис|ь (-и) ж manuscript

рукопожа́ти|е (-я) ср handshake

рукоя́т|ка (-ки; *gen pl* -ок) ж handle

рулев|о́й прил: **~о́е колесо́** steering wheel

руле́т (-а) м (*с дже́мом*) ≈ swiss roll

руле́т|ка (-ки; *gen pl* -ок) ж (*для измере́ния*) tape measure; (*в казино́*) roulette

рул|и́ть (-ю́, -и́шь) несов перех to steer

руло́н (-а) м roll

рул|ь (-я́) м steering wheel

румя́н|а (-) мн blusher ед

румя́н|ец (-ца) м glow

румя́н|ить (-ю, -ишь; *pf* на-) несов перех (*щёки*) to apply blusher; **~ся** (*pf* раз~ся) несов

возв (*to flush*; (*pf* на~ся; *же́нщина*) to apply blusher; (*pf* под~ся; *пиро́г*) to brown

румя́ный прил rosy; (*пиро́г*) browned

РУО́П (-а) ср сокр (= *Региона́льное управле́ние по борьбе́ с организо́ванной престу́пностью*) department fighting organized crime

руо́пов|ец (-ца) м member of the department fighting organized crime

ру́пор (-а) м megaphone

руса́л|ка (-ки; *gen pl* -ок) ж mermaid

ру́сл|о (-ла; *gen pl* -ел) ср bed (of river); (*перен: направле́ние*) course

ру́сск|ий прил Russian ♦ (-ого) м Russian; **~ язы́к** Russian

ру́сый прил (*во́лосы*) light brown

ру́хн|уть (-у) сов to collapse

руча́тельств|о (-а) ср guarantee

руча́|ться (-юсь; *pf* поручи́ться) несов возв: **~ за** +*acc* to guarantee

руч|е́й (-ья́) м stream

ру́ч|ка (-ки; *gen pl* -ек) ж уменьш от рука́; (*две́ри, чемода́на итп*) handle; (*кре́сла, дива́на*) arm; (*для письма́*) pen

ручн|о́й прил hand; (*живо́тное*) tame; **~а́я кладь, ~ бага́ж** hand luggage; **~ы́е часы́** (wrist)watch

РФ ж сокр = **Росси́йская Федера́ция**

ры́б|а (-ы) ж fish; **ни ~ ни мя́со** neither here nor there

рыба́|к (-а́) м fisherman

рыба́л|ка (-ки; *gen pl* -ок) ж fishing

рыба́цкий прил fishing

ры́бий прил fish; **~ жир** cod-liver oil

ры́бный прил (*магази́н*) fish;

(*промышленность*) fishing

рыболо́в (-а) *м* angler, fisherman

Ры́б|ы (-) *мн* (*созвездие*) Pisces *ед*

рыв|о́к (-ка́) *м* jerk; (*в рабо́те*) push

рыда́|ть (-ю) *несов* to sob

ры́жий *прил* (*во́лосы*) ginger; (*челове́к*) red-haired

ры́н|ок (-ка) *м* market

ры́ночник (-а) *м* marketer

ры́ночный *прил* (*КОММ*) market

ры́|скать (-щу, -щешь) *несов* to roam, rove

рысц|а́ (-ы́) *ж* jog trot

рыс|ь (-и) *ж* (*ЗООЛ*) lynx; (*бег ло́шади*) trot

ры|ть (ро́ю, ро́ешь; *pf* вы́~) *несов перех* to dig; **~ться** *несов возв* (*в земле́, в песке́*) to dig; (*иска́ть*) to rummage

ры́хлый *прил* (*земля́*) loose; (*кирпи́ч*) crumbly

ры́цар|ь (-я) *м* knight

рыча́г (-а́) *м* (*управле́ния*) lever; (*перен: рефо́рм*) instrument

рыч|а́ть (-у́, -и́шь) *несов* to growl

рья́ный *прил* zealous

ря́кет (-а) *м* racket

рэкети́р (-а) *м* racketeer

рюкза́к (-а́) *м* rucksack

рю́м|ка (-ки; *gen pl* -ок) *ж* liqueur glass

ряби́н|а (-ы) *ж* (*де́рево*) rowan, mountain ash; (*со́бир: я́годы*) rowan berries *мн*

ряд (-а; *loc sg* -у́, *nom pl* -ы́) *м* row; (*явле́ний*) sequence; (*prp sg* -е; *не́сколько*) ~ +*gen* (*вопро́сов, причи́н*) a number of; **из ря́да вон выходя́щий** extraordinary; *см. та́кже* **ряды́**

рядов|о́й *прил* (*обы́чный*) ordinary; (*член па́ртии*) rank-and-

file ♦ (-о́го) *м* (*ВОЕН*) private

ря́дом *нареч* side by side; (*бли́зко*) nearby; ~ **с** +*instr* next to; **э́то совсе́м** ~ it's really near

ряд|ы́ (-о́в) *мн* (*а́рмии*) ranks *мн*

ря́женк|а (-и) *ж* natural set yoghurt

ря́с|а (-ы) *ж* cassock

С, с

с *сокр* (= **се́вер**) N; (= **секу́нда**) s

с *предл*; +*instr* **1** (*ука́зывает на объе́кт, от кото́рого что-н отделя́ется*) off; **лист упа́л с де́рева** a leaf fell off the tree; **с рабо́ты/ле́кции** from work/a lecture

2 (*сле́дуя чему-н*) from; **перево́д с ру́сского** a translation from Russian

3 (*об исто́чнике*) from; **де́ньги с зака́зчика** money from a customer

4 (*начина́я с*) since; **жду тебя́ с утра́** I've been waiting for you since morning; **с января́ по май** from January to May

5 (*на основа́нии чего-н*) with; **с одобре́ния парла́мента** with the approval of parliament

6 (*по причи́не*) of; **с го́лоду/ хо́лода/го́ря** of hunger/cold/grief; **я уста́л с доро́ги** I was tired from the journey

♦ *предл*; (+*acc*; *приблизи́тельно*) about; **с киломе́тр/то́нну** about a kilometre (*BRIT*) или kilometer (*US*)/ton(ne)

♦ *предл*; +*instr* **1** (*совме́стно*) with; **я иду́ гуля́ть с дру́гом** I am going for a walk with a friend; **он познако́мился с де́вушкой** he

has met a girl; **мы с ним** he and I
2 (*о наличии чего-н в чём-н*):
пиро́г с мя́сом a meat pie; **хлеб с
ма́слом** bread and butter;
челове́к с ю́мором a man with a
sense of humour (*BRIT*) *или* humor
(*US*)
3 (*при указании на образ
де́йствия*) with; **слу́шать** (*impf*) **с
удивле́нием** to listen with *или* in
surprise; **ждём с нетерпе́нием
встре́чи с Ва́ми** we look forward
to meeting you
4 (*при посредстве*): **с курье́ром**
by courier
5 (*при наступлении чего-н*): **с
во́зрастом** with age; **мы вы́ехали
с рассве́том** we left at dawn
6 (*об объекте воздействия*) with;
поко́нчить (*pf*) **с
несправедли́востью** to do away
with injustice; **спеши́ть
(поспеши́ть** *pf*) **с вы́водами** to
draw hasty conclusions; **что с
тобо́й?** what's the matter with
you?

с. *сокр* (= **страни́ца**) p.; = **село́**
са́б|ля (**-ли**; *gen pl* **-ель**) *ж* sabre
(*BRIT*), saber (*US*)
сад (**-а**; *loc sg* **-у́**, *nom pl* **-ы́**) *м*
garden; (*фрукто́вый*) orchard;
(*также*: **де́тский** ~) nursery
(school) (*BRIT*), kindergarten
са|ди́ться (**-жу́сь, -ди́шься**)
несов см **сесть**
садо́вник (**-а**) *м* (professional)
gardener
садово́д (**-а**) *м* (*специалист*)
horticulturalist
садо́вый *прил* garden
са́ж|а (**-и**) *ж* soot
сажа́|ть (**-ю**; *pf* **посади́ть**) *несов
перех* to seat; (*дерево*) to plant;
(*самолёт*) to land; ~ (**посади́ть** *pf*)

кого́-н в тюрьму́ to put sb in
prison
сайт (**-а**) *м* (*КОМП*) site
саксофо́н (**-а**) *м* saxophone
сала́т (**-а**) *м* (*КУЛИН*) salad
сала́тниц|а (**-ы**) *ж* salad bowl
са́л|о (**-а**) *ср* (*живо́тного*) fat;
(*КУЛИН*) lard
сало́н (**-а**) *м* salon; (*авто́буса,
самолёта итп*) passenger section
салфе́т|ка (**-ки**; *gen pl* **-ок**) *ж*
napkin
са́льто *ср нескл* mid-air
somersault
салю́т (**-а**) *м* salute
сам (**-ого́**; *f* **-а́**, *nt* **-о́**, *pl* **са́ми**)
мест myself; (*ты*) yourself; (*он*)
himself; (*как таково́й*) itself; ~ **по
себе́** (*отде́льно*) by itself
сам|а́ (**-о́й**) *мест* (*я*) myself; (*ты*)
yourself; (*она́*) herself; см. *также*
сам
сам|е́ц (**-ца́**) *м* male (*ZOOL*)
са́м|и (**-их**) *мест* (*мы*) ourselves;
(*они́*) themselves; см. *также* **сам**
са́м|ка (**-ки**; *gen pl* **-ок**) *ж* female
(*ZOOL*)
са́ммит (**-а**) *м* summit
сам|о́ (**-ого́**) *мест* itself; ~ **собо́й
(разуме́ется)** it goes without
saying; см. *также* **сам**
самова́р (**-а**) *м* samovar
самоде́льный *прил* home-made
самоде́ятельност|ь (**-и**) *ж*
initiative; (*также*:
худо́жественная ~) amateur
performing arts
самоде́ятельный *прил* (*теа́тр*)
amateur
самока́т (**-а**) *м* scooter
самолёт (**-а**) *м* (aero)plane (*BRIT*),
(air)plane (*US*)
самолюби́вый *прил* self-centred
(*BRIT*), self-centered (*US*)
самооблада́ни|е (**-я**) *ср* self-

possession

самообслу́живани|е (-я) *ср*
self-service

самоокупа́емост|ь (-и) *ж (ЭКОН)*
self-sufficiency

самопоже́ртвенный *прил* self-sacrificing

самостоя́тельный *прил*
independent

самоуби́йств|о (-а) *ср* suicide;
поко́нчить *(pf)* **жизнь ~м** to
commit suicide

самоуби́йц|а (-ы) *м/ж* suicide
(victim)

самоуве́ренный *прил* self-confident, self-assured

самоучи́тел|ь (-я) *м* teach-yourself book

самочу́встви|е (-я) *ср:* **как Ва́ше
~?** how are you feeling?

са́м|ый *мест (+n)* the very; *(+adj)*
вку́сный, краси́вый итп) the
most; **в ~ом нача́ле/конце́** right
at the beginning/end; **в ~ом де́ле**
really; **на ~ом де́ле** in actual fact

санато́ри|й (-я) *м* sanatorium
(BRIT), sanitarium *(US)*

санда́ли|я (-и) *ж (обычно мн)*
sandal

са́н|и (-е́й) *мн* sledge *ед (BRIT)*,
sled *ед (US)*; *(спорти́вные)*
toboggan *ед*

санита́рк|а (-ки; *gen pl* **-ок)** *ж*
nursing auxiliary

санита́рн|ый *прил* sanitary;
(ВОЕН) medical; **~ая те́хника**
collective term for plumbing equipment
and bathroom accessories

са́нки (-ок) *мн* sledge *ед (BRIT)*,
sled *ед (US)*

санкциони́р|овать (-ую) *(не)сов
перех* to sanction

са́нкци|я (-и) *ж* sanction

санте́хник (-а) *м сокр (=
санита́рный те́хник)* plumber

санте́хник|а (-и) *ж сокр =
санита́рная те́хника*

сантиме́тр (-а) *м* centimetre
(BRIT), centimeter *(US)*; *(линейка)*
tape measure

сапо́г (-а́; *nom pl* **-и́,** *gen pl* **-)** *м*
boot

сапо́жник (-а) *м* shoemaker

сапфи́р (-а) *м* sapphire

сара́|й (-я) *м (пла́тье)* shed; *(для сена)*
barn

сарафа́н (-а) *м (пла́тье)* pinafore
(dress) *(BRIT)*, jumper *(US)*

сати́н (-а) *м* sateen

сати́р|а (-ы) *ж* satire

сати́рик (-а) *м* satirist

сау́довск|ий *прил:* **Сау́довская
Ара́вия** Saudi Arabia

са́ун|а (-ы) *ж* sauna

са́хар (-а; *part gen* **-у)** *м* sugar

са́харниц|а (-ы) *ж* sugar bowl

са́харн|ый *прил* sugary; **~ диабе́т**
diabetes; **~ песо́к** granulated sugar

сач|о́к (-ка́) *м (для ло́вли рыб)*
landing net; *(для бабочек)*
butterfly net

сба́в|ить (-лю, -ишь; *impf*
сбавля́ть) *сов перех* to reduce

сбе́га|ть (-ю) *сов (разг):* **~ в
магази́н** to run to the shop

сбежа́ть *(как* бежа́ть; *см. Table
20; impf* **сбега́ть)** *сов (убежа́ть)*
to run away; **сбега́ть** *(pf)* **с +gen
(с горы́ итп)** to run down; **~ся**
(impf **сбега́ться)** *сов возв* to
come running

сберба́нк (-а) *м сокр (=
сберега́тельный банк)* savings
bank

сберега́тельн|ый *прил:* **~ банк**
savings bank; **~ая ка́сса** savings
bank; **~ая кни́жка** savings book

сберега́|ть (-ю) *несов от*
сбере́чь

сбереже́ни|е (-я) *ср (действие)*

сбере́чь (**-егу́, -ежёшь** итп, **-егу́т**; pt **-ёг, -егла́**; impf **сберега́ть**) сов перех (здоровье, любовь, отношение) to preserve; (деньги) to save (up)

сберка́сс|**а** (**-ы**) ж сокр = **сберега́тельная ка́сса**

сберкни́ж|**ка** (**-ки**; gen pl **-ек**) ж сокр = **сберега́тельная кни́жка**

сбить (**собью, собьёшь**; imper **сбе́й(те)**; impf **сбива́ть**) сов перех to knock down; (птицу, самолёт) to shoot down; (сливки, яйца) to beat; **сби́ться** (impf **сбива́ться**) сов возв (шапка, повязка итп) to slip; **сбива́ться** (**сби́ться** с пути́ pf) (также перен) to lose one's way

сбли́з|**ить** (**-жу, -зишь**) impf **сближа́ть** сов перех to bring closer together; **-ся** (impf **сближа́ться**) сов возв (люди, государства) to become closer

сбо́ку нареч at the side

сбор (**-а**) м (урожая, данных) gathering; (налогов) collection; (плата: страховой итп) fee; (прибыль) takings мн, receipts мн; (собрание) assembly, gathering; **тамо́женный/ге́рбовый** ~ customs/stamp duty; **все в сбо́ре** everyone is present

сбо́р|**ка** (**-ки**; gen pl **-ок**) ж (изделия) assembly

сбо́рн|**ая** (**-ой**) ж (разг) = **сбо́рная кома́нда**

сбо́рник (**-а**) м collection (of stories, articles)

сбо́рн|**ый** прил: **~ пункт** assembly point; **~ая ме́бель** kit furniture; **~ая кома́нда (страны́)** national team

сбо́рочный прил assembly

сбра́сыва|**ть(ся)** (**-ю(сь)**) несов

от **сбро́сить(ся)**

сбр|**ить** (**-е́ю, -е́ешь**; impf **сбрива́ть**) сов перех to shave off

сбро́|**сить** (**-шу, -сишь**; impf **сбра́сывать**) сов перех (предмет) to throw down; (свергнуть) to overthrow; (скорость, давление) to reduce; **~ся** (impf **сбра́сываться**) сов возв: **сбра́сываться** (**~ся** pf) с +gen to throw o.s. from

сбру́|**я** (**-и**) ж harness

СБСЕ ср сокр (= Совеща́ние по безопа́сности и сотру́дничеству в Евро́пе) CSCE

сбыт (**-а**) м sale

сбыть (как быть; см. Table 21; impf **сбыва́ть**) сов перех (товар) to sell; **сбы́ться** (impf **сбыва́ться** сов возв (надежды) to come true

СВ сокр (= сре́дние во́лны) MW

св. сокр (= свято́й) St

сва́дь|**ба** (**-ьбы**; gen pl **-еб**) ж wedding

сва́л|**ить(ся)** (**-ю́**) сов от **вали́ть(ся)**

сва́л|**ка** (**-ки**; gen pl **-ок**) ж (место) rubbish dump

свал|**ить** (**-алю́, -а́лишь**) сов от вали́ть ♦ (impf **сва́ливать**) перех to throw down; **~ся** сов от вали́ться

сва́р|**ить(ся)** (**-арю́(сь), -а́ришь(ся)**) сов от **вари́ть(ся)**

сва́рка (**-и**) ж welding

сва́рщик (**-а**) м welder

сва́та|**ть** (**-ю**; pf **по~** или **со~**) несов перех: **~ кого́-н (за +acc)** to try to arrange sb's marriage; **~ся** (pf **по~ся**) несов возв: **~ся к** +dat или **за** +acc to court

сва́|**я** (**-и**) ж (СТРОИТ) pile

све́дени|**е** (**-я**) ср information ед; **доводи́ть (довести́** pf) что́-н до **~я кого́-н** to bring sth to sb's attention

сведе́ни|е (-я) *ср* (пятна́)
removal; (*в табли́цу, в гра́фик
итп*) arrangement

све́жий *прил* fresh; (*журна́л*)
recent

свёкл|а (-ы) *ж* beetroot

свёк|ор (-ра) *м* father-in-law,
husband's father

свекро́вь (-и) *ж* mother-in-law,
husband's mother

сверг|ну́ть (-у́), *impf* **сверга́ть**
сов перех to overthrow

сверже́ние (-я) *ср* overthrow

све́р|ить (-ю, -ишь), *impf*
сверя́ть *сов перех*: ~ (с +*instr*)
to check (against)

сверка́|ть (-ю) *несов* (*звезда́,
глаза́*) to twinkle; (*огни́*) to flicker;
~ (*impf*) *умо́м/красото́й* to sparkle
with intelligence/beauty

сверкн|у́ть (-у́, -ёшь) *сов* to flash

сверл|и́ть (-ю́, -и́шь), *pf* **про~**
несов перех to drill, bore

сверл|о́ (-ерла́; *nom pl* **ёрла**) *ср*
drill

сверн|у́ть (-у́, -ёшь; *impf*
свора́чивать *сов перех*
(*ска́тать: ка́рту*) to roll up ♦ (*impf*
свора́чивать *неперех*
(*поверну́ть*) to turn; ~**ся** (*impf*
свора́чиваться *сов возв*
(*челове́к, живо́тное*) to curl up;
(*молоко́*) to curdle; (*кровь*) to clot

све́рстник (-а) *м* peer; **мы с ней
~и** she and I are the same age

свёрт|ок (-ка) *м* package

сверх *предл*: ~ +*gen* (*но́рмы*) over
and above

сверхзвуково́й *прил* supersonic

све́рху *нареч* (*о направле́нии*)
from the top; (*в ве́рхней ча́сти*)
on the surface

сверхуро́чн|ые (-ых) *мн* (*пла́та*)
overtime pay *ед*

сверхуро́чн|ый *прил*: ~**ая**

рабо́та overtime

сверхъесте́ственный *прил*
supernatural

сверч|о́к (-ка́) *м* (*ЗООЛ*) cricket

сверя́|ть (-ю) *несов от* **све́рить**

све́с|иться (3*sg* -ится), *impf*
све́шиваться *сов возв* (*ве́тви*)
to overhang

св|ести́ (-еду́, -едёшь; *pt* -ёл,
-ела́; *impf* **своди́ть** *сов перех*:
~ **с** +*gen* to lead down; (*пятно́*) to
shift; (*собра́ть*) to arrange;

своди́ть (~) кого́-н **с ума́** to
drive sb mad; ~**сь** (*perf*

свести́сь *сов возв*: ~**сь к** +*dat*
to be reduced to

свет (-а) *м* light; (*Земля́*) the
world; **ни ~ ни заря́** at the crack of
dawn; **выходи́ть** (**вы́йти** *pf*) **в** ~
(*кни́га*) to be published; **ни за что
на све́те не сде́лал бы э́того**
(*разг*) I wouldn't do it for the
world

света́|ть (3*sg* -ет) *несов безл* to
get *или* grow light

свети́льник (-а) *м* lamp

све|ти́ть (-чу́, -тишь) *несов* to
shine; ~ (**по~** *pf*) кому́-н
(*фонарём итп*) to light the way for
sb; ~**ся** *несов возв* to shine

светле́|ть (-ю; *pf* **по~** *или* **про~**
несов to lighten

све́тлый *прил* light; (*ко́мната,
день*) bright; (*ум*) lucid

светофо́р (-а) *м* traffic light

свеч|а́ (-и́; *nom pl* -и, *gen pl* -е́й) *ж*
candle; (*МЕД*) suppository; (*ТЕХ*)
spark(ing) plug; (*СПОРТ*) lob

све́чк|а (-ки; *gen pl* -ек) *ж* candle

све́ша|ться (-юсь) *сов от* **све́шать**

све́шива|ться (-юсь) *несов от*
све́ситься

свива́|ть (-ю; *pf* **свить**) *несов
перех* to weave

свида́ни|е (-я) *ср* rendezvous;

(делово́е) appointment; (с заключённым, с больны́м) visit; (влюблённых) date; до ~я goodbye; до ско́рого ~я see you soon

свиде́тел|**ь** (-**я**) *м* witness

свиде́тельств|**о** (-**а**) *ср* evidence; (докуме́нт) certificate; ~ о бра́ке/рожде́нии marriage/birth certificate

свиде́тельствовать (-**ую**) *несов*: ~ о +*prp* to testify to

свин|е́ц (-**ца́**) *м* lead (*metal*)

свини́н|а (-**ы**) *ж* pork

свинк|а (-**и**) *ж* (*МЕД*) mumps

свин|**о́й** *прил* (*са́ло, корм*) pig; (*из свини́ны*) pork

свин|ья́ (-**ьи́**; *nom pl* -**ьи**, *gen pl* -**е́й**) *ж* pig

свиса́ть (*3sg* -**ет**) *несов* to hang

свист (-**а**) *м* whistle

свисте́ть (-**щу́**, -**сти́шь**; *pf* **про~**) *несов* to whistle

сви́стн|уть (-**у**) *сов* to give a whistle

свист|о́к (-**ка́**) *м* whistle

сви́тер (-**а**) *м* sweater

свить (**совью́**, **совьёшь**) *сов от* **вить**, **свива́ть**

свобо́д|а (-**ы**) *ж* freedom; **лише́ние** ~ imprisonment

свобо́дный *прил* free; (*незаня́тый: ме́сто*) vacant; (*движе́ние, речь*) fluent; **вход** ~ free admission; ~ **уда́р** (*в футбо́ле*) free kick

свод (-**а**) *м* (*пра́вил итп*) set; (*зда́ния*) vaulting

свод|**и́ть(ся)** (-**ожу́(сь)**, -**о́дишь(ся)**) *несов от* **свести́(сь)**

сво́дк|а (-**и**; *gen pl* -**ок**) *ж*: ~ **пого́ды/новосте́й** weather/news summary

сво́дный *прил* (*табли́ца*)

summary; ~ **брат** stepbrother; ~**ая сестра́** stepsister

свое (-**его́**) *мест см.* **свой**

своево́льный *прил* self-willed

своевре́менный *прил* timely

своеобра́зный *прил* original; (*необы́чный*) peculiar

KEYWORD

сво|й (-**его́**; *f* **своя́**, *nt* **своё**, *pl* **свои́**; *как* **мой**; *см. Table 8*) *мест*
1 (*я*) my; (*ты*) your; (*он*) his; (*она́*) her; (*оно́*) its; (*мы*) our; (*вы*) your; (*они́*) their; **я люблю́ свою́ рабо́ту** I love my work; **мы собра́ли свои́ ве́щи** we collected our things
2 (*со́бственный*) one's own; **у неё свой компью́тер** she has her own computer
3 (*своеобра́зный*) its; **э́тот план име́ет свои́ недоста́тки** this plan has its shortcomings
4 (*бли́зкий*): **свой челове́к** one of us

сво́йственный *прил*: ~ +*dat* characteristic of

сво́йств|о (-**а**) *ср* characteristic, feature

свора́чива|ть(ся) (-**ю(сь)**) *несов от* **сверну́ть(ся)**

сво|я́ (-**е́й**) *мест см.* **свой**

СВЧ *сокр* = **сверхвысо́кая частота́**) SHF

свы́ше *предл*: ~ +*gen* (*вы́ше*) beyond; (*бо́льше*) over, more than

свя́занный *прил*: ~ (**с** +*instr*) connected (to *или* with); (*име́ющий свя́зи*): ~ **с** (*с деловы́ми круга́ми*) associated with; (*несвобо́дный*) restricted

свя|за́ть (-**жу́**, -**жешь**) *сов от* **вяза́ть** ♦ (*impf* **свя́зывать**) *перех* (*верёвку итп*) to tie; (*ве́щи*, человека) to tie up; (установить сообщение, зависимость): ~ что-н с +*instr* to connect или link sth to; ~ся (*impf* свя́зываться) *сов возв*: ~ся с +*instr* to contact; (*разг*: с невыгодным делом) to get (o.s.) caught in up

свя́зк|а (**-и**; *gen pl* **-ок**) *ж* (ключей) bunch; (бумаг, дров) bundle; (АНАТ) ligament; (ЛИНГ) copula

связь (**-и**) *ж* tie; (причинная) connection, link; (почтовая итп) communications *мн*; **в ~й с** +*instr* (вследствие) due to; (по поводу) in connection with; **связи с общественностью** public relations

свя|ти́ть (**-щу́, -ти́шь**, *3sg* **-ти́т**, *impf* **о~**) *несов перех* (РЕЛ) to sanctify

свят|о́й *прил* holy; (дело, истина) sacred ♦ (**-о́го**) *м* (РЕЛ) saint

свяще́нник (**-а**) *м* priest

свяще́нн|ый *прил* holy, sacred; (долг) sacred

с.г. *сокр* = сего́ го́да

сгиб (**-а**) *м* bend

сгиба́|ть (**-ю**) *pf* **согну́ть** *несов перех* to bend; ~ся *несов возв* (*pf* **согну́ться**) to bend down

сгни|ть (**-ю́, -ёшь**) *сов от* гнить

сгно|и́ть (**-ю́, -и́шь**) *сов от* гнои́ть

сгора́|ть (**-ю**) *несов от* сгоре́ть ♦ *неперех*: ~ **от** любопытства to be burning with curiosity

сгор|е́ть (**-ю́, -и́шь**, *impf* **сгора́ть** или **горе́ть**) *сов* to burn; (*impf* **сгора́ть**; ЭЛЕК) to fuse; (*на солнце*) to get burnt

сгр|ести́ (**-ебу́, -ебёшь**, *pt* **-ёб, -ебла́**; *impf* **сгреба́ть**) *сов перех* (*собрать*) to rake up

сгр|узи́ть (**-ужу́, -у́зишь**; *impf* **сгружа́ть**) *сов перех*: ~ (**с** +*gen*)

to unload (from)

сгусти́|ться (*impf* **сгуща́ться**) *сов возв* to thicken

сгущённ|ое молоко́ condensed milk

сгущённ|ый *прил*: ~**ое молоко́**

сда|ва́ть (**-ю́, -ёшь**, *imper* **-ва́й(те)**) *несов от* сдать ♦ *перех*: ~ **экза́мен** to sit an exam; ~**ся** *несов от* **сда́ться** ♦ *возв* (*помещение*) to be leased out; "~**ётся внаём**" "to let"

сда́в|ить (**-лю́, -ишь**) *impf* **сда́вливать** *сов перех* to squeeze

сдать (*как* дать; *см.* Table 16; *impf* **сдава́ть**) *сов перех* (*пальто, багаж, работу*) to hand in; (*дом, комнату итп*) to rent out, let; (*город, позицию*) to surrender; (*по impf; экзамен, зачёт итп*) to pass; ~**ся** (*impf* **сдава́ться**) *сов возв* to give up; (*солдат, город*) to surrender

сда́ч|а (**-и**) *ж* (*деньги*) change; (*экзамена*) passing; (*города*) surrender

сдвиг (**-а**) *м* (*в работе*) progress

сдви́н|уть (**-у**; *impf* **сдвига́ть**) *сов перех* (*переместить*) to move; (*сблизить*) to move together; ~**ся** (*impf* **сдвига́ться**) *сов возв*: ~**ся** (**с ме́ста**) to move

сде́ла|ть(ся) (**-ю(сь)**) *сов от* де́лать(ся)

сде́л|ка (**-и**; *gen pl* **-ок**) *ж* deal

сде́ржанный *прил* (*человек*) reserved

сде́рж|ать (**-ержу́, -е́ржишь**; *impf* **сде́рживать**) *сов перех* to contain, hold back; (*смех*) to suppress; (*pf* **сде́рживать**) *сло́во/обеща́ние* to keep one's word/promise; ~**ся** (*impf* **сде́рживаться**) *сов возв* to restrain o.s.

сдёрн|уть (**-у**; *impf* **сдёргивать**)

сов *перех* to pull off

сдира́|ть (-ю) *несов от* **содра́ть**

сдо́бный *прил* (*тесто*) rich

сду|ть (-ю; *impf* **сдува́ть**) *сов перех* to blow away

сеа́нс (-а) *м* (*кино*) show; (*терапии*) session

себе́ *мест см.* **себя́ ♦** *част* (*разг*): **так** ~ so-so; **ничего́** ~ (*сносно*) not bad; (*ирония*) well, I never!

себесто́имост|ь (-и) *ж* cost price

KEYWORD

себя́ *мест* (*я*) myself; (*ты*) yourself; (*он*) himself; (*она*) herself; (*оно*) itself; (*мы*) ourselves; (*вы*) yourselves; (*они*) themselves; **он тре́бователен к себе́** he asks a lot of himself; **она́ вини́т себя́** she blames herself; **к себе́** (*домой*) home; **в свою́ ко́мнату** to one's room; **"к себе́"** (*на двери*) "pull"; **"от себя́"** (*на двери*) "push"; **по себе́** (*по свои́м вку́сам*) to one's taste; **говори́ть** (*impf*)/**чита́ть** (*impf*) **про себя́** to talk/read to o.s.; **она́ себе́ на уме́** (*разг*) she is secretive; **он у себя́** (*в своём до́ме*) he is at home; (*в своём кабине́те*) he is in the office

---

се́вер (-а) *м* north; **Се́вер** (*Аркти́ка*) the Arctic North

се́верн|ый *прил* north; (*ветер, направле́ние*) northerly; (*кли́мат, полуша́рие*) northern; **Се́верный Ледови́тый океа́н** Arctic Ocean; **~ое сия́ние** the northern lights *мн*

се́веро-восто́к (-а) *м* northeast

се́веро-за́пад (-а) *м* northwest

сего́ *мест см.* **сей**

сего́дня *нареч, сущ нескл* today; **~ у́тром/днём/ве́чером** this morning/afternoon/evening

сего́дняшний *прил* today's

седе́|ть (-ю; *pf* **по~**) *несов* to go grey (*BRIT*) *или* gray (*US*)

сед|ина́ (-ины́; *nom pl* -и́ны) *ж* grey (*BRIT*) *или* gray (*US*) hair

седл|о́ (-а́) *ср* saddle

седо́й *прил* (*во́лосы*) grey (*BRIT*), gray (*US*)

седьмо́й *чис* seventh; **сейча́с ~ час** it's after six

сезо́н (-а) *м* season

сезо́нный *прил* seasonal

сей (*сего́*; см. *Table 12*) *мест* this

сейсми́ческий *прил* seismic; (*прибо́р*) seismological

сейф (-а) *м* (*я́щик*) safe

сейча́с *нареч* (*тепе́рь*) now; (*ско́ро*) just now; ~ **же**! right now!

секре́т (-а) *м* secret

секрета́рш|а (-и) *ж* (*разг*) secretary

секрета́р|ь (-я́) *м* secretary; **~-машини́стка** secretary

секре́тный *прил* secret

секс (-а) *м* sex

сексуа́льный *прил* sexual; (*жизнь, образова́ние*) sex; **~ое пресле́дование** *или* **домога́тельство** sexual harassment

се́кт|а (-ы) *ж* sect

секта́нт (-а) *м* sect member

се́ктор (-а) *м* sector

секу́нд|а (-ы) *ж* second

секу́ндный *прил* (*па́уза*) second's; **~ая стре́лка** second hand (*on clock*)

секундоме́р (-а) *м* stopwatch

се́кци|я (-и) *ж* section

сел *итп сов см.* **сесть**

селёдк|а (-ки; *gen pl* -ок) *ж* herring

селезёнк|а (-и) *ж* spleen

селе́ктор (-а) *м* (*ТЕЛ*) intercom

селе́кци|я (-и) *ж* (*БИО*) selective

breeding

селе́ни|е (-я) *ср* village

сел|и́ть (-ю́, -ишь; *pf* по~) *несов перех* (*в местности*) to settle; (*в доме*) to house; **~ся** (*pf* по~ся) *несов возв* to settle

сел|о́ (-а́; *nom pl* сёла) *ср* village

сельдере́|й (-я) *м* celery

сельд|ь (-и; *gen pl* -е́й) *ж* herring

се́льск|ий *прил* (*см сущ*) village; country, rural; **~ое хозя́йство** agriculture

сельскохозя́йственный *прил* agricultural

сёмг|а (-и) *ж* salmon

семе́йный *прил* family

семе́йств|о (-а) *ср* family

семёр|ка (-ки; *gen pl* -ок) *ж* (*цифра, карта*) seven

се́меро| (-ы́х; *как* че́тверо; *см. Table 30b*) *чис* seven

семе́стр (-а) *м* term (*BRIT*), semester (*US*)

се́меч|ко (-ка; *gen pl* -ек) *ср* seed; **~ки** sunflower seeds

семидеся́тый *чис* seventieth

семина́р (-а) *м* seminar

семина́ри|я (-и) *ж* seminary

семна́дцатый *чис* seventeenth

семна́дцат|ь (-и; *как* пять; *см. Table 26*) *чис* seventeen

сем|ь (-и́; *как* пять; *см. Table 26*) *чис* seven

се́м|ьдесят (-и́десяти; *как* пятьдеся́т; *см. Table 26*) *чис* seventy

сем|ьсо́т (-исо́т; *как* пятьсо́т; *см. Table 28*) *чис* seven hundred

сем|ья́ (-и́; *nom pl* -ьи) *ж* family

се́м|я (-ени; *как* вре́мя; *см. Table 4*) *ср* seed; *no pl* БИО) semen

сена́тор (-а) *м* senator

сенн|о́й *прил:* **~а́я лихора́дка** hay fever

се́н|о (-а) *м* hay

сенса́ци|я (-и) *ж* sensation

сентимента́льный *прил* sentimental

сентя́бр|ь (-я́) *м* September

се́р|а (-ы) *ж* sulphur (*BRIT*), sulfur (*US*); (*в ушах*) (ear)wax

серва́нт (-а) *м* buffet unit

се́рвер (-а) *м* (КОМП) server

серви́з (-а) *м*: **столо́вый/ча́йный ~** dinner/tea service

се́рвис (-а) *м* service (*in shop, restaurant etc*)

серде́чный *прил* heart, cardiac; (*человек*) warm-hearted; (*приём, разговор*) cordial; **~ при́ступ** heart attack

серди́тый *прил* angry

серд|и́ть (-жу́, -дишь; *pf* рас~) *несов перех* to anger, make angry; **~ся** (*pf* рас~ся) *несов возв*: **серди́ться (на кого-н/что-н)** to be angry (with sb/about sth)

се́рд|це (-ца; *nom pl* -ца́) *ср* heart; **в глубине́ ~ца** in one's heart of hearts; **от всего́ ~ца** from the bottom of one's heart

сердцебие́ни|е (-я) *ср* heartbeat

серебр|о́ (-а́) *ср, собир* silver

сере́бряный *прил* silver

середи́н|а (-ы) *ж* middle

серёж|ка (-ки; *gen pl* -ек) *ж* уменьш от **серьга́**

сержа́нт (-а) *м* sergeant

сериа́л (-а) *м* (ТЕЛ) series

се́ри|я (-и) *ж* series; (*кинофи́льма*) part

се́рн|ый *прил:* **~ая кислота́** sulphuric (*BRIT*) *или* sulfuric (*US*) acid

серп (-а́) *м* sickle

сертифика́т (-а) *м* certificate; (*товара*) guarantee (certificate)

се́р|ый *прил* grey (*BRIT*), gray (*US*); **~ хлеб** brown bread

серьга́ (-ги́; nom pl -ги, gen pl -ёг, dat pl -га́м) ж earring

серьёзно нареч, вводн сл seriously

серьёзный прил serious

се́ссия (-и) ж (суда, парламента) session; (также: экзаменацио́нная ~) examinations мн

сестра́ (-ы́; nom pl сёстры, gen pl сестёр) ж sister; (также: медици́нская ~) nurse

сесть (ся́ду, ся́дешь; pt сел, се́ла; impf сади́ться) сов to sit down; (птица, самолёт) to land; (солнце, луна) to go down; (одежда) to shrink; (батаре́йка) to run down; **сади́ться** (~ pf) **в по́езд/на самолёт** to get on a train/plane; **сади́ться** (~ pf) **в тюрьму́** to go to prison

сетево́й прил (КОМП) net; (магазин) chain

се́тка (-ки; gen pl -ок) ж net; (су́мка) net bag

сеть (-и; prp sg -и́, gen pl -е́й) ж (для ловли рыб итп) net; (доро́г) network; (магази́нов) chain; (КОМП) the Net

сече́ние (-я) ср section; **ке́сарево ~** Caesarean (BRIT) или Cesarean (US) (section)

сечь (секу́, сечёшь итп, секу́т; pt сёк, секла́) несов перех (руби́ть) to cut up

се́ять (-ю; pf по~) несов перех to sow

сжа́литься (-юсь, -ишься) сов возв: **~ (над** +instr) to take pity (on)

сжа́тый прил (во́здух, газ) compressed; (расска́з) condensed; **в ~ые сро́ки** in a short space of time

сжать (сожму́, сожмёшь; impf

сжима́ть) сов перех to squeeze; (во́здух, газ) to compress; **сжа́ться** (impf **сжима́ться**) сов возв (пружи́на) to contract; (челове́к: от бо́ли, от испу́га) to tense up; (перен: се́рдце) to seize up

сжечь (сожгу́, сожжёшь итп, сожгу́т; pt сжёг, сожгла́; impf **сжига́ть** или **жечь**) сов перех to burn

сжима́ть(ся) (-ю(сь)) несов от **сжа́ть(ся)**

сза́ди нареч (подойти́) from behind; (находи́ться) behind
♦ предл: ~ +gen behind

сзыва́ть (-ю) несов от **созва́ть**

сиби́рский прил Siberian

Сиби́рь (-и) ж Siberia

сибиря́к (-а́) м Siberian

сигаре́та (-ы) ж cigarette

сигна́л (-а) м signal

сигнализа́ция (-и) ж (в кварти́ре) burglar alarm

сигна́лить (-ю, -ишь; pf про~) несов to signal; (АВТ) to honk

сиде́нье (-я) ср seat

сиде́ть (-жу́, -ди́шь) несов to sit; (оде́жда) to fit

си́дя нареч: **рабо́тать/есть** ~ to work/eat sitting down

сидя́чий прил (положе́ние) sitting; **~ие места́** seats мн

си́ла (-ы) ж strength; (то́ка, ве́тра, зако́на) force; (во́ли, сло́ва) power; (обы́чно мн: душе́вные, тво́рческие) energy; **в ~у того́ что ...** owing to the fact that ...; **от ~ы** (разг) at (the) most; **вступа́ть (вступи́ть pf) в ~у** или **входи́ть (войти́ pf) в ~у** to come into или take effect; см. также **си́лы**

си́лой нареч by force

силуэ́т (-а) м (ко́нтур) silhouette

си́л|ы (-) *мн* forces *мн*; **~ами кого́-н** through the efforts of sb; **свои́ми ~ами** by oneself

си́льно *нареч* strongly; *(уда́рить)* hard; *(хоте́ть, понра́виться итп)* very much

си́льный *прил* strong; *(моро́з)* hard; *(впечатле́ние)* powerful; *(дождь)* heavy

си́мвол (-а) *м* symbol; *(КОМП)* character

символизи́р|овать (-ую) *несов перех* to symbolize

симметри́ческий *прил* symmetrical

симметри́|я (-и) *ж* symmetry

симпатизи́р|овать (-ую) *несов*: **~ кому́-н** to like *или* to be fond of sb

симпати́чный *прил* nice, pleasant

симпа́ти|я (-и) *ж* liking, fondness

симпто́м (-а) *м* symptom

симфони́ческий *прил* symphonic; **~ орке́стр** symphony orchestra

симфо́ни|я (-и) *ж (МУЗ)* symphony

синаго́г|а (-и) *ж* synagogue

синдро́м (-а) *м (МЕД)* syndrome

сине́|ть (-ю; *pf* **по~**) *несов* to turn blue

си́ний *прил* blue

сини́ц|а (-ы) *ж* tit *(ZOOL)*

сино́д (-а) *м* synod

сино́ним (-а) *м* synonym

сино́птик (-а) *м* weather forecaster

синта́ксис (-а) *м* syntax

си́нтез (-а) *м (также ХИМ)* synthesis

синтети́ческий *прил* synthetic

синхро́нный *прил* synchronous; *(перево́д)* simultaneous

синя́к (-а́) *м* bruise

сире́н|а (-ы) *ж (гудо́к)* siren

сире́невый *прил* lilac

сире́н|ь (-и) *ж (куста́рник)* lilac

bush ♦ *собир (цветы́)* lilac

сиро́п (-а) *м* syrup

сир|ота́ (-оты́; *nom pl* -о́ты) *м/ж* orphan

систе́м|а (-ы) *ж* system

системати́ческий *прил* regular

си́т|ец (-ца) *м* cotton

си́течк|о (-ка; *gen pl* -ек) *ср (для ча́я)* (tea) strainer

си́т|о (-а) *ср* sieve

ситуа́ци|я (-и) *ж* situation

си́тцевый *прил (ткань)* cotton

СИФ *м сокр* c.i.f.

сия́|ть (-ю) *несов (со́лнце, звезда́)* to shine; *(ого́нь)* to glow

сия́ющий *прил (глаза́)* shining; *(лицо́, улы́бка)* beaming

ск|аза́ть (-ажу́, -а́жешь) *сов от* **говори́ть** ♦ *перех*: **~а́жем** *(разг)* let's say; **~ажи́те!** *(разг)* I say!; **так ~** so to speak; **~ся** *(impf* **ска́зываться)** *сов возв (ум, о́пыт итп)* to show; *(отрази́ться)*: **~ся на** *+prp* to take its toll on

ска́з|ка (-ки; *gen pl* -ок) *ж* fairy tale

ска́зочный *прил* fairy-tale

ска́зуем|ое (-ого) *ср (линг)* predicate

скака́л|ка (-ки; *gen pl* -ок) *ж* skipping rope

ск|ака́ть (-ачу́, -а́чешь) *несов (челове́к)* to skip; *(мяч)* to bounce; *(ло́шадь, вса́дник)* to gallop

скаков́|о́й *прил*: **~а́я ло́шадь** racehorse

скаку́н (-а́) *м* racehorse

ск|ала́ (-алы́; *nom pl* -а́лы) *ж* cliff

скали́стый *прил* rocky

скалола́з (-а) *м* rock-climber

скаме́йк|а (-йки; *gen pl* -ек) *ж* bench

скам|ья́ (-ьи́; *gen pl* -е́й) *ж* bench; **~ подсуди́мых** *(ЮР)* the dock

сканда́л (-а) *м* scandal; *(ссора)* quarrel

сканда́л|**ить** (-ю, -ишь; *pf* по~) *несов* to quarrel

сканда́льный *прил* scandalous

ска́нер (-а) *м* (КОМП) scanner

ска́плива|**ться** (-юсь) *несов от* скопи́ться

скарлати́н|**а** (-ы) *ж* scarlet fever

скат (-а) *м* slope; *(АВТ, колесо)* wheel

ска|**та́ть** (-ю; *impf* ска́тывать) *сов перех* to roll up

ска́терт|**ь** (-и) *ж* tablecloth

ск|**ати́ть** (-ачу́, -а́тишь; *impf* ска́тывать) *сов перех* to roll down; ~**ся** (*impf* ска́тываться) *сов возв (слеза)* to slide towards/into; *(перен)*; ~**ся к** +*dat/*на +*acc* to slide towards/into

скафа́ндр (-а) *м (водолаза)* diving suit; *(космонавта)* spacesuit

ска́ч|**ки** (-ек) *мн* the races *мн*

скач|**о́к** (-ка́) *м* leap

скв *ж сокр* (= свобо́дно конверти́руемая валю́та) convertible currency

сква́жин|**а** (-ы) *ж (нефтяная, газовая)* well; **замо́чная** ~ keyhole

сквер (-а) *м* small public garden

скве́рный *прил* foul

сквоз|**и́ть** (*3sg* -и́т) *несов безл*: **здесь** ~**и́т** it's draughty here

сквозня́к (-а́) *м (в комнате)* draught (BRIT), draft (US)

сквозь *предл*: ~ +*acc* through

скво́р|**ец** (-ца́) *м* starling

скворе́чник (-а) *м* nesting box

скеле́т (-а) *м* skeleton

скепти́ческий *прил* sceptical

ски́д|**ка** (-ки; *gen pl* -ок) *ж (с цены)* discount, reduction

ски́н|**уть** (-у; *сбросить*) *сов перех* to throw down

ски́с|**нуть** (-ну, -нешь; *pt* -, -ла, -ло; *impf* скиса́ть) *сов (молоко)* to turn sour

склад (-а) *м (товарный)* store; *(оружия итп)* cache; *(образ мыслей)* way

скла́д|**ка** (-ки; *gen pl* -ок) *ж (на одежде)* pleat

складно́й *прил* folding

скла́дыва|**ть(ся)** (-ю(сь)) *несов от* сложи́ть(ся)

скле́|**ить** (-ю, -ишь) *сов от* кле́ить (~ *impf* скле́ивать) *перех* to glue together

склеро́з (-а) *м* sclerosis; **рассе́янный** ~ multiple sclerosis

склон (-а) *м* slope

склоне́ни|**е** (-я, -онию) *ср (ЛИНГ)* declension

скл|**они́ть** (-оню́, -о́нишь; *impf* склоня́ть) *сов перех (опустить)* to lower; **склони́ть** (~ *pf*) **кого́-н к побе́гу/на преступле́ние** to persuade sb to escape/commit a crime; ~**ся** (*impf* склоня́ться) *сов возв (нагнуться)* to bend; *(перен)*: ~**ся к** +*dat* to come round to

скло́нност|**ь** (-и) *ж*: ~ **к** +*dat (к му́зыке)* aptitude for *(к меланхо́лии, к полноте́)* tendency to

скло́нный *прил*: ~ **к** +*dat (к про́студам)* prone *или* susceptible to; ~ +*infin (помири́ться)* inclined to do

склоня́емый *прил* declinable

склоня́|**ть** (-ю) *несов от* склони́ть ♦ (*pf* про~) *перех (ЛИНГ)* to decline; ~**ся** *несов от* склони́ться ♦ *возв (ЛИНГ)* to decline

ск|**оба́** (-обы́; *nom pl* -о́бы) *ж (для опоры)* clamp; *(для крепле́ния)* staple

скоб|ка (-ки; gen pl -ок) ж
уменьш от **скоба**; (обычно мн:
в тексте) bracket, parentheses мн
ско́ванный прил inhibited
ск|ова́ть (-ую; impf **ско́вывать**)
сов перех to paralyse
сковород|а́ (-ы́; nom pl
ско́вороды) ж frying-pan (BRIT),
skillet (US)
сколь нареч (как) how;
(возможно) as much as; ~ ...
сто́ль (же) as much ... as ...
скольз|и́ть (-жу́, -зи́шь) несов
to glide; (падая) to slide
ско́льзкий прил slippery;
(ситуация, вопрос) sensitive
скользн|у́ть (-у́, -ёшь) сов to
glide; (быстро пройти) to slip

KEYWORD

ско́льк|о (-их) местоимённое
нареч 1; (+gen): книг, часов, дней
итп) how many; (сахара, сил,
работы итп) how much; **ско́лько
люде́й пришло́?** how many
people came? **ско́лько де́нег
тебе́ на́до?** how much money do
you need? **ско́лько э́то сто́ит?**
how much is it? **ско́лько тебе́
лет?** how old are you?
2 (относительное) as much;
бери́, ско́лько хо́чешь take as
much as you want; **ско́лько
уго́дно** as much as you like
♦ нареч (насколько) as far as;
**ско́лько по́мню, он всегда́ был
агресси́вный** as far as I remember,
he was always aggressive
2 (много): **ско́лько люде́й!** what
a lot of people! **не сто́лько ...
ско́лько ...** not so much ... as ...

ско́мка|ть (-ю) сов от **ко́мкать**
сконча́|ться (-юсь) сов возв to
pass away

скоп|и́ть (-лю́, -ишь) сов от
копи́ть; **~ся** сов от **копи́ться**
♦ (impf **ска́пливаться**) возв
(люди) to gather; (работа) to
mount up
ско́р|ая (-ой) ж (разг: также: ~
по́мощь) ambulance
скорб|ь (-и; gen pl -е́й) ж grief
скоре́е сравн прил от **ско́рый**
♦ сравн нареч от **ско́ро** ♦ част
rather; ~...**чем** или **не́жели** (в
большей степени) more likely ...
than; (лучше, охотнее) rather ...
than; ~ **всего́ они́ до́ма** it's most
likely they'll be (at) home; ~ **бы он
верну́лся** I wish he would come
back soon
скорлуп|а́ (-ы́; nom pl -у́пы) ж
shell
ско́ро нареч soon ♦ как сказ it's
soon; ~ **зима́** it will soon be winter
скоропости́жн|ый прил: ~**ая
смерть** sudden death
скоростно́й прил (поезд) high-
speed
ско́рост|ь (-и; gen pl -е́й) ж speed
скоросшива́тел|ь (-я) м (loose-
leaf) binder
скорпио́н (-а) м scorpion;
(созвездие): **Скорпио́н** Scorpio
ско́р|ый прил (движение) fast;
(разлука, визит) impending; **в
~ом вре́мени** shortly; **~ая
по́мощь** (учреждение)
ambulance service; (автомашина)
ambulance; ~ **по́езд** express (train)
скот (-а́) м собир livestock;
моло́чный/мясно́й ~ dairy/beef
cattle
скрепи́|ть (-лю́, -ишь; impf
скрепля́ть) сов перех
(соединить) to fasten together
скре́п|ка (-ки; gen pl -ок) ж
paperclip
скре|сти́ть (-щу́, -сти́шь; impf

скре́щивать) *сов перех* to cross; *(животных)* to cross-breed; **~ся** *(impf* **скре́щиваться)** *сов возв* to cross

скрип (-а) *м (двери, пола)* creak; *(металла)* grate

скрипа́ч (-а́) *м* violinist

скрип|е́ть (-лю́, -и́шь) *несов* to creak

скрип|ка (-ки; *gen pl* **-ок)** *ж* violin

скро́мность (-и) *ж* modesty

скро́мный *прил* modest; *(служащий, должность)* humble

скр|ути́ть (-учу́, -у́тишь) *сов* **крути́ть ♦** *(impf* **скру́чивать)** *перех (провода, волосы)* to twist together; **~ся** *сов возв* to twist together

скрыва́|ть (-ю) *несов от* **скрыть**; **~ся** *несов от* **скры́ться ♦** *возв (от полиции)* to hide

скры́тный *прил* secretive

скры́тый *прил (возможности)* potent; *(тайный)* hidden

скр|ыть (-о́ю, -о́ешь; *impf* **скрыва́ть)** *сов перех (спрятать)* to hide; *(факты)* to conceal; **скры́ться** *(impf* **скрыва́ться)** *сов возв (от дождя, от погони)* to take cover; *(стать невидимым)* to disappear

ску́дный *прил (запасы)* meagre *(BRIT)*, meager *(US)*

ску́к|а (-и) *ж* boredom

скул|а́ (-ы́; *nom pl* **-ы)** *ж (обычно мн)* cheekbone

скул|и́ть (-ю́, -и́шь) *несов* to whine

ску́льптор (-а) *м* sculptor

скульпту́р|а (-ы) *ж* sculpture

скумбри|я (-и) *ж* mackerel

скуп|и́ть (-уплю́, -у́пишь; *impf* **скупа́ть)** *сов перех* to buy up

скупо́й *прил* mean

скуча́|ть (-ю) *несов* to be bored;

(тосковать): **~ по** *+dat* или **о** *+prp* to miss

ску́чно *нареч (жить, рассказывать итп)* boringly **♦** *как сказ:* **здесь ~** it's boring here; **мне ~** I'm bored

ску́чный *прил* boring, dreary

слабе́|ть (-ю; *pf* **о-)** *несов* to grow weak; *(дисциплина итп)* to slacken

слаби́тельн|ое (-ого) *ср* laxative

сла́бо *нареч (вскрикнуть)* weakly; *(нажать)* lightly; *(знать)* badly

сла́бость (-и) *ж* weakness

сла́бый *прил* weak; *(ветер)* light; *(знания, доказательство итп)* poor; *(дисциплина итп)* slack

сла́в|а (-ы) *ж (героя)* glory; *(писателя, актёра итп)* fame; **~ Бо́гу!** thank God!

славя́н|ин (-ина; *nom pl* **-я́не,** *gen pl* **-я́н)** *м* Slav

славя́нский *прил* Slavonic

слага́|ть (-ю) *несов от* **сложи́ть**

сла́дкий *прил* sweet

сла́дко *нареч (пахнуть)* sweet; *(спать)* deeply

сла́дк|ое (-ого) *ср* sweet things *мн; (разг: десерт)* afters *(BRIT)*, dessert *(US)*

слайд (-а) *м (ФОТО)* slide

сла́лом (-а) *м* slalom

слать (шлю, шлёшь) *несов перех* to send

сла́ще *сравн прил от* **сла́дкий ♦** *сравн нареч от* **сла́дко**

сле́ва *нареч* on the left

слегка́ *нареч* slightly

след (-а; *nom pl* **-ы)** *м* trace; *(ноги)* footprint

сле|ди́ть (-жу́, -ди́шь) *несов:* **~ за** *+instr* to follow; *(заботиться)* to take care of; *(за шпионом)* to watch

сле́довани|е (-я) *ср (моде)*

following; **по́езд/авто́бус да́льнего ~я** long-distance train/ bus

сле́дователь (**-я**) *м* detective

сле́довательно *вводн сл* consequently **♦** *союз* therefore

сле́довать (**-ую**) *pf* **по~** *несов* (вывод, неприятность) to follow **♦** *безл*: **Вам ~ует поду́мать об э́том** you should think about it; **как ~ует** properly

сле́дом *предл*: **~ за** +*instr* following

сле́дственный *прил* investigative

сле́дствие (**-я**) *ср* (последствие) consequence; (ЮР) **♦** investigation

сле́дующий *прил* next **♦** *мест* following; **на ~ день** the next day

слеза́ (**-ы́**; *nom pl* **-ёзы**, *dat pl* **-еза́м**) *ж* tear

слеза́ть (**-ю**) *несов от* **слезть**

слези́ться (3sg **-ится**) *несов возв* (глаза) to water

слезоточи́вый *прил*: **~ газ** tear gas

слезть (**-у**, **-ешь**; *pt* **-**, **ла**) *impf* **слеза́ть** *сов* (кожа, краска) to peel off; **слеза́ть** (*pf*) (**с** +*gen*) (*с дерева*) to climb down

слепи́ть (**-еплю́**, **-е́пишь**) *сов от* **лепи́ть**

сле́пнуть (**-у**; *pf* **о~**) *несов* to go blind

слепо́й *прил* blind **♦** (**-о́го**) *м* blind person

сле́сарь (**-я**; *nom pl* **-я́**, *gen pl* **-е́й**) *м* maintenance man

слете́ть (**-я́**; *nom pl* **-я́**, *gen pl* **-е́й**) *м* maintenance man

слете́ть (**-чу́**, **-ти́шь**; *impf* **слета́ть**) *сов*: **~** (**с** +*gen*) (птица) to fly down (from); **~ся** (*impf* **слета́ться**) *сов возв* (птицы) to flock

сли́ва (**-ы**) *ж* (дерево) plum

(*tree*); (*плод*) plum

слива́ть(ся) (**-ю(сь)**) *несов от* **сли́ть(ся)**

сли́вки (**-ок**) *мн* cream *ед*

сли́вочный *прил* made with cream; **~ое ма́сло** butter

сли́зистый *прил*: **~ая оболо́чка** mucous membrane

слизь (**-и**) *ж* mucus; (*от грязи*) slime

сли́пнуться (3sg **-нется**, *pt* **-ся**, **-лась**; *impf* **слипа́ться**) *сов возв* to stick together

сли́ток (**-ка**) *м* (металлический) bar; (золота, серебра) ingot

слить (**солью́**, **сольёшь**; *pt* **-л**, **-ла́**, *imper* **сле́й(те)**; *impf* **слива́ть**) *сов перех* to pour; (*перен: соединить*) to merge; **сли́ться** (*impf* **слива́ться**) *сов возв* to merge

сли́шком *нареч* too; **э́то уже́ ~** (*разг*) that's just too much

слова́рный *прил* (работа, статья) lexicographic(al); **~ запа́с** vocabulary

слова́рь (**-я́**) *м* (книга) dictionary; (запас слов) vocabulary

слове́сный *прил* oral; (протест) verbal

сло́вно *союз* (как) like; (как будто) as if

сло́во (**-а**; *nom pl* **-а́**) *ср* word

сло́вом *вводн сл* in a word

словосочета́ние (**-я**) *ср* word combination

слог (**-а**; *nom pl* **-и**, *gen pl* **-о́в**) *м* syllable

слоёный *прил*: **~ое те́сто** puff pastry

сложе́ние (**-я**) *ср* (в математике) addition; (фигура) build

сл|**ожи́ть** (**-ожу́**, **-о́жишь**) *impf*

скла́дывать *сов перех* (*вещи*) to put; (*чемодан итп*) to pack; (*придавая форму*) to fold (up); (*impf* **скла́дывать** *или* **слага́ть**; *числа*) to add (up); (*песню, стихи*) to make up; (*impf*) **~ожа́ руки** to sit back and do nothing; **~ся** *impf*

скла́дываться *сов возв* (*ситуация*) to arise; (*характер*) to form; (*зонт, палатка*) to fold up; (*впечатление*) to be formed

сло́жно *нареч* (*делать*) in a complicated way ♦ *как сказ* it's difficult

сло́жность (**-и**) *ж* (*многообразие*) complexity; (*обычно мн: трудности*) difficulty; **в о́бщей ~** all in all

сло́жный *прил* complex; (*узор*) intricate; (*трудный*) difficult

слой (**-я**; *nom pl* **-и́**) *м* layer

слома́|ть(ся) (**-ю(сь)**) *сов от* **лома́ть(ся)**

слом|и́ть (**-лю́, -ишь**) *сов перех* to break; **~я́ го́лову** (*разг*) at breakneck speed; **~ся** *сов возв* (*перен: человек*) to crack

слон (**-а́**) *м* elephant; (ШАХМАТЫ) bishop

слон|ёнок (**-ёнка**; *nom pl* **-я́та**, *gen pl* **-я́т**) *м* elephant calf

слони́х|а (**-ы**) *ж* cow (*elephant*)

слоно́вый *прил* elephant; **~ая кость** ivory

слуг|а́ (**-и́**; *nom pl* **-и**) *м* servant

служа́н|ка (**-ки**; *gen pl* **-ок**) *ж* maid

слу́жащ|ий (**-его**) *м* white collar worker; **госуда́рственный ~** civil servant; **конто́рский ~** clerk

слу́жб|а (**-ы**) *ж* service; (*работа*) work; (*фирма*) agency; **срок ~ы** durability; **Слу́жба бы́та** consumer services; **Слу́жба**

за́нятости ≈ Employment Agency

служе́бный *прил* (*дела итп*) official

служи́тел|ь (**-я**) *м* (*в музее, в зоопарке*) keeper; (*на автозапра́вке*) attendant; **~ це́ркви** clergyman

служи́тельниц|а (**-ы**) *ж* keeper

сл|ужи́ть (**-ужу́, -у́жишь**) *несов* to serve; (*в ба́нке*) to work; **чем могу́ ~?** what can I do for you?

слух (**-а**) *м* hearing; (*музыка́льный*) ear; (*известие*) rumour (*BRIT*), rumor (*US*)

слухово́й *прил* (*нерв, орган*) auditory; **~ аппара́т** hearing aid

слу́ча|й (**-я**) *м* occasion; (*случа́йность*) chance; **в ~е** +*gen* in the event of; **во вся́ком ~е** in any case; **на вся́кий ~** just in case

случа́йно *нареч* by chance ♦ *вводн сл* by any chance

случа́йность (**-и**) *ж* chance

случа́йный *прил* (*встреча*) chance

случ|и́ться (**-у́сь, -и́шься**; *impf* **случа́ться**) *сов возв* to happen

слу́шани|я (**-й**) *мн* hearing *ед*

слу́шател|ь (**-я**) *м* listener; (ПРОСВЕЩ) student

слу́ша|ть (**-ю**) *несов перех* (*музыку, речь*) to listen to; (ЮР) to hear; (*pf* **у~**; *совет*) to listen to; **~ся** (*pf* **по~**) *несов возв*: **~ся** +*gen* to obey; (*совета*) to follow

слы́ш|ать (**-у, -ишь**) *несов* to hear ♦ (*pf* **у~**) *перех* to hear; (*impf*) **о** +*prp* to hear about; **он пло́хо ~ит** he's hard of hearing; **~ся** *несов возв* to be heard

слы́шно *как сказ* it can be heard; **мне ничего́ не ~** I can't hear a thing; **о ней ничего́ не ~** there's no news of her

слы́шный прил audible

слюн|а́ (-ы́) ж saliva

слю́н|ки (-ок) мн: у меня́ ~ теку́т my mouth's watering

сля́коть (-и) ж slush

см сокр (= **сантиме́тр**) cm

см. сокр (= **смотри́**) v., qv

сма́з|ать (-жу, -жешь) impf **сма́зывать** сов перех (ма́слом) to lubricate

сма́зк|а (-и) ж lubrication; (вещество́) lubricant

сма́зыва|ть (-ю) несов от **сма́зать**

смахн|у́ть (-у́, -ёшь) impf **сма́хивать** сов перех to brush off

сме́жный прил (ко́мната) adjoining, adjacent; (предприя́тие) affiliated

смеле́|ть (-ю; pf o~) несов to grow bolder

сме́лост|ь (-и) ж (хра́брость) courage, bravery

сме́лый прил courageous, brave; (иде́я, прое́кт) ambitious

смен|а́ (-ы́) ж (руково́дства) change; (на произво́дстве) shift

см|ени́ть (-еню́, -е́нишь) impf **сменя́ть** сов перех to change; (колле́гу) to relieve; ~**ся** (impf **сменя́ться** сов возв (руково́дство) to change

смерте́льный прил mortal; (ску́ка) deadly; ~ **слу́чай** fatality

сме́ртность (-и) ж death или mortality (US) rate, mortality

сме́ртный прил mortal; (разг: ску́ка) deadly; ~ **пригово́р** death sentence; ~**ая ка́знь** the death penalty, capital punishment

смерт|ь (-и) ж death; **я уста́л до́**~**и** I am dead tired

смеси́тель (-я) м mixer

сме|си́ть (-шу́, -сишь) сов от **меси́ть**

см|ести́ (-ету́, -етёшь; pt -ёл, -ела́, -ело́; impf **смета́ть**) сов перех to sweep

сме|сти́ть (-щу́, -сти́шь; impf **смеща́ть**) сов перех (уво́лить) to remove; ~**ся** (impf **смеща́ться**) сов возв to shift

сме́с|ь (-и) ж mixture; **моло́чная** ~ powdered baby milk

смета́ (-ы) ж (ЭКОН) estimate

смета́н|а (-ы) ж sour cream

смета́|ть (-ю) несов от **смести́**

сме́|ть (-ю; pf **посме́ть**) несов: ~ +infin to dare to do

смех (-а) м laughter

смехотво́рный прил ludicrous

смеша́|ть (-ю) сов от **меша́ть** ♦ (impf **сме́шивать**) перех (спу́тать) to mix up; ~**ся** сов от **меша́ться** ♦ (impf **сме́шиваться**) возв (сли́ться) to mingle; (кра́ски, цвета́) to blend

смеш|и́ть (-у́, -и́шь; pf **на**~ или **рас**~) несов перех: ~ **кого́-н** to make sb laugh

смешно́ нареч (смотре́ться) funny ♦ как сказ it's funny; (глу́по) it's ludicrous

смешно́й прил funny

смеща́|ть(ся) (-ю(сь)) несов от **смести́ть(ся)**

смеще́ни|е (-я) ср (руково́дства) removal; (поня́тий, крите́риев) shift

сме|я́ться (-ю́сь) несов возв to laugh

СМИ сокр (= **сре́дства ма́ссовой информа́ции**) mass media

смир|и́ть (-ю́, -и́шь; impf **смиря́ть**) сов перех to suppress; ~**ся** (impf **смиря́ться**) сов возв (покори́ться) to be tamed; (примири́ться): ~**ся с** +instr to resign o.s. to

сми́рно нареч (сидеть, вести себя) quietly; (ВОЕН): ~! attention!

сми́рный прил docile

смог etc сов см. смочь

смо́жешь etc сов см. смочь

смол|á (-ы́; nom pl -ы) ж (дерево) resin; (дёготь) tar

смо́лк|нуть (-ну; pt -, -ла; impf **смолка́ть**) сов (звуки) to fade away

сморка́|ть (-ю; pf **вы́сморкать** несов перех: ~ нос to blow one's nose; ~ся (pf **вы́сморкаться** несов возв to blow one's nose

сморо́дин|а (-ы) ж: кра́сная ~ (ягоды) redcurrants мн; чёрная ~ (ягоды) blackcurrants мн

смо́рщ|ить(ся) (-у(сь), -ишь(ся)) сов от мо́рщить(ся)

смота́|ть (-ю; impf **сма́тывать**) сов перех to wind

смотр (-а) м presentation; (музыка́льный) festival

см|отре́ть (-отрю́, -о́тришь; pf **по**~) несов ♦ перех (фильм, игру́) to watch; (карти́ну) to look at; (музе́й, вы́ставку) to look round; (следи́ть): ~ за +instr to look after; ~ (impf) в/на +acc to look onto; ~отря́ по +dat depending on; ~ся (pf **по**~ся) несов возв: ~ся в +acc (в зе́ркало) to look at o.s. in

смотри́тел|ь (-я) м attendant

смо́|чь (-гу́, -жешь etc, -гут; pt -г, -гла́, -гло́) сов от мочь

сму́гл|ый прил swarthy

сму́т|а (-ы) ж unrest

смут|и́ть (-щу́, -ти́шь; impf **смуща́ть**) сов перех to embarrass; ~ся (pf **смути́ться** сов возв to get embarrassed

сму́тный прил vague; (вре́мя) troubled

смуще́ни|е (-я) ср embarrassment

смущённый прил embarrassed

смысл (-а) м sense; (назначе́ние) point

смы́|ть (-о́ю, -о́ешь; impf **смыва́ть**) сов перех to wash off; (подлеж: волна́) to wash away; ~ться (impf **смыва́ться**) сов возв to wash off

смыч|о́к (-ка́) м (МУЗ) bow

смягч|и́ть (-у́, -и́шь; impf **смягча́ть**) сов перех (ко́жу, уда́р) to soften; (боль) to ease; (наказа́ние) to mitigate; (челове́ка) to appease; ~ся (impf **смягча́ться**) сов возв to soften

смя́ть(ся) (**сомну́(сь), сомнёшь(ся)**) сов от мя́ть(ся)

сна etc сущ см. сон

снаб|ди́ть (-жу́, -ди́шь; impf **снабжа́ть**) сов перех: ~ кого́-н/ что́-н че́м-н to supply sb/sth with sth

снабже́ни|е (-я) ср supply

сна́йпер (-а) м sniper

снару́жи нареч on the outside; (закры́ть) from the outside

снаря́д (-а) м (ВОЕН) shell; (СПОРТ) apparatus

снаря|ди́ть (-жу́, -ди́шь; impf **снаряжа́ть**) сов перех to equip

снаряже́ни|е (-я) ср equipment

снача́ла нареч at first; (ещё раз) all over again

СНГ м сокр (= Содру́жество Незави́симых Госуда́рств) CIS

снег (-а; loc sg -ý, nom pl -á) м snow; идёт ~ it's snowing

снеги́р|ь (-я́) м bullfinch

снегови́к (-á) м snowman

снегопа́д (-а) м snowfall

Снегу́ро́чк|а (-ки; gen pl -ек) ж Snow Maiden

Снегу́рочка - Snow Maiden. She
accompanies Father Christmas on
his visits to children's New Year
parties, where she organizes
games and helps to give out the
presents.

снежи́н|ка (-ки; gen pl -ок) ж
snowflake
сне́жный прил snow; (зима)
snowy
снеж|о́к (-ка́) м snowball
снести́ (-су́, -сёшь; pt -ёс,
-есла́, -есло́, impf сноси́ть) сов
перех (отнести) to take; (подлеж:
буря) to tear down; (перен) to
take; (дом) to demolish
снижа́|ть(ся (-ю(сь)) несов от
сни́зить(ся)
сниже́ни|е (-я) ср (цен итп)
lowering; (самолёта) descent;
(выдачи) reduction
сни́|зить (-жу, -зишь; impf
снижа́ть) сов перех (цены,
давление итп) to lower;
(скорость) to reduce; **~ся** (impf
снижа́ться) сов возв to fall;
(самолёт) to descend
сни́зу нареч (внизу) at the
bottom; (о направлении) from
the bottom
снима́|ть(ся (-ю(сь)) несов от
снять(ся)
сни́м|ок (-ка) м (ФОТО) snap(shot)
снисходи́тельный прил lenient;
(высокомерный) condescending
сни́|ться (-юсь, -ишься; pf
при~) несов безл: мне ~и́лся
стра́шный сон I was having a
terrible dream; мне ~и́лось, что я
в гора́х I dreamt I was in the
mountains; ты ча́сто ~и́шься мне
I often dream about you
сно́ва нареч again

снос (-а) м demolition
сно́с|ка (-ки; gen pl -ок) ж
footnote
снотво́рн|ое (-ого) ср sleeping
pill
сноха́ (-и́) ж daughter-in-law (of
husband's father)
сня́ть (-иму́, -и́мешь; impf
снима́ть) сов перех to take
down; (плод) to pick; (одежду) to
take off; (запрет,
ответственность) to remove;
(фотографировать) to
photograph; (копию) to make;
(нанять) to rent; (уволить) to
dismiss; **снима́ть** (~ pf)
фотогра́фию to take a picture;
снима́ть (~ pf) **фильм** to shoot a
film; **сня́ться** (impf **снима́ться**)
сов возв (сфотографироваться)
to have one's photograph taken; (в
фильме) to appear
со предл = с
соа́втор (-а) м coauthor
соба́к|а (-и) ж dog
собаково́д (-а) м dog-breeder
соба́чий прил dog's
собе́с (-а) м social security;
(орган) social security department
собесе́дник (-а) м: мой ~
замолча́л the person I was talking
to fell silent
собесе́довани|е (-я) ср interview
собира́тель (-я) м collector
собира́|ть (-ю) несов от
собра́ть; **~ся** несов от
собра́ться ♦ возв: я ~ю́сь пойти́
туда́ I'm going to go there
соблазн|и́ть (-ю́, -и́шь; impf
соблазня́ть) сов перех to
seduce; (прельстить): **~ кого́-н
чем-н** to tempt sb with sth; **~ся**
(impf **соблазня́ться**) сов возв:
~ся +instr/ +infin to be tempted
by/to do

соблюда́|ть (-ю) *несов от* **соблюсти́** ♦ *перех* (дисципли́ну, поря́док) to maintain

соблю|сти́ (-ду́, -дёшь) *сов от* **блюсти́** ♦ *impf* **соблюда́ть** *перех* (зако́н, пра́вила) to observe

соболе́знование (-я) *ср* condolences *мн*

со́бол|ь (-оля; *nom pl* -оля́) *м* sable

собо́р (-а) *м* cathedral

СОБР (-а) *м сокр* (= Сво́дный отря́д бы́строго реаги́рования) flying squad

собра́ни|е (-я) *ср* meeting; (*полит*) assembly; (карти́н *итп*) collection; ~ **сочине́ний** collected works

соб|ра́ть (-еру́, -ерёшь; *pt* -ра́л, -рала́, -ра́ло; *impf* **собира́ть**) *сов перех* to gather (together); (я́годы, грибы́) to pick; (механи́зм) to assemble; (нало́ги, по́дписи) to collect; **~ся** *возв* (го́сти) to assemble, gather; (пригото́виться): **~ся** +*infin* to get ready to do; **собира́ться** (**~ся** *pf*) **с** +*instr* (с си́лами, с мы́слями) to gather

собро́в|ец (-ца) *м* member of the flying squad

со́бственник (-а) *м* owner

со́бственно *част* actually ♦ *вводн сл*: ~ (говоря́) as a matter of fact

со́бственност|ь (-и) *ж* property

со́бственный *прил* (one's) own

собы́ти|е (-я) *ср* event

сов|а́ (-ы́; *nom pl* -ы) *ж* owl

соверша́|ть(ся) (-ю) *несов от* **соверши́ть(ся)**

соверше́ни|е (-я) *ср* (сде́лки) conclusion; (преступле́ния) committing

соверше́нно *нареч* (о́чень хорошо́) perfectly; (совсе́м) absolutely, completely

совершенноле́тн|ий *прил*: **стать ~им** to come of age

соверше́нный *прил* (хоро́ший) perfect; (абсолю́тный) absolute, complete; ~ **вид** (линг) perfective (aspect)

соверше́нств|о (-а) *ср* perfection

соверше́нствовать (-ую; *pf* **у~**) *несов перех* to perfect; **~ся** (*pf* **у~ся**) *несов возв*: **~ся в** +*prp* to perfect

соверш|и́ть (-у́, -и́шь; *impf* **соверша́ть**) *сов перех* to make; (сде́лку) to conclude; (преступле́ние) to commit; (обря́д, по́двиг) to perform; **~ся** (*impf* **соверша́ться**) *сов возв* (собы́тие) to take place

со́вест|ь (-и) *ж* conscience; **на ~** (сде́ланный) very well

сове́т (-а) *м* advice *то́лько ед*; (вое́нный) council

сове́тник (-а) *м* (юсти́ции *итп*) councillor; (президе́нта) adviser

сове́т|овать (-ую; *pf* **по~**) *несов*: **~ кому́-н** +*infin* to advise sb to do; **~ся** (*pf* **по~ся**) *несов возв*: **~ся с ке́м-н** (с дру́гом) to ask sb's advice; (с юри́стом) to consult sb

сове́тский *прил* Soviet

совеща́ни|е (-я) *ср* (собра́ние) meeting; (конгре́сс) conference

совеща́тельный *прил* (о́рган, го́лос) consultative

совеща́|ться (-юсь) *несов возв* to deliberate

совмести́мый *прил* compatible

совме|сти́ть (-щу́, -сти́шь; *impf* **совмеща́ть**) *сов перех* to combine

совме́стный *прил* (о́бщий) joint; **~ое предприя́тие** joint venture

совок **300** сожаление

сов|о́к (-ка́) м (для мусора) dustpan; (для муки) scoop

совоку́пность (-и) ж combination; **в ~и** in total

совоку́пный прил (усилия) joint

совпаде́ни|е (-я) ср coincidence; (данных, цифр) tallying

совпа́|сть (3sg -де́т) сов; impf **совпада́ть** сов (события) to coincide; (данные, цифры итп) to tally; (интересы, вкусы итп) to match

совр|а́ть (-у́, -ёшь) сов от врать

совреме́нник (-а) м contemporary

совреме́нность (-и) ж the present day; (идей) modernity

совреме́нный прил contemporary; (техника) up-to-date; (человек, идеи) modern

совсе́м нареч (новый) completely; (молодой) very; (нисколько: не пригодный, не нужный) totally; **не ~** not quite

согла́си|е (-я) ср consent; (в семье) harmony, accord

согла|си́ться (-шу́сь, -си́шься; impf **соглаша́ться)** сов возв to agree

согла́сно предл: **~** +dat или **с** +instr in accordance with

согла́сн|ый (-ого) м (также: **~ звук)** consonant ♦ прил: **~ на** +асс (на условия) agreeable to; **Вы ~ы (со мной)?** do you agree (with me)?

соглас|ова́ть (-у́ю; impf **согласо́вывать)** сов перех (действия) to coordinate; (обговорить): **~ что-н** +instr (план, цену) to agree sth with; **~ся** (не)сов возв: **~ся с** +instr to correspond with

соглаша́|ться (-юсь) несов от согласи́ться

соглаше́ни|е (-я) ср agreement

согн|у́ть (-у́, -ёшь) сов от гнуть, сгиба́ть

согре́|ть (-ю; impf **согрева́ть)** сов перех (воду) to heat up; (ноги, руки) to warm up; **~ся** (impf **согрева́ться)** сов возв to warm up; (вода) to heat up

со́д|а (-ы) ж soda

соде́йстви|е (-я) ср assistance

соде́йств|овать (-ую) (не)сов: **~** +dat to assist

содержа́ни|е (-я) ср (семьи, детей) upkeep; (магазина, фермы) keeping; (книги) contents мн; (сахара, витаминов) content; (оглавление) (table of) contents мн

содержа́тельный прил (статья, доклад) informative

сод|ержа́ть (-ержу́, -е́ржишь) несов перех (детей, родителей, магазин) to keep; (ресторан) to own; (сахар, ошибки, информацию итп) to contain; **~ся** несов возв (под арестом) to be held

содр|а́ть (сдеру́, сдерёшь; pt **-а́л, -ала́;** impf **сдира́ть)** сов перех (слой, одежду) to tear off

содру́жеств|о (-а) ср (дружба) co-operation; (союз) commonwealth; **Содру́жество Незави́симых Госуда́рств** the Commonwealth of Independent States

со́евый прил soya

соедин|и́ть (-ю́, -и́шь; impf **соединя́ть)** сов перех (силы, детали) to join; (людей) to unite; (провода, трубы, по телефону) to connect; (города) to link; **~ся** (impf **соединя́ться)** сов возв (люди, отряды) to join together

сожале́ни|е (-я) ср (сострадание) pity; **~ (о** +prp) (о

прошлом, о поте́ре) regret
(about); **к ~ю** unfortunately

сожале́ть (**-ю**) *несов*: **о чём-н**/**что** to regret sth/that

созва́ть (**-ову́, -ове́шь**; *pt* **-ва́л, -вала́**; *impf* **созыва́ть** (*пригласи́ть*) *сов перех* to summon; (*impf* **созыва́ть**; *съезд*) to convene

созве́зди|е (**-я**) *ср* constellation

созвони́ться (**-ю́сь, -и́шься**; *impf* **созва́ниваться**) *сов возв*: **~ с +instr** to phone (*BRIT*) или call (*US*)

созда|ва́ть(ся) (**-ю́, -ёшь**) *несов от* **созда́ть(ся)**

созда́ни|е (**-я**) *ср* creation; (*существо*) creature

созда́тел|ь (**-я**) *м* creator

созда́ть (*как* **дать**; *см. Table 16*; *impf* **создава́ть** (*сов перех* to create; (*impf* **создава́ться**) *сов возв* (*обстано́вка*) to emerge; (*впечатле́ние*) to be created

созна|ва́ть (**-ю́, -ёшь**) *несов от* **созна́ть** ♦ *перех* to be aware of; **~ся** *несов от* **созна́ться**

созна́ни|е (**-я**) *ср* consciousness; (*вины, до́лга*) awareness; **приходи́ть** (**прийти́** *pf*) **в ~** to come round

созна́тельн|ость (**-и**) *ж* awareness

созна́тельный *прил* (*челове́к, во́зраст*) mature; (*жизнь*) adult; (*обма́н, посту́пок*) intentional

созна́|ть (**-ю**; *impf* **сознава́ть** (*сов перех* (*вину́, долг*) to realize; **~ся** (*impf* **сознава́ться**) *сов возв* (**в** +*prp*) (*в оши́бке*) to admit (to); (*в преступле́нии*) to confess (to)

созре́|ть (**-ю**) *сов от* **зреть**

созыва́ть (**-ю**) *несов от* **созва́ть**

сойти́ (*как* **идти́**; *см. Table 18*; *impf* **сходи́ть** (*сов* (*с горы́, с*

ле́стницы) to go down; (*с доро́ги*) to leave; (*разг*): **~ +instr** (*с по́езда, с авто́буса*) to get off; (*impf* **сходи́ть**; **~ с ума́** to go mad; **~сь** (*impf* **сходи́ться**) *сов возв* (*собра́ться*) to gather; (*ци́фры, показа́ния*) to tally

сок (**-а**) *м* juice

со́кол (**-а**) *м* falcon

сократи́ть (**-щу́, -ти́шь**; *impf* **сокраща́ть** (*сов перех* to shorten; (*расхо́ды*) to reduce; **~ся** (*impf* **сокраща́ться**) *сов возв* (*расстоя́ние, сро́ки*) to be shortened; (*расхо́ды, снабже́ние*) to be reduced

сокраще́ни|е (**-я**) *ср* (*см глаг*) shortening; reduction; (*сокращённое назва́ние*) abbreviation; (*та́кже*: **~ шта́тов**) staff reduction

сокро́вищ|е (**-а**) *ср* treasure

соку́рсни|к (**-а**) *м*: **он мой ~** he is in my year

сол|га́ть (**-гу́, -жёшь** *etc*, **-гу́т**) *сов от* **лгать**

солда́т (**-а**; *gen pl* **-**) *м* soldier

солда́тик (**-а**) *м* (*игру́шка*) toy soldier

солёный *прил* (*пи́ща*) salty; (*о́вощи*) pickled in brine; (*вода́*) salt

солида́рн|ость (**-и**) *ж* solidarity

соли́дный *прил* (*постро́йка*) solid; (*фи́рма*) established

соли́ст (**-а**) *м* soloist

соли́ть (**-ю́, -ишь**; *pf* **по~**) *несов перех* to salt; (*заса́ливать*) to preserve in brine

со́лнечный *прил* solar; (*день, пого́да*) sunny; **уда́р** sunstroke; **~ые очки́** sunglasses

со́лнц|е (**-а**) *ср* sun

со́ло *ср нескл, нареч* solo

солов|е́й (**-ья́**) *м* nightingale

соло́м|а (-ы) *ж* straw

соло́менный *прил (шля́па)* straw

соло́н|ка (-ки; *gen pl* **-ок)** *ж* saltcellar

сол|ь (-и) *ж* salt

со́льный *прил* solo

сомнева́|ться (-юсь) *несов возв*: ~ в чём-н/, что to doubt sth/that

сомне́ни|е (-я) *ср* doubt

сомни́тельный *прил (де́ло, ли́чность)* shady; *(предложе́ние, знако́мство)* dubious

сон (сна) *м* sleep; *(сновиде́ние)* dream

сона́т|а (-ы) *ж* sonata

со́нный *прил (заспа́нный)* sleepy

сообража́|ть (-ю) *несов от* **сообрази́ть**

соображе́ни|е (-я) *ср (мысль)* idea; *(обычно мн: моти́вы)* reasoning

сообрази́тельный *прил* smart

сообраз|и́ть (-жу́, -зи́шь; *impf* **сообража́ть)** *сов* to work out

сообща́ *нареч* together

сообща́|ть (-ю) *несов от* **сообщи́ть**

сообще́ни|е (-я) *ср (информа́ция)* report; *(прави́тельственное)* announcement; *(связь)* communications *мн*

соо́бществ|о (-а) *ср* association; **мирово́е** или **междунаро́дное ~** international community

сообщ|и́ть (-у́, -и́шь; *impf* **сообща́ть)** *сов*: ~ кому́-н о +*prp* to inform sb of ♦ *перех (но́вости, та́йну)* to tell

сообщ́ник (-а) *м* accomplice

соотве́тственно *предл*: ~ +*dat (обстано́вке)* according to

соотве́тственный *прил (опла́та)* appropriate; *(результа́ты)* fitting

соотве́тстви|е (-я) *ср*

(интере́сов, сти́лей итп) correspondence; **в ~и с** +*instr* in accordance with

соотве́тств|овать (-ую) *несов*: ~ +*dat* to correspond to; *(тре́бованиям)* to meet

соотве́тствующий *прил* appropriate

соофте́чественник (-а) *м* compatriot

соотноше́ни|е (-я) *ср* correlation

сопе́рник (-а) *м* rival; *(в спо́рте)* competitor

сопе́рнича|ть (-ю) *несов*: ~ с кем-н в чём-н to rival sb in sth

сопра́но *нескл* soprano

сопровожда́|ть (-ю; *pf* **сопроводи́ть)** *несов перех* to accompany

сопровожде́ни|е (-я) *ср*: **в ~и** +*gen* accompanied by

сопротивле́ни|е (-я) *ср* resistance

сопротивля́|ться (-юсь) *несов возв*: ~ +*dat* to resist

сор (-а) *м* rubbish

сорв|а́ть (-у́, -ёшь; *impf* **срыва́ть)** *сов перех (цвето́к, я́блоко)* to pick; *(дверь, кры́шу, оде́жду)* to tear off; *(ле́кцию, перегово́ры)* to sabotage; *(пла́ны)* to frustrate; **~ся** *(impf* **срыва́ться)** *сов возв (челове́к)* to lose one's temper; *(пла́ны)* to be frustrated; **срыва́ться** *(~ся pf)* +*gen (с пе́тель)* to come away from

соревнова́ни|е (-я) *ср* competition

соревн|ова́ться (-у́юсь) *несов возв* to compete

сор|и́ть (-ю́, -и́шь; *pf* **на~)** *несов* to make a mess

сорня́к (-á) *м* weed

со́рок (-á; см. Table 27) *чис* forty

соро́к|а (-и) ж magpie

сороково́й чис fortieth

соро́ч|ка (-ки; gen pl **-ек)** ж (мужская) shirt; **ночна́я ~** nightgown

сорт (-а; nom pl **-а́)** м sort; (пшеницы) grade

сорти́р|овать (-у́ю; pf **рас~)** несов перех to sort; (по качеству) to grade

сос|а́ть (-у́, -ёшь) несов перех to suck; (младенец, детёныш) to suckle

сосе́д (-а; nom pl **-и,** gen pl **-ей)** м neighbour (BRIT), neighbor (US)

сосе́дний прил neighbouring (BRIT), neighboring (US)

сосе́дств|о (-а) ср: **жить по ~у** to live nearby; **в ~е с** +instr near

соси́с|ка (-ки; gen pl **-ок)** ж sausage

со́с|ка (-ки; gen pl **-ок)** ж (на бутылке) teat; (пустышка) dummy (BRIT), pacifier (US)

соск|очи́ть (-очу́, -о́чишь) impf **соска́кивать)** сов to jump off

соску́ч|иться (-усь, -ишься) сов возв to be bored; **(** pf **по** +dat (по детям) to miss

сослага́тельн|ый прил: **-ое накло́не́ние** subjunctive mood

со|сла́ть (-шлю́, -шлёшь) impf **ссыла́ть)** сов перех to exile; **~ся (** impf **ссыла́ться)** сов возв: **~ся на** +acc to refer to

сослужи́в|ец (-ца) м colleague

сос|на́ (-ны́; nom pl **-ны,** gen pl **-ен)** ж pine (tree)

сосно́вый прил pine

сос|о́к (-ка́) м nipple

сосредото́ч|ить (-у, -ишь) impf **сосредота́чивать)** сов перех to concentrate; **~ся (** impf **сосредота́чиваться)** сов возв (войска) to be concentrated;

(внимание): **~ся на** +acc to focus on

соста́в (-а) м (классовый) structure; (комитета) members мн of; (вещества) composition of

сост|а́вить (-лю, -ишь) impf **составля́ть)** сов перех (словарь, список) to compile; (план) to draw up; (сумму) to constitute; (команду) to put together; **~ся (** impf **составля́ться)** сов возв to be formed

составн|о́й прил: **~а́я часть** component

соста́р|ить (-ю, -ишь) сов от **ста́рить; ~ся** сов возв (человек) to grow old

состоя́ни|е (-я) ср state; (больного) condition; (собственности) fortune; **быть** (impf) **в ~и** +infin to be able to do

состоя́тельный прил (богатый) well-off

состо|я́ть (-ю́, -и́шь) несов: **~ из** +gen (книга) to consist of; (заключаться): **~ в** +prp to be (в партии) to be a member of; **~** (impf) +instr (директором итп) to be; **~ся** несов возв (собрание) to take place

сострада́ни|е (-я) ср compassion

состяза́ни|е (-я) ср contest

состяза́|ться (-юсь) несов возв to compete

сосу́д (-а) м vessel

сосу́л|ька (-ьки; gen pl **-ек)** ж icicle

сосущество́вани|е (-я) ср coexistence

сот чис см. **сто**

сотворе́ни|е (-я) ср: **~ ми́ра** Creation

со́т|ня (-ни; gen pl **-ен)** ж (сто) a hundred

со́тов|ый прил: ~ телефо́н
mobile phone; ~ая связь network

сотру́дник (-а) м (служащий)
employee; нау́чный ~ research
worker

сотру́дничать (-ю) несов to
cooperate; (работать) to work

сотру́дничеств|о (-а) ср (см
глаг) cooperation; work

сотрясе́ни|е (-я) ср (от взрыва)
shaking; (также: ~ мо́зга)
concussion

сотряс|ти́ (-у́, -ёшь; impf
сотряса́ть) сов перех to shake;
~сь (impf **сотряса́ться**) сов возв
to shake

со́т|ы (-ов) мн: (пчели́ные)
honeycomb ед

со́тый чис hundredth

со́ус (-а) м sauce

соуча́стник (-а) м accomplice

соф|а́ (-ы́; nom pl -ы) ж sofa

со́х|нуть (-ну; pt -, -ла; pf
вы́сохнуть) несов to dry;
(растения) to wither

сохран|и́ть (-ю́, -и́шь; impf
сохраня́ть) сов перех to
preserve; (КОМП) to save; ~ся (impf
сохраня́ться) сов возв to be
preserved

сохра́нность (-и) ж (вкладов,
документов) security; в (по́лной)
~и (fully) intact

социа́л-демокра́т (-а) м social
democrat

социали́зм (-а) м socialism

социалисти́ческий прил socialist

социа́льн|ый прил social; ~ая
защищённость social security

социо́лог (-а) м sociologist

социоло́ги|я (-и) ж sociology

сочета́ни|е (-я) ср combination

сочета́|ть(ся) (-ю(сь)) (не)сов возв
to combine; ~ся (не)сов возв
(соединиться) to combine

(гармонировать) to match

сочине́ни|е (-я) ср
(литературное) work;
(музыкальное) composition;
(ПРОСВЕЩ) essay

сочин|и́ть (-ю́, -и́шь; impf
сочиня́ть) сов перех (музыку)
to compose; (стихи, песню) to
write

со́чный прил (плод) juicy; (трава)
lush; (краски) vibrant

сочу́встви|е (-я) ср sympathy

сочу́ств|овать (-ую) несов: ~
+dat to sympathize with

сошёл(ся) etc сов см. **сойти́(сь)**

сошью́ итп сов см. **сшить**

сою́з (-а) м union; (военный)
alliance; (ЛИНГ) conjunction

сою́зник (-а) м ally

сою́зный прил (армия) allied;
(слово) conjunctive

со́|я (-и) ж собир soya beans мн

спад (-а) м drop; экономи́ческий
~ recession

спада́|ть (3sg -ет) несов от
спасть

спазм (-а) м spasm

спа́льн|ый прил (место) sleeping;
~ ваго́н sleeping car; ~ мешо́к
sleeping bag

спа́льн|я (-ьни; gen pl -ен) ж
(комната) bedroom; (мебель)
bedroom suite

Спас (-а) м (РЕЛ) the Day of the
Saviour (in Orthodox Church)

спаси́тель (-я) м rescuer

спаса́тельн|ый прил (станция)
rescue; ~ая ло́дка lifeboat; ~
жиле́т lifejacket; ~ по́яс lifebelt

спаса́|ть(ся) (-ю(сь)) несов от
спасти́(сь)

спасе́ни|е (-я) ср rescue; (РЕЛ)
Salvation

спаси́бо част: ~ (Вам) thank you;
большо́е ~! thank you very much!;

~ за по́мощь thanks for the help

спаси́тель (-я) м saviour; (РЕЛ) the Saviour

спас|ти́ (-у́, -ёшь; impf спаса́ть) сов перех to save; ~сь (impf спаса́ться сов возв: ~сь (от +gen) to escape

спа|сть (3sg -дёт; impf спада́ть) сов (вода) to drop

спать (-лю, -ишь) несов to sleep; ложи́ться (лечь pf) ~ to go to bed; **спа́ться** несов возв: мне не -и́тся I can't (get to) sleep

СПБ сокр (= Санкт-Петербу́рг) St Petersburg

спекта́кл|ь (-я) м performance

спектр (-а) м spectrum

спекули́р|овать (-ую) несов (дефици́том) to profiteer; (КОММ) ~ +instr (на би́рже) to speculate In

спекуля́нт (-а) м (би́ржевой) speculator; (дефици́том) profiteer

спекуля́ци|я (-и) ж (дефици́том) profiteering; (на би́рже) speculation

спе́лый прил ripe

спе́реди нареч in front

спе́рм|а (-ы) ж sperm

спе|ть (3sg -ёет; pf поспе́ть) несов (фру́кты, о́вощи) to ripen ♦ (-о́ю, -о́ешь) сов от петь

спех (-а) м: мне не к спе́ху (разг) I'm in no hurry

специализи́р|оваться (-уюсь) (не)сов возв: ~ в +prp или по +dat to specialize in

специали́ст (-а) м specialist

специа́льность (-и) ж (профе́ссия) profession

специа́льный прил special

специ́фик|а (-и) ж specific nature

специфи́ческий прил specific

спе́ци|я (-и) ж spice

спецко́р (-а) м сокр (= специа́льный корреспонде́нт)

---

special correspondent

спецку́рс (-а) м сокр (в ву́зе): = специа́льный курс) course of lectures in a specialist field

спецна́з (-а) м special task force

спецназо́вец (-ца) м member of the special task force

спецоде́жд|а (-ы) ж сокр (= специа́льная оде́жда) work clothes мн

спецслу́жб|а (-ы) ж сокр (обы́чно мн: = специа́льная слу́жба) special service

спеши́ть (-у́, -и́шь) несов (часы́) to be fast; (челове́к) to be in a rush; (по~ pf) ~ +inf/c +instr to be in a hurry to do/with; (impf) ~ на по́езд to rush for the train

спе́шк|а (-и) ж (разг) hurry, rush

спе́шно нареч hurriedly

спе́шный прил urgent

СПИД м сокр (= синдро́м приобретённого иммунодефици́та) AIDS

спидо́метр (-а) м speedometer

спи́кер (-а) м speaker

спин|а́ (-ы́; acc sg -у, dat sg -е́, nom pl -ы) ж (челове́ка, живо́тного) back

спи́н|ка (-ки; gen pl -ок) ж уменьш от спина́; (ди́вана, сту́ла итп) back; (крова́ти: ве́рхняя) headboard; (: ни́жняя) foot

спинно́й прил (позвоно́к) spinal; ~ мозг spinal cord

спира́л|ь (-и) ж (ли́ния) spiral; (та́кже: внутрима́точная ~) coil (contraceptive)

спирт (-а) м (ХИМ) spirit

спиртно́|е (-о́го) ср alcohol

спиртно́й прил: ~ напи́ток alcoholic drink

спи|са́ть (-шу́, -шешь; impf спи́сывать) сов перех to copy;

(комм) to write off

спи́с|ок (-ка) м list

спи́ц|а (-ы) ж (для вязания) knitting needle; (колеса) spoke

спи́чечн|ый прил: ~ая коро́бка matchbox; ~ая голо́вка matchhead

спи́чк|а (-ки; gen pl **-ек)** ж match

сплав (-а) м alloy

спла́в|ить (-лю, -ишь; impf **сплавля́ть)** сов перех (металлы) to alloy

спла́чива|ть(ся) (-ю) несов от сплоти́ть(ся)

спле|сти́ (-ту́, -тёшь; pt **-ёл, -ела́)** сов от плести́ ♦ (impf **сплета́ть)** перех to plait; (пальцы) to intertwine

спле́тнича|ть (-ю) несов to gossip

спле́тн|я (-и; gen pl **-ен)** ж gossip

спло|ти́ть (-чу́, -ти́шь; impf **спла́чивать)** сов перех to unite; **~ся** (impf **спла́чиваться)** сов возв to unite

сплошно́й прил (степь) continuous; (перепись) universal; (разг: неудача) utter

сплошь нареч (по всей поверхности) all over; (без исключения) completely; **~ и ря́дом** (разг) everywhere

сплю несов см. спать

споко́йный прил (улица, жизнь) quiet; (море, взгляд) calm

споко́йстви|е (-я) ср calm, tranquillity

сполз|ти́ (-у́, -ёшь; pt **-, -ла́)** impf **сполза́ть)** сов to climb down

спонси́р|овать (-ую) (не)сов to sponsor

спо́нсор (-а) м sponsor

спор (-а) м debate; (юр) dispute; **на́ ~** (разг) as a bet

спо́р|ить (-ю, -ишь; pf **по~)**

несов (вести спор) to argue; (держать пари) to bet; **~** (impf) **с кем-н о чём-н** или **за что-н** (о наследстве) to dispute sth with sb

спо́рный прил (дело) disputed; (победа) doubtful; **~ вопро́с** moot point

спорт (-а) м sport

спортза́л (-а) м сокр (= спорти́вный зал) sports hall

спорти́вный прил sports; (фигура, человек) sporty; **~ костю́м** tracksuit

спортсме́н (-а) м sportsman

спо́соб (-а) м way

спосо́бность (-и) ж ability

спосо́бный прил capable; (тала́нтливый) able

спосо́бств|овать (-ую) сов: **~ +dat** (успеху, развитию) to encourage

спотк|ну́ться (-у́сь, -ёшься; impf **спотыка́ться)** сов возв to trip

спою́ итп несов см. спеть

спра́ва нареч to the right; **от ~ +gen** to the right of

справедли́вость (-и) ж justice

справедли́вый прил fair, just; (вывод) correct

спра́виться (impf **справля́ться)** сов возв: **~ся с** +instr (с работой) to cope with, manage; (с противником) to deal with; (узнавать) **~ся о** +prp to enquire или ask about

спра́в|ка (-ки; gen pl **-ок)** ж (сведения) information; (документ) certificate

спра́вочник (-а) м directory; (грамматический) reference book

спра́вочный прил (литература) reference; **~ое бюро́** information office или bureau

спра́шива|ть(ся) (-ю(сь)) несов от спроси́ть(ся)

спрос (-а) м: ~ **на** +acc (на
товары) demand for;
(требование) ~ с +gen (с
родителей) demands мн on; **без
спро́са** или **спро́су** without
permission

спр|оси́ть (-ошу́, -о́сишь; impf
спра́шивать) сов перех
(дорогу, время) to ask; (совета,
денег) to ask for; (взыскать): ~
что-н с +gen to call sb to account
for sth; (осведомиться): ~ кого-н
о чём-н to ask sb about sth;
спра́шивать (~ pf) ученика́ to
question или test a pupil; **~ся**
(impf **спра́шиваться**) сов возв:
~ен или у +gen (у учителя итп)
to ask permission of

пры́г|нуть (-ну; impf
пры́гивать) сов: с +gen to
jump off

пряга́|ть (-ю; pf про-) несов
перех (линг) to conjugate
пряже́ни|е (-я) ср (линг)
conjugation

пря́|тать(ся) (-чу(сь),
-чешь(ся)) сов от **пря́тать(ся)**

пуск (-а) м (флага) lowering;
(корабля) launch; (воды, газа)
training; (с горы) descent

пуска́|ть (-ю) несов от
пусти́ть ♦ перех: я не ~л глаз
с неё I didn't take my eyes off her;
~ся несов от **спусти́ться**

пу|сти́ть (-щу́, -стишь; impf
пуска́ть) сов перех to lower;
(собаку) to let loose; (газ, воду)
to drain; **~ся** (impf **спуска́ться**)
сов возв to go down

пустя́ нареч: ~ **три дня/год** three
days/a year later

пу́та|ть(ся) (-ю(сь))
сов от ~ть(ся)

пу́тник (-а) м (в пути) travelling
(BRIT) или traveling (US)

---

companion; (АСТРОНОМИЯ)
satellite; (КОСМОС: также)
иску́сственный ~) sputnik,
satellite

спя́чк|а (-и) ж hibernation

сравне́ни|е (-я) ср comparison; **в
~и** или **по ~ю с** +instr compared
with

сра́внива|ть (-ю) несов от
сравни́ть, **сравня́ть**

сравни́тельный прил
comparative

сравн|и́ть (-ю́, -и́шь) impf
сра́внивать) сов перех: ~
что-н/кого́-н (с +instr) to compare
sth/sb (with); **~ся** сов возв: **~ся с**
+instr to compare with

сравн|я́ть (-ю) сов от **равня́ть**
♦ (impf **сра́внивать**) перех: ~
счёт to equalize

сраже́ни|е (-я) ср battle

сра|зи́ть (-жу́, -зи́шь; impf
сража́ть) сов перех (пулей,
ударом) to slay; **~ся** (impf
сража́ться) сов возв: **~ся** (с
+instr) to join battle with; (с
недостатками) to combat

сра́зу нареч (немедленно)
straight away; (в один приём) (all)
at once

сраст|и́сь (3sg **-ётся**; impf
сраста́ться) сов возв (кости) to
knit (together)

сред|а́ (-ы́; nom pl -ы) ж medium;
(no pl; природная, социальная)
environment; (acc sg -у; день
недели) Wednesday; **окружа́ющая ~** = environment;
охра́на окружа́ющей ~ы
conservation

среди́ предл: ~ +gen in the middle
of; (в числе) among

средизе́мный прил:
Средизе́мное мо́ре the
Mediterranean (Sea)

среднеазиа́тский *прил* Central Asian

средневеко́вый *прил* medieval

среднегодово́й *прил* average annual

сре́дний *прил* average; *(размер)* medium; *(в середине)* middle; *(школа)* secondary

---

сре́дняя шко́ла . Children in Russia start school at the age of six or seven. They stay in the same school throughout their education. They can leave school after eight years if they plan to continue into further education. Those who stay on study for a further two or three years before sitting their final exams. On completing the final exams they receive the Certificate of Secondary Education. See also note an **аттеста́т зре́лости**.

сре́дств|о (-а) *ср* means *мн*; *(лекарство)* remedy

срез (-а) *м (место)* cut; *(тонкий слой)* section

сре́|зать (-жу, -жешь; *impf* **среза́ть**) *сов перех* to cut

срок (-а) *м (длительность)* time, period; *(дата)* date; **в ~** *(во время)* in time; **после́дний** *или* **преде́льный ~** deadline; **~ го́дности** *(товара)* sell-by date; **~ де́йствия** period of validity

сро́чный *прил* urgent

срыв (-а) *м* disruption; *(на экзамене итп)* failure

срыва́|ть(ся) (-ю(сь)) *несов от* **сорва́ть(ся)**

сса́дин|а (-ы) *ж* scratch

ссо́р|а (-ы) *ж* quarrel

ссо́р|ить (-ю, -ишь; *pf* **по~**) *несов перех (друзей)* to cause to quarrel; **~ся** *(pf* **по~ся**) *несов*

возв to quarrel

СССР *м сокр (ИСТ: = Сою́з Сове́тских Социалисти́ческих Респу́блик)* USSR

ссу́д|а (-ы) *ж* loan

ссу|жа́ть (-жу́, -дишь; *impf* **ссужа́ть**) *сов перех (деньги)* to lend

ссыла́|ть (-ю) *несов от* **сосла́ть**; **~ся** *несов от* **сосла́ться** ♦ *возв:* **~ясь на** +*acc* with reference to

ссы́л|ка (-ки; *gen pl* **-ок**) *ж* exile; *(цитата)* quotation

ст. *сокр* (= **ста́нция**) sta.

ста *чис см.* **сто**

стабилизи́р|овать (-ую) *(не)сов перех* to stabilize

стаби́льный *прил* stable

ста́в|ить (-лю, -ишь; *pf* **по~**) *несов перех* to put; *(назначать: мини́стром)* to appoint; *(оперу)* to stage; **~ (по~** *pf)* **часы́** to set a clock

ста́в|ка (-ки; *gen pl* **-ок**) *ж (также* КОММ) rate; *(ВОЕН)* headquarters *мн*; *(в ка́ртах)* stake; *(перен):* **~ на** +*acc (расчёт)* reliance on

ставри́д|а (-ы) *ж (ЗООЛ)* horse mackerel, scad

стадио́н (-а) *м* stadium

ста́ди|я (-и) *ж* stage

ста́д|о (-а; *nom pl* **-а́**) *ср (коров)* herd; *(овец)* flock

стаж (-а) *м (рабочий)* experience

стажёр (-а) *м* probationer

стажи́р|оваться (-уюсь) *несов возв* to work on probation

стажиро́в|ка (-ки; *gen pl* **-ок**) *ж* probationary period

стака́н (-а) *м* glass; **бума́жный ~** paper cup

стал *сов от* **стать**

сталева́р (-а) *м* steel-maker

ста́лкива|ть(ся) (-ю(сь)) *несов от* **столкну́ть(ся)**

сталь (-и) ж steel

стам итп чис см. **сто**

стандарт (-а) м standard

стан|овиться (-овлюсь, -овишься) несов от **стать**

становлени|е (-я) ср formation

стан|о́к (-ка́) м machine (tool)

стану итп сов см. **стать**

станци|я (-и) ж station; **телефонная ~** telephone exchange

старани|е (-я) ср effort

стара́тельный прил diligent; (работа) painstaking

стара́|ться (-юсь; pf **по~)** несов возв: **~** +infin to try to do

старе́|ть (-ю; pf **по~)** несов (человек) to grow old(er), age; (pf **у~**; оборудование) to become out of date

стари́к (-а́) м old man

стари́нный прил ancient

стар|и́ть (-ю, -ишь; pf **со~)** несов перех to age

старомо́дный прил old-fashioned

старост|а (-ы) м (курса) senior student; (класса: мальчик) head boy; (: девочка) head girl; (клуба) head, president

старост|ь (-и) ж old age

старт (-а) м (СПОРТ) start; (ракеты) takeoff; (место) takeoff point

старт|ова́ть (-у́ю) (не)сов (СПОРТ) to start; (ракета) to take off

стару́х|а (-и) ж old woman

стару́шк|а (-и; gen pl **-ек)** ж = **стару́ха**

ста́рш|е сравн прил от **ста́рый** ♦ как сказ: **я ~ сестры́ на́ год** I am a year older than my sister

старшекла́ссник (-а) м senior pupil

старшеку́рсник (-а) м senior

student

ста́рший прил senior; (сестра, брат) elder

ста́рый прил old

стати́стик|а (-и) ж statistics

статисти́ческий прил statistical; **Центра́льное ~ое управле́ние** central statistics office

ста́тус (-а) м status

стату́эт|ка (-ки) ж statuette

ста́ту|я (-и) ж statue

ста|ть (-ти) ж: **под ~ кому́-н/чему́-н** like sb/sth ♦ (**-ну, -нешь;** impf **станови́ться**) сов to stand; (no impf: остановиться) to stop; (начать) to begin или start doing ♦ безл (наличествовать): **нас ста́ло бо́льше/тро́е** there are more/three of us; **с како́й ста́ти?** (разг) why?; **станови́ться (~** pf) +instr (учителем) to become; **не ста́ло де́нег/сил** I have no money/energy left; **ста́ло быть** (значит) so; **во что бы то ни ста́ло** no matter what

стат|ья́ (-ьи́; gen pl **-е́й)** ж (в газете) article; (в законе, в договоре) paragraph, clause

ста́|я (-и) ж (птиц) flock; (волков) pack; (рыб) shoal

ствол (-а́) м (дерева) trunk; (ружья, пушки) barrel

сте́б|ель (-ля) м (цветка) stem

стёган|ый прил quilted; **~ое одея́ло** quilt

стега́|ть (-ю; pf **про~)** несов перех (одеяло) to quilt; (no impf; хлыстом) to lash

стеж|о́к (-ка́) м stitch

стека́|ть(ся) (3sg **-ет(ся))** несов от **стечь(ся)**

стекл|и́ть (-ю́, -и́шь; pf **о~)** несов перех (окно) to glaze

стекл|о́ (-а́; nom pl **стёкла,** gen pl

стёкол *ср* glass; (*также*: **око́нное ~**) (window pane; (*для очков*) lenses *мн* ♦ *собир* (*изделия*) glassware

стёклышк|о (-**а**; *gen pl* -**ек**) *ср* (*осколок*) piece of glass

стекля́нный *прил* glass

стел|и́ть (-**ю́**, -**ишь**; *pf* **по~**) *несов перех* (*скатерть, подстилку*) to spread out; (*pf* **на~**; *паркет*) to lay; (**по~** *pf*) **посте́ль** to make up a bed

стемне́|ть (*3sg* -**ет**) *сов от* **темне́ть**

стен|а́ (-**ы́**; *acc sg* -**у**, *dat sg* -**е́**, *nom pl* -**ы**, *gen pl* -**а́м**) *ж* wall

стенд (-**а**) *м* (*выставочный*) display stand; (*испытательный*) test-bed; (*для стрельбы*) rifle range

сте́нк|а (-**и**; *gen pl* -**ок**) *ж уменьш от* **стена́**; (*желудка, также ФУТБОЛ*) wall; (*разг*: *мебель*) wall unit

стенн|о́й *прил* wall; **~а́я ро́спись** mural

стенографи́р|овать (-**ую**; *pf* **за~**) *несов перех*: **~ что-н** to take sth down in shorthand (*BRIT*) *или* stenography (*US*)

стенографи́ст (-**а**) *м* shorthand typist (*BRIT*), stenographer (*US*)

сте́пен|ь (-**и**; *gen pl* -**ей**) *ж* (*также ПРОСВЕЩ*) degree; (*МАТ*) power

степ|ь (-**и**; *gen pl* -**ей**) *ж* the steppe

стереосисте́м|а (-**ы**) *ж* stereo

стереоти́п (-**а**) *м* stereotype

стере́|ть (сотру́, сотрёшь; *pt* **стёр, стёрла**, *impf* **стира́ть**) *сов перех* to wipe off; **~ся** (*impf* **стира́ться**) *сов возв* (*надпись, краска*) to be worn away; (*подошвы*) to wear down

стер|е́чь (-**егу́**, -**ежёшь** *итп*, -**егу́т**; *pt* -**ёг**, -**егла́**) *несов перех*

to watch over

сте́рж|ень (-**ня**) *м* rod; (*шариковой ручки*) (ink) cartridge

стерилиз|ова́ть (-**у́ю**) (*не*)*сов перех* to sterilize

стери́льный *прил* sterile, sterilized

сте́рлинг (-**а**) *м* (*ЭКОН*) sterling; **10 фу́нтов ~ов** 10 pounds sterling

стесне́ни|е (-**я**) *ср* constraints *мн*; (*смущение*) shyness

стесни́тельный *прил* shy

стесн|и́ть (-**ю́**, -**и́шь**; *impf* **стесня́ть**) *сов перех* (*хозяев*) to inconvenience; (*дыхание*) to constrict

стесня́|ться (-**юсь**; *pf* **по~**) *несов возв*: **~** (+*gen*) to be shy (of)

стече́ни|е (-**я**) *ср* (*народа*) gathering; (*случайностей*) combination

сте|чь (*3sg* -**чёт**, *pt* -**ёк**, -**екла́**, *impf* **стека́ть**) *сов*: **~** (**с** +*gen*) to run down (from); **сте́чься** (*impf* **стека́ться**) *сов возв* (*реки*) to flow; (*люди*) to congregate

стили́ст (-**а**) *м* stylist

стилисти́ческий *прил* stylistic

стил|ь (-**я**) *м* style

сти́мул (-**а**) *м* incentive, stimulus

стимули́р|овать (-**ую**) (*не*)*сов перех* to stimulate; (*работу, прогресс*) to encourage

стипе́нди|я (-**и**) *ж* grant

стира́льный *прил* washing

стира́|ть (-**ю**) *несов от* **стере́ть** ♦ (*pf* **вы́стирать** *или* **по~**) *перех* to wash; **~ся** *несов от* **стере́ться**

сти́р|ка (-**ки**) *ж* washing

стисн|уть (-**у**; *impf* **сти́скивать**) *сов перех* (*в руке*) to clench

стиха́|ть (-**ю**) *несов от* **сти́хнуть**

стих|и́ (-**о́в**) *мн* (*поэзия*) poetry *ед*

стихи́йный *прил* (*развитие*) unrestrained; (*протест*) spontaneous; **~ое бе́дствие** natural disaster

стихи́|я (-и) ж (вода, огонь итп) element; (рынка) natural force

сти́х|нуть (-ну; pt **-, -ла;** impf **стиха́ть)** сов to die down

стихотворе́ни|е (-я) ср poem

сто (ста; см: Table 27) чис one hundred

стог (-а; nom pl **-а́) м: ~ се́на** haystack

сто́имост|ь (-и) ж (затраты) cost; (ценность) value

сто́|ить (-ю, -ишь) несов (не)перех; (+acc или +gen); (денег) to cost ♦ неперех; **+gen** (внимания, любви) to be worth ♦ безл; **+infin** to be worth doing; **мне ничего́ не ~ит сде́лать э́то** it's no trouble for me to do it; **спаси́бо! - не ~ит** thank you! – don't mention it; **~ит (то́лько) захоте́ть** you only have to wish

сто́|йка (-йки; gen pl **-ек) ж** (положение тела) stance; (прилавок) counter

сто́йкий прил (человек) steadfast, resilient; (краска) durable, hard-wearing; (запах) stubborn

стол (-а́) м table; (письменный) desk

столб (-а́) м (пограничный) post; (телеграфный) pole; (перен: пыли) cloud

сто́лбик (-а) м уменьш от **столб;** (цифр) column

столбня́к (-а́) м tetanus

столе́ти|е (-я) ср (срок) century; (годовщина) **~ +gen** centenary of

сто́лик (-а) м уменьш от **стол**

столи́ц|а (-ы) ж capital (city)

столи́чн|ый прил: **~ые теа́тры** the capital's theatres

столкнове́ни|е (-я) ср clash; (машин) collision

столкн|у́ть (-у́, -ёшь; impf **ста́лкивать)** сов перех: **~ (с** +gen) to push off; (подлеж: случай) to bring together; **~ся** (impf **ста́лкиваться)** сов возв (машины) to collide; (интересы, характеры) to clash; (встретиться): **~ся с** +instr to come into contact with; (случайно) to bump или run into; (с трудностями) to encounter

столо́в|ая (-ой) ж (заведение) canteen; (комната) dining room

столо́в|ый прил (мебель) dining-room; **~ая ло́жка** tablespoon; **~ая соль** table salt; **~ серви́з** dinner service

столп|и́ться (3sg -и́тся) сов возв to crowd

столь нареч so; **~ же ... ско́лько ... аs ... as ...**

сто́льк|о нареч (книг) so many; (сахара) so much ♦ (**-их**) мест (см нареч) this many; this much

сто́лько-то нареч (книг) X number of; (сахара) X amount of

столя́р (-а́) м joiner

стомато́лог (-а) м dental surgeon

стоматологи́ческий прил dental

стомéтро́в|ый прил: **~ая диста́нция** one hundred metres (BRIT) или meters (US)

стон (-а) м groan

стон|а́ть (-у́, -ешь) несов to groan

стоп межд stop

стоп|а́ (-ы́; nom pl **-ы́) ж** (АНАТ) sole

сто́п|ка (-ки; gen pl **-ок) ж** (бумаг) pile

стоп-кра́н (-а) м emergency handle (on train)

сто́пор (-а) м (ТЕХ) lock

стоп|та́ть (-чу́, -чешь; impf **ста́птывать)** сов перех to wear out; **~ся** (*impf* **ста́пываться**) *сов возв* to wear out

сто́рож (**-а**; *nom pl* **-á**) *м* watchman

сторожев|о́й *прил*: **~áя вы́шка** watchtower

сторож|и́ть (**-ý, -и́шь**) *несов перех* = **стере́чь**

сторон|á (**-ы́**; *acc sg* **-ону**, *dat sg* **-оне́**, *nom pl* **-оны**, *gen pl* **-о́н**, *dat pl* **-она́м**) *ж* side; (*направление*): **ле́вая/пра́вая ~** the left/right; **в ~оне́ а little way** off; **в сто́рону** +*gen* towards; **э́то о́чень любе́зно с Ва́шей ~оны́** that is very kind of you; **с одно́й ~оны́ ... с друго́й ~оны́** on the one hand ... on the other hand ...

сторо́нник (**-а**) *м* supporter

сто́чн|ый *прил*: **~ая кана́ва** gutter (*in street*); **~ая труба́** drainpipe

сто́я *нареч* standing up

стоя́н|ка (**-ки**; *gen pl* **-ок**) *ж* (*остановка*) stop; (*автомобилей*) car park (*BRIT*), parking lot (*US*); (*геологов*) camp; **~ такси́** taxi rank

сто|я́ть (**-ю́, -и́шь**; *imper* **сто́й(те)**) *несов* to stand; (*бездействовать*) to stand idle; (*pf* **по~**; *защищать*): **~ за** +*acc* to stand up for

стоя́щий *прил* (*дело*) worthwhile; (*человек*) worthy

стр. *сокр* = **страни́ца** pg.

страда́ни|е (**-я**) *ср* suffering

страда́тельн|ый *прил* (*линг*): **~ зало́г** passive voice

страда́|ть (**-ю**) *несов* to suffer

стра́ж|а (**-и**) *ж собир* guard; **под ~ей** in custody

стран|á (**-ы́**; *nom pl* **-ы**) *ж* country

страни́ц|а (**-ы**) *ж* page

стра́нно *нареч* strangely ♦ *как*

сказ that is strange *или* odd; **мне ~, что ...** I find it strange that ...

стра́нный *прил* strange

стра́стный *прил* passionate

стра́ст|ь (**-и**) *ж* passion

страте́ги|я (**-и**) *ж* strategy

страх (**-а**) *м* fear

страхова́ни|е (**-я**) *ср* insurance; **госуда́рственное ~** national insurance (*BRIT*); **~ жи́зни** life insurance

страхова́тел|ь (**-я**) *м person taking out insurance*

страх|ова́ть (**-у́ю**; *pf* **за~**) *несов перех*: **~ от** +*gen* (*имущество*) to insure (against); (*принимать меры*) to protect (against); **~ся** (*pf* **за~ся**) *несов возв*: **~ся (от** +*gen*) to insure o.s. (against); (*принимать меры*) to protect o.s. (from)

страхо́в|ка (**-ки**; *gen pl* **-ок**) *ж* insurance

страхов|о́й *прил* (*фирма, аге́нт*) insurance; **~ взнос** *или* **~áя пре́мия** insurance premium

страхо́вщик (**-а**) *м* insurer

стра́шно *нареч* (*крича́ть*) in a frightening way; (*разг: уста́лый, дово́льный*) terribly ♦ *как сказ* it's frightening; **мне ~** I'm frightened *или* scared

стра́шный *прил* (*фильм, сон*) terrifying; (*хо́лод итп*) terrible, awful; **ничего́ ~ого** it doesn't matter

стрек|оза́ (**-озы́**; *nom pl* **-о́зы**) *ж* dragonfly

стрел|á (**-ы́**; *nom pl* **-ы**) *ж* (*для стрельбы́*) arrow; (*поезд*) express (train)

стрел|е́ц (**-ьца́**) *м* (*созве́здие*): **Стреле́ц** Sagittarius

стре́л|ка (**-ки**; *gen pl* **-ок**) *ж* уменьш *от* **стрела́**; (*часо́в*) hand;

(компаса) needle; (знак) arrow

стре́лочник (-а) м signalman

стрельба́ (-ы́) ж shooting, firing

стреля́ть (-ю) несов: ~ (в +acc) to shoot (at) ♦ перех (убивать) to shoot; ~ся несов возв to shoot o.s.

стреми́тельный прил (движение, атака) swift; (изменения) rapid

стреми́ться (-лю́сь, -и́шься) несов возв: ~ в/на +acc (в университет) to aspire to go to; (на родину) to long to go to; (добиваться): ~ к +dat (к славе) to strive for

стремле́ние (-я) ср: ~ (к +dat) striving (for), aspiration (for)

стре́мя (-ени; как вре́мя; см. Table 4) ср stirrup

стремя́нка (-ки; gen pl -ок) ж stepladder

стресс (-а) м stress

стриж (-а́) м swift

стри́жка (-ки; gen pl -ек) ж (см глаг) cutting; mowing; pruning; (причёска) haircut

стри́чь (-гу́, -жёшь итп, -гу́т; pt -г, -гла; pf постри́чь) несов перех (волосы, траву) to cut; (газон) to mow; (кусты) to prune; ~ (постри́чь pf) кого́-н to cut sb's hair; **стри́чься** (pf постри́чься) несов возв (в парикма́херской) to have one's hair cut

стро́гий прил strict; (причёска, наказание) severe

стро́го нареч (воспитывать) strictly; (наказать, сказать) severely

строе́ние (-я) ср (здание) building; (организации, вещества) structure

стро́же сравн прил от стро́гий ♦ сравн нареч от стро́го

строи́тель (-я) м builder

строи́тельный прил building, construction

строи́тельство (-а) ср (зданий) building, construction

стро́ить (-ю, -ишь; pf вы́строить или по~) несов перех to build, construct; (pf по~; общество, семью) to create; (план) to make; (отряд) to draw up; ~ся (pf вы́строиться) несов возв (солдаты) to form up

строй (-я) м (социальный) system; (языка) structure; (loc sg -ю́; ВОЕН, шеренга) line

стро́йка (-ки; gen pl -ек) ж (место) building или construction site

стро́йный прил (фигура) shapely; (человек) well-built

строка́ (-и́; nom pl -и, dut pl -а́м) ж (в тексте) line

стропти́вый прил headstrong

стро́чка (-ки; gen pl -ек) ж уменьш от строка́; (шов) stitch

строчно́й прил: ~я бу́ква lower case или small letter

структу́ра (-ы) ж structure

струна́ (-ы́; nom pl -ы) ж string

стру́нный прил (инструмент) stringed; ~ кварте́т string quartet

стручко́вый прил: ~ пе́рец chilli; ~ая фасо́ль runner beans мн

струя́ (-и́; nom pl -и) ж stream

стряхну́ть (-у́, -ёшь; impf стря́хивать) сов перех to shake off

студе́нт (-а) м student

студе́нческий прил student; ~ биле́т student card

сту́день (-ня) м jellied meat

сту́дия (-и) ж studio; (школа) school for actors, dancers, artists etc); (мастерская) workshop

сту́жа (-и) ж severe cold

стук (-а) *м* (*в дверь*) knock; (*сердца*) thump; (*падающего предмета*) thud

сту́кн|уть (-у) *сов* (*в дверь, в окно*) to knock; (*по столу*) to bang; **~ся** (*impf* **сту́каться**) *сов* to bang o.s.

стул (-а; *nom pl* **-ья**, *gen pl* **-ьев**) *м* chair

ступе́н|ь (-и) *ж* step; (*gen pl* **-е́й**; *процесса*) stage

ступе́н|ька (-ьки; *gen pl* **-ек**) *ж* step

сту́п|ка (-ки; *gen pl* **-ок**) *ж* mortar

ступн|я́ (-и́) *ж* (*стопа*) foot

стуч|а́ть (-у́, -и́шь; *pf* **по~**) *несов* (*в дверь, в окно*) to knock; (*по столу*) to bang; (*сердце*) to thump; (*зубы*) to chatter; **~ся** (*pf* **по~ся**) *несов возв*: **~ся** (*в +acc*) to knock (at); **~ся** (*по~ся pf*) **к кому́-н** to knock at sb's door

стыд (-а́) *м* shame

сты|ди́ть (-жу́, -ди́шь; *pf* **при~**) *несов перех* to (put) to shame; **~ся** (*pf* **по~ся**) *несов возв*: **~ся** (*+gen/ +infin*) to be ashamed of/to do

сты́дно *как сказ* it's a shame; **мне ~** I am ashamed; **как тебе́ не ~!** you ought to be ashamed of yourself!

сты|ть (-ну, -нешь; *pf* **осты́ть**) *несов* to go cold; (*pf* **просты́ть**; *мёрзнуть*) to freeze

стюарде́сс|а (-ы) *ж* air hostess

стян|у́ть (-у́, -ешь; *impf* **стя́гивать**) *сов перех* (*пояс, шнуровку*) to tighten; (*войска*) to round up

суббо́т|а (-ы) *ж* Saturday

субподря́д (-а) *м* subcontract

субподря́дчик (-а) *м* subcontractor

субсиди́р|овать (-ую) (*не*)*сов перех* to subsidize

субси́ди|я (-и) *ж* subsidy

субти́тр (-а) *м* subtitle

субъекти́вный *прил* subjective

сувени́р (-а) *м* souvenir

суверените́т (-а) *м* sovereignty

суверенный *прил* sovereign

сугро́б (-а) *м* snowdrift

суд (-а́) *м* (*орган*) court; (*заседание*) court session; (*процесс*) trial; (*мнение*) judgement, verdict; **отдава́ть (отда́ть** *pf*) **кого́-н под ~** to prosecute sb; **подава́ть (пода́ть** *pf*) **на кого́-н в ~** to take sb to court

судебно-медици́нск|ий *прил*: **~ая эксперти́за** forensics

суде́бный *прил* (*заседание, органы*) court; (*издержки, практика*) legal; **~ое реше́ние** adjudication; **~ое де́ло** court case

суде́йск|ий *прил* (*ЮР*) judge's; **~ая колле́гия** (*ЮР*) the bench; (*СПОРТ*) panel of judges

су|ди́ть (-жу́, -дишь) *несов перех* (*преступника*) to try; (*матч*) to referee; (*укорять*) to judge; **су́дя по** *+dat* judging by; **~ся** *несов возв*: **~ся с кем-н** to be involved in a legal wrangle with sb

су́дн|о (-а; *nom pl* **-á**, *gen pl* **-о́в**) *ср* vessel

судове́рф|ь (-и) *ж сокр* (= **судострои́тельная верфь**) shipyard

судовладе́л|ец (-ьца) *м* shipowner

судов|о́й *прил*: **~áя кома́нда** ship's crew; **~ журна́л** ship's log

судопроизво́дств|о (-а) *ср* legal proceedings *мн*

су́дорог|а (-и) *ж* (*от боли*) spasm

су́дорожный *прил* convulsive; (*перен: приготовления*) feverish

судострое́ни|е (-я) *ср* ship building

судохо́дный *прил* navigable; **~ кана́л** shipping canal

судохо́дств|о (-а) *ср* navigation

судьб|а́ (-ы́; *nom pl* **-ьбы,** *gen pl* **-еб)** *ж* fate; (*будущее*) destiny; **каки́ми ~ми!** what brought you here!

судь|я́ (-и́; *nom pl* **-и,** *gen pl* **-е́й)** *ж* judge; (*СПОРТ*) referee

суеве́ри|е (-я) *ср* superstition

суеве́рный *прил* superstitious

суе|та́ (-ы́) *ж* vanity; (*хлопоты*) commotion

суе|ти́ться (-чу́сь, -ти́шься) *несов возв* to fuss (about)

суетли́вый *прил* fussy; (*жизнь, работа*) busy

су́етный *прил* futile; (*хлопотный*) busy; (*человек*) vain

сужа́|ть (-ю) *несов от* **су́зить**

сужде́ни|е (-я) *ср* (*мнение*) opinion

суждено́ *как сказ:* **(нам) не ~ бы́ло встре́титься** we weren't fated to meet

су́|зить (-жу, -зишь; *impf* **сужа́ть)** *сов перех* to narrow

су|к (-ка́; *loc sg* **-ку́,** *nom pl* **-чья,** *gen pl* **-чьев)** *м* (*дерева*) bough

су́к|а (-и) *ж* bitch; **~ин сын** (*разг*) son of a bitch (!)

сукн|о́ (-а́; *nom pl* **-на,** *gen pl* **-он)** *ср* (*шерстяное*) baize

сумасше́дш|ий *прил* mad; (*разг: успех*) amazing ♦ **(-его)** *м* madman

сумасше́стви|е (-я) *ср* madness, lunacy

сумато́х|а (-и) *ж* chaos

су́мерк|и (-ек) *мн* twilight *ед*, dusk *ед*

суме́|ть (-ю) *сов:* **~ +***infin* to manage to do

су́м|ка (-ки; *gen pl* **-ок)** *ж* bag

су́мм|а (-ы) *ж* sum

сумми́р|овать (-ую) *(не)сов перех* (*затраты итп*) to add up; (*информацию*) to summarize

су́моч|ка (-ки; *gen pl* **-ек)** *ж* *уменьш от* **су́мка**; (*дамская, вечерняя*) handbag

су́мрак (-а) *м* gloom

су́мрачный *прил* gloomy

сунду́к (-а́) *м* trunk, chest

су|п (-а; *nom pl* **-ы́)** *м* soup

суперма́ркет (-а) *м* supermarket

суперобло́ж|ка (-ки; *gen pl* **-ек)** *ж* (dust) jacket

супру́г (-а; *nom pl* **-и)** *м* spouse; **~и** husband and wife

супру́г|а (-и) *ж* spouse

супру́жеский *прил* marital

сургу́ч (-а́) *м* sealing wax

суро́вый *прил* harsh

су́слик (-а) *м* ground squirrel (*BRIT*), gopher (*US*)

суста́в (-а) *м* (*АНАТ*) joint

су́тк|и (-ок) *мн* twenty four hours *мн*; **кру́глые ~** round the clock

су́точный *прил* twenty-four-hour

суту́л|ить (-ю, -ишь; *pf* **с~)** *несов перех* to hunch; **~ся** (*pf* **с~ся)** *несов возв* to stoop

суть (-и) *ж* essence; **~ де́ла** the crux of the matter; **по су́ти (де́ла)** as a matter of fact

суфле́ *ср нескл* soufflé

су́ффикс (-а) *м* suffix

суха́р|ь (-я́) *м* cracker

сухожи́ли|е (-я) *ср* tendon

сухо́й *прил* dry; (*засушенный*) dried; **~ зако́н** prohibition

сухопу́тн|ый *прил* land; **~ые войска́** ground forces *мн*

сухофру́кт|ы (-ов) *мн* dried fruit *ед*

су́ш|а (-и) *ж* (dry) land

су́ше *сравн прил от* **сухо́й**

сушёный *прил* dried

суш|и́ть (-у́, -ишь; *pf* **вы́сушить**) *несов перех* to dry; **~ся** (*pf* **вы́сушиться**) *несов возв* to dry

суще́ственный *прил* essential; (*изменения*) substantial

существи́тельн|ое (-ого) *ср* (*также*: **и́мя ~**) noun

существ|о́ (-а́) *ср* (*вопроса, дела итп*) essence; (*nom pl* -а́; *животного*) creature; **по ~у́** (*говорить*) to the point; (*вводн сл*) essentially

существова́ни|е (-я) *ср* existence; **сре́дства к ~ю** livelihood

существ|ова́ть (-у́ю) *несов* to exist

су́щност|ь (-и) *ж* essence

СФ *м сокр* (= Сове́т Федера́ции) upper chamber of Russian parliament

сфе́р|а (-ы) *ж* sphere; (*производства, науки*) area; **в ~е** +*gen* in the field of; **~ обслу́живания** *или* услу́г service industry

схват|и́ть (-чу́, -тишь) *сов от* **хвата́ть** ♦ (*impf* **схва́тывать**) *перех* (*мысль, смысл*) to grasp; **~ся** *сов от* **хвата́ться**

схва́т|ка (-ки; *gen pl* -ок) *ж* fight; *см. также* **схва́тки**

схва́т|ки (-ок) *мн* (МЕД) contractions *мн*

схе́м|а (-ы) *ж* (*метро, улиц*) plan; (*элек, радио итп*) circuit board

схо|ди́ть (-жу́, -дишь) *сов* (*разг*: *в театр, на прогулку*) to go ♦ *несов от* **сойти́**; **~ся** *несов от* **сойти́сь**

схо́дный *прил* similar

схо́дств|о (-а) *ср* similarity

сце́н|а (-ы) *ж* (*подмостки*) stage; (*в пьесе, на улице*) scene

сцена́ри|й (-я) *м* (*фильма*) script

сцена́ри́ст (-а) *м* scriptwriter

сцеп|и́ть (-лю́, -ишь; *impf* **сцепля́ть**) *сов перех* to couple; (*пальцы*) to clasp

сча́стливо *нареч* (*жить, рассмея́ться*) happily; **~ отде́латься** (*pf*) to have a lucky escape

счастли́во *нареч*: **~! all the best!;** **~ остава́ться!** good luck!

счастли́в|ый *прил* happy; (*уда́чный*) lucky; **~ого пути́!** have a good journey!

сча́сть|е (-я) *ср* happiness; (*удача*) luck; **к ~ю** luckily, fortunately; **на на́ше ~** luckily for us

счесть (сочту́, сочтёшь; *pt* счёл, сочла́) *сов от* **счита́ть**

счёт (-а; *loc sg* -у́, *nom pl* -а́) *м* (*действие*) counting; (*: накладна́я*) invoice; (*рестора́нный, телефо́нный*) bill; (*no pl; СПОРТ*) score; **в ~** +*gen* in lieu of; **за ~** +*gen* (*фирмы*) at the expense of; (*внедрения итп*) due to; **на ~ кого́-н** at sb's expense; **на э́тот ~** in this respect; **э́то не в ~** that doesn't count; **лицево́й ~** (КОММ) personal account; **теку́щий ~** (КОММ) current (BRIT) *или* checking (US) account

счётн|ый *прил*: **~ая маши́на** calculator

счётчик (-а) *м* meter

счёт|ы (-ов) *мн* (*приспособле́ние*) abacus *ед*; (*делов́ые*) dealings *мн*

счи́танный *прил*: **~ые дни/мину́ты** only a few days/minutes; **~ое коли́чество** very few

счита́|ть (-ю) *несов со* count ♦ (*pf* **по~** *или* **со~**) *перех* (*деньги итп*) to count; (*pf* **по~** *или*

счесть): ~ кого-н/что-н +instr to regard sb/sth as; **я ~ю, что ...** I believe или think that ...; **~ся** несов возв to be considered to be; (уважать): **~ся с** +instr to respect

США мн сокр (= **Соединённые Штаты Америки**) USA

сшить (**сошью, сошьёшь**; imper **сшей(те)**; pf **сшивать**) несов перех (соединить шитьём) to sew together

съеда́ть(ся) несов от **съесть(ся)**

съедо́бный прил edible

съезд (-а) м (партийный) congress

съе́здить (-жу, -дишь) сов to go

съезжа́ть(ся) (-ю(сь)) несов от **съе́хать(ся)**

съём сов см. **съесть**

съём|ка (-ки; gen pl -ок) ж (обычно мн: фильма) shooting ед

съёмочн|ый прил: **~ая площа́дка** film set; **~ая гру́ппа** film crew

съёмщик (-а) м tenant

съесть (как **есть**; см. Table 15; impf **есть** или **съеда́ть** сов перех (хлеб, мясо) to eat; (подлеж: моль, тоска) to eat away at

съе́хать (как **е́хать**; см. Table 19; impf **съезжа́ть** сов: ~ (с +gen) (спуститься) to go down; ~ **с** (кварти́ры) to move out of (one's flat); **~ся** (impf **съезжа́ться** сов возв (делегаты) to gather

съешь сов см. **съесть**

сы́ворот|ка (-ки; gen pl -ок) ж (молочная) serum; (мед) serum

сыгра́ть (-ю) сов от **игра́ть**

сын (-а; nom pl -овья́, gen pl

-ове́й, dat pl **-овья́м**) м son

сы́п|ать (-лю, -лешь; imper **~ь(те)**) несов перех to pour; **~ся** несов возв (pf **по~ся**) to pour

сыпу́чий прил crumbly

сыпь (-и) ж rash

сыр (-а; nom pl -ы) м cheese

сыре́|ть (3sg -ет) несов to get damp

сыро́й прил damp; (мясо, овощи) raw

сыро́е́ж|ка (-ки; gen pl -ек) ж russula

сыр|о́к (-ка́) м: **творо́жный ~** sweet curd cheese; **пла́вленный ~** processed cheese

сы́рость (-и) ж dampness

сырь|ё (-я́) ср собир raw materials мн

сыск (-а) м criminal detection

сы́тный прил filling

сы́тый прил (не голодный) full

сэконо́м|ить (-лю, -ишь) сов от **эконо́мить**

сы́щик (-а) м detective

сюда́ нареч here

сюже́т (-а) м plot

сюрпри́з (-а) м surprise

ся́ду итп сов см. **сесть**

Т, т

т сокр (= **то́нна**) t

т. сокр (= **том**) v., vol.; **= ты́сяча**

та (**той**) мест см. **тот**

таба́к (-а́) м tobacco

та́бел|ь (-я) м (просвещ) school report (BRIT), report card (US, SCOTTISH); (график) chart

табле́т|ка (-ки; gen pl -ок) ж tablet

табли́ц|а (-ы) ж table; (спорт) (league) table; **~ умноже́ния**

multiplication table

табло́ *ср нескл* (information) board; (*на стадионе*) scoreboard

табу́н (**-а́**) *м* herd

таёжный *прил* taiga

таз (**-а**; *пот pl* **-ы́**) *м* (*сосуд*) basin; (*АНАТ*) pelvis

тайнственный *прил* mysterious

та́инств|о (**-а**) *ср* (*РЕЛ*) sacrament

та́й|ть (**-ю́, -йшь**) *несов перех* to conceal; **~ся** *несов возв* (*скрываться*) to hide; (*опасность*) to lurk

тайг|а́ (**-и́**) *ж* the taiga

тайко́м *нареч* in secret, secretly

тайм (**-а**) *м* (*СПОРТ*) period; **пе́рвый/второ́й ~** (*ФУТБОЛ*) the first/second half

та́йн|а (**-ы**) *ж* (*личная*) secret; (*события*) mystery

тайни́к (**-а́**) *м* hiding place

та́йный *прил* secret

KEYWORD

так *нареч* 1 (*указательное: таким образом*) like this, this way; **пусть бу́дет так** so be it

2 (*настолько*) so

3 (*разг: без какого-н намерения*) for no (special) reason; **почему́ ты пла́чешь? - да так** why are you crying? - for no reason

♦ *част* 1 (*разг: ничего*) nothing; **что с тобо́й? - так** what's wrong? - nothing

2 (*разг: приблизительно*) about; **дня так че́рез два** in about two days

3 (*например*) for example

4 (*да*) OK; **так, всё хорошо́** OK, that's fine

♦ *союз* 1 (*в таком случае*) then; **е́хать, так е́хать** if we are going, (then) let's go

2 (*таким образом*) so; **так ты**

поедёшь? so, you are going?

3 (*в разделительных вопросах*): **э́то поле́зная кни́га, не так ли?** it's a useful book, isn't it?; **он хоро́ший челове́к, не так ли?** he's a good person, isn't he?

4 (*во фразах*): **и так** (*и без того уже*) anyway; **е́сли** или **раз так** in that case; **так и быть!** so be it!; **так и есть** (*разг*) sure enough; **так ему́!** serves him right!; **так себе́** (*разг*) so-so; **так как** since; **так что** so; **так что́бы** so that

та́кже *союз, нареч* also; **С Но́вым Го́дом! - И Вас ~** Happy New Year! - the same to you

тако́в (**-а́, -о́, -ы́**) *как сказ* such

таково́й *мест*: **как ~** as such

так|о́е (**-о́го**) *ср* (*о чём-л интересном, важном итп*) something; **что тут ~о́го?** what is so special about that?

как|о́й *мест* such; **что ~о́е?** what is it?

та́кс|а (**-ы**) *ж* (*КОММ*) (fixed) rate

такси́ *ср нескл* taxi

такси́ст (**-а**) *м* taxi driver

таксопа́рк (**-а**) *м сокр* (= **таксомото́рный парк**) taxi depot

такт (**-а**) *м* (*тактичность*) tact; (*МУЗ*) bar (BRIT), measure (US)

та́ктик|а (**-и**) *ж* tactic; (*ВОЕН*) tactics *мн*

такти́чный *прил* tactful

тала́нт (**-а**) *м* talent

тала́нтливый *прил* talented

та́ли|я (**-и**) *ж* waist

тало́н (**-а**) *м* ticket; (*на продукты итп*) coupon

там *нареч* there; **~ посмо́трим** (*разг*) we'll see

тамо́женник (**-а**) *м* customs officer

тамо́женн|ый *прил* (*досмотр*)

customs; **~ая по́шлина** customs (duty)

тамо́ж|ня (**-ни**; gen pl **-ен**) ж customs

тампо́н (**-а**) м tampon

та́н|ец (**-ца**) м dance

танк (**-а**) м tank

та́нкер (**-а**) м tanker (ship)

танц|ева́ть (**-у́ю**) несов (не)перех to dance

танцо́вщик (**-а**) м dancer

танцо́р (**-а**) м dancer

та́поч|ка (**-ки**; gen pl **-ек**) ж (обычно мн: домашняя) slipper; (: спортивная) plimsoll (BRIT), sneaker (US)

та́р|а (**-ы**) ж собир containers мн

тарака́н (**-а**) м cockroach

таре́л|ка (**-ки**; gen pl **-ок**) ж plate; **я здесь не в свое́й ~ке** (разг) I feel out of place here

тари́ф (**-а**) м tariff

таска́|ть (**-ю**) несов перех to lug; **~ся** несов возв: **~ся по** +dat (по магазинам итп) to trail around; **~ся** (impf) **за кем-н** to trail around after sb

тас|ова́ть (**-у́ю**; pf **с~**) несов перех to shuffle

ТАСС м сокр (= Телегра́фное аге́нтство Сове́тского Сою́за) Tass (news agency)

татуиро́в|ка (**-ки**; gen pl **-ок**) ж tattoo

та́ч|ка (**-ки**; gen pl **-ек**) ж wheelbarrow

тащ|и́ть (**-у́**, **-ишь**) несов перех to drag; (тянуть) to pull; (нести) to haul; (pf **вы́тащить**; перен: в театр, на прогулку) to drag out; **~ся** несов возв (медленно ехать) to trundle along

та́|ять (**-ю**; pf **рас~**) несов неперех to melt

ТВ м сокр (= телеви́дение) TV

тверде́|ть (3sg **-ет**; pf **за~**) несов

to harden

тве́рдо нареч (верить, сказать) firmly; (запомнить) properly; **я зна́ю, что ...** I know for sure that ...

твёрдый прил (физ) solid; (земля, предмет) hard; (решение, сторонник, тон) firm; (цены, ставки) stable; (знания) solid; (характер) tough; **~ знак** (линг) hard sign

тве́рже сравн прил от **твёрдый** ♦ сравн нареч от **твёрдо**

тво|й (**-его́**; f **-я́**, nt **-ё**, pl **-и́**; как **мой**; см. Table 8) притяж мест your; **как по-тво́ему?** what is your opinion?; **дава́й сде́лаем по-тво́ему** let's do it your way

творе́ни|е (**-я**) ср creation

твори́тельный прил: **~ паде́ж** (линг) the instrumental (case)

твор|и́ть (**-ю́**, **-ишь**) несов to create ♦ (pf **со~**) перех to create; (pf **на~**; разг) to get up to; **~ся** несов возв: **что тут ~и́тся?** what's going on here?

творо́г (**-а́**) м ≈ curd cheese

творо́жный прил curd-cheese

тво́рческий прил creative

тво́рчеств|о (**-а**) ср creative work; (писателя) work

твоя́ (**-ей**) притяж мест см. **твой**

те (**тех**) мест см. **тот**

т.е. сокр (= то есть) i.e.

теа́тр (**-а**) м theatre (BRIT), theater (US)

театра́льный прил (афиша, сезон) theatre (BRIT), theater (US); (деятельность) theatrical; **~ институ́т** drama school

тебя́ итп мест см. **ты**

тёз|ка (**-ки**; gen pl **-ок**) м/ж namesake

текст (**-а**) м text; (песни) words мн, lyrics мн

тексти́льн|ый *прил* textile; **~ые изде́лия** textiles *мн*

теку́чий *прил* fluid

теку́щий *прил* (*год*) current; **~ счёт** (*КОММ*) current (*BRIT*) *или* checking (*US*) account

тел. *сокр* (= **телефо́н**) tel.

телеви́дени|е (**-я**) *ср* television

телевизио́нный *прил* television; **~ фильм** television drama

телеви́зор (**-а**) *м* television (set)

телегра́мм|а (**-ы**) *ж* telegram

телегра́ф (**-а**) *м* (*спо́соб свя́зи*) telegraph; (*учрежде́ние*) telegraph office

телеграфи́р|овать (**-ую**) (*не*)*сов перех* to wire

телегра́фн|ый *прил* telegraphic; **~ое аге́нтство** news agency

теле́ж|ка (**-ки**; *gen pl* **-ек**) *ж* (*для багажа, в суперма́ркете*) trolley

телезри́тел|ь (**-я**) *м* viewer

телека́мер|а (**-ы**) *ж* television camera

те́лекс (**-а**) *м* telex

телёнок (**-ёнка**; *nom pl* **-я́та**) *м* calf

телепереда́ч|а (**-и**) *ж* TV programme (*BRIT*) *или* program (*US*)

телеско́п (**-а**) *м* telescope

телесту́ди|я (**-и**) *ж* television studio

телета́йп (**-а**) *м* teleprinter (*BRIT*), teletypewriter (*US*), Teletype ®

телефо́н (**-а**) *м* telephone

телефо́нн|ый *прил* telephone; **~ая кни́га** telephone book *или* directory

Тел|е́ц (**-ьца́**) *м* (*созве́здие*) Taurus

телеце́нтр (**-а**) *м* television centre (*BRIT*) *или* center (*US*)

те́л|о (**-а**; *nom pl* **-а́**) *ср* body

телогре́й|ка (**-йки**; *gen pl* **-ек**) *ж* body warmer

телохрани́тел|ь (**-я**) *м* bodyguard

теля́тин|а (**-ы**) *ж* veal

тем *мест см.* **тот**; **то** ♦ *союз* (*+comparative*): **чем бо́льше, ~ лу́чше** the more the better; **~ бо́лее** all the more so!; **~ бо́лее что ...** especially as ...; **~ не ме́нее** nevertheless; **~ са́мым** thus

те́м|а (**-ы**) *ж* topic; (*МУЗ, ЛИТЕРАТУ́РА*) theme

те́ми *мест см.* **тот**; **то**

темне́|ть (*3sg* **-ет**; *pf* **по~**) *несов* to darken ♦ (*pf* **с~**) *безл* to get dark

темно́ *как сказ*: **на у́лице ~** it's dark outside

темнот|а́ (**-ы́**) *ж* darkness

тёмный *прил* dark

темп (**-а**) *м* speed; **в те́мпе** (*разг*) quickly

темпера́мент (**-а**) *м* temperament

темпера́ментный *прил* spirited

температу́р|а (**-ы**) *ж* temperature

тенде́нци|я (**-и**) *ж* tendency; (*предвзя́тость*) bias

те́ндер (**-а**) *м* (*КОММ*) tender

теневой *прил* shady; (*перен: сто́роны жи́зни*) shadowy; **~ая эконо́мика** shadow economy; **~ кабине́т** (*ПОЛИТ*) shadow cabinet

те́н|и (**-ей**) *мн* (*также*: **~ для век**) eye shadow *ед*

те́ннис (**-а**) *м* tennis

тенниси́ст (**-а**) *м* tennis player

тен|ь (**-и**; *prp sg* **-и́**, *gen pl* **-е́й**) *ж* (*ме́сто*) shade; (*предме́та, челове́ка*) shadow; (*перен*): **~** *+gen* (*волне́ния, печа́ли*) flicker of; *см. также* **те́ни**

теорети́ческий *прил* theoretical

тео́ри|я (**-и**) *ж* theory

тепе́рь *нареч* now

тепле́|ть (*3sg* **-ет**; *pf* **по~**) *несов*

to get warmer

тепли́ц|а (-ы) ж hothouse

тепли́чный прил (растение) hothouse

тепл|о́ нареч warmly ♦ (-á) ср (также перен) warmth ♦ как сказ it's warm; **мне** ~ I'm warm

теплово́й прил thermal

теплохо́д (-а) м motor ship или vessel

тепло́(электро)центра́л|ь (-и) ж generator plant (supplying central heating systems)

тёплый прил warm

терапе́вт (-а) м ≈ general practitioner

тера́кт (-а) м сокр (= террористи́ческий акт) terrorist attack

терапи́|я (-и) ж (МЕД, наука) (internal) medicine; (лечение) therapy

тере́ть (тру, трёшь; pt тёр, тёрла, тёрло) несов перех to rub; (овощи) to grate

терза́|ть (-ю; pf рас~) несов перех (добычу) to savage; (pf ис~; перен: упрёками, ревностью) to torment; ~**ся** несов возв: ~**ся** +instr (сомнениями) to be racked by

тёр|ка (-ки; gen pl -ок) ж grater

те́рмин (-а) м term

термина́л (-а) м terminal

термо́метр (-а) м thermometer

те́рмос (-а) м Thermos ®

термоя́дерный прил thermonuclear

терпели́вый прил patient

терпе́ни|е (-я) ср patience

терп|е́ть (-лю, -ишь) несов перех (боль, холод) to suffer, endure; (pf по~; неудачу) to suffer; (грубость) to tolerate; ~ (по~ pf) круше́ние (корабль) to

be wrecked; (поезд) to crash; **не могу́ таки́х люде́й** (разг) I can't stand people like that; ~ **не могу́ спо́рить** (разг) I hate arguing; ~**ся** несов безл: **мне не те́рпится** +infin I can't wait to

терпи́мост|ь (-и) ж: ~ (к +dat) tolerance (of)

терпи́мый прил tolerant

терра́с|а (-ы) ж terrace

террито́ри|я (-и) ж territory

терроризи́р|овать (-ую) (не)сов перех to terrorize

террори́зм (-а) м terrorism

террори́ст (-а) м terrorist

террористи́ческий прил terrorist

теря́|ть (-ю; pf по~) несов перех to lose; ~**ся** (pf по~**ся**) несов возв to get lost; (робеть) to lose one's nerve

тесн|и́ть (-ю, -и́шь; pf по~) несов перех (в толпе) to squeeze; (к стене) to press

те́сно нареч (располагать(ся)) close together; (сотрудничать) closely ♦ как сказ: **в кварти́ре о́чень** ~ the flat is very cramped; **мы с ним ~ знако́мы** he and I know each other very well

те́сный прил (проход) narrow; (помещение) cramped; (обувь) tight; (дружба) close; **мир те́сен** it's a small world

тест (-а) м test

тести́р|овать (-ую) (не)сов to test

те́ст|о (-а) ср (дрожжевое) dough; (слоёное, песочное) pastry (BRIT), paste (US)

тест|ь (-я) м father-in-law, wife's father

тесьм|а́ (-ы́) ж tape

тёт|ка (-ки; gen pl -ок) ж auntie

тетра́д|ь (-и) ж exercise book

тёт|я (-и; gen pl -ь) ж aunt; (разг:

же́нщина) lady

те́фтел|и (-ей) *мн* meatballs *мн*

тех *мест см.* **те**

те́хник|а (-и) *ж* technology; *(приёмы)* technique ♦ *собир (маши́ны)* machinery; *(разг: муз)* hi-fi; **~ безопа́сности** industrial health and safety

те́хникум (-а) *м* technical college

техни́ческ|ий *прил* technical; **~ осмо́тр** *(АВТ)* ≈ MOT *(BRIT)* (annual roadworthiness check); **~ое обслу́живание** maintenance, servicing

технологи́ческий *прил* technical

техноло́ги|я (-и) *ж* technology

те́ч|ь (3sg -чёт, *pt* **тёк, ~кла́)** *несов* to flow; *(крыша, лодка итп)* to leak ♦ **(-чи)** *ж* leak

тёщ|а (-и) *ж* mother-in-law, wife's mother

тигр (-а) *м* tiger

ти́ка|ть (3sg -ет) *несов* to tick

ти́н|а (-ы) *ж* slime

тип (-а) *м* type; **ти́па** *+gen (разг)* sort of

типи́чный *прил*: **~ (для** *+gen)* typical (of)

типово́й *прил* standard-type

типогра́фи|я (-и) *ж* press, printing house

типогра́фский *прил* typographical; **~ стано́к** printing press

тир (-а) *м* shooting gallery

тира́ж (-а́) *м (газеты)* circulation; *(кни́ги)* printing; *(лотереи)* drawing

тира́н (-а) *м* tyrant

тирани́|я (-и) *ж* tyranny

тире́ *ср нескл* dash

тиск|и́ (-о́в) *мн*: **в ~а́х** *+gen*

(перен) in the grip of

тита́н (-а) *м (ХИМ)* titanium; *(для нагре́ва воды́)* urn; *(о челове́ке)* giant

титр (-а) *м (обычно мн)* credit (of film)

ти́тул (-а) *м* title

ти́тульный *прил*: **~ лист** title page

тиф (-а) *м* typhus

ти́хий *прил* quiet; **Ти́хий океа́н** the Pacific (Ocean); **~ у́жас!** *(разг)* what a nightmare!

ти́хо *нареч (говорить, жить)* quietly ♦ *как сказ*: **в до́ме ~** the house is quiet; **~!** (be) quiet!

ти́ше *сравн прил от* **ти́хий** ♦ *сравн нареч от* **ти́хо** ♦ *как сказ*: **~!** quiet, hush!

тишин|а́ (-ы́) *ж* quiet

т.к. *сокр* = **так как**

ткан|ь (-и) *ж* fabric, material; *(АНАТ)* tissue

тк|ать (-у, -ёшь; *pf* **сотка́ть)** *несов перех* to weave

тка́цкий *прил*: **~ая фа́брика** mill *(for fabric production)*; **~ стано́к** loom

тле|ть (3sg -ет) *несов (дрова, у́гли)* to smoulder *(BRIT)*, smolder *(US)*

тмин (-а) *м (КУЛИН)* caraway seeds *мн*

т.н. *сокр* = **так называ́емый**

то *союз (условный)*: **е́сли ... ~ ...** if ... then ...; *(разделительный)*: **~ ... ~ ...** sometimes ... sometimes ...; **и ~ ~** even; **то (того́)** *мест см.* **тот**

т.о. *сокр* = **таки́м о́бразом**

-то *част (для выделе́ния)*: **письмо́-то ты получи́л?** did you (at least) receive the letter?

тобо́й *мест см.* **ты**

това́р (-а) *м* product; *(экон)*

commodity

това́рищ (-а) м (прия́тель) friend; (по па́ртии) comrade

това́рищеский прил comradely; ~ **матч** (СПОРТ) friendly (match)

това́рищество (-а) ср (КОММ) partnership

това́рный прил (произво́дство) goods; (ры́нок) commodity; **~ая би́ржа** commodity exchange; **~ знак** trademark

товарообме́н (-а) м barter

товарооборо́т (-а) м turnover

тогда́ нареч then; **~ как** (хотя́) while; (при противопоставле́нии) whereas

того́ мест см. **тот**; **то**

то́же нареч (та́кже) too, as well, also

той мест см. **та**

ток (-а) м (ЭЛЕК) current

тока́рный прил: **~ стано́к** lathe

то́кар|ь (-я; nom pl -я́) м turner

толк (-а) м (в рассужде́ниях) sense; (разг: по́льза) use; **сбива́ть** (сбить pf) **кого́-н с то́лку** to confuse sb

толка́|ть (-ю; pf толкну́ть) несов перех to push; (перен): **~ кого́-н на** +acc to force sb into; **~ся** несов возв to push (one's way)

толк|ова́ть (-у́ю) несов перех to interpret

толко́вый прил intelligent

толп|а́ (-ы́; nom pl -ы) ж crowd

толп|и́ться (3sg -и́тся) несов возв to crowd around

толсте́|ть (-ю; pf по~) несов to get fatter

то́лстый прил thick; (челове́к) fat

толч|о́к (-ка́) м (в спину) shove; (при торможе́нии) jolt; (при землетрясе́нии) tremor; (перен: к +dat) incentive

то́лще сравн прил от **то́лстый**

толщин|а́ (-ы́) ж thickness

KEYWORD

то́лько част 1 only

2 (+pron/+adv, усиливает вырази́тельность): **попро́буй то́лько** just try to refuse!; **поду́мать то́лько!** imagine that!

♦ союз 1 (сра́зу по́сле) as soon as

2 (одна́ко, но) only; **позвони́, то́лько разгова́ривай недо́лго** phone (BRIT) или call (US), only don't talk for long

♦ нареч 1 (неда́вно) (only) just; **ты давно́ здесь?** - нет, то́лько вошла́ have you been here long? - no, I've (only) just come in

2 (во фра́зах): **то́лько лишь** (разг) only; **то́лько и всего́** (разг) that's all; **как или лишь или едва́ то́лько** as soon as; **не то́лько ..., но и ...** not only ... but also ...; **то́лько бы** if only; **то́лько что** only just

том мест см. **тот**; **то** ♦ (-а; nom pl -а́) м volume

тома́тный прил: **~ сок** tomato juice

тому́ мест см. **тот**; **то**

тон (-а) м tone

тонзилли́т (-а) м tonsillitis

тонизи́рующ|ий прил (напи́ток) refreshing; **~ее сре́дство** tonic

то́нкий прил (фигу́ра) slender; (черты́ лица́, рабо́та, ум) fine; (разли́чия, намёк) subtle

то́нн|а (-ы) ж tonne

тонне́л|ь (-я) м tunnel

тон|у́ть (-у́, -ешь; pf у~) несов (челове́к) to drown; (pf за~; кора́бль) to sink

то́ньше сравн прил от **то́нкий**

то́па|ть (-ю) несов: **~ нога́ми** to

stamp one's feet

топ|и́ть (**-лю́, -ишь**) *несов перех* (*печь*) to stoke (up); (*масло, воск*) to melt; (*pf у~ или по~*)(*корабль*) to sink; (*человека*) to drown; **~ся** *несов возв* (*печь*) to burn; (*pf у~*)(*человек*) to drown o.s.

то́пленый *прил* (*масло*) melted

то́плив|о (**-а**) *ср* fuel

то́пол|ь (**-я**) *м* poplar

топо́р (**-а́**) *м* axe (*BRIT*), ax (*US*)

то́пот (**-а**) *м* clatter

топ|та́ть (**-чу́, -чешь**; *pf* **по~**) *несов перех* (*траву*) to trample; **~ся** *несов возв* to shift from one foot to the other

торг (**-а**) *м* trading

торг|и́ (**-о́в**) *мн* (*аукцион*) auction *ед*; (*состязание*) tender *ед*

торг|ова́ть (**-у́ю**) *несов* (*магазин*) to trade; **~** (*impf*) *+instr* (*мясом, мебелью*) to trade in; **~ся** (*pf* **с~ся**) *несов возв* to haggle

торго́в|ец (**-ца**) *м* merchant; (*мелкий*) trader

торго́вл|я (**-и**) *ж* trade

торго́в|ый *прил* trade; (*судно, флот*) merchant; **~ая сеть** retail network; **~ая то́чка** retail outlet; **~ое представи́тельство** trade mission; **~ центр** shopping centre (*BRIT*), mall (*US*)

торгпре́д (**-а**) *м сокр* (= *торго́вый представи́тель*) head of the trade mission

торгпре́дств|о (**-а**) *ср сокр* = *торго́вое представи́тельство*

торже́ственный *прил* (*день, случай*) special; (*собрание*) celebratory; (*вид, обстановка*) festive; (*обещание*) solemn

торжеств|о́ (**-а́**) *ср* celebration; (*в голосе, в словах*) triumph

торжеств|ова́ть (**-у́ю**; *pf* **вос~**) *несов*: **~** (*над* *+instr*) to triumph (over)

то́рмоз (**-а**; *nom pl* **-а́**) *м* brake

тормо|зи́ть (**-жу́, -зи́шь**; *pf* **за~**) *несов перех* (*машину*) to slow down ♦ *неперех* (*машина*) to brake; **~ся** (*pf* **за~ся**) *несов возв* (*работа итп*) to be hindered

тор|опи́ть (**-оплю́, -о́пишь**; *pf* **по~**) *несов перех* to hurry; **~ся** (*pf* **по~ся**) *несов возв* to hurry

торопли́вый *прил* (*человек*) hasty

торпе́д|а (**-ы**) *ж* torpedo

торт (**-а**) *м* cake

торф (**-а**) *м* peat

торч|а́ть (**-у́, -и́шь**) *несов* (*вверх*) to stick up; (*в стороны*) to stick out; (*разг: на улице*) to hang out

торше́р (**-а**) *м* standard lamp

тоск|а́ (**-и́**) *ж* (*на сердце*) anguish; (*скука*) boredom; **~ по ро́дине** homesickness

тоскли́вый *прил* gloomy

тоск|ова́ть (**-у́ю**) *несов* to pine away; (*impf*) **по** *+dat или о +prp* to miss

тост (**-а**) *м* toast

KEYWORD

то|т (**-го́**; *f* **та**, *nt* **то**, *pl* **те**; *см. Table 11*) *мест* **1** that; **тот дом** that house

2 (*о ранее упомянутом*) that; **в тот раз/день** that time/day

3 (*в главных предложениях*): **э́то тот челове́к, кото́рый приходи́л вчера́** it's the man who came yesterday

4 (*о после́днем из на́званных лиц*): **я посмотре́л на дру́га, тот стоя́л мо́лча** I looked at my friend, who stood silently

5 (*обычно с отрица́нием*): **зашёл не в тот дом** I called at the wrong

house
6 (*об одном из перечисляемых предметов*): **ни тот ни друго́й** neither one or the other; **тем или ины́м спо́собом** by some means or other; **тот же** the one or other
7 (*во фразах*): **до того́** so; **мне не до того́** I have no time for that; **к тому́ же** moreover; **ни с того́ ни с сего́** (*разг*) out of the blue; **тому́ наза́д** ago, and **тому́ подо́бное** et cetera, and so on

тоталита́рный *прил* totalitarian
тота́льный *прил* total; (*война*) all-out
то-то *част* (*разг*: вот именно) exactly, that's just it; (*вот почему*) that's why; (*выражает удовлетворение*): **~ же** pleased to hear it; **~ он удиви́тся!** he WILL be surprised!
то́тчас *нареч* immediately
точи́л|**ка** (**-ки**; *gen pl* **-ок**) *ж* pencil sharpener
точи́ть (**-ý, -ишь**; *pf* **на~**) *несов перех* to sharpen; (*no pf*; *подлеж: червь, ржавчина*) to eat away at
то́ч|**ка** (**-ки**; *gen pl* **-ек**) *ж* point; (*пятнышко*) dot; (*линг*) full stop (*BRIT*), period (*esp US*); **~ зре́ния** point of view; **~ с запято́й** semicolon
точне́е *вводн сл* to be exact *или* precise
то́чно *нареч* exactly; (*объяснить*) exactly, precisely; (*подсчитать, перевести*) accurately ♦ *част* (*разг: действительно*) exactly, precisely
то́чност|**ь** (**-и**) *ж* accuracy
то́чный *прил* exact; (*часы, перевод, попадание*) accurate
точь-в-то́чь *нареч* (*разг*) just like
тошни́ть (*3sg* **-и́т**; *pf* **с~**) *несов*

безл: **меня́ ~и́т** I feel sick
тошнот|а́ (**-ы́**) *ж* (*чувство*) nausea
то́щий *прил* (*человек*) skinny
т.п. *сокр* (= *тому́ подо́бное*) etc.
трав|а́ (**-ы́**; *nom pl* **-ы**) *ж* grass; (*лекарственная*) herb
трави́ть (**-лю́, -ишь**) *несов перех* (*также перен*) to poison; (*pf* **за~**; *дичь*) to hunt; (*перен: разг: притеснять*) to harass, hound; **-ся** (*pf* **о~ся**) *несов возв* to poison o.s.
тра́вл|я (**-и**) *ж* hunting; (*демократов*) hounding
тра́вм|а (**-ы**) *ж* (*физическая*) injury; (*психическая*) trauma
травмато́лог (**-а**) *м* doctor working in a casualty department
травматологи́ческий *прил*: **~ отде́л** casualty; **~ пункт** first-aid room
травми́р|овать (**-ую**) (*не*)*сов перех* to injure; (*перен: психически*) to traumatise
травяно́й *прил* (*настойка*) herbal
траге́ди|я (**-и**) *ж* tragedy
траги́ческий *прил* tragic
традицио́нный *прил* traditional
тради́ци|я (**-и**) *ж* tradition
тра́ктор (**-а**) *м* tractor
трактори́ст (**-а**) *м* tractor driver
трамва́|й (**-я**) *м* tram (*BRIT*), streetcar (*US*)
трампли́н (**-а**) *м* springboard; **лы́жный ~** ski jump
транзи́стор (**-а**) *м* (*приёмник*) transistor (radio)
транзи́т (**-а**) *м* in transit
транс (**-а**) *м* (*документ*) transport document
трансге́нный *прил* (*овощи*) genetically modified
трансли́р|овать (**-ую**) (*не*)*сов перех* to broadcast
трансля́ци|я (**-и**) *ж* (*передача*)

broadcast

транспара́нт (-а) м banner

транспланта́ци|я (-и) ж transplant

тра́нспорт (-а) м transport

транспортёр (-а) м (конве́йер) conveyor belt; (ВОЕН) army personnel carrier

транспорти́р (-а) м protractor

транспорти́р|овать (-ую) (не)сов перех to transport

тра́нспортный прил transport

транше́|я (-и) ж trench

трап (-а) м gangway

тра́сс|а (-ы) ж (лыжная) run; (трубопровода) line; **автомоби́льная ~** motorway (BRIT), expressway (US)

тра́т|а (-ы) ж spending; **пуста́я ~ вре́мени/де́нег** a waste of time/ money

тра́|тить (-чу, -тишь; pf ис~ или по~) несов перех to spend

тра́ур (-а) м mourning

трафаре́т (-а) м stencil

тре́бовани|е (-я) ср demand; (правило) requirement

тре́бовательный прил demanding

тре́б|овать (-ую; pf по~) несов перех: **~ что-н/** +infin to demand sth/to do; **~ся** (pf **по~ся**) несов возв to be needed или required

трево́г|а (-и) ж (волнение) anxiety; **возду́шная ~** air-raid warning

трево́ж|ить (-у, -ишь; pf вс~) несов перех to alarm; (мешать) to disturb; **~ся** (pf **вс~ся**) несов возв (за детей) to be concerned

трево́жный прил (голос, взгляд) anxious; (сведения) alarming

трезве́|ть (-ю; pf о~) несов to sober up

тре́звый прил (человек) sober; (перен: идея) sensible

трём etc чис см. **три**

тремста́м etc чис см. **три́ста**

тренажёр (-а) м equipment used for physical training

тре́нер (-а) м coach

тре́ни|е (-я) ср friction

трениp|ова́ть (-у́ю; pf на~) несов перех to train; (спортсменов) to coach; **~ся** (pf **на~ся**) несов возв (спортсмен) to train

трениро́в|ка (-ки; gen pl -ок) ж training; (отдельное занятие) training (session)

трениро́вочный прил training; **~ костю́м** tracksuit

треп|а́ть (-лю́, -лешь; pf по~) несов перех (подлеж: ветер) to blow about; (человека: по плечу) to pat; (pf ис~ или по~; разг: обувь, книги) to wear out; **~ся** (pf **ис~ся** или **по~ся**) несов возв (одежда) to wear out

тре́пет (-а) м (волнение) tremor; (страх) trepidation

трепе|та́ть (-щу́, -щешь) несов (флаги) to quiver; (от ужаса) to quake, tremble

треск (-а) м (сучьев) snapping; (выстрелов) crackling

треск|а́ (-и́) ж cod

тре́ска|ться (3sg -ется; pf по~) несов возв to crack

тресн|у́ть (-ет) сов (ветка) to snap; (стакан, кожа) to crack

трест (-а) м (ЭКОН) trust

тре́т|ий чис third; **~ье лицо́** (ЛИНГ) the third person

тре́т|ь (-и; nom pl -и, gen pl -е́й) ж third

тре́ть|е (-его) ср (КУЛИН) sweet (BRIT), dessert

треуго́льник (-а) м triangle

треуго́льный *прил* triangular

тре́ф|ы (-) *мн (КАРТЫ)* clubs *мн*

трёх *чис см.* **три**

трёхкра́тн|ый *прил*: ~ чемпио́н three-times champion; **в ~ом разме́ре** threefold

трёхме́рный *прил* 3-D, three-dimensional

трёхсо́т *чис см.* **три́ста**

трёхсо́тый *чис* three hundredth

треща́|ть (-у́, -и́шь) *несов (лёд, доски)* to crack; *(кузнечики)* to chip

трещи́н|а (-ы) *ж* crack

три (-ёх; *см. Table 24*) *чис* three
♦ *нескл (ПРОСВЕЩ)* ≈ C *(school mark)*

трибу́н|а (-ы) *ж* platform; *(стадиона)* stand

трибуна́л (-а) *м* tribunal; **вое́нный ~** military court

тридца́тый *чис* thirtieth

три́дцат|ь (-и; *как* **пять**; *см. Table 26*) *чис* thirty

три́жды *нареч* three times

трико́ *ср нескл* leotard

трикота́ж (-а) *м (ткань)* knitted fabric ♦ *собир (одежда)* knitwear

трикота́жный *прил* knitted

трило́ги|я (-и) *ж* trilogy

трина́дцатый *чис* thirteenth

трина́дцат|ь (-и; *как* **пять**; *см. Table 26*) *чис* thirteen

три́о *ср нескл* trio

три́ста (трёхсо́т; *как* **сто**; *см. Table 28*) *чис* three hundred

триу́мф (-а) *м* triumph

тро́гательный *прил* touching

тро́га|ть (-ю; *pf* **тро́нуть**) *несов перех* to touch; *(подлеж: рассказ, событие)* to move; **~ся** *(pf* **тро́нуться**) *несов возв (поезд)* to move off

тро́е (-и́х; *см. Table 30a*) *чис* three

троебо́рь|е (-я) *ср* triathlon

тро́иц|а (-ы) *ж (также:* **Свята́я ~)** the Holy Trinity; *(праздник)* ≈ Trinity Sunday

Тро́ицын *прил*: ~ **день** ≈ Trinity Sunday

тро́|йка (-йки; *gen pl* -ек) *ж (цифра, карта)* three; *(ПРОСВЕЩ)* ≈ C *(school mark)*; *(лошадей)* troika; *(костюм)* three-piece suit

тройни́к (-а́) *м (ЭЛЕК)* (three-way) adaptor

тройно́й *прил* triple

тролле́йбус (-а) *м* trolleybus

тромбо́н (-а) *м* trombone

трон (-а) *м* throne

тро́|нуть(ся) (-у(сь)) *сов от* **тро́гать(ся)**

тропа́ (-ы́; *nom pl* -ы) *ж* pathway

тро́пик (-а) *м*: **се́верный/ю́жный ~** the tropic of Cancer/Capricorn

тропи́н|ка (-ки; *gen pl* -ок) *ж* footpath

тропи́ческий *прил* tropical

трос (-а) *м* cable

тростни́к (-а́) *м* reed; **са́харный ~** sugar cane

трость (-и) *ж* walking stick

тротуа́р (-а) *м* pavement *(BRIT)*, sidewalk *(US)*

трофе́|й (-я) *м* trophy

трою́родн|ый *прил*: ~ **брат** second cousin *(male)*; **~ая сестра́** second cousin *(female)*

тро́йкий *прил* triple

труб|а́ (-ы́; *nom pl* -ы) *ж* pipe; *(дымовая)* chimney; *(МУЗ)* trumpet

труба́ч (-а́) *м* trumpeter

труб|и́ть (-лю́, -и́шь; *pf* **про-)** *несов (труба)* to sound; *(МУЗ)*: **в** +*acc* to blow

тру́б|ка (-ки; *gen pl* -ок) *ж* tube; *(курительная)* pipe; *(телефона)* receiver

трубопрово́д (-а) *м* pipeline

труд (-а́) *м* work; (*ЭКОН*) labour (*BRIT*), labor (*US*); **без ~а́** without any difficulty; **с (больши́м) ~о́м** with (great) difficulty

тру|ди́ться (-жу́сь, -дишься) *несов возв* to work hard

тру́дно *как сказ* it's hard *или* difficult; **у меня́ ~ с деньга́ми** I've got money problems; **мне ~ поня́ть э́то** I find it hard to understand; **(мне) ~ бе́гать/стоя́ть** I have trouble running/standing up; **~ сказа́ть** it's hard to say

тру́дност|ь (-и) *ж* difficulty

тру́дный *прил* difficult

трудово́й *прил* working

трудова́я кни́жка - employment record book. This is a booklet in which all employment details are recorded e.g. employment dates, position and any merits or reprimands received in the course of service. This is an extremely important document, the absence of which can make employment almost impossible.

трудоёмкий *прил* labour-intensive (*BRIT*), labor-intensive (*US*)

трудолюби́вый *прил* hard-working, industrious

трудя́щ|ийся *прил* working
♦ (-егося) *м* worker

труп (-а) *м* corpse

тру́пп|а (-ы) *ж* (*ТЕАТР*) company

трус (-а) *м* coward

тру́сик|и (-ов) *мн* (*детские*) knickers *мн* (*BRIT*), panties *мн* (*US*)

тру́|сить (-шу, -сишь; *pf* с~) *несов* to get scared

трусли́вый *прил* cowardly

трус|ы́ (-о́в) *мн* (*бельё: обычно мужские*) (under)pants *мн*;

(*спортивные*) shorts *мн*

трущо́б|а (-ы) *ж* slum

трюк (-а) *м* trick; (*акробатический*) stunt

трюм (-а) *м* hold (*of ship*)

трюмо́ *ср* (*нескл*) (*мебель*) dresser

трю́фел|ь (-я; *nom pl* -я́) *м* truffle

тря́п|ка (-ки; *gen pl* -ок) *ж* (*половая*) cloth; (*лоскут*) rag; **~ки** (*разг*) clothes *мн*

тряс|ти́ (-у́, -ёшь) *несов перех* to shake; **~сь** *несов возв*: **~сь пе́ред** +*instr* (*перед нача́льством*) to tremble before; **~сь** (*impf*) **над** +*instr* (*разг: над ребёнком*) to fret over *или* about

трях|ну́ть (-у́, -ёшь) *сов перех* to shake

т/с *сокр* (= теку́щий счёт) С/А

ТУ *м сокр* = самолёт констру́кции А.Н.Ту́полева

туале́т (-а) *м* toilet; (*оде́жда*) outfit

туале́тн|ый *прил*: **~ая бума́га** toilet paper; **~ое мы́ло** toilet soap; **~ые принадле́жности** toiletries; **~ сто́лик** dressing table

туберкулёз (-а) *м ТВ*, tuberculosis

туго́й *прил* (*струна, пружина*) taut; (*узел, оде́жда*) tight; **он туг на́ ухо** (*разг*) he's a bit hard of hearing

туда́ *нареч* there; **и обра́тно** there and back; **биле́т ~ и обра́тно** return (*BRIT*) *или* round-trip (*US*) ticket

туда́-сюда́ *нареч* all over the place; (*раска́чиваться*) backwards and forwards

ту́же *сравн прил от* туго́й

туз (-а́) *м* (*КАРТЫ*) ace

тузе́м|ец (-ца) *м* native

ту́ловищ|е (-а) *ср* torso

тума́н (-а) *м* mist

тума́нный *прил* misty; (*иде́и*)

nebulous

ту́мб|а (-ы) ж (причальная, уличная) bollard; (для скульптуры) pedestal

ту́мбоч|ка (-ки; gen pl **-ек)** ж уменьш от **ту́мба**; (мебель) bedside cabinet

ту́ндр|а (-ы) ж tundra

тун|е́ц (-ца́) м tuna (fish)

туне́яд|ец (-ца) м parasite (fig)

тунне́л|ь (-я) м = **тонне́ль**

тупи́к (-а́) м (улица) dead end, cul-de-sac; (для поездов) siding; (перен: в переговорах итп) deadlock

туп|и́ть (-лю́, -ишь; pf **за-)** несов перех to blunt; **-ся** (pf **за~ся)** несов возв to become blunt

тупо́й прил (нож, карандаш) blunt; (человек) stupid; (боль, ум) dull; (покорность) blind

тур (-а) м (этап) round; (в танце) turn

турби́н|а (-ы) ж turbine

тури́зм (-а) м tourism

тури́ст (-а) м tourist; (в походе) hiker

туристи́ческий прил tourist

турне́ ср нескл (ТЕАТР, СПОРТ) tour

турни́р (-а) м tournament

Ту́рци|я (-и) ж Turkey

ту́склый прил (стекло) opaque; (краска) mat(t); (свет, взгляд) dull

тускне́|ть (3sg -ет, pf **по~)** несов (краска, талант) to fade; (серебро, позолота) to tarnish

тус|ова́ться (-у́юсь, pf **по~)** несов (разг) to hang out

тусо́вк|а (-и) ж (разг: на улице) hanging about; (вечеринка) party

тут нареч here; **и всё ~** (разг) and that's that; **не ~-то бы́ло** (разг) it

wasn't to be

ту́ф|ля (-ли; gen pl **-ель)** ж shoe

ту́хлый прил (еда) rotten; (запах) putrid

ту́х|нуть (3sg -нет, pt **-, -ла,** pf **по~)** несов (костёр, свет) to go out; (pf **про~;** мясо) to go off

ту́ч|а (-и) ж rain cloud

ту́ш|а (-и) ж carcass

тушён|ка (-ки; gen pl **-ок)** ж (разг) tinned (BRIT) или canned meat

тушёный прил (КУЛИН) braised

туш|и́ть (-у́, -ишь; pf **за~** или **по~)** несов перех (огонь) to put out, extinguish; (КУЛИН) to braise

туш|ь (-и) ж (для рисования) Indian ink; (для ресниц) mascara

т/ф м сокр = **телевизио́нный фильм**

ТЦ м сокр (= телеви́зионный центр) television centre (BRIT) или center (US)

тща́тельный прил thorough

тщесла́ви|е (-я) ср vanity

тщесла́вный прил vain

тще́тный прил futile

ты (тебя́; см. Table 6а) мест you; **быть** (impf) **с кем-н на ~** to be on familiar terms with sb

ты́|кать (-чу, -чешь; pf ткну́ть) несов перех (разг: ударять): **что-н/кого́-н чем-н** to poke sth/sb with sth

ты́кв|а (-ы) ж pumpkin

тыл (-а; loc sg **-у́,** nom pl **-ы)** м (ВОЕН, территория) the rear

ты́льный прил back

тыс. сокр = **ты́сяча**

ты́сяч|а (-и; см. Table 29) ж чис thousand

ты́сячный чис thousandth; (толпа, армия) of thousands

тьм|а (-ы) ж (мрак) darkness, gloom

ТЭЦ ж сокр = **тепло(электро)-централь**

тюбик (-а) м tube

ТЮЗ (-а) м сокр (= театр юного зрителя) children's theatre (BRIT) или theater (US)

тюлень (-я) (ZOOL) seal

тюльпан (-а) м tulip

тюремный прил prison; **~ое заключение** imprisonment

тюрьма (-ы) ж prison

тяг|а (-и) ж (в печи) draught (BRIT), draft (US); (насоса, пылесоса) suction; **~ к** +dat (перен) attraction

тягостный прил burdensome; (впечатления) depressing

тяготение (-я) ср (ФИЗ) gravity

тягот|ы (-) мн hardships мн

тяжб|а (-ы) ж dispute

тяжеле|ть (-ю), pf о~ или по~) несов to get heavier

тяжело нареч heavily; (больной) seriously ♦ как сказ (нести) it's heavy; (понять) it's hard; **мне ~ здесь** I find it hard here; **больному ~** the patient is suffering

тяжелоатлет (-а) м weightlifter

тяжёл|ый прил heavy; (труд, день) hard; (сон) restless; (запах) strong; (воздух) stale; (преступление, болезнь, рана) serious; (зрелище, мысли, настроение) grim; (трудный: человек, характер) difficult; **~ая атлетика** weightlifting; **~ая промышленность** heavy industry

тяжесть (-и) ж weight, heaviness; (работы) difficulty; (болезни, преступления) seriousness, severity; (обычно мн: тяжёлый предмет) weight

тяжкий прил (труд) arduous; (преступление) grave

тян|уть (-у, -ешь) несов перех (канат, сеть итп) to pull; (шею, руку) to stretch out; (дело) to lay; (pf вытянуть; кабель) to draw ♦ неперех: **~ с** +instr (с ответом, с решением) to delay; **меня тянет в Петербург** I want to go to Petersburg; **~ся** несов возв to stretch; (дело, время) to drag on; (дым, запах) to waft; **~ся** (impf) **к** +dat to be attracted или drawn to

тяпк|а (-ки; gen pl -ок) ж hoe

У, у

у предл; +gen **1** (около) by; **у окна** by the window

2 (обозначает обладателя чего-н): **у меня есть дом/дети** I have a house/children

3 (обозначает объект, с которым соотносится действие): **я живу у друзей** I live with friends; **я учился у него** I was taught by him

4 (указывает на источник получения чего-н) from; **я попросил у друга денег** I asked for money from a friend

♦ межд (выражает испуг, восторг) oh

убега|ть (-ю) несов от убежать

убедительный прил (пример) convincing; (просьба) urgent

убеди|ть (2sg -ишь, 3sg -ит; impf **убеждать**) сов перех: **~ кого-н** +infin to persuade sb to do; **убеждать** (**~** pf) **кого-н в чём-н** to convince sb of sth; **~ся** (impf убежда́ться) *сов возв*: ~ся в чём-н to be convinced of sth

убежа́ть (*как* бежа́ть; *см.* Table 20); *impf* убега́ть) *сов* to run away

убежде́ни|е (-я) *ср* (*взгляд*) conviction

убе́жищ|е (-а) *ср* (*от дождя, от бомб*) shelter; **полити́ческое ~** political asylum

убер|е́чь -егу́, -ежёшь итп, -егу́т; *pt* -ёг, -егла́; *impf* уберега́ть) *сов перех* to protect; **~ся** (*impf* уберега́ться) *сов возв* (*от опасности итп*) to protect o.s.

убива́|ть (-ю) *несов от* уби́ть

уби́йств|о (-а) *ср* murder

уби́йц|а (-ы) *м/ж* murderer

убира́|ть (-ю) *несов от* убра́ть

уби́т|ый (-ого) *ср* dead man

уб|и́ть (-ью, -ьёшь; *impf* убива́ть) *сов перех* to kill; (*о преступлении*) to murder

убо́гий *прил* wretched

убо́|й (-я) *м* slaughter

убо́р (-а) *м*: **головно́й ~** hat

убо́рк|а (-и) *ж* (*помещения*) cleaning; **~ урожа́я** harvest

убо́рн|ая (-ой) *ж* (*артиста*) dressing room; (*туалет*) lavatory

убо́рщиц|а (-ы) *ж* cleaner

убр|а́ть (уберу́, уберёшь; *impf* убира́ть) *сов перех* (*унести: вещи*) to take away; (*комнату*) to tidy; (*урожай*) to gather (in); **убира́ть (~ pf) со стола́** to clear the table

убы́л|ь (-и) *ж* decrease; **идти́** (*impf*) **на ~** to decrease

убы́т|ок (-ка) *м* loss

убы́точный *прил* loss-making

убью́ итп *см. см.* уби́ть

уважа́ем|ый *прил* respected, esteemed; **~ господи́н** Dear Sir; **~ а госпожа́** Dear Madam

уважа́|ть (-ю) *несов перех* to

respect

уваже́ни|е (-я) *ср* respect

УВД *ср сокр* (= Управле́ние вну́тренних дел) administration of internal affairs within a town or region

уве́дом|ить (-лю, -ишь; *impf* уведомля́ть) *сов перех* to notify

уведомле́ни|е (-я) *ср* notification

увез|ти́ (-у́, -ёшь; *pt* увёз, -ла́; *impf* увози́ть) *сов перех* to take away

увеличи́тельн|ый *прил*: **~ое стекло́** magnifying glass

увели́ч|ить (-у, -ишь; *impf* увели́чивать) *сов перех* to increase; (*фотографию*) to enlarge; (*impf* увели́чиваться) *сов возв* to increase

уве́ренност|ь (-и) *ж* confidence

уве́ренный *прил* confident

увертю́р|а (-ы) *ж* overture

уверя́|ть (-ю) *несов перех*: **кого́-н/что-н (в чём-н)** to assure sb/sth (of sth)

ув|ести́ (-еду́, -едёшь; *pt* -ёл, -ела́; *impf* уводи́ть) *сов перех* to lead off

уви́де|ть(ся) (-жу(сь), -дишь(ся)) *сов от* ви́деть(ся)

увлека́тельный *прил* (*рассказ*) absorbing; (*поездка*) entertaining

увлече́ни|е (-я) *ср* passion

увл|е́чь (-еку́, -ечёшь итп, -еку́т; *pt* -ёк, -екла́; *impf* увлека́ть) *сов перех* to lead away; (*перен: захватить*) to captivate; **~ся** (*impf* увлека́ться) *сов возв*: **~ся** *+instr* to get carried away with; (*влюбиться*) to fall for; (*шахматами итп*) to become keen on

ув|оди́ть (-ожу́, -о́дишь) *несов от* увести́

ув|ози́ть (-ожу́, -о́зишь) *несов*

от увезти́

уво́л|**ить** (-ю, -ишь; *impf* **увольня́ть**) *сов перех* (с рабо́ты) to dismiss, sack; **~ся** (*impf* **увольня́ться**) *сов возв*: **~ся** (с рабо́ты) to lose one's job

увольне́ни|**е** (-я) *ср* (со слу́жбы) dismissal; (*ВОЕН*) leave

увы́ *межд* alas

увя́н|**уть** (-у) *сов от* **вя́нуть**

угада́|**ть** (-ю; *impf* **уга́дывать**) *сов перех* to guess

уга́рный *прил*: **~ газ** carbon monoxide

угаса́|**ть** (-ю; *pf* **уга́снуть**) *несов* (*огонь*) to die out

угла́ *итп сущ см.* **у́гол**

углево́д (-а) *м* carbohydrate

углеки́слый *прил*: **~ газ** carbon dioxide

углеро́д (-а) *м* (*ХИМ*) carbon

углово́й *прил* corner (*также*: **~ уда́р**: *СПОРТ*) corner

углуб|**и́ть** (-лю́, -и́шь; *impf* **углубля́ть**) *сов перех* to deepen; **~ся** (*impf* **углубля́ться**) *сов возв* to deepen

угля́ *итп сущ см.* **у́голь**

угна́|**ть** (угоню́, уго́нишь; *impf* **угоня́ть**) *сов перех* to drive off; (*самолёт*) to hijack

угнета́|**ть** (-ю) *несов перех* to oppress; (*тяготить*) to depress

угнете́ни|**е** (-я) *ср* oppression

угово́р|**и́ть** (-ю́, -и́шь; *impf* **угова́ривать**) *сов перех* to persuade

угод|**и́ть** (-жу́, -ди́шь; *сов* (*попасть*) to end up; **угожда́ть** (**~** *pf*) +*dat* to please

уго́дно *част*: **что ~** whatever you like ♦ *как сказ*: **что Вам ~?** what you like; **кто ~** anyone; **когда́/како́й ~** whenever/ whichever you like; **от них мо́жно**

ожида́ть чего́ **~** they might do anything

уго́дный *прил*: **~** +*dat* pleasing to

угожда́|**ть** (-ю) *несов от* **угоди́ть**

у́г|**ол** (-ла́; *loc sg* -лу́) *м* corner; (*ГЕОМ*) angle; **~ зре́ния** perspective

уголо́вник (-а) *м* criminal

уголо́вный *прил* criminal; **~ое преступле́ние** felony; **~ преступник** criminal; **~ ро́зыск** Criminal Investigation Department

у́г|**оль** (-ля́) *м* coal

уго́н (-а) *м* (*самолёта*) hijacking; (*кража*) theft

уго́нщик (-а) *м* (*самолёта*) hijacker

угоня́|**ть** (-ю) *несов от* **угна́ть**

у́г|**орь** (-ря́; *nom pl* -ри́) *м* (*ЗООЛ*) eel; (*на лице́*) blackhead

уго|**сти́ть** (-щу́, -сти́шь; *impf* **угоща́ть**) *сов перех*: **~ кого́-н чем-н** (*пирогом, вином*) to offer sb sth

угоща́|**ться** (-юсь) *несов возв*: **~йтесь!** help yourself!

угрожа́|**ть** (-ю) *несов*: **~ кому́-н (чем-н)** to threaten sb (with sth)

угро́з|**а** (-ы) *ж* (*обычно мн*) threat

угрыза́ни|**е** (-я) *ср*: **~я со́вести** pangs *мн* of conscience

угрю́мый *прил* gloomy

уда|**ва́ться** (*3sg* -ётся) *несов от* **уда́ться**

удал|**и́ть** (-ю́, -и́шь; *impf* **удаля́ть**) *сов перех* (*отослать*) to send away; (*игрока*) to send off; (*пятно, занозу, орган*) to remove

уда́р (-а) *м* blow; (*ногой*) kick; (*инсульт*) stroke; (*сердца*) beat

ударе́ни|**е** (-я) *ср* stress

уда́р|**ить** (-ю, -ишь; *impf* **ударя́ть**) *сов перех* to hit; (*ногой*) to kick; (*подлеж: часы*) to strike; **~ся** (*impf* **ударя́ться**) *сов*

возв: **~ся о** +*acc* to bang (o.s.)
against

уда́рный *прил* (*инструмент*)
percussion; (*слог*) stressed

уда́ться (*как* **дать**; *см.* Table 16;
impf **удава́ться**) *сов возв* (*опыт,
дело*) to be successful, work;
(*пирог*) to turn out well; **нам
удало́сь поговори́ть/зако́нчить
рабо́ту** we managed to talk to
each other/finish the work

уда́ч|а (**-и**) *ж* (good) luck; **жела́ю
~и!** good luck!

уда́чный *прил* successful; (*слова*)
apt

удво́|ить (**-ю, -ишь,** *impf*
удва́ивать) *сов перех* to double

удел|и́ть (**-ю́, -и́шь,** *impf* **уделя́ть**)
сов перех: **~ что-н кому́-н/
чему́-н** to devote sth to sb/sth

удерж|а́ть (**-ержу́, -е́ржишь,**
impf **уде́рживать**) *сов перех* to
restrain; (*деньги*) to deduct;
уде́рживать (**~** *pf*) (**за собо́й**) to
retain; **уде́рживать** (**~** *pf*) **кого́-н
от пое́здки** to keep sb from going
on a journey; **~ся** (*impf*
уде́рживаться) *сов возв* to stop
или restrain o.s.

удиви́тельный *прил* amazing

удив|и́ть (**-лю́, -и́шь,** *impf*
удивля́ть) *сов перех* to surprise;
~ся (*impf* **удивля́ться**) *сов возв:*
~ся +*dat* to be surprised at *или* by

удивле́ни|е (**-я**) *ср* surprise

удл|и́ть (**ужу́, у́дишь,**) *несов ср* to
angle

удлин|и́ть (**-ю́, -и́шь,** *impf*
удлиня́ть) *сов перех* to
lengthen; (*срок*) to extend

удо́бно *нареч* (*сесть*) comfortably
♦ *как сказ* it's comfortable;
(*прилично*) it's proper; **не ~ так
говори́ть/де́лать** it is not proper
to say so/do so; **мне не ~** I feel

awkward; **мне здесь ~** I'm
comfortable here; **мне ~ прийти́
ве́чером** it's convenient for me to
come in the evening

удо́бный *прил* comfortable;
(*время, место*) convenient

удобре́ни|е (**-я**) *ср* fertilizer

удо́бств|о (**-а**) *ср* comfort;
кварти́ра со все́ми ~ами a flat
with all (modern) conveniences

удовлетворе́ни|е (**-я**) *ср*
satisfaction; (*требования*)
fulfilment

удовлетвори́тельный *прил*
satisfactory

удовлетвор|и́ть (**-ю́, -и́шь,** *impf*
удовлетворя́ть) *сов перех* to
satisfy; (*потребности, про́сьбу*) to
meet; (*жалобу*) to respond to; **~ся**
(*impf* **удовлетворя́ться**) *сов
возв:* **~ся** +*instr* to be satisfied with

удово́льстви|е (**-я**) *ср* pleasure

удостовере́ни|е (**-я**) *ср*
identification (card); **~ ли́чности**
identity card

удоч|ери́ть (**-ю́, -и́шь,** *impf*
удочеря́ть) *сов перех* to adopt
(*daughter*)

у́доч|ка (**-ки;** *gen pl* **-ек**) *ж*
(fishing-)rod

удуше́|е (**-я**) *ср* suffocation

уе́хать (*как* **е́хать;** *см.* Table 19;
impf **уезжа́ть**) *сов* to leave, go
away

уж (**-а́**) *м* (ЗООЛ) grass snake ♦ *част*
(*при усилении*): **здесь не так ~
пло́хо** it's not as bad as all that
here

ужа́л|ить (**-ю, -ишь**) *сов от*
жа́лить

у́жас (**-а**) *м* horror; (*страх*) terror
♦ *как сказ* (*разг*): (**э́то**) **~!** it's
awful *или* terrible!; **ти́хий ~!** (*разг*)
what a nightmare!; **до ~а** (*разг*)
terribly

ужасн|у́ть (-у́, -ёшь; *impf*
ужаса́ть) *сов перех* to horrify;
~ся (*impf* **ужаса́ться**) *сов возв* to
be horrified

ужа́сно *нареч* (*разг: очень*)
awfully, terribly ♦ *как сказ*: э́то ~
it's awful *или* terrible

ужа́сный *прил* terrible, horrible,
awful

у́же *сравн прил от* **у́зкий**

уже́ *нареч, част always*; **ты же ~
не ма́ленький** you're not a child
any more

ужива́|ться (-ю́сь) *несов от*
ужи́ться

у́жин (-а) *м* supper

у́жина|ть (-ю; *pf* **по~**) *несов* to
have supper

ужи́|ться (-ву́сь, -вёшься; *impf*
ужива́ться) *сов возв*: ~ **с кем-н**
to get on with sb

узако́н|ить (-ю, -ишь; *impf*
узако́нивать) *сов перех* to
legalize

у́з|ел (-ла́) *м* knot; (*мешок*)
bundle; **телефо́нный ~** telephone
exchange; **железнодоро́жный ~**
railway junction; **санита́рный ~**
bathroom and toilet

у́зкий *прил* narrow; (*тесный*)
tight; (*перен: человек*) narrow-
minded

узна́|ть (-ю; *impf* **узнава́ть**) *сов
перех* to recognize; (*новости*) to
learn

у́зок *прил см.* **у́зкий**

узо́р (-а) *м* pattern

узо́рный *прил* patterned

уйти́ (*как* **идти́**; *см.* Table 18; *impf*
уходи́ть) *сов* (*человек*) to go
away, leave; (*автобус, поезд*) to
go, leave; (*избежать*): ~ **от** +*gen*
(*от опасности итп*) to get away
from; (*потребоваться*): ~ **на** +*acc*
(*деньги, время*) to be spent on

ука́з (-а) *м* (*президента*) decree

указа́ни|е (-я) *ср* indication;
(*разъяснение*) instruction;
(*приказ*) directive

указа́тел|ь (-я) *м* (*дорожный*)
sign; (*книга*) guide; (*список в
книге*) index; (*прибор*) indicator

указа́тельн|ый *прил* **~ое
местоиме́ние** demonstrative
pronoun; **~ па́лец** index finger

ук|аза́ть (-ажу́, -а́жешь; *impf*
ука́зывать) *сов перех* to point
out; (*сообщить*) to indicate

ука́з|ка (-ки; *gen pl* -ок) *ж* pointer

укача́|ть (-ю; *impf* **ука́чивать**)
сов перех (*усыпить*) to rock to
sleep; **его́ ~ло в маши́не/на
парохо́де** he got (car-/sea-)sick

укла́дыва|ть(ся) (-ю) *несов от*
уложи́ть; ~ся *несов от*
уложи́ться ♦ *возв*: **э́то не ~ется
в обы́чные ра́мки** this is out of
the ordinary; **э́то не ~ется в
голове́ или в созна́нии** it's
beyond me

укло́н (-а) *м* slant; **под ~** downhill

укл|они́ться (-оню́сь,
-о́нишься; *impf* **уклоня́ться**)
сов возв (*от удара*) to swerve;
уклоня́ться (**~** *pf*) **от** +*gen* to
dodge; (*от темы, предмета*) to
digress from

укло́нчивый *прил* evasive

уко́л (-а) *м* prick; (*МЕД*) injection

ук|оло́ть (-олю́, -о́лешь) *сов от*
коло́ть

уко́р (-а) *м* (*упрёк*) reproach; **~ы
со́вести** pangs of conscience

укороти́ть (-чу́, -ти́шь; *impf*
укора́чивать) *сов перех* to
shorten; (*impf*
укора́чиваться) *сов возв* to be
shortened

укра́дкой *нареч* furtively

укра́|сить (-шу, -сишь; *impf*

украша́ть (сов перех to decorate; (жизнь итп) to brighten (up)

укра́сть (-ду́, -дёшь) сов от **красть**

украша́ть (-ю) несов от **укра́сить**

украше́ни|е (-я) ср decoration; (коллекции) jewel; (также: ювели́рное ~) jewellery (BRIT), jewelry (US)

укрепи́ть (-лю́, -и́шь; impf **укрепля́ть**) сов перех to strengthen; (стену) to reinforce; **~ся** (impf **укрепля́ться**) сов возв to become stronger

укрепле́ни|е (-я) ср strengthening

укро́п (-а) м, собир dill

укро́ти́ть (-щу́, -ти́шь; impf **укроща́ть**) сов перех to tame

укры́ти|е (-я) ср shelter

укры́ть (-о́ю, -о́ешь; impf **укрыва́ть**) сов перех (закрыть) to cover; (беженца) to shelter; **~ся** (impf **укрыва́ться**) сов возв to cover o.s.; (от дождя) to take cover

у́ксус (-а) м vinegar

уку́с (-а) м bite

укуси́ть (-ушу́, -у́сишь) сов перех to bite

уку́та|ть (-ю; impf **уку́тывать**) сов перех to wrap up; **~ся** (impf **уку́тываться**) сов возв to wrap o.s. up

ул. сокр (= у́лица) St

ула́влива|ть (-ю) несов от **улови́ть**

ула́ди|ть (-жу, -дишь; impf **ула́живать**) сов перех to settle

у́ле|й (-ья) м (bee-)hive

улета́ть (-ю; impf **улете́ть**) сов (птица) to fly away; (самолёт) to leave

улету́ч|иться (-усь, -ишься; impf **улету́чиваться**) сов возв to evaporate

ули́к|а (-и) ж (piece of) evidence

ули́т|ка (-ки; gen pl -ок) ж snail

у́лиц|а (-ы) ж street; на ~е outside

у́личн|ый прил street; **~ое движе́ние** traffic

уло́в (-а) м catch (of fish)

улови́мый прил: едва́ или чуть или е́ле ~ barely perceptible

улови́ть (-овлю́, -о́вишь; impf **ула́вливать**) сов перех to detect; (мысль, связь) to grasp

уложи́ть (-ожу́, -о́жишь; impf **укла́дывать**) сов перех (ребёнка) to put to bed; (вещи, чемодан) to pack; **~ся** (impf **укла́дываться**) сов возв to pack; (**~ся** pf) **в сро́ки** to keep to the time limit

улу́чш|ить (-у, -ишь; impf **улучша́ть**) сов перех to improve

улыба́|ться (-юсь; pf **улыбну́ться**) несов возв: ~ (+dat) to smile (at)

улы́б|ка (-ки; gen pl -ок) ж smile

ультразву́к (-а) м ultrasound

ультрафиоле́тов|ый прил: **~ые лучи́** ultraviolet rays мн

ум (-а́) м mind; быть (impf) **без ~а́ от кого́-н/чего́-н** to be wild about sb/sth; в ~е (счита́ть) in one's head; бра́ться (взя́ться pf) за ~ to see sense; сходи́ть (сойти́ pf) с ~а́ to go mad; своди́ть (свести́ pf) кого́-н с ~а́ to drive sb mad; (перен: увлечь) to drive sb wild; **~а́ не приложу́, куда́/ско́лько/ кто ...** I can't think where/how much/who ...

ума́лчива|ть (-ю) несов от **умолча́ть**

уме́лый прил skilful (BRIT), skillful (US)

уме́ни|е (-я) *ср* ability, skill

уме́ньш|ить (-у, -ишь; *impf* **уменьша́ть)** *сов перех* to reduce; **~ся** (*impf* **уменьша́ться**) *сов возв* to diminish

уме́ренный *прил* moderate; (*климат, характер*) temperate

ум|ере́ть (-ру́, -рёшь; *impf* **умира́ть)** *сов* to die

уме́р|ить (-ю, -ишь; *impf* **умеря́ть)** *сов* to moderate

уме|сти́ть (-щу́, -сти́шь; *impf* **умеща́ть)** *сов перех* to fit; **~ся** (*impf* **умеща́ться**) *сов возв* to fit

уме́|ть (-ю) *несов* can, to be able to; (*иметь способность*) to know how to; **он ~ет пла́вать/чита́ть** he can swim/read

умеща́|ть(ся) (-ю(сь)) *несов от* **умести́ть(ся)**

умира́|ть (-ю) *несов от* **умере́ть** ♦ *неперех* (*перен*): **~ю, как хочу́ есть/спать** I'm dying for something to eat/to go to sleep; **я ~ю от ску́ки** I'm bored to death

умиротвор|и́ть (-ю́, -и́шь; *impf* **умиротворя́ть)** *сов перех* (*враждующих*) to pacify; (*агрессора*) to appease

умне́|ть (-ю; *pf* **по~)** *несов* (*человек*) to grow wiser

у́мниц|а (-ы) *м/ж*: **он/она́ ~** he's/she's a clever one; (*разг*): **вот ~!** good for you!, well done!

у́мно *нареч* (*сделанный*) cleverly; (*вести себя*) sensibly; (*говорить*) intelligently

умножа́|ть (-ю) *несов от* **умно́жить**

умноже́ни|е (-я) *ср* multiplication

умно́ж|ить (-у, -ишь; *impf* **мно́жить** *или* **умножа́ть)** *сов перех* (*МАТ*) to multiply

у́мный *прил* clever, intelligent

умозаключе́ни|е (-я) *ср* (*вывод*) deduction

умол|и́ть (-ю́, -и́шь; *impf* **умоля́ть)** *сов перех*: **~ кого́-н** (+*infin*) to prevail upon sb (to do)

умо́лк *м*: **без ~** incessantly

умо́лкн|уть (-у; *impf* **умолка́ть)** *сов* to fall silent

умолч|а́ть (-у́, -и́шь; *impf* **ума́лчивать)** *сов*: **~ о чём-н** to keep quiet about sth

умоля́|ть (-ю) *несов от* **умоли́ть** ♦ *перех* to implore

умру́ *итп см* **умере́ть**

умо́ю(сь) *сов см* **умы́ть(ся)**

у́мственно *нареч*: **~ отста́лый** mentally retarded

у́мственный *прил* (*способности*) mental; (*труд*) intellectual work

умудр|и́ться (-ю́сь, -и́шься; *impf* **умудря́ться**) *сов возв* to manage

умч|а́ть (-у́, -и́шь) *сов перех* to whisk off *или* away; **~ся** *сов возв* to dash off

умыва́льник (-а) *м* washstand

умы́|ть (-о́ю, -о́ешь; *impf* **умыва́ть)** *сов перех* to wash; **~ся** (*impf* **умыва́ться**) *сов возв* to wash

умы́шленный *прил* deliberate, intentional; (*преступление*) premeditated

ун|ести́ (-есу́, -есёшь; *pt* **-ёс, -есла́;** *impf* **уноси́ть)** *сов перех* to take away; **~сь** (*impf* **уноси́ться**) *сов возв* to speed off

универма́г (-а) *м* = **универса́льный магази́н**

универса́льный *прил* universal; (*образование*) all-round; (*человек, машина*) versatile; **~ магази́н** department store

универса́м (-а) *м* supermarket

университе́т (-а) *м* university

унижа́|ть(ся) (-ю(сь)) несов от
уни́зить(ся)

униже́ние (-я) ср humiliation

уни́женный прил (человек)
humiliated; (взгляд, просьба)
humble

унизи́тельный прил humiliating

уни́з|ить (-жу, -зишь; impf
унижа́ть) (~ pf) себя́ to abase o.s.;
~ся (impf унижа́ться) сов возв:
~ся (пе́ред +instr) to abase o.s.
(before)

уника́льный прил unique

унита́з (-а) м toilet

уничто́ж|ить (-у, -ишь; impf
уничтожа́ть) сов перех to
destroy

ун|ести́(сь) (-осу́(сь),
-осёшь(ся)) несов от
унести́(сь)

уныва́|ть (-ю) несов (человек) to
be downcast или despondent

уны́лый прил despondent

уны́ни|е (-я) ср despondency

уня́|ть (уйму́, уймёшь; pt -л,
-ла́, -ло; impf унима́ть) сов
перех (волнение) to suppress

упа́д|ок (-ка) м decline

упак|ова́ть (-у́ю) сов от
пакова́ть

упако́вк|а (-и) ж packing;
(материал) packaging

упасти́ сов перех: упаси́ Бог или
Бо́же или Го́споди! God forbid!

упа́|сть (-ду́, -дёшь) сов от
па́дать

упере́ть (упру́, упрёшь; pt
упёр, упёрла, упёрло; impf
упира́ть) сов перех: ~ что-н
+acc во что-н итп) to prop sth
against; ~ся (impf упира́ться)
возв: ~ся чем-н в +acc (в зе́млю)
to dig sth into; (натолкнуться):
~ся в +acc (в сте́ну) to come up

against

упива́|ться (-юсь) несов возв
(перен): ~ +instr (сча́стьем) to be
intoxicated by

упира́|ть (-ю) несов от упере́ть;
~ся несов от упере́ться ♦ возв
(иметь причиной): ~ся в +prp to
be down to

упла́т|а (-ы) ж payment

упла|ти́ть (-чу́, -а́тишь) сов от
плати́ть

уплы́|ть (-ву́, -вёшь; impf
уплыва́ть) сов (человек, рыба
итп) to swim away или off;
(корабль) to sail away или off

уподо́б|ить (-лю, -ишь; impf
уподобля́ть) сов перех:
что-н/кого́-н +dat to compare sth/
sb to; ~ся (impf уподобля́ться)
сов возв: ~ся +dat to become like

упол|зти́ (-у́, -ёшь; pt -, -ла́)
(змея) to slither away

уполномо́чи|е (-я) ср: по ~ю
+gen on behalf of

уполномо́ч|ить (-у, -ишь; impf
уполномо́чивать) сов перех: ~
кого́-н +infin to authorize sb to do

упомяну́ть (-яну́, -я́нешь; impf
упомина́ть) сов (не)перех
(назвать): ~ +acc или (о +prp) to
mention

упо́р (-а) м (для ног) rest; в ~
(стреля́ть) point-blank;
(смотре́ть) intently; де́лать
(сде́лать pf) ~ на +prp to put
emphasis on

упо́рный прил persistent

упо́рств|о (-а) ср persistence

употреби́тельный прил
frequently used

употреб|и́ть (-лю́, -и́шь; impf
употребля́ть) сов перех to use

употребле́ни|е (-я) ср (слова)
usage; (лекарства) taking;
(алкоголя, пищи) consumption

упр. сокр (= **управле́ние**) admin

управле́ни|**е** (-**я**) ср (*делами*)
administration; (*фирмой*)
management; (*учреждение*)
office; (*система приборов*)
controls мн

управля́|ть (-**ю**) несов: ~ +instr
(*автомобилем*) to drive; (*судном*)
to navigate; (*государством*) to
govern; (*учреждением, фирмой*)
to manage; (*оркестром*) to
conduct

управля́ющ|ий (-**его**) м
(*хозяйством*) manager;
(*имением*) bailiff

упражне́ни|**е** (-**я**) ср exercise

упражня́|ть (-**ю**) несов перех to
exercise; ~**ся** несов возв to
practise

упраздни́|ть (-**ю**, -**йшь**; impf
упраздня́ть) сов перех to
abolish

упра́шива|ть (-**ю**) несов от
упроси́ть

упрёк (-**а**) м reproach

упрека́|ть (-**ю**; pf **упрекну́ть**)
несов перех: ~ кого́-н (в +prp) to
reproach sb (for)

упро|си́ть (-**ошу́**, -**о́сишь**; impf
упра́шивать) сов перех: ~
кого́-н +infin to persuade sb to do

упро|сти́ть (-**щу́**, -**сти́шь**; impf
упроща́ть) сов перех to simplify

упро́ч|ить (-**у**, -**ишь**; impf
упро́чивать) сов перех to
consolidate; ~**ся**
упро́читься сов возв
(*положение, позиции*) to be
consolidated

упроща́|ть (-**ю**) несов от
упрости́ть

упроще́ни|**е** (-**я**) ср simplification

упру́гий прил (*пружина, тело*)
elastic; (*движения*) springy

упря́ж|ка (-**ки**; gen pl -**ек**) ж team

(of horses, dogs etc); (*упряжь*)
harness

у́пряж|ь (-**и**) ж; no pl harness

упря́мый прил obstinate, stubborn

упуска́|ть (-**ю**) несов от **упусти́ть**

упуще́ни|**е** (-**я**) ср error, mistake

ура́ межд hooray, hurrah

уравне́ни|**е** (-**я**) ср (*МАТ*)
equation

ура́внива|ть (-**ю**) несов от
уравня́ть

уравнове́|сить (-**шу**, -**сишь**; impf
уравнове́шивать) сов перех to
balance; ~**ся** (impf
уравнове́шиваться) сов возв
(*силы*) to be counterbalanced

уравнове́шенный прил balanced

уравня́|ть (-**ю**; impf **ура́внивать**)
сов перех to make equal

урага́н (-**а**) м hurricane

урага́нный прил: ~ **ве́тер** gale

ура́н (-**а**) м uranium

урегули́р|овать (-**ую**) сов перех
to settle

у́рн|а (-**ы**) ж (*погреба́льная*) urn;
(*для мусора*) bin; **избира́тельная**
~ ballot box

у́ров|ень (-**ня**) м level; (*техники*)
standard; (*зарпла́ты*) rate;
встре́ча на вы́сшем ~**не** summit
meeting; ~ **жи́зни** standard of
living

уро́д (-**а**) м person with a deformity

уро́дливый прил (*с уро́дством*)
deformed; (*некраси́вый*) ugly

урожа́|й (-**я**) м harvest

уро́к (-**а**) м lesson; (*задание*) task;
(*обычно мн: дома́шняя рабо́та*)
homework ед; **де́лать** (**сде́лать** pf)
~**и** to do one's homework

ур|они́ть (-**оню́**, -**о́нишь**) сов от
роня́ть

ус (-а) *м* whisker; *см. также* **усы́**

уса́д|**ить** (-ажу́, -а́дишь; *impf* **уса́живать**) *сов перех* (заставить делать): ~ **кого́-н за что-н**/+*infin* to sit sb down to sth/ to do

уса́дьб|**а** (-ы) *ж* (помещичья) country estate; (крестьянская) farmstead

уса́жива|**ть** (-ю) *несов от* усади́ть; ~**ся** *несов от* усе́сться

уса́тый *прил*: ~ **мужчи́на** man with a moustache (*BRIT*) *или* mustache (*US*)

усво́|**ить** (-ю, -ишь; *impf* **усва́ивать**) *сов перех* (пищу, лекарство) to assimilate; (привычку) to acquire; (урок) to master

усе́рдный *прил* diligent

усе́|**сться** (-я́дусь, -я́дешься; *pt* -е́лся, -е́лась; *impf* **уса́живаться**) *сов возв* to settle down; **уса́живаться** (~ *pf*) **за** +*acc* (за работу) to sit down to

уси́ленный *прил* (охрана) heightened; (внимание) increased

уси́лива|**ть** (-ю) *несов от* уси́лить

уси́ли|**е** (-я) *ср* effort

уси́л|**ить** (-ю, -ишь; *impf* **уси́ливать**) *сов перех* to intensify; (охрану) to heighten; (внимание) to increase; ~**ся** (*impf* **уси́ливаться**) *сов возв* (ветер) to get stronger; (волнение) to increase

ускольз|**ну́ть** (-у́, -ёшь; *impf* **ускольза́ть**) *сов* to slip away

ускор|**ить** (-ю, -ишь; *impf* **ускоря́ть**) *сов перех* (шаги) to quicken; (отъезд) to speed up; ~**ся** (*impf* **ускори́ться**) *сов возв* (шаги) to quicken; (решение) to be speeded up

усло́ви|**е** (-я) *ср* condition; (договора) term; (обычно мн: правила) requirement; *см. также* **усло́вия**

усло́в|**иться** (-люсь, -ишься; *impf* **усла́вливаться**) *сов возв*: ~ **о** +*prp* (договориться) to agree on

усло́ви|**я** (-й) *мн* (природные) conditions мн; (задачи) factors мн; **жили́щные** ~ housing, ~ **труда́** working conditions; **в** ~**х** +*gen* in an atmosphere of; **по** ~**м догово́ра** on the terms of the agreement; **на льго́тных** ~**х** on special terms

усло́вный *прил* conditional; (сигнал) signal

усложн|**и́ть** (-ю́, -и́шь; *impf* **усложня́ть**) *сов перех* to complicate; ~**ся** (*impf* **усложня́ться**) *сов возв* to get more complicated

услу́г|**а** (-и) *ж* (одолжение) favour (*BRIT*), favor (*US*); (обычно мн: облуживание) service; **к Ва́шим** ~**м!** at your service!

услы́ш|**ать** (-у, -ишь) *сов от* **слы́шать**

усма́трива|**ть** (-ю) *несов от* **усмотре́ть**

усмех|**ну́ться** (-у́сь, -ёшься; *impf* **усмеха́ться**) *сов возв* to smile slightly

усме́шк|**а** (-и) *ж* slight smile; **зла́я** ~ sneer

усмир|**и́ть** (-ю́, -и́шь; *impf* -я́ть) *сов перех* (зверя) to tame

усмотре́ни|**е** (-я) *ср* discretion

усмо́тр|**еть** (-ю́, -о́трю, -о́тришь; *impf* **усма́тривать**) *сов перех* (счесть): ~ **что-н в** +*prp* to see sth in

усн|**у́ть** (-у́, -ёшь) *сов* to fall asleep, to go to sleep

усовершéнствовани|**е** (-я) *ср* improvement

усомни́ться (-ю́сь, -и́шься) *сов возв*: ~ в +*prp* to doubt

успева́емост|ь (-и) *ж* performance (*in studies*)

успе́|ть (-ю; *impf* **успева́ть**) *сов* (*о работе*) to manage; (*прийти вовремя*) to be *или* make it in time

успе́х (-а) *м* success; (*обычно мн: в спорте, в учёбе*) achievement; **как Ва́ши ~и?** how are you getting on?

успе́шный *прил* successful

успоко́|ить (-ю, -ишь; *impf* **успока́ивать**) *сов перех* to calm (down);

успока́иваться (*impf* **успока́иваться**) *сов возв* (*человек*) to calm down

уста́в (-а) *м* (*партийный*) rules *мн*; (*воинский*) regulations *мн*; (*фирмы*) statute

уста|ва́ть (-ю́, -ёшь) *несов от* **уста́ть**

уста́в|ить (-лю, -ишь; *impf* **уставля́ть**) *сов перех* (*занять*): ~ **что-н чем-н** to cover with sth; (*разг: устремить*): ~ **что-н** +*acc* to fix sth on; **~ся** (*impf* **уставля́ться**) *сов возв* (*разг*): **~ся на/в** +*acc* to stare at

уста́лост|ь (-и) *ж* tiredness, fatigue

уста́лый *прил* tired

у́стал|ь (-и) *ж*: **без** *или* **не зна́я ~и** tirelessly

устан|ови́ть (-овлю́, -о́вишь; *impf* **устана́вливать**) *сов перех* to establish; (*сроки*) to set; (*прибор*) to install; **~ся** (*impf* **устана́вливаться**) *сов возв* to be established

устано́вк|а (-и) *ж* installation

устаре́|ть (-ю) *сов от* **старе́ть**

♦ (*impf* **устарева́ть**) *неперех* (*оборудование*) to become

obsolete

уста́|ть (-ну, -нешь; *impf* **устава́ть**) *сов* to get tired

у́стн|ый *прил* (*экзамен*) oral; (*обещание, приказ*) verbal; **~ая речь** spoken language

усто́йчив|ый *прил* stable; **~ое (сло́во)сочета́ние** set phrase

усто|я́ть (-ю́, -и́шь; *impf* **устоя́ть**) *сов* (*не упасть*) to remain standing; (*в борьбе итп*) to stand one's ground; (*перед соблазном*) to resist

устра́ива|ть(ся) (-ю(сь)) *несов от* **устро́ить(ся)**

устран|и́ть (-ю́, -и́шь; *impf* **устраня́ть**) *сов перех* to remove

устрем|и́ть (-лю́, -и́шь; *impf* **устремля́ть**) *сов перех* to direct; **~ся** (*impf* **устремля́ться**) *сов возв*: **~ся на** +*acc* (*толпа*) to charge at

устремле́ни|е (-я) *ср* aspiration

у́стриц|а (-ы) *ж* oyster

устрои́тел|ь (-я) *м* organizer

устро́|ить (-ю, -ишь; *impf* **устра́ивать**) *сов перех* to organize; (*подлеж: цена*) to suit; **э́то меня́ ~ит** that suits me; **~ся** (*impf* **устра́иваться**) *сов возв* (*расположиться*) to settle down; (*прийти в поря́док*) to work out; **устра́иваться** (**~ся** *pf*) **на рабо́ту** to get a job

устро́йств|о (-а) *ср* (*прибора*) construction; (*техническое*) device, mechanism

усту́п (-а) *м* foothold

уст|упи́ть (-уплю́, -у́пишь; *impf* **уступа́ть**) *сов перех*: ~ **что-н кому́-н** to give sth up for sb; (*победу*) to concede sth to sb ♦ *неперех*: **~ кому́-н/чему́-н** (*силе, жела́нию*) to yield to sb/ sth; **уступа́ть** (**~** *pf*) **в** +*prp* (*в си́ле,* *в уме́*) to be inferior in

усту́п|ка (-**ки**; gen pl -**ок**) ж conciliation; (ски́дка) discount; **пойти́** (pf) **на** ~**ку** to compromise

у́сть|е (-**я**) ср (реки́) mouth

усугуби́|ть (-**лю́**, -**ишь**; impf **усугубля́ть**) сов перех to aggravate

усы́ (-**о́в**) мн (у челове́ка) moustache ед (BRIT), mustache ед (US); (у живо́тных) whiskers мн

усынови́|ть (-**лю́**, -**ишь**; impf **усыновля́ть**) сов перех to adopt (сы́на)

усып|и́ть (-**лю́**, -**и́шь**; impf **усыпля́ть**) сов перех (больно́го) to anaesthetize (BRIT), anesthetize (US); (ребёнка) to lull to sleep

ута́щ|ить (-**у́**, -**ищь**; impf **ута́скивать**) сов перех (унести́) to drag away или off

утверди́тельный прил (та́кже линг) affirmative

утвер|ди́ть (-**жу́**, -**ди́шь**; impf **утвержда́ть**) сов перех (зако́н) to pass; (догово́р) to ratify; (план) to approve; (поря́док) to establish; ~**ся** (impf **утвержда́ться**) сов возв to be established

утвержда́|ть (-**ю**) несов от **утверди́ть** ♦ перех (наста́ивать) to maintain; ~**ся** несов от **утверди́ться**

утвержде́ни|е (-**я**) ср (см глаг) passing; ratification; approval; establishment; (мысль) statement

ут|ёнок (-**ёнка**; nom pl -**я́та**, gen pl -**я́т**) м duckling

утеп|ли́ть (-**лю́**, -**и́шь**; impf **утепля́ть**) сов перех to insulate

утёс (-**а**) м cliff

уте́чк|а (-**и**) ж (та́кже перен) leak; (ка́дров) turnover; ~ **мозго́в** brain drain

ут|е́чь (3sg -**ечёт**, pt -**ёк**, -**екла́**, -**екло́**; impf **утека́ть**) сов (вода́) to leak out

уте́ш|ить (-**у**, -**ишь**; impf **утеша́ть**) сов перех to comfort, console

утих|а́ть (-**а́ю**; impf **утиха́ть**) сов (спор) to calm down; (звук) to die away; (вьюга) to die down

у́т|ка (-**ки**; gen pl -**ок**) ж duck

уткн|у́ть (-**у́**, -**ёшь**) сов перех (разг: лицо́) to bury; ~**ся** сов возв (разг): ~**ся в** +acc (в кни́гу) to bury one's nose in

утол|и́ть (-**ю́**, -**и́шь**; impf **утоля́ть**) сов перех to satisfy; (жа́жду) to quench

утоми́тельный прил tiring

утом|и́ть (-**лю́**, -**и́шь**; impf **утомля́ть**) сов перех to tire; ~**ся** (impf **утомля́ться**) сов возв to get tired

утомле́ни|е (-**я**) ср tiredness

ут|ону́ть (-**ону́**, -**о́нешь**) сов от **тону́ть**

утопа́|ть (-**ю**) несов (тону́ть) to drown

утоп|и́ть(ся) (-**лю́(сь)**, -**о́пишь(ся)**) сов от **топи́ть(ся)**

уточн|и́ть (-**ю́**, -**и́шь**; impf **уточня́ть**) сов перех to clarify

утра́т|а (-**ы**) ж loss

утра́|тить (-**чу**, -**тишь**; impf **утра́чивать**) сов перех (потеря́ть) to lose; утра́чивать (~ pf) си́лу (докуме́нт) to become invalid

у́тренний прил morning; (собы́тие) this morning's

у́тренник (-**а**) м matinée; (для дете́й) children's party

у́тр|о (-**а**; nom pl -**а**, gen pl -**ам**; dat pl -**ам**) ср morning; до́брое ~!, с до́брым ~! good morning!; на ~ next morning; под ~, к утру́ in the early hours of the morning

утро́б|а (-ы) ж (матери) womb

утро́|ить (-ю, -ишь) сов перех to treble, triple; **~ся** сов возв to treble, triple

у́тром нареч in the morning

утружда́|ть (-ю) несов: **~ кого́-н чем-н** to trouble sb with sth; **~ся** несов возв to trouble o.s.

утю́г (-а́) м iron (appliance)

утю́ж|ить (-у, -ишь); pf **вы́тюжить** или **от~)** несов перех to iron

уф межд: **~!** phew!

ух межд: **~!** ooh!

ух|а́ (-и́) ж fish broth

ухажива|ть (-ю) несов: **~ за +instr** (за больным) to nurse (за садом) to tend (за женщиной) to court

ухва|ти́ть (-чу́, -́тишь); impf **ухва́тывать)** сов перех (человека: за руку) to get hold of; (перен: идею, смысл) to grasp; **~ся** (impf ухва́тываться) сов возв: **~ся за** +acc to grab hold of; (за идею) to jump at

у́х|о (-а; nom pl **у́ши**, gen pl **уше́й**) ср ear; (у шапки) flap

ухо́д (-а) м departure; (из семьи) desertion; (со сцены) exit; (за больным, за ребёнком) care; **~ на отста́вку** resignation; **~ на пе́нсию** retirement

ух|оди́ть (-ожу́, -о́дишь) несов от **уйти́**

ухо́женный прил (ребёнок) well-looked-after; (сад) well-kept

ухудш|ить (-у, -ишь); impf **ухудша́ть)** сов перех to make worse; **~ся** (impf **ухудша́ться)** сов возв to deteriorate

уцеле́|ть (-ю) сов to survive

уце́ненный прил reduced

уце́н|ить (-ю, -ишь); impf **уце́нивать)** сов перех to reduce

(the price of)

уце́н|ка (-ки; gen pl **-ок)** ж reduction

уча́ст|вовать (-ую) сов: **~ в** +prp to take part in

уча́сти|е (-я) ср participation; (сочувствие) concern

учаща́|ть (-щу́, -сти́шь) impf **уча́щивать)** сов перех to quicken; (контакты) to make more frequent; **~ся** (impf **учаща́ться)** сов возв to quicken; (контакты) to become more frequent

участко́в|ый прил local **♦ (-ого)** м (разг: также: **~ инспе́ктор)** local policeman; (: также: **~ врач)** local GP или doctor

уча́стник (-а) м participant; (экспедиции) member

уча́ст|ок (-ка) м (земли, кожи итп) area; (реки, фронта) stretch; (врачебный) catchment area; (земельный) plot; (строительный) site; (работы) field; **садо́вый ~** allotment

у́часть (-и) ж lot

учаща́|ть(ся) (-ю) несов от **участи́ть(ся)**

учащ|ийся (-егося) м (школы) pupil; (училища) student

уче́б|а (-ы) ж studies мн

уче́бник (-а) м textbook

уче́бн|ый прил (работа) academic; (фильм) educational; (бой) mock; (судно) training; (методы) teaching; **~ая програ́мма** curriculum; **~ое заведе́ние** educational establishment; **~ год** academic year

уче́ни|е (-я) ср (теория) teachings мн; см. также **уче́ния**

учени́к (-а́) м (школы) pupil; (училища) student; (мастера) apprentice

учени́ческий прил (тетради)

school

уче́ни|я (-й) мн exercises мн

учён|ый прил academic; (труды) scholarly; (человек) learned, scholarly ♦ (-oго) м academic; scholar; (в области точных и естественных наук) scientist

уч|е́сть (-ту́, -тёшь; pt **-ёл, -ла́,** impf **учи́тывать)** сов перех to take into account; **~ти́те, что ...** bear in mind that ...

учёт (-а) м (факторов) consideration; (военный, медицинский) registration; (затрат) record; **брать [взять** pf**] на ~** to register; **вести́** (impf) **~** to keep a record

учётн|ый прил: **~ая ка́рточка** registration form

учи́лищ|е (-а) ср college

учи́тел|ь (-я; nom pl **-я́)** м teacher

учи́тельск|ая (-ой) ж staffroom

учи́тыва|ть (-ю) несов от **уче́сть**

уч|и́ть (-у́, -ишь; pf **вы́учить)** несов перех (урок, роль) to learn; (pf **на~** или **об~**): **~ кого́-н чему́-н/**+infin to teach sb sth/to do; **~ся** несов возв (в школе, в училище) to study; (pf **вы́учиться** или **на~ся**): **~ся чему́-н/**+infin to learn sth/to do

учреди́тел|ь (-я) м founder

учреди́тельн|ый прил: **~ое собра́ние** inaugural meeting

учре|ди́ть (-жу́, -ди́шь; impf **учрежда́ть)** сов перех (организацию) to set up; (контроль, порядок) to introduce

учрежде́ни|е (-я) ср (организации итп) setting up; (научное) establishment; (финансовое, общественное) institution

учти́вый прил courteous

уша́н|ка (-ки; gen pl **-ок)** ж cap with ear-flaps

уша́|ть etc сущ см **у́хо**

уши́ etc сущ см **у́хо**

уши́б (-а) м bruise

уши|би́ть (-бу́, -бёшь; pt **-, -ла,** impf **ушиба́ть)** сов перех to bang; **~ся** сов возв to bruise

уши|ть (-ью, -ьёшь; impf **ушива́ть)** сов перех (одежду) to take in

у́шк|о (-ка; nom pl **-ки,** gen pl **-ек)** ср уменьш от **у́хо;** (иголки) eye

ушла́ etc глаг см **уйти́**

ушн|о́й прил ear; **~а́я боль** earache

уще́ль|е (-я; gen pl **-ий)** ср gorge, ravine

ущем|и́ть (-лю́, -и́шь; impf **ущемля́ть)** сов перех (палец) to trap; (права) to infringe

ущемле́ни|е (-я) ср (прав) limitation

уще́рб (-а) м (материальный) damage; (здоровью) detriment

ущипн|у́ть (-у́, -ёшь) сов перех to nip, pinch

ую́т (-а) м comfort, cosiness

ую́тно нареч (расположиться) comfortably ♦ как сказ: **здесь ~** it's cosy here; **мне здесь ~** I feel comfortable here

ую́тный прил cosy

уязви́мый прил vulnerable

уязв|и́ть (-лю́, -и́шь) сов перех to wound, hurt

уясн|и́ть (-ю́, -и́шь; impf **уясня́ть)** сов перех (значение) to comprehend

Ф, ф

фа́брик|а (-и) ж factory; (ткацкая, бумажная) mill
фабри́чный прил factory
фа́з|а (-ы) ж phase
фаза́н (-а) м pheasant
файл (-а) м (КОМП) file
фа́кел (-а) м torch
факс (-а) м fax
факт (-а) м fact
факти́чески нареч actually, in fact
факти́ческий прил factual
фа́ктор (-а) м factor
факту́р|а (-ы) ж texture; (КОММ) invoice
факультати́вный прил optional
факульте́т (-а) м faculty
фальши́вый прил false; (деньги) counterfeit; (пение) out of tune
фами́ли|я (-и) ж surname; **де́вичья ~** maiden name
фамилья́рный прил over(ly) familiar
фан (-а) м fan
фана́тик (-а) м fanatic
фана́тичный прил fanatical
фане́р|а (-ы) ж plywood; (для облицовки) veneer
фантази́р|овать (-ую) несов (мечтать) to dream; (выдумывать) to make up stories
фанта́зи|я (-и) ж fantasy; (выдумка) fib
фанта́ст (-а) м writer of fantasy; (научный) science-fiction writer
фанта́стик|а (-и) ж, собир (ЛИТЕРАТУРА) fantasy; **нау́чная ~** science fiction
фантасти́ческий прил fantastic
фа́р|а (-ы) ж (АВТ, АВИА) light

фармаце́вт (-а) м chemist, pharmacist
фа́ртук (-а) м apron
фарфо́р (-а) м, собир porcelain, bone china
фарш (-а) м stuffing, forcemeat; (мясной) mince
фаршир| овать (-ую) pf за~) несов перех to stuff
фаса́д (-а) м (передняя сторона) facade, front; за́дний ~ back
фас|ова́ть (-у́ю) pf рас~) несов перех to prepack
фасо́л|ь (-и) ж (растение) bean plant ♦ собир (семена) beans мн
фасо́н (-а) м style
фата́ (-ы́) ж veil
фаши́зм (-а) м fascism
фаши́ст (-а) м fascist
ФБР ср сокр (= Федера́льное бюро́ рассле́дований (США)) FBI
февра́л|ь (-я́) м February

---

23 Февраля́: День защи́тника оте́чества - This is an official celebration of the Russian army, though various sections of the armed forces have their own special holidays. Men of all ages and walks of life receive gifts, mainly from women.

федера́льный прил federal
федерати́вный прил federal
федера́ци|я (-и) ж federation
фейерве́рк (-а) м firework
фе́льдшер (-а) м (в поликли́нике) ≈ practice nurse; ~ **ско́рой по́мощи** ≈ paramedic
фельето́н (-а) м satirical article
фемини́зм (-а) м feminism
фемини́ст|ка (-ки; gen pl -ок) ж feminist
фен (-а) м hairdryer
феода́льный прил feudal

ферз|ь (-я́) м (ШАХМАТЫ) queen
фе́рм|а (-ы) ж farm
фе́рмер (-а) м farmer
фе́рмерск|ий прил: ~ое хозя́йство farm
фестива́л|ь (-я) м festival
фетр (-а) м felt
фехтова́ни|е (-я) ср (СПОРТ) fencing
фе́|я (-и) ж fairy
фиа́лк|а (-ки; gen pl -ок) ж violet
фиа́ско ср нескл fiasco
фи́г|а (-и) ж (БОТ) fig; (разг) fig (gesture of refusal); **иди́ на́ фиг!** get lost!; **ни фига́** nothing at all
фигу́р|а (-ы) ж figure; (ШАХМАТЫ) (chess)piece
фигури́р|овать (-ую) несов to be present; (имя, тема) to feature
фигури́ст (-а) м figure skater
фигу́рн|ый прил (резьба) figured; ~**ое ката́ние** figure skating; ~**ые ско́бки** curly или brace brackets
фи́зик (-а) м physicist
фи́зик|а (-и) ж physics
физиологи́ческий прил physiological
физиотерапи́|я (-и) ж physiotherapy
физи́ческ|ий прил physical; (труд) manual; ~**ая культу́ра** physical education
физкульту́р|а (-ы) ж сокр (= физи́ческая культу́ра) PE
фикс м: **иде́я** ~ idée fixe
фикси́р|овать (-ую; pf за~) несов перех to fix; (отмеча́ть) to record
фикти́вный прил fictitious; ~ **брак** (ЮР) marriage of convenience
фи́кус (-а) м ficus
филармо́ни|я (-и) ж (зал) concert hall; (организация)

philharmonic society
филатели́ст (-а) м philatelist
филе́ ср нескл fillet
фили́н (-а) м eagle owl
фило́лог (-а) м specialist in language and literature
филоло́ги|я (-и) ж language and literature
филологи́ческий прил philological; ~ **факульте́т** department of language and literature
фило́соф (-а) м philosopher
филосо́фи|я (-и) ж philosophy
фильм (-а) м film
фильтр (-а) м filter
фильтр|ова́ть (-у́ю; pf про~) несов перех to filter
фина́л (-а) м finale; (СПОРТ) final
фина́льный прил final
финанси́р|овать (-ую) несов перех to finance
финанси́ст (-а) м financier; (специалист) specialist in financial matters
фина́нсовый прил financial; (год) fiscal; (отдел, инспектор) finance
фина́нс|ы (-ов) мн finances мн; Министе́рство ~ов ≈ the Treasury (BRIT), ≈ the Treasury Department или Department of the Treasury (US)
фи́ник (-а) м (плод) date
фи́ниш (-а) м (СПОРТ) finish
финиши́р|овать (-ую) (не)сов to finish
Финля́нди|я (-и) ж Finland
финн (-а) м Finn
фи́нский прил Finnish; ~ **язы́к** Finnish; ~ **зали́в** Gulf of Finland
Ф.И.О. сокр (= фами́лия, и́мя, о́тчество) surname, first name, patronymic
фиоле́товый прил purple
фи́рм|а (-ы) ж firm

фи́рменный _прил (магазин)_ chain; _(разг: товар)_ quality; **~ знак** brand name

фити́ль (**-я́**) _м_ wick; _(бомбы)_ fuse

ФИ́ФА _ж сокр (= Междунаро́дная федера́ция футбо́ла)_ FIFA

фи́ш|**ка** (**-ки**; _gen pl_ **-ек**) _ж_ counter, chip

флаг (**-а**) _м_ flag

флако́н (**-а**) _м_ bottle

фланг (**-а**) _м_ flank

флане́ль (**-и**) _ж_ flannel

фле́йта (**-ы**) _ж_ flute

флейти́ст (**-а**) _м_ flautist

фли́гель (**-я**) _м (АРХИТ)_ wing

флома́стер (**-а**) _м_ felt-tip (pen)

флот (**-а**) _м (ВОЕН)_ navy; _(МОР)_ fleet; **возду́шный ~** air force

флюс (**-а**) _м_ (dental) abscess, gumboil

фля́г|**а** (**-и**) _ж (бутылка)_ flask; _(канистра)_ churn

фойе́ _ср нескл_ foyer

фокстерье́р (**-а**) _м_ fox terrier

фо́кус (**-а**) _м_ trick; _(ТЕХ, перен)_ focus

фо́кусник (**-а**) _м_ conjurer

фольг|**а́** (**-и́**) _ж_ foil

фолькло́р (**-а**) _м_ folklore

фон (**-а**) _м_ background

фона́рь (**-я́**) _м (уличный)_ lamp; _(карманный)_ torch

фонд (**-а**) _м (организация)_ foundation; _(деньги)_ fund; _(жилищный, земельный)_ resources _мн_; **фо́нды** _(ценные бумаги)_ stocks

фо́ндов|**ый** _прил_: **~ая би́ржа** stock exchange

фоне́тика (**-и**) _ж_ phonetics

фоноте́ка (**-и**) _ж_ record and tape collection

фонта́н (**-а**) _м_ fountain

форе́ль (**-и**) _ж_ trout

фо́рм|**а** (**-ы**) _ж_ form; _(одежда)_ uniform; _(ТЕХ)_ mould _(BRIT)_, mold _(US)_; _(КУЛИН)_ (cake) tin _(BRIT)_ или pan _(US)_

форма́льность (**-и**) _ж_ formality

форма́льн|**ый** _прил_ formal; _(подход)_ bureaucratic

форма́т (**-а**) _м_ format

форма́ци|**я** (**-и**) _ж (общественная)_ system

фо́рменн|**ый** _прил_: **~ бланк** standard form; **~ая оде́жда** uniform

формирова́ни|**е** (**-я**) _ср_ formation; **вое́нное ~** military unit

формир|**ова́ть** (**-у́ю**; _pf_ **c~**) _несов перех_ to form; **~ся** _(pf_ **c~ся**) _несов возв_ to form

фо́рмул|**а** (**-ы**) _ж_ formula

формули́р|**овать** (**-ую**; _pf_ **c~**) _несов перех_ to formulate

формули́ров|**ка** (**-ки**; _gen pl_ **-ок**) _ж (определение)_ definition

фортепья́но _ср нескл_ (grand) piano

фо́рточ|**ка** (**-ки**; _gen pl_ **-ек**) _ж_ hinged, upper pane in window for ventilation

фо́рум (**-а**) _м_ forum

фо́сфор (**-а**) _м_ phosphorous

фотоаппара́т (**-а**) _м_ camera

фото́граф (**-а**) _м_ photographer

фотографи́р|**овать** (**-ую**; _pf_ **c~**) _несов перех_ to photograph; **~ся** _(pf_ **c~ся**) _несов возв_ to have one's photo(graph) taken

фотогра́фи|**я** (**-и**) _ж_ photography; _(снимок)_ photograph

фотока́рточ|**ка** (**-ки**; _gen pl_ **-ек**) _ж_ photo

фрагме́нт (**-а**) _м (отрывок)_ excerpt; _(обломок)_ fragment

фра́з|**а** (**-ы**) _ж_ phrase

фрак (**-а**) _м_ tail coat, tails _мн_

фра́кци|**я** (**-и**) _ж_ faction

Фра́нци|я (-и) ж France

францу́жен|ка (-ки) ж Frenchwoman

францу́з (-а) м Frenchman

францу́зский прил French; ~ **язы́к** French

фрахт (-а) м freight

фрахт|ова́ть (-у́ю; pf **за~)** несов перех to charter

фре́с|ка (-ки; gen pl **-ок)** ж fresco

фрикаде́ль|ка (-ьки; gen pl **-ек)** ж meatball

фронт (-а; nom pl **-ы́)** м front

фронтови́к (-а́) м front line soldier; (ветеран) war veteran

фрукт (-а) м (БОТ) fruit

фрукто́вый прил fruit

ФСБ ж нескл сокр (= Федера́льная слу́жба безопа́сности) Department of State Security

ФСК ж нескл сокр (= Федера́льная слу́жба контрразве́дки) counterespionage intelligence service

фтор (-а) м fluorin(e)

фу межд ~! ugh!

фуже́р (-а) м wineglass; (для шампа́нского) flute

фунда́мент (-а) м (СТРОИТ) foundations мн, base; (перен: семьи, науки) foundation, basis

фундамента́льный прил (здание) sound, solid; (перен: знания) profound

фунду́к (-а) м (плод) hazelnut

функционе́р (-а) м official

функциони́р|овать (-ую) несов to function

фу́нкци|я (-и) ж function

фунт (-а) м pound

фура́ж (-а́) м fodder

фура́ж|ка (-ки; gen pl **-ек)** ж cap; (ВОЕН) forage cap

фурго́н (-а) м (АВТ) van; (повозка) (covered) wagon

фуро́р (-а) м furore

фуру́нкул (-а) м boil

футбо́л (-а) м football (BRIT), soccer

футболи́ст (-а) м football (BRIT) или soccer player

футбо́л|ка (-ки; gen pl **-ок)** ж T-shirt, tee shirt

футбо́льный прил football (BRIT), soccer; ~ **мяч** football

футля́р (-а) м case

фы́рка|ть (-ю) несов (животное) to snort

фыркн|у́ть (-у) сов (животное) to give a snort

фюзеля́ж (-а) м (АВИА) fuselage

Х, х

ха́кер (-а) м (КОМП) hacker

хала́т (-а) м (домашний) dressing gown; (врача) gown

хала́тный прил negligent

хам (-а) м (разг) lout

ха́мств|о (-а) ср rudeness

ха́нжеств|о (-а) ср prudishness

ха́ос (-а) м chaos

хаоти́чный прил chaotic

хара́ктер (-а) м character, nature; (человека) personality

характериз|ова́ть (-у́ю) несов перех to be typical of; (pf **о~**; человека, ситуацию) to characterize

характери́стик|а (-и) ж (документ) (character) reference; (описание) description

характе́рный прил (свойственный): ~ **(для** +gen) characteristic (of); (случай) typical

х/б сокр = **хлопчатобума́жный**

хвале́бный прил complimentary

хвали́ть (-ю́, -ишь; pf по~) несов перех to praise

хва́ста|ться (-юсь; pf по~) несов возв: ~ (+instr) to boast (about)

хвастли́вый прил boastful

хвасту́н (-а́) м (разг) show-off

хвата́|ть (-ю; pf схвати́ть) несов перех to grab (hold of), snatch; (преступника) to arrest; ♦ (pf хвати́ть) безл: ~ +gen (денег, времени) to have enough; мне ~ет де́нег на еду́ I've enough to buy food; э́того ещё не ~ло! (разг) that's the limit!; не ~ет то́лько, что́бы он отказа́лся (разг) now all we need is for him to refuse; ~ся (pf схвати́ться) несов возв: ~ся за +acc (за ру́чку, за ору́жие) to grab

хва|ти́ть (-чу́, -тишь) сов от хвата́ть ♦ безл (разг): хва́тит! that's enough!; с меня́ хва́тит! I've had enough!

хва́т|ка (-ки; gen pl -ок) ж grip; делова́я ~ business acumen

хво́йный прил coniferous; ~ое де́рево conifer

хво́рост (-а) м собир firewood

хвост (-а́) м tail; (по́езда) tail end; (причёска) ponytail

хво́стик (-а) м (мыши, реди́ски) tail; (причёска) pigtail

хво|я́ (-и) ж собир needles мн (of conifer)

хек (-а) м whiting

хе́рес (-а) м sherry

хи́жин|а (-ы) ж hut

хи́лый прил sickly

хи́мик (-а) м chemist

хими́ческий (-а) м chemical

химиотерапи́|я (-и) ж chemotherapy

хими́ческ|ий прил chemical; (факульте́т, кабине́т) chemistry; ~ая чи́стка (процесс) dry-

cleaning; (пункт приёма) dry-cleaner's

хи́ми|я (-и) ж chemistry

химчи́ст|ка (-ки; gen pl -ок) ж сокр = хими́ческая чи́стка

хи́ппи м нескл hippie

хиру́рг (-а) м surgeon

хирурги́ческий прил surgical; (кли́ника) surgery

хирурги́|я (-и) ж surgery

хитре́ц (-а́) м cunning devil

хитр|и́ть (-ю́, -и́шь; pf с~) несов to act slyly

хи́трость (-и) ж cunning

хи́трый прил cunning

хихи́ка|ть (-ю) несов (разг) to giggle

хище́ни|е (-я) ср misappropriation

хи́щник (-а) м predator

хи́щн|ый прил predatory; ~ая пти́ца bird of prey

хладнокро́вный прил composed; (уби́йство) cold-blooded

хлам (-а) м собир junk

хлеб (-а) м bread; (зерно́) grain

хле́бниц|а (-ы) ж bread basket; (для хране́ния) breadbin (BRIT), breadbox (US)

хлебн|у́ть (-у́, -ёшь) сов перех (разг: чай итп) to take a gulp of

хлебозаво́д (-а) м

хлев (-а; nom pl -á) м cowshed

хле|ста́ть (-щу́, -щешь) несов перех (ремнём) to whip; (по щека́м) to slap ♦ непере́х (вода́, кровь) to gush

хлестн|у́ть (-у́, -ёшь) сов перех to whip; (по щеке́) to slap

хло́па|ть (-ю) несов перех (ладо́нью) to slap ♦ непере́х: ~ +instr (две́рью, кры́шкой) to slam; ~ (impf) +dat (арти́сту) to clap

хло́пковый прил cotton

хло́пн|уть (-у) сов перех (по спине́) to slap ♦ непере́х (в

ладони) to clap; (*дверь*) to slam shut

хлоп|ок (**-ка**) *м* cotton

хлоп|о́к (**-ка́**) *м* (*удар в ладоши*) clap

хлопота́ть (**-очу́, -о́чешь**) *несов* (*по дому*) to busy o.s.; ~ (*impf*) **о** +*prp* (*о разрешении*) to request

хлопотли́вый *прил* (*человек*) busy; (*работа*) troublesome

хлоп|о́ты (**-о́т**; *dat pl* **-о́там**) *мн* (*по дому итп*) chores *мн*; (*прося чего-н*) efforts *мн*

хлопу́ш|ка (**-ки**; *gen pl* **-ек**) *ж* (*игрушка*) (Christmas) cracker

хлопчатобума́жный *прил* cotton

хло́пь|я (**-ев**) *мн* (*снега, мыла*) flakes *мн*; **кукуру́зные ~** cornflakes

хлор (**-а**) *м* chlorine

хло́рк|а (**-и**) *ж* (*разг*) bleaching powder

хло́рн|ый *прил*: **~ая и́звесть** bleaching powder

хлы́н|уть (3sg **-ет**) *сов* to flood

хме́ле|ть (**-ю**; *pf* **за~**) *несов* to be drunk

хму́р|ить (**-ю, -ишь**; *pf* **на~**) *несов перех* (*лоб, брови*) to furrow; **~ся** (*pf* **на~ся**) *несов возв* to frown

хму́рый *прил* gloomy

хны́ка|ть (**-ю**) *несов* (*разг*: *плакать*) to whimper

хо́бби *ср нескл* hobby

хо́бот (**-а**) *м* (*слона*) trunk

ход (**-а**; *part gen* **-у**, *loc sg* **-у́**) *м* (*машины, поршня*) movement; (*событий, дела*) course; (*часов, двигателя*) working; (*карты*) go; (*маневр, также* ШАХМАТЫ) move; (*возможность*) (*вход*) entrance; **в хо́де** +*gen* in the course of; **~ мы́слей** train of thought;

идти́ (**пойти́** *pf*) **в ~** to come into use; **быть** (*impf*) **в (большо́м) ~у́** to be (very) popular; **на ~у́** (*есть, разгова́ривать*) on the move; (*пошути́ть*) in passing; **с хо́ду** straight off; **дава́ть** (**дать** *pf*) **~ де́лу** to set things in motion

хода́тайств|о (**-а**) *ср* petition

хода́тайств|овать (**-ую**; *pf* **по~**) *несов*: **~ о чём-н/за кого́-н** to petition for sth/on sb's behalf

хо|ди́ть (**-жу́, -дишь**) *несов* to walk; (*по магазинам, в гости*) to go (on foot); (*поезд, автобус итп*) to go; (*слухи*) to go round; (*часы*) to work; (*носить*): **~ в** +*prp* (*в пальто, в сапога́х итп*) to wear; (*impf*) +*instr* (*тузом итп*) to play; (*конём, пешкой итп*) to move

ходьб|а́ (**-ы́**) *ж* walking

хожу́ *несов см.* **ходи́ть**

хоздогово́р (**-а**) *м сокр* (= *хозя́йственный догово́р*) business deal (*between companies*)

хозрасчёт (**-а**) *м* (= *хозя́йственный расчёт*) system of management based on self-financing and self-governing principles

хозрасчётн|ый *прил*: **-ое предприя́тие** self-financing, self-governing enterprise

хозя́|ин (**-ина**; *nom pl* **-ева**, *gen pl* **-ев**) *м* (*владелец*) owner; (*сдающий жильё*) landlord; (*принимающий гостей*) host; (*перен*: *распорядитель*) master

хозя́йк|а (**-йки**; *gen pl* **-ек**) *ж* (*владелица*) owner; (*сдающая жильё*) landlady; (*принимающая гостей*) hostess; (*в доме*) housewife

хозя́йнича|ть (**-ю**) *несов* (*в доме, на кухне*) to be in charge; (*командовать*) to be bossy

хозя́йственн|ый *прил*

(де́ятельность) economic; **(постро́йка, инвента́рь)** domestic; **(челове́к)** thrifty; **~ые това́ры** hardware; **▪ магази́н** hardware shop

хозя́йств|**о** (-**а**) *ср* (*экон*) economy; (*фе́рмерское*) enterprise; (*предме́ты бы́та*) household goods *мн*; (*дома́шнее*) ~ housekeeping

хозя́йствовать (-**ую**) *несов*: ~ **на предприя́тии** to manage an enterprise

хоккеи́ст (-**а**) *м* hockey player

хокке́|й (-**я**) *м* hockey

холе́р|**а** (-**ы**) *ж* cholera

холл (-**а**) *м* (*теа́тра, гости́ницы*) lobby; (*в кварти́ре, в до́ме*) hall

холм (-**á**) *м* hill

холми́стый *прил* hilly

хо́лод (-**а**; *nom pl* -**á**) *м* cold; (*пого́да*) cold weather *ед*

холода́|ть (*3sg* -**ет**; *pf* **по~**) *несов безл* to turn cold

холоде́|ть (-**ю**; *pf* **по~**) *несов* to get cold; (*от стра́ха*) to freeze

холоди́льник (-**а**) *м* (*дома́шний*) fridge; (*промы́шленный*) refrigerator

хо́лодно *нареч* coldly **♦** *как сказ* it's cold; **мне/ей** ~ I'm/she's cold

холо́дный *прил* cold

холосто́й *прил* (*мужчи́на*) single, unmarried; (*вы́стрел, патро́н*) blank

холостя́к (-**á**) *м* bachelor

холст (-**á**) *м* canvas

хомя́к (-**á**) *м* hamster

хор (-**а**) *м* choir; (*насме́шек*) chorus

Хорва́ти|**я** (-**и**) *ж* Croatia

хорео́граф (-**а**) *м* choreographer

хореогра́фи|**я** (-**и**) *ж* choreography

хо́ром *нареч* in unison

хор|**они́ть** (-**оню́**, -**о́нишь**; *pf* **по~**) *несов перех* to bury

хоро́шенький *прил* (*лицо́*) cute

хоро́шенько *нареч* (*разг*) properly

хороше́|ть (-**ю**; *pf* **по~**) *несов* to become more attractive

хоро́ш|**ий** *прил* good; **он** ~ **(собо́й)** he's good-looking; **всего́ ~его!** all the best!

хорошо́ *нареч* well **♦** *как сказ* it's good; **мне** ~ I feel good **♦** *част*, *вводн сл* okay, all right **♦** *ср нескл* (*ПРОСВЕЩ*) ≈ good (*school mark*); **мне здесь** ~ I like it here; **ну**, ~! (*разг*: *угро́за*) right then!; **~ бы поéсть/поспа́ть** (*разг*) I wouldn't mind a bite to eat/getting some sleep

хо|**те́ть** (*см. Table 14*) *несов перех*: ~ +*infin* to want to do; **как ~ти́те** (*как вам уго́дно*) as you wish; (*а всё-таки*) no matter what you say; **хо́чешь не хо́чешь** whether you like it or not; ~ (*impf*) **есть/пить** to be hungry/thirsty; **~ся** *несов безл*: **мне хо́чется пла́кать/есть** I feel like crying/something to eat

хоть *союз* **1** (*несмотря́ на то, что*) (al)though; **хоть я и оби́жен, я помогу́ тебе́** although I am hurt, I will help you

2 (*до тако́й сте́пени, что*) even if; **не соглаша́ется, хоть до утра́ проси́** he won't agree, even if you ask all night; **хоть убе́й, не могу́ пойти́ на э́то** I couldn't do that to save my life; **хоть..., хоть...** either..., or...; **езжа́й хоть сего́дня, хоть че́рез ме́сяц** go either today, or in a month's time

♦ *част* **1** (*слу́жит для усиле́ния*)

at least; **подвези́ его́ хоть до ста́нции** take him to the station at least; **пойми́ хоть ты** you of all people should understand

2 (*во фразах*): **хоть бы** at least; **хоть бы ты ему́ позвони́л** you could at least phone him!; **хоть бы закончить сего́дня!** if only we could get finished today!; **хоть кто** anyone; **хоть како́й** any; **ему́ хоть бы что** it doesn't bother him; **хоть куда́!** (*разг*) excellent!; **хоть бы и так!** so what!

хотя́ *союз* although; ~ **и** even though; ~ **бы** at least

хо́хот (-а) *м* loud laughter

хох|ота́ть (-очу́, -о́чешь) *несов* to guffaw; ~ (*impf*) (**над** +*instr*) to laugh (at)

хочу́ *etc несов см.* **хоте́ть**

хра́брост|ь (-и) *ж* courage, bravery

хра́брый *прил* courageous, brave

храм (-а) *м* (*РЕЛ*) temple

хране́ни|е (-я) *ср* (*денег*) keeping; ~ **ору́жия** possession of firearms; **ка́мера** ~**я** (*на вокзале*) left-luggage office (*BRIT*) *или* checkroom (*US*)

храни́лищ|е (-а) *ср* store

храни́тел|ь (-я) *м* keeper

хран|и́ть (-ю́, -и́шь) *несов перех* to keep; (*достоинство*) to protect; (*традиции*) to preserve; ~**ся** *несов возв* to be kept

храп (-а) *м* (*во сне*) snoring

храп|е́ть (-лю́, -и́шь) *несов* to snore

хреб|е́т (-та́) *м* (*АНАТ*) spine; (*ГЕО*) ridge; **го́рный** ~ mountain range

хрен (-а) *м* horseradish

хризанте́м|а (-ы) *ж* chrysanthemum

хрип (-а) *м* wheezing

хрип|е́ть (-лю́, -и́шь) *несов* to wheeze

хри́плый *прил* (*голос*) hoarse

хри́пн|уть (-у; *pf* о~) *несов* to become *или* grow hoarse

христиа́н|ин (-ина; *nom pl* -а́не, *gen pl* -а́н) *м* Christian

христиа́нский *прил* Christian

христиа́нств|о (-а) *ср* Christianity

Христ|о́с (-а́) *м* Christ

хром (-а) *м* (*ХИМ*) chrome

хрома́|ть (-ю) *несов* to limp

хромо́й *прил* lame

хромосо́м|а (-ы) *ж* chromosome

хро́ник|а (-и) *ж* chronicle; (*в газеты*) news items

хрони́ческий *прил* chronic

хронологи́ческий *прил* chronological

хру́пкий *прил* fragile; (*печенье, кости*) brittle; (*перен: фигура*) delicate; (: *здоровье, организм*) frail

хруста́лик (-а) *м* (*АНАТ*) lens

хруста́л|ь (-я́) *м, собир* crystal

хруста́льный *прил* crystal

хру|сте́ть (-щу́, -сти́шь) *несов* to crunch

хрустя́щий *прил* crunchy, crisp

хрю́ка|ть (-ю) *несов* to grunt

худе́|ть (-ю) *несов* to grow thin; (*быть на диете*) to slim

худо́жественн|ый *прил* artistic; (*школа, выставка*) art; ~**ая литерату́ра** fiction; ~**ая самоде́ятельность** amateur performing arts; ~ **сало́н** (*выставка*) art exhibition; (*магазин*) art gallery and craft shop; ~**фильм** feature film

худо́жник (-а) *м* artist

худо́й *прил* thin

ху́дший *превос прил* the worst

ху́же *сравн прил, нареч* worse

хулига́н (-а) *м* hooligan

хулига́н|ить (-ю, -ишь; *pf* на~) *несов* to act like a hooligan

хулига́нств|о (-а) *ср* hooliganism

ху́тор (-а; *nom pl* -а́) *м* (*ферма*) croft; (*село*) village

Ц, ц

ца́п|ля (-ли; *gen pl* -ель) *ж* heron

цара́па|ть (-ю; *pf* о~) *несов перех* (*руку*) to scratch; ~**ся** (*pf* о~ся) *несов возв* to scratch

цара́пина (-ы) *ж* scratch

цари́ц|а (-ы) *ж* tsarina (*wife of tsar*)

ца́рский *прил* tsar's, royal; (*режим, правительство*) tsarist

ца́рств|о (-а) *ср* reign

ца́рств|овать (-ую) *несов* to reign

царь (-я́) *м* tsar

цвес|ти́ (-ту́, -тёшь) *несов* (*БОТ*) to blossom, flower

цвет (-а; *nom pl* -а́) *м* (*окраска*) colour (*BRIT*), color (*US*); (*prep sg* -ý; *БОТ*) blossom

цветно́й *прил* (*карандаш*) coloured (*BRIT*), colored (*US*); (*фото, фильм*) colour (*BRIT*), color (*US*)

цвет|о́к (-ка́; *nom pl* -ы́) *м* flower (*bloom*); (*комнатный*) plant

цвето́чный *прил* flower

цвету́щий *прил* blooming

це|ди́ть (-жу́, -дишь; *pf* про~) *несов перех* (*жидкость*) to strain; (*перен: слова*) to force out

це́др|а (-ы) *ж* (dried) peel *ед*

целе́бный *прил* medicinal; (*воздух*) healthy

целево́й *прил* (*финансирование*) targeted

целенапра́вленный *прил*

single-minded; (*политика*) consistent

целесообра́зный *прил* expedient

целеустремлённый *прил* purposeful

целико́м *нареч* (*без ограничений*) wholly, entirely; (*сварить*) whole

цели́н|а (-ы́) *ж* virgin territory

це́л|иться (-юсь, -ишься; *pf* на~) *несов возв*: ~ в +*acc* to (take) aim at

целлофа́н (-а) *м* cellophane ®

цел|ова́ть (-у́ю; *pf* по~) *несов перех* to kiss; ~**ся** (*pf* по~ся) *несов возв* to kiss (each other)

це́л|ое (-ого) *ср* whole

це́лый *прил* whole, entire; (*неповреждённый*) intact; **в ~ом** (*полностью*) as a whole; (*в общем*) on the whole

цель (-и) *ж* (*при стрельбе*) target; (*перен*) aim, goal; **с це́лью** +*infin* with the object *или* aim of doing; **с це́лью** +*gen* for; **в це́лях** +*gen* for the purpose of

це́льный *прил* (*кусок*) solid; (*характер*) complete

цеме́нт (-а) *м* cement

цементи́р|овать (-ую; *pf* за~) *несов перех* to cement

цен|а́ (-ы́; *acc sg* -у, *dat sg* -е́, *nom pl* -ы) *ж* price; (*перен: человека*) value; **-о́й** +*gen* at the expense of

цензу́р|а (-ы) *ж* censorship

цен|и́ть (-ю́, -ишь) *несов перех* (*вещь*) to value; (*помощь*) to appreciate

це́нник (-а) *м* (*бирка*) price tag

це́нность (-и) *ж* value; ~**и** valuables; **материа́льные ~и** commodities

це́нный *прил* valuable; (*письмо*) registered; ~**ые бума́ги** securities

це́нтнер (-а) *м* centner (*100kg*)

центр (-а) *м* centre (*BRIT*), center (*US*); **в це́нтре внима́ния** in the limelight; **торго́вый ~** shopping centre (*BRIT*) *или* mall (*US*)

централизова́ть (-у́ю) *(не)сов перех* to centralize

центра́льный *прил* central

центра́льное отопле́ние - central heating. The vast majority of Russians live in flats for which hot water and central heating are provided by huge communal boiler systems. Each city borough has a boiler system of its own. These systems distribute hot water for domestic use all year round and radiators are heated during the cold months. The heating is controlled centrally and individual home owners do not have any say over it. See also note at **отопи́тельный сезо́н**.

Центроба́нк *м сокр* = *Центра́льный банк (Росси́и)*

центрово́й *прил*: **~ напада́ющий** centre (*BRIT*) *или* center (*US*) forward ♦ (**-ого**) *м* (*в баскетбо́ле*) centre (*BRIT*), center (*US*); (*в футбо́ле*) midfielder

цепля́|ться (-юсь) *несов возв*: **~ за** +*acc* to cling *или* hang on to

цепно́й *прил* chain

цепо́чка (-ки; *gen pl* -ек) *ж* (*тонкая цепь*) chain; (*машин, люде́й*) line

цеп|ь (-и; *loc sg* -и́) *ж* chain; (*ЭЛЕК*) circuit; **го́рная ~** mountain range

церемо́ни|я (-и) *ж* ceremony

церко́вный *прил* church

це́рк|овь (-ви; *instr sg* -овью, *nom pl* -ви, *gen pl* -ве́й) *ж* church

цех (-а; *loc sg* -у́, *nom pl* -а́) *м* (work)shop (*in factory*)

цивилиза́ци|я (-и) *ж* civilization

цивилизо́ванный *прил* civilized

цикл (-а) *м* cycle; (*ле́кций*) series

цикл|ева́ть (-ю́ю; *pf* **от~**) *несов перех* to sand

цикло́н (-а) *м* cyclone

цили́ндр (-а) *м* cylinder; (*шля́па*) top hat

цини́чный *прил* cynical

цинк (-а) *м* zinc

цирк (-а) *м* circus

циркули́р|овать (*3sg* -ует) *несов* to circulate

ци́ркул|ь (-я) *м* (a pair of) compasses *мн*

циркуля́р (-а) *м* decree

цисте́рн|а (-ы) *ж* cistern

цита́т|а (-ы) *ж* quote, quotation

цити́р|овать (-ую; *pf* **про~**) *несов перех* to quote

ци́трусовый *прил* citrus

цифербла́т (-а) *м* dial; (*на часа́х*) face

ци́фр|а (-ы) *ж* number; (*ара́бские, ри́мские*) numeral; (*обы́чно мн*: *расчёт*) figure

ЦРУ *ср сокр* (= *Центра́льное разве́дывательное управле́ние (США)*) CIA

ЦСУ *ср сокр* = *Центра́льное статисти́ческое управле́ние*

ЦТ *ср сокр* = *Центра́льное телеви́дение*

цыга́н (-а; *nom pl* -е) *м* gypsy

цыпл|ёнок (-ёнка; *nom pl* -я́та, *gen pl* -я́т) *м* chick

цы́поч|ки (-ек) *мн*: **на ~ках** on tiptoe

Ч, ч

ча|ди́ть (**-жу́**, **-ди́шь**; *pf* **на-**) *несов* to give off fumes

чаев|ы́е (**-ы́х**) *мн* tip *ед*

ча|й (**-я**; *part gen* **-ю**, *nom pl* **-и́**) *м* tea; **зава́ривать** (**завари́ть** *pf*) ~ to make tea; **дава́ть** (**дать** *pf*) **кому́-н** **на** ~ to give sb a tip

ча́йка (**-йки**; *gen pl* **-ек**) *ж* (sea)gull

ча́йная (**-ой**) *ж* tearoom

ча́йник (**-а**) *м* kettle; (*для заварки*) teapot

ча́йн|ый *прил*: ~**ая ло́жка** teaspoon

ча́ртер (**-а**) *м* (*КОММ*) charter

час (**-а**; *nom pl* **-ы́**) *м* hour; **академи́ческий** ~ (*ПРОСВЕЩ*) period; **кото́рый** ~? what time is it?; **сейча́с 3** ~**á но́чи/дня** it's 3 o'clock in the morning/afternoon; *см. также* **часы́**

часо́в|ня (**-ни**; *gen pl* **-ен**) *ж* chapel

часов|о́й *прил* (*лекция*) one-hour; (*механизм: ручных часов*) watch; (: *стенных часов*) clock ♦ (**-о́го**) *м* sentry; ~**áя стре́лка** the small hand; ~ **по́яс** time zone

части́ц|а (**-ы**) *ж* (*стекла*) fragment; (*желания*) bit; (*количества*) fraction; (*ФИЗ, ЛИНГ*) particle

части́чный *прил* partial

ча́стник (**-а**) *м* (*собственник*) (private) owner

ча́стность (**-и**) *ж* (*деталь*) detail; (*подробность*) particular; **в** ~**и** for instance

ча́стн|ый *прил* private; (*случай*) isolated; ~**ая со́бственность** private property

ча́сто *нареч* (*много раз*) often; (*тесно*) close together

част|ота́ (**-оты́**; *nom pl* **-о́ты**) *ж* (*ТЕХ*) frequency

ча́стый *прил* frequent

част|ь (**-и**; *gen pl* **-éй**) *ж* part; (*симфонии*) movement; (*отдел*) department; (*ВОЕН*) unit; ~ **ре́чи** part of speech; ~ **све́та** continent

час|ы́ (**-о́в**) *мн* (*карманные*) watch *ед*; (*стенные*) clock *ед*

ча́шка (**-ки**; *gen pl* **-ек**) *ж* cup

ча́щ|а (**-и**) *ж* (*лес*) thick forest; (*заросль*) thicket

ча́ще *сравн прил от* **ча́стый** ♦ *сравн нареч от* **ча́сто**

чего́ *мест см.* **что**

чей (**чего́**; *f* **чья**, *nt* **чьё**, *pl* **чьи**) *мест* whose; ~ **бы то ни́ было** no matter whose it is

чей-либо (**чьего́-либо**; *как* **чей**; *см. Table 5*) (*f* **чья́-либо**, *nt* **чьё-либо**, *pl* **чьи-либо**) *мест* = **чей-нибудь**

чей-нибудь (**чьего́-нибудь**; *как* **чей**; *см. Table 5*) (*f* **чья́-нибудь**, *nt* **чьё-нибудь**, *pl* **чьи-нибудь**) *мест* anyone's

чей-то (**чьего́-то**; *как* **чей**; *см. Table 5*) (*f* **чья́-то**, *nt* **чьё-то**, *pl* **чьи-то**) *мест* someone's, somebody's

чек (**-а**) *м* (*банковский*) cheque (*BRIT*), check (*US*); (*товарный, кассовый*) receipt

че́ковый *прил* cheque (*BRIT*), check (*US*)

чёл|ка (**-ки**; *gen pl* **-ок**) *ж* (*человека*) fringe (*BRIT*), bangs *мн* (*US*)

челн|о́к (**-ка́**) *м* shuttle; (*торговец*) small trader buying goods abroad and selling them on their local markets

челове́к (-а; *nom pl* **лю́ди**, *gen pl* **люде́й**) *м* human (being); (*некто, ли́чность*) person

челове́ческий *прил* human; (*челове́чный*) humane

челове́честв|о (-а) *ср* humanity, mankind

челове́чный *прил* humane

че́люст|ь (-и) *ж* (*АНАТ*) jaw

чем *мест см.* **что** ♦ *союз* than; (*разг: вместо того чтобы*) instead of; ~ **бо́льше/ра́ньше, тем лу́чше** the bigger/earlier, the better

чемода́н (-а) *м* suitcase

чемпио́н (-а) *м* champion

чемпиона́т (-а) *м* championship

чему́ *мест см.* **что**

чепуха́ (-и́) *ж* nonsense

че́рв|и (-е́й) *мн* (*КАРТЫ*) hearts *мн*

черви́вый *прил* maggoty

черв|ь (-я́; *nom pl* -и, *gen pl* -е́й) *м* worm; (*личинка*) maggot

червя́к (-а́) *м* worm

черда́к (-а́) *м* attic, loft

черед|ова́ть (-у́ю) *несов перех*: ~ **что-н с** +*instr* to alternate sth with

KEYWORD

че́рез *предл*, +*acc* **1** (*попере́к*) across, over; **переходи́ть** (**перейти́** *pf*) **че́рез доро́гу** to cross the road

2 (*сквозь*) through; **че́рез окно́** through the window

3 (*пове́рх*) over; **че́рез забо́р** over the fence

4 (*спустя́*) in; **че́рез час** in an hour('s time)

5 (*ми́нуя како́е-н простра́нство*): **че́рез три кварта́ла - ста́нция** the station is three blocks away

6 (*при по́мощи*) via; **он пе́редал письмо́ че́рез знако́мого** he sent the letter via a friend

7 (*при повторе́нии де́йствия*) every; **принима́йте табле́тки че́рез ка́ждый час** take the tablets every hour

че́реп (-а) *м* skull

черепа́х|а (-и) *ж* tortoise; (*морска́я*) turtle

черепи́ц|а (-ы) *ж собир* tiles *мн*

чере́ш|ня (-ни; *gen pl* -ен) *ж* cherry

черне́|ть (-ю; *pf* по~) *несов* (*станови́ться чёрным*) to turn black

черни́к|а (-и) *ж* bilberry

черни́л|а (-) *мн* ink *ед*

черн|и́ть (-ю́, -и́шь; *pf* о~) *несов перех* (*имя*) to tarnish

чёрно-бе́лый *прил* black-and-white

чернови́к (-а́) *м* draft

чёрный (-ен, -на́, -но́) *прил* black; (*ход*) back

черп|а́ть (-ю) *несов перех* (*жи́дкость*) to ladle

черст|ве́ть (-ю; *pf* за~) *несов* (*хлеб*) to go stale

чёрствый *прил* (*хлеб*) stale; (*челове́к*) callous

чёрт (-а; *nom pl* **че́рти**, *gen pl* **черте́й**) *м* (*дья́вол*) devil; **иди́ к** ~**у!** (*разг*) go to hell!

черт|а́ (-ы́) *ж* (*ли́ния*) line; (*при́знак*) trait; **в о́бщих** ~**х** in general terms; *см. та́кже* **черты́**

чертёж (-а́) *м* draft

чер|ти́ть (-чу́, -тишь; *pf* на~) *несов перех* (*ли́нию*) to draw; (*гра́фик*) to draw up

черто́чк|а (-и; *gen pl* -ек) *ж* (*дефи́с*) hyphen

черт|ы́ (-) *мн* (*также*: ~ **лица́**) features *мн*

че|са́ть (-шу́, -шешь; *pf* по~) *несов перех* (*спи́ну*) to scratch;

~**ся** (*pf* **по**~**ся**) *несов возв* to scratch o.s.; (*no pf*; *зудеть*) to itch

чесно́к (**-а́**) *м* garlic

че́стно *нареч* (*сказать*) honestly; (*решить*) fairly ♦ *как сказ*: **так бу́дет** ~ that'll be fair

че́стность (**-и**) *ж* honesty

че́стный *прил* honest; ~**ое сло́во** honestly

честолюби́вый *прил* ambitious

честь (**-и**) *ж* honour (*BRIT*), honor (*US*); (*loc sg* **-и́**; *почёт*) glory; **к че́сти кого́-н** to sb's credit; **отдава́ть** (**отда́ть** *pf*) **кому́-н** ~ to salute sb

четве́рг (**-а́**) *м* Thursday

четверёньки (**-ек**) *мн*: **на** ~**ьках** on all fours

четвёрка (**-ки**; *gen pl* **-ок**) *ж* (*цифра, карта*) four; (*ПРОСВЕЩ*) ≈ B (*school mark*)

че́тверо (*см. Table 30a*; **-ы́х**) *чис* four

четвёртый *чис* fourth; **сейча́с** ~ **час** it's after three

че́тверть (**-и**) *ж* quarter; (*ПРОСВЕЩ*) term

четвертьфина́л (**-а**) *м* (*СПОРТ*) quarter final

чёткий *прил* (*движения*) precise

чётный *прил* (*число*) even

четы́ре (**-ёх**; *instr sg* **-ьмя́**; *см. Table 24*) *чис* (*цифра, число*) four; (*ПРОСВЕЩ*) ≈ B (*school mark*)

четы́реста (**-ёхсо́т**; *см. Table 28*) *чис* four hundred

четырёхуго́льник (**-а**) *м* quadrangle

четы́рнадцатый *чис* fourteenth

четы́рнадцать (**-и**; *как* **пять**; *см. Table 26*) *чис* fourteen

Че́хия (**-и**) *ж* the Czech Republic

чехо́л (**-ла́**) *м* (*для мебели*) cover; (*для гитары, для оружия*)

case

чешу́я (**-и́**) *ж собир* scales *мн*

чин (**-а**; *nom pl* **-ы́**) *м* rank

чини́ть (**-ю́, -ишь**; *pf* **по**~) *несов перех* to mend, repair; (*pf* **о**~; *карандаш*) to sharpen

чино́вник (**-а**) *м* (*служащий*) official

чи́псы (**-ов**) *мн* crisps *мн*

чири́кать (**-ю**) *несов* to twitter

чи́сленность (**-и**) *ж* (*армии*) numbers *мн*; (*учащихся*) number; ~ **населе́ния** population

числи́тельное (**-ого**) *ср* numeral

число́ (**-ла́**; *nom pl* **-ла**, *gen pl* **-ел**) *ср* number; (*день месяца*) date; **быть** (*impf*) **в** ~**ле́** +*gen* to be among(st)

чи́стить (**-щу, -стишь**; *pf* **вы́чистить** *или* **по**~) *несов перех* to clean; (*зубы*) to brush, clean; (*pf* **по**~; *яблоко, картошку*) to peel; (*рыбу*) to scale

чи́сто *нареч* (*только*) purely; (*убранный, сделанный*) neatly ♦ *как сказ*: **в до́ме** ~ the house is clean

чистови́к (**-а́**) *м* fair copy

чистосерде́чный *прил* sincere

чистота́ (**-ы́**) *ж* purity; **у него́ в до́ме всегда́** ~ his house is always clean

чи́стый *прил* (*одежда, комната*) clean; (*совесть, небо*) clear; (*золото, спирт*) pure; (*прибыль, вес*) net; (*случайность*) pure; **экологи́чески** ~ organic

чита́льный *прил*: ~ **зал** reading room

чита́тель (**-я**) *м* reader

чита́ть (**-ю**; *pf* **прочёсть** *или* **про**~) *несов перех* to read; (*лекцию*) to give

чиха́ть (**-ю**; *pf* **чихну́ть**) *несов* to sneeze

член (-а) *м* member; (*обычно мн: коне́чности*) limb; **половой ~** penis; **~ предложе́ния** part of a sentence

чо́каться (-юсь; *pf* **чо́кнуться**) *несов возв* to clink glasses (*during toast*)

чрева́тый *прил*: ~ +*instr* fraught with

чрезвыча́йно *нареч* extremely

чрезвыча́йный *прил* (*исключи́тельный*) extraordinary; (*экстренный*) emergency; **~ое положе́ние** state of emergency

чрезме́рный *прил* excessive

чте́ние (-я) *ср* reading

KEYWORD

что (*чего́*; *см. Table 7*) *мест* 1 (*вопроси́тельное*) what; **что ты сказа́л?** what did you say?; **что Вы говори́те!** you don't say! 2 (*относи́тельное*) which; **она́ мне не поздоро́валась, что мне бы́ло неприя́тно** she did not say hello, which wasn't nice for me; **что ни говори́ ...** whatever you say ... 3 (*сто́лько ско́лько*): **она́ закрича́ла что бы́ло сил** she shouted with all her might 4 (*разг: что-нибудь*) anything; **е́сли что случи́тся** if anything happens, **в слу́чае чего́** if anything happens; **чуть что - сра́зу скажи́ мне** get in touch at the slightest thing
♦ *нареч* (*почему́*) why; **что ты грусти́шь?** why are you sad?
♦ *союз* 1 (*при сообще́нии, выска́зывании*): **я зна́ю, что на́до де́лать** I know what must be done; **я зна́ю, что он прие́дет** I know that he will come 2 (*во фра́зах*): **а что?** (*разг*) why (do you ask?); **к чему́** (*зачем*)

why; **не́ за что!** not at all! (*BRIT*), you're welcome! (*US*); **ни за что!** (*разг*) no way!; **ни за что ни про что** (*разг*) for no (good) reason at all; **что ты!** (*при возраже́нии*) what!; **я здесь ни при чём** it has nothing to do with me; **что к чему** (*разг*) what's what

чтоб *союз* = **чтобы**

KEYWORD

чтобы *союз*: **чтобы** +*infin* (*выражает цель*) in order или so as to do
♦ *союз*, +*pt* 1 (*выражает цель*) so that 2 (*выражает жела́тельность*): **я хочу́, чтобы она́ пришла́** I want her to come 3 (*выражает возмо́жность*): **не мо́жет быть, чтобы он так поступи́л** it can't be possible that he could have acted like that
♦ *част* 1 (*выражает пожела́ние*): **чтобы она́ заболе́ла!** I hope she gets ill! 2 (*выражает тре́бование*): **чтобы я его́ здесь бо́льше не ви́дел!** I hope (that) I never see him here again!

что́-либо (*чего́-либо*; *как что; см. Table 7*) *мест* = **что́-нибудь**

что́-нибудь (*чего́-нибудь*; *как что; см. Table 7*) *мест* (*в утвержде́нии*) something; (*в вопро́се*) anything

что́-то (*чего́-то*; *как что; см. Table 7*) *мест* something; (*приблизи́тельно*) something like
♦ *нареч* (*разг: почему́-то*) somehow

чувстви́тельный *прил* sensitive

чу́вство (-а) *ср* feeling; ~ +*gen*

(*юмора, долга*) sense of

чу́вств|**овать** (**-ую**; *pf* **по~**) *несов перех* to feel; (*присутствие, опасность*) to sense; ~ (*impf*) **себя́ хорошо́/нело́вко** to feel good/ awkward; **~ся** *несов возв* (*жара, усталость*) to be felt

чугу́н (**-а́**) *м* cast iron

чуда́к (**-а́**) *м* eccentric

чудеса́ *итп сущ см.* **чу́до**

чуде́сный *прил* (*очень хороший*) marvellous (*BRIT*), marvelous (*US*), wonderful; (*необычный*) miraculous

чу́д|**о** (**-а**; *nom pl* **-еса́**, *gen pl* **-е́с**, *dat pl* **-еса́м**) *ср* miracle

чудо́вищ|**е** (**-а**) *ср* monster

чудо́вищный *прил* monstrous

чу́дом *нареч* by a miracle

чу́ждый *прил* alien

чужо́й *прил* (*вещь*) someone *или* somebody else's; (*речь, обычай*) foreign; (*человек*) strange

чул|**о́к** (**-ка́**; *gen pl* **-о́к**, *dat pl* **-ка́м**) *м* (*обычно мн*) stocking

чум|**а́** (**-ы́**) *ж* plague

чу́ткий *прил* sensitive; (*добрый*) sympathetic

чу́точку *нареч* (*разг*) a tiny bit

чуть *нареч* (*разг: едва*) hardly; (*немного*) a little ♦ *союз* (*как только*) as soon as; ~ (*было*) **не** almost, nearly; ~ **что** (*разг*) at the slightest thing

чуть-чуть *нареч* (*разг*) a little

чу́чел|**о** (**-а**) *ср* scarecrow

чушь (**-и**) *ж* (*разг*) rubbish (*BRIT*), garbage (*US*), nonsense

чу́|**ять** (**-ю**) *несов перех* (*собака*) to scent; (*предвидеть*) to sense

чьё (**чьего́**) *мест см.* **чей**

чьи (**чьих**) *мест см.* **чей**

чья (**чьей**) *мест см.* **чей**

Ш, ш

шаг (**-а**; *nom pl* **-и́**) *м* step

шага́|**ть** (**-ю**) *несов* to march

шагн|**у́ть** (**-у́, -ёшь**) *сов* to step, take a step

ша́йб|**а** (**-ы**) *ж* (*СПОРТ*) puck

ша́|**йка** (**-йки**; *gen pl* **-ек**) *ж* gang

шака́л (**-а**) *м* jackal

шаль (**-и**) *ж* shawl

шампа́нск|**ое** (**-ого**) *ср* champagne

шампиньо́н (**-а**) *м* (*БОТ*) (field) mushroom

шампу́н|**ь** (**-я**) *м* shampoo

шанс (**-а**) *м* chance

шанта́ж (**-а́**) *м* blackmail

шантажи́р|**овать** (**-ую**) *несов перех* to blackmail

ша́п|**ка** (**-ки**; *gen pl* **-ок**) *ж* hat

шар (**-а**; *nom pl* **-ы́**) *м* (*ГЕОМ*) sphere; (*gen sg* **-а**; *бильярдный итп*) ball; **возду́шный ~** balloon

ша́рик (**-а**) *м* (*детский*) balloon

ша́риков|**ый** *прил:* **~ая ру́чка** ballpoint pen

ша́р|**ить** (**-ю, -ишь**) *несов* (*разг*): ~ (**рука́ми**) to grope

ша́рка|**ть** (**-ю**) *несов:* ~ **+***instr* to shuffle

шарф (**-а**) *м* scarf

шасси́ *ср нескл* (*самолёта*) landing gear; (*автомобиля*) chassis

шата́|**ть** (**-ю**) *несов перех* (*раскачивать*) to rock; **~ся** *несов возв* (*зуб*) to be loose *или* wobbly; (*стол*) to shake; (*от ветра*) to shake; (*от усталости*) to reel; (*по улицам*) to hang around

шах (**-а**) *м* (*монарх*) shah; (*в шахматах*) check

ша́хматный *прил* chess

шáхмат|ы (-) мн (игра) chess ед; (фигуры) chessmen мн

шáхт|а (-ы) ж мine; (лифта) shaft

шахтёр (-а) м miner

шáш|ки (-ек) мн (игра) draughts ед (BRIT), checkers ед (US)

шашлы́к (-á) м shashlik, kebab

швабр|а (-ы) ж mop

швартов|áть (-ýю; pf при~) несов перех to moor

швед (-а) м Swede

швéдский прил Swedish

швéйный прил sewing

швейцáр (-а) м doorman

швейцáр|ец (-ца) м Swiss

Швейцáри|я (-и) ж Switzerland

швейцáрский прил Swiss

Швéци|я (-и) ж Sweden

швея́ (-и́) ж seamstress

швыря́|ть (-ю) несов перех to hurl

шевел|и́ть (-ю́, -и́шь; pf по~) несов перех (сено) to turn over; (подлеж: ветер) to stir ♦ неперех: ~ +instr (пальцами, губами) to move; **~ся** (pf по~ся) несов возв to stir

шедéвр (-а) м masterpiece

шёл несов см. **идти́**

шелест|éть (-и́шь) несов to rustle

шёлк (-а; nom pl -á) м silk

шёлковый прил silk

шелуш|и́ться (-ýсь, -и́шься) несов возв to peel

шепн|ýть (-ý, -ёшь) сов перех to whisper

шёпот (-а) м whisper

шёпотом нареч in a whisper

шеп|тáть (-чý, -чешь) несов перех to whisper; **~ся** несов возв to whisper to each other

шерéнг|а (-и) ж (солдат) rank

шерст|ь (-и) ж (животного) hair; (пряжа, ткань) wool

шерстяно́й прил (пряжа, ткань) woollen (BRIT), woolen (US)

шершáвый прил rough

шéстер|о (-ы́х; см. Table 30b) чис six

шестидеся́тый чис sixtieth

шестнáдцатый чис sixteenth

шестнáдцат|ь (-и; как пять; см. Table 26) чис sixteen

шесто́й чис sixth

шест|ь (-и; как пять; см. Table 26) чис six

шест|ьдеся́т (-и́десяти; как пятьдеся́т; см. Table 26) чис sixty

шест|ьсо́т (-исо́т; как пятьсо́т; см. Table 28) чис six hundred

шеф (-а) м (полиции) chief; (разг: начальник) boss; (благотворитель: лицо) patron; (организация) sponsor

шéфств|о (-а) ср: **~ над** +instr (лица) patronage of; (организация) sponsorship of

шéфств|овать (-ую) несов: **~ над** +instr (лицо) to be patron of; (организация) to sponsor

шé|я (-и) ж (АНАТ) neck

шиворот (-а) м (разг): **за ~** by the collar

шизофрéник (-а) м schizophrenic

шизофрéни|я (-и) ж schizophrenia

шикáрный прил (разг) glamorous, chic

шимпанзé м нескл chimpanzee

шин|а (-ы) ж (АВТ) tyre (BRIT), tire (US)

шинéл|ь (-и) ж greatcoat

шинк|овáть (-ýю; pf на~) несов перех (овощи) to shred

шип (-á) м (растения) thorn; (на колесе) stud; (на ботинке) spike

шип|éть (-лю́, -и́шь) несов to hiss; (шампáнское) to fizz

шипýчий прил fizzy

ши́ре *сравн прил от* **широ́кий**
♦ *сравн нареч от* **широко́**

ширин|**а́** (**-ы́**) *ж* width; **доро́жка**
ме́тр ~о́й *или* **в ~у́** a path a metre
(*BRIT*) *или* meter (*US*) wide

ши́рм|**а** (**-ы**) *ж* screen

широ́кий *прил* wide; **степи́,**
пла́ны) extensive; (*перен*:
обще́ственность) general;
(: *смысл*) broad; (: *нату́ра, жест*)
generous; **това́ры ~ого**
потребле́ния (*ЭКОН*) consumer
goods

широко́ *нареч* (*раски́нуться*)
widely; (*улыба́ться*) broadly

широкоэкра́нный *прил* (*фильм*)
wide-screen

широт|**а́** (**-оты́**) *ж* breadth; (*nom pl*
-о́ты; *ГЕО*) latitude

ширпотре́б (**-а**) *м сокр* =
широ́кое потребле́ние) (*разг*: *о*
това́рах) consumer goods *мн*; (: *о*
плохо́м това́ре) shoddy goods *мн*

шить (**шью, шьёшь**; *pf* **с~**)
несов перех (*пла́тье итп*) to sew

ши́фер (**-а**) *м* slate

шифр (**-а**) *м* code, cipher

шиш (**-а́**) *м* (*разг*: *gesture of refusal*;
(**ни**) **-а́** (*разг*: *ничего*) nothing at
all

ши́шк|**а** (**-и**; *gen pl* **-ек**) *ж* (*БОТ*)
cone; (*на лбу*) bump, lump

шкал|**а́** (**-ы́**) *ж* scale

шкату́л|**ка** (**-ки**; *gen pl* **-ок**) *ж*
casket

шкаф (**-а**; *loc sg* **-ý**, *nom pl* **-ы́**) *м*
(*для оде́жды*) wardrobe; (*для*
посу́ды) cupboard; **кни́жный ~**
bookcase

шки́пер (**-а**) *м* (*МОР*) skipper

шко́л|**а** (**-ы**) *ж* school; (*мили́ции*)
academy; **сре́дняя ~** secondary
(*BRIT*) *или* high (*US*) school

шко́ла-интерна́т (**-ы**, **-а́**) *ж*
boarding school

шко́льник (**-а**) *м* schoolboy

шко́льница (**-ы**) *ж* schoolgirl

шко́льный *прил* (*зда́ние*) school

шку́р|**а** (**-ы**) *ж* (*живо́тного*) fur;
(*уби́того живо́тного*) skin;
(: *обрабо́танная*) hide

шла *несов см.* **идти́**

шлагба́ум (**-а**) *м* barrier

шланг (**-а**) *м* hose

шлем (**-а**) *м* helmet

шли *несов см.* **идти́**

шлиф|**ова́ть** (**-у́ю**; *pf* **от~**) *несов*
перех (*ТЕХ*) to grind

шло *несов см.* **идти́**

шлю́п|**ка** (**-ки**; *gen pl* **-ок**) *ж* (*МОР*)
dinghy; **спаса́тельная ~** lifeboat

шля́п|**а** (**-ы**) *ж* hat

шля́п|**ка** (**-ки**; *gen pl* **-ок**) *ж* hat;
(*гвоздя́*) head; (*гриба́*) cap

шмел|**ь** (**-я́**) *м* bumblebee

шмы́га|ть (**-ю**) *несов*: **~ но́сом** to
sniff

шнур (**-а́**; *верёвка*) cord;
(*телефо́нный, ла́мпы*) cable

шнур|**ова́ть** (**-у́ю**; *pf* **за~**) *несов*
перех (*боти́нки*) to lace up

шнур|**о́к** (**-ка́**) *м* (*боти́нка*) lace

шов (**шва**; *швейный*) seam;
(*хирурги́ческий*) stitch, suture;
(*намёточный итп*) stitch

шовини́зм (**-а**) *м* chauvinism

шок (**-а**) *м* (*МЕД, перен*) shock

шоки́р|**овать** (**-ую**) (*не*)*сов*
перех to shock

шокола́д (**-а**) *м* chocolate

шокола́дный *прил* chocolate

шо́рох (**-а**) *м* rustle

шо́рт|**ы** (**-**) *м shorts мн*

шоссе́ *ср нескл* highway

шотла́нд|**ец** (**-ца**) *м* Scotsman

Шотла́ндия (**-и**) *ж* Scotland

шотла́ндский *прил* Scottish,
Scots

шо́у *ср нескл* (*также перен*) show

шофёр (**-а**) *м* driver

шпа́г|а (-и) ж sword

шпага́т (-а) м (бечёвка) string, twine

шпакл|ева́ть (-ю́ю; pf за~) несов перех to fill

шпаклёвк|а (-и) ж (замазка) filler

шпа́л|а (-ы) ж sleeper (RAIL)

шпи́л|ь (-я) м spire

шпи́ль|ка (-ьки; gen pl -ек) ж (для волос) hairpin; (каблук) stiletto (heel)

шпина́т (-а) м spinach

шпингале́т (-а) м (на окне) catch

шпио́н (-а) м spy

шпиона́ж (-а) м espionage

шпио́н|ить (-ю, -ишь) несов (разг) to spy

шприц (-а) м syringe

шпро́т|ы (-ов) мн sprats мн

шрам (-а) м (на теле) scar

шрифт (-а; nom pl -ы́) м type

штаб (-а) м headquarters мн

штамп (-а) м (печать) stamp

штамп|ова́ть (-у́ю; pf про~) несов перех (документы) to stamp; (pf от~; детали) to punch, press

шта́нг|а (-и) ж (СПОРТ, в тяжёлой атлетике) weight; (: ворот) post

штан|ы́ (-о́в) мн trousers мн

штат (-а) м (государства) state; (работники) staff

шта́тный прил (сотрудник) permanent

шта́тск|ий прил (одежда) civilian ♦ (-ого) м civilian

штёмпел|ь (-я) м: почто́вый ~ postmark

штёпсел|ь (-я) м (ЭЛЕК) plug

што́па|ть (-ю; pf за~) несов перех to darn

што́пор (-а) м corkscrew

што́р|а (-ы) ж drape

шторм (-а) м gale

штормов|о́й прил stormy; ~о́е

предупрежде́ние storm warning

штраф (-а) м (денежный) fine; (СПОРТ) punishment

штрафн|о́й прил penal ♦ (-о́го) м (СПОРТ: также: ~ уда́р) penalty (kick)

штраф|ова́ть (-у́ю; pf о~) несов перех to fine; (СПОРТ) to penalize

штрих (-а́) м (черта) stroke

штрихово́й прил: ~ код bar code

шту́к|а (-и) ж (предмет) item

штукату́р|ить (-ю, -ишь; pf от~ или о~) несов перех to plaster

штукату́рк|а (-и) ж plaster

штурм (-а) м (ВОЕН) storm

шту́рман (-а) м navigator

штурм|ова́ть (-у́ю) несов перех (ВОЕН) to storm

штык (-а́) м (ВОЕН) bayonet

шу́б|а (-ы) ж (меховая) fur coat

шум (-а; part gen -у) м (звук) noise

шум|е́ть (-лю́, -и́шь) несов to make a noise

шу́мный прил noisy; (разговор, компания) loud; (оживлённый: улица) bustling

шу́рин (-а) м brother-in-law (wife's brother)

шуру́п (-а) м (ТЕХ) screw

шурш|а́ть (-у́, -и́шь) несов to rustle

шу|ти́ть (-чу́, -тишь; pf по~) несов to joke; (смеяться): ~ над +instr to make fun of; (no pf; пренебрегать): ~ +instr (здоровьем) to disregard

шу́т|ка (-ки; gen pl -ок) ж joke; без ~ок joking apart, seriously

шутли́вый прил humourous (BRIT), humorous (US)

шу́точный прил (рассказ) comic, funny

шучу́ несов см. шути́ть

шху́н|а (-ы) ж schooner

шью итп несов см. шить

Щ, щ

щаве́л|ь (-я́) *м* sorrel

ща|ди́ть (-жу́, -ди́шь; *pf* **по~)** *несов перех* to spare

щебе|та́ть (-чу́, -чешь) *несов* to twitter

ще́дрост|ь (-и) *ж* generosity

ще́дрый *прил* generous

щек|а́ (щеки́; *nom pl* **щёки,** *gen pl* **щёк,** *dat pl* **-а́м)** *ж* cheek

щек|ота́ть (-очу́, -о́чешь; *pf* **по~)** *несов перех* to tickle

щекотли́вый *прил (вопрос итп)* delicate

щёлк|а (-и) *ж* small hole

щёлка|ть (-ю) *несов:* ~ *+instr (языко́м)* to click; *(кнуто́м)* to crack

щёлкн|уть (-у) *сов* to click; ~ *(pf)* *+instr (хлысто́м)* to crack

щёлоч|ь (-и) *ж* alkali

щелч|о́к (-ка́) *м* flick; *(звук)* click

щел|ь (-и; *loc sg* **-и́,** *gen pl* **-е́й)** *ж (в полу́)* crack; **смотрова́я ~** peephole

щен|о́к (-ка́; *nom pl* **-я́та,** *gen pl* **-я́т)** *м (собаки)* pup; *(лисы, волчи́цы)* cub

щепети́льный *прил* scrupulous

ще́п|ка (-ки; *gen pl* **-ок)** *ж* splinter; *(для расто́пки):* **-ки** chippings

щепо́т|ка (-ки; *gen pl* **-ок)** *ж* pinch

щети́н|а (-ы) *ж (живо́тных, щётки)* bristle; *(у мужчи́ны)* stubble

щети́н|иться (3sg -ится; *pf* **о~)** *несов возв* to bristle

щёт|ка (-ки; *gen pl* **-ок)** *ж* brush; ~ **для воло́с** hairbrush

щи (щей; *dat pl* **щам)** *мн* cabbage soup *ед*

щи́колот|ка (-ки; *gen pl* **-ок)** *ж* ankle

щипа́|ть (-лю́, -лешь) *несов перех (до бо́ли)* to nip, pinch; *(no pf; подлеж: моро́з)* to bite; *(pf* **о~;** *воло́сы, ку́рицу)* to pluck; **~ся** *несов возв (разг)* to nip, pinch

щипц|ы́ (-о́в) *мн:* **хирурги́ческие ~** forceps; ~ **для са́хара** sugar-tongs

щи́пчик|и (-ов) *мн (для ногте́й)* tweezers *мн*

щит (-а́) *м* shield; *(рекла́мный, баскетбо́льный)* board; *(TEX)* panel

щитови́дн|ый *прил:* **~ая железа́** thyroid gland

щу́к|а (-и) *ж* pike

щу́пальце (-ьца; *nom pl* **-ьца,** *gen pl* **-ец)** *ср (осьмино́га)* tentacle; *(насеко́мых)* feeler

щу́па|ть (-ю; *pf* **по~)** *несов перех* to feel for

щу́р|ить (-ю, -ишь; *pf* **со~)** *несов перех:* ~ **глаза́** to screw up one's eyes; **~ся** *(pf* **со~ся)** *несов возв (от со́лнца)* to squint

Э, э

эвакуа́ци|я (-и) *ж* evacuation

эвакуи́р|овать (-ую) *(не)сов перех* to evacuate

ЭВМ *ж сокр (= электро́нная вычисли́тельная маши́на)* computer

эволю́ци|я (-и) *ж* evolution

эгои́ст (-а) *м* egoist

эгоисти́чный *прил* egotistic(al)

эква́тор (-а) *м* equator

эквивале́нт (-а) *м* equivalent

экза́мен (-а) *м:* ~ **(по** +dat*) (по исто́рии)* exam(ination) (in);

выпускны́е ~ы Finals; **сдава́ть** (*impf*) ~ to sit (*BRIT*) *или* take an exam(ination); **сдать** (*pf*) ~ to pass an exam(ination)

экзамена́тор (-а) м examiner

экзаменацио́нный *прил* examination; (*вопрос*) exam

экземпля́р (-а) м copy

экзоти́ческий *прил* exotic

экипа́ж (-а) м crew

экологи́ческий *прил* ecological

эколо́ги|я (-и) ж ecology

эконо́мик|а (-и) ж economy; (*наука*) economics

экономи́ст (-а) м economist

эконо́м|ить (-лю, -ишь; *pf* **с-)** *несов перех* (*энергию, деньги*) to save; (*выгадывать*): ~ **на** +*prp* to economize *или* save on

экономи́ческий *прил* economic

эконо́ми|я (-и) ж economy

эконо́мный *прил* (*хозяин*) thrifty; (*метод*) economical

экра́н (-а) м screen

экскава́тор (-а) м excavator, digger

экску́рси|я (-и) ж excursion

экскурсово́д (-а) м guide

экспеди́ци|я (-и) ж (*научная*) field work; (*группа людей*) expedition

экспериме́нт (-а) м experiment

эксперименти́р|овать (-ую) *несов*: ~ (**над** *или* **с** +*instr*) to experiment (on *или* with)

экспе́рт (-а) м expert

эксплуата́ци|я (-и) ж exploitation; (*машин*) utilization

эксплуати́р|овать (-ую) *несов перех* to exploit; (*машины*) to use

экспона́т (-а) м exhibit

экспо́рт (-а) м export

экспортёр (-а) м exporter

экспорти́р|овать (-ую) *несов перех* to export

экстрема́льный *прил* extreme

э́кстренный *прил* urgent; (*заседание*) emergency

эласти́чный *прил* stretchy

элева́тор (-а) м (*С.-Х.*) grain store *или* elevator (*US*)

элега́нтный *прил* elegant

эле́ктрик (-а) м electrician

электри́ческий *прил* electric

электри́честв|о (-а) *ср* electricity

электри́чк|а (-ки; *gen pl* **-ек)** ж (*разг*) electric train

электробытов́ой *прил*: **~ые прибо́ры** electrical appliances мн

электрогита́р|а (-ы) ж electric guitar

электромонтёр (-а) м electrician

электро́н (-а) м electron

электро́ник|а (-и) ж electronics

электро́нный *прил* electronic; ~ **микроско́п** electron microscope; **~ая по́чта** (*КОМП*) e-mail, electronic mail; ~ **а́дрес** e-mail address; **~ая страни́ца** webpage

электропереда́ч|а (-и) ж power transmission; **ли́ния ~и** power line

электропо́езд (-а) м electric train

электроприбо́р (-а) м electrical device

электропрово́дк|а (-и) ж (*electrical*) wiring

электроста́нци|я (-и) ж (*electric*) power station

электроте́хник (-а) м electrical engineer

электроэне́рги|я (-и) ж electric power

элеме́нт (-а) м element

элемента́рный *прил* elementary; (*правила*) basic

эли́т|а (-ы) ж *собир* élite

эли́тный *прил* (*лучший*) élite; (*дом, школа*) exclusive

эма́левый *прил* enamel

эмалиро́ванный *прил* enamelled

эма́л|ь (-и) ж enamel

эмба́рго ср нескл embargo

эмбле́м|а (-ы) ж emblem

эмбрио́н (-а) м embryo

эмигра́нт (-а) м emigrant

эмиграцио́нный прил emigration

эмигра́ци|я (-и) ж emigration

эмигри́р|овать (-ую) (не)сов to emigrate

эмоциона́льный прил emotional

эмо́ци|я (-и) ж emotion

эму́льси|я (-и) ж emulsion

энерге́тик|а (-и) ж power industry

энергети́ческий прил energy

энерги́чный прил energetic

эне́рги|я (-и) ж energy

э́нн|ый прил: ~ое число́/коли́чество X number/amount; **в ~ раз** yet again

энтузиа́зм (-а) м enthusiasm

энциклопе́ди|я (-и) ж encyclopaedia (BRIT), encyclopedia (US)

эпи́граф (-а) м epigraph

эпиде́ми|я (-и) ж epidemic

эпизо́д (-а) м episode

эпизоди́ческий прил (явление) random

эпиле́пси|я (-и) ж epilepsy

эпило́г (-а) м epilogue (BRIT), epilog (US)

эпице́нтр (-а) м epicentre (BRIT), epicenter (US)

эпопе́|я (-и) ж epic

э́пос (-а) м epic literature

эпо́х|а (-и) ж epoch

э́р|а (-ы) ж era; **пе́рвый век на́шей ~ы/до на́шей ~ы** the first century AD/BC

эро́зи|я (-и) ж erosion

эроти́ческий прил erotic

эскала́тор (-а) м escalator

эскала́ци|я (-и) ж escalation

эски́з (-а) м (к карти́не) sketch; (к прое́кту) draft

эскимо́ ср нескл choc-ice, Eskimo (US)

эско́рт (-а) м escort

эссе́нци|я (-и) ж (КУЛИН) essence

эстака́д|а (-ы) ж (на доро́ге) flyover (BRIT), overpass

эстафе́т|а (-ы) ж (СПОРТ) relay (race)

эсте́тик|а (-и) ж aesthetics (BRIT), esthetics (US)

эстети́ческий прил aesthetic (BRIT), esthetic (US)

эсто́н|ец (-ца) м Estonian

Эсто́ни|я (-и) ж Estonia

эстра́д|а (-ы) ж (для орке́стра) platform; (вид иску́сства) variety

эстра́дный прил: ~ конце́рт variety show

э́т|а (-ой) мест см. э́тот

эта́ж (-а́) м floor, storey (BRIT), story (US); **пе́рвый/второ́й/тре́тий ~** ground/first/second floor (BRIT), first/second/third floor (US)

эта́же́р|ка (-ки; gen pl **-ок)** ж stack of shelves

этало́н (-а) м (ме́ры) standard; (перен: красоты́) model

эта́п (-а) м (рабо́ты) stage; (го́нки) lap

э́т|и (-их) мест см. э́тот

э́тик|а (-и) ж ethics

этике́т (-а) м etiquette

этике́т|ка (-ки; gen pl **-ок)** ж label

э́тим мест см. э́тот

э́тими мест см. э́ти

этимоло́ги|я (-и) ж etymology

эти́чный прил ethical

KEYWORD

э́т|о (-ого; см. Table 10**)** мест **1** (указа́тельное) this; **э́то бу́дет тру́дно** this will be difficult; **он на всё соглаша́ется - э́то о́чень стра́нно** he is agreeing to everything, this is most strange

2 (связка в сказуемом): **любо́вь - э́то проще́ние** love is forgiveness

3 (как подлежащее): **с кем ты разгова́ривал? - э́то была́ моя́ сестра́** who were you talking to? - that was my sister; **как э́то произошло́?** how did it happen?

4 (для усиления): **э́то он во всём винова́т** he is the one who is to blame for everything

♦ част 1 (служит для усиления): **кто э́то звони́л?** who was it who phoned (BRIT) или called (US)?

KEYWORD

э́т|от (-ого; f э́та, nt э́то, pl э́ти) (см. Table 10) мест 1 (указательное: о близком предмете) this; (: о близких предметах) these; **э́тот дом** this house; **э́ти кни́ги** these books

2 (о данном времени) this; **э́тот год осо́бенно тру́дный** this year is particularly hard; **в э́ти дни я при́нял реше́ние** in the last few days I have come to a decision; **э́тот са́мый** that very

3 (о чём-то только что упомянутом) this; **он ложи́лся в 10 часо́в ве́чера - э́та привы́чка меня́ всегда́ удивля́ла** he used to go to bed at 10 p.m., this habit always amazed me

♦ ср (как сущ: об одном предмете) this one; (: о многих предметах) these ones; **дай мне вот э́ти** give me these ones; **э́тот на всё спосо́бен** this one is capable of anything; **при э́том** at that

этю́д (-а) м sketch

эфи́р (-а) м (ХИМ) ether; (воздушное пространство) air; **выходи́ть (вы́йти** pf**) в** ~ to go on the air; **прямо́й** ~ live broadcast

эффе́кт (-а) м effect

эффекти́вный прил effective

эффе́ктный прил (одежда) striking; (речь) impressive

э́х|о (-а) ср echo

эшело́н (-а) м echelon; (поезд) special train

Ю, ю

ю. сокр (= юг) S; (= ю́жный) S

юбиле́|й (-я) м (годовщина) anniversary; (празднование) jubilee

ю́б|ка (-ки; gen pl -ок) ж skirt

ювели́р (-а) м jeweller (BRIT), jeweler (US)

ювели́рный прил jewellery (BRIT), jewellery (US)

юг (-а) м south

южа́нин (-а) м southerner

ю́жный прил southern

ю́мор (-а) м humour (BRIT), humor (US)

юмори́ст (-а) м comedian

юмористи́ческий прил humorous

ЮНЕ́СКО ср сокр UNESCO

юнио́р (-а) м (СПОРТ) junior

ю́ность (-и) ж youth

ю́нош|а (-и; nom pl -и, gen pl -ей) м young man

ю́ношеский прил youthful; (организация) youth

ю́ный прил (молодой) young

юриди́ческий прил (сила) juridical; (образование) legal; ~ **факульте́т** law faculty; **~ая консульта́ция** ≈ legal advice office

юрисди́кци|я (-и) ж jurisdiction

юрискóнсульт (-а) *м* ≈ solicitor, ≈ lawyer

юрúст (-а) *м* lawyer

юстúци|**я** (-и) *ж* judiciary; **Министéрство ~и** Ministry of Justice

Я, я

я (меня; *см. Table 6a*) *мест I* ♦ *сущ нескл* (личность) the self, the ego

я́бед|**а** (-ы) *м/ж* sneak

я́беднича|**ть** (-ю; *pf* на~) *несов*: ~ **на** +*acc* (*разг*) to tell tales about

я́блок|**о** (-а; *nom pl* -и) *ср* apple

я́блон|**я** (-и) *ж* apple tree

я́блочный *прил* apple

яв|**úться** (-люсь, -ишься; *impf* явля́ться) *сов возв* to appear; (*домой, в гости*) to arrive; **явля́ться** (~ *pf*) +*instr* (причиной) to be

я́в|**ка** (-ки; *gen pl* -ок) *ж* appearance

явлéни|**е** (-я) *ср* phenomenon; (*РЕЛ*) manifestation

явля́ться (-юсь) *несов от* **яви́ться** ♦ *возв*: ~ +*instr* to be

я́вно *нареч* (очевидно) obviously

я́вный *прил* (вражда) overt; (ложь) obvious

явь (-и) *ж* reality

ягн|**ёнок** (-ёнка; *nom pl* -я́та, *gen pl* -я́т) *м* lamb

я́год|**а** (-ы) *ж* berry

ягоди́ц|**а** (-ы) *ж* (*обычно мн*) buttock

яд (-а) *м* poison

я́дерный *прил* nuclear

ядови́тый *прил* poisonous

яд|**ро́** (-ра́; *nom pl* -ра, *gen pl* -ер) *ср* nucleus; (*Земли, древесины*) core; (*СПОРТ*) shot

я́зв|**а** (-ы) *ж* (*МЕД*) ulcer

язви́тельный *прил* scathing

язв|**úть** (-лю́, -úшь; *pf* съ~) *несов*: ~ +*dat* to sneer at

язы́к (-á) *м* tongue; (*русский, разговорный*) language; **владéть** (*impf*) **языко́м** to speak a language

языково́й *прил* language

язы́ческий *прил* pagan

язы́ч|**о́к** (-ка́) *м* (*ботинка*) tongue

яи́чница (-ы) *ж* fried eggs *мн*

яи́чн|**ый** *прил*: ~ **бело́к** egg white; ~ **скорлупа́** eggshell

яйц|**о́** (яйца́; *nom pl* я́йца, *gen pl* яи́ц, *dat pl* я́йцам) *ср* egg; ~ **всмя́тку/вкруту́ю** soft-boiled/hard-boiled egg

ЯК (*м сокр* = самолёт констру́кции А.С. Я́ковлева

я́кобы *союз* (будто бы) that ♦ *част* supposedly

я́кор|**ь** (-я; *nom pl* -я́) *м* (*МОР*) anchor

я́м|**а** (-ы) *ж* (*в земле*) pit

я́моч|**ка** (-ки; *gen pl* -ек) *ж* dimple

янва́р|**ь** (-я́) *м* January

янта́р|**ь** (-я́) *м* amber

Япо́ни|**я** (-и) *ж* Japan

я́ркий *прил* bright; (*перен*: человек, речь) brilliant

ярлы́к (-á) *м* label

я́рмар|**ка** (-ки; *gen pl* -ок) *ж* fair; **междунаро́дная** ~ international trade fair

я́ростный *прил* (взгляд, слова) furious; (атака, критика) fierce

я́рост|**ь** (-и) *ж* fury

я́рус (-а) *м* (*в теáтре*) circle

я́сл|**и** (-ей) *мн* (также: *де́тские* ~) crèche *ед*, day nursery *ед* (*BRIT*)

я́сно *нареч* clearly ♦ *как сказ* **о пого́де** it's fine; (*поня́тно*) it's clear

я́сност|**ь** (-и) *ж* clarity

я́сный *прил* clear

я́стреб (-а) м hawk

я́хт|**а** (-ы) ж yacht

яхтсме́н (-а) м yachtsman

яче́|**йка** (-йки; gen pl -ек) ж (сотовая) cell; (профсоюзная) branch; (для почты) pigeonhole

ячме́нный прил barley

ячме́н|**ь** (-я́) м barley

я́щериц|**а** (-ы) ж lizard

я́щик (-а) м (вместилище: большой) chest; (: маленький) box; (в письменном столе итп) drawer; **му́сорный** ~ dustbin (BRIT), garbage can (US); **почто́вый** ~ (на улице) postbox; (дома) letterbox

я́щур (-а) м foot-and-mouth disease

А, а
Б, б
В, в
Г, г
Д, д
Е, е
Ж, ж
З, з
И, и
Й, й
К, к
Л, л
М, м
Н, н
О, о
П, п
Р, р
С, с
Т, т
У, у
Ф, ф
Х, х
Ц, ц
Ч, ч
Ш, ш
Щ, щ
Ъ, ъ
Ы, ы
Ь, ь
Э, э
Ю, ю
Я, я

A, a
B, b
C, c
D, d
E, e
F, f
G, g
H, h
I, i
J, j
K, k
L, l
M, m
N, n
O, o
P, p
Q, q
R, r
S, s
T, t
U, u
V, v
W, w
X, x
Y, y
Z, z

A, a

A [eɪ] n (MUS) ля nt ind

KEYWORD

a [ə] (before vowel or silent h: **an**) indef art **1**: **a book** кни́га; **an apple** я́блоко; **she's a student** она́ студе́нтка

2 (instead of the number "one"): **a week ago** неде́лю наза́д; **a hundred pounds** сто фу́нтов

3 (in expressing time) в +acc; **3 a day** 3 в день; **10 km an hour** 10 км в час

4 (in expressing prices): **30p a kilo** 30 пе́нсов килогра́мм; **£5 a person** £5 с ка́ждого

AA n abbr (BRIT) (= Automobile Association) автомоби́льная ассоциа́ция

AAA n abbr (= American Automobile Association) америка́нская автомоби́льная ассоциа́ция

aback [əˈbæk] adv: **I was taken ~** я был поражён

abandon [əˈbændən] vt (person) покида́ть (поки́нуть pf); (search) прекраща́ть (прекрати́ть pf); (hope) оставля́ть (оста́вить pf); (idea) отка́зываться (отказа́ться pf) от +gen

abbey [ˈæbɪ] n абба́тство

abbreviation [əbriːvɪˈeɪʃən] n сокраще́ние

abdomen [ˈæbdəmən] n брюшна́я по́лость f, живо́т

abide [əˈbaɪd] vt: **I can't ~ it/him** я э́того/его́ не выношу́; **~ by** vt fus соблюда́ть (соблюсти́ pf)

ability [əˈbɪlɪtɪ] n (capacity) спосо́бность f; (talent, skill) спосо́бности fpl

ablaze [əˈbleɪz] adj: **to be ~** (on fire) быть (impf) в огне́

able [ˈeɪbl] adj (capable) спосо́бный; (skilled) уме́лый; **he is ~ to ...** он спосо́бен +infin

abnormal [æbˈnɔːml] adj ненорма́льный

aboard [əˈbɔːd] prep (position, NAUT, AVIAT) на борту́ +gen; (: train, bus) в +prp; (motion, NAUT, AVIAT) на борт +gen; (: train, bus) в +acc
♦ adv: **to climb ~** (train) сади́ться (сесть pf) в по́езд

abolish [əˈbɔlɪʃ] vt отменя́ть (отмени́ть pf)

abolition [æbəˈlɪʃən] n отме́на

abortion [əˈbɔːʃən] n або́рт; **to have an ~** де́лать (сде́лать pf) або́рт

KEYWORD

about [əˈbaut] adv **1** (approximately: referring to time, price etc) о́коло +gen, приме́рно +acc; **at about two (o'clock)** приме́рно в два (часа́), о́коло двух (часо́в); **I've just about finished** я почти́ зако́нчил

2 (approximately: referring to height, size etc) о́коло +gen, приме́рно +nom; **the room is about 10 metres wide** ко́мната приме́рно 10 ме́тров в ширину́; **she is about your age** она́ приме́рно Ва́шего во́зраста

3 (referring to place) повсю́ду; **to leave things lying about** разбра́сывать (разбро́сать pf) ве́щи повсю́ду; **to run/walk about** бе́гать (impf)/ходи́ть (impf) вокру́г

4: **to be about to do** собира́ться

(собра́ться *pf*) +*infin*; **he was
about to go to bed** он собра́лся
лечь спать
♦ *prep* **1** (*relating to*) о(б) +*prp*; **a
book about London** кни́га о
Ло́ндоне; **what is it about?** о чём
э́то?; **what** *or* **how about doing
...?** как насчёт того́, что́бы +*infin*
...? **2** (*referring to place*) по +*dat*; **to
walk about the town** ходи́ть
(*impf*) по го́роду; **her clothes were
scattered about the room** её
оде́жда была́ разбро́сана по
ко́мнате

above [ə'bʌv] *adv* (*higher up*)
наверху́ ♦ *prep* (*higher than*) над
+*instr* (: *in rank etc*) вы́ше +*gen*;
from ~ све́рху; **mentioned ~**
вышеупомя́нутый; **~ all** пре́жде
всего́
abrasive [ə'breɪzɪv] *adj* (*manner*)
жёсткий
abroad [ə'brɔːd] *adv* (*to be*) за
грани́цей *or* рубежо́м; (*to go*) за
грани́цу *or* рубе́ж; (*to come from*)
из-за грани́цы *or* рубежа́
abrupt [ə'brʌpt] *adj* (*action, ending*)
внеза́пный; (*person, manner*)
ре́зкий; **~ly** (*leave, end*)
внеза́пно; (*speak*) ре́зко
absence ['æbsəns] *n* отсу́тствие
absent ['æbsənt] *adj* (*person*)
отсу́тствующий
absolute ['æbsəluːt] *adj*
абсолю́тный; **~ly** [æbsə'luːtlɪ] *adv*
абсолю́тно, соверше́нно; (*certainly*) безусло́вно
absorb [əb'zɔːb] *vt* (*liquid,
information*) впи́тывать (впита́ть
pf); (*light, firm*) поглоща́ть
(поглоти́ть *pf*); **he is ~ed in a
book** он поглощён кни́гой; **~ent
cotton** *n* (*US*) гигроскопи́ческая
ва́та; **~ing** *adj* увлека́ющий
absorption [əb'sɔːpʃən] *n* (*see vt*)

впи́тывание; поглоще́ние;
(*interest*) увлечённость *f*
abstract ['æbstrækt] *adj*
абстра́ктный
absurd [əb'sɔːd] *adj* абсу́рдный,
неле́пый
abundant [ə'bʌndənt] *adj*
оби́льный
abuse *n* [ə'bjuːs] *vb* [ə'bjuːz] *n*
(*insults*) брань *f*; (*ill-treatment*)
жесто́кое обраще́ние; (*misuse*)
злоупотребле́ние ♦ *vt* (*see n*)
оскорбля́ть (оскорби́ть *pf*);
жесто́ко обраща́ться (*impf*) с
+*instr*; злоупотребля́ть
(злоупотреби́ть *pf*) +*instr*
abusive [ə'bjuːsɪv] *adj* (*person*)
гру́бый, жесто́кий
AC *abbr* (= *alternating current*)
переме́нный ток
academic [ækə'dɛmɪk] *adj* (*system*)
академи́ческий; (*qualifications*)
учёный; (*work, books*) нау́чный;
(*person*) интеллектуа́льный ♦ *n*
учёный(ая) *m(f) adj*
academy [ə'kædəmɪ] *n* (*learned
body*) акаде́мия; (*college*)
учи́лище; (*in Scotland*) сре́дняя
шко́ла; **~ of music**
консервато́рия
accelerate [æk'sɛləreɪt] *vi* (*AUT*)
разгоня́ться (разогна́ться *pf*)
acceleration [ækselə'reɪʃən] *n* (*AUT*)
разго́н
accelerator [æk'sɛləreɪtər] *n*
акселера́тор
accent ['æksɛnt] *n* акце́нт; (*stress
mark*) знак ударе́ния
accept [ək'sɛpt] *vt* принима́ть
(приня́ть *pf*); (*fact, situation*)
мири́ться (примири́ться *pf*) с
+*instr*; (*responsibility, blame*)
принима́ть (приня́ть *pf*) на себя́;
~able *adj* приёмлемый; **~ance** *n*
приня́тие; (*of fact*) прия́тие
access ['æksɛs] *n* до́ступ; **~ible**

[æk'sesəbl] adj доступный

accessory [æk'sesərɪ] n
принадлежность f; **accessories**
npl (DRESS) аксессуары mpl

accident [ˈæksɪdənt] n (disaster)
несчастный случай; (in car etc)
авария; **by** ~ случайно; ~**al**
[æksɪˈdɛntl] adj случайный; ~**ally**
[æksɪˈdɛntəlɪ] adv случайно

acclaim [əˈkleɪm] n признание

accommodate [əˈkɔmədeɪt] vt
(subj: person) предоставлять
(предоставить pf) жильё +dat;
(: car, hotel etc) вмещать
(вместить pf)

accommodation [əkɔməˈdeɪʃən] n
(to live in) жильё; (to work in)
помещение; ~**s** npl (US: lodgings)
жильё ntsg

accompaniment [əˈkʌmpənɪmənt]
n сопровождение; (MUS)
аккомпанемент

accompany [əˈkʌmpənɪ] vt
сопровождать (сопроводить pf);
(MUS) аккомпанировать (impf)
+dat

accomplice [əˈkʌmplɪs] n
сообщник(ица)

accomplish [əˈkʌmplɪʃ] vt (task)
завершать (завершить pf); (goal)
достигать (достигнуть or
достичь pf) +gen; ~**ed** adj (person)
талантливый

accord [əˈkɔːd] n: **of his own** ~ по
собственному желанию; **of its
own** ~ сам по себе; ~**ance** n: **in
~ance with** в согласии or
соответствии с +instr; ~**ing** prep:
~**ing to** согласно +dat; ~**ingly** adv
соответствующим образом; (as
a result) соответственно

account [əˈkaunt] n (bill) счёт; (in
bank) (расчётный) счёт; (report)
отчёт; ~**s** npl (COMM) счета mpl;
to keep an ~ of вести (impf) счёт

+gen or +dat; **to bring sb to ~ for
sth** призывать (призвать pf)
кого-н к ответу за что-н; **by all
~s** по всем сведениям; **it is of no
~** ни на чём важно; **on ~** в кредит;
on no ~ ни в коем случае; **on ~
of** по причине +gen; **to take
into~, take ~ of** принимать
(принять pf) в расчёт (+acc)
(expenses) отчитываться
(отчитаться pf) за +acc; (absence,
failure) объяснять (объяснить pf);
~**able** adj отчётный; **to be ~able
to sb for sth** отвечать (impf) за
что-н перед кем-н; ~**ancy** n
бухгалтерия, бухгалтерское
дело; ~**ant** n бухгалтер

accumulate [əˈkjuːmjuleɪt] vt
накапливать (накопить pf) ♦ vi
накапливаться (накопиться pf)

accuracy [ˈækjurəsɪ] n точность f

accurate [ˈækjurɪt] adj точный;
(person, device) аккуратный; ~**ly**
adv точно

accusation [ækjuˈzeɪʃən] n
обвинение

accuse [əˈkjuːz] vt: **to ~ sb (of sth)**
обвинять (обвинить pf) кого-н (в
чём-н); ~**d** n (LAW): **the ~d**
обвиняемый(ая)

accustomed [əˈkʌstəmd] adj: **I'm ~
to working late/to the heat** я
привык работать поздно/к жаре

ace [eɪs] n (CARDS) туз; (TENNIS)
выигрыш с подачи

ache [eɪk] n боль f ♦ vi болеть
(impf); **my head ~s** у меня болит
голова

achieve [əˈtʃiːv] vt (result)
достигать (достигнуть or
достичь pf) +gen; (success)
добиваться (добиться pf) +gen;
~**ment** n достижение

acid [ˈæsɪd] adj (CHEM) кислотный;
(taste) кислый ♦ n (CHEM)
кислота; ~ **rain** n кислотный

дождь m

acknowledge [ək'nɒlɪdʒ] vt (letter etc): also: ~ **receipt of**) подтвержда́ть (подтверди́ть pf) получе́ние +gen; (fact) признава́ть (призна́ть pf); **~ment** (of letter etc) подтвержде́ние получе́ния

acne ['æknɪ] n угри́ mpl, прыщи́ mpl

acorn ['eɪkɔːn] n жёлудь m

acquaintance [ə'kweɪntəns] n знако́мый(ая) m(f) adj

acquire [ə'kwaɪə'] vt приобрета́ть (приобрести́ pf)

acquisition [ækwɪ'zɪʃən] n приобрете́ние

acre ['eɪkə'] n акр

across [ə'krɒs] prep (over) че́рез +acc; (on the other side of) на друго́й стороне́ +gen, по ту сто́рону +gen; (crosswise over) че́рез +acc, поперёк +gen ♦ adv где-нибу́дь; (measurement: width) ширино́й; to **walk** ~ **the road** переходи́ть (перейти́ pf) доро́гу; to **take sb** ~ **the road** переводи́ть (перевести́ pf) кого́-н че́рез доро́гу; **the lake is 12 km** ~ ширина́ о́зера - 12 км; ~ **from** напро́тив +gen

act [ækt] n (also LAW) акт; (deed) посту́пок; (of play) де́йствие, акт ♦ vi (do sth) поступа́ть (поступи́ть pf), де́йствовать (impf); (behave) вести́ (повести́ pf) себя́; (have effect) де́йствовать (поде́йствовать pf); (THEAT) игра́ть (сыгра́ть pf); **in the** ~ **of** в проце́ссе +gen; **to** ~ **as** де́йствовать (impf) в ка́честве +gen; **~ing** adj: **~ing director** исполня́ющий обя́занности дире́ктора ♦ n (profession) актёрская профе́ссия

action ['ækʃən] n (deed) посту́пок;

де́йствие; (motion) движе́ние; (MIL) вое́нные де́йствия ntpl; (LAW) иск; **the machine was out of** ~ маши́на вы́шла из стро́я; **to take** ~ принима́ть (приня́ть pf) ме́ры

active ['æktɪv] adj акти́вный; (volcano) де́йствующий; **~ly** adv (participate) акти́вно; (discourage, dislike) си́льно

activist ['æktɪvɪst] n активи́ст(ка)

activity [æk'tɪvɪtɪ] n (being active) акти́вность f; (action) де́ятельность f; (pastime) заня́тие

actor ['æktə'] n актёр

actress ['æktrɪs] n актри́са

actual ['æktjʊəl] adj (real) действи́тельный; **the** ~ **work hasn't begun yet** сама́ рабо́та ещё и не начала́сь; **~ly** adv (really) действи́тельно; (in fact) на са́мом де́ле, факти́чески; (even) да́же

acupuncture ['ækjʊpʌŋktʃə'] n иглоука́лывание, акупункту́ра

acute [ə'kjuːt] adj (anxiety) о́стрый; ~ **accent** аку́т

AD adv abbr (= Anno Domini) н.э.

ad [æd] n abbr (inf) = **advertisement**

adamant ['ædəmənt] adj непрекло́нный

adapt [ə'dæpt] vt (alter) приспоса́бливать (приспосо́бить pf) ♦ vi: **to** ~ **(to)** приспоса́бливаться (приспосо́биться pf) (к +dat), адапти́роваться (impf/pf) (к +dat)

add [æd] vt (to collection etc) прибавля́ть (приба́вить pf); (comment) добавля́ть (доба́вить pf); (figures: also: ~ **up**) скла́дывать (сложи́ть pf) ♦ vi: **to** ~ **to** (workload) увели́чивать (увели́чить pf); (problems) усугубля́ть (усугуби́ть pf)

adder ['ædə'] n гадюка

addict ['ædɪkt] n (also: **drug ~**) наркома́н; **~ed** [ə'dɪktɪd] adj: to be **~ed to** (drugs etc) пристрасти́ться (pf) к +dat; (fig): he's **~ed to football** он за́ядлый люби́тель футбо́ла; **~ion** [ə'dɪkʃən] n пристра́стие; **drug ~ion** наркома́ния; **~ive** [ə'dɪktɪv] adj (drug) вызыва́ющий привыка́ние

addition [ə'dɪʃən] n (sum) сложе́ние; (thing added) добавле́ние; (to collection) пополне́ние; **in ~** вдоба́вок, дополни́тельно; **in ~ to** в дополне́ние к +dat; **~al** adj дополни́тельный

address [ə'drɛs] n а́дрес; (speech) речь f ♦ vt (letter) адресова́ть (impf/pf); (person) обраща́ться (обрати́ться pf) к +dat; (problem) занима́ться (заня́ться pf) +instr; **~ book** n записна́я кни́жка

adept ['ædɛpt] adj: **~ at** иску́сный в +prp

adequate ['ædɪkwɪt] adj (sufficient) доста́точный; (satisfactory) адеква́тный

adhere [əd'hɪə'] vi: to **~ to** (fig) приде́рживаться (impf) +gen

adhesive [əd'hi:zɪv] adj кле́йкий ♦ n клей

ad hoc [æd'hɔk] adj (committee) со́зданный на ме́сте

adjacent [ə'dʒeɪsənt] adj: **~ (to)** сме́жный (c +instr)

adjective ['ædʒɛktɪv] n прилага́тельное nt adj

adjust [ə'dʒʌst] vt (plans, views) приспоса́бливать (приспосо́бить pf); (clothing) поправля́ть (попра́вить pf); (mechanism) регули́ровать (отрегули́ровать pf) ♦ vi: to **~ to** приспоса́бливаться (приспосо́биться pf) (к +dat);

~able adj регули́руемый; **~ment** n (to surroundings) адапта́ция; (of prices, wages) регули́рование; to **make ~ments** вноси́ть (внести́ pf) измене́ния в +acc

administer [əd'mɪnɪstə'] vt (country, department) управля́ть (impf) +instr, руководи́ть (impf) +instr; (justice) отправля́ть (impf); (test) проводи́ть (провести́ pf)

administration [ədmɪnɪs'treɪʃən] n (management) администра́ция

administrative [əd'mɪnɪstrətɪv] adj администрати́вный

admiration [ædmə'reɪʃən] n восхище́ние

admire [əd'maɪə'] vt восхища́ться (восхити́ться pf) +instr; (gaze at) любова́ться (impf) +instr, **~r** n покло́нник(ица)

admission [əd'mɪʃən] n (admittance) до́пуск; (entry fee) входна́я пла́та; **"~ free", "free ~"** "вход свобо́дный"

admit [əd'mɪt] vt (confess, accept) признава́ть (призна́ть pf); (permit to enter) впуска́ть (впусти́ть pf); (to hospital) госпитализи́ровать (impf/pf); to **~ to** fus (crime) сознава́ться (созна́ться pf) в +prp; **~tedly** [əd'mɪtɪdlɪ] adv: **~tedly it is not easy** призна́ться, э́то не легко́

adolescence [ædəu'lɛsns] n подро́стковый во́зраст

adolescent [ædəu'lɛsnt] adj подро́стковый ♦ n подро́сток

adopt [ə'dɔpt] vt (son) усыновля́ть (усынови́ть pf); (daughter) удочеря́ть (удочери́ть pf); (policy) принима́ть (приня́ть pf); **~ed** (child) приёмный; **~ion** [ə'dɔpʃən] n (see vt) усыновле́ние; удочере́ние; приня́тие

adore [ə'dɔ:'] vt обожа́ть (impf)

adrenalin [ə'drɛnəlɪn] n адренали́н

Adriatic [eɪdrɪˈætɪk] n: **the ~** Адриатика

adult [ˈædʌlt] n взрослый(ая) m(f) ♦ adj ♦ adj (grown-up) взрослый; **~ film** фильм для взрослых

adultery [əˈdʌltərɪ] n супружеская неверность f

advance [ədˈvɑːns] n (progress) успех; (MIL) наступление f(m); (money) аванс ♦ adj (booking) предварительный ♦ vt (theory, idea) выдвигать (выдвинуть pf) ♦ vi продвигаться (продвинуться pf), (MIL) наступать (impf); **in ~** заранее, предварительно; **to ~ sb money** платить (заплатить pf) кому-н авансом; **~d** adj (studies) для продвинутого уровня; (course) продвинутый; (child, country) развитой; **~d maths** высшая математика

advantage [ədˈvɑːntɪdʒ] n преимущество; **to take ~ of** (person) использовать (pf); **to our ~** в наших интересах; **~ous** [ædvənˈteɪdʒəs] adj (situation) выгодный; **it's ~ous to us** нам это выгодно

adventure [ədˈventʃəʳ] n приключение

adventurous [ədˈventʃərəs] adj (person) смелый

adverb [ˈædvəːb] n наречие

adversary [ˈædvəsərɪ] n противник(ица)

adverse [ˈædvəːs] adj неблагоприятный

adversity [ədˈvəːsɪtɪ] n беда, несчастье

advert [ˈædvəːt] n abbr (BRIT) = **advertisement**

advertise [ˈædvətaɪz] vti рекламировать (impf); **to ~ on television/in a newspaper** давать (дать pf) объявление по телевидению/в газету; **to ~ a job**

объявлять (объявить pf) конкурс на место; **~ for staff** давать (дать pf) объявление, что требуются работники; **~ment** [ədˈvəːtɪsmənt] n реклама; (classified) объявление

advice [ədˈvaɪs] n совет; **a piece of ~** совет; **to take legal ~** обращаться (обратиться pf) за советом к юристу

advisable [ədˈvaɪzəbl] adj целесообразный

advise [ədˈvaɪz] vt советовать (посоветовать pf) +dat; (professionally) консультировать (проконсультировать pf) +gen; **to ~ sb of sth** извещать (известить pf) кого-н о чём-н; **to ~ (sb) against doing** отсоветовать (pf) (кому-н) +impf infin; **~r** n советник, консультант; **legal ~r** юрисконсульт

advisor [ədˈvaɪzəʳ] n = **adviser; ~y** [ədˈvaɪzərɪ] adj консультативный

advocate vb [ˈædvəkeɪt] n [ˈædvəkɪt] vt выступать (выступить pf) за +acc ♦ n (LAW) защитник, адвокат; (supporter): **~** of сторонник(ица) +gen

Aegean [iːˈdʒiːən] n: **the ~** Эгейское море

aerial [ˈɛərɪəl] n антенна ♦ adj воздушный; **~ photography** аэрофотосъёмка

aerobics [ɛəˈrəubɪks] n аэробика

aeroplane [ˈɛərəpleɪn] n (BRIT) самолёт

aerosol [ˈɛərəsɔl] n аэрозоль m

aesthetic [iːsˈθetɪk] adj эстетический

affair [əˈfɛəʳ] n (matter) дело; (also: **love ~**) роман

affect [əˈfekt] vt (influence) действовать (подействовать pf) or влиять (повлиять pf) на +acc; (afflict) поражать (поразить pf);

(*move deeply*) трóгать (трóнуть *pf*)

affection [əˈfekʃən] *n*
привя́занность *f*; **~ate** *adj*
не́жный

affluent [ˈæfluənt] *adj*
благополу́чный

afford [əˈfɔːd] *vt* позволя́ть
(позво́лить *pf*) себе́; **I can't ~ it**
мне э́то не по карма́ну; **I can't ~
the time** мне вре́мя не
позволя́ет; **~able** *adj* досту́пный

Afghanistan [æfˈɡænɪstæn] *n*
Афганиста́н

afloat [əˈfləut] *adv* (*floating*) на
плаву́

afraid [əˈfreɪd] *adj* испу́ганный; **to
be ~ of sth/sb/of doing** боя́ться
(*impf*) чего́-н/кого́-н/+infin; **to be ~
to** боя́ться (побоя́ться *pf*) +infin; **I
am ~ that** (*apology*) бою́сь, что; **I
am ~ so/not** бою́сь, что да/
нет

Africa [ˈæfrɪkə] *n* А́фрика; **African**
adj африка́нский

after [ˈɑːftə] *prep* (*time*) по́сле +gen,
спустя́ +acc, че́рез +acc; (*place*,
order) за +instr ♦ *adv* пото́м, по́сле
♦ *conj* по́сле того́ как; **~ three
years they divorced** спустя́ *or*
че́рез три го́да они́ развели́сь;
who are you ~? кто Вам ну́жен?;
to name sb ~ sb называ́ть
(назва́ть *pf*) кого́-н в честь кого́-н;
it's twenty ~ eight (*US*) сейча́с
два́дцать мину́т девя́того; **to ask ~
sb** справля́ться (спра́виться *pf*)
о ком-н; **~ all** в конце́ концо́в; **~
he left** по́сле того́ как он ушёл; **~
having done this** сде́лав э́то;
~math *n* после́дствия *ntpl*;
~noon *n* втора́я полови́на дня; **in
the ~noon** днём; **~shave (lotion)**
n одеколо́н по́сле бритья́;
~wards (*US* **~ward**) *adv*
впосле́дствии, пото́м

again [əˈɡen] *adv* (*once more*) ещё

раз, сно́ва; (*repeatedly*) опя́ть; **I
won't go there ~** я бо́льше не
пойду́ туда́; **~ and ~** сно́ва и
сно́ва

against [əˈɡenst] *prep* (*lean*) к +dat;
(*hit*, *rub*) о +acc; (*stand*) у +gen; (*in
opposition to*) про́тив +gen; (*at odds
with*) вопреки́ +dat; (*compared to*)
по сравне́нию с +instr

age [eɪdʒ] *n* во́зраст; (*period in
history*) век

aged[1] [ˈeɪdʒd] *adj*: **a boy ~ ten**
ма́льчик десяти́ лет

aged[2] [ˈeɪdʒɪd] *npl*: **the ~**
престаре́лые *pl adj*

agency [ˈeɪdʒənsɪ] *n* (*COMM*) бюро́
nt ind, аге́нтство; (*POL*)
управле́ние

agenda [əˈdʒendə] *n* (*of meeting*)
пове́стка (дня)

agent [ˈeɪdʒənt] *n* аге́нт; (*COMM*)
посре́дник; (*CHEM*) реакти́в

aggression [əˈɡreʃən] *n* агре́ссия

aggressive [əˈɡresɪv] *adj* (*belligerent*)
агресси́вный

agility [əˈdʒɪlɪtɪ] *n* прово́рство;
mental agility жи́вость *f* ума́

AGM *n abbr* = **annual general
meeting**

ago [əˈɡəu] *adv*: **two days ~** два
дня наза́д; **not long ~** неда́вно;
how long ~? как давно́?

agony [ˈæɡənɪ] *n* мучи́тельная
боль *f*; **to be in ~** му́читься (*impf*)
от бо́ли

agree [əˈɡriː] *vt* согласо́вывать
(согласова́ть *pf*) ♦ *vi*: **to ~ with**
(*have same opinion*) соглаша́ться
(согласи́ться *pf*) с +instr;
(*correspond*) согласо́ваться (*impf*)
с +instr; **to ~ that** соглаша́ться
(согласи́ться *pf*), что; **garlic
doesn't ~ with me** я не
переношу́ чеснока́; **to ~ to sth/to
do** соглаша́ться (согласи́ться *pf*)
на что-н/+infin; **~able** *adj*

(*pleasant*) прия́тный; (*willing*) **I am ~able** я согла́сен; ~**ment** *n* (*consent*) согла́сие; (*arrangement*) соглаше́ние, догово́р; **in ~ment with** в согла́сии с +*instr*; **we are in complete ~ment** ме́жду на́ми по́лное согла́сие

agricultural [ægrɪˈkʌltʃərəl] *adj* сельскохозя́йственный; **~ land** земе́льные уго́дья

agriculture [ˈægrɪkʌltʃəʳ] *n* се́льское хозя́йство

ahead [əˈhed] *adv* впереди́; (*direction*) вперёд; **~ of** впереди́ +*gen* (*earlier than*) ра́ньше +*gen*; **~ of time** *or* **schedule** досро́чно; **go right** *or* **straight ~** иди́те вперёд *or* пря́мо; **go ~!** (*giving permission*) приступа́йте!, дава́йте!

aid [eɪd] *n* (*assistance*) по́мощь *f*; (*device*) приспособле́ние ♦ *vt* помога́ть (помо́чь *pf*) +*dat*; **in ~ of** в по́мощь +*dat*; *see also* **hearing**

aide [eɪd] *n* помо́щник

AIDS [eɪdz] *n abbr* (= *acquired immune deficiency syndrome*) СПИД

aim [eɪm] *n* (*objective*) цель *f* ♦ *vi* (*also*: **take ~**) це́литься (наце́литься *pf*) ♦ *vt*: **to ~** (**at**) (*gun, camera*) наводи́ть (навести́ *pf*) (на +*acc*); (*missile, blow*) це́лить (наце́лить *pf*) (в +*acc*); (*remark*) направля́ть (напра́вить *pf*) (на +*acc*); **to ~ to do** ста́вить (поста́вить *pf*) свое́й це́лью +*infin*; **he has a good ~** он ме́ткий стрело́к

ain't [eɪnt] (*inf*) = **am not, are not, is not**

air [ɛəʳ] *n* (*gen*) во́здух; (*appearance*) вид ♦ *vt* (*room, bedclothes*) прове́тривать (прове́трить *pf*); (*views*) обнаро́довать (*pf*) ♦ *cpd* возду́шный; **by ~** по во́здуху; **on the ~** (*be*) в эфи́ре; (*go*) в эфи́р; **~borne** *adj* (*attack*) возду́шный;

~ conditioning *n* кондициони́рование; **~craft** *n inv* самолёт; **Air Force** *n* Вое́нно-Возду́шные Си́лы *fpl*; **~ hostess** *n* (*BRIT*) бортпроводни́ца, стюарде́сса; **~line** *n* авиакомпа́ния; **~ mail** *n*: **by ~ mail** авиапо́чтой; **~plane** *n* (*US*) самолёт; **~port** *n* аэропо́рт; **~ rage** *n* хулига́нское поведе́ние на борту́ самолёта; **~ raid** *n* возду́шный налёт

airy [ˈɛərɪ] *adj* (*room*) просто́рный

aisle [aɪl] *n* прохо́д

alarm [əˈlɑːm] *n* (*anxiety*) трево́га; (*device*) сигнализа́ция ♦ *vt* трево́жить (встрево́жить *pf*); **~ clock** *n* буди́льник

Albania [ælˈbeɪnɪə] *n* Алба́ния

album [ˈælbəm] *n* альбо́м

alcohol [ˈælkəhɔl] *n* алкого́ль *m*; **~ic** [ælkəˈhɔlɪk] *adj* алкого́льный ♦ *n* алкого́лик(и́чка)

alcove [ˈælkəʊv] *n* алько́в

alert [əˈləːt] *adj* внима́тельный; (*to danger*) бди́тельный ♦ *vt* (*police etc*) предупрежда́ть (предупреди́ть *pf*); **to be on the ~** (*also MIL*) быть (*impf*) начеку́

A levels - квалификацио́нные экза́мены. Шко́льники сдаю́т их в во́зрасте 17-18 лет. Полу́ченные результа́ты определя́ют приём в университе́т. Экза́мены сдаю́тся по трём предме́там. Вы́бор предме́тов дикту́ется специа́льностью, кото́рую выпускни́к плани́рует изуча́ть в университе́те.

Algeria [ælˈdʒɪərɪə] *n* Алжи́р

alias [ˈeɪlɪəs] *n* вы́мышленное и́мя *nt* ♦ *adv*: **~ John** он же Джон

alibi [ˈælɪbaɪ] *n* а́либи *nt ind*

alien ['eɪlɪən] n (extraterrestrial) инопланетя́нин(-я́нка) ♦ adj: ~ (to) чу́ждый (+dat); **~ate** ['eɪlɪəneɪt] vt отчужда́ть (impf), оттáлкивать (оттолкну́ть pf)

alight [ə'laɪt] adj: to be ~ горе́ть (impf); (eyes, face) сия́ть (impf)

alike [ə'laɪk] adj одина́ковый ♦ adv одина́ково; **they look** ~ они́ похо́жи друг на дру́га

alive [ə'laɪv] adj (place) оживлённый; **he is** ~ он жив

KEYWORD

all [ɔ:l] adj весь (f вся, nt всё, pl все); **all day** весь день; **all night** всю ночь; **all five stayed** все пя́теро остáлись; **all the books** все кни́ги; **all the time** всё вре́мя ♦ pron 1 всё; **I ate it all, I ate all of it** я всё съел; **all of us stayed** мы все остáлись; **we all sat down** мы все се́ли; **is that all?** э́то всё?
2 (in phrases): **above all** пре́жде всего́; **after all** в конце́ концо́в; **all in all** в це́лом или о́бщем; **not at all** (in answer to question) совсе́м или во́все нет; (in answer to thanks) не́ за что; **I'm not at all tired** я совсе́м не устáл ♦ adv совсе́м; **I am all alone** я совсе́м оди́н; **I did it all by myself** я всё сде́лал сам; **it's not as hard as all that** э́то во́все не так уж тру́дно; **the more/better** тем бо́лее/лу́чше; **I have all but finished** я почти́ (что) зако́нчил; **the score is two all** счёт 2:2

---

all clear n отбо́й
allegation [ælɪ'geɪʃən] n обвине́ние
allege [ə'ledʒ] vt (claim) утвержда́ть (impf); **~dly** [ə'ledʒɪdlɪ] adv я́кобы
allegiance [ə'li:dʒəns] n ве́рность

f; (to idea) приве́рженность f

allergic [ə'lɜ:dʒɪk] adj: **he is** ~ **to** ... у него́ аллерги́я на +acc ...

allergy ['ælədʒɪ] n (MED) аллерги́я

alleviate [ə'li:vɪeɪt] vt облегча́ть (облегчи́ть pf)

alley ['ælɪ] n переу́лок

alliance [ə'laɪəns] n сою́з; (POL) алья́нс

allied ['ælaɪd] adj сою́зный

alligator ['ælɪgeɪtə] n аллига́тор

all-in ['ɔ:lɪn] adj (BRIT): **it cost me £100** ~ в о́бщей сло́жности мне э́то сто́ило £100

all-night ['ɔ:l'naɪt] adj ночно́й

allocate ['æləkeɪt] vt (money) (вы́делить pf); (tasks) поруча́ть (поручи́ть pf)

all-out ['ɔ:laut] adj (effort) максимáльный; (attack) масси́рованный

allow [ə'lau] vt (permit) разреша́ть (разреши́ть pf); (: claim, goal) признавáть (призна́ть pf); (concede): **to** ~ **that** допускáть (допусти́ть pf), что; **to** ~ **sb to do** разреши́ть (разреши́ть pf) or позволя́ть (позво́лить pf) кому́-+infin; ~ **for** vt fus учи́тывать (уче́сть pf), принимáть (приня́ть pf) в расчёт; **~ance** n (COMM) де́ньги pl на расхо́ды; (pocket money) кармáнные де́ньги; (welfare payment) посо́бие; **to make ~ances for** дéлать (сдéлать pf) ски́дку для +gen

all right adv хорошо́, нормáльно; (positive response) хорошо́, лáдно ♦ adj неплохо́й, нормáльный; **is everything** ~? всё в поря́дке or в поря́дке?; **are you** ~? как ты?, ты в поря́дке? (разг); **do you like him?** - **he's** ~ он Вам нрáвится? - ничего́

all-time ['ɔːl'taɪm] *adj* (*record*) непревзойдённый; **inflation is at an ~ low** инфляция на небывало низком уровне

ally *n* ['ælaɪ] *n* союзник

almighty [ɔːl'maɪtɪ] *adj* (*tremendous*) колоссальный

almond ['ɑːmənd] *n* миндаль *m*

almost ['ɔːlməʊst] *adv* почти; (*all but*) чуть *or* едва не

alone [ə'ləʊn] *adj, adv* один; **to leave sb/sth ~** оставлять (оставить *pf*) кого-н/что-н в покое; **let ~** ... не говоря уже о +*prp* ...

along [ə'lɒŋ] *prep* (*motion*) по +*dat*, вдоль +*gen*; (*position*) вдоль +*gen* ♦ *adv*: **is he coming ~ (with us)?** он идёт с нами?; **he was limping ~** он шёл хромая; **~ with** вместе с +*instr*; **all ~** с самого начала; **~side** *prep* (*position*) рядом с +*instr*, вдоль +*gen*; (*motion*) к +*dat* ♦ *adv* рядом

aloud [ə'laʊd] *adv* (*read, speak*) вслух

alphabet ['ælfəbet] *n* алфавит *m*

alpine ['ælpaɪn] *adj* высокогорный, альпийский

Alps [ælps] *npl*: **the ~** Альпы *pl*

already [ɔːl'redɪ] *adv* уже

alright ['ɔːl'raɪt] *adv* (*BRIT*) = **all right**

also ['ɔːlsəʊ] *adv* (*about subject*) также, тоже; (*about object*) также; (*moreover*) кроме того, к тому же; **he ~ likes apples** он также *or* тоже любит яблоки; **he likes apples ~** он любит также яблоки

altar ['ɔːltə] *n* алтарь *m*

alter ['ɔːltə] *vt* изменять (изменить *pf*) ♦ *vi* изменяться (измениться *pf*); **~ation** [ɔːltə'reɪʃən] *n* изменение

alternate *adj* [ɔl'tɜːnɪt] *vb* ['ɔːltəneɪt] *adj* чередующийся; (*US:*

alternative) альтернативный ♦ *vi*: **to ~ (with)** чередоваться (*impf*) (с +*instr*); **on ~ days** через день

alternative [ɔl'tɜːnətɪv] *adj* альтернативный ♦ *n* альтернатива; **~ly** *adv*: **~ly one could ...** кроме того можно ...

although [ɔːl'ðəʊ] *conj* хотя

altitude ['æltɪtjuːd] *n* (*of plane*) высота; (*of place*) высота над уровнем моря

altogether [ɔːltə'geðə] *adv* (*completely*) совершенно; (*in all*) в общем, в общей сложности

aluminium [ælju'mɪnɪəm] *n* (*BRIT*) алюминий

aluminum [ə'luːmɪnəm] *n* (*US*) = **aluminium**

always ['ɔːlweɪz] *adv* всегда

am [æm] *vb see* **be**

A.M. *n abbr* (= *Assembly Member*) член ассамблеи

a.m. *adv abbr* = *ante meridiem*) до полудня

AMA *n abbr* = *American Medical Association*

amateur ['æmətə] *n* любитель *m*; **~ dramatics** любительский театр; **~ photographer** фотограф-любитель *m*

amazement [ə'meɪzmənt] *n* изумление

amazing [ə'meɪzɪŋ] *adj* (*surprising*) поразительный; (*fantastic*) изумительный, замечательный

ambassador [æm'bæsədə] *n* посол *m*

ambiguity [æmbɪ'gjuɪtɪ] *n* неясность *f*, двусмысленность *f*

ambiguous [æm'bɪgjuəs] *adj* неясный, двусмысленный

ambition [æm'bɪʃən] *n* (*see adj*) честолюбие; амбиция; (*aim*) цель *f*

ambitious [æm'bɪʃəs] *adj* честолюбивый (*positive*); (*negative*) амбициозный

ambivalent [æm'bɪvələnt] *adj*
(*attitude*) двойственный; (*person*)
противоречивый

ambulance [ˈæmbjuləns] *n* скорая
помощь *f*

ambush [ˈæmbuʃ] *n* засада ♦ *vt*
устраивать (устроить *pf*) засаду
+*dat*

amend [əˈmend] *vt* (*law, text*)
пересматривать (пересмотреть
pf) ♦ *n*: **to make** ~ заглаживать
(загладить *pf*) (свою) вину;
~**ment** *n* поправка

amenities [əˈmiːnɪtɪz] *npl* удобства
ntpl

America [əˈmerɪkə] *n* Америка; ~**n**
adj американский ♦ *n*
американец(нка)

amicable [ˈæmɪkəbl] *adj*
(*relationship*) дружеский

amid(st) [əˈmɪd(st)] *prep* посреди
+*gen*

amiss [əˈmɪs] *adj, adv*: **there's
something** ~ здесь что-то
неладно

ammunition [æmjuˈnɪʃən] *n* (*for
gun*) патроны *mpl*

amnesty [ˈæmnɪstɪ] *n* амнистия

among(st) [əˈmʌŋ(st)] *prep* среди
+*gen*

amount [əˈmaʊnt] *n* количество
♦ *vi*: **to amount to** (*total*)
составлять (составить *pf*)

amp(ère) [ˈæmp(eəʳ)] *n* ампер

ample [ˈæmpl] *adj* (*large*)
солидный; (*abundant*) обильный;
(*enough*) достаточный; **to have ~
time/room** иметь (*impf*)
достаточно времени/места

amuse [əˈmjuːz] *vt* развлекать
(развлечь *pf*); ~**ment** *n* (*mirth*)
удовольствие; (*pastime*)
развлечение; ~**ment arcade** *n*
павильон с игровыми
аппаратами

an [æn] *indef art see* **a**

anaemia [əˈniːmɪə] (*US* **anemia**) *n*
анемия, малокровие

anaesthetic [ænɪsˈθetɪk] (*US*
anesthetic) *n*

analyse [ˈænəlaɪz] (*US* **analyze**) *vt*
анализировать
(проанализировать *pf*)

analysis [əˈnæləsɪs] (*pl* **analyses**) *n*
анализ

analyst [ˈænəlɪst] *n* (*political*)
аналитик, комментатор;
(*financial, economic*) эксперт; (*US:
psychiatrist*) психиатр

analytic(al) [ænəˈlɪtɪk(l)] *adj*
аналитический

analyze [ˈænəlaɪz] *vt* (*US*) = **analyse**

anarchy [ˈænəkɪ] *n* анархия

anatomy [əˈnætəmɪ] *n* анатомия;
(*body*) организм

ancestor [ˈænsɪstəʳ] *n* предок

anchor [ˈæŋkəʳ] *n* якорь *m*

anchovy [ˈæntʃəvɪ] *n* анчоус

ancient [ˈeɪnʃənt] *adj* (*civilization,
person*) древний; (*monument*)
старинный

and [ænd] *conj* и; **my father** ~ **I** я и
мой отец, мы с отцом; **bread** ~
butter хлеб с маслом; ~ **so on** и
так далее; **try** ~ **come**
постарайтесь прийти; **he talked**
~ **talked** он всё говорил и
говорил

Andes [ˈændiːz] *npl*: **the** ~ Анды *pl*

anecdote [ˈænɪkdəʊt] *n*
любопытная история

anemia [əˈniːmɪə] *n* (*US*) =
anaemia

anesthetic [ænɪsˈθetɪk] *n* (*US*) =
anaesthetic

angel [ˈeɪndʒəl] *n* ангел

anger [ˈæŋgəʳ] *n* гнев,
возмущение

angle [ˈæŋgl] *n* (*corner*) угол

angler [ˈæŋgləʳ] *n* рыболов

Anglican [ˈæŋglɪkən] *adj*
англиканский ♦ *n*

англича́нец(а́нка)

angling ['æŋglɪŋ] n рыбная ло́вля

angrily ['æŋɡrɪlɪ] adv серди́то, гне́вно

angry ['æŋɡrɪ] adj серди́тый, гне́вный; (wound) воспалённый; **to be ~ with sb/at sth** серди́ться (impf) на кого́-н/что-н; **to get ~** серди́ться (рассерди́ться pf)

anguish ['æŋɡwɪʃ] n му́ка

animal ['ænɪml] n живо́тное nt adj; (wild animal) зверь m (pej: person) зверь, живо́тное ♦ adj живо́тный

animated adj оживлённый, живо́й; (film) мультипликацио́нный

animation [ænɪ'meɪʃən] n (enthusiasm) оживле́ние

ankle ['æŋkl] n лоды́жка

anniversary [ænɪ'vɜːsərɪ] n годовщи́на

announce [ə'nauns] vt (engagement, decision) объявля́ть (объяви́ть pf) (o +prp); (birth, death) извеща́ть (извести́ть pf) о +prp; **~ment** n объявле́ние; (in newspaper etc) сообще́ние

annoy [ə'nɔɪ] vt раздража́ть (раздражи́ть pf); **~ed** adj раздражённый; **~ing** adj (noise) раздража́ющий; (mistake, event) доса́дный; **he is ~ing** он меня́ раздража́ет

annual ['ænjuəl] adj (meeting) ежего́дный; (income) годово́й; **~ly** adv ежего́дно

annum ['ænəm] n see **per**

anonymity [ænə'nɪmɪtɪ] n анони́мность f

anonymous [ə'nɔnɪməs] adj анони́мный

anorak ['ænəræk] n ку́ртка

anorexia [ænə'rɛksɪə] n аноре́ксия

another [ə'nʌðər] pron друго́й ♦ adj: **~ book** (additional) ещё

одна́ кни́га; (different) друга́я кни́га; see also **one**

answer ['ɑːnsər] n отве́т; (to problem) реше́ние ♦ vt отвеча́ть (отве́тить pf) ♦ vt (letter, question) отвеча́ть (отве́тить pf) на +acc; (person) отвеча́ть (отве́тить pf) +dat; **in ~ to your letter** в отве́т на Ва́ше письмо́; **to ~ the phone** подходи́ть (подойти́ pf) к телефо́ну; **to ~ the bell** or **the door** открыва́ть (откры́ть pf) дверь; **~ to** vt fus (description) соотве́тствовать (impf) +dat; **~ing machine** n автоотве́тчик

ant [ænt] n мураве́й

antagonism [æn'tæɡənɪzəm] n антагони́зм

Antarctic [ænt'ɑːktɪk] n: **the ~** Анта́рктика

antelope ['æntɪləup] n антило́па

anthem ['ænθəm] n: **national ~** госуда́рственный гимн

antibiotic ['æntɪbaɪ'ɔtɪk] n антибио́тик

antibody ['æntɪbɔdɪ] n антите́ло

anticipate [æn'tɪsɪpeɪt] vt (expect) ожида́ть (impf) +gen; (foresee) предуга́дывать (предугада́ть pf); (forestall) предвосхища́ть (предвосхи́тить pf)

anticipation [æntɪsɪ'peɪʃən] n (expectation) ожида́ние; (eagerness) предвкуше́ние

antics ['æntɪks] npl (of child) ша́лости fpl

antidepressant ['æntɪdɪ'prɛsnt] n антидепресса́нт

antidote ['æntɪdəut] n противоя́дие

antifreeze ['æntɪfriːz] n антифри́з

antique [æn'tiːk] n анти́кварная вещь f, предме́т старины́ ♦ adj антиква́рный

antiquity [æn'tɪkwɪtɪ] n анти́чность f

anti-Semitism [ˈæntɪˈsemɪtɪzəm] *n*
антисемити́зм

antiseptic [æntɪˈseptɪk] *n*
антисе́птик

anxiety [æŋˈzaɪətɪ] *n* трево́га

anxious [ˈæŋkʃəs] *adj* (*person, look*)
беспоко́йный, озабо́ченный
(*time*) трево́жный; **she is ~ to do**
она́ о́чень хо́чет +*infin*; **to be ~
about** беспоко́иться (*impf*) о +*prp*

any [ˈenɪ] *adj* **1** (*in questions etc*):
have you any butter/children? у
Вас есть ма́сло/де́ти?; **do you
have any questions?** у Вас есть
каки́е-нибудь вопро́сы?; **if there
are any tickets left** е́сли ещё
оста́лись биле́ты

2 (*with negative*): **I haven't any
bread/books** у меня́ нет хле́ба/
книг; **I didn't buy any newspapers**
я не купи́л газе́т

3 (*no matter which*) любо́й; **any
colour will do** любо́й цвет
подойдёт

4 (*in phrases*): **in any case** в
любо́м слу́чае; **any day now** в
любо́й день; **at any moment** в
любо́й моме́нт; **at any rate** во
вся́ком слу́чае; (*anyhow*) так и́ли
ина́че; **any time** (*at any moment*) в
любо́е вре́мя; (*whenever*) в
любо́й моме́нт; (*as response*) не́ за
что

♦ *pron* **1** (*in questions etc*): **I need
some money, have you got any?**
мне нужны́ де́ньги, у Вас есть?;
can any of you sing? кто́-нибудь
из вас уме́ет петь?

2 (*with negative*) ни оди́н (*f* одна́,
nt одно́, *pl* одни́); **I haven't any
(of those)** у меня́ таки́х нет

3 (*no matter which one(s)*) любо́й;
take any you like возьми́те то,
что Вам нра́вится

♦ *adv* **1** (*in questions etc*): **do you
want any more soup?** хоти́те
ещё су́пу?; **are you feeling any
better?** Вам лу́чше?

2 (*with negative*): **I can't hear him
any more** я бо́льше его́ не
слы́шу; **don't wait any longer** не
жди́те бо́льше; **he isn't any
better** ему́ не лу́чше

anybody [ˈenɪbɒdɪ] *pron* = **anyone**

anyhow [ˈenɪhaʊ] *adv* (*at any rate*)
так и́ли ина́че; **the work is done
~** (*haphazardly*) рабо́та сде́лана
ко́е-как; **I shall go ~** я так и́ли
ина́че пойду́

anyone [ˈenɪwʌn] *pron* (*in questions
etc*) кто́-нибудь; (*with negative*)
никто́; (*no matter who*) любо́й,
вся́кий; **can you see ~?** Вы
ви́дите кого́-нибудь?; **I can't see
~** я никого́ не ви́жу; **~ could do it**
любо́й от вся́кий мо́жет э́то
сде́лать; **you can invite ~** Вы
мо́жете пригласи́ть кого́ уго́дно

anything [ˈenɪθɪŋ] *pron* (*in questions
etc*) что́-нибудь; (*with negative*)
ничего́; (*no matter what*) (всё,)
что уго́дно; **can you see ~?** Вы
ви́дите что́-нибудь?; **I can't see ~
я** ничего́ не ви́жу; **~ (at all) will
do** всё, что уго́дно подойдёт

anyway [ˈenɪweɪ] *adv* всё равно́;
(*in brief*): **~, I didn't want to go** в
о́бщем, я не хоте́л идти́; **I will be
there ~** я всё равно́ там бу́ду; **~,
I couldn't stay even if I wanted to**
в любо́м слу́чае, я не мог
оста́ться, да́же е́сли бы я хоте́л;
why are you phoning, ~? а всё-
таки, почему́ Вы звони́те?

anywhere [ˈenɪweəʳ] *adv* **1** (*in
questions etc: position*) где́-нибудь;
(*: motion*) куда́-нибудь; **can you**

see him anywhere? Вы его где-нибудь видите? **did you go anywhere yesterday?** Вы вчера куда-нибудь ходили?
2 (*with negative: position*) нигде; (*: motion*) никуда; **I can't see him anywhere** я нигде его не вижу; **I'm not going anywhere today** сегодня я никуда не иду
3 (*no matter where: position*) где угодно; (*: motion*) куда угодно; **anywhere in the world** где угодно в мире; **put the books down anywhere** положите книги куда угодно

apart [ə'pɑːt] *adv* (*position*) в стороне; (*motion*) в сторону; (*separately*) раздельно, врозь; **they are ten miles ~** они находятся на расстоянии десяти миль друг от друга; **to take ~** разбирать (разобрать *pf*) (на части); **~ from** кроме +*gen*

apartheid [ə'pɑːteɪt] *n* апартеид

apartment [ə'pɑːtmənt] *n* (*US*) квартира; (*room*) комната

apathy ['æpəθɪ] *n* апатия

ape [eɪp] *n* человекообразная обезьяна ♦ *vt* копировать (скопировать *pf*)

aperitif [ə'perɪtɪf] *n* аперитив

apex ['eɪpeks] *n* (*also fig*) вершина

apiece [ə'piːs] *adv* (*each person*) на каждого; (*each thing*) за штуку

apologize [ə'pɒlədʒaɪz] *vi*: **to ~ (for sth to sb)** извиниться *pf* (за что-н перед кем-н)

apology [ə'pɒlədʒɪ] *n* извинение

appalling [ə'pɔːlɪŋ] *adj* (*awful*) ужасный; (*shocking*) возмутительный

apparatus [æpə'reɪtəs] *n* аппаратура; (*in gym*) (гимнастический) снаряд; (*of*

organization) аппарат

apparent [ə'pærənt] *adj* (*seeming*) видимый; (*obvious*) очевидный; **~ly** *adv* по всей видимости

appeal [ə'piːl] *vi* (*LAW*) апеллировать (*impf/pf*), подавать (подать *pf*) апелляцию ♦ *n* (*attraction*) привлекательность *f*; (*plea*) призыв; (*LAW*) апелляция, обжалование; **to ~ (to sb) for** (*help, funds*) обращаться (обратиться *pf*) (к кому-н) за +*instr*; (*calm, order*) призывать (призвать *pf*) (кого-н) к +*dat*; **to ~ to** (*attract*) привлекать (привлечь *pf*), нравиться (понравиться *pf*) +*dat*; **~ing** *adj* привлекательный; (*pleading*) умоляющий

appear [ə'pɪər] *vi* появляться (появиться *pf*); (*seem*) казаться (показаться *pf*); **to ~ in court** представать (предстать *pf*) перед судом; **to ~ on TV** выступать (выступить *pf*) по телевидению; **it would ~ that ...** похоже (на то), что ...; **~ance** *n* (*arrival*) появление; (*look, aspect*) внешность *f*; (*in public, on TV*) выступление

appendices [ə'pendɪsiːz] *npl of* **appendix**

appendicitis [əpendɪ'saɪtɪs] *n* аппендицит

appendix [ə'pendɪks] (*pl* **appendices**) *n* приложение; (*ANAT*) аппендикс

appetite ['æpɪtaɪt] *n* аппетит

applaud [ə'plɔːd] *vi* аплодировать (*impf*), рукоплескать (*impf*) ♦ *vt* аплодировать (*impf*), рукоплескать (*impf*) +*dat*; (*praise*) одобрять (одобрить *pf*)

applause [ə'plɔːz] *n* аплодисменты *pl*

apple ['æpl] *n* яблоко

applicable [ə'plɪkəbl] *adj*: **~ (to)**

примени́мый (к +*dat*)

applicant [ˈæplɪkənt] *n* (*for job, scholarship*) кандида́т; (*for college*) абитурие́нт

application [æplɪˈkeɪʃən] *n* (*for job, grant, scholarship*) заявле́ние; ~ **form** *n* заявле́ние-анке́та

applied [əˈplaɪd] *adj* прикладно́й

apply [əˈplaɪ] *vt* (*paint, make-up*) наноси́ть (нанести́ *pf*) ♦ *vi*: **to ~ to** применя́ться (*impf*) к +*dat*; (*ask*) обраща́ться (обрати́ться *pf*) (с про́сьбой) к +*dat*; **to ~ o.s. to** сосредото́чиваться (сосредото́читься *pf*) на +*prp*; **to ~ for a grant/job** подава́ть (пода́ть *pf*) заявле́ние на стипе́ндию/о приёме на рабо́ту

appoint [əˈpɔɪnt] *vt* назнача́ть (назна́чить *pf*); ~**ed** *adj*: **at the ~ed time** в назна́ченное вре́мя; ~**ment** *n* (*of person*) назначе́ние; (*post*) до́лжность *f*; (*arranged meeting*) приём; **to make an ~ment (with sb)** (кому́-н) встре́чу; **I have an ~ment with the doctor** я записа́лся на приём(е) к врачу́

appraisal [əˈpreɪzl] *n* оце́нка

appreciate [əˈpriːʃɪeɪt] *vt* (*value*) цени́ть (*impf*); (*understand*) оце́нивать (оцени́ть *pf*) ♦ *vi* (*COMM*) повыша́ться (повы́ситься *pf*) в цене́

appreciation [əpriːʃɪˈeɪʃən] *n* (*understanding*) понима́ние; (*gratitude*) призна́тельность *f*

apprehensive [æprɪˈhɛnsɪv] *adj* (*glance etc*) опа́сливый

apprentice [əˈprɛntɪs] *n* учени́к, подмасте́рье; ~**ship** *n* учени́чество

approach [əˈprəʊtʃ] *vi* приближа́ться (прибли́зиться *pf*) ♦ *vt* (*ask, apply to*) обраща́ться (обрати́ться *pf*) к +*dat*; (*come to*)

приближа́ться (прибли́зиться *pf*) к +*dat*; (*consider*) подходи́ть (подойти́ *pf*) к +*dat* с подхо́д; (*advance: also fig*) приближе́ние

appropriate [əˈprəʊprɪɪt] *adj* (*behaviour*) подоба́ющий; (*remarks*) уме́стный; (*tools*) подходя́щий

approval [əˈpruːvəl] *n* одобре́ние; (*permission*) согла́сие; **on ~** (*COMM*) на про́бу

approve [əˈpruːv] *vt* (*motion, decision*) одобря́ть (одо́брить *pf*); (*product, publication*) утвержда́ть (утверди́ть *pf*); ~ **of** *fus* одобря́ть (одо́брить *pf*)

approximate [əˈprɒksɪmɪt] *adj* приблизи́тельный; ~**ly** *adv* приблизи́тельно

apricot [ˈeɪprɪkɒt] *n* абрико́с

April [ˈeɪprəl] *n* апре́ль *m*

apron [ˈeɪprən] *n* фа́ртук

apt [æpt] *adj* уда́чный, уме́стный; **~ to do** скло́нный +*infin*

aquarium [əˈkwɛərɪəm] *n* аква́риум

Aquarius [əˈkwɛərɪəs] *n* Водоле́й

Arab [ˈærəb] *adj* ара́бский ♦ *n* ара́б(ка); ~**ian** [əˈreɪbɪən] *adj* ара́бский; ~**ic** *adj* ара́бский

arbitrary [ˈɑːbɪtrərɪ] *adj* произво́льный

arbitration [ɑːbɪˈtreɪʃən] *n* трете́йский суд; (*INDUSTRY*) арбитра́ж; **the dispute went to ~** спор пе́редан в арбитра́ж

arc [ɑːk] *n* (*also MATH*) дуга́

arch [ɑːtʃ] *n* а́рка, свод; (*of foot*) свод ♦ *vt* (*back*) выгиба́ть (вы́гнуть *pf*)

archaeology [ɑːkɪˈɒlədʒɪ] (*US* **archeology**) *n* археоло́гия

archaic [ɑːˈkeɪɪk] *adj* архаи́ческий

archbishop [ɑːtʃˈbɪʃəp] *n* архиепи́скоп

archeology [ɑːkɪˈɒlədʒɪ] *n* (*US*) = **archaeology**

architect [ˈɑːkɪtekt] n (of building) архите́ктор; **~ure** n архитекту́ра

archive [ˈɑːkaɪv] n архи́в; **~s** npl (documents) архи́в msg

Arctic [ˈɑːktɪk] adj аркти́ческий ♦ n: **the ~** А́рктика

ardent [ˈɑːdənt] adj пы́лкий

arduous [ˈɑːdjʊəs] adj тяжёлый, тя́жкий

are [ɑː] vb see **be**

area [ˈɛərɪə] n (области ?) (: of place) уча́сток m; (: of room) часть f

arena [əˈriːnə] n (also fig) аре́на

aren't [ɑːnt] = **are not**; see **be**

Argentina [ɑːdʒənˈtiːnə] n Аргенти́на

arguably [ˈɑːgjʊəblɪ] adv возмо́жно

argue [ˈɑːgjuː] vi (quarrel) ссо́риться (поссо́риться pf); (reason) дока́зывать (доказа́ть pf)

argument [ˈɑːgjʊmənt] n (quarrel) ссо́ра; (reasons) аргуме́нт, до́вод

Aries [ˈɛərɪz] n Ове́н

arise [əˈraɪz] (pt **arose**, pp **~n**) vi (occur) возника́ть (возни́кнуть pf); **~n** [əˈrɪzn] pp of **arise**

aristocracy [ærɪsˈtɔkrəsɪ] n аристокра́тия

arithmetic [əˈrɪθmətɪk] n (MATH) арифме́тика; (calculation) подсчёт

arm [ɑːm] n рука́; (of chair) ру́чка; (of clothing) рука́в ♦ vt вооружа́ть (вооружи́ть pf); **~s** npl (MIL) вооруже́ние ntsg; (HERALDRY) герб; **~ in ~** по́д руку; **~chair** n кре́сло; **~ed** adj вооружённый

armour [ˈɑːmə[r]] (US **armor**) n (also: **suit of ~**) доспе́хи mpl

army [ˈɑːmɪ] n (also fig) а́рмия

aroma [əˈrəʊmə] n арома́т; **~therapy** [ərəʊməˈθɛrəpɪ] n ароматерапи́я

arose [əˈrəʊz] pt of **arise**

around [əˈraʊnd] adv вокру́г ♦ prep (encircling) вокру́г +gen; (near, about) о́коло +gen

arouse [əˈraʊz] vt (interest, passions) возбужда́ть (возбуди́ть pf)

arrange [əˈreɪndʒ] vt (organize) устра́ивать (устро́ить pf); (put in order) расставля́ть (расста́вить pf) ♦ vi: **we ~d for a car to pick you up** мы договори́лись, что́бы за Ва́ми зае́хала маши́на; **to ~ to do** догова́риваться (договори́ться pf) +infin; **~ment** n (agreement) договорённость f; (order, layout) расположе́ние; **~ments** npl (plans) приготовле́ния ntpl

array [əˈreɪ] n: **~ of** ряд +gen

arrears [əˈrɪəz] npl задо́лженность fsg; **to be in ~ with one's rent** име́ть (impf) задо́лженность по квартпла́те

arrest [əˈrest] vt (LAW: person) аресто́вывать (арестова́ть pf) ♦ n аре́ст; **under ~** под аре́стом

arrival [əˈraɪvl] n (of person, vehicle) прибы́тие; **new ~** нови́чо́к;; (baby) новорождённый(ая) m(f) adj

arrive [əˈraɪv] vi (traveller) прибыва́ть (прибы́ть pf); (letter, news) приходи́ть (прийти́ pf); (baby) рожда́ться (роди́ться pf)

arrogance [ˈærəgəns] n высокоме́рие

arrogant [ˈærəgənt] adj высокоме́рный

arrow [ˈærəʊ] n (weapon) стрела́; (sign) стре́лка

arse [ɑːs] n (BRIT : infl) жо́па (!)

arsenal [ˈɑːsɪnl] n арсена́л

arson [ˈɑːsn] n поджо́г

art [ɑːt] n иску́сство; **Arts** npl (SCOL) гуманита́рные нау́ки fpl

artery [ˈɑːtərɪ] n (also fig) арте́рия

art gallery n (national) карти́нная галере́я; (private) (арт-)галере́я

arthritis [ɑːˈθraɪtɪs] n артри́т

artichoke [ˈɑːtɪtʃəʊk] n (also: **globe**

~) артишо́к; (also: **Jerusalem** ~) земляна́я гру́ша

article ['ɑːtɪkl] n (object) предме́т; (LING) арти́кль m; (in newspaper, document) статья́

articulate vb [ɑː'tɪkjuleɪt] adj [ɑː'tɪkjulɪt] vt (ideas) выража́ть (вы́разить pf) ♦ adj: she is very ~ она́ чётко выража́ет свои́ мы́сли

artificial [ɑːtɪ'fɪʃl] adj иску́сственный; (affected) неесте́ственный

artillery [ɑː'tɪlərɪ] n (corps) артилле́рия

artist ['ɑːtɪst] n худо́жник(ица) (performer) арти́ст(ка); **~ic** [ɑː'tɪstɪk] adj худо́жественный

KEYWORD
---

as [æz, əz] conj 1 (referring to time) когда́; **he came in as I was leaving** он вошёл, когда́ я уходи́л; **as the years went by** с года́ми; **as from tomorrow** с за́втрашнего дня

2 (in comparisons): **as big as** тако́й же большо́й, как; **twice as big as** в два ра́за бо́льше, чем; **as white as snow** бе́лый, как снег; **as much money/many books as** сто́лько же де́нег/книг, ско́лько; **as soon as** как то́лько; **as soon as possible** как мо́жно скоре́е

3 (since, because) поско́льку, так как

4 (referring to manner, way) как; **do as you wish** де́лайте, как хоти́те; **as she said** как она́ сказа́ла

5 (concerning): **as for** or **to** что каса́ется +gen

6: **as if** or **though как бу́дто**; **he looked as if he had been ill** он вы́глядел так, как бу́дто он был бо́лен

♦ prep (in the capacity of): **he works as a waiter** он рабо́тает

официа́нтом; **as chairman of the company, he ...** как глава́ компа́нии он ...; see also **long**; **same**; **such**; **well**

a.s.a.p. adv abbr = **as soon as possible**

ascent [ə'sɛnt] n (slope) подъём; (climb) восхожде́ние

ash [æʃ] n (of fire) зола́, пе́пел; (of cigarette) пе́пел; (wood, tree) я́сень m

ashamed [ə'feɪmd] adj: **to be ~ (of)** стыди́ться (impf) (+gen); **I'm ~ of ...** мне сты́дно за +acc ...

ashore [ə'ʃɔː] adv (be) на берегу́; (swim, go) на бе́рег

ashtray ['æʃtreɪ] n пе́пельница

Asia ['eɪʃə] n А́зия; **~n** adj азиа́тский ♦ n азиа́т(ка)

aside [ə'saɪd] adv в сто́рону ♦ n ре́плика

ask [ɑːsk] vt (inquire) спра́шивать (спроси́ть pf); (invite) звать (позва́ть pf); **to ~ sb for sth/sb to do** проси́ть (попроси́ть pf) что-н у кого́-н/кого́-н +infin; **to ~ sb about** спра́шивать (спроси́ть pf) кого́-н о +prp; **to ~ (sb) a question** задава́ть (зада́ть pf) (кому́-н) вопро́с; **to ~ sb out to dinner** пригласи́ть (пригласи́ть pf) кого́-н в рестора́н; **~ for** vt fus проси́ть (попроси́ть pf) (trouble) напра́шиваться (напроси́ться pf) на +acc

asleep [ə'sliːp] adj: **to be ~** спать (impf); **to fall ~** засыпа́ть (засну́ть pf)

asparagus [əs'pærəgəs] n спа́ржа

aspect ['æspɛkt] n (element) аспе́кт, сторона́; (quality, air) вид

aspirin ['æsprɪn] n аспири́н

ass [æs] n (also fig) осёл; (US : inf!) жо́па (!)

assassin [ə'sæsɪn] n

(полити́ческий) уби́йца *m/f*;
~ation [əsɔːlˈteɪʃən] *n*
(полити́ческое) уби́йство

assault [əˈsɔːlt] *n* нападе́ние; (*MIL,
fig*) ата́ка ♦ *vt* напада́ть (напа́сть
pf) на +*acc*; (*sexually*) наси́ловать
(изнаси́ловать *pf*)

assemble [əˈsɛmbl] *vt* собира́ть
(собра́ть *pf*) ♦ *vi* собира́ться
(собра́ться *pf*)

assembly [əˈsɛmblɪ] *n* (*meeting*)
собра́ние; (*institution*) ассамбле́я,
законода́тельное собра́ние;
(*construction*) сбо́рка

assert [əˈsəːt] *vt* (*opinion, authority*)
утвержда́ть (утверди́ть *pf*);
(*rights, innocence*) отста́ивать
(отстоя́ть *pf*); **~ion** [əˈsəːʃən] *n*
(*claim*) утвержде́ние

assess [əˈsɛs] *vt* оце́нивать
(оцени́ть *pf*); **~ment** *n*: **~ment
(of)** оце́нка (+*gen*)

asset [ˈæsɛt] *n* (*quality*)
досто́инство; **~s** *npl* (*property,
funds*) акти́вы *mpl*; (*COMM*) акти́в
*msg*бала́нса

assignment [əˈsaɪnmənt] *n*
зада́ние

assist [əˈsɪst] *vt* помога́ть (помо́чь
pf) +*dat*; (*financially*)
соде́йствовать
(посоде́йствовать *pf*) +*dat*; **~ance**
n (*see vt*) по́мощь *f*; соде́йствие;
~ant *n* помо́щник(ица); (*in office
etc*) ассисте́нт(ка); (*BRIT: also*:
shop ~ant) продаве́ц(вщи́ца)

associate [*n* əˈsəuʃɪt, *vb* əˈsəuʃɪeɪt]
n (*colleague*) колле́га *m/f* ♦ *adj*
(*member, professor*)
ассоции́рованный ♦ *vt* (*mentally*)
ассоции́ровать (*impf/pf*); **to ~ with
sb** обща́ться (*impf*) с кем-н

association [əsəusɪˈeɪʃən] *n*
ассоциа́ция; (*involvement*) связь *f*

assorted [əˈsɔːtɪd] *adj*
разнообра́зный

assortment [əˈsɔːtmənt] *n* (*of
clothes, colours*) ассортиме́нт; (*of
books, people*) подбо́р

assume [əˈsjuːm] *vt* (*suppose*)
предполага́ть (предположи́ть
pf), допуска́ть (допусти́ть *pf*);
(*responsibility*) принима́ть
(приня́ть *pf*) (на себя́); (*air*)
напуска́ть (напусти́ть *pf*) на
себя́; (*power*) брать (взять *pf*)

assumption [əˈsʌmpʃən] *n*
предположе́ние; (*of responsibility*)
приня́тие на себя́; **~ of power**
прихо́д к вла́сти

assurance [əˈʃuərəns] *n* (*promise*)
завере́ние; (*confidence*)
уве́ренность *f*; (*insurance*)
страхова́ние

assure [əˈʃuə] *vt* (*reassure*)
заверя́ть (заве́рить *pf*);
(*guarantee*) обеспе́чивать
(обеспе́чить *pf*)

asthma [ˈæsmə] *n* а́стма

astonishment [əˈstɔnɪʃmənt] *n*
изумле́ние

astrology [əsˈtrɔlədʒɪ] *n*
астроло́гия

astronomical [æstrəˈnɔmɪkl] *adj*
(*also fig*) астрономи́ческий

astronomy [əsˈtrɔnəmɪ] *n*
астроно́мия

astute [əsˈtjuːt] *adj* (*person*)
проница́тельный

KEYWORD

---

at [æt] *prep* **1** (*referring to position*)
в/на +*prp*; **at school** в шко́ле; **at
the theatre** в теа́тре; **at a concert**
на конце́рте; **at the station** на
ста́нции; **at the top** наверху́; **at
home** до́ма; **they are sitting at
the table** они́ сидя́т за столо́м;
at my friend's (house) у моего́
дру́га; **at the doctor's** у врача́
2 (*referring to direction*) в/на +*acc*;
to look at смотре́ть (посмотре́ть

pf) на +*acc*; **to throw sth at sb**
(*stone*) броса́ть (бро́сить *pf*) что-н
ог чем-н в кого́-н
3 (*referring to time*): **at four o'clock**
в четы́ре часа́; **at half past two** в
полови́не тре́тьего; **at a quarter
to two** без че́тверти два; **at a
quarter past two** в че́тверть
тре́тьего; **at dawn** на заре́; **at
night** но́чью; **at Christmas** на
Рождество́; **at lunch** за обе́дом;
at times времена́ми
4 (*referring to rates*): **at one pound
a kilo** по фу́нту за кило́; **two at
a time** по́ дво́е; **at fifty
km/h** со ско́ростью пятьдеся́т
км/ч; **at full speed** на по́лной
ско́рости
5 (*referring to manner*): **at a stroke**
одни́м ма́хом; **at peace** в ми́ре
6 (*referring to activity*): **to be at
home/work** быть (*impf*) до́ма/на
рабо́те; **to play at cowboys**
игра́ть (*impf*) в ковбо́и; **to be
good at doing** хорошо́ уме́ть
(*impf*) +*infin*
7 (*referring to cause*): **he is
surprised/annoyed at sth** он
удивлён/раздражён чем-н; **I am
surprised at you** Вы меня́
удивля́ете; **I stayed at his
suggestion** я оста́лся по его́
предложе́нию

ate [eɪt] *pt of* **eat**
atheist [ˈeɪθɪɪst] *n* атеи́ст(ка)
Athens [ˈæθɪnz] *n* Афи́ны *pl*
athlete [ˈæθliːt] *n* спортсме́н(ка)
athletic [æθˈlɛtɪk] *adj* спорти́вный;
~s [æθˈlɛtɪks] *n* лёгкая атле́тика
Atlantic [ətˈlæntɪk] *n*: **the ~** (*Ocean*)
Атланти́ческий океа́н
atlas [ˈætləs] *n* а́тлас
atmosphere [ˈætməsfɪəʳ] *n*
атмосфе́ра
atom [ˈætəm] *n* а́том; **~ic** [əˈtɔmɪk]

adj а́томный

attach [əˈtætʃ] *vt* прикрепля́ть
(прикрепи́ть *pf*); (*document, letter*)
прилага́ть (приложи́ть *pf*); **to be
~ed to** (*fond of*) он привя́зан к
+*dat*; **to ~ importance to**
придава́ть (прида́ть *pf*) значе́ние
+*dat*; **~ment** *n* (*device*)
приспособле́ние, наса́дка;
~ment (to sb) (*love*)
привя́занность *f* (к кому́-н)
attack [əˈtæk] *vt* (*MIL, fig*) атакова́ть
(*impf/pf*); (*assault*) напада́ть
(напа́сть *pf*) на +*acc* ♦ *n* (*MIL, fig*)
ата́ка; (*assault*) нападе́ние; (*of
illness*) при́ступ; **~er** *n* his/her
~er напа́вший(ая) *m(f) adj* на
него́/неё
attain [əˈteɪn] *vt* (*happiness, success*)
достига́ть (дости́гнуть *or*
дости́чь *pf*) +*gen*, добива́ться
(доби́ться *pf*) +*gen*
attempt [əˈtɛmpt] *n* попы́тка ♦ *vt*:
to ~ to do пыта́ться (попыта́ться
pf) +*infin*; **to make an ~ on sb's life**
покуше́ние на кого́-н; **~ed** *adj*:
~ed murder покуше́ние на
жизнь; **~ed suicide/burglary**
попы́тка самоуби́йства/
ограбле́ния
attend [əˈtɛnd] *vt* (*school, church*)
посеща́ть (*impf*); **~ to** *vt fus* (*needs,
patient*) занима́ться (заня́ться *pf*)
+*instr*; (*customer*) обслу́живать
(обслужи́ть *pf*); **~ance** *n*
прису́тствие; (*SCOL*)
посеща́емость *f*; **~ant** *n*
сопровожда́ющий(ая) *m(f) adj*; (*in
garage*) служи́тель(ница) *m(f)*
attention [əˈtɛnʃən] *n* внима́ние;
(*care*) ухо́д; **for the ~ of** ... (*ADMIN*)
к све́дению +*gen* ...
attentive [əˈtɛntɪv] *adj* (*audience*)
внима́тельный; (*polite*)
предупреди́тельный

attic [ˈætɪk] n (living space)
мансáрда; (storage space) чердáк

attitude [ˈætɪtjuːd] n: **~ (to** or
towards) отношéние (к +dat)

attorney [əˈtɜːnɪ] n (US: lawyer)
юрúст; **Attorney General** n
(BRIT) минúстр юстúции; (US)
Генерáльный прокурóр

attract [əˈtrækt] vt привлекáть
(привлéчь pf); **~ion** [əˈtrækʃən] n
(appeal) привлекáтельность f;
~ive adj привлекáтельный

attribute n [ˈætrɪbjuːt] vb [əˈtrɪbjuːt]
n прúзнак, атрибýт ♦ vt: **to ~** sth
to (cause) относúть (отнестú pf)
что-то за счёт +gen; (painting,
quality) приписывать (приписáть
pf) что-н +dat

aubergine [ˈəubəʒiːn] n баклажáн

auction [ˈɔːkʃən] n (also: **sale by ~**)
аукциóн ♦ vt продавáть (продáть
pf) на аукциóне

audible [ˈɔːdɪbl] adj слышимый

audience [ˈɔːdɪəns] n аудитóрия,
пýблика

audit [ˈɔːdɪt] vt (COMM) проводúть
(провестú pf) ревúзию +gen

audition [ɔːˈdɪʃən] n
прослýшивание

auditor [ˈɔːdɪtəʳ] n ревизóр,
аудúтор

auditorium [ɔːdɪˈtɔːrɪəm] n зал

August [ˈɔːgəst] n áвгуст

aunt [ɑːnt] n тётя; **~ie** [ˈɑːntɪ] n
dimin of **aunt**

au pair [ˈəuˈpɛəʳ] n (also: **~ girl**)
молодáя нáня-инострáнка,
живýщая в семьé

aura [ˈɔːrə] n (fig: air) орéол

austere [ɔsˈtɪəʳ] adj стрóгий;
(person, manner) сурóвый

Australia [ɔsˈtreɪlɪə] n Австрáлия

Austria [ˈɔstrɪə] n Áвстрия

authentic [ɔːˈθentɪk] adj
пóдлинный

author [ˈɔːθəʳ] n (of text, plan)

áвтор; (profession) писáтель(ница)
m(f)

authoritarian [ɔːθɔrɪˈtɛərɪən] adj
(conduct) авторитáрный

authoritative [ɔːˈθɔrɪtətɪv] adj
авторитéтный

authority [ɔːˈθɔrɪtɪ] n (power)
власть f; (POL) управлéние;
(expert) авторитéт; (official
permission) полномóчие; **the
authorities** npl (ruling body)
влáсти fpl

autobiography [ɔːtəbaɪˈɔgrəfɪ] n
автобиогрáфия

autograph [ˈɔːtəgrɑːf] n автóграф
♦ vt надпúсывать (надписáть pf)

automatic [ɔːtəˈmætɪk] adj
автоматúческий ♦ n (US: gun)
(самозарядный) пистолéт; (car)
автомобúль m с автоматúческим
переключéнием скоростéй;
~ally adv автоматúчески

automobile [ˈɔːtəməbiːl] n (US)
автомобúль m

autonomous [ɔːˈtɔnəməs] adj
(region) автонóмный; (person,
organization) самостоятельный

autonomy [ɔːˈtɔnəmɪ] n
автонóмия, самостоятельность f

autumn [ˈɔːtəm] n óсень f; **in ~**
óсенью

auxiliary [ɔːgˈzɪlɪərɪ] adj
вспомогáтельный ♦ n помóщник

avail [əˈveɪl] n: **to no ~** напрáсно

availability [əveɪləˈbɪlɪtɪ] n налúчие

available [əˈveɪləbl] adj достýпный;
(person) свобóдный

avalanche [ˈævəlɑːnʃ] n лавúна

avenue [ˈævənjuː] n (street) ýлица;
(drive) аллéя

average [ˈævərɪdʒ] n срéднее nt adj
♦ adj срéдний ♦ vt достигáть
(достúчь pf) в срéднем +gen;
(sum) составлять (состáвить pf) в
срéднем; **on ~** в срéднем

avert [əˈvɜːt] vt предотвращáть

(предотврати́ть pf); (blow, eyes) отводи́ть (отвести́ pf)

aviary ['eɪvɪərɪ] n пти́чий вольёр

aviation [eɪvɪ'eɪʃən] n авиа́ция

avid ['ævɪd] adj (keen) стра́стный

avocado [ævə'kɑːdəu] n (also: ~ pear: BRIT) авока́до n ind

avoid [ə'vɔɪd] vt избега́ть (избежа́ть pf) +gen

await [ə'weɪt] vt ожида́ть (impf) +gen

awake [ə'weɪk] (pt **awoke**, pp **awoken** or ~d) adj: he is ~ он просну́лся; he was still ~ он ещё не спал

award [ə'wɔːd] n награ́да ♦ vt награжда́ть (награди́ть pf); (LAW) присужда́ть (присуди́ть pf)

aware [ə'wɛə] adj: to be ~ (of) (realize) сознава́ть (impf) (+acc); to become ~ of sth/that сознава́ть (осозна́ть pf) что-н./, что; ~ness n осозна́ние

away [ə'weɪ] adv (movement) в сто́рону; (position) в стороне́; (far away) далеко́; the holidays are two weeks ~ до кани́кул (оста́лось) две неде́ли; ~ from (movement) от +gen; (position) в стороне́ от +gen; two kilometres ~ from the town в двух киломе́трах от го́рода; two hours ~ by car в двух часа́х езды́ на маши́не; he's ~ for a week он в отъе́зде на неде́лю; to take ~ (from) (remove) забира́ть (забра́ть pf) (у +gen); (subtract) отнима́ть (отня́ть pf) (от +gen); he is working ~ (continuously) он продолжа́ет рабо́тать

awe [ɔː] n благогове́ние

awful ['ɔːful] adj ужа́сный; an ~ lot (of) ужа́сно мно́го (+gen); ~ly adv ужа́сно

awkward ['ɔːkwəd] adj (clumsy) неуклю́жий; (inconvenient)

неудо́бный; (embarrassing) нело́вкий

awoke [ə'wəuk] pt of **awake**; ~n pp of **awake**

axe [æks] (US **ax**) n топо́р ♦ vt (project) отменя́ть (отмени́ть pf); (jobs) сокраща́ть (сократи́ть pf)

axis ['æksɪs] (pl **axes**) n ось f

B, b

B [biː] n (MUS) си nt ind

BA n abbr = **Bachelor of Arts**

baby ['beɪbɪ] n ребёнок; (newborn) младе́нец; ~ **carriage** n (US) коля́ска; ~-**sit** vi смотре́ть (impf) за детьми́; ~-**sitter** n приходя́щая ня́ня

bachelor ['bætʃələ] n холостя́к; **Bachelor of Arts/Science** ≈бакала́вр гуманита́рных/ есте́ственных нау́к

KEYWORD

back [bæk] n 1 (of person, animal) спина́; the back of the hand ты́льная сторона́ ладо́ни 2 (of house, car etc) за́дняя часть f; (of chair) спи́нка; (of page, book) оборо́т 3 (FOOTBALL) защи́тник ♦ vt 1 (candidate: also: **back up**) подде́рживать (поддержа́ть pf) 2 (financially: horse) ста́вить (поста́вить pf) на +acc; (: person) финанси́ровать (impf) 3: he backed the car into the garage он дал за́дний ход и поста́вил маши́ну в гара́ж ♦ vi (car etc: also: **back up**) дава́ть (дать pf) за́дний ход ♦ adv 1 (not forward) обра́тно, наза́д; he ran back он побежа́л обра́тно or наза́д 2 (returned): he's back он

вернулся
3 *(restitution)*: **to throw the ball
back** кидать (кинуть *pf*) мяч
обратно
4 *(again)*: **to call back** *(visit again)*
заходить (зайти *pf*) ещё раз;
(TEL) перезванивать
(перезвонить *pf*)
♦ *cpd* **1** *(payment)* задним числом
2 *(AUT, seat, wheels)* задний
back down *vi* отступать
(отступить *pf*)
back out *vi* *(of promise)*
отступаться (отступиться *pf*)
back up *vt* *(person, theory etc)*
поддерживать (поддержать *pf*)

back: ~**ache** *n* прострел, боль *f* в
пояснице; ~**bencher** *n* *(BRIT)*
заднескамеечник; ~**bone** *n*
позвоночник; **he's the ~bone of
the organization** на нём
держится вся организация;
~**ground** *n* *(of picture)* задний
план; *(of events)* предыстория;
(experience) опыт; **he's from a
working class ~ground** он из
рабочей семьи; **against a
~ground of ...** на фоне *+gen ...*;
~**hand** *n* *(TENNIS)* удар слева;
~**ing** *n* *(support)* поддержка;
~**lash** *n* *(fig)* обратная реакция;
~**log** *n*: ~**log of work**
невыполненная работа; ~**pack** *n*
рюкзак; ~**side** *n* *(inf)* зад;
~**stage** *adv* за кулисами; ~**ward**
adj *(movement)* обратный; *(person,
country)* отсталый; ~**wards** *adv*
назад; *(list)* наоборот; *(fall)*
навзничь; **to walk ~wards**
пятиться (попятиться *pf*); ~**yard**
n *(of house)* задний двор
bacon ['beɪkən] *n* бекон
bacteria [bæk'tɪərɪə] *npl* бактерии
fpl
bad [bæd] *adj* плохой; *(mistake)*

серьёзный; *(injury, crash)*
тяжёлый; *(food)* тухлый; **his ~
leg** его больная нога; **to go ~**
(food) тухнуть (протухнуть *pf*),
портиться (испортиться *pf*)
badge [bædʒ] *n* значок
badger ['bædʒə] *n* барсук
badly ['bædlɪ] *adv* плохо; ~
wounded тяжело раненый; **he
needs it ~** он сильно в этом
нуждается; **to be ~ off** *(for
money)* нуждаться *(impf)* в
деньгах)
badminton ['bædmɪntən] *n*
бадминтон
bad-tempered ['bæd'tempəd] *adj*
вспыльчивый; *(now)*
раздражённый
bag [bæg] *n* сумка; *(paper, plastic)*
пакет; *(handbag)* сумочка;
(satchel) ранец; *(case)* портфель
m; ~ **s of** *(inf)* уйма *+gen*
baggage ['bægɪdʒ] *n* *(US)* багаж
baggy ['bægɪ] *adj* мешковатый
Bahamas [bə'hɑːməz] *npl*: **the ~**
Багамские острова *mpl*
bail [beɪl] *n* *(money)* залог ♦ *vt*
(also: **to grant ~ to**): выпускать
(выпустить *pf*) под залог; **he was
released on ~** он был выпущен
под залог; ~ **out** *vt* *(LAW)*
платить (заплатить *pf*)
залоговую сумму за *+acc*; *(boat)*
вычерпывать (вычерпать *pf*)
воду из *+gen*
bailiff ['beɪlɪf] *n* *(LAW, BRIT)*
судебный исполнитель *m*; *(; US)*
помощник шерифа
bait [beɪt] *n* *(for fish)* наживка; *(for
animal, criminal)* приманка ♦ *vt*
(hook, trap) наживлять (наживить
pf)
bake [beɪk] *vt* печь (испечь *pf*) ♦ *vi*
(bread etc) печься (испечься *pf*);
(make cakes etc) печь *(impf)*; ~**d
beans** *npl* консервированная

фасо́ль *fsg* (в тома́те); **~r** *n* пе́карь *m*; (*also*: **the baker's**) бу́лочная *f adj*; **~ry** *n* пека́рня; (*shop*) бу́лочная *f adj*

baking ['beɪkɪŋ] *n* вы́печка; **she does her ~ once a week** она́ печёт раз в неде́лю; **~ powder** *n* разрыхли́тель *m*

balance ['bæləns] *n* (*equilibrium*) равнове́сие; (*COMM, in account*) бала́нс; (: *remainder*) оста́ток; (*scales*) весы́ *pl* ♦ *vt* (*budget, account*) баланси́ровать (сбаланси́ровать *pf*); (*make equal*) уравнове́шивать (уравнове́сить *pf*); **~ of payments/trade** платёжный/торго́вый бала́нс; **~d** *adj* (*diet*) сбаланси́рованный

balcony ['bælkənɪ] *n* балко́н

bald [bɔːld] *adj* (*head*) лы́сый; (*tyre*) стёртый

bale [beɪl] *n* (*of hay etc*) тюк

ball [bɔːl] *n* (*for football, tennis*) мяч; (*for golf*) мя́чик; (*of wool, string*) клубо́к; (*dance*) бал

ballerina [bælə'riːnə] *n* балери́на

ballet ['bæleɪ] *n* бале́т

balloon [bə'luːn] *n* возду́шный шар; (*also*: **hot air ~**) аэроста́т

ballot ['bælət] *n* голосова́ние, баллотиро́вка

ballroom ['bɔːlrum] *n* ба́льный зал

Baltic ['bɔːltɪk] *n*: **the ~** Балти́йское мо́ре ♦ *adj*: **the ~ States** стра́ны *fpl* Ба́лтии, прибалти́йские госуда́рства *ntpl*

bamboo [bæm'buː] *n* бамбу́к

ban [bæn] *vt* (*prohibit*) запреща́ть (запрети́ть *pf*); (*suspend, exclude*) отстраня́ть (отстрани́ть *pf*) ♦ *n* (*prohibition*) запре́т

banal [bə'nɑːl] *adj* бана́льный

banana [bə'nɑːnə] *n* бана́н

band [bænd] *n* (*group: of people, rock musicians*) гру́ппа; (: *of jazz, military musicians*) орке́стр

bandage ['bændɪdʒ] *n* повя́зка ♦ *vt* бинтова́ть (забинтова́ть *pf*)

bandwagon ['bændwæɡən] *n*: **to jump on the ~** эксплуати́ровать (*impf/pf*) ситуа́цию

bang [bæŋ] *n* стук; (*explosion*) вы́стрел; (*blow*) уда́р ♦ *excl* бах ♦ *vt* (*door*) хло́пать (хло́пнуть *pf*) +*instr*; (*head etc*) уда́рить (уда́рить *pf*) ♦ *vi* (*door*) захло́пываться (захло́пнуться *pf*)

bangs [bæŋz] *npl* (*US*) чёлка *fsg*

banish ['bænɪʃ] *vt* высыла́ть (вы́слать *pf*)

bank [bæŋk] *n* банк; (*of river, lake*) бе́рег; (*of earth*) на́сыпь *f* ♦ **~ on** *vt fus* полага́ться (положи́ться *pf*) на +*acc*; **~ account** *n* ба́нковский счёт; **~ card** *n* ба́нковская ка́рточка; **~ holiday** *n* (*BRIT*) нерабо́чий день *m* (*обы́чно понеде́льник*); **~ note** *n* банкно́т

bankrupt ['bæŋkrʌpt] *adj* обанкро́тившийся; **to go ~** обанкро́титься (*pf*); **I am ~** я - банкро́т, я обанкро́тился (*pf*); **~cy** *n* банкро́тство, несостоя́тельность *f*

bank statement *n* вы́писка с ба́нковского счёта

banner ['bænə*] *n* транспара́нт

bannister ['bænɪstə*] *n* (*usu pl*) пери́ла *pl*

banquet ['bæŋkwɪt] *n* банке́т

baptism ['bæptɪzəm] *n* креще́ние

bar [bɑː*] *n* (*in pub*) бар; (*counter*) сто́йка; (*rod*) прут; (*of soap*) брусо́к; (*of chocolate*) пли́тка; (*MUS*) такт ♦ *vt* (*door, way*) загора́живать (загороди́ть *pf*); (*person*) не допуска́ть (допусти́ть *pf*); **~s** *npl* (*on window*) решётка *fsg*; **behind ~s** за решёткой; **the Bar** адвокату́ра; **~ none** без исключе́ния

barbaric [bɑː'bærɪk] *adj*

ва́рварский

barbecue ['bɑ:bɪkju:] n барбекю́ nt ind

barbed wire ['bɑ:bd-] n колю́чая про́волока

barber ['bɑ:bəʳ] n парикма́хер

bar code n штрихово́й код

bare [bɛəʳ] adj (body) го́лый, обнажённый; (trees) оголённый ♦ vt (one's body) оголи́ть (оголя́ть pf), обнажи́ть (обнажа́ть pf); (teeth) ска́лить (оска́лить pf); in or with ~ feet босико́м; ~**foot** adj босо́й ♦ adv босико́м; ~**ly** adv едва́

bargain ['bɑ:gɪn] n сде́лка; (good buy) вы́годная поку́пка

barge [bɑ:dʒ] n ба́ржа

bark [bɑ:k] n (of tree) кора́ ♦ vi (dog) ла́ять (impf)

barley ['bɑ:lɪ] n ячме́нь m

barman ['bɑ:mən] (irreg) n ба́рмен

barn [bɑ:n] n амба́р

barometer [bə'rɔmɪtəʳ] n баро́метр

baron ['bærən] n баро́н; (of press, industry) магна́т

barracks ['bærəks] npl каза́рма fsg

barrage ['bærɑ:ʒ] n (fig) лави́на

barrel ['bærəl] n (of wine, beer) бо́чка; (of oil) баррéль m; (of gun) ствол

barren ['bærən] adj (land) беспло́дный

barricade [bærɪ'keɪd] n баррика́да ♦ vt баррикади́ровать (забаррикади́ровать pf); to ~ o.s. in баррикади́роваться (забаррикади́роваться pf)

barrier ['bærɪəʳ] n (at entrance) барье́р; (at frontier) шлагба́ум; (fig: to progress) препя́тствие

barring ['bɑ:rɪŋ] prep за исключе́нием +gen

barrister ['bærɪstəʳ] n (BRIT) адвока́т

barrow ['bærəu] n (also: **wheel~**)

та́чка

barter ['bɑ:təʳ] vi производи́ть (произвести́ pf) ба́ртерный обме́н

base [beɪs] n основа́ние; (of monument etc) постаме́нт; (MIL) ба́за; (for organization) местонахожде́ние ♦ adj ни́зкий ♦ vt: ~ **sth on** (opinion) осно́вывать (impf) что-н на +prp; ~**ball** n бейсбо́л; ~**ment** n подва́л;

bases[1] npl of **base**

bases[2] npl of **basis**

basic ['beɪsɪk] adj (fundamental) фундамента́льный; (elementary) нача́льный; (primitive) элемента́рный; ~**ally** adv по существу́; (on the whole) в основно́м; ~**s** npl: **the ~s** осно́вы fpl

basil ['bæzl] n базили́к

basin ['beɪsn] n (also: **wash~**) ра́ковина; (GEO) бассе́йн

basis ['beɪsɪs] (pl **bases**) n основа́ние; **on a part-time ~** на непо́лной ста́вке; **on a trial ~** на испыта́тельный срок

basket ['bɑ:skɪt] n корзи́на; ~**ball** n баскетбо́л

bass [beɪs] n бас ♦ adj ба́ссовый

bastard ['bɑ:stəd] n внебра́чный ребёнок; (inf!) ублю́док (!)

bat [bæt] n (ZOOL) лету́чая мышь f; (SPORT) бита́; (BRIT: TABLE TENNIS) раке́тка

batch [bætʃ] n (of bread) вы́печка; (of papers) па́чка

bath [bɑ:θ] n ва́нна ♦ vt купа́ть (вы́купать pf); **to have a ~** принима́ть (приня́ть pf) ва́нну; see also **baths**

bathe [beɪð] vi (swim) купа́ться (impf); (US: have a bath) принима́ть (приня́ть pf) ва́нну ♦ vt (wound) промыва́ть (промы́ть pf)

bathroom ['bɑ:θrum] n ва́нная f adj

baths [bɑ:ðz] npl (also: **swimming ~**) пла́вательный бассе́йн msg

bath towel n ба́нное полоте́нце

baton ['bætən] n (MUS) дирижёрская па́лочка; (POLICE) дуби́нка; (SPORT) эстафе́тная па́лочка

battalion [bə'tæliən] n батальо́н

batter ['bætə'] vt (person) бить (изби́ть pf); (subj: wind, rain) бить (поби́ть pf) ♦ n жи́дкое те́сто

battery ['bætəri] n (of torch etc) батаре́йка; (AUT) аккумуля́тор

battle ['bætl] n би́тва, бой

bay [beɪ] n зали́в; (smaller) бу́хта; **loading ~** погру́зочная площа́дка; **to hold sb at ~** держа́ть (impf) кого́-н на расстоя́нии

bazaar [bə'zɑ:'] n база́р, ры́нок; (fete) благотвори́тельный база́р

B & B n abbr = **bed and breakfast**

BBC n abbr (= British Broadcasting Corporation) Би-Би-Си́ nt ind

BC adv abbr (= before Christ) до рождества́ Христо́ва

---KEYWORD---

be [bi:] (pt **was, were**, pp **been**) aux vb **1** (with present participle: forming continuous tenses): **what are you doing?** что Вы де́лаете?; **it is raining** идёт дождь; **they're working tomorrow** они́ рабо́тают за́втра; **the house is being built** дом стро́ится; **I've been waiting for you for ages** я жду Вас уже́ це́лую ве́чность

2 (with pp: forming passives): **he was killed** он был уби́т; **the box had been opened** я́щик откры́ли; **the thief was nowhere to be seen** во́ра нигде́ не́ было ви́дно

3 (in tag questions) не так or

пра́вда ли, да; **she's back again, is she?** она́ верну́лась, да or не так or пра́вда ли?; **she is pretty, isn't she?** она́ хоро́шенькая, не пра́вда ли or да

4 (+ to +infin): **the house is to be sold** дом должны́ прода́ть; **you're to be congratulated for all your work** Вас сле́дует поздра́вить за всю Ва́шу рабо́ту; **he's not to open it** он не до́лжен открыва́ть э́то

♦ vb **1** (+ complement: in present tense): **he is English** он англича́нин; (in past/future tense) быть (impf) +instr; **he was a doctor** он был врачо́м; **she is going to be very tall** она́ бу́дет о́чень высо́кой; **I'm tired** я уста́л; **I was hot/cold** мне бы́ло жа́рко/хо́лодно; **two and two are four** два́жды два - четы́ре; **she's tall** она́ высо́кая; **be careful!** бу́дьте осторо́жны!; **be quiet!** ти́хо!, ти́ше!

2 (of health): **how are you feeling?** как Вы себя́ чу́вствуете?; **he's very ill** он о́чень бо́лен; **I'm better now** мне сейча́с лу́чше

3 (of age): **how old are you?** ско́лько Вам лет?; **I'm sixteen (years old)** мне шестна́дцать (лет)

4 (cost): **how much is the wine?** ско́лько сто́ит вино́?; **that'll be £5.75, please** с Вас £5.75, пожа́луйста

♦ vi **1** (exist) быть (impf); **there are people who ...** есть лю́ди, кото́рые ...; **there is one drug that ...** есть одно́ лека́рство, кото́рое ...; **is there a God?** Бог есть?

2 (occur) быва́ть (impf); **there are frequent accidents on this road** на э́той доро́ге ча́сто быва́ют ава́рии; **be that as it may** как бы то ни́ было; **so be it** так и быть, быть по сему́

3 (*referring to place*): **I won't be here tomorrow** меня́ здесь за́втра не бу́дет; **the book is on the table** кни́га на столе́; **there are pictures on the wall** на стене́ карти́ны; **Edinburgh is in Scotland** Эдинбу́рг нахо́дится в Шотла́ндии; **there is someone in the house** в до́ме кто-то есть; **we've been for ages** мы здесь уже́ це́лую ве́чность

4 (*referring to movement*) быть (*impf*); **where have you been?** где Вы бы́ли?; **I've been to the post office** я был на по́чте

♦ *impers vb* **1** (*referring to time*): **it's five o'clock (now)** сейча́с пять часо́в; **it's the 28th of April (today)** сего́дня 28-ое апре́ля

2 (*referring to distance, weather: in present tense*): **it's 10 km to the village** до дере́вни 10 км; (: *in past/future tense*) быть (*impf*); **it's hot/cold (today)** сего́дня жа́рко/хо́лодно; **it was very windy yesterday** вчера́ бы́ло о́чень ве́трено; **it will be sunny tomorrow** за́втра бу́дет со́лнечно

3 (*emphatic*): **it's (only) me/the postman** э́то я/почтальо́н; **it was Maria who paid the bill** и́менно Мари́я оплати́ла счёт

beach [biːtʃ] *n* пляж
beacon ['biːkən] *n* (*marker*) сигна́льный огонь *m*
bead [biːd] *n* бу́сина *f*; (*of sweat*) ка́пля
beak [biːk] *n* клюв
beam [biːm] *n* (*ARCHIT*) ба́лка, стропи́ло, (*of light*) луч
bean [biːn] *n* боб; **French**

фасо́ль *f no pl*; **runner ~** фасо́ль о́гненная; **coffee ~** кофе́йное зерно́

bear [bɛəʳ] (*pt* **bore**, *pp* **borne**) *n* медве́дь/(и́ца) *m(f)* ♦ *vt* (*cost, responsibility*) нести́ (понести́ *pf*); (*weight*) нести́ (*impf*) ♦ *vi*: **to ~ right/left** (*AUT*) держа́ться (*impf*) пра́вого/ле́вого поворо́та; **~ out** *vt* подтвержда́ть (подтверди́ть *pf*)
beard [biəd] *n* борода́; **~ed** *adj* борода́тый
bearing ['bɛərɪŋ] *n* (*connection*) отноше́ние; **~s** *npl* (*also*: **ball ~s**) ша́рики *mpl* подши́пника; **to take a ~** ориенти́роваться (*impf/pf*)
beast [biːst] *n* (*also inf*) зверь *m*
beat [biːt] (*pt* **~**, *pp* **~en**) *n* (*of heart*) бие́ние; (*MUS, rhythm*) ритм; (*POLICE*) уча́сток ♦ *vt* (*wife, child*) бить (поби́ть *pf*); (*eggs etc*) взбива́ть (взбить *pf*); (*opponent, record*) побива́ть (поби́ть *pf*); (*drum*) бить (*impf*) в +*acc* ♦ *vi* (*heart*) би́ться (*impf*); (*rain, wind*) стуча́ть (*impf*); **~ it!** (*inf*) кати́сь!; **off the ~en track** по непроторённому пути́; **~ up** (*person*) избива́ть (изби́ть *pf*); **~ing** *n* избие́ние; (*thrashing*) по́рка
beautiful ['bjuːtɪful] *adj* краси́вый; (*day, experience*) прекра́сный; **~ly** ['bjuːtɪflɪ] *adv* (*play, sing etc*) краси́во, прекра́сно
beauty ['bjuːtɪ] *n* красота́; (*woman*) краса́вица
beaver ['biːvəʳ] *n* (*ZOOL*) бобр
became [bɪ'keɪm] *pt of* **become**
because [bɪ'kɔz] *conj* потому́ что; (*since*) так как; **~ of** из-за +*gen*
become [bɪ'kʌm] (*irreg: like* **come**) *vi* станови́ться (стать *pf*) +*instr*; **to ~ fat** толсте́ть (потолсте́ть *pf*); **to ~ thin** худе́ть (похуде́ть *pf*)

bed [bed] n крова́ть f; (of river, sea) дно; (of flowers) клу́мба; **to go to ~** ложи́ться (лечь pf) спать; **~ and breakfast** n ма́ленькая ча́стная гости́ница с за́втраком; (terms) ночлёг и за́втрак; **~clothes** npl посте́льное бельё ntsg; **~ding** n посте́льные принадле́жности fpl; **~room** n спа́льня; **~side** n: **at sb's ~side** у посте́ли кого́-н; **~spread** n покрыва́ло; **~time** n вре́мя nt ложи́ться спать

bee [biː] n пчела́

beech [biːtʃ] n бук

beef [biːf] n говя́дина; **roast ~** ро́стбиф

been [biːn] pp of **be**

beer [bɪə] n пи́во

beet [biːt] n (vegetable) кормова́я свёкла; (US: also: **red ~**) свёкла

beetle ['biːtl] n жук

beetroot ['biːtruːt] n (BRIT) свёкла

before [bɪ'fɔː] prep пе́ред +instr, до +gen ♦ conj до того́ or пе́ред тем, как ♦ adv (time) ра́ньше, пре́жде; **the day ~ yesterday** позавчера́; **do this ~ you forget** сде́лайте э́то, пока́ Вы не забы́ли; **~ going** пе́ред ухо́дом; **~ she goes** до того́ or пе́ред тем, как она́ уйдёт; **the week ~** неде́лю наза́д, на про́шлой неде́ле; **I've never seen it ~** я никогда́ э́того ра́ньше не ви́дел; **~hand** adv зара́нее

beg [beg] vi попроша́йничать (impf), ни́щенствовать (impf) ♦ vt (also: **~ for**: food, money) проси́ть (impf); (: mercy, forgiveness) умоля́ть (умоли́ть pf) o +prp; **to ~ sb to do** умоля́ть (умоли́ть pf) кого́-н +infin

began [bɪ'ɡæn] pt of **begin**

beggar ['beɡə] n попроша́йка, ни́щий(ая) m(f) adj

begin [bɪ'ɡɪn] (pt **began**, pp **begun**) vt начина́ть (нача́ть pf) ♦ vi начина́ться (нача́ться pf); **to ~ doing** or **to do** начина́ть (нача́ть pf) +impf infin; **~ner** n начина́ющий(ая) m(f) adj; **~ning** n нача́ло

begun [bɪ'ɡʌn] pp of **begin**

behalf [bɪ'hɑːf] n: **on** or (US) **in ~ of** от и́мени +gen; (for benefit of) в по́льзу +gen, в интере́сах +gen; **on my/his ~** от моего́/его́ и́мени

behave [bɪ'heɪv] vi вести́ (impf) себя́; (also: **~ o.s.**) вести́ (impf) себя́ хорошо́

behaviour [bɪ'heɪvjə] (US **behavior**) n поведе́ние

behind [bɪ'haɪnd] prep (at the back of) за +instr, позади́ +gen; (supporting) за +instr; (lower in rank etc) ни́же +gen ♦ adv сза́ди, позади́ ♦ n (buttocks) зад; **to be ~ schedule** отстава́ть (отста́ть pf) от гра́фика

beige [beɪʒ] adj бе́жевый

Beijing ['beɪ'dʒɪŋ] n Пеки́н

Beirut [beɪ'ruːt] n Бейру́т

Belarus [belə'rus] n Белору́сь f

belated [bɪ'leɪtɪd] adj запозда́лый

belfry ['belfrɪ] n колоко́льня

Belgian ['beldʒən] n бельги́ец(и́йка)

Belgium ['beldʒəm] n Бе́льгия

belief [bɪ'liːf] n (conviction) убежде́ние; (trust, faith) ве́ра; **it's beyond ~** э́то невероя́тно; **in the ~ that** полага́я, что

believe [bɪ'liːv] vt ве́рить (пове́рить pf) +dat or в +acc ♦ vi ве́рить (impf); **to ~ in** ве́рить (пове́рить pf) в +acc

bell [bel] n ко́локол; (small) колоко́льчик; (on door) звоно́к

belligerent [bɪ'lɪdʒərənt] adj войнстве́нный

belly ['belɪ] n (of animal) брю́хо; (of

person) живо́т

belong [bɪ'lɒŋ] *vi*: **to ~ to**
принадлежа́ть (*impf*) +*dat*; (*club*)
состоя́ть (*impf*) в +*prp*; **this book**
~s here ме́сто э́той кни́ги здесь;
~ings *npl* ве́щи *fpl*

beloved [bɪ'lʌvɪd] *adj* люби́мый

below [bɪ'ləu] *prep* (*position*) под
+*instr*; (*motion*) под +*acc*; (*less than*)
ни́же +*gen ♦ adv* (*position*) внизу́;
(*motion*) вниз; **see** ~ смотри́ ни́же

belt [bɛlt] *n* (*leather*) реме́нь *m*;
(*cloth*) по́яс; (*of land*) по́яс, зо́на;
(*TECH*) приводно́й реме́нь

bemused [bɪ'mju:zd] *adj*
озада́ченный

bench [bɛntʃ] *n* скамья́; (*BRIT : POL*)
места́ *ntpl* па́ртий в парла́менте;
(*in workshop*) верста́к; (*in*
laboratory) лаборато́рный стол;
the Bench (*LAW*) суде́йская
колле́гия

bend [bɛnd] (*pt, pp* **bent**) *vt* гнуть
(согну́ть *pf*), сгиба́ть (*impf*) ♦ *vi*
(*person*) гну́ться (согну́ться *pf*) ♦ *n*
(*BRIT : in road*) поворо́т; (*in pipe*)
изги́б; (*in river*) излу́чина; ~
down ♦ наклоня́ться
(наклони́ться *pf*), нагиба́ться
(нагну́ться *pf*)

beneath [bɪ'ni:θ] *prep* (*position*) под
+*instr*; (*motion*) под +*acc*; (*unworthy*
of) ни́же +*gen ♦ adv* внизу́

beneficial [bɛnɪ'fɪʃl] *adj*: ~ (**to**)
благотво́рный (для +*gen*)

benefit ['bɛnɪfɪt] *n* (*advantage*)
вы́года; (*money*) посо́бие ♦ *vt*
приноси́ть (принести́ *pf*) по́льзу
+*dat ♦ vi*: **he'll ~ from it** он
полу́чит от э́того вы́году

benevolent [bɪ'nɛvələnt] *adj*
(*person*) доброжела́тельный

benign [bɪ'naɪn] *adj*
доброду́шный; (*MED*)
доброка́чественный

bent [bɛnt] *pt, pp of* **bend** ♦ *adj*

(*wire, pipe*) по́гнутый; **he is ~ on**
doing он настро́ился +*infin*

bereaved [bɪ'ri:vd] *adj* поне́сший
тяжёлую утра́ту ♦ *n*: **the ~**
друзья́ *mpl* и ро́дственники *mpl*
поко́йного

Berlin [bə:'lɪn] *n* Берли́н

Bermuda [bə:'mju:də] *n*
Берму́дские острова́ *mpl*

berry ['bɛrɪ] *n* я́года

berserk [bə'sə:k] *adj*: **to go ~**
чуме́ть (очуме́ть *pf*)

berth [bə:θ] *n* (*in caravan, on ship*)
ко́йка; (*on train*) по́лка; (*mooring*)
прича́л

beset [bɪ'sɛt] (*pt, pp* ~) *vt*: **we have**
been ~ by problems нас
одолева́ли пробле́мы

beside [bɪ'saɪd] *prep* ря́дом с +*instr*,
о́коло +*gen*, у +*gen*; **to be ~ o.s.**
(**with**) быть (*impf*) вне себя́ (от
+*gen*); **that's ~ the point** э́то к
де́лу не отно́сится

besides [bɪ'saɪdz] *adv* кро́ме того́
♦ *prep* кро́ме +*gen*, поми́мо +*gen*

best [bɛst] *adj* лу́чший ♦ *adv* лу́чше
всего́; **the ~ part of** (*quantity*)
бо́льшая часть +*gen*; **at the ~**
в лу́чшем слу́чае; **to make the ~ of**
sth испо́льзовать (*impf*) что-н
наилу́чшим о́бразом; **to do one's**
~ де́лать (сде́лать *pf*) всё
возмо́жное; **to the ~ of my**
knowledge наско́лько мне
изве́стно; **to the ~ of my ability** в
ме́ру мои́х спосо́бностей; ~
man *n* ша́фер; ~**seller** *n*
бестсе́ллер

bet [bɛt] (*pt, pp* ~**ted**) *n* (*wager*)
пари́ *nt ind*; (*in gambling*) ста́вка
♦ *vi* (*wager*) держа́ть (*impf*) пари́;
(*expect, guess*) би́ться (*impf*) об
закла́д ♦ *vt*: **to ~ sb sth** спо́рить
(поспо́рить *pf*) с кем-н на что-н;
to ~ money on sth ста́вить
(поста́вить *pf*) де́ньги на что-н

betray [bɪ'treɪ] vt (friends) предава́ть (преда́ть pf); (trust) обма́нывать (обману́ть pf); **~al** n преда́тельство

better ['betə*] adj лу́чший ♦ adv лу́чше ♦ vt (score) улучша́ть (улу́чшить pf) ♦ n: **to get the ~ of** бра́ть (взя́ть pf) верх над +instr; **I feel** ~ я чу́вствую себя́ лу́чше; **to get ~** (MED) поправля́ться (попра́виться pf); **I had ~ go** мне лу́чше уйти́; **he thought ~ of it** он переду́мал; ~ **off** adj (wealthier) бо́лее состоя́тельный

betting ['betɪŋ] n пари́ nt ind

between [bɪ'twi:n] prep ме́жду +instr ♦ adv: **in** ~ ме́жду тем

beware [bɪ'weə*] vi: **to** ~ (**of**) остерега́ться (остере́чься pf) (+gen)

bewildered [bɪ'wɪldəd] adj изумлённый

beyond [bɪ'ɔnd] prep (position) за +instr; (motion) за +acc; (understanding) вы́ше +gen; (expectations) сверх +gen; (doubt) вне +gen; (age) бо́льше +gen; (date) по́сле +gen ♦ adv (position) вдали́; (motion) вдаль; **it's** ~ **repair** э́то невозмо́жно починить

bias ['baɪəs] n (against) предубежде́ние; (towards) пристра́стие

bib [bɪb] n (child's) нагру́дник

Bible ['baɪbl] n Би́блия

biblical ['bɪblɪkl] adj библе́йский

bicycle ['baɪsɪkl] n велосипе́д

bid [bɪd] (pt **bade** or ~, pp ~(**den**)) n (at auction) предложе́ние цены́; (attempt) попы́тка ♦ vt (offer) предлага́ть (предложи́ть pf) ♦ vi: **to** ~ **for** (at auction) предлага́ть (предложи́ть pf) це́ну за +acc; ~**der** n: **the highest** ~**der** лицо́, предлага́ющее наивы́сшую це́ну

big [bɪg] adj большо́й; (important)

ва́жный; (bulky) кру́пный; (older: brother, sister) ста́рший

bigotry ['bɪgətrɪ] n фанати́зм

bike [baɪk] n (inf: bicycle) вело́к

bikini [bɪ'ki:nɪ] n бики́ни nt ind

bilateral [baɪ'lætərl] adj двусторо́нний

bilingual [baɪ'lɪŋgwəl] adj двуязы́чный

bill [bɪl] n (invoice) счёт; (POL) законопрое́кт; (US: banknote) казначе́йский биле́т, банкно́т; (beak) клюв; ~**board** n доска́ объявле́ний

billion ['bɪljən] n (BRIT) биллио́н; (US) миллиа́рд

bin [bɪn] n (BRIT: also: **rubbish** ~) мусо́рное ведро́; (container) я́щик

bind [baɪnd] (pt, pp **bound**) vt (tie) привя́зывать (привяза́ть pf); (hands, feet) свя́зывать (связа́ть pf); (oblige) обя́зывать (обяза́ть pf); (book) переплета́ть (переплести́ pf); ~**ing** adj обя́зывающий

bingo ['bɪŋgəu] n лото́ nt ind

binoculars [bɪ'nɔkjuləz] npl бино́кль msg

biography [baɪ'ɔgrəfɪ] n биогра́фия

biological [baɪə'lɔdʒɪkl] adj (science) биологи́ческий; (warfare) бактериологи́ческий; (washing powder) содержа́щий биопрепара́ты

biology [baɪ'ɔlədʒɪ] n биоло́гия

birch [bə:tʃ] n берёза

bird [bə:d] n пти́ца

Biro ® ['baɪərəu] n ша́риковая ру́чка

birth [bə:θ] n рожде́ние; **to give** ~ **to** рожа́ть (роди́ть pf); ~ **certificate** n свиде́тельство о рожде́нии; ~ **control** n (policy) контро́ль m рожда́емости;

(methods) противозача́точные ме́ры fpl; **~day** n день m рожде́ния ♦ cpd: **~day card** откры́тка ко дню рожде́ния; see also **happy**; **~place** n ро́дина

biscuit ['biskit] n (BRIT) пече́нье; (US) ≈ кекс

bisexual ['bai'seksjuəl] adj бисексуа́льный

bishop ['biʃəp] n (REL) епи́скоп; (CHESS) слон

bit [bit] pt of **bite** ♦ n (piece) кусо́к, кусо́чек; (COMPUT) бит; **a ~ of** немно́го +gen; **a ~ dangerous** слегка́ опа́сный; **~ by ~** ма́ло-пома́лу, понемно́гу

bitch [bitʃ] n (also infl) су́ка (also !)

bite [bait] (pt **bit**, pp **bitten**) vt куса́ть (укуси́ть pf) ♦ vi куса́ться (impf) ♦ n (insect bite) уку́с; **to ~ one's nails** куса́ть (impf) но́гти; **let's have a ~ (to eat)** (inf) дава́йте переку́сим; **he had a ~ of cake** он откуси́л кусо́к пирога́

bitter ['bitə'] adj го́рький; (wind) пронзи́тельный; (struggle) ожесточённый; **~ness** n (anger, of taste) го́речь f, ожесточённость f

bizarre [bi'zɑ:'] adj стра́нный, причу́дливый

black [blæk] adj чёрный; (tea) без молока́; (person) черноко́жий ♦ n (colour) чёрный цвет, чёрное nt adj; (person): **Black** негр(итя́нка); **~ and blue** в синяка́х; **to be in the ~** (impf) быть в ба́нке; **~berry** n ежеви́ка f no pl; **~bird** n (чёрный) дрозд, **~board** n кла́ссная доска́; **~coffee** n чёрный ко́фе m ind; **~currant** n чёрная сморо́дина; **~ eye** n синя́к под гла́зом; **to give sb a ~ eye** подби́ть (pf) кому́-н глаз; **~mail** n шанта́ж ♦ vt шантажи́ровать (impf); **~**

market n чёрный ры́нок; **~out** n (ELEC) обесто́чка; (TV, RADIO) приостановле́ние переда́ч; (MED) о́бморок; **~ pepper** n чёрный пе́рец; **Black Sea** n: **the Black Sea** Чёрное мо́ре; **~smith** n кузне́ц

bladder ['blædə'] n мочево́й пузы́рь m

blade [bleid] n ле́звие; (of propeller, oar) ло́пасть f; **a ~ of grass** трави́нка

blame [bleim] n вина́ ♦ vt: **to ~ sb for sth** вини́ть (impf) кого́-н в чём-н; **he is to ~ (for sth)** он винова́т (в чём-н)

bland [blænd] adj (food) пре́сный

blank [blæŋk] adj (paper) чи́стый; (look) пусто́й; (of memory) прова́л; (on form) про́пуск; (for gun) холосто́й патро́н

blanket ['blæŋkit] n одея́ло; (of snow) покро́в; (of fog) пелена́

blasé ['blɑ:zei] adj вальяжный

blasphemy ['blæsfimi] n богоху́льство

blast [blɑ:st] n (explosion) взрыв ♦ vt (blow up) взрыва́ть (взорва́ть pf)

blatant ['bleitənt] adj я́вный

blaze [bleiz] n (fire) пла́мя nt; (of colour) полыха́ние

blazer ['bleizə'] n фо́рменный пиджа́к

bleach [bli:tʃ] n (also: **household ~**) отбе́ливатель m ♦ vt (fabric) отбе́ливать (отбели́ть pf)

bleak [bli:k] adj (day, face) уны́лый; (prospect) мра́чный

bleed [bli:d] (pt, pp **bled**) vi кровото́чить (impf); **my nose is ~ing** у меня́ из но́са идёт кровь

blend [blend] n (of tea, whisky) буке́т ♦ vt (CULIN) сме́шивать (смеша́ть pf) ♦ vi (also: **~ in**) сочета́ться (impf)

bless [bles] (*pt, pp* **~ed** *or* **blest**) *vt* благословля́ть (благослови́ть *pf*); **~ you!** бу́дьте здоро́вы!; **~ing** *n* благослове́ние; (*godsend*) Бо́жий дар

blew [bluː] *pt of* **blow**

blind [blaɪnd] *adj* слепо́й ♦ *n* што́ра; (*also:* **Venetian ~**) жалюзи́ *pl ind* ♦ *vt* ослепля́ть (ослепи́ть *pf*); **the ~** *npl* (*blind people*) слепы́е *pl adj*; **to be ~ (to)** (*fig*) не ви́деть (*impf*) (+*acc*); **~ly** *adv* (*without thinking*) сле́по; **~ness** *n* (*physical*) слепота́

blink [blɪŋk] *vi* морга́ть (*impf*); (*light*) мига́ть (*impf*)

bliss [blɪs] *n* блаже́нство

blithely ['blaɪðlɪ] *adv* беспе́чно

blizzard ['blɪzəd] *n* вью́га

bloated ['bləʊtɪd] *adj* (*face, stomach*) взду́тый; **I feel ~** я весь разду́лся

blob [blɔb] *n* (*of glue, paint*) сгу́сток; (*shape*) сму́тное очерта́ние

bloc [blɔk] *n* блок

block [blɔk] *n* (*of buildings*) кварта́л; (*of stone etc*) плита́ ♦ *vt* (*barricade*) блоки́ровать (заблоки́ровать *pf*), загора́живать (загороди́ть *pf*); (*progress*) препя́тствовать (*impf*); **~ of flats** (*BRIT*) многокварти́рный дом; **mental ~** прова́л па́мяти; **~ade** [blɔ'keɪd] *n* блока́да; **~age** ['blɔkɪdʒ] *n* блокиро́вание

bloke [bləʊk] *n* (*BRIT : inf*) па́рень *m*

blond(e) [blɔnd] *adj* белоку́рый ♦ *n*: **~e** (*woman*) блонди́нка

blood [blʌd] *n* кровь *f*; **~ donor** *n* до́нор; **~ pressure** *n* кровяно́е давле́ние; **~shed** *n* кровопроли́тие; **~stream** *n* кровообраще́ние; **~ test** *n* ана́лиз кро́ви; **~y** *adj* (*battle*)

крова́вый; (*BRIT : inf!*): **this ~y weather** э́та прокля́тая пого́да; **~y good** (*inf!*) черто́вски хоро́ший

blossom ['blɔsəm] *n* цвет, цвете́ние

blot [blɔt] *n* (*on text*) кля́кса

blow [bləʊ] (*pt* **blew**, *pp* **~n**) *n* уда́р ♦ *vi* (*wind*) дуть (поду́ть *pf*); (*fuse*) перегора́ть (перегоре́ть *pf*) ♦ *vt* (*subj: wind*) гнать (*impf*); (*instrument*) дуть (*impf*) в +*acc*; **to ~ one's nose** сморка́ться (вы́сморкаться *pf*); **~ away** *vt* сдува́ть (сдуть *pf*); **~ up** *vi* (*storm, crisis*) разража́ться (разрази́ться *pf*) ♦ *vt* (*bridge*) взрыва́ть (взорва́ть *pf*); (*tyre*) надува́ть (наду́ть *pf*)

blue [bluː] *adj* (*colour: light*) голубо́й; (*: dark*) си́ний; (*unhappy*) гру́стный; **the ~s** *npl* (*MUS*) блюз *msg*; **out of the ~** (*fig*) как гром среди́ я́сного не́ба; **~bell** *n* колоко́льчик; **~print** *n* (*fig*): **a ~print (for)** прое́кт (+*gen*)

bluff [blʌf] *vi* блефова́ть (*impf*) ♦ *vt*: **to call sb's ~** заставля́ть (заста́вить *pf*) кого́-н раскры́ть ка́рты

blunder ['blʌndə'] *n* гру́бая оши́бка

blunt [blʌnt] *adj* тупо́й; (*person*) прямолине́йный

blur [bləː'] *n* (*shape*) сму́тное очерта́ние ♦ *vt* (*vision*) затума́нивать (затума́нить *pf*); (*distinction*) стира́ть (стере́ть *pf*)

blush [blʌʃ] *vi* красне́ть (покрасне́ть *pf*)

BNP *n abbr = British National Party*

boar [bɔː'] *n* бо́ров; (*wild pig*) каба́н

board [bɔːd] *n* доска́; (*card*) карто́н; (*committee*) комите́т; (*in firm*) правле́ние ♦ *vt* (*ship, train*) сади́ться (сесть *pf*) на +*acc*; **on ~**

(NAUT, AVIAT) на борту́; **full ~**
(BRIT) по́лный пансио́н; **half ~**
(BRIT) пансио́н с за́втраком и
у́жином; **~ and lodging**
прожива́ние и пита́ние; **~ing
card** (AVIAT, NAUT) посадо́чный
тало́н; **~ing school** n шко́ла-
интерна́т

boast [bəust] vi: **to ~ (about** or **of)**
хва́статься (похва́статься pf)
(+instr)

boat [bəut] n (small) ло́дка; (large)
кора́бль m

bob [bɔb] vi (boat: also: **~ up and
down**) пока́чиваться (impf)

bodily ['bɔdɪlɪ] adj физи́ческий
♦ adv целико́м

body ['bɔdɪ] n те́ло; (of car)
ко́рпус; (torso) ту́ловище; (fig:
group) гру́ппа; (: organization)
о́рган; **~guard** n телохрани́тель
m; **~ language** n язы́к же́стов;
~work n ко́рпус

bog [bɔg] n (GEO) боло́то, тряси́на

bogus ['bəugəs] adj (claim)
фикти́вный

boil [bɔɪl] vt (water) кипяти́ть
(вскипяти́ть pf); (eggs, potatoes)
вари́ть (свари́ть pf) ♦ vi кипе́ть
(вскипе́ть pf) ♦ n фуру́нкул; **to
come to the** (BRIT) or **a** (US) **~**
вскипа́ть (вскипе́ть pf); **~ed egg**
n варёное яйцо́; **~er** n (device)
парово́й котёл, бо́йлер

boisterous ['bɔɪstərəs] adj
разбитно́й

bold [bəuld] adj (brave) сме́лый;
(pej: cheeky) на́глый; (pattern,
colours) бро́ский

bolt [bəult] n (lock) засо́в; (with nut)
болт ♦ adv: **~ upright**
вы́тянувшись в стру́нку

bomb [bɔm] n бо́мба ♦ vt бомби́ть
(impf)

bombardment [bɔm'bɑːdmənt] n
бомбардиро́вка

bomber ['bɔmə^r] n (AVIAT)
бомбардиро́вщик

bombshell ['bɔmʃel] n (fig): **the
news was a real ~** э́то изве́стие
произвело́ эффе́кт
разорва́вшейся бо́мбы

bond [bɔnd] n у́зы pl; (FINANCE)
облига́ция

bone [bəun] n кость f ♦ vt
отделя́ть (отдели́ть pf) от
косте́й; **~ marrow** n ко́стный
мозг

bonfire ['bɔnfaɪə^r] n костёр

bonnet ['bɔnɪt] n (hat) ка́пор;
(BRIT: of car) капо́т

bonus ['bəunəs] n (payment)
пре́мия; (fig) дополни́тельное
преиму́щество

bony ['bəunɪ] adj (person, fingers)
костля́вый; (fish) кости́стый

boo [buː] excl фу ♦ vt освисты́вать
(освиста́ть pf)

book [buk] n кни́га; (of stamps,
tickets) кни́жечка ♦ vt (ticket, table)
зака́зывать (заказа́ть pf); (seat,
room) брони́ровать
(заброни́ровать pf); (subj:
policeman, referee) штрафова́ть
(оштрафова́ть pf); **~s** npl
(accounts) бухга́лтерские кни́ги
fpl; **~case** n кни́жный шкаф; **~let**
n брошю́ра; **~mark** n закла́дка;
~shop n кни́жный магази́н

boom [buːm] n (noise) ро́кот;
(growth) бум

boon [buːn] n бла́го

boost [buːst] n (to confidence)
сти́мул ♦ vt стимули́ровать (impf)

boot [buːt] n (for winter) сапо́г; (for
football) бу́тса; (for walking)
боти́нок; (BRIT: of car) бага́жник

booth [buːð] n (at fair) ларёк;
(TEL, for voting) бу́дка

booze [buːz] (inf) n вы́пивка

border ['bɔːdə^r] n (of country)
грани́ца; (for flowers) бордю́р; (on

cloth etc) кайма́ ♦ vt (road, river etc)
окаймля́ть (окаймля́ть pf);
(country: also: ~ on) грани́чить
(impf) c +instr; ~line n: on the ~line
на гра́ни

bore [bɔ:] pt of **bear** ♦ vt (hole)
сверли́ть (просверли́ть pf);
(person) наскучи́ть (pf) +dat ♦ n
(person) зану́да m/f; **to be ~d**
скуча́ть (impf); ~**dom** n (condition)
ску́ка; (boring quality) заку́дство

boring ['bɔ:rɪŋ] adj скучный

born [bɔ:n] adj рождённый; **to be**
~ рожда́ться (роди́ться pf)

borne [bɔ:n] pp of **bear**

borough ['bʌrə] n
администрати́вный о́круг

borrow ['bɔrəʊ] vt: **to ~ sth from**
sb занима́ть (заня́ть pf) что-н у
кого́-н

Bosnia ['bɒznɪə] n Бо́сния;
~**-Herzegovina** [-,hɜːtsəgəʊ'viːnə]
n Бо́сния-Герцегови́на

bosom ['bʊzəm] n (ANAT) грудь f

boss [bɒs] n (employer)
хозя́ин(я́йка), босс ♦ vt (also: ~
around, ~ about)
распоряжа́ться (impf),
кома́ндовать (impf) +instr; ~**y** adj
вла́стный

both [bəʊθ] adj, pron о́ба f (о́бе)
♦ adv: ~ **A and B** и А, и Б; ~ **of us**
went, we ~ went мы о́ба пошли́

bother ['bɒðə] vt (worry)
беспоко́ить (обеспоко́ить pf);
(disturb) беспоко́ить
(побеспоко́ить pf) ♦ vi (also: ~
o.s.) беспоко́иться (impf) ♦ n
(trouble) беспоко́йство; (nuisance)
хло́поты pl; **to ~ doing** брать
(взять pf) на себя́ труд +infin

bottle ['bɒtl] n (also) буты́лка; ~**-opener**
n што́пор

bottom ['bɒtəm] n (of container,
sea) дно; (ANAT) зад; (of page, list)
низ; (of class) отстаю́щий(ая) m(f)

adj ♦ adj (lowest) ни́жний; (last)
после́дний

bough [baʊ] n сук

bought [bɔ:t] pt, pp of **buy**

boulder ['bəʊldə] n валу́н

bounce [baʊns] vi (ball)
отска́кивать (отскочи́ть pf);
(cheque) верну́ться (pf) (ввиду́
отсу́тствия де́нег на счету́) ♦ vt
(ball) ударя́ть (уда́рить pf); ~**r** n
(inf) вышиба́ла m

bound [baʊnd] pt, pp of **bind** ♦ vi
(leap) пры́гать (пры́гнуть pf)
♦ adj: **he is ~ by law to** ...
обя́зывает зако́н +infin ... ♦ npl: ~**s**
(limits) преде́лы mpl

boundary ['baʊndrɪ] n грани́ца

boundless ['baʊndlɪs] adj
безграни́чный

bouquet ['bʊkeɪ] n буке́т

bourgeois ['bʊəʒwɑ:] adj
буржуа́зный

bout [baʊt] n (of illness) при́ступ;
(of activity) всплеск

boutique [bu:'ti:k] n ла́вка

bow[1] [bəʊ] n (knot) бант; (weapon)
лук; (MUS) смычо́к

bow[2] [baʊ] n (of head, body)
покло́н; (NAUT: also: ~**s**) нос ♦ vi
(with head, body) кла́няться
(поклони́ться pf); (yield): **to ~ to**
or before поддава́ться
(подда́ться pf) +dat or на +acc

bowels ['baʊəlz] npl кише́чник
msg

bowl [baʊl] n (plate, food) ми́ска,
ча́ша; (ball) шар

bowling ['baʊlɪŋ] n (game)
кегельба́н

bowls [baʊlz] n (game) игра́ в
шары́

bow tie [bəʊ-] n ба́бочка

box [bɒks] n я́щик, коро́бка; (also:
cardboard ~) карто́нная
коро́бка; (THEAT) ло́жа; (inf: TV)
я́щик; ~**er** n боксёр; ~**ing** n бокс;

Boxing Day n (BRIT) день после Рождества

> **Boxing Day** - пе́рвый день по́сле Рождества́. Буква́льно "День коробок". Этот день явля́ется пра́здничным. Его́ назва́ние свя́зано с обы́чаем де́лать пода́рки, упако́ванные в рожде́ственские коро́бки, почтальо́нам, разно́счикам газе́т и други́м рабо́тникам, ока́зывающим услу́ги по до́му.

box office n театра́льная ка́сса
boy [bɔɪ] n ма́льчик; (son) сыно́к
boycott ['bɔɪkɔt] n бойко́т ♦ vt бойкоти́ровать (impf/pf)
boyfriend ['bɔɪfrɛnd] n друг
BR abbr (formerly) = **British Rail**
bra [brɑ:] n ли́фчик
brace [breɪs] n (on leg) ши́на; (on teeth) пласти́нка ♦ vt (knees, shoulders) напряга́ть (напря́чь pf); ~**s** npl (BRIT: for trousers) подтя́жки pl; **to ~ o.s.** (for shock) собира́ться (собра́ться pf) с ду́хом
bracelet ['breɪslɪt] n брасле́т
bracing ['breɪsɪŋ] adj бодря́щий
bracken ['brækən] n (BOT) орля́к
bracket ['brækɪt] n (TECH) кронште́йн; (group, range) катего́рия; (also: **brace** ~) ско́бка; (also: **round** ~) кру́глая ско́бка; (also: **square** ~) квадра́тная ско́бка ♦ vt (word, phrase) заключа́ть (заключи́ть pf) в ско́бки
brain [breɪn] n мозг; ~**s** npl (also CULIN) мозги́ mpl; ~**wave** n: **he had a ~wave** на него́ нашло́ озаре́ние; ~**y** adj мозгови́тый
brake [breɪk] n то́рмоз ♦ vi тормози́ть (затормози́ть pf)
bramble ['bræmbl] n ежеви́ка
bran [bræn] n о́труби pl

branch [brɑ:ntʃ] n (of tree) ве́тка, ветвь f; (of bank, firm etc) филиа́л
brand [brænd] n (also: ~ **name**) фи́рменная ма́рка ♦ vt (cattle) клейми́ть (заклейми́ть pf)
brand-new ['brænd'nju:] adj соверше́нно но́вый
brandy ['brændɪ] n бре́нди nt ind, конья́к
brash [bræʃ] adj наха́льный
brass [brɑ:s] n (metal) латунь f; **the** ~ духовы́е инструме́нты mpl
brat [bræt] n (pej) озорни́к
brave [breɪv] adj сме́лый, хра́брый ♦ vt сме́ло или хра́бро встреча́ть (встре́тить pf); ~**ry** ['breɪvərɪ] n сме́лость f, хра́брость f
brawl [brɔ:l] n дра́ка
brazen ['breɪzn] adj (woman) бессты́жий ♦ vt: **to** ~ **it out** выкру́чиваться (вы́крутиться pf)
Brazil [brə'zɪl] n Брази́лия
breach [bri:tʃ] n (of defence, security) пробива́ние (проби́ть pf) ♦ n (gap) брешь f; ~ **of contract/the peace** наруше́ние догово́ра/ обще́ственного поря́дка
bread [brɛd] n (food) хлеб; ~ **and butter** n хлеб с ма́слом; ~**bin** n (BRIT) хле́бница; ~**box** n (US) = **breadbin**; ~**crumbs** npl (CULIN) паниро́вочные сухари́ mpl
breadth [brɛtθ] n ширина́; (fig: of knowledge, subject) широта́
break [breɪk] (pt **broke**, pp **broken**) vt (crockery) разбива́ть (разби́ть pf); (leg, arm) лома́ть (слома́ть pf); (law, promise) наруша́ть (нару́шить pf); (record) побива́ть (поби́ть pf); (crockery) разбива́ться (разби́ться pf); (storm) разража́ться (разрази́ться pf); (weather) по́ртиться (испо́ртиться pf); (dawn) бре́зжить (забре́зжить pf); (story, news) сообща́ть (сообщи́ть pf)

pf) ♦ n (gap) пробе́л; (chance) шанс; (fracture) перело́м; (playtime) переме́на; **to ~ even** (COMM) зака́нчивать (зако́нчить pf) без убы́тка; **to ~ free** или **loose** вырыва́ться (вы́рваться pf) на свобо́ду; **~ down** vi (machine, car) лома́ться (слома́ться pf); (person) сломи́ться (pf); (talks) срыва́ться (сорва́ться pf)

~ in vi (burglar) вла́мываться (вломи́ться pf); (interrupt) вме́шиваться (вмеша́ться pf); **~ into** vt fus (house) вла́мываться (вломи́ться в +acc)

~ off vi (branch) отла́мываться (отломи́ться pf); (speaker) прерыва́ть (прерва́ть pf) речь ♦ vt (engagement) расторга́ть (расто́ргнуть pf)

~ out vi (begin) разража́ться (разрази́ться pf); (escape) сбега́ть (сбежа́ть pf); **to ~ out in spots/a rash** покрыва́ться (покры́ться pf) прыща́ми/сы́пью

~ up vi (ship) разбива́ться (разби́ться pf); (crowd, meeting) расходи́ться (разойти́сь pf); (marriage, partnership) распада́ться (распа́сться pf); (SCOL) закрыва́ться (закры́ться pf) на кани́кулы ♦ vt разла́мывать (разломи́ть pf); (journey) прерыва́ть (прерва́ть pf); (fight) прекраща́ть (прекрати́ть pf)

breakdown ['breɪkdaʊn] n (in communications) наруше́ние, срыв; (of marriage) распа́д; (also: **nervous ~**) не́рвный срыв

breaker ['breɪkə*] n вал

breakfast ['brekfəst] n за́втрак

break-in ['breɪkɪn] n взлом

breakthrough ['breɪkθruː] n (in

technology) перело́мное откры́тие

breakwater ['breɪkwɔːtə*] n мол, волноре́з

breast [brest] n грудь f; (of meat) груди́нка; (of poultry) бе́лое мя́со; **~-feed** (irreg: like **feed**) vt корми́ть (покорми́ть pf) гру́дью ♦ vi корми́ть (impf) гру́дью)

breath [breθ] n вдох; (breathing) дыха́ние; **to be out of ~** запыха́ться (запыха́ться pf)

breathe [briːð] vi дыша́ть (impf); **~ in** vt вдыха́ть (сде́лать pf) ♦ vi де́лать (сде́лать pf) вдох **~ out** vi де́лать (сде́лать pf) вы́дох

breathing ['briːðɪŋ] n дыха́ние; **~ space** n (fig) переды́шка

breathless ['breθlɪs] adj (from exertion) запыха́вшийся

breathtaking ['breθteɪkɪŋ] adj захва́тывающий дух

bred [bred] pt, pp of **breed**

breed [briːd] (pt, pp **bred**) vt (animals, plants) разводи́ть (развести́ pf) ♦ vi размножа́ться (impf) ♦ n (ZOOL) поро́да; **~ing** n (of dogs) разведе́ние

breeze [briːz] n ве́тер

breezy ['briːzɪ] adj (manner, tone) оживлённый; (weather) прохла́дный

brew [bruː] vt (tea) зава́ривать (завари́ть pf); (beer) вари́ть (свари́ть pf) ♦ vi (storm) надвига́ться (надви́нуться pf); (fig: trouble) назрева́ть (назре́ть pf); **~ery** n пивова́ренный заво́д

bribe [braɪb] n взя́тка, по́дкуп ♦ vt (person) подкупа́ть (подкупи́ть pf); (give a bribe) дать (дать pf) взя́тку; **~ry** ['braɪbərɪ] n по́дкуп

brick [brɪk] n (for building) кирпи́ч

bridal ['braɪdl] adj подвене́чный, сва́дебный

bride [braɪd] *n* невеста; **~groom** *n* жених; **~smaid** *n* подружка невесты

bridge [brɪdʒ] *n* мост; (*NAUT*) капитанский мостик; (*CARDS*) бридж; (*of nose*) переносица ♦ *vt* (*fig: gap*) преодолевать (преодолеть *pf*)

bridle ['braɪdl] *n* уздечка, узда

brief [briːf] *adj* (*period of time*) короткий; (*description*) краткий ♦ *n* (*task*) задание ♦ *vt* знакомить (ознакомить *pf*) с +*instr*; **~s** *npl* (*for men*) трусы *pl*; (*for women*) трусики *pl*; **~case** *n* портфель *m*; (*attaché case*) дипломат; **~ing** *n* инструктаж; (*PRESS*) брифинг; **~ly** *adv* (*glance, smile*) бегло; (*explain*) вкратце

bright [braɪt] *adj* (*light, colour*) яркий; (*room, future*) светлый; (*clever: person, idea*) блестящий; (*lively: person*) живой, весёлый; **~en** *vt* (*also*: **~en up**: *room, event*) оживлять (оживить *pf*) ♦ *vi* (*weather*) проясняться (проясниться *pf*); (*person*) оживляться (оживиться *pf*); (*face*) светлеть (просветлеть *pf*)

brilliance ['brɪljəns] *n* яркость *f*, блеск; (*of person*) гениальность *f*

brilliant ['brɪljənt] *adj* блестящий; (*sunshine*) яркий; (*inf: holiday etc*) великолепный

brim [brɪm] *n* (*of cup*) край; (*of hat*) поля *pl*

bring [brɪŋ] (*pt, pp* **brought**) *vt* (*thing*) приносить (принести *pf*); (*person: on foot*) приводить (привести *pf*); (*: by transport*) привозить (привезти *pf*); (*satisfaction, trouble*) доставлять (доставить *pf*); **~ about** *vt* (*cause: unintentionally*) вызывать (вызвать *pf*); (*: intentionally*) осуществлять (осуществить *pf*);

~ back *vt* (*restore*) возрождать (возродить *pf*); (*return*) возвращать (возвратить *pf*), вернуть (*pf*); **~ down** *vt* (*government*) свергать (свергнуть *pf*); (*plane*) сбивать (сбить *pf*); (*price*) снижать (снизить *pf*); **~ forward** *vt* (*meeting*) переносить (перенести *pf*) на более ранний срок; **~ out** *vt* вынимать (вынуть *pf*); (*publish*) выпускать (выпустить *pf*); **~ up** *vt* (*carry up*) приносить (принести *pf*) наверх; (*child*) воспитывать (воспитать *pf*); (*subject*) поднимать (поднять *pf*); **he brought up his food** его стошнило

brink [brɪŋk] *n*: **on the ~ of** (*fig*) на грани +*gen*

brisk [brɪsk] *adj* (*tone*) отрывистый; (*person, trade*) оживлённый; **business is ~** дела идут полным ходом

Britain ['brɪtən] *n* (*also*: **Great ~**) Британия

British ['brɪtɪʃ] *adj* британский; **the ~ пробрание** британцы *mpl*; **the ~ Isles** *npl* Британские острова *mpl*; **~ Rail** *n* (*formerly*) Британская железная дорога

Briton ['brɪtən] *n* британец(нка)

brittle ['brɪtl] *adj* хрупкий, ломкий

broad [brɔːd] *adj* (*wide, general*) широкий; (*strong*) сильный; **in ~ daylight** средь бела дня; **~cast** (*pt, pp* **~cast**) *n* (*радио*)передача, (*TV*) (теле)передача ♦ *vt* транслировать (*impf*) ♦ *vi* вещать (*impf*); **~en** *vt* расширять (расширить *pf*) ♦ *vi* расширяться (расшириться *pf*); **~ly** *adv* вообще

broccoli ['brɔkəlɪ] *n* брокколи *nt ind*

brochure ['brəʊʃjʊə*] *n* брошюра

broke [brəuk] *pt of* **break** ♦ *adj*: **I am ~** (*inf*) я на мели; **~n** *pp of* **break** ♦ *adj* (window, cup etc) разбитый; (machine, leg) сломанный; **in ~n Russian** на ломаном русском

broker ['brəukə*r*] *n* (*in shares*) брокер; (*in insurance*) страховой агент

brolly ['brɒlɪ] *n* (BRIT: *inf*) зонт

bronchitis [brɒŋ'kaɪtɪs] *n* бронхит

bronze [brɒnz] *n* (metal) бронза; (sculpture) бронзовая скульптура

brooch [brəutʃ] *n* брошь *f*

Bros. *abbr* (COMM: = brothers) братья *mpl*

broth [brɒθ] *n* похлёбка

brothel ['brɒθl] *n* публичный дом, бордель *m*

brother ['brʌðə*r*] *n* брат; **~-in-law** *n* (sister's husband) зять *m*; (wife's brother) шурин; (husband's brother) деверь *m*

brought [brɔːt] *pt, pp of* **bring**

brow [brau] *n* лоб, чело; (also: **eye~**) бровь *f*; (of hill) гребень *m*

brown [braun] *adj* коричневый; (hair) тёмно-русый; (eyes) карий; (tanned) загорелый ♦ *n* (colour) коричневый цвет ♦ *vt* (CULIN) подрумянивать (подрумянить *pf*); **~ bread** *n* чёрный хлеб; **~ sugar** *n* неочищенный сахар

browse [brauz] *vi* осматриваться (осмотреться *pf*); **to ~ through a book** пролистывать (пролистать *pf*) книгу; **~r** *n* (COMPUT) браузер

bruise [bruːz] *n* (on face etc) синяк ♦ *vt* ушибать (ушибить *pf*)

brunette [bruː'net] *n* брюнетка

brunt [brʌnt] *n*: **to bear the ~ of** принимать (принять *pf*) на себя основной удар +gen

brush [brʌʃ] *n* (for cleaning) щётка; (for painting) кисть *f*; (for shaving) помазок ♦ *vt* (sweep) подметать

(подмести *pf*); (groom) чистить (почистить *pf*) щёткой; (also: **~ against**) задевать (задеть *pf*)

Brussels ['brʌslz] *n* Брюссель *m*; **~ sprout** *n* брюссельская капуста

brutal ['bruːtl] *adj* жестокий, зверский; (honesty) жёсткий; **~ity** [bruː'tælɪtɪ] *n* (of person, action) жестокость *f*; зверство

brute [bruːt] *n* зверь *m* ♦ *adj*: **by ~ force** грубой силой

bubble ['bʌbl] *n* пузырь *m*; **~ bath** *n* пенистая ванна

buck [bʌk] *n* (US: *inf*) бакс

bucket ['bʌkɪt] *n* ведро

buckle ['bʌkl] *n* пряжка

bud [bʌd] *n* (of tree) почка; (of flower) бутон

Buddhism ['budɪzəm] *n* буддизм

buddy ['bʌdɪ] *n* (US) приятель *m*, дружок

budge [bʌdʒ] *vt* (fig: person) заставлять (заставить *pf*) уступить ♦ *vi* сдвигаться (сдвинуться *pf*) (с места)

budgerigar ['bʌdʒərɪɡɑː*r*] *n* волнистый попугайчик

budget ['bʌdʒɪt] *n* бюджет

budgie ['bʌdʒɪ] *n* = **budgerigar**

buff [bʌf] *adj* желто-коричневый ♦ *n* (inf: enthusiast) спец, знаток

buffalo ['bʌfələu] *n* (pl **~** *or* **~es**) (BRIT) буйвол; (US: bison) бизон

buffer ['bʌfə*r*] *n* буфер

buffet ['bufeɪ] *n* (BRIT: in station) буфет; (food) шведский стол

bug [bʌɡ] *n* (insect) насекомое *nt adj*; (COMPUT) ошибка; (fig: germ) вирус; (hidden microphone) подслушивающее устройство ♦ *vt* (room etc) прослушивать (impf); (inf: annoy): **to ~ sb** действовать (impf) кому-н на нервы

buggy ['bʌɡɪ] *n* (also: **baby ~**) складная (детская) коляска

build [bɪld] (*pt*, *pp* **built**) *n* (*of person*) (тело)сложе́ние ♦ *vt* стро́ить (постро́ить *pf*); (*forces*, *production*) нара́щивать (impf); (*stocks*) нака́пливать (накопи́ть *pf*); **~ up** *vt* ~**er** *n* строи́тель *m*; ~**ing** *n* строе́ние; ~**ing society** *n* (*BRIT*) ≈ "строи́тельное о́бщество"

building society - строи́тельное о́бщество или ипоте́чный ба́нк. Они́ бы́ли со́зданы для предоставле́ния ипоте́чного жили́щного кредитова́ния. Одновре́менно строи́тельные о́бщества функциони́ровали как сберега́тельные ба́нки. В после́дние го́ды они́ ста́ли предоставля́ть бо́лее широ́кий объём ба́нковских услу́г.

built [bɪlt] *pt*, *pp* of **build** ♦ *adj*: ~**-in** встро́енный

bulb [bʌlb] *n* (*BOT*) лу́ковица; (*ELEC*) ла́мпа, ла́мпочка

Bulgaria [bʌlˈɡɛərɪə] *n* Болга́рия

bulimia [bəˈlɪmɪə] *n* були́мия

bulk [bʌlk] *n* грома́да; **in** ~ о́птом; **the ~ of** бо́льшая часть +*gen*; ~**y** *adj* громо́здкий

bull [bul] *n* (*ZOOL*) бык

bulldozer [ˈbuldəʊzəʳ] *n* бульдо́зер

bullet [ˈbulɪt] *n* пу́ля

bulletin [ˈbulɪtɪn] *n* (*journal*) бюллете́нь *m*; **news ~** сво́дка новосте́й; ~ **board** *n* (*COMPUT*) доска́ объявле́ний

bullock [ˈbulək] *n* вол

bully [ˈbulɪ] *n* зади́ра *m/f*, пресле́дователь *m* ♦ *vt* трави́ть (затрави́ть *pf*)

bum [bʌm] *n* (*inf*: *backside*) за́дница; (*esp US*: *tramp*) бродя́га *m/f*; (: *good-for-nothing*) безде́льник

bumblebee [ˈbʌmblbiː] *n* шмель *m*

bump [bʌmp] *n* (*minor accident*) столкнове́ние; (*jolt*) толчо́к; (*swelling*) ши́шка ♦ *vt* (*strike*) ударя́ть (уда́рить *pf*); **~ into** *vt fus* ната́лкиваться (натолкну́ться *pf*) на +*acc*; ~**er** *n* (*AUT*) ба́мпер ♦ *adj*: ~**er crop** or **harvest** небыва́лый урожа́й; ~**y** *adj* (*road*) уха́бистый

bun [bʌn] *n* (*CULIN*) сдо́бная бу́лка; (*of hair*) узел

bunch [bʌntʃ] *n* (*of flowers*) буке́т; (*of keys*) свя́зка; (*of bananas*) гроздь *f*; (*of people*) компа́ния; ~**es** *npl* (*in hair*) хвости́ки *mpl*

bundle [ˈbʌndl] *n* (*of clothes*) узел; (*of sticks*) вяза́нка; (*of papers*) па́чка ♦ *vt* (*also*: ~ **up**) свя́зывать (связа́ть *pf*) в узел; **to ~ sth/sb into** зата́лкивать (затолкну́ть *pf*) что-н/кого́-н в +*acc*

bungalow [ˈbʌŋɡələʊ] *n* бунга́ло *nt indl*

bunk [bʌŋk] *n* (*bed*) ко́йка; ~ **beds** *npl* двухъя́русная крова́ть *fsg*

bunker [ˈbʌŋkəʳ] *n* бу́нкер

bunny [ˈbʌnɪ] *n* (*also*: ~ **rabbit**) за́йчик

buoy [bɔɪ] *n* буй, ба́кен

buoyant [ˈbɔɪənt] *adj* (*fig*: *economy*, *market*) оживлённый; (: *person*) жизнера́достный

burden [ˈbəːdn] *n* (*responsibility*) бре́мя *nt*; (*load*) но́ша ♦ *vt*: **to ~ sb with** обременя́ть (обремени́ть *pf*) кого́-н +*instr*

bureau [ˈbjʊərəʊ] (*pl* ~**x**) *n* (*BRIT*) бюро́ *nt indl*; (*US*) комо́д

bureaucracy [bjʊəˈrɔkrəsɪ] *n* (*POL*, *COMM*) бюрокра́тия; (*system*) бюрократи́зм

bureaucrat [ˈbjʊərəkræt] *n* бюрокра́т

bureaux [ˈbjʊərəʊz] *npl* of **bureau**

burger [ˈbəːɡəʳ] *n* бу́ргер

burglar ['bɜːɡlə'] n взло́мщик; **~ alarm** n сигнализа́ция; **~y** n (crime) кра́жа со взло́мом, кварти́рный разбо́й

burial ['bɛrɪəl] n погребе́ние, по́хороны, pl

burly ['bɜːlɪ] adj дю́жий

burn [bɜːn] (pt, pp **~ed** or **~t**) vt жечь (сжечь pf), сжига́ть (сжечь pf); (intentionally) поджига́ть (подже́чь pf) ♦ vi (house, wood) горе́ть (сгоре́ть pf), сгора́ть (сгоре́ть pf); (cakes) подгора́ть (подгоре́ть pf) ♦ n ожо́г; **~er** n горе́лка; **~ing** adj (building, forest) горя́щий; (issue, ambition) жгу́чий

burst [bɜːst] (pt, pp **~**) vt разрыва́ть (разорва́ть pf) ♦ vi (tyre, balloon, pipe) ло́пнуть (ло́паться pf) ♦ n (of gunfire) залп; (of energy) прили́в; (also: **~ pipe**) проры́в; **to ~ into flames** вспы́хнуть (вспы́хнуть pf); **to ~ into tears** распла́каться (pf); **to ~ out laughing** расхохота́ться (pf); **to be ~ing with** (pride, anger) раздува́ться (разду́ться pf) +gen; **~ into** vt fus (room) врыва́ться (ворва́ться pf)

bury ['bɛrɪ] vt (object) зарыва́ть (зары́ть pf), зака́пывать (закопа́ть pf); (person) хорони́ть (похорони́ть pf); **many people were buried in the rubble** мно́го люде́й бы́ло погребено́ под обло́мками

bus [bʌs] n авто́бус; (double decker) (двухэта́жный) авто́бус

bush [buʃ] n куст; **to beat about the ~** ходи́ть (impf) вокру́г да о́коло

bushy ['buʃɪ] adj пуши́стый

busily ['bɪzɪlɪ] adv делови́то, энерги́чно

business ['bɪznɪs] n (matter) де́ло; (trading) би́знес, де́ло; (firm) предприя́тие; (occupation) заня́тие; **to be away on ~** быть (impf) в командиро́вке; **it's none of my ~** э́то не моё де́ло; **he means ~** он настро́ен серьёзно; **~like** adj делови́тый; **~man** (irreg) n бизнесме́н; **~ trip** n делова́я пое́здка; **~woman** (irreg) n бизнесме́нка

bus stop n авто́бусная остано́вка

bust [bʌst] n бюст, грудь f; (measurement) объём груди́; (sculpture) бюст ♦ adj: **to go ~** (firm) прогора́ть (прогоре́ть pf)

bustle ['bʌsl] n суматоха, суета́

bustling ['bʌslɪŋ] adj оживлённый, шу́мный

busy ['bɪzɪ] adj (person) занято́й; (street) оживлённый, шу́мный; (TEL.): **the line is ~** ли́ния занята́ ♦ vt: **to ~ o.s. with** занима́ться (заня́ться pf) +instr

KEYWORD

but [bʌt] conj 1 (yet) но; (: in contrast) a; **he's not very bright, but he's hard-working** он не о́чень умён, но усе́рден; **I'm tired but Paul isn't** я уста́л, а Па́вел нет

2 (however) но; **I'd love to come, but I'm busy** я бы с удово́льствием пришёл, но я за́нят

3 (showing disagreement, surprise etc) но; **but that's fantastic!** но э́то же потряса́юще!

♦ prep (apart from, except): **no-one but him can do it** никто́, кро́ме него́, не мо́жет э́то сде́лать; **nothing but trouble** сплошны́е or одни́ неприя́тности; **but for you/your help** е́сли бы не Вы/Ва́ша по́мощь; **I'll do anything but that** я сде́лаю всё, что уго́дно, но то́лько не э́то

♦ *adv* (*just, only*): **she's but a child** она всего лишь ребёнок; **I can but try** конечно, я могу попробовать; **the work is all but finished** работа почти закончена

butcher ['butʃər] *n* мясник; (*also:* **~'s (shop)**) мясной магазин

butt [bʌt] *n* (*large barrel*) бочка; (*of rifle*) приклад; (*of pistol*) рукоятка; (*of cigarette*) окурок; (*BRIT: of teasing*) предмет

butter ['bʌtər] *n* (*сливочное*) масло ♦ *vt* намазывать (намазать *pf*) (сливочным маслом); **~cup** *n* лютик

butterfly ['bʌtərflaɪ] *n* бабочка; (*also:* **~ stroke**) баттерфляй

buttocks ['bʌtəks] *npl* ягодицы *fpl*

button ['bʌtn] *n* (*on clothes*) пуговица; (*on machine*) кнопка; (*US: badge*) значок ♦ *vt* (*also:* **~ up**) застёгивать (застегнуть *pf*)

buy [baɪ] (*pt, pp* **bought**) *vt* покупать (купить *pf*) ♦ *n* покупка; **to ~ sb sth/sth from sb** покупать (купить *pf*) кому-н что-н/что-н у кого-н; **to ~ sb a drink** покупать (купить *pf*) кому-н выпить; **~er** *n* покупатель(ница) *m(f)*

buzz [bʌz] *n* жужжание, звонок; **~er** *n* зуммер, звонок

KEYWORD

by [baɪ] *prep* **1** (*referring to cause, agent*): **he was killed by lightning** его убило молнией; **a painting by Van Gogh** картина Ван Гога; **it's by Shakespeare** это Шекспир **2** (*referring to manner, means*): **by bus/train** автобусом/поездом; **by car** на машине; **by phone** по телефону; **to pay by cheque** платить (заплатить *pf*) чеком; **by moonlight** при свете луны; **by**

candlelight при свечах; **by working constantly, he ...** благодаря тому, что он работал без остановки, он ... **3** (*via, through*) через +*acc*; **by the back door** через заднюю дверь; **by land/sea** по суше/морю **4** (*close to*) у +*gen*, около +*gen*; **the house is by the river** дом находится у или около реки; **a holiday by the sea** отпуск на море **5** (*past*) мимо +*gen*; **she rushed by** она пронеслась мимо меня **6** (*not later than*) к +*dat*; **by four o'clock** к четырём часам; **by the time I got here ...** к тому времени, когда я добрался сюда ... **7** (*during*): **by day** днём; **by night** ночью **8** (*amount*): **to sell by the metre/ kilo** продавать (продать *pf*) метрами/килограммами; **she is paid by the hour** у неё почасовая оплата **9** (*MATH, measure*) на +*acc*; **to multiply/divide by three** умножать (умножить *pf*)/делить (разделить *pf*) на три; **a room three metres by four** комната размером три метра на четыре **10** (*according to*) по +*dat*; **to play by the rules** играть (*impf*) по правилам; **it's all right by me** я не возражаю; **by law** по закону **11**: **(all) by oneself** (*alone*) (совершенно) один (*f* одна, *pl* одни); (*unaided*) сам (*f* сама, *pl* сами); **I did it all by myself** я сделал всё один *или* сам; **he was standing by himself** он стоял один **12**: **by the way** кстати, между прочим

♦ *adv* **1** *see* **pass** *etc*

2: by and by вскóре; **by and large** в цéлом

bye(-bye) ['baɪ('baɪ)] excl покá

by-election ['baɪɪlekʃən] n (BRIT) дополни́тельные вы́боры mpl

bygone ['baɪɡɔn] n: **let ~s be ~s** что бы́ло, то прошлó

bypass ['baɪpɑːs] n (AUT) объéзд, окружнáя дорóга; (MED) обходнóе шунти́рование ♦ vt (town) объезжáть (объéхать pf)

by-product ['baɪprɔdʌkt] n (INDUSTRY) побóчный продýкт

bystander ['baɪstændə*] n свидéтель(ница) m(f), прохóжий(ая) m(f)

byte [baɪt] n (COMPUT) байт

C, c

C [siː] n (MUS) до nt ind

C. abbr = **Celsius**, **centigrade**

CA n abbr (BRIT) = **chartered accountant**

cab [kæb] n такси́ nt ind; (of truck etc) каби́на

cabaret ['kæbəreɪ] n кабарé nt ind

cabbage ['kæbɪdʒ] n капýста

cabin ['kæbɪn] n (on ship) каю́та; (on plane) каби́на

cabinet ['kæbɪnɪt] n шкаф; (also: **display ~**) гóрка; (POL) кабинéт (мини́стров)

cable ['keɪbl] n кáбель m; (rope) канáт; (metal) трос m; (message) телеграфи́ровать (impf/pf); ~ **television** n кáбельное телеви́дение

cacti ['kæktaɪ] npl of **cactus**

cactus ['kæktəs] n (pl **cacti**) кáктус

cadet [kə'dɛt] n курсáнт

Caesarean [sɪ'zɛərɪən] n (also: ~ **section**) кéсарево сечéние

café ['kæfeɪ] n кафé nt ind

caffein(e) ['kæfiːn] n кофеи́н

cage [keɪdʒ] n (for animal) клéтка

cagoule [kə'ɡuːl] n дождеви́к

cake [keɪk] n (large) торт; (small) пиро́жное nt adj

calcium ['kælsɪəm] n кáльций

calculate ['kælkjuleɪt] vt (figures, cost) подсчи́тывать (подсчитáть pf); (distance) вычислять (вы́числить pf); (estimate) рассчи́тывать (рассчитáть pf)

calculating ['kælkjuleɪtɪŋ] adj расчётливый

calculation [kælkju'leɪʃən] n (see vb) подсчёт; вычислéние; расчёт

calculator ['kælkjuleɪtə*] n калькуля́тор

calendar ['kæləndə*] n календáрь m

calf [kɑːf] n (pl **calves**) (of cow) телёнок; (ANAT) икрá

calibre ['kælɪbə*] (US **caliber**) n кали́бр

call [kɔːl] vt называ́ть (назвáть pf); (TEL) звони́ть (позвони́ть pf) +dat; (summon) вызывáть (вы́звать pf); (arrange) созывáть (созвáть pf) ♦ vi (shout) кричáть (кри́кнуть pf); (TEL) звони́ть (позвони́ть pf); (visit : also: ~ **in**, ~ **round**) заходи́ть (зайти́ pf) ♦ n (shout) крик; (TEL) звонóк; **she is ~ed Suzanne** её зовýт Сюзáнна; **the mountain is ~ed Ben Nevis** горá называ́ется Бен Нéвис; **to be on ~** дежýрить (impf); ~ **back** vi (return) заходи́ть (зайти́ pf) опя́ть; (TEL) перезвáнивать (перезвони́ть pf) ♦ vt (TEL) перезвáнивать (перезвони́ть pf) +dat; ~ **for** vt fus (demand) призывáть (призвáть pf) к +dat; (fetch) заходи́ть (зайти́ pf) за +instr; ~ **off** vt отменя́ть (отмени́ть pf); ~ **on** vt fus (visit) заходи́ть (зайти́ pf) к +dat; (appeal to) призывáть (призвáть pf) к

+dat; **~ out** vi крича́ть (кри́кнуть pf); **~ centre** n (BRIT) центр приёма комме́рческих итп звонко́в в большо́м объёме

callous ['kæləs] adj безду́шный

calm [kɑ:m] adj споко́йный; (place) ти́хий; (weather) безве́тренный ♦ n тишина́, поко́й ♦ vt успока́ивать (успоко́ить pf); **~ down** vt успока́ивать (успоко́ить pf) ♦ vi успока́иваться (успоко́иться pf)

calorie ['kælərɪ] n кало́рия

calves [kɑ:vz] npl of **calf**

Cambodia [kæm'bəudɪə] n Камбо́джа

camcorder ['kæmkɔ:dər] n видеока́мера

came [keɪm] pt of **come**

camel ['kæməl] n верблю́д

camera ['kæmərə] n фотоаппара́т; (also: **cine~**, **movie ~**) кинока́мера; (TV) телека́мера; **~man** (irreg) n (CINEMA) (кино)опера́тор; (TV) (теле)опера́тор

camouflage ['kæməflɑ:ʒ] n (MIL) камуфля́ж, маскиро́вка ♦ vt маскирова́ть (замаскирова́ть pf)

camp [kæmp] n ла́герь m; (MIL) вое́нный городо́к ♦ vi разбива́ть (разби́ть pf) ла́герь; (go camping) жить (impf) в пала́тках

campaign [kæm'peɪn] n кампа́ния ♦ vi: **to ~ (for/against)** вести́ (impf) кампа́нию (за +acc/про́тив +gen)

camping ['kæmpɪŋ] n ке́мпинг; **to go ~** отправля́ться (отпра́виться pf) в похо́д

camp site n ке́мпинг

campus ['kæmpəs] n студе́нческий городо́к

can¹ [kæn] n (for food) консе́рвная ба́нка ♦ vt консерви́ровать (законсерви́ровать pf)

KEYWORD

can² [kæn] (negative **cannot**, **can't**, conditional, pt **could**) aux vb **1** (be able to) мочь (смочь pf); **you can do it** ты смо́жешь э́то сде́лать; **I'll help you all I can** я помогу́ Вам всем, чем смогу́; **I can't go on any longer** я бо́льше не могу́; **I can't see you** я не ви́жу Вас; **she couldn't sleep that night** в ту ночь она́ не могла́ спать

2 (know how to) уме́ть (impf); **I can swim** я уме́ю пла́вать; **can you speak Russian?** Вы уме́ете говори́ть по-ру́сски?

3 (may) мо́жно; **can I use your phone?** мо́жно от Вас позвони́ть?; **could I have a word with you?** мо́жно с Ва́ми поговори́ть?; **you can smoke if you like** Вы мо́жете кури́ть, е́сли хоти́те; **can I help you with that?** я могу́ Вам в э́том помо́чь?

4 (expressing disbelief, puzzlement): **it can't be true!** (э́того) не мо́жет быть!; **what CAN he want?** что же ему́ ну́жно?

5 (expressing possibility, suggestion): **he could be in the library** он, мо́жет быть и́ли возмо́жно, в библиоте́ке; **she could have been delayed** возмо́жно, что её задержа́ли

Canada ['kænədə] n Кана́да

canal [kə'næl] n кана́л

canary [kə'nɛərɪ] n канаре́йка

cancel ['kænsəl] vt отменя́ть (отмени́ть pf); (contract, cheque, visa) аннули́ровать (impf/pf); **~lation** [kænsə'leɪʃən] n (see vb) отме́на; аннули́рование

cancer ['kænsər] n (MED) рак; **Cancer** Рак

candid ['kændɪd] adj и́скренний

candidate ['kændıdeıt] n
претендент; (in exam)
экзаменуемый(ая) m(f) adj; (POL)
кандидат

candle ['kændl] n свеча; ~stick n
подсвечник

candour ['kændə] (US candor) n
искренность f

candy ['kændı] n (US) конфета

cane [keın] n (BOT) тростник; (stick)
розга ♦ vt (BRIT) наказывать
(наказать pf) розгами

cannabis ['kænəbıs] n гашиш

canned [kænd] adj (fruit etc)
консервированный

cannon ['kænən] (pl ~ or ~s) n
пушка

cannot ['kænɔt] = can not; see
can²

canoe [kə'nu:] n каноэ nt ind

can't [kænt] = cannot; see can²

canteen [kæn'ti:n] n столовая f adj

canter ['kæntə] vi галопировать
(impf)

canvas ['kænvəs] n (also ART)
холст; (for tents) брезент; (NAUT)
парусина ♦ adj парусиновый

canyon ['kænjən] n каньон

cap [kæp] n кепка; (of uniform)
фуражка; (of pen) колпачок; (of
bottle) крышка ♦ vt (outdo)
превосходить (превзойти pf)

capability [keıpə'bılıtı] n
способность f

capable ['keıpəbl] adj (person)
способный; ~ of sth/doing
способный на что-н/+infin

capacity [kə'pæsıtı] n ёмкость f; (of
ship, theatre etc) вместительность
f; (of person: capability)
способность f; (: role) роль f

cape [keıp] n (GEO) мыс; (cloak)
плащ

capital ['kæpıtl] n (also: ~ city)
столица; (money) капитал; (also:
~ letter) заглавная буква; ~ism

n капитализм; ~ist adj
капиталистический ♦ n
капиталист; ~ punishment n
смертная казнь f

Capricorn ['kæprıkɔːn] n Козерог

capsule ['kæpsju:l] n капсула

captain ['kæptın] n командир; (of
team, in army) капитан

caption ['kæpʃən] n подпись f

captive ['kæptıv] n узник(ица),
пленник(ица)

captivity [kæp'tıvıtı] n плен

capture ['kæptʃə] vt захватывать
(захватить pf); (animal) ловить
(поймать pf); (attention)
приковывать (приковать pf) ♦ n
(of person, town) захват; (of
animal) поимка

car [kɑː] n автомобиль m,
машина; (RAIL) вагон

caramel ['kærəməl] n (sweet)
карамель f

carat ['kærət] n карат

caravan ['kærəvæn] n (BRIT) жилой
автоприцеп; ~ site n (BRIT)
площадка для стоянки жилых
автоприцепов

carbohydrate [kɑːbəu'haıdreıt] n
углевод

car bomb n бомба, подложенная
в машину

carbon ['kɑːbən] n углерод; ~
dioxide [-daı'ɔksaıd] n двуокись f
углерода

car boot sale - буквально
"продажа с багажника". Этим
понятием обозначается
продажа подержанных вещей.
Товары выставляются в
багажниках машин или на
столах. Продажи проводятся
на автостоянках, в полях или
любых других открытых
пространствах.

card [kɑːd] n картóн; (also: **playing ~**) (игрáльная) кáрта; (also: **greetings ~**) открытка; (also: **visiting~, business ~**) визитная кáрточка; **~board** n картóн

cardiac [ˈkɑːdɪæk] adj сердéчный; (unit) кардиологи́ческий

cardigan [ˈkɑːdɪɡən] n жакéт (вязаный)

cardinal [ˈkɑːdɪnl] adj (importance, principle) кардинáльный; (number) коли́чественный ♦ n кардинáл

care [kɛəʳ] n (worry) забóта; (of patient) ухóд; (attention) внимáние ♦ vi: **to ~ about** люби́ть (impf); **in sb's ~** на чьём-н попечéнии; **to take ~ (to do)** позабóтиться (pf) (+infin); **to take ~ of** заботиться (позаботиться pf) о +prp; (problem) занимáться (заняться pf) +instr; **of** для передáчи +dat; **I don't ~** мне всё равнó; **I couldn't ~ less** мне наплевáть; **~ for** vt fus заботиться (позаботиться pf) о +prp; **he ~s for her** (like) он неравнодушен к ней

career [kəˈrɪəʳ] n карьéра; **~ woman** (irreg) n деловáя жéнщина

carefree [ˈkɛəfriː] adj беззабóтный

careful [ˈkɛəful] adj осторóжный; (thorough) тщáтельный; (be) **~!** осторóжно!, береги́сь!; **~ly** [ˈkɛəfəlɪ] adv (see adj) осторóжно; тщáтельно

careless [ˈkɛəlɪs] adj (clumsy) невнимáтельный; (casual) небрéжный; (untroubled) беззабóтный

caretaker [ˈkɛəteɪkəʳ] n завхóз

cargo [ˈkɑːɡəu] (pl **~es**) n груз

car hire (BRIT) прокáт автомоби́лей

Caribbean [kærɪˈbiːən] n: **the ~ (Sea)** Кари́бское мóре

caricature [ˈkærɪkətjuəʳ] n карикату́ра

caring [ˈkɛərɪŋ] adj (person etc) забóтливый

carnation [kɑːˈneɪʃən] n гвозди́ка

carnival [ˈkɑːnɪvəl] n карнавáл; (US: funfair) аттракциóнный городóк

carol [ˈkærəl] n (also: **Christmas ~**) рождéственский гимн

car park (BRIT) автостоянка

carpenter [ˈkɑːpɪntəʳ] n плóтник

carpet [ˈkɑːpɪt] n ковёр ♦ vt устилáть (устлáть pf) коврáми

carriage [ˈkærɪdʒ] (BRIT : RAIL) (пассажи́рский) вагóн; (horse-drawn) экипáж; (costs) стóимость f перевóзки; **~way** n (BRIT) проéзжая часть f дорóги

carrier [ˈkærɪəʳ] n (MED) носи́тель m; (COMM) транспортирóвщик; **~ bag** n (BRIT) пакéт (для покýпок)

carrot [ˈkærət] n (BOT) моркóвь f

carry [ˈkærɪ] vt (take) носи́ть/нести́ (impf); (transport) вози́ть/везти́ (impf); (involve) влечь (повлéчь pf) (за собóй); (MED) переноси́ть (impf) ♦ vi (sound) передавáться (impf); **to get carried away (by)** (fig) увлекáться (увлéчься pf) (+instr); **~ on** vi продолжáться (продóлжиться pf) ♦ vt продолжáть (продóлжить pf); **~ out** vt (orders) выполнять (выполнить pf); (investigation) проводи́ть (провести́ pf); **~cot** (BRIT) переноснáя колыбéль f; **~-on** n (inf) суматóха

cart [kɑːt] n телéга, повóзка ♦ vt (inf) таскáть/тащи́ть (impf)

carton [ˈkɑːtən] n картóнная корóбка; (container) пакéт

cartoon [kɑːˈtuːn] n (drawing) карикату́ра; (BRIT: comic strip) кóмикс; (TV) мультфи́льм

cartridge ['kɑːtrɪdʒ] n (in gun) гильза; (of pen) (чернильный) баллончик

carve [kɑːv] vt (meat) нарезать (нарезать pf); (wood, stone) резать (impf) по +dat

carving ['kɑːvɪŋ] n резное изделие

car wash n мойка автомобилей

case [keɪs] n случай; (MED, patient) больной(ая) m(f) adj; (LAW) (судебное) дело; (investigation) расследование; (for spectacles) футляр; (BRIT: also: suit~) чемодан; (of wine) ящик (содержащий 12 бутылок); **in ~ (of)** в случае (+gen); **in any ~** во всяком случае; **just in ~** на всякий случай

cash [kæʃ] n наличные pl adj (деньги) ♦ vt: **to ~ a cheque** обналичивать (обналичить pf); **to pay (in)** ~ платить (заплатить pf) наличными; **~ on delivery** наложенным платежом; **~ card** n банкоматная карточка; **~ desk** n (BRIT) касса; **~ dispenser** n (BRIT) банкомат; **~ flow** n движение денежной наличности; **~ier** [kæ'ʃɪə] n кассир

cashmere ['kæʃmɪə] n кашемир

casino [kə'siːnəu] n казино nt ind

casserole ['kæsərəul] n рагу nt ind; (also: ~ **dish**) латка

cassette [kæ'set] n кассета

cast [kɑːst] (pt, pp ~) vt (light, shadow, glance) бросать (бросить pf); (doubts) сеять (посеять pf); (FISHING) забрасывать (забросить pf); (doubts) сеять (посеять pf) в (THEAT) состав (исполнителей) ♦ (MED: also: plaster ~) гипс; **to ~ one's vote** отдавать (отдать pf) свой голос

caster sugar ['kɑːstə-] n (BRIT) сахарная пудра

castle ['kɑːsl] n замок; (fortified)

крепость f; (CHESS) ладья, тура

casual ['kæʒjul] adj (meeting) случайный; (attitude) небрежный; (clothes) повседневный; (dress) просто; **~ly** adv (behave) небрежно; (dress) просто

casualty ['kæʒjultɪ] n (sb injured) пострадавший(ая) m(f) adj; (sb killed) жертва; (department) травматология

cat [kæt] n (pet) кошка; (tomcat) кот; **big ~s** (ZOOL) кошачьи pl adj

catalogue ['kætəlɔg] (US **catalog**) n каталог

catalyst ['kætəlɪst] n катализатор

catapult ['kætəpʌlt] n (BRIT) рогатка

catarrh [kə'tɑː] n катар

catastrophe [kə'tæstrəfɪ] n катастрофа

catastrophic [kætə'strɔfɪk] adj катастрофический

catch [kætʃ] (pt, pp **caught**) vt (ball etc) ловить (поймать pf); (bus etc) садиться (сесть pf) на +acc; (breath: in shock) затаивать (затаить pf); (: after running) передохнуть (pf); (attention) привлекать (привлечь pf); (hear) улавливать (уловить pf); (illness) подхватывать (подхватить pf) ♦ vi (become trapped) застревать (застрять pf) ♦ n (of fish) улов; (of ball) захват; (hidden problem) подвох; (of lock) защёлка; **to ~ sight of** увидеть (pf); **to ~ fire** загораться (загореться pf) ♦ vi приживаться (прижиться pf); **~ up** vi (fig) нагонять (нагнать pf) ♦ vt (also: **~ up with**) догонять (догнать pf); **~ing** adj (MED) заразный

category ['kætɪgərɪ] n категория

cater ['keɪtə] vi: **to ~ (for)** организовать (impf/pf) питание (для +gen); **~ for** vt fus (BRIT: needs, *tastes*) удовлетворя́ть (удовлетвори́ть *pf*); (: *readers etc*) обслу́живать (обслужи́ть *pf*)

cathedral [kəˈθiːdrəl] *n* собо́р

Catholic [ˈkæθəlɪk] *adj* католи́ческий ♦ *n* като́лик(и́чка)

cattle [ˈkætl] *npl* скот *msg*

catwalk [ˈkætwɔːk] *n* помо́ст (*для пока́за мод*)

caught [kɔːt] *pt, pp of* **catch**

cauliflower [ˈkɒlɪflauə] *n* цветна́я капу́ста

cause [kɔːz] *n* (*reason*) причи́на; (*aim*) де́ло ♦ *vt* явля́ться (яви́ться *pf*) причи́ной +gen

caution [ˈkɔːʃən] *n* осторо́жность *f*; (*warning*) предупрежде́ние, предостереже́ние ♦ *vt* предупрежда́ть (предупреди́ть *pf*)

cautious [ˈkɔːʃəs] *adj* осторо́жный; ~**ly** *adv* осторо́жно

cavalry [ˈkævəlrɪ] *n* кавале́рия; (*mechanized*) мотопехо́та

cave [keɪv] *n* пеще́ра; ~ **in** *vi* (*roof*) обва́ливаться (обвали́ться *pf*)

caviar(e) [ˈkævɪɑː] *n* икра́

cavity [ˈkævɪtɪ] *n* (*in tooth*) дупло́

CBI *n abbr* (= *Confederation of British Industries*) Конфедера́ция брита́нской промы́шленности

cc *abbr* (= *cubic centimetre*) куби́ческий сантиме́тр

CCTV *n abbr* (= *closed-circuit television*) за́мкнутая телевизио́нная систе́ма

CD *n abbr* (= *compact disc*); ~ **player** прои́грыватель *m* для компа́кт-ди́сков; ~-**ROM** *n* компа́кт-ди́ск ПЗУ

cease [siːs] *vi* прекраща́ться (прекрати́ться *pf*); ~-**fire** *n* прекраще́ние огня́

cedar [ˈsiːdər] *n* кедр

ceiling [ˈsiːlɪŋ] *n* (*also fig*) потоло́к

celebrate [ˈsɛlɪbreɪt] *vt*

пра́здновать (отпра́здновать *pf*) ♦ (: *readers etc*) обслу́живать (обслужи́ть *pf*)

пра́здновать (отпра́здновать *pf*); (: *readers etc*) повеселя́ться (повесели́ться *pf*); **to ~ Mass** соверша́ть (соверши́ть *pf*) прича́стие; ~**d** *adj* знамени́тый

celebration [sɛlɪˈbreɪʃən] *n* (*event*) пра́здник; (*of anniversary etc*) пра́зднование

celebrity [sɪˈlɛbrɪtɪ] *n* знамени́тость *f*

celery [ˈsɛlərɪ] *n* сельдере́й

cell [sɛl] *n* (*in prison*) ка́мера; (*BIO*) кле́тка

cellar [ˈsɛlər] *n* подва́л; (*also: wine ~*) ви́нный по́греб

cello [ˈtʃɛləu] *n* виолонче́ль *f*

cellulose [ˈsɛljuləus] *n* клетча́тка, целлюло́за

Celsius [ˈsɛlsɪəs] *adj*: **30 degrees ~** 30 гра́дусов по Це́льсию

Celtic [ˈkɛltɪk] *adj* ке́льтский

cement [səˈmɛnt] *n* цеме́нт

cemetery [ˈsɛmɪtrɪ] *n* кла́дбище

censor [ˈsɛnsər] *n* це́нзор ♦ *vt* подверга́ть (подве́ргнуть *pf*) цензу́ре; ~**ship** *n* цензу́ра

census [ˈsɛnsəs] *n* пе́репись *f*

cent [sɛnt] *n* цент; *see also* **per cent**

centenary [sɛnˈtiːnərɪ] *n* столе́тие

center *etc* (*US*) *see* **centre** *etc*

centigrade [ˈsɛntɪgreɪd] *adj*: **30 degrees ~** 30 гра́дусов по Це́льсию

centimetre [ˈsɛntɪmiːtər] (*US* **centimeter**) *n* сантиме́тр

centipede [ˈsɛntɪpiːd] *n* многоно́жка

central [ˈsɛntrəl] *adj* центра́льный; **this flat is very ~** эта кварти́ра располо́жена бли́зко к це́нтру; **Central America** *n* Центра́льная Аме́рика; ~ **heating** *n* центра́льное отопле́ние

centre [ˈsɛntər] (*US* **center**) *n* центр ♦ *vt* (*PHOT, TYP*) центри́ровать (*impf/pf*); ~ **forward** *n* центра́льный напада́ющий *m adj*, центр-фо́рвард

century ['sɛntjʊrɪ] *n* век

ceramic [sɪ'ræmɪk] *adj* керами́ческий; **~s** *npl* кера́мика *fsg*

cereal ['sɪːrɪəl] *n*: **~s** зерновы́е *pl adj*; (*also*: **breakfast ~**) хло́пья *pl* к за́втраку

ceremony ['sɛrɪmənɪ] *n* церемо́ния; (*behaviour*) церемо́нии *fpl*; **with ~** со все́ми форма́льностями

certain ['səːtən] *adj* определённый; **I'm ~ (that)** я уве́рен(, что); **~ days** определённые дни; **a ~ pleasure** не́которое удово́льствие; **it's ~ (that)** несомне́нно, что); **in ~ circumstances** при определённых обстоя́тельствах; **a ~ Mr Smith** не́кий Ми́стер Смит; **for ~** наверняка́; **~ly** *adv* (*undoubtedly*) несомне́нно; (*of course*) коне́чно; **~ty** *n* (*assurance*) уве́ренность *f*; (*inevitability*) несомне́нность *f*

certificate [sə'tɪfɪkɪt] *n* свиде́тельство; (*doctor's etc*) спра́вка; (*diploma*) дипло́м

cervix ['səːvɪks] *n* ше́йка ма́тки

cf. *abbr* = **compare**

CFC *n abbr* (= *chlorofluorocarbon*) хлорфторуглеро́д

ch. *abbr* = **chapter** гл.

chain [tʃeɪn] *n* цепь *f*; (*decorative, on bicycle*) цепо́чка; (*of shops, hotels*) сеть *f*; (*of events, ideas*) верени́ца *f* ♦ *vt* (*also*: **~ up**: *person*) прико́вывать (прикова́ть *pf*); (: *dog*) сажа́ть (посади́ть *pf*) на цепь; **a ~ of mountains** го́рная цепь

chair [tʃɛəʳ] *n* стул; (*also*: **arm~**) кре́сло; (*of university*) ка́федра; (*also*: **~person**) председа́тель *m*

♦ *vt* председа́тельствовать (*impf*) на +*prp*; **~ lift** *n* кана́тный подъёмник; **~man** (*irreg*) *n* председа́тель *m*; (*BRIT : COMM*) президе́нт

chalet ['ʃæleɪ] *n* шале́ *m ind*

chalk [tʃɔːk] *n* мел

challenge ['tʃælɪndʒ] *n* вы́зов; (*task*) испыта́ние ♦ *vt* (*also SPORT*) броса́ть (бро́сить *pf*) вы́зов +*dat*; (*authority, right etc*) оспа́ривать (оспо́рить *pf*); **to ~ sb to** вызыва́ть (вы́звать *pf*) кого́-н на +*acc*

challenging ['tʃælɪndʒɪŋ] *adj* (*tone, look*) вызыва́ющий; (*task*) тру́дный

chamber ['tʃeɪmbəʳ] *n* ка́мера; (*POL*) пала́та; **~ of commerce** Торго́вая Пала́та

champagne [ʃæm'peɪn] *n* шампа́нское *nt adj*

champion ['tʃæmpɪən] *n* чемпио́н; (*of cause*) побо́рник(ица); (*of person*) защи́тник(ица); **~ship** *n* (*contest*) чемпиона́т; (*title*) зва́ние чемпио́на

chance [tʃɑːns] *n* шанс; (*opportunity*) возмо́жность *f*; (*risk*) риск ♦ *vt* рискова́ть (*impf*) +*instr* ♦ *adj* случа́йный; **to take a ~** рискну́ть (*pf*); **by ~** случа́йно; **to leave to ~** оставля́ть (оста́вить *pf*) на во́лю слу́чая

chancellor ['tʃɑːnsələʳ] *n* (*POL*) ка́нцлер; **Chancellor of the Exchequer** *n* (*BRIT*) Ка́нцлер казначе́йства

Chancellor of the Exchequer - ка́нцлер казначе́йства. В Великобрита́нии он выполня́ет фу́нкции мини́стра фина́нсов.

---

chandelier [ʃændə'lɪəʳ] *n* лю́стра

change [tʃeɪndʒ] *vt* меня́ть

(поменя́ть pf); (money: to other currency) обме́нивать (обменя́ть pf); (: for smaller currency) разме́нивать (разменя́ть pf) ♦ vi (alter) меня́ться (impf), изменя́ться (impf); (one's clothes) переодева́ться (переоде́ться pf); (change trains etc) де́лать (сде́лать pf) переса́дку ♦ n (alteration) измене́ние; (difference) переме́на; (replacement) сме́на; (also: **small** or **loose ~**) ме́лочь f; (money returned) сда́ча; **to ~ sb into** превраща́ть (преврати́ть pf) кого́-н в +acc ♦ adj; **to ~ one's mind** переду́мывать (переду́мать pf); **to ~ gear** переключа́ть (переключи́ть pf) ско́рость; **for a ~** для разнообра́зия

channel ['tʃænl] n кана́л; (NAUT) тра́сса ♦ vt: **to ~ into** направля́ть (напра́вить pf) на +acc ♦ adj: **the C~ Islands** Норма́ндские острова́ mpl; **the (English) C~** Ла-Ма́нш; **the C~ Tunnel** тунне́ль m под Ла-Ма́ншем

chant [tʃɑːnt] n сканди́рование; (REL) пе́ние

chaos ['keɪɒs] n ха́ос

chaotic [keɪ'ɒtɪk] adj хаоти́чный

chap [tʃæp] n (BRIT: inf) па́рень m

chapel ['tʃæpl] n (in church) приде́л n; (in prison etc) часо́вня n; (BRIT: also: **non-conformist ~**) протеста́нтская нон-конформи́стская це́рковь

chaplain ['tʃæplɪn] n капелла́н

chapter ['tʃæptə*] n глава́; (in life, history) страни́ца

character ['kærɪktə*] n (personality) ли́чность f; (nature) хара́ктер; (in novel, film) персона́ж; (letter, symbol) знак; **~istic** ['kærɪk'rɪstɪk] n характе́рная черта́ ♦ adj: **~istic (of)** характе́рный (для +gen)

charcoal ['tʃɑːkəul] n (fuel) древе́сный у́голь m

charge [tʃɑːdʒ] n (fee) пла́та; (LAW) обвине́ние; (responsibility) отве́тственность f; (MIL) ата́ка ♦ vt атакова́ть (impf/pf) ♦ vi (battery, gun) заряжа́ть (заряди́ть pf); (LAW): **to ~ sb with** предъявля́ть (предъяви́ть pf) кому́-н обвине́ние в +prp; **~s** npl (COMM) де́нежный сбор msg; (TEL) телефо́нный тари́ф msg; **to reverse the ~s** (BRIT) звони́ть (позвони́ть pf) по колле́кту; **to take ~ of** (child) брать (взять pf) на попече́ние; (company) брать (взять pf) на себя́ руково́дство +instr; **to be in ~ of** отвеча́ть (impf) за +acc; **who's in ~ here?** кто здесь гла́вный?; **to ~ (sb) (for)** проси́ть (попроси́ть pf) (у кого́-н) пла́ту (за +acc); **how much do you ~ for?** ско́лько Вы про́сите за +acc?; **~ card** n креди́тная ка́рточка (определённого магази́на)

charisma [kæ'rɪzmə] n обая́ние, хари́зма

charitable ['tʃærɪtəbl] adj благотвори́тельный

charity ['tʃærɪtɪ] n (organization) благотвори́тельная организа́ция; (kindness) милосе́рдие; (money, gifts) ми́лостыня

charity shop - благотвори́тельный магази́н. В э́тих магази́нах рабо́тают волонтёры, продаю́щие поде́ржанную оде́жду, ста́рые кни́ги, предме́ты дома́шнего обихо́да. Получа́емая при́быль направля́ется в благотвори́тельные о́бщества, кото́рые э́ти магази́ны подде́рживают.

charm [tʃɑːm] n очарова́ние, обая́ние; (on bracelet etc) брело́к ♦ vt очаро́вывать (очарова́ть pf); ~**ing** adj очарова́тельный

chart [tʃɑːt] n гра́фик; (of sea) навигацио́нная ка́рта; (of stars) ка́рта звёздного не́ба ♦ vt наноси́ть (нанести́ pf) на ка́рту; (progress) следи́ть (impf) за +instr, ~s npl (MUS) хит-пара́д msg

charter ['tʃɑːtə] vt фрахтова́ть (зафрахтова́ть pf) ♦ n ха́ртия; (COMM) уста́в; ~**ed accountant** n (BRIT) бухга́лтер вы́сшей квалифика́ции; ~ **flight** n ча́ртерный рейс

chase [tʃeɪs] vt гоня́ться (impf) or гна́ться (impf) за +instr ♦ n пого́ня; **to ~ away** or **off** прогоня́ть (прогна́ть pf)

chasm ['kæzəm] n (GEO) про́пасть f

chassis ['ʃæsɪ] n шасси́ nt ind

chat [tʃæt] vi болта́ть (поболта́ть pf) ♦ n бесе́да; ~ **show** n (BRIT) шóу с уча́стием знамени́тостей

chatter ['tʃætə] n (gossip) болтовня́

chauffeur ['ʃəufə] n (персона́льный) шофёр

cheap [tʃiːp] adj дешёвый ♦ adv дёшево; ~**er** adj деше́вле; ~**ly** adv дёшево

cheat [tʃiːt] vi (at cards) жу́льничать (impf); (in exam) спи́сывать (списа́ть pf) ♦ n жу́лик ♦ vt: **to ~ sb (out of £10)** надува́ть (наду́ть pf) кого́-н (на £10)

check [tʃek] vt проверя́ть (прове́рить pf); (halt) уде́рживать (удержа́ть pf); (curb) сде́рживать (сдержа́ть pf); (US: items) отмеча́ть (отме́тить pf) ♦ n (inspection) прове́рка; (US: bill) счёт; (: COMM) = **cheque**; (pattern)

кле́тка ♦ adj кле́тчатый; ~ **in** vi (at hotel etc) регистри́роваться (зарегистри́роваться pf) ♦ vt (luggage) сдава́ть (сдать pf); ~ **out** vi выпи́сываться (вы́писаться pf); ~ **up** vi: **to ~ up on** наводи́ть (навести́ pf) спра́вки о +prp; ~**ing account** n (US) теку́щий счёт; ~**out** n контро́ль m, ка́сса; ~**room** n (US) ка́мера хране́ния; ~**up** n осмо́тр

cheek [tʃiːk] n щека́; (impudence) на́глость f; (nerve) де́рзость f; ~**y** adj наха́льный, на́глый

cheer [tʃɪə] vt приве́тствовать (поприве́тствовать pf) ♦ vi одобри́тельно восклица́ть (impf); ~**s** npl (of welcome) приве́тственные во́згласы mpl; (of approval) одобри́тельные во́згласы mpl; ~**s!** (за) Ва́ше здоро́вье!; ~ **up** vi развесели́ться (pf), повесле́ть (pf) ♦ vt развесели́ть (pf); ~ **up!** не грусти́те!; ~**ful** adj весёлый

cheese [tʃiːz] n сыр

cheetah ['tʃiːtə] n гепа́рд

chef [ʃef] n шеф-по́вар

chemical ['kemɪkl] adj хими́ческий ♦ n химика́т; (in laboratory) реакти́в

chemist ['kemɪst] n (BRIT: pharmacist) фармаце́вт; (scientist) хи́мик; ~**ry** n хи́мия

chemotherapy [kiːməuˈθerəpɪ] n химиотерапи́я

cheque [tʃek] n (BRIT) чек; ~**book** n (BRIT) че́ковая кни́жка; ~ **card** n (BRIT) ка́рточка, подтвержда́ющая платёжеспосо́бность владе́льца

cherish ['tʃerɪʃ] vt леле́ять (взлеле́ять pf)

cherry ['tʃerɪ] n чере́шня; (sour variety) ви́шня

chess [tʃɛs] n ша́хматы pl
chest [tʃɛst] n грудь f; (box) сунду́к
chestnut [ˈtʃɛsnʌt] n кашта́н
chest of drawers n комо́д
chew [tʃuː] vt жева́ть (impf); ~**ing
gum** n жева́тельная рези́нка
chic [ʃiːk] adj шика́рный,
элега́нтный
chick [tʃɪk] n цыплёнок; (of wild
bird) птене́ц
chicken [ˈtʃɪkɪn] n ку́рица; (inf:
coward) труси́шка m/f; ~**pox** n
ветря́нка
chief [tʃiːf] n (of organization etc)
нача́льник ♦ adj гла́вный,
основно́й; ~ **executive** (US ~
executive officer) n гла́вный
исполни́тельный дире́ктор; ~**ly**
adv гла́вным о́бразом
child [tʃaɪld] (pl ~**ren**) n ребёнок;
do you have any ~ren? у Вас есть
де́ти?; ~**birth** n ро́ды pl; ~**hood** n
де́тство; ~**ish** adj (games, attitude)
ребя́ческий; (person)
ребя́чливый; ~**like** adj де́тский; ~
minder n (BRIT) ня́ня; ~**ren**
[ˈtʃɪldrən] npl of **child**
Chile [ˈtʃɪlɪ] n Чи́ли ind
chili [ˈtʃɪlɪ] n (US) = **chilli**
chill [tʃɪl] n (MED) просту́да ♦ vt
охлади́ть (охлади́ть pf); **to
catch a ~** простуди́ться
(простуди́ться pf)
chilli [ˈtʃɪlɪ] (US **chili**) n кра́сный
стручко́вый пе́рец
chilly [ˈtʃɪlɪ] adj холо́дный
chimney [ˈtʃɪmnɪ] n (дымова́я)
труба́
chimpanzee [tʃɪmpænˈziː] n
шимпанзе́ m ind
chin [tʃɪn] n подборо́док
China [ˈtʃaɪnə] n Кита́й
china [ˈtʃaɪnə] n фарфо́р
Chinese [tʃaɪˈniːz] adj кита́йский
♦ n inv кита́ец(а́йнка)
chip [tʃɪp] n (of wood) ще́пка; (of

stone) оско́лок; (also: **micro~**)
микросхе́ма, чип ♦ vt отбива́ть
(отби́ть pf); ~**s** npl (BRIT)
карто́фель msg-фри; (US: also:
potato ~) чи́псы mpl
chiropodist [kɪˈrɔpədɪst] n (BRIT)
мозо́льный опера́тор m/f
chisel [ˈtʃɪzl] n (for wood) долото́;
(for stone) зуби́ло
chives [tʃaɪvz] npl лук-ре́занец msg
chlorine [ˈklɔːriːn] n хлор
chocolate [ˈtʃɔklɪt] n шокола́д;
(sweet) шокола́дная конфе́та
choice [tʃɔɪs] n вы́бор
choir [ˈkwaɪə] n хор; (area) хо́ры pl
choke [tʃəuk] vi (подави́ться pf);
(with smoke,
anger) задыха́ться (задохну́ться
pf) ♦ vt (strangle) души́ть
(задуши́ть or удуши́ть pf)
cholesterol [kəˈlɛstərɔl] n
холестери́н; **high** ~ с высо́ким
содержа́нием холестери́на
choose [tʃuːz] (pt **chose**, pp
chosen) vt выбира́ть (вы́брать
pf); **to ~ to do** реша́ть (реши́ть pf)
+infin
chop [tʃɔp] vt (wood) руби́ть
(наруби́ть pf); (also: ~ **up**:
vegetables, meat) ре́зать
(наре́зать or поре́зать pf) ♦ n
(CULIN) отбивна́я (котле́та)
chord [kɔːd] n (MUS) акко́рд
chore [tʃɔːr] n (burden)
повседне́вная обя́занность f;
household ~s дома́шние
хло́поты
choreographer [kɔrɪˈɔgrəfəʳ] n
хорео́граф; (of ballet)
балетме́йстер
chorus [ˈkɔːrəs] n хор; (refrain)
припе́в
chose [tʃəuz] pt of **choose**; ~**n**
[ˈtʃəuzn] pp of **choose**
Christ [kraɪst] n Христо́с
Christian [ˈkrɪstɪən] adj

христиа́нский ♦ *n* христиани́н(а́нка); **~ity** [krɪstɪˈænɪtɪ] *n* христиа́нство; **~ name** *n* и́мя *nt*

Christmas [ˈkrɪsməs] *n* Рождество́; **Happy** or **Merry ~!** Счастли́вого Рождества́!; **~ card** *n* рожде́ственская откры́тка

> **Christmas cracker** - рожде́ственская хлопу́шка. В отли́чие от обы́чной хлопу́шки в неё завора́чиваются бума́жная коро́на, шу́тка и ма́ленький пода́рок. Механи́зм хлопу́шки приво́дится в де́йствие, е́сли дёрнуть за о́ба её конца́ одновре́менно. Раздаётся хлопо́к и из хлопу́шки выпада́ет пода́рок.

Christmas Day *n* день *m* Рождества́
Christmas Eve *n* Соче́льник

> **Christmas pudding** - рожде́ственский пу́динг. Кекс, пригото́вленный на па́ру и содержа́щий большо́е коли́чество сушёных фру́ктов.

Christmas tree *n* (рожде́ственская) ёлка
chrome [krəʊm] *n* хром
chronic [ˈkrɒnɪk] *adj* хрони́ческий
chronological [krɒnəˈlɒdʒɪkl] *adj* (*order*) хронологи́ческий
chubby [ˈtʃʌbɪ] *adj* пу́хлый
chuck [tʃʌk] *vt* (*inf*) швыря́ть (швырну́ть *pf*)
chuckle [ˈtʃʌkl] *vi* посме́иваться (*impf*)
chunk [tʃʌŋk] *n* (*of meat*) кусо́к
church [tʃəːtʃ] *n* це́рковь *f*; **~yard** *n* пого́ст
CIA *n abbr* (*US*) (= Central Intelligence

Agency) ЦРУ
CID *n abbr* (*BRIT*: = Criminal Investigation Department) уголо́вный ро́зыск
cider [ˈsaɪdə*r*] *n* сидр
cigar [sɪˈɡɑː*r*] *n* сига́ра
cigarette [sɪɡəˈrɛt] *n* сигаре́та
cinema [ˈsɪnəmə] *n* кинотеа́тр
cinnamon [ˈsɪnəmən] *n* кори́ца
circle [ˈsəːkl] *n* круг; (*THEAT*) балко́н
circuit [ˈsəːkɪt] *n* (*ELEC*) цепь *f*; (*tour*) турне́ *nt ind*; (*track*) трек
circular [ˈsəːkjulə*r*] *adj* (*plate, pond etc*) кру́глый ♦ *n* циркуля́р
circulate [ˈsəːkjuleɪt] *vi* циркули́ровать (*impf*) ♦ *vt* передава́ть (переда́ть *pf*)
circulation [səːkjuˈleɪʃən] *n* (*PRESS*) тира́ж; (*MED*) кровообраще́ние; (*COMM*) обраще́ние; (*of air, traffic*) циркуля́ция
circumstances [ˈsəːkəmstənsɪz] *npl* обстоя́тельства *ntpl*
circus [ˈsəːkəs] *n* (*show*) цирк
cite [saɪt] *vt* цити́ровать (процити́ровать *pf*); (*LAW*) вызыва́ть (вы́звать *pf*) в суд
citizen [ˈsɪtɪzn] *n* (*of country*) граждани́н(а́нка); (*of town*) жи́тель(ница) *m(f)*; **~ship** *n* гражда́нство
city [ˈsɪtɪ] *n* го́род; **the City** Си́ти *nt ind*

> **the City** - Си́ти. Э́тот райо́н Ло́ндона явля́ется его́ фина́нсовым це́нтром.

civic [ˈsɪvɪk] *adj* муниципа́льный; (*duties, pride*) гражда́нский
civil [ˈsɪvl] *adj* гражда́нский; (*authorities*) госуда́рственный; (*polite*) учти́вый; **~ian** [sɪˈvɪlɪən] *adj* (*life*) обще́ственный ♦ *n*

ми́рный(ая) жи́тель(ница) m(f);
~ian casualties же́ртвы среди́
ми́рного населе́ния

civilization [sɪvɪlaɪˈzeɪʃən] n
цивилиза́ция

civilized [ˈsɪvɪlaɪzd] adj
культу́рный; (society)
цивилизо́ванный

civil: ~ liberties fpl гражда́нские
свобо́ды fpl; ~ servant n
госуда́рственный служащий m
adj; Civil Service n
госуда́рственная слу́жба; ~ war
n гражда́нская война́

clad [klæd] adj: ~ (in) облачённый
(в +acc)

claim [kleɪm] vt (responsibility)
брать (взять pf) на себя́; (credit)
припи́сывать (приписа́ть pf)
себе́; (rights, inheritance)
претендова́ть (impf) или притяза́ть
(impf) на +acc ♦ vi (for insurance)
де́лать (сде́лать pf) страхову́ю
зая́вку ♦ n (assertion)
утвержде́ние; (for compensation)
зая́вка; (to inheritance, land)
прете́нзия, притяза́ние; to ~
(that) или to утвержда́ть (impf),
что

clamour [ˈklæmə] (US clamor) vi:
to ~ for шу́мно тре́бовать (impf)
+gen

clamp [klæmp] n зажи́м ♦ vt
зажима́ть (зажа́ть pf)

clan [klæn] n клан

clandestine [klænˈdɛstɪn] adj
подпо́льный

clap [klæp] vi хло́пать (impf)

claret [ˈklærət] n бордо́ nt ind

clarify [ˈklærɪfaɪ] vt (fig)
разъясня́ть (разъясни́ть pf)

clarinet [klærɪˈnɛt] n кларне́т

clarity [ˈklærɪtɪ] n (fig) я́сность f

clash [klæʃ] n столкнове́ние; (of
events etc) совпаде́ние; (of metal
objects) звяка́нье ♦ vi

ста́лкиваться (столкну́ться pf);
(colours) не совмеща́ться (impf);
(events etc) совпада́ть (совпа́сть
pf) (по вре́мени); (metal objects)
звяка́ть (impf)

class [klɑːs] n класс; (lesson) уро́к;
(of goods: type) разря́д; (: quality)
сорт ♦ vt классифици́ровать
(impf/pf)

classic [ˈklæsɪk] adj класси́ческий
♦ n класси́ческое произведе́ние;
~al adj класси́ческий

classification [klæsɪfɪˈkeɪʃən] n
классифика́ция; (category)
разря́д

classified [ˈklæsɪfaɪd] adj
засекре́ченный

classless [ˈklɑːslɪs] adj
бескла́ссовый

classroom [ˈklɑːsrum] n класс

clatter [ˈklætə] n звя́канье; (of
hooves) цо́канье

clause [klɔːz] n (LAW) пункт

claustrophobic [klɔːstrəˈfəubɪk] adj:
she is ~ она́ страда́ет
клаустрофо́бией

claw [klɔː] n ко́готь m; (of lobster)
клешня́

clay [kleɪ] n гли́на

clean [kliːn] adj чи́стый; (edge,
fracture) ро́вный ♦ vt (hands, face)
мыть (вы́мыть pf); (car, room)
чи́стить (почи́стить pf); ~ out
(tidy) вычища́ть (вы́чистить pf); ~
up (room) убира́ть (убра́ть pf);
(child) мыть (помы́ть pf); ~er n
убо́рщик(ица); (substance)
мо́ющее сре́дство; ~liness
[ˈklɛnlɪnɪs] n чистопло́тность f

cleanse [klɛnz] vt очища́ть
(очи́стить pf); (face) мыть
(вы́мыть pf); (wound)
(промы́ть pf); ~r n очища́ющий
лосьо́н

clean-shaven [ˈkliːnˈʃeɪvn] adj
чи́сто вы́бритый

clear [klɪəʳ] adj ясный; (footprint, writing) чёткий; (glass, water) прозрачный; (road) свободный; (conscience, profit) чистый ♦ vt (space, room) освобождать (освободить pf); (suspect) оправдывать (оправдать pf); (fence etc) брать (взять pf) ♦ vi (sky) проясняться (проясниться pf); (fog, smoke) рассеиваться (рассеяться pf) ♦ adv: ~ of подальше от +gen; to make it ~ to sb that ... давать (дать pf) кому-н понять, что ...; to ~ the table убирать (убрать pf) со стола; ~ up vt убирать (убрать pf); (mystery, problem) разрешать (разрешить pf); ~ance n расчистка; (permission) разрешение; ~-cut adj ясный, чёткий; ~ing n поляна; ~ly adv ясно; (obviously) явно, очевидно

cleft [kleft] n расселина

clergy ['klɜːdʒɪ] n духовенство; ~man (irreg) n священник

clerical ['klerɪkl] adj канцелярский; (REL) церковный

clerk [klɑːk, (US) klɜːrk] n (BRIT) клерк, делопроизводитель(ница) m(f); (US: sales person) продавец(вщица)

clever ['klevəʳ] adj (intelligent) умный

cliché ['kliːʃeɪ] n клише nt ind, штамп

click [klɪk] vt (tongue, heels) щёлкать (щёлкнуть pf) +instr ♦ vi (device, switch) щёлкать (щёлкнуть pf); ~ on vt fus (COMPUT) щёлкать (щёлкнуть pf) по +dat

client ['klaɪənt] n клиент

cliff [klɪf] n скала, утёс

climate ['klaɪmɪt] n климат

climax ['klaɪmæks] n кульминация

climb [klaɪm] vi подниматься (подняться pf); (plant) ползти (impf); (plane) набирать (набрать pf) высоту ♦ vt (stairs) взбираться (взобраться pf) по +prp; (tree, hill) взбираться (взобраться pf)+acc ♦ n подъём; to ~ over a wall перелезать (перелезть pf) через стену; ~er n альпинист(ка)

clinch [klɪntʃ] vt (deal) заключать (заключить pf); (argument) разрешать (разрешить pf)

cling [klɪŋ] (pt, pp clung) vi (clothes) прилегать (impf); to ~ to вцепляться (вцепиться pf) в +acc; (fig) цепляться (impf) за +acc

clinic ['klɪnɪk] n клиника; ~al adj клинический; (fig: attitude) бесстрастный

clip [klɪp] n (also: **paper** ~) скрепка; (for hair) заколка; (TV, CINEMA) клип ♦ vt (fasten) прикреплять (прикрепить pf); (cut) подстригать (подстричь pf); ~ping n (PRESS) вырезка

clique [kliːk] n клика

cloak [kləʊk] n (cape) плащ; ~room n гардероб; (BRIT: WC) уборная f adj

clock [klɒk] n (timepiece) часы pl; ~wise adv по часовой стрелке; ~work adj (toy) заводной

clone [kləʊn] n (BIO) клон

close¹ [kləʊs] adj близкий; (writing) убористый; (contact, ties) тесный; (watch, attention) пристальный; (weather, room) душный ♦ adv близко; to ~ (near) близкий к +dat; to ~ or on (almost) близко к +dat; ~ by or at hand рядом

close² [kləʊz] vt закрывать (закрыть pf); (finalize) заключать (заключить pf); (end) завершать (завершить pf) ♦ vi закрываться (закрыться pf); (end)

завершáться (завершúться pf)
♦ в концé; ~ **down** vt
закрывáть (закрыть pf) ♦ vi
закрывáться (закрыться pf); ~**d**
adj закрытый

closely ['kləuslɪ] adv пристáльно;
(connected, related) тéсно

closet ['klɔzɪt] n (cupboard) шкаф

close-up ['kləusʌp] n крýпный
план

closure ['kləuʒər] n (of factory, road)
закрытие

clot [klɔt] n сгýсток; (in vein)
тромб

cloth [klɔθ] n ткань f; (for cleaning
etc) трápка

clothes [kləuðz] npl одéжда fsg; ~
brush n одéжная щётка; ~ **peg**
(US = **pin**) n прищéпка

clothing ['kləuðɪŋ] n = **clothes**

cloud [klaud] n óблако; ~**y** adj (sky)
óблачный; (liquid) мýтный

clout [klaut] vt (inf) долбанýть (pf)

clove [kləuv] n гвоздúка; ~ **of**
garlic дóлька чеснокá

clover ['kləuvər] n клéвер

clown [klaun] n клóун

club [klʌb] n клуб; (weapon)
дубúнка; (also: **golf** ~) клюшка;
~**s** npl (CARDS) трéфы fpl

clue [klu:] n ключ; (for police)
улúка; **I haven't a** ~ (я) понятия
не имéю

clump [klʌmp] n зáросли fpl

clumsy ['klʌmzɪ] adj неуклюжий;
(object) неудóбный

clung [klʌŋ] pt, pp of **cling**

cluster ['klʌstər] n скоплéние

clutch [klʌtʃ] n хвáтка; (AUT)
сцеплéние ♦ vt сжимáть (сжать
pf)

clutter ['klʌtər] vt (also: ~ **up**)
захламлять (захламúть pf)

cm abbr (= **centimetre**) см

CND n abbr = Campaign for Nuclear
Disarmament

Co. abbr = **company, county**

coach [kəutʃ] n (bus) автóбус;
(horse-drawn) экипáж; (of train)
вагóн; (SPORT) трéнер; (SCOL)
репетúтор ♦ vt (SPORT)
тренировáть (натренировáть pf);
(SCOL): **to ~ sb for** подготáвливать
(подготóвить pf) когó-н +dat

coal [kəul] n ýголь m

coalition [kəuə'lɪʃən] n коалúция

coarse [kɔ:s] adj грýбый

coast [kəust] n бéрег; (area)
побережье; ~**al** adj прибрéжный;
~**guard** n офицéр берегово́й
слýжбы; ~**line** n береговáя
лúния

coat [kəut] n пальтó nt ind; (on
animal: fur) мех; (: wool) шерсть
f; (of paint) слой ♦ vt покрывáть
(покрыть pf); ~ **hanger** n
вéшалка

cobweb ['kɔbwɛb] n паутúна

cocaine [kə'keɪn] n кокаúн

cock [kɔk] n петýх ♦ vt (gun)
взводúть (взвестú pf); ~**erel**
['kɔkərl] n петýх

---

cockney - кóкни. Так называ́ют
выходцев из восто́чного
райо́на Ло́ндона. Они́ говоря́т
на осо́бом диале́кте
англи́йского языка́. Кóкни
та́кже обознача́ет э́тот
диале́кт.

---

cockpit ['kɔkpɪt] n кабúна

cockroach ['kɔkrəutʃ] n тарака́н

cocktail ['kɔkteɪl] n кокте́йль m;
(with fruit, prawns) сала́т

cocoa ['kəukəu] n кака́о nt ind

coconut ['kəukənʌt] n коко́совый
оре́х; (flesh) коко́с

COD abbr = **cash on delivery**; (US:
= **collect on delivery**) нало́женный
платёж

cod [kɔd] n треска́ f no pl

code [kəud] *n* код; (*of behaviour*) кόдекс; **post ~** (*BRIT*) почтόвый и́ндекс

coffee ['kɔfɪ] *n* кόфе *m ind*; **~ table** *n* кофéйный стόлик

coffin ['kɔfɪn] *n* гроб

cognac ['kɔnjæk] *n* коньáк

coherent [kəu'hɪərənt] *adj* свя́зный, стрόйный; **she was very ~** её речь былá όчень свя́зной

coil [kɔɪl] *n* мотόк ♦ *vt* смáтывать (смотáть *pf*)

coin [kɔɪn] *n* монéта ♦ *vt* приду́мывать (приду́мать *pf*)

coincide [kəuɪn'saɪd] *vi* совпадáть (совпáсть *pf*); **~nce** [kəu'ɪnsɪdəns] *n* совпадéние

coke [kəuk] *n* кокс

colander ['kɔləndə] *n* дуршлáг

cold [kəuld] *adj* холόдный ♦ *n* хόлод; (*MED*) простýда; **it's ~** хόлодно; **I am** *or* **feel ~** мне хόлодно; **to catch ~** *or* **a ~** простужáться (простуди́ться *pf*); **in ~ blood** хладнокрόвно; **~ly** *adv* хόлодно; **~ sore** *n* лихорáдка (на губé и́ли носý)

colic ['kɔlɪk] *n* кόлики *pl*

collaboration [kəlæbə'reɪʃən] *n* сотрýдничество

collapse [kə'læps] *vi* (*building, system, plans*) рýшиться (рýхнуть *pf*); (*table etc*) склáдываться (сложи́ться *pf*); (*company*) разори́ться (разори́ться *pf*); (*government*) развáливаться (развали́ться *pf*); (*MED, person*) свали́ться (*pf*) ♦ *n* (*of building*) обвáл; (*of system, plans*) крушéние; (*of company*) разорéние; (*of government*) падéние; (*MED*) упáдок сил, коллáпс

collar ['kɔlə] *n* воротни́к; (*for dog etc*) ошéйник; **~bone** *n* ключи́ца

colleague ['kɔliːg] *n* коллéга *m/f*

collect [kə'lɛkt] *vt* собирáть (собрáть *pf*); (*stamps etc*) коллекциони́ровать (*impf*); (*BRIT: fetch*) забирáть (забрáть *pf*); (*debts etc*) взы́скивать (взыскáть *pf*) ♦ *vi* (*crowd*) собирáться (собрáться *pf*); **to call ~** (*US*) звони́ть (*impf*) по коллéкту; **~ion** [kə'lɛkʃən] *n* (*of stamps etc*) коллéкция; (*for charity, also REL*) пожéртвования *ntpl*; (*of mail*) вы́емка; **~ive** *adj* коллекти́вный; **~or** *n* коллекционéр; (*of taxes etc*) сбόрщик

college ['kɔlɪdʒ] *n* учи́лище; (*of university*) кόлледж; (*of technology etc*) институ́т

colliery ['kɔlɪərɪ] *n* (*BRIT*) ýгольная шáхта

collision [kə'lɪʒən] *n* столкновéние

colon ['kəulən] *n* (*LING*) двоетόчие; (*ANAT*) пряма́я кишкá

colonel ['kə:nl] *n* полкόвник

colony ['kɔlənɪ] *n* колόния

color *etc* (*US*) = **colour** *etc*

colossal [kə'lɔsl] *adj* колоссáльный

colour ['kʌlə] (*US* **color**) *n* цвет ♦ *vt* раскрáшивать (раскрáсить *pf*); (*dye*) крáсить (покрáсить *pf*); (*fig: opinion*) окрáшивать (окрáсить *pf*) ♦ *vi* краснéть (покраснéть *pf*); **skin ~** цвет кόжи; **in ~** в цвéте; **~ in** *vt* раскрáшивать (раскрáсить *pf*); **~ed** *adj* цветнόй; **~ film** *n* цветнáя плёнка; **~ful** *adj* крáсочный; (*character*) я́ркий; **~ing** *n* (*of skin*) цвет лицá; (*in food*) краси́тель *m*; **~ scheme** *n* цветовáя гáмма; **~ television** *n* цветнόй телеви́зор

column ['kɔləm] *n* колόнна; (*of smoke*) столб; (*PRESS*) рубрика

coma ['kəumə] *n*: **to be in a ~** находи́ться (*impf*) в кόме

comb [kəum] *n* расчёска;
(*ornamental*) гребень *m* ♦ *vt*
расчёсывать (расчесать *pf*); (*fig*)
прочёсывать (прочесать *pf*)

combat [ˈkɔmbæt] *n* бой; (*battle*)
битва ♦ *vt* бороться (*impf*) против
+*gen*

combination [kɔmbɪˈneɪʃən] *n*
сочетание, комбинация; (*code*)
код

combine [kəmˈbaɪn] *vt*
комбинировать
(скомбинировать *pf*) ♦ *vi* (*groups*)
объединяться (объединиться *pf*)

KEYWORD

come [kʌm] (*pt* **came**, *pp* **come**) *vi*
1 (*move towards: on foot*)
подходить (подойти *pf*); (: *by
transport*) подъезжать
(подъехать *pf*); **to come running**
подбегать (подбежать *pf*)
2 (*arrive: on foot*) приходить
(прийти *pf*); (: *by transport*)
приезжать (приехать *pf*); **he
came running to tell us** он
прибежал, сказать нам; **are you
coming to my party?** Вы придёте
ко мне на вечеринку?; **I've only
come for an hour** я зашёл только
на час
3 (*reach*) доходить (дойти *pf*) до
+*gen*; **to come to** (*power, decision*)
приходить (прийти *pf*) к +*dat*
4 (*occur*): **an idea came to me** мне
в голову пришла идея
5 (*be, become*): **to come into being**
возникать (возникнуть *pf*); **to
come loose** отходить (отойти *pf*);
I've come to like him он стал мне
нравиться

come about *vi*: **how did it come
about?** каким образом это
произошло?, как это
получилось?; **it came about
through ...** это получилось из-за

+*gen* ...

come across *vt fus*
натыкаться (натолкнуться *pf*)
на +*acc*

come away *vi* уходить (уйти *pf*);
(*come off*) отходить (отойти *pf*)

come back *vi* возвращаться
(возвратиться *pf*), вернуться (*pf*)

come by *vt fus* доставать
(достать *pf*)

come down *vi* (*price*)
понижаться (понизиться *pf*); **the
tree came down in the storm**
дерево снесло бурей; **the
building will have to come down
soon** здание должны скоро
снести **come forward** *vi*
(*volunteer*) вызываться
(вызваться *pf*)

come from *vt fus*: **she comes
from India** она из Индии

come in *vi* (*person*) входить
(войти *pf*); **to come in on** (*deal*)
вступать (вступить *pf*) в +*acc*;
where does he come in? в чём
его роль?

come in for *vt fus* подвергаться
(подвергнуться *pf*) +*dat*

come into *vt fus* (*fashion*)
входить (войти *pf*) в +*acc*; (*money*)
наследовать (унаследовать *pf*)

come off *vi* (*button*) отрываться
(оторваться *pf*); (*handle*)
отламываться (отломаться *pf*);
(*can be removed*) сниматься (*impf*);
(*attempt*) удаваться (удаться *pf*)

come on *vi* (*pupil*) делать
(сделать *pf*) успехи; (*work*)
продвигаться (продвинуться *pf*);
(*lights etc*) включаться
(включиться *pf*); **come on!** ну!,
давайте!

come out *vi* выходить (выйти
pf); (*stain*) сходить (сойти *pf*)

come round *vi* очнуться (*pf*),
приходить (прийти *pf*) в себя

come to vi = **come round**

come up vi (sun) всходи́ть (взойти́ pf); (event) приближа́ться (прибли́зиться pf); (questions) возника́ть (возни́кнуть pf)

something important has come up случи́лось что-то ва́жное

come up against vt fus ста́лкиваться (столкну́ться pf) с +instr

come up with vt fus (idea, solution) предлага́ть (предложи́ть pf)

come upon vt fus ната́лкиваться (натолкну́ться pf) на +acc

comeback ['kʌmbæk] n: **to make a ~** (actor etc) обрета́ть (обрести́ pf) но́вую популя́рность

comedian [kə'miːdɪən] n ко́мик

comedy ['kɒmɪdɪ] n коме́дия

comet ['kɒmɪt] n коме́та

comfort ['kʌmfət] n комфо́рт; (relief) утеше́ние ♦ vt утеша́ть (уте́шить pf); **~s** npl (luxuries) удо́бства; **~able** adj комфорта́бельный, удо́бный; **to be ~able** (physically) чу́вствовать (impf) себя́ удо́бно; (financially) жить (impf) в доста́тке; (patient) чу́вствовать (impf) себя́ норма́льно; **~ably** adv удо́бно

comic ['kɒmɪk] adj коми́ческий, смешно́й ♦ n (comedian) ко́мик; (BRIT: magazine) ко́микс

coming ['kʌmɪŋ] adj приближа́ющийся

comma ['kɒmə] n запята́я f adj

command [kə'mɑːnd] n кома́нда; (control) контро́ль m; (mastery) владе́ние ♦ vt (MIL) кома́ндовать (impf) +instr

commemorate [kə'mɛmərəɪt] vt (with statue etc) увекове́чивать (увекове́чить pf); (with event etc) отмеча́ть (отме́тить pf)

commence [kə'mɛns] vt приступа́ть (приступи́ть pf) к +dat ♦ vi начина́ться (нача́ться pf)

commend [kə'mɛnd] vt хвали́ть (похвали́ть pf); (recommend): **to ~ sth to sb** рекомендова́ть (порекомендова́ть pf) что-н кому́-н

comment ['kɒmɛnt] n замеча́ние ♦ vi: **to ~ (on)** комменти́ровать (прокомменти́ровать pf); **"no ~"** "возде́рживаюсь от коммента́риев"; **~ary** ['kɒməntərɪ] n (SPORT) репорта́ж; **~ator** ['kɒmənteɪtə'] n коммента́тор

commerce ['kɒməːs] n комме́рция

commercial [kə'məːʃəl] adj комме́рческий ♦ n рекла́ма

commission [kə'mɪʃən] n зака́з; (COMM) комиссио́нные pl adj; (committee) коми́ссия ♦ vt зака́зывать (заказа́ть pf); **out of ~** неиспра́вный

commit [kə'mɪt] vt (crime) соверша́ть (соверши́ть pf); (money) выделя́ть (вы́делить pf); (entrust) вверя́ть (вве́рить pf); **to ~ o.s.** принима́ть (приня́ть pf) на себя́ обяза́тельство; **to ~ suicide** поко́нчить (pf) жизнь самоуби́йством; **~ment** n (belief) пре́данность f; (obligation) обяза́тельство

committee [kə'mɪtɪ] n комите́т

commodity [kə'mɔdɪtɪ] n това́р

common ['kɒmən] adj о́бщий; (usual) обы́чный; (vulgar) вульга́рный ♦ npl: **the Commons** (also: **the House of Commons**: BRIT) Пала́та fsg о́бщин; **to have sth in (with sb)** име́ть (impf) что-н о́бщее (с кем-н); **it's ~ knowledge that** общеизве́стно, что; **to** or **for the ~ good** для всео́бщего бла́га; **~ law** n

обы́чное пра́во; **~ly** adv обы́чно;
Common Market n: **the
Common Market** О́бщий ры́нок;
~place adj обы́чный, обы́денный

House of Commons - Пала́та
общин. Одна́ из пала́т
брита́нского парла́мента. В
ней заседа́ет 650 вы́борных
чле́нов парла́мента.

common sense n здра́вый
смысл
Commonwealth n (BRIT): **the
Commonwealth** Содру́жество
commotion [kə'məʊʃən] n
сумато́ха
communal ['kɒmju:nl] adj (shared)
о́бщий; (flat) коммуна́льный
commune ['kɒmju:n] n комму́на
communicate [kə'mju:nɪkeɪt] vt
передава́ть (переда́ть pf) ♦ vi: to
~ (with) обща́ться (impf) (с +instr)
communication [kəmju:nɪ'keɪʃən]
n коммуника́ция
communion [kə'mju:nɪən] n (also:
Holy Communion) Свято́е
Прича́стие
communism ['kɒmjunɪzəm] n
коммуни́зм
communist ['kɒmjunɪst] adj
коммунисти́ческий ♦ n
коммуни́ст(ка)
community [kə'mju:nɪtɪ] n
обще́ственность f; (within larger
group) общи́на; **the business ~**
деловы́е круги́; **~ centre** (BRIT)
≈ обще́ственный центр

community service - трудова́я
пови́нность. Для не́которых
наруши́телей зако́на така́я
фо́рма наказа́ния заменя́ет
тюре́мное заключе́ние.

commuter [kə'mju:tə*r*] n челове́к,

кото́рый е́здит на рабо́ту из
при́города в го́род

compact [kəm'pækt] adj компа́кт-
ный; **~ disc** n компа́кт-диск
companion [kəm'pænjən] n
спу́тник(ица)
company ['kʌmpənɪ] n компа́ния;
(THEAT) тру́ппа; (companionship)
компа́ния, о́бщество; **to keep sb
~** составля́ть (соста́вить pf)
кому́-н компа́нию
comparable ['kɒmpərəbl] adj (size)
сопостави́мый
comparative [kəm'pærətɪv] adj (also
LING) сравни́тельный; **~ly** adv
сравни́тельно
compare [kəm'peə*r*] vt: to ~ sb/sth
with or to сра́внивать (сравни́ть
pf) кого́-н/что-н с +instr (set side by
side) сопоставля́ть (сопоста́вить
pf) кого́-н/что-н с +instr ♦ vi: to ~
(with) соотноси́ться (impf) (с
+instr)
comparison [kəm'pærɪsn] n (see vt)
сравне́ние; сопоставле́ние; **in ~
(with)** по сравне́нию or в
сравне́нии (с +instr)
compartment [kəm'pɑ:tmənt] n
купе́ nt ind; (section) отделе́ние
compass ['kʌmpəs] n ко́мпас; **~es**
npl (also: **pair of ~es**) ци́ркуль
msg
compassion [kəm'pæʃən] n
сострада́ние; **~ate** adj
сострада́тельный
compatible [kəm'pætɪbl] adj
совмести́мый
compel [kəm'pel] vt вынужда́ть
(вы́нудить pf); **~ling** adj
(argument) убеди́тельный;
(reason) настоя́тельный
compensate ['kɒmpənseɪt] vt: to ~
sb for sth компенси́ровать (impf/
pf) кому́-н что-н ♦ vi: to ~ for
(distress, loss) компенси́ровать
(impf/pf)

compensation [kɒmpən'seɪʃən] *n*
компенсация

compete [kəm'piːt] *vi (in contest etc)* соревноваться *(impf)*; **to ~ (with)** *(companies)* конкурировать *(impf)* (с *+instr*); *(rivals)* соперничать *(impf)* (с *+instr*)

competence ['kɒmpɪtəns] *n*
компетенция

competent ['kɒmpɪtənt] *adj (person)*
компетентный

competing [kəm'piːtɪŋ] *adj (claims, explanations)* противоположный

competition [kɒmpɪ'tɪʃən] *n*
соревнование; *(between firms)* конкуренция; *(between rivals)* соперничество

competitive [kəm'petɪtɪv] *adj (person)* честолюбивый; *(price)* конкурентоспособный

competitor [kəm'petɪtəʳ] *n (rival)* соперник, конкурент; *(participant)* участник(ица) соревнования

compile [kəm'paɪl] *vt* составлять (составить *pf*)

complacent [kəm'pleɪsnt] *adj*
безразличие

complain [kəm'pleɪn] *vi*: **to ~ (about)** жаловаться (пожаловаться *pf*) (на *+acc*); **~t** *n* жалоба; **to make a ~t against** подавать (подать *pf*) жалобу на *+acc*

complement ['kɒmplɪmənt] *vt*
дополнять (дополнить *pf*)

complete [kəm'pliːt] *adj* полный; *(finished)* завершённый ♦ *vt (building, task)* завершать (завершить *pf*); *(set)* комплектовать (укомплектовать *pf*); *(form)* заполнять (заполнить *pf*); **~ly** *adv* полностью, совершенно

completion [kəm'pliːʃən] *n (of building, task)* завершение

complex ['kɒmpleks] *adj* сложный

♦ *n* комплекс

complexion [kəm'plekʃən] *n (of face)* цвет лица

complexity [kəm'pleksɪtɪ] *n*
сложность *f*

compliance [kəm'plaɪəns] *n (submission)* послушание; **~ with** следование *+dat*

complicate ['kɒmplɪkeɪt] *vt*
усложнять (усложнить *pf*); **~d** *adj* сложный

complication [kɒmplɪ'keɪʃən] *n*
осложнение

compliment *n* ['kɒmplɪmənt] *vb* ['kɒmplɪment] *n* комплимент, хвала ♦ *vt* хвалить (похвалить *pf*); **~s** *npl (regards)* наилучшие пожелания *ntpl*; **to ~ sb, pay sb a ~** делать (сделать *pf*) кому-н комплимент; **~ary** [kɒmplɪ'mentərɪ] *adj (remark)* лестный; *(ticket etc)* дарственный

comply [kəm'plaɪ] *vi*: **to ~ (with)** подчиняться (подчиниться *pf*) *(+dat)*

component [kəm'pəunənt] *adj* составной ♦ *n* компонент

compose [kəm'pəuz] *vt* сочинять (сочинить *pf*); **to be ~d of** состоять *(impf)* из *+gen*; **to ~ o.s.** успокаиваться (успокоиться *pf*); **~d** *adj* спокойный; **~r** *n* композитор

composition [kɒmpə'zɪʃən] *n (structure)* состав; *(essay)* сочинение; *(MUS)* композиция

compost ['kɒmpɒst] *n* компост

composure [kəm'pəuʒəʳ] *n*
самообладание

compound ['kɒmpaund] *n (CHEM)* соединение; *(LING)* сложное слово; *(enclosure)* комплекс

comprehend [kɒmprɪ'hend] *vt*
постигать (постигнуть *or* постичь *pf*)

comprehension [kɒmprɪ'henʃən] *n*

понимáние

comprehensive [kɔmprɪ'hensɪv] adj
исчéрпывающий ♦ n (BRIT: also:
~ **school**)
общеобразовáтельная шкóла

comprehensive school -
общеобразовáтельная шкóла.
В Великобритáнии это
госудáрственная шкóла для
детéй в вóзрасте 11-18 лет.

comprise [kəm'praɪz] vt (also: **be
~d of**) включáть (impf) в себя,
состоя́ть (impf) из +gen; (constitute)
составля́ть (состáвить pf)

compromise ['kɔmprəmaɪz] n
компромúсс ♦ vt
компрометúровать
(скомпрометúровать pf) ♦ vi идти́
(пойти́ pf) на компромúсс

compulsion [kəm'pʌlʃən] n (desire)
влечéние; (force) принуждéние

compulsive [kəm'pʌlsɪv] adj
патологúческий; (reading etc)
захвáтывающий

compulsory [kəm'pʌlsərɪ] adj
(attendance) обязáтельный;
(redundancy) принудúтельный

computer [kəm'pju:tə*] n
компью́тер; ~ **game** n
компью́терная игрá

computing [kəm'pju:tɪŋ] n (as
subject) компью́терное дéло

comrade ['kɔmreɪd] n товáрищ

con [kɔn] vt надувáть (надýть pf)
♦ n (trick) обмáн, надувáтельство

conceal [kən'si:l] vt укрывáть
(укры́ть pf); (keep back) скрывáть
(скрыть pf)

concede [kən'si:d] vt признавáть
(признáть pf)

conceited [kən'si:tɪd] adj
высокомéрный

conceivable [kən'si:vəbl] adj
мы́слимый

conceive [kən'si:v] vt (idea)
задýмывать (задýмать pf) ♦ vi
забеременеть (pf)

concentrate ['kɔnsəntreɪt] vi
сосредотáчиваться
(сосредотóчиться pf),
концентрúроваться
(сконцентрúроваться pf) ♦ vt: **to
~ (on)** (energies) сосредотáчивать
(сосредотóчить pf or
концентрúровать
(сконцентрúровать pf) (на +prp)

concentration [kɔnsən'treɪʃən] n
сосредотóчение, концентрáция;
(attention) сосредотóченность f;
(CHEM) концентрáция

concept ['kɔnsept] n поня́тие;
~ion [kən'sepʃən] n (idea)
концéпция; (BIO) зачáтие

concern [kən'sɜ:n] n (affair) дéло;
(worry) тревóга, озабóченность f;
(care) учáстие; (COMM)
предприя́тие ♦ vt (worry)
беспокóить (impf), тревóжить
(impf); (involve) вовлекáть
(вовлéчь pf); **to be ~ed (about)**
беспокóиться (impf) (о +prp); **~ing**
prep относúтельно +gen

concert ['kɔnsət] n концéрт

concerted [kən'sə:tɪd] adj
совмéстный

concession [kən'seʃən] n
(compromise) устýпка; (right)
концéссия; (reduction) льгóта

concise [kən'saɪs] adj крáткий

conclude [kən'klu:d] vt
закáнчивать (закóнчить pf);
(treaty, deal etc) заключáть
(заключúть pf); (decide)
приходúть (прийтú pf) к
заключéнию or вы́воду

concluding [kən'klu:dɪŋ] adj
заключúтельный

conclusion [kən'klu:ʒən] n
заключéние; (of speech)
окончáние; (of events)

завершéние

conclusive [kənˈkluːsɪv] adj
(evidence) неопровержи́мый

concrete [ˈkɒŋkriːt] n бетóн ♦ adj
бетóнный; (fig) конкрéтный

concussion [kənˈkʌʃən] n
сотрясéние мóзга

condemn [kənˈdɛm] vt осужда́ть
(осуди́ть pf); (building) бракова́ть
(забракова́ть pf); **~ation**
[kɒndɛmˈneɪʃən] n осуждéние

condensation [kɒndɛnˈseɪʃən] n
конденсáция

condition [kənˈdɪʃən] n состоя́ние;
(requirement) усло́вие ♦ vt
формирова́ть (сформирова́ть
pf); (hair, skin) обраба́тывать
(обрабо́тать pf); **~s** npl
(circumstances) усло́вия ntpl; **on ~
that** при усло́вии, что; **~al** adj
усло́вный; **~er** n (for hair)
бальзáм; (for fabrics)
смягча́ющий раство́р

condom [ˈkɒndəm] n презервати́в

condone [kənˈdəun] vt
потво́рствовать (impf) +dat

conduct n [ˈkɒndʌkt] vb [kənˈdʌkt] n
(of person) поведéние ♦ vt (survey
etc) проводи́ть (провести́ pf);
(MUS) дирижи́ровать (impf); (PHYS)
проводи́ть (impf); **to ~ o.s.** вести́
(повести́ pf) себя́; **~or** [kənˈdʌktə*]
n (MUS) дирижёр; (US : RAIL)
контролёр; (on bus) конду́ктор

cone [kəun] n кóнус; (also : traffic
~) конусообрáзное доро́жное
загражде́ние; (BOT) ши́шка; (ice-
cream) моро́женое nt adj
(тру́бочка)

confectionery [kənˈfɛkʃənə*] n
конди́терские изде́лия ntpl

confederation [kənfɛdəˈreɪʃən] n
конфедерáция

confer [kənˈfɜː*] vi совеща́ться
(impf) ♦ vt: **to ~ sth (on sb)**
(honour) оказывать (оказа́ть pf)

что-н (кому́-н); (degree)
присужда́ть (присуди́ть pf) что-н
(кому́-н)

conference [ˈkɒnfərəns] n
конферéнция

confess [kənˈfɛs] vt (guilt,
ignorance) признава́ть (призна́ть
pf); (sin) испове́доваться
(испове́даться pf) в +prp ♦ vi (to
crime) признава́ться (призна́ться
pf); **~ion** [kənˈfɛʃən] n призна́ние;
(REL) и́споведь f

confide [kənˈfaɪd] vi: **to ~ in**
доверя́ться (дове́риться pf) +dat

confidence [ˈkɒnfɪdns] n
увéренность f; (in self)
увéренность в себе́; **in ~**
конфиденциа́льно

confident [ˈkɒnfɪdənt] adj (see n)
увéренный; увéренный в себе́

confidential [kɒnfɪˈdɛnʃəl] adj
конфиденциа́льный; (tone)
довери́тельный

confine [kənˈfaɪn] vt (lock up)
запира́ть (запере́ть pf); (limit): **to
~ (to)** ограни́чивать (ограни́чить
pf) (+instr); **~d** adj закры́тый;
~ment n (in jail) тюре́много
заключéние; **~s** [ˈkɒnfaɪnz] npl
предéлы mpl

confirm [kənˈfɜːm] vt
подтвержда́ть (подтверди́ть pf);
~ation [kɒnfəˈmeɪʃən] n
подтвержде́ние; **~ed** adj
убеждённый

conflict [ˈkɒnflɪkt] n конфли́кт; (of
interests) столкнове́ние; **~ing** adj
противоречи́вый; (interests)
противополóжный

conform [kənˈfɔːm] vi: **to ~ (to)**
подчиня́ться (подчини́ться pf)
(+dat)

confront [kənˈfrʌnt] vt (problems)
ста́лкиваться (столкну́ться pf) с
+instr; (enemy) противостоя́ть
(impf) +dat; **~ation** [kɒnfrənˈteɪʃən]

n конфронта́ция

confuse [kən'fju:z] *vt* запу́тывать (запу́тать *pf*); (*mix up*) пу́тать (спу́тать *pf*); **~d** *adj* (*person*) озада́ченный

confusing [kən'fju:zɪŋ] *adj* запу́танный

confusion [kən'fju:ʒən] *n* (*perplexity*) замеша́тельство; (*mix-up*) пу́таница; (*disorder*) беспоря́док

congested [kən'dʒestɪd] *adj* (*see n*) перегру́женный; перенаселённый

congestion [kən'dʒestʃən] *n* (*on road*) перегру́женность *f*; (*in area*) перенаселённость *f*

congratulate [kən'grætjuleɪt] *vt*: **to ~ sb** (**on**) поздравля́ть (поздра́вить *pf*) кого́-н (с +*instr*)

congratulations [kəngrætju'leɪʃənz] *npl* поздравле́ния *ntpl*; **~** (**on**) (*from one person*) поздравля́ю (с +*instr*); (*from several people*) поздравля́ем (с +*instr*)

congregation [kɔŋgrɪ'geɪʃən] *n* прихожа́не *mpl*, прихо́д

congress ['kɔŋgres] *n* конгре́сс; (*US*): **Congress** конгре́сс США; **~man** (*irreg*) *n* (*US*) конгрессме́н

conjunctivitis [kəndʒʌŋktɪ'vaɪtɪs] *n* конъюнктиви́т

conjunction [kən'dʒʌŋkʃən] *n* (*LING*) сою́з

conjure ['kʌndʒəʳ] *vt* (*fig*) сообража́ть (сообрази́ть *pf*); **~ up** *vt* (*memories*) пробужда́ть (пробуди́ть *pf*)

connect [kə'nekt] *vt* (*ELEC*) подсоединя́ть (подсоедини́ть *pf*), подключа́ть (подключи́ть *pf*); (*fig: associate*) свя́зывать (связа́ть *pf*) ♦ *vi*: **to ~ with** согласо́вываться (согласова́ться *pf*) по расписа́нию с +*instr*; **to ~ sb/sth** (**to**) соединя́ть (соедини́ть

pf) кого́-н/что-н (с +*instr*); **he is ~ed with ...** он свя́зан с +*instr* ...; **I am trying to ~ you** (*TEL*) я пыта́юсь подключи́ть Вас; **~ion** [kə'nekʃən] *n* связь *f*; (*train etc*) переса́дка

connoisseur [kɔnɪ'sə:ʳ] *n* знато́к

conquer ['kɔŋkəʳ] *vt* (*MIL*) завоёвывать (завоева́ть *pf*); (*overcome*) поборо́ть (*pf*)

conquest ['kɔŋkwest] *n* (*MIL*) завоева́ние

cons [kɔnz] *npl see* **convenience**; **pro**

conscience ['kɔnʃəns] *n* со́весть *f*

conscientious [kɔnʃɪ'enʃəs] *adj* добросо́вестный

conscious ['kɔnʃəs] *adj* (*deliberate*) созна́тельный; (*aware*) **to be ~ of sth/that** сознава́ть (*impf*) что-н/, что; **the patient was ~** пацие́нт находи́лся в созна́нии; **~ness** *n* созна́ние; (*of group*) самосозна́ние

consecutive [kən'sekjutɪv] *adj*: **on three ~ occasions** в трёх слу́чаях подря́д; **on three ~ days** три дня подря́д

consensus [kən'sensəs] *n* еди́ное мне́ние; **~ of opinion** консе́нсус

consent [kən'sent] *n* согла́сие

consequence ['kɔnsɪkwəns] *n* сле́дствие; **of ~** (*significant*) значи́тельный; **it's of little ~** э́то не име́ет большо́го значе́ния; **in ~** (*consequently*) сле́довательно, всле́дствие э́того

consequently ['kɔnsɪkwəntlɪ] *adv* сле́довательно

conservation [kɔnsə'veɪʃən] *n* (*also*: **nature ~**) охра́на приро́ды, природоохра́на

conservative [kən'sə:vətɪv] *adj* консервати́вный; (*estimate*) скро́мный; (*BRIT*: *POL*): **Conservative** консервати́вный

♦ n (BRIT): **Conservative**
консерва́тор

conservatory [kən'sə:vətri] n
застеклённая вера́нда

conserve [kən'sə:v] vt сохраня́ть
(сохрани́ть pf); (energy) сберега́ть
(сбере́чь pf) **♦** n варе́нье

consider [kən'sidə*] vt (believe)
счита́ть (посчита́ть pf); (study)
рассма́тривать (рассмотре́ть pf);
(take into account) учи́тывать
(уче́сть pf); (regard): **to ~ that** ...
полага́ть (impf) or счита́ть (impf),
что ...; **to ~ sth** (think about)
ду́мать (impf) о чём-н; **~able** adj
значи́тельный; **~ably** adv
значи́тельно; **~ate** adj (person)
забо́тливый; (action)
внима́тельный; **~ation**
[kənsidə'reiʃən] n рассмотре́ние,
обду́мывание; (factor)
соображе́ние; (thoughtfulness)
внима́ние; **~ing** prep учи́тывая
+acc

consignment [kən'sainmənt] n
(COMM) па́ртия

consist [kən'sist] vi: **to ~ of**
состоя́ть (impf) из +gen

consistency [kən'sistənsi] n
после́довательность f; (of yoghurt
etc) консисте́нция

consistent [kən'sistənt] adj
после́довательный

consolation [kɔnsə'leiʃən] n
утеше́ние

console [kən'səul] vt утеша́ть
(уте́шить pf)

consolidate [kən'sɔlideit] vt
(position, power) укрепля́ть
(укрепи́ть pf)

consonant ['kɔnsənənt] n
согла́сный m adj

consortium [kən'sɔ:tiəm] n
консо́рциум

conspicuous [kən'spikjuəs] adj
заме́тный

conspiracy [kən'spirəsi] n за́говор

constable ['kʌnstəbl] (BRIT: also:
police ~) n (участко́вый)
полице́йский m adj

constant ['kɔnstənt] adj
постоя́нный; (fixed)
неизме́нный; **~ly** adv постоя́нно

constipation [kɔnsti'peiʃən] n
запо́р

constituency [kən'stitjuənsi] n
(area) избира́тельный о́круг

constituent [kən'stitjuənt] n
избира́тель(ница) m(f);
(component) составна́я часть f

constitute ['kɔnstitju:t] vt
(represent) явля́ться (яви́ться pf)
+instr; (make up) составля́ть
(соста́вить pf)

constitution [kɔnsti'tju:ʃən] n (of
country, person) конститу́ция; (of
organization) строе́ние; **~al** adj
конституцио́нный

constraint [kən'streint] n
(restriction) ограниче́ние

construct [kən'strʌkt] vt
сооружа́ть (сооруди́ть pf); **~ion**
[kən'strʌkʃən] n (of building etc)
сооруже́ние; (structure)
констру́кция, **~ive** adj
конструкти́вный

consul ['kɔnsl] n ко́нсул; **~ate**
['kɔnsjulit] n ко́нсульство

consult [kən'sʌlt] vt (friend)
сове́товаться (посове́товаться
pf) с +instr; (book, map)
справля́ться (спра́виться pf) в
+prp; **to ~ sb (about)** (expert)
консульти́роваться
(проконсульти́роваться pf) с
кем-н (о +prp); **~ant** n
консульта́нт; (MED) врач-
консульта́нт; **~ation**
[kɔnsəl'teiʃən] n (MED)
консульта́ция; (discussion)
совеща́ние

consume [kən'sju:m] vt

потребля́ть (потреби́ть *pf*); ~r n
потреби́тель *m*; ~ **goods** *npl*
потреби́тельские това́ры *mpl*
consumption [kənˈsʌmpʃən] *n*
потребле́ние; *(amount)* расхо́д
cont. *abbr* = **continued**; ~ **on**
продолже́ние на +*prp*
contact [ˈkɔntækt] *n*
(communication) конта́кт; *(touch)*
соприкоснове́ние; *(person)*
делово́й(а́я) знако́мый(ая) *m(f)*
adj ♦ *vt* свя́зываться (связа́ться
pf) с +*instr*; ~ **lenses** *npl*
конта́ктные ли́нзы *fpl*
contagious [kənˈteɪdʒəs] *adj*
зара́зный; *(fig)* зарази́тельный
contain [kənˈteɪn] *vt (hold)*
вмеща́ть (вмести́ть *pf*); *(include)*
содержа́ть *(impf)*; *(curb)*
сде́рживать (сдержа́ть *pf*); **to ~
o.s.** сде́рживаться (сдержа́ться
pf); ~er *n* конте́йнер
contamination [kənˌtæmɪˈneɪʃən] *n*
загрязне́ние
contemplate [ˈkɔntəmpleɪt] *vt*
(consider) размышля́ть *(impf)* о
+*prp*; *(look at)* созерца́ть *(impf)*
contemporary [kənˈtɛmpərərɪ] *adj*
совреме́нный ♦ *n*
совреме́нник(ица)
contempt [kənˈtɛmpt] *n*
презре́ние; ~ **of court**
оскорбле́ние суда́; ~uous *adj*
презри́тельный
contend [kənˈtɛnd] *vt*: **to ~ that**
утвержда́ть *(impf)*, что ♦ *vi*: **to ~
with** *(problem etc)* боро́ться *(impf)*
с +*instr*; **to ~ for** *(power)* боро́ться
(impf) за +*acc*; ~er *n*
претенде́нт(ка)
content *n* [ˈkɔntɛnt] *adj*, *vb*
[kənˈtɛnt] *n* содержа́ние ♦ *adj*
дово́льный ♦ *vt (satisfy)*
удовлетворя́ть (удовлетвори́ть
pf); ~s *npl (of bottle etc)*
содержи́мое *ntsg adj*; *(of book)*

содержа́ние *ntsg*; **(table of)** ~s
оглавле́ние; ~ed *adj* дово́льный
contention [kənˈtɛnʃən] *n*
(assertion) утвержде́ние;
(argument) разногла́сие
contest *n* [ˈkɔntɛst] *vb* [kənˈtɛst] *n*
(sport) соревнова́ние; *(beauty)*
ко́нкурс; *(for power etc)* борьба́
♦ *vt* оспа́ривать (оспо́рить *pf*);
(election, competition) боро́ться
(impf) на +*prp*; ~ant [kənˈtɛstənt] *n*
уча́стник(ница)
context [ˈkɔntɛkst] *n* конте́кст
continent [ˈkɔntɪnənt] *n*
контине́нт, матери́к; **the
Continent** *(BRIT)* Евро́па *(кроме
британских островов)*
continental [kɔntɪˈnɛntl] *adj (BRIT)*
европе́йский

continental breakfast -
европе́йский за́втрак. В
европе́йский за́втрак вхо́дят
хлеб, ма́сло и джем. Его́
подаю́т в гости́ницах вме́сто
традицио́нного за́втрака из
беко́на и яи́чницы.

continental quilt *n (BRIT)*
стёганое одея́ло
contingency [kənˈtɪndʒənsɪ] *n*
возмо́жность *f*
contingent [kənˈtɪndʒənt] *n (also
MIL)* континге́нт
continual [kənˈtɪnjuəl] *adj*
непреры́вный, постоя́нный; ~ly
adv (constantly) непреры́вно,
постоя́нно
continuation [kənˌtɪnjuˈeɪʃən] *n*
продолже́ние
continue [kənˈtɪnju:] *vi (carry on)*
продолжа́ться *(impf)*; *(after
interruption: talk)* продолжа́ть
(продо́лжиться *pf*); *(: person)*
продолжа́ть (продо́лжить *pf*) ♦ *vt*
(carry on) продолжа́ть

(продо́лжить pf)

continuity [kɒntɪ'njuːɪtɪ] n
прее́мственность f

continuous [kən'tɪnjuəs] adj
непреры́вный; (line) сплошно́й

contraception [kɒntrə'sɛpʃən] n
предупрежде́ние бере́менности

contraceptive [kɒntrə'sɛptɪv] n
противозача́точное сре́дство,
контрацепти́в

contract n ['kɒntrækt] vb [kən'trækt]
n догово́р, контра́кт ♦ vi
сжима́ться (сжа́ться pf) ♦ vt (MED)
заболева́ть (заболе́ть pf) +instr;
~ion [kən'trækʃən] n (MED)
родова́я поту́га; **~or** [kən'træktər]
n подря́дчик

contradict [kɒntrə'dɪkt] vt (person)
возража́ть (возрази́ть pf) +dat;
(statement) возража́ть (возрази́ть
pf) на +acc; **~ion** [kɒntrə'dɪkʃən] n
противоре́чие; **~ory** adj
противоречи́вый

contrary ['kɒntrərɪ] adj
противополо́жный ♦ n
противополо́жность f; **on the ~**
напро́тив, наоборо́т; **unless you
hear to the ~** е́сли не бу́дет
други́х инстру́кций

contrast n ['kɒntrɑːst] vb [kən'trɑːst]
n контра́ст ♦ vt сопоставля́ть
(сопоста́вить pf); **in ~ to** или **with**
по контра́сту с +instr; **~ing**
[kən'trɑːstɪŋ] adj (colours)
контрасти́рующий; (views)
противополо́жный

contribute [kən'trɪbjuːt] vi (give)
де́лать (сде́лать pf) вклад ♦ vt
(money, an article) вноси́ть
(внести́ pf); **to ~ to** (to charity)
же́ртвовать (поже́ртвовать pf)
на +acc или для +gen; (to paper)
писа́ть (написа́ть pf) для +gen; (to
discussion) вноси́ть (внести́ pf)
вклад в +prp; (to problem)

усугубля́ть (усугуби́ть pf)

contribution [kɒntrɪ'bjuːʃən] n
(donation) поже́ртвование,
вклад; (to debate, campaign)
вклад; (to journal) публика́ция

contributor [kən'trɪbjuːtər] n (to
appeal) же́ртвователь m; (to
newspaper) а́втор

control [kən'trəul] vt
контроли́ровать (impf) ♦ n (of
country, organization) контро́ль m;
(of o.s.) самооблада́ние; **~s** npl (of
vehicle) управле́ние; (on radio etc)
ру́чки fpl настро́йки; **to ~ o.s.**
сохраня́ть (сохрани́ть pf)
самооблада́ние; **to be in ~ of**
контроли́ровать (impf);
everything is under ~ всё под
контро́лем; **out of ~**
неуправля́емый

controversial [kɒntrə'vəːʃl] adj
спо́рный; (person, writer)
неоднозна́чный

controversy ['kɒntrəvəːsɪ] n
диску́ссия, спор

convene [kən'viːn] vt созыва́ть
(созва́ть pf) ♦ vi собира́ться
(собра́ться pf)

convenience [kən'viːnɪəns] n
удо́бство; **at your ~** когда́ Вам
бу́дет удо́бно; **a flat with all
modern ~s** или (BRIT) **all mod cons**
кварти́ра со все́ми удо́бствами

convenient [kən'viːnɪənt] adj
удо́бный

convent ['kɒnvənt] n (REL)
(же́нский) монасты́рь m

convention [kən'vɛnʃən] n (custom)
усло́вность f; (conference)
конфере́нция; (agreement)
конве́нция; **~al** adj
традицио́нный; (methods,
weapons) обы́чный

converge [kən'vəːdʒ] vi (people)
съезжа́ться (съе́хаться pf)

conversation [kɒnvə'seɪʃən] n

беседа, разговор; **to have a ~ with sb** разговаривать (impf) or беседовать (побеседовать pf) с кем-н

conversely [kən'vɜːslɪ] *adv* наоборот

conversion [kən'vɜːʃən] *n* обращение; (*of weights*) перевод; (*of substances*) превращение

convert *vb* [kən'vɜːt] *n* ['kɒnvɜːt] *vt* (*person*) обращать (обратить pf) ♦ *n* новообращённ(ая)*m(f) adj*; **to ~ sth into** превращать (превратить pf) что-н в +acc

convey [kən'veɪ] *vt* передавать (передать pf); (*cargo, goods*) перевозить (перевезти pf)

convict *vb* [kən'vɪkt] *n* ['kɒnvɪkt] *vt* осуждать (осудить pf) ♦ *n* каторжник; **~ion** [kən'vɪkʃən] *n* (*belief*) убеждение; (*certainty*) убеждённость f; (*LAW*) осуждение; (: *previous*) судимость f

convince [kən'vɪns] *vt* (*assure*) уверять (уверить pf); (*persuade*) убеждать (убедить pf); **~d** *adj*: **~d of/that** убеждённый в +prp/, что

convincing [kən'vɪnsɪŋ] *adj* убедительный

convoy ['kɒnvɔɪ] *n* (*of trucks*) колонна; (*of ships*) конвой

cook [kuk] *vt* готовить (приготовить pf) ♦ *vi* (*person*) готовить (impf); (*food*) готовиться (impf) ♦ *n* повар; **~er** *n* плита; **~ery** *n* кулинария; **~ery book** (*BRIT*) поваренная *n* и кулинарная книга; **~ie** *n* (*esp US*) печенье; **~ing** *n* готовка; **I like ~ing** я люблю готовить

cool [kuːl] *adj* прохладный; (*dress, clothes*) лёгкий; (*person*: *calm*) невозмутимый; (: *hostile*) холодный; (*inf*: *great*) крутой ♦ *vi* (*water, air*) остывать (остыть pf);

~! (*inf*) здорово!

cooperate [kəu'ɒpəreɪt] *vi* (*collaborate*) сотрудничать (impf); (*assist*) содействовать (impf)

cooperation [kəuɒpə'reɪʃən] *n* (*see vi*) кооперация, сотрудничество; содействие

cooperative [kəu'ɒpərətɪv] *n* кооператив ♦ *adj*: **he is very ~** он всегда готов оказать помощь

coordinate *vb* [kəu'ɔːdɪneɪt] *n* [kəu'ɔːdɪnət] *vt* (*activity, attack*) согласовывать (согласовать pf), координировать (impf/pf) ♦ *n* (*MATH*) координата

coordination [kəuɔːdɪ'neɪʃən] *n* координация

cop [kɒp] *n* (*BRIT*: *inf*) мент

cope [kəup] *vi*: **to ~ with** справляться (справиться pf) с +instr

copper ['kɒpə] *n* (*metal*) медь f

copy ['kɒpɪ] *n* (*duplicate*) копия; (*of book etc*) экземпляр ♦ *vt* копировать (скопировать pf); **~right** *n* авторское право, копирайт

coral ['kɒrəl] *n* коралл

cord [kɔːd] *n* (*string*) верёвка; (*ELEC*) шнур; (*fabric*) вельвет

cordial ['kɔːdɪəl] *adj* сердечный

cordon ['kɔːdn] *n* кордон, оцепление

corduroy ['kɔːdərɔɪ] *n* вельвет

core [kɔː] *n* (*of fruit*) сердцевина; (*of problem*) суть f ♦ *vt* вырезать (вырезать pf) сердцевину у +gen

coriander [kɒrɪ'ændə] *n* (*spice*) кинза, кориандр

cork [kɔːk] *n* пробка; **~screw** *n* штопор

corn [kɔːn] *n* (*BRIT*) зерно; (*US*: *maize*) кукуруза; (*on foot*) мозоль f; **~ on the cob** початок кукурузы

corner ['kɔːnə] *n* угол; (*SPORT*: *also*: **~ kick**) угловой *m adj* (удар

cornflour [ˈkɔːnflaʊə] n (BRIT) кукуру́зная мука́

coronary [ˈkɔrənərɪ] n (also: ~ **thrombosis**) корона́рный тромбо́з

coronation [kɔrəˈneɪʃən] n корона́ция

coroner [ˈkɔrənə] n (LAW) ко́ронер (судья́, рассле́дующий причи́ны сме́рти, происше́дшей при подозри́тельных обстоя́тельствах)

corporal [ˈkɔːpərl] adj: ~ **punishment** теле́сное наказа́ние

corporate [ˈkɔːpərɪt] adj корпорацио́нный; (ownership) о́бщий; (identity) корпорати́вный

corporation [kɔːpəˈreɪʃən] n (COMM) корпора́ция

corps [kɔːʳ] (pl ~) n (also MIL) ко́рпус

corpse [kɔːps] n труп

correct [kəˈrekt] adj пра́вильный; (proper) соотве́тствующий ♦ vt исправля́ть (испра́вить pf); (exam) проверя́ть (прове́рить pf); ~**ion** [kəˈrekʃən] n исправле́ние; (mistake corrected) попра́вка

correspond [kɔrɪsˈpɔnd] vi: **to ~ (with)** (write) перепи́сываться (impf) (c +instr); (tally) согласо́вываться (impf) (c +instr); (equate): **to ~ (to)** соотве́тствовать (impf) (+dat); ~**ence** n (letters) перепи́ска; (: in business) корреспонде́нция; (: relationship) соотноше́ние; ~**ent** n (PRESS) корреспонде́нт(ка)

corridor [ˈkɔrɪdɔːʳ] n коридо́р; (in train) прохо́д

corrosion [kəˈrəuʒən] n (damage) ржа́вчина

corrugated [ˈkɔrəgeɪtɪd] adj рифлёный

corrupt [kəˈrʌpt] adj прода́жный, коррумпи́рованный ♦ vt

развраща́ть (разврати́ть pf); ~**ion** [kəˈrʌpʃən] n корру́пция, прода́жность f

cosmetic [kozˈmetɪk] n (usu pl) косме́тика

cosmopolitan [kozməˈpɔlɪtn] adj (place) космополити́ческий

cost [kost] (pt, pp ~) n (price) сто́имость f ♦ vt сто́ить (impf); (pt, pp ~**ed**; find out cost of) рассчи́тывать (рассчита́ть pf) сто́имость +gen; ~**s** npl (COMM) расхо́ды mpl; (LAW) суде́бные изде́ржки fpl; **how much does it ~?** ско́лько э́то сто́ит?; **to ~ sb sth** (time, job) сто́ить (impf) кому́-н чего́-н; **at all ~s** любо́й цено́й; ~**ly** adj (expensive) дорогосто́ящий; ~ **of living** n сто́имость f жи́зни

costume [ˈkostjuːm] n костю́м; (BRIT: also: **swimming ~**) купа́льник, купа́льный костю́м

cosy [ˈkəuzɪ] (US **cozy**) adj (room, atmosphere) ую́тный

cot [kot] n (BRIT) де́тская крова́тка; (US: camp bed) ко́йка; ~ **death** n внеза́пная смерть здоро́вого младе́нца во сне

cottage [ˈkotɪdʒ] n котте́дж

cotton [ˈkotn] n (fabric) хло́пок, хлопчатобума́жная ткань f; (thread) (шве́йная) ни́тка; ~ **wool** n (BRIT) ва́та

couch [kautʃ] n куше́тка, дива́н

cough [kof] vi ка́шлять (impf) ♦ n ка́шель m

could [kud] pt of **can²**; ~**n't** [ˈkudnt] = **could not**; see **can²**

council [ˈkaunsl] n сове́т; **city** or **town ~** муниципалите́т, городско́й сове́т; ~ **house** n (BRIT) дом, принадлежа́щий муниципалите́ту; ~**lor** n член (BRIT) муниципалите́та; ~ **tax** n (BRIT) муниципа́льный нало́г

council estate - муниципа́льный жило́й микрорайо́н. Дома́ в таки́х райо́нах стро́ятся на сре́дства муниципалите́та. Типовы́е постро́йки включа́ют многоэта́жные дома́ и ряд однотипных примыка́ющих друг к дру́гу домо́в с сада́ми.

counsel ['kaunsl] *n* (advice) сове́т; (lawyer) адвока́т ♦ *vt*: **to ~ sth/sb to do** сове́товать (посове́товать *pf*) что-н/кому́-н +infin; **~lor** *n* сове́тник; (US: lawyer) адвока́т

count [kaunt] *vt* счита́ть (посчита́ть *pf*); (include) счита́ть (impf) ♦ *vi* счита́ть (сосчита́ть *pf*); (qualify) счита́ться (impf); (matter) име́ть (impf) значе́ние ♦ *n* подсчёт; (level) у́ровень *m*; **~ on** *vt fus* рассчи́тывать (impf) на +acc; **~down** *n* обра́тный счёт

counter ['kaunta] *n* (in shop, café) прила́вок; (in bank, post office) сто́йка; (in game) фи́шка ♦ *vt* опроверга́ть (опрове́ргнуть *pf*) ♦ *adv*: **to в** противове́с +dat

counterpart ['kauntapa:t] *n* (of person) колле́га *m/f*

countless ['kauntlis] *adj* несчётный, бесчи́сленный

country ['kʌntrɪ] *n* (nation) страна́; (native land) ро́дина; (rural area) дере́вня; **~side** *n* дере́вня, се́льская ме́стность *f*

county ['kauntɪ] *n* гра́фство

---

county - гра́фство. В Великобрита́нии, Ирла́ндии и США э́то - администрати́вно-территориа́льная едини́ца эквивале́нтная о́бласти и управля́емая ме́стным прави́тельством.

---

coup [ku:] *n* (*pl* **~s**) (also: **~ d'état**) госуда́рственный переворо́т

couple ['kʌpl] *n* (married couple) (супру́жеская) па́ра; (of people, things) па́ра; **a ~ of** (some) па́ра +gen

coupon ['ku:pɔn] *n* (voucher) купо́н; (form) тало́н

courage ['kʌrɪdʒ] *n* сме́лость *f*, хра́брость *f*; **~ous** [kə'reɪdʒəs] *adj* сме́лый, хра́брый

courgette [kuə'ʒet] *n* (BRIT) молодо́й кабачо́к

courier ['kurɪə] *n* курье́р; (for tourists) руководи́тель *m* гру́ппы

course [kɔ:s] *n* курс; (of events, time) ход; (of action) направле́ние; (of river) тече́ние; **first/last ~** пе́рвое/сла́дкое блю́до; **of ~** коне́чно

court [kɔ:t] *n* (LAW) суд; (SPORT) корт; (royal) двор; **to take sb to ~** подава́ть (пода́ть *pf*) на кого́-н в суд

courteous ['kə:tɪəs] *adj* ве́жливый

courtesy ['kə:təsɪ] *n* ве́жливость *f*; **(by) ~ of** благодаря́ любе́зности +gen

courtroom ['kɔ:trum] *n* зал суда́

courtyard ['kɔ:tja:d] *n* вну́тренний двор

cousin ['kʌzn] *n* (also: **first ~**: male) двою́родный брат; (: female) двою́родная сестра́

cove [kəuv] *n* (bay) бу́хта

cover ['kʌvə] *vt* закрыва́ть (закры́ть *pf*); (with cloth) укрыва́ть (укры́ть *pf*); (distance) покрыва́ть (покры́ть *pf*); (topic) рассма́тривать (рассмотре́ть *pf*); (include) охва́тывать (охвати́ть *pf*); (PRESS) освеща́ть (освети́ть *pf*) ♦ *n* (for furniture, machinery) чехо́л; (of book etc) обло́жка; (shelter)

крытие; **~s** npl (for bed)
остельное бельё ntsg; **he was
  ...ed in** or **with** (mud) он был
  ...крыт +instr; **to take ~**
  ...крываться (укрыться pf); **under
  ...**в укрытии; **under ~ of darkness**
  ...од покровом темноты; **~ up for sb** покрывать
  ...покрыть pf) кого-л; **~age** n
  ...свещение; **~ing** n пласт; (of
  snow, dust etc) слой; (on floor)
  ...настил; **~-up** n ширма,
  прикрытие

...**ow** [kau] n (also inf!) корова (also !)

...**oward** ['kauəd] n трус(иха); **~ice**
['kauədıs] n трусость f; **~ly** adj
трусливый

...**owboy** ['kaubɔı] n ковбой

...**oy** [kɔı] adj (shy) застенчивый

...**ozy** ['kəuzı] adj (US) = **cosy**

...**ab** [kræb] n краб

...**ack** [kræk] n (noise) треск; (gap)
цель f; (in dish, wall) трещина ♦ vt
(whip, twig) щёлкать (щёлкнуть
pf) +instr; (dish etc) раскалывать
(расколоть pf; (nut) колоть
(расколоть pf; (problem) решать
(решить pf); (code) разгадывать
(разгадать pf); (joke) отпускать
(отпустить pf)

crackle ['krækl] vi потрескивать
(impf)

cradle ['kreıdl] n (crib) колыбель
f

craft [krɑːft] n (trade) ремесло;
(boat: pl inv) корабль f; **~sman**
(irreg) n ремесленник;
~smanship n (quality) выделка;
(skill) мастерство; **~y** adj лукавый

cram [kræm] vt: **to ~ sth with**
набивать (набить pf) что-н +instr;
to ~ sth into втискивать
(втиснуть pf) что-н в +acc

cramp [kræmp] n судорога; **~ed**
adj тесный

crane [kreın] n (TECH)
(подъёмный) кран

crank [kræŋk] n (person) чудак;
(handle) заводная рукоятка

crash [kræʃ] n (noise) грохот; (of
car) авария; (of plane, train)
крушение ♦ vt разбивать
(разбить pf) ♦ vi разбиваться
(разбиться pf); (two cars)
сталкиваться (столкнуться pf); **~
course** n интенсивный курс; **~
helmet** n защитный шлем

crass [kræs] adj тупой

crate [kreıt] n деревянный ящик;
(for bottles) упаковочный ящик

crater ['kreıtə] n (of volcano)
кратер; (of bomb) воронка

crave [kreıv] vti: **to ~ sth** or **for
sth** жаждать (impf) чего-н

crawl [krɔːl] vi (move) ползать/
ползти (impf) ♦ n (SPORT) кроль f

craze [kreız] n повальное
увлечение

crazy ['kreızı] adj сумасшедший;
he's ~ about skiing (inf) он
помешан на лыжах; **to go ~**
помешаться (pf)

cream [kriːm] n сливки pl;
(cosmetic) крем ♦ n (colour)
кремовый; **~y** adj (taste)
сливочный

crease [kriːs] n (fold) складка; (: in
trousers) стрелка; (in dress, on
brow) морщина

create [kriː'eıt] vt создавать
(создать pf); (invent) творить
(impf), создавать
(создать pf)

creation [kriː'eıʃən] n создание;
(REL) сотворение

creative [kriː'eıtıv] adj творческий

creature ['kriːtʃə] n (animal)
существо; (person) создание

crèche [krɛʃ] n (детские) ясли pl

credentials [krı'dɛnʃlz] npl
(references) квалификация fsg; (for

identity) рекоменда́тельное
письмо́ ntsg, рекоменда́ция fsg
credibility [krɛdɪˈbɪlɪtɪ] n (*see adj*)
правдоподо́бность f; авторите́т
credible [ˈkrɛdɪbl] adj вероя́тный,
правдоподо́бный; (*person*)
авторите́тный
credit [ˈkrɛdɪt] n (COMM) креди́т;
(*recognition*) до́лжное nt adj ♦ vt
(COMM) кредитова́ть (*impf/pf*); **to ~
sb with sth** (*sense*) припи́сывать
(*приписа́ть pf*) кому́-н что-н; **~s**
npl (CINEMA, TV) ти́тры mpl; **~
card** n креди́тная ка́рточка; **~or**
n кредито́р
creed [kri:d] n (REL) (веро)уче́ние
creek [kri:k] n у́зкий зали́в; (US:
stream) руче́й
creep [kri:p] (*pt, pp* **crept**) vi
(*person, animal*) кра́сться (*impf*) ♦ n
(*inf*) подхали́м(ка); **~y** adj
жу́ткий
crept [krɛpt] pt, pp of **creep**
crescent [ˈkrɛsnt] n полуме́сяц
cress [krɛs] n кресс-сала́т
crest [krɛst] n (*of hill*) гре́бень m;
(*of bird*) хохоло́к, гребешо́к; (*coat
of arms*) герб
crew [kru:] n экипа́ж; (TV, CINEMA)
съёмочная гру́ппа
cricket [ˈkrɪkɪt] n (*game*) крике́т;
(*insect*) сверчо́к
crime [kraɪm] n преступле́ние;
(*illegal activity*) престу́пность f
criminal [ˈkrɪmɪnl] n
престу́пник(ица) ♦ adj (*illegal*)
престу́пный
crimson [ˈkrɪmzn] adj мали́новый,
тёмно-кра́сный
cripple [ˈkrɪpl] n кале́ка m/f ♦ vt
(*person*) кале́чить (искале́чить
pf)
crisis [ˈkraɪsɪs] (*pl* **crises**) n кри́зис
crisp [krɪsp] adj (*food*) хрустя́щий;
(*weather*) све́жий; (*reply*) чёткий;
~s npl (BRIT) чи́псы mpl

criterion [kraɪˈtɪərɪən] (*pl* **criteria**) n
крите́рий
critic [ˈkrɪtɪk] n кри́тик; **~al** adj
крити́ческий; (*person, opinion*)
крити́чный; **he is ~al** (MED) он в
крити́ческом состоя́нии; **~ally**
adv (*speak, look*) крити́чески; **~ism**
[ˈkrɪtɪsɪzəm] n кри́тика; (*of book,
play*) крити́ческий разбо́р; **~ize**
[ˈkrɪtɪsaɪz] vt критикова́ть
(*impf*)
Croatia [krəʊˈeɪʃə] n Хорва́тия
crockery [ˈkrɔkərɪ] n посу́да
crocodile [ˈkrɔkədaɪl] n (ZOOL)
крокоди́л
crocus [ˈkrəʊkəs] n шафра́н
crook [kruk] n (*criminal*) жу́лик;
~ed [ˈkrukɪd] adj криво́й;
(*dishonest*) жуликова́тый;
(*business*) жу́льнический
crop [krɔp] n (*сельско-
хозя́йственная*) культу́ра;
(*harvest*) урожа́й; (*also*: **riding**
~) плеть f
cross [krɔs] n крест; (*mark*)
кре́стик; (BIO) по́месь f ♦ vt
пересека́ть (пересе́чь pf),
переходи́ть (перейти́ pf); (*cheque*)
кросси́ровать (*impf/pf*); (*arms etc*)
скре́щивать (скрести́ть pf) ♦ adj
серди́тый; **~ out** vt вычёркивать
(вы́черкнуть pf); **~ing** n
перепра́ва; (*also*: **pedestrian
crossing**) перехо́д; **~roads** n
перекрёсток; **~ section** n (*of
population*) про́филь m; (*of object*)
попере́чное сече́ние; **~word** n
кроссво́рд
crotch [krɔtʃ] n промежность f;
the trousers are tight in the ~
брю́ки жмут в шагу́
crouch [krautʃ] vi приседа́ть
(присе́сть pf)
crow [krəʊ] n (*bird*) воро́на
crowd [kraud] n толпа́; **~ed** adj
(*area*) перенаселённый; **the room**

was ~ed ко́мната была́ полна́
люде́й

crown [kraun] n коро́на; (of head)
маку́шка; (of hill) верши́на; (of
tooth) коро́нка ♦ vt коронова́ть
(impf/pf); **the Crown** (Брита́нская)
Коро́на

crucial ['kru:ʃl] adj реша́ющий;
(work) ва́жный

crucifixion [kru:sɪ'fɪkʃən] n
распя́тие (на кресте́)

crude [kru:d] adj (materials) сыро́й;
(fig: basic) примити́вный;
(: vulgar) гру́бый

cruel ['kruəl] adj жесто́кий; ~**ty** n
жесто́кость f

cruise [kru:z] n круи́з ♦ vi
крейси́ровать (impf)

crumb [krʌm] n (of cake etc)
кро́шка

crumble ['krʌmbl] vt кроши́ть
(раскроши́ть pf) ♦ vi осыпа́ться
(осы́паться pf); (fig) ру́шиться
(ру́хнуть pf)

crunch [krʌntʃ] vt (food etc) грызть
(разгры́зть pf) ♦ n (fig): **the ~**
крити́ческий or реша́ющий
моме́нт; ~**y** adj хрустя́щий

crusade [kru:'seɪd] n (campaign)
кресто́вый похо́д

crush [krʌʃ] vt (squash) выжима́ть
(вы́жать pf); (crumple) мять
(смять pf); (defeat) сокруша́ть
(сокруши́ть pf); (upset)
уничтожа́ть (уничто́жить pf) ♦ n
(crowd) да́вка; **to have a ~ on sb**
сходи́ть (impf) с ума́ по кому́-н

crust [krʌst] n (of bread) ко́рка; (of earth)
кора́

crutch [krʌtʃ] n (MED) косты́ль m

crux [krʌks] n суть f

cry [kraɪ] vi пла́кать (impf); (also: ~
out) крича́ть (кри́кнуть pf) ♦ n
крик

crypt [krɪpt] n склеп

cryptic ['krɪptɪk] adj зага́дочный

crystal ['krɪstl] n (glass) хруста́ль;
(CHEM) криста́лл

cub [kʌb] n детёныш

Cuba ['kju:bə] n Ку́ба

cube [kju:b] n (also MATH) куб ♦ vt
возводи́ть (возвести́ pf) в куб

cubic ['kju:bɪk] adj куби́ческий

cubicle ['kju:bɪkl] n (at pool)
каби́на

cuckoo ['kuku:] n куку́шка

cucumber ['kju:kʌmbər] n огуре́ц

cuddle ['kʌdl] vt обнима́ть
(обня́ть pf) ♦ vi обнима́ться
(обня́ться pf) ♦ n ла́ска

cue [kju:] n кий; (THEAT) ре́плика

cuff [kʌf] n (of sleeve) манже́та; (US:
of trousers) отворо́т; (blow)
шлепо́к; **off the ~** экспро́мтом

cuisine [kwɪ'zi:n] n ку́хня
(кушанья)

cul-de-sac ['kʌldəsæk] n тупи́к

culinary ['kʌlɪnərɪ] adj кулина́рный

culmination [kʌlmɪ'neɪʃən] n
кульмина́ция

culprit ['kʌlprɪt] n (person)
вино́вник(вни́ца)

cult [kʌlt] n (also REL) культ

cultivate ['kʌltɪveɪt] vt (crop, feeling)
культиви́ровать (impf); (land)
возде́лывать (impf)

cultural ['kʌltʃərəl] adj культу́рный

culture ['kʌltʃə'] n культу́ра; ~**d** adj
культу́рный

cumbersome ['kʌmbəsəm] adj
громо́здкий

cumulative ['kju:mjulətɪv] adj
(effect, result) сумма́рный; (process)
нараста́ющий

cunning ['kʌnɪŋ] n хи́трость f ♦ adj
(crafty) хи́трый

cup [kʌp] n ча́шка; (as prize) ку́бок;
(of bra) ча́шечка

cupboard ['kʌbəd] n шкаф

curate ['kjuərɪt] n вика́рий

curator [kjuə'reɪtə'] n храни́тель m

curb [kə:b] vt (powers etc)

обуздывать (обуздáть pf) ♦ n (US: kerb) бордюр

cure [kjuə^r] vt вылéчивать (вылечить pf); (CULIN) обрáбатывать (обработáть pf) ♦ n лекáрство; (solution) срéдство

curfew ['kə:fju:] n комендáнтский час

curiosity [kjuərɪ'ɔsɪtɪ] n (see adj) любопытство; любознáтельность f

curious ['kjuərɪəs] adj любопытный; (interested) любознáтельный

curl [kə:l] n (of hair) лóкон, завитóк ♦ vt завивáть (завить pf); (: tightly) закрýчивать (закрутить pf) ♦ vi (hair) виться (impf); **~y** adj вьющийся

currant ['kʌrnt] n (dried grape) изюминка; **~s** (dried grapes) кишмиш

currency ['kʌrnsɪ] n валюта

current ['kʌrnt] n (of air, water) потóк; (ELEC) ток ♦ adj (present) текущий, совремéнный; (accepted) общепринятый; **~ account** n (BRIT) текущий счёт; **~ affairs** npl текущие событ́ия ntpl; **~ly** adv в дáнный or настоящий момéнт

curriculum [kə'rɪkjuləm] (pl **~s** or **curricula**) n (SCOL) (учéбная) прогрáмма

curriculum vitae [kərɪkjuləm'vi:taɪ] n (BRIT) автобиогрáфия

curry ['kʌrɪ] n блюдо с кáрри

curse [kə:s] n проклят́ие; (swearword) ругáтельство

curt [kə:t] adj рéзкий

curtain ['kə:tn] n зáнавес; (light) занавéска

curve [kə:v] n изгиб

cushion ['kuʃən] n подýшка ♦ vt смягчáть (смягчить pf)

custard ['kʌstəd] n заварнóй крем

custody ['kʌstədɪ] n опéка; **to take into ~** брать (взять pf) под стрáжу

custom ['kʌstəm] n (traditional) традиция; (convention) обычай; (habit) привычка; **~ary** adj обычный, традициóнный

customer ['kʌstəmə^r] n (of shop) покупáтель(ница) m(f); (of business) клиéнт, закáзчик

customs ['kʌstəmz] npl тамóжня fsg

cut [kʌt] (pt, pp **~**) vt (bread, meat) рéзать (разрéзать pf); (hand, knee) рéзать (порéзать pf); (grass, hair) стричь (постричь pf); (text) сокращáть (сократить pf); (spending, supply) урéзывать (урéзать pf); (prices) снижáть (снизить pf) or рéзать (impf) ♦ n (in skin) порéз; (in salary, spending) снижéние; (of meat) кусóк; **~ down** vt (tree) срубáть (срубить pf); (consumption) сокращáть (сократить pf); **~ off** vt отрезáть (отрéзать pf); (electricity, water) отключáть (отключить pf); (TEL) разъединять (разъединить pf); **~ out** vt (remove) вырезáть (вырезать pf); (stop) прекращáть (прекратить pf); **~ up** vt разрезáть (разрéзать pf)

cute [kju:t] adj (sweet) милый, прелéстный

cutlery ['kʌtlərɪ] n столóвый прибóр

cut-price (US **cut-rate**) adj по сниженной ценé

cut-rate adj (US) = **cut-price**

cutting ['kʌtɪŋ] adj (edge) острый; (remark etc) язвительный; (BRIT: PRESS) вырезка; (from plant) черенóк

CV n abbr (BRIT) = **curriculum vitae**

cybercafé ['saɪbəkæfeɪ] n

интерне́т-кафе́ *nt ind*

cyberspace ['saɪbəspeɪs] *n* киберпростра́нство

cycle ['saɪkl] *n* цикл; (*bicycle*) велосипе́д

cyclone ['saɪkləun] *n* цикло́н

cylinder ['sɪlɪndə*] *n* цили́ндр; (*of gas*) балло́н

cymbals ['sɪmblz] *npl* таре́лки *fpl*

cynical ['sɪnɪkl] *adj* цини́чный

cynicism ['sɪnɪsɪzəm] *n* цини́зм

Cyprus ['saɪprəs] *n* Кипр

cystitis [sɪs'taɪtɪs] *n* цисти́т

Czech [tʃɛk] *adj* че́шский ♦ *n* чех (че́шка); ~ **Republic** *n*: the ~ **Republic** Че́шская Респу́блика

D, d

D [di:] *n* (*MUS*) ре

dab [dæb] *vt* (*eyes, wound*) промокну́ть (*pf*); (*paint, cream*) наноси́ть (нанести́ *pf*)

dad [dæd] *n* (*inf*) па́па *m*, па́почка *m*; ~**dy** *n* (*inf*) = **dad**

daffodil ['dæfədɪl] *n* нарци́сс

daft [dɑ:ft] *adj* (*ideas*) дура́цкий; (*person*) чо́кнутый

dagger ['dægə*] *n* кинжа́л

daily ['deɪlɪ] *adj* (*dose*) су́точный; (*routine*) повседне́вный; (*wages*) дневно́й ♦ *n* (*also*: ~ **paper**) ежедне́вная газе́та ♦ *adv* ежедне́вно

dainty ['deɪntɪ] *adj* изя́щный

dairy ['dɛərɪ] *n* (*BRIT: shop*) моло́чный магази́н; (*for making butter*) маслоде́льня; (*for making cheese*) сырова́рня; ~ **farm** моло́чная фе́рма; ~ **products** моло́чные проду́кты *mpl*

daisy ['deɪzɪ] *n* маргари́тка

dam [dæm] *n* да́мба ♦ *vt* перекрыва́ть (перекры́ть *pf*) да́мбой

damage ['dæmɪdʒ] *n* (*harm*) уще́рб; (*dents etc*) поврежде́ние; (*fig*) вред ♦ *vt* поврежда́ть (повреди́ть *pf*); (*fig*) вреди́ть (повреди́ть *pf*) +*dat*; ~**s** *npl* (*LAW*) компенса́ция *fsg*

damn [dæm] *vt* осужда́ть (осуди́ть *pf*) ♦ *adj* (*inf*: *also*: ~**ed**) прокля́тый ♦ *n* (*inf*): **I don't give a** ~ мне плева́ть; (**it**)! чёрт возьми́ и́ли побери́!; ~**ing** *adj* обличи́тельный

damp [dæmp] *adj* (*building, wall*) сыро́й; (*cloth*) вла́жный ♦ *n* сы́рость *f* ♦ *vt* (*also*: ~**en**) сма́чивать (смочи́ть *pf*); (: *fig*) охлажда́ть (охлади́ть *pf*)

damson ['dæmzən] *n* терносли́ва

dance [dɑ:ns] *n* та́нец; (*social event*) та́нцы *mpl* ♦ *vi* танцева́ть (*impf*); ~**r** *n* танцо́вщик(ица); (*for fun*) танцо́р

dandelion ['dændɪlaɪən] *n* одува́нчик

danger ['deɪndʒə*] *n* опа́сность *f*; "~!" "опа́сно!"; **in/out of** ~ в/вне опа́сности; **he is in** ~ **of losing his job** ему́ грози́т поте́ря рабо́ты; ~**ous** *adj* опа́сный

Danish ['deɪnɪʃ] *adj* да́тский ♦ *npl*: **the** ~ датча́не

dare [dɛə*] *vt*: **to** ~ **sb to do** вызыва́ть (вы́звать *pf*) кого́-н +*infin* ♦ *vi*: **to** ~ (**to**) **do** сметь (посме́ть *pf*) +*infin*; **I** ~ **say** смею́ заме́тить

daring ['dɛərɪŋ] *adj* (*audacious*) де́рзкий; (*bold*) сме́лый

dark [dɑ:k] *adj* тёмный; (*complexion*) сму́глый ♦ *n*: **in the** ~ в темноте́; ~ **blue** etc тёмно-си́ний etc; **after** ~ по́сле наступле́ния темноты́; ~**ness** *n* темнота́; ~**room** *n* тёмная ко́мната, проявительная лаборато́рия

darling ['dɑ:lɪŋ] *adj* дорого́й(а́я) *m(f) adj*

dart [dɑ:t] *n* (*in game*) дро́тик (*для игры в дарт*); (*in sewing*) вы́тачка; ~**s** *n* дарт

dash [dæʃ] *n* (*drop*) ка́пелька; (*sign*) тире́ *nt ind* ♦ *vt* (*throw*) швыря́ть (швырну́ть *pf*); (*shatter: hopes*) разруша́ть (разру́шить *pf*); ♦ *vi*: **to** ~ **towards** рвану́ться (*pf*) к +*dat*

dashboard ['dæʃbɔ:d] *n* (AUT) прибо́рная пане́ль *f*

data ['deɪtə] *npl* да́нные *pl*; ~**base** *n* ба́за да́нных

date [deɪt] *n* (*day*) число́, да́та; (*with friend*) свида́ние; (*fruit*) фи́ник ♦ *vt* дати́ровать (*impf/pf*); (*person*) встреча́ться (*impf*) с +*instr*; ~ **of birth** да́та рожде́ния; **to** ~ на сего́дняшний день; **out of** ~ устаре́лый; (*expired*) просро́ченный; **up to** ~ совреме́нный; ~**d** *adj* устаре́лый

daughter ['dɔ:tə] *n* дочь *f*; ~**-in-law** *n* сноха́

daunting ['dɔ:ntɪŋ] *adj* устраша́ющий

dawn [dɔ:n] *n* (*of day*) рассве́т

day [deɪ] *n* (*period*) су́тки *pl*, день *m*; (*daylight*) день *m*; (*heyday*) вре́мя *nt*; **the** ~ **after** накану́не; **the** ~ **after tomorrow** послеза́втра; **the** ~ **before yesterday** позавчера́; **the following** ~ на сле́дующий день; **by** ~ днём; ~**light** *n* дневно́й свет; ~ **return** *n* (BRIT) обра́тный биле́т (*действи́тельный в тече́ние одного́ дня*); ~**time** *n* день *m*

daze [deɪz] *vt* (*stun*) ошеломля́ть (ошеломи́ть *pf*) ♦ *n*: **in a** ~ в тума́не

dazzle ['dæzl] *vt* (*blind*) ослепля́ть (ослепи́ть *pf*)

DC *abbr* (= direct current) постоя́нный ток

dead [ded] *adj* мёртвый; (*arm, leg*) онеме́лый ♦ *adv* (inf: completely) абсолю́тно; (inf: directly) пря́мо ♦ *npl*: **the** ~ мёртвые *pl adj*; (*in accident, war*) поги́бшие *pl adj*; **the battery is** ~ батаре́йка се́ла; **the telephone is** ~ телефо́н отключи́лся; **to shoot sb** ~ застрели́ть (*pf*) кого́-н; ~ **tired** смерте́льно уста́лый, уста́вший; ~ **end** *n* тупи́к; ~**line** *n* после́дний и преде́льный срок; ~**lock** *n* тупи́к; ~**ly** *adj* (*lethal*) смертоно́сный; **Dead Sea** *n*: **the Dead Sea** Мёртвое мо́ре

deaf [def] *adj* (*totally*) глухо́й

deal [di:l] (*pt, pp* ~**t**) *n* (*agreement*) сде́лка ♦ *vt* (*blow*) наноси́ть (нанести́ *pf*); (*cards*) сдава́ть (сдать *pf*); **a great** ~ (**of**) о́чень мно́го (+*gen*); ~ **in** *vt fus* (COMM, *drugs*) торгова́ть (*impf*) +*instr*; ~ **with** *vt fus* име́ть (*impf*) де́ло с +*instr*; (*problem*) реша́ть (реши́ть *pf*); (*subject*) занима́ться (заня́ться *pf*) +*instr*; ~**t** [delt] *pt, pp of* **deal**

dean [di:n] *n* (SCOL) дека́н

dear [dɪə] *adj* дорого́й ♦ *n*: (**my**) ~ (*to man, boy*) дорого́й (мой); (*to woman, girl*) дорога́я (моя́) ♦ *excl*: ~ **me!** о, Го́споди!; **Dear Sir** уважа́емый господи́н; **Dear Mrs Smith** дорога́я *or* уважа́емая ми́ссис Смит; ~**ly** *adv* (*love*) о́чень; (*pay*) до́рого

death [deθ] *n* смерть *f*; ~ **penalty** *n* сме́ртная казнь *f*; ~ **toll** *n* число́ поги́бших

debatable [dɪ'beɪtəbl] *adj* спо́рный

debate [dɪ'beɪt] *n* деба́ты *pl* ♦ *vt* (*topic*) обсужда́ть (обсуди́ть *pf*)

debit ['debɪt] *vt*: **to** ~ **a sum to sb** *or*

to sb's account дебетовать *(impf/ pf)* сумму с кого-н *or* с чьего-н счёта; *see also* **direct debit**

debris ['debri:] *n* обломки *mpl*, развалины *fpl*

debt [det] *n (sum)* долг; **to be in ~** быть *(impf)* в долгу; **~or** *n* должник

decade ['dekeɪd] *n* десятилетие

decaffeinated [dɪ'kæfɪneɪtɪd] *adj:* **~ coffee** кофе без кофеина

decay [dɪ'keɪ] *n* разрушение

deceased [dɪ'si:st] *n:* **the ~** покойный(ая) *m(f) adj*

deceit [dɪ'si:t] *n* обман

deceive [dɪ'si:v] *vt* обманывать (обмануть *pf*)

December [dɪ'sembə^r] *n* декабрь *m*

decency ['di:sənsɪ] *n (propriety)* благопристойность *f*

decent ['di:sənt] *adj (wages, meal)* приличный; *(behaviour, person)* порядочный

deception [dɪ'sepʃən] *n* обман

deceptive [dɪ'septɪv] *adj* обманчивый

decide [dɪ'saɪd] *vt (settle)* решать (решить *pf*) ♦ *vi:* **to ~ to do/that** решать (решить *pf*) +*infin*/, что; **to ~ on** останавливаться (остановиться *pf*) на +*prp*; **~dly** *adv (distinctly)* несомненно; *(emphatically)* решительно

deciduous [dɪ'sɪdjuəs] *adj* лиственный, листопадный

decision [dɪ'sɪʒən] *n* решение

decisive [dɪ'saɪsɪv] *adj* решительный

deck [dek] *n (NAUT)* палуба; *(of cards)* колода; *(also:* **record ~)** проигрыватель *m*; **top ~** *(of bus)* верхний этаж; **~ chair** *n* шезлонг

declaration [deklə'reɪʃən] *n (statement)* декларация; *(of war)* объявление

declare [dɪ'kleə^r] *vt (state)* объявлять (объявить *pf*); *(for tax)* декларировать *(impf/pf)*

decline [dɪ'klaɪn] *n (drop)* падение; *(in strength)* упадок; *(lessening)* уменьшение; **to be in** *or* **on the ~** быть *(impf)* в упадке

décor ['deɪkɔ:^r] *n* отделка

decorate ['dekəreɪt] *vt (room etc)* отделывать (отделать *pf*); *(adorn):* **to ~ (with)** украшать (украсить *pf*) +*instr*

decoration [dekə'reɪʃən] *n (on tree, dress)* украшение; *(medal)* награда

decorative ['dekərətɪv] *adj* декоративный

decorator ['dekəreɪtə^r] *n* обойщик

decrease [dɪ'kri:s] *vt* уменьшать (уменьшить *pf*) ♦ *vi* уменьшаться (уменьшиться *pf*) ♦ *n:* **~ (in)** уменьшение (+*gen*)

decree [dɪ'kri:] *n* постановление

dedicate ['dedɪkeɪt] *vt:* **to ~ to** посвящать (посвятить *pf*) +*dat*

dedication [dedɪ'keɪʃən] *n (devotion)* преданность *f*; *(in book etc)* посвящение

deduction [dɪ'dʌkʃən] *n (conclusion)* умозаключение; *(subtraction)* вычитание; *(amount)* вычет

deed [di:d] *n (feat)* деяние, поступок; *(LAW)* акт

deep [di:p] *adj* глубокий; *(voice)* низкий ♦ *adv:* **the spectators stood 20 ~** зрители стояли в 20 рядов; **the lake is 4 metres ~** глубина озера - 4 метра; **~ blue** *etc* тёмно-синий *etc*; **~en** *vi (crisis, mystery)* углубляться (углубиться *pf*); **~ly** *adv* глубоко; **~-sea** *cpd (fishing)* глубоководный; **~-sea diver** водолаз; **~-seated** *adj* закоренелый

deer [dɪə^r] *n inv* олень *m*

defeat [dɪ'fi:t] *n* поражение ♦ *vt*

defect [ˈdiːfekt] n (in product)
дефе́кт; (of plan) недоста́ток;
~**ive** [dɪˈfektɪv] adj (goods)
дефе́ктный

defence [dɪˈfens] (US **defense**) n
защи́та; (MIL) оборо́на; ~**less** adj
беззащи́тный

defend [dɪˈfend] vt защища́ть
(защити́ть pf); (LAW) защища́ть
(impf); ~**ant** n подсуди́мый(ая)
m(f) adj, обвиня́емый(ая) m(f) adj;
(in civil case) отве́тчик(ица) m(f);
~**er** n
защи́тник

defense etc (US) = **defence**

defensive [dɪˈfensɪv] adj (weapons,
measures) оборони́тельный;
(behaviour, manner) вызыва́ющий
♦ n: he was on the ~ он был
гото́в к оборо́не

defer [dɪˈfɜː] vt отсро́чивать
(отсро́чить pf)

deference [ˈdefərəns] n почте́ние

defiance [dɪˈfaɪəns] n вы́зов; **in ~
of** вопреки́ +dat

defiant [dɪˈfaɪənt] adj (person, reply)
де́рзкий; (tone) вызыва́ющий

deficiency [dɪˈfɪʃənsɪ] n (lack)
нехва́тка

deficient [dɪˈfɪʃənt] adj: **to be ~ in**
(lack) испы́тывать (impf)
недоста́ток в +prp

deficit [ˈdefɪsɪt] n (COMM) дефици́т

define [dɪˈfaɪn] vt определя́ть
(определи́ть pf); (word etc) дава́ть
(дать pf) определе́ние +dat

definite [ˈdefɪnɪt] adj
определённый; **he was ~ about**
it его́ мне́ние на э́тот счёт бы́ло
определённым; ~**ly** adv
(certainly)
несомне́нно

definition [defɪˈnɪʃən] n (of word)
определе́ние

definitive [dɪˈfɪnɪtɪv] adj

оконча́тельный

deflate [diːˈfleɪt] vt (tyre, balloon)
спуска́ть (спусти́ть pf)

deflect [dɪˈflekt] vt (shot) отража́ть
(отрази́ть pf); (criticism)
отклоня́ть (отклони́ть pf);
(attention) отвлека́ть (отвле́чь pf)

deformed [dɪˈfɔːmd] adj
дефо́рми́рованный

deft [deft] adj ло́вкий

defuse [diːˈfjuːz] vt разряжа́ть
(разряди́ть pf)

defy [dɪˈfaɪ] vt (resist) оспа́ривать
(оспо́рить pf); (fig: description etc)
не поддава́ться (impf) +dat; **to ~
sb to do** (challenge) призыва́ть
(призва́ть pf) кого́-н +infin

degenerate vb [dɪˈdʒenəreɪt] adj
[dɪˈdʒenərɪt] vi вырожда́ться
(вы́родиться pf) ♦ adj
вы́родившийся

degrading [dɪˈɡreɪdɪŋ] adj
унизи́тельный

degree [dɪˈɡriː] n (extent) сте́пень f;
(unit of measurement) гра́дус;
(SCOL) (учёная) сте́пень; **by ~s**
постепе́нно; **to some~, to a
certain ~** до не́которой сте́пени

delay [dɪˈleɪ] vt (decision, event)
откла́дывать (отложи́ть pf);
(person, plane etc) заде́рживать
(задержа́ть pf) ♦ vi ме́длить (impf)
♦ n заде́ржка; **to be ~ed**
заде́рживаться (impf); **without ~**
незамедли́тельно

delegate n [ˈdelɪɡɪt] vb [ˈdelɪɡeɪt] n
делега́т ♦ vt (task) поруча́ть
(поручи́ть pf)

delegation [delɪˈɡeɪʃən] n (group)
делега́ция; (of task) переда́ча

deliberate adj [dɪˈlɪbərɪt] vb
[dɪˈlɪbəreɪt] adj (intentional)
наме́ренный; (slow)
неторопли́вый ♦ vi совеща́ться
(impf); (person) разду́мывать
(impf); ~**ly** adv (see adj)

наме́ренно, наро́чно;
неторопли́во

delicacy ['delɪkəsɪ] n то́нкость f;
(food) деликате́с

delicate ['delɪkɪt] adj то́нкий;
(problem) делика́тный; (health)
хру́пкий

delicatessen [delɪkə'tesn] n
гастроно́мия, магази́н
деликате́сов

delicious [dɪ'lɪʃəs] adj о́чень
вку́сный; (smell) восхити́тельный

delight [dɪ'laɪt] n (feeling) восто́рг
♦ vt ра́довать (пора́довать pf); to
take (a) ~ in находи́ть (impf)
удово́льствие в +prp; **~ed** adj (to
be) **~ed (at** or **with)** (быть (impf)) в
восто́рге (от +gen); **he was ~ed to
see her** он был рад ви́деть её;
~ful ♦ adj восхити́тельный

delinquent [dɪ'lɪŋkwənt] adj
престу́пный

delirious [dɪ'lɪrɪəs] adj: **to be ~** (with
fever) быть (impf) в бреду́; (with
excitement) быть (impf) в упое́нии

deliver [dɪ'lɪvə'] vt (goods)
доставля́ть (доста́вить pf); (letter)
вруча́ть (вручи́ть pf); (message)
передава́ть (переда́ть pf);
(speech) произноси́ть
(произнести́ pf); (baby)
принима́ть (приня́ть pf); **~y** n (of
goods) доста́вка; (of baby) ро́ды
pl; **to take ~y of** получа́ть
(получи́ть pf)

deluge ['deljuːdʒ] n (fig) лави́на

delusion [dɪ'luːʒən] n
заблужде́ние

demand [dɪ'mɑːnd] vt тре́бовать
(потре́бовать pf) +gen ♦ n (request,
claim) тре́бование; (ECON): **~ (for)**
спрос (на +acc); **to be in ~**
(commodity) по́льзоваться (impf)
спро́сом; **on ~** по тре́бованию;
~ing adj (boss) тре́бовательный;
(child) тру́дный; (work: requiring

effort) тяжёлый

demeanour [dɪ'miːnə'] (US
demeanor) n мане́ра поведе́ния

demented [dɪ'mentɪd] adj
поме́шанный

demise [dɪ'maɪz] n (fig) упа́док

demo ['deməu] n abbr (inf) =
demonstration

democracy [dɪ'mɔkrəsɪ] n (system)
демокра́тия; (country)
демократи́ческая страна́

democrat ['deməkræt] n демокра́т;
Democrat (US) член па́ртии
демокра́тов; **~ic** [demə'krætɪk] adj
демократи́ческий; **Democratic
Party** (US) па́ртия демокра́тов

demolish [dɪ'mɔlɪʃ] vt сноси́ть
(снести́ pf); (argument)
разгроми́ть (pf)

demolition [demə'lɪʃən] n (see vb)
снос; разгро́м

demon ['diːmən] n де́мон

demonstrate ['demənstreɪt] vt
демонстри́ровать
(продемонстри́ровать pf) ♦ vi: **to
~ (for/against)** демонстри́ровать
(impf) (за +acc/про́тив +gen)

demonstration [demən'streɪʃən] n
демонстра́ция

den [den] n (of animal, person)
ло́гово

denial [dɪ'naɪəl] n отрица́ние;
(refusal) отка́з

denim ['denɪm] n джи́нсовая
ткань f; **~s** npl (jeans) джи́нсы pl

Denmark ['denmɑːk] n Да́ния

denote [dɪ'nəut] vt (indicate)
ука́зывать (указа́ть pf) на +acc

denounce [dɪ'nauns] vt (condemn)
осужда́ть (осуди́ть pf); (inform on)
доноси́ть (донести́ pf) на +acc

dense [dens] adj (smoke, foliage etc)
густо́й; (inf: person) тупо́й; **~ly**
adv: **~ly populated** гу́сто
населённый

density ['densɪtɪ] n пло́тность f;

single/double-~ disk диск с одина́рной/двойно́й пло́тностью

dent [dent] n (in metal) вмя́тина
♦ vt (also): **make a ~ in**: car etc) оставля́ть (оста́вить pf) вмя́тину на +acc

dental ['dentl] adj зубно́й

dentist ['dentist] n зубно́й врач, стомато́лог

dentures ['dentʃəz] npl зубно́й проте́з msg

denunciation [dɪnʌnsɪ'eɪʃən] n осужде́ние

deny [dɪ'naɪ] vt отрица́ть (impf); (allegation) отверга́ть (отве́ргнуть pf); (refuse): **to ~ sb sth** отка́зывать (отказа́ть pf) кому́-н в чём-н

deodorant [diː'əudərənt] n дезодора́нт

depart [dɪ'pɑːt] vi (person) отбыва́ть (отбы́ть pf); (bus, train) отправля́ться (отпра́виться pf); (plane) улета́ть (улете́ть pf); **to ~ from** (fig) отклоня́ться (отклони́ться pf) от +gen

department [dɪ'pɑːtmənt] n (in shop) отде́л; (SCOL) отделе́ние; (POL) ве́домство, департа́мент; **~ store** n универса́льный магази́н, универма́г

departure [dɪ'pɑːtʃə*] n (see vb) отъе́зд; отправле́ние; вы́лет; **~ lounge** n зал вы́лета

depend [dɪ'pend] vi: **to ~ on** зави́сеть (impf) от +gen; (trust) полага́ться (положи́ться pf) на +acc; **it ~s** смотря́ по обстоя́тельствам, как полу́чится; **~ing on ...** в зави́симости от +gen ...; **~able** adj надёжный; **~ence** n зави́симость f; **~ent** adj: **~ent (on)** зави́симый (от +gen) ♦ n иждиве́нец(нка)

depict [dɪ'pɪkt] vt изобража́ть

(изобрази́ть pf)

deplorable [dɪ'plɔːrəbl] adj (behaviour) возмути́тельный; (conditions) плаче́вный

deploy [dɪ'plɔɪ] vt дислоци́ровать (impf/pf)

deport [dɪ'pɔːt] vt депорти́ровать (impf/pf), высыла́ть (вы́слать pf)

deposit [dɪ'pɔzɪt] n (in account) депози́т, вклад; (down payment) пе́рвый взнос, зада́ток; (of ore, oil) за́лежь f ♦ vt (money) помеща́ть (помести́ть pf); (bag) сдава́ть (сдать pf); **~ account** n депози́тный счёт

depot ['depəu] n (storehouse) склад; (for buses) парк; (for trains) депо́ nt ind; (US: station) ста́нция

depreciation [dɪpriːʃɪ'eɪʃən] n обесце́нивание

depress [dɪ'pres] vt (PSYCH) подавля́ть (impf), угнета́ть (impf); **~ed** adj (person) пода́вленный, угнетённый; (prices) сни́женный; **~ed area** райо́н, переживаю́щий экономи́ческий упа́док; **~ing** adj (news, outlook) удруча́ющий; **~ion** [dɪ'preʃən] n депре́ссия; (METEOROLOGY) о́бласть f ни́зкого давле́ния

deprivation [deprɪ'veɪʃən] n (poverty) нужда́

deprive [dɪ'praɪv] vt: **to ~ sb of** лиша́ть (лиши́ть pf) кого́-н +gen; **~d** adj (family, child) обездо́ленный

depth [depθ] n глубина́; **in the ~s of despair** в глубо́ком отча́янии; **to be out of one's ~** (in water) не достава́ть (impf) до дна

deputy ['depjuti] n замести́тель m; (POL) депута́т ♦ cpd: **~ chairman** замести́тель председа́теля; **~ head** (BRIT : SCOL) замести́тель дире́ктора

deranged [dɪ'reɪndʒd] adj

психически расстроенный; **he is ~** у него расстроена психика

derelict ['derɪlɪkt] *adj* заброшенный

derive [dɪ'raɪv] *vt*: **to ~ (from)** (*pleasure*) получать (получить *pf*) (от +*gen*); (*benefit*) извлекать (извлечь *pf*) (из +*gen*)

descend [dɪ'send] *vt* (*stairs*) спускаться (спуститься *pf*) по +*dat*; (*hill*) спускаться (спуститься *pf*) с +*gen* ♦ *vi* (*go down*) спускаться (спуститься *pf*); **~nt** *n* потомок

descent [dɪ'sent] *n* спуск; (*AVIAT*) снижение; (*origin*) происхождение

describe [dɪs'kraɪb] *vt* описывать (описать *pf*)

description [dɪs'krɪpʃən] *n* описание; (*sort*) род

descriptive [dɪs'krɪptɪv] *adj* (*writing*) описательный

desert *n* ['dezət] *vb* [dɪ'zə:t] *n* пустыня ♦ *vt* покидать (покинуть *pf*) ♦ *vi* (*MIL*) дезертировать (*impf/pf*); **~ island** *n* необитаемый остров

deserve [dɪ'zə:v] *vt* заслуживать (заслужить *pf*)

deserving [dɪ'zə:vɪŋ] *adj* достойный

design [dɪ'zaɪn] *n* дизайн; (*process: of dress*) моделирование; (*sketch: of building*) проект; (*pattern*) рисунок ♦ *vt* (*house, kitchen*) проектировать (спроектировать *pf*); (*product, test*) разрабатывать (разработать *pf*)

designate ['dezɪɡneɪt] *vt* (*nominate*) назначать (назначить *pf*); (*indicate*) обозначать (обозначить *pf*)

designer [dɪ'zaɪnə*r*] *n* (*also: fashion designer*) модельер; (*ART*) дизайнер; (*of machine*) конструктор

desirable [dɪ'zaɪərəbl] *adj* (*proper*) желательный

desire [dɪ'zaɪə*r*] *n* желание ♦ *vt* (*want*) желать (*impf*)

desk [desk] *n* (*in office, study*) (письменный) стол; (*for pupil*) парта; (*in hotel, at airport*) стойка; (*BRIT: also: cash-~*) касса; **~top** *adj* настольный

desolate ['desəlɪt] *adj* (*place*) заброшенный; (*person*) покинутый

despair [dɪs'peə*r*] *n* отчаяние ♦ *vi*: **to ~ of sth/doing** отчаиваться (отчаяться *pf*) в чём-н/+*infin*

despatch [dɪs'pætʃ] *n, vt* = **dispatch**

desperate ['despərɪt] *adj* (*action, situation*) отчаянный; (*criminal*) отъявленный; **to be ~** (*person*) быть (*impf*) в отчаянии; **to be ~ to do** жаждать (*impf*) +*infin*; **to be ~ for money** крайне нуждаться (*impf*) в деньгах; **~ly** *adv* отчаянно; (*very*) чрезвычайно

desperation [despə'reɪʃən] *n* отчаяние

despicable [dɪs'pɪkəbl] *adj* презренный

despise [dɪs'paɪz] *vt* презирать (*impf*)

despite [dɪs'paɪt] *prep* несмотря на +*acc*

dessert [dɪ'zə:t] *n* десерт

destination [destɪ'neɪʃən] *n* (*of person*) цель f; (*of mail*) место назначения

destined ['destɪnd] *adj*: **he is ~ to do** ему суждено +*infin*; **to be ~ for** предназначаться (*impf*) для +*gen*

destiny ['destɪnɪ] *n* судьба

destitute ['destɪtju:t] *adj* обездоленный

destroy [dɪs'trɔɪ] *vt* уничтожать (уничтожить *pf*), разрушать (разрушить *pf*)

destruction [dɪsˈtrʌkʃən] n
уничтоже́ние, разруше́ние

destructive [dɪsˈtrʌktɪv] adj
(capacity, force) разруши́тельный;
(criticism) сокруши́тельный;
(emotion) губи́тельный

detached [dɪˈtætʃt] adj
беспристра́стный; ~ **house**
особня́к

detachment [dɪˈtætʃmənt] n
отстранённость f; (MIL) отря́д

detail [ˈdiːteɪl] n подро́бность f,
дета́ль f ♦ vt перечисля́ть
(перечи́слить pf); **in** – подро́бно,
в дета́лях; ~**ed** adj дета́льный,
подро́бный

detain [dɪˈteɪn] vt заде́рживать
(задержа́ть pf); (in hospital)
оставля́ть (оста́вить pf)

detect [dɪˈtekt] vt обнару́живать
(обнару́жить pf); (sense)
чу́вствовать (почу́вствовать pf);
~**ion** [dɪˈtekʃən] n (discovery)
обнаруже́ние; ~**ive** n сы́щик,
детекти́в

detention [dɪˈtenʃən] n
(imprisonment) содержа́ние под
стра́жей; (arrest) задержа́ние;
(SCOL): **to give sb** – оставля́ть
(оста́вить pf) кого́-н по́сле
уро́ков

> **detention** - в брита́нских
> шко́лах дете́й, наруша́ющих
> дисципли́ну, в ка́честве
> наказа́ния мо́гут оста́вить
> по́сле уро́ков в шко́ле.

deter [dɪˈtəː] vt уде́рживать
(удержа́ть pf)

detergent [dɪˈtəːdʒənt] n мо́ющее
сре́дство

deteriorate [dɪˈtɪərɪəreɪt] vi
уху́дшаться (уху́дшиться pf)

deterioration [dɪtɪərɪəˈreɪʃən] n
уху́дшение

determination [dɪtəːmɪˈneɪʃən] n
(resolve) реши́мость f;
(establishment) установле́ние

determine [dɪˈtəːmɪn] vt (find out)
устана́вливать (установи́ть pf);
(establish, dictate) определя́ть
(определи́ть pf); ~**d** adj
реши́тельный, волево́й; ~**d to do**
по́лный реши́мости +infin

deterrent [dɪˈterənt] n сре́дство
сде́рживания, сде́рживающее
сре́дство; **nuclear** ~ сре́дство
я́дерного сде́рживания

detour [ˈdiːtuə] n (also US) объе́зд

detract [dɪˈtrækt] vi: **to** ~ **from**
умаля́ть (умали́ть pf)

detriment [ˈdetrɪmənt] n: **to the** ~
of в уще́рб +dat; ~**al** [detrɪˈmentl]
adj: ~**al to** вре́дный для +gen

devaluation [dɪvæljuˈeɪʃən] n
(ECON) девальва́ция

devalue [ˈdiːˈvæljuː] vt (ECON)
обесце́нивать (обесце́нить pf);
(person, work) недооце́нивать
(недооцени́ть pf)

devastating [ˈdevəsteɪtɪŋ] adj
(weapon, storm) разруши́тельный;
(news, effect) ошеломля́ющий

develop [dɪˈveləp] vt (idea, industry)
развива́ть (разви́ть pf); (plan,
resource) разраба́тывать
(разрабо́тать pf); (land)
застра́ивать (застро́ить pf);
(PHOT) проявля́ть (прояви́ть pf)
♦ vi (evolve, advance) развива́ться
(разви́ться pf); (appear)
проявля́ться (прояви́ться pf);
~**ment** n разви́тие; (of resources)
разрабо́тка; (of land) застро́йка

deviation [diːvɪˈeɪʃən] n: ~ **(from)**
отклоне́ние (от +gen)

device [dɪˈvaɪs] n (apparatus)
устро́йство, прибо́р

devil [ˈdevl] n дья́вол, чёрт

devious [ˈdiːvɪəs] adj (person)
лука́вый

devise [dɪ'vaɪz] vt разраба́тывать (разрабо́тать pf)

devoid [dɪ'vɔɪd] adj: ~ of лишённый +gen

devolution [di:və'lu:ʃən] n переда́ча вла́сти (ме́стным о́рганам)

devote [dɪ'vəut] vt: to ~ sth to посвяща́ть (посвяти́ть pf) что-н +dat; ~d adj (admirer, partner) пре́данный; **his book is ~d to Scotland** его́ кни́га посвящена́ Шотла́ндии

devotion [dɪ'vəuʃən] n пре́данность f; (REL) поклоне́ние

devout [dɪ'vaut] adj (REL) благочести́вый

dew [dju:] n роса́

diabetes [daɪə'bi:ti:z] n диабе́т

diabetic [daɪə'betɪk] n диабе́тик

diabolical [daɪə'bɒlɪkl] adj (inf) жу́ткий

diagnose [daɪəg'nəuz] vt (illness) диагности́ровать (impf/pf); (problem) определя́ть (определи́ть pf)

diagnosis [daɪəg'nəusɪs] (pl **diagnoses**) n диа́гноз

diagonal [daɪ'ægənl] adj диагона́льный

diagram ['daɪəgræm] n схе́ма

dial ['daɪəl] n (of clock) цифербла́т; (of radio) регуля́тор настро́йки ♦ vt (number) набира́ть (набра́ть pf)

dialect ['daɪəlekt] n диале́кт

dialling tone ['daɪəlɪŋ-] (US **dial tone**) n непреры́вный гудо́к

dialogue ['daɪəlɒg] (US **dialog**) n диало́г

dial tone n (US) = **dialling tone**

diameter [daɪ'æmɪtəʳ] n диа́метр

diamond ['daɪəmənd] n алма́з; (cut diamond) бриллиа́нт; (shape) ромб; ~s npl (CARDS) бу́бны fpl

diaper ['daɪəpəʳ] n (US) подгу́зник

diaphragm ['daɪəfræm] n диафра́гма

diarrhoea [daɪə'ri:ə] (US **diarrhea**) n поно́с

diary ['daɪərɪ] n (journal) дневни́к; (engagements book) ежедне́вник

dice [daɪs] npl of **die**; (in game) ку́бик ♦ vt ре́зать (наре́зать pf) ку́биками

dictate [dɪk'teɪt] vt диктова́ть (продиктова́ть pf)

dictator [dɪk'teɪtəʳ] n дикта́тор; ~**ship** n диктату́ра

dictionary ['dɪkʃənrɪ] n слова́рь m

did [dɪd] pt of **do**

didn't ['dɪdnt] = **did not**

die [daɪ] vi (person, emotion) умира́ть (умере́ть pf); (smile, light) угаса́ть (уга́снуть pf); **to be dying for sth/to do** до́ смерти хоте́ть (impf) чего́-н/+infin

diesel ['di:zl] n ди́зель m; (also: ~ **oil**) ди́зельное то́пливо

diet ['daɪət] n дие́та

differ ['dɪfəʳ] vi: to ~ (from) отлича́ться (impf) (от +gen); (disagree): to ~ about расходи́ться (разойти́сь pf) в вопро́се +gen; ~**ence** n разли́чие; (in size, age) ра́зница; (disagreement) разногла́сие; ~**ent** adj друго́й, ино́й; (various) разли́чный, ра́зный; to be ~**ent from** отлича́ться (impf) от +gen; ~**entiate** [dɪfə'renʃɪeɪt] vi: to ~**entiate (between)** проводи́ть (провести́ pf) разли́чие (ме́жду +instr); ~**ently** adv (otherwise) ина́че, по-друго́му; (in different ways) по-ра́зному

difficult ['dɪfɪkəlt] adj тру́дный, тяжёлый; ~**y** n тру́дность f, затрудне́ние

diffuse [dɪ'fju:s] vt (information) распространя́ть (распространи́ть pf)

dig [dɪg] (pt, pp **dug**) vt (hole) копа́ть (вы́копать pf), рыть (вы́рыть pf); (garden) копа́ть (вскопа́ть pf) ♦ vt (prod) толчо́к; (excavation) раско́пки fpl; **to ~ one's nails into** впива́ться (впи́ться pf) ногтя́ми в +acc; **~ up** vt (plant) выка́пывать (вы́копать pf); (information) раска́пывать (раскопа́ть pf)

digest [daɪˈdʒɛst] vt (food) перева́ривать (перевари́ть pf); (facts) усва́ивать (усво́ить pf); **~ion** [dɪˈdʒɛstʃən] n пищеваре́ние

digit [ˈdɪdʒɪt] n (number) ци́фра; **~al** adj: **~al watch** электро́нные часы́ mpl; **~al camera** цифрова́я ка́мера; **~al TV** цифрово́е телеви́дение

dignified [ˈdɪgnɪfaɪd] adj по́лный досто́инства

dignity [ˈdɪgnɪtɪ] n досто́инство

dilapidated [dɪˈlæpɪdeɪtɪd] adj ве́тхий

dilemma [daɪˈlɛmə] n диле́мма

diligent [ˈdɪlɪdʒənt] adj (worker) усе́рдный, приле́жный

dilute [daɪˈluːt] vt (liquid) разбавля́ть (разба́вить pf)

dim [dɪm] adj (outline, memory) сму́тный; (light) ту́склый; (room) пло́хо освещённый ♦ vt (light) приглуша́ть (приглуши́ть pf)

dimension [daɪˈmɛnʃən] n (measurement) измере́ние; (also pl: scale, size) разме́ры mpl; (aspect) аспе́кт

diminish [dɪˈmɪnɪʃ] vi уменьша́ться (уме́ньшиться pf)

din [dɪn] n гро́хот

dine [daɪn] vi обе́дать (пообе́дать pf); **~r** n (person) обе́дающий m(f) adj; (US) дешёвый рестора́н

dinghy [ˈdɪŋgɪ] n (also: **sailing ~**) шлю́пка; (also: **rubber ~**) надувна́я ло́дка

dingy [ˈdɪndʒɪ] adj (streets, room) мра́чный; (clothes, curtains etc) замы́зганный

dining room [ˈdaɪnɪŋ-] n столо́вая f adj

dinner [ˈdɪnər] n (evening meal) у́жин; (lunch, banquet) обе́д; **~ jacket** n смо́кинг; **~ party** n зва́ный обе́д

dinosaur [ˈdaɪnəsɔːr] n диноза́вр

dip [dɪp] n (depression) впа́дина; (CULIN) со́ус ♦ vt (immerse) погружа́ть (погрузи́ть pf), окуна́ть (окуну́ть pf); (: in liquid) мака́ть (макну́ть pf), обма́кивать (обмакну́ть pf); (BRIT: AUT, lights) приглуша́ть (приглуши́ть pf) ♦ vi (ground, road) идти́ (пойти́ pf) под укло́н; **to go for a ~** окуна́ться (окуну́ться pf)

diploma [dɪˈpləumə] n дипло́м

diplomacy [dɪˈpləuməsɪ] n диплома́тия

diplomat [ˈdɪpləmæt] n диплома́т; **~ic** [dɪpləˈmætɪk] adj (POL) дипломати́ческий; (tactful) дипломати́чный

dire [daɪər] adj (consequences) злове́щий; (poverty, situation) жу́ткий

direct [daɪˈrɛkt] adj прямо́й ♦ adv пря́мо ♦ vt (company, project etc) руководи́ть (impf) +instr; (play, film) ста́вить (поста́вить pf); **to ~ (towards или at)** (attention, remark) направля́ть (напра́вить pf) (на +acc); **to ~ sb to do** (order) веле́ть (impf) кому́-н +infin; **can you ~ me to ...?** Вы не ука́жете, где нахо́дится ...?; **~ debit** n (BRIT: COMM) прямо́е дебети́рование; **~ion** [dɪˈrɛkʃən] n (way) направле́ние; **~ions** npl (instructions) указа́ния ntpl; **to have a good sense of ~ion** хорошо́ ориенти́роваться (pf);

~ions for use инстру́кция; ~ly
[dɪ'rɛktlɪ] adv пря́мо; (at once)
сейча́с же; (as soon as)
то́лько; ~or [dɪ'rɛktər] n (COMM)
дире́ктор; (of project)
руководи́тель m; (TV, CINEMA)
режиссёр; (of play) диспетчер m
спра́вочник

dirt [dəːt] n грязь f; ~y adj гря́зный
♦ vt па́чкать (испа́чкать pf)

disability [dɪsə'bɪlɪtɪ] n (physical) –
инвали́дность f no pl; mental ~
у́мственная неполноце́нность f

disabled [dɪs'eɪbld] adj (mentally)
у́мственно неполноце́нный;
(physically): ~ person инвали́д
♦ npl: the ~ инвали́ды mpl

disadvantage [dɪsəd'vɑːntɪdʒ] n
недоста́ток

disagree [dɪsə'griː] vi (differ)
расходи́ться (разойти́сь pf); to ~
(with) (oppose) не соглаша́ться
(согласи́ться pf) (с +instr); I ~ with
you я с Ва́ми не согла́сен;
~ment n разногла́сие;
(opposition): ~ment with
несогла́сие с +instr

disappear [dɪsə'pɪər] vi исчеза́ть
(исче́знуть pf); ~ance n
исчезнове́ние

disappoint [dɪsə'pɔɪnt] vt
разочаро́вывать (разочарова́ть
pf); ~ed adj разочаро́ванный;
~ing adj: the film is rather ~ing
э́тот фильм не́сколько
разочаро́вывает; ~ment n
разочарова́ние

disapproval [dɪsə'pruːvəl] n
неодобре́ние

disapprove [dɪsə'pruːv] vi: to ~ (of)
не одобря́ть (impf) (+acc)

disarm [dɪs'ɑːm] vt (MIL)
разоружа́ть (разоружи́ть pf);
~ament n разоруже́ние

disarray [dɪsə'reɪ] n: in ~ в
смяте́нии; (hair, clothes) в

беспоря́дке

disaster [dɪ'zɑːstər] n (natural)
бе́дствие; (man-made, also fig)
катастро́фа

disastrous [dɪ'zɑːstrəs] adj
губи́тельный

disband [dɪs'bænd] vt распуска́ть
(распусти́ть pf) ♦ vi
расформиро́вываться
(расформирова́ться pf)

disbelief [dɪsbə'liːf] n неве́рие

disc [dɪsk] n (ANAT)
межпозвоно́чный хрящ;
(COMPUT) = **disk**

discard [dɪs'kɑːd] vt (object)
выбра́сывать (вы́бросить pf);
(idea, plan) отбра́сывать
(отбро́сить pf)

discern [dɪ'səːn] vt (see) различа́ть
(различи́ть pf); (identify)
определя́ть (определи́ть pf);
~ing adj разбо́рчивый

discharge [dɪs'tʃɑːdʒ] vt (waste)
выбра́сывать (вы́бросить pf);
(patient) выпи́сывать (вы́писать pf);
(employee) увольня́ть (уво́лить
pf); (soldier) демобилизова́ть
(impf/pf) ♦ n [dɪstʃɑːdʒ] (MED)
выделе́ние; (of
patient) вы́писка; (of employee)
увольне́ние; (of soldier)
демобилиза́ция

disciple [dɪ'saɪpl] n (REL) апо́стол;
(fig) учени́к(и́ца)

discipline ['dɪsɪplɪn] n дисципли́на
♦ vt дисциплини́ровать (impf/pf);
(punish) налага́ть (наложи́ть pf)
дисциплина́рное взыска́ние на
+acc

disclose [dɪs'kləuz] vt раскрыва́ть
(раскры́ть pf)

disclosure [dɪs'kləuʒər] n
раскры́тие

disco ['dɪskəu] n abbr (= discotheque)
дискоте́ка

discomfort [dɪs'kʌmfət] n (unease)

нело́вкость f; (pain) недомога́ние

discontent [dɪskən'tɛnt] n недово́льство

discord ['dɪskɔːd] n разла́д

discount n ['dɪskaʊnt] vb [dɪs'kaʊnt] n ски́дка ♦ vt (COMM) снижа́ть (сни́зить pf) це́ну на +acc; (idea, fact) не принима́ть (приня́ть pf) в расчёт

discourage [dɪs'kʌrɪdʒ] vt (dishearten) препя́тствовать (воспрепя́тствовать pf); **to ~ sb from doing** отгова́ривать (отговори́ть pf) кого́-н +infin

discover [dɪs'kʌvə*] vt обнару́живать (обнару́жить pf); **~y** n откры́тие

discredit [dɪs'krɛdɪt] vt дискредити́ровать (impf/pf)

discreet [dɪs'kriːt] adj (tactful) такти́чный; (careful) осмотри́тельный; (barely noticeable) неприме́тный

discrepancy [dɪs'krɛpənsɪ] n расхожде́ние

discretion [dɪs'krɛʃən] n (tact) такти́чность f; **use your (own) ~** поступа́йте по своему́ усмотре́нию

discriminate [dɪs'krɪmɪneɪt] vi: **to ~ between** различа́ть (различи́ть pf); **to ~ against** дискримини́ровать (impf/pf)

discrimination [dɪskrɪmɪ'neɪʃən] n (bias) дискримина́ция; (discernment) разбо́рчивость f

discuss [dɪs'kʌs] vt обсужда́ть (обсуди́ть pf); **~ion** [dɪs'kʌʃən] n (talk) обсужде́ние; (debate) диску́ссия

disdain [dɪs'deɪn] n презре́ние

disease [dɪ'ziːz] n боле́знь f

disgrace [dɪs'greɪs] n позо́р ♦ vt позо́рить (опозо́рить pf); **~ful** adj позо́рный

disgruntled [dɪs'grʌntld] adj

недово́льный

disguise [dɪs'ɡaɪz] n маскиро́вка ♦ vt (object) маскирова́ть (замаскирова́ть pf); **to ~** (as) (dress up) переодева́ть (переоде́ть pf) (+instr); (make up) гримирова́ть (загримирова́ть pf) (под +acc); **in ~** (person) переоде́тый

disgust [dɪs'ɡʌst] n отвраще́ние ♦ vt внуша́ть (внуши́ть pf) отвраще́ние +dat; **~ing** adj отврати́тельный

dish [dɪʃ] n блю́до; **to do** or **wash the ~es** мыть (вы́мыть pf) посу́ду

dishevelled [dɪ'ʃɛvəld] (US **disheveled**) adj растрёпанный

dishonest [dɪs'ɔnɪst] adj нече́стный; **~y** n нече́стность f

dishwasher ['dɪʃwɔʃə*] n посудомо́ечная маши́на

disillusion [dɪsɪ'luːʒən] vt разочаро́вывать (разочарова́ть pf)

disinfectant [dɪsɪn'fɛktənt] n дезинфици́рующее сре́дство

disintegrate [dɪs'ɪntɪɡreɪt] vi (break up) распада́ться (распа́сться pf)

disinterested [dɪs'ɪntrɪstɪd] adj (impartial) бескоры́стный

disk [dɪsk] n диск

dislike [dɪs'laɪk] n (feeling) неприя́знь f ♦ vt не люби́ть (impf); **I ~ the idea** мне не нра́вится э́та иде́я; **he ~s cooking** он не лю́бит гото́вить

dislodge [dɪs'lɔdʒ] vt смеща́ть (смести́ть pf)

dismal ['dɪzml] adj уны́лый, мра́чный; (failure, performance) жа́лкий

dismantle [dɪs'mæntl] vt разбира́ть (разобра́ть pf)

dismay [dɪs'meɪ] n трево́га, смяте́ние ♦ vt приводи́ть (привести́ pf) в смяте́ние

dismiss [dɪs'mɪs] vt (worker)
увольня́ть (уво́лить pf); (pupils,
soldiers) распуска́ть (распусти́ть
pf); (LAW) прекраща́ть
(прекрати́ть pf); (possibility, idea)
отбра́сывать (отбро́сить pf); **~al**
n (sacking) увольне́ние

disobedience [dɪsə'biːdɪəns] n
непослуша́ние

disorder [dɪs'ɔːdə'] n беспоря́док;
(MED) расстро́йство; **civil** ~
социа́льные беспоря́дки

dispatch [dɪs'pætʃ] vt (send)
отправля́ть (отпра́вить pf) ♦ n
(sending) отпра́вка; (PRESS)
сообще́ние; (MIL) донесе́ние

dispel [dɪs'pɛl] vt рассе́ивать
(рассе́ять pf)

dispense [dɪs'pɛns] vt (medicines)
приготовля́ть (пригото́вить pf);
~ **with** vt fus обходи́ться
(обойти́сь pf) без +gen; **~r** n
торго́вый автома́т

disperse [dɪs'pəːs] vt (objects)
рассе́ивать (рассе́ять pf); (crowd)
разгоня́ть (разогна́ть pf) ♦ vi
рассе́иваться (рассе́яться pf)

display [dɪs'pleɪ] n демонстра́ция;
(exhibition) вы́ставка ♦ vt (emotion,
quality) выка́зывать (вы́казать pf);
(goods, exhibits) выставля́ть
(вы́ставить pf)

displeasure [dɪs'plɛʒə'] n
неудово́льствие

disposable [dɪs'pəuzəbl] adj
однора́зовый

disposal [dɪs'pəuzl] n (of goods)
реализа́ция; (of rubbish)
удале́ние; **to have sth at one's** ~
располага́ть (impf) чем-н

dispose [dɪs'pəuz] vi: ~ **of**
избавля́ться (изба́виться pf) от
+gen; (problem, task) справля́ться
(спра́виться pf) c +instr

disposed [dɪs'pəuzd] adj: **to be well
~ towards sb** хорошо́ относи́ться

(impf) к кому́-н

disposition [dɪspə'zɪʃən] n (nature)
нрав

disproportionate [dɪsprə'pɔːʃənət]
adj (excessive) неопра́вданно
большо́й; ~ **to** несоизмери́мый с
+instr

dispute [dɪs'pjuːt] n спор;
(domestic) ссо́ра; (LAW) тя́жба ♦ vt
оспа́ривать (оспо́рить pf)

disregard [dɪsrɪ'gɑːd] vt
пренебрега́ть (пренебре́чь pf)

disrupt [dɪs'rʌpt] vt наруша́ть
(нару́шить pf); **~ion** [dɪs'rʌpʃən] n
(interruption) наруше́ние

dissatisfaction [dɪssætɪs'fækʃən] n
неудовлетворённость f,
недово́льство

dissatisfied [dɪs'sætɪsfaɪd] adj
неудовлетворённый; ~ **(with)**
недово́льный (+instr)

dissent [dɪ'sɛnt] n инакомы́слие

dissident ['dɪsɪdnt] n дисиде́нт
♦ adj диссиде́нтский

dissolve [dɪ'zɔlv] vt (substance)
растворя́ть (раствори́ть pf);
(organization, parliament)
распуска́ть (распусти́ть pf);
(marriage) растяга́ть
(расто́ргнуть pf) ♦ vi
растворя́ться (раствори́ться pf);
to ~ in(to) tears залива́ться
(зали́ться pf) слеза́ми

dissuade [dɪ'sweɪd] vt: **to ~ sb
(from sth)** отгова́ривать
(отговори́ть pf) кого́-н (от
чего́-н)

distance ['dɪstns] n (in space)
расстоя́ние; (in sport) диста́нция;
(in time) отдалённость f; **in the ~**
вдалеке́, вдали́; **from a ~**
издалека́, и́здали

distant ['dɪstnt] adj (place, time)
далёкий; (relative) да́льний;
(manner) отчуждённый

distaste [dɪs'teɪst] n неприя́знь f,

~ful adj неприя́тный

distinct [dɪs'tɪŋkt] adj (clear)
отчётливый; (unmistakable)
определённый; (different): ~
(from) отли́чный (от +gen); **as** ~
from в отли́чие от +gen; **~ion**
[dɪs'tɪŋkʃən] n (difference) отли́чие;
(honour) честь f; (SCOL) ≈
"отли́чно"; **~ive** adj
своеобра́зный, характе́рный;
(feature) отличи́тельный

distinguish [dɪs'tɪŋgwɪʃ] vt
различа́ть (различи́ть pf); **to ~**
o.s. отлича́ться (отличи́ться pf);
~ed adj ви́дный; **~ing** adj (feature)
отличи́тельный

distort [dɪs'tɔːt] vt искажа́ть
(искази́ть pf); **~ion** [dɪs'tɔːʃən] n
искаже́ние

distract [dɪs'trækt] vt отвлека́ть
(отвле́чь pf); **~ed** adj (dreaming)
невнима́тельный; (anxious)
встрево́женный; **~ion**
[dɪs'trækʃən] n (diversion)
отвлече́ние; (amusement)
развлече́ние

distraught [dɪs'trɔːt] adj: ~ **(with)**
обезу́мевший (от +gen)

distress [dɪs'trɛs] n отча́яние;
(through suffering) страда́ние ♦ vt
расстра́ивать (расстро́ить pf);
приводи́ть (привести́ pf) в
отча́яние

distribute [dɪs'trɪbjuːt] vt (prizes)
раздава́ть (разда́ть pf); (leaflets)
распространя́ть
(распространи́ть pf); (profits,
weight) распределя́ть
(распредели́ть pf)

distribution [dɪstrɪ'bjuːʃən] n (of
goods) распростране́ние; (of
profits, weight) распределе́ние

distributor [dɪs'trɪbjutər] n (COMM)
дистрибью́тер

district ['dɪstrɪkt] n райо́н

distrust [dɪs'trʌst] n недове́рие

♦ vt не доверя́ть (impf) +dat

disturb [dɪs'tɜːb] vt (person)
беспоко́ить (побеспоко́ить pf);
(thoughts, peace) меша́ть
(помеша́ть pf) +dat; (disorganize)
наруша́ть (нару́шить pf); ~
расстро́йство; (violent event)
беспоря́дки mpl; **~ed** adj (person:
upset) расстро́енный; **emotionally**
~ed психи́чески
неуравнове́шенный; **~ing** adj
трево́жный

disused [dɪs'juːzd] adj
забро́шенный

ditch [dɪtʃ] n ров, кана́ва; (for
irrigation) кана́л ♦ vt (inf: person,
car) броса́ть (бро́сить pf); (: plan)
забра́сывать (забро́сить pf)

dive [daɪv] n (from board) прыжо́к
(в во́ду); (underwater) ныря́ние
♦ vi ныря́ть (impf); **to ~ into** (bag,
drawer etc) запуска́ть (запусти́ть
pf) ру́ку в +acc; (shop, car etc)
ныря́ть (нырну́ть pf) в +acc; **~r** n
водола́з

diverse [daɪ'vɜːs] adj
разнообра́зный

diversion [daɪ'vɜːʃən] n (BRIT : AUT)
объе́зд; (of attention, funds)
отвлече́ние

diversity [daɪ'vɜːsɪti] n
разнообра́зие, многообра́зие

divert [daɪ'vɜːt] vt (traffic) отводи́ть
(отвести́ pf); (funds, attention)
отвлека́ть (отвле́чь pf)

divide [dɪ'vaɪd] vt (split) разделя́ть
(раздели́ть pf); (MATH) дели́ть
(раздели́ть pf); (share out) дели́ть
(подели́ть pf) ♦ vi дели́ться
(раздели́ться pf); (road)
разделя́ться (раздели́ться pf);
~d highway n (US) автотра́сса

dividend ['dɪvɪdɛnd] n (COMM)
дивиде́нд; (fig): **to pay ~s**
приноси́ть (принести́ pf)
дивиде́нды

divine [dɪ'vaɪn] *adj* боже́ственный

diving ['daɪvɪŋ] *n* ныря́ние; прыжки́ *mpl* в во́ду; **~ board** *n* вы́шка (*для прыжко́в в во́ду*)

divinity [dɪ'vɪnɪtɪ] *n* (*SCOL*) богосло́вие

division [dɪ'vɪʒən] *n* (*also MATH*) деле́ние; (*sharing out*) разделе́ние; (*disagreement*) разногла́сие; (*COMM*) подразделе́ние; (*MIL*) диви́зия; (*SPORT*) ли́га

divorce [dɪ'vɔːs] *n* разво́д ♦ *vt* (*LAW*) развести́сь (*развести́ pf*) с +*instr*; **~d** *adj* разведённый; **~e** [dɪvɔː'siː] *n* разведённый(ая) *m(f) adj*

divulge [daɪ'vʌldʒ] *vt* разглаша́ть (разгласи́ть *pf*)

DIY *n abbr* (*BRIT*) (= *do-it-yourself*) сде́лай сам

dizzy ['dɪzɪ] *adj*: **~ turn** *or* **spell** при́ступ головокруже́ния

DJ *n abbr* (= *disc jockey*) диск-жоке́й

KEYWORD

---

do [duː] (*pt* **did**, *pp* **done**) *aux vb* **1** (*in negative constructions and questions*); **I don't understand** я не понима́ю; **she doesn't want it** она́ не хо́чет э́того; **didn't you know?** ра́зве Вы не зна́ли?; **what do you think?** что Вы ду́маете?

2 (*for emphasis*) действи́тельно; **she does look rather pale** она́ действи́тельно вы́глядит о́чень бле́дной; **oh do shut up!** да, замолчи́ же!

3 (*in polite expressions*) пожа́луйста; **do sit down** пожа́луйста, сади́тесь; **do take care!** пожа́луйста, береги́ себя́!

4 (*used to avoid repeating vb*): **she swims better than I do** она́ пла́вает лу́чше меня́ *or*, чем я; **do you read newspapers? - yes, I**

do/no, I don't Вы чита́ете газе́ты? - да(, чита́ю)/нет(, не чита́ю); **she lives in Glasgow - so do I** она́ живёт в Гла́зго - и я то́же; **he didn't like it and neither did we** ему́ э́то не понра́вилось, и нам то́же; **who made this mess? - I did** кто здесь насори́л? - я; **he asked me to help him and I did** он попроси́л меня́ помо́чь ему́, что я и сде́лал

5 (*in tag questions*) не так *or* пра́вда ли; **you like him, don't you?** он Вам нра́вится, не так *or* пра́вда ли?; **I don't know him, do I?** я его́ не зна́ю, не так *or* пра́вда ли?

♦ *vt* **1** де́лать (сде́лать *pf*); **what are you doing tonight?** что Вы де́лаете сего́дня ве́чером?; **I've got nothing to do** мне не́чего де́лать; **what can I do for you?** чем могу́ быть поле́зен?; **we're doing "Othello" at school** (*studying*) мы прохо́дим "Оте́лло" в шко́ле; (*performing*) мы ста́вим "Оте́лло" в шко́ле; **to do one's teeth** (почи́стить *pf*) зу́бы; **to do one's hair** причёсываться (причеса́ться *pf*); **to do the washing-up** (*BRIT*) мыть (помы́ть *pf*) посу́ду

2 (*AUT etc*): **the car was doing 100 (km/h)** маши́на шла со ско́ростью 100 км/ч; **we've done 200 km already** мы уже́ прое́хали 200 км; **he can do 100 km/h in that car** он мо́жет е́хать со ско́ростью 100 км/ч

♦ *vi* **1** (*act, behave*) де́лать (сде́лать *pf*); **do as I do** де́лайте, как я; **you did well to react so quickly** ты молоде́ц, что так бы́стро среаги́ровал

2 (*get on, fare*): **he's doing well/badly at school** он хорошо/плохо учится; **the firm is doing well** дела в фирме идут успешно; **how do you do?** очень приятно **3** (*be suitable*) подходить (подойти *pf*); **will it do?** это подойдёт? **4** (*be sufficient*) хватать (хватить *pf* +*gen*); **will ten pounds do?** десяти фунтов хватит?; **that'll do** этого достаточно; **that'll do!** (*in annoyance*) довольно!, хватит!; **to make do (with)** удовлетворяться (удовлетвориться *pf*) (+*instr*)

♦ *n* (*inf*): **we're having a bit of a do on Saturday** у нас будет вечеринка в субботу; **it was a formal do** это был официальный приём

do away with *vt fus* (*abolish*) покончить (*pf*) с +*instr*

do up *vt* (*laces*) завязывать (завязать *pf*); (*dress, buttons*) застёгивать (застегнуть *pf*); (*room, house*) ремонтировать (отремонтировать *pf*)

do with *vt fus*: **I could do with a drink** я бы выпил чего-нибудь; **I could do with some help** помощь мне бы не помешала; **what has it got to do with you?** какое это имеет к Вам отношение?; **I won't have anything to do with it** я не желаю иметь к этому никакого отношения; **it has to do with money** это касается денег

do without *vt fus* обходиться (обойтись *pf*) без +*gen*

docile ['dəusaɪl] *adj* кроткий
dock [dɒk] *n* (NAUT) скамья подсудимых; **~s** *npl* (NAUT) док *msg*, верфь *fsg*; **~yard**

n док, верфь *f*
doctor ['dɒktə*r*] *n* (MED) врач; (SCOL) доктор
doctrine ['dɒktrɪn] *n* доктрина
document ['dɒkjumənt] *n* документ; **~ary** [dɒkju'mɛntərɪ] *n* документальный фильм; **~ation** [dɒkjumən'teɪʃən] *n* документация
dodge [dɒdʒ] *vt* увёртываться (увернуться *pf*) от +*gen*
dodgy ['dɒdʒɪ] *adj* (*inf*): **~ character** подозрительный тип
does [dʌz] *vb see* **do**; **~n't** ['dʌznt] = **does not**
dog [dɒg] *n* собака ♦ *vt* преследовать (*impf*)
dogged ['dɒgɪd] *adj* упорный
dogma ['dɒgmə] *n* догма; **~tic** [dɒg'mætɪk] *adj* догматический
dole [dəul] *n* (BRIT) пособие по безработице; **to be on the ~** получать (*impf*) пособие по безработице
doll [dɒl] *n* (*also US*: *inf*) кукла
dollar ['dɒlə*r*] *n* доллар
dolphin ['dɒlfɪn] *n* дельфин
dome [dəum] *n* купол
domestic [də'mɛstɪk] *adj* домашний; (*trade, politics*) внутренний; (*happiness*) семейный
dominant ['dɒmɪnənt] *adj* (*share, role*) преобладающий, доминирующий; (*partner*) властный
dominate ['dɒmɪneɪt] *vt* доминировать (*impf*) над +*instr*
dominoes ['dɒmɪnəuz] *n* (*game*) домино *nt and sing*
donate [də'neɪt] *vt*: **to ~ (to)** жертовать (пожертвовать *pf*) (+*dat* или на +*acc*)
donation [də'neɪʃən] *n* пожертвование
done [dʌn] *pp of* **do**
donkey ['dɒŋkɪ] *n* осёл

donor ['dəunə*] n (MED) до́нор; (to charity) же́ртвователь(ница) m(f)

don't [dəunt] = **do not**

donut ['dəunʌt] n (US) = **doughnut**

doom [du:m] n рок ♦ vt: **the plan was ~ed to failure** план был обречён на прова́л

door [dɔ:*] n дверь f; ~**bell** n (дверно́й) звоно́к; ~ **handle** n дверна́я ру́чка; (of car) ру́чка две́ри; (of car) ру́чка две́ри; ~**mat** n полови́к; ~**step** n поро́г; ~**way** n дверно́й проём

dope [dəup] n (inf: drug) гаши́ш; (: person) приду́рок ♦ vt вводи́ть (ввести́ pf) нарко́тик +dat

dormitory ['dɔ:mɪtri] n о́бщая спа́льня; (US: building) общежи́тие

DOS [dɒs] n abbr (COMPUT: = disk operating system) ДОС, DOS

dosage ['dəusɪdʒ] n до́за

dose [dəus] n (of medicine) до́за

dossier ['dɒsɪeɪ] n досье́ nt ind

dot [dɒt] n то́чка; (speck) кра́пинка, пя́тнышко ♦ vt: ~**ted with** усе́янный +instr; **on the** ~ мину́та в мину́ту

double ['dʌbl] adj двойно́й ♦ adv: **to cost** ~ сто́ить (impf) вдво́е доро́же ♦ n двойни́к ♦ vt удва́ивать (удво́ить pf) ♦ vi (increase) удва́иваться (удво́иться pf); **at the** ~ бего́м; ~ **bass** n контраба́с; ~ **bed** n двуспа́льная крова́ть f; ~**-decker** n (also: ~-decker bus) двухэта́жный авто́бус; ~ **glazing** n (BRIT) двойны́е ра́мы fpl; ~ **room** n (in hotel) двухме́стный но́мер; ~**s** n (TENNIS) па́ры fpl

doubly ['dʌblɪ] adv вдвойне́

doubt [daut] n сомне́ние ♦ vt сомнева́ться (impf); (mistrust) сомнева́ться (impf) в +prp, не доверя́ть (impf) +dat; **I** ~ **whether** или **if she'll come** я сомнева́юсь,

что она́ придёт; ~**ful** adj сомни́тельный; ~**less** adv несомне́нно

dough [dəu] n (CULIN) те́сто; ~**nut** (US **donut**) n по́нчик

dove [dʌv] n го́лубь m

down [daun] n (feathers) пух ♦ adv (motion) вниз; (position) внизу́ ♦ prep (towards lower level) вниз с +gen или +dat; (along) (вдоль) по +dat ♦ vt (inf: drink) прогла́тывать (проглоти́ть pf); ~ **with the government!** доло́й прави́тельство!; ~**fall** n паде́ние; (from drinking etc) ги́бель f; ~**hill** adv (face, look) вниз; **to go** ~**hill** (person, business) идти́ (пойти́ pf) под го́ру; (road) идти́ (пойти́ pf) под укло́н; ~**pour** n ли́вень m; ~**right** adj я́вный; (refusal) по́лный ♦ adv соверше́нно;

Down's syndrome n синдро́м Да́уна; ~**stairs** adv (position) внизу́; (motion) вниз; ~**stream** adv вниз по тече́нию; ~**-to-earth** adj (person) просто́й; (solution) практи́чный; ~**town** adv (position) в це́нтре; (motion) в центр; ~**ward** adj напра́вленный вниз ♦ adv вниз; ~**ward trend** тенде́нция к пониже́нию; ~**wards** adv = **downward**

dozen ['dʌzn] n дю́жина; **a** ~ **books** дю́жина книг; ~**s of** деся́тки +gen

Dr abbr = **doctor**

drab [dræb] adj уны́лый

draft [drɑ:ft] n (first version) чернови́к; (US: MIL) призы́в ♦ vt набра́сывать (наброса́ть pf); (proposal) составля́ть (соста́вить pf); see also **draught**

drag [dræg] vt тащи́ть (impf); (lake, pond) проче́сывать (прочеса́ть pf) ♦ vi (time, event etc) тяну́ться (impf)

dragon ['drægn] n драко́н; **~fly** n
стрекоза́

drain [dreɪn] n водосто́к,
водоотво́д; (fig): ~ on (on
resources) уте́чка +gen; (on health,
energy) расхо́д +gen ♦ vt (land,
glass) осуша́ть (осуши́ть pf);
(vegetables) сли́вать (слить pf);
(wear out) утомля́ть (утоми́ть pf)
♦ vi (liquid) стека́ть (стечь pf);
~age ['dreɪnɪdʒ] n (system)
канализа́ция; (process) дрена́ж,
осуше́ние; **~ing board** (US
~board) n су́шка

drama ['drɑːmə] n (also fig) дра́ма;
~tic [drə'mætɪk] adj
драмати́ческий; (increase etc)
ре́зкий; (change) рази́тельный;
~tist n драмату́рг

drank [dræŋk] pt of **drink**

drastic ['dræstɪk] adj (measure)
реши́тельный; (change)
коренно́й

draught [drɑːft] (US **draft**) n (of air)
сквозня́к; **on** ~ (beer) бо́чковое;
~s n (BRIT) ша́шки pl

draw [drɔː] (pt drew, pp ~n) vt
(ART) рисова́ть (нарисова́ть pf);
(TECH) черти́ть (начерти́ть pf);
(pull: cart) тащи́ть (impf);
(: curtains) задёргивать
(задёрнуть pf); (gun, tooth)
вырыва́ть (вы́рвать pf); (attention)
привлека́ть (привле́чь pf);
(crowd) собира́ть (собра́ть pf);
(money) снима́ть (снять pf);
(wages) получа́ть (получи́ть pf)
♦ vi (SPORT) игра́ть (сыгра́ть pf) в
ничью́ ♦ n (SPORT) ничья́; (lottery)
лотере́я; **to ~ near**
приближа́ться (прибли́зиться
pf); ~ **up** vi (train, bus etc)
подъезжа́ть (подъе́хать pf) ♦ vt
(chair etc) придвига́ть
(придви́нуть pf); (document)
составля́ть (соста́вить pf); **~back**

n недоста́ток; **~er** n я́щик; **~ing**
n (picture) рису́нок; **~ing pin** n
(BRIT) (канцеля́рская) кно́пка;
~ing room n гости́ная f adj

drawl [drɔːl] n протя́жное
произноше́ние

drawn [drɔːn] pp of **draw**

dread [drɛd] n у́жас ♦ vt
страши́ться (impf) +gen; **~ful** adj
ужа́сный, стра́шный

dream [driːm] (pt, pp ~ed or ~t) n
сон; (ambition) мечта́ ♦ vt: **I must
have** ~**t it** мне э́то, наве́рное,
присни́лось ♦ vi ви́деть (impf)
сон; (wish) мечта́ть (impf); **~y**
adj (expression, person etc)
мечта́тельный

dreary ['drɪərɪ] adj тоскли́вый

dress [drɛs] n (frock) пла́тье; (no pl:
clothing) оде́жда ♦ vt одева́ть
(оде́ть pf); (wound) перевя́зывать
(перевяза́ть pf) ♦ vi одева́ться
(оде́ться pf); **to get ~ed**
одева́ться (оде́ться pf); ~ **up** vi
наряжа́ться (наряди́ться pf); **~er**
n (BRIT) буфе́т; (US: chest of
drawers) туале́тный сто́лик; **~ing**
n (MED) повя́зка; (CULIN)
запра́вка; **~ing gown** n (BRIT)
хала́т; **~ing room** n (THEAT)
(артисти́ческая) убо́рная f adj;
(SPORT) раздева́лка; **~ing table** n
туале́тный сто́лик

drew [druː] pt of **draw**

dried [draɪd] adj (fruit) сушёный;
(milk) сухо́й

drift [drɪft] n (of current) ско́рость f;
(of snow) зано́с, сугро́б;
(meaning) смысл ♦ vi
дрейфова́ть (impf); **snow had ~ed
over the road** доро́гу занесло́
сне́гом

drill [drɪl] n (drill bit) сверло́;
(machine) дрель f; (: for mining etc)
бура́в; (MIL) уче́ние ♦ vt (hole)
сверли́ть (просверли́ть pf) ♦ vi

(*for oil*) бури́ть (*impf*)

drink [drɪŋk] (*pt* **drank**, *pp* **drunk**) *n* напи́ток; (*alcohol*) (спиртно́й) напи́ток; (*sip*) глото́к ♦ *vt* пить (вы́пить *pf*) ♦ *vi* пить (*impf*); **to have a ~** попи́ть (*pf*); (*alcoholic*) вы́пить (*pf*); **I had a ~ of water** я вы́пил воды́; **~-driving** *n* вожде́ние в нетре́звом состоя́нии; **~er** *n* пью́щий(ая) *m(f) adj*; **~ing water** *n* питьева́я вода́

drip [drɪp] *n* ка́панье; (*one drip*) ка́пля; (*MED*) ка́пельница ♦ *vi* (*water, rain*) ка́пать (*impf*); **the tap is ~ping** кран течёт

drive [draɪv] (*pt* **drove**, *pp* **~n**) *n* (*journey*) пое́здка; (*also: ~way*) подъе́зд; (*energy*) напо́р; (*campaign*) кампа́ния; (*COMPUT*: *also: ~ disk ~*) дисково́д ♦ *vt* (*vehicle*) води́ть/вести́ (*impf*); (*motor, wheel*) приводи́ть (привести́ *pf*) в движе́ние ♦ *vi* води́ть (вести́ *pf*) (маши́ну); (*travel*) е́здить/е́хать (*impf*); **right-/left-hand ~** право-/левосторо́нее управле́ние; **to ~ sb to the airport** отвози́ть (отвезти́ *pf*) кого́-н в аэропо́рт; **to ~ sth into** (*nail, stake*) вбива́ть (вбить *pf*) что-н в +*acc*; **to ~ sb mad** своди́ть (свести́ *pf*) кого́-н с ума́; **~n** [drɪvn] *pp of* **drive**; **~r** *n* води́тель *m* (*в транзит*) маши́нист; **~r's license** *n* (*US*) (води́тельские) права́ *ntpl* ~way *n* подъе́зд

driving [ˈdraɪvɪŋ] *n* вожде́ние; **~ licence** *n* (*BRIT*) (води́тельские) права́ *ntpl*

drizzle [ˈdrɪzl] *n* и́зморось *f* ♦ *vi* мороси́ть (*impf*)

drone [drəʊn] *n* (*noise*) гуде́ние

drop [drɒp] *n* (*of water*) ка́пля; (*reduction*) паде́ние; (*fall: distance*)

расстоя́ние (*све́рху вниз*) ♦ *vt* (*object*) роня́ть (урони́ть *pf*); (*eyes*) опуска́ть (опусти́ть *pf*); (*voice, price*) понижа́ть (пони́зить *pf*); (*also: ~ off: passenger*) выса́живать (вы́садить *pf*) ♦ *vi* па́дать (упа́сть *pf*); (*wind*) стиха́ть (сти́хнуть *pf*); **~s** *npl* (*MED*) ка́пли *fpl*; **~ off** *vi* (*go to sleep*) засыпа́ть (засну́ть *pf*); **~ out** *vi* (*of game, deal*) выходи́ть (вы́йти *pf*) (*from society*) отщепе́нец(нка); **~pings** *npl* помёт *msg*

drought [draʊt] *n* за́суха

drove [drəʊv] *pt of* **drive**

drown [draʊn] *vt* топи́ть (утопи́ть *pf*); (*also: ~ out: sound*) заглуша́ть (заглуши́ть *pf*) ♦ *vi* тону́ть (утону́ть *pf*)

drug [drʌg] *n* (*MED*) лека́рство; (*narcotic*) нарко́тик ♦ *vt* (*person, animal*) вводи́ть (ввести́ *pf*) нарко́тик +*dat*; **to be on ~s** быть (*impf*) на нарко́тиках; **hard/soft ~s** си́льные/сла́бые нарко́тики

drugstore – апте́ка.
Америка́нские апте́ки сочета́ют в себе́ апте́ки и кафе́. В них продаю́т не то́лько лека́рства, но и космети́ческие това́ры, напи́тки и заку́ски.

drum [drʌm] *n* бараба́н; (*for oil*) бо́чка; **~s** *npl* (*kit*) уда́рные инструме́нты *mpl*; **~mer** *n* (*in rock group*) уда́рник

drunk [drʌŋk] *pp of* **drink** ♦ *adj* пья́ный ♦ *n* пья́ный(ая) *m(f) adj*; (*also: ~ard*) пья́ница *m/f*; **~en** *adj* пья́ный

dry [draɪ] *adj* сухо́й; (*lake, riverbed*) вы́сохший; (*humour*) сде́ржанный; (*lecture, subject*) ску́чный ♦ *vt* (*clothes, ground*) сушить (высушить pf); (surface) вытирать (вытереть pf); ♦ vi сохнуть (высохнуть pf); **~-cleaner's** n химчистка

DSS n abbr (BRIT: = Department of Social Security) Министерство социального обеспечения

dual ['djuəl] adj двойной; (function) двойственный; ♦ **carriageway** n (BRIT) автотрасса

dubious ['dju:bɪəs] adj сомнительный

Dublin ['dʌblɪn] n Дублин

duchess ['dʌtʃɪs] n герцогиня

duck [dʌk] n утка ♦ vi (also: ~ **down**) пригибаться (пригнуться pf)

due [dju:] adj (expected) предполагаемый; (attention, consideration) должный: **I am ~ £20** ♦ мне должны or полагается £20 ♦ n: **to give sb his** (or her) **~** отдавать (отдать pf) кому-н должное ♦ adv: **~ north** прямо на север; **~s** npl (for club etc) взносы mpl; **in ~ course** в своё время; **~ to** из-за +gen; **he is ~ to go** он должен идти

duel ['djuəl] n дуэль f

duet [dju:'et] n дуэт

dug [dʌg] pt, pp of **dig**

duke [dju:k] n герцог

dull [dʌl] adj (light, colour) тусклый, мрачный; (sound) глухой; (pain, wit) тупой; (event) скучный; ♦ vt (pain) притуплять (притупить pf)

duly ['dju:lɪ] adv (properly) должным образом; (on time) своевременно

dumb [dʌm] adj (mute) немой; (inf: pej: person) тупой; (: idea) дурацкий

dummy ['dʌmɪ] n (tailor's model) манекен; (BRIT: for baby) соска, пустышка ♦ adj (bullet) холостой

dump [dʌmp] n (also: **rubbish ~**)

свалка; (inf: pej: place) дыра ♦ vt (put down) сваливать (свалить pf), выбрасывать (выбросить pf); (car) бросать (бросить pf)

dung [dʌŋ] n навоз

dungarees [dʌŋgə'ri:z] npl комбинезон msg

duplicate n, adj ['dju:plɪkət] vb ['dju:plɪkeɪt] n дубликат, копия ♦ adj запасной ♦ vt копировать (скопировать pf); (repeat) дублировать (продублировать pf); **in ~** в двойном экземпляре

durable ['djuərəbl] adj прочный

duration [djuə'reɪʃən] n продолжительность f

during ['djuərɪŋ] prep (in the course of) во время +gen, в течение +gen; (from beginning to end) в течение +gen

dusk [dʌsk] n сумерки pl

dust [dʌst] n пыль f ♦ vt вытирать (вытереть pf) пыль с +gen; **to ~ with** (cake etc) посыпать (посыпать pf) +instr; **~bin** n (BRIT) мусорное ведро; **~y** adj пыльный

Dutch [dʌtʃ] adj голландский ♦ npl: **the ~** голландцы mpl; **they decided to go ~** (inf) они решили, что каждый будет платить за себя

duty ['dju:tɪ] n (responsibility) обязанность f; (obligation) долг; (tax) пошлина; **on ~** на дежурстве; **off ~** вне службы; **~-free** adj (drink etc) беспошлинный

duvet [du:'veɪ] n (BRIT) одеяло

dwarf [dwɔ:f] (pl **dwarves**) n карлик ♦ vt делать (сделать pf) крохотным; (achievement) умалять (умалить pf)

dwarves [dwɔ:vz] npl of **dwarf**

dwell [dwel] (pt, pp **dwelt**) vi проживать (impf); **~ on** vt fus задéрживаться (задержáться *pf*) на +*prp*

dye [daɪ] *n* красúтель *m*, крáска ♦ *vt* крáсить (покрáсить *pf*)

dying ['daɪɪŋ] *adj* (*person, animal*) умирáющий

dyke [daɪk] *n* (*BRIT: wall*) дáмба

dynamic [daɪ'næmɪk] *adj* (*leader, force*) динамúчный

dynamite ['daɪnəmaɪt] *n* динамúт

dynamo ['daɪnəməʊ] *n* (*ELEC*) динáмо-машúна

E, e

E [iː] *n* (*MUS*) ми *nt ind*

each [iːtʃ] *adj, pron* кáждый; ~ **other** друг дрýга; **they hate ~ other** онú ненавúдят друг дрýга; **they think about ~ other** онú дýмают друг о дрýге; **they have two books** ~ у кáждого из них по две кнúги

eager ['iːgə*r*] *adj* (*keen*) увлечённый; (*excited*) возбуждённый; **to be ~ for/to do** жáждать (*impf*) +*gen*/+*infin*

eagle ['iːgl] *n* орёл

ear [ɪə*r*] *n* (*ANAT*) ýхо; (*of corn*) кóлос; **~ache** *n* ушнáя боль *f*; **I have ~ache** у меня болúт ýхо

earl [əːl] *n* (*BRIT*) граф

earlier ['əːlɪə*r*] *adj* бóлее рáнний ♦ *adv* рáньше, ранéе

early ['əːlɪ] *adv* рáно ♦ *adj* рáнний; (*quick: reply*) незамедлúтельный; (*settlers*) пéрвый; ~ **in the morning** рáно ýтром; **to have an ~ night** рáно ложúться (лечь *pf*) спать; **in the ~ spring**, **in the spring** рáнней веснóй; **in the ~ 19th century**, ~ **in the 19th century** в начáле 19-го вéка; ~ **retirement** *n*: **to take ~ retirement** рáно уходúть (уйтú *pf*) на пéнсию

earn [əːn] *vt* (*salary*) зарабáтывать (заработáть *pf*); (*interest*) приносúть (принестú *pf*); (*praise*) заслýживать (заслужúть *pf*)

earnest ['əːnɪst] *adj* (*person, manner*) серьёзный; (*wish, desire*) úскренний; **in ~** всерьёз

earnings ['əːnɪŋz] *npl* зáработок *msg*

earring ['ɪərɪŋ] *n* серьгá

earth [əːθ] *n* земля; (*BRIT: ELEC*) заземлéние ♦ *vt* (*BRIT: ELEC*) заземлять (заземлúть *pf*); **Earth** (*planet*) Земля; **~enware** *n* керáмика; **~quake** *n* землетрясéние

ease [iːz] *n* лёгкость *f*; (*comfort*) покóй ♦ *vt* (*pain, problem*) облегчáть (облегчúть *pf*); (*tension*) ослаблять (осла́бить *pf*); **to ~ sth into** вставлять (вставить *pf*) что-н в +*acc*; **to ~ sth out of** вынимáть (вынуть *pf*) что-н из +*gen*; **to ~ o.s. into** опускáться (опустúться *pf*) в +*acc*; **at ~!** (*MIL*) вóльно!

easily ['iːzɪlɪ] *adv* (*see adj*) легкó; непринуждённо; (*without doubt*) несомнéнно

east [iːst] *n* востóк ♦ *adj* востóчный ♦ *adv* на востóк; **the East Восток**

Easter ['iːstə*r*] *n* Пáсха; ~ **egg** (*chocolate*) пасхáльное яйцó

eastern ['iːstən] *adj* востóчный

East Germany *n* (*formerly*) Восточная Германия

easy ['iːzɪ] *adj* лёгкий; (*manner*) непринуждённый ♦ *adv*: **to take it** *or* **things** ~ не напрягáться (*impf*); **~-going** *adj* (*person*) уживчивый, покладистый

eat [iːt] (*pt* **ate**, *pp* **~en**) *vt* есть (съесть *pf*) ♦ *vi* есть (*impf*)

ebony ['ebənɪ] *n* эбéновое *or* чёрное дéрево

EC n abbr (= European Community) EC

ECB n abbr = European Central Bank

eccentric [ɪkˈsɛntrɪk] adj эксцентри́чный

ecclesiastic(al) [ɪkliːziˈæstɪk(l)] adj духо́вный

echo [ˈɛkəʊ] (pl **~es**) n э́хо ♦ vt (repeat) вторя́ть (impf) +dat ♦ vi (sound) отдава́ться (отда́ться pf); **the room ~ed with her laughter** в ко́мнате раздава́лся её смех

eclipse [ɪˈklɪps] n затме́ние

ecological [iːkəˈlɒdʒɪkəl] adj экологи́ческий

ecology [ɪˈkɒlədʒɪ] n эколо́гия

economic [iːkəˈnɒmɪk] adj экономи́ческий; (profitable) рента́бельный; **~al** adj (financial) экономи́чный; (thrifty) эконо́мный; **~s** n (SCOL) эконо́мика

economist [ɪˈkɒnəmɪst] n экономи́ст

economy [ɪˈkɒnəmɪ] n эконо́мика, хозя́йство; (financial prudence) эконо́мия; **~ class** n (AVIAT) дешёвые посадочные места́

ecstasy [ˈɛkstəsɪ] n экста́з

ecstatic [ɛksˈtætɪk] adj восто́рженный

eczema [ˈɛksɪmə] n экзе́ма

edge [ɛdʒ] n край; (of knife etc) остриё ♦ vt (trim) окаймля́ть (окайми́ть pf); **on ~** (fig) нерво́зный; **to ~ away from** отходи́ть (отойти́ pf) бочко́м от +gen

edgy [ˈɛdʒɪ] adj нерво́зный

edible [ˈɛdɪbl] adj съедо́бный

Edinburgh [ˈɛdɪnbərə] n Эдинбу́рг

edit [ˈɛdɪt] vt редакти́ровать (отредакти́ровать pf); (broadcast, film) монти́ровать (смонти́ровать pf); **~ion** [ɪˈdɪʃən] n (of book) изда́ние; (of newspaper, programme) вы́пуск; **~or** n

реда́ктор; (PRESS, TV) обозрева́тель m; **~orial** [ɛdɪˈtɔːrɪəl] adj редакцио́нный ♦ n редакцио́нная f adj (статья́)

educate [ˈɛdjʊkeɪt] vt (teach) дава́ть (дать pf) образова́ние +dat; (instruct) просвеща́ть (просвети́ть pf)

education [ɛdjʊˈkeɪʃən] n (schooling) просвеще́ние, образова́ние; (teaching) обуче́ние; (knowledge) образова́ние; **~al** adj (institution) уче́бный; (staff) преподава́тельский; **~al policy** поли́тика в о́бласти просвеще́ния; **~al system** систе́ма образова́ния or просвеще́ния

EEC n abbr (= European Economic Community) ЕЭС

eel [iːl] n у́горь m

eerie [ˈɪərɪ] adj жу́ткий

effect [ɪˈfɛkt] n (result) эффе́кт; **to take ~** (drug) де́йствовать (поде́йствовать pf); (law) вступа́ть (вступи́ть pf) в си́лу; **in ~** в су́щности; **~ive** adj (successful) эффекти́вный; (actual) действи́тельный; **~ively** adv (successfully) эффекти́вно; (in reality) в су́щности, факти́чески; **~iveness** n эффекти́вность f

efficiency [ɪˈfɪʃənsɪ] n (see adj) эффекти́вность f; де́льность f

efficient [ɪˈfɪʃənt] adj эффекти́вный; (person) де́льный

effort [ˈɛfət] n уси́лие; (attempt) попы́тка; **~less** adj (achievement) лёгкий

e.g. adv abbr (for example: = exempli gratia) наприме́р

egg [ɛg] n яйцо́; **hard-boiled/soft-boiled ~** яйцо́ вкруту́ю/всмя́тку; **~ cup** n рю́мка для яйца́; **~plant** n (esp US) баклажа́н

ego ['i:gəʊ] n самолюбие

Egypt ['i:dʒɪpt] n Египет

eight [eɪt] n восемь; **~een**
восемнадцать; **~eenth** [eɪ'ti:nθ]
adj восемнадцатый; **~h** [eɪtθ]
восьмой; **~ieth** adj
восьмидесятый; **~y** n
восемьдесят

Eire ['eərə] n Эйре int nd

either ['aɪðər] adj (one or other)
любой (из двух); (both, each)
каждый ♦ adv также ♦ pron: ~ (of
them) любой (из них) ♦ conj: ~
yes or no либо да, либо нет; on
~ side на обеих сторонах; I don't
smoke - I don't ~ я не курю - я
тоже; I don't like ~ мне не
нравится ни тот, ни другой;
there was no sound from ~ of the
flats ни из одной из квартир не
доносилось ни звука

elaborate adj [ɪ'læbərɪt] vb
[ɪ'læbəreɪt] adj сложный ♦ vt
(expand) развивать (развить pf);
(refine) разрабатывать
(разработать pf) ♦ vi: to ~ on
(idea, plan) рассматривать
(рассмотреть pf) в деталях

elastic [ɪ'læstɪk] n резинка ♦ adj
(stretchy) эластичный

elated [ɪ'leɪtɪd] adj: to be ~
ликовать (impf)

elation [ɪ'leɪʃən] n ликование

elbow ['elbəʊ] n локоть m

elder ['eldər] adj старший ♦ n (tree)
бузина; (older person): ~s старшие
pl adj; **~ly** adj пожилой ♦ npl: the
~ly престарелые pl adj

eldest ['eldɪst] adj (самый)
старший ♦ n старший(ая) m(f) adj

elect [ɪ'lekt] vt избирать (избрать
pf) ♦ adj: the president ~
избранный президент; to ~ to
do предпочитать (предпочесть
pf) +infin; **~oral** adj
избирательный; **~orate** n: the

~orate электорат, избиратели
mpl

electric [ɪ'lektrɪk] adj
электрический; **~al** adj
электрический; ~ **blanket** n
одеяло-грелка; **~ian**
[ɪlek'trɪʃən] n
электромонтёр, электрик; **~ity**
[ɪlek'trɪsɪtɪ] n электричество

electronic [ɪlek'trɔnɪk] adj
электронный; **~s** n электроника
f

elegance ['elɪgəns] n элегантность
f

elegant ['elɪgənt] adj элегантный

element ['elɪmənt] n (also CHEM)
элемент; (of heater, kettle etc)
(электронагревательный)
элемент; **the ~s** npl стихия fsg;
he is in his ~ он в своей стихии;
~ary [elɪ'mentərɪ] adj
элементарный; (school, education)
начальный

elephant ['elɪfənt] n слон(иха)

elevation [elɪ'veɪʃən] n (height)
возвышенность f

elevator ['elɪveɪtər] n (US) лифт

eleven [ɪ'levn] n одиннадцать; **~th**
adj одиннадцатый

eligible ['elɪdʒəbl] adj (for marriage)
подходящий; to be ~ for
(qualified) иметь (impf) право на
+acc; (suitable) подходить
(подойти pf)

eliminate [ɪ'lɪmɪneɪt] vt исключать
(исключить pf); (team, contestant)
выбивать (выбить pf)

elimination [ɪlɪmɪ'neɪʃən] n (see vt)
исключение; устранение

élite [eɪ'li:t] n элита

elm [elm] n вяз

eloquent ['eləkwənt] adj
(description, person)
красноречивый; (speech) яркий

else [els] adv (other) ещё; **nothing ~**
больше ничего; **somewhere ~**
(be) где-нибудь ещё; (go) куда-
нибудь ещё; (come from) откуда-

нибудь ещё; **everywhere ~**
везде; **where ~?** (position) где
ещё?; (motion) куда ещё?;
everyone ~ все остальные;
nobody ~ spoke больше никто
не говорил; **or ~** ... а не то ...;
~where adv (be) в другом or
ином месте; (go) в другое or
иное место

elusive [ɪˈluːsɪv] adj неуловимый

e-mail [ˈiːmeɪl] n электронная
почта ♦ vt (message) посылать
(послать pf) по электронной
почте; **to ~ sb** писать (написать
pf) кому-н по электронной
почте; **~ address** адрес
электронной почты,
электронный адрес

emancipation [ɪmænsɪˈpeɪʃən] n
освобождение; (of women)
эмансипация

embankment [ɪmˈbæŋkmənt] n (of
road, railway) насыпь f; (of river)
набережная f adj

embargo [ɪmˈbɑːgəu] (pl **~es**) n
эмбарго nt ind

embark [ɪmˈbɑːk] vi: **to ~ on**
(journey) отправляться
(отправиться pf) в +acc; (task)
браться (взяться pf); (course of
action) предпринимать
(предпринять pf)

embarrass [ɪmˈbærəs] vt смущать
(смутить pf); (POL) ставить
(поставить pf) в
затруднительное положение;
~ed adj смущённый; **~ing** adj
(position) неловкий, неудобный;
~ment n (feeling) смущение;
(problem) затруднение

embassy [ˈembəsɪ] n посольство

embedded [ɪmˈbedɪd] adj (object)
вделанный

emblem [ˈembləm] n эмблема

embody [ɪmˈbɔdɪ] vt (incarnate)
воплощать (воплотить pf);

(include) содержать (impf) (в себе)

embrace [ɪmˈbreɪs] vt обнимать
(обнять pf); (include) охватывать
(охватить pf) ♦ vi обниматься
(impf)

embroidery n (stitching) вышивка;
(activity) вышивание

embryo [ˈembrɪəu] n (BIO) эмбрион

emerald [ˈemərəld] n изумруд

emerge [ɪˈmɜːdʒ] vi (fact)
всплывать (всплыть pf); (industry,
society) появляться (появиться
pf); **to ~ from** (from room,
imprisonment) выходить (выйти
pf) из +gen

emergency [ɪˈmɜːdʒənsɪ] n
экстремальная ситуация; **in an ~**
в экстремальной ситуации; **state
of ~** чрезвычайное положение; **~
talks** экстренные переговоры; **~
exit** n аварийный выход

emigrate [ˈemɪgreɪt] vi
эмигрировать (impf/pf)

emigration [emɪˈgreɪʃən] n
эмиграция

eminent [ˈemɪnənt] adj видный,
знатный

emission [ɪˈmɪʃən] n (of gas)
выброс; (of radiation) излучение

emotion [ɪˈməuʃən] n (feeling)
чувство; **~al** adj эмоциональный;
(issue) волнующий

emotive [ɪˈməutɪv] adj волнующий

emphasis [ˈemfəsɪs] (pl **emphases**)
n значение; (in speaking)
ударение, акцент

emphasize [ˈemfəsaɪz] vt
подчёркивать (подчеркнуть pf)

emphatic [ɪmˈfætɪk] adj (statement,
denial) категорический,
решительный; (person) твёрдый,
категоричный; **~ally** adv
категорически; (certainly)
решительно

empire [ˈempaɪəʳ] n империя

empirical [emˈpɪrɪkl] adj

эмпири́ческий

employ [ɪm'plɔɪ] vt нанима́ть
(наня́ть pf); (tool, weapon)
применя́ть (примени́ть pf); **~ee**
[ɪmplɔɪ'iː] n рабо́тник; **~er** n
работода́тель m; **~ment** n
рабо́та; (availability of jobs)
за́нятость f

emptiness ['ɛmptɪnɪs] n пустота́

empty ['ɛmptɪ] adj пусто́й ♦ vt
(container) опоражнивать
(опорожни́ть pf); (place, house etc)
опустоша́ть (опустоши́ть pf) ♦ vi
(house) пусте́ть (опусте́ть pf);
~-handed adj с пусты́ми рука́ми

EMU n abbr = economic and
monetary union

emulate ['ɛmjuleɪt] vt подража́ть
(impf) +dat

emulsion [ɪ'mʌlʃən] n (also: ~
paint) эму́льсия, эмульсио́нная
кра́ска

enable [ɪ'neɪbl] vt (make possible)
спосо́бствовать (impf) +dat; **to ~**
sb to do (allow) дава́ть (дать pf)
возмо́жность кому́-н +infin

enact [ɪ'nækt] vt (play)
разы́грывать (разыгра́ть pf)

enamel [ɪ'næməl] n эма́ль f

enchanting [ɪn'tʃɑːntɪŋ] adj
обворожи́тельный

encl. abbr (on letters etc: = enclosed,
enclosure) приложе́ние

enclose [ɪn'kləuz] vt (land, space)
огора́живать (огороди́ть pf);
(object) заключа́ть (заключи́ть pf);
to ~ (with) (letter) прилага́ть
(приложи́ть pf) (к +dat); **please**
find ~d a cheque for £100 здесь
прилага́ется чек на £100

enclosure [ɪn'kləuʒəʳ] n
огоро́женное ме́сто

encompass [ɪn'kʌmpəs] vt (include)
охва́тывать (охвати́ть pf)

encore [ɔŋ'kɔːʳ] excl бис ♦ n: **as an**
~ на бис

encounter [ɪn'kauntəʳ] n встре́ча
♦ vt встреча́ться (встре́титься pf)
с +instr; (problem) ста́лкиваться
(столкну́ться pf) с +instr

encourage [ɪn'kʌrɪdʒ] vt поощря́ть
(поощри́ть pf); (growth)
спосо́бствовать (impf) +dat; **to ~**
sb to do убежда́ть (impf) кого́-н
+infin; **~ment** n (see vb)
поощре́ние; подде́ржка

encyclop(a)edia [ensaɪkləu'piːdɪə] n
энциклопе́дия

end [end] n коне́ц; (aim) цель f ♦ vt
(also: **bring to an~, put an ~ to**)
класть (положи́ть pf) коне́ц +dat,
прекраща́ть (прекрати́ть pf) ♦ vi
(situation, activity, period)
конча́ться (ко́нчиться pf); **in the**
~ в конце́ концо́в; **on ~** (object)
стоймя́; **for hours on ~** часа́ми; **~**
up vi: **to ~ up in** (place)
ока́зываться (оказа́ться pf) в
+prp; (in prison) угожда́ть
(угоди́ть pf) в +prp; **we ~ed up**
taking a taxi в конце́ концо́в мы
взя́ли такси́

endanger [ɪn'deɪndʒəʳ] vt
подверга́ть (подве́ргнуть pf)
опа́сности; **an ~ed species**
вымира́ющий вид

endearing [ɪn'dɪərɪŋ] adj (smile)
покоря́ющий; (person, behaviour)
располага́ющий

endeavour [ɪn'dɛvəʳ] (US
endeavor) n (attempt) попы́тка

ending ['endɪŋ] n (of book etc)
коне́ц

endless ['endlɪs] adj бесконе́чный;
(forest, beach) бескра́йний

endorse [ɪn'dɔːs] vt (cheque)
распи́сываться (расписа́ться pf)
на +prp; (document) де́лать
(сде́лать pf) отме́тку на +prp;
(proposal, candidate)
подде́рживать (поддержа́ть pf);
~ment n (approval) подде́ржка;

(BRIT : AUT) отме́тка

endurance [ɪn'djʊərəns] n
вы́носливость f

endure [ɪn'djʊər] vt переноси́ть
(перенести́ pf) ♦ vi вы́стоять (pf)

enemy ['ɛnəmɪ] adj вра́жеский,
неприя́тельский ♦ n враг;
(opponent) проти́вник

energetic [ɛnə'dʒɛtɪk] adj
энерги́чный

energy ['ɛnədʒɪ] n эне́ргия

enforce [ɪn'fɔ:s] vt (law) следи́ть
(impf) или проследи́ть (pf) за
соблюде́нием +gen

engage [ɪn'geɪdʒ] vt (attention,
interest) привлека́ть (привле́чь
pf); (person) нанима́ть (наня́ть pf)
♦ vi: **to ~ in** занима́ться (заня́ться
pf) +instr; **~d** adj (couple)
обручённый; (BRIT: busy): **the line
is ~d** ли́ния занята́; **he is ~d** to
он обручён с +instr; **to get ~d**
обруча́ться (обручи́ться pf); **~d
tone** n (BRIT : TEL) гудки́ pl
"за́нято"; **~ment** n (appointment)
договорённость f; (to marry)
обруче́ние; **~ment ring** n
обруча́льное кольцо́

engine ['ɛndʒɪn] n (AUT) дви́гатель
m, мото́р; (RAIL) локомоти́в

engineer [ɛndʒɪ'nɪər] n (designer)
инжене́р; (for repairs) меха́ник;
(US : RAIL) машини́ст; **~ing** n
(SCOL) инжене́рное де́ло; (design)
техни́ческий диза́йн

England ['ɪŋglənd] n А́нглия

English ['ɪŋglɪʃ] adj англи́йский ♦ n
(LING) англи́йский язы́к; **the ~** npl
(people) англича́не mpl; **~man**
(irreg) n англича́нин

enhance [ɪn'hɑ:ns] vt (enjoyment,
beauty) уси́ливать (уси́лить pf);
(reputation) повыша́ть (повы́сить
pf)

enigmatic [ɛnɪg'mætɪk] adj
зага́дочный

enjoy [ɪn'dʒɔɪ] vt люби́ть (impf);
(have benefit of) облада́ть (impf)
+instr; **to ~ o.s.** хорошо́
проводи́ть (провести́ pf) вре́мя;
to ~ doing люби́ть (impf) +infin;
~able adj прия́тный; **~ment** n
удово́льствие

enlarge [ɪn'lɑ:dʒ] vt увели́чивать
(увели́чить pf) ♦ vi: **to ~ on**
распространя́ться (impf) о +prp;
~ment n (PHOT) увеличе́ние

enlightened [ɪn'laɪtnd] adj
просвещённый

enlist [ɪn'lɪst] vt (person) вербова́ть
(заверова́ть pf); (support)
заруча́ться (заручи́ться pf) +instr
♦ vi: **to ~ in** (MIL) вербова́ться
(заверова́ться pf) в +acc

enormous [ɪ'nɔ:məs] adj
грома́дный

enough [ɪ'nʌf] adj доста́точно
+gen ♦ pron доста́точно ♦ adv: **big
~** доста́точно большо́й; **I've had
~!** с меня́ хва́тит!;
have you got ~ work to do? у Вас
доста́точно рабо́ты?; **have you
had ~ to eat?** Вы нае́лись?;
that's~, thanks доста́точно,
спаси́бо; **I've had ~ of him** он
мне надое́л; **~! дово́льно!;
strangely** или **oddly ~** ... как э́то ни
стра́нно ...

enquire [ɪn'kwaɪər] vti = **inquire**

enrich [ɪn'rɪtʃ] vt обогаща́ть
(обогати́ть pf)

en route [ɔn'ru:t] adv (to place) по
пути́

ensure [ɪn'ʃʊər] vt обеспе́чивать
(обеспе́чить pf)

entail [ɪn'teɪl] vt влечь (повле́чь pf)
за собо́й

enter ['ɛntər] vt (room, building)
входи́ть (войти́ pf) в +acc;
(university, college) поступа́ть
(поступи́ть pf) в +acc; (club,
profession, contest) вступа́ть

(вступи́ть pf) в +acc; (in book)
заноси́ть (занести́ pf); (COMPUT)
вводи́ть (ввести́ pf) ♦ vi входи́ть
(войти́ pf) в +acc; ~ **to** ~ **sb in** (competition)
запи́сывать (записа́ть pf) кого́-н
в +acc; ~ **into** (вступи́ть pf) в +acc

enterprise ['entəpraɪz] n (company,
undertaking) предприя́тие;
(initiative) предприи́мчивость f;
free/private ~ свобо́дное/ча́стное
предпринима́тельство

enterprising ['entəpraɪzɪŋ] adj
(person) предприи́мчивый;
(scheme) предпринима́тельский

entertain [entə'teɪn] vt (amuse)
развлека́ть (развле́чь pf); (play
host to) принима́ть (приня́ть pf);
(idea) разду́мывать (impf) над
+instr; ~**er** n эстра́дный арти́ст;
~**ing** adj занима́тельный,
развлека́тельный; ~**ment** n
развлече́ние; (show)
представле́ние

enthusiasm [ɪn'θu:zɪæzəm] n
энтузиа́зм

enthusiastic [ɪnθu:zɪ'æstɪk] adj:
~ **(about)** по́лный энтузиа́зма (по
по́воду +gen)

entice [ɪn'taɪs] vt соблазня́ть
(соблазни́ть pf); (to place)
зама́нивать (замани́ть pf)

entire [ɪn'taɪə'] adj весь; ~**ly** adv
по́лностью; (for emphasis)
соверше́нно

entitled adj: **to be** ~ **to sth/to do**
име́ть (impf) пра́во на что-н/+infin

entourage [ɔntu'rɑ:ʒ] n антура́ж,
окруже́ние

entrance n ['entrns] vb [ɪn'trɑ:ns] n
(way in) вход; (arrival) появле́ние
♦ vt обвора́живать (обворожи́ть
pf); **to gain** ~ **to** (university)
поступа́ть (поступи́ть pf) в +acc;
(profession) вступа́ть (вступи́ть pf)
в +acc; **to make an** ~ появля́ться

(появи́ться pf)

entrepreneur ['ɔntrəprə'nə:'] n
предпринима́тель(ница) m(f)

entry ['entrɪ] n (way in; in register,
accounts) вход; (in reference
book; arrival: in country)
въезд; **"no** ~**"** "нет вхо́да"; (AUT)
"нет въе́зда"; ~ **form** n зая́вка
на уча́стие

envelope ['envələup] n конве́рт

envious ['envɪəs] adj зави́стливый

environment [ɪn'vaɪərnmənt] n
среда́; **the** ~ окружа́ющая среда́;
~**al** [ɪnvaɪərn'mentl] adj
экологи́ческий

envisage [ɪn'vɪzɪdʒ] vt предви́деть
(impf)

envoy ['envɔɪ] n посла́нник

envy ['envɪ] n за́висть f ♦ vt
зави́довать (позави́довать pf)
+dat; **to** ~ **sb sth** зави́довать
(позави́довать pf) кому́-н из-за
чего́-н

epic ['epɪk] n эпопе́я; (poem)
эпи́ческая поэ́ма ♦ adj
эпоха́льный

epidemic [epɪ'demɪk] n эпиде́мия

epilepsy ['epɪlepsɪ] n эпиле́псия

episode ['epɪsəud] n эпизо́д

epitaph ['epɪtɑ:f] n эпита́фия

epoch ['i:pɔk] n эпо́ха

equal ['i:kwl] adj ра́вный; (intensity,
quality) одина́ковый ♦ n
ра́вный(ая) m(f) adj ♦ vt (number)
равня́ться (impf) +dat; **he is** ~ **to**
(task) ему́ по си́лам or по плечу́;
~**ity** [i:'kwɔlɪtɪ] n ра́венство,
равнопра́вие; ~**ly** adv
одина́ково; (share) по́ровну

equate [ɪ'kweɪt] vt: ~ **sth with**
sth, ~ **sth to sth** прира́внивать
(приравня́ть pf) что-н к чему́-н

equation [ɪ'kweɪʒən] n (MATH)
уравне́ние

equator [ɪ'kweɪtə'] n эква́тор

equilibrium [i:kwɪ'lɪbrɪəm] n

равновесие

equinox ['iːkwɪnɒks] n
равноденствие

equip [ɪ'kwɪp] vt: to ~ (with)
(person, army) снаряжать
(снарядить pf) (+instr); (room, car)
оборудовать (impf/pf) (+instr); to ~
sb for (prepare) готовить
(подготовить pf) кого-н к +dat;
~ment n оборудование

equivalent [ɪ'kwɪvələnt] n
эквивалент ♦ adj: ~ (to)
эквивалентный (+dat)

era ['ɪərə] n эра

eradicate [ɪ'rædɪkeɪt] vt
искоренять (искоренить pf)

erase [ɪ'reɪz] vt стирать (стереть
pf); ~r n резинка, ластик

erect [ɪ'rekt] adj (posture) прямой
♦ vt (build) воздвигать
(воздвигнуть pf), возводить
(возвести pf); (assemble) ставить
(поставить pf); ~ion n
(see vb) возведение; установка;
(PHYSIOL) эрекция

erosion [ɪ'rəʊʒən] n эрозия

erotic [ɪ'rɒtɪk] adj эротический

erratic [ɪ'rætɪk] adj (attempts)
беспорядочный; (behaviour)
сумасбродный

error ['erə] n ошибка

erupt [ɪ'rʌpt] vi (war, crisis)
разражаться (разразиться pf);
the volcano ~ed произошло
извержение вулкана; ~ion
[ɪ'rʌpʃən] n (of volcano)
извержение; (of fighting) взрыв

escalator ['eskəleɪtə] n эскалатор

escape [ɪs'keɪp] n (from prison)
побег; (from person) бегство; (of
gas) утечка ▷ vi убегать (убежать
pf); (from jail) бежать (impf/pf);
(leak) утекать (утечь pf) ♦ vt
(consequences etc) избегать
(избежать pf) +gen; **his name ~s
me** его имя выпало у меня из

памяти; **to ~ from** (place) сбегать
(сбежать pf) из/с +gen; (person)
сбегать (сбежать pf) от +gen; **he
~d with minor injuries** он
отделался лёгкими ушибами

escort [n 'eskɔːt; vb ɪs'kɔːt] n
сопровождение; (MIL, POLICE)
конвой; (: one person) конвоир
♦ vt сопровождать (сопроводить
pf)

especially [ɪs'peʃlɪ] adv особенно

espionage ['espɪənɑːʒ] n шпионаж

essay ['eseɪ] n (SCOL) сочинение

essence ['esns] n сущность f;
(CULIN) эссенция

essential [ɪ'senʃl] adj
обязательный, необходимый;
(basic) существенный ♦ n
необходимое nt adj; ~s (of subject)
основы; **it is ~ to ...** необходимо
+infin ...; ~ly adv в сущности

establish [ɪs'tæblɪʃ] vt (organization)
учреждать (учредить pf); (facts,
contact) устанавливать
(установить pf); (reputation)
утверждать (утвердить pf) за
собой; ~ed (business)
признанный; (custom, practice)
установившийся; ~ment n (see
vb) учреждение; установление;
утверждение; (shop etc)
заведение; **the Establishment**
истеблишмент

estate [ɪs'teɪt] n (land) поместье;
(BRIT: also: ~ housing) жилой
комплекс; ~ **agent** n (BRIT) агент
по продаже недвижимости,
риэлтор

esteem [ɪs'tiːm] n: **to hold sb in
high ~** относиться (impf) к кому-н
с большим почтением, чтить
(impf) кого-н

estimate [vb 'estɪmeɪt; n 'estɪmət] n
(reckon) предварительно
подсчитывать (подсчитать pf);
(: cost) оценивать (оценить pf)

♦ *n* (*calculation*) подсчёт; (*assessment*) оценка; (*builder's etc*) смета

estranged [ɪs'treɪndʒd] *adj* (*from spouse, family*) ставший чужим

estuary ['estjuəri] *n* устье

etc. *abbr* (= et cetera) и т.д.

eternal [ɪ'tɜːnl] *adj* вечный

eternity [ɪ'tɜːnɪtɪ] *n* вечность *f*

ethical ['eθɪkl] *adj* (*relating to ethics*) этический; (*morally right*) этичный

ethics ['eθɪks] *n, npl* этика *fsg*

Ethiopia [iːθɪ'əupɪə] *n* Эфиопия

ethnic ['eθnɪk] *adj* этнический

etiquette ['etɪket] *n* этикет

EU *n abbr* (= European Union) ЕС, Евросоюз

euphemism ['juːfəmɪzəm] *n* эвфемизм

euphoria [juː'fɔːrɪə] *n* эйфория

euro ['juərəu] *n* евро *m ind*

Europe ['juərəp] *n* Европа; **~an** [juərə'piːən] *adj* европейский; **~an Community** *n* Европейское сообщество; **~an Union** *n* Европейский Союз

euthanasia [juːθə'neɪzɪə] *n* эвтаназия

evacuate [ɪ'vækjueɪt] *vt* (*people*) эвакуировать (*impf/pf*); (*place*) освобождать (освободить *pf*)

evacuation [ɪvækju'eɪʃən] *n* (*see vb*) эвакуация; освобождение

evade [ɪ'veɪd] *vt* (*duties, question*) уклоняться (уклониться *pf*) от +*gen*; (*person*) избегать (*impf*) +*gen*

evaluate [ɪ'væljueɪt] *vt* оценивать (оценить *pf*)

evasion [ɪ'veɪʒən] *n* (*of responsibility, tax etc*) уклонение

evasive [ɪ'veɪsɪv] *adj* (*reply, action*) уклончивый

eve [iːv] *n*: **on the ~ of** накануне +*gen*

even ['iːvn] *adj* (*level, smooth*) ровный; (*equal*) равный;

(*number*) чётный ♦ *adv* даже; **~ if** даже если; **~ though** хотя даже; **~ more** ещё больше; (+*adj*) ещё более; **~ so** (и) всё же; **not ~** даже не; **I am ~ more likely to leave now** теперь ещё более вероятно, что я уеду; **to break ~** заканчивать (закончить *pf*) без убытка; **to get ~ with sb** (*inf*) расквитаться (*pf*) с кем-н

evening ['iːvnɪŋ] *n* вечер; **in the ~** вечером; **~ dress** *n* (*no pl: formal clothes*) вечерний туалет

event [ɪ'vent] *n* (*occurrence*) событие; (*SPORT*) вид (соревнования); **in the ~ of** в случае +*gen*

eventual [ɪ'ventʃuəl] *adj* конечный; **~ly** *adv* в конце концов

ever ['evə^r] *adv* (*always*) всегда; (*at any time*) когда-либо, когда-нибудь; **why ~ not?** почему же нет?; **the best ~** самый лучший; **have you ~ been to Russia?** Вы когда-нибудь были в России?; **better than ~** лучше, чем когда-либо; **~ since** с тех пор; **~ since our meeting** со дня нашей встречи; **~ since we met** с тех пор как мы встретились; **~ since that day** с того дня; **~-green** *adj* вечнозелёный

KEYWORD

every ['evri] *adj* **1** (*each*) каждый; (*all*) все; **every one of them** каждый из них; **every shop in the town was closed** все магазины города были закрыты
2 (*all possible*) всякий, всяческий; **we wish you every success** мы желаем Вам всяческих успехов; **I gave you every assistance** я помог Вам всем, чем только возможно; **I tried every option** я испробовал все варианты; **I**

have every confidence in him я в нём соверше́нно уве́рен; **he's every bit as clever as his brother** он столь же умён, как и его́ брат

3 (showing recurrence) ка́ждый; **every week** ка́ждую неде́лю; **every other car** ка́ждая втора́я маши́на; **she visits me every other/third day** она́ прихо́дит ко мне че́рез день/ка́ждые два дня; **every now and then** вре́мя от вре́мени

everybody ['evrɪbɒdɪ] pron (each) ка́ждый; (all) все pl
everyday ['evrɪdeɪ] adj (daily) ежедне́вный; (common) повседне́вный
everyone ['evrɪwʌn] pron = **everybody**
everything ['evrɪθɪŋ] pron всё
everywhere ['evrɪwɛə] adv везде́, повсю́ду
eviction [ɪ'vɪkʃən] n высе́ление
evidence ['evɪdns] n (proof) доказа́тельство; (testimony) показа́ния mpl; (indication) при́знаки mpl; **to give** ~ дава́ть (дать pf) (свиде́тельские) показа́ния
evident ['evɪdnt] adj очеви́дный; ~**ly** adv очеви́дно
evil ['iːvl] adj (person, spirit) злой; (influence) дурно́й; (system) ги́бельный ♦ n зло
evocative [ɪ'vɒkətɪv] adj навева́ющий чу́вства и воспомина́ния
evoke [ɪ'vəuk] vt вызыва́ть (вы́звать pf)
evolution [iːvə'luːʃən] n эволю́ция
evolve [ɪ'vɒlv] vi (animal, plant) эволюциони́ровать (impf/pf); (plan, idea) развива́ться (разви́ться pf)
ex- [eks] prefix (former) экс-,

бы́вший
exacerbate [eks'æsəbeɪt] vt усугубля́ть (усугуби́ть pf)
exact [ɪg'zækt] adj то́чный ♦ vt: **to ~ sth from** (payment) взы́скивать (взыска́ть pf) что-н +gen; ~**ing** adj (task) тру́дный; (person) взыска́тельный; ~**ly** adv то́чно
exaggerate [ɪg'zædʒəreɪt] vti преувели́чивать (преувели́чить pf)
exaggeration [ɪgzædʒə'reɪʃən] n преувеличе́ние
exam [ɪg'zæm] n abbr = **examination**
examination [ɪgzæmɪ'neɪʃən] n (inspection) изуче́ние; (consideration) рассмотре́ние; (SCOL) экза́мен; (MED) осмо́тр
examine [ɪg'zæmɪn] vt (scrutinize) рассма́тривать (рассмотре́ть pf), изуча́ть (изучи́ть pf); (inspect) осма́тривать (осмотре́ть pf); (SCOL) экзаменова́ть (проэкзаменова́ть pf); (MED) осма́тривать (осмотре́ть pf); ~**r** n (SCOL) экзамена́тор
example [ɪg'zɑːmpl] n приме́р; **for** ~ наприме́р
exasperation [ɪgzɑːspə'reɪʃən] n раздраже́ние
exceed [ɪk'siːd] vt превыша́ть (превы́сить pf); ~**ingly** adv весьма́, чрезвыча́йно
excel [ɪk'sel] vi: **to ~ (in** or **at)** отлича́ться (отличи́ться pf) (в +prp); ~**lence** ['eksələns] n (in sport, business) мастерство́; (superiority) превосхо́дство; **Excellency** ['eksələnsɪ] n: **His Excellency** его́ превосходи́тельство; ~**lent** ['eksələnt] adj отли́чный, превосхо́дный
except [ɪk'sept] prep (also: ~ **for**) кро́ме +gen ♦ vt: **to ~ sb (from)** исключа́ть (исключи́ть pf) кого́-н

(из +*gen*); ~ **if/when** кро́ме тех
слу́чаев, е́сли/когда́; ~ **that**
кро́ме того́, что; **~ion** [ɪkˈseʃən]
n исключе́ние; **to take ~ion to**
обижа́ться (оби́деться *pf*) на
+*acc*; **~ional** [ɪkˈsepʃənl] *adj*
исключи́тельный

excess [ɪkˈses] *n* избы́ток; ~
baggage *n* изли́шек багажа́;
~ive *adj* чрезме́рный

exchange [ɪksˈtʃeɪndʒ] *n* (*argument*)
перепа́лка ♦ *vt*: **to ~ (for)** (*goods
etc*) обме́нивать (обменя́ть *pf*)
(на +*acc*); **(of)** обме́н (+*instr*); ~
rate *n* (COMM) валю́тный *or*
обме́нный курс

Exchequer [ɪksˈtʃekə*r*] *n* (BRIT): **the
~ казначе́йство**

excise [ˈeksaɪz] *n* акци́з, акци́зный
сбор

excite [ɪkˈsaɪt] *vt* возбужда́ть
(возбуди́ть *pf*), волнова́ть
(взволнова́ть *pf*); **to get ~d**
возбужда́ться (возбуди́ться *pf*),
волнова́ться (взволнова́ться *pf*);
~ment *n* (*agitation*)
возбужде́ние; (*exhilaration*)
волне́ние

exciting [ɪkˈsaɪtɪŋ] *adj* (*news,
opportunity*) волну́ющий

exclude [ɪksˈkluːd] *vt* исключа́ть
(исключи́ть *pf*)

exclusion [ɪksˈkluːʒən] *n*
исключе́ние

exclusive [ɪksˈkluːsɪv] *adj* (*hotel,
interview*) эксклюзи́вный; (*use,
right*) исключи́тельный; **~ of**
исключа́я +*acc*; **~ly** *adv*
исключи́тельно

excruciating [ɪksˈkruːʃɪeɪtɪŋ] *adj*
мучи́тельный

excursion [ɪksˈkəːʃən] *n* экску́рсия

excuse *n* [ɪksˈkjuːs] *vb* [ɪksˈkjuːz]
оправда́ние ♦ *vt* (*justify*)
опра́вдывать (оправда́ть *pf*);
(*forgive*) проща́ть (прости́ть *pf*);

to make ~s for sb опра́вдываться
(*impf*) за кого́-н; **that's no** ~
не оправда́ние!; **to ~ sb from sth**
освобожда́ть (освободи́ть *pf*)
кого́-н от чего́-н; ~ **me!**
извини́те!, прости́те!; (*as
apology*) извини́те *or* прости́те
(меня́)!; **if you will ~ me, I have
to ...** с Ва́шего разреше́ния я
до́лжен ...

execute [ˈeksɪkjuːt] *vt* (*kill*) казни́ть
(*impf/pf*); (*carry out*) выполня́ть
(вы́полнить *pf*)

execution [eksɪˈkjuːʃən] *n* (*see vb*)
казнь *f*; выполне́ние

executive [ɪgˈzekjutɪv] *n* (*person*)
руководи́тель *m*; (*committee*)
исполни́тельный о́рган ♦ *adj*
(*board, role*) руководя́щий

exemplary [ɪgˈzempləri] *adj*
приме́рный

exempt [ɪgˈzempt] *adj*: ~ **from**
освобождённый от +*gen* ♦ *vt*: **to ~
sb from** освобожда́ть
(освободи́ть *pf*) кого́-н от +*gen*;
~ion [ɪgˈzempʃən] *n*
освобожде́ние

exercise [ˈeksəsaɪz] *n* (SPORT)
заря́дка, гимна́стика; (: *for legs,
stomach etc*) (физи́ческое)
упражне́ние; (*also* SCOL, MUS)
упражне́ние; ♦ *vt* (*patience*)
проявля́ть (прояви́ть *pf*);
(*authority, right*) применя́ть
(примени́ть *pf*); (*dog*)
выгу́ливать (*impf*) ♦ *vi* (*also*:
to take ~) упражня́ться
(*impf*); **military ~s** вое́нные
уче́ния; ~ **bike** *n* велосипе́д-
тренажёр

exert [ɪgˈzəːt] *vt* (*influence, pressure*)
ока́зывать (оказа́ть *pf*); (*authority*)
применя́ть (примени́ть *pf*); **to ~
o.s.** напряга́ться (напря́чься *pf*);
~ion [ɪgˈzəːʃən] *n* (*effort*) уси́лие

exhaust [ɪgˈzɔːst] *n* (*also*: ~ **pipe**)

exhibit 474 explain

выхлопная труба; (*fumes*)
выхлопные газы *mpl* ♦ *vt* (*person*)
изнурять (изнурить *pf*); (*money,
resources*) истощать (истощить
pf); (*topic*) исчерпывать
(исчерпать *pf*); ~**ed** *adj*
изнурённый, изможённый;
~**ion** [ɪɡˈzɔːstʃən] *n* изнеможение;
nervous ~ion нервное
истощение; ~**ive** *adj*
исчерпывающий

exhibit [ɪɡˈzɪbɪt] *n* экспонат ♦ *vt*
(*paintings*) экспонировать (*impf/
pf*), выставлять (выставить *pf*);
(*quality, emotion*) проявлять
(проявить *pf*); ~**ion** [eksɪˈbɪʃən] *n*
(*of paintings etc*) выставка

exhilarating [ɪɡˈzɪləreɪtɪŋ] *adj*
волнующий

exile [ˈeksaɪl] *n* (*banishment*)
ссылка, изгнание; (*person*)
ссыльный(ая) *m(f) adj*, изгнанник
♦ *vt* (*abroad*) высылать (выслать
pf)

exist [ɪɡˈzɪst] *vi* существовать
(*impf*); ~**ence** *n* существование;
~**ing** *adj* существующий

exit [ˈeksɪt] *n* (*way out*) выход; (*on
motorway*) выезд; (*departure*) уход

exodus [ˈeksədəs] *n* массовое
бегство, исход

exotic [ɪɡˈzɔtɪk] *adj* экзотический

expand [ɪksˈpænd] *vt* (*area, business,
influence*) расширять (расширить
pf) ♦ *vi* (*gas, metal, business*)
расширяться (расшириться *pf*)

expanse [ɪksˈpæns] *n*: **an ~ of sea/
sky** морской/небесный простор

expansion [ɪksˈpænʃən] *n*
расширение; (*of economy*) рост

expatriate [eksˈpætrɪət] *n*
эмигрант(ка)

expect [ɪksˈpekt] *vt* ожидать (*impf*);
(*baby*) ждать (*impf*); (*suppose*)
полагать (*impf*) ♦ *vi*: **to be ~ing** (*be
pregnant*) ждать (*impf*) ребёнка;

~**ancy** *n* предвкушение; **life**
~**ancy** продолжительность *f*
жизни; ~**ation** [ekspekˈteɪʃən] *n*
(*hope*) ожидание

expedient [ɪksˈpiːdɪənt] *adj*
целесообразный

expedition [ekspɪˈdɪʃən] *n*
экспедиция; (*for pleasure*) поход

expel [ɪksˈpel] *vt* (*from school etc*)
исключать (исключить *pf*); (*from
place*) изгонять (изгнать *pf*)

expenditure [ɪksˈpendɪtʃə*] *n*
(*money spent*) затраты *fpl*; (*of
energy, time, money*) затрата,
расход

expense [ɪksˈpens] *n* (*cost*)
стоимость *f*; ~**s** *npl* (*travelling etc
expenses*) расходы *mpl*;
(*expenditure*) затраты *fpl*; **at the ~
of** за счёт +*gen*

expensive [ɪksˈpensɪv] *adj* дорогой

experience [ɪksˈpɪərɪəns] *n* (*in job,
of situation*) опыт; (*event, activity*)
случай; (: *difficult, painful*)
испытание ♦ *vt* испытывать
(испытать *pf*), переживать
(пережить *pf*); ~**d** *adj* опытный

experiment [ɪksˈperɪmənt] *n*
эксперимент, опыт ♦ *vi*: **to ~
(with/on)** экспериментировать
(*impf*) (с +*instr*/на +*prp*); ~**al**
[ɪksperɪˈmentl] *adj* (*methods, tests*)
экспериментальный; (*tests*)
пробный

expert [ˈekspəːt] *n* эксперт,
специалист; ~ **opinion/advice**
мнение/совет эксперта *or*
специалиста; ~**ise** [ekspəːˈtiːz] *n*
знания *ntpl* и опыт

expire [ɪksˈpaɪə*] *vi* (*run out*)
истекать (истечь *pf*); **my passport
~s in January** срок действия
моего паспорта истекает в
январе

explain [ɪksˈpleɪn] *vt* объяснять
(объяснить *pf*)

explanation [eksplə'neɪʃən] n объяснение

explanatory [ɪks'plænətrɪ] adj объяснительный, пояснительный

explicit [ɪks'plɪsɪt] adj явный, очевидный; (sex, violence) откровенный

explode [ɪks'pləud] vi (bomb, person) взрываться (взорваться pf); (population) резко возрастать (возрасти pf)

exploit vb [ɪks'plɔɪt] n ['eksplɔɪt] vt эксплуатировать (impf); (opportunity) использовать (impf/ pf) ♦ n деяние; ~ation [eksplɔɪ'teɪʃən] (see vb) эксплуатация; использование

exploratory [ɪks'plɔrətrɪ] adj (expedition) исследовательский; (talks) предварительный

explore [ɪks'plɔ:r] vt (place) исследовать (impf/pf) (idea, suggestion) изучать (изучить pf); ~r n исследователь(ница) m(f)

explosion [ɪks'pləuʒən] n взрыв; **population ~** демографический взрыв

explosive [ɪks'pləusɪv] adj (device, effect) взрывной; (situation) взрывоопасный; (person) вспыльчивый ♦ n (substance) взрывчатое вещество; (device) взрывное устройство

exponent [ɪks'pəunənt] n (of idea, theory) поборник(ица)

export n, cpd ['ekspɔ:t] vb [eks'pɔ:t] n (process) экспорт, вывоз; (product) предмет экспорта ♦ vt экспортировать (impf/pf), вывозить (вывезти pf) ♦ cpd (duty, licence) экспортный

expose [ɪks'pəuz] vt (object) обнажать (обнажить pf); (truth, plot) раскрывать (раскрыть pf); (person) разоблачать

(разоблачить pf); **to ~ sb to sth** подвергать (подвергнуть pf) кого-н чему-н; **~d** adj (place): **~d (to)** открытый (+dat)

exposure [ɪks'pəuʒər] n (of culprit) разоблачение; (PHOT) выдержка, экспозиция; **to suffer from ~** (MED) страдать (пострадать pf) от переохлаждения

express [ɪks'pres] adj (clear) чёткий; (BRIT: service) срочный ♦ n экспресс ♦ vt выражать (выразить pf); ~**ion** [ɪks'preʃən] n выражение; ~**ive** adj выразительный

expulsion [ɪks'pʌlʃən] n (from school etc) исключение; (from place) изгнание

exquisite [ɪks'kwɪzɪt] adj (perfect) изысканный

extend [ɪks'tend] vt (visit, deadline) продлевать (продлить pf); (building) расширять (расширить pf); (hand) протягивать (протянуть pf); (welcome) оказывать (оказать pf) ♦ vi (land, road) простираться (impf); (period) продолжаться (продолжиться pf); **to ~ an invitation to sb** приглашать (пригласить pf) кого-н

extension [ɪks'tenʃən] n (of building) пристройка; (of time) продление; (ELEC) удлинитель m; (TEL, in house) параллельный телефон; (: in office) добавочный телефон

extensive [ɪks'tensɪv] adj обширный; (damage) значительный; **~ly** adv: **he has travelled ~ly** он много путешествовал

extent [ɪks'tent] n (of area etc) протяжённость f; (of problem etc) масштаб; **to some ~** до некоторой степени; **to go to the**

~ **of** ... доходи́ть (дойти́ pf) до
того́, что ...; **to such an** ~ **that** ...
до тако́й сте́пени, что ...

exterior [eks'tɪərɪə] adj нару́жный
♦ n (outside) вне́шняя сторона́

external [eks'tə:nl] adj вне́шний

extinct [ɪks'tɪŋkt] adj (animal)
вы́мерший; (plant) исче́знувший;
to become ~ (animal) вымира́ть
(вы́мереть pf); (plant) исчеза́ть
(исче́знуть pf); ~**ion** [ɪks'tɪŋkʃən] n
(of animal) вымира́ние; (of plant)
исчезнове́ние

extortion [ɪks'tɔ:ʃən] n
вымога́тельство

extortionate [ɪks'tɔ:ʃnɪt] adj (price)
граби́тельский; (demands)
вымога́тельский

extra ['ekstrə] adj (additional)
дополни́тельный; (spare) ли́шний
♦ adv (in addition) дополни́тельно;
(especially) осо́бенно ♦ n (luxury)
изли́шество; (surcharge) допла́та

extract vb [ɪks'trækt] n ['ekstrækt] vt
извлека́ть (извле́чь pf); (tooth)
удаля́ть (удали́ть pf); (mineral)
добыва́ть (добы́ть pf); (money,
promise) выта́гивать (вы́тянуть pf)
♦ n (from novel, recording)
отры́вок

extradition [ekstrə'dɪʃən] n вы́дача
(престу́пника)

extraordinary [ɪks'trɔ:dnrɪ] adj
незауря́дный, необыча́йный

extravagance [ɪks'trævəgəns] n
(with money) расточи́тельство

extravagant [ɪks'trævəgənt] adj
(lavish) экстравага́нтный;
(wasteful: person) расточи́тельный

extreme [ɪks'tri:m] adj кра́йний;
(situation) экстрема́льный; (heat,
cold) си́льне́йший ♦ n (of
behaviour) кра́йность f; ~**ly** adv
кра́йне

extrovert ['ekstrəvə:t] n экстрове́рт

exuberant [ɪg'zju:bərnt] adj (person,

behaviour) экспанси́вный

eye [aɪ] n (ANAT) глаз; (of needle)
у́шко ♦ vt разгля́дывать
(разгляде́ть pf); **to keep an** ~ **on**
(person, object) присма́тривать
(присмотре́ть pf) за +instr; (time)
следи́ть (impf) за +instr; ~**brow** n
бровь f; ~**lash** n ресни́ца; ~**lid** n
ве́ко; ~**liner** n каранда́ш для век;
~ **shadow** n те́ни fpl (для век);
~**sight** n зре́ние; ~**witness** n
очеви́дец

F, f

F [ef] n (MUS) фа

F abbr = **Fahrenheit**

fabric ['fæbrɪk] n (cloth) ткань
f

fabulous ['fæbjuləs] adj (inf)
ска́зочный; (extraordinary)
невероя́тный

façade [fə'sɑ:d] n фаса́д; (pretence)
види́мость f

face [feɪs] n (of person, organization)
лицо́; (of clock) цифербла́т; (of
mountain, cliff) склон ♦ vt (fact)
признава́ть (призна́ть pf); **the
house** ~**s the sea** дом обращён к
мо́рю; **he was facing the door** он
был обращён лицо́м к две́ри;
we are facing difficulties нам
предстоя́т тру́дности; ~ **down**
лицо́м вниз; **to lose/save** ~
теря́ть (потеря́ть pf)/спаса́ть
(спасти́ pf) репута́цию или лицо́; **to
make** or **pull a** ~ де́лать (сде́лать
pf) грима́су; **in the** ~ **of** (difficulties
etc) пе́ред лицо́м +gen; **on the** ~
of it на пе́рвый взгляд; ~ **to** ~
лицо́м к лицу́ (с +instr); ~
up to vt fus признава́ть
(призна́ть pf); (difficulties)
справля́ться (спра́виться pf) с
+instr; ~ **cloth** n (BRIT) махро́вая

салфетка (для лица); ~ **value** n номинальная стоимость f; **to take sth at** ~ **value** принимать (принять pf) что-н за чистую монету

facial ['feɪʃl] adj: ~ **expression** выражение лица; ~ **hair** волосы, растущие на лице

facilitate [fə'sɪlɪteɪt] vt способствовать (impf/pf) +dat

facilities [fə'sɪlɪtɪz] npl условия ntpl; (buildings) помещение ntsg; (equipment) оборудование ntsg; **cooking** ~ условия для приготовления пищи

facing ['feɪsɪŋ] prep напротив +gen

fact [fækt] n факт; **in** ~ фактически

faction ['fækʃən] n (group) фракция

factor ['fæktər] n (of problem) фактор

factory ['fæktərɪ] n (for textiles) фабрика; (for machinery) завод

factual ['fæktjuəl] adj фактический

faculty ['fækəltɪ] n способность f; (of university) факультет

fad [fæd] n причуда

fade [feɪd] vi (colour) выцветать (выцвести pf); (light, hope, smile) угасать (угаснуть pf); (sound) замирать (замереть pf); (memory) тускнеть (потускнеть pf)

fag [fæg] n (BRIT: inf) сигарета

Fahrenheit ['færənhaɪt] n Фаренгейт

fail [feɪl] vt (exam, candidate) проваливать (провалить pf); (subj: memory) изменять (изменить pf) +dat; (: person) подводить (подвести pf); (: courage) покидать (покинуть pf) ♦ vi (candidate, attempt) проваливаться (провалиться pf); (brakes) отказывать (отказать pf); **my eyesight/health is** ~**ing** у меня слабеет зрение/здоровье;

to ~ **to do** (be unable) не мочь (смочь pf) +infin; without ~ обязательно, непременно; ~**ing** n недостаток ♦ prep за неимением +gen; ~**ure** n провал, неудача; (TECH) авария, выход из строя; (person) неудачник(ица)

faint [feɪnt] adj слабый; (recollection) смутный; (mark) едва заметный ♦ vi (MED) падать (упасть pf) в обморок; **to feel** ~ чувствовать (почувствовать pf) слабость; ~**est** adj: **I haven't the** ~**est idea** я не имею ни малейшего понятия

fair [feər] adj (person, decision) справедливый; (size, number) изрядный; (chance, guess) хороший; (skin, hair) светлый; (weather) хороший, ясный ♦ n (also: **trade** ~) ярмарка; (BRIT: also: **fun**~) аттракционы mpl ♦ adv: **to play** ~ вести (impf) дела честно; ~**-ground** n ярмарочная площадь f; ~**ly** adv (justly) справедливо; (quite) довольно; ~ **play** n честная игра

fairy ['feərɪ] n фея; ~ **tale** n сказка

faith [feɪθ] n (also REL) вера; ~**ful** adj: ~**ful (to)** верный (+dat); ~**fully** adv верно

fake [feɪk] n (painting, document) подделка ♦ adj фальшивый, поддельный ♦ vt (forge) подделывать (подделать pf); (feign) симулировать (impf)

fall [fɔːl] (pt **fell**, pp ~**en**) n падение; (US: autumn) осень f ♦ vi падать (упасть pf); (government) пасть (pf); (rain, snow) падать (impf), выпадать (выпасть pf); ~**s** npl (waterfall) водопад msg; **a** ~ **of snow** снегопад; **to** ~ **flat** (plan) проваливаться (провалиться pf); **to** ~ **flat (on one's face)** падать (упа́сть pf) ничко́м; ~ **back on** vt fus прибега́ть (прибе́гнуть pf) к +dat; ~ **down** vi (person) па́дать (упа́сть pf); (building) ру́шиться (ру́хнуть pf); ~ **for** fus (trick, story) ве́рить (пове́рить pf) +dat; (person) влюбля́ться (влюби́ться pf) в +acc; ~ **in** vi (roof) обва́ливаться (обвали́ться pf); ~ **off** vi па́дать (упа́сть pf); (handle, button) отва́ливаться (отвали́ться pf); ~ **out** vi (hair, teeth) выпада́ть (вы́пасть pf); **to ~ out with sb** ссо́риться (поссо́риться pf) с кем-н

fallacy ['fæləsɪ] n заблужде́ние

fallen ['fɔːlən] pp of **fall**

false [fɔːls] adj (untrue, wrong) ло́жный; (insincere, artificial) фальши́вый; ~ **teeth** npl (BRIT) иску́сственные зу́бы mpl

fame [feɪm] n сла́ва

familiar [fə'mɪlɪə] adj (well-known) знако́мый; (intimate) дру́жеский; **he is ~ with** (subject) он знако́м с +instr

family ['fæmɪlɪ] n семья́; (children) де́ти pl

famine ['fæmɪn] n го́лод

famous ['feɪməs] adj знамени́тый

fan [fæn] n (folding) ве́ер; (ELEC) вентиля́тор; (of famous person) покло́нник(ица); (of sports team) боле́льщик(ица); (: inf) фан ♦ vt (face) обма́хивать (обмахну́ть pf); (fire) раздува́ть (разду́ть pf)

fanatic [fə'nætɪk] n (extremist) фана́тик

fanciful ['fænsɪful] adj причу́дливый

fan club n клуб покло́нников, фан-клу́б (разг)

fancy ['fænsɪ] n (whim) при́хоть f ♦ adj шика́рный ♦ vt (want) хоте́ть (захоте́ть pf); (imagine) вообража́ть (вообрази́ть pf); **to**

take a ~ to увлека́ться (увле́чься pf) +instr; **he fancies her** (inf) она́ ему́ нра́вится; ~ **that!** представля́ете!; ~ **dress** n маскара́дный костю́м

fanfare ['fænfeə] n фанфа́ра

fang [fæŋ] n (of wolf) клык

fantastic [fæn'tæstɪk] adj фантасти́ческий!; **that's ~!** замеча́тельно!, потряса́юще!

fantasy ['fæntəsɪ] n фанта́зия

far [fɑː] adj (distant) да́льний ♦ adv (a long way) далеко́; (much) гора́здо; **at the ~ end** в да́льнем конце́; **at the ~ side** на друго́й стороне́; **the ~ left/right** (POL) кра́йне ле́вый/пра́вый; ~ **away**, ~ **off** далеко́; **he was ~ from poor** он был далеко́ от отню́дь не бе́ден; **by ~** намно́го; **go as ~ as the post office** дойди́те до по́чты; **as ~ as I know** наско́лько мне изве́стно; **how ~?** (distance) как далеко́?; ~**away** adj (place) да́льний, далёкий; (look) отсу́тствующий

farce [fɑːs] n фарс

farcical ['fɑːsɪkl] adj (fig) неле́пый

fare [feə] n (in taxi, train, bus) сто́имость f прое́зда; **half/full** ~ полсто́имости/по́лная сто́имость прое́зда

Far East n: **the** ~ Да́льний Восто́к

farm [fɑːm] n фе́рма ♦ vt (land) обраба́тывать (обрабо́тать pf); ~**er** n фе́рмер; ~**house** n фе́рмерская уса́дьба; ~**ing** n (agriculture) се́льское хозя́йство; (of crops) выра́щивание; (of animals) разведе́ние; ~**land** n земе́льные уго́дья ntpl; ~**yard** n фе́рмерский двор

far-reaching ['fɑː'riːtʃɪŋ] adj (reform) далеко́ иду́щий; (effect) глубо́кий

fascinating ['fæsɪneɪtɪŋ] adj (story)

захва́тывающий; (person)
очарова́тельный

fascination [fæsɪˈneɪʃən] n
очарова́ние

fascism [ˈfæʃɪzəm] n (POL) фаши́зм

fashion [ˈfæʃən] n (trend) мо́да;
in/out of ~ в/не в мо́де; **in a
friendly ~** по-дру́жески; **~able** adj
мо́дный; **~ show** n пока́з or
демонстра́ция мод

fast [fɑːst] adv (quickly) бы́стро;
(firmly: stick) про́чно; (: hold)
кре́пко ♦ n (REL) пост ♦ adj
(быстрый); (progress)
стреми́тельный; (car)
скоростно́й; (colour) про́чный; **to
be ~** (clock) спеши́ть (impf); **he is ~
asleep** он кре́пко спит

fasten [ˈfɑːsn] vt закрепля́ть
(закрепи́ть pf); (door) запира́ть
(запере́ть pf); (shoe) завя́зывать
(завяза́ть pf); (coat, dress)
застёгивать (застегну́ть pf); (seat
belt) пристёгивать (пристегну́ть
pf) ♦ vi (coat, belt) застёгиваться
(застегну́ться pf); (door)
запира́ться (запере́ться pf)

fast food n бы́стро
пригото́вленная еда́

fat [fæt] adj то́лстый ♦ n жир

fatal [ˈfeɪtl] adj (mistake)
фата́льный, роково́й; (injury,
illness) смерте́льный; **~ly** adv
(injured) смерте́льно

fate [feɪt] n судьба́, рок; **~ful** adj
роково́й

father [ˈfɑːðər] n оте́ц; **~-in-law**
(wife's father) свёкор; (husband's
father) тесть m

fathom [ˈfæðəm] n фа́том,
морска́я са́жень f ♦ vt (also: ~
out) пости́гнуть (пости́чь pf)

fatigue [fəˈtiːg] n утомле́ние

fatty [ˈfætɪ] adj (food) жи́рный

fault [fɔːlt] n (blame) вина́; (defect:
in person) недоста́ток; (: in

machine) дефе́кт; (GEO) разло́м
♦ vt (criticize) придира́ться (impf) к
+dat; **it's my ~** э́то моя́ вина́; **to
find ~ with** придира́ться
(придра́ться pf) к +dat; **I am at ~** я
винова́т; **~y** adj (goods)
испо́рченный; (machine)
повреждённый

fauna [ˈfɔːnə] n фа́уна

favour [ˈfeɪvər] (US **favor**) n
(approval) расположе́ние; (help)
одолже́ние ♦ vt (prefer: solution)
ока́зывать (оказа́ть pf)
предпочте́ние +dat; (: pupil etc)
выделя́ть (вы́делить pf); (assist)
благоприя́тствовать (impf) +dat;
to do sb a ~ ока́зывать (оказа́ть
pf) кому́-н услу́гу; **in ~ of** в
по́льзу +gen; **~able** (US
favorable) adj благоприя́тный;
~ite (US **favorite**) adj люби́мый
♦ n люби́мец; (SPORT) фавори́т

fawn [fɔːn] n молодо́й оле́нь m

fax [fæks] n факс ♦ vt посыла́ть
(посла́ть pf) фа́ксом

FBI n abbr (US) (= Federal Bureau of
Investigation) ФБР

FE abbr (= Further Education) ≈
профессиона́льно-техни́ческое
образова́ние

fear [fɪər] n страх; (less strong)
боя́знь f; (worry) опасе́ние ♦ vt
боя́ться (impf) +gen; **for ~ of
missing my flight** боя́сь
опозда́ть на самолёт; **~ful** adj
(person): **to be ~ful of** боя́ться
(impf) or страши́ться (impf) +gen;
~less adj бесстра́шный

feasible [ˈfiːzəbl] adj
осуществи́мый

feast [fiːst] n (banquet) пир; (REL :
also: ~ **day**) пра́здник

feat [fiːt] n по́двиг

feather [ˈfeðər] n перо́

feature [ˈfiːtʃər] n осо́бенность f,
черта́; (PRESS) о́черк; (TV, RADIO)

переда́ча ♦ vi: **to ~ in** фигури́ровать (impf) в +prp; **~s** npl (of face) черты́ fpl (лица́); **~ film** n худо́жественный фильм

February ['februarı] n февра́ль m

fed [fed] pt, pp of **feed**

federal ['fedərəl] adj федера́льный

federation [fedə'reıʃən] n федера́ция

fed up adj: **he is ~** он сыт по го́рло, ему́ надое́ло

fee [fi:] n пла́та; **school ~s** пла́та за обуче́ние

feeble ['fi:bl] adj хи́лый; (excuse) сла́бый

feed [fi:d] (pt, pp **fed**) n (fodder) корм ♦ vt корми́ть (накорми́ть pf); **~ sth into** (data) загружа́ть (загрузи́ть pf) что-н в +acc; (paper) подава́ть (пода́ть pf) что-н в +acc; **~ on** vt fus пита́ться (impf) +instr

feel [fi:l] (pt, pp **felt**) vt (touch) тро́гать (потро́гать pf); (experience) чу́вствовать (impf), ощуща́ть (ощути́ть pf); **to ~ (that)** (believe) счита́ть (impf), что; **he ~s hungry** он го́лоден; **she ~s cold** ей хо́лодно; **to ~ lonely/better** чу́вствовать (impf) себя́ одино́ко/лу́чше; **I don't ~ well** я пло́хо себя́ чу́вствую; **the material ~s like velvet** э́тот материа́л на о́щупь как ба́рхат; **I ~ like ...** (want) мне хо́чется ...; **~ about** vi: **to ~ about for sth** иска́ть (impf) что-н о́щупью; **~ing** n чу́вство; (physical) ощуще́ние

feet [fi:t] npl of **foot**

fell [fel] pt of **fall**

fellow ['feləu] n (man) па́рень m; (of society) действи́тельный член ♦ cpd: **their ~ prisoners/students** их сока́мерники/соку́рсники; **~ship** n (SCOL) стипе́ндия (для иссле́довательской рабо́ты)

felt [felt] pt, pp of **feel** ♦ n фетр

female ['fi:meıl] n са́мка ♦ adj же́нский; (child) же́нского по́ла

feminine ['femının] adj (clothes, behaviour) же́нственный; (LING) же́нского ро́да

feminist ['femınıst] n фемини́ст(ка)

fence [fens] n (barrier) забо́р, и́згородь f

fencing ['fensıŋ] n (SPORT) фехтова́ние

fend [fend] vi: **to ~ for o.s.** забо́титься (позабо́титься pf) о себе́; **~ off** vt отража́ть (отрази́ть pf)

fender ['fendə] n (US: of car) крыло́

fern [fə:n] n па́поротник

ferocious [fə'rəuʃəs] adj (animal, attack) свире́пый; (behaviour, heat) ди́кий

ferocity [fə'rɔsıtı] n свире́пость f, жесто́кость f

ferry ['feri] n (also: **~boat**) паро́м ♦ vt перевози́ть (перевезти́ pf)

fertile ['fə:taıl] adj (land, soil) плодоро́дный; (imagination) бога́тый; (woman) спосо́бный к зача́тию

fertility [fə'tılıtı] n (of land, soil) плодоро́дие; (of woman) спосо́бность f к зача́тию

fertilizer ['fə:tılaızə] n удобре́ние

fervent ['fə:vənt] adj пы́лкий

fervour ['fə:və] (US **fervor**) n пыл

festival ['festıvəl] n (REL) пра́здник; (ART, MUS) фестива́ль m

festive ['festıv] adj (mood) пра́здничный; **the ~ season** (BRIT) = Свя́тки pl

festivities [fes'tıvıtız] npl пра́зднества ntpl

fetch [fetʃ] vt (object) приноси́ть (принести́ pf); (person) приводи́ть (привести́ pf); (by car) привози́ть (привезти́ pf)

fête [feɪt] n благотвори́тельный база́р

fetus ['fiːtəs] n (US) = **foetus**

feud [fjuːd] n вражда́

fever ['fiːvə'] n (temperature) жар; (disease) лихора́дка; **~ish** adj лихора́дочный; (person: with excitement) возбуждённый; **he is ~ish** у него́ жар, его́ лихора́дит

few [fjuː] adj (not many) немно́гие (some) не́которые pl adj ♦ pron: **(a) ~** немно́гие pl adj; **a ~** (several) не́сколько +gen; **~er** adj ме́ньше +gen

fiancé [fɪˈɑːnseɪ] n жени́х; **~e** n неве́ста

fiasco [fɪˈæskəu] n фиа́ско nt ind

fibre ['faɪbə'] (US **fiber**) n волокно́; (dietary) клетча́тка

fickle ['fɪkl] adj непостоя́нный

fiction ['fɪkʃən] n (LITERATURE) худо́жественная литерату́ра; **~al** adj (event, character) вы́мышленный

fictitious [fɪkˈtɪʃəs] adj (invented) фикти́вный; (imaginary) вы́мышленный

fiddle ['fɪdl] n (MUS) скри́пка; (swindle) надува́тельство ♦ vt (BRIT: accounts) подде́лывать (подде́лать pf)

fidelity [fɪˈdɛlɪtɪ] n (loyalty) ве́рность f

field [fiːld] n по́ле nt; (fig) о́бласть f

fierce [fɪəs] adj свире́пый; (fighting) я́ростный

fiery ['faɪərɪ] adj (sunset) о́гненный; (temperament) горя́чий

fifteen [fɪfˈtiːn] n пятна́дцать; **~th** adj пятна́дцатый

fifth [fɪfθ] adj пя́тый ♦ n (fraction) пя́тая f adj; (AUT: also: **~ gear**) пя́тая ско́рость f

fiftieth ['fɪftɪɪθ] adj пятидеся́тый

fifty ['fɪftɪ] n пятьдеся́т

fig [fɪg] n инжи́р

fight [faɪt] (pt, pp **fought**) n дра́ка; (campaign, struggle) борьба́ ♦ vt (person) дра́ться (подра́ться pf) +instr; (MIL) воева́ть (impf) c +instr; (illness, problem, emotion) боро́ться (impf) c +instr ♦ vi (people) дра́ться (impf); (MIL) воева́ть (impf); **to ~ an election** уча́ствовать (impf) в предвы́борной борьбе́; **~er** n (also fig) боре́ц; **~ing** n (battle) бой; (brawl) дра́ка

figure ['fɪgə'] n фигу́ра; (number) ци́фра ♦ vt (think) счита́ть (impf) ♦ vi (appear) фигури́ровать (impf); **~ out** vt понима́ть (поня́ть pf); **~head** n (fig, pej) номина́льный глава́ m

file [faɪl] n (dossier) де́ло; (folder) скоросшива́тель m; (COMPUT) файл ♦ vt (papers, document) подшива́ть (подши́ть pf); (LAW, claim) подава́ть (пода́ть pf); (wood, fingernails) шлифова́ть (отшлифова́ть pf) ♦ vi: **to ~ in/ past** проходи́ть (пройти́ pf) коло́нной; **in single ~** в коло́нну по одному́

fill [fɪl] vi (room etc) наполня́ться (напо́лниться pf) ♦ vt (vacancy) заполня́ть (запо́лнить pf); (need) удовлетворя́ть (удовлетвори́ть pf) ♦ n: **to eat one's ~** наеда́ться (нае́сться pf); **to ~ (with)** (container) наполня́ть (напо́лнить pf) (+instr); (space, area) заполня́ть (запо́лнить pf) (+instr); **~ in** vt заполня́ть (запо́лнить pf); **~ up** vt (container) наполня́ть (напо́лнить pf); (space) заполня́ть (запо́лнить pf) ♦ vi (AUT) заправля́ться (запра́виться pf)

fillet ['fɪlɪt] n филе́ nt ind

filling ['fɪlɪŋ] n (for tooth) пло́мба; (of pie) начи́нка; (of cake) прослойка

film [fɪlm] n (CINEMA) фильм;
(PHOT) плёнка; (of powder, liquid
etc) тонкий слой ♦ vti снимать
(снять pf); ~ **star** n кинозвезда
m/f

Filofax ® ['faɪləʊfæks] n ≈
ежедневник

filter ['fɪltə*] n фильтр ♦ vt
фильтровать (профильтровать
pf)

filth [fɪlθ] n грязь f; ~**y** adj
грязный

fin [fɪn] n (of fish) плавник

final ['faɪnl] adj (last) последний;
(SPORT) финальный; (ultimate)
заключительный; (definitive)
окончательный ♦ n (in SPORT)
финал; ~**s** npl (SCOL) выпускные
экзамены mpl; ~**e** [fɪ'nɑːlɪ] n
финал; ~**ist** n финалист; ~**ly** adv
(eventually) в конце концов;
(lastly) наконец

finance [faɪ'næns] n финансы pl
♦ vt финансировать (impf/pf); ~**s**
npl (personal) финансы pl

financial [faɪ'nænʃəl] adj
финансовый

find [faɪnd] (pt, pp **found**) vt
находить (найти pf); (discover)
обнаруживать (обнаружить pf)
♦ n находка; to ~ **sb at home**
заставать (застать pf) кого-н
дома; to ~ **sb guilty** (LAW)
признавать (признать pf) кого-н
виновным(ой); ~ **out** vt (fact,
truth) узнавать (узнать pf);
(person) разоблачать
(разоблачить pf) ♦ vi: to ~ **out**
about узнавать (узнать pf) о +prp;
~**ings** npl (LAW) заключение ntsg;
(in research) результаты mpl

fine [fam] adj прекрасный;
(delicate: hair, features) тонкий;
(sand, powder, detail) мелкий;
(adjustment) точный ♦ adv (well)

прекрасно ♦ n штраф ♦ vt
штрафовать (оштрафовать pf);
he's ~ (well) он чувствует себя
хорошо; (happy) у него всё в
порядке; **the weather is** ~ погода
хорошая; **to cut it** ~ (of time)
оставлять (оставить pf) слишком
мало времени

finger ['fɪŋgə*] n палец ♦ vt (touch)
трогать (потрогать pf); **little** ~
мизинец

finish ['fɪnɪʃ] n конец; (SPORT)
финиш; (polish etc) отделка ♦ vt
заканчивать (закончить pf),
кончать (кончить pf) ♦ vi
заканчиваться (закончиться pf);
(person) заканчивать (закончить
pf); to ~ **doing** кончать (кончить
pf) +infin; **he** ~**ed third** (in race etc)
он закончил третьим; ~ **off** vt
(kill)
приканчивать (прикончить pf); ~
up vt (food) доедать (доесть pf);
(drink) допивать (допить pf) ♦ vi
(end up) кончать (кончить pf)

Finland ['fɪnlənd] n Финляндия;
Gulf of ~ Финский залив

Finn [fɪn] n финн; ~**ish** adj
финский

fir [fəː*] n ель f

fire ['faɪə*] n (flames) огонь m,
пламя nt; (in hearth) огонь m;
(accidental) пожар; (bonfire)
костёр ♦ vt (gun etc) выстрелить
(pf) из +gen; (arrow) выпускать
(выпустить pf); (stimulate)
разжигать (разжечь pf); (inf:
dismiss) увольнять (уволить pf)
♦ vi (shoot) выстрелить (pf); **the**
house is on ~ дом горит or в
огне; ~ **alarm** n пожарная
сигнализация; ~**arm** n
огнестрельное оружие nt no pl; ~
brigade n пожарная команда; ~
engine n пожарная машина; ~
escape n пожарная лестница

~-extinguisher n огнетуши́тель m; **~-man** (irreg) n пожа́рный ♦ adj, пожа́рный; **~place** n ками́н; **~ station** n пожа́рное депо́ nt ind; **~wood** n дрова́ pl; **~works** npl фейерве́рк msg

firm [fə:m] adj (ground, decision, faith) твёрдый; (mattress) жёсткий; (grasp, body, muscles) кре́пкий ♦ n фи́рма; **~ly** adv (believe, stand) твёрдо; (grasp, shake hands) кре́пко

first [fə:st] adj пе́рвый ♦ adv (before all others) пе́рвый; (firstly) во-пе́рвых ♦ n (AUT: also: ~ **gear**) пе́рвая ско́рость f; (BRIT : SCOL, degree) дипло́м пе́рвой сте́пени; **at ~** снача́ла; **~ of all** пре́жде всего́; **~ aid** n пе́рвая по́мощь f; **~-aid kit** n паке́т пе́рвой по́мощи; **~-class** adj (excellent) первокла́ссный; **~-class ticket** биле́т пе́рвого кла́сса; **~-class stamp** ма́рка пе́рвого кла́сса

first-hand adj непосре́дственный; **a ~ account** расска́з очеви́дца
first lady n (US) пе́рвая ле́ди f ind
firstly adv во-пе́рвых
first name n и́мя nt
first-rate adj первокла́ссный
fiscal ['fɪskl] adj фиска́льный
fish [fɪʃ] n inv ры́ба ♦ vt (river, area) лови́ть (impf) ры́бу в +prp, рыба́чить (impf) в +prp ♦ vi (commercially) занима́ться (impf)

рыбо́ловством; (as sport, hobby) занима́ться (impf) ры́бной ло́влей; **to go ~ing** ходи́ть/идти́ (пойти́ pf) на рыба́лку; **~erman** (irreg) n рыба́к; **~ing rod** n у́дочка; **~ slice** n ры́бный нож

fist [fɪst] n кула́к

fit [fɪt] adj (suitable) приго́дный; (healthy) в хоро́шей фо́рме ♦ vt (subj: clothes etc) подходи́ть (подойти́ pf) по разме́ру +dat, быть (impf) впо́ру +dat ♦ vi (clothes) подходи́ть (подойти́ pf) по разме́ру, быть (impf) впо́ру; (parts) подходи́ть (подойти́ pf) ♦ n (MED) припа́док; (of coughing, giggles) при́ступ; **~ to do** (ready) гото́вый +infin; **~ for** (suitable for) приго́дный для +gen; **a ~ of anger** при́ступ гне́ва; **this dress is a good ~** э́то пла́тье хорошо́ сиди́т; **by ~s and starts** уры́вками; **~ in** vi (person, object) впи́сываться (вписа́ться pf); **~ness** n (MED) состоя́ние здоро́вья; **~ting** adj (thanks) надлежа́щий; **~tings** npl: **fixtures and ~tings** обору́дование ntsg

five [faɪv] n пять; **~r** n (inf: BRIT) пять фу́нтов; (: US) пять до́лларов

fix [fɪks] vt (arrange: date) назнача́ть (назна́чить pf); (: amount) устана́вливать (установи́ть pf); (mend) нала́живать (нала́дить pf) ♦ n (inf): **to be in a ~** влипа́ть (влипнуть pf); ~ed adj (price) твёрдый; (ideas) навязчивый; (smile) застывший

fixture ['fɪkstʃə⁰] n see **fittings**

fizzy ['fɪzɪ] adj шипучий, газированный

flabby ['flæbɪ] adj дряблый

flag [flæg] n флаг; ~ship n флагман

flair [fleə⁰] n (style) стиль m; **a ~ for** (talent) дар or талант к +dat; **political ~** политический талант

flak [flæk] n (inf) нахлобучка

flake [fleɪk] n (of snow, soap powder) хлопья pl; (of rust, paint) слой

flamboyant [flæm'bɔɪənt] adj яркий, броский; (person) колоритный

flame [fleɪm] n (of fire) пламя nt

flank [flæŋk] n (of animal) бок; (MIL) фланг ♦ vt: ~ed by между +instr

flannel ['flænl] n (fabric) фланель f; (BRIT: also: **face ~**) махровая салфетка (для лица)

flap [flæp] n (of envelope) отворот; (of pocket) клапан ♦ vt (wings) хлопать (impf) +instr

flare [fleə⁰] n (signal) сигнальная ракета; **~ up** vi вспыхивать (вспыхнуть pf)

flash [flæʃ] n вспышка; (also: **news ~**) "молния" ♦ vt (light) (внезапно) освещать (осветить pf); (news, message) посылать (послать pf) молнией; (look) метать (метнуть pf) ♦ vi (lightning, light, eyes) сверкать (сверкнуть pf); (light on ambulance etc) мигать (impf); **in a ~** в мгновенно; **to ~ by** or **past** (sth) (person) мчаться (промчаться pf) мимо (чего-н); **~light** n фонарь m, прожектор; **~y** adj (pej) кричащий

flask [flɑːsk] n (also: **vacuum ~**) термос

flat [flæt] adj (surface) плоский; (tyre) спущенный; (battery) севший; (beer) выдохшийся; (refusal, denial) категорический; (MUS, note) бемольный ♦ n (BRIT: apartment) квартира; (AUT: also: ~ **tyre**) спущенная шина; (MUS) бемоль m; **to work ~ out** выкладываться (выложиться pf) полностью; **~ly** adv (deny) начисто; (refuse) наотрез

flatter ['flætə⁰] vt льстить (польстить pf) +dat

flavour ['fleɪvə⁰] (US **flavor**) vt (soup) приправлять (приправить pf) ♦ n (taste) вкус; (of ice-cream etc) привкус; **strawberry-~ed** adj клубничным привкусом

flaw [flɔː] n (in argument, character) недостаток, изъян; (in cloth, glass) дефект; **~less** adj безупречный

flea [fliː] n блоха

fleck [flek] n (mark) крапинка

flee [fliː] (pt, pp **fled**) vt (danger, famine) бежать (impf) от +gen; (country) бежать (impf/pf) из +gen ♦ vi спасаться (impf) бегством

fleece [fliːs] n (sheep's coat) (овечья) шкура; (sheep's wool) овечья шерсть f

fleet [fliːt] n (of ships) флот; (of lorries, cars) парк

fleeting ['fliːtɪŋ] adj мимолётный

Flemish ['flemɪʃ] adj фламандский

flesh [fleʃ] n (ANAT) плоть f; (of fruit) мякоть f

flew [fluː] pt of **fly**

flex [fleks] n гибкий шнур ♦ vt (leg, muscles) разминать (размять pf); **~ibility** n гибкость f; **~ible** adj гибкий

flick [flɪk] vt (with finger) смахивать (смахнуть pf); (ash) стряхивать (стряхнуть pf); (whip) хлестну́ть (pf) +instr; (switch) щёлкать (щёлкнуть pf) +instr

flicker ['flɪkə'] vi (light, flame) мерца́ть (impf)

flight [flaɪt] n полёт; (of steps) пролёт (ле́стницы)

flimsy ['flɪmzɪ] adj (shoes, clothes) лёгкий; (structure) непро́чный; (excuse, evidence) сла́бый

fling [flɪŋ] (pt, pp flung) vt (throw) швыря́ть (швырну́ть pf)

flip [flɪp] vt (coin) подбра́сывать (подбро́сить pf) щелчко́м

float [fləʊt] n (for fishing) поплаво́к; (for swimming) пенопла́стовая доска́ для обуча́ющихся пла́вать; (money) разме́нные де́ньги pl ♦ vi (object, person: on water) пла́вать (impf); (sound, cloud) плыть (impf) ♦ vt (idea, plan) пуска́ть (пусти́ть pf) в ход; **to ~ a company** выпуска́ть (вы́пустить pf) а́кции компа́нии на ры́нок

flock [flɒk] n (of sheep) ста́до; (of birds) ста́я ♦ vi: **to ~ to** стека́ться (сте́чься pf) в +prp

flood [flʌd] n (of water) наводне́ние; (of letters, imports etc) пото́к ♦ vt (subj: water) залива́ть (зали́ть pf); (: people) наводня́ть (наводни́ть pf) ♦ vi (place) наполня́ться (напо́лниться pf) водо́й; **to ~ into** (people, goods) хлы́нуть (pf) в/на +acc; **~ing** n наводне́ние

floor [flɔː'] n (of room: also: storey) эта́ж; (of sea, valley) дно ♦ vt (subj: question, remark) сража́ть (срази́ть pf); **ground** or (US) **first ~** пе́рвый эта́ж; **~board** n полови́ца

flop [flɒp] n (failure) прова́л

floppy ['flɒpɪ] adj ♦ n (also: ~ **disk**) диске́та, ги́бкий диск

flora ['flɔːrə] n фло́ра; **~l** ['flɔːrl] adj

(pattern) цвети́стый

flour ['flaʊə'] n мука́

flourish ['flʌrɪʃ] vi (business) процвета́ть (impf); (plant) пы́шно расти́ (impf) ♦ n (bold gesture): **with a ~** демонстрати́вно; **~ing** adj (company, trade) процвета́ющий

flow [fləʊ] n (also ELEC) пото́к; (of blood, river) тече́ние ♦ vi течь (impf)

flower ['flaʊə'] n цвето́к ♦ vi (plant, tree) цвести́ (impf); **~s** цветы́; **~bed** n клу́мба; **~pot** n цвето́чный горшо́к; **~y** adj (perfume) цвето́чный

flown [fləʊn] pp of **fly**

flu [fluː] n (MED) грипп

fluent ['fluːənt] adj (linguist) свобо́дно говоря́щий; (speech) бе́глый; (writing) свобо́дный; **he speaks ~ Russian, he's ~ in Russian** он свобо́дно говори́т по-ру́сски

fluff [flʌf] n (on jacket, carpet) ворс; **~y** adj (soft) пуши́стый

fluid ['fluːɪd] adj (movement) теку́чий; (situation) переме́нчивый ♦ n жи́дкость f

fluke [fluːk] n (inf) уда́ча, везе́ние

flung [flʌŋ] pt, pp of **fling**

fluorescent [fluə'rɛsnt] adj (dial, light) флюоресци́рующий

fluoride ['fluəraɪd] n фтори́д

flurry ['flʌrɪ] n (of snow) вихрь m; **a ~ of activity** бу́рная де́ятельность f

flush [flʌʃ] n (on face) румя́нец ♦ vt (drains, pipe) промыва́ть (промы́ть pf) ♦ vi (redden) зарде́ться (pf) ♦ adj: **~ with** (level) на одно́м у́ровне с +instr; **to ~ the toilet** спуска́ть (спусти́ть pf) во́ду в туале́те; **~ed** adj раскрасне́вшийся

flustered ['flʌstəd] adj смущённый

flute [fluːt] n фле́йта

flutter ['flʌtə'] n (of wings) взмах

flux [flʌks] n: **in a state of ~** в состоянии непрерывного изменения

fly [flaɪ] (pt **flew**, pp **flown**) n (insect) муха; (on trousers: also: **flies**) ширинка ♦ vt (plane) летать (impf) на +prp; (passengers, cargo) перевозить (перевезти pf); (distances) пролетать (пролететь pf); (obstacles) преодолевать (преодолеть pf) ♦ vi (also fig) летать/лететь (impf); (flag) развеваться (impf); **~ing** n (activity) лётное дело ♦ adj: **a ~ing visit** краткий визит; **with ~ing colours** блестяще

foal [fəul] n жеребёнок

foam [fəum] n пена; (also: **~ rubber**) поролон

focal point ['fəukl-] n средоточие

focus ['fəukəs] (pl **~es**) n (PHOT) фокус; (of attention, argument) средоточие ♦ vt (camera) настраивать (настроить pf) ♦ vi: **to ~ (on)** (PHOT) настраивать (настроиться pf) (на +acc); **to ~ on** (fig) сосредотачиваться (сосредоточиться pf) на +prp; **in ~** в фокусе; **out of ~** не в фокусе

fodder ['fɒdə'] n корм, фураж

foetus ['fiːtəs] (US **fetus**) n плод, зародыш

fog [fɔg] n туман; **~gy** adj туманный; **it's ~gy** туманно

foil [fɔɪl] vt срывать (сорвать pf) ♦ n (metal) фольга

fold [fəuld] n (crease) складка; (: in paper) сгиб ♦ vt (clothes, paper) складывать (сложить pf); (arms) скрещивать (скрестить pf) ♦ **~er** n папка; (ring-binder) скоросшиватель m; **~ing** adj складной

foliage ['fəulɪdʒ] n (of tree etc) листва

folk [fəuk] npl люди pl, народ msg

♦ cpd (art, music) народный; **~s** npl (inf: relatives) близкие pl adj; **~lore** n фольклор

follow ['fɔləu] vt (leader, person) следовать (последовать pf) за +instr; (example, advice) следовать (последовать pf) +dat; (event, story) следить (impf) за +instr; (route, path) держаться (impf) +gen ♦ vi следовать (последовать pf); **to ~ suit** (fig) следовать (последовать pf) примеру; **~ up** vt (letter, offer) рассматривать (рассмотреть pf); (case) расследовать (impf/pf); **~er** n (of person, belief, cause) последователь(ница) m(f); **~ing** adj следующий ♦ n (followers) последователи mpl

fond [fɔnd] adj (smile, look, parents) ласковый; (memory) приятный; **to be ~ of** любить (impf)

food [fuːd] n еда, пища; **~ poisoning** n пищевое отравление; **~ processor** n кухонный комбайн

fool [fuːl] n дурак ♦ vt (deceive) обманывать (обмануть pf), одурачивать (одурачить pf); **~ish** adj (stupid) глупый; (rash) неосмотрительный

foot [fut] (pl **feet**) n (of person) нога, ступня; (of animal) нога; (of bed) конец; (of cliff) подножие; (measure) фут ♦ vt: **to ~ the bill** платить (заплатить pf); **on ~** пешком

foot - фут. Мера длины равная 30.4 см.

footage ['futɪdʒ] n (CINEMA, material) кадры mpl

foot: **~ball** n футбольный мяч; (game: BRIT) футбол; (: US) американский футбол; **~baller** n

(BRIT) футболи́ст; **~hills** npl предго́рья ntpl; **~hold** n (on rock etc) опо́ра; **~ing** n (fig) осно́ва; **to lose one's ~ing** (fall) теря́ть (потеря́ть pf) опо́ру; **~note** n сно́ска; **~path** n тропи́нка, доро́жка; **~print** n след; **~wear** n о́бувь f

KEYWORD

for [fɔːr] prep **1** (indicating destination) в/на +acc; (indicating intention) за +instr; **the train for London** по́езд в ог на Ло́ндон; **he left for work** он уе́хал на рабо́ту; **he went for the paper/the doctor** он пошёл за газе́той/врачо́м; **is this for me?** э́то мне ог для меня́?; **there's a letter for you** Вам письмо́; **it's time for lunch/bed** пора́ обе́дать/спать

2 (indicating purpose) для +gen; **what's it for?** для чего́ э́то?; **give it to me – what for?** да́йте мне э́то – заче́м ог для чего́?; **to pray for peace** моли́ться (impf) за мир

3 (on behalf of, representing): **to speak for sb** говори́ть (impf) от лица́ кого́-н; **MP for Brighton** член парла́мента от Бра́йтона; **he works for the government** он на госуда́рственной слу́жбе; **he works for a local firm** он рабо́тает на ме́стную фи́рму; **I'll ask him for you** я спрошу́ его́ от Ва́шего и́мени; **to do sth for sb** (on behalf of) де́лать (сде́лать pf) что-н за кого́-н

4 (because of) из-за +gen; **for lack of funds** из-за отсу́тствия средств; **for this reason** по э́той причи́не; **for some reason, for whatever reason** по како́й-то причи́не; **for fear of being criticized** боя́сь кри́тики; **to be**

famous for sth быть (impf) изве́стным чем-н

5 (with regard to) для +gen; **it's cold for July** для ию́ля сейча́с хо́лодно; **he's tall for his age** для своего́ во́зраста он высо́кий; **a gift for languages** спосо́бности к языка́м; **for everyone who voted yes, 50 voted no** на ка́ждый го́лос "за", прихо́дится 50 голосо́в "про́тив"

6 (in exchange for, in favour of) +acc; **I sold it for £5** я про́дал э́то за £5; **I'm all for it** я целико́м и по́лностью за э́то

7 (referring to distance): **there are roadworks for five miles** на протяже́нии пяти́ миль произво́дятся доро́жные рабо́ты; **to stretch for miles** простира́ться (impf) на мно́го миль; **we walked for miles/for ten miles** мы прошли́ мно́го миль/де́сять миль

8 (referring to time) +acc; (: in past): **he was away for 2 years** он был в отъе́зде 2 го́да, его́ не́ было 2 го́да; (: in future): **she will be away for a month** она́ уезжа́ет на ме́сяц; **can you do it for tomorrow?** Вы мо́жете сде́лать э́то к за́втрашнему дню?; **it hasn't rained for 3 weeks** уже́ 3 неде́ли не́ было дождя́; **for hours** часа́ми

9 (with infinite clause): **it is not for me to decide** не мне реша́ть; **there is still time for you to do it** у Вас ещё есть вре́мя сде́лать э́то; **for this to be possible ...** что́бы э́то осуществи́ть, ...

10 (in spite of) несмотря́ на +acc; **for all his complaints** несмотря́ на все его́ жа́лобы

11 (in phrases): **for the first/last time** в пе́рвый/после́дний раз;

for the time being пока
♦ *conj* (*rather formal*) ибо

forbid [fə'bɪd] (*pt* **forbad(e)**, *pp*
forbidden) *vt* запрещать
(запретить *pf*); **to ~sb to do**
запрещать (запретить *pf*) кому-н
+*infin*; **~ding** *adj* враждебный

force [fɔ:s] *n* (*also PHYS*) сила
♦ *vt* (*compel*) вынуждать (вынудить
pf), принуждать (принудить *pf*);
(*push*) толкать (толкнуть *pf*);
(*break open*) взламывать
(взломать *pf*); **the Forces** *npl*
(*BRIT : MIL*) вооружённые силы
fpl; **in ~** в большом количестве;
to ~ o.s. to заставлять
(заставить *pf*) себя +*infin*; **~d** *adj*
(*landing*) вынужденный; (*smile*)
принуждённый; **~ful** *adj*
сильный

forcibly ['fɔ:səblɪ] *adv* насильно

fore [fɔ:ʳ] *n*: **to come to the ~**
выдвигаться (выдвинуться *pf*)

forecast ['fɔ:ka:st] (*irreg: like* **cast**) *n*
прогноз ♦ *vt* предсказывать
(предсказать *pf*)

forecourt ['fɔ:kɔ:t] *n* (*of garage*)
передняя площадка

forefinger ['fɔ:fɪŋgəʳ] *n*
указательный палец

forefront ['fɔ:frʌnt] *n*: **in** or **at the ~
of** (*movement*) в авангарде +*gen*

foreground ['fɔ:graund] *n*
передний план

forehead ['fɔrɪd] *n* лоб

foreign ['fɔrɪn] *adj* (*language, tourist,
firm*) иностранный; (*trade*)
внешний; (*country*) зарубежный;
~ person *n* иностранец(нка); **~er** *n*
иностранец(нка); **~ exchange** *n*
(*system*) обмен валюты; **Foreign
Office** *n* (*BRIT*) министерство
иностранных дел; **Foreign
Secretary** *n* (*BRIT*) министр
иностранных дел

foreman ['fɔ:mən] (*irreg*) *n*
(*INDUSTRY*) мастер

foremost ['fɔ:məust] *adj* (*most
important*) важнейший ♦ *adv*: **first
and ~** в первую очередь,
прежде всего

forensic [fə'rɛnsɪk] *adj* (*medicine,
test*) судебный

forerunner ['fɔ:rʌnəʳ] *n*
предшественник(ница)

foresee [fɔ:'si:] (*irreg: like* **see**) *vt*
предвидеть (*impf/pf*); **~able** *adj*: **in
the ~able future** в обозримом
будущем

foresight ['fɔ:saɪt] *n*
предусмотрительность *f*

forest ['fɔrɪst] *n* лес; **~ry** *n*
лесоводство, лесничество

forever [fə'rɛvəʳ] *adv* (*for good*)
навсегда, навек; (*endlessly*)
вечно

foreword ['fɔ:wə:d] *n* предисловие

forgave [fə'geɪv] *pt of* **forgive**

forge [fɔ:dʒ] *vt* (*signature, money*)
подделывать (подделать *pf*); **~ry**
n подделка

forget [fə'gɛt] (*pt* **forgot**, *pp*
forgotten) *vt* забывать (забыть
pf); (*appointment*) забывать
(забыть *pf*) о +*prp* ♦ *vi* забывать
(забыть *pf*); **~ful** *adj* забывчивый;
~-me-not *n* незабудка

forgive [fə'gɪv] (*pt* **forgave**, *pp* **~n**)
vt (*pardon*) прощать (простить
pf); **to ~ sb sth** прощать
(простить *pf*) кому-н что-н; **to ~
sb for sth** (*excuse*) прощать
(простить *pf*) кого-н за что-н; **I
forgave him for doing it** я
простил его за то, что он
сделал это; **~ness** *n* прощение

forgot [fə'gɔt] *pt of* **forget**; **~ten** *pp*
of **forget**

fork [fɔ:k] *n* вилка; (*for gardening*)
вилы *pl*; (*in road etc*)
разветвление

forlorn [fəˈlɔːn] adj покину́тый; (hope, attempt) тще́тный

form [fɔːm] n (type) вид; (shape) фо́рма; (SCOL) класс; (questionnaire) анке́та; (also: **booking** ~) бланк ♦ vt (make) образо́вывать (образова́ть pf); (organization, group) формирова́ть (сформирова́ть pf); (idea, habit) выраба́тывать (вы́работать pf); **in top** ~ в прекра́сной фо́рме

formal [ˈfɔːml] adj форма́льный; (person, behaviour) церемо́нный; (occasion) официа́льный; ~ **clothes** официа́льная фо́рма оде́жды; ~**ities** [fɔːˈmælɪtɪz] npl форма́льности fpl; ~**ity** [fɔːˈmælɪtɪ] n форма́льность f; (of person, behaviour) церемо́нность f; (of occasion) официа́льность f; ~**ly** adv (behave) форма́льно; (behave) церемо́нно

format [ˈfɔːmæt] n форма́т

formation [fɔːˈmeɪʃən] n формирова́ние

formative [ˈfɔːmətɪv] adj: **in his** ~ **years** в го́ды становле́ния его́ ли́чности

former [ˈfɔːmər] adj бы́вший; (earlier) пре́жний ♦ n: **the** ~ ... **the latter** ... пе́рвый ... после́дний ...; ~**ly** adv ра́нее, ра́ньше

formidable [ˈfɔːmɪdəbl] adj (opponent) гро́зный; (task) серьёзнейший

formula [ˈfɔːmjulə] (pl ~**e** or ~**s**) n (MATH, CHEM) фо́рмула; (plan) схе́ма; ~**te** [ˈfɔːmjuleɪt] vt (plan, strategy) выраба́тывать (вы́работать pf); (opinion, thought) формули́ровать (сформули́ровать pf)

fort [fɔːt] n кре́пость f, форт

forte [ˈfɔːtɪ] n си́льная сторона́

forth [fɔːθ] adv: **to go back and** ~ ходи́ть (impf) взад и вперёд; **and**

so ~ и так да́лее; ~**coming** adj предстоя́щий; (person) общи́тельный; ~**right** adj (condemnation, opposition) откры́тый

fortieth [ˈfɔːtɪɪθ] adj сороково́й

fortnight [ˈfɔːtnaɪt] (BRIT) n две неде́ли; ~**ly** adv раз в две неде́ли ♦ adj: ~**ly magazine** журна́л, выходя́щий раз в две неде́ли

fortress [ˈfɔːtrɪs] n кре́пость f

fortunate [ˈfɔːtʃənɪt] adj (event, choice) счастли́вый; (person) уда́чливый; **he was** ~ **to get a job** на его́ сча́стье, он получи́л рабо́ту; **it is** ~ **that** ... к сча́стью ...; ~**ly** adv к сча́стью; ~**ly for him** на его́ сча́стье

fortune [ˈfɔːtʃən] n (wealth) состоя́ние; (also: **good** ~) сча́стье, уда́ча; **ill** ~ невезе́ние, неуда́ча

forty [ˈfɔːtɪ] n со́рок

forum [ˈfɔːrəm] n фо́рум

forward [ˈfɔːwəd] adv вперёд ♦ n (SPORT) напада́ющий(ая) m(f) adj, фо́рвард ♦ vt (letter, parcel) пересыла́ть (пересла́ть pf) ♦ adj (position) пере́дний; (not shy) де́рзкий; **to move** ~ (progress) продвига́ться (продви́нуться pf); ~**s** adv вперёд

fossil [ˈfɔsl] n окамене́лость f, ископа́емое m adj

foster [ˈfɔstər] vt (child) брать (взять pf) на воспита́ние

fought [fɔːt] pt, pp of **fight**

foul [faul] adj га́дкий, мёрзкий; (language) непристо́йный; (temper) жу́ткий ♦ n (SPORT) наруше́ние ♦ vt (dirty) га́дить (зага́дить pf)

found [faund] pt, pp of **find** ♦ vt (establish) осно́вывать (основа́ть pf); ~**ation** n (base) осно́ва;

(organization) общество, фонд; (also: ~ation cream) крем под макияж; ~ations npl (of building) фундамент msg; ~er n основатель(ница) m(f)

fountain ['fauntɪn] n фонтан

four [fɔːʳ] n четыре; on all ~s на четвереньках

fourteen ['fɔː'tiːn] n четырнадцать; ~th adj четырнадцатый

fourth ['fɔːθ] adj четвёртый ♦ n (AUT: also: ~ gear) четвёртая скорость f

fowl [faul] n птица

fox [fɔks] n лиса ♦ vt озадачивать (озадачить pf)

foyer ['fɔɪeɪ] n (in hotel etc) фойе nt ind

fraction ['frækʃən] n (portion) частица; (MATH) дробь f; a ~ of a second доля секунды

fracture ['fræktʃəʳ] n перелом ♦ vt (bone) ломать (сломать pf)

fragile ['frædʒaɪl] adj хрупкий

fragment ['frægmənt] n фрагмент; (of glass) осколок, обломок

fragrance ['freɪgrəns] n благоухание

fragrant ['freɪgrənt] adj душистый

frail [freɪl] adj (person) слабый, немощный; (structure) хрупкий

frame [freɪm] n (of building, structure) каркас, остов; (of person) сложение; (of picture, window) рама; (of spectacles: also: ~s) оправа ♦ vt обрамлять (обрамить pf); ~ of mind настроение; ~ n каркас; (fig) рамки fpl

France [frɑːns] n Франция

franchise ['fræntʃaɪz] n (POL) право голоса; (COMM) франшиза

frank [fræŋk] adj (discussion, person) откровенный; (look) открытый; ~ly adv откровенно

frantic ['fræntɪk] adj иступлённый; (hectic) лихорадочный

fraternity [frə'tɜːnɪtɪ] n (club) содружество

fraud [frɔːd] n (person) мошенник; (crime) мошенничество; ~ulent adj (scheme, claim) мошеннический

fraught [frɔːt] adj: ~ with чреватый +instr

fray [freɪ] vi трепаться (истрепаться pf); tempers were ~ed все были на грани срыва

freak [friːk] adj странный, ненормальный ♦ n: he is a ~ он ненормальный

freckle ['frekl] n (usu pl) веснушка

free [friː] adj свободный; (costing nothing) бесплатный ♦ vt (prisoner etc) освобождать (освободить pf), выпускать (выпустить pf) (на свободу); (object) высвобождать (высвободить pf); ~ (of charge), for ~ бесплатно; ~dom n свобода; ~ kick n (FOOTBALL) свободный удар; ~lance adj внештатный, работающий по договору; ~ly adv (without restriction) свободно; (liberally) обильно; ~range adj (of hens: eggs) яйца от кур на свободном выгуле; ~ will n: of one's own ~ will по (своей) доброй воле

freeze [friːz] (pt froze, pp frozen) vi (weather) холодать (похолодать pf); (liquid, pipe, person) замерзать (замёрзнуть pf); (person: stop moving) застывать (застыть pf) ♦ vt (food) замораживать (заморозить pf) ♦ n (on arms, wages) замораживание; ~r n морозильник

freezing ['friːzɪŋ] adj: ~ (cold) ледяной ♦ n: 3 degrees below ~ 3 градуса мороза или ниже нуля; I'm ~ я замёрз; it's ~ очень хо́лодно

freight [freɪt] n фрахт

French [frentʃ] adj францу́зский; **the ~** npl (people) францу́зы mpl; **~ fries** npl (US) карто́фель msg-фри; **~man** (irreg) n францу́з

frenzy ['frenzɪ] n (of violence) остервене́ние, бе́шенство

frequency ['friːkwənsɪ] n частота́

frequent adj ['friːkwənt] vb [frɪ'kwent] adj ча́стый ♦ vt посеща́ть (impf); **~ly** adv ча́сто

fresh [freʃ] adj све́жий; (instructions, approach) но́вый; **to make a ~ start** начина́ть (нача́ть pf) за́ново; **in one's mind** свежо́ в па́мяти; **~er** n (BRIT : inf) первоку́рсник; **~ly** adv: **~ly made** свежеприготовленный; **~ly painted** свежевыкрашенный; **~water** adj (lake) пре́сный; (fish) пресново́дный

fret [fret] vi волнова́ться (impf)

friction ['frɪkʃən] n тре́ние; (fig) тре́ния ntpl

Friday ['fraɪdɪ] n пя́тница

fridge [frɪdʒ] n (BRIT) холоди́льник

fried [fraɪd] pt, pp of **fry** ♦ adj жа́реный

friend [frend] n (male) друг; (female) подру́га; **~ly** adj (person, smile etc) дружелю́бный; (government, country) дру́жественный; (place, restaurant) прия́тный ♦ n (also: **~ly match**) това́рищеский матч; **to be ~ly with** дружи́ть (impf) +instr; **to be ~ly to** относи́ться (отнести́сь pf) к кому́-н дружелю́бно; **~ship** n дру́жба

fright [fraɪt] n испу́г; **to take ~** испуга́ться (pf); **~en** vt пуга́ть (испуга́ть pf); **~ened** adj испу́ганный; **to be ~ened (of)** боя́ться (impf) (+gen); **he is ~ened by change** его́ пуга́ют

измене́ния; **~ening** adj стра́шный, устраша́ющий

frilly adj: **~ dress** пла́тье с обо́рками

fringe [frɪndʒ] n (BRIT: of hair) чёлка; (on shawl, lampshade etc) бахрома́; (of forest etc) край, окра́ина

frivolous ['frɪvələs] adj (conduct, person) легкомы́сленный; (object, activity) пустя́чный

fro [frəu] adv: **to and ~** туда́-сюда́

frog [frɒg] n лягу́шка

KEYWORD

---

from [frɒm] prep 1 (indicating starting place, origin etc) из +gen, с +gen; (from a person) от +gen; **he is from Cyprus** он с Ки́пра; **from London to Glasgow** из Ло́ндона в Гла́зго; **a letter from my sister** письмо́ от мое́й сестры́; **a quotation from Dickens** цита́та из Ди́ккенса; **to drink from the bottle** пить (impf) из буты́лки; **where do you come from?** Вы отку́да?

2 (indicating movement: from inside) из +gen; (: away from) от +gen; (: off) с +gen; (: from behind) из-за +gen; **she ran from the house** она́ вы́бежала из до́ма; **the car drove away from the house** маши́на отъе́хала от до́ма; **he took the magazine from the table** он взял журна́л со стола́; **they got up from the table** они́ вста́ли из-за стола́

3 (indicating time) с +gen; **from two o'clock to** или **until** или **till three (o'clock)** с двух часо́в до трёх (часо́в); **from January (to August)** с января́ (по а́вгуст)

4 (indicating distance: position) от +gen; (: motion) до +gen; **the hotel is one kilometre from the beach**

гости́ница нахо́дится в
киломе́тре от пля́жа; **we're still a
long way from home** мы ещё
далеко́ от до́ма
5 (*indicating price, number etc:
range*) от +*gen*; (: *change*) с +*gen*;
prices range from £10 to £50
це́ны коле́блются от £10 до £50;
**the interest rate was increased
from nine per cent to ten per cent**
проце́нтные ста́вки повы́сились
с девяти́ до десяти́ проце́нтов
6 (*indicating difference*) от +*gen*; **to
be different from sb/sth**
отлича́ться (*impf*) от кого́-н/
чего́-н
7 (*because of, on the basis of*): **from
what he says** су́дя по тому́, что
он говори́т; **from what I
understand** как я понима́ю; **to
act from conviction** де́йствовать
(*impf*) по убежде́нию; **he is weak
from hunger** он слаб от го́лода

front [frʌnt] *n* (*of house, also fig*)
фаса́д; (*of dress*) пе́ред; (*of train,
car*) пере́дняя часть *f*; (*also:* **sea
~**) на́бережная *f adj*; (*MIL,
METEOROLOGY*) фронт ♦ *adj*
пере́дний; **in ~** впереди́; **in ~
of** пе́ред +*instr*; **~ door** входна́я
дверь *f*; **~ier** [ˈfrʌntɪə] *n* грани́ца;
~ page пе́рвая страни́ца
(*газе́ты*)

frost [frɔst] *n* моро́з; (*also:* **hoar-
~**) и́ней; **~bite** *n* обмороже́ние; **~y**
adj (*weather, night*) моро́зный;
(*welcome, look*) ледяно́й

froth [ˈfrɔθ] *n* (*on liquid*) пе́на

frown [fraun] *n* нахму́ренный
взгляд

froze [frauz] *pt of* **freeze**; **~n** *pp of*
freeze

fruit [fruːt] *n inv* фрукт; (*fig*) плод;
~ful *adj* плодотво́рный; **~ion**
[fruːˈɪʃən] *n*: **to come to ~ion**

дава́ть (дать *pf*) плоды́; **~
machine** *n* (*BRIT*) игрово́й
автома́т

frustrate [frʌsˈtreɪt] *vt* (*person, plan*)
расстра́ивать (расстро́ить *pf*)

frustration [frʌsˈtreɪʃən] *n* доса́да

fry [fraɪ] (*pt, pp* **fried**) *vt* жа́рить
(пожа́рить *pf*); **~ing pan** (*US*
~-pan) *n* сковорода́

ft. *abbr* = **feet, foot**

fudge [fʌdʒ] *n* ≈ сли́вочная
пома́дка

fuel [ˈfjuəl] *n* (*for heating*) то́пливо;
(*for plane, car etc*) горю́чее *nt adj*

fugitive [ˈfjuːdʒɪtɪv] *n*
бегле́ц(ля́нка)

fulfil [fulˈfil] (*US* **fulfill**) *vt* (*function,
desire, promise*) исполня́ть
(испо́лнить *pf*); (*ambition*)
осуществля́ть (осуществи́ть *pf*);
~ment (*US* **~lment**) *n* (*of promise,
desire*) исполне́ние; (*satisfaction*)
удовлетворе́ние; (*of ambitions*)
осуществле́ние

full [ful] *adj* по́лный; (*skirt*)
широ́кий ♦ *adv*: **to know ~ well
that** прекра́сно знать (*impf*), что;
at ~ volume/power на по́лную
гро́мкость/мо́щность; **I'm ~ (up)**
я сыт; **he is ~ of enthusiasm/hope**
он по́лон энтузиа́зма/наде́жды;
~ details все дета́ли; **at ~ speed**
на по́лной ско́рости; **a two
hours** це́лых два часа́; **in ~**
по́лностью; **~-length** *adj* (*film,
novel*) полнометра́жный; (*coat*)
дли́нный; (*mirror*) высо́кий; **~
moon** *n* по́лная луна́; **~-scale**
adj (*attack, war, search etc*)
широкомасшта́бный; **~-time** *adj,
adv* (*study*) на дневно́м
отделе́нии; (*work*) на по́лной
ста́вке; **~y** *adv* (*completely*)
по́лностью, вполне́; **~y as big as**
по кра́йней ме́ре тако́й же
по величине́, как; **~y fledged** *adj*

(*teacher, barrister*) вполне́
сложи́вшийся

fumes [fju:mz] *npl* испаре́ния *ntpl*,
пары́ *mpl*

fun [fʌn] *n*: **what** ~! как ве́село!;
to have ~ весели́ться
(повесели́ться *pf*); **he's good** ~ (**to
be with**) с ним ве́село; **for** ~ для
заба́вы; **to make** ~ **of**
подшу́чивать (подшути́ть *pf*) над
+*instr*

function [ˈfʌŋkʃən] *n* фу́нкция;
(*product*) произво́дная *f adj*; (*social
occasion*) приём ♦ *vi* (*operate*)
функциони́ровать (*impf*); ~**al** *adj*
(*operational*) де́йствующий;
(*practical*) функциона́льный

fund [fʌnd] *n* фонд; (*of knowledge
etc*) запа́с; ~**s** *npl* (*money*)
(де́нежные) сре́дства *ntpl*,
фо́нды *mpl*

fundamental [fʌndəˈmɛntl] *adj*
фундамента́льный

funding [ˈfʌndɪŋ] *n*
финанси́рование

funeral [ˈfjuːnərəl] *n* по́хороны
pl

fungus [ˈfʌŋgəs] (*pl* **fungi**) *n* (*plant*)
гриб; (*mould*) плéсень *f*

funnel [ˈfʌnl] *n* (*for pouring*)
воро́нка; (*of ship*) труба́

funny [ˈfʌnɪ] *adj* (*amusing*)
заба́вный; (*strange*) стра́нный,
чудно́й

fur [fəː] *n* мех

furious [ˈfjuərɪəs] *adj* (*person*)
взбешённый; (*exchange,
argument*) бу́рный; (*effort, speed*)
нейстовый

furnace [ˈfəːnɪs] *n* печь *f*

furnish [ˈfəːnɪʃ] *vt* (*room, building*)
обставля́ть (обста́вить *pf*); **to** ~
sb with sth (*supply*)
предоставля́ть (предоста́вить *pf*)
что-н кому́-н; ~**ings** *npl*
обстано́вка *fsg*

furniture [ˈfəːnɪtʃər] *n* ме́бель *f*;
piece of ~ предме́т ме́бели

furry [ˈfəːrɪ] *adj* пуши́стый

further [ˈfəːðər] *adj*
дополни́тельный ♦ *adv* (*farther*)
да́льше; (*moreover*) бо́лее того́
♦ *vt* (*career, project*) продвига́ть
(продви́нуть *pf*), соде́йствовать
(*impf/pf*) +*dat*; ~ **education** *n*
(*BRIT*) сре́днее специа́льное
образова́ние

further education - сре́днее
специа́льное образова́ние. Его́
мо́жно получи́ть в колле́джах.
Обуче́ние прово́дится на
осно́ве по́лного дневно́го
ку́рса, почасово́го или
вече́рнего ку́рса.

furthermore *adv* бо́лее того́

furthest [ˈfəːðɪst] *superl of* **far**

furtive [ˈfəːtɪv] *adj*: ~ **movement/
glance** движе́ние/взгляд
украдкой

fury [ˈfjuərɪ] *n* я́рость *f*, бе́шенство

fuse [fjuːz] (*US* **fuze**) *n* (*ELEC*)
предохрани́тель *m*; (*on bomb*)
фити́ль *m*

fusion [ˈfjuːʒən] *n* (*of ideas, qualities*)
слия́ние; (*also*: **nuclear** ~)
я́дерный си́нтез

fuss [fʌs] *n* (*excitement*) сумато́ха;
(*anxiety*) суета́; (*trouble*) шум; **to
make** *or* **kick up a** ~ (*impf*)
(подня́ть *pf*) шум; **to make a** ~ **of
sb** носи́ться (*impf*) с кем-н; ~**y** *adj*
(*nervous*) суетли́вый; (*choosy*)
мéлочный, сýетный; (*elaborate*)
вы́чурный

futile [ˈfjuːtaɪl] *adj* (*attempt*)
тще́тный; (*comment*) беспло́дный

future [ˈfjuːtʃər] *adj* бу́дущий ♦ *n*
бу́дущее *nt adj*; (*LING*: *also*: ~
tense) бу́дущее вре́мя *nt*; **in
(the)** ~ в бу́дущем; **in the near/**

immediate ~ в недалёком/ближайшем бу́дущем

fuze [fjuːz] n (US) = **fuse**

fuzzy ['fʌzɪ] adj (thoughts, picture) расплы́вчатый; (hair) пуши́стый

G, g

g. abbr = **gram** г

gadget ['gædʒɪt] n приспособле́ние

Gaelic ['geɪlɪk] n (LING) га́льский язы́к

gag [gæg] n (on mouth) кляп ♦ vt вставля́ть (вста́вить pf) кляп +dat

gain [geɪn] n (increase) приро́ст ♦ vt (confidence, experience) приобрета́ть (приобрести́ pf); (speed) набира́ть (набра́ть pf) ♦ vi (benefit): **to ~ from sth** извлека́ть (извле́чь pf) вы́году из чего́-н; **to ~ 3 pounds (in weight)** поправля́ться (попра́виться pf) на 3 фу́нта; **~ on sb** догоня́ть (догна́ть pf) кого́-н

gala ['gɑːlə] n (festival) пра́зднество

galaxy ['gæləksɪ] n гала́ктика

gale [geɪl] n (wind) си́льный ве́тер; (at sea) штормово́й ве́тер

gallery ['gælərɪ] n (also: **art ~**) галере́я; (in hall, church) балко́н; (in theatre) галёрка

gallon ['gælən] n галло́н (4,5 ли́тра)

gallop ['gæləp] vi (horse) скака́ть (impf) (гало́пом), галопи́ровать (impf)

galore [gə'lɔː] adv в изоби́лии

gamble ['gæmbl] n риско́ванное предприя́тие, риск ♦ vt (money) ста́вить (поста́вить pf) ♦ vi (take a risk) рискова́ть (рискну́ть pf); (bet) игра́ть (impf) в аза́ртные и́гры; **to ~ on sth** (also fig) де́лать (сде́лать pf) ста́вку на что-н; **~r** n

игро́к

gambling ['gæmblɪŋ] n аза́ртные и́гры fpl

game [geɪm] n игра́; (match) матч; (esp TENNIS) гейм; (also: **board ~**) насто́льная игра́; (CULIN) дичь f ♦ adj (willing): **~ (for)** гото́вый (на +acc); **big ~** кру́пный зверь

gammon ['gæmən] n (bacon) о́корок; (ham) ветчина́

gang [gæŋ] n ба́нда; (of friends) компа́ния

gangster ['gæŋstə'] n га́нгстер

gap [gæp] n (space) промежу́ток; (: between teeth) щербина; (: in time) интерва́л; (difference) расхожде́ние; **generation ~** разногла́сия ме́жду поколе́ниями

gaping ['geɪpɪŋ] adj (hole) зия́ющий

garage ['gærɑːʒ] n гара́ж; (petrol station) запра́вочная ста́нция, бензоколо́нка

garbage ['gɑːbɪdʒ] n (US: rubbish) му́сор; (inf: nonsense) ерунда́; **~ can** n (US) помо́йный я́щик

garden ['gɑːdn] n сад; **~s** npl (park) парк msg; **~er** n садо́вод; (employee) садо́вник(ица); **~ing** n садово́дство

garish ['gɛərɪʃ] adj (light) ре́зкий; (dress, colour) крича́щий

garland ['gɑːlənd] n гирля́нда

garlic ['gɑːlɪk] n чесно́к

garment ['gɑːmənt] n наря́д

garnish ['gɑːnɪʃ] vt украша́ть (укра́сить pf)

garrison ['gærɪsn] n гарнизо́н

gas [gæs] n газ; (US: gasoline) бензи́н ♦ vt (kill) удуша́ть (удуши́ть pf) (га́зом)

gash [gæʃ] n (wound) глубо́кая ра́на; (cut) глубо́кий поре́з ♦ vt распа́рывать (распоро́ть pf)

gasoline ['gæsəliːn] n (US) бензи́н

gasp [gɑːsp] n (breath) вдох

gas station n (US) заправочная станция, бензоколонка

gastric ['gæstrɪk] adj (MED) желудочный

gate [geɪt] n калитка; (at airport) выход; **~s** ворота; **~way** n ворота pl

gather ['gæðə²] vt собирать (собрать pf); (understand) полагать (impf) ♦ vi собираться (собраться pf); **to ~ speed** набирать (набрать pf) скорость; **~ing** n собрание

gaudy ['gɔːdɪ] adj пёстрый

gauge [geɪdʒ] n (instrument) измерительный прибор ♦ vt (amount, quantity) измерять (измерить pf); (fig) оценивать (оценить pf)

gaunt [gɔːnt] adj изможденный

gauntlet ['gɔːntlɪt] n (fig): **to run the ~** подвергаться (подвергнуться pf) нападкам; **to throw down the ~** бросать (бросить pf) перчатку

gauze [gɔːz] n (fabric) марля

gave [geɪv] pt of **give**

gay [geɪ] adj (cheerful) весёлый; (homosexual): **~ bar** бар для голубых или гомосексуалистов ♦ n гомосексуалист, голубой m adj; **he is ~** он гомосексуалист или голубой

gaze [geɪz] n (пристальный) взгляд ♦ vi: **to ~ at sth** разглядывать (impf) что-н

GB abbr = **Great Britain**

GCSE n abbr (BRIT) = General Certificate of Secondary Education

GCSE - аттестат о среднем образовании. Школьники сдают экзамены для получения этого аттестата в возрасте 15-16 лет.

Часть предметов, по которым сдаются экзамены, обязательна, часть - по выбору. Однако этого аттестата не достаточно для поступления в университет.

gear [gɪə²] n (equipment, belongings etc) принадлежности fpl; (AUT) скорость f; (: mechanism) передача f ♦ vt (fig): **to ~ sth to** приспосабливать (приспособить pf) что-н к +dat; **top** или (US) **high/low ~** высшая/низкая скорость; **in ~** в зацеплении; **~box** n коробка передач или скоростей; **~ lever** (US **~ shift**) n переключатель n скоростей

geese [giːs] npl of **goose**

gelatin(e) ['dʒɛlətiːn] n желатин

gem [dʒɛm] n (stone) драгоценный камень m, самоцвет

Gemini ['dʒɛmɪnaɪ] n Близнецы mpl

gender ['dʒɛndə²] n (sex) пол; (LING) род

gene [dʒiːn] n ген

general ['dʒɛnərl] n (MIL) генерал ♦ adj общий; (movement, interest) всеобщий; **in ~** в общем; **~ election** n всеобщие выборы mpl; **~ly** adv вообще; (+vb) обычно; **to become ~ly available** становиться (стать pf) общедоступным(ой); **it is ~ly accepted that ...** общепризнанно, что ...

generate ['dʒɛnəreɪt] vt (power, electricity) генерировать (impf), вырабатывать (выработать pf); (excitement, interest) вызывать (вызвать pf); (+vb) создавать (создать pf)

generation [dʒɛnə'reɪʃən] n поколение; (of power) генерирование; **for ~s** из поколе́ния в поколе́ние

generator ['dʒenəreɪtə^r] n
генера́тор

generosity [dʒenə'rɔsɪtɪ] n
ще́дрость f

generous ['dʒenərəs] adj (person:
lavish) ще́дрый; (: unselfish)
великоду́шный; (amount of
money) значи́тельный

genetics [dʒɪ'netɪks] n гене́тика

Geneva [dʒɪ'niːvə] n Жене́ва

genial ['dʒiːnɪəl] adj (smile,
expression) приве́тливый; (host)
раду́шный

genitals ['dʒenɪtlz] npl половы́е
о́рганы mpl

genius ['dʒiːnɪəs] n (skill) тала́нт;
(person) ге́ний

gent [dʒent] n abbr (BRIT : inf) =
gentleman

gentle ['dʒentl] adj не́жный,
ла́сковый; (nature, movement,
landscape) мя́гкий

gentleman ['dʒentlmən] (irreg) n
(man) джентльме́н

gently ['dʒentlɪ] adv (smile, treat,
speak) не́жно, ла́сково; (curve,
slope, move) мя́гко

gentry ['dʒentrɪ] n inv: **the ~**
дворя́нство

gents [dʒents] n: **the ~** мужско́й
туале́т

genuine ['dʒenjuɪn] adj (sincere)
и́скренний; (real) по́длинный

geographic(al) [dʒɪə'ɡræfɪk(l)] adj
географи́ческий

geography [dʒɪ'ɔɡrəfɪ] n
геогра́фия

geology [dʒɪ'ɔlədʒɪ] n геоло́гия

geometry [dʒɪ'ɔmɪtrɪ] n геоме́трия

Georgia ['dʒɔːdʒə] n Гру́зия; **~n** adj
грузи́нский

geranium [dʒɪ'reɪnɪəm] n гера́нь f

geriatric [dʒerɪ'ætrɪk] adj
гериатри́ческий

germ [dʒəːm] n (MED) микро́б

German ['dʒəːmən] adj неме́цкий
♦ n не́мец(мка); **~ measles** n
(BRIT) красну́ха

Germany ['dʒəːmənɪ] n Герма́ния

gesture ['dʒestjə^r] n жест

KEYWORD

get [get] (pt, pp **got**; US pp **gotten**)
vi 1 (become) станови́ться (стать
pf); **it's getting late** стано́вится
по́здно; **to get old** старе́ть
(постаре́ть pf); **to get tired**
устава́ть (уста́ть pf); **to get cold**
мёрзнуть (замёрзнуть pf); **to get
annoyed easily** легко́
раздража́ться (impf); **he was
getting bored** ему́ ста́ло ску́чно;
he gets drunk every weekend он
напива́ется ка́ждый выходно́й
2 (be): **he got killed** его́ уби́ли;
when do I get paid? когда́ мне
запла́тят?
3 (go): **to get to/from**
добира́ться (добра́ться pf) до
+gen/из +gen/c +gen; **how did you
get here?** как Вы сюда́
добра́ли́сь?
4 (begin): **to get to know sb**
узнава́ть (узна́ть pf) кого́-н; **I'm
getting to like him** он начина́ет
мне нра́виться; **let's get started**
дава́йте начнём
♦ modal aux vb: **you've got to do it**
Вы должны́ э́то сде́лать
♦ vt 1: **to get sth done** сде́лать
(pf) что-н; **to get the washing
done** стира́ть (постира́ть pf); **to
get the dishes done** мыть
(помы́ть или вы́мыть pf) посу́ду; **to
get the car started** or **to start**
заводи́ть (завести́ pf) маши́ну; **to
get sb to do** заставля́ть
(заста́вить pf) кого́-н +infin; **to get
sb ready** собира́ть (собра́ть pf)
кого́-н; **to get sth ready** гото́вить
(пригото́вить pf) что-н; **to get sth**

drunk напáивать (напои́ть pf) когó-н; **she got me into trouble** онá вовлеклá меня́ в неприя́тности

2 (obtain: permission, results) получáть (получи́ть pf); (find: job, flat) находи́ть (найти́ pf); (person: call) звать (позвáть pf); (: pick up) забирáть (забрáть pf); (call out: doctor, plumber etc) вызывáть (вы́звать pf); (object: carry) приноси́ть (принести́ pf); (: buy) покупáть (купи́ть pf); (: deliver) доставля́ть (достáвить pf); **we must get him to hospital** мы должны́ достáвить егó в больни́цу; **do you think we'll get the piano through the door?** как Вы ду́маете, как мы протáщим пиани́но чéрез дверь?; **I'll get the car** я схожу́ за маши́ной; **can I get you something to drink?** Позвóльте предложи́ть Вам чтó-нибудь вы́пить?

3 (receive) получáть (получи́ть pf); **to get a reputation for** приобретáть (приобрести́ pf) +instr; **what did you get for your birthday?** что Вам подари́ли на день рождéния?

4 (grab) хватáть (схвати́ть pf); (hit): **the bullet got him in the leg** пу́ля попáла ему́ в нóгу

5 (catch, take): **we got a taxi** мы взя́ли такси́; **did she get her plane?** онá успéла на самолёт?; **what train are you getting?** каки́м пóездом Вы éдете?; **where do I get the train?** где мне сесть на пóезд?

6 (understand) понимáть (поня́ть pf); (hear) расслы́шать (pf); (do you) **get it?** (inf) (тебé) поня́тно?; **I've got it!** тепéрь поня́тно!; **I'm sorry, I didn't get**

your name прости́те, я не расслы́шал Вáше и́мя

7 (have, possess): **how many children have you got?** скóлько у Вас детéй?; **I've got very little time** у меня́ óчень мáло врéмени

get about vi (news) распространя́ться (распространи́ться pf); **I don't get about much now** (go places) тепéрь я мáло где бывáю

get along vi: **get along with** лáдить (impf) с +instr; (manage) = **get by**; **I'd better be getting along** мне, пожáлуй, порá (идти́)

get at vt fus (criticize) придирáться (придрáться pf) к +dat; (reach) дотя́гиваться (дотяну́ться pf) до +gen

get away vi (leave) уходи́ть (уйти́ pf); (escape) убегáть (убежáть pf)

get away with vt fus: **he gets away with everything** ему́ всё схóдит с рук

get back vi (return) возвращáться (возврати́ться pf), верну́ться (pf) ♦ vt получáть (получи́ть pf) назáд or обрáтно

get by vi (pass) проходи́ть (пройти́ pf); (manage): **to get by without** обходи́ться (обойти́сь pf) без +gen; **I will get by** (manage) я спрáвлюсь

get down vt (depress) угнетáть (impf) ♦ vi: **to get down from** слезáть (слезть pf) с +gen

get down to vt fus садиться (сесть pf) or брáться (взя́ться pf) за +acc

get in vi (train) прибывáть (прибы́ть pf), приходи́ть (прийти́ pf); (arrive home) приходи́ть (прийти́ pf); (to concert, building) попадáть (попáсть pf), проходи́ть (пройти́ pf); **he got in by ten votes** он прошёл с большинство́м в де́сять голосо́в; **as soon as the bus arrived we all got in** как то́лько авто́бус подошёл, мы се́ли в него́

get into vt fus (building) входи́ть (войти́ pf) в +acc; (vehicle) сади́ться (сесть pf) в +acc; (clothes) влеза́ть (влезть pf) в +acc; (fight, argument) вступа́ть (вступи́ть pf) в +acc; (university, college) поступа́ть (поступи́ть pf) в +acc; (subj: train) прибыва́ть (прибы́ть pf) в/на +acc; **to get into bed** ложи́ться (лечь pf) в посте́ль

get off vi (escape): **to get off lightly/with sth** отде́лываться (отде́латься pf) легко́/чем-н ♦ vt (clothes) снима́ть (снять pf) ♦ vt fus (train, bus) сходи́ть (сойти́ pf) с +gen; (horse, bicycle) слеза́ть (слезть pf) с +gen

get on vi (age) старе́ть (impf); **how are you getting on?** как Ва́ши успе́хи?

get out vi (leave) выбира́ться (вы́браться pf); (socialize) выбира́ться (вы́браться pf) из до́ма

get out of vt fus (duty) отде́лываться (отде́латься pf) от +gen

get over vt fus (illness) преодолева́ть (преодоле́ть pf)

get round vt fus (law, rule) обходи́ть (обойти́ pf); (fig: person) угова́ривать (уговори́ть pf)

get through vi (TEL) дозва́ниваться (дозвони́ться pf)

get through to vt fus (TEL) дозва́ниваться (дозвони́ться pf) до +gen

get together vi (several people) собира́ться (собра́ться pf) ♦ vt (people) собира́ть (собра́ть pf)

get up vi вставать (встать pf)

get up to vt fus (BRIT) затева́ть (зате́ять pf); **they're always getting up to mischief** они́ всегда́ прока́зничают

ghastly ['gɑːstlɪ] adj ме́рзкий, омерзи́тельный

gherkin ['gəːkɪn] n марино́ванный огуре́ц

ghetto ['gɛtəu] n ге́тто nt ind

ghost [gəust] n (spirit) привиде́ние, при́зрак

giant ['dʒaɪənt] n (in myths) велика́н; (fig, COMM) гига́нт ♦ adj огро́мный

Gibraltar [dʒɪ'brɔːltə] n Гибралта́р

giddy ['gɪdɪ] adj: **I feel ~** (dizzy) у меня́ кру́жится голова́

gift [gɪft] n (present) пода́рок; (ability) дар, тала́нт; **~ed** adj одарённый

gigantic [dʒaɪ'gæntɪk] adj гига́нтский

giggle ['gɪgl] vi хихи́кать (impf)

gills [gɪlz] npl (of fish) жа́бры fpl

gilt [gɪlt] adj позоло́ченный

gimmick ['gɪmɪk] n уло́вка, трюк

gin [dʒɪn] n джин

ginger ['dʒɪndʒə] n (spice) имби́рь m; **~bread** n (cake) имби́рный пиро́г; (biscuit) имби́рное пече́нье

gingerly ['dʒɪndʒəlɪ] adv опа́сливо

giraffe [dʒɪ'rɑːf] n жира́ф

girl [gəːl] n (child) де́вочка; (young unmarried woman) де́вушка; (daughter) до́чка; **an English ~** молода́я англича́нка; **~friend** n подру́га

giro ['dʒaɪrəu] n (BRIT: welfare cheque) чек, по кото́рому получа́ют посо́бие по безрабо́тице

gist [dʒɪst] n суть f

KEYWORD

give [gɪv] (pt **gave**, pt **given**) vt 1
(hand over): **to give sb sth** or **sth
to sb** давать (дать pf) кому-н
что-н; **they gave her a book for
her birthday** они подарили ей
книгу на день рождения
2 (used with noun to replace verb):
to give a sigh вздыхать
(вздохнуть pf); **to give a shrug**
передёргивать (передёрнуть pf)
плечами; **to give a speech**
выступать (выступить pf) с
речью; **to give a lecture** читать
(прочитать pf) лекцию; **to give
three cheers** трижды прокричать
(pf) "ура"
3 (tell: news) сообщать
(сообщить pf); (advice) давать
(дать pf); **could you give him a
message for me please? tell her
that ...** передайте ему,
пожалуйста, от меня, что ...; **I've
got a message to give you from
your brother** я должен передать
тебе что-то от твоего брата
4: **to give sb sth** (clothing, food,
right) давать (дать pf) кому-н
что-н; (title) присваивать
(присвоить pf) кому-н что-н;
(honour, responsibility) возлагать
(возложить pf) на кого-н что-н;
to give sb a surprise удивлять
(удивить pf) кого-н; **that's given
me an idea** это навело меня на
мысль
5 (dedicate: one's life) отдавать
(отдать pf); **you'll need to give
me more time** Вы должны дать
мне больше времени; **she gave
it all her attention** она отнеслась
к этому с большим вниманием
6 (organize: dinner etc) давать
(дать pf)
♦ vi 1 (stretch: fabric)

растягиваться (растянуться pf)
2 (break, collapse) = **give way**
give away vt (money, object)
отдавать (отдать pf); (bride)
отдавать (отдать pf) замуж
give back vt отдавать (отдать
pf) обратно
give in vi (yield) сдаваться
(сдаться pf)
♦ vt (essay etc) сдавать (сдать pf)
give off vt (smoke, heat)
выделять (impf)
give out vt (distribute) раздавать
(раздать pf)
give up vi (stop trying) сдаваться
(сдаться pf)
♦ vt (job, boyfriend) бросать
(бросить pf); (idea, hope)
оставлять (оставить pf); **to give
up smoking** бросать (бросить pf)
курить; **to give o.s. up** сдаваться
(сдаться pf)
give way vi (rope, ladder) не
выдерживать (выдержать pf);
(wall, roof) обваливаться
(обвалиться pf); (floor)
проваливаться (провалиться pf);
(chair) рухнуть (pf); (BRIT : AUT)
уступать (уступить pf) дорогу;
his legs gave way beneath him у
него подкосились ноги

glacier ['glæsɪə*r*] n ледник
glad [glæd] adj: **I am ~** я рад; **~ly**
adv (willingly) с радостью
glamorous ['glæmərəs] adj
шикарный, роскошный
glance [glɑːns] n (look) взгляд ♦ vi:
to ~ at бросать (бросить pf)
взгляд (взглянуть pf) на +acc
glancing ['glɑːnsɪŋ] adj боковой
gland [glænd] n железа
glare [glɛə*r*] n взгляд; (of light)
сияние
glaring ['glɛərɪŋ] adj явный,
вопиющий

glass [glɑːs] n (substance) стекло́; (container, contents) стака́н; **~es** npl (spectacles) очки́ ntpl

glaze [gleɪz] n (on pottery) глазу́рь f; **~d** adj (eyes) му́тный, ту́склый

gleam [gliːm] vi мерца́ть (impf)

glee [gliː] n (joy) ликова́ние

glen [glen] n речна́я доли́на

glib [glɪb] adj (promise, response) бо́йкий

glide [glaɪd] vi скользи́ть (impf); (AVIAT) плани́ровать (impf); (bird) пари́ть (impf); **~r** n пла́нер

gliding ['glaɪdɪŋ] n плани́рование

glimmer ['glɪmə*] n (of interest, hope) про́блеск; (of light) мерца́ние

glimpse [glɪmps] n: **~ of** взгляд на +acc ♦ vt ви́деть (уви́деть pf) ме́льком, взгляну́ть (pf) на +acc

glint [glɪnt] vi блесте́ть (блесну́ть pf), мерца́ть (impf)

glitter ['glɪtə*] vi сверка́ть (сверкну́ть pf)

global ['gləʊbl] adj (interest, attention) глоба́льный; **~ warming** n глоба́льное потепле́ние

globe [gləʊb] n (world) земно́й шар; (model of world) гло́бус

gloom [gluːm] n мрак; (fig) уны́ние

glorified ['glɔːrɪfaɪd] adj несча́стный; **she is merely a ~ secretary** она́ всего́-на́всего несча́стная секрета́рша

glorious ['glɔːrɪəs] adj (sunshine, flowers) великоле́пный

glory ['glɔːrɪ] n (prestige) сла́ва

gloss [glɒs] n (shine) гля́нец, лоск; (also: **~ paint**) гля́нцевая кра́ска

glossary ['glɒsərɪ] n глосса́рий

glossy ['glɒsɪ] adj (photograph, magazine) гля́нцевый; (hair) блестя́щий

glove [glʌv] n перча́тка; **~**

compartment n перча́точный я́щик, барда́чок (разг)

glow [gləʊ] vi свети́ться (impf)

glucose ['gluːkəʊs] n глюко́за

glue [gluː] n клей ♦ vt: **to ~ sth onto sth** прикле́ивать (прикле́ить pf) что-н на что-н

glum [glʌm] adj мра́чный

glut [glʌt] n избы́ток

gnarled [nɑːld] adj (tree) сучкова́тый; (hand) скрю́ченный

gnat [næt] n мо́шка

go [gəʊ] (pt **went**, pp **gone**, pl **goes**) vi **1** (move: on foot) ходи́ть/идти́ (пойти́ pf); (travel: by transport) е́здить/е́хать (пое́хать pf); **she went into the kitchen** она́ пошла́ на ку́хню; **he often goes to China** он ча́сто е́здит в Кита́й; **they are going to the theatre tonight** сего́дня ве́чером они́ иду́т в теа́тр

2 (depart: on foot) уходи́ть (уйти́ pf); (: by plane) улета́ть (улете́ть pf); (: by train, car) уезжа́ть (уе́хать pf); **the plane goes at 6am** самолёт улета́ет в 6 часо́в утра́; **the train/bus goes at 6pm** по́езд/авто́бус ухо́дит в 6 часо́в; **I must go now** мне на́до идти́

3 (attend): **to go to** ходи́ть (impf) в/на +acc; **she doesn't go to lectures/school** она́ не хо́дит на ле́кции/в шко́лу; **she went to university** она́ учи́лась в университе́те

4 (take part in activity): **to go dancing** ходи́ть/идти́ (пойти́ pf) танцева́ть

5 (work): **is your watch going?** Ва́ши часы́ иду́т?; **the bell went** прозвене́л звоно́к; **the tape recorder was still going** магнитофо́н всё ещё рабо́тал

6 (*become*): **to go pale** бледне́ть (побледне́ть *pf*); **to go mouldy** пле́сневеть (запле́сневеть *pf*)

7 (*be sold*) расходи́ться (разойти́сь *pf*); **the books went for £10** кни́ги разошли́сь по £10

8 (*fit, suit*): **to go with** подходи́ть (подойти́ *pf*) к +*dat*

9 (*be about to, intend to*): **to go to do** собира́ться (собра́ться *pf*) +*infin*

10 (*time*) идти́ (*impf*)

11 (*event, activity*) проходи́ть (пройти́ *pf*); **how did it go?** как всё прошло́?

12 (*be given*): **the proceeds will go to charity** при́быль пойдёт на благотвори́тельные це́ли; **the job is to go to someone else** рабо́ту даду́т кому́-то друго́му

13 (*break etc*): **the fuse went** предохрани́тель перегоре́л; **the leg of the chair went** но́жка сту́ла слома́лась

14 (*be placed*): **the milk goes in the fridge** молоко́ быва́ет в холоди́льнике

♦ *n* 1 (*try*) попы́тка; **to have a go (at doing)** де́лать (сде́лать *pf*) попы́тку (+*infin*)

2 (*turn*): **whose go is it?** (*in board games*) чей ход?

3 (*move*): **to be on the go** быть (*impf*) на нога́х

go about *vi* (*also*: **go around**: *rumour*) идти́ (*impf*)

go ahead *vi* (*event*) продолжа́ться (продо́лжиться *pf*); **to go ahead with** (*project*) приступа́ть (приступи́ть *pf*) к +*dat*; **may I begin? - yes, go ahead!** мо́жно начина́ть? - да, дава́йте!

go along *vi* идти́ (пойти́ *pf*); **to go along with sb** (*accompany*)

идти́ (пойти́ *pf*) с кем-н; (*agree*) соглаша́ться (согласи́ться *pf*) с кем-н

go away *vi* (*leave: on foot*) уходи́ть (уйти́ *pf*); (: *by transport*) уезжа́ть (уе́хать *pf*); **go away and think about it for a while** иди́ и поду́май об э́том

go back *vi* (*return, go again*) возвраща́ться (возврати́ться *pf*), верну́ться (*pf*); **we went back into the house** мы верну́лись в дом; **I am never going back to her house again** я никогда́ бо́льше не пойду́ к ней

go for *vt fus* (*fetch: paper, doctor*) идти́ (пойти́ *pf*) за +*instr*; (*choose, like*) выбира́ть (вы́брать *pf*); (*attack*) набра́сываться (набро́ситься *pf*) на +*acc*; **that goes for me too** ко мне э́то то́же отно́сится

go in *vi* (*enter*) входи́ть (войти́ *pf*), заходи́ть (зайти́ *pf*)

go in for *vt fus* (*enter*) принима́ть (приня́ть *pf*) уча́стие в +*prp*; (*take up*) набра́сываться (набро́ситься *pf*) на +*acc*

go into *vt fus* (*enter*) входи́ть (войти́ *pf*) в +*acc*; (*take up*) заня́ться (*pf*) +*instr*; **to go into details** входи́ть (*impf*) *or* вдава́ться (*impf*) в подро́бности

go off *vi* (*leave: on foot*) уходи́ть (уйти́ *pf*); (: *by transport*) уезжа́ть (уе́хать *pf*); (*food*) по́ртиться (испо́ртиться *pf*); (*bomb*) взрыва́ться (взорва́ться *pf*); (*gun*) выстре́ливать (вы́стрелить *pf*); (*alarm*) звене́ть (зазвене́ть *pf*); (*event*) проходи́ть (пройти́ *pf*); (*lights*) выключа́ться (вы́ключиться *pf*)

♦ *vt fus* разлюби́ть (*pf*)

go on *vi* (*discussion*) продолжа́ться (*impf*); (*continue*): **to go on (doing)** продолжа́ть

(impf) (+infin); life goes on жизнь продолжа́ется; **what's going on here?** что здесь происхо́дит?; **we don't have enough information to go on** у нас недоста́точно информа́ции, что́бы продолжа́ть (продо́лжить pf)

go on with vt fus продолжа́ть (продо́лжить pf)

go out vi (fire, light) га́снуть (пога́снуть pf); (leave): **to go out of** выходи́ть (вы́йти pf) из +gen; **are you going out tonight?** Вы сего́дня ве́чером куда́-нибудь идёте?

go over vi идти́ (пойти́ pf) ♦ vt просма́тривать (просмотре́ть pf)

go through vt fus (town etc: by transport) проезжа́ть (прое́хать pf) че́рез +acc; (files, papers) просма́тривать (просмотре́ть pf)

go up vi (ascend) поднима́ться (подня́ться pf); (price, level, buildings) расти́ (вы́расти pf)

go without vt fus обходи́ться (обойти́сь pf) без +gen

---

go-ahead ['gəʊəhed] n добро́

goal [gəʊl] n (SPORT) гол; (aim) цель f; **~keeper** n врата́рь m, голки́пер; **~ post** n бокова́я шта́нга, сто́йка воро́т

goat [gəʊt] n (billy) козёл; (nanny) коза́

go-between ['gəʊbɪtwiːn] n посре́дник(ица)

god [gɒd] n (fig) божество́, бог; **God** Бог; **~child** n кре́стник(ица); **~daughter** n кре́стница; **~dess** n боги́ня; **~father** n крёстный оте́ц; **~mother** n крёстная мать f; **~son** n кре́стник

goggles ['gɒglz] npl защи́тные очки́ ntpl

going ['gəʊɪŋ] adj: **the ~ rate** теку́щие расце́нки fpl

gold [gəʊld] n (metal) зо́лото ♦ adj золото́й; **~ reserves** золото́й запа́с; **~fish** n серебря́ный кара́сь m

golf [gɒlf] n гольф; **~ club** n (stick) клю́шка (в го́льфе); **~ course** n по́ле для игры́ в гольф

gone [gɒn] pp of **go**

gong [gɒŋ] n гонг

good [gʊd] adj хоро́ший; (pleasant) прия́тный; (kind) до́брый ♦ n (virtue) добро́; (benefit) по́льза; **~s** npl (COMM) това́ры mpl; **~!** хорошо́!; **to be ~ at** име́ть (impf) спосо́бности к +dat; **it's ~ for you** э́то поле́зно (для здоро́вья); **would you be ~ enough to ...?** не бу́дете ли Вы так добры́ +pf infin ...?; **a ~ deal (of)** большо́е коли́чество (+gen); **a ~ many** мно́го (+gen); **~ afternoon/evening!** до́брый день/ве́чер!; **~ morning!** до́брое у́тро!; **~ night!** (on leaving) до свида́ния!; (on going to bed) споко́йной or до́брой но́чи!; **it's no ~ complaining** жа́ловаться бесполе́зно; **for ~** навсегда́; **~bye** excl до свида́ния; **to say ~bye (to)** проща́ться (попроща́ться pf) (c +instr); **Good Friday** n Страстна́я пя́тница; **~-looking** adj краси́вый; **~-natured** adj доброду́шный; (pet) послу́шный; **~ness** n доброта́; **for ~ness sake!** ра́ди Бо́га!; **~ness gracious!** Бо́же!, Го́споди!; **~will** n (of person) до́брая во́ля

goose [guːs] n (pl **geese**) гусь m(f)

gooseberry ['gʊzbərɪ] n крыжо́вник

goose pimples npl гуси́ная ко́жа fsg

gore [gɔː] vt бода́ть (забода́ть pf)

gorge [gɔːdʒ] n тесни́на, (у́зкое)

ущелье [vt: **to ~ o.s. (on)** наедаться (наесться pf) (+gen)

gorgeous ['gɔːdʒəs] adj прелестный

gorilla [gə'rɪlə] n горилла

gorse [gɔːs] n (BOT) утёсник

gospel ['gɔspl] n (REL) Евангелие

gossip ['gɔsɪp] n (rumours) сплетня; (chat) разговоры mpl; (person) сплетник(ица)

got [gɔt] pt, pp of **get**; **~ten** pp (US) of **get**

gout [gaut] n (MED) подагра

govern ['gʌvn] vt (country) управлять (impf) +instr, (event, conduct) руководить (impf) +instr

governess ['gʌvənɪs] n гувернантка

government ['gʌvnmənt] n правительство; (act) управление

governor ['gʌvənər] n (of state, colony) губернатор; (of school etc) член правления

gown [gaun] n (dress) платье; (of teacher, judge) мантия

GP n abbr (= general practitioner) участковый терапевт

grab [græb] vt хватать (схватить pf) ♦ vi: **to ~ at** хвататься (схватиться pf) за +acc

grace [greɪs] n грация, изящество; (REL) молитва (перед едой); **5 days' ~** 5 дней отсрочки; **~ful** adj (animal, person) грациозный

gracious ['greɪʃəs] adj (person, smile) любезный ♦ excl: **(good) ~!** Боже правый!

grade [greɪd] n (COMM, quality) сорт, (SCOL, mark) оценка; (US: school year) класс ♦ vt (rank, class) распределять (распределить pf); (products) сортировать (рассортировать pf); **~ crossing** n (US) железнодорожный переезд; **~ school** n (US) начальная школа

gradient ['greɪdɪənt] n (of hill) уклон

gradual ['grædjuəl] adj постепенный; **~ly** adv постепенно

graduate [n 'grædjuɪt, vb 'grædjueɪt] n выпускник(ица) ♦ vi: **to ~ from** заканчивать (закончить pf); **I ~d last year** я закончил университет в прошлом году

graduation [grædju'eɪʃən] n (ceremony) выпускной вечер

graffiti [grə'fiːtɪ] n, npl графити nt ind

grain [greɪn] n (seed) зерно; (no pl: cereals) хлебные злаки mpl; (of sand) песчинка; (of salt) крупинка; (of wood) волокно

gram [græm] n грамм

grammar ['græmər] n грамматика; **~ school** n (BRIT) ≈ гимназия

<hr>

grammar school - гимназия. В Великобритании гимназии дают среднее образование. Ученики поступают в них на конкурсной основе. Число их невелико. Однако в США **grammar school** называются начальные школы.

<hr>

grammatical [grə'mætɪkl] adj грамматический

gramme [græm] n = **gram**

grand [grænd] adj грандиозный; (gesture) величественный; **~child** (pl **~children**) n внук(учка); **~dad** n (inf) дедушка; **~daughter** n внучка; **~eur** ['grændʒər] n великолепие; **~father** n дед; **~iose** ['grændɪəus] adj грандиозный; **~ma** n (inf) бабуля, бабушка; **~mother** n бабушка; **~parents** npl дедушка m и бабушка f; **~ piano** n рояль _m_; **~son** _n_ внук; **~stand** _n_ (SPORT) центральная трибуна

granite ['grænɪt] _n_ гранит

granny ['grænɪ] _n_ (inf) = **grandma**

grant [grɑːnt] _vt_ (money, visa) выдавать (выдать pf); (request) удовлетворять (удовлетворить pf); (admit) признавать (признать pf) ♦ _n_ (SCOL) стипендия; (ADMIN) грант; **to take sb/sth for ~ed** принимать (принять pf) кого-н/что-н как должное

grape [greɪp] _n_ виноград _m no pl_; **~fruit** (_pl_ **~fruit** _or_ **~fruits**) _n_ грейпфрут

graph [grɑːf] _n_ (diagram) график; **~ic** _adj_ (explicit) выразительный; (design) изобразительный; **~ics** _n_ графика

grapple ['græpl] _vi_: **to ~ with sb** схватываться (схватиться pf) с кем-н

grasp [grɑːsp] _vt_ хватать (схватить pf) ♦ _n_ (grip) хватка; (understanding) понимание; **~ing** _adj_ (greedy) алчный

grass [grɑːs] _n_ трава; (lawn) газон; **~hopper** _n_ кузнечик; **~roots** _adj_ (support, organization) низовой

grate [greɪt] _n_ камінная решётка ♦ _vt_ (CULIN) тереть (натереть pf) ♦ _vi_ (metal, chalk): **to ~ (on)** скрежетать (impf) (по +dat)

grateful ['greɪtful] _adj_ благодарный

grater ['greɪtər] _n_ тёрка

gratifying ['grætɪfaɪɪŋ] _adj_ приятный

grating ['greɪtɪŋ] _n_ решётка ♦ _adj_ (noise) скрипучий

gratitude ['grætɪtjuːd] _n_ благодарность f

grave [greɪv] _n_ могила ♦ _adj_ серьёзный

gravel ['grævl] _n_ гравий

gravestone ['greɪvstəun] _n_

надгробие

graveyard ['greɪvjɑːd] _n_ кладбище

gravity ['grævɪtɪ] _n_ тяготение, притяжение; (seriousness) серьёзность f

gravy ['greɪvɪ] _n_ (sauce) соус

gray [greɪ] _adj_ (US) = **grey**

graze [greɪz] _vi_ пастись (impf) ♦ _vt_ (scrape) царапать (оцарапать pf)

grease [griːs] _n_ (lubricant) смазка; (fat) жир ♦ _vt_ смазывать (смазать pf); **~proof paper** _n_ (BRIT) жиронепроницаемая бумага

greasy ['griːsɪ] _adj_ жирный

great [greɪt] _adj_ (large) большой; (heat, pain) сильный; (city, man) великий; (inf: terrific) замечательный; **Great Britain** _n_ Великобритания

> **Great Britain** - Великобритания. В Великобританию входят Англия, Шотландия и Уэльс. Эти страны вместе с Северной Ирландией образуют United Kingdom - Соединённое Королевство (Великобритании).

great- _prefix_ пра-

greatly _adv_ очень; (influenced) весьма, в значительной степени

Greece [griːs] _n_ Греция

greed [griːd] _n_ жадность f; (for power, wealth) жажда; **~y** _adj_ жадный

Greek [griːk] _adj_ греческий

green [griːn] _adj_ зелёный ♦ _n_ (colour) зелёный цвет; (grass) лужайка; **~s** _npl_ (vegetables) зелень fsg; **~ belt** _n_ зелёная зона, зелёный пояс; **~ery** _n_ зелень f; **~grocer** _n_ (BRIT) зеленщик; (shop) овощной магазин; **~house** _n_ теплица;

~house effect n: the **~house effect** парниковый эффект
Greenland ['gri:nlənd] n Гренландия
greet [gri:t] vt приветствовать (поприветствовать pf); здороваться (поздороваться pf); (news) встречать (встретить pf); **~ing** n приветствие
gregarious [grə'geəriəs] adj общительный
grenade [grə'neid] n (also: **hand ~**) (ручная) граната
grew [gru:] pt of **grow**
grey [grei] (US **gray**) adj серый; (hair) седой; **~hound** n борзая f adj
grid [grid] n (pattern) сетка; (grating) решётка, (ELEC) единая энергосистема
grief [gri:f] n горе n
grievance ['gri:vəns] n жалоба
grieve [gri:v] vi горевать (impf); **to ~ for** горевать (impf) о +prp
grievous ['gri:vəs] adj: **~ bodily harm** тяжёлые телесные повреждения ntpl
grill [gril] n (on cooker) гриль m; (grilled food: also: **mixed ~**) жаренные на гриле продукты mpl ♦ vt (BRIT) жарить (пожарить pf) (на гриле)
grim [grim] adj (place, person) мрачный, угрюмый; (situation) тяжёлый
grimace [gri'meis] n гримаса
grime [graim] n (from soot, smoke) копоть f; (from mud) грязь f
grin [grin] n широкая улыбка ♦ vi: **to ~ (at)** широко улыбаться (улыбнуться pf) (+dat)
grind [graind] (pt, pp **ground**) vt (coffee, pepper) молоть (смолоть pf); (US: meat) прокручивать (прокрутить pf); (knife) точить (наточить pf)

grip [grip] n хватка; (of tyre) сцепление ♦ vt (object) схватывать (схватить pf); (audience, attention) захватывать (захватить pf); **to come to ~s with** +instr, **~ping** adj захватывающий
grisly ['grizli] adj жуткий
grit [grit] n (stone) щебень m ♦ vt (road) посыпать (посыпать pf) щебнем; **to ~ one's teeth** стискивать (стиснуть pf) зубы
groan [grəun] n (of person) стон
grocer ['grəusə*] n бакалейщик; **~ies** npl бакалея fsg; **~'s (shop)** n бакалейный магазин, бакалея
groin [grɔin] n пах
groom [gru:m] n (for horse) конюх; (also: **bride~**) жених ♦ vt (horse) ухаживать (impf) за +instr; **to ~ sb for** (job) готовить (подготовить pf) кого-н к +dat
groove [gru:v] n канавка
gross [grəus] adj вульгарный; (neglect, injustice) вопиющий; (COMM, income) валовой; **~ly** adv чрезмерно
grotesque [grə'tesk] adj гротескный
ground [graund] pt, pp of **grind** ♦ n (earth, land) земля; (floor) пол; (US: also: **~ wire**) заземление; (usu pl: reason) основание ♦ vt (US: ELEC) заземлять (заземлить pf); **~s** npl (of coffee) гуща fsg; **school ~** школьная площадка; **sports ~** спортивная площадка; **on the ~** на земле; **to the ~** (burnt) дотла; **the plane was ~ed by the fog** самолёт не мог подняться в воздух из-за тумана; **~ing** n (in education) подготовка; **~work** n (in preparation) фундамент, основа; **to do the ~work** закладывать (заложить pf) фундамент

group [gru:p] *n* гру́ппа

grouse [graus] *n inv* (*bird*) (шотла́ндская) куропа́тка

grow [grəu] (*pt* **grew**, *pp* **~n**) *vi* расти́ (вы́расти *pf*); (*become*) станови́ться (стать *pf*) ♦ *vt* (*roses, vegetables*) выра́щивать (вы́растить *pf*); (*beard, hair*) отра́щивать (отрасти́ть *pf*); **~ up** *vi* (*child*) расти́ (вы́расти *pf*); взросле́ть (повзросле́ть *pf*)

growl [graul] *vi* (*dog*) рыча́ть (*impf*)

grown [grəun] *pp of* **grow**; **~-up** *n* (*adult*) взро́слый *m(f) adj* ♦ *adj* (*son, daughter*) взро́слый

growth [grəuθ] *n* рост; (*increase*) приро́ст; (*MED*) о́пухоль *f*

grub [grʌb] *n* (*larva*) личи́нка; (*inf: food*) жратва́

grubby ['grʌbɪ] *adj* гря́зный

grudge [grʌdʒ] *n* недово́льство; **to bear sb a ~** зата́ивать (затаи́ть *pf*) на кого́-н оби́ду

gruelling ['gruəlɪŋ] (*US* **grueling**) *adj* изнури́тельный, тя́жкий

gruesome ['gru:səm] *adj* жу́ткий

gruff [grʌf] *adj* (*voice*) хри́плый; (*manner*) ре́зкий

grumble ['grʌmbl] *vi* ворча́ть (*impf*)

grumpy ['grʌmpɪ] *adj* сварли́вый

grunt [grʌnt] *vi* (*pig*) хрю́кать (хрю́кнуть *pf*); (*person*) бурча́ть (бу́ркнуть *pf*)

guarantee [gærən'ti:] *n* (*assurance*) поручи́тельство; (*warranty*) гара́нтия ♦ *vt* гаранти́ровать (*impf/pf*); **he can't ~ (that) he'll come** он не мо́жет поручи́ться, что он придёт

guard [ɡɑːd] *n* (*one person*) охра́нник; (*squad*) охра́на; (*BRIT: RAIL*) конду́ктор; (*TECH*) предохрани́тельное устро́йство; (*also:* **fire~**) предохрани́тельная решётка (*пе́ред ками́ном*) ♦ *vt* (*prisoner*) охраня́ть (*impf*); (*secret*)

храни́ть (*impf*); **to ~ (against)** (*protect*) охраня́ть (*impf*) (от *+gen*); **to be on one's ~** быть (*impf*) насторо́же *or* начеку́; **~ against** *vt fus* (*prevent*) предохраня́ть (*impf*) от *+gen*; **~ed** *adj* (*statement, reply*) осторо́жный; **~ian** *n* (*LAW*) опеку́н

guerrilla [ɡəˈrɪlə] *n* партиза́н(ка)

guess [ges] *vt* (*estimate*) счита́ть (сосчита́ть *pf*) приблизи́тельно; (*correct answer*) уга́дывать (угада́ть *pf*) ♦ *vi* дога́дываться (догада́ться *pf*) ♦ *n* дога́дка; **to take** *or* **have a ~** отга́дывать (отгада́ть *pf*)

guest [ɡest] *n* (*visitor*) гость(я) *m(f)*; (*in hotel*) постоя́лец(лица); **~house** *n* гости́ница

guidance ['ɡaɪdəns] *n* (*advice*) сове́т

guide [ɡaɪd] *n* (*in museum, on tour*) гид, экскурсово́д; (*also:* **~book**) путеводи́тель *m*; (*handbook*) руково́дство ♦ *vt* (*show around*) води́ть (*impf*); (*direct*) направля́ть (напра́вить *pf*); **~book** *n* путеводи́тель *m*; **~ dog** *n* соба́ка-поводы́рь *f*; **~lines** *npl* руково́дство *ntsg*

guild [ɡɪld] *n* ги́льдия

guilt [ɡɪlt] *n* (*remorse*) вина́; (*culpability*) вино́вность *f*; **~y** *adj* (*person, expression*) винова́тый; (*of crime*) вино́вный

guinea pig ['ɡɪnɪ-] *n* морска́я сви́нка; (*fig*) подо́пытный кро́лик

guise [ɡaɪz] *n*: **in** *or* **under the ~ of** под ви́дом *or* личи́ной *+gen*

guitar [ɡɪˈtɑː^r] *n* гита́ра

gulf [ɡʌlf] *n* (*GEO*) зали́в; (*fig*) про́пасть *f*

gull [ɡʌl] *n* ча́йка

gullible ['ɡʌlɪbl] *adj* легкове́рный

gully ['ɡʌlɪ] *n* (*ravine*) лощи́на

gulp [gʌlp] *vi* нéрвно сглáтывать (сглотнýть *pf*) ♦ *vt* (*also*: ~ **down**) проглáтывать (проглотить *pf*)

gum [gʌm] *n* (*ANAT*) деснá; (*glue*) клей; (*also*: **chewing-~**) жвáчка (*разг*), жевáтельная резинка

gun [gʌn] *n* пистолéт; (*rifle, airgun*) ружьё; (*artillery*) стрельбá; **~man** (*irreg*) *n* вооружённый бандит; **~point**: **at ~point** под дýлом пистолéта; **~shot** *n* выстрел

guru ['guru:] *n* гурý *m ind*

gust [gʌst] *n* (*of wind*) порыв

gusto ['gʌstəu] *n*: **with ~** (*eat*) с удовóльствием; (*work*) с жáром

gut [gʌt] *n* (*ANAT*) кишкá; **~s** *npl* (*ANAT*) кишки *fpl*, внýтренности *fpl*; (*inf*: *courage*) мýжество *ntsg*

gutter ['gʌtə*r*] *n* (*in street*) стóчная канáва; (*of roof*) водостóчный жёлоб

guy [gaɪ] *n* (*inf*: *man*) пáрень *m*; (*also*: **~rope**) палáточный шнур

gym [dʒɪm] *n* (*also*: **~nasium**) гимнастический зал; (*also*: **~nastics**) гимнáстика; **~nastics** [dʒɪm'næstɪks] *n* гимнáстика

gynaecologist [gaɪnɪ'kɔlədʒɪst] (*US* **gynecologist**) *n* гинекóлог

gypsy ['dʒɪpsɪ] *n* цыгáн(ка)

H, h

habit ['hæbɪt] *n* (*custom*) привычка; (*addiction*) пристрáстие; (*REL*) облачéние

habitat ['hæbɪtæt] *n* средá обитáния

habitual [hə'bɪtjuəl] *adj* (*action*) привычный; (*liar, drinker*) отъявленный

hack [hæk] *vt* отрубáть (отрубить *pf*) ♦ *n* (*pej*: *writer*) писáка *m/f*

had [hæd] *pt, pp of* **have**

haddock ['hædək] (*pl* ~ *or* ~**s**) *n* трескá

hadn't ['hædnt] = **had not**

haemorrhage ['hemərɪdʒ] (*US* **hemorrhage**) *n* кровотечéние; **brain ~** кровоизлияние (в мозг)

haggard ['hægəd] *adj* (*face, look*) измождённый

Hague [heɪg] *n*: **The ~** Гáага

hail [heɪl] *n* град ♦ *vt* (*flag down*) подзывáть (подозвáть *pf*) ♦ *vi*: **it's ~ing** идёт град; **~stone** *n* грáдина

hair [hεə*r*] *n* вóлосы *pl*; (*of animal*) волосянóй покрóв; **to do one's ~** причёсываться (причесáться *pf*); **~brush** *n* щётка для волóс; **~cut** *n* стрижка; **~dresser** *n* парикмáхер; **~ dryer** *n* фен; **~spray** *n* лак для волóс; **~style** *n* причёска; **~y** *adj* (*person*) волосáтый; (*animal*) мохнáтый

half [hɑ:f] (*pl* **halves**) *n* половина; (*also*: ~ **pint**) (*of beer etc*) полпинты *f*; (*on train, bus*) билéт за полцены ♦ *adv* наполовину; **one and a ~** (*with m noun*) полторá *+gen sg*; (*with f noun*) полторы *+gen sg*; **three and a ~** три с половиной; **a dozen (of)** полдюжины *f* (*+gen*); **a pound (of)** полфýнта *m* (*+gen*); **a week and a ~** полторы недéли; ~ (**of**) половина *m* (*+gen*); **the amount of** половина *+gen*; **to cut sth in ~** разрезáть (разрéзать *pf*) что-н попопáм; **~-hearted** *adj* лени́вый; **~-hour** *n* полчасá *m*; **~-price** *adj, adv* за полцены; **~-time** *n* перерыв между тáймами; **~-way** *adv* на полпути

---

half-term - корóткие каникулы. В середине триместров шкóльникам дают корóткий перерыв в 3-4 дня.

hall [hɔːl] n (in house) прихо́жая f adj, холл; (for concerts, meetings etc) зал

hallmark ['hɔːlmɑːk] n про́ба; (fig) отличи́тельная черта́

Hallowe'en ['hæləʊ'iːn] n кану́н Дня всех святы́х

> **Hallowe'en** – кану́н Дня всех святы́х. Этот пра́здник отмеча́ют ве́чером 31 октября́. По тради́ции э́то день ведьм и ду́хов. Де́ти наряжа́ются в костю́мы ведьм и вампи́ров, де́лают ла́мпы из тыкв. С наступле́нием темноты́ они́ хо́дят по дома́м, игра́я в игру́ подо́бную ру́сским Коробе́йникам. Если хозя́ева не даю́т де́тям конфе́т, они́ мо́гут сыгра́ть над ни́ми шу́тку.

hallucination [həluːsɪ'neɪʃən] n галлюцина́ция

hallway ['hɔːlweɪ] n прихо́жая f adj, холл

halo ['heɪləʊ] n (REL) нимб

halt [hɔːlt] n остано́вка ♦ vt остана́вливать (останови́ть pf) ♦ vi остана́вливаться (останови́ться pf)

halve [hɑːv] vt (reduce) сокраща́ть (сократи́ть pf) наполови́ну; (divide) дели́ть (раздели́ть pf) попола́м

halves [hɑːvz] pl of **half**

ham [hæm] n (meat) ветчина́; **~burger** n га́мбургер

hammer ['hæmə'] n молото́к ♦ vt (on door etc) колоти́ть (impf) ♦ vt (nail): **to ~ in** забива́ть (заби́ть pf), вбива́ть (вбить pf); **to ~ sth into sb** (fig) вда́лбливать (вдолби́ть pf) что-н кому́-н

hamper ['hæmpə'] vt меша́ть (помеша́ть pf) +dat ♦ n (basket) больша́я корзи́на с кры́шкой

hamster ['hæmstə'] n хомя́к

hand [hænd] n (ANAT) рука́, кисть f; (of clock) стре́лка; (worker) рабо́чий m adj ♦ vt (give) вруча́ть (вручи́ть pf); **to give** или **lend sb a ~** протя́гивать (протяну́ть pf) кому́-н ру́ку (по́мощи); **at ~** под руко́й; **in ~** (situation) под контро́лем; (time) в распоряже́нии; **on ~** (person, services etc) в распоряже́нии; **I have the information to ~** я располага́ю информа́цией; **on the one ~..., on the other ~...** с одно́й стороны́ ..., с друго́й стороны́ ...; **~ in** vt (work) сдава́ть (сдать pf); **~ out** vt раздава́ть (разда́ть pf); **~ over** vt передава́ть (переда́ть pf), вруча́ть (вручи́ть pf); **~bag** n (да́мская) су́мочка; **~brake** n ручно́й то́рмоз; **~cuffs** npl нару́чники mpl; **~ful** n (fig: of people) го́рстка; **~-held** adj ручно́й

handicap ['hændɪkæp] n (disability) физи́ческая неполноце́нность f; (disadvantage) препя́тствие ♦ vt препя́тствовать (воспрепя́тствовать pf) +dat; **mentally/ physically ~ped** у́мственно/ физи́чески неполноце́нный

handkerchief ['hæŋkətʃɪf] n носово́й плато́к

handle ['hændl] n (touch) держа́ть (impf) в рука́х; (deal with) занима́ться (impf) +instr; (: successfully) справля́ться (спра́виться pf) с +instr; (treat: people) обраща́ться (impf) с +instr; **to fly off the ~** (inf) срыва́ться (сорва́ться pf); **"~ with care"** "обраща́ться осторо́жно"

hand luggage n ручна́я кладь f

handmade ['hænd'meɪd] adj

ручной работы; **it's ~** это ручная работа

hand-out ['hændaut] *n* благотворительная помощь *f*; (*summary: of lecture*) краткое изложение

handshake ['hændʃeɪk] *n* рукопожатие

handsome ['hænsəm] *adj* (*man*) красивый; (*woman*) интересный; (*building, profit*) внушительный

handwriting ['hændraɪtɪŋ] *n* почерк

handy ['hændɪ] *adj* (*useful*) удобный; (*close at hand*) поблизости

hang [hæŋ] (*pt, pp* hung) *vt* вешать (повесить *pf*); (*pt, pp* ~ed; *execute*) вешать (повесить *pf*) ♦ *vi* висеть (*impf*) ♦ *n*: **to get the ~ of sth** (*inf*) разбираться (разобраться *pf*) в чём-н; **~ around** *vi* слоняться (*impf*), болтаться (*impf*); **~ on** *vi* (*wait*) подождать (*impf*); **~ up** *vi* (*TEL*) вешать (повесить *pf*) трубку ♦ *vt* вешать (повесить *pf*)

hangar ['hæŋəʳ] *n* ангар

hangover ['hæŋəuvəʳ] *n* (*after drinking*) похмелье

hanky ['hæŋkɪ] *n abbr* = **handkerchief**

haphazard [hæp'hæzəd] *adj* бессистемный

happen ['hæpən] *vi* случаться (случиться *pf*), происходить (произойти *pf*); **I ~ed to meet him in the park** я случайно встретил его в парке; **~ as it ~s** кстати

happily ['hæpɪlɪ] *adv* (*luckily*) к счастью; (*cheerfully*) радостно

happiness ['hæpɪnɪs] *n* счастье

happy ['hæpɪ] *adj* (*pleased*) счастливый; (*cheerful*) весёлый; **I am ~ (with it)** (*content*) я доволен (этим); **he is always ~ to help** он

всегда рад помочь; **~ birthday!** с днём рождения!

harassment ['hærəsmənt] *n* преследование

harbour ['hɑːbəʳ] (*US* **harbor**) *n* гавань *f* ♦ *vt* (*hope, fear*) затаивать (затаить *pf*); (*criminal, fugitive*) укрывать (укрыть *pf*)

hard [hɑːd] *adj* (*surface, object*) твёрдый; (*question, problem*) трудный; (*work, life*) тяжёлый; (*person*) суровый; (*facts, evidence*) неопровержимый ♦ *adv*: **to work ~** много и усердно работать (*impf*); **I don't have any ~ feelings** я не держу зла; **he is ~ of hearing** он туг на ухо; **to think ~** хорошо подумать (*pf*); **to try ~ to win** упорно добиваться (*impf*) победы; **to look ~ at** смотреть (посмотреть *pf*) пристально на +*acc*; **~back** *n* книга в твёрдом переплёте; **~ disc** *n* жёсткий диск; **~en** *vt* (*substance*) делать (сделать *pf*) твёрдым(ой); (*attitude, person*) ожесточать (ожесточить *pf*) ♦ *vi* (*see vt*) твердеть (затвердеть *pf*); ожесточаться (ожесточиться *pf*)

hardly ['hɑːdlɪ] *adv* едва; **~ ever/ anywhere** почти никогда/нигде

hardship ['hɑːdʃɪp] *n* тяготы *fpl*, трудности *fpl*

hard up *adj* (*inf*) нуждающийся; **I am ~** я нуждаюсь

hardware ['hɑːdwɛəʳ] *n* (*tools*) скобяные изделия *ntpl*

hard-working [hɑːd'wəːkɪŋ] *adj* усердный

hardy ['hɑːdɪ] *adj* выносливый; (*plant*) морозоустойчивый

hare [hɛəʳ] *n* заяц

harm [hɑːm] *n* (*injury*) телесное повреждение, травма; (*damage*) ущерб ♦ *vt* (*thing*) повреждать (повредить *pf*); (*person*) наносить

(нанести pf) вред +dat; **~ful** adj
вредный; **~less** adj безобидный

harmonica [hɑːˈmɒnɪkə] n губная
гармоника

harmonious [hɑːˈməunɪəs] adj
гармоничный

harmony [ˈhɑːmənɪ] n гармония

harness [ˈhɑːnɪs] n (for horse)
упряжь f; (for child) постромки
fpl; (safety harness) привязные
ремни mpl ♦ vt (horse) запрягать
(запрячь pf); (resources, energy)
ставить (поставить pf) себе на
службу

harp [hɑːp] n арфа

harrowing [ˈhærəuɪŋ] adj
душераздирающий

harsh [hɑːʃ] adj (sound, light,
criticism) резкий; (person, remark)
жёсткий; (life, winter) суровый

harvest [ˈhɑːvɪst] n (time) жатва;
(of barley, fruit) урожай ♦ vt
собирать (собрать pf) урожай
+gen

has [hæz] vb see **have**

hash [hæʃ] n: to make a ~ of sth
запарывать (запороть pf) что-н

hasn't [ˈhæznt] = **has not**

hassle [ˈhæsl] (inf) n морока

haste [heɪst] n спешка; **~n** [heɪsn]
vt торопить (поторопить pf) ♦ vi:
to **~n to do** торопиться
(поторопиться pf) +infin

hastily [ˈheɪstɪlɪ] adv (see adj)
поспешно; опрометчиво

hasty [ˈheɪstɪ] adj поспешный;
(rash) опрометчивый

hat [hæt] n шляпа; (woolly) шапка

hatch [hætʃ] n (NAUT: also: **~way**)
люк; (also: **service ~**)
раздаточное окно ♦ vi (also: **~
out**) вылупляться (вылупиться
pf)

hatchet [ˈhætʃɪt] n (axe) топорик

hate [heɪt] vt ненавидеть (impf)

hatred [ˈheɪtrɪd] n ненависть f

haul [hɔːl] vt (pull) таскать/тащить
(impf) ♦ n (of stolen goods etc)
добыча; **~age** n перевозка

haunt [hɔːnt] vt (fig)
преследовать (impf); **to ~ sb/a
house** являться (явиться pf)
кому-н/в доме; **~ed** adj: **this
house is ~ed** в этом доме есть
привидения

have [hæv] (pt, pp **had**) aux vb **1**: to
have already eaten? ты уже поел?;
he has been kind to me он был
добр ко мне; **he has been
promoted** он получил
повышение по службе; **has he
told you?** он Вам сказал?; **having
or when he had finished ...**
закончив огкогда он закончил ...
2 (in tag questions) не так ли;
you've done it, haven't you? Вы
сделали это, не так ли?
3 (in short answers and questions):
**you've made a mistake - no I
haven't/so I have** Вы ошиблись -
нет, не ошибся/да, ошибся; **we
haven't paid - yes we have!** мы
не заплатили - нет, заплатили!;
I've been there before, have you?
я там уже был, а Вы?
♦ modal aux vb (be obliged): **I have
(got) to finish this work** я должен
закончить эту работу; **I haven't
got** or **I don't have to wear
glasses** мне не надо носить
очки; **this has to be a mistake** это,
наверика, ошибка
♦ vt **1** (possess): **I etc have** у меня
(есть) etc +nom; **he has (got) blue
eyes/dark hair** у него голубые
глаза/тёмные волосы; **do you
have** or **have you got a car?** у Вас
есть машина?
2 (referring to meals etc): to have

dinner обéдать (пообéдать pf); **to have breakfast** зáвтракать (позáвтракать pf); **to have a cigarette** выкýривать (выкурить pf) сигарéту; **to have a glass of wine** выпивáть (выпить pf) бокáл винá

3 (receive, obtain etc): **may I have your address?** Вы мóжете дать мне свой áдрес?; **you can have the book for £5** берите кнúгу за £5; **I must have the report by tomorrow** доклáд дóлжен быть у меня к зáвтрашнему дню; **she is having a baby in March** онá бýдет рожáть в мáрте

4 (allow) допускáть (допустить pf); **I won't have it!** я этого не допущý!

5: **I am having my television repaired** мне дóлжны починить телевизор; **to have sb do** просить (попросить pf) когó-н +infin; **he soon had them all laughing** вскóре он застáвил всех смеяться

6 (experience, suffer): **I have flu/a headache** у меня грипп/болит головá; **to have a cold** простужáться (простудиться pf); **she had her bag stolen** у неё укрáли сýмку; **he had an operation** емý сдéлали опéрацию

7 (+n): **to have a swim** плáвать (поплáвать pf); **to have a rest** отдыхáть (отдохнýть pf); **let's have a look** давáйте посмóтрим; **we are having a meeting tomorrow** зáвтра у нас бýдет собрáние; **let me have a try** дáйте мне попрóбовать

have out vt: **to have it out with sb** объясняться (объясниться pf) с кем-н; **she had her tooth out** ей удалили зуб; **she had her tonsils**

out ей вырезали глáнды

haven ['heɪvn] n (fig) убéжище

haven't ['hævnt] = **have not**

havoc ['hævək] n (chaos) хáос

hawk [hɔːk] n я́стреб

hay [heɪ] n сéно; **~ fever** n сеннáя лихорáдка; **~stack** n стог сéна

hazard ['hæzəd] n опáсность f ♦ vt: **to ~ a guess** осмéливаться (осмéлиться pf) предположить; **~ous** adj опáсный

haze [heɪz] n дымка; **heat ~** мáрево

hazy ['heɪzɪ] adj тумáнный

he [hiː] pron он

head [hed] n (ANAT) головá; (mind) ум; (of list, queue) начáло; (of table) главá; (COMM) руководитель(ница) m(f); (SCOL) дирéктор ♦ vt возглавлять (возглáвить pf); **~s or tails** орёл или рéшка; **he is ~ over heels in love** он влюблён по ýши; **~ for** vt fus (place) направляться (напрáвиться pf) в/на +acc or к +dat; (disaster) обрекáть (обрéчь pf) себя на +acc; **~ache** n (MED) головнáя боль f; **~ing** n заголóвок; **~land** n мыс; **~light** n фáра; **~line** n заголóвок; **~long** adv (headfirst) головóй вперёд; (hastily) опромéтчиво; **~master** n дирéктор шкóлы; **~mistress** n дирéктор шкóлы; **~ office** n управлéние; **~-on** adj лобовóй ♦ adv нос к нóсу; **~phones** npl наýшники mpl; **~quarters** npl штаб-квартира fsg; **~scarf** n косынка, (головнóй) платóк; **~ teacher** n дирéктор шкóлы; **~way** n: **to make ~way** продвигáться (продвинуться pf) вперёд; **~y** adj (experience) головокружительный;

(atmosphere) пьяный

heal [hi:l] vt вылечивать
(вылечить pf); (damage)
поправлять (поправить pf) ♦ vi
(injury) заживать (зажить pf);
(damage) восстанавливаться
(восстановиться pf)

health [helθ] n здоровье; ~ **care** n
здравоохранение; **Health
Service** n (BRIT): the Health
Service служба
здравоохранения; **~y** adj
здоровый; (pursuit) полезный;
(profit) достаточно хороший

heap [hi:p] n (small) куча; (large)
груда ♦ vt: to ~ (up) (stones, sand)
сваливать (свалить pf) в кучу; to
~ with sth (plate, sink) наполнять
(наполнить pf) чем-н; ~s of (inf)
куча fsg +gen

hear [hɪə] (pt, pp ~d) vt слышать
(услышать pf); (lecture, concert,
case) слушать (impf); to ~ about
слышать (услышать pf) о +prp; to
~ from sb слышать (услышать pf)
от кого-н; I can't ~ you Вас не
слышно; ~d [hɜːd] pt, pp of hear;
~ing n (sense) слух; (LAW, POL)
слушание; ~ing aid n слуховой
аппарат

heart [hɑːt] n сердце; (of problem,
matter) суть f; ~s npl (CARDS)
черви fpl; to lose/take ~ пасть
(pf)/не падать (impf) духом; at ~ в
глубине души; (off) by ~
наизусть; ~ache n сердечная
боль f; ~ attack n сердечный
приступ, инфаркт; ~beat n
(rhythm) сердцебиение; ~broken
adj: he is ~broken он убит горем;
~ failure n (fatal) остановка
сердца; ~felt adj искренний

hearth [hɑːθ] n очаг

heartless [ˈhɑːtlɪs] adj
бессердечный

hearty [ˈhɑːtɪ] adj (person, laugh)

задорный, весёлый; (welcome,
support) сердечный; (appetite)
здоровый

heat [hi:t] n тепло; (extreme) жар;
(of weather) жара; (excitement)
пыл; (: also: qualifying ~: in race)
забег; (: in swimming) заплыв ♦ vt
(water, food) греть (нагреть pf);
(house) отапливать (отопить pf);
~ up vi (water, house) согреваться
(согреться pf) ♦ vt (food, water)
подогревать (подогреть pf);
(room) согревать (обогреть pf);
~ed adj (argument) горячий;
(pool) обогреваемый; ~er n
обогреватель m

heath [hi:θ] n (BRIT) (вересковая)
пустошь f

heather [ˈhɛðə] n вереск

heating [ˈhi:tɪŋ] n отопление

heat wave n период сильной
жары

heaven [ˈhɛvn] n рай; ~**ly** adj (fig)
райский

heavily [ˈhɛvɪlɪ] adv (fall, sigh)
тяжело; (drink, smoke, depend)
сильно; (sleep) крепко

heavy [ˈhɛvɪ] adj тяжёлый; (rain,
blow, fall) сильный; (build: of
person) грузный; he is a ~
drinker/smoker он много пьёт/
курит

Hebrew [ˈhi:bru:] adj
древнееврейский

Hebrides [ˈhɛbrɪdi:z] npl: the ~
Гебридские острова mpl

hectic [ˈhɛktɪk] adj (day)
суматошный; (activities)
лихорадочный

he'd [hi:d] = he would, he had

hedge [hɛdʒ] n живая изгородь f

hedgehog [ˈhɛdʒhɔg] n ёж

heed [hi:d] vt (also: take ~ of)
принимать (принять pf) во
внимание

heel [hi:l] n (of foot) пятка; (of shoe)

каблу́к

hefty ['heftɪ] adj (person, object)
здорове́нный; (profit, fine)
изря́дный

height [haɪt] n (of tree, of plane)
высота́; (of person) рост; (of
power) верши́на; (of season)
разга́р; (of luxury, taste) верх; **~en**
vt усили́вать (уси́лить pf)

heir [ɛəʳ] n насле́дник; **~ess** n
насле́дница

held [held] pt, pp of **hold**

helicopter ['helɪkɔptəʳ] n вертолёт

helium ['hiːlɪəm] n ге́лий

hell [hel] n (also fig) ад; **~!** (inf)
чёрт!

he'll [hiːl] = **he will, he shall**; see
will

hello [hə'ləu] excl здра́вствуйте;
(informal) приве́т; (TEL) алло́

helmet ['helmɪt] n (of policeman,
miner) ка́ска; (also: **crash ~**)
шлем

help [help] n по́мощь f ♦ vt
помога́ть (помо́чь pf) +dat; **~!** на
по́мощь!, помоги́те!; **~ yourself**
угоща́йтесь; **he can't ~ it** он
ничего́ не мо́жет поде́лать с
э́тим; **~er** n помо́щник(ица); **~ful**
adj поле́зный; **~less** adj
беспо́мощный; **~line** n телефо́н
дове́рия

hem [hem] n (of dress) подо́л

hemorrhage ['hemərɪdʒ] n (US) =
haemorrhage

hen [hen] n (chicken) ку́рица

hence [hens] adv (therefore)
сле́довательно, всле́дствие
э́того; **2 years ~** (from now) по
истече́нии двух лет

hepatitis [hepə'taɪtɪs] n гепати́т,
боле́знь f Бо́ткина

her [həːʳ] pron (direct) её; (indirect)
ей; (after prep: +gen) неё; (: +instr,
+dat, +prp) ней; see also **me** ♦ adj
её; (referring to subject of sentence)

свой; see also **my**

herald ['herəld] vt (event)
предвеща́ть (impf)

herb [həːb] n (as medicine)
лека́рственная трава́; **~s** npl
(CULIN) зе́лень fsg

herd [həːd] n ста́до

here [hɪəʳ] adv (location) здесь;
(destination) сюда́; (at this point: in
past) тут; **from ~** отсю́да; **"~!"**
(present) "здесь!"; **~ is..., ~ are ...**
вот ...

hereditary [hɪ'redɪtrɪ] adj
насле́дственный

heresy ['herəsɪ] n е́ресь f

heritage ['herɪtɪdʒ] n насле́дие

hermit ['həːmɪt] n отше́льник(ица)

hernia ['həːnɪə] n гры́жа

hero ['hɪərəu] (pl **~es**) n геро́й; **~ic**
[hɪ'rəuɪk] adj геро́йческий

heroin ['herəuɪn] n герои́н

heroine ['herəuɪn] n геро́иня

heron ['herən] n ца́пля

herring ['herɪŋ] n (ZOOL) сельдь f;
(CULIN) селёдка

hers [həːz] pron её; (referring to
subject of sentence) свой; see also
mine¹

herself [həː'self] pron (reflexive, after
prep: +acc, +gen) себя́; (: +dat,
+prp) себе́; (: +instr) собо́й;
(emphatic) сама́; (alone): **by ~**
одна́; see also **myself**

he's [hiːz] = **he is, he has**

hesitant ['hezɪtənt] adj
нереши́тельный; **to be ~ to do**
не реша́ться (impf) +infin

hesitate ['hezɪteɪt] vi колеба́ться
(поколеба́ться pf); (be unwilling)
не реша́ться (impf)

hesitation [hezɪ'teɪʃən] n
колеба́ние

heterosexual ['hetərəu'seksjuəl] adj
гетеросексуа́льный

heyday ['heɪdeɪ] n: **the ~ of**
расцве́т +gen

hi [haɪ] *excl* (*as greeting*) приве́т

hiccoughs ['hɪkʌps] *npl* = **hiccups**

hiccups ['hɪkʌps] *npl*: **she's got (the)** ~ у неё икóта

hide [haɪd] (*pt* **hid**, *pp* **hidden**) (*skin*) шкýра ♦ *vt* (*object, person*) прýтать (спрýтать *pf*); (*feeling, information*) скрыва́ть (скрыть *pf*); (*sun, view*) закрыва́ть (закры́ть *pf*)
♦ *vi*: **to** ~ (**from sb**) прýтаться (спря́таться *pf*) (от когó-н);
~**away** *n* убе́жище

hideous ['hɪdɪəs] *adj* жýткий; (*face*) омерзи́тельный

hiding ['haɪdɪŋ] *n* (*beating*) пóрка;
to be in ~ скрыва́ться (*impf*)

hierarchy ['haɪərɑːkɪ] *n* иера́рхия

hi-fi ['haɪfaɪ] *n* (*system*) стерео-систе́ма

high [haɪ] *adj* высóкий; (*wind*) сильный ♦ *adv* высóко; **the building is 20 m** ~ высота́ зда́ния - 20 м; **to be** ~ (*inf: on drugs etc*) кайфова́ть (*impf*); ~ **risk** высóкая сте́пень ри́ска; ~ **in the air** (*position*) высóко в вóздухе;
~**chair** *n* высóкий стýльчик (*для ма́леньких дете́й*); ~**er education** *n* вы́сшее образова́ние; ~ **jump** *n* прыжóк в высотý; **Highlands** *npl*: **the Highlands** Высокогóрья *ntpl* (*Шотла́ндии*); ~**light** *n* (*of event*) кульмина́ция ♦ *vt* (*problem, need*) выявля́ть (вы́явить *pf*); ~**ly** *adv* óчень; (*paid*) высóко; **to speak** ~**ly of** высóко отзыва́ться (отозва́ться *pf*) о +*prp*; **to think** ~**ly of** быть (*impf*) высóкого мне́ния о +*prp*; ~**ness** *n*: **Her/His Highness** Её/Егó Высóчество; ~-**pitched** *adj* пронзи́тельный; ~-**rise** *adj* высóтный; ~ **school** *n* (*BRIT*) сре́дняя шкóла (*для 11-18ти ле́тних*); (*US*) сре́дняя шкóла (*для 14-18ти ле́тних*)

high school - сре́дняя шкóла. В Брита́нии де́ти посеща́ют сре́днюю шкóлу в вóзрасте от 11 до 18 лет. В США шкóльники внача́ле посеща́ют мла́дшую сре́днюю шкóлу, а зате́м, в вóзрасте от 14 до 18 лет, сре́днюю шкóлу. Шкóльное образова́ние обяза́тельно до 16 лет.

high: ~ **season** *n* (*BRIT*) разга́р сезóна; ~ **street** *n* (*BRIT*) центра́льная ýлица; ~**way** *n* (*US*) тра́сса, автостра́да; (*main road*) автостра́да

hijack ['haɪdʒæk] *vt* (*plane, bus*) угоня́ть (угна́ть *pf*)

hike [haɪk] *n*: **to go for a** ~ идти́ (пойти́ *pf*) в похóд

hilarious [hɪ'lɛərɪəs] *adj* чрезвыча́йно смешнóй

hill [hɪl] *n* (*small*) холм; (*fairly high*) гора́; (*slope*) склон; ~**side** *n* склон; ~**y** *adj* холми́стый

him [hɪm] *pron* (*direct*) егó; (*indirect*) емý; (*after prep: +gen*) негó; (: +*dat*) немý; (: +*instr*) ним; (: +*prp*) нём; *see also* **me**; ~**self** *pron* (*reflexive, after prep: +acc, +gen*) себя́; (: +*dat*, +*prp*) себе́; (: +*instr*) собóй; (*emphatic*) сам; (*alone*): **by** ~**self** оди́н; *see also* **myself**

hinder ['hɪndə^r] *vt* препя́тствовать (воспрепя́тствовать *pf*) *or* меша́ть (помеша́ть *pf*) +*dat*

hindrance ['hɪndrəns] *n* помéха

hindsight ['haɪndsaɪt] *n*: **with** ~ ретроспекти́вным взгля́дом

Hindu ['hɪnduː] *adj* инди́йский

hinge [hɪndʒ] *n* (*on door*) петля́

hint [hɪnt] *n* (*suggestion*) намёк; (*tip*) совéт; (*sign, glimmer*) подóбие

hip [hɪp] n бедро́

hippopotami [hɪpə'pɒtəmaɪ] npl of **hippopotamus**

hippopotamus [hɪpə'pɒtəməs] (pl ~es or hippopotami) n гиппопота́м

hire ['haɪər] vt (BRIT: car, equipment) брать (взять pf) напрока́т; (venue) снима́ть (снять pf), арендова́ть (impf/pf); (worker) нанима́ть (наня́ть pf); (BRIT: of car) прока́т; **for** ~ напрока́т; **~-purchase** n (BRIT): **to buy sth on ~-purchase** покупа́ть (купи́ть pf) что-н в рассро́чку

his [hɪz] adj его́; (referring to subject of sentence) свой; see also **my** ♦ pron его́; see also **mine¹**

hiss [hɪs] vi (snake, gas) шипе́ть (impf)

historian [hɪ'stɔːrɪən] n исто́рик

historic [hɪ'stɒrɪk] adj (agreement, achievement) истори́ческий; **~al** adj (event, film) истори́ческий

history ['hɪstərɪ] n (of town, country) исто́рия

hit [hɪt] (pt ~) vt ударя́ть (уда́рить pf); (target) попада́ть (попа́сть pf) в +acc; (collide with: car) ста́лкиваться (столкну́ться pf) с +instr; (affect: person, services) ударя́ть (уда́рить pf) по +dat ♦ n (COMPUT) посеще́ние; (success): **the play was a big ~** пье́са по́льзовалась больши́м успе́хом; **to ~ it off (with sb)** (inf) находи́ть (найти́ pf) о́бщий язы́к (с кем-н)

hitch [hɪtʃ] vt (also: ~ **up**: trousers, skirt) подтя́гивать (подтяну́ть pf) ♦ n (difficulty) поме́ха; **to ~ sth to** (fasten) привя́зывать (привяза́ть pf) что-н к +dat; (hook) прицепля́ть (прицепи́ть pf) что-н к +dat; **to ~ (a lift)** лови́ть (пойма́ть pf) попу́тку

hi-tech ['haɪtɛk] adj высокотехни́чный

hitherto [hɪðə'tuː] adv (formal) до настоя́щего вре́мени

HIV n abbr (= human immuno-deficiency virus) ВИЧ; **~-negative/positive** с отрица́тельной/положи́тельной реа́кцией на ВИЧ

hive [haɪv] n (of bees) у́лей

HMS abbr (BRIT) = His (or Her) Majesty's Ship

hoard [hɔːd] n (of food) (та́йный) запа́с; (of treasure) клад ♦ vt (provisions) запаса́ть (запасти́ pf); (money) копи́ть (скопи́ть pf)

hoarse [hɔːs] adj (voice) хри́плый

hoax [həʊks] n (false alarm) ло́жная трево́га

hob [hɒb] n ве́рхняя часть плиты́ с конфо́рками

hobby ['hɒbɪ] n хо́бби nt ind

hockey ['hɒkɪ] n хокке́й (на траве́)

hog [hɒg] vt (inf) завладева́ть (завладе́ть pf) +instr

hoist [hɔɪst] n подъёмник, лебёдка ♦ vt поднима́ть (подня́ть pf); **to ~ sth on to one's shoulders** взва́ливать (взвали́ть pf) что-н на пле́чи

hold [həʊld] (pt, pp held) vt (grip) держа́ть (impf); (contain) вмеща́ть (impf); (detain) содержа́ть (impf); (power, qualification) облада́ть (impf) +instr; (post) занима́ть (заня́ть pf); (conversation, meeting) вести́ (провести́ pf); (party) устра́ивать (устро́ить pf) ♦ vi (withstand pressure) выде́рживать (вы́держать pf); (be valid) остава́ться (оста́ться pf) в си́ле ♦ n (grasp) захва́т; (NAUT) трюм; (AVIAT) грузово́й отсе́к; **to ~ one's head up** высоко́ держа́ть (impf) го́лову; **to ~ sb hostage** держа́ть (impf) кого́-н в ка́честве заложника; **~ the line!** (TEL) не кладите or вешайте трубку!; **he ~s you responsible for her death** он считает Вас виновным в её смерти; **to catch** or **grab ~ of** хвататься (схватиться pf) за +acc; **to have a ~ over sb** держать (impf) кого-н в руках; **~ back** vt (thing) придержать (придержать pf); (person) удерживать (удержать pf); (information) скрывать (скрыть pf); **~ down** vt (person) удерживать (удержать pf); **to ~ down a job** удерживаться (удержаться pf) на работе; **~ on** vi (grip) держаться (impf); (wait) ждать (подождать pf); **~ on!** (TEL) не кладите or вешайте трубку!; **~ on to** vt fus (for support) держаться (impf) за +acc; (keep: object) придерживать (придержать pf); (: beliefs) сохранять (сохранить pf); **~ out** vt протягивать (протянуть pf); (hope, prospect) сохранять (сохранить pf) ♦ vi (resist) держаться (продержаться pf); **~ up** vt (raise) поднимать (поднять pf); (support) поддерживать (поддержать pf); (delay) задерживать (задержать pf); (rob) грабить (ограбить pf); **~er** n (container) держатель m; (of ticket, record) обладатель(ница) m(f); (title ~) носящий(ая) m(f) титул; **~up** n (robbery) ограбление; (delay) задержка; (BRIT: in traffic) пробка

hole [həul] n (in wall) дыра; (in road) яма; (burrow) нора; (in clothing) дырка; (in argument) брешь f

holiday ['hɔlɪdeɪ] n (BRIT: from school) каникулы pl; (: from work) отпуск; (day off) выходной день

m; (also: **public ~**) праздник; **on ~** (from school) на каникулах; (from work) в отпуске

Holland ['hɔlənd] n Голландия

hollow ['hɔləu] adj (container) полый; (log, tree) дуплистый; (cheeks) впалый; (laugh) неискренний; (claim, sound) пустой ♦ n (in ground) впадина; (in tree) дупло ♦ vt: **to ~ out** выкапывать (выкопать pf)

holly ['hɔlɪ] n остролист

holocaust ['hɔləkɔːst] n (nuclear) истребление; (Jewish) холокост

holy ['həulɪ] adj святой

homage ['hɔmɪdʒ] n: **to pay ~ to** воздавать (воздать pf) почести +dat

home [həum] n дом; (area, country) родина ♦ cpd домашний; (ECON, POL) внутренний; (SPORT): **~ team** хозяева mpl поля ♦ adv (go, come) домой; (hammer etc) в точку; **at ~** дома; (in country) на родине; (in situation) как у себя дома; **make yourself at ~** чувствуйте себя как дома; **~land** n родина; **~less** adj бездомный ♦ npl: **the ~less** бездомные pl; **~ly** adj уютный; **~-made** adj (food) домашний; (bomb) самодельный; **Home Office** n (BRIT): **the Home Office** ≈ Министерство внутренних дел

homeopathy [həumɪ'ɔpəθɪ] n (US) = **homoeopathy**

home: ~ page n электронная страница or страничка; **Home Secretary** n (BRIT) ≈ министр внутренних дел; **~sick** adj: **to be ~sick** (for family) скучать (impf) по дому; (for country) скучать (impf) по родине; **~ town** n родной город; **~work** n домашняя работа, домашнее задание

homicide ['hɔmɪsaɪd] n (esp US)

убийство

homoeopathy [həumɪˈɒpəθɪ] (US **homeopathy**) n гомеопатия

homogeneous [həməˈdʒiːnɪəs] adj однородный

homosexual [həməˈseksjuəl] adj гомосексуальный ♦ n гомосексуалист(ка)

honest [ˈɒnɪst] adj честный; **~ly** adv честно; **~y** n честность f

honey [ˈhʌnɪ] n (food) мёд; **~moon** n медовый месяц; **~suckle** n жимолость f

honorary [ˈɒnərərɪ] adj почётный

honour [ˈɒnəʳ] (US **honor**) n (person) почитать (impf), чтить (impf); (commitment) выполнять (выполнить pf) ♦ n (pride) честь f; (tribute, distinction) почесть f; **~able** (person, action) благородный

---

honours degree - (учёная) степень. Студенты университетов получают учёную степень. Такая степень выше по уровню, чем так называемая "обычная степень" или "зачёт".

---

hood [hud] n капюшон; (US : AUT) капот; (of cooker) вытяжной колпак

hoof [huːf] (pl **hooves**) n копыто

hook [huk] n крючок ♦ vt прицеплять (прицепить pf)

hooligan [ˈhuːlɪgən] n хулиган

hoop [huːp] n обруч

hoover ® [ˈhuːvəʳ] (BRIT) n пылесос ♦ vt пылесосить (пропылесосить pf)

hooves [huːvz] npl of **hoof**

hop [hɒp] n скакать (impf) на одной ноге

hope [həup] vti надеяться (impf)

♦ n надежда; **to ~ that/to do** надеяться (impf), что/+infin; **I ~ so/not** надеюсь, что да/нет; **~ful** adj (person) полный надежд; (situation) обнадёживающий; **to be ~ful of sth** надеяться (impf) на что-н; **~fully** adv (expectantly) с надеждой; **~fully, he'll come back** будем надеяться, что он вернётся; **~less** adj (situation, person) безнадёжный; **I'm ~less at names** я не в состоянии запоминать имена

hops [hɒps] npl хмель msg

horizon [həˈraɪzn] n горизонт; **~tal** [hɒrɪˈzɒntl] adj горизонтальный

hormone [ˈhɔːməun] n гормон

horn [hɔːn] n (of animal) рог; (also : French ~) валторна; (AUT) гудок

horoscope [ˈhɒrəskəup] n гороскоп

horrendous [həˈrendəs] adj ужасающий

horrible [ˈhɒrɪbl] adj ужасный

horrid [ˈhɒrɪd] adj противный, мерзкий

horror [ˈhɒrəʳ] n (alarm) ужас; (dislike) отвращение; (of war) ужасы mpl

horse [hɔːs] n лошадь f; **~back** adv: on **~back** верхом; **~power** n лошадиная сила; **~ racing** n скачки fpl; **~radish** n хрен; **~shoe** n подкова

horticulture [ˈhɔːtɪkʌltʃəʳ] n растениеводство

hose [həuz] n (also : **~pipe**) шланг

hospice [ˈhɒspɪs] n больница (для безнадёжно больных)

hospitable [ˈhɒspɪtəbl] adj (person, behaviour) гостеприимный

hospital [ˈhɒspɪtl] n больница

hospitality [hɒspɪˈtælɪtɪ] n гостеприимство

host [həust] n (at party, dinner)

хозя́ин; (TV, RADIO) веду́щий m
adj; **a ~ of** ма́сса +gen, мно́жество
+gen

hostage ['hɒstɪdʒ] n
зало́жник(ица)

hostel ['hɒstl] n общежи́тие; (for
homeless) прию́т; (also: **youth ~**)
молодёжная гости́ница

hostess ['həustɪs] n (at party, dinner
etc) хозя́йка; (TV, RADIO) веду́щая
f adj; (BRIT: also: **air ~**)
стюарде́сса

hostile ['hɒstaɪl] adj (person,
attitude) вражде́бный; (conditions,
environment) неблагоприя́тный;
(troops) вра́жеский

hostility [hɒ'stɪlɪtɪ] n
вражде́бность f

hot [hɒt] adj (object, temper,
argument) горя́чий; (weather)
жа́ркий; (spicy: food) о́стрый; **she
is ~** ей жа́рко; **it's ~** (weather)
жа́рко

hotel [həu'tɛl] n гости́ница, оте́ль
m

hotly ['hɒtlɪ] adv горячо́

hot-water bottle [hɒt'wɔːtə-] n
гре́лка

hound [haund] vt трави́ть
(затрави́ть pf) ♦ n го́нчая f
adj

hour ['auə'] n час; **~ly** adj (rate)
почасово́й; (service) ежечасны́й

house n [haus] vb [hauz] n дом;
(THEAT) зал ♦ vt (person) сели́ть
(посели́ть pf); (collection)
размеща́ть (размести́ть pf); **at
my ~** у меня́ до́ма; **the House of
Commons/Lords** (BRIT) Пала́та
о́бщин/ло́рдов; **on the ~** (inf)
беспла́тно; **~hold** n (inhabitants)
домоча́дцы mpl; (home) дом;
~keeper n эконо́мка; **~wife**
(irreg) n дома́шняя хозя́йка,
домохозя́йка; **~work** n
дома́шние дела́ ntpl

housing ['hauzɪŋ] n жильё; **~
estate** (US **~ project**) n
жили́щный ко́мплекс; (larger)
жило́й масси́в

hover ['hɒvə'] vi (bird, insect)
пари́ть (impf); **~craft** n су́дно на
возду́шной поду́шке

KEYWORD

how [hau] adv 1 (in what way) как;
to know how to do уме́ть (impf)
+infin, знать (impf), как +infin; **how
did you like the film?** как Вам
понра́вился фильм?; **how are
you?** как дела́ or Вы?
2 (to what degree): **how much milk/many
people?** ско́лько молока́/
челове́к?; **how long?** как до́лго?,
ско́лько вре́мени?; **how old are
you?** ско́лько Вам лет?; **how tall
is he?** како́го он ро́ста?; **how
lovely/awful!** как чуде́сно/
ужа́сно!

howl [haul] vi (animal, wind) выть
(impf); (baby, person) реве́ть (impf)

HP n abbr (BRIT) = **hire-purchase**

h.p. abbr (AUT: = **horsepower**) л.с.

HQ abbr = **headquarters**

HTML abbr (= hypertext markup
language) гиперте́кст

hub [hʌb] n (of wheel) ступи́ца;
(fig) средото́чие

hue [hjuː] n тон, отте́нок

hug [hʌg] vt обнима́ть (обня́ть pf);

(object) обхва́тывать (обхвати́ть *pf*)

huge [hjuːdʒ] *adj* огро́мный, грома́дный; **~ly** *adv* чрезвыча́йно

hull [hʌl] *n* (NAUT) ко́рпус

hum [hʌm] *vt* напева́ть (*impf*) (без слов) ♦ *vi* (*person*) напева́ть (*impf*); (*machine*) гуде́ть (прогуде́ть *pf*)

human ['hjuːmən] *adj* челове́ческий ♦ *n* (*also*: **~ being**) челове́к

humane [hjuː'meɪn] *adj* (*treatment*) челове́чный

humanitarian [hjuːmænɪ'tɛərɪən] *adj* (*aid*) гуманита́рный; (*principles*) гума́нный

humanity [hjuː'mænɪtɪ] *n* (*mankind*) челове́чество; (*humaneness*) челове́чность *f*, гума́нность *f*

human rights *npl* права́ *ntpl* челове́ка

humble ['hʌmbl] *adj* скро́мный ♦ *vt* сбива́ть (сбить *pf*) спесь с +*gen*

humidity [hjuː'mɪdɪtɪ] *n* вла́жность *f*

humiliate [hjuː'mɪlɪeɪt] *vt* унижа́ть (уни́зить *pf*)

humiliation [hjuːmɪlɪ'eɪʃən] *n* униже́ние

humility [hjuː'mɪlɪtɪ] *n* (*modesty*) скро́мность *f*

humming bird *n* коли́бри *m/f ind*

humor ['hjuːmər] (US) = **humour**

humorous ['hjuːmərəs] *adj* (*book*) юмористи́ческий; (*remark*) шутли́вый; **~ person** челове́к с ю́мором

humour ['hjuːmə*r*] (US **humor**) *n* ю́мор; (*mood*) настрое́ние ♦ *vt* ублажа́ть (ублажи́ть *pf*)

hump [hʌmp] *n* (*in ground*) буго́р; (*on back*) горб

hunch [hʌntʃ] *n* дога́дка

hundred ['hʌndrəd] *n* сто; **~th** *adj* со́тый

hung [hʌŋ] *pt, pp of* **hang**

Hungarian [hʌŋ'gɛərɪən] *adj* венге́рский

Hungary ['hʌŋgərɪ] *n* Ве́нгрия

hunger ['hʌŋgə*r*] *n* го́лод; **~ strike** *n* голодо́вка

hungry ['hʌŋgrɪ] *adj* голо́дный; (*keen*): **~ for** жа́ждущий +*gen*; **he is ~** он го́лоден

hunk [hʌŋk] *n* (большо́й) кусо́к

hunt [hʌnt] *vt* (*animal*) охо́титься (*impf*) на +*acc*; (*criminal*) охо́титься (*impf*) за +*instr* ♦ *vi* (SPORT) охо́титься (*impf*) ♦ *n* охо́та; (*for criminal*) ро́зыск; **to ~ (for)** (*search*) иска́ть (*impf*); **~er** *n* охо́тник(ица); **~ing** *n* охо́та

hurdle ['həːdl] *n* препя́тствие; (SPORT) барье́р

hurricane ['hʌrɪkən] *n* урага́н

hurried ['hʌrɪd] *adj* (*departure*) поспе́шный; (*action*) торопли́вый

hurry ['hʌrɪ] *n* спе́шка ♦ *vi* спеши́ть (поспеши́ть *pf*), торопи́ться (потороти́ться *pf*) ♦ *vt* (*person*) подгоня́ть (подогна́ть *pf*), торопи́ть (потороти́ть *pf*); **to be in a ~** спеши́ть (*impf*), торопи́ться (*impf*); **~ up** *vt* (*person*) подгоня́ть (подогна́ть *pf*), торопи́ть (поторопи́ть *pf*); (*process*) ускоря́ть (уско́рить *pf*) ♦ *vi* торопи́ться (поторопи́ться *pf*); **~ up!** поторопи́сь!, скоре́е!

hurt [həːt] (*pt, pp* **~**) *vt* причиня́ть (причини́ть *pf*) боль +*dat*; (*injure*) ушиба́ть (ушиби́ть *pf*); (*feelings*) задева́ть (заде́ть *pf*) ♦ *vi* (*be painful*) боле́ть (*impf*) ♦ *adj* (*offended*) оби́женный; (*injured*) уши́бленный; **to ~ o.s.** ушиба́ться (ушиби́ться *pf*); **~ful** *adj* оби́дный

husband ['hʌzbənd] *n* муж

hush [hʌʃ] *n* тишина́; ~! ти́хо!, ти́ше!

husky ['hʌskɪ] *adj* (*voice*) хри́плый
♦ *n* ездова́я соба́ка

hut [hʌt] *n* (*house*) избу́шка, хи́жина; (*shed*) сара́й

hyacinth ['haɪəsɪnθ] *n* гиаци́нт

hydraulic [haɪ'drɔ:lɪk] *adj* гидравли́ческий

hydrogen ['haɪdrədʒən] *n* водоро́д

hyena [haɪ'i:nə] *n* гие́на

hygiene ['haɪdʒi:n] *n* гигие́на

hygienic [haɪ'dʒi:nɪk] *adj* (*product*) гигиени́ческий

hymn [hɪm] *n* церко́вный гимн

hype [haɪp] *n* (*inf*) ажиота́ж

hypnosis [hɪp'nəʊsɪs] *n* гипно́з

hypocrisy [hɪ'pɒkrɪsɪ] *n* лицеме́рие

hypocritical [hɪpə'krɪtɪkl] *adj* лицеме́рный

hypothermia [haɪpəʊ'θə:mɪə] *n* гипотерми́я

hypotheses [haɪ'pɒθɪsi:z] *npl of* **hypothesis**

hypothesis [haɪ'pɒθɪsɪs] (*pl* **hypotheses**) *n* гипо́теза

hypothetic(al) [haɪpəʊ'θetɪk(l)] *adj* гипотети́ческий

hysteria [hɪ'stɪərɪə] *n* исте́рия

I, i

I [aɪ] *pron* я

ice [aɪs] *n* лёд; (*ice cream*) моро́женое *nt adj* ♦ *vt* покрыва́ть (покры́ть *pf*) глазу́рью; **~berg** *n* а́йсберг; **~ cream** *n* моро́женое *nt adj*; **~ hockey** *n* хокке́й (на льду)

Iceland ['aɪslənd] *n* Исла́ндия

icicle ['aɪsɪkl] *n* сосу́лька

icing ['aɪsɪŋ] *n* глазу́рь *f*; **~ sugar** *n* (*BRIT*) са́харная пу́дра (*для приготовле́ния глазу́ри*)

icon ['aɪkɒn] *n* (*REL*) ико́на; (*COMPUT*) ико́нка

icy ['aɪsɪ] *adj* (*cold*) ледяно́й; (*road*) обледене́лый

I'd [aɪd] = **I would, I had**

idea [aɪ'dɪə] *n* иде́я

ideal [aɪ'dɪəl] *n* идеа́л ♦ *adj* идеа́льный; **~ist** *n* идеали́ст(ка)

identical [aɪ'dentɪkl] *adj* иденти́чный

identification [aɪdentɪfɪ'keɪʃən] *n* определе́ние, идентифика́ция; (*of person, body*) опозна́ние; (*means of*) ~ удостовере́ние ли́чности

identify [aɪ'dentɪfaɪ] *vt* определя́ть (определи́ть *pf*); (*person*) узнава́ть (узна́ть *pf*); (*body*) опознава́ть (опозна́ть *pf*); (*distinguish*) выявля́ть (вы́явить *pf*)

identity [aɪ'dentɪtɪ] *n* (*of person*) ли́чность *f*; (*of group, nation*) самосозна́ние

ideology [aɪdɪ'ɒlədʒɪ] *n* идеоло́гия

idiom ['ɪdɪəm] *n* (*phrase*) идио́ма

idiot ['ɪdɪət] *n* идио́т(ка)

idle ['aɪdl] *adj* пра́здный; (*lazy*) лени́вый; (*unemployed*) безрабо́тный; (*machinery, factory*) безде́йствующий; **to be ~** безде́йствовать (*impf*)

idol ['aɪdl] *n* куми́р; (*REL*) и́дол

idyllic [ɪ'dɪlɪk] *adj* идилли́ческий

i.e. *abbr* (*that is: = id est*) т.е.

KEYWORD

if [ɪf] *conj* **1** (*conditional use*) е́сли; **if I finish early, I will ring you** е́сли я зако́нчу ра́но, я тебе́ позвоню́; **if I were you (I would ...)** на Ва́шем ме́сте (я бы ...)
2 (*whenever*) когда́
3 (*although*): (**even**) **if** да́же е́сли; **I'll get it done, (even) if it takes all night** я сде́лаю э́то, да́же

если э́то займёт у меня́ всю
ночь
4 (whether) ли; **I don't know if he
is here** я не зна́ю, здесь ли он;
ask him if he can stay спроси́те,
смо́жет ли он оста́ться
5: if so/not если да/нет; **if only**
если бы; **if only I could**
если бы я то́лько мог; see also **as**

ignite [ɪɡˈnaɪt] vt (set fire to)
зажига́ть (заже́чь pf) ♦ vi
загора́ться (загоре́ться pf)
ignition [ɪɡˈnɪʃən] n (AUT)
зажига́ние
ignorance [ˈɪɡnərəns] n
неве́жество
ignorant [ˈɪɡnərənt] adj
неве́жественный; **~ of** (a subject)
несве́дущий в +prp; **he is ~ of
that fact** (unaware of) он не зна́ет
об э́том
ignore [ɪɡˈnɔːr] vt игнори́ровать
(impf/pf); (disregard) пренебрега́ть
(пренебре́чь pf)
I'll [aɪl] = **I will**, **I shall**
ill [ɪl] adj больно́й; (effects) дурно́й
♦ adv: **to speak ~ of** (sb) ду́рно
говори́ть (impf) (о ком-н); **he is ~**
он бо́лен; **to be taken ~**
заболева́ть (заболе́ть pf)
illegal [ɪˈliːɡl] adj незако́нный;
(organization) нелега́льный
illegible [ɪˈlɛdʒɪbl] adj
неразбо́рчивый
illegitimate [ɪlɪˈdʒɪtɪmət] adj (child)
внебра́чный; (activities)
незако́нный, нелегити́мный
ill-fated [ɪlˈfeɪtɪd] adj злополу́чный
ill-health [ɪlˈhɛlθ] n плохо́е
здоро́вье
illicit [ɪˈlɪsɪt] adj (substance)
незако́нный; (affair)
предосуди́тельный
illiterate [ɪˈlɪtərət] adj
негра́мотный

illness [ˈɪlnɪs] n боле́знь f
illogical [ɪˈlɔdʒɪkl] adj нелоги́чный
illuminate [ɪˈluːmɪneɪt] vt (light up)
освеща́ть (освети́ть pf)
illusion [ɪˈluːʒən] n (false idea)
иллю́зия f; (trick) обма́н
illustrate [ˈɪləstreɪt] vt
иллюстри́ровать
(проиллюстри́ровать pf)
illustration [ɪləˈstreɪʃən] n
иллюстра́ция
illustrious [ɪˈlʌstrɪəs] adj (person)
просла́вленный; (career)
блестя́щий
I'm [aɪm] = **I am**
image [ˈɪmɪdʒ] n (picture) о́браз;
(public face) и́мидж; (reflection)
изображе́ние
imaginary [ɪˈmædʒɪnərɪ] adj
(creature, land) вообража́емый
imagination [ɪmædʒɪˈneɪʃən] n
воображе́ние
imaginative [ɪˈmædʒɪnətɪv] adj
(solution) хитроу́мный; **he is very
~** он облада́ет бога́тым
воображе́нием
imagine [ɪˈmædʒɪn] vt (visualize)
представля́ть (предста́вить pf)
(себе́), вообража́ть (вообрази́ть pf);
(dream) вообража́ть
(вообрази́ть pf); (suppose)
предполага́ть (предположи́ть pf)
imitate [ˈɪmɪteɪt] vt подража́ть
(impf) +dat, имити́ровать (impf)
imitation [ɪmɪˈteɪʃən] n
подража́ние, имита́ция
immaculate [ɪˈmækjulət] adj
безупре́чный
immaterial [ɪməˈtɪərɪəl] adj
несуще́ственный
immature [ɪməˈtjuər] adj незре́лый
immediate [ɪˈmiːdɪət] adj (reaction,
answer) неме́дленный; (need)
безотлага́тельный; (family)
ближа́йший; **~ly** adv (at once)
неме́дленно; (directly) сра́зу

immense [ɪ'mɛns] adj огро́мный, грома́дный

immigrant ['ɪmɪɡrənt] n иммигра́нт(ка)

immigration [ɪmɪ'ɡreɪʃən] n иммигра́ция; (also: ~ control) иммиграцио́нный контро́ль

imminent ['ɪmɪnənt] adj (arrival, departure) немину́емый

immobile [ɪ'məubaɪl] adj неподви́жный

immoral [ɪ'mɔrl] adj амора́льный, безнра́вственный

immortal [ɪ'mɔːtl] adj бессме́ртный

immune [ɪ'mjuːn] adj: **he is ~ to** (disease) у него́ иммуните́т про́тив +gen; (flattery, criticism etc) он невосприи́мчив к +dat; ~ **system** n имму́нная систе́ма

immunity [ɪ'mjuːnɪtɪ] n (to disease) иммуните́т; (to criticism) невосприи́мчивость f; (from prosecution) неприкоснове́нность f

immunize ['ɪmjunaɪz] vt: **to ~ sb (against)** де́лать (сде́лать pf) кому́-н приви́вку (про́тив +gen)

impact ['ɪmpækt] n (of crash) уда́р; (force) уда́рная си́ла; (of law, measure) возде́йствие

impaired [ɪm'pɛəd] adj (hearing, speech) затруднённый

impart [ɪm'pɑːt] vt: **to ~ (to)** (skills) передава́ть (переда́ть pf) (+dat); (news) ве́дать (пове́дать pf) (+dat); (flavour) придава́ть (прида́ть pf) (+dat)

impartial [ɪm'pɑːʃl] adj беспристра́стный

impatience [ɪm'peɪʃəns] n нетерпе́ние

impatient [ɪm'peɪʃənt] adj нетерпели́вый; **to get** or **grow ~** теря́ть (потеря́ть pf) терпе́ние; **she was ~ to leave** ей не

impeccable [ɪm'pɛkəbl] adj безупре́чный

impediment [ɪm'pɛdɪmənt] n: **speech ~** дефе́кт ре́чи

impending [ɪm'pɛndɪŋ] adj гряду́щий

imperative [ɪm'pɛrətɪv] adj: **it is ~ that ...** необходи́мо, что́бы ...

imperceptible [ɪmpə'sɛptɪbl] adj неощути́мый

imperfect [ɪm'pəːfɪkt] adj (system) несоверше́нный; (goods) дефе́ктный

imperial [ɪm'pɪərɪəl] adj (history, power) импе́рский; (BRIT: measure): ~ **system** брита́нская систе́ма едини́ц измере́ния и ве́са

impersonal [ɪm'pəːsənl] adj (organization, place) безли́кий

impersonate [ɪm'pəːsəneɪt] vt выдава́ть (вы́дать pf) себя́ за +acc

impertinent [ɪm'pəːtɪnənt] adj де́рзкий

impetuous [ɪm'pɛtjuəs] adj поры́вистый

implement vb ['ɪmplɪment] ['ɪmplɪmənt] vt проводи́ть (провести́ pf) в жизнь ♦ n (for gardening) ору́дие

implication [ɪmplɪ'keɪʃən] n (inference) сле́дствие

implicit [ɪm'plɪsɪt] adj (inferred) невы́раженный, имплици́тный; (unquestioning) безогово́рочный

implore [ɪm'plɔː] vt умоля́ть (умоли́ть pf)

imply [ɪm'plaɪ] vt (hint) намека́ть (намекну́ть pf); (mean) означа́ть (impf)

import vb [ɪm'pɔːt] n, cpd ['ɪmpɔːt] vt импорти́ровать (impf/pf), ввози́ть (ввезти́ pf) ♦ n (article) импорти́руемый това́р;

(*importation*) импорт ♦ *cpd*: ~ **duty/licence** пошлина/лицензия на ввоз

importance [ɪmˈpɔːtns] *n* важность *f*

important [ɪmˈpɔːtnt] *adj* важный; **it's not ~** это неважно

impose [ɪmˈpəuz] *vt* (*restrictions, fine*) налагать (наложить *pf*); (*discipline, rules*) вводить (ввести *pf*) ♦ *vi* навязываться (навязаться *pf*)

imposing [ɪmˈpəuzɪŋ] *adj* величественный

impossible [ɪmˈpɔsɪbl] *adj* (*task, demand*) невыполнимый; (*situation, person*) невыносимый

impotent [ˈɪmpətnt] *adj* бессильный

impractical [ɪmˈpræktɪkl] *adj* (*plan etc*) нереальный; (*person*) непрактичный

impress [ɪmˈpres] *vt* (*person*) производить (произвести *pf*) впечатление на +*acc*; **to ~ sth on sb** внушать (внушить *pf*) что-н кому-н

impression [ɪmˈpreʃən] *n* впечатление *n*; (*of stamp, seal*) отпечаток; (*imitation*) имитация; **he is under the ~ that ...** у него создалось впечатление, что ...; **~able** *adj* впечатлительный

impressive [ɪmˈpresɪv] *adj* впечатляющий

imprint [ˈɪmprɪnt] *n* отпечаток

imprison [ɪmˈprɪzn] *vt* заключать (заключить *pf*) в тюрьму; **~ment** *n* (тюремное) заключение

improbable [ɪmˈprɔbəbl] *adj* невероятный

impromptu [ɪmˈprɔmptjuː] *adj* (*party*) импровизированный

improve [ɪmˈpruːv] *vt* улучшать (улучшить *pf*) ♦ *vi* улучшаться (улучшиться *pf*); (*pupil*)

становиться (стать *pf*) лучше; **the patient ~d** больному стало лучше; **~ment** *n* ~**ment (in)** улучшение (+*gen*)

improvise [ˈɪmprəvaɪz] *vti* импровизировать (*impf*)

impudent [ˈɪmpjudnt] *adj* бесстыдный

impulse [ˈɪmpʌls] *n* (*urge*) порыв; **to act on ~** поддаться (поддаться *pf*) порыву

impulsive [ɪmˈpʌlsɪv] *adj* (*person*) импульсивный; (*gesture*) порывистый

KEYWORD

in [ɪn] *prep* 1 (*indicating position*) в/на +*prp*; **in the house/garden** в доме/саду; **in the street/Ukraine** на улице/Украине; **in London/ Canada** в Лондоне/Канаде; **in the country** в деревне; **in town** в городе; **in here** здесь; **in there** там

2 (*indicating motion*) в/на +*acc*; **in the house/room** в дом/комнату

3 (*indicating time: during*) в; **in spring/summer/autumn/winter** весной/летом/осенью/зимой; **in the morning/afternoon/evening** утром/днём/вечером; **in the evenings** по вечерам; **at 4 o'clock in the afternoon** в 4 часа дня

4 (*indicating time: in the space of*) за +*acc*; (*: after a period of*) через +*acc*; **I did it in 3 hours** я сделал это за 3 часа; **I'll see you in 2 weeks** увидимся через 2 недели

5 (*indicating manner etc*): **in a loud/quiet voice** громким/тихим голосом; **in English/Russian** по-английски/по-русски, на английском/русском языке

6 (*wearing*) в +*prp*; **the boy in the blue shirt** мальчик в голубой рубашке

7 (*indicating circumstances*): **in the sun** на со́лнце; **in the rain** под дождём; **in the shade** в тени́; **a rise in prices** повыше́ние цен
8 (*indicating mood, state*) в +*prp*; **in despair** в отча́янии
9 (*with ratios, numbers*): **one in ten households** одна́ из десяти́ семе́й; **20 pence in the pound** 20 пе́нсов с ка́ждого фу́нта; **they lined up in twos** они́ вы́строились по́ дво́е; **a gradient of one in five** укло́н оди́н к пяти́
10 (*referring to people, works*) у +*gen*; **the disease is common in children** э́то заболева́ние ча́сто встреча́ется у дете́й; **in Dickens** у Ди́ккенса; **you have a good friend in him** он тебе́ хоро́ший друг
11 (*indicating profession etc*): **to be in publishing/advertising** занима́ться (*impf*) изда́тельским де́лом/рекла́мным би́знесом; **to be in teaching** рабо́тать (*impf*) учи́телем; **to be in the army** быть (*impf*) в а́рмии
12 (*with present participle*): **in saying this** говоря́ э́то, она́ ...; **in behaving like this, she ...** поступа́я таки́м о́бразом, она́ ...
♦ *adv*: **to be in** (*train, ship, plane*) прибыва́ть (прибы́ть *pf*); (*in fashion*) быть (*impf*) в мо́де; **is he in today?** он сего́дня здесь?; **he is not in today** его́ сего́дня нет; **he wasn't in yesterday** его́ вчера́ не́ было; **he'll be in later today** он бу́дет по́зже сего́дня; **to ask sb in** предлага́ть (предложи́ть *pf*) кому́-н войти́; **to walk in** входи́ть (войти́ *pf*)
♦ *n*: **to know all the ins and outs** знать (*impf*) все ходы́ и вы́ходы

in. *abbr* = **inch**

inability [ɪnə'bɪlɪtɪ] *n*: ~ **(to do)** неспосо́бность *f* (+*infin*)
inaccessible [ɪnək'sesɪbl] *adj* (*also fig*) недосту́пный
inaccurate [ɪn'ækjurət] *adj* нето́чный
inactivity [ɪnæk'tɪvɪtɪ] *n* безде́ятельность *f*
inadequate [ɪn'ædɪkwət] *adj* недоста́точный; (*work*) неудовлетвори́тельный; (*person*) некомпете́нтный; **to feel** ~ чу́вствовать (*impf*) себя́ не на у́ровне
inadvertently [ɪnəd'vɜ:tntlɪ] *adv* неча́янно, неумы́шленно
inanimate [ɪn'ænɪmət] *adj* (*object*) неодушевлённый
inappropriate [ɪnə'prəuprɪət] *adj* (*unsuitable*) неподходя́щий; (*improper*) неуме́стный
inarticulate [ɪnɑ:'tɪkjulət] *adj* (*person*) косноязы́чный
inasmuch as [ɪnəz'mʌtʃ-] *adv* (*in that*) поско́льку; (*insofar as*) насто́лько
inaudible [ɪn'ɔ:dɪbl] *adj* невня́тный
inauguration [ɪnɔ:gju'reɪʃən] *n* (*of person*) вступле́ние в до́лжность; (*of a president*) инаугура́ция
Inc. *abbr* = **incorporated**
incapable [ɪn'keɪpəbl] *adj* (*helpless*) беспо́мощный; ~ **of sth/doing** неспосо́бный на что-н/+*infin*
incense *n* ['ɪnsens] *vb* [ɪn'sens] *n* ла́дан ♦ *vt* приводи́ть (привести́ *pf*) в я́рость
incentive [ɪn'sentɪv] *n* сти́мул
incessant [ɪn'sesnt] *adj* бесконе́чный, постоя́нный
incest ['ɪnsest] *n* кровосмеше́ние
inch [ɪntʃ] *n* (*measurement*) дюйм

inch - дюйм. Ме́ра длины́ ра́вная 2.54 см.

incidence ['ɪnsɪdns] n число; **high ~** высо́кий у́ровень

incident ['ɪnsɪdnt] n (event) слу́чай; **without ~** без происше́ствий; **~ally** [ɪnsɪ'dentəlɪ] adv (by the way) кста́ти, ме́жду про́чим

incite [ɪn'saɪt] vt (violence, hatred) возбужда́ть (возбуди́ть pf); (people) подстрека́ть (impf)

inclination [ɪnklɪ'neɪʃən] n (desire) располо́женность f; (tendency) скло́нность f

incline n ['ɪnklaɪn] vb [ɪn'klaɪn] (slope) укло́н, накло́н ♦ vi: **he is ~d to ...** он скло́нен +infin ...; **he is ~d to depression** он скло́нен к депре́ссии

include [ɪn'kluːd] vt включа́ть (включи́ть pf)

including [ɪn'kluːdɪŋ] prep включа́я +acc

inclusion [ɪn'kluːʒən] n включе́ние

inclusive [ɪn'kluːsɪv] adj: **~ of** включа́я +acc; **the price is fully ~** цена́ включа́ет в себя́ всё; **from March 1st to 5th ~** с 1-ого до 5-ого ма́рта включи́тельно

incoherent [ɪnkəʊ'hɪərənt] adj (argument) непосле́довательный; (speech) несвя́зный; (person) косноязы́чный

income ['ɪnkʌm] n дохо́д; **~ support** n де́нежное посо́бие (се́мьям с ни́зким дохо́дом); **~ tax** n подохо́дный нало́г

incomparable [ɪn'kɔmpərəbl] adj несравне́нный

incompatible [ɪnkəm'pætɪbl] adj несовмести́мый

incompetence [ɪn'kɔmpɪtns] n некомпете́нтность f

incompetent [ɪn'kɔmpɪtnt] adj (person) некомпете́нтный; (work) неуме́лый

incomplete [ɪnkəm'pliːt] adj (unfinished) незавершённый;

(partial) непо́лный

incomprehensible [ɪnkɔmprɪ'hensɪbl] adj непоня́тный

inconceivable [ɪnkən'siːvəbl] adj немы́слимый

inconsistency [ɪnkən'sɪstənsɪ] n (of actions) непосле́довательность f; (of statement) противоречи́вость f

inconsistent [ɪnkən'sɪstnt] adj (see n) непосле́довательный; противоречи́вый; (work) неро́вный; **~ with** (beliefs, values) несовмести́мый с +instr

inconvenience [ɪnkən'viːnjəns] n (problem) неудо́бство ♦ vt причиня́ть (причини́ть pf) беспоко́йство +dat

inconvenient [ɪnkən'viːnjənt] adj неудо́бный

incorporate [ɪn'kɔːpəreɪt] vt (contain) включа́ть (impf) в себя́, содержа́ть (impf); **to ~ (into)** включа́ть (включи́ть pf) (в +acc)

incorrect [ɪnkə'rekt] adj неве́рный, непра́вильный

increase [ɪn'kriːs] vb [ɪn'kriːs] n: **~ (in), ~ (of)** увеличе́ние (+gen) ♦ vi увели́чиваться (увели́читься pf) ♦ vt увели́чивать (увели́чить pf); (price) поднима́ть (подня́ть pf)

increasingly adv (with comparative) всё; (more intensely) всё бо́лее; (more often) всё ча́ще

incredible [ɪn'kredɪbl] adj невероя́тный

incredulous [ɪn'kredjuləs] adj недове́рчивый

incur [ɪn'kəː] vt (expenses, loss) нести́ (понести́ pf); (debt) нака́пливать (накопи́ть pf); (disapproval, anger) навлека́ть (навле́чь pf) на себя́

incurable [ɪn'kjuərəbl] adj (disease) неизлечи́мый

indebted [ɪn'detɪd] adj: **I am ~ to you** (grateful) я Вам обя́зан

indecent [ɪnˈdiːsnt] adj
непристойный
indecisive [ɪndɪˈsaɪsɪv] adj
нерешительный
indeed [ɪnˈdiːd] adv (certainly)
действительно, в самом деле;
(in fact, furthermore) более того;
this book is very interesting ~ эта
книга весьма интересная; **thank
you very much** ~ большое Вам
спасибо; **he is** ~ **very talented** он
на самом деле очень талантлив;
yes ~! да, действительно или
конечно!
indefinite [ɪnˈdefɪnɪt] adj (answer,
view) неопределённый; (period,
number) неограниченный; ~**ly**
adv (continue, wait) бесконечно;
(be closed, delayed) на
неопределённое время
independence [ɪndɪˈpendns] n
независимость f
independent [ɪndɪˈpendnt] adj
независимый
in-depth [ˈɪndepθ] adj глубокий
indestructible [ɪndɪsˈtrʌktəbl] adj
(object) прочный; (friendship,
alliance) нерушимый
index [ˈɪndeks] (pl ~**es**) n (in book)
указатель m; (in library etc)
каталог; **price** ~ индекс цен; ~
finger n указательный палец
India [ˈɪndɪə] n Индия; ~**n** adj
индийский ♦ n индиец; **Red** ~**n**
индеец
indicate [ˈɪndɪkeɪt] vt указывать
(указать pf) на +acc; (mention)
указывать (указать pf)
indication [ɪndɪˈkeɪʃən] n знак; **all
the** ~**s are that** ... всё указывает
на то, что ...
indicative [ɪnˈdɪkətɪv] adj: **to be** ~
of свидетельствовать (impf) о
+prp, указывать (impf) на +acc
indicator [ˈɪndɪkeɪtə*] n (AUT)
указатель m поворота; (fig)

indifference [ɪnˈdɪfrəns] n
безразличие, равнодушие
indifferent [ɪnˈdɪfrənt] adj
безразличный, равнодушный;
(mediocre) посредственный
indigestion [ɪndɪˈdʒestʃən] n
несварение желудка
indignant [ɪnˈdɪɡnənt] adj: ~ **at
sth/with sb** возмущённый
чем-н/кем-н
indignation [ɪndɪɡˈneɪʃən] n
возмущение, негодование
indirect [ɪndɪˈrekt] adj (way)
окольный, обходной; (answer)
уклончивый; (effect) побочный; ~
object (LING) косвенное
дополнение
indiscriminate [ɪndɪsˈkrɪmɪnət] adj
(bombing) беспорядочный
indispensable [ɪndɪsˈpensəbl] adj
(object) необходимый; (person)
незаменимый
indisputable [ɪndɪsˈpjuːtəbl] adj
(undeniable) неоспоримый
individual [ɪndɪˈvɪdjuəl] n
личность f, индивидуум ♦ adj
индивидуальный; (certain) ~**s**
отдельные личности; ~**ly** adv в
отдельности; (responsible) лично
indoctrination [ɪndɒktrɪˈneɪʃən] n
идеологическая обработка
indoor [ˈɪndɔː*] adj (plant)
комнатный; (pool) закрытый; ~**s**
adv (go) в помещение; (be) в
помещении; **he stayed** ~**s all
morning** он просидел дома всё
утро
induce [ɪnˈdjuːs] vt (cause)
вызывать (вызвать pf); (persuade)
побуждать (побудить pf); (MED,
birth) стимулировать (impf/pf)
indulge [ɪnˈdʌldʒ] vt (desire, whim
etc) потворствовать (impf) +dat,
потакать (impf) +dat; (person, child)
баловать (избаловать pf) ♦ vi: **to**

~ **in** баловаться (побаловаться
pf) +instr; ~**nce** n (pleasure)
прихоть f; (leniency) потворство
industrial [ɪnˈdʌstrɪəl] adj
индустриальный,
промышленный; ~ **accident**
несчастный случай на
производстве; ~ **action** n
забастовка; ~ **estate** n (BRIT)
индустриальный парк
industry [ˈɪndəstrɪ] n
(manufacturing) индустрия,
промышленность f;
industries отрасли pl
промышленности; **tourist/
fashion** ~ индустрия туризма/
моды
inedible [ɪnˈɛdɪbl] adj
несъедобный
ineffective [ɪnɪˈfɛktɪv] adj
неэффективный
inefficiency [ɪnɪˈfɪʃənsɪ] n (see adj)
неэффективность f;
непроизводительность f
inefficient [ɪnɪˈfɪʃənt] adj
неэффективный; (machine)
непроизводительный
inept [ɪˈnɛpt] adj неумелый
inequality [ɪnɪˈkwɔlɪtɪ] n (of system)
неравенство
inert [ɪˈnəːt] adj (still)
неподвижный
inescapable [ɪnɪˈskeɪpəbl] adj
неизбежный
inevitable [ɪnˈɛvɪtəbl] adj
неизбежный, неотвратимый
inevitably [ɪnˈɛvɪtəblɪ] adv
неизбежно
inexcusable [ɪnɪksˈkjuːzəbl] adj
непростительный
inexpensive [ɪnɪkˈspɛnsɪv] adj
недорогой
inexperienced [ɪnɪksˈpɪərɪənst] adj
неопытный
inexplicable [ɪnɪkˈsplɪkəbl] adj
необъяснимый

infamous [ˈɪnfəməs] adj (person)
бесчестный
infant [ˈɪnfənt] n (baby) младенец;
(young child) ребёнок
infantry [ˈɪnfəntrɪ] n пехота

---

infant school -
подготовительная школа. В
Великобритании такую школу
посещают дети в возрасте от 5
(иногда 4) до 7 лет.

---

infatuation [ɪnfætjuˈeɪʃən] n
страсть f
infect [ɪnˈfɛkt] vt заражать
(заразить pf); ~**ion** [ɪnˈfɛkʃən] n
зараза, инфекция; ~**ious**
[ɪnˈfɛkʃəs] adj (disease)
инфекционный; (fig)
заразительный
inference [ˈɪnfərəns] n заключение
inferior [ɪnˈfɪərɪər] adj (position,
status) подчинённый; (goods)
низкого качества
infertile [ɪnˈfəːtaɪl] adj бесплодный
infertility [ɪnfəːˈtɪlɪtɪ] n бесплодие
infested [ɪnˈfɛstɪd] adj: **the house is
~ with rats** дом кишит крысами
infidelity [ɪnfɪˈdɛlɪtɪ] n неверность
f
infinite [ˈɪnfɪnɪt] adj бесконечный
infinitive [ɪnˈfɪnɪtɪv] n инфинитив,
неопределённая форма глагола
infinity [ɪnˈfɪnɪtɪ] n бесконечность
f
infirm [ɪnˈfəːm] adj немощный;
~**ary** n больница
inflammable [ɪnˈflæməbl] adj
(fabric) легко
воспламеняющийся; (chemical)
горючий
inflammation [ɪnfləˈmeɪʃən] n
воспаление
inflation [ɪnˈfleɪʃən] n инфляция
inflexible [ɪnˈflɛksɪbl] adj (rule,
timetable) жёсткий; (person)

негибкий

inflict [ɪnˈflɪkt] vt: **to ~ sth on sb** причинять (причинить pf) что-н кому-н

influence [ˈɪnfluəns] n (power) влияние; (effect) воздействие ♦ vt влиять (повлиять pf) на +acc; **under the ~ of alcohol** под воздействием алкоголя

influential [ɪnfluˈɛnʃl] adj влиятельный

influx [ˈɪnflʌks] n приток

inform [ɪnˈfɔːm] vt: **to ~ sb of sth** сообщать (сообщить pf) кому-н о чём-н ♦ vi: **to ~ on sb** доносить (донести pf) на кого-н

informal [ɪnˈfɔːml] adj (visit, invitation) неофициальный; (discussion, manner) непринуждённый; (clothes) будничный

information [ɪnfəˈmeɪʃən] n информация, сообщение; **a piece of ~** сообщение

informative [ɪnˈfɔːmətɪv] adj содержательный

informer [ɪnˈfɔːmə*] n (also: **police ~**) осведоми́тель(ница) m(f)

infrastructure [ˈɪnfrəstrʌktʃə*] n инфраструктура

infringe [ɪnˈfrɪndʒ] vt (law) преступать (преступить pf) ♦ vi: **to ~ on** ущемлять (ущемить pf), посягать (посягнуть pf) на +acc

infuriating [ɪnˈfjuərɪeɪtɪŋ] adj возмутительный

ingenious [ɪnˈdʒiːnjəs] adj хитроумный; (person) изобретательный

ingenuity [ɪndʒɪˈnjuːɪtɪ] n (see adj) хитроумие f; изобретательность f

ingredient [ɪnˈɡriːdɪənt] n ингредиент; (fig) составная часть f

inhabit [ɪnˈhæbɪt] vt населять

inhale [ɪnˈheɪl] vt вдыхать (вдохнуть pf) ♦ vi (сделать pf) вдох; (when smoking) затягиваться (затянуться pf)

inherent [ɪnˈhɪərənt] adj: **~ in** присущий +dat

inherit [ɪnˈhɛrɪt] vt наследовать (impf/pf), унаследовать (pf); **~ance** n наследство

inhibit [ɪnˈhɪbɪt] vt сковывать (сковать pf); (growth) задерживать (задержать pf); **~ed** adj скованный; **~ion** [ɪnhɪˈbɪʃən] n скованность f

inhospitable [ɪnhɔsˈpɪtəbl] adj (person, place) неприветливый

inhuman [ɪnˈhjuːmən] adj (behaviour) бесчеловечный

initial [ɪˈnɪʃl] adj первоначальный, начальный ♦ n (also: **~ letter**) начальная буква ♦ vt ставить (поставить pf) инициалы на +prp; **~s** npl (of name) инициалы mpl; **~ly** adv (at first) вначале, сначала

initiate [ɪˈnɪʃɪeɪt] vt (talks etc) класть (положить pf) начало +dat, зачинать (impf); (new member) посвящать (посвятить pf)

initiation [ɪnɪʃɪˈeɪʃən] n начало; (into secret etc) посвящение

initiative [ɪˈnɪʃətɪv] n инициатива, начинание; (enterprise) инициативность f; **to take the ~** брать (взять pf) на себя инициативу

inject [ɪnˈdʒɛkt] vt (drugs, poison) вводить (ввести pf); (patient): **to ~ sb with sth** делать (сделать pf) укол чего-н кому-н; **to ~ into** (money) вливать (влить pf) в +acc; **~ion** [ɪnˈdʒɛkʃən] n укол; (of money) вливание

injunction [ɪnˈdʒʌnkʃən] n (LAW) судебный запрет

injure ['ɪndʒər] vt (person, limb, feelings) ра́нить (impf/pf); **~d** adj ра́неный

injury ['ɪndʒərɪ] n ра́на; (industrial, sports) тра́вма

injustice [ɪn'dʒʌstɪs] n несправедли́вость f

ink [ɪŋk] n (in pen) черни́ла pl

inland ['ɪnlənd] adv (travel) вглубь; **Inland Revenue** n (BRIT) ≈ (Гла́вное) нало́говое управле́ние

in-laws ['ɪnlɔːz] npl (of woman) родня́ со стороны́ му́жа; (of man) родня́ со стороны́ жены́

inlet ['ɪnlɛt] n (у́зкий) зали́в

inmate ['ɪnmeɪt] n (of prison) заключённый(ая) m(f); (of asylum) пацие́нт(ка)

inn [ɪn] n тракти́р

inner ['ɪnər] adj вну́тренний; **~ city** n центра́льная часть f го́рода

innocence ['ɪnəsns] n неви́нность f; (naivety) неви́нность

innocent ['ɪnəsnt] adj неви́нный; (naive) неви́нный

innovation [ɪnəu'veɪʃən] n но́вшество

innumerable [ɪ'njuːmrəbl] adj бесчи́сленный

inoculation [ɪnɔkju'leɪʃən] n приви́вка

input ['ɪnput] n (resources, money) вложе́ние

inquest ['ɪnkwest] n (into death) (суде́бное) рассле́дование

inquire [ɪn'kwaɪər] vi: **to ~ (about)** наводи́ть (навести́ pf) спра́вки (о +prp); (health) справля́ться (спра́виться pf) о +prp; **to ~ when/where** осведомля́ться (осведоми́ться pf) когда́/где; **~ into** vt fus рассле́довать (impf/pf)

inquisitive [ɪn'kwɪzɪtɪv] adj

любопы́тный

ins abbr = **inches**

insane [ɪn'seɪn] adj безу́мный, сумасше́дший

insatiable [ɪn'seɪʃəbl] adj ненасы́тный

inscription [ɪn'skrɪpʃən] n на́дпись f

insect ['ɪnsɛkt] n насеко́мое nt adj; **~icide** [ɪn'sɛktɪsaɪd] n инсектици́д

insecure [ɪnsɪ'kjuər] adj (person) неуве́ренный в себе́

insecurity [ɪnsɪ'kjuərɪtɪ] n неуве́ренность f в себе́

insensitive [ɪn'sɛnsɪtɪv] adj бесчу́вственный

inseparable [ɪn'sɛprəbl] adj (ideas, elements) нераздели́мый; (friends) неразлу́чный

insert [ɪn'səːt] vt: **to ~ (into)** вставля́ть (вста́вить pf) (в +acc); (piece of paper) вкла́дывать (вложи́ть pf) (в +acc); **~ion** [ɪn'səːʃən] n (in book, file) вста́вка; (of needle) введе́ние

inside ['ɪn'saɪd] n вну́тренняя часть f ♦ adj вну́тренний ♦ adv (be) внутри́; (go) внутрь ♦ prep (position) внутри́ +gen; (motion) внутрь +gen; **~ ten minutes** в преде́лах десяти́ мину́т; **~s** npl (inf: stomach) вну́тренности fpl; **~ out** adv наизна́нку; (know) вдоль и поперёк

insight ['ɪnsaɪt] n: **~ (into)** понима́ние

insignificant [ɪnsɪg'nɪfɪknt] adj незначи́тельный

insist [ɪn'sɪst] vi: **to ~ (on)** наста́ивать (настоя́ть pf) (на +prp); **he ~ed that I came** он настоя́л на том, что́бы я пришёл; **he ~ed that all was well** он утвержда́л, что всё в поря́дке; **~ence** n настоя́ние; **~ent** ♦ adj насто́йчивый

insofar as [ɪnsəʊ'faː(r)-] adv поскольку

insolent ['ɪnsələnt] adj (attitude, remark) наглый

insomnia [ɪn'sɒmnɪə] n бессонница

inspect [ɪn'spekt] vt (equipment, premises) осмотреть (осмотреть pf); **~ion** [ɪn'spekʃən] n осмотр m; **~or** n (ADMIN, POLICE) инспектор; (BRIT: on buses, trains) контролёр

inspiration [ɪnspə'reɪʃən] n вдохновение

inspire [ɪn'spaɪə(r)] vt (workers, troops) вдохновлять (вдохновить pf); **to ~ sth (in sb)** внушать (внушить pf) что-н (кому-н)

instability [ɪnstə'bɪlɪtɪ] n нестабильность f

install [ɪn'stɔːl] vt (machine) устанавливать (установить pf); (official) ставить (поставить pf); **~ation** [ɪnstə'leɪʃən] n (of machine, plant) установка

instalment [ɪn'stɔːlmənt] (US **installment**) n (of payment) взнос; (of story) часть f; **to pay in ~s** платить (заплатить pf) в рассрочку

instance ['ɪnstəns] n пример; **for ~** например; **in the first ~** в первую очередь

instant ['ɪnstənt] n мгновение, миг ♦ adj (reaction, success) мгновенный; (coffee) растворимый; **come here this ~!** иди сюда сию же минуту!; **~ly** adv немедленно, сразу

instead [ɪn'sted] adv взамен ♦ prep: **~ of** вместо или взамен +gen

instep ['ɪnstep] n подъём (ноги, туфли)

instil [ɪn'stɪl] vt: **to ~ sth in(to) sb** вселять (вселить pf) что-н в кого-н

instinct ['ɪnstɪŋkt] n инстинкт; **by ~** инстинктивно; **~ive** [ɪn'stɪŋktɪv] adj инстинктивный

institute ['ɪnstɪtjuːt] n (for research, teaching) институт; (professional body) ассоциация ♦ vt (system, rule) учреждать (учредить pf)

institution [ɪnstɪ'tjuːʃən] n учреждение; (custom, tradition) институт

instruct [ɪn'strʌkt] vt: **to ~ sb in sth** обучать (обучить pf) кого-н чему-н; **to ~ sb to do** поручать (поручить pf) кому-н +infin; **~ion** [ɪn'strʌkʃən] n (teaching) обучение; **~ions** npl (orders) указания ntpl; **~ions (for use)** инструкция или руководство (по применению); **~or** n (for driving etc) инструктор

instrument ['ɪnstrəmənt] n инструмент; **~al** [ɪnstru'mentl] adj: **to be ~al in** играть (сыграть pf) существенную роль в +prp

insufficient [ɪnsə'fɪʃənt] adj недостаточный

insulation [ɪnsju'leɪʃən] n (against cold) (тепло)изоляция

insulin ['ɪnsjulɪn] n инсулин

insult vb [ɪn'sʌlt] n ['ɪnsʌlt] vt оскорблять (оскорбить pf) n оскорбление; **~ing** [ɪn'sʌltɪŋ] adj оскорбительный

insurance [ɪn'ʃʊərəns] n страхование; **~ policy** n страховой полис

insure [ɪn'ʃʊə(r)] vt: **to ~ (against)** страховать (застраховать pf) (от +gen); **to ~ (o.s.) against** страховаться (застраховаться pf) от +gen

intact [ɪn'tækt] adj (unharmed) неповреждённый; (whole) нетронутый

intake ['ɪnteɪk] n (of food, drink) потребление; (BRIT: of pupils, recruits) набор

integral ['ɪntɪɡrəl] *adj*
неотъёмлемый

integrate ['ɪntɪɡreɪt] *vt*
интегрировать (*impf/pf*) ♦ *vi*
(*groups, individuals*) объединяться
(объединиться *pf*)

integrity [ɪn'tɛɡrɪtɪ] *n* (*morality*)
честность *f*, порядочность *f*

intellect ['ɪntɪlɛkt] *n* интеллект;
~ual [ɪntə'lɛktjuəl] *adj*
интеллектуальный ♦ *n*
интеллектуал

intelligence [ɪn'tɛlɪdʒəns] *n* ум;
(*thinking power*) умственные
способности *fpl*; (*MIL etc*)
разведка; **~ service**
разведывательная служба

intelligent [ɪn'tɛlɪdʒənt] *adj* умный;
(*animal*) разумный

intend [ɪn'tɛnd] *vt*: **to ~ sth for**
предназначать (предназначить
pf) что-н для +*gen*; **to do**
намереваться (*impf*) +*infin*; **~ed**
adj (*effect*) запланированный;
(*victim*) предполагаемый

intense [ɪn'tɛns] *adj* (*heat, emotion*)
сильный; (*noise, activity*)
интенсивный; **~ly** *adv* сильно,
интенсивно

intensify [ɪn'tɛnsɪfaɪ] *vt* усиливать
(усилить *pf*)

intensity [ɪn'tɛnsɪtɪ] *n* (*of effort, sun*)
интенсивность *f*

intensive [ɪn'tɛnsɪv] *adj*
интенсивный; **~ care**
интенсивная терапия

intent [ɪn'tɛnt] *n* ♦ **~** (**on**)
сосредоточенный (на +*prp*); **to
be ~ on doing** (*determined*)
стремиться (*impf*) +*infin*

intention [ɪn'tɛnʃən] *n* намерение;
~al *adj* намеренный

interact [ɪntər'ækt] *vi*: **to ~** (**with**)
взаимодействовать (*impf*) (с
+*instr*); **~ion** [ɪntər'ækʃən] *n*
взаимодействие

interchangeable [ɪntə'tʃeɪndʒəbl]
adj взаимозаменяемый

intercom ['ɪntəkɔm] *n* селектор

intercourse ['ɪntəkɔːs] *n* (*sexual*)
половое сношение

interest ['ɪntrɪst] *n*: **~** (**in**) интерес
(к +*dat*); (*COMM, sum of money*)
проценты *mpl* ♦ *vt* интересовать
(*impf*); **to ~ sb in sth**
заинтересовывать
(заинтересовать *pf*) кого-н в
чём-н; **~ed** *adj*
заинтересованный; **to be ~ed in
sth** (*music etc*) интересоваться
(*impf*) (чем-н); **~ing** *adj*
интересный; **~ rate** *n*
процентная ставка

interfere [ɪntə'fɪə'] *vi*: **to ~ in**
вмешиваться (вмешаться *pf*) в
+*acc*; **to ~ with** (*hinder*) мешать
(помешать *pf*) +*dat*; **~nce** *n*
вмешательство

interim ['ɪntərɪm] *adj* (*government*)
временный; (*report*)
промежуточный ♦ *n*: **in the ~** тем
временем

interior [ɪn'tɪərɪə'] *n* (*of building*)
интерьер; (*of car, box etc*)
внутренность *f* ♦ *adj* (*door, room
etc*) внутренний; **~ department/
minister** департамент/министр
внутренних дел

intermediate [ɪntə'miːdɪət] *adj*
(*stage*) промежуточный

internal [ɪn'tɜːnl] *adj* внутренний

international [ɪntə'næʃənl] *adj*
международный

Internet ['ɪntənɛt] *n* Интернет; **~
café** *n* интернет-кафе *nt ind*; **~
Service Provider** *n* интернет-
провайдер

interpret [ɪn'tɜːprɪt] *vt* (*explain*)
интерпретировать (*impf/pf*),
толковать (*impf*); (*translate*)
переводить (перевести *pf*)
(устно) ♦ *vi* переводить

(перевести pf) (устно); **~ation**
[ɪntɜ:prɪˈteɪʃən] n интерпретация,
толкование; **~er** [-]
n переводчик(ица) (устный)

interrogation [ɪnterəˈgeɪʃən] n
допрос

interrupt [ɪntəˈrʌpt] vti прерывать
(прервать pf); **~ion** [ɪntəˈrʌpʃən] n
(act) прерывание

interval [ˈɪntəvl] n интервал;
(BRIT : SPORT) (: THEAT)
антракт; **at ~s** время от времени

intervene [ɪntəˈvi:n] vi (in
conversation, situation)
вмешиваться (вмешаться pf);
(event) мешать (помешать pf)

intervention [ɪntəˈvɛnʃən] n
(interference) вмешательство;
(mediation) посредничество

interview [ˈɪntəvju:] n собеседование; интервью nt ind
♦ vt (for job) проводить
(провести pf) собеседование с
+instr; (RADIO, TV etc)
интервьюировать (impf/pf), брать
(взять pf) интервью у +gen

intestine [ɪnˈtɛstɪn] n кишка; **~s**
кишечник msg

intimacy [ˈɪntɪməsɪ] n интимность
f, близость f

intimate [ˈɪntɪmət] adj (friend,
relationship) близкий; (conversation,
atmosphere) интимный;
(knowledge) глубокий,
непосредственный

intimidate [ɪnˈtɪmɪdeɪt] vt
запугивать (запугать pf)

intimidation [ɪntɪmɪˈdeɪʃən] n
запугивание

KEYWORD
---

into [ˈɪntu] prep 1 (indicating motion)
в/на +acc; **into the house/garden**
в дом/сад; **into the post office/
factory** на почту/фабрику;
research into cancer

исследования в области
раковых заболеваний; **he
worked late into the night** он
работал до поздней ночи
2 (indicating change of condition,
result): **she has translated the
letter into Russian** она перевела
письмо на русский язык; **the
vase broke into pieces** ваза
разбилась на мелкие кусочки;
they got into trouble for it им
попало за это; **he lapsed into
silence** он погрузился в
молчание; **to burst into tears**
расплакаться (pf); **to burst into
flames** вспыхивать (вспыхнуть
pf)

intolerable [ɪnˈtɔlərəbl] adj
невыносимый

intolerance [ɪnˈtɔlərns] n
нетерпимость f

intolerant [ɪnˈtɔlərnt] adj
нетерпимый

intranet [ˈɪntrənɛt] n интранет,
локальная вычислительная сеть

intricate [ˈɪntrɪkət] adj (pattern)
замысловатый; (relationship)
сложный

intriguing [ɪnˈtri:gɪŋ] adj
(fascinating) интригующий

introduce [ɪntrəˈdju:s] vt (new idea,
measure etc) вводить (ввести pf);
(speaker, programme)
представлять (представить pf);
to ~ sb (to sb) представлять
(представить pf) кого-н (кому-н);
to ~ sb to (pastime etc) знакомить
(познакомить pf) кого-н с
+instr

introduction [ɪntrəˈdʌkʃən] n
введение; (to person, new
experience) знакомство

introductory [ɪntrəˈdʌktərɪ] adj
(lesson) вступительный

introvert [ˈɪntrəuvɜ:t] n интроверт

intrude [ɪn'truːd] vi: **to ~ (on)**
вторга́ться (вто́ргнуться pf)
(в/на +acc); **~r n: there is an ~r in
our house** к нам в дом кто-то
вто́ргся

intrusion [ɪn'truːʒən] n вторже́ние

intuition [ɪntjuː'ɪʃən] n интуи́ция

intuitive [ɪn'tjuːɪtɪv] adj
интуити́вный

inundate ['ɪnʌndeɪt] vt: **to ~ with**
(calls etc) засыпа́ть (засы́пать pf)
+instr

invade [ɪn'veɪd] vt (MIL) вторга́ться
(вто́ргнуться pf) в +acc

invalid n ['ɪnvəlɪd] инвали́д ♦ adj [ɪn'vælɪd]
недействи́тельный

invaluable [ɪn'væljuəbl] adj
неоцени́мый

invariably [ɪn'vɛərɪəblɪ] adv
неизме́нно

invasion [ɪn'veɪʒən] n (MIL)
вторже́ние

invent [ɪn'vɛnt] vt изобрета́ть
(изобрести́ pf); (fabricate)
выду́мывать (вы́думать pf); **~ion**
[ɪn'vɛnʃən] n (see vt) изобрете́ние;
вы́думка; **~ive** adj
изобрета́тельный; **~or** n
изобрета́тель m

inventory ['ɪnvəntrɪ] n (of house
etc) (инвентаризацио́нная) о́пись
f

invertebrate [ɪn'vəːtɪbrət] n
беспозвоно́чное nt adj

inverted commas [ɪn'vəːtɪd-] npl
(BRIT : LING) кавы́чки fpl

invest [ɪn'vɛst] vt вкла́дывать
(вложи́ть pf) ♦ vi: **to ~ in**
вкла́дывать (вложи́ть pf) де́ньги
в +acc

investigate [ɪn'vɛstɪgeɪt] vt
(accident, crime) рассле́довать
(impf/pf)

investigation [ɪnvɛstɪ'geɪʃən] n
рассле́дование

investment [ɪn'vɛstmənt] n

(activity) инвести́рование;
(amount of money) инвести́ция,
вклад

investor [ɪn'vɛstər] n инве́стор,
вкла́дчик

---

invigilator - экзаменацио́нный
наблюда́тель. Он раздаёт
экзаменацио́нные листы и
следи́т за тем, что́бы студе́нты
не спи́сывали.

---

invigorating [ɪn'vɪgəreɪtɪŋ] adj (air)
бодря́щий

invincible [ɪn'vɪnsɪbl] adj (army,
team) непобеди́мый

invisible [ɪn'vɪzɪbl] adj неви́димый

invitation [ɪnvɪ'teɪʃən] n
приглаше́ние

invite [ɪn'vaɪt] vt приглаша́ть
(пригласи́ть pf); (discussion,
criticism) побужда́ть (побуди́ть
pf) к +dat; **to ~ sb to do** предла-
га́ть (предложи́ть pf) кому́-н
+infin

inviting [ɪn'vaɪtɪŋ] adj
соблазни́тельный

invoice ['ɪnvɔɪs] n счёт, факту́ра
♦ vt выпи́сывать (вы́писать pf)
счёт e факту́ру +dat

involuntary [ɪn'vɔləntrɪ] adj (action,
reflex) непроизво́льный

involve [ɪn'vɔlv] vt (include)
вовлека́ть (вовле́чь pf); (concern,
affect) каса́ться (impf) +gen; **to ~ sb
(in sth)** вовлека́ть (вовле́чь pf)
кого́-н (во что-н); **~ment** n
(participation) прича́стность f;
(enthusiasm) увлече́ние

iodine ['aɪədiːn] n йод

ion ['aɪən] n (ELEC) ио́н

IOU n abbr (= I owe you) долгова́я
распи́ска

IQ n abbr (= intelligence quotient)
коэффицие́нт у́мственного
разви́тия

IRA n abbr (= Irish Republican Army) ИРА

Iran [ɪ'rɑːn] n Ира́н; **~ian** [ɪ'reɪnɪən] adj ира́нский

Iraq [ɪ'rɑːk] n Ира́к; **~i** [ɪ'rɑːkɪ] adj ира́кский

Ireland ['aɪələnd] n Ирла́ндия

iris ['aɪrɪs] n (pl **~es**) (ANAT) ра́дужная оболо́чка (гла́за)

Irish ['aɪrɪʃ] adj ирла́ндский ♦ npl: **the ~** ирла́ндцы; **~man** (irreg) n ирла́ндец

iron ['aɪən] n (metal) желе́зо; (for clothes) утю́г ♦ cpd желе́зный ♦ vt (clothes) гла́дить (погла́дить pf); **~ out** vt (fig: problems) ула́живать (ула́дить pf)

ironic(al) [aɪ'rɔnɪk(l)] adj ирони́ческий

ironing board n гла́дильная доска́

ironmonger ['aɪənmʌŋgə*] n (BRIT) торго́вец скобяны́ми изде́лиями

irony ['aɪrənɪ] n иро́ния

irrational [ɪ'ræʃənl] adj неразу́мный, нерациона́льный

irreconcilable [ɪrekən'saɪləbl] adj (ideas, conflict) непримири́мый

irregular [ɪ'rɛɡjulə*] adj (pattern) непра́вильной фо́рмы; (surface) неро́вный; (LING) непра́вильный

irrelevant [ɪ'rɛləvənt] adj: **this fact is ~** э́тот факт к де́лу не отно́сится

irreparable [ɪ'rɛprəbl] adj (damage) непоправи́мый

irreplaceable [ɪrɪ'pleɪsəbl] adj незамени́мый

irrepressible [ɪrɪ'prɛsəbl] adj неудержи́мый

irresistible [ɪrɪ'zɪstɪbl] adj (urge, desire) непреодоли́мый; (person, thing) неотрази́мый

irrespective [ɪrɪ'spɛktɪv] prep: **~ of** незави́симо от +gen

irresponsible [ɪrɪ'spɔnsɪbl] adj безотве́тственный

irreverent [ɪ'rɛvərnt] adj (person, behaviour) непочти́тельный

irrevocable [ɪ'rɛvəkəbl] adj (action, decision) бесповоро́тный

irrigation [ɪrɪ'ɡeɪʃən] n ороше́ние, иррига́ция

irritable [ɪrɪtəbl] adj раздражи́тельный

irritate ['ɪrɪteɪt] vt раздража́ть (раздражи́ть pf)

irritating ['ɪrɪteɪtɪŋ] adj (sound etc) доса́дный; (person) неприя́тный

irritation [ɪrɪ'teɪʃən] n раздраже́ние

is [ɪz] vb see **be**

ISA n abbr (= individual savings account) индивидуа́льный сберега́тельный счёт (вид вкла́да)

Islam ['ɪzlɑːm] n (REL) исла́м; **~ic** [ɪz'læmɪk] adj исла́мский, мусульма́нский

island ['aɪlənd] n (GEO) о́стров

isn't ['ɪznt] = **is not**

isolate ['aɪsəleɪt] vt (set apart) изоли́ровать (impf/pf); **~d** adj (place, person) изоли́рованный; (incident) отде́льный

isolation [aɪsə'leɪʃən] n изоля́ция

ISP n abbr = **Internet Service Provider**

Israel ['ɪzreɪl] n Изра́иль m; **~i** [ɪz'reɪlɪ] adj изра́ильский

issue ['ɪʃuː] n (problem, subject) вопро́с, пробле́ма; (of book, stamps etc) вы́пуск; (most important part): **the ~** суть f ♦ vt (newspaper) выпуска́ть (вы́пустить pf); (statement) де́лать (сде́лать pf); (equipment, documents) выдава́ть (вы́дать pf); **to be at ~** быть (impf) предме́том обсужде́ния; **to make an ~ of sth** де́лать (сде́лать pf) пробле́му из чего́-н

it [ɪt] pron **1** (specific subject) он (f
она́; nt оно́); (direct object) его́ (f
её); (indirect object) ему́ (f ей);
(after prep: +gen) него́ (f неё);
(: +dat) нему́ (f ней); (: +instr)
ним (f ней); (: +prp) нём (f ней);
**where is your car? - it's in the
garage** где Ва́ша маши́на? - она́
в гараже́; **I like this hat, whose is
it?** мне нра́вится э́та шля́па, чья
она́?

2 э́то; (: indirect object) э́тому; **what
kind of car is it? - it's a Lada** кака́я
э́то маши́на? - э́то Ла́да; **who is
it? - it's me** кто э́то? - э́то я

3 (after prep: +gen) э́того; (: +dat)
э́тому; (: +instr) э́тим; (: +prp)
э́том; **I spoke to him about it** я
говори́л с ним об э́том; **why is it
that ...?** отчего́ ...?; **what is it?**
(what's wrong) что тако́е?

4 (impersonal): **it's raining** идёт
дождь; **it's cold today** сего́дня
хо́лодно; **it's interesting that ...**
интере́сно, что ...; **it's 6 o'clock**
сейча́с 6 часо́в; **it's the 10th of
August** сего́дня 10-ое а́вгуста

Italian [ɪ'tæljən] adj италья́нский
italics [ɪ'tælɪks] npl (TYP) курси́в
msg
Italy ['ɪtəlɪ] n Ита́лия
itch [ɪtʃ] vi чеса́ться (impf); **he was
~ing to know our secret** ему́ не
терпе́лось узна́ть наш секре́т;
~y adj: **I feel all ~y** у меня́ всё
че́шется
it'd ['ɪtd] = **it had, it would**
item ['aɪtəm] n предме́т; (on
agenda) пункт; (also: **news ~**)
сообще́ние
itinerary [aɪ'tɪnərərɪ] n маршру́т
it'll ['ɪtl] = **it shall, it will**
its [ɪts] adj, pron (f её) (referring

to subject of sentence) свой (f своя́,
nt своё) see also **my; mine**[1]
it's [ɪts] = **it has, it is**
itself [ɪt'sɛlf] pron (reflexive) себя́;
(emphatic: masculine) сам по себе́;
(: feminine) сама́ по себе́;
(: neuter) само́ по себе́
ITV n abbr (BRIT : TV) = Independent
Television
I've [aɪv] = **I have**
ivory ['aɪvərɪ] n (substance)
слоно́вая кость f
ivy ['aɪvɪ] n (BOT) плющ

J, j

jab [dʒæb] n (BRIT : inf : MED) уко́л
jack [dʒæk] n (AUT) домкра́т;
(CARDS) вале́т
jackal ['dʒækl] n шака́л
jackdaw ['dʒækdɔ:] n га́лка
jacket ['dʒækɪt] n ку́ртка; (of suit)
пиджа́к; (of book) суперобло́жка
jackpot ['dʒækpɔt] n джэк-пот, куш
jaded ['dʒeɪdɪd] adj утомлённый
jagged ['dʒægɪd] adj зубча́тый
jail [dʒeɪl] n тюрьма́ ♦ vt сажа́ть
(посади́ть pf) (в тюрьму́)
jam [dʒæm] n (preserve) джем; (also:
traffic ~) про́бка ♦ vt (passage)
забива́ть (заби́ть pf); (mechanism)
закли́нивать (закли́нить pf) ♦ vi
(drawer) застрева́ть (застря́ть pf);
to ~ sth into запи́хивать
(запихну́ть pf) что-н в +acc
janitor ['dʒænɪtə*] n вахтёр
January ['dʒænjuərɪ] n янва́рь m
Japan [dʒə'pæn] n Япо́ния
Japanese [dʒæpə'ni:z] adj
япо́нец(нка)
jar [dʒɑ:*] n ба́нка
jargon ['dʒɑ:gən] n жарго́н
jasmine ['dʒæzmɪn] n жасми́н
jaunt [dʒɔ:nt] n вы́лазка; **~y** adj
(tone, step) бо́йкий

javelin ['dʒævlɪn] n копьё

jaw [dʒɔː] n чёлюсть f

jazz [dʒæz] n джаз

jealous ['dʒɛləs] adj ревнивый; **to be ~ of** (possessive) ревновать (impf) к +dat; (envious) завидовать (impf) +dat; **~y** n (resentment) ревность f; (envy) зависть f

jeans [dʒiːnz] npl джинсы pl

jelly ['dʒɛlɪ] n желе nt ind; (US) джем; **~fish** n медуза

jeopardy ['dʒɛpədɪ] n: **to be in ~** быть (impf) в опасности

jerk [dʒəːk] n (jolt) рывок ♦ vt дёргать (дёрнуть pf), рвануть (pf) ♦ vi дёргаться (дёрнуться pf); **the car ~ed to a halt** машина резко затормозила

jersey ['dʒəːzɪ] n (pullover) свитер

Jesus ['dʒiːzəs] n (REL) Иисус

jet [dʒɛt] n (of gas, liquid) струя; (AVIAT) реактивный самолёт; **~ lag** n нарушение суточного режима организма после длительного полёта

jetty ['dʒɛtɪ] n причал

Jew [dʒuː] n еврей(ка)

jewel ['dʒuːəl] n драгоценный камень m; **~ler** (US **~er**) n ювелир; **~lery** (US **~ry**) n драгоценности fpl, ювелирные изделия ntpl

Jewess ['dʒuːɪs] n еврейка

Jewish ['dʒuːɪʃ] adj еврейский

jibe [dʒaɪb] n насмешка

jiffy ['dʒɪfɪ] n (inf): **in a ~** мигом

jig [dʒɪg] n джига

jigsaw ['dʒɪgsɔː] n (also: **~ puzzle**) головоломка

job [dʒɔb] n работа; (task) дело; (inf: difficulty): **I had a ~ getting here!** я с трудом добрался сюда!; **it's not my ~** это не моё дело; **it's a good ~ that ...** хорошо ещё, что ...; **Jobcentre** n (BRIT) биржа труда; **~less** adj

безработный

jockey ['dʒɔkɪ] n жокей

jog [dʒɔg] vt толкать (толкнуть pf) ♦ vi бегать (impf) трусцой; **to ~ sb's memory** подстёгивать (подстегнуть pf) чью-н память; **~ging** n бег трусцой

join [dʒɔɪn] vt (organization) вступать (вступить pf) в +acc; (put together) соединять (соединить pf); (group, queue) присоединяться (присоединиться pf) к +dat; (rivers) сливаться (слиться pf); (roads) сходиться (сойтись pf); **~ in** vi присоединяться (присоединиться pf) ♦ vt fus (work, discussion etc) принимать (принять pf) участие в +prp; **~ up** vi (meet) соединяться (соединиться pf); (MIL) поступать (поступить pf) на военную службу

joiner ['dʒɔɪnər] n (BRIT) столяр

joint [dʒɔɪnt] n (TECH) стык; (ANAT) сустав; (BRIT: CULIN) кусок (мяса); (inf: place) притон; (: of cannabis) скрутка с марихуаной, косяк ♦ adj совместный

joke [dʒəuk] n (gag) шутка, анекдот; (also: **practical ~**) розыгрыш ♦ vi шутить (пошутить pf); **to play a ~ on** шутить (пошутить pf) над +instr, сыграть (pf) шутку с +instr; **~r** n шутник; (CARDS) джокер

jolly ['dʒɔlɪ] adj весёлый ♦ adv (BRIT: inf) очень

jolt [dʒəult] n (jerk) рывок ♦ vt встряхивать (встряхнуть pf); (emotionally) потрясать (потрясти pf)

journal ['dʒəːnl] n журнал; (diary) дневник; **~ism** n журналистика; **~ist** n журналист(ка)

journey ['dʒəːnɪ] n поездка;

(distance covered) путь *m*, дорóга

jovial ['dʒəʊvɪəl] *adj* бóдрый, жизнерáдостный

joy [dʒɔɪ] *n* рáдость *f*; **~ful** *adj* рáдостный; **~rider** *n* человéк, угоня́ющий маши́ны рáди развлечéния

JP *n abbr* (= *Justice of the Peace*) мировóй судья́ *m*

Jr. *abbr* (*in names*) = **junior**

jubilant ['dʒuːbɪlənt] *adj* лику́ющий

jubilee ['dʒuːbɪliː] *n* юбилéй

judge [dʒʌdʒ] *n* судья́ *m* ♦ *vt* (*competition, person etc*) суди́ть (*impf*); (*estimate*) оцéнивать (оцени́ть *pf*); **~ment** *n* (*LAW*) верд́икт, решéние судá; (*view*) суждéние; (*discernment*) рассуди́тельность

judicial [dʒuː'dɪʃl] *adj* судéбный

judiciary [dʒuː'dɪʃɪərɪ] *n*: **the ~** судéбные óрганы *mpl*

judo ['dʒuːdəʊ] *n* дзюдó *nt ind*

jug [dʒʌg] *n* кувши́н

juggle ['dʒʌgl] *vi* жонгли́ровать (*impf*) ♦ *vt* (*fig*) жонгли́ровать (*impf*) +*instr*

juice [dʒuːs] *n* сок

juicy ['dʒuːsɪ] *adj* сóчный

jukebox ['dʒuːkbɒks] *n* музыкáльный автомáт

July [dʒuː'laɪ] *n* ию́ль *m*

jumble ['dʒʌmbl] *n* (*muddle*) нагромождéние ♦ *vt* (*also*: **~ up**) перемéшивать (перемешáть *pf*); **~ sale** *n* благотвори́тельная распродáжа подéржанных вещéй

jumbo ['dʒʌmbəʊ] *n* (*also*: **~ jet**) реакти́вный аэрóбус

jump [dʒʌmp] *vi* прыгать (прыгнуть *pf*); (*start*) подпры́гивать (подпры́гнуть *pf*); (*increase*) подскáкивать (подскочи́ть *pf*) ♦ *vt* (*fence*) перепры́гивать (перепры́гнуть

pf) (чéрез +*acc*), перескáкивать (перескочи́ть *pf*) (чéрез +*acc*) ♦ *n* прыжóк; (*increase*) скачóк; **to ~ the queue** (*BRIT*) идти́ (пойти́ *pf*) без óчереди

jumper ['dʒʌmpə*r*] *n* (*BRIT*) сви́тер, джéмпер; (*US: dress*) сарафáн

junction ['dʒʌŋkʃən] *n* (*BRIT*: *of roads*) перекрёсток; (: *RAIL*) ýзел

June [dʒuːn] *n* ию́нь *m*

jungle ['dʒʌŋgl] *n* джýнгли *pl*

junior ['dʒuːnɪə*r*] *adj* млáдший ♦ *n* млáдший(ая) *m(f) adj*; **he's ~ to me (by 2 years), he's my ~ (by 2 years)** он млáдше меня́ (на 2 гóда)

junk [dʒʌŋk] *n* барахлó, хлам; **~ food** *n* едá, *содержáщая мáло питáтельных вещéств*; **~ie** (*inf*) наркомáн; **~ mail** *n* незапрóшенная почтóвая реклáма

jurisdiction [dʒuərɪs'dɪkʃən] *n* (*LAW*) юрисди́кция; (*ADMIN*) сфéра полномóчий

juror ['dʒuərə*r*] *n* прися́жный заседáтель *m*

jury ['dʒuərɪ] *n* прися́жные *pl adj* (заседáтели)

just [dʒʌst] *adj* справедли́вый ♦ *adv* (*exactly*) как раз, и́менно; (*only*) тóлько; (*barely*) едвá; **he's ~ left** он тóлько что ушёл; **it's ~ right** как раз то, что нáдо; **it's ~ two o'clock** рóвно два часá; **she's ~ as clever as you** онá столь же умнá, как и ты; **it's ~ as well (that) ...** и хорошó, (что) ...; **~ as he was leaving** как раз когдá он собрáлся уходи́ть; **~ before Christmas** пéред сáмым Рождествóм; **there was ~ enough petrol** бензи́на едвá хвати́ло; **~ here** вот здесь; **he (only) missed** он чуть не попáл; **~ listen!** ты тóлько послýшай!

justice ['dʒʌstɪs] n (LAW, system) правосудие; (fairness) справедливость f n; (US: judge) судья m; **to do ~ to** (fig) отдавать (отдать pf) должное +dat

justification [dʒʌstɪfɪ'keɪʃən] n основание; (of action) оправдание

justify ['dʒʌstɪfaɪ] vt оправдывать (оправдать pf); **to ~ o.s.** оправдываться (оправдаться pf)

juvenile ['dʒu:vənaɪl] n несовершеннолетний(яя) m(f) adj, подросток ♦ adj детский

K, k

K abbr = one thousand; (COMPUT: = kilobyte) K

kangaroo [kæŋgə'ru:] n кенгуру m ind

karaoke [kɑːrə'əʊkɪ] n кариоки ind

karate [kə'rɑːtɪ] n карате nt ind

kebab [kə'bæb] n = шашлык

keel [kiːl] n киль m

keen [kiːn] adj острый; (eager) страстный, увлечённый; (competition) напряжённый; **to be ~ to do** or **on doing** очень хотеть (impf) +infin; **to be ~ on sth** увлекаться (impf) чем-н

keep [kiːp] (pt, pp **kept**) vt (receipt, money) оставлять (оставить pf) себе; (store) хранить (impf); (preserve) сохранять (сохранить pf); (house, shop, family) содержать (impf); (prisoner, chickens) держать (impf); (accounts, diary) вести (impf); (promise) сдерживать (сдержать pf) ♦ vi (in certain state or place) оставаться (остаться pf); (food) сохраняться (impf); (continue): **to ~ doing** продолжать (impf) +impf infin ♦ n:

he has enough for his ~ ему достаточно на прожитие; **where do you ~ the salt?** где у вас соль?; **he tries to ~ her happy** он делает всё для того, чтобы она была довольна; **to ~ the house tidy** содержать (impf) дом в порядке; **to ~ sth to o.s.** держать (impf) что-н при себе; **to ~ sth (back) from sb** скрывать (скрыть pf) что-н от кого-н; **to ~ sth from happening** не давать (дать pf) чему-н случиться; **to ~ time** (clock) идти (impf) точно; **~ on** vi: **to ~ on doing** продолжать (impf) +impf infin; **to ~ on (about)** не переставать говорить (impf) (о +prp); **~ out** vt не впускать (впустить pf); "**~ out**" "посторонним вход воспрещён"; **~ up** vt (payments, standards) поддерживать (impf) ♦ vi: **to ~ up (with)** поспевать (поспеть pf) (за +instr), идти (impf) в ногу (с +instr); **~ fit** n аэробика

kennel ['kɛnl] n конура; **~s** npl гостиница fsg для собак

Kenya ['kɛnjə] n Кения

kept [kɛpt] pt, pp of **keep**

kerb [kə:b] n (BRIT) бордюр

kettle ['kɛtl] n чайник

key [kiː] n ключ; (of piano, computer) клавиша ♦ cpd ключевой ♦ vt (also: **~ in**) набирать (набрать pf) (на клавиатуре); **~board** n клавиатура; **~ring** n брелок

khaki ['kɑːkɪ] n, adj хаки nt, adj ind

kick [kɪk] vt (person, table) ударять (ударить pf) ногой; (ball) ударять (ударить pf) ногой по +dat; (inf: habit, addiction) побороть (pf) ♦ vi (horse) лягаться (impf) ♦ n удар; **~ off** vi: **the match ~s off at 3pm** матч начинается в 3 часа (в футболе)

kid [kɪd] n (inf: child) ребёнок; (goat) козлёнок

kidnap ['kɪdnæp] vt похищать (похитить pf)

kidney ['kɪdnɪ] n (MED) почка; (CULIN) почки fpl

kill [kɪl] vt убивать (убить pf); to ~ o.s. покончить (pf) с собой; to be ~ed (in war, accident) погибнуть (погибнуть pf); ~er n убийца m/f

kilo ['kiːləu] n килограмм, кило nt ind (разг); ~gram(me) ['kiːləugræm] n килограмм; ~metre ['kɪləmiːtər] (US ~meter) n километр

kind [kaɪnd] adj добрый ♦ n тип, род; in ~ (COMM) натурой; a ~ of род +gen; two of a ~ две вещи одного типа; what ~ of ...? какой ...?

kindergarten ['kɪndəgɑːtn] n детский сад

kind-hearted [kaɪnd'hɑːtɪd] adj добрый, добросердечный

kindly ['kaɪndlɪ] adj (smile) добрый; (person, tone) доброжелательный ♦ adv (smile, behave) любезно, доброжелательно; will you ~ give me his address будьте добры, дайте мне его адрес

kindness ['kaɪndnɪs] n (quality) доброта

king [kɪŋ] n король m; ~dom n королевство; the animal/plant ~dom животное/растительное царство; ~fisher n зимородок

kiosk ['kiːɔsk] n киоск; (BRIT: TEL) телефонная будка

kipper ['kɪpər] n ≈ копчёная селёдка

kiss [kɪs] n поцелуй ♦ vt целовать (поцеловать pf) ♦ vi целоваться (поцеловаться pf)

kit [kɪt] n (also: sports ~) (спортивный) костюм; (equipment) снаряжение; (set of tools) набор; (for assembly) комплект

kitchen ['kɪtʃɪn] n кухня

kite [kaɪt] n (toy) воздушный змей

kitten ['kɪtn] n котёнок

kitty ['kɪtɪ] n (pool of money) общая касса

kiwi ['kiːwiː] n киви f ind

km abbr (= kilometre) км

knack [næk] n способность f

knee [niː] n колено

kneel [niːl] (pt, pp knelt) vi (also: ~ down) вставать (встать pf) на колени; (: state) стоять (impf) на коленях

knew [njuː] pt of know

knickers ['nɪkəz] npl (BRIT) (женские) трусики mpl

knife [naɪf] (pl knives) n нож ♦ vt ранить (impf) ножом

knight [naɪt] n рыцарь m; (CHESS) конь m

knit [nɪt] vt (garment) вязать (связать pf) ♦ vi вязать (impf); (bones) срастаться (срастись pf); to ~ one's brows хмурить (нахмурить pf) брови; ~ting n вязание; ~ting needle n вязальная спица

knives [naɪvz] npl of knife

knob [nɔb] n (on door) ручка; (on radio etc) кнопка

knock [nɔk] vt (strike) ударять (ударить pf); (bump into) сталкиваться (столкнуться pf) с +instr; (inf: criticize) критиковать (impf) ♦ n (blow, bump) удар, толчок; (on door) стук; to ~ some sense into sb учить (научить pf) кого-н уму-разуму; he ~ed at or on the door he постучал в дверь; ~ down vt (person, price) сбивать (сбить pf); ~ out vt (subj: person, drug) оглушать (оглушить pf); (BOXING) нокаутировать (pf); (defeat) выбива́ть (вы́бить pf); ~ **over** vt сбива́ть (сбить pf)

knot [nɔt] n (also NAUT) у́зел; (in wood) сучо́к ♦ vt завя́зывать (завяза́ть pf) узло́м

know [nəu] (pt knew, pp ~n) vt (facts, people) знать (impf); **to ~ how to do** уме́ть (impf) +infin; **to ~ about** or **of** знать (impf) о +prp; **~-all** n (BRIT: inf: pej) всезна́йка m/f; **~-how** n но́у-ха́у nt ind; **~ingly** adv (purposely) созна́тельно; (smile, look) понима́

knowledge ['nɔlɪdʒ] n зна́ние; (things learnt) зна́ния ntpl; (awareness) представле́ние; **~able** adj зна́ющий; **he is very ~able about art** он большо́й знато́к иску́сства

known [nəun] pp of **know**

knuckle ['nʌkl] n костя́шка

KO n abbr (= knockout) нока́ут

Korea [kə'rɪə] n Коре́я

Kosovan ['kɔsəvən] n косова́р

Kosovar ['kɔsəvɑː] n косова́р

Kosovo ['kɔsəvəu] n Ко́сово

L, l

L abbr (BRIT : AUT: = learner) учени́к

l. abbr (= litre) л

lab [læb] n abbr = **laboratory**

label ['leɪbl] n эти́кетка, ярлы́к; (on suitcase) би́рка ♦ vt (see n) прикрепля́ть (прикрепи́ть pf) ярлы́к на +acc; прикрепля́ть (прикрепи́ть pf) би́рку к +dat

labor ['leɪbə] n (US) = **labour**

laboratory [lə'bɔrətərɪ] n лаборато́рия

labour ['leɪbə] (US labor) n (work) труд; (workforce) рабо́чая си́ла; (MED) ро́ды mpl; **to be in ~** рожа́ть (impf); **~er** n неквалифици́рованный рабо́чий

lace [leɪs] n (fabric) кру́жево; (of shoe) шнуро́к ♦ vt (shoe : also: ~ up) шнурова́ть (зашнурова́ть pf)

lack [læk] n (absence) отсу́тствие; (shortage) нехва́тка ♦ vt: **she ~ed self-confidence** ей не хвата́ло уве́ренности в себе́; **through** or **for ~ of** из-за недоста́тка +gen

lacquer ['lækə] n лак

lad [læd] n па́рень m

ladder ['lædə] n ле́стница; (BRIT: in tights) спусти́вшиеся пе́тли fpl

laden ['leɪdn] adj: **to be ~ (with)** ломи́ться (impf) от +gen; (person): **~ (with)** нагру́женный (+instr)

ladle ['leɪdl] n поло́вник

lady ['leɪdɪ] n (woman) да́ма; **ladies and gentlemen ...** да́мы и господа́ ...; **young/old ~** молода́я/пожила́я же́нщина; **the ladies' (room)** же́нский туале́т; **~bird** n бо́жья коро́вка; **~bug** n (US) = **ladybird**

lag [læg] n (period of time) заде́ржка

lager ['lɑːgə] n све́тлое пи́во

laid [leɪd] pt, pp of **lay**

lain [leɪn] pp of **lie**

lake [leɪk] n о́зеро

lamb [læm] n (ZOOL) ягнёнок; (CULIN: (молода́я) бара́нина

lame [leɪm] adj (person, animal) хромо́й; (excuse, argument) сла́бый

lament [lə'mɛnt] n плач ♦ vt опла́кивать (опла́кать pf)

lamp [læmp] n ла́мпа; (street lamp) фона́рь m; **~post** n (BRIT) фона́рный столб; **~shade** n абажу́р

land [lænd] n земля́ ♦ vi (from ship) выса́живаться (вы́садиться pf); (AVIAT) приземля́ться (приземли́ться pf) ♦ vt (plane)

сажа́ть (посади́ть *pf*); (*goods*)
выгружа́ть (вы́грузить *pf*); **to ~
sb with sth** (*inf*) нава́ливать
(навали́ть *pf*) что-н на кого́-н;
~ing *n* (*of house*) ле́стничная
площа́дка; (*of plane*) поса́дка,
приземле́ние; **~lady** *n* (*of house,
flat*) домовладе́лица, хозя́йка; (*of
pub*) хозя́йка; **~lord** *n* (*of house,
flat*) домовладе́лец, хозя́ин; (*of
pub*) хозя́ин; **~mark** *n*
(назе́мный) ориенти́р; (*fig*) ве́ха;
~owner *n* землевладе́лец(лица);
~scape *n* (*view, painting*) пейза́ж;
(*terrain*) ландша́фт; **~slide** *n* (*GEO*)
о́ползень *m*; (*POL*: *also*: **landslide
victory**) реши́тельная побе́да

lane [leɪn] *n* (*in country*) тропи́нка;
(*of road*) полоса́; (*SPORT*) доро́жка

language [ˈlæŋgwɪdʒ] *n* язы́к; **bad
~** скверносло́вие

lantern [ˈlæntən] *n* фона́рь *m*

lap [læp] *n* коле́ни *ntpl*; (*SPORT*)
круг

lapel [ləˈpel] *n* ла́цкан

lapse [læps] *n* (*bad behaviour*)
про́мах; (*of time*) промежу́ток; (*of
concentration*) поте́ря

laptop [ˈlæptɔp] *n* лапто́п, лэпто́п

larch [lɑːtʃ] *n* ли́ственница

lard [lɑːd] *n* свино́й жир

larder [ˈlɑːdəʳ] *n* кладова́я *f adj*

large [lɑːdʒ] *adj* большо́й; (*major*)
кру́пный; **as ~** (*as a whole*) в
це́лом; (*at liberty*) на во́ле; **~ly**
adv по бо́льшей ча́сти; **~ly
because ...** в основно́м, потому́
что ...; **~-scale** *adj*
крупномасшта́бный

lark [lɑːk] *n* (*bird*) жа́воронок

larva [ˈlɑːvə] (*pl* **~e**) *n* личи́нка

laryngitis [lærɪnˈdʒaɪtɪs] *n*
ларинги́т

laser [ˈleɪzəʳ] *n* ла́зер; **~ printer**
ла́зерный при́нтер

lash [læʃ] *n* (*eyelash*) ресни́ца; (*of*
whip) уда́р (хлыста́); ♦ *vt* (*also*: **~
against**: *subj: rain, wind*) хлеста́ть
(*impf*) о +*acc*; (*tie*): **to ~ to**
привя́зывать (привяза́ть *pf*) к
+*dat*

last [lɑːst] *adj* (*most recent*)
про́шлый; (*final*) после́дний
♦ *adv* в после́дний раз; (*finally*) в
конце́ ♦ *vi* (*continue*) дли́ться
(продли́ться *pf*), продолжа́ться
(*impf*); (*keep*: *thing*) сохраня́ться
(сохрани́ться *pf*); (: *person*)
держа́ться (продержа́ться *pf*);
(*suffice*): **we had enough money to
~ us** нам хвати́ло де́нег; **~ year** в
про́шлом году́; **~ week** на
про́шлой неде́ле; **~ night** (*early*)
вчера́ ве́чером; (*late*) про́шлой
но́чью; **at ~** наконе́ц; **~ but one**
предпосле́дний; **~ing** *adj*
(*friendship*) продолжи́тельный,
дли́тельный; (*solution*)
долговре́менный; **~ly** *adv*
наконе́ц; **~-minute** *adj*
после́дний

latch [lætʃ] *n* (*on gate*) задви́жка;
(*on front door*) замо́к *m*

late [leɪt] *adj* (*dead*)
поко́йный ♦ *adv* по́здно; (*behind
time*) с опозда́нием; **to be ~**
опа́здывать (опозда́ть *pf*); **of ~** в
после́днее вре́мя; **in ~ May** в
конце́ ма́я; **~comer** *n*
опозда́вший(ая)*m(f) adj*; **~ly** *adv* в
после́днее вре́мя

later [ˈleɪtəʳ] *adj* (*time, date*) бо́лее
по́здний; (*meeting, version*)
после́дующий ♦ *adv* по́зже,
по́зднее; ♦ *на* впосле́дствии,
по́зже; **he arrived ~ than me** он
пришёл по́зже меня́

latest [ˈleɪtɪst] *adj* са́мый по́здний;
(*most recent*) (са́мый) после́дний;
(*news*) после́дний; **at the ~** са́мое
по́зднее

lathe [leɪð] *n* тока́рный стано́к

lather ['lɑːðəʳ] n (мыльная) пена

Latin ['lætɪn] n (LING) латинский язык ♦ adj: **~ languages** романские языки; **~ countries** страны Южной Европы; **~ America** n Латинская Америка

latitude ['lætɪtjuːd] n (GEO) широта

latter ['lætəʳ] adj последний ♦ n: **the ~** последний(яя) m(f) adj

Latvia ['lætvɪə] n Латвия; **~n** adj латвийский ♦ n (LING) латышский язык

laugh [lɑːf] n смех ♦ vi смеяться (impf); **for a ~** (inf) для смеха; **~ at** vt fus смеяться (посмеяться pf) над +instr; **~able** adj смехотворный; **~ing stock** n: **to be the ~ing stock of** служить (impf) посмешищем для +gen; **~ter** n смех

launch [lɔːntʃ] n (of rocket, product) запуск ♦ vt (ship) спускать (спустить pf) на воду; (rocket) запускать (запустить pf); (attack, campaign) начинать (начать pf); (product) пускать (пустить pf) в продажу, запускать (запустить pf)

Laundrette® [lɔːn'drɛt] n (BRIT) прачечная f adj самообслуживания

laundry ['lɔːndrɪ] n (washing) стирка

laurel ['lɔrl] n лавр, лавровое дерево

lava ['lɑːvə] n лава

lavatory ['lævətərɪ] n туалет

lavender ['lævəndəʳ] n лаванда

lavish ['lævɪʃ] adj (amount, hospitality) щедрый ♦ vt: **to ~ sth on sb** осыпать (осыпать pf) кого-н чем-н

law [lɔː] n закон; (professions): **(the) ~** юриспруденция; (SCOL) право; **it's against the ~** это противозаконно; **~-abiding** adj

законопослушный; **~ and order** n правопорядок; **~ful** adj законный

lawn [lɔːn] n газон; **~ mower** n газонокосилка

lawsuit ['lɔːsuːt] n судебный иск

lawyer ['lɔːjəʳ] n (solicitor, barrister) юрист

lax [læks] adj (discipline) слабый; (standards) низкий; (morals, behaviour) распущенный

laxative ['læksətɪv] n слабительное nt adj

lay [leɪ] (pt, pp laid) pt of **lie** ♦ adj (not expert) непрофессиональный; (REL) мирской ♦ vt (place) класть (положить pf); (table) накрывать (накрыть pf) (на +acc); (carpet) стлать (постелить pf); (cable) прокладывать (проложить pf); (egg) откладывать (отложить pf); **~ down** vt (object) класть (положить pf); (rules etc) устанавливать (установить pf); (weapons) складывать (сложить pf); **to ~ down the law** приказывать (приказать pf); **~ off** vt (workers) увольнять (уволить pf); **~ on** vt (meal etc) устраивать (устроить pf); **~ out** vt раскладывать (разложить pf); **~by** (BRIT) площадка для временной стоянки (на автодороге)

layer ['leɪəʳ] n слой

layout ['leɪaut] n (of garden, building) планировка

laziness ['leɪzɪnɪs] n лень f

lazy ['leɪzɪ] adj ленивый

lb. abbr (= pound (weight)) фунт

---
lb. - фунт. Мера веса равная 0.454 кг.
---

lead¹ [liːd] (pt, pp led) n (front

position) пе́рвенство, ли́дерство; (*clue*) нить f; (*in play, film*) гла́вная роль f; (*for dog*) поводо́к; (*ELEC*) про́вод ♦ vt (*competition, market*) лиди́ровать (*impf*) в +prp; (*opponent*) опережа́ть (*impf*); (*person, group: guide*) вести́ (*повести́* pf); (*activity, organization etc*) руководи́ть (*impf*) +instr ♦ vi (*road, pipe*) вести́ (*impf*); (*SPORT*) лиди́ровать (*impf*); **to ~ the way** ука́зывать (указа́ть pf) путь; **~ away** vt уводи́ть (увести́ pf); **~ on** vt води́ть (*impf*) за́ нос; **to ~ to** fus вести́ (привести́ pf) к +dat; **~ up to** vt fus (*events*) приводи́ть (привести́ pf) к +dat; (*topic*) подводи́ть (подвести́ pf) к +dat

lead² [lɛd] n (*metal*) свине́ц; (*in pencil*) графи́т

leader ['li:dər] n (*of group, SPORT*) ли́дер; **~ship** n руково́дство; (*quality*) ли́дерские ка́чества ntpl

lead-free ['lɛdfri:] adj не содержа́щий свинца́

leading ['li:dɪŋ] adj (*most important*) веду́щий; (*first, front*) пере́дний

lead singer [li:d-] n соли́ст(ка)

leaf [li:f] (pl **leaves**) n лист

leaflet ['li:flɪt] n листо́вка

league [li:g] n ли́га; **to be in ~ with sb** быть (*impf*) в сго́воре с кем-н

leak [li:k] n уте́чка; (*hole*) течь f ♦ vi протека́ть (проте́чь pf); (*liquid, gas*) проса́чиваться (просочи́ться pf) ♦ vt (*information*) разглаша́ть (разгласи́ть pf)

lean [li:n] (pt, pp **~ed** or **~t**) adj (*person*) сухоща́вый; (*meat*) по́стный ♦ vt: **to ~ sth on** or **against** прислоня́ть (прислони́ть pf) что-н к +dat ♦ vi: **to ~ forward/back** наклоня́ться (наклони́ться pf) вперёд/наза́д; **to ~ against** (*wall*) прислоня́ться

(прислони́ться pf) к +dat; (*person*) опира́ться (опере́ться pf) на +acc; **to ~ on** (*chair*) опира́ться (опере́ться pf) о +acc; (*rely on*) опира́ться (опере́ться pf) на +acc; **~t** [lɛnt] pt, pp of **lean**

leap [li:p] (pt, pp **~ed** or **~t**) n скачо́к ♦ vi пры́гать (пры́гнуть pf); (*price, number*) подска́кивать (подскочи́ть pf); **~ year** n високо́сный год

learn [lə:n] (pt, pp **~ed** or **~t**) vt (*skill*) учи́ться (научи́ться pf) +dat; (*facts, poem*) учи́ть (вы́учить pf) ♦ vi учи́ться (*impf*); **to ~ about** or **of/that ...** (*hear, read*) узнава́ть (узна́ть pf) о +prp, что ...; **to ~ about sth** (*study*) изуча́ть (изучи́ть pf) что-н; **to ~ (how) to do** учи́ться (научи́ться pf) +impf infin; **~ed** ['lə:nɪd] adj учёный; **~t** [lə:nt] pt, pp of **learn**

lease [li:s] n аре́ндный догово́р, аре́нда ♦ vt: **to ~ sth (to sb)** сдава́ть (сдать pf) что-н в аре́нду (кому́-н); **to ~ sth from sb** арендова́ть (*impf/pf*) о́рбрать (взять pf) в аре́нду у кого́-н

leash [li:ʃ] n поводо́к

least [li:st] adj: **the ~** (+noun: *smallest*) наиме́ньший ((*slightest*): *difficulty*) мале́йший ♦ adv (+vb) ме́ньше всего́; (+adj): **the ~** наиме́нее; **at ~** по кра́йней ме́ре; **not in the ~** (as response) отню́дь нет; (+vb, +adj) ниско́лько or во́все не

leather ['lɛðər] n ко́жа

leave [li:v] (pt, pp **left**) vt оставля́ть (оста́вить pf), покида́ть (поки́нуть pf); (*go away from: on foot*) уходи́ть (уйти́ pf) из +gen; (: *by transport*) уезжа́ть (уе́хать pf) из +gen; (*party, committee*) выходи́ть (вы́йти pf) из +gen ♦ vi (*on foot*) уходи́ть (уйти́ pf); (*by*)

transport) уезжа́ть (уе́хать *pf)*;
(bus, train) уходи́ть (уйти́ *pf)* ♦ *n*
о́тпуск; **to ~ sth to sb** *(money,
property)* оставля́ть (оста́вить *pf)*
что-н кому́-н; **to be left (over)**
остава́ться (оста́ться *pf)*; **on ~** в
о́тпуске; **~ behind** *vt* оставля́ть
(оста́вить *pf)*; **~ out** *vt (omit)*
пропуска́ть (пропусти́ть *pf)*; **he
was left out** его́ пропусти́ли
leaves [li:vz] *npl of* **leaf**
lecture ['lektʃə*r*] *n* ле́кция ♦ *vi*
чита́ть *(impf)* ле́кции ♦ *vt (scold)*:
to ~ sb on *or* **about** чита́ть
(прочита́ть *pf)* кому́-н ле́кцию по
по́воду +gen; **to give a ~** on
+prp; читать (прочитать pf) ле́кцию о
+prp; **~r** *n (BRIT : SCOL)*
преподава́тель(ница) *m(f)*
led [led] *pt, pp of* **lead**[1]
ledge [ledʒ] *n* вы́ступ; *(of window)*
подоко́нник
leech [li:tʃ] *n (also fig)* пия́вка
leek [li:k] *n* лук-поре́й *no pl*
left [left] *pt, pp of* **leave** ♦ *adj (of
direction, position)* ле́вый ♦ *n* ле́вая
сторона́ ♦ *adv (motion)*: **(to the) ~**
нале́во; *(position)*: **(on the) ~**
сле́ва; **the Left** *(POL)* ле́вые *pl adj*;
~-handed *adj*: **he/she is ~-handed**
он/она́ левша́; **~-wing** *adj (POL)*
ле́вый
leg [leg] *n (ANAT)* нога́; *(of insect,
furniture)* но́жка; *(also: ~ trouser ~)*
штани́на; *(of journey, race)* эта́п
legacy ['legəsɪ] *n (in will)*
насле́дство; *(fig)* насле́дие
legal ['li:gl] *adj (advice, requirement)*
юриди́ческий; *(system, action)*
суде́бный; *(lawful)* зако́нный; **~ity**
[lɪ'gælɪtɪ] *n* зако́нность *f*; **~ize**
vt узако́нивать (узако́нить *pf)*;
~ly *adv* юриди́чески; *(by law)* по
зако́ну
legend ['ledʒənd] *n (story)* леге́нда;
(person) легенда́рная ли́чность *f*;

~ary *adj* легенда́рный
legislation [ledʒɪs'leɪʃən] *n*
законода́тельство
legislative ['ledʒɪslətɪv] *adj (POL)*
законода́тельный
legitimate [lɪ'dʒɪtɪmət] *adj*
зако́нный, легити́мный
leisure ['leʒə*r*] *n (also: ~ time)*
досу́г, свобо́дное вре́мя *nt*; **at
(one's) ~** не спеша́; **~ centre** *n*
спорти́вно-оздорови́тельный
ко́мплекс; **~ly** *adj* неторопли́вый
lemon ['lemən] *n (fruit)* лимо́н; **~ade**
[lemə'neɪd] *n* лимона́д
lend [lend] *(pt, pp* **lent)** *vt*: **to ~ sth
to sb, ~ sb sth** ода́лживать
(одолжи́ть *pf)* что-н кому́-н
length [leŋθ] *n (measurement)*
длина́; *(distance)* протяжённость
f; *(piece: of wood, cloth etc)*
отре́зок; *(duration)*
продолжи́тельность *f*; **at ~** *(for a
long time)* простра́нно; **~y** *adj
(text)* дли́нный; *(meeting)*
продолжи́тельный; *(explanation)*
простра́нный
lenient ['li:nɪənt] *adj* мя́гкий
lens [lenz] *n (of glasses, camera)*
ли́нза
Lent [lent] *n* Вели́кий Пост
lent [lent] *pt, pp of* **lend**
lentil ['lentl] *n* чечеви́ца *no pl*
Leo ['li:əʊ] *n* Лев
leopard ['lepəd] *n* леопа́рд
leotard ['li:ətɑːd] *n* трико́ *nt ind*
lesbian ['lezbɪən] *adj* лесби́йский
♦ *n* лесбия́нка
less [les] *adj (attention, money)*
ме́ньше +gen ♦ *adv (beautiful,
clever)* ме́нее ♦ *prep* ми́нус +nom;
~ than ме́ньше +gen *or* ме́нее +gen;
~ than half ме́ньше полови́ны; **~
than ever** ме́ньше, чем когда́-
либо; **~ and ~** ме́ньше и
ме́ньше; *(+adj)* всё ме́нее и
ме́нее; **the ~ ... the more ~** чем

ме́ньше ..., тем бо́льше ...; **~er** *adj:* **to a ~er extent** в ме́ньшей сте́пени

lesson ['lesn] *n* уро́к; **to teach sb a ~** (*fig*) проучи́ть (*pf*) кого́-н

let [let] (*pt, pp* **~**) *vt* (*BRIT: lease*) сдава́ть (сдать *pf*) (внаём); (*allow*): **to ~ sb do** разреша́ть (разреши́ть *pf*) *or* позволя́ть (позво́лить *pf*) кому́-н +*infin*; **~ me try** да́йте я попро́бую; **to ~ sb know about ...** дава́ть (дать *pf*) кому́-н знать о +*prp* ...; **~'s go there** дава́й(те) пойдём туда́; **~'s do it!** дава́й(те) сде́лаем э́то; **"to ~"** "сдаётся внаём"; **~ go of** отпуска́ть (отпусти́ть *pf*); **~ down** *vt* (*tyre etc*) спуска́ть (спусти́ть *pf*); (*fig: person*) подводи́ть (подвести́ *pf*); **~ in** *vt* (*water, air*) пропуска́ть (пропусти́ть *pf*); (*person*) впуска́ть (впусти́ть *pf*); **~ off** *vt* (*culprit, child*) отпуска́ть (отпусти́ть *pf*); (*bomb*) взрыва́ть (взорва́ть *pf*); **~ out** *vt* выпуска́ть (вы́пустить *pf*); (*sound*) издава́ть (изда́ть *pf*)

lethal ['li:θl] *adj* (*weapon, chemical*) смертоно́сный; (*dose*) смерте́льный

lethargic [lɛ'θɑ:dʒɪk] *adj* вя́лый, со́нный

letter ['lɛtər] *n* письмо́; (*of alphabet*) бу́ква; **~ box** *n* (*BRIT*) почто́вый я́щик

letter box - почто́вый я́щик. Поми́мо почто́вого я́щика да́нное сло́во та́кже обознача́ет про́резь во входно́й две́ри, в кото́рую опуска́ется корреспонде́нция.

lettuce ['lɛtɪs] *n* сала́т лату́к
leukaemia [lu:'ki:mɪə] (*US* **leukemia**) *n* белокро́вие,

лейкеми́я

level ['lɛvl] *adj* (*flat*) ро́вный ♦ *n* у́ровень *m* ♦ *adv:* **to draw ~** (*with person, vehicle*) поравня́ться (*pf*) (*c* +*instr*); **to be ~ with** быть (*impf*) на одно́м у́ровне с +*instr*

lever ['li:vər] *n* рыча́г; (*bar*) лом; **~age** *n* (*fig: influence*) влия́ние

levy ['lɛvɪ] *n* нало́г ♦ *vt* налага́ть (наложи́ть *pf*)

liability [laɪə'bɪlɪtɪ] *n* (*responsibility*) отве́тственность *f*; (*person, thing*) обу́за *m/f*; **liabilities** *npl* (*COMM*) обяза́тельства *ntpl*

liable ['laɪəbl] *adj:* **~ for** (*legally responsible*) подсу́дный за +*acc*; **to be ~ to** подлежа́ть (*impf*) +*dat*; **he's ~ to take offence** возмо́жно, что он оби́дится

liaison [li:'eɪzɒn] *n* (*cooperation*) взаимоде́йствие, коопера́ция

liar ['laɪər] *n* лжец, лгун(ья)

libel ['laɪbl] *n* клевета́

liberal ['lɪbərl] *adj* (*also POL*) либера́льный; (*large, generous*) ще́дрый; **Liberal Democrat** *n* либера́л-демокра́т; **the Liberal Democrats** (*party*) па́ртия либера́л-демокра́тов

liberate ['lɪbəreɪt] *vt* освобожда́ть (освободи́ть *pf*)

liberation [lɪbə'reɪʃən] *n* освобожде́ние

liberty ['lɪbətɪ] *n* свобо́да; **to be at ~** (*criminal*) быть (*impf*) на свобо́де; **I'm not at ~ to comment** я не во́лен комменти́ровать; **to take the ~ of doing** позво́лить (*pf*) себе́ +*infin*

Libra ['li:brə] *n* Весы́ *pl*

librarian [laɪ'brɛərɪən] *n* библиоте́карь *m*

library ['laɪbrərɪ] *n* библиоте́ка

lice [laɪs] *npl of* **louse**

licence ['laɪsns] (*US* **license**) *n*

(*permit*) лицéнзия; (*AUT*: *also*: **driving ~**) (водúтельские) правá *ntpl*

license ['laɪsns] *n* (*US*) = **licence** ♦ *vt* выдавáть (вы́дать *pf*) лицéнзию на +*acc*; **~d** *adj* (*restaurant*) с лицéнзией на продáжу спиртны́х напúтков

lick [lɪk] *vt* (*stamp, fingers etc*) лизáть (*impf*), облúзывать (облизáть *pf*); **to ~ one's lips** облúзываться (облизáться *pf*)

lid [lɪd] *n* крýшка; (*also*: **eye~**) вéко

lie [laɪ] (*pt* **lay**, *pp* **lain**) *vi* (*be horizontal*) лежáть (*impf*); (*be situated*) лежáть (*impf*), находúться (*impf*); (*problem, cause*) заключáться (*impf*); (*pt, pp* **~d**; *be untruthful*) лгать (солгáть *pf*), врать (соврáть *pf*) ♦ *n* (*untrue statement*) ложь *f no pl*; **to ~** or **be lying in first/last place** занимáть (*impf*) пéрвое/послéднее мéсто; **~ down** *vi* (*motion*) ложúться (лечь *pf*); (*position*) лежáть (*impf*); **~-in** (*BRIT*): **to have a ~-in** вставáть (встать *pf*) попóзже

lieutenant [lef'tenənt, (*US*) luːˈtenənt] *n* лейтенáнт

life [laɪf] (*pl* **lives**) *n* жизнь *f*; **~ belt** *n* (*BRIT*) спасáтельный круг; **~boat** *n* спасáтельное сýдно; (*on ship*) спасáтельная шлю́пка; **~guard** *n* спасáтель *m*; **~ jacket** *n* спасáтельный жилéт; **~less** *adj* безжúзненный; **~line** *n* (*fig*) срéдство выживáния; **~long** ♦ *adj* (*friend, habit*) неизмéнный; **it was a ~long ambition of his** э́то бы́ло мечтóй всей егó жúзни; **~ preserver** *n* (*US*) = **life jacket**; **~style** *n* óбраз жúзни; **~time** *n* (*of person*) жизнь *f*; (*of institution*) врéмя *nt* существовáния

lift [lɪft] *vt* поднимáть (подня́ть

pf); (*ban, sanctions*) снимáть (снять *pf*) ♦ *vi* (*fog*) рассéиваться (рассéяться *pf*) ♦ *n* (*BRIT*) лифт; **to give sb a ~** (*BRIT*: *AUT*) подвозúть (подвезтú *pf*) когó-н

ligament ['lɪgəmənt] *n* свя́зка

light [laɪt] (*pt, pp* **lit**) *n* свет; (*AUT*) фáра ♦ *vt* (*candle, fire*) зажигáть (заже́чь *pf*); (*place*) освещáть (освети́ть *pf*) ♦ *adj* (*pale, bright*) свéтлый; (*not heavy*) лёгкий; **~s** *npl* (*also*: **traffic ~s**) светофóр *msg*; **have you got a ~?** (*for cigarette*) мóжно у Вас прикурúть?; **to come to ~** выясня́ться (вы́ясниться *pf*); **in the ~ of** (*discussions etc*) в свéте +*gen*; **~ up** *vi* (*face*) светлéть (просветлéть *pf*) ♦ *vt* (*illuminate*) освещáть (освети́ть *pf*); **~-hearted** *adj* (*person*) беспéчный; (*question, remark*) несерьёзный; **~house** *n* мая́к; **~ing** *n* освещéние; **~ly** *adv* (*touch, kiss*) слегкá; (*eat, treat*) слегкá; (*sleep*) чýтко; **to get off ~ly** легкó отдéлываться (отдéлаться *pf*)

lightning ['laɪtnɪŋ] *n* мóлния

like [laɪk] *prep* как +*acc*; (*similar to*) похóжий на +*acc* ♦ *vt* (*sweets, reading*) любúть (*impf*) ♦ *n*: **and the ~** и томý подóбное; **he looks ~ his father** он похóж на своегó отцá; **what does she look ~** как онá вы́глядит?; **what's he ~?** что он за человéк?; **there's nothing ~ ...** ничтó не мóжет сравнúться с +*instr* ...; **do it ~ this** дéлайте э́то так; **that's just ~ him** (*typical*) э́то на негó похóже; **it is nothing ~ ...** э́то совсéм не то, чтó ...; **I ~/d him** он мне нрáвится/ понрáвился; **I would~, I'd ~** мне хотéлось бы, я бы хотéл; **would you ~ a coffee?** хотúте кóфе?; **his ~s and dislikes** егó вкýсы; **~able**

adj симпати́чный

likelihood ['laɪklɪhud] *n* вероя́тность *f*

likely ['laɪklɪ] *adj* вероя́тный; **she is ~ to agree** она́, вероя́тно, согласи́тся; **not ~!** (*inf*) ни за что!

likeness ['laɪknɪs] *n* схо́дство

likewise ['laɪkwaɪz] *adv* та́кже; **to do ~** поступа́ть (поступи́ть *pf*) таки́м же о́бразом

lilac ['laɪlək] *n* сире́нь *f no pl*

lily ['lɪlɪ] *n* ли́лия

limb [lɪm] *n* (*ANAT*) коне́чность *f*

lime [laɪm] *n* (*fruit*) лайм; (*tree*) ли́па; (*chemical*) и́звесть *f*

limelight ['laɪmlaɪt] *n*: **to be in the ~** (*impf*) в це́нтре внима́ния

limestone ['laɪmstəun] *n* известня́к

limit ['lɪmɪt] *n* преде́л; (*restriction*) лими́т, ограниче́ние ♦ *vt* (*production, expense etc*) лимити́ровать (*impf/pf*); ограни́чивать (ограни́чить *pf*); **~ation** [lɪmɪ'teɪʃən] *n* ограниче́ние; **~ed** *adj* ограни́ченный

limousine ['lɪməziːn] *n* лимузи́н

limp [lɪmp] *vi* хрома́ть (*impf*) ♦ *adj* (*person, limb*) бесси́льный; (*material*) мя́гкий

line [laɪn] *n* ли́ния; (*row*) ряд; (*of writing, song*) строка́, стро́чка; (*wrinkle*) морщи́на; (*wire*) про́вод; (*fig: of thought*) ход; (*of business, work*) о́бласть *f* ♦ *vt* (*road*) выстра́иваться (вы́строиться *pf*) вдоль +*gen*; (*clothing*) подбива́ть (подби́ть *pf*); (*container*) выкла́дывать (вы́ложить *pf*) изнутри́; **hold the ~ please!** (*TEL*) пожа́луйста, не клади́те тру́бку!; **to cut in ~** (*US*) идти́ (пойти́ *pf*) без о́череди; **in ~ with** (*in keeping with*) в соотве́тствии с +*instr*; **~ up** *vi* выстра́иваться (вы́строиться *pf*) ♦ *vt* (*order*) выстра́ивать (вы́строить *pf*)

lined [laɪnd] *adj* (*paper*) лино́ванный; (*face*) морщи́нистый

linen ['lɪnɪn] *n* (*sheets etc*) бельё

liner ['laɪnə*] *n* (*ship*) ла́йнер; (*also*: **bin~**) целофа́новый мешо́к для му́сорного ведра́

linesman ['laɪnzmən] *n* судья́ *m* на ли́нии

linger ['lɪŋɡə*] *vi* удержи́ваться (удержа́ться *pf*); (*person*) заде́рживаться (задержа́ться *pf*)

lingerie ['lænʒəriː] *n* же́нское (ни́жнее) бельё

linguist ['lɪŋɡwɪst] *n* (*language specialist*) лингви́ст; **~ics** [lɪŋ'ɡwɪstɪks] *n* языкозна́ние, лингви́стика

lining ['laɪnɪŋ] *n* (*cloth*) подкла́дка

link [lɪŋk] *n* связь *f*; (*of chain*) звено́ ♦ *vt* (*join*) соединя́ть (соедини́ть *pf*); (*associate*): **to ~ with** *or* **to** свя́зывать (связа́ть *pf*) с +*instr*; **~ up** (*systems*) соединя́ть (соедини́ть *pf*) ♦ *vi* соединя́ться (соедини́ться *pf*)

lino ['laɪnəu] *n* = **linoleum**

linoleum [lɪ'nəulɪəm] *n* лино́леум

lion ['laɪən] *n* лев

lip [lɪp] *n* (*ANAT*) губа́; **~-read** *vi* чита́ть с губ; **~stick** *n* (губна́я) пома́да

liqueur [lɪ'kjuə*] *n* ликёр

liquid ['lɪkwɪd] *n* жи́дкость *f* ♦ *adj* жи́дкий

liquor ['lɪkə*] *n* (*esp US*) спиртно́е *nt adj*, спиртно́й напи́ток

Lisbon ['lɪzbən] *n* Лиссабо́н

lisp [lɪsp] *n* шепеля́вость *f*

list [lɪst] *n* спи́сок ♦ *vt* (*enumerate*) перечисля́ть (перечи́слить *pf*); (*write down*) составля́ть (соста́вить *pf*) спи́сок +*gen*

listen ['lɪsn] *vi*: **to ~ (to sb/sth)**
слу́шать (*impf*) (кого́-н/что-н)

lit [lɪt] *pt, pp of* **light**

liter ['li:tə*r*] *n* (*US*) = **litre**

literacy ['lɪtərəsɪ] *n* гра́мотность *f*

literal ['lɪtərl] *adj* буква́льный; **~ly**
adv буква́льно

literary ['lɪtərərɪ] *adj* литерату́рный

literate ['lɪtərət] *adj* (*able to read
and write*) гра́мотный

literature ['lɪtrɪtʃə*r*] *n* литерату́ра

Lithuania [lɪθju'eɪnɪə] *n* Литва́; **~n**
adj лито́вский

litre ['li:tə*r*] (*US* **liter**) *n* литр

litter ['lɪtə*r*] *n* (*rubbish*) му́сор;
(*ZOOL*) помёт, вы́водок

little ['lɪtl] *adj* ма́ленький;
(*younger*) мла́дший; (*short*)
коро́ткий ♦ *adv* ма́ло; **a ~ (bit)**
немно́го; **~ by ~** понемно́гу;
~-known *adj* малоизве́стный

live *vb* [lɪv] *adj* [laɪv] *vi* жить (*impf*)
♦ *adj* (*animal, plant*) живо́й;
(*broadcast*) прямо́й; (*performance*)
пе́ред пу́бликой; (*bullet*) боево́й;
(*ELEC*) под напряже́нием; **to ~
with sb** жить (*impf*) с кем-н; **he ~d
to (be) a hundred** он до́жил до
ста лет; **~ on** *vt fus* (*food*) жить
(*impf*) на +*prp*; (*salary*) жить на
+*acc*; **~ up to** *vt fus*
опра́вдывать (оправда́ть *pf*)

livelihood ['laɪvlɪhud] *n* сре́дства
ntpl к существова́нию

lively ['laɪvlɪ] *adj* живо́й; (*place,
event*) оживлённый

liver ['lɪvə*r*] *n* (*ANAT*) пе́чень *f*;
(*CULIN*) печёнка

lives [laɪvz] *npl of* **life**

livestock ['laɪvstɔk] *n* скот

living ['lɪvɪŋ] *adj* живо́й ♦ *n*:
earn *or* **make a ~** зараба́тывать
(зарабо́тать *pf*) на жизнь; **~
conditions** *npl* усло́вия *ntpl*
жи́зни; **~ room** *n* гости́ная *f adj*;
~ standards *npl* жи́зненный

у́ровень *msg*

lizard ['lɪzəd] *n* я́щерица

load [ləud] *n* (*of person, animal*)
но́ша; (*of vehicle*) груз; (*weight*)
нагру́зка ♦ *vt* (*also*: **~ up**: *goods*)
грузи́ть (погрузи́ть *pf*); (*gun,
camera*) заряжа́ть (заряди́ть *pf*);
to ~ (with) (*also*: **~ up**: *vehicle,
ship*) загружа́ть (загрузи́ть *pf*)
(+*instr*); **~s of, a ~ of** (*inf*) ку́ча
+*gen*; **a ~ of rubbish** (*inf*)
сплошна́я чепуха́; **~ed** *adj* (*gun*)
заря́женный; **~ed question**
вопро́с с подте́кстом или
подво́хом

loaf [ləuf] (*pl* **loaves**) *n* буха́нка

loan [ləun] *n* заём; (*money*) ссу́да
♦ *vt* дава́ть (дать *pf*) взаймы́;
(*money*) ссужа́ть (ссуди́ть *pf*); **to
take sth on ~** брать (взять *pf*)
что-н на вре́мя

loathe [ləuð] *vt* ненави́деть (*impf*)

loaves [ləuvz] *npl of* **loaf**

lobby ['lɔbɪ] *n* (*of building*)
вестибю́ль *m*; (*pressure group*)
ло́бби *nt ind* ♦ *vt* склоня́ть
(склони́ть *pf*) на свою́ сто́рону;
(*POL*) лобби́ровать (*impf*)

lobster ['lɔbstə*r*] *n* ома́р

local ['ləukl] *adj* ме́стный; **the ~s**
npl ме́стные *pl adj* (жи́тели); **~
authorities** *npl* ме́стные вла́сти
fpl; **~ government** *n* ме́стное
управле́ние; **~ly** *adv* (*live, work*)
поблизости

locate [ləu'keɪt] *vt* (*find*)
(определя́ть (определи́ть *pf*)
местонахожде́ние или
местонахожде́ние +*gen*; **to be ~d
in** (*situated*) располага́ться (*impf*),
находи́ться (*impf*) в/на +*prp*

location [ləu'keɪʃən] *n* (*place*)
расположе́ние,
местонахожде́ние; **on ~** (*CINEMA*)
на нату́ре

loch [lɔx] *n* (*SCOTTISH*) о́зеро

lock [lɔk] *n* (*on door etc*) замо́к; (*on*

canal) шлюз; (of hair) ло́кон ♦ vt запира́ть (запере́ть pf) vi (door) запира́ться (запере́ться pf); (wheels) тормози́ть (затормози́ть pf); ~ **in** vt: to ~ **sb in** запира́ть (запере́ть pf) кого́-н; ~ **up** vt (criminal etc) упря́тывать (упря́тать pf); (house) запира́ть (запере́ть pf) ♦ vi запира́ться (запере́ться pf) в систе́му

locker ['lɔkə⁴] n шка́фчик

locomotive [ləukə'məutɪv] n локомоти́в

locust ['ləukəst] n саранча́ f no pl

lodge [lɔdʒ] n привра́тницкая f adj; ~ **r** n квартира́нт(ка)

lodgings ['lɔdʒɪŋz] npl кварти́ра fsg

loft [lɔft] n черда́к

log [lɔg] n бревно́; (for fire) поле́но; (account) журна́л ♦ vt (event, fact) регистри́ровать (зарегистри́ровать pf); ~ **off** vi (COMPUT) выходи́ть (вы́йти pf) из систе́мы; ~ **on** vi (COMPUT) входи́ть (войти́ pf) в систе́му

logic ['lɔdʒɪk] n ло́гика; ~**al** (based on logic) логи́ческий; (reasonable) логи́чный

logo ['ləugəu] n эмбле́ма

London ['lʌndən] n Ло́ндон

lone [ləun] adj (person) одино́кий

loneliness ['ləunlɪnɪs] n одино́чество

lonely ['ləunlɪ] adj (person, childhood) одино́кий; (place) уединённый

long [lɔŋ] adj дли́нный; (in time) до́лгий ♦ adv (see adj) дли́нно; до́лго ♦ vi: to ~ **for sth/to do** жа́ждать (impf) чего́-н/+infin; **so or as ~ as** you don't delay е́сли то́лько Вы не возража́ете; **don't be ~!** не заде́рживайтесь!; **how ~ is the street?** какова́ длина́ э́той у́лицы?; **how ~ is the lesson?** ско́лько дли́тся уро́к?; **6**

metres ~ длино́й в 6 ме́тров; **6 months ~** продолжи́тельностью в 6 ме́сяцев; **all night (~)** всю ночь (напролёт); **he no ~er comes** он бо́льше не прихо́дит; ~ **before** до́лго до +gen; ~ **after** до́лгое вре́мя по́сле +gen; **before ~** вско́ре; **at ~ last** наконе́ц; **~-distance** adj (travel) да́льний

longitude ['lɔŋgɪtju:d] n долгота́

long: ~ **jump** n прыжо́к в длину́; **~-life** adj консерви́рованный; (battery) продлённого де́йствия; **~-lost** adj (relative etc) давно́ поте́рянный; **~-standing** adj долголе́тний; **~-suffering** adj многострада́льный; **~-term** adj долгосро́чный

look [luk] vi (see) смотре́ть (посмотре́ть pf); (glance) взгляну́ть (pf); (seem, appear) вы́глядеть (impf) ♦ n (glance) взгляд; (appearance) вид; (expression) выраже́ние; **~s** npl: **good ~s** краси́вая вне́шность fsg; **to ~ south/(out) onto the sea** (face) выходи́ть (impf) на юг/на мо́ре; ~ **after** vt fus (care for) уха́живать (impf) за +instr; (deal with) забо́титься (impf) o +prp; ~ **around** vt fus = **look round**; ~ **at** vt fus (посмотре́ть pf) на +acc; (read quickly) просма́тривать (просмотре́ть pf) на +acc; ~ **back** vi (turn around): **to ~ back (at)** огля́дываться (огляну́ться pf) (на +acc); ~ **down on** vt fus (fig) смотре́ть (impf) свысока́ на +acc; ~ **for** vt fus иска́ть (impf); ~ **forward to** vt fus: **to ~ forward to sth** ждать (impf) чего́-н с нетерпе́нием; **we ~ forward to hearing from you** (с нетерпе́нием) ждём Ва́шего отве́та; ~ **into** vt fus рассле́довать (impf/pf); ~ **on** vi (watch) наблюда́ть (impf); ~ out vi (beware): to ~ out (for) остерега́ться (impf) (+gen); to ~ out (of) (glance out) вы́глядывать (вы́глянуть pf) в +acc; ~ out for vt (search for) стара́ться (постара́ться pf) найти́; ~ round vt fus (museum etc) осма́тривать (осмотре́ть pf); ~ through vt fus (papers) просма́тривать (просмотре́ть pf); (window) смотре́ть (посмотре́ть pf) в +acc; ~ to vt fus (rely on) жда́ть (impf) от +gen; ~ up vi поднима́ть (подня́ть pf) глаза́; (situation) идти́ (пойти́ pf) к лу́чшему ♦ vt (fact) смотре́ть (посмотре́ть pf; ~out n (person) наблюда́тель(ница) m(f); (point) наблюда́тельный пункт; to be on the ~out for sth присма́тривать (impf) что-л.

loop [lu:p] n пе́тля ♦ vt: to ~ sth round sth завя́зывать (завяза́ть pf) что-н пе́тлей вокру́г чего́-н.

loose [lu:s] adj свобо́дный (knot, grip, connection) сла́бый; (hair) распу́щенный ♦ adj: to be on the ~ быть (impf) в бега́х; the handle is ~ ру́чка расшата́лась; to set ~ (prisoner) освобожда́ть (освободи́ть pf); ~ly adv (fit, translate) свобо́дно; ~n vt (belt, screw, grip) ослабля́ть (осла́бить pf)

loot [lu:t] n (inf) награ́бленное nt adj ♦ vt (shops, homes) разграбля́ть (разгра́бить pf)

lord [lɔ:d] n (BRIT: peer) лорд; (REL): the Lord Госпо́дь m; my Lord мило́рд; good Lord! Бо́же пра́вый!

lorry ['lɔrɪ] n (BRIT) грузови́к

lose [lu:z] (pt, pp lost) vt теря́ть (потеря́ть pf); (contest, argument) прои́грывать (проигра́ть pf ♦ vi (in contest, argument) прои́грывать (проигра́ть pf); ~r n (in

(in contest, competition) проигра́вший(ая) m(f) adj

loss [lɔs] n поте́ря; (sense of bereavement) утра́та; (COMM) убы́ток; heavy ~es тяжёлые поте́ри fpl; to be at a ~ теря́ться (растеря́ться pf)

lost [lɔst] pt, pp of lose ♦ adj пропа́вший; to be ~ заблуди́ться (pf)

lot [lɔt] n (of people, goods) па́ртия; (at auction) лот; a ~ (of) (many) мно́го; the ~ (everything) всё; ~s of ... мно́го +gen ...; I see a ~ of him мы с ним ча́сто ви́димся; I read/don't read a ~ я мно́го/ма́ло чита́ю; a ~ bigger/ more expensive намно́го or гора́здо бо́льше/доро́же; to draw ~s (for sth) тяну́ть (impf) жре́бий (для чего́-н)

lotion ['ləʊʃən] n лосьо́н

lottery ['lɔtərɪ] n лотере́я

loud [laud] adj (noise, voice, laugh) гро́мкий; (support, condemnation) громогла́сный; (clothes) крича́щий ♦ adj (speak, laugh) вслух; ~ly adv (speak, laugh) гро́мко; (support) громогла́сно; ~speaker n громкоговори́тель m

lounge [laundʒ] n (in house, hotel) гости́ная f adj; (at airport) зал ожида́ния

louse [laus] (pl lice) n (insect) вошь f

lovable ['lʌvəbl] adj ми́лый

love [lʌv] vt люби́ть (impf) ♦ n: ~ (for) любо́вь f (к +dat); to ~ to do люби́ть (impf) +infin; I'd ~ to pf; (pt, pp lost) я бы с удово́льствием пришёл; "~ (from) Anne" "лю́бящая Вас А́нна"; to fall in ~ with влюбля́ться (влюби́ться pf) в +acc; he is ~ with her он в неё влюблён; to make ~ занима́ться (заня́ться pf) любо́вью; "fifteen

~" (TENNIS) "пятна́дцать - ноль";
~ **affair** n рома́н; ~ **life** n
инти́мная жизнь f

lovely ['lʌvlɪ] adj (beautiful)
краси́вый; (delightful) чуде́сный

lover ['lʌvə'] n (sweetheart)
любо́вник(ица); (of art etc)
люби́тель(ница) m(f)

loving ['lʌvɪŋ] adj не́жный

low [ləu] adj ни́зкий; (quiet) ти́хий;
(depressed) пода́вленный ♦ adv
(fly) ни́зко; (sing: quietly) ти́хо ♦ n
(METEOROLOGY) ни́зкое давле́ние;
we are (running) ~ on milk
у нас оста́лось ма́ло молока́; **an
all-time ~** небыва́ло ни́зкий
у́ровень

lower ['ləuə'] adj (bottom: of two
things) ни́жний; (less important)
ни́зший ♦ vt (object) спуска́ть
(спусти́ть pf); (level, price)
снижа́ть (сни́зить pf); (voice)
понижа́ть (пони́зить pf); (eyes)
опуска́ть (опусти́ть pf)

lower sixth - ни́жняя ступе́нь
шко́льного
квалификацио́нного ку́рса.
Этот ку́рс дли́тся два го́да, в
тече́ние кото́рых шко́льники
гото́вятся к
квалификацио́нным
экза́менам, даю́щим пра́во на
поступле́ние в университе́т.

low-fat ['ləu'fæt] adj (food, drink)
обезжи́ренный

loyal ['lɔɪəl] adj ве́рный; (POL)
лоя́льный; ~**ty** n ве́рность f;
(POL) лоя́льность f; ~**ty card** n ≈
диско́нтная ка́рта

L-plates ['elpleɪts] - бе́лая табли́чка, на
кото́рую нанесена́ кра́сная
бу́ква 'L', обознача́ющая
"**Learner**" - Учени́к.

Таки́е табли́чки помеща́ются
на за́днем или ветрово́м
стекле́ автомоби́лей, води́тели
кото́рых прохо́дят курс по
вожде́нию.

Ltd abbr (COMM: = limited (liability)
company) компа́ния с
ограни́ченной
отве́тственностью

lucid ['lu:sɪd] adj (writing, speech)
я́сный

luck [lʌk] n (also: **good ~**) уда́ча;
bad ~ неуда́ча; **good ~!** уда́чи
(Вам)!; **hard** or **tough ~!** не
повезло́!; ~**ily** adv к сча́стью; ~**y**
adj (object) счастли́вый; (person)
уда́чливый; **he is ~y at cards/
in love** ему́ везёт в ка́ртах/
любви́

lucrative ['lu:krətɪv] adj
при́быльный, дохо́дный; (job)
высокоопла́чиваемый

ludicrous ['lu:dɪkrəs] adj
смехотво́рный

luggage ['lʌgɪdʒ] n бага́ж

lukewarm ['lu:kwɔ:m] adj слегка́
тёплый; (fig) прохла́дный

lull [lʌl] n зати́шье ♦ vt: **to ~ sb to
sleep** убаю́кивать (убаю́кать pf)
кого́-н; **to ~ sb into a false sense
of security** усыпля́ть (усыпи́ть pf)
чью-н бди́тельность

lullaby ['lʌləbaɪ] n колыбе́льная f
adj

luminous ['lu:mɪnəs] adj (digit, star)
светя́щийся

lump [lʌmp] n (of clay, snow) ком;
(of butter, sugar) кусо́к; (bump)
ши́шка; (growth) о́пухоль f ♦ vt:
to ~ together меша́ть (смеша́ть
pf) в (одну́) ку́чу; **a ~ sum**
единовре́менно выпла́чиваемая
су́мма; ~**y** adj (sauce) комкова́тый

lunar ['lu:nə'] adj лу́нный

lunatic ['lu:nətɪk] adj безу́мный

lunch [lʌntʃ] n обéд; ~ **time** n обéденное врéмя nt, обéд

lung [lʌŋ] n лёгкое nt adj; ~ **cancer** рак лёгких

lurch [lɜːtʃ] vi: **the car ~ed forward** машину брóсило вперёд

lure [luə'] vt замáнивать (заманить pf); **to ~ sb away from** отвлекáть (отвлéчь pf) когó-н от +gen

lush [lʌʃ] adj (healthy) пышный

lust [lʌst] n (sexual desire) пóхоть f; (greed): ~ (**for**) жáжда (к +dat)

lustre ['lʌstə'] (US **luster**) n блеск

Luxembourg ['lʌksəmbɜːg] n Люксембýрг

luxurious [lʌg'zjuəriəs] adj роскóшный

luxury ['lʌkʃəri] n (great comfort) рóскошь f; (treat) роскóшество

lyrical ['lɪrɪkl] adj (fig) востóрженный

lyrics ['lɪrɪks] npl текст msg (пéсни)

M, m

m. abbr (= metre) м; = **mile**, **million**

MA n abbr = **Master of Arts**

mac [mæk] n (BRIT: inf) макинтóш

macabre [mə'kɑːbrə] adj жýткий

macaroni [mækə'rəunɪ] n макарóны pl

Macedonia [mæsɪ'dəunɪə] n Македóния

machine [mə'ʃiːn] n машина; (also: sewing ~) машинка; ~ **gun** n пулемёт; (POL) механизм

mackerel ['mækrl] n inv скýмбрия

mackintosh ['mækɪntɔʃ] n = **mac**

mad [mæd] adj сумасшéдший, помéшанный; (angry) бéшеный; (keen): **he is ~ about** он помéшан на +prp

madam ['mædəm] n (form of address) мадáм f ind, госпожá

made [meɪd] pt, pp of **make**

madman ['mædmən] n (irreg) m сумасшéдший m adj

madness ['mædnɪs] n безýмие

Madrid [mə'drɪd] n Мадрид

Mafia ['mæfɪə] n: **the** ~ мáфия

magazine [mægə'ziːn] n журнáл

maggot ['mægət] n личинка (насекóмых)

magic ['mædʒɪk] n мáгия; ~**al** adj магический; (experience, evening) волшéбный; ~**ian** [mə'dʒɪʃən] n (conjurer) фóкусник

magistrate ['mædʒɪstreɪt] n (LAW) мировóй судьá m

magnet ['mægnɪt] n магнит; ~**ic** [mæg'netɪk] adj магнитный; (personality) притягáтельный

magnificent [mæg'nɪfɪsnt] adj великолéпный

magnify ['mægnɪfaɪ] vt увеличивать (увеличить pf); (sound) усиливать (усилить pf); ~**ing glass** n увеличительное стеклó, лýпа

magnitude ['mægnɪtjuːd] n (size) величинá; (importance) масштáб

mahogany [mə'hɔgənɪ] n крáсное дéрево

maid [meɪd] n (in house) служáнка; (in hotel) гóрничная f adj

maiden ['meɪdn] adj (first) пéрвый; ~ **name** n дéвичья фамилия

mail [meɪl] n пóчта ♦ vt отправлять (отпрáвить pf) по пóчте; (COMPUT): **to ~ sb** писáть (написáть pf) комý-н по электрóнной пóчте; ~**box** n (US: letter box) почтóвый ящик; ~ **order** n закáз товáров по пóчте

maim [meɪm] vt калéчить (искалéчить pf)

main [meɪn] adj глáвный ♦ n: gas/ water ~ газопровóдная/

водопрово́дная магистра́ль f;
the ~s npl сеть fsg; **~ meal** обе́д;
~land n: **the ~land** матери́к; **~ly**
adv гла́вным о́бразом; **~stay** n
гла́вная опо́ра; **~stream** n
госпо́дствующее направле́ние

maintain [meɪn'teɪn] vt (friendship,
system, momentum) подде́рживать
(поддержа́ть pf); (building)
обслу́живать (impf); (affirm: belief,
opinion) утвержда́ть (impf)

maintenance ['meɪntənəns] n (of
friendship, system) подде́ржка f;
(of building) обслу́живание n; (LAW,
alimony) алиме́нты pl

maize [meɪz] n кукуру́за, маи́с

majestic [mə'dʒestɪk] adj
вели́чественный

majesty ['mædʒɪstɪ] n: **Your
Majesty** Ва́ше Вели́чество

major ['meɪdʒəʳ] adj (important)
суще́ственный

majority [mə'dʒɒrɪtɪ] n
большинство́

make [meɪk] (pt, pp **made**) vt
де́лать (сде́лать pf); (clothes)
шить (сшить pf); (manufacture)
изготовля́ть (изгото́вить pf);
(meal) гото́вить (пригото́вить pf);
(money) зараба́тывать
(зарабо́тать pf); (profit) получа́ть
(получи́ть pf); (brand) ма́рка f;
to ~ sb do (force) заставля́ть
(заста́вить pf) кого́-н +infin; **2 and
2 ~ 4** (equal) 2 плюс 2 равня́ется
четырём; **to ~ sb unhappy**
расстра́ивать (расстро́ить pf)
кого́-н; **to ~ a noise** шуме́ть
(impf); **to ~ the bed** стели́ть
(постели́ть pf) посте́ль; **to ~ a
fool of sb** де́лать (сде́лать pf) из
кого́-н дурака́; **to ~ a profit**
получа́ть (получи́ть pf) при́быль;
to ~ a loss нести́ (понести́ pf)
убы́ток; **to ~ it** (arrive) успева́ть
(успе́ть pf); **let's ~ it Monday**

дава́йте договори́мся на
понеде́льник; **to ~ do with/
without** обходи́ться (обойти́сь
pf) +instr/без +gen; **~ for** vt fus
(place) направля́ться
(напра́виться pf) +dat/в +acc; **~
out** vt (decipher) разбира́ть
(разобра́ть pf); (see) различа́ть
(различи́ть pf); (write out)
выпи́сывать (вы́писать pf);
(understand) разбира́ться
(разобра́ться pf) в +prp; **~ up** vt
fus (constitute) составля́ть
(соста́вить pf) ♦ vt (invent)
выду́мывать (вы́думать pf) ♦ vi
(after quarrel) мири́ться
(помири́ться pf); (with cosmetics):
to ~ (o.s.) up де́лать (сде́лать pf)
макия́ж; **~ up for** vt fus (mistake)
загла́живать (загла́дить pf); (loss)
восполня́ть (воспо́лнить pf); **~r** n
(of goods) изготови́тель m; **~shift**
adj вре́менный; **~up** n
косме́тика, макия́ж; (THEAT) грим

making ['meɪkɪŋ] n (of programme)
созда́ние n; **to have the ~s of**
име́ть (impf) зада́тки pl

malaria [mə'lɛərɪə] n маляри́я

male [meɪl] n (human) мужчи́на m;
(animal) саме́ц ♦ adj мужско́й;
(child) мужско́го по́ла

malice ['mælɪs] n зло́ба

malicious [mə'lɪʃəs] adj зло́бный,
злой

malignant [mə'lɪgnənt] adj (MED)
злока́чественный

mall [mɔːl] n (also: **shopping ~**)
≈ торго́вый центр

mallet ['mælɪt] n деревя́нный
молото́к

malnutrition [mælnju:'trɪʃən] n
недоеда́ние

malt [mɔːlt] n (grain) со́лод; (also:
~ whisky) соло́довое ви́ски nt
ind

mammal ['mæml] n

млекопита́ющее nt adj
mammoth ['mæməθ] adj (task)
колосса́льный

man [mæn] (pl **men**) n мужчи́на m;
(person, mankind) челове́к ♦ vt
(machine) обслу́живать (impf);
(post) занима́ть (заня́ть pf); **an
old ~** стари́к; **~ and wife** муж и
жена́

manage ['mænɪdʒ] vi (get by)
обходи́ться (обойти́сь pf) ♦ vt
(business, organization) руководи́ть
(impf) +instr, управля́ть (impf) +instr;
(shop, restaurant) заве́довать
(impf) +instr; (economy) управля́ть
(impf) +instr; (workload, task)
справля́ться (спра́виться (impf)) с
+instr; **I ~d to convince him** мне
удало́сь убеди́ть его́; **~ment** n
(body) руково́дство; (act): **~ment
(of)** управле́ние (+instr); **~r** n (of
business, organization)
управля́ющий m adj, ме́неджер;
(of shop) заве́дующий m adj; (of
pop star) ме́неджер; (SPORT)
гла́вный тре́нер; **~ress** ['mænɪdʒ
n (of shop) заве́дующая f adj; **~rial**
[mænɪ'dʒɪərɪəl] adj (role)
руководя́щий; **~rial staff**
руководя́щий аппара́т

managing director ['mænɪdʒɪŋ-] n
управля́ющий дире́ктор

mandarin ['mændərɪn] n (also: **~
orange**) мандари́н

mandate ['mændeɪt] n (POL)
полномо́чие

mandatory ['mændətərɪ] adj
обяза́тельный

mane [meɪn] n гри́ва

maneuver [mə'nu:və'] n, vb (US) =
manoeuvre

mango ['mæŋgəʊ] (pl **~es**) n ма́нго
nt ind

mania ['meɪnɪə] n (also PSYCH)
ма́ния

maniac ['meɪnɪæk] n манья́к

manic ['mænɪk] adj безу́мный,
маниака́льный

manifest ['mænɪfest] vt проявля́ть
(прояви́ть pf) ♦ adj очеви́дный,
я́вный

manifesto [mænɪ'festəʊ] n
манифе́ст

manipulate [mə'nɪpjuleɪt] vt
манипули́ровать (impf) +instr

mankind [mæn'kaɪnd] n
челове́чество

manly ['mænlɪ] adj му́жественный

man-made ['mæn'meɪd] adj
иску́сственный

manner ['mænə'] n (way) о́браз;
(behaviour) мане́ра; **~s** npl
(conduct) мане́ры fpl; **all ~ of
things/people** всевозмо́жные
ве́щи/лю́ди; **in a ~ of speaking** в
не́котором ро́де; **~ism** n
мане́ры fpl

manoeuvre [mə'nu:və'] (US
maneuver) vt передвига́ть
(передви́нуть pf); (manipulate)
маневри́ровать (impf) +instr ♦ vi
маневри́ровать (impf) ♦ n манёвр

manpower ['mænpauə'] n рабо́чая
си́ла

mansion ['mænʃən] n особня́к

manslaughter ['mænslɔ:tə'] n
непреднаме́ренное уби́йство

mantelpiece ['mæntlpi:s] n
ками́нная доска́

manual ['mænjuəl] adj ручно́й ♦ n
посо́бие; **~ worker**
черноробо́чий(ая) m(f) adj

manufacture [mænju'fæktʃə'] vt
(goods) изготовля́ть (изгото́вить
pf), производи́ть (произвести́ pf)
♦ n изготовле́ние,
произво́дство; **~r** n
изготови́тель m, производи́тель
m

manure [mə'njuə'] n наво́з

manuscript ['mænjuskrɪpt] n (old
text) ма́нускрипт; (before printing)

рукопись f

many ['mɛnɪ] adj (a lot of) мно́го
+gen ♦ pron (several) мно́гие pl adj;
a great ~ о́чень мно́го +gen,
мно́жество +gen; **how ~?**
ско́лько?; **~ a time** мно́го раз; **in
~ cases** во мно́гих слу́чаях; **~ of
us** мно́гие из нас

map [mæp] n ка́рта; (of town) план

maple ['meɪpl] n клён

mar [mɑ:ʳ] vt по́ртить (испо́ртить
pf)

marathon ['mærəθən] n марафо́н

marble ['mɑ:bl] n (stone) мра́мор

March [mɑ:tʃ] n март

march [mɑ:tʃ] vi маршировать
(промаршировать pf) ♦ n
марш

mare [mɛəʳ] n кобы́ла

margarine [mɑ:dʒə'ri:n] n
маргари́н

margin ['mɑ:dʒɪn] n (on page) поля́
ntpl; (of victory) преиму́щество; (of
defeat) меньшинство́; (also: **profit
~**) ма́ржа, чи́стая при́быль f no
pl; **~al** adj незначи́тельный

marigold ['mærɪɡəuld] n ноготки́
mpl

marijuana [mærɪ'wɑ:nə] n
марихуа́на

marina [mə'ri:nə] n мари́на,
при́стань f для яхт

marine [mə'ri:n] adj морско́й;
(engineer) судово́й; (in BRIT)
слу́жащий m вое́нно-
морско́го фло́та; (US) морско́й
пехоти́нец

marital ['mærɪtl] adj супру́жеский;
~ status семе́йное положе́ние

maritime ['mærɪtaɪm] adj морско́й

mark [mɑ:k] n (symbol) значо́к,
поме́тка; (stain) пятно́; (of shoes
etc) след; (token) знак; (in BRIT :
SCOL) отме́тка, оце́нка ♦ vt
(occasion) отмеча́ть (отме́тить pf);
(with pen) помеча́ть (поме́тить

pf); (subj: shoes, tyres) оставля́ть
(оста́вить pf) след на +prp;
(furniture) повреждать
(повреди́ть pf); (clothes, carpet)
ста́вить (поста́вить pf) пятно́ на
+prp; (place, time) указывать
(указа́ть pf); (in BRIT : SCOL)
проверя́ть (прове́рить pf); **~ed**
adj заме́тный; **~er** n (sign) знак;
(bookmark) закла́дка; (pen)
фломастер

market ['mɑ:kɪt] n ры́нок ♦ vt
(promote) реклами́ровать (impf);
(sell) выпуска́ть (вы́пустить pf) в
прода́жу; **~ing** n ма́ркетинг; **~
research** n маркетинговые
иссле́дования ntpl

marmalade ['mɑ:məleɪd] n джем
(ци́трусовый)

maroon [mə'ru:n] vt: **we were ~ed**
мы бы́ли отре́заны от вне́шнего
ми́ра

marquee [mɑ:'ki:] n марки́за,
пала́точный павильо́н

marriage ['mærɪdʒ] n брак;
(wedding) сва́дьба; **~ certificate**
n свиде́тельство о бра́ке

married ['mærɪd] adj (man)
жена́тый; (woman) заму́жняя;
(couple) жена́тые; (life)
супру́жеский

marrow ['mærəu] n (BOT) кабачо́к;
(also: **bone ~**) ко́стный мозг

marry ['mærɪ] vt (subj: man)
жени́ться (impf/pf) на +prp;
(: woman) выдава́ть (вы́дать pf)
за́муж за +acc; (: priest) венча́ть
(обвенча́ть pf); (also: **~ off**: son)
жени́ть (impf/pf); (: daughter)
выдава́ть (вы́дать pf) за́муж ♦ vi:
to get married (man) жени́ться
(impf); (woman) выходи́ть (вы́йти
pf) за́муж; (couple) жени́ться
(пожени́ться pf)

Mars [mɑ:z] n Марс

marsh [mɑ:ʃ] n боло́то

marshal ['mɑːʃl] n (at public event) распоряди́тель(ница) m(f) ♦ vt (support) упоря́дочивать (упоря́дочить pf); **police ~** (US) нача́льник полице́йского уча́стка

marshy ['mɑːʃɪ] adj боло́тистый

martial law ['mɑːʃəl-] n вое́нное положе́ние

martyr ['mɑːtər] n му́ченик(ица)

marvellous (US **marvelous**) ['mɑːvləs] adj восхити́тельный, изуми́тельный

Marxist ['mɑːksɪst] adj маркси́стский ♦ n маркси́ст(ка)

marzipan ['mɑːzɪpæn] n марципа́н

mascara [mæsˈkɑːrə] n тушь f для ресни́ц

mascot ['mæskət] n талисма́н

masculine ['mæskjulɪn] adj мужско́й; (LING) мужско́го ро́да

mash [mæʃ] vt де́лать (сде́лать pf) пюре́ из +gen

mask [mɑːsk] n ма́ска ♦ vt (feelings) маскирова́ть (impf)

mason ['meɪsn] n (also: **stone~**) ка́менщик; (also: **free~**) масо́н, во́льный ка́менщик; **~ic** [məˈsɔnɪk] adj масо́нский; **~ry** n (ка́менная) кла́дка

mass [mæs] n (also PHYS) ма́сса; (REL): **Mass** прича́стие ♦ cpd ма́ссовый; **the ~es** npl (наро́дные) ма́ссы fpl; **~es of** (inf) ма́сса fsg +gen, у́йма fsg +gen

massacre ['mæsəkər] n ма́ссовое уби́йство, резня́

massage ['mæsɑːʒ] n масса́ж ♦ vt (rub) масси́ровать (impf)

massive ['mæsɪv] adj масси́вный; (support, changes) огро́мный

mass media n inv сре́дства ntpl ма́ссовой информа́ции

mast [mɑːst] n ма́чта

master ['mɑːstər] n (also fig) хозя́ин ♦ vt (control) владе́ть (овладе́ть pf) +instr; (learn, understand) овладева́ть (овладе́ть pf) +instr; **Master Smith** (title) господи́н or ма́стер Смит; **Master of Arts/Science** ≈ маги́стр гуманита́рных/ есте́ственных нау́к; **~piece** n шеде́вр

masturbation [mæstəˈbeɪʃən] n мастурба́ция

mat [mæt] n ко́врик; (also: **door~**) дверно́й ко́врик; (also: **table ~**) подста́вка ♦ adj = **matt**

match [mætʃ] n спи́чка; (SPORT) матч; (equal) ро́вня m/f ♦ vt (subj: colours) сочета́ться (impf) с +instr; (correspond to) соотве́тствовать (impf) +dat ♦ vi (colours, materials) сочета́ться (impf); **to be a good ~** (colours, clothes) хорошо́ сочета́ться (impf); **they make or are a good ~** — они́ хоро́шая па́ра; **~ing** adj сочета́ющийся

mate [meɪt] n (inf: friend) друг; (animal) саме́ц(мка); (NAUT) помо́щник капита́на ♦ vi спа́риваться (спа́риться pf)

material [məˈtɪərɪəl] n материа́л ♦ adj материа́льный; **~s** npl (equipment) принадле́жности fpl; **building ~s** строи́тельные материа́лы; **~ize** vi материализова́ться (impf/pf), осуществля́ться (осуществи́ться pf)

maternal [məˈtəːnl] adj матери́нский

maternity [məˈtəːnɪtɪ] n матери́нство

mathematics [mæθəˈmætɪks] n матема́тика

maths [mæθs] n abbr = **mathematics**

matron ['meɪtrən] n (in hospital) ста́ршая медсестра́; (in school) (шко́льная) медсестра́

matt [mæt] *adj* ма́товый

matter ['mætər] *n* де́ло, вопро́с;
(*substance, material*) вещество́ ♦ *vi*
име́ть (*impf*) значе́ние; ~s *npl*
(*affairs, situation*) дела́ *ntpl*; **reading**
~ (*BRIT*) материа́л для чте́ния;
what's the ~? в чём де́ло?; **no** ~
what несмотря́ ни на что́; **as a ~**
of course как само́ собо́й
разуме́ющееся; **as a ~ of**
fact со́бственно говоря́, **it doesn't** ~
э́то не ва́жно; ~**-of-fact** *adj* (*tone*)
бесстра́стный

mattress ['mætrɪs] *n* матра́с

mature [mə'tjʊər] *adj* (*person*)
зре́лый; (*cheese, wine*)
вы́держанный ♦ *vi* (*develop*)
развива́ться (разви́ться *pf*);
(*grow up*) взросле́ть
(повзросле́ть *pf*); (*cheese*) зреть *or*
созрева́ть (созре́ть *pf*); (*wine*)
выста́иваться (вы́стояться *pf*)

maturity [mə'tjʊərɪtɪ] *n* зре́лость
f

maximum ['mæksɪməm] (*pl*
maxima *or* ~**s**) *adj*
максима́льный ♦ *n* ма́ксимум

May [meɪ] *n* май

> May Day - Первома́й. По
> тради́ции в э́тот день
> пра́зднуется нача́ло весны́.

may [meɪ] (*conditional* **might**) *vi* (*to*
show possibility): **I ~ go to Russia** я,
мо́жет быть, пое́ду в Росси́ю; (*to*
show permission): **I ~ smoke/come?**
мо́жно закури́ть/мне прийти́?; **it**
~ **or might rain** мо́жет пойти́
дождь; **you ~ or might as well go**
now Вы, пожа́луй, мо́жете идти́
сейча́с; **come what ~** будь что
бу́дет

maybe ['meɪbiː] *adv* (*perhaps*)
мо́жет быть

mayhem ['meɪhɛm] *n* погро́м

mayonnaise [meɪə'neɪz] *n*
майоне́з

mayor [mɛər] *n* мэр

> KEYWORD

me [miː] *pron* **1** (*direct*) меня́; **he**
loves me он лю́бит меня́; **it's me**
э́то я

2 (*indirect*) мне; **give me them** *or*
them to me да́йте их мне

3 (*after prep: +gen*) меня́; (: +*dat,*
+prp) мне; (: +*instr*) мной; **it's for**
me (*on answering phone*) э́то мне

4 (*referring to subject of sentence:*
after prep: +gen) себя́; (: +*dat*)
себе́; (: +*instr*) собо́й; (: +*prp*)
себе́; **I took him with me** я взял
его́ с собо́й

meadow ['mɛdəʊ] *n* луг

meagre ['miːgər] (*US* **meager**) *adj*
ску́дный

meal [miːl] *n* еда́ *no pl*; (*afternoon*)
обе́д; (*evening*) у́жин; **during ~s**
во вре́мя еды́, за едо́й

mean [miːn] (*pt, pp* ~**t**) *adj* (*miserly*)
скупо́й; (*unkind*) вре́дный;
(*vicious*) по́длый ♦ *vt* (*signify*)
зна́чить (*impf*), означа́ть (*impf*);
(*refer to*) име́ть (*impf*) в виду́ ♦ *n*
(*average*) середи́на; ~**s** *npl* (*way*)
спо́соб *msg*, сре́дство *ntsg*;
(*money*) сре́дства *ntpl*; **by ~s of**
посре́дством, с по́мощью
+*gen*; **by all ~s!** пожа́луйста!; **do**
you ~ it? вы э́то серьёзно?; **to ~**
to do (*intend*) намерева́ться
(*impf*) +*infin*; **to be ~t for**
предназнача́ться (*impf*) для +*gen*;
~**ing** *n* (*purpose, value*) смысл;
(*definition*) значе́ние; ~**ingful** *adj*
(*result, occasion*) значи́тельный;
(*glance, remark*) много-
значи́тельный; ~**ingless** *adj*
бессмы́сленный; ~**t** [mɛnt] *pt, pp*
of **mean**; ~**time** *adv* (*also:* **in the**

~time тем временем, между тем; **~while** adv = **meantime**

measles ['mi:zlz] n корь f

measure ['meʒə'] vt измерять (измерить pf) ♦ n мера; (of whisky etc) порция; (also: **tape ~**) рулетка, сантиметр ♦ vi: **the room ~s 10 feet by 20** площадь комнаты 10 футов на 20; **~d** adj (tone) сдержанный; (step) размеренный; (opinion) взвешенный; **~ments** npl мерки fpl, размеры mpl

meat [mi:t] n мясо; **cold ~s** (BRIT) холодные мясные закуски fpl

mechanic [mɪ'kænɪk] n механик; **~al** adj механический; **~s** npl (of government) механика fsg

mechanism ['mekənɪzəm] n механизм

medal ['medl] n медаль f; **~list** (US **~ist**) n медалист(ка)

meddle ['medl] vi: **to ~ in** вмешиваться (вмешаться pf) в +acc; **to ~ with** sth вторгаться (вторгнуться pf) во что-н

media ['mi:dɪə] n or npl: **the ~** средства ntpl массовой информации, медия ♦ npl see **medium**

mediaeval [medɪ'i:vl] adj = **medieval**

mediate ['mi:dɪeɪt] vi (arbitrate) посредничать (impf)

mediator ['mi:dɪeɪtə'] n посредник(ица)

medical ['medɪkl] adj медицинский ♦ n медосмотр

medication [medɪ'keɪʃən] n лекарство, лекарственный препарат

medicinal [me'dɪsɪnl] adj (substance, qualities) лекарственный

medicine ['medsɪn] n (science) медицина; (drug) лекарство

medieval [medɪ'i:vl] adj

средневековый

mediocre [mi:dɪ'əukə'] adj заурядный, посредственный

meditation [medɪ'teɪʃən] n (REL) медитация

Mediterranean [medɪtə'reɪnɪən] adj: **the ~ (Sea)** Средиземное море

medium ['mi:dɪəm] (pl **media** or **~s**) adj средний ♦ n средство

meek [mi:k] adj кроткий

meet [mi:t] (pt, pp **met**) vt встречать (встретить pf); (obligations) выполнять (выполнить pf); (problem) сталкиваться (столкнуться pf) с +instr; (need) удовлетворять (удовлетворить pf) ♦ vi (people) встречаться (встретиться pf); (lines, roads) пересекаться (пересечься pf); **~ with** vt fus (difficulty) сталкиваться (столкнуться pf) с +instr; (success) пользоваться (impf) +instr; (approval) находить (найти pf); **~ing** n встреча; (at work, of committee etc) заседание, собрание; (POL: also: **mass ~ing**) митинг; **she's at a ~ing** она на заседании

melancholy ['melənkəlɪ] adj (smile) меланхолический

mellow ['meləu] adj (sound) бархатистый; (taste) мягкий ♦ vi смягчаться (смягчиться pf)

melodrama ['meləudrɑ:mə] n мелодрама

melody ['melədɪ] n мелодия

melon ['melən] n дыня

melt [melt] vi таять (растаять pf) ♦ vt (snow, butter) топить (растопить pf)

member ['membə'] n (also ANAT) член; **Member of Parliament** (BRIT) член парламента; **~ship** n (members) члены mpl; (status)

чле́нство; **~ship card** n
чле́нский биле́т

membrane ['membreɪn] n
мембра́на

memento [mə'mentəʊ] n сувени́р

memo ['meməʊ] n (ADMIN,
instruction) директи́ва

memoirs ['memwɑːz] npl мемуа́ры
pl

memorable ['memərəbl] adj
па́мятный

memorial [mɪ'mɔːrɪəl] n па́мятник
♦ cpd (service) мемориа́льный

memorize ['meməraɪz] vt
зау́чивать (заучи́ть pf) (наизу́сть)

memory ['memərɪ] n па́мять f;
(recollection) воспомина́ние; **in ~
of** в па́мять о +prp

men [men] npl of **man**

menace ['menɪs] n (threat) угро́за

menacing ['menɪsɪŋ] adj
угрожа́ющий

mend [mend] vt ремонти́ровать
(отремонти́ровать pf), чини́ть
(почини́ть pf); (clothes) чини́ть
(почини́ть pf) ♦ n: **to be on the ~**
идти́ (impf) на попра́вку; **to ~
one's ways** исправля́ться
(испра́виться pf)

menial ['miːnɪəl] adj чёрный

meningitis [menɪn'dʒaɪtɪs] n
менинги́т

menopause ['menəʊpɔːz] n: **the ~**
климактери́ческий пери́од,
кли́макс

menstruation [menstru'eɪʃən] n
менструа́ция

menswear ['menzweər] n мужска́я
оде́жда

mental ['mentl] adj (ability,
exhaustion) у́мственный; (image)
мы́сленный; (illness) душе́вный,
психи́ческий; (arithmetic,
calculation) в уме́; **~ity** [men'tælɪtɪ]
n менталите́т, умонастрое́ние

mention ['menʃən] n упомина́ние

♦ vt упомина́ть (упомяну́ть pf);
don't ~ it! не́ за что!

mentor ['mentɔːr] n наста́вник

menu ['menjuː] n (also COMPUT)
меню́ nt ind

MEP n abbr (BRIT) (= Member of the
European Parliament) член
Европе́йского парла́мента

mercenary ['məːsɪnərɪ] adj
коры́стный ♦ n наёмник

merchant ['məːtʃənt] n торго́вец

merciful ['məːsɪful] adj
милосе́рдный; (fortunate) благо́й

merciless ['məːsɪlɪs] adj
беспоща́дный

mercury ['məːkjurɪ] n (metal) ртуть
f

mercy ['məːsɪ] n милосе́рдие; **to
be at sb's ~** быть (impf) во вла́сти
кого́-л

mere [mɪər] adj: **she's a ~ child** она́
всего́ лишь ребёнок; **his ~
presence irritates her** само́ его́
прису́тствие раздража́ет её; **~ly**
adv (simply) про́сто; (just) то́лько

merge [məːdʒ] vt слива́ть (слить
pf), объединя́ть (объедини́ть pf)
♦ vi (also COMM) слива́ться
(сли́ться pf); (roads) сходи́ться
(сойти́сь pf); **~r** n (COMM)
слия́ние

meringue [mə'ræŋ] n безе́ nt ind

merit ['merɪt] n досто́инство ♦ vt
заслу́живать (заслужи́ть pf)

merry ['merɪ] adj весёлый; **Merry
Christmas!** С Рождество́м!,
Счастли́вого Рождества́!

mesh [meʃ] n (net) сеть f

mess [mes] n (in room)
беспоря́док; (of situation)
неразбери́ха; (MIL) столо́вая f
adj; **to be in a ~** (untidy) быть
(impf) в беспоря́дке; **~ up** vt
(spoil) по́ртить (испо́ртить pf)

message ['mesɪdʒ] n сообще́ние;
(note) запи́ска; (of play, book)

идёя; **to leave sb a ~** (note)
оставля́ть (оста́вить pf) кому́-н
запи́ску; **can I give him a ~?** ему́
что́-нибудь переда́ть?

messenger ['mesɪndʒə^r] n курье́р,
посы́льный m

Messrs abbr (on letters: = messieurs)
гг.

messy ['mesɪ] adj (untidy)
неубранный

met [met] pt, pp of **meet**

metabolism [me'tæbəlɪzəm] n
метаболи́зм, обме́н веще́ств

metal ['metl] n мета́лл

metaphor ['metəfə^r] n мета́фора

meteor ['mi:tɪə^r] n метео́р

meteorology [mi:tɪə'rɒlədʒɪ] n
метеороло́гия

meter ['mi:tə^r] n (instrument)
счётчик; (US: unit) = **metre**

method ['meθəd] n (way) ме́тод,
спо́соб; **~ical** [mɪ'θɒdɪkl] adj
методи́чный; **Methodist** n (REL)
методи́ст(ка)

meticulous [me'tɪkjuləs] adj
тща́тельный

metre ['mi:tə^r] n (US **meter**) n метр

metric ['metrɪk] adj метри́ческий

metropolitan [metrə'pɒlɪtn] adj
столи́чный

Mexico ['meksɪkəu] n Ме́ксика

mice [maɪs] npl of **mouse**

micro: **~phone** n микрофо́н;
~scope n микроско́п; **~scopic**
adj микроскопи́ческий; **~wave** n
(also: **~wave oven**)
микроволно́вая печь f

mid [mɪd] adj: **in ~ May/afternoon**
в середи́не ма́я/дня; **in ~ air** в
во́здухе; **~day** n по́лдень m

middle ['mɪdl] n середи́на ♦ adj
сре́дний; **in the ~ of** посреди́
+gen; **~-aged** adj сре́дних
лет; **Middle Ages** npl: **the Middle
Ages** сре́дние века́ mpl; **~-class**
adj: **~-class people/values** лю́ди/

це́нности сре́днего кла́сса;
Middle East n: **the Middle East**
Бли́жний Восто́к

midge [mɪdʒ] n мо́шка

midnight ['mɪdnaɪt] n по́лночь f

midst [mɪdst] n: **in the ~ of**
посреди́ +gen

midway [mɪd'weɪ] adv: **~ (between)**
на полпути́ (ме́жду +instr); **~
through** в середи́не +gen

midweek [mɪd'wi:k] adv в
середи́не неде́ли

midwife ['mɪdwaɪf] (pl **midwives**)
n акуше́рка

might [maɪt] vb see **may**; **~y** adj
могу́чий

migraine ['mi:greɪn] n мигре́нь f

migrant ['maɪgrənt] adj: **~ worker**
рабо́чий-мигра́нт

migration [maɪ'greɪʃən] n
мигра́ция

mike [maɪk] n abbr = **microphone**

mild [maɪld] adj мя́гкий; (interest)
сла́бый; (infection) лёгкий

mildew ['mɪldju:] n (mould)
пле́сень f

mildly ['maɪldlɪ] adv (see adj)
мя́гко; слегка́; легко́; **to put it ~**
мя́гко говоря́

mile [maɪl] n ми́ля, **~age** n
коли́чество миль; **~stone** n
≈ киломе́тро́вый столб; (fig)
ве́ха

mile - ми́ля. В Великобрита́нии
и Аме́рике расстоя́ние
измеря́ется в ми́лях, а не в
киломе́трах. Одна́ ми́ля
равня́ется 1,609 ме́трам.

militant ['mɪlɪtnt] adj
вои́нствующий

military ['mɪlɪtərɪ] adj вое́нный ♦ n:
the ~ вое́нные pl adj; **~ service**
вое́нная слу́жба

militia [mɪ'lɪʃə] n (наро́дное)

ополчение

milk [mɪlk] *n* молоко́ ♦ *vt* (*cow*) дои́ть (подои́ть *pf*); (*fig*) эксплуати́ровать (*impf*); **~y** *adj* моло́чный

mill [mɪl] *n* (*factory: making cloth*) фа́брика; (*: making steel*) заво́д; (*for coffee, pepper etc*) ме́льница

millimetre (*US* **millimeter**) [ˈmɪlɪmiːtəʳ] *n* миллиме́тр

million [ˈmɪljən] *n* миллио́н; **~aire** [mɪljəˈnɛəʳ] *n* миллионе́р

mime [maɪm] *n* пантоми́ма ♦ *vt* изобража́ть (изобрази́ть *pf*) же́стами

mimic [ˈmɪmɪk] *vt* (*subj: comedian*) пароди́ровать (*impf/pf*)

min. *abbr* (= **minute**) мин(.)

mince [mɪns] *vt* (*meat*) пропуска́ть (пропусти́ть *pf*) че́рез мясору́бку ♦ *n* (*BRIT*) (мясно́й) фарш

---

mince pie - пирожо́к с сухофру́ктами. Хотя́ э́то выраже́ние буква́льно означа́ет "пирожо́к с фа́ршем", начи́нка тако́го пирожка́ состои́т из сухофру́ктов, а не из мя́са.

---

mind [maɪnd] *n* (*intellect*) ум ♦ *vt* (*look after*) смотре́ть (*impf*) за +*instr*; **I don't ~ the noise** шум меня́ не беспоко́ит; **it's always on my ~** э́то не выхо́дит у меня́ из головы́; **to keep** *or* **bear sth in ~** име́ть (*impf*) что-н. в виду́; **to make up one's ~** реша́ться (реши́ться *pf*); **to my ~ ...** по моему́ мне́нию ...; **I don't ~** мне всё равно́; **~ you, ...** име́йте в виду́ ...; **never ~!** ничего́!; **~ful** *adj*: **~ful of** име́ть (*impf*) в виду́; **~less** *adj* (*violence*) безду́мный; (*job*) механи́ческий

KEYWORD

mine¹ [maɪn] *pron* **1** мой (*f* моя́, *nt* моё, *pl* мои́); **that book is mine** э́та кни́га моя́; **that house is mine** э́то мой дом; **this is mine** э́то моё; **an uncle of mine** мой дя́дя

2 (*referring back to subject*) свой (*f* своя́, *nt* своё, *pl* свои́); **may I borrow your pen? I have forgotten mine** мо́жно взять Ва́шу ру́чку? я забы́л свою́

---

mine² [maɪn] *n* (*for coal*) ша́хта; (*explosive*) ми́на ♦ *vt* (*coal*) добыва́ть (добы́ть *pf*); **~field** *n* ми́нное по́ле; **~r** *n* шахтёр

mineral [ˈmɪnərəl] *n* минера́л; (*ore*) поле́зное ископа́емое *nt adj*; **~ water** *n* минера́льная вода́

miniature [ˈmɪnətʃəʳ] *adj* миниатю́рный

minibus [ˈmɪnɪbʌs] *n* микроавто́бус

---

minicab - такси́. Э́тот тип такси́ регули́руется зако́ном в ме́ньшей сте́пени. В отли́чие от традицио́нного чёрного такси́ его́ вызыва́ют по телефо́ну, а не остана́вливают на у́лице.

Minidisc® [ˈmɪnɪdɪsk] *n* ми́ни-диск

minimal [ˈmɪnɪml] *adj* минима́льный

minimize [ˈmɪnɪmaɪz] *vt* (*reduce*) своди́ть (свести́ *pf*) к ми́нимуму; (*play down*) преуменьша́ть (преуме́ньшить *pf*)

minimum [ˈmɪnɪməm] (*pl* **minima**) *n* ми́нимум ♦ *adj* минима́льный

mining [ˈmaɪnɪŋ] *n* (*industry*) у́гольная промы́шленность *f*

minister [ˈmɪnɪstəʳ] *n* (*BRIT*)

минúстр; (REL) свящéнник; **~ial**
[mɪnɪsˈtɪərɪəl] adj (BRIT)
министéрский

ministry [ˈmɪnɪstrɪ] n (BRIT : POL)
министéрство

minor [ˈmaɪnəʳ] adj (injuries)
незначúтельный; (repairs)
мéлкий ♦ n (LAW)
несовершеннолéтний(яя) m(f)
adj; **~ity** [maɪˈnɔrɪtɪ] n
меньшинствó

mint [mɪnt] n (BOT) мя́та; (sweet)
мя́тная конфéта ♦ vt чекáнить
(отчекáнить pf); **in ~ condition** в
прекрáсном состоя́нии

minus [ˈmaɪnəs] n (also: ~ **sign**)
мúнус ♦ prep: **12 – 6 equals 6** 12
мúнус 6 равня́ется 6; **~ 24**
(degrees) мúнус 24 грáдуса

minute¹ [maɪˈnjuːt] adj (search)
тщáтельный

minute² [ˈmɪnɪt] n (of time)
минýта; **~s** npl (of meeting)
протокóл msg; **at the**
last ~ в послéднюю минýту

miracle [ˈmɪrəkl] n чýдо

miraculous [mɪˈrækjʊləs] adj
чудéсный

mirror [ˈmɪrəʳ] n зéркало

misbehave [mɪsbɪˈheɪv] vi плóхо
себя́ вести́ (impf)

miscarriage [ˈmɪskærɪdʒ] n (MED)
вы́кидыш; **~ of justice** судéбная
ошúбка

miscellaneous [mɪsɪˈleɪnɪəs] adj
(subjects, items) разнообрáзный

mischief [ˈmɪstʃɪf] n озорствó;
(maliciousness) зло

mischievous [ˈmɪstʃɪvəs] adj
(naughty, playful) озорнóй

misconception [ˈmɪskənˈsepʃən] n
заблуждéние, лóжное
представлéние

misconduct [mɪsˈkɔndʌkt] n
дурнóе поведéние; **professional**
~ нарушéние служéбной
дисциплúны

miserable [ˈmɪzərəbl] adj (unhappy)
несчáстный; (unpleasant)
сквéрный; (donation, conditions)
жáлкий; (failure) позóрный

misery [ˈmɪzərɪ] n (unhappiness)
невзгóда; (wretchedness) жáлкое
существовáние

misfortune [mɪsˈfɔːtʃən] n
несчáстье

misguided [mɪsˈgaɪdɪd] adj (person)
невéрно ориентúрованный;
(ideas) ошúбочный

misinterpret [mɪsɪnˈtəːprɪt] vt
невéрно интерпретúровать
(impf/pf) или толковáть
(истолковáть pf)

mislead [mɪsˈliːd] n (irreg: like lead¹)
vt вводúть (ввести́ pf) в
заблуждéние; **~ing** adj
обмáнчивый

misprint [ˈmɪsprɪnt] n опечáтка

Miss [mɪs] n мисс f ind

miss [mɪs] vt (train, bus etc)
пропускáть (пропустúть pf);
(target) не попадáть (попáсть pf)
в +acc; (person, home) скучáть
(impf) no +dat; (chance, opportunity)
упускáть (упустúть pf) ♦ vi
(person) промáхиваться
(промахнýться pf) ♦ n промáх;
you can't ~ my house мой дом
невозмóжно не замéтить; **~ out**
vt (BRIT) пропускáть (пропустúть
pf)

missile [ˈmɪsaɪl] n (MIL) ракéта

missing [ˈmɪsɪŋ] adj (tooth, wheel)
недостáющий; **to**
be ~ (absent) отсýтствовать (impf);
to be~, go ~ пропадáть
(пропáсть pf) бéз вести

mission [ˈmɪʃən] n (also POL, REL)
мúссия; **~ary** n миссионéр(ка)

mist [mɪst] n (light) дымкá

mistake [mɪsˈteɪk] n (irreg: like take)
ошúбка ♦ vt (be wrong about)
ошибáться (ошибúться pf) в +prp;

by ~ по оши́бке; **to make a ~**
ошиба́ться (ошиби́ться pf),
де́лать (сде́лать pf) оши́бку; **to ~**
A for B принима́ть (приня́ть pf) A
за Б; **~n** pp of **mistake** ♦ adj: **to**
be ~n ошиба́ться (ошиби́ться pf)

mistletoe - оме́ла. В
Великобрита́нии и США э́то
расте́ние испо́льзуется как
рожде́ственское украше́ние.
По обы́чаю под оме́лой
полага́ется целова́ться.

mistook [mɪsˈtuk] pt of **mistake**
mistress [ˈmɪstrɪs] n (also fig)
хозя́йка; (lover) любо́вница
mistrust [mɪsˈtrʌst] vt не доверя́ть
(impf) +dat ♦ n: ~ **(of)** недове́рие (к
+dat)
misty [ˈmɪstɪ] adj (day) тума́нный
misunderstand [mɪsʌndəˈstænd] n
(irreg: like **understand**) vt
непра́вильно понима́ть (поня́ть
pf) ♦ vi не понима́ть (поня́ть pf);
~ing n недоразуме́ние
misuse n [mɪsˈjuːs] vb [mɪsˈjuːz] n (of
power, funds) злоупотребле́ние
♦ vt злоупотребля́ть
(злоупотреби́ть pf) +instr
mix [mɪks] vt (cake, cement)
заме́шивать (замеси́ть pf) ♦ n
смесь f ♦ vi (people): **to ~ (with)**
обща́ться (с +instr); **to ~ sth**
(with sth) сме́шивать (смеша́ть
pf) что-н (с чем-н); **~ up** vt
(combine) переме́шивать
(перемеша́ть pf); (confuse: people)
пу́тать (спу́тать pf); (: things)
пу́тать (перепу́тать pf); **~er** n (for
food) ми́ксер; **~ture** [ˈmɪkstʃəʳ] n
смесь f; **~up** n пу́таница
mm abbr (= **millimetre**) мм
moan [məun] n (cry) стон ♦ vi (inf:
complain): **to ~ (about)** ныть (impf)
(о +prp)

mistletoe   563   **modify**

moat [məut] n ров
mob [mɒb] n (crowd) толпа́
mobile [ˈməubaɪl] adj подви́жный
♦ n (toy) подвесно́е
декорати́вное украше́ние;
(phone) моби́льный телефо́н,
моби́льник (разг); **~ phone** n
моби́льный телефо́н
mobility [məuˈbɪlɪtɪ] n
подви́жность f
mobilize [ˈməubɪlaɪz] vt
мобилизова́ть (impf/pf)
mock [mɒk] vt (ridicule) издева́ться
(impf) над +instr ♦ adj (fake)
ло́жный; (pretended)
притво́рный; **to make a ~ery of sb/sth**
выставля́ть (вы́ставить pf)
кого́-н/что-н на посмеша́ище
mod cons npl abbr (BRIT) =
modern conveniences
mode [məud] n (of life) о́браз; (of
transport) вид
model [ˈmɒdl] n моде́ль f, маке́т;
(also: **fashion ~**) моде́ль,
манеке́нщик(ица); (also: **artist's**
~) нату́рщик(ица) ♦ adj (ideal)
образцо́вый
modem [ˈməudem] n (COMPUT)
моде́м
moderate adj, n [ˈmɒdərət] vb
[ˈmɒdəreɪt] adj (views, amount)
уме́ренный; (change)
незначи́тельный ♦ vt умеря́ть
(уме́рить pf)
moderation [mɒdəˈreɪʃən] n
уме́ренность f
modern [ˈmɒdən] adj
совреме́нный
modest [ˈmɒdɪst] adj скро́мный;
~y n скро́мность f
modification [mɒdɪfɪˈkeɪʃən] n (see
vb) модифика́ция;
видоизмене́ние
modify [ˈmɒdɪfaɪ] vt (vehicle, engine)
модифици́ровать (impf/pf); (plan)
видоизменя́ть (видоизмени́ть pf)

moist [mɔɪst] *adj* вла́жный; **~en** *vt* (*lips*) увлажня́ть (увлажни́ть *pf*); (*sponge*) мочи́ть (смочи́ть *pf*); **~ure** *n* вла́га

mold [məʊld] *n, vb* (*US*) = **mould**

mole [məʊl] *n* (*spot*) ро́динка; (*ZOOL*) крот

molecule ['mɔlɪkjuːl] *n* моле́кула

molt [məʊlt] *vi* (*US*) = **moult**

mom [mɔm] *n* (*US*) = **mum**

moment ['məʊmənt] *n* моме́нт, мгнове́ние; **for a ~** на мгнове́ние; **at that ~** в э́тот моме́нт; **at the ~** в настоя́щий моме́нт; **~ary** *adj* мгнове́нный

momentous [məʊ'mentəs] *adj* знамена́тельный

momentum [məʊ'mentəm] *n* (*fig*) дви́жущая си́ла; **to gather** *or* **gain ~** набира́ть (набра́ть *pf*) си́лу

mommy ['mɔmɪ] *n* (*US*) = **mummy**

monarch ['mɔnək] *n* мона́рх; **~y** *n* мона́рхия

monastery ['mɔnəstərɪ] *n* монасты́рь *m*

Monday ['mʌndɪ] *n* понеде́льник

monetary ['mʌnɪtərɪ] *adj* де́нежный

money ['mʌnɪ] *n* де́ньги *pl*; **to make ~** (*person*) зараба́тывать (зарабо́тать *pf*) де́ньги; (*make a profit*) де́лать (сде́лать *pf*) де́ньги

mongrel ['mʌŋgrəl] *n* дворня́га

monitor ['mɔnɪtə] *n* монито́р ♦ *vt* (*broadcasts, pulse*) следи́ть (*impf*) за +*instr*

monk [mʌŋk] *n* мона́х

monkey ['mʌŋkɪ] *n* обезья́на

monopoly [mə'nɔpəlɪ] *n* монопо́лия

monotonous [mə'nɔtənəs] *adj* однообра́зный, моното́нный

monster ['mɔnstə] *n* чудо́вище, монстр

monstrous ['mɔnstrəs] *adj* чудо́вищный

month [mʌnθ] *n* ме́сяц; **~ly** *adj* ежеме́сячный; (*ticket*) ме́сячный ♦ *adv* ежеме́сячно

monument ['mɔnjumənt] *n* (*memorial*) па́мятник, монуме́нт; **~al** [mɔnju'mentl] *adj* (*important*) монумента́льный; (*terrific*) колосса́льный

mood [muːd] *n* настрое́ние; (*of crowd*) настро́й; **to be in a good/ bad ~** быть (*impf*) в хоро́шем/ плохо́м настрое́нии; **~y** *adj* (*temperamental*): **she is a very ~y person** у неё о́чень переме́нчивое настрое́ние

moon [muːn] *n* луна́; **~light** *n* лу́нный свет

moor [muə] *n* вереско́вая пу́стошь *f*

moose [muːs] *n inv* лось *m*

mop [mɔp] *n* (*for floor*) шва́бра; (*hair*) копна́ ♦ *vt* (*floor*) мыть (вы́мыть *or* помы́ть *pf*) (шва́брой); (*eyes, face*) вытира́ть (вы́тереть *pf*)

moped ['məʊped] *n* мопе́д

moral ['mɔrl] *adj* мора́льный; (*person*) нра́вственный ♦ *n* (*of story*) мора́ль *f*; **~s** *npl* (*values*) нра́вы *mpl*

morale [mɔ'rɑːl] *n* мора́льный дух

morality [mə'rælɪtɪ] *n* нра́вственность *f*

morbid ['mɔːbɪd] *adj* (*imagination*) ненорма́льный; (*ideas*) жу́ткий

<hr>

KEYWORD

<hr>

more [mɔː] *adj* **1** (*greater in number etc*) бо́льше +*gen*; **I have more friends than enemies** у меня́ бо́льше друзе́й, чем враго́в **2** (*additional*) ещё; **do you want (some) more tea?** хоти́те ещё ча́ю?; **is there any more wine?** вино́ ещё есть?; **I have no** *or* **I don't have any more money** у

меня́ бо́льше нет де́нег; **it'll take a few more weeks** э́то займёт ещё не́сколько неде́ль
♦ *pron* 1 (*greater amount*): **more than ten** бо́льше десяти́; **we've sold more than a hundred tickets** мы прода́ли бо́лее ста биле́тов; **it costs more than we expected** э́то сто́ит бо́льше, чем мы ожида́ли
2 (*further or additional amount*): **is there any more?** ещё есть?; **there's no more** бо́льше ничего́ нет; **a little more** ещё немно́го *or* чуть-чуть; **many/much more** намно́го/гора́здо бо́льше
♦ *adv* 1 (+*vb*) бо́льше; **I like this picture more** мне э́та карти́на нра́вится бо́льше
2: **more dangerous/difficult (than)** бо́лее опа́сный/тру́дный(, чем)
3: **more economically (than)** бо́лее экономи́чно(, чем); **more easily/quickly (than)** ле́гче/ бы́стрее(, чем); **more and more** (*excited, friendly*) всё бо́лее и бо́лее; **he grew to like her more and more** она́ нра́вилась ему́ всё бо́льше и бо́льше; **more or less** бо́лее и́ли ме́нее; **she is more beautiful than ever** она́ прекра́снее, чем когда́-либо; **he loved her more than ever** он люби́л её бо́льше, чем когда́-либо; **the more..., the better** чем бо́льше ..., тем лу́чше; **once more** ещё раз; **I'd like to see more of you** мне хоте́лось бы ви́деть тебя́ ча́ще

moreover [mɔːˈrəʊvə] *adv* бо́лее того́
morgue [mɔːg] *n* морг
morning [ˈmɔːnɪŋ] *n* у́тро; (*between midnight and 3 a.m.*) ночь
n ♦ *cpd* у́тренний; **in the ~** у́тром;

3 o'clock in the ~ 3 часа́ но́чи; **7 o'clock in the ~** 7 часо́в утра́
Morse [mɔːs] *n* (*also*: **~ code**) а́збука Мо́рзе
mortal [ˈmɔːtl] *adj* (*man, sin*) сме́ртный; (*deadly*) смерте́льный; **~ity** [mɔːˈtælɪtɪ] *n* сме́ртность *f*
mortar [ˈmɔːtə] *n* (*cement*) цеме́нтный раство́р
mortgage [ˈmɔːgɪdʒ] *n* ипоте́чный креди́т ♦ *vt* закла́дывать (заложи́ть *pf*)
Moscow [ˈmɒskəʊ] *n* Москва́
Moslem [ˈmɒzləm] *adj*, *n* = **Muslim**
mosque [mɒsk] *n* мече́ть *f*
mosquito [mɒsˈkiːtəʊ] *n* (*pl* **~es**) кома́р
moss [mɒs] *n* мох

KEYWORD

most [məʊst] *adj* 1 (*almost all: countable nouns*) большинство́ +*gen*; (: *uncountable and collective nouns*) бо́льшая часть +*gen*; **most cars** большинство́ маши́н; **most milk** бо́льшая часть молока́; **in most cases** в большинстве́ слу́чаев
2 (*largest, greatest*): **who has the most money?** у кого́ бо́льше всего́ де́нег?; **this book has attracted the most interest among the critics** э́та кни́га вы́звала наибо́льший интере́с у кри́тиков
♦ *pron* (*greatest quantity, number: countable nouns*) большинство́; (: *uncountable and collective nouns*) бо́льшая часть *f*; **most of the houses** большинство́ домо́в; **most of the cake** бо́льшая часть то́рта; **do the most you can** де́лайте всё, что Вы мо́жете; **I ate the most** я съел бо́льше всех; **to make the most of sth** максима́льно испо́льзовать

(impf/pf) что-н; **at the (very) most** са́мое бо́льшее
♦ adv (+vb: with inanimate objects) бо́льше всего́; (: with animate objects) бо́льше всех; (+adv) исключи́тельно; (+adj) са́мый, наибо́лее; **I liked him the most** он понра́вился мне бо́льше всех; **what do you value most, wealth or health?** что Вы бо́льше всего́ це́ните, бога́тство и́ли здоро́вье?

mostly ['məʊstlɪ] adv бо́льшей ча́стью, в основно́м
MOT n abbr (BRIT) = Ministry of Transport; **~ (test)** техосмо́тр

MOT - техосмо́тр. По зако́ну автомоби́ли, кото́рым бо́льше трёх лет, должны́ ежего́дно проходи́ть техосмо́тр.

motel [məʊ'tɛl] n моте́ль m
moth [mɒθ] n мотылёк
mother ['mʌðə] n мать f ♦ vt (pamper) ня́нчиться (impf) c +instr ♦ adj: **~ country** ро́дина, родна́я страна́; **~hood** n матери́нство; **~-in-law** n (wife's mother) тёща; (husband's mother) свекро́вь f; **~ tongue** n родно́й язы́к

Mother's Day - День Ма́тери. Отмеча́ется в четвёртое воскресе́нье Вели́кого Поста́. В э́тот день поздравле́ния и пода́рки получа́ет то́лько ма́ма.

motif [məʊ'tiːf] n (design) орна́мент
motion ['məʊʃən] n (movement, gesture) движе́ние; (proposal) предложе́ние; **~less** adj неподви́жный

motivated ['məʊtɪveɪtɪd] adj (inspired) целеустремлённый; **~ by envy/greed** дви́жимый за́вистью/жа́дностью
motivation [məʊtɪ'veɪʃən] n (drive) целеустремлённость f
motive ['məʊtɪv] n моти́в, побужде́ние
motor ['məʊtə] n мото́р ♦ cpd (trade) автомоби́льный; **~bike** n мотоци́кл; **~cycle** n мотоци́кл; **~ist** n автомобили́ст; **~way** n (BRIT) автомагистра́ль f, автостра́да
motto ['mɒtəʊ] (pl **~es**) n деви́з
mould [məʊld] (US **mold**) n (cast) фо́рма; (mildew) пле́сень f ♦ vt (substance) лепи́ть (вы́лепить pf); (fig: opinion, character) формирова́ть (сформирова́ть pf); **~y** adj (food) заплесневе́лый
moult [məʊlt] (US **molt**) vi линя́ть (impf)
mound [maʊnd] n (heap) ку́ча
mount [maʊnt] vt (horse) сади́ться (сесть pf) на +acc; (display) устра́ивать (устро́ить pf); (jewel) оправля́ть (опра́вить pf); (picture) обрамля́ть (обра́мить pf); (stair) всходи́ть (взойти́ pf) по +dat ♦ vi (increase) расти́ (impf) ♦ n: **Mount Ararat** гора́ Арара́т; **~ up** vi нака́пливаться (накопи́ться pf)
mountain ['maʊntɪn] n гора́ ♦ cpd го́рный; **~ bike** n велосипе́д, для езды́ по пересечённой ме́стности; **~ous** adj го́рный, гори́стый
mourn [mɔːn] vt (death) опла́кивать (impf) ♦ vi: **to ~ for** скорбе́ть (impf) по +dat or o +prp; **~ful** adj скорбный; **~ing** n тра́ур; **in ~ing** в тра́уре
mouse [maʊs] (pl **mice**) n мышь f; **~ mat, ~ pad** n ко́врик для мы́ши

moustache [məs'taːʃ] (US **mustache**) n усы́ mpl

mouth [mauθ] (pl **~s**) n рот; (of cave, hole) вход; (of river) у́стье; **~ful** n (of food) кусо́чек; (of drink) глото́к; **~ organ** n губна́я гармо́шка; **~piece** n (MUS) мундшту́к; (of telephone) микрофо́н

move [muːv] n (movement) движе́ние; (in game) ход; (of house) перее́зд; (of job) перехо́д ♦ vt передвига́ть (передви́нуть pf); (piece: in game) ходи́ть (пойти́ pf) +instr; (arm etc) дви́гать (дви́нуть pf) +instr; (person: emotionally) тро́гать (тро́нуть pf), растро́гать (pf) ♦ vi дви́гаться (дви́нуться pf); (things) дви́гаться (impf); (also: ~ **house**) переезжа́ть (перее́хать pf); **get a ~ on!** потора́пливайтесь!; **~ about** vi (change position) передвига́ться (передви́нуться pf), перемеща́ться (перемести́ться pf); (travel) переезжа́ть (impf) с ме́ста на ме́сто; **~ around** vi = **move about**; **~ away** vi: **~ away (from)** (leave) уезжа́ть (уе́хать pf) (из +gen) (step away) отходи́ть (отойти́ pf) (от +gen); **~ in** vi (police, soldiers) входи́ть (войти́ pf); **to ~ in/to** (house) въезжа́ть (въе́хать pf) (в +acc); **~ out** vi (of house) выезжа́ть (вы́ехать pf); **~ over** vi (to make room) подвига́ться (подви́нуться pf); **~ up** vi (be promoted) продвига́ться (продви́нуться pf) по слу́жбе; **~ment** n движе́ние; (between fixed points) передвиже́ние; (in attitude, policy) сдвиг

movie ['muːvɪ] n (esp US) n (кино)фи́льм; **to go to the ~s** ходи́ть/идти́ (пойти́ pf) в кино́

moving ['muːvɪŋ] adj (emotional) тро́гательный; (mobile) подвижно́й

mow [məu] (pt **~ed**, pp **~ed** or **~n**) vt (grass) подстрига́ть (подстри́чь pf)

MP n abbr = **Member of Parliament**

mph abbr = **miles per hour**

MP3 abbr **MP3**

Mr ['mɪstə*] n: **~ Smith** (informal) ми́стер Смит; (formal) г-н Смит

Mrs ['mɪsɪz] n: **~ Smith** (informal) ми́ссис Смит; (formal) г-жа Смит

> **Ms** - да́нное сокраще́ние употребля́ется гла́вным о́бразом в пи́сьменном языке́ и заменя́ет "мисс" и "ми́ссис". Употребля́я его́, вы не ука́зываете, за́мужем же́нщина или нет.

MSP n abbr (= Member of the Scottish Parliament) член шотла́ндского парла́мента

KEYWORD

---

much [mʌtʃ] adj мно́го +gen; **we haven't got much time** у нас не так мно́го вре́мени; **how much** ско́лько +gen; **how much money do you need?** ско́лько де́нег Вам ну́жно?; **he's spent so much money today** он сего́дня потра́тил так мно́го де́нег; **I have as much money as you (do)** у меня́ сто́лько же де́нег, ско́лько у Вас; **I don't have as much time as you (do)** у меня́ нет сто́лько вре́мени, ско́лько у Вас

♦ pron мно́го, мно́гое; **much is still unclear** мно́гое ещё нея́сно;

there isn't much to do here здесь нечего делать; **how much does it cost? - too much** сколько это стоит? - слишком дорого; **how much is it?** сколько это стоит?, почём это? (*разг*)

♦ *adv* 1 (*greatly, a great deal*) очень; **thank you very much** большое спасибо; **we are very much looking forward to your visit** мы очень ждём Вашего приезда; **he is very much a gentleman** он настоящий джентльмен; **however much he tries** сколько бы он ни старался; **I try to help as much as possible** or **I can** я стараюсь помогать как можно больше *or* сколько могу; **I read as much as ever** я читаю столько же, сколько прежде; **he is as much a member of the family as you** он такой же член семьи, как и Вы

2 (*by far*) намного, гораздо; **I'm much better now** мне сейчас намного *or* гораздо лучше; **it's much the biggest publishing company in Europe** это самое крупное издательство в Европе

3 (*almost*) почти; **the view today is much as it was 10 years ago** вид сегодня почти такой же, как и 10 лет назад; **how are you feeling? - much the same** как Вы себя чувствуете? - всё так же

muck [mʌk] *n* (*dirt*) грязь *f*
mud [mʌd] *n* грязь *f*
muddle ['mʌdl] *n* (*mix-up*) путаница, неразбериха; (*mess*) беспорядок ♦ *vt* (*also*: ~ **up**: *person*) запутывать (запутать *pf*); (: *things*) перемешивать (перемешать *pf*)
muddy ['mʌdɪ] *adj* грязный
muffled ['mʌfld] *adj* приглушённый

mug [mʌg] *n* кружка; (*inf*: *face*) морда; (: *fool*) дурень *m* ♦ *vt* грабить (ограбить *pf*) (*на улице*)
mule [mju:l] *n* (*ZOOL*) мул
multilevel ['mʌltɪlɛvl] *adj* (*US*) = **multistorey**
multinational [mʌltɪ'næʃənl] *adj* международный
multiple ['mʌltɪpl] *adj* (*injuries*) многочисленный ♦ *n* (*MATH*) кратное число; ~ **collision** столкновение нескольких автомобилей; ~ **sclerosis** рассеянный склероз
multiplication [mʌltɪplɪ'keɪʃən] *n* умножение
multiply ['mʌltɪplaɪ] *vt* умножать (умножить *pf*) ♦ *vi* размножаться (размножиться *pf*)
multistorey [mʌltɪ'stɔːrɪ] *adj* (*BRIT*) многоэтажный
multitude ['mʌltɪtjuːd] *n* (*large number*): **a ~ of** множество +*gen*
mum [mʌm] (*BRIT* : *inf*) *n* мама ♦ *adj*: **to keep ~ about sth** помалкивать (*impf*) о чём-н
mumble ['mʌmbl] *vt* бормотать (пробормотать *pf*) ♦ *vi* бормотать (*impf*)
mummy ['mʌmɪ] *n* (*BRIT* : *inf*) мамуля, мама; (*corpse*) мумия
mumps [mʌmps] *n* свинка
munch [mʌntʃ] *vt* жевать (*impf*)
mundane [mʌn'deɪn] *adj* обыденный
municipal [mjuː'nɪsɪpl] *adj* муниципальный
mural ['mjuərl] *n* фреска, настенная роспись *f*
murder ['mɜːdə] *n* убийство (умышленное) ♦ *vt* убивать (убить *pf*) (умышленно); ~**er** *n* убийца *m/f*
murky ['mɜːkɪ] *adj* (*street, night*) мрачный; (*water*) мутный

murmur ['mə:mə*] n (of voices, waves) ро́пот ♦ vti шепта́ть (impf)

muscle ['mʌsl] n мы́шца, му́скул

muscular ['mʌskjulə*] adj (pain, injury) мы́шечный; (person) му́скулистый

museum [mju:'zɪəm] n музе́й

mushroom ['mʌʃrum] n гриб

music ['mju:zɪk] n му́зыка; ~al adj музыка́льный; (sound, tune) мелоди́чный ♦ n мю́зикл; ~ian [mju:'zɪʃən] n музыка́нт

Muslim ['mʌzlɪm] n мусульма́нин(нка) ♦ adj мусульма́нский

mussel ['mʌsl] n ми́дия

must [mʌst] n (need) необходи́мость ♦ aux vb (necessity): **I ~ go** мне на́до or ну́жно идти́; (obligation): **I ~ do it** я до́лжен э́то сде́лать; (probability): **he ~ be there by now** он до́лжен уже́ быть там; **you ~ come and see me soon** Вы обяза́тельно должны́ ско́ро ко мне зайти́; **why ~ he behave so badly?** отчего́ он так пло́хо себя́ ведёт?

mustache ['mʌstæʃ] n (US) = **moustache**

mustard ['mʌstəd] n горчи́ца

muster ['mʌstə*] vt (support, energy) собира́ть (собра́ть pf); (troops) набира́ть (набра́ть pf)

mustn't ['mʌsnt] = **must not**

mute [mju:t] adj (silent) безмо́лвный

mutilate ['mju:tɪleɪt] vt (person) уве́чить (изуве́чить pf); (thing) уро́довать (изуро́довать pf)

mutiny ['mju:tɪnɪ] n мяте́ж, бунт

mutter ['mʌtə*] vti бормота́ть (impf)

mutton ['mʌtn] n бара́нина

mutual ['mju:tʃuəl] adj (feeling, help) взаи́мный; (friend, interest)

о́бщий; **~ understanding** взаимопонима́ние; **~ly** adv взаи́мно

muzzle ['mʌzl] n (of dog) мо́рда; (of gun) ду́ло; (for dog) намо́рдник ♦ vt надева́ть (наде́ть pf) намо́рдник на +acc

KEYWORD

my [maɪ] adj мой; (referring back to subject of sentence) свой; **this is my house/car** э́то мой дом/моя́ маши́на; **is this my pen or yours?** э́то моя́ ру́чка или Ва́ша?; **I've lost my key** я потеря́л свой ключ
2 (with parts of the body etc): **I've washed my hair/cut my finger** я помы́л го́лову/поре́зал па́лец

KEYWORD

myself [maɪ'self] pron 1 (reflexive): **I've hurt myself** я уши́бся; **I consider myself clever** я счита́ю себя́ у́мным; **I am ashamed of myself** мне сты́дно за моё поведе́ние
2 (complement): **she's the same age as myself** она́ одного́ во́зраста со мной
3 (after prep: +gen) себя́; (: +dat, +prp) себе́; (: +instr) собо́й; **I wanted to keep the book for myself** я хоте́л оста́вить кни́гу себе́; **I sometimes talk to myself** иногда́ я сам с собо́й разгова́риваю; **(all) by myself** (alone) сам; **I made it all by myself** я всё э́то сде́лал сам
4 (emphatic) сам; **I myself chose the flowers** я сам выбира́л цветы́

KEYWORD

mysterious [mɪs'tɪərɪəs] adj таи́нственный

mystery ['mɪstərɪ] n (puzzle)

зага́дка

mystical ['mɪstɪkl] adj мисти́ческий

myth [mɪθ] n миф; **~ology** n мифоло́гия

N, n

n/a abbr (= not applicable) не применя́ется

nag [næg] vt (scold) пили́ть (impf)

nail [neɪl] n но́готь m; (TECH) гвоздь m ♦ vt: to ~ sth to прибива́ть (приби́ть pf) что-н к +dat; ~ **polish** n лак для ногте́й

naive [naɪ'iːv] adj наи́вный

naked ['neɪkɪd] adj го́лый

name [neɪm] n (of person) и́мя nt; (of place, object) назва́ние; (of pet) кли́чка n называ́ть (назва́ть pf); **what's your ~** как Вас зову́т?; **my ~ is Peter** меня́ зову́т Пи́тер; **what's the ~ of this place?** как называ́ется э́то ме́сто?; **by ~** по и́мени; **in the ~ of** (for the sake of) во и́мя +gen; (representing) от и́мени +gen; **~less** adj (unknown) безымя́нный; (anonymous) неизве́стный; **~ly** adv и́менно

nanny ['nænɪ] n ня́ня

nap [næp] n (sleep) коро́ткий сон

napkin ['næpkɪn] n (also: table ~) салфе́тка

nappy ['næpɪ] n (BRIT) подгу́зник

narrative ['nærətɪv] n исто́рия, по́весть f

narrator [nə'reɪtə*] n (in book) расска́зчик(ица); (in film) ди́ктор

narrow ['nærəu] adj у́зкий; (majority, advantage) незначи́тельный ♦ vi (road) сужа́ться (су́зиться pf); (gap, difference) уменьша́ться (уме́ньшиться pf) ♦ vt: to ~ sth **down to** своди́ть (свести́ pf) что-н к +dat; **to have a ~ escape**

едва́ спасти́сь (pf)

nasal ['neɪzl] adj (voice) гнуса́вый

nasty ['nɑːstɪ] adj (unpleasant) проти́вный; (malicious) злóбный; (situation, wound) скве́рный

nation ['neɪʃən] n наро́д; (state) страна́; (native population) на́ция

national ['næʃənl] adj национа́льный; **National Health Service** n (BRIT) госуда́рственная слу́жба здравоохране́ния; **National Insurance** n (BRIT) госуда́рственное страхова́ние; **~ism** n национали́зм; **~ist** adj националисти́ческий ♦ n (status) [ˌnæʃəˈnælɪtɪ] n (status) гражда́нство; (ethnic group) наро́дность f

nationwide ['neɪʃənwaɪd] adj общенаро́дный ♦ adv по всей стране́

native ['neɪtɪv] n (local inhabitant) ме́стный(ая) жи́тель(ница) m(f) ♦ adj (indigenous) коренно́й, иско́нный; (of one's birth) родно́й; (innate) врождённый; **a ~ of Russia** урожéнец(нка) Росси́и; **a ~ speaker of Russian** носи́тель(ница) m(f) ру́сского языка́

NATO ['neɪtəu] n abbr (= North Atlantic Treaty Organization) НАТО

natural ['nætʃrəl] adj (behaviour) есте́ственный; (aptitude, materials) приро́дный; (disaster) стихи́йный; **~ist** n натурали́ст; **~ly** adv есте́ственно; (innately) от приро́ды; (in nature) есте́ственным о́бразом; **~ly, I refused** есте́ственно, я отказа́лся

nature ['neɪtʃə*] n (also: Nature) приро́да; (character) нату́ра; (sort) хара́ктер; **by ~** (person) по нату́ре; (event, thing) по приро́де

naughty ['nɔːtɪ] adj (child)

непослу́шный, озорно́й

nausea ['nɔːsɪə] *n* тошнота́

nautical ['nɔːtɪkl] *adj* морско́й

naval ['neɪvl] *adj* вое́нно-морско́й

navel ['neɪvl] *n* пупо́к

navigate ['nævɪgeɪt] *vt* (NAUT, AVIAT) управля́ть *(impf)* +*instr* ♦ *vi* определя́ть (определи́ть *pf*) маршру́т

navigation [nævɪ'geɪʃən] *n* (science) навига́ция; (action): ~ (of) управле́ние (+*instr*)

navigator ['nævɪgeɪtər] *n* шту́рман

navy ['neɪvɪ] *n* вое́нно-морско́й флот; **~(-blue)** *adj* тёмно-си́ний

Nazi ['nɑːtsɪ] *n* наци́ст(ка)

NB *abbr* (note well: = nota bene) NB, нота́бене

near [nɪər] *adj* бли́зкий ♦ *adv* бли́зко ♦ *prep* (also: ~ to: space) во́зле +*gen*, о́коло +*gen*; (: time) к +*dat*, о́коло +*gen*; **~by** *adj* близлежа́щий ♦ *adv* побли́зости; **~ly** *adv* почти́; **I ~ly fell** я чуть (бы́ло) не упа́л

neat [niːt] *adj* (person, place) опря́тный; (work) аккура́тный; (clear: categories) чёткий; (esp US: inf) кре́пкий; **~ly** *adv* (dress) опря́тно; (work) аккура́тно; (sum up) чётко

necessarily ['nesɪsrɪlɪ] *adv* неизбе́жно

necessary ['nesɪsrɪ] *adj* необходи́мый; (inevitable) обяза́тельный, неизбе́жный; **it's not ~** – э́то не обяза́тельно; **it is ~ to/that ...** необходи́мо +*infin* чтобы ...

necessity [nɪ'sesɪtɪ] *n* необходи́мость *f*; **necessities** *npl* (essentials) предме́ты *mpl* пе́рвой необходи́мости

neck [nek] *n* (ANAT) ше́я; (of garment) во́рот; (of bottle) го́рлышко; **~lace** ['neklɪs] *n*

ожере́лье

need [niːd] *n* потре́бность *f*; (deprivation) нужда́; (necessity): ~ (for) нужда́ (в +*prp*) ♦ *vt*: **I ~ time/ money** мне ну́жно вре́мя/нужны́ де́ньги; **there's no ~ to** ~ не́зачем волнова́ться; **I ~ to see him** мне на́до *or* ну́жно с ним уви́деться; **you don't ~ to leave yet** Вам ещё не пора́ уходи́ть

needle ['niːdl] *n* игла́, иго́лка; (for knitting) спи́ца ♦ *vt* (fig : inf) подка́лывать (подколо́ть *pf*)

needless ['niːdlɪs] *adj* изли́шний; **~ to say** само́ собо́й разуме́ется

needn't ['niːdnt] = **need not**

needy ['niːdɪ] *adj* нужда́ющийся

negative ['negətɪv] *adj* (also ELEC) отрица́тельный ♦ *n* (PHOT) негати́в

neglect [nɪ'glekt] *vt* (child, work) забра́сывать (забро́сить *pf*); (garden, health) запуска́ть (запусти́ть *pf*); (duty) пренебрега́ть (пренебре́чь *pf*) ♦ *n*: ~ (of) невнима́ние (к +*dat*); **in a state of** ~ в запусте́нии

negligence ['neglɪdʒəns] *n* хала́тность *f*

negligible ['neglɪdʒɪbl] *adj* ничто́жный

negotiate [nɪ'gəuʃɪeɪt] *vt* (treaty, deal) заключа́ть (заключи́ть *pf*); (obstacle) преодолева́ть (преодоле́ть *pf*); (corner) огиба́ть (обогну́ть *pf*) ♦ *vi*: **to ~ (with sb for sth)** вести́ (impf) перегово́ры (с кем-н о чём-н)

negotiation [nɪgəuʃɪ'eɪʃən] *n* (of treaty, deal) заключе́ние; (of obstacle) преодоле́ние; **~s** перегово́ры *mpl*

negotiator [nɪ'gəuʃɪeɪtər] *n* уча́стник перегово́ров

neigh [neɪ] *vi* ржать (impf)

neighbour ['neɪbər] *n* (US **neighbor**)

n сосе́д(ка); **~hood** *n* (place) райо́н; (people) сосе́ди *mpl*; **~ing** *adj* сосе́дний

neither ['naɪðə'] *adj* ни тот, ни друго́й ♦ *conj*: **I didn't move and ~ did John** ни я, ни Джон не дви́нулись с ме́ста ♦ *pron*: **~ of them came** ни тот ни друго́й не пришли́, ни оди́н из них не пришёл; **~ version is true** ни та ни друга́я ве́рсия не верна́; **~ ... nor ... ** ни ..., ни ...; **~ good nor bad** ни хоро́шо, ни пло́хо

neon ['niːɔn] *n* нео́н

nephew ['nevjuː] *n* племя́нник

nerve [nɜːv] *n* (ANAT) нерв; (courage) вы́держка; (impudence) на́глость *f*

nervous ['nɜːvəs] *adj* не́рвный; **to be** *or* **feel ~** не́рвничать (impf); **~ breakdown** *n* не́рвный срыв; **~ness** *n* не́рвность *f*

nest [nest] *n* гнездо́

nestle ['nesl] *vi* приюти́ться (pf)

net [net] *n* (also fig) сеть *f*; (SPORT) се́тка; (COMPUT): **the Net** Сеть *f* ♦ *adj* (COMM) чи́стый ♦ *vt* (fish): (profit) приноси́ть (принести́ pf)

Netherlands ['neðələndz] *npl*: **the ~** Нидерла́нды *pl*

nett [net] *adj* = **net**

nettle ['netl] *n* крапи́ва

network ['netwɜːk] *n* сеть *f*

neurotic [njuə'rɔtɪk] *adj* неврастени́чный

neutral ['njuːtrəl] *adj* нейтра́льный ♦ *n* (AUT) холосто́й ход

never ['nevə'] *adv* никогда́; **~ in my life** никогда́ в жи́зни; **~theless** *adv* тем не ме́нее

new [njuː] *adj* (brand new) но́вый; (recent) неда́вний; **~-born** *adj* новорождённый; **~comer** *n* новичо́к; **~ly** *adv* неда́вно

news [njuːz] *n* (good, bad)

но́вость *f*, изве́стие; **a piece of ~** но́вость *f*; **the ~** (RADIO, TV) но́вости *fpl*; **~ agency** *n* информацио́нное аге́нтство; **~letter** *n* информацио́нный бюллете́нь *m*; **~reader** *n* ди́ктор (програ́ммы новосте́й)

New Year *n* Но́вый год; **Happy ~!** С Но́вым го́дом!; **~'s Day** *n* пе́рвое января́; **~'s Eve** *n* кану́н Но́вого го́да

New Zealand [njuː'ziːlənd] *n* Но́вая Зела́ндия

next [nekst] *adj* сле́дующий; (adjacent) сосе́дний ♦ *adv* пото́м, зате́м ♦ *prep*: **~ to** ря́дом с +*instr*, во́зле +*gen*; **~ time** в сле́дующий раз; **the ~ day** на сле́дующий день; **~ year** в бу́дущем *or* сле́дующем году́; **in the ~ 15 minutes** в ближа́йшие 15 мину́т; **~ to nothing** почти́ ничего́; **~ please!** сле́дующий, пожа́луйста!; **~ door** *adv* по сосе́дству, ря́дом *adj* (neighbour) ближа́йший; **~ of kin** *n* ближа́йший ро́дственник

NHS *n abbr* (BRIT) = **National Health Service**

nib [nɪb] *n* перо́

nibble ['nɪbl] *vt* надку́сывать (надкуси́ть pf)

nice [naɪs] *adj* прия́тный, хоро́ший; (attractive) симпати́чный; **to look ~** хорошо́ вы́глядеть (impf); **that's very ~ of you** о́чень ми́ло с Ва́шей стороны́

nick [nɪk] *n* (in skin) поре́з; (in surface) зару́бка ♦ *vt* (inf: steal) утаска́ивать (утащи́ть pf); **in the ~ of time** как раз во́время

nickel ['nɪkl] *n* ни́кель *m*; (US: coin) моне́та в 5 це́нтов

nickname ['nɪkneɪm] *n* кли́чка, про́звище ♦ *vt* прозыва́ть

(прозва́ть pf)

nicotine ['nɪkətiːn] n никоти́н

niece [niːs] n племя́нница

niggling ['nɪglɪŋ] adj навя́зчивый

night [naɪt] n ночь f; (evening) ве́чер; at~, by ~ но́чью; all ~ long всю ночь напролёт; in or during the ~ но́чью; last ~ вчера́ но́чью; (evening) вчера́ ве́чером; the ~ before last позапро́шлой но́чью; (evening) позавчера́ ве́чером; ~club n ночно́й клуб; ~dress n ночна́я руба́шка; ~fall n су́мерки pl; ~gown n = nightdress

nightingale ['naɪtɪŋgeɪl] n солове́й

nightlife ['naɪtlaɪf] n ночна́я жизнь f

nightly ['naɪtlɪ] adj (every night) ежено́щный ♦ adv ежено́щно

nightmare ['naɪtmɛə] n кошма́р

nil [nɪl] n нуль m; (BRIT: score) ноль m

nimble ['nɪmbl] adj (agile) шу́стрый; (alert) сообрази́тельный

nine [naɪn] n де́вять; ~teen n девятна́дцать; ~teenth adj девятна́дцатый; ~tieth adj девяно́стый; ~ty n девяно́сто

ninth [naɪnθ] adj девя́тый

nip [nɪp] vt (pinch) щипа́ть (ущипну́ть pf); (bite) куса́ть (укуси́ть pf) ♦ vi (BRIT: inf): to ~ out выска́кивать (вы́скочить pf)

nipple ['nɪpl] n (ANAT) сосо́к

nitrogen ['naɪtrədʒən] n азо́т

KEYWORD

no [nəu] (pl **noes**) adv (opposite of "yes") нет; **are you coming? - no (I'm not)** Вы придёте? - нет(, не приду́); **no thank you** нет, спаси́бо

♦ adj (not any): **I have no money/ books** у меня́ нет де́нег/книг; **there is no one here** здесь

никого́ нет; **it is of no importance at all** э́то не име́ет никако́го значе́ния; **no system is totally fair** никака́я систе́ма не явля́ется по́лностью справедли́вой; **"no entry"** "вход воспрещён"; **"no smoking"** "не кури́ть"

♦ n: **there were twenty noes** два́дцать голосо́в бы́ли "про́тив"

---

nobility [nəu'bɪlɪtɪ] n (class) знать f, дворя́нство

noble ['nəubl] adj (aristocratic) дворя́нский, зна́тный; (high-minded) благоро́дный

nobody ['nəubədɪ] pron никто́

nocturnal [nɔk'təːnl] adj ночно́й

nod [nɔd] vi кива́ть (impf) ♦ n киво́к ♦ vt: to ~ one's head кива́ть (кивну́ть pf) голово́й; ~ off vi задрема́ть (pf)

noise [nɔɪz] n шум

noisy ['nɔɪzɪ] adj шу́мный

nominal ['nɔmɪnl] adj номина́льный

nominate ['nɔmɪneɪt] vt (propose): to ~ sb (for) выставля́ть (вы́ставить pf) кандидату́ру кого́-н (на +acc); (appoint): to ~ sb (to/as) назнача́ть (назна́чить pf) кого́-н (на +acc/+instr)

nomination [nɔmɪ'neɪʃən] n (see vb) выставле́ние; назначе́ние

nominee [nɔmɪ'niː] n кандида́т

non- [nɔn] prefix не-

none [nʌn] pron (person) никто́, ни оди́н; (thing: countable) ничто́, ни оди́н; (: uncountable) ничего́; ~ of you никто́ or ни оди́н из вас; I've ~ left у меня́ ничего́ не оста́лось

nonetheless ['nʌnðə'les] adv тем не ме́нее, всё же

nonfiction [nɔn'fɪkʃən] n докумета́льная литерату́ра

nonsense ['nɔnsəns] n ерунда́,

чепуха

non-smoker [nɒn'sməʊkə^r] *adj*
некурящий *m adj*

nonstop *adj* (*conversation*)
беспрерывный; (*flight*)
беспосадочный ♦ (*speak*)
беспрерывно; (*fly*) без посадок

noodles ['nu:dlz] *npl* вермишель
fsg

noon [nu:n] *n* полдень *m*

no-one ['nəʊwʌn] *pron* = **nobody**

noose [nu:s] *n* петля

nor [nɔ:^r] *conj* = **neither** ♦ *adv see*
neither

norm [nɔ:m] *n* норма

normal ['nɔ:məl] *adj* нормальный;
~ly *adv* (*usually*) обычно; (*properly*)
нормально

north [nɔ:θ] *n* север ♦ *adj*
северный ♦ *adv* (*go*) на север;
(*be*) к северу; **North Africa** *n*
Северная Африка; **North
America** *n* Северная Америка;
~east *n* северо-восток; **~erly**
['nɔ:ðəlɪ] *adj* северный; **~ern**
['nɔ:ðən] *adj* северный; **Northern
Ireland** *n* Северная Ирландия;
North Pole *n* Северный полюс;
North Sea *n* Северное море;
~west *n* северо-запад

Norway ['nɔ:weɪ] *n* Норвегия

Norwegian [nɔ:'wi:dʒən] *adj*
норвежский

nose [nəʊz] *n* нос; (*sense of smell*)
нюх, чутьё; **~ (a)** *vi* (*go*) лезть;
~bleed *n* носовое
кровотечение; **~y** ['nəʊzɪ] *adj*
(*inf*) = **nosy**

nostalgia [nɒs'tældʒɪə] *n*
ностальгия

nostalgic [nɒs'tældʒɪk] *adj* (*memory,
film*) ностальгический; **to be ~
(for)** испытывать (*impf*)
ностальгию (по +*dat*), тосковать
(*impf*) по +*dat*

nostril ['nɒstrɪl] *n* ноздря

nosy ['nəʊzɪ] *adj* (*inf*): **to be ~**

совать (*impf*) нос в чужие дела

not [nɒt] *adv* нет; (*before verbs*) не;
he is ~ или isn't at home его нет
дома; **he asked me ~ to do it** он
попросил меня не делать этого;
you must ~ do that (*forbidden*) этого нельзя
делать; **it's too late, isn't it?** уже
слишком поздно, не правда ли?;
~ that ... не то, чтобы ...; ~ yet
нет ещё, ещё нет; **~ now** не
сейчас; *see also* **all**; **only**

notably ['nəʊtəblɪ] *adv* (*particularly*)
особенно; (*markedly*) заметно

notch [nɒtʃ] *n* насечка

note [nəʊt] *n* (*record*) запись *f*;
(*letter*) записка; (*also*: **foot~**)
сноска; (*also*: **bank~**) банкнота;
(*MUS*) нота; (*tone*) тон ♦ *vt*
(*observe*) замечать (заметить *pf*);
(*also*: **~ down**) записывать
(записать *pf*); **~book** *n* записная
книжка; **~d** *adj* известный; **~pad**
n блокнот; **~paper** *n* писчая
бумага

nothing ['nʌθɪŋ] *n* ничто; (*zero*)
ноль *m*; **he does ~** он ничего не
делает; **there is ~ to do/be said**
делать/сказать нечего; **~ new/
much/of the sort** ничего нового/
особенного/подобного; **for ~** за
даром

notice ['nəʊtɪs] *n* (*announcement*)
объявление; (*warning*)
предупреждение ♦ *vt* замечать
(заметить *pf*); **to take ~ of**
обращать (обратить *pf*)
внимание на +*acc*; **at short ~** без
предупреждения; **until further ~**
впредь до дальнейшего
уведомления; **~able** *adj*
заметный; **~ board** *n* доска
объявлений

notify ['nəʊtɪfaɪ] *vt*: **to ~ sb (of sth)**
уведомлять (уведомить *pf*)
кого-н (о чём-н)

notion ['nəʊʃən] n (idea) поня́тие; (opinion) представле́ние

notorious [nəʊ'tɔːrɪəs] adj печа́льно изве́стный

noun [naʊn] n (и́мя nt) существи́тельное nt adj

nourish ['nʌrɪʃ] vt пита́ть (impf); (fig) взра́щивать (взрасти́ть pf); **~ing** adj пита́тельный; **~ment** (food) пита́ние

novel ['nɒvl] n рома́н ♦ adj оригина́льный; **~ist** n романи́ст(ка); (newness) новизна́; (object) нови́нка

November [nəʊ'vembə] n ноя́брь m

novice ['nɒvɪs] n (in job) новичо́к

now [naʊ] adv тепе́рь, сейча́с ♦ conj: ~ (that) ... тепе́рь, когда́ ...; **right** ~ пря́мо сейча́с; **by** ~ к настоя́щему вре́мени; **and then** или **again** вре́мя от вре́мени; **from** ~ **on** отны́не, впредь; **until** ~ до сих пор; **~adays** adv в на́ши дни

nowhere ['nəʊweə] adv (be) нигде́; (go) никуда́

nuclear ['njuːklɪə] adj я́дерный

nucleus ['njuːklɪəs] (pl **nuclei**) n ядро́

nude [njuːd] adj обнажённый, наго́й ♦ n: **in the** ~ в обнажённом ви́де

nudge [nʌdʒ] vt подта́лкивать (подтолкну́ть pf)

nudity ['njuːdɪtɪ] n нагота́

nuisance ['njuːsns] n доса́да; (person) зану́да; **what a** ~! кака́я доса́да!

numb [nʌm] adj: ~ (with) онеме́вший (от +gen); **to go** ~ неме́ть (онеме́ть pf)

number ['nʌmbə] n но́мер m; (MATH) число́; (written figure) ци́фра; (quantity) коли́чество ♦ vt (pages etc) нумерова́ть (пронумерова́ть pf); (amount to) насчи́тывать (impf); **a** ~ **of** не́сколько +gen, ряд +gen; **~plate** n (BRIT) номерно́й знак

numeral ['njuːmərəl] n ци́фра

numerical [njuː'merɪkl] adj (value) числово́й; **in** ~ **order** по номера́м

numerous ['njuːmərəs] adj многочи́сленный; **on** ~ **occasions** многокра́тно

nun [nʌn] n мона́хиня

nurse [nɜːs] n медсестра́; (also: **male** ~) медбра́т ♦ vt (patient) уха́живать (impf) за +instr

nursery ['nɜːsərɪ] n (institution) я́сли pl; (room) де́тская f adj; (for plants) пито́мник; ~ **rhyme** n де́тская пе́сенка; ~ **school** n де́тский сад

nursing ['nɜːsɪŋ] n (profession) профе́ссия медсестры́; ~ **home** n ча́стный дом для престаре́лых

nurture ['nɜːtʃə] vt (child, plant) выра́щивать (вы́растить pf)

nut [nʌt] n (BOT) оре́х; (TECH) га́йка; ~**meg** n муска́тный оре́х

nutrient ['njuːtrɪənt] n пита́тельное вещество́

nutrition [njuː'trɪʃən] n (nourishment) пита́тельность f; (diet) пита́ние

nutritious [njuː'trɪʃəs] adj пита́тельный

nylon ['naɪlɒn] n нейло́н ♦ adj нейло́новый

O, o

oak [əʊk] n дуб ♦ adj дубо́вый

OAP n abbr (BRIT) = **old age pensioner**

oar [ɔː] n весло́

oasis [əʊ'eɪsɪs] (pl **oases**) n оа́зис

oath [əʊθ] n (promise) кля́тва; (: LAW) прися́га; (swear word) прокля́тие; **on** (BRIT) or **under** ~

под прися́гой
oats [əuts] *npl* овёс *msg*
obedience [ə'bi:diəns] *n*
повинове́ние, послуша́ние
obedient [ə'bi:diənt] *adj*
послу́шный
obey [ə'beɪ] *vt* подчиня́ться
(подчини́ться *pf*) +*dat*,
повинова́ться (*impf/pf*) +*dat*
obituary [ə'bɪtjuarɪ] *n* некроло́г
object *n* ['ɔbdʒɪkt] *vb* [əb'dʒekt] *n*
(thing) предме́т; (aim, purpose)
цель *f*; (of affection, desires)
объе́кт; (LING) дополне́ние ♦ *vi*:
to ~ (to) возража́ть (возрази́ть
pf) (про́тив +*gen*); **money is no ~**
де́ньги - не пробле́ма; **I have**
no ~ion to ... я не име́ю никаки́х
возраже́ний про́тив +*gen* ...;
~ionable [əb'dʒekʃənəbl] *adj*
(language, conduct)
возмути́тельный; (person)
гну́сный; **~ive** [əb'dʒektɪv] *adj*
объекти́вный ♦ *n* цель *f*
obligation [ɔblɪ'geɪʃən] *n*
обяза́тельство
obligatory [ə'blɪgətərɪ] *adj*
обяза́тельный
oblige [ə'blaɪdʒ] *vt* обя́зывать
(обяза́ть *pf*); (force): **to ~ sb to do**
обя́зывать (обяза́ть *pf*) кого́-н
+*infin*; **I'm much ~d to you for**
your help (grateful) я о́чень
обя́зан Вам за Ва́шу по́мощь
obliging [ə'blaɪdʒɪŋ] *adj* любе́зный
oblivion [ə'blɪvɪən] *n* забве́ние
oblivious [ə'blɪvɪəs] *adj*: **to be ~ of**
or **to** не сознава́ть (*impf*) +*gen*
obnoxious [əb'nɔkʃəs] *adj*
отврати́тельный
oboe ['əubəu] *n* гобо́й
obscene [əb'si:n] *adj*
непристо́йный
obscure [əb'skjuə] *adj* (little known)

неприме́тный; (incomprehensible)
сму́тный ♦ *vt* (view etc)
загора́живать (загороди́ть *pf*);
(truth etc) затемня́ть (затемни́ть
pf)
observant [əb'zə:vnt] *adj*
наблюда́тельный
observation [ɔbzə'veɪʃən] *n*
наблюде́ние; (remark) замеча́ние
observe [əb'zə:v] *vt* (watch)
наблюда́ть (*impf*) за +*instr*;
(comment) замеча́ть (заме́тить
pf); (abide by) соблюда́ть
(соблюсти́ *pf*); **~r** *n* наблюда́тель
m
obsession [əb'seʃən] *n* страсть *f*,
одержи́мость *f*
obsessive [əb'sesɪv] *adj* страстный,
одержи́мый
obsolete ['ɔbsəli:t] *adj* устаре́вший
obstacle ['ɔbstəkl] *n* препя́тствие
obstinate ['ɔbstɪnɪt] *adj* упря́мый
obstruct [əb'strʌkt] *vt* (road, path)
загора́живать (загороди́ть *pf*);
(traffic, progress) препя́тствовать
(воспрепя́тствовать *pf*) +*dat*;
~ion [əb'strʌkʃən] *n* (of law)
обстру́кция; (object) препя́тствие
obtain [əb'teɪn] *vt* приобрета́ть
(приобрести́ *pf*)
obvious ['ɔbvɪəs] *adj* очеви́дный;
~ly *adv* очеви́дно; (of course)
разуме́ется; **~ly not** разуме́ется,
нет
occasion [ə'keɪʒən] *n* (time) раз;
(case, opportunity) слу́чай; (event)
собы́тие; **~al** *adj* ре́дкий,
нечастый; **~ally** *adv* изредка
occupant ['ɔkjupənt] *n* (long-term)
обита́тель(ница) *m(f)*
occupation [ɔkju'peɪʃən] *n*
заня́тие; (MIL) оккупа́ция
occupy ['ɔkjupaɪ] *vt* занима́ть
(заня́ть *pf*); (country, attention)
захва́тывать (захвати́ть *pf*); **to ~**
o.s. with sth занима́ться

(заня́ться *pf*) чем-н
occur [ə'kз:] *vi* происходи́ть
(произойти́ *pf*), случа́ться
(случи́ться *pf*); (*exist*) встреча́ться
(встре́титься *pf*); **to ~ to sb**
приходи́ть (прийти́ *pf*) кому́-н в
го́лову; **~rence** *n* (*event*)
происше́ствие

ocean ['əuʃən] *n* океа́н

o'clock [ə'klɒk] *adv*: **it is five ~**
сейча́с пять часо́в

October [ɒk'təubə] *n* октя́брь *m*

octopus ['ɒktəpəs] *n* осьмино́г

odd [ɒd] *adj* (*strange*) стра́нный,
необы́чный; (*uneven*) нечётный;
(*not paired*) непа́рный; **60-~**
шестьдеся́т с ли́шним; **at ~ times**
времена́ми; **I was the ~ one out**
я был ли́шний; **~ly** *adv* (*behave,
dress*) стра́нно; *see also* **enough**;
~s *npl* (*in betting*) ста́вки *fpl*; **to be
at ~s (with)** быть (*impf*) не в
лада́х (с +*instr*)

odour ['əudə] (*US* **odor**) *n* за́пах

KEYWORD

of [ɒv, əv] *prep* **1** (*expressing
belonging*): **the history of Russia**
исто́рия Росси́и; **a friend of ours**
наш друг; **a boy of 10** ма́льчик
десяти́ лет; **that was kind of you**
э́то бы́ло о́чень любе́зно с
Ва́шей стороны́; **a man of great
ability** челове́к больши́х
спосо́бностей; **the city of New
York** го́род Нью-Йо́рк; **south of
London** к ю́гу от Ло́ндона
2 (*expressing quantity, amount,
dates etc*): **a kilo of flour**
килогра́мм муки́; **how much of
this material do you need?**
ско́лько тако́й тка́ни Вам
ну́жно?; **there were three of them**
(*people*) их бы́ло тро́е; (*objects*)
бы́ло три; **three of us stayed**
тро́е из нас оста́лись; **the 5th of**

July 5-ое ию́ля; **on the 5th of
July** 5-ого ию́ля
3 (*from*) из +*gen*; **the house is
made of wood** дом сде́лан из
де́рева

KEYWORD

off [ɒf] *adv* **1** (*referring to distance,
time*): **it's a long way off** э́то
далеко́ отсю́да; **the city is 5
miles off** до го́рода 5 миль; **the
game is 3 days off** до игры́
оста́лось 3 дня
2 (*departure*): **to go off to Paris/
Italy** уезжа́ть (уе́хать *pf*) в
Пари́ж/Ита́лию; **I must be off** мне
пора́ (идти́)
3 (*removal*): **to take off one's hat/
clothes** снима́ть (снять *pf*)
шля́пу/оде́жду; **the button came
off** пу́говица оторвала́сь; **ten
percent off** (*COMM*) ски́дка в
де́сять проце́нтов
4: to be off (*on holiday*) быть (*impf*)
в о́тпуске; **I'm off on Fridays** (*day
off*) у меня́ выходно́й по
пя́тницам; **he was off on Friday**
(*absent*) в пя́тницу его́ не́ было
на рабо́те; **I have a day off** у
меня́ отгу́л; **to be off sick** не
рабо́тать (*impf*) по боле́зни
♦ *adj* **1** (*not on*) вы́ключенный;
(: *tap*) закры́тый; (*disconnected*)
отключённый
2 (*cancelled: meeting, match*)
отменённый; (: *agreement*)
расто́ргнутый
3 (*BRIT*): **to go off** (*milk*)
прокиса́ть (проки́снуть *pf*);
(*cheese, meat*) по́ртиться
(испо́ртиться *pf*)
4: on the off chance на вся́кий
слу́чай; **to have an off day**
встава́ть (встать *pf*) с ле́вой ноги́
♦ *prep* **1** (*indicating motion*) с +*gen*;

to fall off a cliff упа́сть (pf) со скалы́ 2 (distant from) от +gen; it's just off the M1 э́то недалеко́ от автостра́ды M1; it's five km off the main road э́то в пяти́ км от шоссе́; to be off meat (dislike) разлюби́ть (pf) мя́со

offence [əˈfɛns] (US **offense**) n (crime) правонаруше́ние; **to take ~ at** обижа́ться (оби́деться pf) на +acc

offend [əˈfɛnd] vt (person) обижа́ть (оби́деть pf); **~er** n правонаруши́тель(ница) m(f); **~ing** adj соотве́тствующий

offense [əˈfɛns] n (US) = **offence**

offensive [əˈfɛnsɪv] adj (remark, behaviour) оскорби́тельный ♦ n (MIL) наступле́ние; **~ weapon** ору́дие нападе́ния

offer [ˈɒfəʳ] n предложе́ние ♦ vt предлага́ть (предложи́ть pf)

office [ˈɒfɪs] n о́фис; (room) кабине́т; **doctor's ~** (US) кабине́т врача́; **to take ~** (person) вступа́ть (вступи́ть pf) в до́лжность

officer [ˈɒfɪsəʳ] n (MIL) офице́р; (also: **police ~**) полице́йский m adj; (: in Russia) милиционе́р

official [əˈfɪʃl] adj официа́льный ♦ n (of organization) должностно́е лицо́; **government ~** официа́льное лицо́

off-licence [ˈɒflaɪsns] n (BRIT) ви́нный магази́н

off-line [ˈɒflaɪn] adj (COMPUT) автоно́мный; (switched off) отключённый

off-peak [ˈɒfˈpiːk] adj (heating, electricity) непи́ковый

offset [ˈɒfsɛt] (irreg) vt уравнове́шивать (уравнове́сить pf)

offshore [ɒfˈʃɔːʳ] adj (oilrig, fishing) морско́й; (COMM) оффшо́рный; ~

wind ве́тер с бе́рега

offspring [ˈɒfsprɪŋ] n inv отпрыск

often [ˈɒfn] adv ча́сто; **how ~ ...?** как ча́сто ...?; **more ~ than not** ча́ще всего́; **as ~ as not** дово́льно ча́сто; **every so ~** вре́мя от вре́мени

oil [ɔɪl] n ма́сло; (petroleum) нефть f; (for heating) печно́е то́пливо ♦ vt сма́зывать (сма́зать pf); **~y** adj (rag) промасленный; (skin) жи́рный

ointment [ˈɔɪntmənt] n мазь f

O.K. [ˈəʊˈkeɪ] excl (inf) хорошо́, ла́дно

old [əʊld] adj ста́рый; **how ~ are you?** ско́лько Вам лет?; **he's 10 years ~** ему́ 10 лет; **~ man** стари́к; **~ woman** стару́ха; **~er brother** ста́рший брат; **~ age** ста́рость f; **~-fashioned** adj старомо́дный

olive [ˈɒlɪv] n (fruit) масли́на, оли́вка ♦ adj оли́вковый; **~ oil** n оли́вковое ма́сло

Olympic Games npl: **the ~ Games** (also: **the ~s**) Олимпи́йские и́гры fpl

omelet(te) [ˈɒmlɪt] n омле́т

omen [ˈəʊmən] n предзнаменова́ние

ominous [ˈɒmɪnəs] adj злове́щий

omission [əʊˈmɪʃən] n про́пуск

omit [əʊˈmɪt] vt пропуска́ть (пропусти́ть pf)

KEYWORD

on [ɒn] prep 1 (position) на +prp; (motion) на +acc; **the book is on the table** кни́га на столе́; **to put the book on the table** класть (положи́ть pf) кни́гу на стол; **on the left** сле́ва; **the house is on the main road** дом стои́т у шоссе́ 2 (indicating means, method, condition etc): **on foot** пешко́м; **on**

the plane/train (go) на
самолёте/пóезде; (be) в
самолёте/пóезде; **on the radio/
television** по рáдио/телевúзору;
she's on the telephone онá
разговáривает по телефóну; **to
be on medication** принимáть
(impf) лекáрства; **to be on
holiday/business** быть (impf) в
óтпуске/командирóвке
3 (referring to time): **on Friday** в
пя́тницу; **on Fridays** по
пя́тницам; **on June 20th** 20-ого
úюня; **a week on Friday** чéрез
недéлю, считáя с пя́тницы; **on
arrival** по приéзде; **on seeing this**
уви́дев э́то
4 (about, concerning) о +prp;
information on train services
информáция о расписáнии
поездóв; **a book on physics**
кни́га по фúзике
♦ adv **1** (referring to dress) в +prp;
to have one's coat on быть (impf) в
пальтó; **what's she got on?** во
что онá былá одéта?; **she put
her boots/hat on** онá надéла
сапогú/шля́пу
2 (further, continuously) дáльше,
дáлее; **to walk on** идтú (impf)
дáльше
♦ adj **1** (functioning, in operation)
включённый; (: tap) откры́тый; **is
the meeting still on?** (not
cancelled) собрáние состои́тся?;
**there's a film on at the
cinema** в кинотеáтре идёт
хорóший фильм
2: that's not on! так не пойдёт! **or** не годи́тся!

once [wʌns] adv (один) раз;
(formerly) когдá-то, однáжды
♦ conj как тóлько; **at ~** срáзу же;
(simultaneously) вмéсте; **~ a week**
(один) раз в недéлю); **~ more**

ещё раз; **~ and for all** раз и
навсегдá

oncoming ['ɔnkʌmɪŋ] adj
встрéчный

one [wʌn] n один (f однá, nt однó,
pl одни́); **one hundred and fifty**
сто пятьдеся́т; **one day there
was a knock at the door**
однáжды раздáлся стук в дверь;
one by one один за други́м
♦ adj **1** (sole) еди́нственный; **the
one book which** ... еди́нственная
кни́га, котóрая ...
2 (same) один; **they all belong to
the one family** они́ все из однóй
семьи́
♦ pron **1: I'm the one who told
him** э́то я сказáл ему́; **this one**
э́тот (f э́та, nt э́то); **that one** тот (f
та, nt то); **I've already got one** у
меня́ ужé есть
2: one another друг дрýга; **do
you ever see one another?** Вы
когдá-нибудь ви́дитесь?; **they
didn't dare look at one another**
они́ не смéли взгляну́ть друг на
дрýга
3 (impersonal): **one never knows**
никогдá не знáешь; **one has to
do it** нáдо сдéлать э́то; **to cut
one's finger** порéзать (pf) (себé)
пáлец

one: ~-man adj (business)
индивидуáльный; **~-off** n (BRIT:
inf) едини́чный слýчай; **~'s** adj:
to dry ~'s hands вытирáть
(вы́тереть pf) рýки; **naturally
loves ~'s children** человéку
свóйственно люби́ть свои́х
детéй; **~self** pron (reflexive) себя́;
(emphatic) сам; (after prep: +acc,
+gen) себя́; (: +dat) себé; (: +instr)
собóй; (: +prp) себé; **to hurt ~self**

ушибáться (ушибíться pf); to keep sth for ~self держáть (impf) что-н при себé; to talk to ~self разговáривать (impf) с (сами́м) собóй; ~-sided adj односторóнний; (contest) нерáвный; ~-way adj: ~-way street ýлица с односторóнним движéнием

on-line ['ɒn'laɪn] adj онлáйновый; **to go ~** включáться (включи́ться pf) в сеть

ongoing ['ɒngəʊɪŋ] adj продолжáющаяся

onion ['ʌnjən] n лук

only ['əʊnlɪ] adv тóлько ♦ adj еди́нственный ♦ conj тóлько; **not ~ ... but also ...** не тóлько ..., но и ...

onset ['ɒnsɛt] n наступлéние

onshore ['ɒnʃɔ:ʳ] adj: ~ **wind** вéтер с мóря

onward(s) ['ɒnwəd(z)] adv вперёд, дáльше; **from that time ~** с тех пор

opal ['əupl] n опáл

opaque [əu'peɪk] adj мáтовый

OPEC n abbr (= Organization of Petroleum-Exporting Countries) ОПЕК

open ['əupn] adj откры́тый ♦ vt открывáть (откры́ть pf) ♦ vi открывáться (откры́ться pf); (book, debate etc) начинáться (начáться pf); **in the ~** (air) на откры́том воздýхе; ~ **up** ♦ vi открывáться (откры́ться pf); ~**ing** adj (speech, remarks etc) вступи́тельный ♦ n (gap, hole) отвéрстие; (job) вакáнсия; ~**ly** adv откры́то; ~-**minded** adj (person) откры́тый; ~-**plan** adj: ~-**plan office** óфис с откры́той плани́ровкой

opera ['ɒpərə] n óпера

operate ['ɒpəreɪt] vt управля́ть (impf) +instr ♦ vi дéйствовать (impf); (MED): **to ~ (on sb)** опери́ровать (проопери́ровать pf) (когó-н)

operation [ɒpə'reɪʃən] n опéрация; (of machine: functioning) рабóта; (: controlling) управлéние; **to be in ~** дéйствовать (impf); (MED) ему́ сдéлали опéрацию; ~**al** [ɒpə'reɪʃənl] adj: **the machine was ~al** маши́на функциони́ровала

operative ['ɒpərətɪv] adj (law etc) дéйствующий

operator ['ɒpəreɪtəʳ] n (TEL) телефони́ст(ка); (TECH) оператóр

opinion [ə'pɪnjən] n мнéние; **in my ~** по моему́ мнéнию, по-мóему; ~ **poll** n опрóс обществéнного мнéния

opponent [ə'pəunənt] n оппонéнт, проти́вник(ница); (SPORT) проти́вник

opportunity [ɒpə'tju:nɪtɪ] n возмóжность f; **to take the ~ of doing** пóльзоваться (воспóльзоваться pf) слýчаем, чтóбы +infin

oppose [ə'pəuz] vt проти́виться (воспроти́виться pf) +dat; **to be ~d to sth** проти́виться (impf) чему́-н; **as ~d to** в проти́воположность +dat

opposing [ə'pəuzɪŋ] adj (ideas, forces) проти́воборствующий; **the ~ team** комáнда проти́вника

opposite ['ɒpəzɪt] adj проти́воположный ♦ adv напро́тив ♦ prep напро́тив +gen ♦ n: **the ~** проти́воположное nt adj

opposition [ɒpə'zɪʃən] n оппози́ция; **the Opposition** (POL) оппозицио́нная пáртия

oppress [ə'prɛs] vt угнетáть (impf); ~**ion** [ə'prɛʃən] n угнетéние; ~**ive**

adj (*régime*) угнетательский; (*weather, heat*) гнетущий

opt [ɔpt] *vi*: **to ~ for** избирать (избрать *pf*); **to ~ to do** решать (решить *pf*) +*infin*; **~ out** *vi*: **to ~ out of** выходить (выйти *pf*) из +*gen*

optical ['ɔptɪkl] *adj* оптический

optician [ɔp'tɪʃən] *n* окулист

optimism ['ɔptɪmɪzəm] *n* оптимизм

optimistic [ɔptɪ'mɪstɪk] *adj* оптимистичный

optimum ['ɔptɪməm] *adj* оптимальный

option ['ɔpʃən] *n* (*choice*) возможность *f*, вариант; **~al** *adj* необязательный

or [ɔːr] *conj* или; (*otherwise*): **~ (else)** а то, иначе; (*with negative*): **he hasn't seen ~ heard anything** он ничего не видел и не слышал

oral ['ɔːrl] *adj* устный; (*medicine*) оральный ♦ *n* устный экзамен

orange ['ɔrɪndʒ] *n* апельсин ♦ *adj* (*colour*) оранжевый

orbit ['ɔːbɪt] *n* орбита ♦ *vt* обращаться (обратиться *pf*) вокруг +*gen*

orchard ['ɔːtʃəd] *n* сад (фруктовый)

orchestra ['ɔːkɪstrə] *n* (*MUS*) оркестр

orchid ['ɔːkɪd] *n* орхидея

ordeal [ɔː'diːl] *n* испытание

order ['ɔːdər] *n* заказ; (*command*) приказ; (*sequence, discipline*) порядок ♦ *vt* заказывать (заказать *pf*); (*command*) приказывать (приказать *pf*) +*dat*; (*also*: **put in ~**) располагать (расположить *pf*) по порядку; **in ~** в порядке; **in ~ to do** для того чтобы +*infin*; **out of ~** (*not in sequence*) не по порядку; (*not working*) неисправный; **to ~ sb to**

do приказывать (приказать *pf*) кому-н +*infin*; **~ form** *n* бланк заказа; **~ly** *n* (*MED*) санитар ♦ *adj* (*room*) опрятный; (*system*) упорядоченный

ordinary ['ɔːdnrɪ] *adj* обычный, обыкновенный; (*mediocre*) заурядный; **out of the ~** необычайный

ore [ɔːr] *n* руда

organ ['ɔːgən] *n* (*ANAT*) орган; (*MUS*) орган; **~ic** [ɔː'gænɪk] *adj* (*fertilizer*) органический; (*food*) экологически чистый; **~ism** *n* организм

organization [ɔːgənaɪ'zeɪʃən] *n* организация

organize ['ɔːgənaɪz] *vt* организовывать (impf/*pf*), устраивать (устроить *pf*)

orgasm ['ɔːgæzm] *n* оргазм

Orient ['ɔːrɪənt] *n*: **the ~** Восток

oriental [ɔːrɪ'entl] *adj* восточный

origin ['ɔrɪdʒɪn] *n* происхождение; **~al** [ə'rɪdʒɪnl] *adj* первоначальный; (*new*) оригинальный; (*genuine*) подлинный; (*imaginative*) самобытный ♦ *n* подлинник, оригинал; **~ally** *adv* первоначально; **~ate** [ə'rɪdʒɪneɪt] *vi*: **to ~ate from** происходить (произойти *pf*) от/из +*gen*; **to ~ate in** зарождаться (зародиться *pf*) в +*prp*

ornament ['ɔːnəmənt] *n* (*decorative object*) украшение; **~al** [ɔːnə'mentl] *adj* декоративный

ornate [ɔː'neɪt] *adj* декоративный

orphan ['ɔːfn] *n* сирота *m/f*; **~age** *n* детский дом

orthodox ['ɔːθədɔks] *adj* ортодоксальный; **the Russian Orthodox Church** Русская православная церковь

orthopaedic [ɔːθə'piːdɪk] (*US*

orthopedic; *adj* ортопеди́ческий
ostrich ['ɒstrɪtʃ] *n* стра́ус
other ['ʌðə] *adj* друго́й ♦ *pron:* **the ~ (one)** друго́й(а́я) *m(f) adj*, друго́е *nt adj* ♦ *adv:* **~ than** кро́ме +*gen;* **~s** (*other people*) други́е *pl adj;* **the ~s** остальны́е *pl adj;* **the ~ day** на днях; **~wise** *adv* (*differently*) ина́че, по-друго́му; (*apart from that*) в остально́м ♦ *conj* а то, ина́че
otter ['ɒtə] *n* вы́дра
ought [ɔːt] (*pt ~*) *aux vb:* **I ~ to do it** мне сле́дует э́то сде́лать; **this ~ to have been corrected** э́то сле́довало испра́вить; **he ~ to win** он до́лжен вы́играть

ounce [auns] *n* у́нция

> **ounce** – у́нция. Ме́ра ве́са ра́вная 28.349 гр.

our ['auə] *adj* наш; *see also* **my;** **~s** *pron* наш; (*referring to subject of sentence*) свой; *see also* **mine**[1]; **~selves** *pl pron* (*reflexive, complement*) себя́; (*after prep:* +*acc,* +*gen*) себя́; (*:* +*dat,* +*prp*) себе́; (*:* +*instr*) собо́й; (*emphatic*) са́ми; (*alone*) **(all) by ~selves** са́ми; **let's keep it between ~selves** дава́йте оста́вим э́то ме́жду на́ми; *see also* **myself**

oust [aust] *vt* изгоня́ть (изгна́ть *pf*)

KEYWORD

out [aut] *adv* **1** (*not in*): **they're out in the garden** они́ в саду́; **out in the rain/snow** под дождём/ сне́гом; **out here** здесь; **out there** там; **to go out** выходи́ть (вы́йти *pf*); **out loud** гро́мко

2 (*not at home, absent*): **he is out at the moment** его́ сейча́с нет (до́ма); **let's have a night out on Friday** дава́йте пойдём куда́-

нибудь в пя́тницу ве́чером!

3 (*indicating distance*) в +*prp;* **the boat was ten km out (from the shore)** кора́бль находи́лся в десяти́ км от бе́рега

4 (*SPORT*): **the ball is out** мяч за преде́лами по́ля

♦ *adj* **1** *be out* (*unconscious*) быть (*impf*)без созна́ния; (*out of game*) выбыва́ть (вы́быть *pf*); (*flowers*) распуска́ться (распусти́ться *pf*); (*news, secret*) станови́ться (стать *pf*) изве́стным(ой); (*fire, light, gas*) ту́хнуть (поту́хнуть *pf*), га́снуть (пога́снуть *pf*); **to go out of fashion** выходи́ть (вы́йти *pf*) из мо́ды

2 (*finished*): **before the week was out** до оконча́ния неде́ли
3: to be out to do (*intend*) намерева́ться (*impf*) +*infin;* **to be out in one's calculations** (*wrong*) ошиба́ться (ошиби́ться *pf*) в расчётах

♦ *prep* **1** (*outside, beyond*) из +*gen;* **to go out of the house** выходи́ть (вы́йти *pf*) из до́ма; **to be out of danger** (*safe*) быть (*impf*) вне опа́сности

2 (*cause, motive*) **out of curiosity** из любопы́тства; **out of fear/joy/ boredom** от стра́ха/ра́дости/ ску́ки; **out of grief** с го́ря; **out of necessity** по необходи́мости
3 (*from, from among*) из +*gen*
4 (*without*): **we are out of sugar/ petrol** у нас ко́нчился са́хар/ бензи́н

out-and-out ['autəndaut] *adj* (*villain*) отъя́вленный
outbreak ['autbreɪk] *n* (*of disease, violence*) вспы́шка; (*of war*) нача́ло
outburst ['autbəːst] *n* взрыв

outcast ['autkɑːst] n изгой

outcome ['autkʌm] n исход

outcry ['autkraɪ] n негодование, протест

outdated [aut'deɪtɪd] adj (customs, ideas) отживший; (technology) устарелый

outdo [aut'duː] (irreg) vt превзойти pf

outdoor [aut'dɔːʳ] adj на открытом воздухе; (pool) открытый; ~s adv на улице, на открытом воздухе

outer ['autəʳ] adj наружный; ~ space n космическое пространство

outfit ['autfɪt] n (clothes) костюм

outgoing ['autgəuɪŋ] adj (extrovert) общительный; (president, mayor etc) уходящий

outing ['autɪŋ] n поход

outlandish [aut'lændɪʃ] adj диковинный

outlaw ['autlɔː] vt объявлять (объявить pf) вне закона

outlay ['autleɪ] n затраты fpl

outlet ['autlet] n (hole) выходное отверстие; (pipe) сток; (COMM : also : retail ~) торговая точка; (for emotions) выход

outline ['autlaɪn] n (shape) контур, очертания ntpl; (sketch, explanation) набросок ♦ vt (fig) описывать (описать pf)

outlook ['autluk] n (attitude) взгляды mpl; (prospects) перспективы fpl

outlying ['autlaɪɪŋ] adj отдалённый

outnumber [aut'nʌmbəʳ] vt численно превосходить (превзойти pf)

out-of-date [autəv'deɪt] adj (clothes) немодный; (equipment) устарелый

out-of-the-way ['autəvðə'weɪ] adj (place) глубинный

outpatient ['autpeɪʃənt] n

амбулаторный(ая) пациент(ка)

output ['autput] n выработка, продукция; (COMPUT) выходные данные fpl

outrage ['autreɪdʒ] n (emotion) возмущение ♦ vt возмущать (возмутить pf); ~ous [aut'reɪdʒəs] adj возмутительный

outright [aut'raɪt] adv (win, own) абсолютно; (refuse, deny) наотрез; (ask) прямо ♦ adj (winner, victory) абсолютный; (refusal, hostility) открытый; to be killed ~ погибать (погибнуть pf) сразу

outset ['autset] n начало

outside [aut'saɪd] n наружная сторона ♦ adj наружный, внешний ♦ adv (be) снаружи; (go) наружу ♦ prep вне +gen, за пределами +gen; (building) у +gen; (city) под +instr; ~r n (stranger) посторонний(яя) m(f) adj

outskirts ['autskəːts] npl окраины fpl

outspoken [aut'spəukən] adj откровенный

outstanding [aut'stændɪŋ] adj (exceptional) выдающийся; (unfinished) незаконченный; (unpaid) неоплаченный

outward ['autwəd] adj внешний; the ~ journey поездка туда

outweigh [aut'weɪ] vt перевешивать (перевесить pf)

outwit [aut'wɪt] vt перехитрить (pf)

oval ['əuvl] adj овальный

ovary ['əuvərɪ] n яичник

ovation [əu'veɪʃən] n овация

oven ['ʌvn] n (domestic) духовка

KEYWORD

over ['əuvəʳ] adv 1 (across): to cross over переходить (перейти pf); over here здесь; over there там;

to ask sb over (to one's house) приглашать (пригласить pf) кого-н в гости or к себе

2 (indicating movement from upright): **to knock/turn sth over** сбивать (сбить pf)/ переворачивать (перевернуть pf) что-н; **to fall over** падать (упасть pf); **to bend over** нагибаться (нагнуться pf)

3 (finished): **the game is over** игра окончена; **his life is over** жизнь его закончилась

4 (excessively) слишком, чересчур

5 (remaining: money, food etc): **there are 3 over** осталось 3

6: **all over** (everywhere) везде, повсюду; **over and over** (again) снова и снова

♦ prep 1 (on top of) на +prp; (above, in control of) над +instr

2 (on(to) the other side of) через +acc; **the pub over the road** паб через дорогу

3 (more than) свыше +gen, больше+gen; **she is over 40** ей больше 40; **over and above** намного больше, чем

4 (in the course of) в течение +gen, за +acc; **over the winter** зá зиму, в течение зимы; **let's discuss it over dinner** давайте обсудим это за обедом; **the work is spread over two weeks** работа рассчитана на две недели

overall ['əʊvərɔːl] adj общий ♦ adv (in general) в целом or общем; (altogether) целиком ♦ n (BRIT) халат; ~s npl (clothing) комбинезон msg; **~ majority** подавляющее большинство

overboard ['əʊvəbɔːd] adv: **to fall ~** падать (упасть pf) зá борт

overcast ['əʊvəkɑːst] adj хмурый,

пáсмурный

overcoat ['əʊvəkəut] n пальто nt ind

overcome [əʊvə'kʌm] (irreg) vt (problems) преодолевать (преодолеть pf)

overcrowded [əʊvə'kraudɪd] adj переполненный

overdo [əʊvə'duː] (irreg) vt (work, exercise) перестараться (pf) в +prp; (interest, concern) утрировать (impf)

overdose ['əʊvədəus] n передозировка

overdraft ['əʊvədrɑːft] n перерасход, овердрафт

overdrawn [əʊvə'drɔːn] adj: **he is ~** он превысил кредит своего текущего счёта

overdue [əʊvə'djuː] adj (change, reform etc) запоздалый

overgrown [əʊvə'grəun] adj (garden) заросший

overhead adv ['əʊvəhɛd] adj, n ['əʊvəhɛd] adv наверху, над головой; (in the sky) в небе ♦ adj (lighting) верхний; (cable, railway) надземный ♦ n (US) **~s** npl (expenses) накладные расходы mpl

overhear [əʊvə'hɪər] (irreg) vt (случайно) подслушать (pf)

overjoyed [əʊvə'dʒɔɪd] adj: **to be ~ (at)** радоваться (обрадоваться pf) (+dat); **she was ~ to see him** она была очень рада видеть его

overlap [əʊvə'læp] vi находить (impf) один на другой; (fig) частично совпадать (совпасть pf)

overleaf [əʊvə'liːf] adv на обороте

overload [əʊvə'ləud] vt (also ELEC, fig) перегружать (перегрузить pf)

overlook [əʊvə'luk] vt (place)

выходи́ть (impf) на +acc; (problem) упуска́ть (упусти́ть pf) из ви́ду; (behaviour) закрыва́ть (закры́ть pf) глаза́ на +acc

overnight [əuvə'naɪt] adv (during the night) за́ ночь; (fig) в одноча́сье, сра́зу; **to stay ~** ночева́ть (переночева́ть pf)

overpowering [əuvə'pauərɪŋ] adj (heat, stench) невыноси́мый

overriding [əuvə'raɪdɪŋ] adj (factor, consideration) реша́ющий

overrun [əuvə'rʌn] (irreg) vi (meeting) затя́гиваться (затяну́ться pf)

overseas [əuvə'si:z] adv (live, work) за рубежо́м or грани́цей; (go) за рубе́ж or грани́цу ♦ adj (market, trade) вне́шний; (student, visitor) иностра́нный

oversee [əuvə'si:] vt следи́ть (impf) за +instr

overshadow [əuvə'ʃædəu] vt (place, building etc) возвыша́ться (impf) над +instr; (fig) затмева́ть (затми́ть pf)

oversight ['əuvəsaɪt] n недосмо́тр

overt [əu'və:t] adj откры́тый

overtake [əuvə'teɪk] (irreg) vt (AUT) обгоня́ть (обогна́ть pf)

overthrow [əuvə'θrəu] (irreg) vt сверга́ть (све́ргнуть pf)

overtime ['əuvətaɪm] n сверхуро́чное вре́мя nt

overture ['əuvətʃuə] n (MUS) увертю́ра; (fig) вступле́ние

overturn [əuvə'tə:n] vt (car, chair) перевора́чивать (переверну́ть pf); (decision, plan) отменя́ть (отмени́ть pf); (government, system) сверга́ть (све́ргнуть pf)

overweight [əuvə'weɪt] adj ту́чный

overwhelm [əuvə'wɛlm] vt (subj: feelings, emotions) переполня́ть (перепо́лнить pf); **~ing** adj (victory, defeat) по́лный; (majority)

подавля́ющий; (feeling, desire) всепобежда́ющий

owe [əu] vt: **she ~s me £500** она́ должна́ мне £500; **he ~s his life to that man** он обя́зан свое́й жи́знью э́тому челове́ку

owing to ['əuɪŋ-] prep всле́дствие +gen

owl [aul] n сова́

own [əun] vt владе́ть (impf) +instr ♦ adj со́бственный; **he lives on his ~** он живёт оди́н; **to get one's ~ back** отыгрыва́ться (отыгра́ться pf); **~ up** vi: **to ~ up to sth** признава́ться (призна́ться pf) в чём-н; **~er** n владе́лец(лица); **~ership** n: **~ership (of)** владе́ние (+instr)

ox [ɔks] (pl **~en**) n бык

oxygen ['ɔksɪdʒən] n кислоро́д

oyster ['ɔɪstə] n у́стрица

oz. abbr = **ounce**

ozone ['əuzəun] n озо́н; **~ hole** n озо́новая дыра́

P, p

p abbr (BRIT) = **penny**, **pence**

PA n abbr (= personal assistant) рефере́нт, ли́чный секрета́рь m

pa [pɑ:] n (inf) па́па m

p.a. abbr = **per annum**

pace [peɪs] n (step) шаг; (speed) темп ♦ vi: **to ~ up and down** ходи́ть (impf) взад вперёд; **to keep ~ with** идти́ (impf) в но́гу с +instr; **~maker** n (MED) ритмиза́тор се́рдца

Pacific [pə'sɪfɪk] n: **the ~ (Ocean)** Ти́хий океа́н

pacifist ['pæsɪfɪst] n пацифи́ст(ка)

pack [pæk] n (packet) па́чка; (of wolves) ста́я; (also: **~back**) рюкза́к; (of cards) коло́да ♦ vt (fill) накова́ть (упакова́ть pf);

(*cram*): **to ~ into** набива́ть (наби́ть *pf*) в +*acc* ♦ *vi*: **to ~ (one's bags)** укла́дываться (уложи́ться *pf*)

package ['pækɪdʒ] *n* паке́т; (*also:* **~ deal** (*COMM*)) паке́т предложе́ний; **~ holiday** *n* (*BRIT*) организо́ванный о́тдых по путёвке

packet ['pækɪt] *n* (*of cigarettes etc*) па́чка; (*of crisps*) паке́т

packing ['pækɪŋ] *n* прокла́дочный материа́л; (*act*) упако́вка

pact [pækt] *n* пакт

pad [pæd] *n* (*of paper*) блокно́т; (*soft material*) прокла́дка ♦ *vt* (*cushion, soft toy etc*) набива́ть (наби́ть *pf*)

paddle ['pædl] *n* (*oar*) байда́рочное весло́; (*US: bat*) раке́тка ♦ *vt* управля́ть (*impf*) +*instr* ♦ *vi* (*in sea*) шлёпать (*impf*)

paddock ['pædək] *n* (*field*) вы́гон

padlock ['pædlɔk] *n* (*висячий*) замо́к

paedophile ['pi:dəufaɪl] (*US* **pedophile**) *n* педофи́л

pagan ['peɪgən] *adj* язы́ческий

page [peɪdʒ] *n* страни́ца; (*also:* **~boy**) паж ♦ *vt* (*in hotel etc*) вызыва́ть (вы́звать *pf*) (по селе́ктору)

paid [peɪd] *pt, pp* of **pay**

pain [peɪn] *n* боль *f*; **to be in ~** страда́ть (*impf*) от бо́ли; **to take ~s to do** стара́ться (постара́ться *pf*) изо всех сил +*infin*; **~ful** *adj* мучи́тельный; **my back is ~ful** у меня́ боли́т спина́; **~fully** *adv* (*fig: very*) глубоко́; (*: aware, familiar*) бо́льно; **~killer** *n* болеутоля́ющее сре́дство (сре́дство); **~less** *adj* безболе́зненный; **~staking** *adj* кропотли́вый

paint [peɪnt] *n* кра́ска ♦ *vt* кра́сить

(покра́сить *pf*); (*picture, portrait*) рисова́ть (нарисова́ть *pf*), писа́ть (написа́ть *pf*); **to ~ the door blue** кра́сить (покра́сить *pf*) дверь в голубо́й цвет; **~er** *n* (*artist*) худо́жник(ица); (*decorator*) маля́р; **~ing** *n* карти́на; (*activity: of artist*) жи́вопись *f*; (*: of decorator*) маля́рное де́ло; **~work** *n* кра́ска

pair [pɛə] *n* па́ра

pajamas [pə'dʒɑ:məz] *npl* (*US*) пижа́ма *fsg*

pal [pæl] *n* (*inf*) дружо́к

palace ['pæləs] *n* дворе́ц

pale [peɪl] *adj* бле́дный

Palestine ['pælɪstaɪn] *n* Палести́на

pallet ['pælɪt] *n* (*for goods etc*) поддо́н

palm [pɑ:m] *n* (*also:* **~ tree**) па́льма; (*of hand*) ладо́нь *f* ♦ *vt*: **to ~ sth off on sb** (*inf*) подсо́вывать (подсу́нуть *pf*) что-н кому́-н

palpable ['pælpəbl] *adj* ощути́мый

pamphlet ['pæmflət] *n* брошю́ра; (*political, literary etc*) памфле́т

pan [pæn] *n* (*also:* **~ sauce-**) кастрю́ля; (*also:* **frying ~**) сковорода́

pancake ['pænkeɪk] *n* (*thin*) блин; (*thick*) ола́дья

panda ['pændə] *n* па́нда, бамбу́ковый медве́дь *m*

pane [peɪn] *n*: **~ (of glass)** (*in window*) око́нное стекло́

panel ['pænl] *n* (*of wood, glass etc*) пане́ль *f*; (*of experts*) коми́ссия; **~ of judges** жюри́ *nt ind*; **~ling** (*US* **~ing**) *n* деревя́нная обши́вка

pang [pæŋ] *n* (*of jealousy*) уко́л; **~s of conscience** упрёки со́вести; **~s of regret** му́ки сожале́ния; **hunger ~s** голо́дные бо́ли

panic ['pænɪk] *n* па́ника ♦ *vi* паникова́ть (*impf*)

panorama [pænəˈrɑːmə] *n* панора́ма

pansy [ˈpænzɪ] *n* аню́тины гла́зки *pl*

panther [ˈpænθər] *n* панте́ра

pantihose [ˈpæntɪhəuz] *npl* (*US*) колго́тки *pl*

> **pantomime** – рождественское представле́ние. Коме́дии с бога́тым музыка́льным оформле́нием, напи́санные по моти́вам изве́стных ска́зок, таки́х как "Зо́лушка", "Кот в сапога́х" и др. Они́ предназна́чены гла́вным о́бразом для дете́й. Теа́тры ста́вят их в Рождество́.

pants [pænts] *npl* (*BRIT: underwear*) трусы́ *pl*; (*US: trousers*) брю́ки *pl*

paper [ˈpeɪpər] *n* бума́га; (*also:* **news~**) газе́та; (*exam*) пи́сьменный экза́мен; (*essay: at conference*) докла́д; (: *in journal*) статья́; (*also:* **wall~**) обо́и *pl* ♦ *adj* бума́жный ♦ *vt* окле́ивать (окле́ить *pf*) обо́ями; **~s** *npl* (*also:* **identity ~s**) докуме́нты *mpl*; **~back** *n* кни́га в мя́гкой обло́жке; **~clip** *n* (канцеля́рская) скре́пка; **~work** *n* бума́жная воло́кита

papier-mâché [ˈpæpjeɪˈmæʃeɪ] *n* папье́-маше́ *nt ind*

paprika [ˈpæprɪkə] *n* кра́сный мо́лотый пе́рец

par [pɑː] *n*: **to be on a ~ with** быть (*impf*) на ра́вных *c* +*instr*

parachute [ˈpærəʃuːt] *n* парашю́т

parade [pəˈreɪd] *n* ше́ствие; (*MIL*) пара́д ♦ *vi* (*MIL*) идти́ (*impf*) стро́ем

paradise [ˈpærədaɪs] *n* (*also fig*) рай

paradox [ˈpærədɔks] *n* парадо́кс; **~ically** [pærəˈdɔksɪklɪ] *adv* как э́то ни парадокса́льно

paraffin [ˈpærəfɪn] *n* (*BRIT: also:* **~ oil**) кероси́н

paragraph [ˈpærəɡrɑːf] *n* абза́ц

parallel [ˈpærəlel] *adj* паралле́льный; (*fig: similar*) аналоги́чный ♦ *n* паралле́ль *f*

paralyse [ˈpærəlaɪz] *vt* (*BRIT: also fig*) парализова́ть (*impf/pf*); **he is ~d** он парализо́ван

paralysis [pəˈrælɪsɪs] *n* (*MED*) парали́ч

paramilitary [pærəˈmɪlɪtərɪ] *adj* военизи́рованный

paramount [ˈpærəmaunt] *adj* первостепе́нный

paranoia [pærəˈnɔɪə] *n* парано́йя

paranoid [ˈpærənɔɪd] *adj* (*person*) парано́идный

paraphrase [ˈpærəfreɪz] *vt* перефрази́ровать (*impf/pf*)

parasite [ˈpærəsaɪt] *n* парази́т

parcel [ˈpɑːsl] *n* (*package*) свёрток; (*sent by post*) посы́лка

pardon [ˈpɑːdn] *n* (*LAW*) поми́лование ♦ *vt* (*LAW*) ми́ловать (поми́ловать *pf*); **~ me!, I beg your ~!** прошу́ проще́ния!; (**I beg your**) **~?**, (*US*) **~ me?** (*what did you say?*) прости́те, не расслы́шал

parent [ˈpɛərənt] *n* роди́тель(ница) *m(f)*; **~s** *npl* (*mother and father*) роди́тели *mpl*; **~al** [pəˈrentl] *adj* роди́тельский

parenthesis [pəˈrenθɪsɪs] (*pl* **parentheses**) *n* (*phrase*) вво́дное предложе́ние

Paris [ˈpærɪs] *n* Пари́ж

parish [ˈpærɪʃ] *n* (*REL*) прихо́д

parity [ˈpærɪtɪ] *n* (*of pay etc*) парите́т

park [pɑːk] *n* парк ♦ *vt* ста́вить (поста́вить *pf*), паркова́ть

(припаркова́ть pf) ♦ vi
парко́ваться (припаркова́ться pf)

parking ['pɑːkɪŋ] n (of vehicle)
парко́вка; (space to park) стоя́нка;
"no ~" "стоя́нка запрещена́"; **~ lot** n (US) (авто)стоя́нка

parliament ['pɑːləmənt] n
парла́мент; **~ary** [pɑːlə'mentərɪ] adj парла́ментский

parody ['pærədɪ] n паро́дия

parole [pə'rəʊl] n: **he was released on ~** (LAW) он был освобождён под че́стное сло́во

parrot ['pærət] n попуга́й

parry ['pærɪ] vt (blow) отража́ть (отрази́ть pf)

parsley ['pɑːslɪ] n петру́шка

parsnip ['pɑːsnɪp] n пастерна́к (посевно́й)

part [pɑːt] n (section, division) часть f; (component) дета́ль f; (role) роль f; (episode) се́рия; (US: in hair) пробо́р ♦ adv = **partly** ♦ vt разделя́ть (раздели́ть pf); (hair) расчёсывать (расчеса́ть pf) на пробо́р ♦ vi (people) расстава́ться (расста́ться pf); (crowd) расступа́ться (расступи́ться pf); **to take ~ in** принима́ть (приня́ть pf) уча́стие в +prp; **to take sb's ~** (support) станови́ться (стать pf) на чью-н. сто́рону; **for my ~** с мое́й стороны́; **for the most ~** бо́льшей ча́стью; **~ with** vt fus расстава́ться (расста́ться pf) с +instr

partial ['pɑːʃl] adj (incomplete) части́чный; **I am ~ to chocolate** (like) у меня́ пристра́стие к шокола́ду

participant [pɑː'tɪsɪpənt] n уча́стник(ица)

participate [pɑː'tɪsɪpeɪt] vi: **to ~ in** уча́ствовать (impf) в +prp

participation [pɑːtɪsɪ'peɪʃən] n уча́стие

particle ['pɑːtɪkl] n части́ца

particular [pə'tɪkjulə°] adj (distinct, special) осо́бый; (fussy) приве́редливый; **~s** npl (personal details) да́нные pl adj; **in ~** в ча́стности; **~ly** adv осо́бенно

parting ['pɑːtɪŋ] n разделе́ние; (farewell) проща́ние; (BRIT: in hair) пробо́р ♦ adj проща́льный

partisan [pɑːtɪ'zæn] adj (politics) пристра́стный; (views) пы́лкий ♦ n (supporter) приве́рженец

partition [pɑː'tɪʃən] n (wall, screen) перегоро́дка

partly ['pɑːtlɪ] adv части́чно

partner ['pɑːtnə°] n партнёр(ша); (spouse) супру́г(а); (COMM, SPORT, CARDS) партнёр; **~ship** n (COMM, company) това́рищество; (: with person) партнёрство; (POL) сою́з

part-time ['pɑːt'taɪm] adj (work) почасово́й; (: staff) на почасово́й ста́вке ♦ adv: **to work ~** быть (impf) на почасово́й ста́вке; **to study ~** обуча́ться (impf) по неполно́й програ́мме

party ['pɑːtɪ] n па́ртия; (celebration: formal) ве́чер; (: informal) вечери́нка; (group: rescue) отря́д; (: of tourists etc) гру́ппа ♦ cpd (POL) парти́йный; **birthday ~** пра́зднование дня рожде́ния, день рожде́ния

pass [pɑːs] vt (time) проводи́ть (провести́ pf); (hand over) передава́ть (переда́ть pf); (go past: on foot) проходи́ть (пройти́ pf); (: by transport) проезжа́ть (прое́хать pf); (overtake: vehicle) обгоня́ть (обогна́ть pf); (exam) сдава́ть (сдать pf); (law, proposal) принима́ть (приня́ть pf) ♦ vi (go past: on foot) проходи́ть (пройти́ pf); (: by transport) проезжа́ть (прое́хать pf); (in exam) сдава́ть (сдать pf) экза́мен ♦ n (permit) про́пуск; (GEO) перева́л; (SPORT) пас, переда́ча; (SCOL: also: ~ **mark**): **to get a ~** получа́ть (получи́ть pf) зачёт; **~ by** vi (on foot) проходи́ть (пройти́ pf); (by transport) проезжа́ть (прое́хать pf); **~ on** vt передава́ть (переда́ть pf)

passage ['pæsɪdʒ] n (also ANAT) прохо́д; (in book) отры́вок; (journey) путеше́ствие

passenger ['pæsɪndʒə*] n пассажи́р(ка)

passer-by [pɑːsə'baɪ] (pl **passers-by**) n прохо́жий(ая) m(f) adj

passing ['pɑːsɪŋ] adj мимолётный ♦ n: **in ~** мимохо́дом

passion ['pæʃən] n страсть f; **~ate** adj стра́стный

passive ['pæsɪv] adj пасси́вный

passport ['pɑːspɔːt] n па́спорт

password ['pɑːswɜːd] n паро́ль m

past [pɑːst] prep ми́мо +gen; (beyond) за +instr; (later than) по́сле +gen ♦ adj (government etc) пре́жний; (week, month etc) про́шлый ♦ n (also LING): **the ~ (tense)** проше́дшее вре́мя ♦ adv: **to run ~** пробега́ть (пробежа́ть pf) ми́мо; **ten/quarter ~ eight** де́сять мину́т/че́тверть девя́того; **for the ~ few days** за после́дние не́сколько дней

pasta ['pæstə] n макаро́нные изде́лия ntpl

paste [peɪst] n (wet mixture) па́ста; (glue) клейстер; (CULIN) паште́т ♦ vt (paper etc) наноси́ть (нанести́ pf) клей на +acc

pastel ['pæstl] adj пасте́льный

pastime ['pɑːstaɪm] n времяпрепровожде́ние

pastoral ['pɑːstərl] adj (REL) па́сторский

pastry ['peɪstrɪ] n (dough) те́сто

pasture ['pɑːstʃə*] n па́стбище

pat [pæt] vt (dog) ласка́ть (приласка́ть pf) ♦ n: **to give sb/ o.s. a ~ on the back** (fig) хвали́ть (похвали́ть pf) кого́-н/себя́

patch [pætʃ] n (of material) запла́та; (eye ~) повя́зка; (area) пятно́; (repair) запла́та ♦ vt (clothes) лата́ть (залата́ть pf); **to go through a bad ~** пережива́ть (impf) тру́дные времена́; **bald ~** лы́сина; **~work** n (SEWING) лоску́тная рабо́та; **~y** adj (colour) пятни́стый; (information, knowledge etc) отры́вочный

pâté ['pæteɪ] n (CULIN) паште́т

patent ['peɪtnt] n пате́нт ♦ vt (COMM) патентова́ть (запатентова́ть pf)

paternal [pə'tɜːnl] adj (love, duty) отцо́вский

path [pɑːθ] n (trail, track) тропа́, тропи́нка; (concrete, gravel etc) доро́жка; (trajectory) путь m движе́ния

pathetic [pə'θetɪk] adj жа́лостный; (very bad) жа́лкий

pathological [pæθə'lɒdʒɪkl] adj (liar, hatred) патологи́ческий

pathology [pə'θɒlədʒɪ] n патоло́гия

patience ['peɪʃns] n (quality) терпе́ние

patient ['peɪʃnt] n пацие́нт(ка) ♦ adj терпели́вый

patio ['pætɪəu] n па́тио m ind, вну́тренний дво́рик

patriot ['peɪtrɪət] n патрио́т(ка); **~ic** [pætrɪ'ɒtɪk] adj патриоти́чный; (song etc) патриоти́ческий; **~ism** n патриоти́зм

patrol [pə'trəul] n патру́ль m ♦ vt патрули́ровать (impf)

patron ['peɪtrən] n (client) (постоя́нный) клие́нт; (benefactor: of charity) шеф, покрови́тель m; **~ of the arts** покрови́тель(ница) *m(f)* искусств; **~age** *n (of charity)* шéфство, покрови́тельство; **~ize** ['pætrənaiz] *vt (pej: look down on)* трети́ровать *(impf)*; **~ saint** *n (REL)* засту́пник(ица)

pattern ['pætən] *n (design)* узóр; *(SEWING)* выкрóйка

pause [pɔːz] *n* переры́в; *(in speech)* пáуза ♦ *vi* дéлать (сдéлать *pf)* переры́в; *(in speech)* дéлать (сдéлать *pf)* пáузу

pave [peɪv] *vt* мости́ть (вы́мостить *pf)*; **to ~ the way for** *(fig)* прокла́дывать (проложи́ть *pf)* путь для +*gen*; **~ment** *n (BRIT)* тротуáр

pavilion [pə'vɪlɪən] *n (SPORT)* павильóн

paw [pɔː] *n (of animal)* лáпа

pawn [pɔːn] *n (CHESS, fig)* пéшка ♦ *vt* закла́дывать (заложи́ть *pf)*; **~broker** *n* ростóвщик(ица)

pay [peɪ] *(pt, pp* **paid)** *n* зарплáта ♦ *vt (sum of money, wage)* плати́ть (заплати́ть *pf)*; *(debt, bill)* плати́ть (уплати́ть *pf)* ♦ *vi (be profitable)* окупáться (окупи́ться *pf)*; **to ~ attention to** обращáть (обрати́ть *pf)* внимáние (на +*acc*); **to ~ sb a visit** наноси́ть (нанести́ *pf)* комý-н визи́т; **~ back** *vt* возвращáть (возврати́ть *pf)*; *(person)* отпла́чивать (отплати́ть *pf)*; **~ for** *vt fus* плати́ть (заплати́ть *pf)* за +*acc*; *(fig)* поплáтиться (*pf)* за +*acc*; **~ in** *vt* вноси́ть (внести́ *pf)*; **~ off** *vt (debt)* выпла́чивать (вы́платить *pf)*; *(creditor)* расплáчиваться (расплати́ться *pf)* с +*instr*; *(person)* расплáчивать ♦ *vi* окупáться (окупи́ться *pf)*; **~ up** *vi* расплáчиваться (расплати́ться *pf)* (сполнá); **~able** *adj (cheque)*: **~able to** подлежáщий уплáте на

и́мя +*gen*; **~ment** *n (act)* платёж, уплáта; *(amount)* вы́плата

PC *n abbr* = **personal computer** ПК; *(BRIT)* = **police constable**; = **politically correct**

pc *abbr* = **per cent**

pea [piː] *n (BOT, CULIN)* горóх *m no pl*

peace [piːs] *n (not war)* мир; *(calm)* покóй; **~ful** *adj (calm)* ми́рный

peach [piːtʃ] *n* пéрсик

peacock ['piːkɔk] *n* павли́н

peak [piːk] *n* верши́на, пик; *(of cap)* козырёк

peanut ['piːnʌt] *n* арáхис

pear [pɛə] *n* грýша

pearl [pɜːl] *n* жемчýжина, **~s** жéмчуг

peasant ['pɛznt] *n* крестья́нин(ка)

peat [piːt] *n* торф

pebble ['pɛbl] *n* гáлька *no pl*

peck [pɛk] *vt (subj: bird)* клевáть *(impf)*; *(: once)* клю́нуть *(pf)* ♦ *n (kiss)* поцелýй

peculiar [pɪ'kjuːlɪə] *adj (strange)* своеобрáзный; *(unique)*: **~ to** свóйственный +*dat*

pedal ['pɛdl] *n* педáль *f* ♦ *vi* крути́ть *(impf)* педáли

pedantic [pɪ'dæntɪk] *adj* педанти́чный

pedestal ['pɛdəstl] *n* пьедестáл

pedestrian [pɪ'dɛstrɪən] *n* пешехóд

pedigree ['pɛdɪgriː] *n* родослóвная *f adj* ♦ *cpd* порóдистый

pedophile ['piːdəʊfaɪl] *n (US)* = **paedophile**

pee [piː] *vi (inf)* пи́сать (попи́сать *pf)*

peel [piːl] *n* кожурá ♦ *vt (vegetables, fruit)* чи́стить (почи́стить *pf)* ♦ *vi (paint)* лупи́ться (облупи́ться *pf)*; *(wallpaper)* отставáть (отстáть *pf)*; *(skin)* шелуши́ться *(impf)*

peep [piːp] *n (look)* взгляд

укра́дкой ♦ *vi* взгля́дывать
(взгляну́ть *pf*)

peer [pɪəʳ] *n* (*BRIT*: *noble*) пэр;
(*equal*) ро́вня *m/f*; (*contemporary*)
рове́сник(ица) ♦ *vi*: **to ~ at**
всма́триваться (всмотре́ться *pf*)
в +*acc*

peg [peg] *n* (*for coat rack*) крючо́к;
(*BRIT*: *also*: **clothes ~**) прище́пка

pejorative [pɪ'dʒɔrətɪv] *adj*
уничижи́тельный

pelvis ['pelvɪs] *n* таз

pen [pen] *n* ру́чка; (*felt-tip*)
флома́стер; (*enclosure*) заго́н

penal ['piːnl] *adj* (*colony, institution*)
исправи́тельный; (*system*)
кара́тельный; **~ code** уголо́вный
ко́декс; **~ize** *vt* нака́зывать
(наказа́ть *pf*); (*SPORT*)
штрафова́ть (оштрафова́ть *pf*)

penalty ['penltɪ] *n* наказа́ние;
(*fine*) штраф; (*SPORT*) пена́льти *m*
ind

pence [pens] *npl of* **penny**

pencil ['pensl] *n* каранда́ш

pending ['pendɪŋ] *prep* впредь до
+*gen*, в ожида́нии +*gen* ♦ *adj*
(*lawsuit, exam etc*) предстоя́щий

pendulum ['pendjuləm] *n* ма́ятник

penetrate ['penɪtreɪt] *vt* (*subj*:
person, light) проника́ть
(прони́кнуть *pf*) в +*acc*

penetration [penɪ'treɪʃən] *n*
проникнове́ние

penguin ['pengwɪn] *n* пингви́н

penicillin [penɪ'sɪlɪn] *n*
пеницилли́н

peninsula [pə'nɪnsjulə] *n*
полуо́стров

penis ['piːnɪs] *n* пе́нис, половой
член

penknife ['pennaɪf] *n* перочи́нный
нож

penniless ['penɪlɪs] *adj* без гроша́

penny ['penɪ] (*pl* **pennies** *or* (*BRIT*)
pence) *n* (*BRIT*) пе́нни *nt ind*, пенс

pension ['penʃən] *n* пе́нсия; **~er** (*BRIT*: *also*: **old age ~er**)
пенсионе́р(ка)

pentagon ['pentəgən] *n* (*US*): **the
Pentagon** Пентаго́н

pent-up ['pentʌp] *adj* зада́вленный

penultimate [pe'nʌltɪmət] *adj*
предпосле́дний

people ['piːpl] *npl* (*persons*) лю́ди
pl; (*nation, race*) наро́д; **several ~
came** пришло́ не́сколько
челове́к; **~ say that ...** говоря́т,
что ...

pepper ['pepəʳ] *n* пе́рец ♦ *vt* (*fig*):
to ~ with забра́сывать
(заброса́ть *pf*) +*instr*; **~mint** *n*
(*sweet*) мя́тная конфе́та

per [pəːʳ] *prep* (*of amounts*) на +*acc*;
(*of price*) за +*acc*; (*of charge*) с +*gen*;
~ annum/day в год/день; **~
person** на челове́ка

perceive [pə'siːv] *vt* (*realize*)
осознава́ть (осозна́ть *pf*)

per cent *n* проце́нт

percentage [pə'sentɪdʒ] *n* проце́нт

perception [pə'sepʃən] *n* (*insight*)
понима́ние

perceptive [pə'septɪv] *adj*
проница́тельный

perch [pəːtʃ] *vi*: **to ~ (on)** (*bird*)
сади́ться (сесть *pf*) (на +*acc*);
(*person*) присе́живаться
(присе́сть *pf*) (на +*acc*)

percolator ['pəːkəleɪtəʳ] *n* (*also*:
coffee ~) кофева́рка

percussion [pə'kʌʃən] *n* уда́рные
инструме́нты *mpl*

perennial [pə'renɪəl] *adj* (*fig*)
ве́чный

perfect *adj* ['pəːfɪkt] *vb* [pə'fekt] *adj*
соверше́нный, безупре́чный;
(*weather*) прекра́сный; (*utter*:
nonsense etc) соверше́нный ♦ *vt*
(*technique*) соверше́нствовать
(усоверше́нствовать *pf*); **~ion**
[pə'fekʃən] *n* соверше́нство;

~ionist [pə'fekʃənist] n
взыскательный человек; **~ly**
['pə:fiktli] adv (well, all right)
вполне

perform [pə'fɔ:m] vt (task,
operation) выполнять (выполнить
pf); (piece of music) исполнять
(исполнить pf), (play) играть
(сыграть pf) ♦ vi (well, badly)
справляться (справиться pf);
~ance n (of actor, athlete etc)
выступление; (of musical work)
исполнение; (of play, show)
представление; (of car, engine,
company) работа; **~er** n
исполнитель(ница) m(f)

perfume ['pə:fju:m] n духи pl

perhaps [pə'hæps] adv может
быть, возможно

peril ['peril] n опасность f

perimeter [pə'rimitə'] n периметр

period ['piəriəd] n (length of time)
период; (SCOL) урок; (esp US: full
stop) точка; (MED) менструация
♦ adj (costume, furniture)
старинный; **~ic** [piəri'ɔdik] adj
периодический; **~ical** [piəri'ɔdikl]
n (magazine) периодическое
издание ♦ adj периодический

periphery [pə'rifəri] n периферия

perish ['periʃ] vi (person) погибать
(погибнуть pf)

perk [pə:k] n (inf)
дополнительное преимущество

perm [pə:m] n перманент,
химическая завивка

permanent ['pə:mənənt] adj
постоянный; (dye, ink) стойкий

permissible [pə'misibl] adj
допустимый, позволительный

permission [pə'miʃən] n
позволение, разрешение

permit vb [pə'mit] n ['pə:mit] vt
позволять (позволить pf) ♦ n
разрешение

perpetual [pə'petjuəl] adj (motion,

questions) вечный; (darkness, noise)
постоянный

persecute ['pə:sikju:t] vt
преследовать (impf)

persecution [pə:si'kju:ʃən] n
преследование

perseverance [pə:si'viərns] n
настойчивость f

persevere [pə:si'viə'] vi
упорствовать (impf)

persist [pə'sist] vi: **to ~ (in doing)**
настаивать (настоять pf) (на том,
чтобы +infin); **~ence** n упорство;
~ent adj непрекращающийся;
(smell) стойкий; (person) упорный

person ['pə:sn] n человек; **in ~**
лично; **~al** adj личный; **~al**
computer n персональный
компьютер; **~ality** [pə:sə'næliti] n
характер; (famous person)
знаменитость f; **~ally** adv лично;
to take sth ~ally принимать
(принять pf) что-н на свой счёт

personnel [pə:sə'nel] n персонал,
штат; (MIL) личный состав

perspective [pə'spektiv] n (ARCHIT,
ART) перспектива; (way of
thinking) видение; **to get sth into**
~ (fig) смотреть (посмотреть pf)
на что-н в истинном свете

perspiration [pə:spi'reiʃən] n пот

persuade [pə'sweid] vt: **to ~ sb to**
do убеждать (убедить pf) or
уговаривать (уговорить pf)
кого-н +infin

persuasion [pə'sweiʒən] n
убеждение

persuasive [pə'sweisiv] adj
(argument) убедительный;
(person) настойчивый

pertinent ['pə:tinənt] adj уместный

Peru [pə'ru:] n Перу f ind

perverse [pə'və:s] adj (contrary)
вредный

perversion [pə'və:ʃən] n
извращение

pervert vb [pə'vɜːt] vt [pə'vɜːt] vt (person, mind) развраща́ть (разврати́ть pf), растлева́ть (растли́ть pf); (truth, sb's words) извраща́ть (изврати́ть pf) ♦ n (also: **sexual ~**) (полово́й) извраще́нец

pessimism ['pesɪmɪzəm] n пессими́зм

pessimistic [pesɪ'mɪstɪk] adj пессимисти́чный

pest [pest] n (insect) вреди́тель m; (fig: nuisance) зану́да m/f

pester ['pestə] vt пристава́ть (приста́ть pf) к +dat

pesticide ['pestɪsaɪd] n пестици́д

pet [pet] n дома́шнее живо́тное nt adj

petal ['petl] n лепесто́к

petite [pə'tiːt] adj миниатю́рный

petition [pə'tɪʃən] n (signed document) пети́ция

petrified ['petrɪfaɪd] adj (fig) оцепене́вший; **I was ~** я оцепене́л

petrol ['petrəl] (BRIT) n бензи́н

petroleum [pə'trəulɪəm] n нефть f

petty ['petɪ] adj (trivial) ме́лкий; (small-minded) ограни́ченный

pew [pjuː] n скамья́ (в це́ркви)

phantom ['fæntəm] n (ghost) фанто́м

pharmaceutical [fɑːmə'sjuːtɪkl] adj фармацевти́ческий

pharmacist ['fɑːməsɪst] n фармаце́вт

pharmacy ['fɑːməsɪ] n (shop) апте́ка

phase [feɪz] n фа́за ♦ vt: **to ~ sth in** поэта́пно вводи́ть (ввести́ pf) что-н; **to ~ sth out** поэта́пно ликвиди́ровать (impf/pf) что-н

PhD n abbr (= Doctor of Philosophy) до́ктор филосо́фии

pheasant ['feznt] n фаза́н

phenomena [fɪ'nɔmɪnə] npl of **phenomenon**

phenomenal [fɪ'nɔmɪnl] adj феномена́льный

phenomenon [fɪ'nɔmɪnən] (pl **phenomena**) n явле́ние, феноме́н

philosopher [fɪ'lɔsəfə] n фило́соф

philosophical [fɪlə'sɔfɪkl] adj филосо́фский

philosophy [fɪ'lɔsəfɪ] n филосо́фия

phobia ['fəubjə] n фо́бия, страх

phone [fəun] n телефо́н ♦ vi звони́ть (позвони́ть pf) +dat; **to be on the ~** говори́ть (impf) по телефо́ну; (possess phone) име́ть (impf) телефо́н; **~ back** vt перезва́нивать (перезвони́ть pf) +dat ♦ vi перезва́нивать (перезвони́ть pf); **~ up** vt звони́ть (позвони́ть pf) +dat; **~ book** n телефо́нная кни́га; **~ box** n (BRIT) телефо́нная бу́дка; **~ call** n телефо́нный звоно́к; **~ card** n телефо́нная ка́рта

phonetics [fə'netɪks] n фоне́тика

phoney ['fəunɪ] adj фальши́вый

photo ['fəutəu] n фотогра́фия; **~copier** ['fəutəukɔpɪə] n (machine) ксе́рокс, копирова́льная маши́на; **~copy** n ксероко́пия, фотоко́пия ♦ vt фотокопи́ровать (сфотокопи́ровать pf), ксероко́пировать (impf/pf); **~genic** [fəutəu'dʒenɪk] adj фотогени́чный; **~graph** n фотогра́фия ♦ vt фотографи́ровать (сфотографи́ровать pf); **~grapher** [fə'tɔgrəfə] n фото́граф; **~graphy** [fə'tɔgrəfɪ] n фотогра́фия

phrase [freɪz] n фра́за ♦ vt формули́ровать (сформули́ровать pf)

physical ['fɪzɪkl] adj физи́ческий;

(world, object) материа́льный; **~ly** adv физи́чески

physician [fɪ'zɪʃən] n (esp US) врач

physicist ['fɪzɪsɪst] n фи́зик

physics ['fɪzɪks] n фи́зика

physiotherapy [fɪzɪəʊ'θerəpɪ] n физиотерапи́я

physique [fɪ'ziːk] n (of person) телосложе́ние

pianist ['pɪənɪst] n пиани́ст(ка)

piano [pɪ'ænəʊ] n пиани́но, фортепья́но nt ind

pick [pɪk] n (also: **~axe**) кирка́ ♦ vt (select) выбира́ть (вы́брать pf); (gather: fruit, flowers) собира́ть (собра́ть pf); (remove) рвать (impf); (lock) взла́мывать (взлома́ть pf); **take your ~** выбира́йте; **to ~ one's nose/teeth** ковыря́ть (impf) в носу́/зуба́х; **to ~ a quarrel (with sb)** иска́ть (impf) по́вод для ссо́ры (с кем-н); **~ out** vt (distinguish) разгляде́ть (pf); (select) отбира́ть (отобра́ть pf); **~ up** vi (improve) улучша́ться (улу́чшиться pf) ♦ vt (lift) поднима́ть (подня́ть pf); (arrest) забира́ть (забра́ть pf); (collect: person: by car) заезжа́ть (зае́хать pf) за +instr; (passenger) подбира́ть (подобра́ть pf); (language, skill etc) усва́ивать (усво́ить pf); (RADIO) лови́ть (пойма́ть pf); **to ~ up speed** набира́ть (набра́ть pf) ско́рость; **to ~ o.s. up** (after falling) поднима́ться (подня́ться pf)

picket ['pɪkɪt] n пике́т ♦ vt пикети́ровать (impf)

pickle ['pɪkl] n (also: **~s**) соле́нья ntpl ♦ vt (in vinegar) маринова́ть (замаринова́ть pf); (in salt water) соли́ть (засоли́ть pf)

pickpocket ['pɪkpɔkɪt] n вор-карма́нник

picnic ['pɪknɪk] n пикни́к

picture ['pɪktʃər] n карти́на; (photo) фотогра́фия; (TV) изображе́ние ♦ vt (imagine) рисова́ть (нарисова́ть pf) карти́ну +gen; **the ~s** npl (BRIT : inf) кино́ nt ind

picturesque [pɪktʃə'resk] adj живопи́сный

pie [paɪ] n пиро́г; (small) пирожо́к

piece [piːs] n (portion, part) кусо́к; (component) дета́ль f ♦ vt: **to ~ together** (information) свя́зывать (связа́ть pf); (object) соединя́ть (соедини́ть pf); **a ~ of clothing** вещь f, предме́т оде́жды; **a ~ of advice** сове́т; **to take to ~s** (dismantle) разбира́ть (разобра́ть pf)

pier [pɪər] n пирс

pierce [pɪəs] vt протыка́ть (проткну́ть pf), прока́лывать (проколо́ть pf)

pig [pɪg] n (also fig) свинья́

pigeon ['pɪdʒən] n го́лубь m; **~hole** n (in office, bureau) яче́йка (для корреспонде́нции)

pigment ['pɪgmənt] n пигме́нт

pigtail ['pɪgteɪl] n коси́чка

pike [paɪk] n (fish) щу́ка

pile [paɪl] n (large heap) ку́ча, гру́да; (neat stack) сто́пка; (of carpet) ворс ♦ vi: **to ~ into** (vehicle) набива́ться (наби́ться pf) в +acc; **to ~ out of** (vehicle) выва́ливаться (вы́валиться pf) из +gen; **~ up** vi (objects) сва́ливаться (свали́ть pf) в ку́чу ♦ vi громозди́ться (impf); (problems, work) нака́пливаться (накопи́ться pf)

piles [paɪlz] npl (MED) геморро́й msg

pilgrimage ['pɪlgrɪmɪdʒ] n пало́мничество

pill [pɪl] n табле́тка; **the ~** (contraceptive) противозача́точные pl adj (табле́тки)

pillar ['pɪlər] n (ARCHIT) столб,

колонна

pillow ['pɪləʊ] *n* подушка; **~case** *n* наволочка

pilot ['paɪlət] *n* (AVIAT) пилот, лётчик ♦ *cpd* (*scheme, study etc*) экспериментальный ♦ *vt* (*aircraft*) управлять (*impf*) +instr

pimple ['pɪmpl] *n* прыщ, прыщик

PIN [pɪn] *n* (= *personal identification number*; *also*: **~ number**) персональный идентификационный номер

pin [pɪn] *n* (*for clothes, papers*) булавка ♦ *vt* прикалывать (приколоть *pf*); **~s and needles** (*fig*) колоть; **to ~ sth on sb** (*fig*) возлагать (возложить *pf*) что-н. на кого-н.; **~ down** *vt*: **to ~ sb down** (*fig*) принуждать (принудить *pf*) кого-н.

pinch [pɪntʃ] *n* (*small amount*) щепотка ♦ *vt* щипать (ущипнуть *pf*); (*inf: steal*) стащить (*pf*); **at a ~** = в крайнем случае

pine [paɪn] *n* (*tree, wood*) сосна

pineapple ['paɪnæpl] *n* ананас

pink [pɪŋk] *adj* розовый

pint [paɪnt] *n* пинта

---

pint - пинта. Одна пинта равна 0.568 л.

---

pioneer [paɪə'nɪə*] *n* (*of science, method*) первооткрыватель *m*, новатор

pious ['paɪəs] *adj* набожный

pip [pɪp] *n* (*of grape, melon*) косточка; (*of apple, orange*) зёрнышко

pipe [paɪp] *n* (*for water, gas*) труба; (*for smoking*) трубка ♦ *vt* (*water, gas, oil*) подавать (подать *pf*); **~s** *npl* (*also*: **bag~s**) волынка *fsg*

pirate ['paɪərət] *n* (*sailor*) пират ♦ *vt* (*video tape, cassette*) незаконно распространять

Pisces ['paɪsiːz] *n* Рыбы *fpl*

pistol ['pɪstl] *n* пистолет

pit [pɪt] *n* (*in ground*) яма; (*also*: **coal ~**) шахта; (*quarry*) карьер ♦ *vt*: **to ~ one's wits against sb** состязаться (*impf*) в уме с кем-н.

pitch [pɪtʃ] *n* (BRIT : SPORT) поле; (MUS) высота; (*level*) уровень *m*

pitiful ['pɪtɪful] *adj* жалкий

pitiless ['pɪtɪlɪs] *adj* безжалостный

pity ['pɪtɪ] *n* жалость *f* ♦ *vt* жалеть (пожалеть *pf*)

pivot ['pɪvət] *n* (*fig*) центр

pizza ['piːtsə] *n* пицца

placard ['plækɑːd] *n* плакат

place [pleɪs] *vt* (*put*) помещать (поместить *pf*); (*identify: person*) вспоминать (вспомнить *pf*) ♦ *n* место; (*home*): **at his ~** у него (дома); **to ~ an order with sb for sth** (COMM) заказывать (заказать *pf*) что-н. у кого-н.; **to take ~** происходить (произойти *pf*); **out of ~** (*inappropriate*) неуместный; **in the first ~** (*first of all*) во-первых; **to change ~s with sb** меняться (поменяться *pf*) местами с кем-н.

placid ['plæsɪd] *adj* (*person*) тихий

plague [pleɪg] *n* (MED) чума; (*fig: of locusts etc*) нашествие ♦ *vt* (*subj: problems*) осаждать (осадить *pf*)

plaice [pleɪs] *n inv* камбала

plain [pleɪn] *adj* простой; (*unpatterned*) гладкий; (*clear*) ясный, понятный ♦ *adv* (*wrong, stupid etc*) явно ♦ *n* (GEO) равнина; **~ly** *adv* ясно

plan [plæn] *n* план ♦ *vt* планировать (запланировать *pf*); (*draw up plans for*) планировать (*impf*) ♦ *vi* планировать (*impf*)

plane [pleɪn] *n* (AVIAT) самолёт; (*fig: level*) план

planet ['plænɪt] n планета
plank [plæŋk] n (of wood) доска
planner ['plænər] n (of towns)
планировщик
planning ['plænɪŋ] n (of future,
event) планирование; (also: **town
~**) планировка
plant [plɑːnt] n (BOT) растение;
(factory) завод; (machinery)
установка ♦ vt (seed, garden)
сажать (посадить pf); (field)
засеивать (засеять pf); (bomb,
evidence) подкладывать
(подложить pf); **~ation**
[plænˈteɪʃən] n (of tea, sugar etc)
плантация; (of trees)
лесонасаждение
plaque [plæk] n (on teeth) налёт;
(on building) мемориальная доска
plaster ['plɑːstər] n (for walls)
штукатурка; (also: **~ of Paris**)
гипс; (BRIT: also: **sticking ~**)
пластырь m ♦ vt (wall, ceiling)
штукатурить (оштукатурить pf);
(cover): **to ~ with**
заштукатуривать
(заштукатурить pf) +instr
plastic ['plæstɪk] n пластмасса
♦ adj (made of plastic)
пластмассовый
plate [pleɪt] n (dish) тарелка
plateau ['plætəu] (pl **~s** or **~x**) n
плато nt ind
platform ['plætfɔːm] n (at meeting)
трибуна; (at concert) помост; (for
landing, loading on etc) площадка;
(RAIL, POL) платформа
platonic [pləˈtɔnɪk] adj
платонический
plausible ['plɔːzɪbl] adj
убедительный
play [pleɪ] n пьеса ♦ vt (subj:
children: game) играть (impf) в
+acc; (sport, cards) играть
(сыграть pf) в +acc; (opponent)
играть (сыграть pf) с +instr; (part,

piece of music) играть (сыграть pf);
(instrument) играть (impf) на +prp;
(tape, record) ставить (поставить
pf) ♦ vi играть (impf); **~ down** vt
не заострять (impf) внимание на
+prp; **~er** n (SPORT) игрок; **~ful** adj
(person) игривый; **~ground** n (in
park) детская площадка; (in
school) игровая площадка;
~group n детская группа; **~pen**
n (child's) манеж; **~time** n
(SCOL) перемена; **~wright** n
драматург
plc abbr (BRIT) (= public limited
company) публичная компания с
ограниченной
ответственностью
plea [pliː] n (personal request)
мольба; (public request) призыв;
(LAW) заявление
plead [pliːd] vt (ignorance, ill health
etc) ссылаться (сослаться pf) на
+acc ♦ vi (LAW): **to ~ guilty/not
guilty** признавать (признать pf)
себя виновным(ой)/
невиновным(ой); (beg): **to ~ with
sb** умолять (impf) кого-н
pleasant ['plɛznt] adj приятный
please [pliːz] excl пожалуйста ♦ vt
угождать (угодить pf) +dat; **~
yourself!** (inf) как Вам угодно!;
do as you ~ делайте как хотите;
he is difficult/easy to ~ ему
трудно/легко угодить; **~d** adj: **~d
(with)** довольный (+instr); **~d to
meet you** очень приятно
pleasure ['plɛʒər] n удовольствие;
it's a ~ не стоит; **to take ~ in**
получать (получить pf)
удовольствие от +gen
pleat [pliːt] n складка
pledge [plɛdʒ] n обязательство
♦ vt (money) обязываться
(обязаться pf); (support)
обязываться (обязаться pf)
оказать

plentiful ['plentɪful] adj обильный

plenty ['plentɪ] n (enough) изобилие; ~ of (food, money etc) много +gen; (jobs, people, houses) множество +gen; we've got ~ of time to get there у нас вполне достаточно времени, чтобы туда добраться

pliable ['plaɪəbl] adj (material) гибкий

pliers ['plaɪəz] npl плоскогубцы pl

plight [plaɪt] n муки fpl

plot [plɒt] n (conspiracy) заговор; (of story) сюжет; (of land) участок ♦ vt (plan) замышлять (замыслить impf); (MATH) наносить (нанести pf) ♦ vi (conspire) составлять (составить pf) заговор

plough [plaʊ] (US **plow**) n плуг ♦ vt пахать (вспахать pf)

ploy [plɔɪ] n уловка

pluck [plʌk] vt (eyebrows) выщипывать (выщипать pf); (instrument) перебирать (impf) струны +gen; to ~ up courage набираться (набраться pf) храбрости или мужества

plug [plʌg] n (ELEC) вилка, штепсель m; (in sink, bath) пробка ♦ vt (hole) затыкать (заткнуть pf); (inf: advertise) рекламировать (разрекламировать pf); ~ in vt (ELEC) включать (включить pf) в розетку

plum [plʌm] n слива

plumber ['plʌmə'] n водопроводчик, слесарь-сантехник

plumbing ['plʌmɪŋ] n (piping) водопровод и канализация; (trade, work) слесарное дело

plummet ['plʌmɪt] vi: to ~ (down) (price, amount) резко падать (упасть pf)

plump [plʌmp] adj полный, пухлый ♦ vi: to ~ for (inf) выбирать (выбрать pf)

plunge [plʌndʒ] n (of prices etc) резкое падение ♦ vt (knife) метать (метнуть pf); (hand) выбрасывать (выбросить pf) ♦ vi (fall) рухнуть (pf); (dive) бросаться (броситься pf); (fig: prices etc) резко падать (упасть pf); to take the ~ (fig) отваживаться (отважиться pf)

plural ['pluərl] n множественное число

plus [plʌs] n, adj плюс ind ♦ prep: **ten ~ ten is twenty** десять плюс десять - двадцать; **ten/twenty ~** (more than) десять/двадцать с лишним

plush [plʌʃ] adj шикарный

plutonium [plu:'təunɪəm] n плутоний

plywood ['plaɪwud] n фанера

PM abbr (BRIT) = **Prime Minister**

p.m. adv abbr (= post meridiem) после полудня

pneumonia [nju:'məunɪə] n воспаление лёгких, пневмония

PO Box n abbr (= Post Office Box) абонентский или почтовый ящик

pocket ['pɒkɪt] n карман; (fig: small area) уголок ♦ vt класть (положить pf) себе в карман; **to be out of ~** (BRIT) быть (impf) в убытке

pod [pɒd] n (BOT) стручок

poem ['pəuɪm] n (long) поэма; (short) стихотворение

poet ['pəuɪt] n поэт(есса); ~**ic** [pəu'etɪk] adj поэтический; ~**ry** поэзия

poignant ['pɔɪnjənt] adj пронзительный

point [pɔɪnt] n (of needle, knife etc) остриё, кончик; (purpose) смысл; (significant part) суть f; (particular

position) то́чка; (detail, moment)
моме́нт; (stage in development)
ста́дия; (score) очко́; ♦ vt (show,
mark) ука́зывать (указа́ть pf) ♦ vi:
to ~ at ука́зывать (указа́ть pf) на
+acc; ~s npl (RAIL) стре́лка fsg; to
be on the ~ of doing собира́ться
(impf) +infin; I made a ~ of visiting
him я счёл необходи́мым
посети́ть его́; to get/miss the ~
понима́ть (поня́ть pf)/не
понима́ть (поня́ть pf) суть; to
come to the ~ доходи́ть (дойти́
pf) до су́ти; there's no ~ +infin; to ~ sth at sb
(gun etc) наце́ливать (наце́лить
pf) что-н на кого́-н; ~ out vt
ука́зывать (указа́ть pf) на +acc;
to ~ to vt fus ука́зывать (указа́ть
pf) на +acc; ~-blank adv (refuse)
наотре́з; (say, ask) напрямы́к
♦ adj: at ~-blank range в упо́р;
~ed adj о́стрый; (fig: remark)
язви́тельный; ~less adj
бессмы́сленный; ~ of view n
то́чка зре́ния

poise [pɔɪz] n равнове́сие

poison ['pɔɪzn] n яд ♦ vt отравля́ть
(отрави́ть pf); ~ous adj (toxic)
ядови́тый

poke [pəʊk] vt (with stick etc)
ты́кать (ткнуть pf); to ~ sth in(to)
(put) втыка́ть (воткну́ть pf) что-н
в +acc

poker ['pəʊkə*] n кочерга́; (CARDS)
по́кер

Poland ['pəʊlənd] n По́льша

polar ['pəʊlə*] adj поля́рный; ~
bear n бе́лый медве́дь m

pole [pəʊl] n (stick) шест; (telegraph
pole) столб; (GEO) по́люс; ~ **vault**
n прыжки́ mpl с шесто́м

police [pə'li:s] npl поли́ция fsg; (in
Russia) мили́ция fsg ♦ vt
патрули́ровать (impf); ~**man**

(irreg) n полице́йский m adj; ~
station n полице́йский уча́сток;
(in Russia) отделе́ние мили́ции;
~**woman** (irreg) n
(же́нщина-)полице́йский m adj

policy ['pɔlɪsɪ] n поли́тика; (also:
insurance ~) по́лис

polio ['pəʊlɪəʊ] n полиомиели́т

Polish ['pəʊlɪʃ] adj по́льский

polish ['pɔlɪʃ] n (for furniture)
(полирова́льная) па́ста; (for
shoes) гутали́н; (for floor)
масти́ка; (shine, also fig) лоск ♦ vt
(furniture etc) полирова́ть
(отполирова́ть pf); (floors, shoes)
натира́ть (натере́ть pf); ~**ed** adj
(style) отто́ченный

polite [pə'laɪt] adj ве́жливый

political [pə'lɪtɪkl] adj
полити́ческий; (person)
полити́чески акти́вный,
политизи́рованный; ~**ly** adv
полити́чески; ~**ly correct**
полити́чески корре́ктный

politician [pɔlɪ'tɪʃn] n поли́тик,
полити́ческий де́ятель m

politics ['pɔlɪtɪks] n поли́тика n;
(SCOL) политоло́гия

poll [pəʊl] n (also: **opinion** ~)
опро́с; (usu pl: election) вы́боры
mpl ♦ vt (number of votes)
набира́ть (набра́ть pf)

pollen ['pɔlən] n пыльца́

pollute [pə'lu:t] vt загрязня́ть
(загрязни́ть pf)

pollution [pə'lu:ʃən] n
загрязне́ние; (substances)
загрязни́тель m

polo neck ['pəʊləʊ-] n (also:
sweater or **jumper**) сви́тер с
кру́глым воротнико́м

polyester [pɔlɪ'estə*] n (fabric)
полиэфи́рное волокно́

polystyrene [pɔlɪ'staɪri:n] n
пенопла́ст

polytechnic [pɔlɪ'teknɪk] n (college)

≈ политехни́ческий институ́т

polythene [ˈpɒliθiːn] n полиэтиле́н

pomegranate [ˈpɒmɪɡrænɪt] n (BOT) грана́т

pompous [ˈpɒmpəs] adj (pej: person, style) напы́щенный, чва́нный

pond [pɒnd] n пруд

ponder [ˈpɒndəʳ] vt обду́мывать (обду́мать pf)

pony [ˈpəʊnɪ] n по́ни m ind; **~tail** n (hairstyle) хвост, хво́стик m

poodle [ˈpuːdl] n пу́дель m

pool [puːl] n (in puddle) лу́жа; (pond) пруд; (also: **swimming ~**) бассе́йн; (fig: of light, paint) пятно́; (SPORT, COMM) пул ♦ vt объединя́ть (объедини́ть pf); **~s** npl (also: **football ~s**) футбо́льный тотализа́тор; **typing~**, (US) **secretary ~** машинопи́сное бюро́ nt ind

poor [pʊəʳ] adj (not rich) бе́дный; (bad) плохо́й; **the ~** npl (people) бедно́та fsg, бе́дные pl adj; **in (resources etc)** бе́дный +instr; **~ly** adv пло́хо ♦ adj: **she is feeling ~ly** она́ пло́хо себя́ чу́вствует

pop [pɒp] n (also: **~ music**) поп-му́зыка f; (inf: US: father) па́па m; (sound) хлопо́к ♦ vi ло́паться (ло́пнуть pf) ♦ vt (put quickly): **to ~ sth into/onto** забра́сывать (забро́сить pf) что-н в +acc/на +acc; **~ in** vi загля́дывать (загляну́ть pf), заска́кивать (заскочи́ть pf); **~ up** vi вылеза́ть (вы́лезти pf); **~corn** n возду́шная кукуру́за, попко́рн

pope [pəʊp] n: **the Pope** Па́па m ри́мский

poplar [ˈpɒpləʳ] n то́поль m

poppy [ˈpɒpɪ] n мак

pop star n поп-звезда́ m/f

populace [ˈpɒpjʊləs] n: **the ~** наро́д

popular [ˈpɒpjʊləʳ] adj

популя́рный; **~ity** [pɒpjuˈlærɪtɪ] n популя́рность f

population [pɒpjuˈleɪʃən] n (of town, country) населе́ние

porcelain [ˈpɔːslɪn] n фарфо́р

porch [pɔːtʃ] n крыльцо́; (US) вера́нда

pore [pɔːʳ] n по́ра

pork [pɔːk] n свини́на

porn [pɔːn] n (inf) порногра́фия

pornographic [pɔːnəˈɡræfɪk] adj порнографи́ческий

pornography [pɔːˈnɔɡrəfɪ] n порногра́фия

porpoise [ˈpɔːpəs] n бу́рый дельфи́н

porridge [ˈpɒrɪdʒ] n овся́ная ка́ша

port [pɔːt] n (harbour) порт; (wine) портве́йн; **~ of call** порт захо́да

portable [ˈpɔːtəbl] adj портати́вный

porter [ˈpɔːtəʳ] n (doorkeeper) портье́ m ind, швейца́р; (for luggage) носи́льщик

portfolio [pɔːtˈfəʊlɪəʊ] n (ART) па́пка

portion [ˈpɔːʃən] n (part) часть f; (equal part) до́ля; (of food) по́рция

portrait [ˈpɔːtreɪt] n портре́т

portray [pɔːˈtreɪ] vt изобража́ть (изобрази́ть pf); **~al** n изображе́ние

Portugal [ˈpɔːtjʊɡl] n Португа́лия

Portuguese [pɔːtjuˈɡiːz] adj португа́льский

pose [pəʊz] n по́за ♦ vt (question) ста́вить (поста́вить pf); (problem, danger) создава́ть (созда́ть pf) ♦ vi (pretend): **to ~ as** выдава́ть (вы́дать pf) себя́ за +acc; **to ~ for** пози́ровать (impf) для +gen

posh [pɒʃ] adj (inf: hotel etc) фешене́бельный; (: person, behaviour) великосве́тский

position [pəˈzɪʃən] n положе́ние; (of house, thing) расположе́ние, ме́сто; (job) до́лжность f; (in competition, race) ме́сто; (attitude) пози́ция ♦ vt располага́ть (расположи́ть pf)

positive ['pozɪtɪv] adj (affirmative) положи́тельный; (certain) уве́ренный, убеждённый; (definite: decision, policy) определённый

possess [pə'zɛs] vt владе́ть (impf) +instr; (quality, ability) облада́ть (impf) +instr; **~ion** [pə'zɛʃən] n (state of possessing) владе́ние; **~ions** npl (belongings) ве́щи fpl; **to take ~ion of** вступа́ть (вступи́ть pf) во владе́ние +instr; **~ive** (quality) со́бственнический; (person) ревни́вый; (LING) притяжа́тельный

possibility [posɪ'bɪlɪtɪ] n возмо́жность f

possible ['posɪbl] adj возмо́жный; **it's ~** э́то возмо́жно; **as soon as ~** как мо́жно скоре́е

possibly ['posɪblɪ] adv (perhaps) возмо́жно; **if you ~ can** е́сли то́лько Вы мо́жете; **I cannot ~ come** я никáк не смогу́ прийти́

post [pəust] n (BRIT: mail) по́чта; (pole) столб; (job, situation) пост ♦ vt (BRIT: mail) посыла́ть (посла́ть pf), отправля́ть (отпра́вить pf) (по по́чте); **~age** n почто́вые расхо́ды mpl; **~al** adj почто́вый; **~card** n (почто́вая) откры́тка; **~code** n (BRIT) почто́вый и́ндекс

poster ['pəustər] n афи́ша, плака́т; (for advertising) по́стер

postgraduate ['pəust'grædʒuət] n аспира́нт(ка) ♦ adj: **~ study** аспиранту́ра

posthumous ['pɔstjuməs] adj посме́ртный

postman ['pəustmən] (irreg) n почтальо́н

post office n почто́вое отделе́ние, отделе́ние свя́зи; (organization): **the Post Office** ≈ Министе́рство свя́зи

postpone [pəus'pəun] vt откла́дывать (отложи́ть pf); **~ment** n отсро́чка

postscript ['pəustskrɪpt] n (in letter) постскри́птум

posture ['pɔstʃər] n (of body) оса́нка

postwar [pəust'wɔːr] adj послевое́нный

posy ['pəuzɪ] n буке́тик

pot [pɔt] n (for cooking, flowers) горшо́к; (also: **tea~**) (зава́рочный) ча́йник; (also: **coffee~**) кофе́йник; (bowl, container) ба́нка ♦ vt (plant) сажа́ть (посади́ть pf); **a ~ of tea** ча́йник ча́я

potato [pə'teɪtəu] (pl **~es**) n карто́фель m no pl, карто́шка (разг); (single potato) картофели́на

potent ['pəutnt] adj мо́щный; (drink) кре́пкий

potential [pə'tɛnʃl] adj потенциа́льный ♦ n потенциа́л; **~ly** adv потенциа́льно

pottery ['pɔtərɪ] n кера́мика; (factory) фа́брика керами́ческих изде́лий; (small) керами́ческий цех

potty ['pɔtɪ] adj (inf: mad) чо́кнутый ♦ n (for child) горшо́к

pouch [pautʃ] n (for tobacco) кисе́т; (for coins) кошелёк; (ZOOL) су́мка

poultry ['pəultrɪ] n (birds) дома́шняя пти́ца; (meat) пти́ца

pounce [pauns] vi: **to ~ on** набра́сываться (набро́ситься pf) на +acc

pound [paund] n (money, weight) фунт; **~ sterling** n фунт сте́рлингов

pound - фунт. Ме́ра ве́са ра́вная 0.454 кг.

pour [pɔːʳ] vt (liquid) налива́ть (нали́ть pf); (dry substance) насыпа́ть (насы́пать pf) ♦ vi (water etc) ли́ться (impf); (rain) лить (impf); **to ~ sb some tea** налива́ть (нали́ть pf) кому́-н чай; **~ in** vi (people) вали́ть (повали́ть pf); (news, letters etc) сы́паться (посы́паться pf); **~ out** vi (people) вали́ть (повали́ть pf) ♦ vt (drink) налива́ть (нали́ть pf); (fig: thoughts etc) излива́ть (изли́ть pf)

pout [paut] vi надува́ть (наду́ть pf) гу́бы, ду́ться (impf)

poverty ['pɒvətɪ] n бе́дность f

powder ['paudəʳ] n порошо́к; (also: **face ~**) пу́дра

power ['pauəʳ] n (authority) власть f; (ability, opportunity) возмо́жность f; (legal right) полномо́чие; (of engine) мо́щность f; (electricity) (электро)эне́ргия; **to be in ~** находи́ться (impf) у вла́сти; **~ful** adj могу́чий; (person, organization) могу́щественный; (argument, engine) мо́щный; **~less** adj бесси́льный; **~ station** n электроста́нция

pp abbr = **pages**

PR n abbr = **public relations**

practicable ['præktɪkəbl] adj осуществи́мый

practical ['præktɪkl] adj (not theoretical) практи́ческий; (sensible, viable) практи́чный; (good with hands) уме́лый; **~ity** [præktɪ'kælɪtɪ] n практи́чность f; **~ities** npl (of situation etc) практи́ческая сторона́ fsg; **~ly** adv практи́чески

practice ['præktɪs] n пра́ктика;

(custom) привы́чка ♦ vti (US) = **practise**; **in ~** на пра́ктике; **I am out of ~** я разучи́лся

practise ['præktɪs] (US **practice**) vt (piano etc) упражня́ться (impf) на +acc; (sport, language) отраба́тывать (отрабо́тать pf); (custom) приде́рживаться (impf) +gen; (craft) занима́ться (impf) +instr; (religion) испове́довать (impf) ♦ vi (MUS) упражня́ться (impf); (SPORT) тренирова́ться (impf); (lawyer, doctor) практикова́ть (impf); **to ~ law/ medicine** занима́ться (impf) адвока́тской/враче́бной пра́ктикой

practising ['præktɪsɪŋ] adj (Christian etc) на́божный; (doctor, lawyer) практику́ющий

practitioner [præk'tɪʃənəʳ] n терапе́вт

pragmatic [præg'mætɪk] adj (reason etc) прагмати́ческий

praise [preɪz] n (approval) похвала́ ♦ vt хвали́ть (похвали́ть pf)

pram [præm] n (BRIT) де́тская коля́ска

prawn [prɔːn] n креве́тка

pray [preɪ] vi моли́ться (помоли́ться pf); **to ~ for/that** моли́ться (impf) за +acc/, что́бы; **~er** [preəʳ] n моли́тва

preach [priːtʃ] vi пропове́довать (impf) ♦ vt (sermon) произноси́ть (произнести́ pf) ♦ vi пропове́довать; **~er** n пропове́дник(ица)

precarious [prɪ'kɛərɪəs] adj риско́ванный

precaution [prɪ'kɔːʃən] n предосторо́жность f

precede [prɪ'siːd] vt предше́ствовать (impf) +dat; **~nce** ['prɛsɪdəns] n (priority) первоочере́дность f; **~nt** ['prɛsɪdənt] n прецеде́нт

preceding [prɪ'siːdɪŋ] *adj*
предшествующий

precinct ['priːsɪŋkt] *n* (*US: in city*)
район, префектура; **pedestrian ~**
(*BRIT*) пешеходная зона; **shopping ~** (*BRIT*) торговый центр

precious ['prɛʃəs] *adj* ценный;
(*stone*) драгоценный

precise [prɪ'saɪs] *adj* точный; **~ly**
adv (*accurately*) точно; (*exactly*)
ровно

precision [prɪ'sɪʒən] *n* точность *f*

precocious [prɪ'kəʊʃəs] *adj*: **a ~
child** не по годам развитой
ребёнок

precondition ['priːkən'dɪʃən] *n*
предпосылка

predator ['predətəʳ] *n* хищник

predecessor ['priːdɪsesəʳ] *n*
предшественник(ица)

predicament [prɪ'dɪkəmənt] *n*
затруднительное положение

predict [prɪ'dɪkt] *vt* предсказывать
(предсказать *pf*); **~able** *adj*
предсказуемый; **~ion** [prɪ'dɪkʃən]
n предсказание

predominantly [prɪ'dɒmɪnəntlɪ] *adv*
преимущественно

preface ['prefəs] *n* предисловие

> **prefect** - староста школы.
> Старостами могут быть только
> старшеклассники. Они
> помогают учителям
> поддерживать в школе
> дисциплину.

prefer [prɪ'fɜːʳ] *vt* предпочитать
(предпочесть *pf*); **~able** *adj*
предпочтительный; **~ably** *adv*
предпочтительно; **~ence**
['prefrəns] *n* (*liking*): **to have a
~ence for** предпочитать;
~ential [prefə'renʃəl] *adj*: **~ential
treatment** особое отношение

prefix ['priːfɪks] *n* приставка

pregnancy ['pregnənsɪ] *n*
беременность *f*

pregnant ['pregnənt] *adj*
беременная; (*remark, pause*)
многозначительный; **she is 3
months ~** она на четвёртом
месяце беременности

prehistoric ['priːhɪs'tɒrɪk] *adj*
доисторический

prejudice ['predʒudɪs] *n* (*dislike*)
предрассудок; (*preference*)
предвзятость *f*, предубеждение

preliminary [prɪ'lɪmɪnərɪ] *adj*
предварительный

prelude ['preljuːd] *n* прелюдия

premature ['premətʃuəʳ] *adj*
преждевременный; (*baby*)
недоношенный

premier ['premɪəʳ] *adj* лучший ♦ *n*
премьер(-министр)

première ['premɪeəʳ] *n* премьера

premise ['premɪs] *n* предпосылка;
~s *npl* (*of business*) помещение
ntsg; **on the ~s** в помещении

premium [priːmɪəm] *n* премия; **to
be at a ~** пользоваться (*impf*)
большим спросом

premonition [premə'nɪʃən] *n*
предчувствие

preoccupation [priːɒkjuˈpeɪʃən] *n*:
~ with озабоченность *f* +*instr*

preoccupied [priːˈɒkjupaɪd] *adj*
озабоченный

preparation [prepə'reɪʃən] *n*
(*activity*) подготовка; (*of food*)
приготовление; **~s** *npl*
(*arrangements*) приготовления *ntpl*

preparatory [prɪ'pærətərɪ] *adj*
подготовительный

prepare [prɪ'peəʳ] *vt*
подготавливать (подготовить
pf); (*meal*) готовить (приготовить
pf) ♦ *vi*: **to ~** готовиться
(подготовиться *pf*) к +*dat*; **~d** *adj*
готовый; **~d for** (*ready*) готовый к
+*dat*

preposition [prepə'zɪʃən] n
предло́г

preposterous [prɪ'pɔstərəs] adj
ди́кий

prescribe [prɪ'skraɪb] vt (MED)
пропи́сывать (прописа́ть pf)

prescription [prɪ'skrɪpʃən] n (MED,
slip of paper) реце́пт; (: medicine)
лека́рство (назна́ченное
врачо́м)

presence ['prezns] n прису́тствие;
(fig) нару́жность f; **in sb's** ~ в
прису́тствии кого́-н

present adj, n ['preznt] vb [prɪ'zent]
adj (current) ны́нешний,
настоя́щий; (in attendance)
прису́тствующий ♦ n (gift)
пода́рок ♦ vt представля́ть
(предста́вить pf); (RADIO, TV)
вести́ (impf); **to ~ sth to sb, ~ sb
with sth** (prize etc) вруча́ть
(вручи́ть pf) что-н кому́-н; (gift)
преподноси́ть (преподнести́ pf)
что-н кому́-н; **to ~ sb (to)**
(introduce) представля́ть
(предста́вить pf) кого́-н (+dat);
the ~ (time) настоя́щее nt adj; **at** ~
в настоя́щее вре́мя; **to give sb a**
~ дари́ть (подари́ть pf) кому́-н
пода́рок; **~ation** [prezn'teɪʃən] n
(of report etc) изложе́ние;
(appearance) вне́шний вид; (also:
~ation ceremony) презента́ция;
~-day adj сего́дняшний,
ны́нешний; **~er** [prɪ'zentə'] n
(RADIO, TV) веду́щий(ая) m(f) adj;
(: of news) ди́ктор; **~ly** adv
вско́ре; (now) в настоя́щее
вре́мя

preservation [prezə'veɪʃən] n
(act: of building, democracy)
сохране́ние

preservative [prɪ'zə:vətɪv] n (for
food) консерва́нт; (for wood)
пропи́точный соста́в

preserve [prɪ'zə:v] vt сохраня́ть

(сохрани́ть pf); (food)
консерви́ровать
(законсерви́ровать pf) ♦ n (usu pl:
jam) варе́нье

preside [prɪ'zaɪd] vi: **to ~ (over)**
председа́тельствовать (impf) (на
+prp)

presidency ['prezɪdənsɪ] n
президе́нтство

president ['prezɪdənt] n (POL,
COMM) президе́нт; **~ial**
[prezɪ'denʃl] adj президе́нтский;
~ial candidate кандида́т в
президе́нты; **~ial adviser**
сове́тник президе́нта

press [pres] n (also: **printing ~**)
печа́тный стано́к ♦ vt (hold
together) прижима́ть (прижа́ть
pf); (push) нажима́ть (нажа́ть pf);
(iron) гла́дить (погла́дить pf);
(pressurize: person) вынужда́ть
(вы́нудить pf); **the** ~ (newspapers,
journalists) пре́сса; **to ~ sth on sb**
(insist) навя́зывать (навяза́ть pf)
что-н кому́-н; **to ~ sb to do** or
into doing вынужда́ть (вы́нудить
pf) +infin; ~ **for** (change
etc) наста́ивать (настоя́ть pf) на
+prp; ~ **on** vi продолжа́ть (impf)
~ **ahead** vi: **to ~ ahead with**
продолжа́ть (продо́лжить pf); ~
conference n пресс-
конфере́нция; ~ **ing** adj (urgent)
неотло́жный

pressure ['preʃə'] n давле́ние;
(stress) напряже́ние; **to put ~ on
sb (to do)** ока́зывать (оказа́ть pf)
давле́ние or нажи́м на кого́-н
(+infin); ~ **group** n инициати́вная
гру́ппа

prestige [pres'ti:ʒ] n прести́ж

prestigious [pres'tɪdʒəs] adj
прести́жный

presumably [prɪ'zju:məblɪ] adv
на́до полага́ть

presume [prɪ'zju:m] vt: **to ~ (that)**

(*suppose*) предполага́ть (предположи́ть *pf*), что
presumption [prɪˈzʌmpʃən] *n* предположе́ние
presumptuous [prɪˈzʌmpʃəs] *adj* самонаде́янный
pretence [prɪˈtens] (*US* **pretense**) *n* притво́рство; **under false ~s** под ло́жным предло́гом
pretend [prɪˈtend] *vi*: **to ~ that** притворя́ться (притвори́ться *pf*), что; **he ~ed to help** он сде́лал вид, что помога́ет; **he ~ed to be asleep** он притвори́лся, что спит
pretense [prɪˈtens] *n* (*US*) = **pretence**
pretentious [prɪˈtenʃəs] *adj* претенцио́зный
pretext [ˈpriːtekst] *n* предло́г
pretty [ˈprɪtɪ] *adj* (*person*) хоро́шенький; (*thing*) краси́вый ♦ *adv* (*quite*) дово́льно
prevail [prɪˈveɪl] *vi* (*be current*) преобладать (*impf*), превали́ровать (*impf*); (*gain influence*) оде́рживать (одержа́ть *pf*) верх; **~ing** *adj* (*wind*) преоблада́ющий
prevent [prɪˈvent] *vt* (*accident etc*) предотвраща́ть (предотврати́ть *pf*), предупрежда́ть (предупреди́ть *pf*); **to ~ sb from doing** меша́ть (помеша́ть *pf*) кому́-н +*infin*; **~ative** *adj* = **preventive**; **~ion** [prɪˈvenʃən] *n* предотвраще́ние, предупрежде́ние; **~ive** *adj* (*POL, measures*) превенти́вный; (*medicine*) профилакти́ческий
preview [ˈpriːvjuː] *n* (*of film*) (закры́тый) просмо́тр; (*of exhibition*) вернисаж
previous [ˈpriːvɪəs] *adj* предыду́щий; **~ to** до +*gen*; **~ly** *adv* (*before*) ра́нее; (*in the past*) пре́жде

prey [preɪ] *n* добы́ча
price [praɪs] *n* цена́ ♦ *vt* оце́нивать (оцени́ть *pf*); **~less** *adj* (*diamond, painting etc*) бесце́нный; **~ list** *n* прейскура́нт
prick [prɪk] *n* (*pain*) уко́л ♦ *vt* (*make hole in*) прока́лывать (проколо́ть *pf*); (*finger*) коло́ть (уколо́ть *pf*); **to ~ up one's ears** навостри́ть (*pf*) у́ши
prickly [ˈprɪklɪ] *adj* колю́чий
pride [praɪd] *n* го́рдость *f*; (*pej: arrogance*) горды́ня ♦ *vt*: **to ~ o.s. on** горди́ться (*impf*) +*instr*
priest [priːst] *n* свяще́нник; **~hood** *n* свяще́нство
prim [prɪm] *adj* чо́порный
primarily [ˈpraɪmərɪlɪ] *adv* в пе́рвую о́чередь
primary [ˈpraɪmərɪ] *adj* (*task*) первостепе́нный, первоочередно́й ♦ *n* (*US : POL*) предвари́тельные вы́боры *mpl*; **~ school** *n* (*BRIT*) нача́льная шко́ла
prime [praɪm] *adj* (*most important*) гла́вный, основно́й; (*best quality*) первосо́ртный; (*example*) я́ркий ♦ *n* расцве́т ♦ *vt* (*fig: person*) подгота́вливать (подгото́вить *pf*); **Prime Minister** *n* премье́р-мини́стр
primitive [ˈprɪmɪtɪv] *adj* (*early*) первобы́тный; (*unsophisticated*) примити́вный
primrose [ˈprɪmrəuz] *n* первоцве́т
prince [prɪns] *n* принц; (*Russian*) князь *m*; **~ss** [prɪnˈses] *n* принце́сса; (*Russian: wife*) княги́ня; (*: daughter*) княжна́
principal [ˈprɪnsɪpl] *adj* гла́вный, основно́й ♦ *n* (*of school, college*) дире́ктор; (*of university*) ре́ктор
principle [ˈprɪnsɪpl] *n* при́нцип; (*scientific law*) зако́н; **in ~** в при́нципе; **on ~** из при́нципа
print [prɪnt] *n* (*TYP*) шрифт; (*ART*)

эста́мп, гравю́ра; (PHOT, fingerprint) отпеча́ток; (footprint) след ♦ vt (book etc) печа́тать (напеча́тать pf); (cloth) набива́ть (наби́ть pf); (write in capitals) писа́ть (написа́ть pf) печа́тными бу́квами; **this book is out of ~** э́та кни́га бо́льше не изда́ётся; **~ er** n (machine) при́нтер; (firm : also : **~er's**) типогра́фия

prior ['praɪər] adj (previous) пре́жний; (more important) гла́вный; **~ knowledge of sth** знать (impf) о чём-н зара́нее; **to ~ to** do +gen

priority [praɪˈɒrɪtɪ] n (most urgent task) первоочередна́я зада́ча; (most important thing, task) приорите́т; **to have ~ (over)** име́ть (impf) преиму́щество (пе́ред +instr)

prison ['prɪzn] n тюрьма́ ♦ cpd тюре́мный; **~er** n (in prison) заключённый(ая) m(f) adj; (captured person) пле́нный(ая) m(f) adj; **~er of war** n военнопле́нный m adj

privacy ['prɪvəsɪ] n уедине́ние

private ['praɪvɪt] adj (property, industry) ча́стный; (discussion, club) закры́тый; (belongings, life) ли́чный; (thoughts, affairs) скры́тый; (secluded) уединённый; (secretive, reserved) за́мкнутый; (confidential) конфиденциа́льный; **"~"** (on door) "посторо́нним вход воспрещён"; **in ~** конфиденциа́льно

privatize ['praɪvɪtaɪz] vt приватизи́ровать (impf/pf)

privilege ['prɪvɪlɪdʒ] n привиле́гия; **~d** adj привилегиро́ванный

prize [praɪz] n приз ♦ adj первокла́ссный ♦ vt (высоко́) цени́ть (impf)

pro [prəʊ] prep (in favour of) за +acc

♦ n: **the ~s and cons** за и про́тив

probability [prɒbəˈbɪlɪtɪ] n: **~ of/ that** вероя́тность f +gen/того́, что; **in all ~** по всей вероя́тности

probable ['prɒbəbl] adj вероя́тный

probably ['prɒbəblɪ] adv вероя́тно

probation [prəˈbeɪʃən] n (LAW) усло́вное осужде́ние; (employee) испыта́тельный срок

probe [prəʊb] vt (investigate) рассле́довать (impf/pf); (poke) прощу́пывать (прощу́пать pf)

problem ['prɒbləm] n пробле́ма

procedure [prəˈsiːdʒər] n процеду́ра

proceed [prəˈsiːd] vi (activity, event, process) продолжа́ться (продо́лжиться pf); (person) продвига́ться (продви́нуться pf); **to ~ with** (continue) продолжа́ть (продо́лжить pf); **to ~ to do** продолжа́ть (продо́лжить pf) +infin; **~ings** npl (events) мероприя́тия ntpl; (LAW) суде́бное разбира́тельство ntsg

process ['prəʊses] n проце́сс ♦ vt обраба́тывать (обрабо́тать pf); **in the ~** в проце́ссе

procession [prəˈseʃən] n проце́ссия

proclaim [prəˈkleɪm] vt провозглаша́ть (провозгласи́ть pf)

proclamation [prɒkləˈmeɪʃən] n провозглаше́ние

prod [prɒd] vt (push) ты́кать (ткнуть pf) ♦ n тычо́к

prodigy ['prɒdɪdʒɪ] n: **child ~** вундерки́нд

produce vb [prəˈdjuːs] n ['prɒdjuːs] vt (manufacture) производи́ть (произвести́ pf); (CHEM) выраба́тывать (вы́работать pf); (evidence, argument) представля́ть (предста́вить pf); (bring or take out) предъявля́ть (предъяви́ть *pf*); (*play, film*) ста́вить (поста́вить *pf*) ♦ *n* (*AGR*) (сельско-хозя́йственная) проду́кция; ~**r** *n* (*of film, play*) режиссёр-постано́вщик, продю́сер; (*of record*) продю́сер

product ['prɔdʌkt] *n* (*thing*) изде́лие; (*food, result*) проду́кт

production [prə'dʌkʃən] *n* (*process*) произво́дство; (*amount produced*) проду́кция; (*THEAT*) постано́вка

productive [prə'dʌktɪv] *adj* производи́тельный, продукти́вный

productivity [prɔdʌk'tɪvɪtɪ] *n* производи́тельность *f*, продукти́вность *f*

profess [prə'fes] *vt* (*claim*) претендова́ть (*impf*) на +*acc*

profession [prə'feʃən] *n* профе́ссия; ~**al** *adj* профессиона́льный

professor [prə'fesə*r*] *n* (*BRIT*) профе́ссор; (*US*) преподава́тель(ница) *m(f)*

proficient [prə'fɪʃənt] *adj* уме́лый

profile ['prəufaɪl] *n* (*of face*) про́филь *m*; (*article*) о́черк

profit ['prɔfɪt] *n* при́быль *f*, дохо́д ♦ *vi*: **to** ~ **by** *or* **from** (*fig*) извлека́ть (извле́чь *pf*) вы́году из +*gen*; ~**ability** [prɔfɪtə'bɪlɪtɪ] *n* при́быльность *f*; ~**able** *adj* при́быльный; (*fig*) вы́годный

profound [prə'faund] *adj* глубо́кий

prognosis [prɔg'nausɪs] (*pl* **prognoses**) *n* прогно́з

program(me) ['prəugræm] *n* програ́мма ♦ *vt* программи́ровать (запрограмми́ровать *pf*); ~**r** *n* программи́ст(ка)

progress *n* ['prəugres] ♦ *vb* [prə'gres] *n* (*advances, changes*) прогре́сс; (*development*) разви́тие ♦ *vi* прогресси́ровать (*impf*); (*continue*)

продолжа́ться (продо́лжиться *pf*); **the match is in** ~ матч идёт; ~**ion** [prə'greʃən] *n* (*gradual development*) продвиже́ние; ~**ive** [prə'gresɪv] *adj* прогресси́вный; (*gradual*) постепе́нный

prohibit [prə'hɪbɪt] *vt* запреща́ть (запрети́ть *pf*); ~**ion** [prəuɪ'bɪʃən] *n* запреще́ние, запре́т

project *n* ['prɔdʒekt] *vb* [prə'dʒekt] *n* прое́кт ♦ *vt* (*plan, estimate*) проекти́ровать (запроекти́ровать *pf*) ♦ *vi* (*jut out*) выступа́ть (вы́ступить *pf*)

projection [prə'dʒekʃən] *n* (*estimate*) перспекти́вная оце́нка

projector [prə'dʒektə*r*] *n* (*CINEMA*) кинопрое́ктор; (*also*: **slide** ~) прое́ктор

prolific [prə'lɪfɪk] *adj* плодови́тый

prologue ['prəulɔg] (*US* **prolog**) *n* проло́г

prolong [prə'lɔŋ] *vt* продлева́ть (продли́ть *pf*)

promenade [prɔmə'nɑːd] *n* променя́д

prominence ['prɔmɪnəns] *n* (*of person*) ви́дное положе́ние; (*of issue*) ви́дное ме́сто

prominent ['prɔmɪnənt] *adj* выдаю́щийся

promiscuous [prə'mɪskjuəs] *adj* развра́тный

promise ['prɔmɪs] *n* (*vow*) обеща́ние; (*talent*) потенциа́л; (*hope*) наде́жда ♦ *vi* (*vow*) дава́ть (дать *pf*) обеща́ние ♦ *vt*: **to** ~ **sb sth**, ~ **sth to sb** обеща́ть (пообеща́ть *pf*) что-н кому́-н; **to** ~ (**sb**) **to do/that** обеща́ть (пообеща́ть *pf*) (кому́-н) +*infin*/, что; **to** ~ **well** подава́ть (*impf*) больши́е наде́жды

promising ['prɔmɪsɪŋ] *adj* многообеща́ющий

promote [prə'məut] *vt* (*employee*)

повыша́ть (повы́сить pf) (в до́лжности); (product, pop-star) реклами́ровать (impf/pf); (ideas) подде́рживать (поддержа́ть pf); ~**r** n (of event) аге́нт; (of cause, idea) пропаганди́ст(ка)

promotion [prə'məʊʃən] n (at work) повыше́ние (в до́лжности); (of product, event) рекла́ма

prompt [prɒmpt] adj незамедли́тельный ♦ vt (cause) побужда́ть (побуди́ть pf); (when talking) подска́зывать (подсказа́ть pf) ♦ adv: at 8 o'clock ~ ро́вно в 8 часо́в; to ~ sb to do побужда́ть (побуди́ть pf) кого́-н +infin; ~**ly** adv (immediately) незамедли́тельно; (exactly) то́чно

prone [prəʊn] adj: ~ to (inclined to) скло́нный к +dat

pronoun ['prəʊnaʊn] n местоиме́ние

pronounce [prə'naʊns] vt (word) произноси́ть (произнести́ pf); (declaration, verdict) объявля́ть (объяви́ть pf); (opinion) выска́зывать (вы́сказать pf); ~**d** adj отчётливый

pronunciation [prənʌnsɪ'eɪʃən] n (of word) произноше́ние

proof [pruːf] n (evidence) доказа́тельство ♦ adj: this vodka is 70% ~ э́то семидесятигра́дусная во́дка

prop [prɒp] n (support) подпо́рка ♦ vt (also: ~ **up**) подпира́ть (подпере́ть pf); to ~ sth against прислоня́ть (прислони́ть pf) что-н к +dat; ~s npl (THEAT) реквизи́т msg

propaganda [prɒpə'gændə] n пропага́нда

propel [prə'pel] vt (vehicle, machine) приводи́ть (привести́ pf) в движе́ние; ~**ler** n пропе́ллер

proper ['prɒpər] adj (real)

настоя́щий; (correct) до́лжный; надлежа́щий; (socially acceptable) прили́чный; ~**ly** adv (eat, study) как сле́дует; (behave) прили́чно, до́лжным о́бразом

property ['prɒpətɪ] n (possessions) со́бственность f; (building and land) недви́жимость f; (quality) сво́йство

prophecy ['prɒfɪsɪ] n проро́чество

proportion [prə'pɔːʃən] n (part) часть f, до́ля; (ratio) пропо́рция, соотноше́ние; ~**al** adj: ~**al to** пропорциона́льный (+dat)

proposal [prə'pəʊzl] n предложе́ние

propose [prə'pəʊz] vt (plan, toast) предлага́ть (предложи́ть pf); (motion) выдвига́ть (вы́двинуть pf) ♦ vi (offer marriage) де́лать (сде́лать pf) предложе́ние (кому́-н); to ~ sth/to do or doing предполага́ть (impf) что-н/+infin

proposition [prɒpə'zɪʃən] n (statement) утвержде́ние; (offer) предложе́ние

proprietor [prə'praɪətər] n владе́лец(лица)

prose [prəʊz] n (not poetry) про́за

prosecute ['prɒsɪkjuːt] vt: to ~ sb пресле́довать (impf) кого́-н в суде́бном поря́дке

prosecution [prɒsɪ'kjuːʃən] n (LAW, action) суде́бное пресле́дование; (: accusing side) обвине́ние

prosecutor ['prɒsɪkjuːtər] n обвини́тель m

prospect ['prɒspekt] n перспекти́ва; ~**s** npl (for work etc) перспекти́вы fpl; ~**ive** [prə'spektɪv] adj (future) бу́дущий; (potential) возмо́жный; ~**us** [prə'spektəs] n проспе́кт

prosper ['prɒspər] vi преуспева́ть (преуспе́ть pf); ~**ity** [prɒ'sperɪtɪ] n

процветáние; **~ous** adj
преуспевáющий

prostitute ['prɒstɪtjuːt] n
проститýтка

protagonist [prə'tægənɪst] n
(supporter) привéрженец

protect [prə'tekt] vt защищáть
(защитить pf); **~ion** [prə'tekʃən] n
защита; **~ive** adj защитный;
(person) забóтливый, бéрежный

protein ['prəutiːn] n белóк,
протеин

protest n [prəutest] vb [prə'test] n
протéст ♦ vi: **to ~ about/against**
протестовáть (impf) по пóводу
+gen/прóтив +gen ♦ vt (insist): **to ~
that** заявлять (заявить pf), что

Protestant ['prɒtɪstənt] n
протестáнт(ка)

protocol ['prəutəkɔl] n протокóл

prototype ['prəutətaɪp] n прототип

proud [praud] adj: **~ (of)** гóрдый
(+instr)

prove [pruːv] vt докáзывать
(доказáть pf) ♦ vi: **to ~ (to be)**
оказáться (impf/pf) +instr; **to ~ o.s.**
проявлять (проявить pf) себя

proverb ['prɒvəːb] n послóвица;
~ial [prə'vəːbɪəl] adj легендáрный

provide [prə'vaɪd] vt обеспéчивать
(обеспéчить pf) +instr; **to ~ sb
with sth** обеспéчивать
(обеспéчить pf) когó-н чем-н; **~
for** vt fus (person) обеспéчивать
(обеспéчить pf); (condition)
при услóвии, что

providing [prə'vaɪdɪŋ] conj =
provided (that)

province ['prɒvɪns] n óбласть f

provincial [prə'vɪnʃəl] adj
провинциáльный

provision [prə'vɪʒən] n (supplying)
обеспéчение; (of contract,
agreement) положéние; **~s** npl
(food) провизия fsg; **~al** adj
врéменный

provocation [prɒvə'keɪʃən] n
провокáция

provocative [prə'vɔkətɪv] adj
(remark, gesture) провокациóнный

provoke [prə'vəuk] vt
провоцировать
(спровоцировать pf)

proximity [prɔk'sɪmɪtɪ] n блúзость
f

proxy ['prɒksɪ] n: **by ~** по
довéренности

prudent ['pruːdnt] adj
благоразýмный

prune [pruːn] n черносли́в m no pl
♦ vt обрезáть (обрéзать pf)

PS abbr = **postscript**

pseudonym ['sjuːdənɪm] n
псевдонúм

psychiatric [saɪkɪ'ætrɪk] adj
психиатрúческий

psychiatrist [saɪ'kaɪətrɪst] n
психиáтр

psychic ['saɪkɪk] adj (also: **~al**:
person) ясновúдящий

psychological [saɪkə'lɔdʒɪkl] adj
психологúческий

psychologist [saɪ'kɔlədʒɪst] n
психóлог

psychology [saɪ'kɔlədʒɪ] n
психолóгия

psychopath ['saɪkəupæθ] n
психопáт(ка)

psychotic [saɪ'kɔtɪk] adj
психúчески бóльной

PTO abbr (= please turn over)
смотри на оборóте

pub [pʌb] n паб, пивнáя f adj

puberty ['pjuːbətɪ] n половáя
зрéлость f

public ['pʌblɪk] adj общéственный;
(statement, action etc) публичный
♦ n: **the ~** (everyone)
общéственность f, нарóд; **to
make ~** публиковáть (предáть pf)
глáсности; **in ~** публично

publication [pʌblɪ'keɪʃən] n

публика́ция, изда́ние

publicity [pʌb'lɪsɪtɪ] n (information) рекла́ма, па́блисити nt ind; (attention) шуми́ха

publicize ['pʌblɪsaɪz] vt предава́ть (преда́ть pf) гла́сности

public: ~ly adv публи́чно; ~ **opinion** n обще́ственное мне́ние; ~ **relations** npl вне́шние свя́зи fpl, свя́зи с обще́ственностью; ~ **school** n (BRIT) ча́стная шко́ла; (US) госуда́рственная шко́ла

publish ['pʌblɪʃ] vt издава́ть (изда́ть pf); (PRESS, letter, article) публикова́ть (опубликова́ть pf); ~**er** n (company) изда́тельство; ~**ing** n (profession) изда́тельское де́ло

pudding ['pudɪŋ] n пу́динг, (BRIT: dessert) сла́дкое nt adj; **black**~, (US) **blood** ~ кровяна́я колбаса́

puddle ['pʌdl] n лу́жа

puff [pʌf] n (of wind) дунове́ние; (of cigarette, pipe) затя́жка; (of smoke) клуб

pull [pul] vt тяну́ть (потяну́ть pf); (trigger) нажима́ть (нажа́ть pf) на +acc; (curtains etc) задёргивать (задёрнуть pf) ♦ vi (tug) тяну́ть (impf) ♦ n: **to give sth a ~** (tug) тяну́ть (потяну́ть pf) что-н; **to ~ to pieces** разрыва́ть (разорва́ть pf) на ча́сти; **to ~ o.s. together** брать (взять pf) себя́ в ру́ки; **to ~ sb's leg** (fig) разы́грывать (разыгра́ть pf) кого́-н; ~ **down** vt (building) сноси́ть (снести́ pf); ~ **in** vt (crowds, people) привлека́ть (привле́чь pf); ~ **out** vt (extract) выта́скивать (вы́тащить pf) ♦ vi: **to ~ out (from)** (AUT: from kerb) отъезжа́ть (отъе́хать pf) (от +gen); ~ **up** vi (stop) остана́вливаться (останови́ться pf) ♦ vt (plant) вырыва́ть (вы́рвать

pf) (с ко́рнем)

pulley ['pulɪ] n шкив

pullover ['puləuvər] n сви́тер, пуло́вер

pulpit ['pulpɪt] n ка́федра

pulse [pʌls] n (ANAT) пульс

puma ['pjuːmə] n пу́ма

pump [pʌmp] n насо́с; pf; (also: **petrol** ~) бензоколо́нка ♦ vt кача́ть (накача́ть pf); (extract: oil, water, gas) выка́чивать (вы́качать pf)

pumpkin ['pʌmpkɪn] n ты́ква

pun [pʌn] n каламбу́р

punch [pʌntʃ] n уда́р; (for making holes) дыроко́л; (drink) пунш ♦ vt (hit): **to ~ sb/sth** ударя́ть (уда́рить pf) кого́-н/что-н кулако́м

punctual ['pʌŋktjuəl] adj пунктуа́льный

punctuation [pʌŋktju'eɪʃən] n пунктуа́ция

puncture ['pʌŋktʃər] n (AUT) проко́л ♦ vt прока́лывать (проколо́ть pf)

punish ['pʌnɪʃ] vt: **to ~ sb (for sth)** нака́зывать (наказа́ть pf) кого́-н (за что-н); ~**ment** n наказа́ние

punter ['pʌntər] n (inf: customer) клие́нт(ка)

pupil ['pjuːpl] n (SCOL) учени́к(и́ца); (of eye) зрачо́к

puppet ['pʌpɪt] n марионе́тка

puppy ['pʌpɪ] n (young dog) щено́к

purchase ['pəːtʃɪs] n поку́пка ♦ vt покупа́ть (купи́ть pf)

pure [pjuər] adj чи́стый; ~**ly** adv чи́сто

purify ['pjuərɪfaɪ] vt очища́ть (очи́стить pf)

purity ['pjuərɪtɪ] n чистота́

purple ['pəːpl] adj фиоле́товый

purpose ['pəːpəs] n цель f; **on** ~ наме́ренно; ~**ful** adj целеустремлённый

purr [pə:ʳ] vi мурлыкать (impf)
purse [pə:s] n (BRIT) кошелёк; (US: handbag) сумка ♦ vt: **to ~ one's lips** поджимать (поджать pf) губы
pursue [pə'sju:] vt преследовать (impf); (fig: policy) проводить (impf); (: interest) развивать (impf)
pursuit [pə'sju:t] n (of person, thing) преследование; (of happiness, wealth etc) поиски mpl; (pastime) занятие
push [puʃ] n (shove) толчок ♦ vt (press) нажимать (нажать pf); (shove) толкать (толкнуть pf); (promote) проталкивать (протолкнуть pf) ♦ vi (press) нажимать (нажать pf); (shove) толкаться (impf); (fig): **to ~ for** требовать (потребовать pf) +acc or +gen; **~ through** vt (measure, scheme) проталкивать (протолкнуть pf); **~ up** vt (prices) повышать (повысить pf); **~y** adj настырный
put [put] (pt, pp ~) vt ставить (поставить pf); (thing: horizontally) класть (положить pf); (person: in institution) помещать (поместить pf); (: in prison) сажать (посадить pf); (idea, feeling) выражать (выразить pf); (case, view) излагать (изложить pf); **I ~ it to you that** ... я говорю Вам, что ...; **~ across** vt (ideas etc) объяснять (объяснить pf); **~ away** vt (store) убирать (убрать pf); **~ back** vt (replace) класть (положить pf) на место; (postpone) откладывать (отложить pf); (delay) задерживать (задержать pf); **~ by** vt откладывать (отложить pf); **~ down** vt (place) ставить (поставить pf); (: horizontally) класть (положить pf); (note down) записывать (записать pf);

(suppress, humiliate) подавлять (подавить pf); (animal: kill) умерщвлять (умертвить pf); **to ~ sth down to** (attribute) объяснить (объяснить pf) что-н +instr; **~ forward** vt (ideas) выдвигать (выдвинуть pf); **~ in** vt (application, complaint) подавать (подать pf); (time, effort) вкладывать (вложить pf); **~ off** vt (delay) откладывать (отложить pf); (discourage) отталкивать (оттолкнуть pf); (switch off) выключать (выключить pf); **~ on** vt (clothes) надевать (надеть pf); (make-up, ointment etc) накладывать (наложить pf); (light etc) включать (включить pf); (kettle, record, dinner) ставить (поставить pf); (assume: look) напускать (напустить pf) на себя; (behaviour) принимать (принять pf); **to ~ on weight** поправляться (поправиться pf); **~ out** vt (fire) тушить (потушить pf); (candle, cigarette, light) гасить (погасить pf); (rubbish) выносить (вынести pf); (one's hand) вытягивать (вытянуть pf); **~ through** vt (person, call) соединять (соединить pf); (plan, agreement) выполнять (выполнить pf); **~ up** vt (building, tent) ставить (поставить pf); (umbrella) раскрывать (раскрыть pf); (hood) надевать (надеть pf); (poster, sign) вывешивать (вывесить pf); (price, cost) поднимать (поднять pf); (guest) помещать (поместить pf); **~ up with** vt fus мириться (impf) с +instr
putty ['pʌtɪ] n замазка
puzzle ['pʌzl] n (game, toy) головоломка
puzzling ['pʌzlɪŋ] adj запутанный
pyjamas [pɪ'dʒɑ:məz] (US **pajamas**)

npl: **(a pair of)** ~ пижа́ма *fsg*

pylon ['paɪlən] *n* пило́н, опо́ра

pyramid ['pɪrəmɪd] *n* (*GEOM*) пирами́да

python ['paɪθən] *n* пито́н

Q, q

quadruple [kwɔ'dru:pl] *vt* увели́чивать (увели́чить *pf*) в четы́ре ра́за ♦ *vi* увели́чиваться (увели́читься *pf*) в четы́ре ра́за

quaint [kweɪnt] *adj* чудно́й

quake [kweɪk] *vi* трепета́ть (*impf*)

qualification [kwɔlɪfɪ'keɪʃən] *n* (*usu pl: academic, vocational*) квалифика́ция; (*skill, quality*) ка́чество; **what are your ~s?** кака́я у Вас квалифика́ция?

qualified ['kwɔlɪfaɪd] *adj* (*trained*) квалифици́рованный; **I'm not ~ to judge that** я не компете́нтен суди́ть об э́том

qualify ['kwɔlɪfaɪ] *vt* (*modify: make more specific*) уточня́ть (уточни́ть *pf*); (*: express reservation*) огова́ривать (оговори́ть *pf*) ♦ *vi*: **to ~ as an engineer** получа́ть (получи́ть *pf*) квалифика́цию инжене́ра; **to ~ (for)** (*benefit etc*) име́ть (*impf*) пра́во (на +*acc*); (*in competition*) выходи́ть (вы́йти *pf*) в +*acc*

quality ['kwɔlɪtɪ] *n* ка́чество; (*property: of wood, stone etc*) сво́йство

quantity ['kwɔntɪtɪ] *n* коли́чество

quarantine ['kwɔrntiːn] *n* каранти́н

quarrel ['kwɔrl] *n* ссо́ра ♦ *vi*: **to ~ (with)** ссо́риться (поссо́риться *pf*) (с +*instr*); **~some** *adj* вздо́рный

quarry ['kwɔrɪ] *n* карье́р; (*for stone*) каменоло́мня

quarter ['kwɔːtə'] *n* че́тверть *f*; (*of year, town*) кварта́л; (*US: coin*)

два́дцать пять це́нтов ♦ *vt* дели́ть (раздели́ть *pf*) на четы́ре ча́сти; **~s** *npl* (*: for living*) помеще́ние *ntsg*; (*: MIL*) каза́рмы *fpl*; **a ~ of an hour** че́тверть *f* ча́са; **~ly** *adj* (*meeting*) (еже)кварта́льный; (*payment*) (по)кварта́льный ♦ *adv* (*see adj*) ежекварта́льно; покварта́льно

quartz [kwɔːts] *n* кварц

quash [kwɔʃ] *vt* (*verdict, judgement*) отменя́ть (отмени́ть *pf*)

quay [kiː] *n* (*also:* **~side**) при́стань *f*

queasy ['kwiːzɪ] *adj*: **I feel a bit ~** меня́ немно́го мути́т

queen [kwiːn] *n* короле́ва; (*CARDS*) да́ма; (*CHESS*) ферзь *m*

queer [kwɪə'] *adj* (*odd*) стра́нный ♦ *n* (*pej: homosexual*) го́мик, голубо́й *m adj*

quell [kwel] *vt* подавля́ть (подави́ть *pf*)

quench [kwentʃ] *vt*: **to ~ one's thirst** утоля́ть (утоли́ть *pf*) жа́жду

query ['kwɪərɪ] *n* вопро́с ♦ *vt* подверга́ть (подве́ргнуть *pf*) сомне́нию

quest [kwest] *n* по́иск

question ['kwestʃən] *n* вопро́с; (*doubt*) сомне́ние ♦ *vt* (*interrogate*) допра́шивать (допроси́ть *pf*); (*doubt*) усомни́ться (*pf*) в +*prp*; **beyond ~** бесспо́рно; **that's out of the ~** об э́том не мо́жет быть и ре́чи; **~able** *adj* сомни́тельный; **~ mark** *n* вопроси́тельный знак; **~naire** [kwestʃə'neə'] *n* анке́та

queue [kjuː] (*BRIT*) *n* о́чередь *f* ♦ *vi* (*also:* **~ up**) стоя́ть (*impf*) в о́череди

quibble ['kwɪbl] *vi*: **to ~ about** *or* **over** спо́рить (поспо́рить *pf*) о +*prp*

quick [kwɪk] *adj* бы́стрый; (*clever:*

person) сообрази́тельный;
(*: mind*) живо́й; (*brief*) кра́ткий;
be ~ бы́стро; ~**ly** adv бы́стро;
~**sand** n зыбу́чий песо́к;
~**-witted** adj сообрази́тельный

quid [kwɪd] n inv (*BRIT: inf*) фунт
(*сте́рлингов*)

quiet ['kwaɪət] adj ти́хий; (*peaceful,
not busy*) споко́йный; (*without
fuss*) сде́ржанный ♦ n (*silence*)
тишина́; (*peace*) поко́й; ~**en**, vi
(*also*: ~**en down**) затиха́ть
(зати́хнуть pf); ~**ly** adv ти́хо;
(*calmly*) споко́йно

quilt [kwɪlt] n (*also*: **continental** ~)
стёганое одея́ло

quirk [kwə:k] n причу́да, при́хоть
f

quit [kwɪt] (*pt, pp* ~ *or* ~**ted**) vt
броса́ть (бро́сить pf) ♦ vi (*give up*)
сдава́ться (сда́ться pf);
(*resign*)
увольня́ться (уво́литься pf)

quite [kwaɪt] adv (*rather*)
дово́льно; (*entirely*) соверше́нно;
(*almost*): **the flat's not ~ big
enough** кварти́ра недоста́точно
больша́я; ~ **a few** дово́льно
мно́го; ~ (**so**)! ве́рно!, (вот)
и́менно!

quits [kwɪts] adj: **let's call it ~**
бу́дем кви́ты

quiver ['kwɪvər] vi (*shake*)
трепета́ть (*impf*)

quiz [kwɪz] n (*game*) виктори́на
♦ vt расспра́шивать
(расспроси́ть pf)

quota ['kwəutə] n кво́та

quotation [kwəu'teɪʃən] n цита́та;
(*estimate*) цена́ (*продавца́*)

quote [kwəut] n цита́та; (*estimate*)
цена́ ♦ vt цити́ровать
(процити́ровать pf); (*figure,
example*) приводи́ть (привести́
pf); (*price*) назнача́ть (назна́чить
pf); ~**s** npl (*quotation marks*)
кавы́чки fpl

rabbi ['ræbaɪ] n равви́н

rabbit ['ræbɪt] n (*male*) кро́лик;
(*female*) кро́льчи́ха

rabble ['ræbl] n (*pej*) сброд

rabies ['reɪbiːz] n бе́шенство,
водобоя́знь f

RAC n abbr (*BRIT: = Royal Automobile
Club*) Короле́вская
автомоби́льная ассоциа́ция

race [reɪs] n (*species*) ра́са;
(*competition*) го́нки fpl; (*: running*)
забе́г; (*: swimming*) заплы́в;
(*: horse race*) ска́чки fpl; (*for power,
control*) борьба́ ♦ vt (*horse*) гнать
(*impf*) ♦ vi (*compete*) принима́ть
(приня́ть pf) уча́стие в
соревнова́нии; (*hurry*) мча́ться
(*impf*); (*pulse*) учаща́ться
(участи́ться pf); ~**course** n
ипподро́м; ~**horse** n скакова́я
ло́шадь f

racial ['reɪʃl] adj ра́совый

racing ['reɪsɪŋ] n (*horse racing*)
ска́чки fpl; (*motor racing*) го́нки fpl

racism ['reɪsɪzəm] n раси́зм

racist ['reɪsɪst] adj раси́стский ♦ n
раси́ст(ка)

rack [ræk] n (*shelf*) по́лка; (*also*:
luggage ~) бага́жная по́лка;
(*also*: **roof** ~) бага́жник (*на
кры́ше автомоби́ля*); (*for dishes*)
суши́лка для посу́ды ♦ vt: **she
was** ~**ed by pain** её терза́ла
боль; **to** ~ **one's brains** лома́ть
(*impf*) го́лову

racket ['rækɪt] n (*SPORT*) раке́тка;
(*noise*) гвалт; (*con*) жу́льничество;
(*extortion*) рэ́кет

radar ['reɪdɑː] n рада́р

radiance ['reɪdɪəns] n (*glow*)
сия́ние

radiant ['reɪdɪənt] adj (*smile, person*)

сия́ющий

radiation [reɪdɪˈeɪʃən] n (radioactive) радиа́ция, радиоакти́вное излуче́ние; (of heat, light) излуче́ние

radiator [ˈreɪdɪeɪtə'] n радиа́тор, батаре́я; (AUT) радиа́тор

radical [ˈrædɪkl] adj радика́льный

radii [ˈreɪdɪaɪ] npl of **radius**

radio [ˈreɪdɪəu] n (broadcasting) ра́дио nt ind; (for transmitting and receiving) радиопереда́тчик ♦ vt (person) связа́ться (связа́ться pf) по ра́дио с +instr; **on the ~** по ра́дио; **~active** adj радиоакти́вный; **~ station** n радиоста́нция

radish [ˈrædɪʃ] n реди́ска; **~es** npl (pl **radii**) n ра́диус

radius [ˈreɪdɪəs] (pl **radii**) n ра́диус

RAF n abbr (BRIT: = Royal Air Force) ≈ ВВС

raffle [ˈræfl] n (вещева́я) лотере́я

raft [rɑːft] n плот

rag [ræg] n тря́пка; (pej: newspaper) газете́нка; **~s** npl (clothes) лохмо́тья pl

rage [reɪdʒ] n (fury) бе́шенство, я́рость f ♦ vi (person) свирепе́ть (impf); (storm, debate) бушева́ть (impf); **it's all the ~** (in fashion) все помеша́лись на э́том

ragged [ˈrægɪd] adj (edge) зазу́бренный; (clothes) потрёпанный

raid [reɪd] n (MIL) рейд; (criminal) налёт; (by police) обла́ва, рейд ♦ vt (see n) соверша́ть (соверши́ть pf) рейд на +acc; соверша́ть (соверши́ть pf) налёт на +acc

rail [reɪl] n (on stairs, bridge etc) пери́ла pl; (pl **railings**) ре́льсы mpl; **by ~** по́ездом; **~ings** n(pl) (iron fence) решётка fsg; **~road** n

(US) = **railway**; **~way** n (BRIT) желе́зная доро́га ♦ cpd железнодоро́жный; **~way line** n (BRIT) железнодоро́жная ли́ния; **~way station** n (BRIT: large) железнодоро́жный вокза́л; (: small) железнодоро́жная ста́нция

rain [reɪn] n дождь m ♦ vi: **it's ~ing** идёт дождь; **in the ~** под дождём, в дождь; **~bow** n ра́дуга; **~coat** n плащ; **~fall** n (measurement) у́ровень m оса́дков; **~y** adj (day) дождли́вый

raise [reɪz] n (esp US) повыше́ние ♦ vt (lift, produce) поднима́ть (подня́ть pf); (increase, improve) повыша́ть (повы́сить pf); (doubts: subj: person) выска́зывать (вы́сказать pf); (: results) вызыва́ть (вы́звать pf); (rear: family) воспи́тывать (воспита́ть pf); (get together: army, funds) собира́ть (собра́ть pf); (: loan) изы́скивать (изыска́ть pf); **to ~ one's voice** повыша́ть (повы́сить pf) го́лос

raisin [ˈreɪzn] n изю́минка; **~s** изю́м m no pl

rake [reɪk] n (tool) гра́бли pl ♦ vt (garden) разра́внивать (разровня́ть pf) (гра́блями); (leaves, hay) сгреба́ть (сгрести́ pf)

rally [ˈrælɪ] n (POL etc) манифеста́ция; (AUT) (а́вто)ра́лли nt ind; (TENNIS) ра́лли nt ind ♦ vt (supporters) спла́чивать (сплоти́ть pf) ♦ vi (supporters) спла́чиваться (сплоти́ться pf)

RAM n abbr (COMPUT: = random access memory) ЗУПВ

ram [ræm] n бара́н ♦ vt (crash into) тара́нить (протара́нить pf); (push: bolt) задвига́ть (задви́нуть pf); (: fist) дви́нуть (pf) +instr

ramble [ˈræmbl] vi (walk) броди́ть

rambling *(impf)*; *(talk: also:* ~ **on)** занудствовать *(impf)*

rambling ['ræmblɪŋ] *adj (speech)* несвязный

ramp [ræmp] *n* скат, уклон; **on** ~ *(US: AUT)* въезд на автостраду; **off** ~ *(US: AUT)* съезд с автострады

rampage [ræm'peɪdʒ] *n:* **to be on the** ~ буйствовать *(impf)*

rampant ['ræmpənt] *adj:* **to be** ~ *(crime)* свирепствовать *(impf)*

ramshackle ['ræmʃækl] *adj* ветхий

ran [ræn] *pt of* **run**

ranch [rɑ:ntʃ] *n* ранчо *nt ind*

random ['rændəm] *adj* случайный ♦ *n:* **at** ~ наугад

rang [ræŋ] *pt of* **ring**

range [reɪndʒ] *n (series: of proposals)* ряд; *(: of products)* ассортимент *no pl*; *(: of colours)* гамма; *(of mountains)* цепь f; *(of missile)* дальность f, радиус действия; *(of voice)* диапазон; *(MIL: also: shooting* ~) стрельбище ♦ *vt (place in a line)* выстраивать (выстроить *pf*) ♦ *vi:* **to** ~ **over** *(extend)* простираться *(impf)*; **to** ~ **from ...** **to** ... колебаться *(impf)* от +*gen* ... до +*gen* ...

ranger ['reɪndʒə*r*] *n (in forest)* лесник; *(in park)* смотритель(ница) *m(f)*

rank [ræŋk] *n (in row)* ряд; *(MIL)* шеренга; *(status)* чин, ранг; *(BRIT: also:* **taxi** ~) стоянка такси ♦ *vi:* **to** ~ **among** числиться *(impf)* среди +*gen* ♦ *vt:* **I** ~ **him sixth** я ставлю его на шестое место; **the** ~ **and file** *(fig)* рядовые члены *mpl*

ransom ['rænsəm] *n* выкуп; **to hold to** ~ *(fig)* держать *(impf)* в заложниках

rant [rænt] *vi:* **to** ~ **and rave** рвать *(impf)* и метать *(impf)*

rap [ræp] *vi:* **to** ~ **on a door/table** стучать (постучать *pf*) в дверь/по столу

rape [reɪp] *n* изнасилование ♦ *vt* насиловать (изнасиловать *pf*)

rapid ['ræpɪd] *adj* стремительный; ~**ly** *adv* стремительно

rapist ['reɪpɪst] *n* насильник

rapport [ræ'pɔ:*r*] *n* взаимопонимание

rapturous ['ræptʃərəs] *adj* восторженный

rare [reə*r*] *adj* редкий; *(steak)* кровавый; ~**ly** *adv* редко, нечасто

rash [ræʃ] *adj* опрометчивый ♦ *n (MED)* сыпь f *no pl*

raspberry ['rɑ:zbərɪ] *n* малина f *no pl*

rat [ræt] *n (also fig)* крыса

rate [reɪt] *n (speed)* скорость f; *(: of change, inflation)* темп; *(of interest)* ставка; *(ratio)* уровень *m*; *(price: at hotel etc)* расценка ♦ *vt (value)* оценивать (оценить *pf*); *(estimate)* расценивать (расценить *pf*); ~**s** *npl (BRIT: property tax)* налог *msg* на недвижимость; **to** ~ **sb as** считать (счесть *pf*) кого-н +*instr*; **to** ~ **sth as** расценивать (расценить *pf*) что-н как

rather ['rɑ:ðə*r*] *adv (quite, somewhat)* довольно; *(to some extent)* несколько; *(more accurately)* **or** ~ вернее сказать; **it's** ~ **expensive** *(quite)* это довольно дорого; **there's a lot** довольно много; **I would** ~ **go** я, пожалуй, пойду; **I'd** ~ **not leave** я бы не хотел уходить; ~ **than** +*n* а не +*nom*, вместо +*gen*; ~ **than go to the park, I went to the cinema** вместо того чтобы идти в парк, я пошёл в кино

ratify ['rætɪfaɪ] *vt* ратифицировать *(impf/pf)*

rating ['reɪtɪŋ] n оце́нка, рейтинг; ~s npl (RADIO, TV) рейтинг msg

ratio ['reɪʃɪəʊ] n соотноше́ние; **in the ~ of one hundred to one** в соотноше́нии сто к одному́

ration ['ræʃən] n (allowance: of food) рацио́н, паёк; (: of petrol) но́рма ♦ vt норми́ровать (impf/pf); ~s npl (MIL) рацио́н msg

rational ['ræʃənl] adj разу́мный, рациона́льный; ~ly adv рациона́льно

rattle ['rætl] n дребезжа́ние; (of train, car) громыха́ние; (for baby) погрему́шка ♦ vi (small objects) дребезжа́ть (impf) ♦ vt (shake noisily) сотряса́ть (сотрясти́ pf); (fig: unsettle) нерви́ровать (impf); **to ~ along** (car, bus) громыха́ть (impf); **the wind ~d the windows** о́кна дребезжа́ли от ве́тра; ~**snake** n грему́чая змея́

raucous ['rɔːkəs] adj рокочущий

rave [reɪv] vi (in anger) беснова́ться (impf), бушева́ть (impf); (MED) бре́дить (impf); (with enthusiasm): **to ~ about** восторга́ться (impf) +instr

raven ['reɪvən] n во́рон

ravine [rə'viːn] n уще́лье

raw [rɔː] adj сыро́й; (unrefined: sugar) нерафини́рованный; (sore) све́жий; (inexperienced) зелёный; (weather, day) промо́зглый; ~ **material** n сырьё nt pl

ray [reɪ] n луч; (of heat) пото́к

razor ['reɪzə²] n бри́тва; **safety ~** безопа́сная бри́тва; **electric ~** электробри́тва

Rd abbr = **road**

re [riː] prep относи́тельно +gen

reach [riːtʃ] vt (place, end, agreement) достига́ть (дости́гнуть or дости́чь pf) +gen; (conclusion, decision) приходи́ть (прийти́ pf) к +dat; (be able to touch) достава́ть (доста́ть pf); (by telephone) свя́зываться (связа́ться pf) с +instr ♦ vi: **to ~ into** запуска́ть (запусти́ть pf) ру́ку в +acc; **out of/within ~** вне/в преде́лах досяга́емости; **within ~ of the shops** недалеко́ от магази́нов; **"keep out of the ~ of children"** "бере́чь от дете́й"; **to ~ for** протя́гивать (протяну́ть pf) ру́ку к +dat; **to ~ up** протя́гивать (протяну́ть pf) ру́ку вверх; ~ vt протя́гивать (протяну́ть pf) ♦ vi: **to ~ out for sth** протя́гивать (протяну́ть pf) ру́ку за чем-н

react [riː'ækt] vi (CHEM): **to ~ (with)** вступа́ть (вступи́ть pf) в реа́кцию (c +instr); (MED): **to ~ (to)** реаги́ровать (impf) (на +acc); (respond) реаги́ровать (отреаги́ровать pf) (на +acc); (rebel): **to ~ (against)** восстава́ть (восста́ть pf) (про́тив +gen); ~**ion** [riː'ækʃən] n (CHEM) реа́кция; (also MED, POL): ~**ion (to/against)** реа́кция (на +acc/про́тив +gen); ~**ions** npl (reflexes) реа́кция fsg; ~**ionary** [riː'ækʃənrɪ] adj реакцио́нный; ~**or** n (also: **nuclear ~or**) реа́ктор

read¹ [red] pt, pp of **read²**

read² [riːd] (pt, pp ~) vt чита́ть (прочита́ть or проче́сть pf); (mood) определя́ть (определи́ть pf); (thermometer etc) снима́ть (снять pf) показа́ния с +gen; (SCOL) изуча́ть (impf) ♦ vi (person) чита́ть (impf); (text etc) чита́ться (impf); ~ **out** vt зачи́тывать (зачита́ть pf); ~**er** n (of book, newspaper etc) чита́тель(ница) m(f); ~**ership** n (of newspaper etc) круг чита́телей

readily ['redɪlɪ] adv (willingly) с гото́вностью; (easily) легко́

readiness ['redɪnɪs] n гото́вность f; **in ~** нагото́ве

reading ['riːdɪŋ] n (of books etc) чте́ние; (on thermometer etc) показа́ние

ready ['redɪ] adj гото́вый ♦ vt: **to get sb/sth ~** гото́вить (подгото́вить pf) кого́-н/что-н; **to get ~** гото́виться (пригото́виться pf)

real [rɪəl] adj настоя́щий; (leather) натура́льный; **in ~ terms** реа́льно; **~ estate** n недви́жимость f; **~ism** n реали́зм; **~istic** [rɪə'lɪstɪk] adj реалисти́ческий; **~ity** [riː'ælɪtɪ] n реа́льность f, действи́тельность f; **in ~ity** на са́мом де́ле, в реа́льности

realization [rɪəlaɪ'zeɪʃən] n (see vt) осозна́ние; осуществле́ние

realize ['rɪəlaɪz] vt (understand) осознава́ть (осозна́ть pf); (fulfil) осуществля́ть (осуществи́ть pf)

really ['rɪəlɪ] adv (very) о́чень; (actually): **what ~ happened?** что произошло́ в действи́тельности or на са́мом де́ле?; **~?** (with interest) действи́тельно?, пра́вда?; (expressing surprise) неуже́ли?

realm [relm] n (fig: of activity, study) о́бласть f, сфе́ра

reap [riːp] vt (fig) пожина́ть (пожа́ть pf)

reappear [riːə'pɪəʳ] vi сно́ва появля́ться (появи́ться pf)

rear [rɪəʳ] adj за́дний ♦ n (back) за́дняя часть f ♦ vt (cattle, family) выра́щивать (вы́растить pf) ♦ vi (also: ~ up) станови́ться (стать pf) на дыбы́

rearrange [riːə'reɪndʒ] vt (objects) переставля́ть (переста́вить pf); (order) изменя́ть (измени́ть pf)

reason ['riːzn] n (cause) причи́на; (ability to think) ра́зум, рассу́док; (sense) смысл ♦ vi: **to ~ with sb** убежда́ть (impf) кого́-н; **it stands to ~ that ...** разуме́ется, что ...; **~able** adj разу́мный; (quality) неплохо́й; (price) уме́ренный; **~ably** adv (sensibly) разу́мно; (fairly) дово́льно; **~ing** n рассужде́ние

reassurance [riːə'ʃuərəns] n (comfort) подде́ржка

reassure [riːə'ʃuəʳ] vt (comfort) утеша́ть (уте́шить pf); **to ~ sb of** заверя́ть (заве́рить pf) кого́-н в +prp

reassuring [riːə'ʃuərɪŋ] adj ободря́ющий

rebate ['riːbeɪt] n обра́тная вы́плата

rebel ['rebl] vb [rɪ'bel] n бунта́рь(рка) m(f) ♦ vi восстава́ть (восста́ть pf); **~lion** [rɪ'beljən] n восста́ние; **~lious** [rɪ'beljəs] adj (child, behaviour) стропти́вый; (troops) мяте́жный

rebound vb [rɪ'baund] n [rɪ'baund] vi: **to ~ (off)** отска́кивать (отскочи́ть pf) (от +gen) ♦ n: **he married her on the ~** он жени́лся на ней по́сле разочарова́ния в любви́ к друго́й

rebuild [riː'bɪld] (irreg: like build) vt (town, building) перестра́ивать (перестро́ить pf); (fig) восстана́вливать (восстанови́ть pf)

rebuke [rɪ'bjuːk] vt де́лать (сде́лать pf) вы́говор +dat

recall [rɪ'kɔːl] vt вспомина́ть (вспо́мнить pf); (parliament, ambassador, territory) отзыва́ть (отозва́ть pf)

recapture [riː'kæptʃəʳ] vt (town, territory) сно́ва захва́тывать (захвати́ть pf); (atmosphere etc)

воссоздавать (воссоздать pf)
receding [rɪ'siːdɪŋ] adj (hair)
редеющий
receipt [rɪ'siːt] n (document)
квитанция; (act of receiving)
получение; **~s** npl (COMM)
денежные поступления ntpl,
платежи mpl
receive [rɪ'siːv] vt получать
(получить pf); (criticism)
встречать (встретить pf); (visitor,
guest) принимать (принять pf); **~r**
n (TEL) (телефонная) трубка;
(COMM) ликвидатор
(неплатёжеспособной
компании)
recent ['riːsnt] adj недавний; **~ly**
adv недавно
reception [rɪ'sepʃən] n (in hotel)
регистрация; (in office, hospital)
приёмная f adj; (in health centre)
регистратура; (party, also RADIO,
TV) приём; **~ist** n (in hotel,
hospital) регистратор; (in office)
секретарь m
receptive [rɪ'septɪv] adj
восприимчивый
recess [rɪ'ses] n (POL) каникулы pl
recession [rɪ'seʃən] n (ECON) спад
recipe ['resɪpɪ] n (also fig) рецепт
recipient [rɪ'sɪpɪənt] n получатель
m
reciprocal [rɪ'sɪprəkl] adj
взаимный, обоюдный
recital [rɪ'saɪtl] n (concert) сольный
концерт
recite [rɪ'saɪt] vt (poem)
декламировать
(продекламировать pf)
reckless ['rekləs] adj
безответственный
reckon ['rekən] vt (calculate)
считать (посчитать или сосчитать
pf); (think): **I ~ that ...** я считаю,
что ...
reclaim [rɪ'kleɪm] vt (demand back)

требовать (потребовать pf)
обратно; (land: from sea)
отвоёвывать (отвоевать pf)
recognition [rekəg'nɪʃən] n
признание; (of person, place)
узнавание; **he has changed
beyond ~** он изменился до
неузнаваемости
recognize ['rekəgnaɪz] vt
признавать (признать pf);
(symptom) распознавать
(распознать pf); **to ~ (by)** (person,
place) узнавать (узнать pf) (по
+dat)
recollect [rekə'lekt] vt
припоминать (припомнить pf),
вспоминать (вспомнить pf); **~ion**
[rekə'lekʃən] n воспоминание,
память f
recommend [rekə'mend] vt
рекомендовать
(порекомендовать pf); **~ation**
[rekəmen'deɪʃən] n рекомендация
reconcile ['rekənsaɪl] vt (people)
мирить (помирить pf); (facts,
beliefs) примирять (примирить
pf); **to ~ o.s. to sth** смиряться
(смириться pf) с чем-н
reconciliation [rekənsɪlɪ'eɪʃən] n
примирение
reconsider [riːkən'sɪdər] vt
пересматривать (пересмотреть pf)
reconstruct [riːkən'strʌkt] vt
перестраивать (перестроить pf);
(event, crime) воспроизводить
(воспроизвести pf),
реконструировать (impf/pf); **~ion**
[riːkən'strʌkʃən] n (of building)
реконструкция; (of country)
перестройка; (of crime)
воспроизведение
record vb [rɪ'kɔːd] n, adj ['rekɔːd] vt
(in writing, on tape) записывать
(записать pf); (register:
temperature, speed etc)

регистри́ровать
(зарегистри́ровать pf) ♦ n (written account) за́пись f; (of meeting) протоко́л; (of attendance) учёт; (MUS) пласти́нка; (history: of person, company) репута́ция; (also: **criminal ~**) суди́мость f; (SPORT) реко́рд ♦ adj: **in ~ time** в реко́рдное вре́мя; **off the ~** (speak) неофициа́льно; **~er** [rɪ'kɔːdə] n (MUS) англи́йская фле́йта; **~ holder** ['-'həʊldə] (SPORT) n рекордсме́н(ка); **~ing** [rɪ'kɔːdɪŋ] n за́пись f; **~ player** ['-'pleɪə] n прои́грыватель m

recount [rɪ'kaʊnt] vt (story) пове́дать (pf); (event) пове́дать (pf) о +prp

recoup [rɪ'kuːp] vt (losses) компенси́ровать (impf/pf)

recover [rɪ'kʌvə] vt получа́ть (получи́ть pf) обра́тно; (COMM) возмеща́ть (возмести́ть pf) ♦ vi (get better): **to ~ (from)** поправля́ться (попра́виться pf) (по́сле +gen); **~y** n (MED) выздоровле́ние; (COMM) подъём; (of stolen items) возвраще́ние; (of lost items) обнаруже́ние

recreation [rekrɪ'eɪʃən] n (leisure activities) развлече́ние

recruit [rɪ'kruːt] n (MIL) новобра́нец, призывни́к ♦ vt (into organization, army) вербова́ть (завербова́ть pf); (into company) нанима́ть (наня́ть pf); (new) n (in company) но́вый сотру́дник; (in organization) но́вый член; **~ment** n (MIL) вербо́вка; (by company) набо́р (на рабо́ту)

rectangle ['rektæŋgl] n прямоуго́льник

rectangular [rek'tæŋgjʊlə] adj прямоуго́льный

rectify ['rektɪfaɪ] vt исправля́ть (испра́вить pf)

recuperate [rɪ'kjuːpərət] vi оправля́ться (опра́виться pf)

recur [rɪ'kəː] vi повторя́ться (повтори́ться pf); **~rence** n повторе́ние; **~rent** adj повторя́ющийся

recycle [riː'saɪkl] vt перераба́тывать (перерабо́тать pf)

red [red] n кра́сный цвет; (pej: POL) кра́сный(ая) m(f) adj ♦ adj кра́сный; (hair) ры́жий; **to be in the ~** име́ть (impf) задо́лженность; **Red Cross** n Кра́сный Крест; **~currant** n кра́сная сморо́дина f no pl

redeem [rɪ'diːm] vt (situation, reputation) спаса́ть (спасти́ pf); (debt) выпла́чивать (вы́платить pf)

redefine [riːdɪ'faɪn] vt пересма́тривать (пересмотре́ть pf)

redhead ['redhed] n ры́жий(ая) m(f) adj

redress [rɪ'dres] vt (error, wrong) исправля́ть (испра́вить pf)

red tape n (fig) бюрокра́тия, волоки́та

reduce [rɪ'djuːs] vt сокраща́ть (сократи́ть pf); **to ~ sb to tears** доводи́ть (довести́ pf) кого́-н до слёз; **to ~ sb to silence** заставля́ть (заста́вить pf) кого́-н замолча́ть; **he was ~d to stealing** он дошёл до того́, что стал ворова́ть

reduction [rɪ'dʌkʃən] n (in price) ски́дка; (in numbers) сокраще́ние

redundancy [rɪ'dʌndənsɪ] (BRIT) n сокраще́ние (шта́тов)

redundant [rɪ'dʌndnt] adj (BRIT: unemployed) уво́ленный; (useless) изли́шний; **he was made ~** его́ сократи́ли

reed [riːd] n (BOT) тростни́к

reef [ri:f] n риф

reel [ri:l] n катушка; (of film, tape) бобина

ref [ref] n abbr (SPORT : inf) = **referee**

refer [rɪˈfəːʳ] vt: to ~ sb to (book etc) отсылáть (отослáть pf) когó-н к +dat; (doctor) направля́ть (напра́вить pf) когó-н к +dat; ~ to vt fus упомина́ть (упомяну́ть pf) о +prp; (relate to) относи́ться (impf) к +dat; (consult) обраща́ться (обрати́ться pf) к +dat

referee [refəˈriː] n (SPORT) рефери́ m ind, судья́ m; (BRIT: for job) лицо́, даю́щее рекоменда́цию ♦ vt суди́ть (impf)

reference [ˈrefrəns] n (mention) упомина́ние; (in book, paper) ссы́лка; (for job: letter) рекоменда́ция; with ~ to (in letter) ссыла́ясь на +acc; ~ book n спра́вочник

referendum [refəˈrendəm] n (pl **referenda**) n рефере́ндум

referral [rɪˈfəːrəl] n направле́ние

refine [rɪˈfaɪn] vt (sugar) рафини́ровать (impf/pf); (oil) очища́ть (очи́стить pf); (theory, task) соверше́нствовать (усоверше́нствовать pf); ~d adj (person, taste) утончённый; ~ment n (of person) утончённость f; (of system) усоверше́нствование

reflect [rɪˈflekt] vt отража́ть (отрази́ть pf) ♦ vi (think) разду́мывать (impf); ~ on vt (discredit) отража́ться (отрази́ться pf) на +acc; ~ion [rɪˈflekʃən] n отраже́ние; (thought) разду́мье; (comment): ~ion on сужде́ние о +prp; on ~ion взве́сив все обстоя́тельства

reflex [ˈriːfleks] n рефле́кс

reform [rɪˈfɔːm] n (of law, system)

рефо́рма ♦ vt (character) преобразова́ть (impf/pf); (system) реформи́ровать (impf/pf)

refrain [rɪˈfreɪn] n (of song) припе́в ♦ vi: to ~ from commenting возде́рживаться (возде́ржа́ться pf) от коммента́риев

refresh [rɪˈfreʃ] vt (subj: sleep) освежа́ть (освежи́ть pf); ~ing adj (sleep) освежа́ющий; (drink) тонизи́рующий; ~ments npl заку́ски fpl и напи́тки mpl

refrigerator [rɪˈfrɪdʒəreɪtəʳ] n холоди́льник

refuge [ˈrefjuːdʒ] n (shelter) убе́жище, прибе́жище; to take ~ in находи́ться (найти́ pf) прибе́жище в +prp

refugee [refjuˈdʒiː] n бе́женец(нка)

refund [ˈriːfʌnd] vb [rɪˈfʌnd] n возмеще́ние ♦ vt возмеща́ть (возмести́ть pf)

refurbish [riːˈfəːbɪʃ] vt ремонти́ровать (отремонти́ровать pf); ~ment n ремо́нт

refusal [rɪˈfjuːzəl] n отка́з

refuse¹ [rɪˈfjuːz] vt (offer, gift) отка́зываться (отказа́ться pf) от +gen; (permission) отка́зывать (отказа́ть pf) в +prp ♦ vi отка́зываться (отказа́ться pf); to ~ to do отка́зываться (отказа́ться pf) +infin

refuse² [ˈrefjuːs] n му́сор

refute [rɪˈfjuːt] vt опроверга́ть (опрове́ргнуть pf)

regain [rɪˈgeɪn] vt (power, position) вновь обрета́ть (обрести́ pf)

regard [rɪˈgɑːd] n (esteem) уваже́ние ♦ vt (consider) счита́ть (impf); (view, look on): to ~ with относи́ться (отнести́сь pf) с +instr; to give one's ~s to передава́ть (переда́ть pf) покло́ны +dat; as ~s, with ~ to что касается +gen, относительно +gen; **~ing** prep относительно +gen; **~less** adv (continue) несмотря ни на что; **~less of** несмотря на +acc, не считаясь с +instr

reggae ['regeı] n рэгги m ind

regime [reı'ʒiːm] n (POL) режим

regiment ['redʒımənt] n полк

region ['riːdʒən] n (area: of country) регион; (: smaller) район; (ADMIN, ANAT) область f; **in the ~ of** (fig) в районе +gen; **~al** adj (organization) областной, региональный; (accent) местный

register ['redʒıstə'] n (census, record) запись f; (SCOL) журнал; (also: **electoral ~**) список избирателей ♦ vt регистрировать (зарегистрировать pf); (subj: meter etc) показывать (показать pf) ♦ vi регистрироваться (зарегистрироваться pf); (as student) записываться (записаться pf); (make impression) запечатлеваться (запечатлеться pf) в памяти; **~ed** adj (letter) заказной; **Registered Trademark** n зарегистрированный товарный знак

registrar ['redʒıstrɑː'] n регистратор

registration [redʒıs'treıʃən] n регистрация; (AUT : also: **~ number**) (регистрационный) номер автомобиля

registry office ['redʒıstrı-] n (BRIT) ≈ ЗАГС (отдел записей гражданского состояния)

regret [rı'gret] n сожаление ♦ vt сожалеть (impf) о +prp; (death) скорбеть (impf) о +prp; **~table** adj прискорбный, достойный сожаления

regular ['regjulə'] adj регулярный;

(even) ровный; (symmetrical) правильный; (usual: time) обычный ♦ n (in cafe, restaurant) завсегдатай; (in shop) клиент; **~ly** adv регулярно; (symmetrically: shaped etc) правильно

regulate ['regjuleıt] vt регулировать (отрегулировать pf)

regulation [regju'leıʃən] n регулирование; (rule) правило

rehabilitation ['riːəbılı'teıʃən] n (of addict) реабилитация; (of criminal) интеграция

rehearsal [rı'həːsəl] n репетиция

rehearse [rı'həːs] vt репетировать (отрепетировать pf)

reign [reın] n царствование ♦ vi (monarch) царствовать (impf); (fig) царить (impf)

reimburse [riːım'bəːs] vt возмещать (возместить pf)

rein [reın] n (for horse) вожжа

reincarnation [riːınkɑː'neıʃən] n (belief) переселение душ

reindeer ['reındıə'] n inv северный олень m

reinforce [riːın'fɔːs] vt (strengthen) укреплять (укрепить pf); (back up) подкреплять (подкрепить pf); **~ment** n укрепление; **~ments** npl (MIL) подкрепление ntsg

reinstate [riːın'steıt] vt восстанавливать (восстановить pf) в прежнем положении

reject vb [rı'dʒekt] n ['riːdʒekt] отклонять (отклонить pf), отвергать (отвергнуть pf); (political system) отвергать (отвергнуть pf); (candidate) отклонять (отклонить pf); (goods) браковать (забраковать pf) ♦ n (product) некондиционное изделие, отклонение; **~ion** [rı'dʒekʃən] n отклонение

rejoice [rı'dʒɔıs] vi: **to ~ at** or **over**

ликова́ть *(impf)* по по́воду +*gen*

rejuvenate [rɪ'dʒuːvəneɪt] *vt*
(person) омола́живать
(омолоди́ть *pf*)

relapse [rɪ'læps] *n (MED)* рециди́в

relate [rɪ'leɪt] *vt (tell)*
переска́зывать (пересказа́ть *pf*);
(connect): **to ~ sth to** относи́ть
(отнести́ *pf*) что-н к +*dat* ♦ *vi*: **to ~
to** *(person)* сходи́ться (сойти́сь *pf*)
с +*instr*; *(subject, thing)* относи́ться
(отнести́сь *pf*) к +*dat*; **~d** *adj*: **~d
(to)** состоя́щий в
родстве́ (с +*instr*); *(animal,
language)* ро́дственный (с +*instr*);
they are ~d они́ состоя́т в
родстве́

relating to [rɪ'leɪtɪŋ-] *prep*
относи́тельно +*gen*

relation [rɪ'leɪʃən] *n (member of
family)* ро́дственник(ица);
(connection) отноше́ние *nt*; **~s** *npl*
(dealings) сноше́ния *ntpl*; *(relatives)*
ро́дственники *mpl*, родня́ *fsg*;
~ship *n (between two people,
countries)* (взаимо)отноше́ния
ntpl; *(between two things, affair)*
связь *f*

relative ['relətɪv] *n (family member)*
ро́дственник(ица) ♦ *adj*
(comparative) относи́тельный; **~
to** *(in relation to)* относя́щийся к
+*dat*; **~ly** *adv* относи́тельно

relax [rɪ'læks] *vi* расслабля́ться
(рассла́биться *pf*) ♦ *vt (grip, rule,
control)* ослабля́ть (осла́бить *pf*);
(person) расслабля́ть (рассла́бить
pf); **~ation** [riːlæk'seɪʃən] *n* о́тдых;
(of muscle) расслабле́ние; *(of grip,
rule, control)* ослабле́ние; **~ed** *adj*
непринуждённый,
рассла́бленный; **~ing** *adj*
(holiday) расслабля́ющий

relay *n* ['riːleɪ] *vb* [rɪ'leɪ] *n (race)*
эстафе́та ♦ *vt* передава́ть
(переда́ть *pf*)

release [rɪ'liːs] *n (from prison)*
освобожде́ние; *(of gas, book, film)*
вы́пуск ♦ *vt (see n)* освобожда́ть
(освободи́ть *pf*); выпуска́ть
(вы́пустить *pf*); *(TECH, catch, spring
etc)* отпуска́ть (отпусти́ть *pf*)

relentless [rɪ'lentlɪs] *adj (effort)*
неосла́бный; *(rain)*
продолжи́тельный; *(determined)*
неуста́нный

relevance ['relɪvəns] *n (of remarks,
question)* уме́стность *f*; *(of
information)* актуа́льность *f*

relevant ['relɪvənt] *adj*
актуа́льный; **~ to** относя́щийся к
+*dat*

reliability [rɪlaɪə'bɪlɪtɪ] *n (see adj)*
надёжность *f*; достове́рность *f*

reliable [rɪ'laɪəbl] *adj* надёжный;
(information) достове́рный

reliance [rɪ'laɪəns] *n*: **~ (on)** *(person,
drugs)* зави́симость *f* (от +*gen*)

relic ['relɪk] *n (of past etc)* рели́квия

relief [rɪ'liːf] *n* облегче́ние; *(aid)*
по́мощь *f*

relieve [rɪ'liːv] *vt (pain, suffering)*
облегча́ть (облегчи́ть *pf*); *(fear,
worry)* уменьша́ть (уме́ньшить
pf); *(colleague, guard)* сменя́ть
(смени́ть *pf*); **to ~ sb of sth**
освобожда́ть (освободи́ть *pf*)
кого́-н от чего́-н

relieved *adj*: **to feel ~** чу́вствовать
(почу́вствовать *pf*) облегче́ние

religion [rɪ'lɪdʒən] *n* рели́гия

religious [rɪ'lɪdʒəs] *adj*
религио́зный

relinquish [rɪ'lɪŋkwɪʃ] *vt (authority)*
отка́зываться (отказа́ться *pf*)
от +*gen*

relish ['relɪʃ] *n (CULIN)* припра́ва;
(enjoyment) наслажде́ние ♦ *vt*
наслажда́ться (наслади́ться *pf*)
+*instr*, смакова́ть *(impf)*

reluctance [rɪ'lʌktəns] *n*
нежела́ние

reluctant [rɪ'lʌktənt] adj неохо́тный; (person): **he is ~ to go there** он идёт туда́ неохо́тно; **~ly** adv неохо́тно

rely on [rɪ'laɪ-] vt fus (count on) рассчи́тывать (impf) на +acc; (trust) полага́ться (положи́ться pf) на +acc

remain [rɪ'meɪn] vi остава́ться (оста́ться pf); **~der** n оста́ток; **~ing** adj сохрани́вшийся, оста́вшийся; **~s** npl (of meal) оста́тки mpl; (of building) развали́ны fpl; (of body) оста́нки mpl

remand [rɪ'mɑːnd] n: **on ~** взя́тый под стра́жу ♦ vt: **he was ~ed in custody** он был взят под стра́жу

remark [rɪ'mɑːk] n замеча́ние ♦ vt замеча́ть (заме́тить pf); **~able** adj замеча́тельный

remedial [rɪ'miːdɪəl] adj (classes) исправи́тельный, корректи́вный

remedy ['rɛmədɪ] n (cure) сре́дство ♦ vt исправля́ть (испра́вить pf)

remember [rɪ'mɛmbəʳ] vt (recall) вспомина́ть (вспо́мнить pf); (bear in mind) по́мнить (impf)

remembrance [rɪ'mɛmbrəns] n па́мять f

Remembrance day - День па́мяти. Отмеча́ется в ближа́йшее к 11 ноября́ воскресе́нье. В э́тот день лю́ди чтят па́мять поги́бших в двух мировы́х во́йнах. Они́ покупа́ют кра́сные бума́жные ма́ки и но́сят их в петли́цах. Де́ньги, вы́рученные от прода́жи ма́ков иду́т на благотвори́тельные це́ли.

remind [rɪ'maɪnd] vt: **to ~ sb to do** напомина́ть (напо́мнить pf) кому́-н +infin; **to ~ sb of sth**

напомина́ть (напо́мнить pf) кому́-н о чём-н; **she ~s me of her mother** она́ напомина́ет мне свою́ мать; **~er** n напомина́ние

reminisce [rɛmɪ'nɪs] vi вспомина́ть (вспо́мнить pf); **~nt** adj: **to be ~nt of sth** напомина́ть (напо́мнить pf) что-н

remit [rɪ'mɪt] vt (send) пересыла́ть (пересла́ть pf)

remnant ['rɛmnənt] n оста́ток

remorse [rɪ'mɔːs] n раска́яние

remote [rɪ'məut] adj (place, time) отдалённый; **~ control** n дистанцио́нное управле́ние; **~ly** adv отдалённо; **I'm not ~ly interested** я ниско́лько не заинтересо́ван

removable [rɪ'muːvəbl] adj съёмный

removal [rɪ'muːvəl] n удале́ние; (BRIT: of furniture) перево́зка

remove [rɪ'muːv] vt (take away) убира́ть (убра́ть pf); (clothing, employee) снима́ть (снять pf); (stain) удаля́ть (удали́ть pf); (problem, doubt) устраня́ть (устрани́ть pf)

Renaissance [rɪ'neɪsɑːs] n: **the ~** (HISTORY) Возрожде́ние

render ['rɛndəʳ] vt (assistance) ока́зывать (оказа́ть pf); (harmless, useless) де́лать (сде́лать pf) +instr

rendezvous ['rɒndɪvuː] n (meeting) свида́ние; (place) ме́сто свида́ния

renew [rɪ'njuː] vt возобновля́ть (возобнови́ть pf); **~al** n возобновле́ние

renounce [rɪ'nauns] vt отка́зываться (отказа́ться pf) от +gen; (belief, throne) отрека́ться (отре́чься pf) от +gen

renovate ['rɛnəveɪt] vt модернизи́ровать (impf/pf); (building) де́лать (сде́лать pf) капита́льный ремо́нт в +prp

renovation [renəˈveɪʃən] n
модерниза́ция; (of work of art)
реставра́ция; (of building)
капита́льный ремо́нт

renowned [rɪˈnaund] adj
просла́вленный

rent [rent] n кварти́рная пла́та ♦ vt
(take for rent: house) снима́ть
(снять pf); (: television, car) брать
(взять pf) напрока́т; (also: ~ out:
house) сдава́ть (сдать pf) (внаём);
(: television, car) дава́ть (дать pf)
напрока́т; **~al** n (charge) пла́та за
прока́т

rep [rep] n abbr (COMM) =
representative

repair [rɪˈpeə^r] n ремо́нт ♦ vt
(clothes, shoes) чини́ть (почин─
и́ть pf); (car) ремонти́ровать
(отремонти́ровать pf); **in good/
bad ~** в хоро́шем/плохо́м
состоя́нии

repay [ri:ˈpeɪ] (irreg) vt (money, debt)
выпла́чивать (вы́платить pf);
(person) упла́чивать (уплати́ть pf)
+dat; **to ~ sb (for sth)** (favour)
отпла́чивать (отплати́ть pf)
кому́-н (за что-н); **~ment** n
вы́плата

repeat [rɪˈpiːt] vt повторя́ть
(повтори́ть pf) ♦ vi повторя́ться
(повтори́ться pf) ♦ n (RADIO, TV)
повторе́ние; **~edly** adv
неоднокра́тно

repel [rɪˈpel] vt (disgust)
отта́лкивать (оттолкну́ть pf);
~lent n: **insect ~lent** репелле́нт

repent [rɪˈpent] vi: **to ~ (of)** ка́яться
(пока́яться pf) (в +prp); **~ance** n
покая́ние

repercussions [ri:pəˈkʌʃənz] npl
после́дствия ntpl

repertoire [ˈrepətwɑː^r] n
репертуа́р

repetition [repɪˈtɪʃən] n (repeat)

повторе́ние

repetitive [rɪˈpetɪtɪv] adj
повторя́ющийся

replace [rɪˈpleɪs] vt (put back)
класть (положи́ть pf) обра́тно;
(: vertically) ста́вить (поста́вить pf)
обра́тно; (take the place of)
заменя́ть (замени́ть pf); **~ment** n
заме́на

replay n [ˈriːpleɪ] vb [riːˈpleɪ] n (of
match) переигро́вка; (of film)
повто́рный пока́з ♦ vt (match,
game) переи́грывать (переигра́ть
pf); (part of tape) повто́рно
прои́грывать (проигра́ть pf)

replenish [rɪˈplenɪʃ] vt (stock etc)
пополня́ть (попо́лнить pf)

replica [ˈreplɪkə] n (copy) ко́пия

reply [rɪˈplaɪ] n отве́т ♦ vi отвеча́ть
(отве́тить pf)

report [rɪˈpɔːt] n (account) докла́д,
отчёт; (PRESS, TV etc) репорта́ж;
(statement) сообще́ние; (BRIT:
also: **school ~**) отчёт об
успева́емости ♦ vt (state)
сообща́ть (сообщи́ть pf) о +prp; (event,
meeting) докла́дывать (доложи́ть
pf) о +prp; (person) доноси́ть
(донести́ pf) на +acc ♦ vi (make a
report) докла́дывать (доложи́ть
pf); **to ~ to sb** (present o.s.)
явля́ться (яви́ться pf) к
кому́-н; (be responsible to) быть
(impf) под нача́лом кого́-н; **to ~
that** сообща́ть (сообщи́ть pf),
что; **~edly** adv как сообща́ют;
~er n репортёр

represent [reprɪˈzent] vt (person,
nation) представля́ть
(предста́вить pf); (view, belief)
излага́ть (изложи́ть pf);
(constitute) представля́ть (impf)
собо́й; (idea, emotion)
символизи́ровать (impf/pf);
(describe): **to ~ sth as** изобража́ть
(изобрази́ть pf) что-н как; **~ation**

[rɪprɪzen'teɪʃən] n (state)
представительство; (picture,
statue) изображение; ~ative n
представитель m ♦ adj
представительный

repress [rɪ'pres] vt подавлять
(подавить pf); ~ion [rɪ'preʃən] n
подавление; ~ive adj
репрессивный

reprieve [rɪ'priːv] n (LAW)
отсрочка (в исполнении
приговора); (fig: delay)
передышка

reprimand ['reprɪmɑːnd] n
выговор ♦ vt делать (сделать pf)
выговор +dat

reprisal [rɪ'praɪzl] n расправа

reproach [rɪ'prəutʃ] n упрёк ♦ vt: to
~ sb for sth/with sth упрекать
(упрекнуть pf) кого-н за что-н/в
чём-н

reproduce [riːprə'djuːs] vt
воспроизводить (воспроизвести
pf) ♦ vi размножаться
(размножиться pf)

reproduction [riːprə'dʌkʃən] n
воспроизведение; (ART)
репродукция

reptile ['reptaɪl] nt adj
пресмыкающееся nt adj
(животное)

republic [rɪ'pʌblɪk] n республика;
~an n (US: POL): **Republican**
республиканец(нка)

repulsive [rɪ'pʌlsɪv] adj
отвратительный

reputable ['repjutəbl] adj (person)
уважаемый; ~ **company**
компания с хорошей
репутацией

reputation [repju'teɪʃən] n
репутация

reputed [rɪ'pjuːtɪd] adj (rumoured)
предполагаемый; ~**ly** adv по
общему мнению

request [rɪ'kwest] n (polite demand)

просьба; (formal demand) заявка
♦ vt: to ~ sth of or from sb
просить (попросить pf) что-н у
кого-н

require [rɪ'kwaɪə'] vt (subj: person)
нуждаться (impf) в +prp; (: thing,
situation) требовать (impf); (order):
to ~ sth of sb требовать
(потребовать pf) что-н от кого-н;
we ~ you to complete the task
мы требуем, чтобы Вы
завершили работу; ~**ment** n
(need, want) потребность f

requisite ['rekwɪzɪt] n требование
♦ adj необходимый

rescue ['reskjuː] n спасение ♦ vt: to
~ (**from**) спасать (спасти pf) (от
+gen); **to come to sb's ~**
приходить (прийти pf) кому-н на
помощь

research [rɪ'səːtʃ] n исследование
♦ vt исследовать (impf/pf); ~**er** n
исследователь m

resemblance [rɪ'zembləns] n
сходство

resemble [rɪ'zembl] vt походить
(impf) на +acc

resent [rɪ'zent] vt (fact) негодовать
(impf) против +gen; (person)
негодовать (impf) на +acc; ~**ful** adj
негодующий; **I am ~ful of his
behaviour** его поведение
приводит меня в негодование;
~**ment** n негодование

reservation [rezə'veɪʃən] n
(booking) предварительный
заказ; (doubt) сомнение; (for
tribe) резервация

reserve [rɪ'zəːv] n (store) резерв,
запас; (also: **nature ~**) запасной
заповедник; (SPORT) запасной
игрок; (restraint) сдержанность f
♦ vt (look, tone) сохранять
(сохранить pf); (seats, table etc)
заказывать (заказать pf); **in ~** в
резерве or запасе; ~**d** adj

(restrained) сде́ржанный

reservoir [ˈrezəvwɑːʳ] n (of water)
водохрани́лище

reshuffle [riːˈʃʌfl] n: **Cabinet ~**
перетасо́вка or перестано́вки fpl
в кабине́те мини́стров

reside [rɪˈzaɪd] vi (live) прожива́ть
(impf); **~nce** [ˈrezɪdəns] n (home)
резиде́нция; (length of stay)
пребыва́ние; **~nt** [ˈrezɪdənt] n (of
country, town) (постоя́нный(ая))
жи́тель(ница) m(f); (in hotel)
прожива́ющий(ая) m(f) adj ♦ adj
(population) постоя́нный; **~ntial**
[rezɪˈdenʃəl] adj (area) жило́й;
(course, college) с прожива́нием

resign [rɪˈzaɪn] vi (from post)
уходи́ть (уйти́ pf) в отста́вку ♦ vt
(one's post) оставля́ть (оста́вить
pf) c +gen; **to ~ o.s. to** смиря́ться
(смири́ться pf) c +instr; **~ation**
[rezɪɡˈneɪʃən] n отста́вка;
(acceptance) поко́рность f,
смире́ние; **~ed** adj (to situation
etc) смири́вшийся

resilience [rɪˈzɪlɪəns] n сто́йкость f

resilient [rɪˈzɪlɪənt] adj сто́йкий

resin [ˈrezɪn] n смола́

resist [rɪˈzɪst] vt сопротивля́ться
(impf) +dat; (temptation) устоя́ть
(pf) пе́ред +instr; **~ance** n
(opposition) сопротивле́ние; (to
illness) сопротивля́емость f

resolute [ˈrezəluːt] adj (faith)
твёрдый; (opposition)
реши́тельный

resolution [rezəˈluːʃən] n (decision)
реше́ние; (: formal) резолю́ция;
(determination) реши́мость f; (of
problem, difficulty) разреше́ние

resolve [rɪˈzɔlv] n реши́тельность f
♦ vt (problem, difficulty) разреши́ть
(разреши́ть pf) ♦ vi: **to ~ to do**
реша́ть (реши́ть pf) +infin; **~d** adj
реши́тельный

resonant [ˈrezənənt] adj звуча́щий

resort [rɪˈzɔːt] n (town) куро́рт;
(recourse) прибега́ние ♦ vi: **to ~ to**
прибега́ть (прибе́гнуть pf) к +dat;
the last ~ после́дняя наде́жда; **in
the last ~** в кра́йнем слу́чае

resounding [rɪˈzaundɪŋ] adj (noise)
звучный; (fig: success) гро́мкий

resource [rɪˈsɔːs] n ресу́рс; **~ful** adj
изобрета́тельный

respect [rɪsˈpekt] n уваже́ние ♦ vt
уважа́ть (impf); **~s** npl (greetings)
почте́ние ntsg; **with ~ to**, **in ~ of** в
отноше́нии +gen; **in this ~** в э́том
отноше́нии; **~ability**
[rɪspektəˈbɪlɪtɪ] n
респекта́бельность f, **~able** adj
прили́чный; (morally correct)
респекта́бельный; **~ful** adj
почти́тельный

respective [rɪsˈpektɪv] adj: **he drove
them to their ~ homes** он отвёз
их обо́их по дома́м; **~ly** adv
соотве́тственно

respond [rɪsˈpɔnd] vi (answer)
отвеча́ть (отве́тить pf); (react): **to
~ to** (pressure, criticism)
реаги́ровать (отреаги́ровать pf)
на +acc

response [rɪsˈpɔns] n (answer)
отве́т; (reaction) резона́нс, о́тклик

responsibility [rɪspɔnsɪˈbɪlɪtɪ] n
(liability) отве́тственность f; (duty)
обя́занность f

responsible [rɪsˈpɔnsɪbl] adj: **~ (for)**
отве́тственный (за +acc)

responsive [rɪsˈpɔnsɪv] adj (child,
nature) отзы́вчивый; **~ to**
(demand, treatment)
восприи́мчивый к +dat

rest [rest] n (relaxation, pause)
о́тдых; (stand, support) подста́вка
♦ vi (relax, stop) отдыха́ть
(отдохну́ть pf) ♦ vt (head, eyes etc)
дава́ть (дать pf) о́тдых +dat;
(lean): **to ~ sth against**
прислоня́ть (прислони́ть pf)
что-н к +dat; **the ~** (remainder)

остально́е nt adj; **the ~ of them** остальны́е (из них); **to ~ on** (person) опира́ться (опере́ться pf) на +acc; (idea) опира́ться (impf) на +acc; (object) лежа́ть (impf) на +prp; **~ assured that ...** бу́дьте уве́рены, что ...; **it ~s with him to ...** на нём лежи́т обя́занность +infin ...; **to ~ one's eyes** or **gaze on** остана́вливать (останови́ть pf) (свой) взгляд на +acc

restaurant ['restərɒn] n рестора́н

restful ['restful] adj ми́рный, поко́йный

restless ['restlɪs] adj беспоко́йный

restoration [restə'reɪʃən] n (of building etc) реставра́ция; (of order, health) восстановле́ние

restore [rɪ'stɔː] vt (see n) реставри́ровать (отреставри́ровать pf); восстана́вливать (восстанови́ть pf); (stolen property) возвраща́ть (возврати́ть pf); (to power) верну́ть (pf)

restrain [rɪs'treɪn] vt сде́рживать (сдержа́ть pf); (person): **to ~ sb from doing** не дава́ть (дать pf) кому́-н +infin; **~ed** adj сде́ржанный; **~t** n (moderation) сде́ржанность f; (restriction) ограниче́ние

restrict [rɪs'trɪkt] vt ограни́чивать (ограни́чить pf); **~ion** [rɪs'trɪkʃən] n: **~ion (on)** ограниче́ние (на +acc); **~ive** adj ограничи́тельный; (clothing) стесня́ющий

result [rɪ'zʌlt] n результа́т ♦ vi: **to ~ in** зака́нчиваться (зако́нчиться pf) +instr; **as a ~ of** в результа́те +gen

resume [rɪ'zjuːm] vt (work, journey) возобновля́ть (возобнови́ть pf) ♦ vi продолжа́ть (продо́лжить pf)

résumé ['reɪzjuːmeɪ] n резюме́ nt ind; (US: for job) автобиогра́фия

resumption [rɪ'zʌmpʃən] n возобновле́ние

resurgence [rɪ'səːdʒəns] n всплеск

retail ['riːteɪl] adj ро́зничный ♦ adv в ро́зницу; **~er** n ро́зничный торго́вец; **~ price** n ро́зничная цена́

retain [rɪ'teɪn] vt (keep) сохраня́ть (сохрани́ть pf)

retaliate [rɪ'tælɪeɪt] vi: **to ~ (against)** (attack) наноси́ть (нанести́ pf) отве́тный уда́р (+dat); (illtreatment) отпла́чивать (отплати́ть pf) (за +acc)

retaliation [rɪtælɪ'eɪʃən] n (see vi) отве́тный уда́р; отпла́та

retarded [rɪ'tɑːdɪd] adj (growth, development) заме́дленный

reticent ['retɪsnt] adj сде́ржанный

retina ['retɪnə] n сетча́тка

retire [rɪ'taɪə] vi (give up work) уходи́ть (уйти́ pf) на пе́нсию; (withdraw) удаля́ться (удали́ться pf); (go to bed) удаля́ться (удали́ться pf) на поко́й; **~d** adj: **he is ~d** он на пе́нсии; **~ment** n вы́ход or ухо́д на пе́нсию

retiring [rɪ'taɪərɪŋ] adj (shy) засте́нчивый

retreat [rɪ'triːt] n (place) убе́жище; (withdrawal) ухо́д; (MIL) отступле́ние ♦ vi отступа́ть (отступи́ть pf)

retribution [retrɪ'bjuːʃən] n возме́здие

retrieval [rɪ'triːvəl] n восстановле́ние

retrieve [rɪ'triːv] vt (object) получа́ть (получи́ть pf) обра́тно; (honour) восстана́вливать (восстанови́ть pf); (situation) спаса́ть (спасти́ pf)

retrospect ['retrəspekt] n: **in ~** в ретроспе́кции; **~ive** [retrə'spektɪv] adj (law, tax) име́ющий обра́тную си́лу

return [rɪ'tɜːn] n (from, to place)
возвращение; (of sth stolen etc)
возврат; (COMM) доход ♦ cpd
(journey, ticket) обратный ♦ vi
возвращаться (возвратиться pf),
вернуться (pf) ♦ vt возвращать
(возвратить pf, вернуть (pf);
(LAW, verdict) выносить (вынести
pf); (POL, candidate) избирать
(избрать pf); (ball) отбивать
(отбить pf); **in ~ (for)** в ответ (на
+acc); **many happy ~s (of the day)!**
с днём рождения!; **to ~ to**
(consciousness) приходить
(прийти pf) в +acc; (power)
вернуться (pf) к +dat

reunion [riː'juːnɪən] n (reuniting)
воссоединение; (party) встреча

rev [rev] n abbr (AUT) = **revolution**

Rev. abbr (REL) = **Reverend**

revamp [riː'væmp] vt обновлять
(обновить pf)

reveal [rɪ'viːl] vt (make known)
обнаруживать (обнаружить pf);
(make visible) открывать (открыть
pf); **~ing** adj (action, statement)
показательный; (dress) открытый

revel ['revl] vi: **to ~ in sth**
упиваться (impf) чем-н; **to ~ in
doing** обожать (impf) +infin

revelation [revə'leɪʃən] n (fact)
открытие

revenge [rɪ'vendʒ] n месть f; **to
take ~ on, ~ o.s. on** мстить
(отомстить pf) +dat

revenue ['revənjuː] n доходы
mpl

reverence ['revərəns] n почтение

Reverend ['revərənd] adj: **the
Reverend** его преподобие

reversal [rɪ'vɜːsl] n радикальное
изменение; (of roles) перемена

reverse [rɪ'vɜːs] n (opposite)
противоположное f; (of coin,
medal) оборотная сторона; (of
paper) оборот; (AUT: also: ~

gear) обратный ход ♦ adj
(opposite) обратный ♦ vt (order,
position, decision) изменять
(изменить pf); (process, policy)
поворачивать (повернуть pf) в
вспять ♦ vi (BRIT : AUT) давать
(дать pf) задний ход; **in ~ order** в
обратном порядке; **to ~ a car**
давать (дать pf) задний ход; **to ~
roles** меняться (поменяться pf)
ролями

revert [rɪ'vɜːt] vi: **to ~ to** (to former
state) возвращаться
(возвратиться pf) к +dat; (LAW:
money, property) переходить
(перейти pf) к +dat

review [rɪ'vjuː] n (of situation, policy
etc) пересмотр; (of book, film etc)
рецензия; (magazine) обозрение
♦ vt (situation, policy etc)
пересматривать (пересмотреть
pf); (book, film etc) рецензировать
(отрецензировать pf)

revise [rɪ'vaɪz] vt (manuscript)
перерабатывать (переработать
pf); (opinion, law) пересматривать
(пересмотреть pf) ♦ vi (SCOL)
повторять (повторить pf)

revision [rɪ'vɪʒən] n (see vb)
переработка; пересмотр;
повторение

revival [rɪ'vaɪvl] n (recovery)
оживление; (of interest, faith)
возрождение

revive [rɪ'vaɪv] vt (person)
возвращать (возвратить pf) к
жизни; (economy, industry)
оживлять (оживить pf); (tradition,
interest etc) возрождать
(возродить pf) ♦ vi (see vt)
приходить (прийти pf) в
сознание; оживляться
(оживиться pf); возрождаться
(возродиться pf)

revolt [rɪ'vəult] n (rebellion)
восстание ♦ vi (rebel) восставать

(восста́ть *pf*) ♦ *vt* вызыва́ть (вы́звать *pf*) отвраще́ние у +*gen*; **~ing** *adj* отврати́тельный

revolution [rɛvə'luːʃən] *n* револю́ция; (*of wheel, earth etc*) оборо́т; **~ary** *adj* революцио́нный ♦ *n* революционе́р(ка)

revolve [rɪ'vɔlv] *vi* (*turn*) враща́ться (*impf*); (*fig*): to ~ (a)round враща́ться (*impf*) вокру́г +*gen*

revolver [rɪ'vɔlvə] *n* револьве́р

revulsion [rɪ'vʌlʃən] *n* отвраще́ние

reward [rɪ'wɔːd] *n* награ́да ♦ *vt*: to ~ (for) (*effort*) вознагражда́ть (вознагради́ть *pf*) (за +*acc*); **~ing** *adj*: this work is **~ing** э́та рабо́та прино́сит удовлетворе́ние

rewind [riː'waɪnd] (*irreg*) *vt* перема́тывать (перемота́ть *pf*)

rewrite [riː'raɪt] (*irreg*) *vt* (*rework*) перепи́сывать (переписа́ть *pf*)

rhetorical [rɪ'tɔrɪkl] *adj* ритори́ческий

rheumatism ['ruːmətɪzəm] *n* ревмати́зм

rhinoceros [raɪ'nɔsərəs] *n* носоро́г

rhubarb ['ruːbɑːb] *n* реве́нь *m*

rhyme [raɪm] *n* ри́фма; (*in poetry*) разме́р

rhythm ['rɪðm] *n* ритм

rib [rɪb] *n* (*ANAT*) ребро́

ribbon ['rɪbən] *n* ле́нта; **in ~s** (*torn*) в кло́чья

rice [raɪs] *n* рис

rich [rɪtʃ] *adj* бога́тый; (*clothes, jewels*) роско́шный; (*food, colour, life*) насы́щенный; (*abundant*): **~ in** бога́тый +*instr*; **the ~** *npl* (*rich people*) бога́тые *pl adj*; **~es** *npl* (*wealth*) бога́тство *ntsg*; **~ly** *adv* (*dressed, decorated*) бога́то; (*rewarded*) ще́дро; (*deserved, earned*) вполне́

rickets ['rɪkɪts] *n* (*MED*) рахи́т

ricochet ['rɪkəʃeɪ] *vi* рикошети́ровать (*impf*)

rid [rɪd] (*pt, pp* ~) *vt*: to ~ **sb of sth** избавля́ть (изба́вить *pf*) кого́-н от чего́-н; **to get ~ of** избавля́ться (изба́виться *pf*) or отде́лываться (отде́латься *pf*) от +*gen*

ridden ['rɪdn] *pp of* **ride**

riddle ['rɪdl] *n* (*conundrum*) зага́дка ♦ *vt*: **~d with** (*holes, bullets*) изрешечённый +*instr*; (*guilt, doubts*) по́лный +*gen*; (*corruption*) прони́занный +*instr*

ride [raɪd] (*pt* **rode**, *pp* **ridden**) *n* пое́здка ♦ *vi* (*as sport*) е́здить (*impf*) верхо́м; (*go somewhere, travel*) е́здить/е́хать (пое́хать *pf*) ♦ *vt* (*horse*) е́здить/е́хать (*impf*) верхо́м на +*prp*; (*bicycle, motorcycle*) е́здить/е́хать (*impf*) на +*prp*; (*distance*) проезжа́ть (прое́хать *pf*); **a 5 mile ~** пое́здка в 5 миль; **to take sb for a ~** (*fig*) прокати́ть (*pf*) кого́-н; **~r** *n* (*on horse*) нае́здник(ица); (*on bicycle*) велосипеди́ст(ка); (*on motorcycle*) мотоцикли́ст(ка)

ridge [rɪdʒ] *n* (*of hill*) гре́бень *m*

ridicule [rɪ'dɪkjuːl] *vt* высме́ивать (вы́смеять *pf*)

ridiculous [rɪ'dɪkjuləs] *adj* смехотво́рный; **it's ~** э́то смешно́

riding ['raɪdɪŋ] *n* верхова́я езда́

rife [raɪf] *adj*: **to be ~** (*corruption*) процвета́ть (*impf*); **to be ~ with** (*rumours, fears*) изоби́ловать (*impf*) +*instr*

rifle ['raɪfl] *n* (*MIL*) винто́вка; (*for hunting*) ружьё

rift [rɪft] *n* (*also fig*) тре́щина

rig [rɪg] *n* (*also*: **oil ~**) бурова́я устано́вка ♦ *vt* подтасо́вывать (подтасова́ть *pf*) результа́ты +*gen*; **~ging** *n* (*NAUT*) такела́ж

right [raɪt] *adj* пра́вильный;
(*person, time, size*) подходя́щий;
(*fair, just*) справедли́вый; (*not left*)
пра́вый ♦ *n* (*entitlement*) пра́во ♦ *adv*
(*correctly*) пра́вильно; (*not to the
left*) напра́во ♦ *vt* (*ship*)
выра́внивать (вы́ровнять *pf*);
(*car*) ста́вить (поста́вить *pf*) на
колёса; (*fault, situation*)
исправля́ть (испра́вить *pf*);
(*wrong*) устраня́ть (устрани́ть *pf*)
♦ *excl* так, хорошо́; **she's ~** она́
права́; **that's ~!** (*answer*)
пра́вильно!; **is that clock ~?** э́ти
часы́ пра́вильно иду́т?; **on the ~**
спра́ва; **you are in the ~** пра́вда
за Ва́ми; **by ~s** по
справедли́вости; **~ and wrong**
хоро́шее и дурно́е; **~ now**
сейча́с же; **~ away** сра́зу же;
~eous ['raɪtʃəs] *adj* пра́ведный;
~ful *adj* зако́нный; **~-handed** *adj*:
he is ~-handed он правша́; **~ly**
adv (*with reason*) справедли́во; **~
of way** (*path etc*) пра́во
прохо́да; (*AUT*) пра́во прое́зда;
~-wing *adj* (*POL*) пра́вый

rigid ['rɪdʒɪd] *adj* (*structure, control*)
жёсткий; (*fig: attitude etc*) косный

rigor ['rɪɡə] *n* (*US*) = **rigour**

rigorous ['rɪɡərəs] *adj* жёсткий;
(*training*) серьёзный

rigour ['rɪɡə] (*US* **rigor**) *n*
жёсткость *f*; **~s** *npl* (*severity*)
тя́готы *fpl*, тру́дности *fpl*

rim [rɪm] *n* (*of glass, dish*) край; (*of
spectacles*) обо́док; (*of wheel*)
о́бод

rind [raɪnd] *n* (*of bacon, cheese*)
ко́рка; (*of lemon, orange etc*)
кожура́

ring [rɪŋ] (*pt* **rang**, *pp* **rung**) *n* (*of
metal, smoke*) кольцо́; (*of people,
objects, light*) круг; (*of spies, drug
dealers etc*) сеть *f*; (*for boxing*)

ринг; (*of circus*) аре́на; (*of doorbell,
telephone*) звоно́к ♦ *vi* звони́ть
(позвони́ть *pf*); (*doorbell*) звене́ть
(*impf*); (*also:* **~ out**: *voice, shot*)
раздава́ться (разда́ться *pf*) ♦ *vt*
(*BRIT : TEL*) звони́ть (позвони́ть *pf*)
+*dat*; **to give sb a ~** (*BRIT : TEL*)
звони́ть (позвони́ть *pf*) кому́-н;
my ears are ~ing у меня́ звени́т в
уша́х; **to ~ the bell** звони́ть (*impf*)
в звоно́к; **~ up** (*BRIT*) звони́ть
(позвони́ть *pf*) +*dat*; **~ing** *n* (*of
telephone, doorbell*) звоно́к; (*of
church bell, in ears*) звон

rink [rɪŋk] *n* (*also:* **ice-~**, **roller
skating ~**) като́к

rinse [rɪns] *vt* полоска́ть
(прополоска́ть *pf*) ♦ *n*: **to give sth
a ~** опола́скивать (ополосну́ть *pf*)
что-н

riot ['raɪət] *n* (*disturbance*)
беспоря́дки *mpl*, бесчи́нства *ntpl*
♦ *vi* бесчи́нствовать (*impf*); **to run
~** бу́йствовать (*impf*); **~ous** *adj*
(*mob, behaviour*)
бесчи́нствующий; (*living*)
разгу́льный; (*welcome*) бу́рный

rip [rɪp] *n* разры́в ♦ *vt* (*paper, cloth*)
разрыва́ть (разорва́ть *pf*) ♦ *vi*
разрыва́ться (разорва́ться *pf*)

ripe [raɪp] *adj* спе́лый, зре́лый; **~n**
vi спеть (поспе́ть *pf*), зреть *or*
созрева́ть (созре́ть *pf*) ♦ *vt*: **the
sun will ~n them** они́ созре́ют на
со́лнце

ripple ['rɪpl] *n* рябь *f no pl*, зыбь *f
no pl*; (*of laughter, applause*) волна́

rise [raɪz] (*pt* **rose**, *pp* **~n**) *n* (*slope*)
подъём; (*increase*) повыше́ние;
(*fig: of state, leader*) возвыше́ние
♦ *vi* поднима́ться (подня́ться *pf*);
(*prices, numbers, voice*)
повыша́ться (повы́ситься *pf*);
(*sun, moon*) всходи́ть (взойти́ *pf*);
(*also:* **~ up**: *rebels*) восстава́ть
(восста́ть *pf*); (*in rank*)

продвига́ться (продви́нуться *pf*);
~ **to power** прихо́д к вла́сти; **to
give** ~ **to** вызыва́ть (вы́звать *pf*);
to ~ **to the occasion** оказа́ться
(оказа́ться *pf*) на высоте́
положе́ния; ~**n** [rɪzn] *pp of* **rise**

rising ['raɪzɪŋ] *adj* (*number, prices*)
расту́щий; (*sun, moon*)
восходя́щий

risk [rɪsk] *n* риск ♦ *vt* (*endanger*)
рискова́ть (*impf*) +*instr*; (*chance*)
рискова́ть (рискну́ть *pf*) +*instr*; **to
take a** ~ рискова́ть (рискну́ть *pf*),
идти́ (пойти́ *pf*) на риск; **to run
the** ~ **of doing** рискова́ть (*impf*)
+*infin*; **to put sb/sth at** ~ подверга́ть
(подве́ргнуть *pf*) кого́-н/что-н
ри́ску; **at one's own** ~ на свой
(страх и) риск; ~**y** *adj*
риско́ванный

rite [raɪt] *n* обря́д; **last** ~**s**
после́днее прича́стие

ritual ['rɪtjuəl] *adj* ритуа́льный ♦ *n*
(*REL*) обря́д; (*procedure*) ритуа́л

rival ['raɪvl] *n* сопе́рник(ица); (*in
business*) конкуре́нт ♦ *adj* (*business*)
конкури́рующий ♦ *vt* сопе́р-
ничать (*impf*) с +*instr*; ~
team кома́нда сопе́рника; ~**ry** *n*
(*in sport, love*) сопе́рничество; (*in
business*) конкуре́нция

river ['rɪvə*] *n* река́ ♦ *cpd* (*port,
traffic*) речно́й; **up/down** ~
вверх/вниз по реке́

road [rəud] *n* доро́га, путь *m*; (*in
town*) доро́га; (*motorway etc*)
шоссе́ *nt ind* ♦ *cpd*
(*accident*) доро́жный; **major/
minor** ~ гла́вная/второстепе́нная
доро́га; ~ **sense** чу́вство доро́ги; ~
junction пересече́ние доро́г,
перекрёсток; ~**block** *n*
доро́жное загражде́ние; ~ **rage** *n*
хулига́нское поведе́ние на
автодоро́ге; ~**side** *n* обо́чина

roam [rəum] *vi* скита́ться (*impf*)

roar [rɔ:*] *n* рёв; (*of laughter*)
взрыв ♦ *vi* реве́ть (*impf*); **to** ~ **with
laughter** хохота́ть (*impf*)

roast [rəust] *n* (*of meat*) жарко́е *nt
adj* ♦ *vt* (*meat, potatoes*) жа́рить
(зажа́рить *pf*)

rob [rɔb] *vt* гра́бить (огра́бить *pf*);
to ~ **sb of sth** лиша́ть (лиши́ть *pf*)
что-н у кого́-н; (*fig*) лиша́ть
(лиши́ть *pf*) кого́-н чего́-н; ~**ber**
n граби́тель *m*; ~**bery** *n*
ограбле́ние, грабёж

robe [rəub] *n* (*for ceremony etc*)
ма́нтия; (*also*: **bath** ~) ба́нный
хала́т; (*US*) плед

robin ['rɔbɪn] *n* (*ZOOL*: *also*: ~
redbreast) заря́нка

robot ['rəubɔt] *n* ро́бот

robust [rəu'bʌst] *adj* (*person*)
кре́пкий

rock [rɔk] *n* (*substance*) (го́рная)
поро́да; (*boulder*) валу́н; (*US*:
small stone) ка́мешек; (*MUS*: *also*:
~ **music**) рок ♦ *vt* (*swing*) кача́ть
(*impf*); (*shake*) шата́ть (*impf*) ♦ *vi*
(*object*) кача́ться (*impf*), шата́ться
(*impf*); (*person*) кача́ться (*impf*); **on
the** ~**s** (*drink*) со льдо́м; (*marriage
etc*) на гра́ни распа́да; ~ **and
roll** *n* рок-н-ро́лл

rocket ['rɔkɪt] *n* раке́та

rocky ['rɔkɪ] *adj* (*hill*) скали́стый;
(*path, soil*) камени́стый; (*unstable*)
ша́ткий

rod [rɔd] *n* прут; (*also*: **fishing** ~)
у́дочка

rode [rəud] *pt of* **ride**

rodent ['rəudnt] *n* грызу́н

rogue [rəug] *n* плут

role [rəul] *n* роль *f*; ~ **model** *n*
приме́р (для подража́ния)

roll [rəul] *n* (*of paper, cloth etc*)
руло́н; (*of banknotes*) сви́ток;
(*also*: **bread** ~) бу́лочка; (*register,
list*) спи́сок; (*of drums*) бой; (*of

thunder) раскат ♦ vt (ball, stone etc) катать/катить (impf); (also: ~ up: string) скручивать (скрутить pf); (: sleeves, eyes) закатывать (закатать pf); (cigarette) свёртывать (свернуть pf); (also: ~ out: pastry) раскатывать (раскатать pf) ♦ vi (also: ~ along: ball, car etc) катиться (impf); (ship) качаться (impf); ~ up vt (carpet, newspaper) сворачивать (свернуть pf); ~er n (for hair) бигуди pl ind; ~er skates npl ролики mpl, роликовые коньки mpl; ~ing pin n скалка; ~ing stock n (RAIL) подвижной состав

ROM [rɒm] n abbr (COMPUT: = read-only memory) ПЗУ

Roman ['rəumən] adj римский; ~ **Catholic** adj (римско-) католический ♦ n католик(ичка)

romance [rə'mæns] n (love affair, novel) роман; (charm) романтика

Romania [rəu'meɪnɪə] n Румыния; ~n adj румынский

romantic [rə'mæntɪk] adj романтичный; (play, story etc) романтический

Rome [rəum] n Рим

roof [ru:f] (pl ~s) n крыша; **the ~ of the mouth** нёбо

room [ru:m] n (in house) комната; (in school) класс; (in hotel) номер; (space) место; ~ npl (lodging) квартира fsg; "~s to let", (US) "~s for rent" (сдаются комнаты"; **single/double** (in hotel) одноместный/двухместный номер

roost [ru:st] vi усаживаться (усесться pf) на ночлег

root [ru:t] n корень m; ~s npl (family origins) корни mpl

rope [rəup] n верёвка ♦ vt (also: ~ off: area) отгораживать (отгородить pf) верёвкой; **to ~ to**

привязывать (привязать pf) верёвкой к +dat; **to ~ together** связывать (связать pf) верёвкой; **to know the ~s** (fig) знать (impf), что к чему

rose [rəuz] pt of **rise** ♦ n роза

rosemary ['rəuzmərɪ] n розмарин

roster ['rɒstə*] n: **duty ~** расписание дежурств

rosy ['rəuzɪ] adj (face, cheeks) румяный; (situation) радостный; (future) радужный

rot [rɒt] n (result) гниль f ♦ vi гнить (сгнить pf)

rota ['rəutə] n расписание дежурств

rotary ['rəutərɪ] adj (motion) вращательный; (engine) ротóрно-поршневой

rotate [rəu'teɪt] vt вращать (impf); (crops, jobs) чередовать (impf) ♦ vi вращаться (impf)

rotation [rəu'teɪʃən] n вращение; (of crops) севооборот

rotten ['rɒtn] adj гнилой; (meat, eggs) тухлый; (fig: unpleasant) мерзкий; (inf: bad) поганый; **to feel ~** (ill) чувствовать (impf) себя погано

rouble ['ru:bl] (US **ruble**) n рубль m

rough [rʌf] adj грубый; (surface) шероховатый; (terrain) пересечённый; (person, manner) резкий; (sea) бурный; (town, area) опасный; (plan, work) черновой; (guess) приблизительный ♦ vt: **to ~ it** ограничивать (ограничить pf) удобствами ♦ adv: **to sleep ~** (BRIT) ночевать (impf) где придётся; **~ly** adv грубо; (approximately) приблизительно

Roumania etc = **Romania** etc

round [raund] adj круглый; (duty: of policeman, doctor) обход; (game: of cards, golf) партия; (in competition) тур; (of ammunition) комплéкт; (of talks, also BOXING) рáунд ♦ vt огибáть (обогнýть pf) ♦ prep (surrounding) вокрýг +gen; (approximately): ~ **about three hundred** где-то óколо трёхсот ♦ adv: **all** ~ кругóм, вокрýг; **a** ~ **of applause** взрыв аплодисмéнтов; **a** ~ **of drinks** по бокáлу на кáждого; ~ **his neck/the table** вокрýг егó шéи/столá; **the shop is just** ~ **the corner** (fig) до магазíна рукóй подáть; **to go** ~ **the back** обходить (обойти́ pf) сзáди; **to walk** ~ **the room** ходи́ть (impf) по кóмнате; **to go** ~ **to sb's (house)** ходи́ть/идти́ (impf) к комý-н; **there's enough to go** ~ хвáтит на всех; ~ **off** vt (speech etc) завершáть (завершить pf); ~ **up** vt (cattle, people) сгонять (согнáть pf); (price, figure) округлять (округли́ть pf); ~**about** n (BRIT: AUT) кольцевáя трáнспортная развязка; (: at fair) карусéль f ♦ adj: **in a** ~**about way** окóльным путём; ~**up** n (of information) свóдка

rouse [rauz] vt (wake up) буди́ть (разбуди́ть pf); (stir up) возбуждáть (возбуди́ть pf)

rousing ['rauzɪŋ] adj (cheer) бýрный

route [ruːt] n (way) путь m, дорóга; (of bus, train etc) маршрýт

routine [ruːˈtiːn] adj (work) повседнéвный; (procedure) обы́чный ♦ n (habits) распорядок; (drudgery) рути́на; (THEAT) нóмер

row[1] [rəu] n ряд ♦ vi грести́ (impf) ♦ vt управлять (impf) +instr; **in a** ~ (fig) подряд

row[2] [rau] n (noise) шум; (dispute) скандáл; (inf: scolding) нагоняй

♦ vi скандáлить (поскандáлить pf)

rowdy ['raudɪ] adj бýйный

rowing ['rəuɪŋ] n грéбля

royal ['rɔɪəl] adj королéвский; ≈ **Royal Air Force** (BRIT) Воéнно-воздýшные си́лы fpl Великобритáнии; ~**ty** n (royal persons) члéны mpl королéвской семьи́; (payment) (áвторский) гонорáр

rpm abbr (= revolutions per minute) оборóты в минýту

RSVP abbr (= répondez s'il vous plaît) прóсим отвéтить на приглашéние

rub [rʌb] vt (part of body) терéть (потерéть pf); (object: to clean) терéть (impf); (: to dry) вытирáть (вы́тереть pf; hands: also: ~ **together**) потирáть (потерéть pf) ♦ n: **to give sth a** ~ (polish) натирáть (натерéть pf) что-н; **to** ~ **sb up** or (US) ~ **sb the wrong way** раздражáть (раздражи́ть pf) когó-н

rubber ['rʌbər] n (substance) рези́на, каучýк; (BRIT: eraser) рези́нка, лáстик

rubbish ['rʌbɪʃ] n мýсор; (junk) хлам, (fig • pej: nonsense) ерундá, чушь f; (: goods) дрянь f

rubble ['rʌbl] n облóмки mpl

ruble ['ruːbl] n (US) = **rouble**

ruby ['ruːbɪ] n руби́н

rucksack ['rʌksæk] n рюкзáк

rudder ['rʌdər] n руль m

ruddy ['rʌdɪ] adj (face) румя́ный

rude [ruːd] adj (impolite) грýбый; (unexpected) жестóкий

rudimentary [ruːdɪˈmɛntərɪ] adj элементáрный

rug [rʌg] n кóврик; (BRIT: blanket) плед

rugby ['rʌgbɪ] n (also: ~ **football**) рéгби nt ind

rugged ['rʌgɪd] *adj* (*landscape*) скалистый; (*features*) грубый; (*character*) прямой

ruin ['ru:ɪn] *n* (*destruction: of building, plans*) разрушение; (*downfall: financial*) разорение; (*bankruptcy*) гибель f; *vt* (*building, hopes, plans*) разрушать (разрушить *pf*); (*future, health, reputation*) губить (погубить *pf*); (*person: financially*) разорять (разорить *pf*); (*spoil: clothes*) портить (испортить *pf*); **~s** *npl* (*of building*) развалины *fpl*, руины *fpl*

rule [ru:l] *n* (*norm, regulation*) правило; (*government*) правление *vt* (*country, people*) править (*impf*) +*instr vi* (*leader, monarch etc*) править (*impf*); **as a ~** как правило; **~ out** *vt* (*exclude*) исключать (исключить *pf*); **~d** *adj* (*paper*) линованый; **~r** *n* правитель(ница) *m(f)*; (*instrument*) линейка

ruling ['ru:lɪŋ] *adj* (*party*) правящий *n* (*LAW*) постановление

rum [rʌm] *n* ром

Rumania *etc* = **Romania** *etc*

rumble ['rʌmbl] *n* (*of traffic, thunder*) гул

rumour ['ru:mər] (*US* **rumor**) *n* слух *vt*: **it is ~ed that ...** ходят слухи, что ...

rump [rʌmp] *n* (*of horse*) круп; (*of cow*) зад

run [rʌn] (*pt* **ran**, *pp* **~**) *n* (*fast pace*) бег; (*journey*) поездка; (*SKIING*) трасса; (*CRICKET, BASEBALL*) очко; (*in tights etc*) спустившиеся петли *fpl vi* бегать/бежать *pf* (*flee*) бежать (*impf/pf*); (*work: machine*) работать (*impf*); (*bus, train*) ходить (*impf*); (*play, show*) идти (*impf*); (*: contract*) длиться (*impf*); (*in election*) баллотироваться (*pf*)

vt (*race, distance*) пробегать (пробежать *pf*); (*business, hotel*) управлять (*impf*) +*instr*; (*competition, course*) организовать (*impf/pf*); (*house*) вести (*impf*); (*COMPUT, program*) выполнять (выполнить *pf*); (*water*) пускать (пустить *pf*); (*bath*) наполнять (наполнить *pf*); (*PRESS, article*) печатать (напечатать *pf*); **to ~ sth along** *or* **over** (*hand, fingers*) проводить (провести *pf*) чем-н по +*dat*; **in the long ~** в конечном итоге; **to be on the ~** скрываться (*impf*); **I'll ~ you to the station** я подвезу Вас до станции; **~ about** *vi* бегать (*impf*); **~ around** *vi* = **run about**; **~ away** *vi* убегать (убежать *pf*); **~ down** *vt* (*production, industry*) сворачивать (свернуть *pf*); (*AUT, hit*) сбивать (сбить *pf*); (*criticize*) поносить (*impf*); **to be ~ down** (*person*) выбиваться (выбиться *pf*) из сил; **~ in** *vt* (*BRIT: car*) обкатывать (обкатать *pf*); **~ into** *vt fus* (*meet: person*) сталкиваться (столкнуться *pf*) с +*instr*; (*: trouble*) наталкиваться (натолкнуться *pf*) на +*acc*; (*collide with*) врезаться (врезаться *pf*) в +*acc*; **~ off** *vt* (*copies*) делать (сделать *pf*), отснять (*pf*) *vi* (*person, animal*) сбегать (сбежать *pf*); **~ out** *vi* (*person*) выбегать (выбежать *pf*); (*liquid*) вытекать (вытечь *pf*); (*lease, visa*) истекать (истечь *pf*); (*money*) иссякать (иссякнуть *pf*); **my passport ~s out in July** срок действия моего паспорта истекает в июле; **~ out of** *vt fus*: **I've ~ out of money/petrol** *or* (*US*) **gas** у меня кончились деньги/ кончился бензин; **~ over** *vt* (*AUT*) давить (задавить *pf*); **~ through** *vt fus* пробегать (пробежать *pf*);

(*rehearse*) прогоня́ть (прогна́ть *pf*); **~ up** *vt*: **to ~ up a debt** аккумули́ровать (*impf/pf*) долги́; **to ~ up against** (*difficulties*) ста́лкиваться (столкну́ться *pf*) с +*instr*; **~away** *adj* (*truck, horse etc*) потеря́вший управле́ние

rung [rʌŋ] *pp of* **ring** ♦ *n* (*of ladder*) ступе́нька

runner ['rʌnə*r*] *n* (*in race: person*) бегу́н(ья); (: *horse*) скаку́н; (*on sledge, for drawer etc*) по́лоз; **~up** *n* финали́ст (заня́вший второ́е ме́сто)

running ['rʌnɪŋ] *n* (*sport*) бег; (*of business*) руково́дство ♦ *adj* (*water: to house*) водопрово́дный; **he is in/out of the ~ for sth** ему́ су́лит/ не су́лит что-л; **6 days ~** 6 дней подря́д; **~ costs** *npl* (*of business*) операцио́нные изде́ржки *fpl*; (*of car*) содержа́ние *ntsg*

runny ['rʌnɪ] *adj* (*honey, egg*) жи́дкий; (*nose*) сопли́вый

run-up ['rʌnʌp] *n* (*to event*) преддве́рие

runway ['rʌnweɪ] *n* взлётно-поса́дочная полоса́

rupture ['rʌptʃə*r*] *n* (*MED*) гры́жа

rural ['rʊərl] *adj* се́льский

rush [rʌʃ] *n* (*hurry*) спе́шка; (*COMM, sudden demand*) большо́й спрос; (*of water*) пото́к; (*of emotion*) прили́в ♦ *vt*: **to ~ one's meal/ work** второпя́х съеда́ть (съесть *pf*)/де́лать (сде́лать *pf*) рабо́ту ♦ *vi* (*person*) бежа́ть (*impf*); (*air, water*) хлыну́ть (*pf*); **~es** *npl* (*BOT*) камыши́ *mpl*; **~ hour** *n* час пик

Russia ['rʌʃə] *n* Росси́я; **~n** *adj* (*native Russian*) ру́сский; (*belonging to Russian Federation*) росси́йский ♦ *n* ру́сский(ая) *m(f)* *adj*; (*LING*) ру́сский язы́к

rust [rʌst] *n* ржа́вчина ♦ *vi* ржаве́ть (заржаве́ть *pf*)

rustic ['rʌstɪk] *adj* дереве́нский

rusty ['rʌstɪ] *adj* ржа́вый; (*fig: skill*) подзабы́тый

rut [rʌt] *n* (*groove*) колея́, борозда́; **to get into a ~** (*fig*) заходи́ть (зайти́ *pf*) в тупи́к

ruthless ['ruːθlɪs] *adj* беспоща́дный

rye [raɪ] *n* рожь *f*

S, s

Sabbath ['sæbəθ] *n* (*Christian*) воскресе́нье

sabotage ['sæbətɑːʒ] *n* сабота́ж ♦ *vt* (*machine, building*) выводи́ть (вы́вести *pf*) из стро́я; (*plan, meeting*) саботи́ровать (*impf/pf*)

sachet ['sæʃeɪ] *n* паке́тик

sack [sæk] *n* (*bag*) мешо́к ♦ *vt* (*dismiss*) увольня́ть (уво́лить *pf*); **to give sb the ~** увольня́ть (уво́лить *pf*) кого́-н (с рабо́ты); **I got the ~** меня́ уво́лили (с рабо́ты); **~ing** *n* (*dismissal*) увольне́ние

sacred ['seɪkrɪd] *adj* свяще́нный; (*place*) свято́й

sacrifice ['sækrɪfaɪs] *n* же́ртва; (*REL*) жертвоприноше́ние ♦ *vt* (*fig*) же́ртвовать (поже́ртвовать *pf*) +*instr*

sad [sæd] *adj* печа́льный

saddle ['sædl] *n* седло́

sadistic [sə'dɪstɪk] *adj* сади́стский

sadly ['sædlɪ] *adv* (*unhappily*) печа́льно, гру́стно; (*unfortunately*) к сожале́нию; (*seriously: mistaken, neglected*) серьёзно

sadness ['sædnɪs] *n* печа́ль *f*, грусть *f*

sae *abbr* (*BRIT*: = *stamped addressed envelope*) надпи́санный конве́рт с ма́ркой

safari [sə'fɑːrɪ] *n*: **to go on ~**

проводи́ть (провести́ *pf*) о́тпуск в сафа́ри

safe [seɪf] *adj* (place, subject) безопа́сный; (return, journey) благополу́чный; (bet) надёжный ♦ *n* сейф; **to be ~** находи́ться (*impf*) в безопа́сности; **~ from** (attack) защищённый *+gen*; **~ and sound** цел и невреди́м; (just) **to be on the ~ side** на вся́кий слу́чай; **~guard** *n* гара́нтия ♦ *vt* (life, interests) охраня́ть (*impf*); **~ly** *adv* (assume, say) с уве́ренностью; (drive, arrive) благополу́чно; **~ty** *n* безопа́сность; **~ty pin** *n* англи́йская була́вка

saga [ˈsɑːgə] *n* са́га

sage [seɪdʒ] *n* (herb) шалфе́й

Sagittarius [sædʒɪˈtɛərɪəs] *n* Стреле́ц

said [sed] *pt*, *pp* of **say**

sail [seɪl] *n* па́рус ♦ *vt* (boat) пла́вать/плыть (*impf*) на *+prp* ♦ *vi* (passenger, ship) пла́вать/плыть (*impf*); (also: **set ~**) отплыва́ть (отплы́ть *pf*); **to go for a ~** е́хать (пое́хать *pf*) ката́ться на ло́дке; **~ing** *n* (SPORT) па́русный спорт; **~or** *n* моря́к, матро́с

saint [seɪnt] *n* свято́й(а́я) *m(f) adj*; **~ly** *adj* свято́й

sake [seɪk] *n*: **for the ~ of sb/sth**, **for sb's/sth's ~** ра́ди кого́-н/ чего́-н

salad [ˈsæləd] *n* сала́т

salami [səˈlɑːmɪ] *n* сала́ми *f ind*

salary [ˈsælərɪ] *n* зарпла́та

sale [seɪl] *n* (act) прода́жа; (with discount) распрода́жа; (auction) то́рги *mpl*; **~s** *npl* (amount sold) объём *msg* прода́ж; **"for ~"** "продаётся"; **on ~** в прода́же; **~sman** (irreg) *n* (also: **travelling ~sman**) торго́вый аге́нт

salient [ˈseɪlɪənt] *adj* суще́ственный

saliva [səˈlaɪvə] *n* слюна́

salmon [ˈsæmən] *n inv* (ZOOL) лосо́сь *m*; (CULIN) лососи́на

salon [ˈsælɔn] *n* сало́н; **beauty ~** космети́ческий сало́н

salt [sɔːlt] *n* соль *f*; **~y** *adj* солёный

salute [səˈluːt] *n* (MIL) салю́т ♦ *vt* (MIL) отдава́ть (отда́ть *pf*) честь *+dat*; (fig) приве́тствовать (*impf*)

salvage [ˈsælvɪdʒ] *n* (saving) спасе́ние ♦ *vt* (also fig) спаса́ть (спасти́ *pf*)

salvation [sælˈveɪʃən] *n* спасе́ние

same [seɪm] *adj* тако́й же; (identical) одина́ковый ♦ *pron*: **the ~** тот же (са́мый) (f та же (са́мая), nt то же (са́мое), pl те же (са́мые)); **the ~ book** за та же (са́мая) кни́га, что и; **at the ~ time** (simultaneously) в э́то же вре́мя; (yet) в то же вре́мя; **all or just the ~** всё равно́; **to do the ~ (as sb)** де́лать (сде́лать *pf*) то же (са́мое) (, что и кто-н); **Happy New Year! - the ~ to you!** С Но́вым Го́дом! - Вас та́кже!

sample [ˈsɑːmpl] *n* (of work, goods) образе́ц ♦ *vt* (food, wine) про́бовать (попро́бовать *pf*); **to take a blood/urine ~** брать (взять *pf*) кровь/мочу́ на ана́лиз

sanction [ˈsæŋkʃən] *n* (approval) са́нкция ♦ *vt* (approve) санкциони́ровать (*impf/pf*); **~s** (severe measures) са́нкции *fpl*

sanctuary [ˈsæŋktjuərɪ] *n* (for animals) запове́дник; (for people) убе́жище

sand [sænd] *n* песо́к ♦ *vt* (also: **~ down**) ошку́ривать (ошку́рить *pf*)

sandal [ˈsændl] *n* санда́лия

sandpaper [ˈsændpeɪpə*] *n* нажда́чная бума́га

sandstone [ˈsændstəun] *n* песча́ник

sandwich ['sændwɪtʃ] n бутербро́д
♦ vt: ~ed between зажа́тый
между +instr; **cheese/ham** ~
бутербро́д с сы́ром/ветчино́й
sandy ['sændɪ] adj песча́ный
sane [seɪn] adj разу́мный
sang [sæŋ] pt of **sing**
sanitary ['sænɪtərɪ] adj
санита́рный; (clean) гигиени́чный
sanitation [sænɪ'teɪʃən] n
санита́рия
sanity ['sænɪtɪ] n (of person)
рассу́док; (sense) разу́мность f
sank [sæŋk] pt of **sink**
Santa Claus ['sæntə'klɔːz] n (in
Britain etc) Са́нта-Кла́ус; (in Russia)
≈ Дед Моро́з
sap [sæp] n (BOT) сок ♦ vt (strength)
выса́сывать (вы́сосать pf); (confidence) отбира́ть (отобра́ть pf)
sapling ['sæplɪŋ] n молодо́е
де́рево
sapphire ['sæfaɪə*] n сапфи́р
sarcasm ['sɑːkæzm] n сарка́зм
sarcastic [sɑː'kæstɪk] adj
саркасти́чный
sardine [sɑː'diːn] n сарди́на
sash [sæʃ] n (around waist) куша́к;
(over shoulder) ле́нта
sat [sæt] pt, pp of **sit**
Satan ['seɪtn] n Сатана́ m
satellite ['sætəlaɪt] n спу́тник; (POL,
country) сателли́т; ~ **dish** n
спу́тниковая анте́нна
satin ['sætɪn] adj атла́сный
satire ['sætaɪə*] n сати́ра
satirical [sə'tɪrɪkl] adj
сатири́ческий
satisfaction [sætɪs'fækʃən] n
(pleasure) удовлетворе́ние;
(refund, apology etc) возмеще́ние
satisfactory [sætɪs'fæktərɪ] adj
удовлетвори́тельный
satisfy ['sætɪsfaɪ] vt удовлетворя́ть
(удовлетвори́ть pf); (convince)
убежда́ть (убеди́ть pf); **to ~ sb**

(that) убежда́ть (убеди́ть pf)
кого́-н (в том, что); ~**ing** adj
прия́тный
saturation [sætʃə'reɪʃən] n (process)
насыще́ние; (state)
насы́щенность f
Saturday ['sætədɪ] n суббо́та

Saturday job - суббо́тняя
рабо́та. Брита́нские шко́льники
в суббо́ту не у́чатся, поэ́тому
мно́гие подро́стки
устра́иваются на суббо́тнюю
рабо́ту в кафе́ и́ли магази́н.

---

sauce [sɔːs] n со́ус; ~**pan** n
кастрю́ля
saucer ['sɔːsə*] n блю́дце
Saudi Arabia [saʊdɪ'reɪbɪə] n
Сау́довская Ара́вия
sauna ['sɔːnə] n са́уна, фи́нская
ба́ня
sausage ['sɔsɪdʒ] n (for cooking)
сарде́лька, соси́ска
savage ['sævɪdʒ] adj свире́пый
save [seɪv] vt (rescue) спаса́ть
(спасти́ pf); (economize on)
эконо́мить (сэконо́мить pf); (put
by) сберега́ть (сбере́чь pf); (:
receipts, file) сохраня́ть
(сохрани́ть pf); (: seat, place)
занима́ть (заня́ть pf); (work,
trouble) избавля́ть (изба́вить pf)
от +gen; (SPORT) отбива́ть (отби́ть
pf), отража́ть (отрази́ть pf) ♦ vi
(also: ~ **up**) копи́ть (скопи́ть pf)
де́ньги ♦ prep поми́мо +gen
saving ['seɪvɪŋ] n эконо́мия ♦ adj:
the ~ grace of спасе́ние +gen; ~**s**
npl (money) сбереже́ния ntpl
saviour ['seɪvjə*] (US **savior**) n
спаси́тель(ница) m(f); (REL)
Спаси́тель m
savour ['seɪvə*] (US **savor**) vt (food,
drink) смакова́ть (impf);
(experience) наслажда́ться

(наслади́ться pf) +instr; **~y** (US
savory) adj неслáдкий

saw [sɔː] (pt **~ed**, pp **~ed** or **~n**) vt
пили́ть (impf) ♦ n пилá ♦ pt of **see**;
~dust n опи́лки fpl; **~mill** n
лесопи́льный заво́д

saxophone ['sæksəfəʊn] n
саксофóн

say [seɪ] (pt, pp **said**) vt говори́ть
(сказáть pf) ♦ n: **to have one's ~**
выража́ть (вы́разить pf) своё
мнéние; **to ~ yes** соглашáться
(согласи́ться pf); **to ~ no**
отка́зываться (отказáться pf);
could you ~ that again?
повтори́те, пожáлуйста; **that is
to ~** то есть; **that goes without
~ing** э́то самó собóй разумéется;
~ing n поговóрка

scab [skæb] n (on wound) струп

scaffolding ['skæfəldɪŋ] n лесá mpl

scald [skɔːld] n ожóг ♦ vt
ошпáривать (ошпáрить pf)

scale [skeɪl] n шкалá; (usu pl: of
fish) чешуя́ f no pl; (MUS) гáмма;
(of map, project etc) масштáб ♦ vt
взбирáться (взобрáться pf) на
+acc; **~s** npl (for weighing) весы́ pl;
on a large ~ в широ́ком
масштáбе

scalp [skælp] n скальп

scalpel ['skælpl] n скáльпель m

scampi ['skæmpɪ] npl (BRIT)
пани́рованные крéветки fpl

scan [skæn] vt (examine)
обслéдовать (pf); (read quickly)
просмáтривать (просмотрéть pf);
(RADAR) сканировать (impf) ♦ n
(MED) скани́рование; **ultrasound
~** ультразву́к

scandal ['skændl] n сканда́л;
(gossip) сплéтни fpl; (disgrace)
позóр; **~ous** adj (behaviour, story)
сканда́льный

Scandinavia [skændɪ'neɪvɪə] n
Скандинáвия

scant [skænt] adj (attention)
поверхностный

scapegoat ['skeɪpɡəʊt] n козёл
отпущéния

scar [skɑː] n шрам; (fig) трáвма
♦ vt травми́ровать (impf/pf); **his
face is ~red** у негó на лицé шрам

scarce [skɛəs] adj рéдкий; **to make
o.s. ~** (inf) исчезáть (исчéзнуть
pf); **~ly** adv (hardly) едвá ли; (with
numbers) тóлько

scare [skɛə] n (fright) испýг; (public
fear) тревóга, пáника ♦ vt пугáть
(испугáть pf); **there was a bomb ~
at the station** опасáлись, что на
стáнции подложéна бóмба;
~crow n (огорóдное) чýчело; **~d**
adj испýганный, напýганный; **he
was ~d** он испугáлся ogбыл
испýган

scarf [skɑːf] (pl **~s** or **scarves**) n
шарф; (also: head~) платóк

scarves [skɑːvz] npl of **scarf**

scary ['skɛərɪ] adj (inf) стрáшный

scathing ['skeɪðɪŋ] adj
уничтожáющий

scatter ['skætə] vt (papers, seeds)
разбрáсывать (разбросáть pf)
♦ vi рассыпáться (рассы́паться
pf)

scenario [sɪ'nɑːrɪəʊ] n сценáрий

scene [siːn] n (THEAT, fig) сцéна;
(of crime, accident) мéсто; (sight,
view) карти́на; **~ry** n (THEAT)
декорáции fpl; (landscape) пейзáж

scenic ['siːnɪk] adj живопи́сный

scent [sɛnt] n (smell) зáпах; (track,
also fig) след; (perfume) духи́ n pl

sceptical ['skɛptɪkl] (US **skeptical**)
adj (person) скепти́ческий; (remarks)
скепти́ческий

scepticism ['skɛptɪsɪzəm] (US
skepticism) n скептици́зм

schedule ['ʃɛdjuːl], (US) 'skɛdjuːl] n
(timetable) расписáние, грáфик;
(list of prices, details etc) перéчень

scheme 638 scrape

m ♦ *vt* (*timetable*) расписывать (расписа́ть *pf*); (*visit*) назнача́ть (назна́чить *pf*); **on ~** по расписа́нию *or* гра́фику; **to be ahead of ~** опережа́ть (опереди́ть *pf*) гра́фик; **to be behind ~** отстава́ть (отста́ть *pf*) от гра́фика

scheme [skiːm] *n* (*plan*, *idea*) за́мысел; (*plot*) про́иски *pl*, ко́зни *pl*; (*pension plan etc*) план

schizophrenic [skɪtsəˈfrɛnɪk] *adj* шизофрени́ческий

scholar [ˈskɔlə*r*] *n* (*learned person*) учёный *m adj*; **~ship** *n* (*grant*) стипе́ндия

school [skuːl] *n* шко́ла; (*US* : *inf*) университе́т; (*BRIT*: *college*) институ́т ♦ *cpd* шко́льный; **~boy** *n* шко́льник; **~children** *npl* шко́льники *mpl*; **~girl** *n* шко́льница; **~ing** *n* шко́льное образова́ние

science [ˈsaɪəns] *n* нау́ка; (*in school*) естествозна́ние; **~ fiction** *n* нау́чная фанта́стика

scientific [saɪənˈtɪfɪk] *adj* нау́чный

scientist [ˈsaɪəntɪst] *n* учёный *m adj*

scintillating [ˈsɪntɪleɪtɪŋ] *adj* (*fig*: *conversation, wit*) блестя́щий

scissors [ˈsɪzəz] *npl*: **(a pair of) ~** но́жницы *pl*

scoff [skɔf] *vi*: **to ~ (at)** насмеха́ться (*impf*) (над +*instr*)

scold [skəuld] *vt* брани́ть (вы́бранить *pf*), руга́ть (отруга́ть *pf*)

scone [skɔn] *n* (*CULIN*) кекс

scooter [ˈskuːtə*r*] *n* (*also*: **motor ~**) мопе́д; (*toy*) самока́т

scope [skəup] *n* (*opportunity*) просто́р; (*of plan, undertaking*) масшта́б

scorch [skɔːtʃ] *vt* (*clothes*) сжига́ть (сжечь *pf*); (*earth, grass*) выжига́ть (вы́жечь *pf*)

score [skɔː*r*] *n* (*in game, test*) счёт ♦ *vt* (*goal*) забива́ть (заби́ть *pf*); (*point*) набира́ть (набра́ть *pf*); (*in test*) получа́ть (получи́ть *pf*) ♦ *vi* (*in game*) набира́ть (набра́ть *pf*) очки́; (*FOOTBALL*) забива́ть (заби́ть *pf*) гол; **~s of** деся́тки +*gen*; **on that ~** на э́тот счёт; **to ~ six out of ten** набра́ть (набра́ть *pf*) шесть ба́ллов из десяти́; **~ out** *vt* вычёркивать (вы́черкнуть *pf*); **~board** *n* табло́ *nt ind*

scorn [skɔːn] *n* презре́ние ♦ *vt* презира́ть (*impf*); **~ful** *adj* презри́тельный

Scorpio [ˈskɔːpɪəu] *n* Скорпио́н

scorpion [ˈskɔːpɪən] *n* скорпио́н

Scot [skɔt] *n* шотла́ндец(дка)

Scotch [skɔtʃ] *n* (*шотла́ндское*) ви́ски *nt ind*

Scotland [ˈskɔtlənd] *n* Шотла́ндия

Scots [skɔts] *adj* шотла́ндский

Scottish [ˈskɔtɪʃ] *adj* шотла́ндский

scout [skaut] *n* (*MIL*) разве́дчик; (*also*: **boy ~**) (бой)ска́ут

scramble [ˈskræmbl] *vi*: **to ~ out of** выка́рабкиваться (вы́карабкаться *pf*) из +*gen*; **to ~ for** дра́ться (подра́ться *pf*) за +*acc*; **~d eggs** *npl* яи́чница-болту́нья

scrap [skræp] *n* (*of paper*) клочо́к; (*of information*) обры́вок; (*of material*) лоску́т; (*also*: **~ metal**) металло́лом, металли́ческий лом ♦ *vt* (*machines etc*) отдава́ть (отда́ть *pf*) на слом; (*plans etc*) отка́зываться (отказа́ться *pf*) от +*gen*; **~s** *npl* (*of food*) объе́дки *mpl*

scrape [skreɪp] *vt* (*remove*) соска́бливать (соскобли́ть *pf*); (*rub against*) цара́пать (поцара́пать *pf*), обдира́ть (ободра́ть *pf*) ♦ *vi*: **to ~ through** (*exam etc*) пролеза́ть (проле́зть *pf*) на +*prp*

scratch [skrætʃ] n цара́пина ♦ vt
цара́пать (поцара́пать pf); (an
itch) чеса́ть (почеса́ть pf) ♦ vi
чеса́ться (почеса́ться pf); from ~
с нуля́; to be up to ~ быть (impf)
на до́лжном у́ровне

scrawl [skrɔ:l] n кара́кули fpl ♦ vt
цара́пать (нацара́пать pf)

scream [skri:m] n вопль m, крик
♦ vi вопи́ть (impf), крича́ть (impf)

screech [skri:tʃ] vi визжа́ть (impf)

screen [skri:n] n экра́н; (barrier,
also fig) ши́рма ♦ vt (protect,
conceal) заслоня́ть (заслони́ть
pf); (film: show) пока́зывать
(выпустить pf) на экра́н; (check:
candidates etc) проверя́ть
(прове́рить pf); ~ing n (MED)
профилакти́ческий осмо́тр;
~play n сцена́рий; ~ saver n
скринсейвер

screw [skru:] n винт m; (for fasten)
приви́нчивать (привинти́ть pf);
to ~ sth in зави́нчивать
(завинти́ть pf) что-н; ~driver n
отвёртка

scribble [ˈskrɪbl] vt черкну́ть (pf)
♦ vi исчёркивать (исчёркать pf)

script [skrɪpt] n (CINEMA etc)
сцена́рий; (Arabic etc) шрифт

Scripture(s) [ˈskrɪptʃəʳ(-əz)] n(pl)
Свяще́нное Писа́ние ntsg

scroll [skrəul] n сви́ток ♦ vi: to ~
up/down перемеща́ть
(перемести́ть pf) наве́рх/вниз

scrub [skrʌb] vt скрести́ (impf)

scruffy [ˈskrʌfɪ] adj потрёпанный

scrupulous [ˈskru:pjuləs] adj
(painstaking) тща́тельный,
скрупулёзный; (fair-minded)
щепети́льный

scrutiny [ˈskru:tɪnɪ] n тща́тельное
изуче́ние или рассмотре́ние

scuffle [ˈskʌfl] n потасо́вка

sculptor [ˈskʌlptəʳ] n ску́льптор

sculpture [ˈskʌlptʃəʳ] n скульпту́ра

scum [skʌm] n пе́на; (inf : pej:
people) подо́нки mpl

scythe [saɪð] n серп

sea [si:] n мо́ре ♦ cpd морско́й; by
~ (travel) мо́рем; on the ~ (town)
на мо́ре; out to~, out at ~ в
мо́ре; ~food n ры́бные блю́да
ntpl; ~front n на́бережная f adj;
~gull n ча́йка

sea level n у́ровень m мо́ря

sea lion n морско́й лев

seam [si:m] n (of garment) шов

search [sə:tʃ] n по́иск; (for criminal)
ро́зыск; (of sb's home etc) о́быск
♦ vt обы́скивать (обыска́ть pf)
♦ vi: to ~ for иска́ть (impf); in ~ of
в по́исках +gen; ~ing adj (look)
пытли́вый; (question) наводя́щий

seasick [ˈsi:sɪk] adj: to be ~
страда́ть (impf) морско́й
боле́знью

seaside [ˈsi:saɪd] n взмо́рье

season [ˈsi:zn] n вре́мя nt го́да;
(for football, of films etc) сезо́н ♦ vt
(food) заправля́ть (запра́вить pf);
~al adj сезо́нный; ~ed adj
(traveller) закалённый; ~ing n
припра́ва

seat [si:t] n (chair, place) сиде́нье;
(in theatre, parliament) ме́сто; (of
trousers) зад ♦ vt (subj: venue)
вмеща́ть (вмести́ть pf); to be ~ed
сиде́ть (impf); ~ belt n привязно́й
реме́нь m

seaweed [ˈsi:wi:d] n во́доросли fpl

sec. abbr = **second²**

secluded [sɪˈklu:dɪd] adj
уединённый

second¹ [sɪˈkɔnd] vt (BRIT:
employee) командирова́ть (impf)

second² [ˈsɛkənd] adj второ́й

♦ adv (come) вторы́м; (when listing) во-вторы́х ♦ n (unit of time) секу́нда; (AUT: also: ~ **gear**) втора́я ско́рость f; (COMM) некондицио́нный това́р; (BRIT: SCOL) дипло́м второ́го кла́сса ♦ vt (motion) подде́рживать (поддержа́ть pf); ~**ary** adj втори́чный; ~**ary school** n сре́дняя шко́ла; ~**class** adj второразря́дный; ~**class stamp** ма́рка второ́го кла́сса

second-class postage - в Великобрита́нии мо́жно приобрести́ почто́вые ма́рки пе́рвого и второ́го кла́сса. Ма́рки второ́го кла́сса деше́вле. Пи́сьма с таки́ми ма́рками доставля́ются по ме́сту назначе́ния че́рез 2-3 дня.

second: ['sekənd] ~ **hand** n (on clock) секу́ндная стре́лка; ~**-hand** adj поде́ржанный, сэ́конд-хэнд ind; ~**ly** adv во-вторы́х; ~**-rate** adj (film) посре́дственный; (restaurant) второразря́дный; ~ **thoughts** npl: **to have** ~ **thoughts (about doing)** сомнева́ться (impf) (сле́дует ли +infin); **on** ~ **thoughts** or (US) **thought** по зре́лом размышле́нии

secrecy ['si:krəsı] n секре́тность f
secret ['si:krıt] adj секре́тный, та́йный; (admirer) та́йный ♦ n секре́т, та́йна; **in** ~ (do, meet) секре́тно, та́йно
secretarial [sekrı'tɛərıəl] adj секрета́рский; ~ **course** ку́рсы mpl секретаре́й
secretary ['sekrətərı] n секрета́рь m; **Secretary of State (for)** (BRIT) ≈ мини́стр (+gen)
secretive ['si:krətıv] adj (pej: person)

скры́тный; **he is** ~ **about his plans** он де́ржит свои́ пла́ны в секре́те
secretly ['si:krıtlı] adv (do, meet) секре́тно
secret service n секре́тная слу́жба
sect [sekt] n се́кта
sectarian [sek'tɛərıən] adj секта́нтский
section ['sekʃən] n (part) часть f; (of population, company) се́ктор; (of document, book) разде́л
sector ['sektə*] n (part) се́ктор
secular ['sekjulə*] adj све́тский
secure [sı'kjuə*] adj (safe: person, money, job) надёжный; (firmly fixed: rope, shelf) про́чный ♦ vt (fix: rope, shelf etc) (про́чно) закрепля́ть (закрепи́ть pf); (get: job, loan etc) обеспе́чивать (обеспе́чить pf)
security [sı'kjuərıtı] n (protection) безопа́сность f; (for one's future) обеспе́ченность f
sedate [sı'deıt] adj (person) степе́нный; (pace) разме́ренный ♦ vt дава́ть (дать pf) седати́вное or успокои́тельное сре́дство
sedative ['sedıtıv] n седати́вное or успокои́тельное сре́дство
sediment ['sedımənt] n оса́док
seduce [sı'dju:s] vt соблазня́ть (соблазни́ть pf)
seduction [sı'dʌkʃən] n (act) обольще́ние
seductive [sı'dʌktıv] adj (look, voice) обольсти́тельный; (offer) соблазни́тельный
see [si:] (pt **saw**, pp ~n) vt ви́деть (уви́деть pf) ♦ vi ви́деть (impf); (find out) выясня́ть (вы́яснить pf); **to** ~ **that** (ensure) следи́ть (проследи́ть pf), что́бы; ~ **you soon!** пока́!, до ско́рого!; ~ **off** vt провожа́ть (проводи́ть pf);

through vt доводи́ть (довести́ pf) до конца́ ♦ vt fus ви́деть (impf) наскво́зь +acc; **~ to** vt fus позабо́титься (pf) о +prp

seed [si:d] n се́мя nt; **to go to ~** (fig) сдать (pf); **~ling** n расса́да no pl; **~y** adj (place) захуда́лый

seeing ['si:ɪŋ] conj: **~ (that)** поско́льку, так как

seek [si:k] (pt, pp **sought**) vt иска́ть (impf)

seem [si:m] vi каза́ться (показа́ться pf); **there ~s to be ...** ка́жется, что име́ется ...; **he ~s to be tired** он ка́жется уста́лым; **~ingly** adv по-ви́димому; (important) как представля́ется

seen [si:n] pp of **see**

see-through ['si:θru:] adj прозра́чный

segment ['segmənt] n (of population) се́ктор; (of orange) до́лька

seize [si:z] vt хвата́ть (схвати́ть pf); (power, hostage, territory) захва́тывать (захвати́ть pf); (opportunity) по́льзоваться (воспо́льзоваться pf) +instr

seizure ['si:ʒəʳ] n (MED) при́ступ; (of power) захва́т; (of goods) конфиска́ция

seldom ['seldəm] adv ре́дко

select [sɪ'lekt] adj (school, area) эли́тный ♦ vt (choose) выбира́ть (вы́брать pf); **~ion** [sɪ'lekʃən] n (process) отбо́р; (range) вы́бор; (medley) подбо́рка; **~ive** adj (person) разбо́рчивый; (not general) избира́тельный

self [self] (pl **selves**) n: **he became his usual ~ again** он стал опя́ть сами́м собо́й

self- [self] prefix само-; **~assured** adj самоуве́ренный; **~catering** adj (BRIT): **~catering holiday**

туристи́ческая путёвка, в кото́рую включа́ется прое́зд и жильё; **~centred** (US **~centered**) adj эгоцентри́чный; **~confidence** n уве́ренность f в себе́; **~conscious** adj (nervous) засте́нчивый; **~control** n самооблада́ние; **~defence** (US **~defense**) n самозащи́та, самооборо́на; **in ~defence** защища́я себя́; **~discipline** n самодисципли́на; **~employed** adj рабо́тающий на себя́; **~evident** adj самоочеви́дный; **~interest** n коры́сть f; **~ish** adj эгоисти́ческий; (of person) эгои́зм; **~ishness** n (of person) эгои́зм; **~less** adj самоотве́рженный; **~pity** n жа́лость f к (самому́) себе́; **~portrait** n автопортре́т; **~respect** n самоуваже́ние; **~righteous** adj убеждённый в свое́й правоте́; **~satisfied** adj самодово́льный; **~service** adj: **~service restaurant** кафе́ nt ind с самообслу́живанием; **~sufficient** adj самостоя́тельный

sell [sel] (pt, pp **sold**) vt продава́ть (прода́ть pf) ♦ vi продава́ться (impf); **to ~ at** or **for 10 pounds** продава́ться (impf) по 10 фу́нтов; **~ off** vt распрода́ть (распрода́ть pf); **~ out** vi (book etc) расхо́диться (разойти́сь pf); (shop): **to ~ out of sth** распрода́ть (распрода́ть pf) что-л; **the tickets are sold out** все биле́ты про́даны

Sellotape ® ['seləuteɪp] n (BRIT) кле́йкая ле́нта

selves [selvz] pl of **self**

semblance ['semblns] n ви́димость f

semester [sɪ'mestəʳ] n (esp US) семе́стр

semi- ['semɪ] prefix полу-

semi - полусособня́к. В Великобрита́нии мно́гие се́мьи живу́т в полусособня́ках - два двухэта́жных до́ма име́ют одну́ о́бщую сте́ну, но отде́льный вход и сад.

semi: ~**circle** n полукру́г; ~**colon** n то́чка с запято́й; ~**final** n полуфина́л

seminar ['semɪnɑːʳ] n семина́р

senate ['senɪt] n сена́т

senator ['senɪtəʳ] n (US etc) сена́тор

send [send] (pt, pp **sent**) vt посыла́ть (посла́ть pf); ~ **away** vt (letter, goods) отсыла́ть (отосла́ть pf); (visitor) прогоня́ть (прогна́ть pf); ~ **back** vt посыла́ть (посла́ть pf) обра́тно; ~ **for** vt fus (by post) зака́зывать (заказа́ть pf); (person) посыла́ть (посла́ть pf) за +instr; ~ **off** vt (letter) отправля́ть (отпра́вить pf); (BRIT: SPORT) удаля́ть (удали́ть pf); ~ **out** vt (invitation) рассыла́ть (разосла́ть pf); (signal) посыла́ть (посла́ть pf); ~**er** n отправи́тель m

senile ['siːnaɪl] adj маразмати́ческий

senior ['siːnɪəʳ] adj (staff, officer) ста́рший; (manager, consultant) гла́вный; **to be ~ to sb** (in rank) быть (impf) вы́ше кого́-н по положе́нию; **she is 15 years his ~** она́ ста́рше его́ на 15 лет; ~ **citizen** n (esp BRIT) пожило́й челове́к, челове́к пенсио́нного во́зраста; ~**ity** [siːnɪˈɔrɪtɪ] n старшинство́

sensation [senˈseɪʃən] n (feeling) ощуще́ние; (great success) сенса́ция; ~**al** adj (wonderful) потряса́ющий; (dramatic) сенсацио́нный

sense [sens] vt чу́вствовать (почу́вствовать pf), ощуща́ть (ощути́ть pf) ♦ n (feeling) чу́вство, ощуще́ние; **it makes** ~ в э́том есть смысл; **the** ~**s** пять чувств; ~**less** adj бессмы́сленный; (unconscious) бесчу́вственный; ~ **of humour** (US ~ **of humor**) n чу́вство ю́мора

sensible ['sensɪbl] adj разу́мный

sensitive ['sensɪtɪv] adj чувстви́тельный; (understanding) чу́ткий; (issue) щекотли́вый

sensitivity [sensɪˈtɪvɪtɪ] n (see adj) чувстви́тельность f; чу́ткость f; щекотли́вость f

sensual ['sensjuəl] adj чу́вственный

sensuous ['sensjuəs] adj (lips) чу́вственный; (material) не́жный

sent [sent] pt, pp of **send**

sentence ['sentns] n (LING) предложе́ние; (LAW) пригово́р ♦ vt: **to** ~ **sb to** приговори́вать (приговори́ть pf) кого́-н к +dat

sentiment ['sentɪmənt] n (tender feelings) чу́вство; (opinion) настрое́ние; ~**al** [sentɪˈmentl] adj сентимента́льный

sentry ['sentrɪ] n часово́й m adj, карау́льный m adj

separate adj ['seprɪt] adj отде́льный; (ways) ра́зный ♦ vt (split up: people) разлуча́ть (разлучи́ть pf); (: things) разделя́ть (раздели́ть pf); (distinguish) различа́ть (различи́ть pf) ♦ vi расходи́ться (разойти́сь pf); ~**ly** ['seprɪtlɪ] adv отде́льно, по отде́льности

separation [sepəˈreɪʃən] n (being apart) разлу́ка; (LAW) разде́льное прожива́ние

September [sepˈtembəʳ] n сентя́брь m

septic ['septɪk] adj заражённый

sequel ['siːkwl] n продолже́ние

sequence ['siːkwəns] n после́довательность f

Serbia ['səːbɪə] n Се́рбия

Serbo-Croat ['səːbəuˈkrəuæt] adj се́рбо-хорва́тский

serene [sɪˈriːn] adj безмяте́жный

sergeant ['saːdʒənt] n сержа́нт

serial ['sɪərɪəl] n (TV, RADIO) сериа́л; (PRESS) публика́ция в не́скольких частя́х

series ['sɪərɪz] n inv се́рия

serious ['sɪərɪəs] adj серьёзный; **are you ~ (about it)?** Вы (э́то) серьёзно?; **~ly** adv серьёзно; **~ness** n серьёзность f

sermon ['səːmən] n про́поведь f

servant ['səːvənt] n слуга́(уж́анка) m(f)

serve [səːv] vt (company, country) служи́ть (impf) +dat; (customer) обслу́живать (обслужи́ть pf); (subj: train etc) обслу́живать (impf); (apprenticeship) проходи́ть (пройти́ pf); (prison term) отбыва́ть (отбы́ть pf) ♦ vi (TENNIS) подава́ть (пода́ть pf) ♦ n (TENNIS) пода́ча; **it ~s him right** подело́м ему́; **to ~ on** (jury, committee) состоя́ть (impf) в +prp; **to ~ as/for** служи́ть (послужи́ть pf) +instr/ вме́сто +gen

service ['səːvɪs] n (help) услу́га; (in hotel) обслу́живание, се́рвис; (REL) слу́жба; (AUT) техобслу́живание; (TENNIS) пода́ча ♦ vt (car) проводи́ть (провести́ pf) техобслу́живание +gen; **the Services** npl (MIL) Вооружённые си́лы fpl; **military** or **national** ~ вое́нная слу́жба; **train** ~ железнодоро́жное сообще́ние; **postal** ~ почто́вая связь

serviette [səːvɪˈɛt] n (BRIT) салфе́тка

session ['sɛʃən] n (of treatment) сеа́нс; **recording** ~ за́пись f; **to be in** ~ (court etc) заседа́ть (impf)

set [sɛt] (pt, pp ~) n (collection) набо́р; (of pans, clothes) компле́кт; (also: **television** ~) телеви́зор; (TENNIS) сет; (MATH) мно́жество; (CINEMA, THEAT, stage) сце́на ♦ adj (fixed) устано́вленный; (ready) гото́вый ♦ vt (place: vertically) ста́вить (поста́вить pf); (: horizontally) класть (положи́ть pf); (table) накрыва́ть (накры́ть pf); (time) назнача́ть (назна́чить pf); (price, record) устана́вливать (установи́ть pf); (alarm, task) ста́вить (поста́вить pf); (exam) составля́ть (соста́вить pf) ♦ vi (sun) сади́ться (сесть pf), заходи́ть (зайти́ pf); (jam, jelly, concrete) застыва́ть (засты́ть pf); **to ~ to music** класть (положи́ть pf) на му́зыку; **to ~ on fire** поджига́ть (поджечь pf); **to ~ free** освобожда́ть (освободи́ть pf); ~ **about** vt fus (task) приступа́ть (приступи́ть pf) к +dat; ~ **aside** vt (money) откла́дывать (отложи́ть pf); (time) выделя́ть (вы́делить pf); ~ **back** vt (progress) заде́рживать (задержа́ть pf); **to ~ sb back £5** обходи́ться (обойти́сь pf) кому́-н в £5; ~ **off** vi отправля́ться (отпра́виться pf) ♦ vt (bomb) взрыва́ть (взорва́ть pf); (alarm) приводи́ть (привести́ pf) в де́йствие; (events) повлека́ть (повле́чь pf) за собо́й); ~ **out** vi (depart): **to ~ out (from)** отправля́ться (отпра́виться pf) (из +gen); **to ~ out to do** намерева́ться (impf) +infin; ~ **up** vt (organization) учрежда́ть (учреди́ть pf); ~**back** n неуда́ча

settee [sɛˈtiː] n диван
setting [ˈsɛtɪŋ] n (background) обстановка; (position: of controls) положение
settle [ˈsɛtl] vt (argument, problem) разрешать (разрешить pf); (matter) улаживать (уладить pf); (bill) рассчитываться (рассчитаться pf) с +instr ♦ vi (dust, sediment) оседать (осесть pf); (also: ~ **down**) обосновываться (обосноваться pf); (: live sensibly) остепеняться (остепениться pf); (calm down) успокаиваться (успокоиться pf); **to ~ for sth** соглашаться (согласиться pf) на что-н; **to ~ on sth** останавливаться (остановиться pf) на чём-н; **~ in** vi осваиваться (освоиться pf); **~ment** n (payment) уплата; (agreement) соглашение; (village, colony) поселение; (of conflict) урегулирование

seven [ˈsɛvn] n семь; **~teen** n семнадцать; **~teenth** adj семнадцатый; **~th** adj седьмой; **~tieth** adj семидесятый; **~ty** n семьдесят

several [ˈsɛvərəl] adj несколько +gen ♦ pron некоторые pl adj; **~ of us** некоторые из нас

severe [sɪˈvɪəʳ] adj (shortage, pain, winter) жестокий; (damage) серьёзный; (stern) жёсткий

severity [sɪˈvɛrɪtɪ] n жестокость f; (of damage) серьёзность

sew [səu] (pt **~ed**, pp **~n**) vti шить (impf)

sewage [ˈsuːɪdʒ] n сточные воды fpl; **~ system** канализация

sewer [ˈsuːəʳ] n канализационная труба

sewing [ˈsəuɪŋ] n шитьё; **~ machine** n швейная машинка

sewn [səun] pp of **sew**

sex [sɛks] n (gender) пол; (lovemaking) секс; **to have ~ with sb** переспать (pf) с кем-н; **~ist** adj сексистский; he is **~ist** он — сексист; **~ual** adj половой; **~ual equality** равенство полов; **~ual harassment** сексуальное преследование; **~y** adj сексуальный; (woman) сексопильная

shabby [ˈʃæbɪ] adj потрёпанный; (treatment) недостойный

shack [ʃæk] n лачуга

shade [ʃeɪd] n (shelter) тень f; (for lamp) абажур; (of colour) оттенок ♦ vt (shelter) затенять (затенить pf); (eyes) заслонять (заслонить pf)

shadow [ˈʃædəu] n тень f ♦ vt (follow) следовать (impf) как тень за +instr; **~ cabinet** n (BRIT) теневой кабинет

shady [ˈʃeɪdɪ] adj (place, trees) тенистый; (fig: dishonest) тёмный

shaft [ʃɑːft] n (of mine, lift) шахта; (of light) сноп

shake [ʃeɪk] (pt **shook**, pp **~n**) vt трясти (impf); (bottle) взбалтывать (взболтать pf); (building) сотрясать (сотрясти pf); (weaken: beliefs, resolve) пошатнуть (pf); (upset, surprise) потрясать (потрясти pf) ♦ vi (voice) дрожать (impf); **to ~ one's head** качать (impf) головой; **to ~ hands with sb** жать (пожать pf) кому-н руку; **to ~ with** трястись (impf) от +gen; **~ off** vt стряхивать (стряхнуть pf); (fig: pursuer) избавляться (избавиться pf) от +gen; **~ up** vt (fig: organization) встряхивать

(встряхну́ть *pf*)

shaky ['ʃeɪkɪ] *adj* (hand, voice) дрожа́щий

shall [ʃæl] *aux vb*: **I ~ go** я пойду́; **~ I open the door?** (мне) откры́ть дверь?; **I'll get some water; ~ I?** я принесу́ воды́, хорошо́?

shallow ['ʃæləʊ] *adj* (water) ме́лкий; (box) неглубо́кий; (breathing, also fig) пове́рхностный

sham [ʃæm] *n* притво́рство

shambles ['ʃæmblz] *n* неразбери́ха

shame [ʃeɪm] *n* (embarrassment) стыд; (disgrace) позо́р ♦ *vt* позо́рить (опозо́рить *pf*); **it is a ~ that/to do sth** что́/+infin; **what a ~!** кака́я жа́лость!, как жаль!; **~ful** *adj* позо́рный; **~less** *adj* бессты́дный

shampoo [ʃæm'puː] *n* шампу́нь *m* ♦ *vt* мыть (помы́ть *или* вы́мыть *pf*) шампу́нем

shan't [ʃɑːnt] = **shall not**

shape [ʃeɪp] *n* фо́рма ♦ *vt* (ideas, events) формирова́ть (сформирова́ть *pf*); (clay) лепи́ть (слепи́ть *pf*); **to take ~** обрета́ть (обрести́ *pf*) фо́рму; **~-d** *suffix*: **heart~~d** сердцеви́дный; **~less** *adj* бесфо́рменный; **~ly** *adj* стро́йный

share [ʃeə⁽ʳ⁾] *n* до́ля; (COMM) а́кция ♦ *vt* (books, cost) дели́ть (подели́ть *pf*); (toys) дели́ться (поделиться *pf*) +instr; (features, qualities) разделя́ть (impf); (opinion, concern) разделя́ть (раздели́ть *pf*); **~ out** *vt* дели́ть (подели́ть *pf*); **~holder** *n* акционе́р

shark [ʃɑːk] *n* аку́ла

sharp [ʃɑːp] *adj* о́стрый; (sound) ре́зкий; (MUS) дие́з *ind* ♦ *adv* (precisely): **at 2 o'clock ~** ро́вно в

два часа́; **he is very ~** у него́ о́чень о́стрый ум; **~en** *vt* (pencil, knife) точи́ть (поточи́ть *pf*); **~ener** *n* (also: **pencil ~ener**) точи́лка; **~ly** *adv* ре́зко

shatter ['ʃætə⁽ʳ⁾] *vt* (vase, hopes) разбива́ть (разби́ть *pf*); (upset: person) потряса́ть (потрясти́ *pf*) ♦ *vi* би́ться (разби́ться *pf*)

shave [ʃeɪv] *vt* брить (побри́ть *pf*) ♦ *vi* бри́ться (побри́ться *pf*) ♦ *n*: **to have a ~** бри́ться (побри́ться *pf*)

shaving ['ʃeɪvɪŋ] *n* бритьё; **~s** (of wood etc) стру́жки *fpl*

shawl [ʃɔːl] *n* шаль *f*

she [ʃiː] *pron* она́

sheaf [ʃiːf] (*pl* **sheaves**) *n* (of papers) сто́пка

shears ['ʃɪəz] *npl* (for hedge) садо́вые но́жницы *pl*

sheaves [ʃiːvz] *npl* of **sheaf**

shed [ʃed] (*pt, pp* **~**) *n* (in garden) сара́й ♦ *vt* (skin, load) сбра́сывать (сбро́сить *pf*); (tears) лить (impf)

she'd [ʃiːd] = **she had, she would**

sheen [ʃiːn] *n* лоск

sheep [ʃiːp] *n inv* овца́; **~dog** *n* овча́рка

sheer [ʃɪə⁽ʳ⁾] *adj* (utter) су́щий; (steep) отве́сный

sheet [ʃiːt] *n* (on bed) простыня́; (of paper, glass etc) лист; (of ice) полоса́

sheik(h) [ʃeɪk] *n* шейх

shelf [ʃelf] (*pl* **shelves**) *n* по́лка

shell [ʃel] *n* (of mollusc) ра́ковина; (of egg, nut) скорлупа́; (explosive) снаря́д; (of building) карка́с; (of ship) ко́рпус ♦ *vt* (peas) лущи́ть (облущи́ть *pf*); (MIL) обстре́ливать (обстреля́ть *pf*)

she'll [ʃiːl] = **she will, she shall**

shellfish ['ʃelfɪʃ] *n inv* (crab) рачки́ *pl*; (scallop) моллю́ски *mpl*

shelter ['ʃeltə⁽ʳ⁾] *n* (refuge) прию́т;

(*protection*) укрытие ♦ *vt* (*protect*) укрывать (укрыть *pf*); (*hide*) давать (дать *pf*) приют +*dat* ♦ *vi* укрываться (укрыться *pf*); ~**ed** *adj* (*life*) беззаботный; (*spot*) защищённый

shelves [ʃelvz] *npl of* **shelf**

shepherd [ˈʃepəd] *n* пастух

sheriff [ˈʃerɪf] *n* (*US*) шериф

sherry [ˈʃerɪ] *n* херес

she's [ʃiːz] = **she is, she has**

shield [ʃiːld] *n* щит; (*trophy*) трофей ♦ *vt*: **to** ~ **(from)** заслонять (заслонить *pf*) (от +*gen*)

shift [ʃɪft] *n* (*in direction, conversation*) перемена; (*in policy, emphasis*) сдвиг; (*at work*) смена ♦ *vt* передвигать (передвинуть *pf*), перемещать (переместить *pf*) ♦ *vi* перемещаться (переместиться *pf*)

shimmer [ˈʃɪməʳ] *vi* мерцать (*impf*)

shin [ʃɪn] *n* голень *f*

shine [ʃaɪn] (*pt, pp* **shone**) *n* блеск ♦ *vi* (*sun, light*) светить (*impf*); (*eyes, hair*) блестеть (*impf*) ♦ *vt*: **to** ~ **a torch on sth** направлять (направить *pf*) фонарь на что-н

shiny [ˈʃaɪnɪ] *adj* блестящий

ship [ʃɪp] *n* корабль *m* ♦ *vt* (*by ship*) перевозить (перевезти *pf*) по морю; (*send*) отправлять (отправить *pf*), экспедировать (*impf/pf*); ~**building** *n* кораблестроение, судостроение; ~**ment** *n* (*goods*) партия; (*of cargo*) перевозка; ~**ping** *n* (*ship*) судно, потерпевшее крушение ♦ *vt*: **to be** ~**wrecked** терпеть (потерпеть *pf*) кораблекрушение; ~**yard** *n* (судостроительная) верфь *f*

shirt [ʃəːt] *n* (*man's*) рубашка; (*woman's*) блузка; **in (one's)** ~

sleeves в одной рубашке

shit [ʃɪt] *excl* (*infl*) чёрт!, блин!

shiver [ˈʃɪvəʳ] *n* дрожь *f* ♦ *vi* дрожать (*impf*)

shoal [ʃəʊl] *n* (*of fish*) косяк

shock [ʃɒk] *n* (*start, impact*) толчок; (*ELEC, MED*) шок; (*emotional*) потрясение ♦ *vt* (*upset*) потрясать (потрясти *pf*); (*offend*) возмущать (возмутить *pf*), шокировать (*impf/pf*); ~ **absorber** *n* амортизатор; ~**ing** *adj* (*outrageous*) возмутительный; (*dreadful*) кошмарный

shoddy [ˈʃɒdɪ] *adj* (*goods*) дрянной; (*workmanship*) кустарный

shoe [ʃuː] *n* (*for person*) туфля; (*for horse*) подкова; ~**s** (*footwear*) обувь *fsg*; ~**lace** *n* шнурок

shone [ʃɒn] *pt, pp of* **shine**

shook [ʃʊk] *pt, pp of* **shake**

shoot [ʃuːt] (*pt, pp* **shot**) *n* (*BOT*) росток, побег ♦ *vt* (*gun*) стрелять (*impf*) из +*gen*; (*bird, robber etc: kill*) застреливать (застрелить *pf*); (*: wound*) выстрелить (*pf*) в +*acc*; (*film*) снимать (снять *pf*) ♦ *vi*: **to** ~ **(at)** стрелять (выстрелить *pf*) в +*acc*; (*FOOTBALL etc*) бить (*impf*) (по +*dat*); ~ **down** *vt* (*plane*) сбивать (сбить *pf*); ~**ing** *n* (*shots, attack*) стрельба; (*HUNTING*) охота

shop [ʃɒp] *n* магазин; (*also*: ~ **work**) мастерская *f adj* ♦ *vi* (*also*: **go** ~**ping**) ходить (*impf*) по магазинам, делать (сделать *pf*) покупки; ~**keeper** *n* владелец(лица) магазина; ~**lifting** *n* кража товаров (*из магазинов*); ~**ping** *n* (*goods*) покупки *fpl*; ~**ping centre** (*US* ~**ping center**) *n* торговый центр; ~**ping mall** *n* (*esp US*) торговый центр

shore [ʃɔːʳ] *n* берег

short [ʃɔːt] adj коро́ткий; (in height)
невысо́кий; (curt) ре́зкий;
(insufficient) ску́дный; **we are ~ of
milk** у нас ма́ло молока́; **in ~**
коро́че говоря́; **it is ~ for ...** э́то
сокраще́ние от +gen ...; **to cut ~**
(speech, visit) прерыва́ть
(прерва́ть pf); **everything ~ of ...**
всё, кро́ме +gen ...; **~ of doing**
кро́ме как +infin; **to fall ~ of**
выполня́ть (вы́полнить pf); **we're
running ~ of time** у нас
зака́нчивается вре́мя; **to stop ~**
застыва́ть (засты́ть pf) на ме́сте;
to stop ~ of doing не
осме́ливаться (осме́литься pf)
+infin; **~age** n: **a ~age of** нехва́тка
+gen, дефици́т +gen; **~ cut** n (on
journey) коро́ткий путь m; **~fall** n
недоста́ча; **~hand** n (BRIT)
стеногра́фия; **~lived** adj
кратковре́менный, недо́лгий;
~ly adv вско́ре; **~s** npl: **(a pair of)
~s** шо́рты pl; **~sighted** adj (BRIT)
близору́кий; **~ story** n расска́з;
~-term adj (effect)
кратковре́менный

shot [ʃɔt] pt, pp of **shoot** ♦ n (of
gun) вы́стрел; (FOOTBALL) уда́р;
(injection) уко́л; (PHOT) сни́мок; **a
good/poor ~** (person) ме́ткий/
плохо́й стрело́к; **like a ~** мигом;
~gun n дробови́к

should [ʃud] aux vb: **I ~ go now** я
до́лжен идти́; **I ~ go if I were you**
на Ва́шем ме́сте я бы пошёл; **I ~
like to** я бы хоте́л

shoulder [ˈʃəuldəʳ] n (ANAT) плечо́
♦ vt (fig) принима́ть (приня́ть pf)
на себя́; **~ blade** n лопа́тка

shouldn't [ˈʃudnt] = **should not**

shout [ʃaut] n крик ♦ vt
выкри́кивать (вы́крикнуть pf) ♦ vi
(also: **~ out**) крича́ть (impf)

shove [ʃʌv] vt толка́ть (толкну́ть pf);
(inf: put): **to ~ sth in**

запи́хивать (запиха́ть or
запихну́ть pf) что-н +acc

shovel [ˈʃʌvl] n лопа́та ♦ vt (snow,
coal) грести́ (impf) (лопа́той)

show [ʃəu] (pt **~ed**, pp **~n**) n (of
emotion) проявле́ние; (semblance)
подо́бие; (exhibition) вы́ставка;
(THEAT) спекта́кль m; (TV)
програ́мма, шо́у nt ind ♦ vt
пока́зывать (показа́ть pf);
(courage etc) проявля́ть
(прояви́ть pf) ♦ vi (be evident)
проявля́ться (прояви́ться pf); **for
~** для ви́ду; **to be on ~** (exhibits
etc) выставля́ться (impf); **~ in** vt
(person) проводи́ть (провести́ pf);
~ off vi хва́статься (impf) ♦ vt
(display) хва́статься
(похва́статься pf) +instr; **~ out** vt
(person) провожа́ть (проводи́ть
pf) к вы́ходу; **~ up** vi (against
background) видне́ться (impf);
(fig) обнару́живаться
(обнару́житься pf); (inf: turn up)
явля́ться (яви́ться pf) ♦ vt
(uncover) выявля́ть (вы́явить pf);
~ business n шо́у-би́знес

shower [ˈʃauəʳ] n (also: **~ bath**)
душ; (of rain) кратковре́менный
дождь m ♦ vi принима́ть
(приня́ть pf) душ ♦ vt: **to ~ sb
with** (gifts, abuse etc) осыпа́ть
(осы́пать pf) кого́-н +instr; **to have
or take a ~** принима́ть (приня́ть
pf) душ

show: **~ing** n (of film) пока́з,
демонстра́ция; **~ jumping** n
ко́нкур; **~n** pp of **show**; **~-off** n
(inf) хвастуни́шка; **~room** n
демонстрацио́нный зал

shrank [ʃræŋk] pt of **shrink**

shrapnel [ˈʃræpnl] n шрапне́ль f

shred [ʃred] n (usu pl) клочо́к ♦ vt
кроши́ть (накроши́ть pf)

shrewd [ʃruːd] adj
проница́тельный

shriek [ʃriːk] n визг ♦ vi визжáть (impf)

shrill [ʃrɪl] adj визглúвый

shrimp [ʃrɪmp] n (мéлкая) кревéтка

shrine [ʃraɪn] n святúня; (tomb) рáка

shrink [ʃrɪŋk] (pt **shrank**, pp **shrunk**) vi (cloth) садúться (сесть pf); (profits, audiences) сокращáться (сократúться pf); (also: ~ **away**) отпрянуть (pf)

shrivel [ʃrɪvl] (also: ~ **up**) vt высýшивать (высушить pf) ♦ vi высыхáть (высохнуть pf)

shroud [ʃraʊd] vt: ~**ed in mystery** окýтанный тáйной

Shrove Tuesday - Мáсленица. За Мáсленицей слéдует пéрвый день Велúкого Постá. По традúции на Мáсленицу пекýт блины.

---

shrub [ʃrʌb] n куст

shrug [ʃrʌg] vi: **to ~ (one's shoulders)** пожимáть (пожáть pf) плечáми; ~ **off** vt отмáхиваться (отмахнýться pf) от +gen

shrunk [ʃrʌŋk] pp of **shrink**

shudder [ʃʌdə] vi содрогáться (содрогнýться pf)

shuffle [ʃʌfl] vt тасовáть (стасовáть pf) ♦ vi: **to ~ (one's feet)** волочúть (impf) нóги

shun [ʃʌn] vt избегáть (impf) +gen

shut [ʃʌt] (pt, pp ~) vt закрывáть (закрыть pf) ♦ vi (factory) закрывáться (закрыться pf); ~ **down** vt (factory etc) закрывáть (закрыть pf) ♦ vi (factory) закрывáться (закрыться pf); ~ **off** vt (supply etc) перекрывáть (перекрыть pf); ~ **up** vi (keep quiet) заткнýться (pf) ♦ vt (keep quiet) затыкáть (заткнýть pf) рот

+dat; ~**ter** n (on window) стáвень m; (PHOT) затвóр

shuttle [ʃʌtl] n (plane) самолёт-челнóк; (also: **space ~**) шатл; (also: ~ **service**) регулярное сообщéние

shy [ʃaɪ] adj (timid) застéнчивый, стеснúтельный; (reserved) осторóжный; ~**ness** n (see adj) застéнчивость f, стеснúтельность f, осторóжность f

Siberia [saɪbɪərɪə] n Сибúрь f

sibling [sɪblɪŋ] n (brother) роднóй брат; (sister) роднáя сестрá

sick [sɪk] adj (ill) больнóй; (humour) сквéрный; **he is/was ~** (vomiting) егó рвёт/вырвало; **I feel ~** меня тошнúт; **I'm ~ of arguing/school** меня тошнúт от спóров/шкóлы; ~**en** vt вызывáть (вызвать pf) отвращéние у +gen; ~**ening** adj протúвный, тошнотвóрный

sickly [sɪklɪ] adj (child) хúлый; (smell) тошнотвóрный

sickness [sɪknɪs] n (illness) болéзнь f; (vomiting) рвóта

side [saɪd] n (of body) сторонá f; (of body) бок; (team) комáнда, сторонá f; (of hill) склон pf; (door etc) боковóй; ~**board** n буфéт; ~**burns** npl бакенбáрды pl; ~**effect** n побóчное дéйствие; ~**street** n переýлок; ~**walk** n (US) тротуáр; ~**ways** adv (go in, lean) бóком; (look) úскоса

siding [saɪdɪŋ] n запаснóй путь m

siege [siːdʒ] n осáда

sieve [sɪv] n (CULIN) сúто ♦ vt просéивать (просéять pf)

sift [sɪft] vt просéивать (просéять pf)

sigh [saɪ] n вздох ♦ vi вздыхáть (вздохнýть pf)

sight [saɪt] n (faculty) зрéние;

(spectacle) зрелище, вид; (on gun) прицел; **in** ~ в поле зрения; **out of** ~ из виду; ~**seeing** n: **to go** ~**seeing** осматривать (осмотреть pf) достопримечательности

sign [saɪn] n (notice) вывеска; (with hand) знак; (indication, evidence) признак; (document) подписывать (подписать pf); **to** ~ **sth over to sb** передавать (передать pf) что-н кому-н; ~ **on** vi (BRIT: as unemployed) отмечаться (отметиться pf) как безработный; (for course) регистрироваться (зарегистрироваться pf); ~ **up** vi (MIL) наниматься (наняться pf); (for course) регистрироваться (зарегистрироваться pf) ♦ vt нанимать (нанять pf)

signal ['sɪɡnl] n сигнал ♦ vi сигнализировать (impf/pf); **to** ~ **to sb** подавать (подать pf) знак +dat

signature ['sɪɡnətʃə'] n подпись f

significance [sɪɡ'nɪfɪkəns] n значение

significant [sɪɡ'nɪfɪkənt] adj (amount, discovery) значительный

signify ['sɪɡnɪfaɪ] vt означать (impf)

silence ['saɪləns] n тишина ♦ vt заставлять (заставить pf) замолчать

silent ['saɪlənt] adj безмолвный; (taciturn) молчаливый; (film) немой; **to remain** ~ молчать (impf)

silhouette [sɪlu:'ɛt] n силуэт

silk [sɪlk] n шёлк ♦ adj шёлковый; ~**y** adj шелковистый

silly ['sɪlɪ] adj глупый

silt [sɪlt] n ил

silver ['sɪlvə'] n серебро ♦ adj серебряный; ~**y** adj серебристый

similar ['sɪmɪlə'] adj: ~ **(to)** сходный (с +instr), подобный

(+dat); ~**ity** [sɪmɪ'lærɪtɪ] n сходство; ~**ly** adv (in a similar way) подобным образом

simmer ['sɪmə'] vi тушиться (impf)

simple ['sɪmpl] adj простой; (foolish) недалёкий

simplicity [sɪm'plɪsɪtɪ] n (see adj) простота; недалёкость f

simplify ['sɪmplɪfaɪ] vt упрощать (упростить pf)

simply ['sɪmplɪ] adv просто

simulate ['sɪmjuleɪt] vt изображать (изобразить pf)

simultaneous [sɪml'teɪnɪəs] adj одновременный; ~**ly** adv одновременно

sin [sɪn] n грех ♦ vi грешить (согрешить pf)

since [sɪns] adv с тех пор ♦ conj (time) с тех пор как; (because) так как ♦ prep: ~ **July** с июля; ~ **then**, **ever** ~ с тех пор; **it's two weeks** ~ **I wrote** две недели с (тех пор) как я написал; ~ **our last meeting** со времени нашей последней встречи

sincere [sɪn'sɪə'] adj искренний

sincerity [sɪn'sɛrɪtɪ] n искренность f

sing [sɪŋ] (pt **sang**, pp **sung**) vti петь (спеть pf)

singe [sɪndʒ] vt палить (опалить pf)

singer ['sɪŋə'] n певец(вица)

singing ['sɪŋɪŋ] n пение

single ['sɪŋɡl] adj (person) одинокий; (individual) одиночный; (not double) одинарный ♦ n (BRIT: also: ~ **ticket**) билет в один конец; **not a** ~ **person** ни один человек; ~ **out** vt (choose) выделять (выделить pf); ~**-minded** adj целеустремлённый; ~ **room** n (in hotel) одноместный номер

singly ['sɪŋɡlɪ] adv врозь, по

отдéльности

singular ['sɪŋgjulə'] *adj*
необыкновéнный ♦ *n* (LING)
еди́нственное число́

sinister ['sɪnɪstə'] *adj* злове́щий

sink [sɪŋk] (*pt* sank, *pp* sunk) *n*
рáковина ♦ *vt* (ship) топи́ть
(потопи́ть *pf*); (well) рыть
(вы́рыть *pf*); (foundations)
врывáть (врыть *pf*) ♦ *vi* (ship)
тону́ть (потону́ть *pf* or затону́ть
pf); (heart, spirits) пáдать (упáсть
pf); (also: ~ **back**, ~ **down**)
откидываться (откину́ться *pf*); to
~ **sth into** (teeth, claws etc)
вонзáть (вонзи́ть *pf*) что-н +*acc*;
~ **in** *vi* (fig): **it took a long time
for her words to** ~ до меня́ нескоро
дошло́ значе́ние её слов

sinus ['saɪnəs] *n* (ANAT) пáзуха

sip [sɪp] *n* мáленький глотóк ♦ *vt*
потя́гивать *impf*

sir [sə'] *n* сэр, господи́н; **Sir John
Smith** Сэр Джон Смит

siren ['saɪərn] *n* сирéна

sister ['sɪstə'] *n* сестрá; (BRIT : MED)
(медицинская or мед.) сестрá;
~-in-law *n* (brother's wife)
невéстка; (husband's sister)
зо́ловка; (wife's sister)
своя́ченица

sit [sɪt] (*pt*, *pp* sat) *vi* (sit down)
сади́ться (сесть *pf*); (be sitting)
сидéть *impf*; (assembly) заседáть
(impf) ♦ *vt* (exam) сдавáть (сдать
pf); ~ **down** *vi* (after standing)
сади́ться (сесть *pf*); ~ **up** *vi* (after lying) сади́ться
(сесть *pf*)

sitcom ['sɪtkɔm] *n abbr* (TV: =
situation comedy) комéдия
положéний

site [saɪt] *n* (place) мéсто; (also:
building ~) строи́тельная
плóщадка

sit-in ['sɪtɪn] *n* сидя́чая
демонстрáция

sitting ['sɪtɪŋ] *n* (of assembly etc)
заседáние; (in canteen) смéна; ~
room *n* гости́ная *f adj*

situated ['sɪtjueɪtɪd] *adj*: **to be** ~
находи́ться (impf), располагáться
(impf)

situation [sɪtju'eɪʃən] *n* ситуáция,
положéние; (job) мéсто; (location)
положéние; **"~s vacant"** (BRIT)
"вакáнтные местá"

six [sɪks] *n* шесть; ~**teen** *n*
шестнáдцать; ~**teenth** *adj*
шестнáдцатый; ~**th** *adj* шестóй;
~**tieth** *adj* шестидеся́тый; ~**ty** *n*
шестьдеся́т

sixth form - квалификацио́нный
курс. Этот курс состои́т из
двух ступенéй - ни́жней и
вéрхней. Курс дли́тся два гóда
и предлагáется на вы́бор
шко́льникам, кото́рые к 16
годáм заверши́ли
обязáтельную шко́льную
програ́мму. В течéние двух лет
ученики́ готóвятся к
выпускны́м экзáменам,
даю́щим прáво на поступлéние
в университéт.

size [saɪz] *n* размéр; (extent)
величинá, масштáб; ~**able** *adj*
поря́дочный

skate [skeɪt] *n* (also: **ice** ~) конёк;
(also: **roller** ~) ро́ликовый конёк,
ро́лик ♦ *vi* катáться (impf) на
конькáх

skating ['skeɪtɪŋ] *n* (for pleasure)
катáние на конькáх

skeleton ['skelɪtn] *n* (ANAT) скелéт;
(outline) схéма

skeptical etc (US) = **sceptical** etc

sketch [sketʃ] *n* эски́з, набро́сок;
(outline) набро́сок; (THEAT, TV)
сцéнка, скетч ♦ *vt* (draw)
набросáть (impf); (also: ~ **out**)

обрисо́вывать (обрисова́ть pf) в
о́бщих черта́х; ~y adj
обрисо́вочный

ski [skiː] n лы́жа ♦ vi ката́ться
(impf) на лы́жах

skid [skɪd] vi (AUT) идти́ (пойти́ pf)
ю́зом

skier [ˈskiːəʳ] n лы́жник(ица)

skiing [ˈskiːɪŋ] n (for pleasure)
ката́ние на лы́жах

skilful [ˈskɪlful] (US **skillful**) adj
иску́сный, уме́лый; (player)
техни́чный

skill [skɪl] n (ability, dexterity)
мастерство́; (in computing etc)
на́вык; ~**ed** adj (able) иску́сный;
(worker) квалифици́рованный;
~**ful** adj (US) = **skilful**

skim [skɪm] vt (milk) снима́ть
(снять pf) сли́вки с +gen; (glide
over) скользи́ть (impf) над +instr
♦ vi: **to ~ through** пробега́ть
(пробежа́ть pf)

skin [skɪn] n (of person) ко́жа; (of
animal) шку́ра; (of fruit, vegetable)
кожура́; (of grape, tomato) ко́жица
♦ vt (animal) снима́ть (снять pf)
шку́ру с +gen; ~**ny** adj (thin)
то́щий

skip [skɪp] n (BRIT: container) скип
♦ vi подпры́гивать (подпры́гнуть
pf); (with rope) скака́ть (impf) ♦ vt
(miss out) пропуска́ть
(пропусти́ть pf)

skipper [ˈskɪpəʳ] n (NAUT) шки́пер,
капита́н; (SPORT) капита́н

skirt [skəːt] n ю́бка ♦ vt обходи́ть
(обойти́ pf)

skull [skʌl] n че́реп

skunk [skʌŋk] n (animal) скунс

sky [skaɪ] n не́бо; ~**light** n
слуховое окно́; ~**scraper** n
небоскрёб

slab [slæb] n плита́

slack [slæk] adj (rope) прови́сший;
(discipline) сла́бый; (security)

плохо́й

slag [slæg] vt (BRIT: inf): **to ~ sb
(off)** поноси́ть (impf) кого́-н

slam [slæm] vt (door) хло́пать
(хло́пнуть pf) +instr ♦ vi (door)
захло́пываться (захло́пнуться
pf)

slang [slæŋ] n (informal language)
сленг; (jargon) жарго́н

slant [slɑːnt] n накло́н; (fig:
approach) укло́н

slap [slæp] n шлепо́к ♦ vt шлёпать
(шлёпнуть pf); **to ~ sb across the
face** дава́ть (дать pf) кому́-н
пощёчину; **to ~ sth on sth** (paint
etc) ля́пать (наля́пать pf) что-н
на что-н

slash [slæʃ] vt ре́зать (поре́зать
pf); (fig: prices) уреза́ть
(уре́зать pf)

slate [sleɪt] n (material) сла́нец;
(tile) кро́вельная пли́тка (из
гли́нистого сла́нца) ♦ vt (fig)
разноси́ть (разнести́ pf) в пух и
прах

slaughter [ˈslɔːtəʳ] n (see vt) убо́й;
резня́, бо́йня ♦ vt (animals)
забива́ть (заби́ть pf); (people)
истребля́ть (истреби́ть pf)

slave [sleɪv] n раб(ы́ня); ~**ry** n
ра́бство

Slavonic [sləˈvɔnɪk] adj славя́нский

sleazy [ˈsliːzɪ] adj (place)
запу́щенный

sledge [slɛdʒ] n са́ни pl; (for
children) са́нки pl; ~**hammer** n
кува́лда

sleek [sliːk] adj (fur) лосня́щийся;
(hair) блестя́щий

sleep [sliːp] (pt, pp **slept**) n сон ♦ vi
спать (impf); (spend night)
ночева́ть (переночева́ть pf); **to
go to ~** засыпа́ть (засну́ть pf); ~
in vi просыпа́ть (проспа́ть pf);
~**er** n (RAIL, train) по́езд со
спа́льными ваго́нами; (: berth)

sleet [sli:t] n мокрый снег

sleeve [sli:v] n (of jacket etc) рукав; (of record) конверт

slender ['slɛndər] adj (figure) стройный; (majority) небольшой

slept [slɛpt] pt, pp of **sleep**

slice [slaɪs] n (of meat) кусок; (of bread, lemon) ломтик ♦ vt (bread, meat etc) нарезать (нарезать pf)

slick [slɪk] adj (performance) гладкий; (salesman, answer) бойкий ♦ n (also: **oil ~**) плёнка нефти

slide [slaɪd] (pt, pp **slid**) n (in playground) детская горка; (PHOT) слайд; (BRIT: also: **hair ~**) заколка ♦ vt задвигать (задвинуть pf) ♦ vi скользить (impf)

slight [slaɪt] adj хрупкий; (small) незначительный; (: error) мелкий; (accent, pain) слабый ♦ n унижение; **not in the ~est** нисколько; **~ly** adv (rather) слегка

slim [slɪm] adj (figure) стройный; (chance) слабый ♦ vi худеть (похудеть pf)

slimy ['slaɪmɪ] adj (pond) илистый

sling [slɪŋ] (pt, pp **slung**) n (MED) перевязь f ♦ vt (throw) швырять (швырнуть pf)

slip [slɪp] n (mistake) промах; (underskirt) нижняя юбка; (of paper) полоска ♦ vt совать (сунуть pf) ♦ vi (slide) скользить (скользнуть f); (lose balance) поскользнуться (pf); (decline) снижаться (снизиться pf); **to give sb the ~** ускользать (ускользнуть pf) от кого-н; **a ~ of the tongue** оговорка; **to ~ sth**

on/off надевать (надеть pf)/ сбрасывать (сбросить pf) что-н; **to ~ into** (room etc) скользнуть (pf) в +acc; **to ~ out of** (room etc) выскальзывать (выскользнуть pf) из +gen; **to ~ away** vi улизнуть (ускользнуть pf); **~ in** vt совать (сунуть pf) ♦ vi вкрасться; **~ up** vi закрадываться (закрасться f)

slipper ['slɪpər] n тапочка

slippery ['slɪpərɪ] adj скользкий

slit [slɪt] (pt, pp ~) n (cut) разрез; (in skirt) шлица; (opening) щель f ♦ vt разрезать (разрезать f)

slither ['slɪðər] vi (person) скользить (impf); (snake) извиваться (impf)

sliver ['slɪvər] n (of glass) осколок

slog [slɔg] n: **it was a hard ~** это была тяжёлая работа

slogan ['sləugən] n лозунг

slope [sləup] n склон; (gentle rise) уклон; (slant) наклон

sloppy ['slɔpɪ] adj (work) халтурный

slot [slɔt] n (in machine) прорезь f, паз ♦ vt: **to ~ into** опускать (опустить pf) что-н в +acc

Slovakia [sləu'vækɪə] n Словакия

Slovakian adj словацкий

slow [sləu] adj медленный; (stupid) тупой ♦ adv медленно ♦ vt (also: **~ down, ~ up**: vehicle) замедлять (замедлить pf); (traffic) замедляться (замедлиться pf); (car, train etc) сбавлять (сбавить pf) ход; **my watch is (20 minutes)** ~ мои часы отстают (на 20 минут); **~ly** adv медленно; **~ motion** ♦ n: **in ~ motion** в замедленном действии

slug [slʌg] n (ZOOL) слизень m

sluggish ['slʌgɪʃ] adj вялый

slum [slʌm] n трущоба

slump [slʌmp] n (economic) спад; (in profits, sales) падение

спальное место; **~ing bag** n спальный мешок; **~less** adj (night) бессонный; **~walker** n лунатик; **~y** adj сонный

slung [slʌŋ] *pt, pp of* **sling**

slur [slɜːʳ] *vt* (words) мя́млить (промя́млить *pf*) ♦ *n* (fig): ~ **(on)** пятно́ (на +*prp*)

sly [slaɪ] *adj* лука́вый

smack [smæk] *n* (slap) шлепо́к ♦ *vt* хло́пать (хло́пнуть *pf*); (child) шлёпать (отшлёпать *pf*) ♦ *vi*: **to ~ of** отдава́ть (*impf*) +*instr*

small [smɔːl] *adj* ма́ленький; (quantity, amount) небольшо́й, ма́лый; **~pox** *n* о́спа; **~ talk** *n* све́тская бесе́да

smart [smɑːt] *adj* (neat, tidy) опря́тный; (clever) толко́вый ♦ *vi* (also fig) жечь (*impf*); **my eyes are ~ing** у меня́ щи́плет глаза́

smash [smæʃ] *n* (collision - also: **~-up**) ава́рия ♦ *vt* разбива́ть (разби́ть *pf*); (SPORT, record) побива́ть (поби́ть *pf*) ♦ *vi* (break) разбива́ться (разби́ться *pf*); **to ~ against** *or* **into** разбива́ться (вре́заться *pf*) в +*acc*; **~ing** *adj* (inf) потряса́ющий

smear [smɪəʳ] *n* (trace) след; (MED - also: ~ **test**) мазо́к ♦ *vt* (spread) ма́зать (нама́зать *pf*)

smell [smel] (*pt, pp* **smelt** *or* **~ed**) *n* за́пах; (sense) обоня́ние ♦ *vt* чу́вствовать (почу́вствовать *pf*) за́пах +*gen* ♦ *vi* (food etc) па́хнуть (*impf*); **to ~ (of)** (unpleasant) воня́ть (*impf*) (+*instr*); **~y** *adj* воню́чий, злово́нный

smelt [smelt] *pt, pp of* **smell**

smile [smaɪl] *n* улы́бка ♦ *vi* улыба́ться (улыбну́ться *pf*)

smirk [smɜːk] *n* (pej) ухмы́лка

smog [smɔɡ] *n* смог

smoke [sməuk] *n* дым ♦ *vi* (person) кури́ть (*impf*); (chimney) дыми́ться (*impf*) ♦ *vt* (cigarettes) кури́ть (вы́курить *pf*); **~d** *adj* (bacon, fish) копчёный; (glass) дымча́тый; **~r** *n* (person) куря́щий(ая) *m(f) adj*,

кури́льщик(щица)

smoking ['sməukɪŋ] *n* (act) куре́ние; **"no ~"** "не кури́ть"

smoky ['sməukɪ] *adj* (room) ды́мный

smolder ['sməuldəʳ] *vi* (*US*) = **smoulder**

smooth [smuːð] *adj* гла́дкий; (sauce) одноро́дный; (flavour) мя́гкий; (movement) пла́вный

smother ['smʌðəʳ] *vt* (fire) туши́ть (потуши́ть *pf*); (person) души́ть (задуши́ть *pf*); (emotions) подавля́ть (подави́ть *pf*)

smoulder ['sməuldəʳ] (*US* **smolder**) *vi* (fire) тлеть (*impf*); (fig: anger) таи́ться (*impf*)

smudge [smʌdʒ] *n* пятно́ ♦ *vt* разма́зывать (разма́зать *pf*)

smug [smʌɡ] *adj* дово́льный

smuggle ['smʌɡl] *vt* (goods) провози́ть (провезти́ *pf*) (контраба́ндой)

smuggling ['smʌɡlɪŋ] *n* контраба́нда

snack [snæk] *n* заку́ска

snag [snæɡ] *n* поме́ха

snail [sneɪl] *n* ули́тка

snake [sneɪk] *n* змея́

snap [snæp] *adj* (decision etc) момента́льный ♦ *vt* (break) разла́мывать (разломи́ть *pf*); (fingers) щёлкать (щёлкнуть *pf*) +*instr* ♦ *vi* (break) разла́мываться (разломи́ться *pf*); (speak sharply) крича́ть (*impf*); **to ~ shut** (trap, jaws etc) защёлкиваться (защёлкнуться *pf*); **~ up** *vt* расхва́тывать (расхвата́ть *pf*); **~shot** *n* сни́мок

snare [snɛəʳ] *n* сило́к

snarl [snɑːl] *vi* рыча́ть (*impf*)

snatch [snætʃ] *n* обры́вок ♦ *vt* (grab) хвата́ть (схвати́ть *pf*); (handbag) вырыва́ть (вы́рвать *pf*); (child) похища́ть (похи́тить pf); (opportunity) урыва́ть (урва́ть pf)

sneak [sniːk] vi: to ~ into проска́льзывать (проскользну́ть pf) в +acc; to ~ out of выска́льзывать (вы́скользнуть pf) из +gen; to ~ up on абедничать (набедничать pf) на +acc; **~ers** npl кроссо́вки fpl

sneer [snɪəʳ] vi (mock): to ~ at глуми́ться (impf) над +instr

sneeze [sniːz] vi чиха́ть (чихну́ть pf)

sniff [snɪf] n (sound) сопе́ние ♦ vi шмы́гать (шмыгну́ть pf) но́сом; (when crying) всхли́пывать (impf) ♦ vt ню́хать (impf)

snip [snɪp] vt ре́зать (поре́зать pf)

sniper [ˈsnaɪpəʳ] n сна́йпер

snob [snɔb] n сноб; **~bish** adj сноби́стский

snooker [ˈsnuːkəʳ] n сну́кер

snore [snɔːʳ] vi храпе́ть (impf)

snorkel [ˈsnɔːkl] n тру́бка (ныря́льщика)

snow [snəu] n снег ♦ vi: it's ~ing идёт снег; **~ball** n снежо́к; **~drift** n сугро́б; **~drop** n подсне́жник; **~fall** n снегопа́д; **~flake** n снежи́нка; **~man** (irreg) n снегови́к, снежная ба́ба

SNP n abbr = Scottish National Party

snub [snʌb] vt пренебрежи́тельно обходи́ться (обойти́сь pf) с +instr

snug [snʌg] adj (place) ую́тный; (well-fitting) облега́ющий

KEYWORD

so [səu] adv 1 (thus, likewise) так; if this is so е́сли э́то так; if so е́сли так; while she was so doing, he … пока́ она́ э́то де́лала, он …; I didn't do it - you did so! я не де́лал э́того - а вот и сде́лал!; you weren't there - I was so! тебя́ там не́ было - а вот и был!; I like him - so do I он мне

нра́вится - мне то́же; I'm still at school - so is he я ещё учу́сь в шко́ле - он то́же; so it is! и действи́тельно!, и пра́вда!; I hope/think so наде́юсь/ду́маю, что так; so far пока́; do you like the book so far? ну, как Вам кни́га?

2 (in comparisons: +adv) насто́лько, так; (: +adj) насто́лько, тако́й; (: +adj) насто́лько, тако́й; so quickly (that) насто́лько or так бы́стро(, что); so big (that) тако́й большо́й(, что); she's not so clever as her brother она́ не так умна́, как её брат

3 (describing degree, extent) так; I've got so much work у меня́ так мно́го рабо́ты; I love you so much я Вас так люблю́; thank you so much спаси́бо Вам большо́е; I'm so glad to see you я так рад Вас ви́деть; there are so many books I would like to read есть так мно́го книг, кото́рые я бы хоте́л проче́сть; so … that … так … что …

4 (about) о́коло +gen; ten or so о́коло десяти́; I only have an hour or so у меня́ есть о́коло ча́са

5 (phrases): so long! (inf: bye) пока́!

♦ conj 1 (expressing purpose): so as to do что́бы +infin; I brought this wine so that you could try it я принёс э́то вино́, что́бы Вы могли́ его́ попро́бовать

2 (expressing result) так что; so I was right так что я был прав; so you see, I could have stayed так что, ви́дите, я мог бы оста́ться

soak [səuk] vt (drench) промочи́ть (pf); (steep) зама́чивать (замочи́ть pf) ♦ vi (steep) отмока́ть (impf); ~ up впи́тывать (впита́ть pf) (в себя́)

soap [səʊp] n мы́ло; ~ **opera** n (TV) мы́льная о́пера

soar [sɔː] vi (price, temperature) подска́кивать (подскочи́ть pf)

sob [sɒb] n рыда́ние ♦ vi рыда́ть (impf)

sober ['səʊbə] adj тре́звый; (colour, style) сде́ржанный

soccer ['sɒkə] n футбо́л

sociable ['səʊʃəbl] adj общи́тельный

social ['səʊʃl] adj (history, structure etc) обще́ственный, социа́льный; **he has a good ~ life** он мно́го обща́ется с людьми́; ~**ism** n социали́зм; ~**ist** n социали́ст ♦ adj социалисти́ческий; ~**ize** vi: **to ~ize (with)** обща́ться (impf) (с +instr); ~**ly** adv: **to visit sb ~ly** заходи́ть (зайти́ pf) к кому́-н по-дру́жески; ~**ly acceptable** социа́льно прие́млемый; ~ **security** (BRIT) n социа́льная защи́та; ~ **work** n социа́льная рабо́та

society [sə'saɪətɪ] n о́бщество

sociology [səʊsɪ'ɒlədʒɪ] n социоло́гия

sock [sɒk] n носо́к

socket ['sɒkɪt] n глазни́ца; (BRIT : ELEC, in wall) розе́тка

soda ['səʊdə] n (also: ~ **water**) со́довая f adj; (US: also: ~ **pop**) газиро́вка

sodden ['sɒdn] adj (very wet) вы́мокший

sodium ['səʊdɪəm] n на́трий

sofa ['səʊfə] n дива́н

soft [sɒft] adj мя́гкий; ~ **drink** n безалкого́льный напи́ток; ~**ly** adv (gently) мя́гко; (quietly) ти́хо; ~**ness** n мя́гкость f; ~**ware** n програ́мма, програ́ммное обеспе́чение

soggy ['sɒgɪ] adj (ground) сыро́й

soil [sɔɪl] n (earth) по́чва; (territory)

земля́ ♦ vt па́чкать (запа́чкать pf)

solar ['səʊlə] adj со́лнечный

sold [səʊld] pt, pp of **sell**

solder ['səʊldə] vt спа́ивать (спая́ть pf)

soldier ['səʊldʒə] n (MIL) солда́т

sole [səʊl] n (of foot) подо́шва; (of shoe) подо́шва, подмётка ♦ n inv (fish) па́лтус ♦ adj (unique) еди́нственный; ~**ly** adv то́лько

solemn ['sɒləm] adj торже́ственный

solicitor [sə'lɪsɪtə] n (BRIT) адвока́т

solid ['sɒlɪd] adj (not hollow) це́льный; (not liquid) твёрдый; (reliable) про́чный; (entire) це́лый; (gold) чи́стый ♦ n твёрдое те́ло; ~**s** npl (food) твёрдая пи́ща fsg

solidarity [sɒlɪ'dærɪtɪ] n солида́рность f

solitary ['sɒlɪtərɪ] adj одино́кий; (empty) уединённый; (single) едини́чный; ~ **confinement** n одино́чное заключе́ние

solitude ['sɒlɪtjuːd] n уедине́ние, одино́чество

solo ['səʊləʊ] n со́ло nt ind ♦ adv (fly) в одино́чку; (play) со́ло; ~**ist** n соли́ст(ка)

soluble ['sɒljʊbl] adj раствори́мый

solution [sə'luːʃən] n (answer) реше́ние; (liquid) раство́р

solve [sɒlv] vt (problem) разреша́ть (разреши́ть pf); (mystery) раскрыва́ть (раскры́ть pf)

solvent ['sɒlvənt] adj платёжеспосо́бный ♦ n раствори́тель m

sombre ['sɒmbə] (US **somber**) adj мра́чный

───────────────
KEYWORD
───────────────

some [sʌm] adj 1 (a certain amount or number of): **would you like some tea/biscuits?** хоти́те ча́ю/

печéнья?; **there's some milk in the fridge** в холоди́льнике есть молоко́; **he asked me some questions** он зáдал мне нéсколько вопро́сов; **there are some people waiting to see you** Вас ждут каки́е-то лю́ди

2 (*certain*: *in contrasts*) нéкоторый; **some people say that** ... нéкоторые говоря́т, что ...

3 (*unspecified*) како́й-то; **some woman phoned you** Вам звони́ла кака́я-то жéнщина; **we'll meet again some day** мы когда́-нибудь опя́ть встрéтимся; **shall we meet some day next week?** дава́йте встрéтимся ка́к-нибудь на слéдующей недéле?

♦ *pron* (*a certain number*: *people*) нéкоторые *pl*, одни́ *pl*; **some took the bus, and some walked** нéкоторые поéхали на авто́бусе, а нéкоторые пошли́ пешко́м; **I've got some** (*books etc*) у меня́ есть нéсколько; **who would like a piece of cake? - I'd like some** кто хо́чет кусо́к то́рта? - я хочу́; **I've read some of the book** я прочёл часть кни́ги

♦ *adv* óколо; **some ten people** óколо десяти́ челове́к

somebody ['sʌmbədɪ] *pron* = **someone**
somehow ['sʌmhaʊ] *adv* (*in some way*: *in future*) ка́к-нибудь; (: *in past*) ка́к-то; (*for some reason*) почему́-то, каки́м-то о́бразом
someone ['sʌmwʌn] *pron* (*specific person*) кто́-то; (*unspecified person*) кто́-нибудь; **I saw ~ in the garden** я ви́дел кого́-то в саду́; **~ will help you** Вам кто́-нибудь помо́жет
somersault ['sʌməsɔːlt] *n* (*in air*) са́льто *nt ind*; (*on ground*)

куворо́к
something ['sʌmθɪŋ] *pron* (*something specific*) что́-то; (*something unspecified*) что́-нибудь; **there's ~ wrong with my car** что́-то случи́лось с мое́й маши́ной; **would you like ~ to eat/drink?** хоти́те чего́-нибудь поéсть/вы́пить?; **I have ~ for you** у меня́ ко́е-что для Вас есть
sometime ['sʌmtaɪm] *adv* (*in future*) когда́-нибудь; (*in past*) когда́-то, ка́к-то
sometimes ['sʌmtaɪmz] *adv* иногда́
somewhat ['sʌmwɔt] *adv* нéсколько
somewhere ['sʌmwɛəʳ] *adv* (*be*: *somewhere specific*) где́-то; (: *anywhere*) где́-нибудь; (*go*: *somewhere specific*) куда́-то; (: *anywhere*) куда́-нибудь; (*come from*) отку́да-то; **it's ~ or other in Scotland** э́то где́-то в Шотла́ндии; **is there a post office ~ around here?** здесь где́-нибудь есть по́чта?; **let's go ~ else** дава́йте поéдем куда́-нибудь в друго́е мéсто
son [sʌn] *n* сын
song [sɔŋ] *n* пéсня
son-in-law ['sʌnɪnlɔː] *n* зять *m*
soon [suːn] *adv* (*in a short time*) ско́ро; (*early*) ра́но; **~ (afterwards)** вско́ре; *see also* **as**; **~ er** скорéе; **I would ~er do that** я бы скорéе сдéлал э́то; **~er or later** ра́но или по́здно
soot [sʊt] *n* са́жа
soothe [suːð] *vt* успока́ивать (успоко́ить *pf*)
sophisticated [sə'fɪstɪkeɪtɪd] *adj* изощрённый; (*refined*) изы́сканный
soprano [sə'prɑːnəʊ] *n* сопра́но *find*
sordid ['sɔːdɪd] *adj* (*place*) убо́гий; (*story etc*) гну́сный

sore [sɔːʳ] n я́зва, боля́чка ♦ adj (esp US: offended) оби́женный; (painful): my arm is~, I've got a ~ arm у меня́ боли́т рука́; it's a ~ point (fig) э́то больно́е ме́сто; ~ly adv: I am ~ly tempted to я испы́тываю большу́ю собла́зн (+infin)

sorrow ['sɔrəu] n печа́ль f, грусть f

sorry ['sɔrɪ] adj плаче́вный; I'm ~ мне жаль; ~! извини́те, пожа́луйста!; ~? (pardon) прости́те?; I feel ~ for him мне его́ жаль

sort [sɔːt] n (type) сорт ♦ vt (mail) сортирова́ть (рассортирова́ть pf); (also: ~ out: papers, belongings etc) разбира́ть (разобра́ть pf); (: problems) разбира́ться (разобра́ться pf) в +prp

SOS n abbr (= save our souls) SOS

so-so ['səusəu] adv так себе́

sought [sɔːt] pt, pp of **seek**

soul [səul] n (spirit, person) душа́

sound [saund] adj (healthy) здоро́вый; (safe, not damaged) це́лый; (secure: investment) надёжный; (reliable, thorough) соли́дный; (sensible: advice) разу́мный ♦ n звук ♦ vt (alarm) поднима́ть (подня́ть pf) ♦ vi звуча́ть (impf) ♦ vt: he is ~ asleep он кре́пко спит; I don't like the ~ of it мне э́то не нра́вится; ~ly adv (sleep) кре́пко; (beat etc) здо́рово; ~track n му́зыка (из кинофи́льма)

soup [suːp] n суп

sour ['sauəʳ] adj ки́слый; (fig: bad-tempered) угрю́мый

source [sɔːs] n (also fig) исто́чник

south [sauθ] n юг ♦ adj ю́жный ♦ adv (go) на юг; (be) на ю́ге; **South America** n Ю́жная

Аме́рика; ~**east** n юго-восто́к; ~**erly** ['sʌðəlɪ] adj обращённый к ю́гу; (wind) ю́жный; ~**ern** ['sʌðən] adj ю́жный; **South Pole** n: the **South Pole** Ю́жный по́люс; ~**west** n юго-за́пад

souvenir [suːvə'nɪəʳ] n сувени́р

sovereign ['sɔvrɪn] n (ruler) госуда́рь(рыня) m(f); ~**ty** n суверените́т

Soviet ['səuvɪət] adj сове́тский; the ~ **Union** (formerly) Сове́тский Сою́з

sow¹ [sau] n (pig) свинья́

sow² [səu] (pt ~ed, pp ~n) vt (also fig) се́ять (посе́ять pf)

soya ['sɔɪə] (US **soy**) adj со́евый

spa [spɑː] n (US: also: health ~) во́ды fpl

space [speɪs] n простра́нство; (small place, room) ме́сто; (beyond Earth) ко́смос; (interval, period) промежу́ток ♦ cpd косми́ческий ♦ vt (also: ~ out: payments, visits) распределя́ть (распредели́ть pf); ~**craft** n косми́ческий кора́бль m; ~**ship** n = **spacecraft**

spacious ['speɪʃəs] adj просто́рный

spade [speɪd] n (tool) лопа́та; (child's) лопа́тка; ~**s** npl (CARDS) пи́ки fpl

spaghetti [spə'gɛtɪ] n спаге́тти pl ind

Spain [speɪn] n Испа́ния

spam [spæm] n (COMPUT) рекла́ма на Интерне́те

span [spæn] pt of **spin** ♦ n (of hand, wings) разма́х; (in time) промежу́ток ♦ vt охва́тывать (охвати́ть pf)

Spanish ['spænɪʃ] adj испа́нский; the ~ npl испа́нцы mpl

spank [spæŋk] vt шлёпать (отшлёпать pf)

spanner ['spænəʳ] n (BRIT) (га́ечный) ключ

spare [spɛəʳ] *adj* (*free: time, seat*) свобо́дный; (*surplus*) ли́шний; (*reserve*) запасно́й ♦ *vt* (*trouble, expense*) избавля́ть (изба́вить *pf*) от +*gen*; (*make available*) выделя́ть (вы́делить *pf*); (*refrain from hurting*) щади́ть (пощади́ть *pf*); **I have some time to** ~ у меня́ есть немно́го свобо́дного вре́мени; **to have money to** ~ име́ть (*impf*) ли́шние де́ньги; ~ **time** *nt* свобо́дное вре́мя *nt*

sparingly [ˈspɛərɪŋlɪ] *adv* эконо́мно

spark [spɑːk] *n* (*also fig*) и́скра

sparkle [ˈspɑːkl] *n* блеск ♦ *vi* (*diamonds, water, eyes*) сверка́ть (*impf*)

sparkling [ˈspɑːklɪŋ] *adj* (*wine*) игри́стый

sparrow [ˈspærəu] *n* воробе́й

sparse [spɑːs] *adj* ре́дкий

spartan [ˈspɑːtən] *adj* спарта́нский

spasm [ˈspæzəm] *n* (*MED*) спазм

spat [spæt] *pt, pp of* **spit**

spate [speɪt] *n* (*fig*): **a** ~ **of** пото́к +*gen*

speak [spiːk] (*pt* **spoke**, *pp* **spoken**) *vi* говори́ть (*impf*); (*make a speech*) выступа́ть (вы́ступить *pf*) ♦ *vt* (*truth*) говори́ть (сказа́ть *pf*); **to** ~ **to** *or* **with** разгова́ривать (*impf*) *or* говори́ть (*impf*) с кем-н; **to** ~ **of** *or* **about** говори́ть (*impf*) о +*prp*; ~ **er** *n* (*in public*) ора́тор; (*also:* **loudspeaker**) громкоговори́тель *m*

spear [spɪəʳ] *n* копьё

special [ˈspɛʃl] *adj* (*important*) осо́бый, осо́бенный; (*edition, adviser, school*) специа́льный; ~**ist** *n* специали́ст; ~**ity** [spɛʃɪˈælɪtɪ] *n* (*dish*) фи́рменное блю́до; (*subject*) специализа́ция; ~**ize** *vi*: **to** ~**ize** (**in**) специализи́роваться (*impf/pf*) (в/на +*prp*); ~**ly** *adv* (*especially*) осо́бенно

species [ˈspiːʃiːz] *n inv* вид

specific [spəˈsɪfɪk] *adj* специфи́ческий, определённый; ~**ally** *adv* (*exactly*) точне́е; (*specially*) специа́льно; ~**ation** [spɛsɪfɪˈkeɪʃən] *n* (*TECH*) специфика́ция; (*requirement*) тре́бование

specify [ˈspɛsɪfaɪ] *vt* уточня́ть (уточни́ть *pf*)

specimen [ˈspɛsɪmən] *n* (*example*) экземпля́р; (*sample*) образе́ц; **a** ~ **of urine** моча́ для ана́лиза

specs [spɛks] *npl* (*inf: glasses*) очки́ *pl*

spectacle [ˈspɛktəkl] *n* (*scene, event*) зре́лище; ~**s** *npl* (*glasses*) очки́ *pl*

spectacular [spɛkˈtækjuləʳ] *adj* впечатля́ющий, порази́тельный

spectator [spɛkˈteɪtəʳ] *n* зри́тель(ница) *m(f)*

spectrum [ˈspɛktrəm] *n* (*pl* **spectra**) *n* спектр

speculate [ˈspɛkjuleɪt] *vi* (*COMM*) спекули́ровать (*impf*); (*guess*): **to** ~ **about** стро́ить (*impf*) предположе́ния о +*prp*

speculation [spɛkjuˈleɪʃən] *n* (*see vb*) спекуля́ция; предположе́ние

sped [spɛd] *pt, pp of* **speed**

speech [spiːtʃ] *n* речь *f*; ~**less** *adj*: **I was** ~**less with anger** от гне́ва я лиши́лся да́ра ре́чи; **she looked at him** ~**less** она́ посмотре́ла на него́ в онеме́нии

speed [spiːd] (*pt, pp* **sped**) *n* (*rate*) ско́рость *f*; (*promptness*) быстрота́ ♦ *vi* (*move*): **to** ~ **along/by** мча́ться (промча́ться *pf*) +*dat*/ми́мо +*gen*; **at full** *or* **top** ~ на по́лной *or* преде́льной ско́рости; ~ **up** (*pt, pp* ~ **ed up**) *vi* ускоря́ться (уско́риться *pf*) ♦ *vt* ускоря́ть (уско́рить *pf*); ~**ily** *adv* бы́стро,

~ing n превышéние скóрости; **~ limit** n предéл скóрости; **~ometer** [spɪˈdɔmɪtə^r] n спидóметр; **~y** adj (prompt) скóрый

spell [spɛl] (pt, pp **spelt** (BRIT) or **~ed**) n (also: **magic ~**) колдовствó; (period of time) перйод ♦ vt (also: **~ out**) произносить (произнести pf) по буквам; (fig: explain) разъяснять (разъяснить pf) ♦ vi: **he can't ~** у негó плохáя орфогрáфия; **~bound** adj зачарóванный; **~ing** n орфогрáфия, правописáние

spend [spɛnd] (pt, pp **spent**) vt (money) трáтить (потрáтить pf); (time, life) проводить (провести pf)

sperm [spə:m] n спéрма

sphere [sfɪə^r] n сфéра

spice [spaɪs] n (pepper, salt etc) спéция

spicy [ˈspaɪsɪ] adj (food) óстрый; (: with a strong flavour) прáный

spider [ˈspaɪdə^r] n паýк

spike [spaɪk] n (point) остриé

spill [spɪl] (pt, pp **spilt** or **~ed**) vt (liquid) проливáть (пролить pf), разливáть (разлить pf) ♦ vi (liquid) проливáться (пролиться pf), разливáться (разлиться pf); **~age** n (of oil) выброс

spin [spɪn] (pt **spun** or **span**, pp **spun**) n (trip in car) катáние; (AVIAT) штóпор; (POL) уклóн, тендéнция ♦ vt (BRIT: clothes) выжимáть (выжать pf) (в стирáльной машине) ♦ vi (make thread) прясть (impf); (person, head) кружиться (impf)

spinach [ˈspɪnɪtʃ] n шпинáт

spinal [ˈspaɪnl] adj (relating to the spine) позвонóчный; (relating to the spinal cord) спинномозговóй; **~ injury** поврежде́ние

позвонóчника; **~ cord** n спиннóй мозг

spine [spaɪn] n (ANAT) позвонóчник; (thorn) колю́чка, иглá

spinning [ˈspɪnɪŋ] n (craft) прядéние

spinster [ˈspɪnstə^r] n стáрая дéва

spiral [ˈspaɪərl] n спирáль f

spire [ˈspaɪə^r] n шпиль m

spirit [ˈspɪrɪt] n дух; (soul) душá; **~s** npl (alcohol) спиртны́е напитки mpl, спиртнóе ntsg adj; **in good/low ~s** в хорóшем/подáвленном настрóении; **~ed** adj энергичный; (performance) воодушевлённый

spiritual [ˈspɪrɪtjuəl] adj духóвный

spit [spɪt] (pt, pp **spat**) n вéртел; (saliva) слюнá ♦ vi (person) плевáть (плю́нуть pf); (fire, hot oil) брызгать (impf); (inf: rain) морóсить (impf)

spite [spaɪt] n злóба, злость f ♦ vt досаждáть (досадить pf) +dat; **in ~ of** несмотря́ на +acc; **~ful** adj злóбный

splash [splæʃ] n (sound) всплеск ♦ vt брызгать (брызнуть pf) ♦ vi (also: **~ about**) плескáться (impf)

splendid [ˈsplɛndɪd] adj великолéпный

splint [splɪnt] n (MED) ши́на

splinter [ˈsplɪntə^r] n (of wood) щéпка; (of glass) оскóлок; (in finger) занóза

split [splɪt] (pt, pp **~**) n (crack, tear) трéщина; (POL, fig) раскóл ♦ vt (atom, piece of wood) расщеплять (расщепить pf); (POL, fig) раскáлывать (расколóть pf); (work, profits) делить (разделить pf) ♦ vi (divide) расщепляться (расщепиться pf), разделяться (разделиться pf); **~ up** vi (couple) расходиться (разойтись pf);

(*group*) разделя́ться
(раздели́ться *pf*)
splutter ['splʌtər] *vi* (*engine*) чиха́ть
(*impf*); (*person*) лепета́ть (*impf*)
spoil [spɔɪl] (*pt, pp* ~**t** *or* ~**ed**) *vt*
по́ртить (испо́ртить *pf*)
spoke [spəuk] *pt of* **speak** ♦ *n* (*of
wheel*) спи́ца; ♦ *pp of* **speak**
spokesman ['spəuksmən] (*irreg*) *n*
представи́тель *m*
spokeswoman ['spəukswumən]
(*irreg*) *n* представи́тельница
sponge [spʌndʒ] *n* гу́бка; (*also:* ~
cake) бискви́т
sponsor ['spɒnsə*ʳ*] *n* спо́нсор ♦ *vt*
финанси́ровать (*impf/pf*),
спонси́ровать (*impf/pf*); (*applicant*)
поруча́ться (поручи́ться *pf*) за
+*acc*; ~**ship** *n* спо́нсорство

sponsorship - В
Великобрита́нии
спонси́рование явля́ется
распространённым спо́собом
сбо́ра де́нег на
благотвори́тельность. При́нято
выполня́ть ра́зного ро́да
зада́чи, наприме́р, пла́вание,
ходьба́ на дли́нную диста́нцию
и́ли да́же похуде́ние.
Предполо́жим, вы хоти́те
собра́ть де́ньги для
благотвори́тельной
организа́ции, финанси́рующей
иссле́дования ра́ковых
заболева́ний. Вы заявля́ете,
что пройдёте пешко́м 10 миль
и про́сите знако́мых, друзе́й
и тд спонси́ровать ва́ше
реше́ние, же́ртвуя де́ньги в
по́льзу э́той
благотвори́тельной
организа́ции.

spontaneous [spɒn'teɪnɪəs] *adj*
(*gesture*) спонта́нный,

непосре́дственный;
(*demonstration*) стихи́йный
spool [spuːl] *n* (*for thread*)
кату́шка; (*for film, tape etc*)
боби́на
spoon [spuːn] *n* ло́жка; ~**ful** *n*
(по́лная) ло́жка
sporadic [spə'rædɪk] *adj*
спорадчи́еский
sport [spɔːt] *n* (*game*) спорт *m no
pl*; (*individual event etc*)
спорти́вный; ~**ing** *n* (*event etc*)
спортсме́н; ~**sman** (*irreg*) *n*
спортсме́нка; ~**y** *adj* спорти́вный
spot [spɒt] *n* (*mark*) пятно́; (*dot: on
pattern*) кра́пинка; (*on skin*)
прыщи́к; (*place*) ме́сто ♦ *vt*
замеча́ть (заме́тить *pf*); **a** ~ **of
bother** ме́лкая неприя́тность *f*;
~**s of rain** ка́пли дождя́; **on the** ~
(*in that place*) на ме́сте;
(*immediately*) в тот же моме́нт;
~**less** *adj* чисте́йший; ~**light** *n*
проже́ктор; ~**ted** *adj* (*pattern*)
пятни́стый; ~**ty** *adj* (*face, youth*)
прыща́вый
spouse [spaus] *n* супру́г(а)
spout [spaut] *n* (*of jug*) но́сик
sprang [spræŋ] *pt of* **spring**
sprawl [sprɔːl] *vi* (*person*)
разва́ливаться (развали́ться *pf*);
(*place*) раски́дываться
(раски́нуться *pf*)
spray [spreɪ] *n* (*drops of water*)
бры́зги *pl*; (*hair spray*) аэрозо́ль *m*
♦ *vt* опры́скивать (опры́скать *pf*)
spread [spred] (*pt, pp* ~) *n* (*range*)
спектр; (*distribution*)
распростране́ние; (*CULIN, butter*)
бутербро́дный маргари́н; (*inf:
food*) пир ♦ *vt* (*lay out*)
расстила́ть (разостла́ть *pf*);
(*scatter*) разбра́сывать
(разброса́ть *pf*); (*butter*)
нама́зывать (нама́зать *pf*);
(*wings*) расправля́ть (распра́вить

pf); (arms) раскрыва́ть (раскры́ть
pf); (workload, wealth)
распределя́ть (распредели́ть pf)
♦ vi (disease, news etc)
распространя́ться
(распространи́ться pf); ~ out vi
(move apart) рассыпа́ться
(рассы́паться pf); ~sheet n
(крупноформа́тная) электро́нная
табли́ца

spree [spriː] n разгу́л

sprightly ['spraɪtlɪ] adj бо́дрый

spring [sprɪŋ] (pt **sprang**, pp
sprung) n (coiled metal) пружи́на;
(season) весна́; (of water)
исто́чник, родни́к ♦ vi (leap)
пры́гать (пры́гнуть pf); **in ~**
весно́й; **to ~ from** (stem from)
происходи́ть (произойти́ pf) из
+gen; ~**time** n весе́нняя пора́

sprinkle ['sprɪŋkl] vt (salt, sugar)
посыпа́ть (посы́пать pf) +instr; **to**
~ water on sth, ~ sth with water
опры́скивать (опры́скать pf)
что-н водо́й

sprint [sprɪnt] n (race) спринт ♦ vi
(run fast) стреми́тельно бе́гать/
бежа́ть (impf)

sprout [spraʊt] vi (BOT) пуска́ть
(пусти́ть pf) ростки́; ~**s** npl (also:
Brussels ~s) брюссе́льская
капу́ста fsg

spruce [spruːs] n inv (BOT) ель f
♦ adj (neat) опря́тный

sprung [sprʌŋ] pp of **spring**

spun [spʌn] pt, pp of **spin**

spur [spəːʳ] n (fig) сти́мул ♦ vt
(also: ~ **on**) пришпо́ривать
(пришпо́рить pf); **to ~ sb on to**
побужда́ть (побуди́ть pf) кого́-н
к +dat; **on the ~ of the moment**
вдруг, не разду́мывая

spurn [spəːn] vt отверга́ть
(отве́ргнуть pf)

spy [spaɪ] n шпио́н ♦ vi: **to ~ on**
шпио́нить (impf) за +instr; ~**ing** n

шпиона́ж

sq. abbr = **square**

squabble ['skwɒbl] vi вздо́рить
(повздо́рить pf)

squad [skwɒd] n (MIL, POLICE)
отря́д; (SPORT) кома́нда

squadron ['skwɒdrn] n (AVIAT)
эскадри́лья

squalid ['skwɒlɪd] adj (place)
убо́гий

squalor ['skwɒləʳ] n убо́гость f

square [skwɛəʳ] n (shape) квадра́т;
(in town) пло́щадь f ♦ adj
квадра́тный ♦ vt (reconcile, settle)
ула́живать (ула́дить pf); **a ~ meal**
соли́дный обе́д; **2 metres ~** = 2
ме́тра в ширину́, 2 ме́тра в
длину́; **2 ~ metres** 2 квадра́тных
ме́тра; ~**ly** adv пря́мо

squash [skwɒʃ] n (BRIT: drink)
напи́ток; (SPORT) сквош ♦ vt
дави́ть (разда́вить pf)

squat [skwɒt] adj приземи́стый ♦ vi
(also: ~ **down**: position) сиде́ть
(impf) на ко́рточках; (: motion)
сади́ться (сесть pf) на ко́рточки

squeak [skwiːk] vi (door) скрипе́ть
(скри́пнуть pf); (mouse) пища́ть
(пи́скнуть pf)

squeal [skwiːl] vi визжа́ть (impf)

squeamish ['skwiːmɪʃ] adj
брезгли́вый

squeeze [skwiːz] n (of hand)
пожа́тие; (ECON) ограниче́ние
♦ vt сжима́ть (сжать pf); (juice)
выжима́ть (вы́жать pf)

squid [skwɪd] n кальма́р

squint [skwɪnt] n (MED) косогла́зие

squirrel ['skwɪrəl] n бе́лка

squirt [skwəːt] vi брызгать
(бры́знуть pf) ♦ vt бры́згать
(бры́знуть pf) +instr

Sr abbr (in names) = **senior**

St abbr = **saint** св.; = **street** ул.

stab [stæb] vt наноси́ть (нанести́
pf) уда́р +dat; (kill): **to ~ sb** (to

death) зарезать (pf) кого-н ♦ n (of pain) укол; (inf: try): **to have a ~ at doing** пытаться (попытаться pf) +infin

stability [stə'bɪlɪtɪ] n устойчивость f, стабильность f

stabilize ['steɪbəlaɪz] vt (prices) стабилизировать (impf/pf) ♦ vi стабилизироваться (impf/pf)

stable ['steɪbl] adj стабильный, устойчивый ♦ n (for horse) конюшня

stack [stæk] n (of wood, plates) штабель m; (of papers) кипа ♦ vt (also: ~ **up**: chairs etc) складывать (сложить pf)

stadium ['steɪdɪəm] n (pl **stadia** or **~s**) (SPORT) стадион

staff [stɑːf] n (workforce) штат, сотрудники mpl; (BRIT : SCOL : also: **teaching ~**) преподавательский состав or коллектив ♦ vt: **the firm is ~ed by 5 people** на фирму работает 5 человек

stag [stæg] n (ZOOL) самец оленя

stage [steɪdʒ] n (in theatre) сцена; (platform) подмостки pl; (point, period) стадия ♦ vt (play) ставить (поставить pf); (demonstration) устраивать (устроить pf); **in ~s** поэтапно, по этапам

stagger ['stægə'] vt (amaze) потрясать (потрясти pf); (holidays etc) распи́сывать (расписать pf) ♦ vi: **he ~ed along the road** он шёл по дороге шатаясь; **~ing** adj потрясающий, поразительный

stagnant ['stægnənt] adj (water) стоячий; (economy) застойный

staid [steɪd] adj чинный

stain [steɪn] n пятно ♦ vt (mark) ставить (поставить pf) пятно на +acc; **~less steel** n нержавеющая сталь f

stair [steə'] n (step) ступень f,

ступенька; **~s** npl (steps) лестница fsg; **~case** n лестница; **~way** n staircase

stake [steɪk] n (post) кол; (investment) доля ♦ vt (money, reputation) рисковать (impf/pf) +instr; **his reputation was at ~** его репутация была поставлена на карту; **to ~ a claim (to)** притязать (impf) (на +acc)

stale [steɪl] adj (bread) чёрствый; (food) несвежий; (air) затхлый

stalemate ['steɪlmeɪt] n (fig) тупик

stalk [stɔːk] n (of flower) стебель m; (of fruit) черешок

stall [stɔːl] n (in market) прилавок; (in stable) стойло ♦ vi (AUT): **I ~ed the car** у меня заглохла машина; **~s** npl (BRIT : THEAT) партер msg

stamina ['stæmɪnə] n стойкость f, выдержка

stammer ['stæmə'] n заикание

stamp [stæmp] n (POST) марка; (rubber stamp) печать f, штамп; (mark, also fig) печать f ♦ vi (also: ~ **one's foot**) топать (топнуть pf) (ногой) ♦ vt (mark) клеймить (заклеймить pf); (: with rubber stamp) штамповать (проштамповать pf)

stampede [stæm'piːd] n давка

stance [stæns] n (also fig) позиция

stand [stænd] (pt, pp **stood**) n (stall) ларёк, киоск; (at exhibition) стенд; (SPORT) трибуна; (for umbrellas) стойка; (for coats, hats) вешалка ♦ vi (be upright) стоять (impf); (rise) вставать (встать pf); (remain: decision, offer) оставаться (остаться pf) в силе; (in election etc) баллотироваться (impf) ♦ vt (place: object) ставить (поставить pf); (tolerate, withstand) терпеть (стерпеть pf), выносить (вынести pf); **to make a ~ against sth** выступать (выступить pf) против чего́-н; **to ~ for parliament** (BRIT) баллоти́роваться (impf) в парла́менте; **to ~ at** (value, score etc) составля́ть (соста́вить pf); **to ~ by** vi (be ready) быть (impf) наготове ♦ vt fus не отступа́ть (отступи́ть pf) от +gen; **~ for** vt fus (signify) обознача́ть (impf); (represent) представля́ть (impf); **I won't ~ for it** я э́того не потерплю́; **~ out** vi (be obvious) выделя́ться (вы́делиться pf); **~ up** vi (rise) встава́ть (встать pf); **~ up for** vt fus (defend) стоя́ть (постоя́ть pf) за +acc; **~ up to** vt fus (withstand) выде́рживать (вы́держать pf); (resist) ока́зывать (оказа́ть pf) сопротивле́ние +dat

standard ['stændəd] n (level) у́ровень m; (norm, criterion) станда́рт ♦ adj (normal: size etc) станда́ртный; **~s** npl (morals) нра́вы mpl; **~ of living** n у́ровень m жи́зни

stand-by ['stændbaɪ] n: **to be on ~** (doctor etc) быть (impf) наготове

stand-in ['stændɪn] n замести́тель m

standpoint ['stændpɔɪnt] n пози́ция

standstill ['stændstɪl] n: **to be at a ~** (negotiations) быть (impf) в тупике́; **to come to a ~** (negotiations) заходи́ть (зайти́ pf) в тупи́к; (traffic) стать (pf)

stank [stæŋk] pt of **stink**

staple ['steɪpl] n (for papers) скоба́ ♦ adj (food etc) основно́й ♦ vt (fasten) сшива́ть (сшить pf)

star [stɑːʳ] n звезда́ ♦ vi: **to ~ in** игра́ть (сыгра́ть pf) гла́вную роль в +prep ♦ vt: **the film ~ my brother** гла́вную роль в фи́льме игра́ет мой брат; **the ~s** npl (horoscope) звёзды fpl

starch [stɑːtʃ] n (also CULIN) крахма́л

stare [steəʳ] vi: **to ~ at** (deep in thought) при́стально смотре́ть (impf) на +acc; (amazed) тара́щиться (impf) на +acc

stark [stɑːk] adj (bleak) го́лый ♦ adv: **~ naked** соверше́нно го́лый

starling ['stɑːlɪŋ] n скворе́ц

starry ['stɑːrɪ] adj звёздный

start [stɑːt] n (beginning) старт; (in fright) вздра́гивание; (advantage) преиму́щество ♦ vt (begin, found) начина́ть (нача́ть pf); (cause) вызыва́ть (вы́звать pf); (engine) заводи́ть (завести́ pf) ♦ vi (begin) начина́ться (нача́ться pf); (begin moving) отправля́ться (отпра́виться pf); (engine, car) заводи́ться (завести́сь pf); (jump: in fright) вздра́гивать (вздро́гнуть pf); **~ to** or **doing** начина́ть (нача́ть pf) +impf infin; **~ off** vi (begin) начина́ться (нача́ться pf); (begin moving) тро́гаться (тро́нуться pf); (leave) отправля́ться (отпра́виться pf); **~ out** vi (leave) отправля́ться (отпра́виться pf); **~ up** vi (engine, car) заводи́ться (завести́сь pf) ♦ vt (business) начина́ть (нача́ть pf); (car, engine) заводи́ть (завести́ pf); **~er** n (BRIT : CULIN) заку́ска; **~ing point** n (for journey) отправно́й пункт

startle ['stɑːtl] vt вспу́гивать (вспугну́ть pf)

startling ['stɑːtlɪŋ] adj порази́тельный

starvation [stɑːˈveɪʃən] n го́лод

starve [stɑːv] vi (to death) умира́ть (умере́ть pf) от го́лода; (be very hungry) голода́ть (impf) ♦ vt (person, animal) мори́ть (замори́ть pf) го́лодом

state [steɪt] n (condition) состоя́ние; (government) госуда́рство ♦ vt (say, declare)

констати́ровать (*impf/pf*); **the
States** *npl* (*GEO*) Соединённые
Шта́ты *mpl*; **to be in a ~** быть
(*impf*) в па́нике; **~ly** *adj*: **~ly home**
дом-уса́дьба
statement ['steɪtmənt] *n*
(*declaration*) заявле́ние
statesman ['steɪtsmən] (*irreg*) *n*
госуда́рственный де́ятель *m*
static ['stætɪk] *adj* (*not moving*)
стати́чный, неподви́жный
station ['steɪʃən] *n* ста́нция; (*larger
railway station*) вокза́л *m*; (*also:*
police ~) полице́йский уча́сток
♦ *vt* (*position: guards etc*)
выставля́ть (вы́ставить *pf*)
stationary ['steɪʃnərɪ] *adj* (*vehicle*)
неподви́жный
stationery ['steɪʃnərɪ] *n*
канцеля́рские принадле́жности
fpl
statistic [stə'tɪstɪk] *n* стати́стик;
~al *adj* статисти́ческий; **~s** *n*
(*science*) стати́стика
statue ['stætjuː] *n* ста́туя
stature ['stætʃər] *n* (*size*) рост
status ['steɪtəs] *n* ста́тус;
(*importance*) значе́ние; **the ~ quo**
ста́тус-кво *m ind*
statutory ['stætjutrɪ] *adj*
устано́вленный зако́ном
staunch [stɔːntʃ] *adj* пре́данный,
непоколеби́мый
stay [steɪ] *n* пребыва́ние ♦ *vi*
(*remain*) остава́ться (оста́ться *pf*);
(*with sb, as guest*) гости́ть (*impf*);
(*in place*) остана́вливаться
(останови́ться *pf*); **to ~ at home**
остава́ться (оста́ться *pf*) до́ма; **to
~ put** не дви́гаться (дви́нуться
pf) с ме́ста; **to ~ the night**
ночева́ть (переночева́ть *pf*); **~ in**
vi (*at home*) остава́ться (оста́ться
pf) до́ма; **~ on** *vi* остава́ться
(оста́ться *pf*); **~ out** *vi* (*of house*)
отсу́тствовать (*impf*); **~ up** *vi* (*at*

night) не ложи́ться (*impf*) (спать)
steadfast ['stɛdfɑːst] *adj* сто́йкий
steadily ['stɛdɪlɪ] *adv* (*firmly*)
про́чно; (*constantly, fixedly*)
постоя́нно
steady ['stɛdɪ] *adj* (*constant*)
стаби́льный; (*boyfriend, speed*)
постоя́нный; (*person*)
уравнове́шенный; (*firm: hand etc*)
твёрдый; (*look, voice*) ро́вный ♦ *vt*
(*object*) придава́ть (прида́ть *pf*)
усто́йчивость +*dat*; (*nerves, voice*)
совлада́ть (*pf*) с +*instr*
steak [steɪk] *n* филе́ *nt ind*; (*fried
beef*) бифште́кс
steal [stiːl] (*pt* **stole**, *pp* **stolen**) *vt*
ворова́ть (сворова́ть *pf*), красть
(укра́сть *pf*) ♦ *vi* ворова́ть (*impf*),
красть (*impf*); (*creep*) кра́сться
(*impf*)
steam [stiːm] *n* пар ♦ *vt* (*CULIN*)
па́рить (*impf*) ♦ *vi* (*give off steam*)
выделя́ть (*impf*) пар; **~er** *n* (*ship*)
парохо́д
steel [stiːl] *n* сталь *f* ♦ *adj* стально́й
steep [stiːp] *adj* круто́й; (*price*)
высо́кий ♦ *vt* (*food*) выма́чивать
(вы́мочить *pf*); (*clothes*)
зама́чивать (замочи́ть *pf*)
steeple ['stiːpl] *n* шпиль *m*
steer [stɪər] *vt* направля́ть
(напра́вить *pf*) ♦ *vi*
маневри́ровать (*impf*); **~ing
wheel** *n* руль *m*
stem [stɛm] *n* (*of plant*) сте́бель *m*;
(*of glass*) но́жка ♦ *vt* (*stop*)
остана́вливать (останови́ть *pf*); **~
from** *vt fus* происходи́ть /
(произойти́ *pf*) из +*gen*
stench [stɛntʃ] *n* (*pej*) смрад
stencil ['stɛnsl] *n* трафаре́т
step [stɛp] *n* (*also fig*) шаг; (*of
stairs*) ступе́нь *f*, ступе́нька ♦ *vi*
(*forward, back*) ступа́ть (ступи́ть
pf); **~s** *npl* (*BRIT*) = **stepladder**; **to
be in/out of ~ (with)** идти́ (*impf*) в

но́гу/не в но́гу (c +instr); ~ **down**
vi (fig: resign) уходи́ть (уйти́ pf) в
отста́вку; ~ **on** vt fus (walk on)
наступа́ть (наступи́ть pf) на +acc; ~
up vt (increase) уси́ливать
(уси́лить pf); ~**brother** n
сво́дный брат; ~**daughter** n
па́дчерица; ~**father** n о́тчим;
~**ladder** n (BRIT) стремя́нка;
~**mother** n ма́чеха; ~**sister** n
сво́дная сестра́; ~**son** n па́сынок

stereo ['steriəu] n (system)
стереосисте́ма

stereotype ['stiərətaip] n
стереоти́п

sterile ['sterail] adj беспло́дный;
(clean) стери́льный

sterilize ['sterilaiz] vt
стерилизова́ть (impf/pf)

sterling ['stə:liŋ] n (ECON) фунт
сте́рлингов; ~ **silver** серебро́
925-ой пробы

stern [stə:n] adj суро́вый

stew [stju:] n (meat) тушёное мя́со
♦ vt туши́ть (потуши́ть pf)

steward ['stju:əd] n (on plane)
бортпроводни́к; ~**ess** n (on
plane) стюарде́сса,
бортпроводни́ца

stick [stik] (pt, pp **stuck**) n (of
wood) па́лка; (walking stick)
трость f ♦ vt (with glue etc) кле́ить
(прикле́ить pf); (inf: put) сова́ть
(су́нуть pf); (thrust) втыка́ть
(воткну́ть pf) ♦ vi (become
attached) прикле́иваться
(прикле́иться pf); (in mind)
засе́сть (pf); ~ **out** vi (ears)
торча́ть (impf); ~ **up for** vt fus
(person) заступа́ться
(заступи́ться pf) за +acc; (principle)
отста́ивать (отстоя́ть pf); ~**er** n
накле́йка; ~**y** adj (hands etc)
ли́пкий; (label) кле́йкий; (fig:
situation) щекотли́вый

stiff [stif] adj (brush) жёсткий;

(person) деревя́нный; (zip) туго́й;
(manner, smile) натя́нутый;
(competition) жёсткий; (severe:
sentence) суро́вый; (strong: drink)
кре́пкий; (: breeze) си́льный ♦ adv
до сме́рти

stifle ['staifl] vt (yawn) подавля́ть
(подави́ть pf)

stifling ['staifliŋ] adj (heat)
удуши́вый

stigma ['stigmə] n (fig) клеймо́

still [stil] adj ти́хий ♦ adv (up to this
time) всё ещё; (even, yet) ещё;
(nonetheless) всё-таки, тем не
ме́нее; ~ **life** n (ART) натюрмо́рт

stimulant ['stimjulənt] n
стимули́рующее or
возбужда́ющее сре́дство

stimulate ['stimjuleit] vt
стимули́ровать (impf/pf)

stimulating ['stimjuleitiŋ] adj
вдохновля́ющий

stimulus ['stimjuləs] (pl **stimuli**) n
(encouragement) сти́мул

sting [stiŋ] (pt, pp **stung**) n (from
insect) уку́с; (from plant) ожо́г;
(organ: of wasp etc) жа́ло ♦ vt (also
fig) уязвля́ть (уязви́ть pf) ♦ vi
(insect, animal) жа́литься (impf);
(plant) жёчься (impf); (eyes,
ointment etc) жечь (impf)

stink [stiŋk] (pt, pp **stunk**) vi
смерде́ть (impf), воня́ть (impf)
(разг)

stir [stə:] n (fig) шум, сенса́ция
♦ vt (tea etc) меша́ть (помеша́ть pf);
(fig: emotions) волнова́ть
(взволнова́ть pf) ♦ vi (move)
шевели́ть (пошевели́ть pf); ~
up vt (trouble) вызыва́ть (вы́звать
pf); ~**fry** vt бы́стро обжа́ривать
(обжа́рить pf)

stitch [stitʃ] n (SEWING) стежо́к;
(KNITTING) петля́; (MED) шов ♦ vt
(sew) шить (сшить pf); (MED)
зашива́ть (заши́ть pf); **I have a ~**

in my side у меня́ ко́лет в боку́

stoat [stəut] n горноста́й

stock [stɔk] n (supply) запа́с; (AGR) поголо́вье; (CULIN) бульо́н; (FINANCE, usu pl) це́нные бума́ги fpl ♦ adj (reply, excuse etc) дежу́рный ♦ vt (have in stock) име́ть (impf) в нали́чии; **~s and shares** а́кции и це́нные бума́ги; **to be in/out of ~** име́ться (impf)/ не име́ться (impf) в нали́чии; **to take ~ of** (fig) оце́нивать (оцени́ть pf); **~broker** n (COMM) фо́ндовый бро́кер; **~ exchange** n фо́ндовая би́ржа

stocking ['stɔkɪŋ] n чуло́к

stock market n (BRIT) фо́ндовая би́ржа

stocky ['stɔkɪ] adj корена́стый

stoke [stəuk] vt (fire) подде́рживать (impf); (boiler, furnace) подде́рживать (impf) ого́нь в +prp

stole [stəul] pt of **steal**; **~n** pp of **steal**

stomach ['stʌmək] n (ANAT) желу́док; (belly) живо́т ♦ vt (fig) переноси́ть (перенести́ pf)

stone [stəun] n (also MED) ка́мень m; (pebble) ка́мешек; (in fruit) ко́сточка; (BRIT: weight) стоун (14 фу́нтов) ♦ adj ка́менный

stone - сто́ун. Ме́ра ве́са ра́вная 6.35 кг.

stony ['stəunɪ] adj (ground) камени́стый; (silence) холо́дный; (glance) ка́менный

stood [stud] pt, pp of **stand**

stool [stu:l] n табуре́т(ка)

stoop [stu:p] vi (also: **~ down**: bend) наклоня́ться (наклони́ться pf), нагиба́ться (нагну́ться pf)

stop [stɔp] n остано́вка; (LING: also: **full ~**) то́чка ♦ vt

остана́вливать (останови́ть pf); (prevent: also: **put a ~ to**) прекраща́ть (прекрати́ть pf) ♦ vi (person, clock) остана́вливаться (останови́ться pf); (rain, noise etc) прекраща́ться (прекрати́ться pf); **to ~ doing** перестава́ть (переста́ть pf) +infin; **~ by** vi заходи́ть (зайти́ pf); **~page** ['stɔpɪdʒ] n (strike) забасто́вка; **~watch** n секундоме́р

storage ['stɔ:rɪdʒ] n хране́ние

store [stɔ:r] n (stock, reserve) запа́с; (depot) склад; (BRIT: large shop) универма́г; (esp US: shop) магази́н ♦ vt храни́ть (impf); **in ~** в бу́дущем; **~room** n кладова́я f adj

storey ['stɔ:rɪ] n (US **story**) n эта́ж

stork [stɔ:k] n а́ист

storm [stɔ:m] n (also fig) бу́ря; (of criticism, laughter) взрыв ♦ vt (attack: place) штурмова́ть (impf); **~y** adj бу́рный; **~y weather** нена́стье

story ['stɔ:rɪ] n исто́рия; (lie) вы́думка, ска́зка; (US) = **storey**

stout [staut] adj (strong: branch etc) кре́пкий; (fat) доро́дный; (resolute: friend, supporter) сто́йкий

stove [stəuv] n печь f, пе́чка

St Petersburg [sənt'pi:təzbə:g] n Санкт-Петербу́рг

straight [streɪt] adj прямо́й; (simple: choice) я́сный ♦ adv пря́мо; **to put** или **get sth ~** (make clear) вноси́ть (внести́ pf) я́сность во что-н; **~ away**, **~ off** (at once) сра́зу (же); **~en** vt (skirt, tie, bed) поправля́ть (попра́вить pf); **~forward** adj (simple) просто́й; (honest) прямо́й

strain [streɪn] n (pressure) нагру́зка; (MED, physical) растяже́ние; (: mental) напряже́ние ♦ vt (back etc) растя́гивать (растяну́ть pf);

(*voice*) напряга́ть (напря́чь *pf*);
(*stretch: resources*) перенапряга́ть
(перенапря́чь *pf*); (*CULIN*)
проце́живать (процеди́ть *pf*);
~**ed** *adj* (*muscle*) растя́нутый;
(*laugh, relations*) натя́нутый

strand [strænd] *n* нить *f*; (*of hair*)
прядь *f*; ~**ed** *adj*: **to be ~ed**
застрева́ть (застря́ть *pf*)

strange [streɪndʒ] *adj* стра́нный;
(*not known*) незнако́мый; ~**ly** *adv*
(*act, laugh*) стра́нно; *see also*
enough; ~**r** *n* (*unknown person*)
незнако́мец, посторо́нний(яя)
m(f) adj

strangle ['stræŋgl] *vt* (*also fig*)
души́ть (задуши́ть *pf*)

strap [stræp] *n* реме́нь *m*; (*of dress*)
брете́лька; (*of watch*) ремешо́к

strategic [strə'tiːdʒɪk] *adj*
стратеги́ческий

strategy ['strætɪdʒɪ] *n* страте́гия

straw [strɔː] *n* соло́ма; (*drinking
straw*) соло́минка; **that's the last
~!** э́то после́дняя ка́пля!

strawberry ['strɔːbərɪ] *n* клубни́ка *f
no pl*; (*wild*) земляни́ка *f no pl*

stray [streɪ] *adj* (*animal*) бродя́чий;
(*bullet*) шально́й ♦ *vi* заблуди́ться
(*pf*); (*thoughts*) блужда́ть (*impf*)

streak [striːk] *n* (*stripe*) полоса́

stream [striːm] *n* руче́й; (*of people,
vehicles, questions*) пото́к ♦ *vi*
(*liquid*) течь (*impf*), ли́ться (*impf*);
to ~ in/out (*people*) вали́ть
(повали́ть *pf*) толпо́й в +*acc*/из
+*gen*

street [striːt] *n* у́лица

strength [streŋθ] *n* си́ла; (*of girder,
knot etc*) про́чность *f*; ~**en** *vt*
(*building, machine*) укрепля́ть
(укрепи́ть *pf*); (*fig: group*)
пополня́ть (попо́лнить *pf*);
(*: argument*) подкрепля́ть
(подкрепи́ть *pf*)

strenuous ['strenjuəs] *adj* (*exercise*)

уси́ленный; (*efforts*)
напряжённый

stress [stres] *n* (*pressure*) давле́ние,
напряже́ние; (*mental strain*)
стресс; (*emphasis*) ударе́ние ♦ *vt*
(*point, need etc*) де́лать (сде́лать
pf) ударе́ние на +*acc*; (*syllable*)
ста́вить (поста́вить *pf*) ударе́ние
на +*acc*

stretch [stretʃ] *n* (*area*) отре́зок,
простра́нство ♦ *vt* (*pull*)
натя́гивать (натяну́ть *pf*) ♦ *vi*
(*person, animal*) потя́гиваться
(потяну́ться *pf*); (*extend*): **to ~ to**
or **as far as** простира́ться (*impf*)
до +*gen*; ~ **out** *vi* растя́гиваться
(растяну́ться *pf*) ♦ *vt* (*arm etc*)
протя́гивать (протяну́ть *pf*)

stretcher ['stretʃər] *n* носи́лки *pl*

strewn [struːn] *adj*: ~ **with**
усы́панный +*instr*

stricken ['strɪkən] *adj*: ~ **with**
(*arthritis, disease*) поражённый
+*instr*

strict [strɪkt] *adj* стро́гий; (*precise:
meaning*) то́чный; ~**ly** *adv*
(*severely*) стро́го; (*exactly*) то́чно

stride [straɪd] (*pt* **strode**, *pp*
stridden) *n* (*step*) шаг ♦ *vi* шага́ть
(*impf*)

strike [straɪk] (*pt, pp* **struck**) *n* (*of
workers*) забасто́вка; (*MIL, attack*)
уда́р ♦ *vt* (*hit: person, thing*)
ударя́ть (уда́рить *pf*); (*subj: idea,
thought*) осеня́ть (осени́ть *pf*); (*oil
etc*) открыва́ть (откры́ть *pf*)
месторожде́ние +*gen*; (*bargain,
deal*) заключа́ть (заключи́ть *pf*)
♦ *vi* (*workers*) бастова́ть (*impf*);
(*disaster, illness*) обру́шиваться
(обру́шиться *pf*); (*clock*) бить
(проби́ть *pf*); **to be on ~** (*workers*)
бастова́ть (*impf*); **to ~ a match**
зажига́ть (заже́чь *pf*) спи́чку; ~**r**
n забасто́вщик(ица); (*SPORT*)
напада́ющий(ая) *m(f) adj*

striking ['straɪkɪŋ] adj поразительный

string [strɪŋ] (pt, pp **strung**) n верёвка; (MUS, for guitar etc) струна; (of beads) нитка ♦ vt: **to ~ together** связывать (связать pf); **the ~s** npl (MUS) струнные инструменты mpl; **to ~ out** растягивать (растянуть pf)

strip [strɪp] n полоса, полоска ♦ vt (undress) раздевать (раздеть pf); (paint) обдирать (ободрать pf), сдирать (содрать pf); (also: **~ down**: machine) разбирать (разобрать pf) ♦ vi раздеваться (раздеться pf)

stripe [straɪp] n полоска; (POLICE, MIL) петлица; **~d** adj полосатый

stripper ['strɪpər] n стриптизёрка

strive [straɪv] (pt **strove**, pp **~n**) vi: **to ~ for sth/to do** стремиться (impf) к чему-н/+infin

strode [strəʊd] pt of **stride**

stroke [strəʊk] n (also MED) удар; (SWIMMING) стиль m ♦ vt гладить (погладить pf); **at a ~** одним махом

stroll [strəʊl] n прогулка ♦ vi прогуливаться (прогуляться pf), прохаживаться (пройтись pf)

strong [strɒŋ] adj сильный; **they are 50 ~** их 50, **~hold** n (fig) оплот, твердыня

strove [strəʊv] pt of **strive**

struck [strʌk] pt, pp of **strike**

structural ['strʌktʃrəl] adj структурный

structure ['strʌktʃər] n структура

struggle ['strʌɡl] n (fight) борьба ♦ vi (try hard) силиться (impf), прилагать (приложить pf) большие усилия; (fight) бороться (impf); (: to free o.s.) сопротивляться (impf)

strung [strʌŋ] pt, pp of **string**

stub [stʌb] n (of cheque, ticket etc)

корешок; (of cigarette) окурок ♦ vt: **to ~ one's toe** больно спотыкаться (споткнуться pf)

stubble ['stʌbl] n (on chin) щетина

stubborn ['stʌbən] adj (determination, child) упрямый, упорный

stuck [stʌk] pt, pp of **stick** ♦ adj: **to be ~** застрять (pf)

stud [stʌd] n (on clothing etc) кнопка, заклёпка; (earring) серьга со штифтом; (on sole of boot) шип ♦ vt (fig): **~ded with** усыпанный +instr

student ['stjuːdənt] n (at university) студент(ка); (at school) учащийся(аяся) m(f) adj ♦ adj студенческий; (at school) ученический

studio ['stjuːdɪəʊ] n студия

study ['stʌdɪ] n (activity) учёба; (room) кабинет ♦ vt изучать (изучить pf) ♦ vi учиться (pf)

stuff [stʌf] n (things) вещи fpl; (substance) вещество ♦ vt набивать (набить pf); (CULIN) начинять (начинить pf), фаршировать (нафаршировать pf); (inf: push) запихивать (запихать pf); **~ing** n набивка; (CULIN) начинка, фарш; **~y** adj (room) душный; (person, ideas) чопорный

stumble ['stʌmbl] vi спотыкаться (споткнуться pf); **to ~ across** or **on** (fig) натыкаться (наткнуться pf) на +acc

stump [stʌmp] n (of tree) пень m; (of limb) обрубок ♦ vt озадачивать (озадачить pf)

stun [stʌn] vt (subj: news) потрясать (потрясти pf), ошеломлять (ошеломить pf); (: blow on head) оглушать (оглушить pf)

stung [stʌŋ] pt, pp of **sting**

stunk [stʌŋk] pp of **stink**

stunning ['stʌnɪŋ] adj (fabulous) потрясающий

stunted ['stʌntɪd] adj (trees) подрубленный; (growth) замедленный

stupendous [stju:'pendəs] adj (large) колоссальный; (impressive) изумительный

stupid ['stju:pɪd] adj глупый; ~**ity** [stju:'pɪdɪtɪ] n глупость f

sturdy ['stə:dɪ] adj крепкий

stutter ['stʌtə*] n заикание ♦ vi заикаться (impf)

style [staɪl] n стиль m

stylish ['staɪlɪʃ] adj стильный, элегантный

subconscious [sʌb'kɔnʃəs] adj подсознательный

subdue [səb'dju:] vt подавлять (подавить pf); ~**d** (light) приглушённый; (person) подавленный

subject n ['sʌbdʒɪkt] vb [səb'dʒekt] n (topic) тема; (SCOL) предмет; (LING) подлежащее nt adj ♦ vt: to ~ sb to sth подвергать (подвергнуть pf) кого-н чему-н; **to be** ~ **to** (tax) подлежать (impf) +dat; (law) подчиняться (impf) +dat; ~**ive** [səb'dʒektɪv] adj субъективный

submarine [sʌbmə'ri:n] n подводная лодка

submerge [səb'mə:dʒ] vt погружать (погрузить pf) (в воду) ♦ vi погружаться (погрузиться pf) (в воду)

submission [səb'mɪʃən] n (state) подчинение, повиновение; (of plan etc) подача

submissive [səb'mɪsɪv] adj покорный

submit [səb'mɪt] vt (proposal, application etc) представлять (представить pf) на

рассмотрение ♦ vi: to ~ to sth подчиняться (подчиниться pf) чему-н

subordinate [sə'bɔ:dɪnət] adj: to be ~ to (in rank) подчинённый +dat ♦ n подчинённый m(f) adj

subscribe [səb'skraɪb] vi: to ~ to (opinion, fund) поддерживать (поддержать pf); (magazine etc) подписываться (подписаться pf) на +acc

subscription [səb'skrɪpʃən] n (to magazine etc) подписка

subsequent ['sʌbsɪkwənt] adj последующий; ~ **to** вслед +dat; ~**ly** adv впоследствии

subside [səb'saɪd] vi (feeling, wind) утихать (утихнуть pf); (flood) убывать (убыть pf); ~**nce** [səb'saɪdns] n оседание

subsidiary [səb'sɪdɪərɪ] n (also: ~ company) дочерняя компания

subsidy ['sʌbsɪdɪ] n субсидия, дотация

substance ['sʌbstəns] n (product, material) вещество

substantial [səb'stænʃl] adj (solid) прочный, основательный; (fig: reward, meal) солидный; (by a lot) значительный; ~**ly** adv (in essence) существенно, основательно

substitute ['sʌbstɪtju:t] n (person) замена; (: FOOTBALL etc) запасной m adj (игрок); (thing) заменитель m ♦ vt: to ~ A for B заменять (заменить pf) A на Б

substitution [sʌbstɪ'tju:ʃən] n (act) замена

subtitle ['sʌbtaɪtl] n (in film) субтитр

subtle ['sʌtl] adj (change) тонкий, едва уловимый; (person) тонкий, искусный; ~**ty** n (detail) тонкость f; (of person) искусность f

subtract [səb'trækt] vt вычитать (вычесть pf)

suburb ['sʌbə:b] n при́город; the ~s npl (area) при́город msg; ~an [sə'bə:bən] adj при́городный

subversive [səb'və:siv] adj подрывно́й

subway ['sʌbwei] n (US) метро́ nt ind, подзе́мка (разг); (BRIT: underpass) подзе́мный перехо́д

succeed [sək'si:d] vi (plan etc) удава́ться (уда́ться pf), име́ть (impf) успе́х; (person: in career etc) преуспева́ть (преуспе́ть pf) ♦ vt (in job, order) сменя́ть (смени́ть pf); he ~ed in finishing the article ему́ удало́сь зако́нчить статью́

success [sək'ses] n успе́х, уда́ча; the book was a ~ кни́га име́ла успе́х; he was a ~ он доби́лся успе́ха; ~ful adj (venture) успе́шный; he was ~ful in convincing her ему́ удало́сь убеди́ть её; ~fully adv успе́шно

succession [sək'sefən] n (series) череда́, ряд; (to throne etc) насле́дование; in ~ подря́д

successive [sək'sesiv] adj (governments) сле́дующий оди́н за други́м

successor [sək'sesə*] n прее́мник(ица); (to throne) насле́дник(ица)

succinct [sək'siŋkt] adj сжа́тый

succulent ['sʌkjulənt] adj (fruit, meat) со́чный

succumb [sə'kʌm] vi (to temptation) поддава́ться (подда́ться pf)

such [sʌtʃ] adj тако́й ♦ adv: ~ a long trip така́я дли́нная пое́здка; ~ a book така́я кни́га; ~ books таки́е кни́ги; ~ a lot of тако́е мно́жество +gen; ~ as (like) таки́е как; as ~ как таково́й; ~-and-~ adj таки́е-то и таки́е-то

suck [sʌk] vt (bottle, sweet) соса́ть (impf)

suction ['sʌkʃən] n вса́сывание

sudden ['sʌdn] adj внеза́пный; all of a ~ внеза́пно, вдруг; ~ly adv внеза́пно, вдруг

sue [su:] vt предъявля́ть (предъяви́ть pf) иск +dat

suede [sweid] n за́мша

suet ['suit] n жир

suffer ['sʌfə*] vt (hardship etc) переноси́ть (перенести́ pf); (pain) страда́ть (impf) от +gen ♦ vi (person, results etc) страда́ть (пострада́ть pf); to ~ from страда́ть (impf) +instr; ~er n (MED) страда́ющий(ая) m(f) adj; ~ing n (hardship) страда́ние

suffice [sə'fais] vi: this ~s ... э́того доста́точно, ...

sufficient [sə'fiʃənt] adj доста́точный; ~ly adv доста́точно

suffocate ['sʌfəkeit] vi задыха́ться (задохну́ться pf)

sugar ['fugə*] n са́хар; ~ cane n са́харный тростни́к

suggest [sə'dʒest] vt (propose) предлага́ть (предложи́ть pf); (indicate) предполага́ть (предположи́ть pf); ~ion [sə'dʒestfən] n (see vt) предложе́ние; предположе́ние; ~ive adj (remarks, looks) непристо́йный

suicide ['suisaid] n (death) самоуби́йство; see also **commit**

suit [su:t] n костю́м; (LAW) иск; (CARDS) масть f ♦ vt (be convenient, appropriate) подходи́ть (подойти́ pf) +dat; (colour, clothes) идти́ (impf) +dat; to ~ sth to (adapt) приспоса́бливать (приспосо́бить pf) что-н к +dat; they are well (couple) они́ хорошо́ друг дру́гу подхо́дят; ~able adj подходя́щий; ~ably adv надлежа́щим о́бразом

suitcase ['su:tkeis] n чемода́н

suite [swiːt] n (of rooms)
апартаме́нты mpl; (furniture):
bedroom/dining room ~
спа́льный/столо́вый гарниту́р

sulfur ['sʌlfər] n (US) = **sulphur**

sulk [sʌlk] vi зло́бствовать (impf),
ду́ться (impf) (разг)

sullen ['sʌlən] adj угрю́мый

sulphur ['sʌlfər] (US **sulfur**) n се́ра

sultana [sʌl'tɑːnə] n кишми́ш

sultry ['sʌltrɪ] adj (weather)
ду́шный

sum [sʌm] n (calculation)
арифме́тика, вычисле́ние;
(amount) су́мма; **~ up** vt (describe)
сумми́ровать (impf/pf) ♦ vi
подводи́ть (подвести́ pf) ито́г

summarize ['sʌməraɪz] vt
сумми́ровать (impf/pf)

summary ['sʌmərɪ] n (of essay etc)
кра́ткое изложе́ние

summer ['sʌmər] n ле́то ♦ adj
ле́тний; **in ~** ле́том; **~time** n
(season) ле́то, ле́тняя пора́

summit ['sʌmɪt] n (of mountain)
верши́на, пик; (also: **~ meeting**)
встре́ча на вы́сшем у́ровне,
са́ммит

sumptuous ['sʌmptjʊəs] adj
роско́шный

sun [sʌn] n со́лнце; **~bathe** vi
загора́ть (impf); **~burn** n
со́лнечный ожо́г

Sunday ['sʌndɪ] n воскресе́нье

sunflower ['sʌnflaʊər] n (BOT)
подсо́лнечник

sung [sʌŋ] pp of **sing**

sunglasses ['sʌnɡlɑːsɪz] npl
солнцезащи́тные очки́ pl

sunk [sʌŋk] pp of **sink**

sun: ~light n со́лнечный свет;
~ny adj (weather, place)
со́лнечный; **~rise** n восхо́д
(со́лнца); **~set** n зака́т, захо́д
(со́лнца); **~shine** n со́лнечный
свет; **in the ~shine** на со́лнце

~stroke n со́лнечный уда́р; **~tan**
n зага́р

super ['suːpər] adj мирово́й,
потряса́ющий

superb [suː'pɜːb] adj
превосхо́дный, великоле́пный

superficial [suːpə'fɪʃl] adj
пове́рхностный; (wound) лёгкий

superfluous [su'pɜːfluəs] adj
изли́шний, нену́жный

superintendent [suːpərɪn'tendənt]
n (POLICE) нача́льник

superior [su'pɪərɪər] adj (better)
лу́чший; (more senior)
вышестоя́щий; (smug)
высокоме́рный ♦ n нача́льник;
~ity [supɪərɪ'ɔrɪtɪ] n
превосхо́дство

supermarket ['suːpəmɑːkɪt] n
суперма́ркет, универса́м

supernatural [suːpə'nætʃərəl] adj
сверхъесте́ственный

superpower ['suːpəpauər] n (POL)
вели́кая держа́ва, сверхдержа́ва

superstition [suːpə'stɪʃən] n
суеве́рие

superstitious [suːpə'stɪʃəs] adj
суеве́рный

supervise ['suːpəvaɪz] vt (person,
activity) кури́ровать (impf);
(dissertation) руководи́ть (impf)

supervision [suːpə'vɪʒən] n
руково́дство, надзо́р

supervisor ['suːpəvaɪzər] n (of
workers) нача́льник; (SCOL)
нау́чный(ая)
руководи́тель(ница) m(f)

supper ['sʌpər] n у́жин

supple ['sʌpl] adj (person, body)
ги́бкий; (leather) упру́гий

supplement n ['sʌplɪmənt] n (of
vitamins) доба́вка, дополне́ние;
(of book, newspaper etc)
приложе́ние ♦ vt добавля́ть
(доба́вить pf) к +dat; **~ary**
[sʌplɪ'mentərɪ] adj (question)

дополни́тельный

supplier [sə'plaɪə^r] n поставщи́к

supply [sə'plaɪ] n (see vt) поста́вка; снабже́ние; (stock) запа́с ♦ vt (goods) поставля́ть (поста́вить pf); (gas) снабжа́ть (снабди́ть pf); **to ~ sb/sth with sth** (see vt) поставля́ть (поста́вить pf) кому́-н/чему́-н; снабжа́ть (снабди́ть pf) кого́-н/что-н чем-н; **supplies** npl (food) запа́сы mpl продово́льствия

support [sə'pɔːt] n (moral, financial etc) подде́ржка; (TECH) опо́ра ♦ vt (morally) подде́рживать (поддержа́ть pf); (financially: family etc) содержа́ть (impf); (football team etc) боле́ть (impf) за +acc; (hold up) подде́рживать (impf); (theory etc) подтвержда́ть (подтверди́ть pf); **~er** n (POL etc) сторо́нник(ица); (SPORT) боле́льщик(ица); **~ive** adj: **to be ~ive of sb** подде́рживать (поддержа́ть pf) кого́-н

suppose [sə'pəuz] vt полага́ть (impf), предполага́ть (предположи́ть pf); **he was ~d to do it** (duty) он до́лжен был э́то сде́лать; **~dly** [sə'pəuzɪdlɪ] adv я́кобы

supposing [sə'pəuzɪŋ] conj предположи́м, допусти́м

suppress [sə'prɛs] vt (revolt) подавля́ть (подави́ть pf); **~ion** [sə'prɛʃən] n подавле́ние

supremacy [su'prɛməsɪ] n госпо́дство, превосхо́дство

supreme [su'priːm] adj (in titles) Верхо́вный; (effort, achievement) велича́йший

surcharge ['sɜːtʃɑːdʒ] n дополни́тельный сбор

sure [ʃuə^r] adj (certain) уве́ренный; (reliable) ве́рный; **to make ~ of sth/that** удостовери́ться

(удостове́риться pf) в чём-н/, что; **~!** (okay) коне́чно!; **~ enough** и пра́вда or впра́вду; **~ly** adv (certainly) наверняка́

surf [sɜːf] vt (COMPUT) ла́зить (impf) по +dat

surface ['sɜːfɪs] n пове́рхность f ♦ vi всплыва́ть (всплыть pf)

surfing ['sɜːfɪŋ] n сёрфинг

surge [sɜːdʒ] n (increase) рост; (fig: of emotion) прили́в

surgeon ['sɜːdʒən] n (MED) хиру́рг

surgery ['sɜːdʒərɪ] n (treatment) хирурги́я, хирурги́ческое вмеша́тельство; (BRIT: room) кабине́т; (: time) приём; **to undergo ~** переноси́ть (перенести́ pf) опера́цию

surgical ['sɜːdʒɪkl] adj хирурги́ческий

surly ['sɜːlɪ] adj угрю́мый

surname ['sɜːneɪm] n фами́лия

surpass [sɜː'pɑːs] vt (person, thing) превосходи́ть (превзойти́ pf)

surplus ['sɜːpləs] n избы́ток, изли́шек; (of trade, payments) акти́вное са́льдо nt ind ♦ adj (stock, grain) избы́точный

surprise [sə'praɪz] n удивле́ние; (unexpected event) неожи́данность f ♦ vt (astonish) удивля́ть (удиви́ть pf); (catch unawares) застава́ть (заста́ть pf) враспло́х

surprising [sə'praɪzɪŋ] adj (situation, announcement) неожи́данный; **~ly** adv удиви́тельно

surrender [sə'rɛndə^r] n сда́ча, капитуля́ция ♦ vi (army, hijackers etc) сдава́ться (сда́ться pf)

surround [sə'raund] vt (subj: walls, hedge etc) окружа́ть (impf); (MIL, POLICE etc) окружа́ть (окружи́ть pf); **~ing** adj (countryside) окружа́ющий, окре́стный; **~ings** npl (place) окре́стности fpl; (conditions) окруже́ние ntsg

surveillance [sə'veɪləns] n наблюде́ние

survey vb [sə:'veɪ] n ['sə:veɪ] vt (scene, work etc) осма́тривать (осмотре́ть pf) ♦ n (of land) геодези́ческая съёмка; (of house) инспе́кция; (of habits etc) обзо́р; ~**or** [sə'veɪə] n (of land) геоде́зист; (of house) инспе́ктор

survival [sə'vaɪvl] n выжива́ние

survive [sə'vaɪv] vi (выжить pf), уцеле́ть (pf); (custom etc) сохрани́ться (сохрани́ться pf) ♦ vt (person) пережива́ть (пережи́ть pf); (illness) переноси́ть (перенести́ pf)

survivor [sə'vaɪvə] n (of illness, accident) выживший(ая) m(f) adj

susceptible [sə'sεptəbl] adj: ~ (to) (injury) подве́рженный (+dat); **to be** ~ **to flattery** легко́ поддава́ться лести

suspect vb [səs'pεkt] n, adj ['sʌspεkt] vt подозрева́ть (impf) ♦ n подозрева́емый(ая) m(f) adj ♦ adj подозри́тельный

suspend [səs'pεnd] vt (delay) приостана́вливать (приостанови́ть pf); (stop) прерыва́ть (прерва́ть pf); (from employment) отстраня́ть (отстрани́ть pf); ~**ers** npl (BRIT) подвя́зки fpl; (US) подтя́жки fpl

suspense [səs'pεns] n трево́га, напряже́ние; **to keep sb in** ~ держа́ть (impf) кого́-н во взве́шенном состоя́нии

suspension [səs'pεnʃən] n (from job, team) отстране́ние; (AUT) амортиза́тор; (of payment) приостановле́ние

suspicion [səs'pɪʃən] n подозре́ние

suspicious [səs'pɪʃəs] adj подозри́тельный

sustain [səs'teɪn] vt подде́рживать (поддержа́ть pf); (losses) нести́

(понести́ pf); (injury) получа́ть (получи́ть pf); ~**able** adj (development, progress) стаби́льный, усто́йчивый; ~**ed** adj неослабева́ющий; (interest) неосла́бный

swagger ['swægə] vi ше́ствовать (impf)

swallow ['swɔləʊ] n (ZOOL) ла́сточка ♦ vt (food, pills) глота́ть (проглоти́ть pf); (fig) подавля́ть (подави́ть pf)

swam [swæm] pt of **swim**

swamp [swɔmp] n топь f ♦ vt (with water) залива́ть (зали́ть pf); (fig: person) зава́ливать (завали́ть pf)

swan [swɔn] n ле́бедь m

swap [swɔp] n обме́н ♦ vt: **to** ~ (**for**) (exchange for)) меня́ть (обменя́ть pf) (на +acc) (replace (with)) меня́ть (поменя́ть pf) (на +acc)

swarm [swɔ:m] n (of bees) рой; (of people) тьма

sway [sweɪ] vi кача́ться (качну́ться pf) ♦ vt: **to be ~ed by** поддава́ться (подда́ться pf) на +acc

swear [swɛə] (pt **swore**, pp **sworn**) vi (curse) скверносло́вить (impf), руга́ться (вы́ругаться pf) ♦ vt кля́сться (покля́сться pf)

sweat [swεt] n пот ♦ vi поте́ть (вспоте́ть pf); ~**er** n сви́тер; ~**shirt** n спорти́вный сви́тер; ~**y** adj (clothes) пропоте́вший; (hands) по́тный

swede [swi:d] n (BRIT) брю́ква

Sweden ['swi:dn] n Шве́ция

Swedish ['swi:dɪʃ] adj шве́дский; **the** ~ npl шве́ды

sweep [swi:p] (pt, pp **swept**) vt (with brush) мести́ or подмета́ть (подмести́ pf); (with arm) сма́хивать (смахну́ть pf); (subj: current) сноси́ть (снести́ pf), смыва́ть (смыть pf) ♦ vi (wind) бушева́ть (*impf*); **~ing** *adj* (*gesture*) широ́кий; (*statement*) огу́льный

sweet [swiːt] *n* (*candy*) конфе́та; (*BRIT : CULIN*) сла́дкое *adj* *no pl*; сла́дости *fpl* ♦ *adj* сла́дкий; (*kind, attractive*) ми́лый; **~ corn** *n* кукуру́за; **~ness** *n* сла́дость *f*; (*kindness*) любе́зность *f*

swell [swel] (*pt* **~ed**, *pp* **swollen** *or* **~ed**) *n* (*of sea*) волне́ние ♦ *adj* (*US : inf*) мирово́й ♦ *vi* (*numbers*) расти́ (вы́расти *pf*); (*also:* **~ up**: *face, ankle etc*) опуха́ть (опу́хнуть *pf*), вздува́ться (взду́ться *pf*); **~ing** *n* (*MED*) о́пухоль *f*, взду́тие *nt*

sweltering ['sweltərɪŋ] *adj* ду́шный

swept [swept] *pt*, *pp* of **sweep**

swift [swɪft] *adj* стреми́тельный; **~ly** *adv* стреми́тельно

swim [swɪm] (*pt* **swam**, *pp* **swum**) *vi* пла́вать/плыть (*impf*); (*as sport*) пла́вать (*impf*); (*head*) плыть (поплы́ть *pf*) кру́гом; (*room*) плыть (поплы́ть *pf*) ♦ *vt* переплыва́ть (переплы́ть *pf*); (*a length*) проплыва́ть (проплы́ть *pf*); **~mer** *n* плове́ц(вчи́ха); **~ming** *n* пла́вание; **~ming costume** *n* (*BRIT*) купа́льный костю́м; **~ming pool** *n* пла́вательный бассе́йн; **~ming trunks** *npl* пла́вки *pl*; **~suit** *n* купа́льник

swing [swɪŋ] (*pt*, *pp* **swung**) *n* (*in playground*) каче́ли *pl*; (*change: in opinions etc*) крен, поворо́т ♦ *vt* (*arms*) разма́хивать (*impf*) +*instr*; (*legs*) болта́ть (*impf*) +*instr*; (*also:* **~ round**: *vehicle etc*) развора́чивать (разверну́ть *pf*) ♦ *vi* кача́ться (*impf*); (*also:* **~ round**: *vehicle etc*) развора́чиваться (разверну́ться *pf*); **to be in full ~** (*party etc*) быть (*impf*) в по́лном разга́ре

swirl [swɜːl] *vi* кружи́ться (*impf*)

Swiss [swɪs] *adj* швейца́рский

switch [swɪtʃ] *n* (*for light, radio etc*)

выключа́тель *m*; (*change*) переключе́ние ♦ *vt* (*change*) переключа́ть (переключи́ть *pf*); **~ off** *vt* выключа́ть (вы́ключить *pf*); **~ on** *vt* включа́ть (включи́ть *pf*); **~board** *n* (*TEL*) коммута́тор

Switzerland ['swɪtsələnd] *n* Швейца́рия

swivel ['swɪvl] *vi* (*also:* **~ round**) повора́чиваться (*impf*)

swollen ['swəulən] *pp* of **swell**

sword [sɔːd] *n* меч

swore [swɔːr] *pt* of **swear**

sworn [swɔːn] *pp* of **swear** ♦ *adj* (*statement, evidence*) да́нный под прися́гой; (*enemy*) закля́тый

swum [swʌm] *pp* of **swim**

swung [swʌŋ] *pt*, *pp* of **swing**

sycamore ['sɪkəmɔːr] *n* я́вор

syllable ['sɪləbl] *n* слог

syllabus ['sɪləbəs] *n* (уче́бная) програ́мма

symbol ['sɪmbl] *n* (*sign*) знак; (*representation*) си́мвол; **~ic(al)** [sɪm'bɔlɪk(l)] *adj* символи́ческий

symmetrical [sɪ'metrɪkl] *adj* симметри́чный

symmetry ['sɪmɪtrɪ] *n* симме́трия

sympathetic [sɪmpə'θetɪk] *adj* (*person*) уча́стливый; (*remark, opinion*) сочу́вственный; (*likeable: character*) прия́тный, симпати́чный; **to be ~ to(wards)** (*supportive of*) сочу́вствовать (*impf*) +*dat*

sympathize ['sɪmpəθaɪz] *vi*: **to ~ with** сочу́вствовать (*impf*) +*dat*

sympathy ['sɪmpəθɪ] *n* (*pity*) сочу́вствие, уча́стие; **with our deepest ~** с глубоча́йшими соболе́знованиями; **to come out in ~** (*workers*) бастова́ть (*impf*) в знак солида́рности

symphony ['sɪmfənɪ] *n* симфо́ния

symptom ['sɪmptəm] *n* симпто́м

synagogue ['sɪnəgɔg] *n* синаго́га

syndicate ['sɪndɪkɪt] n (of people, businesses) синдика́т

syndrome ['sɪndrəum] n синдро́м

synonym ['sɪnənɪm] n сино́ним

synthetic [sɪn'θetɪk] adj (materials) синтети́ческий, иску́сственный

syringe [sɪ'rɪndʒ] n шприц

syrup ['sɪrəp] n (juice) сиро́п; (also: **golden ~**) (све́тлая or жёлтая) па́тока

system ['sɪstəm] n систе́ма; **~atic** [sɪstə'mætɪk] adj системати́ческий

T, t

ta [tɑː] excl (BRIT: inf) спаси́бо

table ['teɪbl] n (furniture) стол; (MATH, CHEM etc) табли́ца; **to lay** or **set the ~** накрыва́ть (накры́ть pf) на стол; **~ of contents** оглавле́ние; **~cloth** n ска́терть f; **~ lamp** n насто́льная ла́мпа; **~mat** n подста́вка (под столо́вые прибо́ры); **~spoon** n столо́вая ло́жка; **~ tennis** n насто́льный те́ннис

tabloid ['tæblɔɪd] n табло́ид, малоформа́тная газе́та

taboo [tə'buː] n табу́ nt ind ♦ adj запрещённый

tacit ['tæsɪt] adj молчали́вый

tack [tæk] n (nail) гвоздь m с широ́кой шля́пкой ♦ vt (nail) прибива́ть (приби́ть pf); (stitch)

tackle ['tækl] n (for fishing etc) снасть f; (for lifting) сло́жный блок; (SPORT) блокиро́вка ♦ vt (difficulty) справля́ться (спра́виться pf) с +instr; (fight, challenge) схвати́ться (pf) с +instr; (SPORT) блокирова́ть (impf/pf)

tacky ['tækɪ] adj (sticky) ли́пкий; (pej: cheap) дешёвый

tact [tækt] n такт, такти́чность f; **~ful** adj такти́чный

tactical ['tæktɪkl] adj такти́ческий

tactics ['tæktɪks] npl та́ктика fsg

tactless ['tæktlɪs] adj беста́ктный

tag [tæg] n (label) этике́тка, ярлы́к

tail [teɪl] n (of animal, plane) хвост; (of shirt) коне́ц; (of coat) пола́ ♦ vt сади́ться (сесть pf) на хвост +dat; **~s** npl (suit) фрак msg; **~back** n (BRIT: AUT) хвост

tailor ['teɪlə*] n (мужско́й) портно́й m adj

take [teɪk] (pt **took**, pp **~n**) vt брать (взять pf); (photo, measures) снима́ть (снять pf); (shower, decision, drug) принима́ть (приня́ть pf); (notes) де́лать (сде́лать pf); (grab: sb's arm etc) хвата́ть (схвати́ть pf); (require: courage, time) тре́бовать (потре́бовать pf); (tolerate: pain etc) переноси́ть (перенести́ pf); (hold: passengers etc) вмеща́ть (вмести́ть pf); (on foot: person) отводи́ть (отвести́ pf); (: thing) относи́ть (отнести́ pf); (by transport: person, thing) отвози́ть (отвезти́ pf); (exam) сдава́ть (сдать pf); **to ~ sth from** (drawer etc) вынима́ть (вы́нуть pf) что-л из +gen; (steal from) брать (взять pf) что-л у +gen; **I ~ it that ...** как я понима́ю, ...; **~ apart** vt разбира́ть (разобра́ть pf); **~ away** vt (remove) убира́ть (убрáть pf); (carry off) забирáть (забрáть pf); (MATH) отнимáть (отня́ть pf); ~ **back** vt (return: thing) относи́ть (отнести́ pf) обрáтно; (: person) отводи́ть (отвести́ pf) обрáтно; (one's words) брать (взять pf) назáд; ~ **down** vt (building) сноси́ть (снести́ pf); (note) запи́сывать (записáть pf); ~ **in** vt (deceive) обмáнывать (обманýть pf); (understand) воспринимáть (восприня́ть pf); (lodger, orphan) брать (взять pf); ~ **off** vi (AVIAT) взлетáть (взлетéть pf) ♦ vt (remove) снимáть (снять pf); ~ **on** vt (work, employee) брать (взять pf); (opponent) сражáться (срази́ться pf) с +instr; (invite) води́ть/вести́ (повести́ pf); (remove) вынимáть (вы́нуть pf); **to ~ sth out of** (drawer, pocket etc) вынимáть (вы́нуть pf) что-н из +gen; **don't ~ your anger out on me!** не вымещáй свой гнев на мне!; ~ **over** vt (business) поглощáть (поглоти́ть pf); (country) захвáтывать (захвати́ть pf) ♦ vi: **to ~ over from sb** сменя́ть (смени́ть pf) когó-н; ~ **to** vt fus: **she took to him** он ей срáзу понрáвился; ~ **up** vt (hobby) заня́ться (pf) +instr; (job) брáться (взя́ться pf) за +acc; (idea, story) подхвáтывать (подхвати́ть pf); (time, space) занимáть (заня́ть pf); **I'll ~ you up on that!** ловлю́ Вас на слóве!; ~**away** n (BRIT: food) едá на вы́нос; ~**off** n (AVIAT) взлёт; ~**over** n (COMM) поглощéние

takings ['teɪkɪŋz] npl (COMM) вы́ручка fsg

tale [teɪl] n рассказ; **to tell ~s** (fig) я́бедничать (наябедничать pf)

talent ['tælnt] n талáнт; ~**ed** adj талáнтливый

talk [tɔ:k] n (speech) доклáд; (conversation, interview) бесéда, разговóр; (gossip) разговóры mpl ♦ vi (speak) говори́ть (impf); (: chat) разговáривать (impf); ~**s** npl (POL etc) переговóры pl; **to ~ about** говори́ть (поговори́ть pf) или разговáривать (impf) о +prp; **to ~ sb into doing** уговáривать (уговори́ть pf) когó-н +infin; **to ~ sb out of sth** отговáривать (отговори́ть pf) когó-н от чегó-н; **to ~ shop** говори́ть (impf) о делáх; ~ **over** vt (problem) обговáривать (обговори́ть pf); ~**ative** adj разговóрчивый, болтли́вый

tall [tɔ:l] adj высóкий; **he is 6 feet ~** егó рост - 6 фýтов

tally ['tælɪ] n счёт

tambourine [tæmbə'ri:n] n (MUS) тамбури́н, бýбен

tame [teɪm] adj ручнóй; (fig) вя́лый

tampon ['tæmpɔn] n тампóн

tan [tæn] n (also: sun~) загáр

tandem ['tændəm] n (cycle) тандéм; **in ~** (together) совмéстно, вмéсте

tang [tæŋ] n си́льный зáпах

tangerine [tændʒə'ri:n] n мандари́н

tangible ['tændʒəbl] adj (benefits) ощути́мый, осязáемый; (proof) реáльный

tank [tæŋk] n (water tank) бак; (: large) цистéрна; (for fish) аквáриум; (MIL) танк

tanker ['tæŋkə'] n (ship) тáнкер; (truck, RAIL) цистéрна

tanned [tænd] adj загорéлый

tantrum ['tæntrəm] n истéрика

tap [tæp] n (водопровóдный) кран; (gentle blow) стук ♦ vt (hit)

стуча́ть (постуча́ть pf) по +dat;
(resources) испо́льзовать (impf/pf);
(telephone, conversation)
прослу́шивать (impf)

tape [teɪp] n (also: **magnetic ~**)
(магни́тная) плёнка; (cassette)
кассе́та; (sticky tape) кле́йкая
ле́нта ♦ vt (record) запи́сывать
(записа́ть pf); (stick) закле́ивать
(закле́ить pf) кле́йкой ле́нтой

taper ['teɪpər] vi (narrow) сужа́ться
(су́зиться pf)

tape recorder n магнитофо́н

tapestry ['tæpɪstrɪ] n (object)
гобеле́н

tar [tɑː] n дёготь m

tarantula [təˈræntjʊlə] n тара́нтул

target ['tɑːgɪt] n цель f

tariff ['tærɪf] n (on goods) тари́ф;
(BRIT: in hotels etc) прейскура́нт

tarmac ['tɑːmæk] n (BRIT: on road)
асфа́льт

tarot ['tærəʊ] adj: **~ cards**
гада́льные ка́рты fpl

tart [tɑːt] n (CULIN, large) пиро́г
♦ adj (flavour) те́рпкий

tartan ['tɑːtn] adj (rug, scarf etc)
кле́тчатый

tartar ['tɑːtə] n (on teeth) зубно́й
ка́мень m

task [tɑːsk] n зада́ча; **to take sb to
~** отчи́тывать (отчита́ть pf)
кого́-н

taste [teɪst] n вкус; (sample) про́ба;
(fig: glimpse, idea) представле́ние
♦ vt пробова́ть (попро́бовать pf)
♦ vi: **to ~ of** or **like** име́ть (impf)
вкус +gen; **you can ~ the garlic (in
the dish)** в блю́де чу́вствуется
чесно́к; **in bad/good ~** в дурно́м/
хоро́шем вку́се; **~ful** adj
элега́нтный; **~less** adj
безвку́сный

tasty ['teɪstɪ] adj (food) вку́сный

tatters ['tætəz] npl: **in ~** (clothes)
изо́рванный в клочья

tattoo [təˈtuː] n (on skin)
татуиро́вка

taught [tɔːt] pt, pp of **teach**

taunt [tɔːnt] n издева́тельство ♦ vt
(person) издева́ться (impf) над
+instr

Taurus ['tɔːrəs] n Теле́ц

taut [tɔːt] adj (thread etc) туго́й;
(skin) упру́гий

tax [tæks] n нало́г ♦ vt (earnings,
goods etc) облага́ть (обложи́ть pf)
нало́гом; (fig: memory, patience)
напряга́ть (напря́чь pf); **~ation**
[tækˈseɪʃən] n (system)
налогообложе́ние; (money paid)
разме́р нало́га; **~-free** adj (goods,
services) не облага́емый нало́гом

taxi ['tæksɪ] n такси́ nt ind

taxpayer ['tækspeɪə] n
налогоплате́льщик(щица)

TB n abbr = **tuberculosis**

tea [tiː] n чай; (BRIT: meal) у́жин;
high ~ (BRIT) (по́здний) обе́д

teach [tiːtʃ] (pt, pp **taught**) vi
преподава́ть (impf) ♦ vt: **to ~ sb
sth, ~ sth to sb** учи́ть (научи́ть
pf) кого́-н чему́-н; (in school)
преподава́ть (impf) что-н кому́-н;
~er n учи́тель(ница) m(f); **~ing** n
(work) преподава́ние

teak [tiːk] n тик

team [tiːm] n (of people) кома́нда;
~work n коллекти́вная рабо́та

teapot ['tiːpɔt] n (зава́рочный)
ча́йник

tear [tɪə] (pt **tore**, pp **torn**) n
дыра́, ды́рка ♦ vt (rip) рвать
(порва́ть pf) ♦ vi (rip) рва́ться
(порва́ться pf)

tear [tɪə] n слеза́; **in ~s** в
слеза́х; **~ful** adj запла́канный

tease [tiːz] vt дразни́ть (impf)

teaspoon ['tiːspuːn] n ча́йная
ло́жка

teatime ['tiːtaɪm] n у́жин

tea towel n (BRIT) посу́дное

полоте́нце

technical ['teknɪkl] adj (terms, advances) техни́ческий; **~ly** adv (strictly speaking) форма́льно; (regarding technique) с техни́ческой то́чки зре́ния

technician [tek'nɪʃən] n те́хник

technique [tek'ni:k] n те́хника

technological [teknə'lɔdʒɪkl] adj технологи́ческий

technology [tek'nɔlədʒɪ] n те́хника; (in particular field) техноло́гия

teddy (bear) ['tedɪ(-)] n (плю́шевый) ми́шка

tedious ['ti:dɪəs] adj ну́дный

tee [ti:] n подста́вка для мяча́ (в го́льфе)

teenage ['ti:neɪdʒ] adj (problems) подростко́вый; (fashion) тинэ́йджеровский; **~ children** подро́стки mpl; **~r** n подро́сток, тинэ́йджер

teens [ti:nz] npl: **to be in one's ~** быть (impf) в подростко́вом во́зрасте

teeth [ti:θ] npl of **tooth**

teetotal ['ti:'təutl] adj непью́щий, тре́звый

telecommunications ['telɪkəmju:nɪ'keɪʃənz] n телекоммуника́ции fpl

teleconferencing ['telɪkɔnfərənsɪŋ] n телеконфере́нция

telegram ['telɪɡræm] n телегра́мма

telegraph ['telɪɡrɑ:f] n телегра́ф

telepathy [tɪ'lepəθɪ] n телепа́тия

telephone ['telɪfəun] n телефо́н
♦ vt (person) звони́ть (позвони́ть pf) +dat; **he is on the ~** (talking) он говори́т по телефо́ну; **are you on the ~?** (possessing phone) у Вас есть телефо́н?; **~ call** n телефо́нный звоно́к; **there is a ~ call for Peter** Пи́тера про́сят к телефо́ну; **~ directory** n

телефо́нный спра́вочник; **~ number** n но́мер телефо́на, телефо́н (разг)

telesales ['telɪseɪlz] n телефо́нная рекла́ма

telescope ['telɪskəup] n телеско́п

television ['telɪvɪʒən] n телеви́дение; (set) телеви́зор; **on ~** по телеви́дению

telex ['teleks] n те́лекс

tell [tel] (pt, pp **told**) vt (say) говори́ть (сказа́ть pf); (relate) расска́зывать (рассказа́ть pf); (distinguish): **to ~ sth from** отлича́ть (отличи́ть pf) что-н от +gen ♦ vi (have an effect): **to ~ (on)** ска́зываться (сказа́ться pf) (на +prp); **to ~ sb to do** говори́ть (сказа́ть pf) кому́-н +infin; **~ off** vt: **to ~ sb off** отчи́тывать (отчита́ть pf) кого́-н; **~er** n (in bank) касси́р; **~ing** adj (remark, detail) показа́тельный

telly ['telɪ] n abbr (BRIT : inf = **television**) те́лик

temper ['tempər] n (nature) нрав; (mood) настрое́ние; (fit of anger) гнев; **to be in a ~** быть (impf) в раздражённом состоя́нии; **to lose one's ~** выходи́ть (вы́йти pf) из себя́

temperament ['temprəmənt] n темпера́мент; **~al** [temprə'mentl] adj темпера́ментный; (fig) капри́зный

temperate ['temprət] adj уме́ренный

temperature ['temprətʃər] n температу́ра; **he has or is running a ~** у него́ температу́ра, он температу́рит (разг)

tempi ['tempi:] npl of **tempo**

temple ['templ] n (REL) храм; (ANAT) висо́к

tempo ['tempəu] (pl **~s** or **tempi**) n темп

emporarily ['tempərərılı] *adv* временно

emporary ['tempərəri] *adj* временный

empt [tempt] *vt* соблазнять (соблазнить *pf*), искушать *(impf)*; **to ~ sb into doing** соблазнять (соблазнить *pf*) кого-н +*infin*; **~ation** [temp'teɪʃən] *n* соблазн, искушение; **~ing** *adj* (offer) соблазнительный

ten [ten] *n* десять

tenacity [tə'næsɪtɪ] *n* упорство

tenancy ['tenənsɪ] *n* (of room, land etc) владение на правах аренды; *(period)* срок аренды *or* найма

tenant ['tenənt] *n* съёмщик(мщица)

tend [tend] *vt* (crops, patient) ухаживать *(impf)* за +*instr* ♦ *vi*: **to ~ to do** иметь *(impf)* склонность +*infin*

tendency ['tendənsɪ] *n* (habit) склонность *f*; (trend) тенденция

tender ['tendə'] *adj* нежный; (sore) чувствительный ♦ *n* (COMM, offer) предложение ♦ *vt* (apology) приносить (принести *pf*); **legal ~** (money) законное платёжное средство; **to ~ one's resignation** подавать (подать *pf*) в отставку; **~ness** *n* нежность *f*

tendon ['tendən] *n* сухожилие

tennis ['tenɪs] *n* теннис

tenor ['tenə'] *n* (MUS) тенор

tense [tens] *adj* напряжённый

tension ['tenʃən] *n* напряжение

tent [tent] *n* палатка

tentative ['tentətɪv] *adj* (person, smile) осторожный; (conclusion, plans) сдержанный

tenth [tenθ] *adj* десятый ♦ *n* (fraction) одна десятая *f adj*

tenuous ['tenjuəs] *adj* слабый

tepid ['tepɪd] *adj* (liquid) тепловатый

term [tə:m] *n* (expression) термин; (period in power etc) срок; (SCOL, in school) четверть *f*; (: at university) триместр ♦ *vt* (call) называть (назвать *pf*); **~s** *npl* (conditions) условия *ntpl*; **in abstract ~s** в абстрактных выражениях; **in the short ~** в ближайшем будущем; **in the long ~** в перспективе; **to be on good ~s with sb** быть *(impf)* в хороших отношениях с кем-н; **to come to ~s with** примиряться (примириться *pf*) с +*instr*

terminal ['tə:mɪnl] *adj* неизлечимый ♦ *n* (ELEC) клемма, зажим; (COMPUT) терминал; *(also:* **air ~**) аэровокзал, терминал; (BRIT: *also:* **coach ~**) автобусный вокзал

terminate ['tə:mɪneɪt] *vt* прекращать (прекратить *pf*)

terminology [tə:mɪ'nɔlədʒɪ] *n* терминология

terrace ['terəs] *n* терраса; **the ~s** *npl* (BRIT: standing areas) трибуны *fpl*; **~d** *adj* (garden) террасный; **~d house** дом в ряду примыкающих друг к другу однотипных домов

terrain [te'reɪn] *n* ландшафт

terrible ['terɪbl] *adj* ужасный

terribly ['terɪblɪ] *adv* ужасно

terrific [tə'rɪfɪk] *adj* (thunderstorm, speed etc) колоссальный; (time, party etc) потрясающий

terrify ['terɪfaɪ] *vt* ужасать (ужаснуть *pf*)

territorial [terɪ'tɔ:rɪəl] *adj* территориальный

territory ['terɪtərɪ] *n* территория; (fig) область *f*

terror ['terə'] *n* ужас; **~ism** *n* терроризм; **~ist** *n* террорист(ка); **~ize** *vt* терроризировать *(impf/pf)*

terse [tə:s] *adj* сжатый, краткий

test [test] *n* (trial, check) проверка, тест; (of courage etc) испытание;

(MED) анализ; (CHEM) о́пыт; (SCOL) контро́льная рабо́та, тест; (also: **driving ~**) экза́мен на води́тельские права́ ♦ vt проверя́ть (прове́рить pf); (courage) испы́тывать (испыта́ть pf); (MED) анализи́ровать (проанализи́ровать pf)

testament ['testəmənt] n: **the Old/ New Testament** Ве́тхий/Но́вый Заве́т

testicle ['testikl] n яи́чко

testify ['testifaɪ] vi (LAW) дава́ть (дать pf) показа́ния; **to ~ to sth** свиде́тельствовать (impf) о чём-н

testimony ['testɪmənɪ] n (LAW) показа́ние, свиде́тельство; (clear proof): **to be (a) ~** явля́ться (яви́ться pf) свиде́тельством +gen

test tube n проби́рка

text [tekst] n текст; **~book** n уче́бник

textiles ['tekstaɪlz] npl (fabrics) тексти́льные изде́лия ntpl; (textile industry) тексти́льная промы́шленность fsg

texture ['tekstʃə'] n (structure) строе́ние, структу́ра; (feel) факту́ра

than [ðæn] conj чем; (with numerals) бо́льше +gen, бо́лее +gen; **I have less work ~ you** у меня́ ме́ньше рабо́ты, чем у Вас; **more ~ once** не раз; **more ~ three times** бо́лее ого́льше трёх раз

thank [θæŋk] vt благодари́ть (поблагодари́ть pf); **~ you (very much)** спаси́бо; **~ God!** сла́ва Бо́гу!; **~ful** adj: **~ful (for)** благода́рный (за +acc); **~less** adj неблагода́рный; **~s npl** благода́рность fsg ♦ excl спаси́бо; **many ~s**, **~s a lot** большо́е спаси́бо; **~s to** благодаря́ +dat

that [ðæt] (pl **those**) adj (demonstrative) тот (f та, nt то); **that man** тот мужчи́на; **which book would you like? - that one over there** каку́ю кни́гу Вы хоти́те? - вон ту; **I like this film better than that** мне э́тот фильм нра́вится бо́льше, чем тот

♦ pron **1** (demonstrative) э́то; **who's/what's that?** кто/что э́то?; **is that you?** э́то Вы?; **we talked of this and that** мы говори́ли об э́том и о том и о сём; **that's what he said** вот что он сказа́л; **what happened after that?** а что произошло́ по́сле э́того?; **that is (to say)** то́ есть

2 (direct object) кото́рый (f кото́рую, nt кото́рое, pl кото́рые); (indirect object) кото́рому (f кото́рой, pl кото́рым); (after prep: +acc) кото́рый (f кото́рую, nt кото́рое, pl кото́рые); (: +gen) кото́рого (f кото́рой, pl кото́рых); (: +dat) кото́рому (f кото́рой, pl кото́рым); (: +instr) кото́рым (f кото́рой, pl кото́рыми); (: +prp) кото́ром (f кото́рой, pl кото́рых); **the theory that we discussed** тео́рия, кото́рую мы обсужда́ли; **all (that) I have** всё, что у меня́ есть

3 (of time) когда́; **the day (that) he died** день, когда́ он у́мер

♦ conj что; (introducing purpose) что́бы; **he thought that I was ill** он ду́мал, что я был бо́лен; **she suggested that I phone you** она́ предложи́ла, что́бы я Вам позвони́л

♦ adv (demonstrative): **I can't work that much** я не могу́ так мно́го работать; **it can't be that bad** не так уж всё плóхо; **the wall's about that high** стенá примéрно вот такóй высоты́

haw [θɔ:] n óттепель f

the [ði:; ðə] def art **1**: **the books/ children are at home** кни́ги/дéти дóма; **the rich and the poor** богáтые pl adj и бéдные pl adj; **to attempt the impossible** пытáться (попытáться pf) сдéлать невозмóжное
2 (in titles): **Elizabeth the First** Елизавéта Пéрвая
3 (in comparisons): **the more ... the more ...** чем бóльше ..., тем бóльше ...; (+adj) чем бóлее ..., тем бóлее ...

theatre ['θɪətər] (US **theater**) n теáтр; (MED: also: **operating ~**) операцибнная f adj
theatrical [θɪ'ætrɪkl] adj театрáльный
theft [θeft] n крáжа
their [ðeər] adj их; (referring to subject of sentence) свой; see also **my**; **~s** pron их; (referring to subject of sentence) свой; see also **mine**[1]
them [ðem] pron (direct) их; (indirect) им; (after prep: +gen) них; (: +dat) ним; (: +instr) ни́ми; **a few of ~** нéкоторые из них; **give me a few of ~** дáйте мне нéсколько из них; see also **me**
theme [θi:m] n тéма
themselves [ðəm'selvz] pl pron (reflexive) себя́; (emphatic) сáми; (after prep: +gen) себя́; (: +dat, +prp) себé; (: +instr) собóй; (alone): **(all) by ~** одни́; **they shared the money between ~** они́

раздели́ли дéньги мéжду собóй; see also **myself**

then [ðen] adv потóм; (at that time) тогдá ♦ conj (therefore) тогдá ♦ adj (at the time) тогдáшний; **from ~ on** с тех пор; **by ~** к тому́ врéмени; **if ... ~ ...** éсли ... то ...
theology [θɪ'ɒlədʒɪ] n теолóгия, богослóвие
theoretical [θɪə'retɪkl] adj теорети́ческий
theory ['θɪərɪ] n теóрия; **in ~** теорети́чески
therapeutic(al) [θerə'pju:tɪk(l)] adj терапевти́ческий
therapist ['θerəpɪst] n врач
therapy ['θerəpɪ] n терапи́я

there [ðeər] adv **1**: **there is some milk in the fridge** в холоди́льнике есть молокó; **there is someone in the room** в кóмнате ктó-то есть; **there were many problems** бы́ло мнóго проблéм; **there will be a lot of people at the concert** на концéрте бýдет мнóго нарóду; **there was a book/there were flowers on the table** на столé лежáла кни́га/стоя́ли цветы́; **there has been an accident** произошлá авáрия
2 (referring to place: motion) тудá; (: position) там; (: closer) тут; **I agree with you there** тут он в э́том я с тобóй соглáсен; **there you go!** (inf) вот!; **there he is!** вот он!; **get out of there!** уходи́ оттýда!

thereabouts ['ðeərə'bauts] adv (place) поблизости; (amount) óколо э́того
thereafter [ðeər'ɑ:ftər] adv с тогó врéмени

thereby ['ðɛəbaɪ] adv таки́м о́бразом

therefore ['ðɛəfɔ:ʳ] adv поэ́тому

there's ['ðɛəz] = there is, there has

thermal ['θə:ml] adj (springs) горя́чий; (underwear) утеплённый

thermometer [θə'mɔmɪtəʳ] n термо́метр, гра́дусник

Thermos ® ['θə:məs] n (also: ~ flask) те́рмос

these [ði:z] pl adj, pron э́ти

thesis ['θi:sɪs] (pl theses) n (SCOL) диссерта́ция

they [ðeɪ] pron они́; ~ say that ... говоря́т, что ...; ~'d = they had, they would; ~'ll = they shall, they will; ~'re = they are; ~'ve = they have

thick [θɪk] adj (in shape) то́лстый; (in consistency) густо́й; (inf: stupid) тупо́й ♦ n: in the ~ of the battle в са́мой гу́ще би́твы; the wall is 20 cm ~ толщина́ стены́ – 20 см; ~en vi (plot) усложня́ться (усложни́ться pf) ♦ vt (sauce etc) де́лать (сде́лать pf) гу́ще; ~ness n (size) толщина́; ~-skinned adj (fig) толстоко́жий

thief [θi:f] (pl thieves) n вор(о́вка)

thigh [θaɪ] n бедро́

thimble ['θɪmbl] n напёрсток

thin [θɪn] adj (person, animal) худо́й; (soup, sauce) жи́дкий ♦ vt: to ~ (down) (sauce, paint) разбавля́ть (разба́вить pf)

thing [θɪŋ] n вещь f; ~s npl (belongings) ве́щи fpl; poor ~ бедня́жка m/f; the best ~ would be to ... са́мое лу́чшее бы́ло бы +infin ...; how are ~s? как дела́?

think [θɪŋk] (pt, pp thought) vt (reflect, believe) ду́мать (impf); to ~ of (come up with) приводи́ть (привести́ pf); (consider) ду́мать

(поду́мать pf) o +prp; what did you ~ of them? что Вы о них ду́маете?; to ~ about ду́мать (поду́мать pf) o +prp; I'll ~ about it я поду́маю об э́том; I am ~ing of starting a business я ду́маю нача́ть би́знес; I ~ so/not я ду́маю, что да/нет; to ~ well of sb ду́мать (impf) o ком-н хорошо́; ~ over vt обду́мывать (обду́мать pf); ~ up vt приду́мывать (приду́мать pf)

thinly ['θɪnlɪ] adv то́нко

third [θə:d] adj тре́тий ♦ n (fraction) треть f, одна́ тре́тья f; (AUT: also: ~ gear) тре́тья ско́рость f; (BRIT: SCOL) дипло́м тре́тьей сте́пени; ~ly adv в-тре́тьих; **Third World** n: **the Third World** Тре́тий мир

thirst [θə:st] n жа́жда; ~y adj: **I am** ~ я хочу́ or мне хо́чется пить

thirteen [θə:'ti:n] n трина́дцать; ~th adj трина́дцатый

thirtieth ['θə:tɪɪθ] adj тридца́тый

thirty ['θə:tɪ] n три́дцать

KEYWORD

---

this [ðɪs] (pl these) adj (demonstrative) э́тот (f э́та, nt э́то); **this man** э́тот мужчи́на; **which book would you like?** - **this one please** каку́ю кни́гу Вы хоти́те? - вот э́ту, пожа́луйста ♦ pron (demonstrative) э́тот (f э́та, nt э́то); **who/what is this?** кто/что э́то?; **this is where I live** здесь я живу́; **this is what he said** вот, что он сказа́л; **this is Mr Brown** э́то ми́стер Бра́ун ♦ adv (demonstrative): **high/long** вот тако́й высоты́/длины́; **the dog was about this big** соба́ка была́ вот така́я больша́я; **we can't stop now we've gone this far** тепе́рь, когда́ мы так далеко зашли, мы не мо́жем останови́ться

thistle ['θɪsl] n чертополо́х

thorn [θɔːn] n шип, колю́чка

thorough ['θʌrə] adj (search, wash) тща́тельный; (knowledge, research) основа́тельный; (person) скрупулёзный; **~bred** n чистокро́вная or чистопоро́дная ло́шадь f; **~ly** adv по́лностью, тща́тельно; (very: satisfied) соверше́нно, вполне́; (: ashamed) соверше́нно

those [ðəuz] adj pl, pron те

though [ðəu] conj хотя́ ♦ adv впро́чем, одна́ко

thought [θɔːt] pt, pp of **think** ♦ n мысль f; (reflection) размышле́ние; (opinion) соображе́ние; **~ful** adj (deep in thought) заду́мчивый; (serious) проду́манный, глубо́кий; (considerate) внима́тельный; **~less** adj безду́мный

thousand ['θauzənd] n ты́сяча; **two** ~ две ты́сячи; **five** ~ пять ты́сяч; **~s of** ты́сячи +gen; **~th** adj ты́сячный

thrash [θræʃ] vt поро́ть (вы́пороть pf); (inf: defeat) громи́ть (разгроми́ть pf)

thread [θred] n (yarn) нить f, ни́тка; (of screw) резьба́ ♦ vt (needle) продева́ть (проде́ть pf) ни́тку в +acc

threat [θret] n угро́за; **~en** vi (storm, danger) грози́ть (impf) ♦ vt: **to ~en sb with** угрожа́ть (impf) or грози́ть (пригрози́ть pf) кому́-л +instr; **to ~en to do** угрожа́ть (impf) or грози́ть (пригрози́ть pf) +infin

three [θriː] n три; **~-dimensional** adj (object) трёхме́рный; **~-piece suite** n мя́гкая ме́бель f

threshold ['θreʃhəuld] n поро́г

threw [θruː] pt of **throw**

thrifty ['θrɪftɪ] adj бережли́вый

thrill [θrɪl] n (excitement) восто́рг; (fear) тре́пет ♦ vt приводи́ть (привести́ pf) в тре́пет, восхища́ть (восхити́ть pf); **to be ~ed** быть (impf) в восто́рге; **~er** n три́ллер; **~ing** adj захва́тывающий

thrive [θraɪv] (pt **~d** or **throve**, pp **~d**) vi процвета́ть (impf); (plant) разраста́ться (разрасти́сь pf); **to ~ on** процвета́ть (impf) на +prp

throat [θrəut] n го́рло; **I have a sore ~** у меня́ боли́т го́рло

throes [θrəuz] npl: **in the ~ of** в лихора́дке +gen

throne [θrəun] n трон

throng [θrɒŋ] n толпа́ ♦ vt заполня́ть (запо́лнить pf)

throttle ['θrɒtl] n (AUT) дро́ссель m ♦ vt души́ть (задуши́ть pf)

through [θruː] prep (space) че́рез +acc; (time) в тече́ние +gen; (by means of) че́рез +acc, посре́дством +gen; (because of) из-за +gen ♦ adj (ticket, train) прямо́й ♦ adv наскво́зь; **he's absent ~ illness** он отсу́тствовал по боле́зни; **to put sb ~ to sb** (TEL) соединя́ть (соедини́ть pf) кого́-л с кем-л; **to be ~ with** поко́нчить (pf) с +instr; **"no-road"** (BRIT) "нет сквозно́го прое́зда"; **~out** prep (place) по +dat; (time) в тече́ние +gen ♦ adv везде́, повсю́ду

throve [θrəuv] pt of **thrive**

throw [θrəu] (pt **threw**, pp **~n**) n бросо́к ♦ vt (object) броса́ть (бро́сить pf); (fig: person) сбива́ть (сбить pf) с то́лку; **to ~ a party** зака́тывать (закати́ть pf) ве́чер; **~ away** vt (rubbish) выбра́сывать (вы́бросить pf); (money) броса́ть (impf) на ве́тер; **~ off** vt

сбра́сывать (сбро́сить pf); ~ **out** vt (rubbish, person) выбра́сывать (вы́бросить pf); (idea) отверга́ть (отве́ргнуть pf); ~ **up** vi (vomit): **he threw up** его́ вы́рвало; ~**in** n вбра́сывание

thrush [θrʌʃ] n (ZOOL) дрозд

thrust [θrʌst] (pt, pp ~) n (TECH) дви́жущая си́ла ♦ vt толка́ть (толкну́ть pf)

thud [θʌd] n глухо́й стук

thug [θʌg] n (criminal) хулига́н

thumb [θʌm] n (ANAT) большо́й па́лец (кисти́); ~ **to: to ~ a lift** (inf) голосова́ть (impf) (на доро́ге)

thump [θʌmp] n (blow) уда́р; (sound) глухо́й стук ♦ vt (person) сту́кнуть (pf) ♦ vi (heart etc) стуча́ть (impf)

thunder [ˈθʌndəʳ] n гром; ~**storm** n гроза́

Thursday [ˈθəːzdɪ] n четве́рг

thus [ðʌs] adv и́так, таки́м о́бразом

thwart [θwɔːt] vt (person) чини́ть (impf) препя́тствия +dat; (plans) расстра́ивать (расстро́ить pf)

thyme [taɪm] n тимья́н, чабре́ц

thyroid [ˈθaɪrɔɪd] n (also: ~ **gland**) щитови́дная железа́

tick [tɪk] n (of clock) ти́канье; (mark) га́лочка, пти́чка; (ZOOL) клещ ♦ vi (clock) ти́кать (impf) ♦ vt отмеча́ть (отме́тить pf) га́лочкой; **in a** ~ (BRIT: inf) ми́гом

ticket [ˈtɪkɪt] n биле́т; (price tag) этике́тка; (for: **parking** =) штраф за наруше́ние пра́вил парко́вания

tickle [ˈtɪkl] vt щекота́ть (пощекота́ть pf) ♦ vi щекота́ть (impf)

ticklish [ˈtɪklɪʃ] adj (problem) щекотли́вый; (person): **to be** ~ боя́ться (impf) щеко́тки

tidal [ˈtaɪdl] adj (estuary) прили́во-

отли́вный; ~ **wave** n прили́вная волна́

tide [taɪd] n прили́в и отли́в; (fig: of events) волна́; (of fashion, opinion) направле́ние; **high** ~ по́лная вода́, вы́сшая то́чка прили́ва; **low** ~ ма́лая вода́, ни́зшая то́чка отли́ва; ~ **over** vt: **this money will** ~ **me over till Monday** на э́ти де́ньги я смогу́ продержа́ться до понеде́льника

tidy [ˈtaɪdɪ] adj опря́тный; (mind) аккура́тный ♦ vt (also: ~ **up**) прибира́ть (прибра́ть pf)

tie [taɪ] n (string etc) шнуро́к; (BRIT: also: **neck**~) га́лстук; (fig: link) связь f; (SPORT) ничья́ ♦ vt завя́зывать (завяза́ть pf) ♦ vi (SPORT) игра́ть (сыгра́ть pf) вничью́; **to** ~ **sth in a bow** завя́зывать (завяза́ть pf) что-л ба́нтом; **to** ~ **a knot in sth** завя́зывать (завяза́ть pf) что-л узло́м; ~ **up** vt (dog, boat) привя́зывать (привяза́ть pf); (prisoner, parcel) свя́зывать (связа́ть pf); **I'm** ~**d up at the moment** (busy) сейча́с я за́нят

tier [tɪəʳ] n (of stadium etc) я́рус; (of cake) слой

tiger [ˈtaɪgəʳ] n тигр

tight [taɪt] adj (rope) туго́й; (shoes, bend, clothes) у́зкий; (security) уси́ленный; (schedule, budget) жёсткий ♦ adv (hold, squeeze) кре́пко; (shut) пло́тно; **money is** ~ у меня́ ту́го с деньга́ми; ~**en** vt (rope) натя́гивать (натяну́ть pf); (screw) затя́гивать (затяну́ть pf); (grip) сжима́ть (сжать pf); (security) уси́ливать (уси́лить pf) ♦ vi (grip) сжима́ться (сжа́ться pf); (rope) натя́гиваться (натяну́ться pf); ~**lipped** adj скры́тный; (fig: through anger) серди́тый; ~**ly** adv (grasp) кре́пко; ~**rope** n

натя́нутый кана́т; ~s npl (BRIT)
колго́тки pl

ile [taɪl] n (on roof) черепи́ца; (on floor) пли́тка

ill [tɪl] n ка́сса ♦ prep, conj = **until**

ilt [tɪlt] vt наклоня́ть (наклони́ть pf); (head) склоня́ть (склони́ть pf) ♦ vi наклоня́ться (наклони́ться pf)

timber ['tɪmbə'] n (wood) древеси́на

time [taɪm] n вре́мя nt; (occasion) раз ♦ vt (measure time of) засека́ть (засе́чь pf) вре́мя +gen; (fix moment for) выбира́ть (вы́брать pf) вре́мя для +gen; **a long ~** до́лго; **a long ~ ago** давно́; **for the ~ being** пока́; **four at a ~** по четы́ре; **from ~ to ~** вре́мя от вре́мени; **at ~s** времена́ми; **in ~** (soon enough) во́время; (after some time) со вре́менем; (MUS, play) в такт; **in a week's ~** че́рез неде́лю; **in no ~** в два счёта; **any ~** (whenever) в любо́е вре́мя; (as response) не́ за что; **on ~** во́время; **five ~s five** пя́тью пять; **what ~ is it?** кото́рый час?; **to have a good ~** хорошо́ проводи́ть (провести́ pf) вре́мя; **~ bomb** n (device) бо́мба с часовы́м механи́змом; **~less** adj ве́чный; **~ limit** n преде́льный срок; **~ly** adj своевре́менный; **~ off** n свобо́дное вре́мя nt; (break) выходно́й m adj; **~r** n (time switch) та́ймер; (period of time) пери́од вре́мени; **~table** n расписа́ние

timid ['tɪmɪd] adj ро́бкий

timing ['taɪmɪŋ] n: **the ~ of his resignation was unfortunate** вы́бор вре́мени для его́ отста́вки был неуда́чен

tin [tɪn] n (material) о́лово; (container) (жестяна́я) ба́нка

(: BRIT: can) консе́рвная ба́нка; **~foil** n фольга́

tinge [tɪndʒ] n отте́нок ♦ vt: **~d with** с отте́нком +gen

tinker ['tɪŋkə'] n бродя́чий луди́льщик

tinned [tɪnd] adj (BRIT) консерви́рованный

tin-opener ['tɪnəupnə'] n (BRIT) консе́рвный нож

tinted ['tɪntɪd] adj (hair) подкра́шенный; (spectacles, glass) дымча́тый

tiny ['taɪnɪ] adj кро́шечный

tip [tɪp] n (of pen etc) ко́нчик; (gratuity) чаевы́е pl adj; (BRIT: for rubbish) сва́лка; (advice) сове́т ♦ vt (waiter) дава́ть (дать pf) на чай +dat; (tilt) наклоня́ть (наклони́ть pf); (also: ~ **over**) опроки́дывать (опроки́нуть pf); (also: ~ **out**) выва́ливать (вы́валить pf); **~-off** n предупрежде́ние

tiptoe ['tɪptəu] n: **on ~** на цы́почках

tire ['taɪə'] n (US) = **tyre** ♦ vt утомля́ть (утоми́ть pf) ♦ vi устава́ть (уста́ть pf); **~d** adj уста́лый; **to be ~d of sth** устава́ть (уста́ть pf) от чего́-н; **~less** adj (worker) неутоми́мый; (efforts) неуста́нный; **~some** adj надое́дливый, зану́дный; **tiring** adj утоми́тельный

tissue ['tɪʃuː] n бума́жная салфе́тка; (ANAT, BIO) ткань f

tit [tɪt] n (ZOOL) сини́ца; **~ for tat** зуб за зуб

title ['taɪtl] n (of book etc) назва́ние; (rank, in sport) ти́тул

KEYWORD

to [tuː, tə] prep 1 (direction) в/на +acc; **to drive to school/the station** е́здить/е́хать (пое́хать pf) в шко́лу/на ста́нцию; **to the left**

налéво; **to the right** напрáво
2 (*as far as*) до +*gen*; **from Paris to London** от Парúжа до Лóндона; **to count to ten** считáть (посчитáть *pf*) до десятú
3 (*with expressions of time*): **a quarter to five** без чéтверти пять
4 (*for, of*) к +*dat*; **the key to the front door** ключ (к) входнóй двéри; **a letter to his wife** письмó женé; **she is secretary to the director** онá секретáрь дирéктора
5 (*expressing indirect object*): **to give sth to sb** давáть (дать *pf*) что-н комý-н; **to talk to sb** разговáривать (*impf*) or говорúть (*impf*) с кем-н; **what have you done to your hair?** что Вы сдéлали со своúми волосáми?
6 (*in relation to*) к +*dat*; **three goals to two** три: два; **X miles to the gallon** ≈ Х лúтров на киломéтр; **30 roubles to the dollar** 30 рублéй за дóллар
7 (*purpose, result*) к +*dat*; **to my surprise** к моемý удивлéнию; **to come to sb's aid** приходúть (прийтú *pf*) комý-н на пóмощь
♦ **with vb** 1: **to want/try to do** хотéть (захотéть *pf*)/пытáться (попытáться *pf*) +*infin*; **he has nothing to lose** емý нéчего терять; **I am happy to** я счáстлив +*infin* ...; **ready to use** готóвый к употреблéнию; **too old/young to ...** слúшком стар/ мóлод, чтóбы +*infin* ...
2 (*with vb omitted*): **I don't want to** я не хочý; **I don't feel like going - you really ought to** мне не хóчется идтú - но, Вы должны
3 (*purpose, result*) чтóбы +*infin*; **I did it to help you** я сдéлал э́то, чтóбы помóчь Вам
♦ **adv**: **to push the door to, pull**

the door to закрывáть (закрыть *pf*) дверь

---

toad [təud] *n* (ZOOL) жáба; **~stool** *n* (BOT) поганка

toast [təust] *n* тост ♦ *vt* (CULIN) поджáривать (поджáрить *pf*); (*drink to*) пить (выпить *pf*) за +*acc*; **~er** *n* тóстер

tobacco [tə'bækəu] *n* табáк

today [tə'deɪ] *adv, n* сегóдня

toddler ['tɔdlə*] *n* малыш

toe [təu] *n* (*of foot*) пáлец (ногú); (*of shoe, sock*) носóк; **to ~ the line** (*fig*) подчинáться (*impf*)

toffee ['tɔfɪ] *n* ирúска, тянýчка

together [tə'gɛðə*] *adv* вмéсте; (*at same time*) одноврéменно; **~ with** вмéсте с +*instr*

toilet ['tɔɪlət] *n* унитáз; (BRIT: *room*) туалéт ♦ *cpd* туалéтный; **~ries** *npl* туалéтные принадлéжности *fpl*

token ['təukən] *n* (*sign, souvenir*) знак; (*substitute coin*) жетóн ♦ *adj* (*strike, payment etc*) символúческий; **book/gift ~** (BRIT) книжный/подарóчный талóн; **record ~** (BRIT) талóн на пластúнку

told [təuld] *pt, pp of* **tell**

tolerable ['tɔlərəbl] *adj* (*bearable*) терпúмый; (*fairly good*) снóсный

tolerance ['tɔlərns] *n* (*patience*) терпúмость *f*

tolerant ['tɔlərnt] *adj*: **~ (of)** терпúмый (к +*dat*)

tolerate ['tɔləreɪt] *vt* терпéть (*impf*)

toll [təul] *n* (*of casualties etc*) числó; (*tax, charge*) сбор, плáта

tomato [tə'mɑːtəu] *n* (*pl* **~es**) *n* помидóр

tomb [tuːm] *n* могúла; **~stone** *n* надгрóбная плитá, надгрóбие

tomorrow [tə'mɔrəu] *adv, n* зáвтра; **the day after ~** послезáвтра; **~ morning** зáвтра ýтром

on [tʌn] n (BRIT) дли́нная то́нна; (US: also: **short ~**) коро́ткая то́нна; (also: **metric ~**) метри́ческая то́нна; **~s of** (inf) у́йма +gen

one [taun] n (of voice, colour) тон ♦ vi (colours : also: **~ in**) сочета́ться (impf); **~ up** vt (muscles) укрепля́ть (укрепи́ть pf)

tongue [tʌn] n язы́к

tonic ['tɒnɪk] n (MED) тонизи́рующее сре́дство; (also: **~ water**) то́ник

tonight [tə'naɪt] adv (this evening) сего́дня ве́чером; (this night) сего́дня но́чью ♦ n (see adv) сего́дняшний ве́чер; сего́дняшняя ночь f

tonsil ['tɒnsl] n (usu pl) минда́лина; **~litis** [tɒnsɪ'laɪtɪs] n тонзилли́т

too [tu:] adv (excessively) сли́шком; (also: referring to subject) та́кже, то́же; (: referring to object) та́кже; **~ much**, **~ many** сли́шком мно́го

took [tuk] pt of **take**

tool [tu:l] n (instrument) инструме́нт

tooth [tu:θ] (pl **teeth**) n (ANAT) зуб; (TECH) зубе́ц; **~ache** n зубна́я боль f; **~brush** n зубна́я щётка; **~paste** n зубна́я па́ста

top [tɒp] n (of mountain) верши́на; (of tree) верху́шка; (of head) маку́шка; (of page, list etc) нача́ло; (of ladder, cupboard, table, box) верх; (lid: of box, jar) кры́шка; (: bottle) про́бка; (also: spinning **~**) юла́, волчо́к ♦ adj (shelf, step) ве́рхний; (highest) вы́сший; (scientist) веду́щий ♦ vt (poll, vote) лиди́ровать (impf) в +prp; (list) возглавля́ть (возгла́вить pf); (exceed: estimate etc) превыша́ть (превы́сить pf); **on ~ of** (above: be)

на +prp; (: put) на +acc; (in addition to) сверх +gen; **from ~ to bottom** све́рху до́низу; **~ up**, (US) **top off** vt (bottle) долива́ть (доли́ть pf)

topic ['tɒpɪk] n те́ма; **~al** adj актуа́льный

topless ['tɒplɪs] adj обнажённый до по́яса

topple ['tɒpl] vt (overthrow) ски́дывать (ски́нуть pf) ♦ vi опроки́дываться (опроки́нуться pf)

top-secret ['tɒp'si:krɪt] adj сверхсекре́тный

torch [tɔ:tʃ] n (with flame) фа́кел; (BRIT: electric) фона́рь m

tore [tɔ:*] pt of **tear** [1]

torment [n 'tɔ:mɛnt vb tɔ:'mɛnt] n муче́ние ♦ vt му́чить (impf)

torn [tɔ:n] pp of **tear** [1]

tornado [tɔ:'neɪdəu] (pl **~es**) n смерч

torpedo [tɔ:'pi:dəu] (pl **~es**) n торпе́да

torrent ['tɒrnt] n пото́к; **~ial** [tɒ'rɛnʃl] adj проливно́й

torso ['tɔ:səu] n ту́ловище, торс

tortoise ['tɔ:təs] n черепа́ха

torture ['tɔ:tʃə*] n пы́тка ♦ vt пыта́ть (impf)

Tory ['tɔ:rɪ] (BRIT : POL) adj консервати́вный ♦ n то́ри m/f ind, консерва́тор

toss [tɒs] vt (throw) подки́дывать (подки́нуть pf), подбра́сывать (подбро́сить pf); (head) отки́дывать (отки́нуть pf) ♦ vi: to **~ and turn** воро́чаться (impf); to **~ a coin** подбра́сывать (подбро́сить pf) моне́ту; to **~ up** to do подбра́сывать (подбро́сить pf) моне́ту, что́бы +infin

total ['təutl] adj (number, workforce etc) о́бщий; (failure, wreck etc)

по́лный ♦ *n* о́бщая су́мма ♦ *vt*
(*add up*) скла́дывать (сложи́ть *pf*);
(*add up to*) составля́ть (соста́вить *pf*)

totalitarian [təutælɪ'tɛərɪən] *adj*
(POL) тоталита́рный

totally ['təutəlɪ] *adv* по́лностью;
(*unprepared*) соверше́нно

touch [tʌtʃ] *n* (*sense*) осяза́ние;
(*approach*) мане́ра; (*detail*) штрих;
(*contact*) прикоснове́ние ♦ *vt* (*with
hand, foot*) каса́ться (косну́ться
pf) +gen, тро́гать (тро́нуть *pf*);
(*tamper with*) тро́гать (impf); (*make
contact with*) прикаса́ться
(прикосну́ться *pf*) к +dat,
дотра́гиваться (дотро́нуться *pf*)
до +gen; (*emotionally*)
тро́гать (тро́нуть *pf*); **there's been
a ~** of frost подморо́зило; **to get
in ~ with sb** свя́зываться
(связа́ться *pf*) с кем-н; **to lose ~**
(*friends*) теря́ть (потеря́ть *pf*)
связь; **~ on** *vt fus* каса́ться
(косну́ться *pf*) +gen; **~ed** *adj*
(*moved*) тро́нутый; **~ing** *adj*
тро́гательный; **~line** *n* боковая
ли́ния; **~y** *adj* (*person*) оби́дчивый

tough [tʌf] *adj* (*hard-wearing*)
кре́пкий, про́чный; (*person:
physically*) выно́сливый; (*:
mentally*) сто́йкий; (*difficult*)
тяжёлый

tour [tuə'] *n* (*journey*) экску́рсия; (*of
town, factory etc*) экску́рсия; (*by
pop group etc*) гастро́ли *pl* ♦ *vt*
(*country, city*) объезжа́ть
(объе́хать *pf*); (*factory*) обходи́ть
(обойти́ *pf*)

tourism ['tuərɪzm] *n* тури́зм

tourist ['tuərɪst] *n* тури́ст(ка) ♦ *cpd*
(*attractions, season*) туристи́ческий

tournament ['tuənəmənt] *n*
турни́р

tow [tau] *vt* вози́ть/везти́ (impf) на
букси́ре; **"on** or (US) **in ~"** (AUT)

"на букси́ре"

toward(s) [tə'wɔːd(z)] *prep* к +dat;
toward(s) doing с тем что́бы
+infin

towel ['tauəl] *n* (*also:* **hand ~**)
полоте́нце для рук; (*also:* **bath
~**) ба́нное полоте́нце

tower ['tauə'] *n* ба́шня; **~ block** *n*
(BRIT) ба́шня, высо́тный дом

town [taun] *n* го́род; **to go to ~**
(*fig*) разоря́ться (разори́ться *pf*);
~ centre *n* центр (го́рода); **~
council** *n* городско́й сове́т; **~
hall** *n* ра́туша

towrope ['tauraup] *n* букси́рный
трос

toxic ['tɒksɪk] *adj* токси́чный

toy [tɔɪ] *n* игру́шка

trace [treɪs] *n* след ♦ *vt* (*draw*)
переводи́ть (перевести́ *pf*);
(*follow*) просле́живать
(проследи́ть *pf*); (*find*)
разы́скивать (разыска́ть *pf*)

track [træk] *n* след; (*path*) тропа́;
(*of bullet etc*) траекто́рия; (RAIL)
(железнодоро́жный) путь *m*;
(*song, also* SPORT) доро́жка ♦ *vt*
(*follow*) идти́ (impf) по сле́ду +gen;
to keep ~ of следи́ть (impf) за
+instr; **~ down** *vt* (*prey*)
высле́живать (вы́следить *pf*);
(*person*) оты́скивать (отыска́ть
pf); **~suit** *n* тренирово́чный
костю́м

tract [trækt] *n* (GEO) простра́нство

tractor ['træktə'] *n* тра́ктор

trade [treɪd] *n* (*activity*) торго́вля;
(*skill, job*) ремесло́ ♦ *vi* (*do
business*) торгова́ть (impf) ♦ *vt*: **to
~ sth (for sth)** обме́нивать
(обменя́ть *pf*) что-н (на что-н); **~
in** *vt* (*car etc*) предлага́ть
(предложи́ть *pf*) для встре́чной
прода́жи; **~mark** *n* торго́вый
знак; **~r** *n* торго́вец; **~sman**
(*irreg*) *n* (*shopkeeper*) торго́вец

ла́вочник; ~ **union** n (BRIT)
профсою́з

radition [trə'dɪʃən] n тради́ция; ~**al** adj (also fig) традицио́нный

raffic ['træfɪk] n движе́ние; (of drugs) нелега́льная торго́вля; ~ **jam** n про́бка, зато́р; ~ **lights** npl светофо́р msg; ~ **warden** n (BRIT) регули́ровщик парко́вки маши́н на городски́х у́лицах

tragedy ['trædʒədɪ] n траге́дия

tragic ['trædʒɪk] adj траги́ческий

trail [treɪl] n (path) доро́жка, тропи́нка; (track) след; (of smoke, dust) шлейф ♦ vt (drag) воло́чить (impf); (follow) сле́довать (impf) по пята́м за +instr ♦ vi (hang loosely) воло́читься (impf); (in game, contest) воло́чи́ться (impf) в хвосте́, отстава́ть (impf); ~**er** n (AUT) прице́п; (US: caravan) автоприце́п; (CINEMA) рекла́мный ро́лик, ано́нс

train [treɪn] n по́езд; (of dress) шлейф ♦ vt (apprentice, doctor etc) обуча́ть (обучи́ть pf), гото́вить (impf); (athlete, mind) тренирова́ть (impf); (dog) дрессирова́ть (выдрессировать pf) ♦ vi учи́ться (обучи́ться pf); (SPORT) тренирова́ться (impf); one's ~ of thought ход мы́сли чьих-н мы́слей; to ~ sb as учи́ть (обучи́ть pf) кого́-н на +acc; to ~ sth on (camera etc) направля́ть (напра́вить pf) что-н на +acc; ~**ed** adj (worker) квалифици́рованный; (animal) дрессиро́ванный; ~**ee** n (hairdresser) учени́к; ~**ee teacher** практика́нт(ка); ~**er** n (coach) тре́нер; (of animals) дрессиро́вщик(щица); ~**ers** npl (shoes) кроссо́вки fpl; ~**ing** n (for occupation) обуче́ние, подгото́вка; (SPORT) трениро́вка; to be in ~**ing** (SPORT)

trait [treɪt] n черта́

traitor ['treɪtə] n преда́тель(ница) m(f)

tram [træm] n (BRIT) трамва́й

tramp [træmp] n (person) бродя́га m/f

trample ['træmpl] vt: to ~ (underfoot) раста́птывать (растопта́ть pf)

trampoline ['træmpəliːn] n бату́т

trance [trɑːns] n (also fig) транс

tranquil ['træŋkwɪl] adj безмяте́жный; ~**lity** [træŋ'kwɪlɪtɪ] (US ~**ity**) n безмяте́жность f

transaction [træn'zækʃən] n опера́ция

transatlantic ['trænzət'læntɪk] adj трансатланти́ческий

transcend [træn'sɛnd] vt переступа́ть (переступи́ть pf)

transcript ['trænskrɪpt] n (typed) распеча́тка; (hand-written) ру́копись f

transfer ['trænsfə] n перево́д; (POL, of power) переда́ча; (SPORT) перехо́д; (design) переводна́я карти́нка ♦ vt (employees, money) переводи́ть (перевести́ pf); (POL, power) передава́ть (переда́ть pf)

transform [træns'fɔːm] vt (completely) преобразо́вывать (преобразова́ть pf); (alter) преобража́ть (преобрази́ть pf); ~**ation** [trænsfə'meɪʃən] n (see vt) преобразова́ние; преображе́ние

transfusion [træns'fjuːʒən] n (also: blood ~) перелива́ние кро́ви

transient ['trænzɪənt] adj мимолётный

transit ['trænzɪt] n транзи́т; in ~ (people, things) при перево́зке, в транзи́те

transition [træn'zɪʃən] n перехо́д; ~**al** adj перехо́дный

translate [trænz'leɪt] vt: to ~

(from/into) переводить
(перевести pf) (с +gen/на +acc)

translation [trænz'leɪʃən] n
перевод

translator [trænz'leɪtə^r] n
переводчик(ица)

transmission [trænz'mɪʃən] n
передача

transmit [trænz'mɪt] vt передавать
(передать pf); **~ter** n передатчик

transparency [trænz'pɛərnsɪ] n (of
glass etc) прозрачность f

transparent [træns'pærnt] adj
прозрачный

transplant n ['trænsplɑːnt] vb
[træns'plɑːnt] n пересадка ♦ vt
(MED, BOT) пересаживать
(пересадить pf)

transport n ['trænspɔːt] vb
[træns'pɔːt] n транспорт ♦ (of people,
goods) перевозка ♦ vt (carry)
перевозить (перевезти pf)

transportation ['trænspɔː'teɪʃən] n
транспортировка, перевозка
(means of transport) транспорт

transvestite [trænz'vɛstaɪt] n
трансвестит

trap [træp] n ловушка, западня
♦ vt ловить (поймать pf) в
ловушку; (confine) запирать
(запереть pf)

trash [træʃ] n мусор; (pej, fig)
дрянь f

trauma ['trɔːmə] n травма; **~tic**
[trɔː'mætɪk] adj (fig) мучительный

travel ['trævl] n (travelling)
путешествия ntpl ♦ vi (for pleasure)
путешествовать (impf); (commute)
ездить (impf); (news, sound)
распространяться
(распространиться pf) ♦ (distance: by transport) проезжать
(проехать pf); **~s** npl (journeys)
разъезды mpl; **~ agent** n
турагент; **~ler** (US **~er**) n
путешественник(ица); **~ler's**

cheque (US **~er's check**) n
дорожный чек

travesty ['trævəstɪ] n пародия

trawler ['trɔːlə^r] n траулер

tray [treɪ] n (for carrying) поднос;
(on desk) корзинка

treacherous ['trɛtʃərəs] adj (person)
вероломный; (look, action)
предательский; (ground, tide)
коварный

treachery ['trɛtʃərɪ] n
предательство, вероломство

treacle ['triːkl] n патока

tread [trɛd] (pt **trod**, pp **trodden**) n
(of stair) ступень f; (of tyre)
протектор ♦ vi ступать (impf)

treason ['triːzn] n измена

treasure ['trɛʒə^r] n сокровище ♦ vt
дорожить (impf) +instr; (thought)
лелеять (impf); **~s** npl (art treasures
etc) сокровища ntpl; **~r** n
казначей

treasury ['trɛʒərɪ] n: **the Treasury**,
(US) **the Treasury Department**
Государственное Казначейство

treat [triːt] n (present)
удовольствие ♦ vt (person, object)
обращаться (impf) с +instr;
(patient, illness) лечить (impf); **to ~
sb to sth** угощать (угостить pf)
кого-н чем-н; **~ment** n (attention,
handling) обращение; (MED)
лечение

treaty ['triːtɪ] n соглашение

treble ['trɛbl] vt утраивать
(утроить pf) ♦ vi утраиваться
(утроиться pf)

tree [triː] n дерево

trek [trɛk] n (trip) поход, переход

tremble ['trɛmbl] vi дрожать (impf)

tremendous [trɪ'mɛndəs] adj
(enormous) громадный; (excellent)
великолепный

tremor ['trɛmə^r] n (trembling)
дрожь f, содрогание; (also: **earth
~**) толчок (при землетрясении)

ench [trentʃ] n кана́ва; (MIL) транше́я, око́п

rend [trend] n (tendency) тенде́нция; (of events, fashion) направле́ние; **~y** adj мо́дный

respass ['trespəs] vi: **to ~ on** (private property) вторга́ться (вто́ргнуться pf) в +acc; **"no "~ing"** "прохо́д воспрещён"

rial ['traɪəl] n (LAW) проце́сс, суд; (of machine etc) испыта́ние; (bad experiences) перипети́и fpl; **on ~** (LAW) под судо́м; **by ~ and error** ме́тодом проб и оши́бок

riangle ['traɪæŋgl] n (MATH, MUS) треуго́льник

riangular [traɪ'æŋgjʊlər] adj треуго́льный

ribal ['traɪbl] adj племенно́й

ribe [traɪb] n пле́мя nt

ribunal [traɪ'bjuːnl] n трибуна́л

ributary ['trɪbjutərɪ] n прито́к

ribute ['trɪbjuːt] n (compliment) дань f; **to pay ~ to** отдава́ть (отда́ть pf) дань +dat

trick [trɪk] n (magic trick) фо́кус; (prank) подво́х; (skill, knack) приём ♦ vt проводи́ть (провести́ pf); **to play a ~ on sb** разы́грывать (разыгра́ть pf) кого́-н; **that should do the ~** э́то должно́ срабо́тать

trickle ['trɪkl] n (of water etc) стру́йка ♦ vi (water, rain etc) струи́ться (impf)

tricky ['trɪkɪ] adj (job) непросто́й; (business) хи́трый; (problem) ка́верзный

trifle ['traɪfl] n (small detail) пустя́к ♦ adv: **a ~ long** чуть длиннова́т

trigger ['trɪgər] n (of gun) куро́к

trim [trɪm] adj (house, garden) ухо́женный; (figure) подтя́нутый ♦ vt (cut) подра́внивать (подровня́ть pf); (decorate): **to ~ (with)** отде́лывать (отде́лать pf)

(+instr) ♦ n: **to give sb a ~** подра́внивать (подровня́ть pf) во́лосы кому́-н

trip [trɪp] n (journey) пое́здка; (outing) экску́рсия ♦ vi (stumble) спотыка́ться (споткну́ться pf); **on a ~** на экску́рсии; **~ up** vi (stumble) спотыка́ться (споткну́ться pf) ♦ vt (person) ста́вить (подста́вить pf) подно́жку +dat

tripe [traɪp] n (CULIN) требуха́

triple ['trɪpl] adj тройно́й; **~ jump** n тройно́й прыжо́к

tripod ['traɪpɔd] n трено́га

trite [traɪt] adj (pej) изби́тый

triumph ['traɪʌmf] n (satisfaction) торжество́; (achievement) триу́мф ♦ vi: **to ~ (over)** торжествова́ть (восторжествова́ть pf) (над +instr); **~ant** [traɪ'ʌmfənt] adj (team, wave) торжеству́ющий; (return) побе́дный

trivial ['trɪvɪəl] adj тривиа́льный

trod [trɔd] pt of **tread**; **~den** pp of **tread**

trolley ['trɔlɪ] n (also: **~ bus**) тележ́ка; (also: **~ bus**) тролле́йбус

trombone [trɔm'bəun] n тромбо́н

troop [truːp] n (of soldiers) отря́д; (of people) гру́ппа; **~s** npl (MIL) войска́ ntpl

trophy ['trəufɪ] n трофе́й

tropical ['trɔpɪkl] adj тропи́ческий

trot [trɔt] n рысь f (спо́соб бе́га)

trouble ['trʌbl] n (difficulty) затрудне́ние; (worry, unrest) беспоко́йство; (bother, effort) хло́поты pl ♦ vt (worry) беспоко́ить (impf); (disturb) беспоко́ить (побеспоко́ить pf) ♦ vi: **to ~ to do** побеспоко́иться (pf) +infin; **~s** npl (personal) неприя́тности fpl; **to be in ~** (ship, climber etc) быть (impf) в беде́; **I am in ~** у меня́ неприя́тности; **to**

have ~ doing с трудо́м +infin; **~d** adj (person) встрево́женный; (times) сму́тный; (country) многострада́льный; **~maker** n смутья́н; **~some** adj (child) озорно́й

trough [trɔf] n (also: **drinking ~**) коры́то; (also: **feeding ~**) корму́шка; (low point) впа́дина

trousers ['trauzəz] npl брю́ки pl; **short ~** шо́рты pl

trout [traut] n inv (ZOOL) форе́ль f

truant ['truːənt] n: **to play ~** прогу́ливать (прогуля́ть pf) уро́ки

truce [truːs] n переми́рие

truck [trʌk] n (lorry) грузови́к; (RAIL) платфо́рма

true [truː] adj и́стинный; (accurate: likeness) то́чный; (loyal) ве́рный; **to come ~** сбыва́ться (сбы́ться pf); **it is ~** э́то пра́вда or ве́рно

truly ['truːlɪ] adv по-настоя́щему; (truthfully) по пра́вде говоря́; **yours ~** (in letter) и́скренне Ваш

trump [trʌmp] n (also: **~ card**) ко́зырь m, кози́рная ка́рта

trumpet ['trʌmpɪt] n (MUS) труба́

truncheon ['trʌntʃən] n (BRIT) дуби́нка

trunk [trʌŋk] n (of tree) ствол; (of elephant) хо́бот; (case) доро́жный сунду́к; (US: AUT) бага́жник; **~s** npl (also: **swimming ~s**) пла́вки pl

trust [trʌst] n (faith) дове́рие; (responsibility) долг; (LAW) довери́тельная со́бственность f ♦ vt (rely on, have faith in) доверя́ть (impl) +dat; (hope): **to ~ (that)** полага́ть (impf); (entrust): **to ~ sth to sb** доверя́ть (дове́рить pf) что-н кому́-н; **to take sth on ~** принима́ть (приня́ть pf) что-н на ве́ру; **~ed** adj пре́данный; **~ee** [trʌs'tiː] n

попечи́тель m; **~ing** adj дове́рчивый; **~worthy** adj надёжный

truth [truːθ] (pl **~s**) n пра́вда; (principle) и́стина; **~ful** adj правди́вый

try [traɪ] n (attempt) попы́тка; (RUGBY) прохо́д с мячо́м ♦ vt (test) про́бовать (попро́бовать pf); (LAW) суди́ть (impf); (patience) испы́тывать (impf); (key, door) про́бовать (попро́бовать pf); (attempt): **to ~ to do** стара́ться (постара́ться pf) or пыта́ться (попыта́ться pf) +infin ♦ vi (make effort) стара́ться (impf); **to have a ~** про́бовать (попро́бовать pf); **~ on** vt (dress etc) примеря́ть (приме́рить pf); **~ing** adj утоми́тельный

tsar [zɑː] n царь m

T-shirt ['tiː.ʃəːt] n футбо́лка

tub [tʌb] n (container) бо́чка; (bath) ва́нна

tube [tjuːb] n (pipe) тру́бка; (container) тю́бик; (BRIT: metro) метро́ nt ind; (for tyre) ка́мера

tuberculosis [tjubəːkju'ləusɪs] n туберкулёз

TUC n abbr (BRIT: = Trades Union Congress) Конгре́сс (брита́нских) профсою́зов

tuck [tʌk] vt (put) су́нуть (pf)

Tuesday ['tjuːzdɪ] n вто́рник

tug [tʌɡ] n (ship) букси́р ♦ vt дёргать (дёрнуть pf)

tuition [tjuː'ɪʃən] n (BRIT) обуче́ние; (US: fees) пла́та за обуче́ние; **private ~** ча́стные уро́ки

tulip ['tjuːlɪp] n тюльпа́н

tumble ['tʌmbl] n паде́ние ♦ vi (fall: person) вали́ться (свали́ться pf)

tumbler ['tʌmblə] n бока́л

tummy ['tʌmɪ] n (inf) живо́т

tumour ['tjuːməʳ] (*US* **tumor**) *n* (*MED*) о́пухоль *f*

tuna ['tjuːnə] *n inv* (*also*: ~ **fish**) туне́ц

tune [tjuːn] *n* (*melody*) моти́в ♦ *vt* настра́ивать (настро́ить *pf*); (*AUT*) нала́живать (нала́дить *pf*); **the guitar is in/out of ~** гита́ра настро́ена/расстро́ена; **to sing in ~** петь (*impf*) в лад; **to sing out of ~** фальши́вить (*impf*); **to be in/out of ~ with** (*fig*) быть (*impf*) в ладу́/не в ладу́ с +*instr*; **~ in** *vi* (*RADIO, TV*) **to ~ in (to)** настра́иваться (настро́иться *pf*) (на +*acc*); **~ful** *adj* мелоди́чный; **~r** *n*: **piano ~** настро́йщик фортепья́но

tunic ['tjuːnɪk] *n* ту́ника

tunnel ['tʌnl] *n* (*passage*) тунне́ль *m*

turbine ['təːbaɪn] *n* (*TECH*) турби́на

turbulent ['təːbjulənt] *adj* бу́рный

turf [təːf] *n* (*grass*) дёрн

Turkey ['təːkɪ] *n* Ту́рция

turkey ['təːkɪ] *n* инде́йка

Turkish ['təːkɪʃ] *adj* туре́цкий

turmoil ['təːmɔɪl] *n* смяте́ние; **in ~** в смяте́нии

turn [təːn] *n* поворо́т; (*chance*) о́чередь *f*; (*inf*: *MED*) вы́вих ♦ *vt* повора́чивать (поверну́ть *pf*) ♦ *vi* (*object*) повора́чиваться (поверну́ться *pf*); (*person: look back*) обора́чиваться (оберну́ться *pf*); (*reverse direction*) развора́чиваться (разверну́ться *pf*); (*become*): **he's ~ed forty** ему́ испо́лнилось со́рок; **a good/bad ~** до́брая/плоха́я услу́га; **"no left ~"** (*AUT*) "нет ле́вого поворо́та"; **it's your ~** – твоя́ о́чередь; **in ~** по о́череди; **to take ~s at sth** де́лать (*impf*) что-н по о́череди; **to ~** nasty озлобля́ться (озлоби́ться *pf*); **~ away** *vi* отвора́чиваться

(отверну́ться *pf*) ♦ *vt* (*business, applicant*) отклоня́ть (отклони́ть *pf*); **~ back** *vi* повора́чивать (поверну́ть *pf*) наза́д ♦ *vt* (*person*) развора́чивать (разверну́ть *pf*); (*vehicle*) **to ~ back the clock** (*fig*) поверну́ть (*pf*) вре́мя вспять; **~ down** *vt* (*request*) отклоня́ть (отклони́ть *pf*); (*heating*) уменьша́ть (уме́ньшить *pf*); ♦ *vi* (*person*) сора́чивать (сверну́ть *pf*) ♦ *vt* выключа́ть (вы́ключить *pf*); **~ on** *vt* включа́ть (включи́ть *pf*); **~ out** *vt* (*light, gas*) выключа́ть (вы́ключить *pf*); (*produce*) выпуска́ть (вы́пустить *pf*) ♦ *vi* (*troops, voters*) прибыва́ть (прибы́ть *pf*); **to ~ out to be** ока́зываться (оказа́ться *pf*) +*instr*; **~ over** *vi* (*person*) повора́чиваться (поверну́ться *pf*) ♦ *vt* (*object, page*) перевора́чивать (переверну́ть *pf*); **~ round** *vi* (*person, vehicle*) развора́чиваться (разверну́ться *pf*); **~ up** *vi* (*person*) объявля́ться (объяви́ться *pf*); (*lost object*) находи́ться (найти́сь *pf*) ♦ *vt* (*collar*) поднима́ть (подня́ть *pf*); (*radio*) де́лать (сде́лать *pf*) гро́мче; (*heater*) увели́чивать (увели́чить *pf*) подачу +*gen*; **~ing** *n* поворо́т; **~ing point** *n* (*fig*) поворо́тный пункт, перело́мный моме́нт

turnip ['təːnɪp] *n* (*BOT, CULIN*) ре́па

turnout ['təːnaut] *n*: **there was a high ~ for the local elections** в ме́стных вы́борах при́няло уча́стие мно́го люде́й

turnover ['təːnəuvəʳ] *n* (*COMM*) оборо́т; (*: of staff*) теку́честь *f*

turn-up ['təːnʌp] *n* (*BRIT*) манже́та

turquoise ['tɜ:kwɔɪz] *adj (colour)* бирюзо́вый

turtle ['tɜ:tl] *n* черепа́ха

tussle ['tʌsl] *n (fight, scuffle)* пота́совка

tutor ['tju:tə^r] *n (SCOL)* преподава́тель(ница) *m(f)*; (: *private tutor*) репети́тор; **~ial** [tju:'tɔ:rɪəl] *n (SCOL)* семина́р

TV *n abbr* (= **television**) ТВ

tweed [twi:d] *n* твид

twelfth [twelfθ] *adj* двена́дцатый

twelve [twelv] *n* двена́дцать; **at ~ (o'clock)** в двена́дцать (часо́в)

twentieth ['twentɪɪθ] *adj* двадца́тый

twenty ['twentɪ] *n* два́дцать

twice [twaɪs] *adv* два́жды; **~ as much** вдво́е бо́льше

twig [twɪg] *n* сучо́к

twilight ['twaɪlaɪt] *n (evening)* су́мерки *mpl*

twin [twɪn] *adj (towers)* па́рный ♦ *n* близне́ц ♦ *vt*: **to be ~ned with** *(towns etc)* быть *(impf)* побрати́мами с +*instr*; **~ sister** сестра́-близне́ц; **~ brother** брат-близне́ц

twinkle ['twɪŋkl] *vi* мерца́ть *(impf)*; *(eyes)* сверка́ть *(impf)*

twist [twɪst] *n (action)* закру́чивание; *(in road, coil, flex)* вито́к; *(in story)* поворо́т ♦ *vt (turn)* изгиба́ть (изогну́ть *pf)*; *(injure: ankle etc)* выви́хивать (вы́вихнуть *pf)*; *(fig: meaning, words)* искажа́ть (искази́ть *pf)*, коверка́ть (исковерка́ть *pf)* ♦ *vi (road, river)* извива́ться *(impf)*

twitch [twɪtʃ] *n (nervous)* подёргивание

two [tu:] *n* два *m/n f* (две); **to put ~ and ~ together** *(fig)* сообража́ть (сообрази́ть *pf)* что к чему́; **~-faced** *adj (pej)* двули́чный

tycoon [taɪ'ku:n] *n*: **(business) ~** магна́т

type [taɪp] *n* тип; *(TYP)* шрифт ♦ *vt (letter etc)* печа́тать (напеча́тать *pf)*; **~writer** *n* пи́шущая маши́нка

typhoid ['taɪfɔɪd] *n* брюшно́й тиф

typhoon [taɪ'fu:n] *n* тайфу́н

typical ['tɪpɪkl] *adj*: **~ (of)** типи́чный *(для +gen)*

typing ['taɪpɪŋ] *n* маши́нопись *f*

typist ['taɪpɪst] *n* машини́стка

tyranny ['tɪrənɪ] *n* тирани́я

tyrant ['taɪərnt] *n* тира́н

tyre ['taɪə^r] *(US* **tire***) n* ши́на

tzar [zɑ:^r] *n* = **tsar**

U, u

udder ['ʌdə^r] *n* вы́мя *nt*

UFO *n abbr* (= **unidentified flying object**) НЛО

ugly ['ʌglɪ] *adj (person, dress etc)* уро́дливый, безобра́зный; *(dangerous: situation)* скве́рный

UK *n abbr* = **United Kingdom**

Ukraine [ju:'kreɪn] *n* Украи́на

Ukrainian [ju:'kreɪnɪən] *adj* украи́нский

ulcer ['ʌlsə^r] *n* я́зва

ultimata [ʌltɪ'meɪtə] *npl of* **ultimatum**

ultimate ['ʌltɪmət] *adj (final)* оконча́тельный, коне́чный; *(greatest)* преде́льный; **~ly** *adv* в коне́чном ито́ге; *(basically)* в преде́льном счёте

ultimatum [ʌltɪ'meɪtəm] *(pl* **~s** *or* **ultimata***) n* ультима́тум

ultraviolet ['ʌltrə'vaɪəlɪt] *adj (light etc)* ультрафиоле́товый

umbrella [ʌm'brelə] *n (for rain, sun)* зонт, зо́нтик

umpire ['ʌmpaɪə^r] *n* судья́ *m*, рефери́ *m ind*

UN *n abbr* = **United Nations**

nable [ʌnˈeɪbl] *adj* неспособный;
he is ~ to pay он неспособен
заплатить

naccompanied [ʌnəˈkʌmpənɪd]
adj (child, bag) без
сопровождения

naccustomed [ʌnəˈkʌstəmd] *adj*:
he is ~ to ... он непривычен к
+*dat* ...

nanimous [juːˈnænɪməs] *adj*
единодушный

narmed [ʌnˈɑːmd] *adj*
безоружный

nashamed [ʌnəˈʃeɪmd] *adj*
бесстыдный

nassuming [ʌnəˈsjuːmɪŋ] *adj*
непритязательный

nattached [ʌnəˈtætʃt] *adj* (person)
одинокий

nattractive [ʌnəˈtræktɪv] *adj*
непривлекательный

unauthorized [ʌnˈɔːθəraɪzd] *adj*
неразрешённый; (actions)
несанкционированный

unavoidable [ʌnəˈvɔɪdəbl] *adj*
(delay) неизбежный

unaware [ʌnəˈweəᵊ] *adj*: **to be ~ of**
не подозревать (*impf*) о +*prp*; (fail
to notice) не осознавать (*impf*)

unbalanced [ʌnˈbælənst] *adj*
(report) несбалансированный;
(person) неуравновешенный

unbearable [ʌnˈbeərəbl] *adj*
невыносимый

unbeatable [ʌnˈbiːtəbl] *adj* (price,
quality) непревзойдённый

unbelievable [ʌnbɪˈliːvəbl] *adj*
невероятный

unbias(s)ed [ʌnˈbaɪəst] *adj* (report)
непредвзятый; (person)
беспристрастный

unbroken [ʌnˈbrəukən] *adj* (silence)
непрерывный; (series)
непрерывный; (SPORT, record)
непобитый

uncanny [ʌnˈkænɪ] *adj* (resemblance,

knack) необъяснимый; (silence)
жуткий

uncertain [ʌnˈsəːtn] *adj* (unsure): ~
about неуверенный
относительно +*gen*; **in no ~ terms**
без обиняков, вполне
определённо; **~ty** *n* (not knowing)
неопределённость f; (often pl:
doubt) сомнение

unchanged [ʌnˈtʃeɪndʒd] *adj*
(orders, habits) неизменный

unchecked [ʌnˈtʃekt] *adv*
беспрепятственно

uncle [ˈʌŋkl] *n* дядя *m*

uncomfortable [ʌnˈkʌmfətəbl] *adj*
неудобный; (unpleasant)
гнетущий

uncommon [ʌnˈkɔmən] *adj* (rare,
unusual) необычный

uncompromising [ʌnˈkɔmprə-
maɪzɪŋ] *adj* бескомпромиссный

unconditional [ʌnkənˈdɪʃənl] *adj*
(acceptance, obedience)
безусловный; (discharge,
surrender) безоговорочный

unconscious [ʌnˈkɔnʃəs] *adj* без
сознания; (unaware): ~ **of** не
сознающий +*gen*; ~**ly** *adv*
(unawares) подсознательно

uncontrollable [ʌnkənˈtrəuləbl] *adj*
(child, animal) неуправляемый;
(laughter) неудержимый

unconventional [ʌnkənˈvenʃənl]
adj нетрадиционный

uncover [ʌnˈkʌvəᵊ] *vt* открывать
(открыть *pf*); (plot, secret)
раскрывать (раскрыть *pf*)

undecided [ʌndɪˈsaɪdɪd] *adj* (person)
колеблющийся; **he is ~ as to
whether he will go** он не решил
пойдёт ли он

undeniable [ʌndɪˈnaɪəbl] *adj* (fact,
evidence) неоспоримый

under [ˈʌndəᵊ] *adv* (go, fly etc) вниз
♦ *prep* (position) под +*instr*; (motion)
под +*acc*; (less than: cost, pay)

ме́ньше +gen; (according to) по +dat; (during) при +prp; **children ~ 16** де́ти до 16-ти лет; **~ there** там внизу́; **~ repair** в ремо́нте

undercover [ʌndəˈkʌvəʳ] adj та́йный

underestimate [ˈʌndərˈestɪmeɪt] vt недооце́нивать (недооцени́ть pf)

undergo [ʌndəˈɡəu] (irreg) vt (repair) проходи́ть (пройти́ pf); (operation) переноси́ть (перенести́ pf); (change) претерпева́ть (претерпе́ть pf)

undergraduate [ʌndəˈɡrædjuɪt] n студе́нт(ка)

underground [ˈʌndəɡraund] adv (work) под землёй ♦ adj (car park) подзе́мный; (activities) подпо́льный ♦ n: **the ~** (BRIT : RAIL) метро́ nt ind (POL) подпо́лье

underline [ʌndəˈlaɪn] vt подчёркивать (подчеркну́ть pf)

undermine [ʌndəˈmaɪn] vt (authority) подрыва́ть (подорва́ть pf)

underneath [ʌndəˈniːθ] adv внизу́ ♦ prep (position) под +instr; (motion) под +acc

underpants [ˈʌndəpænts] npl (men's) трусы́ pl

underprivileged [ʌndəˈprɪvɪlɪdʒd] adj (family) неиму́щий

understand [ʌndəˈstænd] (irreg: like **stand**) vt понима́ть (поня́ть pf); (believe): **to ~ that** полага́ть (impf), что; **~able** adj поня́тный; **~ing** adj понима́ющий ♦ n понима́ние; (agreement) договорённость f

understatement [ˈʌndəsteɪtmənt] n: **that's an ~!** э́то сли́шком мя́гко ска́зано!

understood [ʌndəˈstud] pt, pp of **understand** ♦ adj (agreed) согласо́ванный; (implied) подразумева́емый

undertake [ʌndəˈteɪk] (irreg: like **take**) vt (task, duty) брать (взять pf) на себя́; **to ~ to do** обя́зываться (обяза́ться pf) +infin

undertaker [ˈʌndəteɪkəʳ] n владе́лец похоро́нного бюро́

underwater [ʌndəˈwɔːtəʳ] adv под водо́й ♦ adj подво́дный

underwear [ˈʌndəwɛəʳ] n ни́жнее бельё

underworld [ˈʌndəwəːld] n (of crime) престу́пный мир

undesirable [ʌndɪˈzaɪərəbl] adj нежела́тельный

undisputed [ˈʌndɪsˈpjuːtɪd] adj неоспори́мый

undo [ʌnˈduː] (irreg: like **do**) vt (laces, strings) развя́зывать (развяза́ть pf); (buttons) расстёгивать (расстегну́ть pf); (spoil) губи́ть (погуби́ть pf)

undoubted [ʌnˈdautɪd] adj несомне́нный, бесспо́рный; **~ly** adv несомне́нно, бесспо́рно

undress [ʌnˈdrɛs] vt раздева́ть (разде́ть pf) ♦ vi раздева́ться (разде́ться pf)

undue [ʌnˈdjuː] adj изли́шний

undulating [ˈʌndjuleɪtɪŋ] adj волни́стый

unduly [ʌnˈduːlɪ] adv изли́шне

uneasy [ʌnˈiːzɪ] adj (feeling) трево́жный; (peace, truce) напряжённый; **he is** or **feels ~** он неспоко́ен

uneducated [ʌnˈedjukeɪtɪd] adj необразо́ванный

unemployed [ʌnɪmˈplɔɪd] adj безрабо́тный ♦ npl: **the ~** безрабо́тные pl adj

unemployment [ʌnɪmˈplɔɪmənt] n безрабо́тица

unending [ʌnˈendɪŋ] adj несконча́емый

uneven [ʌnˈiːvn] adj неро́вный

unexpected [ʌnɪksˈpektɪd] adj

неожи́данный; **~ly** *adv*
неожи́данно

unfair [ʌn'feəʳ] *adj*: **~ (to)**
несправедли́вый (к +*dat*)

unfaithful [ʌn'feɪθful] *adj*
неве́рный

unfamiliar [ʌnfə'mɪlɪəʳ] *adj*
незнако́мый

unfashionable [ʌn'fæʃnəbl] (US
unfavorable) *adj*
немо́дный

unfavourable [ʌn'feɪvrəbl] (US
unfavorable) *adj*
неблагоприя́тный

unfinished [ʌn'fɪnɪʃt] *adj*
незако́нченный

unfit [ʌn'fɪt] *adj* (*physically*): **she is ~**
она́ в плохо́й спорти́вной
фо́рме; **he is ~ for the job** он
неприго́ден для э́той рабо́ты

unfold [ʌn'fəuld] *vt* (*sheets, map*)
развора́чивать (разверну́ть *pf*)
♦ *vi* (*situation*) развора́чиваться
(разверну́ться *pf*)

unforeseen ['ʌnfɔ:'si:n] *adj*
непредви́денный

unforgettable [ʌnfə'gɛtəbl] *adj*
незабыва́емый

unforgivable [ʌnfə'gɪvəbl] *adj*
непрости́тельный

unfortunate [ʌn'fɔ:tʃənət] *adj*
(*unlucky*) несча́стный; (*regrettable*)
неуда́чный; **~ly** *adv* к сожале́нию

unfounded [ʌn'faundɪd] *adj*
необосно́ванный

unfriendly [ʌn'frɛndlɪ] *adj*
недружелю́бный

ungrateful [ʌn'greɪtful] *adj*
неблагода́рный

unhappy [ʌn'hæpɪ] *adj*
несча́стный; **~ with** (*dissatisfied*)
недово́льный +*instr*

unharmed [ʌn'hɑ:md] *adj* (*person*)
невреди́мый

unhealthy [ʌn'hɛlθɪ] *adj*
нездоро́вый

unhurt [ʌn'hə:t] *adj* невреди́мый

unidentified [ʌnaɪ'dɛntɪfaɪd] *adj*
(*unnamed*) анони́мный; *see also*
UFO

uniform ['ju:nɪfɔ:m] *n* фо́рма ♦ *adj*
(*length, width*) единообра́зный;
(*temperature*) постоя́нный

unilateral [ju:nɪ'lætərəl] *adj*
(*disarmament etc*) односторо́нний

uninhabited [ʌnɪn'hæbɪtɪd] *adj*
необита́емый

unintentional [ʌnɪn'tɛnʃənəl] *adj*
неумы́шленный

union ['ju:njən] *n* (*unification*)
объедине́ние; (*also*: **trade ~**)
профсою́з ♦ *cpd* профсою́зный

unique [ju:'ni:k] *adj* уника́льный

unison ['ju:nɪsn] *n*: **in ~** (*say*) в
оди́н го́лос; (*sing*) в унисо́н

unit ['ju:nɪt] *n* (*single whole*) це́лое
nt adj; (*measurement*) едини́ца;
(*section: of furniture etc*) се́кция

unite [ju:'naɪt] *vt* объедини́ть
(объедини́ть *pf*) ♦ *vi*
объедини́ться (объедини́ться
pf); **~d** *adj* объединённый; (*effort*)
совме́стный; **United Kingdom** *n*
Соединённое Короле́вство;
United Nations (Organization)
n (Организа́ция) Объединённых
На́ций; **United States (of
America)** *n* Соединённые
Шта́ты (Аме́рики)

unity ['ju:nɪtɪ] *n* еди́нство

universal [ju:nɪ'və:sl] *adj*
универса́льный

universe ['ju:nɪvə:s] *n* вселе́нная *f
adj*

university [ju:nɪ'və:sɪtɪ] *n*
университе́т

unjust [ʌn'dʒʌst] *adj*
несправедли́вый

unkind [ʌn'kaɪnd] *adj* недо́брый;
(*behaviour*) зло́бный

unknown [ʌn'nəun] *adj*
неизве́стный

unlawful [ʌn'lɔ:ful] *adj*

незако́нный

unleash [ʌn'liːʃ] *vt* (*fig: feeling*) дава́ть (дать *pf*) во́лю +*dat*; (: *force*) развя́зывать (развяза́ть *pf*)

unless [ʌn'lɛs] *conj* е́сли не; **he won't come, ~ we ask** он не придёт, е́сли мы не попро́сим

unlike [ʌn'laɪk] *adj* (*not alike*) непохо́жий ♦ *prep* (*different from*) в отли́чие от +*gen*; **he is ~ his brother** (*not like*) он не похо́ж на бра́та

unlikely [ʌn'laɪklɪ] *adj* (*not likely*) малове́роятный

unlimited [ʌn'lɪmɪtɪd] *adj* неограни́ченный

unload [ʌn'ləud] *vt* (*box, car*) разгружа́ть (разгрузи́ть *pf*)

unlucky [ʌn'lʌkɪ] *adj* невезу́чий; (*object*) несчастли́вый; **he is ~ on** невезу́чий, ему́ не везёт

unmarried [ʌn'mærɪd] *adj* (*man*) нежена́тый, холосто́й; (*woman*) незаму́жняя

unmistak(e)able [ʌnmɪs'teɪkəbl] *adj* (*voice, sound*) характе́рный

unnatural [ʌn'nætʃrəl] *adj* неесте́ственный

unnecessary [ʌn'nɛsəsərɪ] *adj* нену́жный

unnoticed [ʌn'nəutɪst] *adj* незаме́ченный

UNO *n abbr* (= *United Nations Organization*) ООН

unobtrusive [ʌnəb'truːsɪv] *adj* (*person*) ненавя́зчивый

unofficial [ʌnə'fɪʃl] *adj* неофициа́льный

unorthodox [ʌn'ɔːθədɔks] *adj* (*also REL*) неортодокса́льный

unpack [ʌn'pæk] *vi* распако́вываться (распакова́ться *pf*) ♦ *vt* распако́вывать (распакова́ть *pf*)

unparalleled [ʌn'pærəleld] *adj*

непревзойдённый; (*crisis*) небыва́лый

unpleasant [ʌn'plɛznt] *adj* неприя́тный

unpopular [ʌn'pɔpjuləʳ] *adj* непопуля́рный

unprecedented [ʌn'prɛsɪdəntɪd] *adj* беспрецеде́нтный

unpredictable [ʌnprɪ'dɪktəbl] *adj* непредсказу́емый

unprofessional [ʌnprə'fɛʃənl] *adj* непрофессиона́льный

unqualified [ʌn'kwɔlɪfaɪd] *adj* неквалифици́рованный; (*total*) соверше́нный

unravel [ʌn'rævl] *vt* (*fig: mystery*) разга́дывать (разгада́ть *pf*)

unreal [ʌn'rɪəl] *adj* (*not real*) нереа́льный

unrealistic ['ʌnrɪə'lɪstɪk] *adj* нереалисти́чный

unreasonable [ʌn'riːznəbl] *adj* неразу́мный; (*length of time*) нереа́льный

unrelated [ʌnrɪ'leɪtɪd] *adj* (*incident*) изоли́рованный, отде́льный; **to be ~** (*people*) не состоя́ть (*impf*) в родстве́

unreliable [ʌnrɪ'laɪəbl] *adj* ненадёжный

unrest [ʌn'rɛst] *n* волне́ния *ntpl*

unruly [ʌn'ruːlɪ] *adj* неуправля́емый

unsafe [ʌn'seɪf] *adj* опа́сный

unsatisfactory ['ʌnsætɪs'fæktərɪ] *adj* неудовлетвори́тельный

unscathed [ʌn'skeɪðd] *adj* невреди́мый

unscrupulous [ʌn'skruːpjuləs] *adj* бессо́вестный, беспринци́пный

unsettled [ʌn'sɛtld] *adj* (*person*) беспоко́йный; **the weather is ~** пого́да не установи́лась

unshaven [ʌn'ʃeɪvn] *adj* небри́тый

unsightly [ʌn'saɪtlɪ] *adj* непригля́дный

nskilled [ʌnˈskɪld] adj
неквалифици́рованный

nstable [ʌnˈsteɪbl] adj (government) нестаби́льный; (person: mentally) неуравнове́шенный

nsteady [ʌnˈstedɪ] adj нетвёрдый

nsuccessful [ʌnsəkˈsesful] adj (attempt) безуспе́шный; (writer) неуда́вшийся; **to be ~ (in sth)** терпе́ть (потерпе́ть pf) неуда́чу (в чём-н); **your application was ~** Ва́ше заявле́ние не при́нято; **~ly** adv безуспе́шно

nsuitable [ʌnˈsuːtəbl] adj неподходя́щий

nsure [ʌnˈʃuəʳ] adj неуве́ренный; **he is ~ of himself** он неуве́рен в себе́

nsuspecting [ʌnsəsˈpektɪŋ] adj ничего́ не подозрева́ющий

nsympathetic [ˈʌnsɪmpəˈθetɪk] adj безуча́стный

nthinkable [ʌnˈθɪŋkəbl] adj немы́слимый

ntidy [ʌnˈtaɪdɪ] adj неопря́тный

until [ənˈtɪl] prep до +gen ♦ conj пока́ не; **~ he comes** пока́ он не придёт; **~ now/then** до сих/тех пор

untimely [ʌnˈtaɪmlɪ] adj (moment) неподходя́щий; (arrival) неуме́стный; (death) безвре́менный

untold [ʌnˈtəuld] adj (joy, suffering) несказа́нный

unused¹ [ʌnˈjuːzd] adj (not used) неиспо́льзованный

unused² [ʌnˈjuːst] adj: **he is ~ to it** он к э́тому не привы́к; **she is ~ to flying** она́ не привы́кла лета́ть

unusual [ʌnˈjuːʒuəl] adj необы́чный; (exceptional) необыкнове́нный

unveil [ʌnˈveɪl] vt (statue) открыва́ть (откры́ть pf)

unwanted [ʌnˈwɒntɪd] adj (child,

pregnancy) нежела́нный

unwavering [ʌnˈweɪvərɪŋ] adj (faith) непоколеби́мый; (gaze) твёрдый

unwelcome [ʌnˈwelkəm] adj (guest) незва́ный, непро́шеный; (news) неприя́тный

unwell [ʌnˈwel] adj: **to feel ~** чу́вствовать (impf) себя́ пло́хо; **he is ~** он пло́хо себя́ чу́вствует, он нездоро́в

unwilling [ʌnˈwɪlɪŋ] adj: **to be ~ to do sth** не хоте́ть (impf) +infin

unwind [ʌnˈwaɪnd] (irreg: like **wind²**) vi (relax) расслабля́ться (рассла́биться pf)

unwise [ʌnˈwaɪz] adj неблагоразу́мный

unwitting [ʌnˈwɪtɪŋ] adj нево́льный

unworthy [ʌnˈwəːðɪ] adj недосто́йный

KEYWORD

up [ʌp] prep (motion) на +acc; (position) на +prp; **he went up the stairs/the hill** он подня́лся по ле́стнице/на́ гору; **the cat was up a tree** ко́шка была́ на де́реве; **they live further up this street** они́ живу́т да́льше на э́той у́лице; **he has gone up to Scotland** он пое́хал в Шотла́ндию
♦ adv 1 (upwards, higher): **up in the sky/the mountains** высоко́ в не́бе/в гора́х; **put the picture a bit higher up** пове́сьте карти́ну повы́ше; **up there** (up above) там наверху́
2: **to be up** (out of bed) встава́ть (встать pf); (prices, level) поднима́ться (подня́ться pf); **the tent is up** пала́тка устано́влена
3: **up to** (as far as) до +gen; **up to now** до сих пор

4: to be up to (*depending on*)
зави́сеть (*impf*) от +*gen*; **it's not
up to me to decide** не мне
реша́ть; **it's up to you** э́то на
Ва́ше усмотре́ние

5: to be up to (*inf: be doing*)
затева́ть (*impf*); (*be satisfactory*)
соотве́тствовать (*impf*) +*dat*,
отвеча́ть (*impf*) +*dat*; **he's not up
to the job** он не справля́ется с
э́той рабо́той; **his work is not up
to the required standard** его́
рабо́та не соотве́тствует
тре́буемым станда́ртам; **what's
she up to these days?** а что она́
тепе́рь поде́лывает?

♦ *n*: **ups and downs** (*in life, career*)
взлёты *mpl* и паде́ния *ntpl*

upbringing [ˈʌpbrɪŋɪŋ] *n*
воспита́ние

update [ʌpˈdeɪt] *vt* (*records*)
обновля́ть (обнови́ть *pf*)

upgrade [ʌpˈɡreɪd] *vt* (*house,
equipment*) модернизи́ровать
(*impf/pf*); (*employee*) повыша́ть
(повы́сить *pf*; **в до́лжности**)

upheaval [ʌpˈhiːvl] *n* переворо́т

uphill [ʌpˈhɪl] *adj* (*fig*) тяжёлый,
напряжённый ♦ *adv* вверх; **to go
~** поднима́ться (подня́ться *pf*) в
го́ру

uphold [ʌpˈhəuld] (*irreg: like* **hold**)
vt подде́рживать (поддержа́ть
pf)

upholstery [ʌpˈhəulstəri] *n* оби́вка

upkeep [ˈʌpkiːp] *n* содержа́ние

upon [əˈpɔn] *prep* (*position*) на +*prp*;
(*motion*) на +*acc*

upper [ˈʌpəʳ] *adj* ве́рхний ♦ *n* верх;
~most *adj* ве́рхний; **what was
~most in my mind** что бо́льше
всего́ занима́ло мои́ мы́сли

upright [ˈʌpraɪt] *adj* (*vertical*)
вертика́льный; (*honest*)
безупре́чный

uprising [ˈʌpraɪzɪŋ] *n* восста́ние

uproar [ˈʌprɔːʳ] *n* (*protest*)
возмуще́ние; (*shouts*) го́мон,
кри́ки *mpl*

upset *vb, adj* [ʌpˈset] *n* [ˈʌpset] (*irreg:
like* **set**) *vt* (*glass etc*)
опроки́дывать (опроки́нуть *pf*);
(*routine*) наруша́ть (нару́шить *pf*);
(*person, plan*) расстра́ивать
(расстро́ить *pf*) ♦ *adj*
расстро́енный ♦ *n*: **I have a
stomach ~** (*BRIT*) у меня́
расстро́йство желу́дка

upside down [ˈʌpsaɪd-] *adv* (*hang,
hold*) вверх нога́ми; (*turn*) вверх
дном

upstairs [ʌpˈstɛəz] *adv* (*be*)
наверху́; (*go*) наве́рх ♦ *adj*
ве́рхний ♦ *n* ве́рхний эта́ж

upstream [ʌpˈstriːm] *adv* про́тив
тече́ния

uptight [ʌpˈtaɪt] *adj* (*inf*)
натя́нутый

up-to-date [ˈʌptəˈdeɪt] *adj*
(*information*) после́дний;
(*equipment*) нове́йший

upturn [ˈʌptəːn] *n* (*ECON*) подъём

upward [ˈʌpwəd] *adj*:
movement/glance движе́ние/
взгляд вверх ♦ *adv* = **upwards**;
~s *adv* вверх; (*more than*): **~s of**
свы́ше +*gen*

uranium [juəˈreɪnɪəm] *n* ура́н

urban [ˈəːbən] *adj* городско́й

urge [əːdʒ] *n* потре́бность *f* ♦ *vt*: **to
~ sb to do** настоя́тельно проси́ть
(попроси́ть *pf*) кого́-н +*infin*

urgency [ˈəːdʒənsɪ] *n* (*of task etc*)
неотло́жность *f*; (*of tone*)
насто́йчивость *f*

urgent [ˈəːdʒənt] *adj* (*message*)
сро́чный; (*need*) насу́щный,
неотло́жный; (*voice*)
насто́йчивый

urinate [ˈjuərɪneɪt] *vi* мочи́ться
(помочи́ться *pf*)

urine ['juərın] n моча́

urn [əːn] n (also: **tea ~**) тита́н

Uruguay ['juərəgwaı] n Уругва́й

US n abbr (= United States) США

us [ʌs] pron (direct) нас; (indirect) нам; (after prep: +gen, +prp) нас; (: +dat) нам; (: +instr) на́ми; **a few of ~** не́которые из нас; see also **me**

USA n abbr (= United States of America) США

use vb [juːz] n [juːs] vt (object, tool) по́льзоваться (impf) +instr, испо́льзовать (impf/pf); (phrase) употребля́ть (употреби́ть pf) ♦ n (using) испо́льзование, употребле́ние; (usefulness) по́льза; (purpose) примене́ние; **she ~d to do it** она́ когда́-то занима́лась э́тим; **what's this ~d for?** для чего́ э́то испо́льзуется?; **to be ~d to** привы́кнуть (pf) к +dat; **to be in ~** употребля́ться (impf), быть (impf) в употребле́нии; **to be out of ~** не употребля́ться (impf); **of ~** поле́зный; **it's no ~** (э́то) бесполе́зно; **~ up** vt (food) расхо́довать (израсхо́довать pf); **~d** [juːzd] adj (car) поде́ржанный; **~ful** ['juːsful] adj поле́зный; **~fulness** ['juːsfəlnɪs] n по́льза; **~less** ['juːslɪs] adj (unusable) непригодный; (pointless) бесполе́зный; **~r** ['juːzə'] n по́льзователь m; **~r-friendly** ['juːzə'frendlɪ] adj просто́й в испо́льзовании

USSR n abbr (formerly: = Union of Soviet Socialist Republics) СССР

usual ['juːʒual] adj (time, place etc) обы́чный; **as ~** как обы́чно; **~ly** adv обы́чно

utensil [juː'tensl] n инструме́нт; (for cooking) принадле́жность f

utility [juː'tɪlɪtɪ] n: **public utilities**

коммуна́льные услу́ги fpl

utilize ['juːtılaız] vt утилизи́ровать (impf/pf)

utmost ['ʌtməust] adj велича́йший ♦ n: **to do one's ~** де́лать (сде́лать pf) всё возмо́жное

utter ['ʌtə'] adj (amazement) по́лный; (conviction) глубо́кий; (rubbish) соверше́нный ♦ vt (words) произноси́ть (произнести́ pf); **~ly** adv соверше́нно

U-turn ['juː'təːn] n (AUT) разворо́т на 180 гра́дусов

V, v

vacancy ['veɪkənsɪ] n (BRIT: job) вака́нсия; (room) свобо́дный но́мер

vacant ['veɪkənt] adj (room, seat) свобо́дный; (look) пусто́й

vacation [və'keɪʃən] n (esp US: holiday) о́тпуск; (BRIT: SCOL) кани́кулы pl

vaccinate ['væksɪneɪt] vt: **to ~ sb (against sth)** де́лать (сде́лать pf) приви́вку кому́-н (от чего́-н)

vaccine ['væksiːn] n вакци́на

vacuum ['vækjum] n (empty space) ва́куум ♦ vt пылесо́сить (пропылесо́сить pf); **~ cleaner** n пылесо́с

vagina [və'dʒaɪnə] n влага́лище

vague [veɪg] adj (blurred: memory, outline) сму́тный; (look) рассе́янный; (idea, instructions, answer) неопределённый; **he was ~ about it** он не сказа́л ничего́ определённого об э́том; **~ly** adv (say) неопределённо; (look) рассе́янно; (suspect) сму́тно; (slightly) слегка́

vain [veɪn] adj (useless) тще́тный; (person) тщесла́вный; **in ~** тще́тно, напра́сно

valid ['vælɪd] adj (ticket, document) действи́тельный; (reason, argument) ве́ский; **~ity** [və'lɪdɪtɪ] n (see adj) действи́тельность f; ве́скость f

valley ['vælɪ] n доли́на

valuable ['væljuəbl] adj це́нный; (time) драгоце́нный; **~s** npl (jewellery etc) це́нности fpl

valuation [vælju'eɪʃən] n оце́нка

value ['vælju:] n це́нность f ♦ vt оце́нивать (оцени́ть pf); (appreciate) цени́ть (impf); **~s** npl (principles) це́нности fpl; **~d** (customer, advice) це́нный

valve [vælv] n (also MED) кла́пан

vampire ['væmpaɪə²] n вампи́р

van [væn] n (AUT) фурго́н

vandalism ['vændəlɪzəm] n вандали́зм

vanilla [və'nɪlə] n вани́ль f

vanish ['vænɪʃ] vi исчеза́ть (исче́знуть pf)

vanity ['vænɪtɪ] n тщесла́вие

vapour ['veɪpə²] (US **vapor**) n пар

variable ['veərɪəbl] adj (likely to change) изме́нчивый; (able to be changed: speed) переме́нный

variation [veərɪ'eɪʃən] n (change) измене́ние; (different form) вариа́ция

varied ['veərɪd] adj разнообра́зный

variety [və'raɪətɪ] n разнообра́зие; (type) разнови́дность f

various ['veərɪəs] adj (different, several) разли́чный

varnish ['vɑːnɪʃ] n (product) лак; (also: **nail ~**) лак для ногте́й ♦ vt (wood, table) лакирова́ть (отлакирова́ть pf); (nails) кра́сить (покра́сить pf)

vary ['veərɪ] vt разнообра́зить (impf) ♦ vi (sizes, colours) различа́ться (impf); (become different): **to ~ with** (weather etc) меня́ться (impf) в зави́симости от

+gen

vase [vɑːz] n ва́за

vast [vɑːst] adj (knowledge, area) обши́рный; (expense) грома́дный

VAT [væt] n abbr (BRIT: = value-added tax) НДС

vat [væt] n ка́дка

Vatican ['vætɪkən] n: **the ~** Ватика́н

vault [vɔːlt] n (tomb) склеп; (in bank) сейф, храни́лище ♦ vt (also: **~ over**) перепры́гивать (перепры́гнуть pf) (че́рез +acc)

VCR n abbr = **video cassette recorder**

veal [viːl] n (CULIN) теля́тина

veer [vɪə²] vi (vehicle) свора́чивать (сверну́ть pf); (wind) меня́ть (поменя́ть pf) направле́ние

vegetable ['vedʒtəbl] n (BOT) о́вощ ♦ adj (oil etc) расти́тельный; (dish) овощно́й

vegetarian [vedʒɪ'teərɪən] n вегетариа́нец(-нка) ♦ adj вегетариа́нский

vegetation [vedʒɪ'teɪʃən] n (plants) расти́тельность f

vehement ['viːɪmənt] adj (attack, denial) я́ростный, гне́вный

vehicle ['viːɪkl] n автотра́нспортное сре́дство; (fig) сре́дство, ору́дие

veil [veɪl] n вуа́ль f

vein [veɪn] n (of leaf) жи́лка; (ANAT) ве́на; (of ore) жи́ла

velocity [vɪ'lɒsɪtɪ] n ско́рость f

velvet ['velvɪt] n ба́рхат ♦ adj ба́рхатный

vendor ['vendə²] n: **street ~** у́личный(-ая) торго́вец(-вка)

veneer [və'nɪə²] n (on furniture) фане́рка

vengeance ['vendʒəns] n мще́ние, возме́здие; **with a ~** (fig) отча́янно

venison ['venɪsn] n олени́на

venom ['venəm] n (also fig) яд

vent [vent] n (also: **air ~**) вентиляцио́нное отве́рстие ♦ vt (fig) дава́ть (дать pf) вы́ход +dat

ventilate ['ventɪleɪt] vt (room, building) прове́тривать (прове́трить pf)

ventilation [ventɪ'leɪʃən] n вентиля́ция

ventilator ['ventɪleɪtə'] n вентиля́тор

venture ['ventʃə'] n предприя́тие ♦ vt (opinion) осме́ливаться (осме́литься pf) на +acc ♦ vi осме́ливаться (осме́литься pf); **business ~** предприя́тие

venue ['venjuː] n ме́сто проведе́ния

veranda(h) [və'rændə] n вера́нда

verb [vɜːb] n глаго́л

verbal ['vɜːbl] adj (spoken) у́стный

verdict ['vɜːdɪkt] n (LAW) верди́кт; (fig: opinion) заключе́ние

verge [vɜːdʒ] n (BRIT: of road) обо́чина; **to be on the ~ of sth** быть (impf) на гра́ни чего́-н

verify ['verɪfaɪ] vt (confirm) подтвержда́ть (подтверди́ть pf); (check) сверя́ть (све́рить pf)

veritable ['verɪtəbl] adj и́стинный, су́щий

vermin ['vɜːmɪn] npl вреди́тели mpl

versatile ['vɜːsətaɪl] adj (person) разносторо́нний; (substance, machine etc) универса́льный

verse [vɜːs] n (poetry, in Bible) стих; (part of poem) строфа́

version ['vɜːʃən] n (form) вариа́нт; (account: of events) ве́рсия

versus ['vɜːsəs] prep про́тив +gen

vertical ['vɜːtɪkl] adj вертика́льный

vertigo ['vɜːtɪgəu] n головокруже́ние

verve [vɜːv] n воодушевле́ние

very ['verɪ] adv о́чень ♦ adj са́мый;

the **~ book which ...** та са́мая кни́га, кото́рая ...; **thank you ~ much** большо́е (Вам) спаси́бо; **~ much better** гора́здо лу́чше; **I ~ much hope so** я о́чень наде́юсь; the **~ last** са́мый после́дний; **at the ~ least** как ми́нимум

vessel ['vesl] n су́дно; (bowl) сосу́д; **blood ~** кровено́сный сосу́д

vest [vest] n (BRIT: underwear) ма́йка; (US: waistcoat) жиле́т

vet [vet] n abbr (BRIT: = veterinary surgeon) ветерина́р ♦ vt (check) проверя́ть (прове́рить pf); (approve) одобря́ть (одо́брить pf)

veteran ['vetərn] n (of war) ветера́н

veterinary ['vetrɪnərɪ] adj ветерина́рный

veto ['viːtəu] (pl **~es**) n ве́то nt ind ♦ vt (POL, LAW) налага́ть (наложи́ть pf) ве́то на +acc

vetting ['vetɪŋ] n прове́рка

via ['vaɪə] prep че́рез +acc

viable ['vaɪəbl] adj жизнеспосо́бный

viaduct ['vaɪədʌkt] n виаду́к

vibrant ['vaɪbrnt] adj (lively) жизнера́достный; (light) я́ркий; (colour) со́чный; (voice) стра́стный

vibrate [vaɪ'breɪt] vi вибри́ровать (impf)

vibration [vaɪ'breɪʃən] n вибра́ция

vicar ['vɪkə'] n (REL) прихо́дский свяще́нник

vice [vaɪs] n поро́к; (TECH) тиски́ pl

vice-chairman [vaɪs'tʃeəmən] (irreg) n замести́тель m председа́теля

vice president n ви́це-президе́нт

vice versa ['vaɪsɪ'vɜːsə] adv наоборо́т

vicinity [vɪ'sɪnɪtɪ] n: **in the ~ (of)** вблизи́ (от +gen)

vicious ['vɪʃəs] adj (attack, blow)

жесто́кий; (words, look, dog) злой;
~ **circle** n поро́чный круг
victim ['vɪktɪm] n же́ртва
victor ['vɪktə'] n победи́тель(ница)
m(f)
victorious [vɪk'tɔːrɪəs] adj (team)
победоно́сный; (shout)
победный
victory ['vɪktərɪ] n побе́да
video ['vɪdɪəu] cpd ви́део ind ♦ n
(also: ~ **film**) видеофи́льм; (also:
~ **cassette**) видеокассе́та; (also:
~ **cassette recorder**)
видеомагнитофо́н; (also: ~
camera) видеока́мера; ~ **game**
n видеоигра́; ~ **recorder** n
видеомагнитофо́н; ~ **tape** n
видеоле́нта
vie [vaɪ] vi: to ~ with sb/for sth
состяза́ться (impf) с кем-н/в
чём-н
Vienna [vɪ'ɛnə] n Ве́на
view [vjuː] n (sight, outlook) вид;
(opinion) взгляд ♦ vt
рассма́тривать (рассмотре́ть pf);
in full ~ **(of)** на виду́ (у +gen); **in** ~
of the bad weather/the fact that
ввиду́ плохо́й пого́ды/того́, что;
in my ~ на мой взгляд; ~
(person) зри́тель(ница) m(f);
~**finder** n (PHOT) видоиска́тель
m; ~**point** n (attitude) то́чка
зре́ния; (place) ме́сто обозре́ния
vigil ['vɪdʒɪl] n бде́ние; ~**ant** adj
бди́тельный
vigor ['vɪgə'] (US) n = **vigour**
vigorous ['vɪgərəs] adj (action,
campaign) энерги́чный
vigour ['vɪgə'] (US **vigor**) n си́ла,
мощь f
vile [vaɪl] adj гну́сный,
омерзи́тельный
villa ['vɪlə] n ви́лла
village ['vɪlɪdʒ] n дере́вня
villain ['vɪlən] n (in novel etc)
злоде́й; (BRIT: criminal)

престу́пник
vindicate ['vɪndɪkeɪt] vt (actions)
опра́вдывать (оправда́ть pf);
(person) реабилити́ровать (impf/
pf)
vine [vaɪn] n (with grapes)
(виногра́дная) лоза́
vinegar ['vɪnɪgə'] n у́ксус
vineyard ['vɪnjɑːd] n виногра́дник
vintage ['vɪntɪdʒ] cpd (comedy,
performance etc) класси́ческий;
(wine) ма́рочный
vinyl ['vaɪnl] n вини́л
viola [vɪ'əulə] n (MUS) альт
violation [vaɪə'leɪʃən] n (of
agreement etc) наруше́ние
violence ['vaɪələns] n (brutality)
наси́лие
violent ['vaɪələnt] adj (behaviour)
жесто́кий; (death)
наси́льственный; (debate,
criticism) ожесточённый
violet ['vaɪələt] adj фиоле́товый
♦ n (plant) фиа́лка
violin [vaɪə'lɪn] n (MUS) скри́пка;
~**ist** n скрипа́ч(ка)
VIP n abbr (= very important person)
осо́бо ва́жное лицо́
virgin ['vəːdʒɪn] n де́вственница
♦ adj (snow, forest etc)
де́вственный; ~**ity** [vəː'dʒɪnɪti] n
де́вственность f
Virgo ['vəːgəu] n Де́ва
virile ['vɪraɪl] adj мужско́й
virtually ['vəːtjuəlɪ] adv
факти́чески, практи́чески
virtual reality ['vəːtjuəl-] n
(COMPUT) виртуа́льная
реа́льность f
virtue ['vəːtjuː] n (moral correctness)
доброде́тель f; (advantage)
преиму́щество; (good quality)
досто́инство; **by** ~ **of** благодаря́
+dat
virtuous ['vəːtjuəs] adj (morally
correct) доброде́тельный

virus ['vaɪərəs] n (MED) ви́рус

visa ['viːzə] n (for travel) ви́за

visibility [vɪzɪ'bɪlɪtɪ] n ви́димость f

visible ['vɪzəbl] adj (results, growth) очеви́дный; (foresight) провиде́ние, ви́дение

vision ['vɪʒən] n (sight) зре́ние; (foresight) провиде́ние, ви́дение

visit ['vɪzɪt] n посеще́ние, визи́т ♦ vt (person, place) посеща́ть (посети́ть pf); (elderly, disabled) навеща́ть (навести́ть pf); **~or** n (person visiting) гость m/f; (in public place) посети́тель(ница) m(f); (in town etc) прие́зжий(ая) m(f) adj

visual ['vɪzjuəl] adj (image) зри́тельный; **~ize** vt представля́ть (предста́вить pf)

vital ['vaɪtl] adj (question) жи́зненный; (problem) насу́щный; (full of life: person) де́ятельный, по́лный жи́зни; (organization) жизнеде́ятельный; **it is ~ ...** необходи́мо ...; **~ity** [vaɪ'tælɪtɪ] n (liveliness) жи́вость f; **~ly** adv: **~ly important** жи́зненно ва́жный

vitamin ['vɪtəmɪn] n витами́н

vivid ['vɪvɪd] adj (description, colour) я́ркий; (memory) отчётливый; (imagination) живо́й; **~ly** adv (describe) я́рко; (remember) отчётливо

vocabulary [vəu'kæbjulərɪ] n (words known) слова́рный запа́с

vocal ['vəukl] adj (articulate) речи́стый

vocation [vəu'keɪʃən] n призва́ние; **~al** adj профессиона́льный

vodka ['vɔdkə] n во́дка

vogue [vəug] n мо́да; **in ~** в мо́де

voice [vɔɪs] n го́лос ♦ vt (opinion) выска́зывать (вы́сказать pf); **~mail** n устное сообще́ние

void [vɔɪd] n (emptiness) пустота́; (hole) прова́л ♦ adj (invalid) недействи́тельный

volatile ['vɔlətaɪl] adj (situation) изме́нчивый; (person) неусто́йчивый; (liquid) лету́чий

volcanic [vɔl'kænɪk] adj вулкани́ческий

volcano [vɔl'keɪnəu] (pl **~es**) n вулка́н

volley ['vɔlɪ] n (of gunfire) залп; (of questions) град; (TENNIS etc) уда́р с лёта; **~ball** n (SPORT) волейбо́л

voltage ['vəultɪdʒ] n (ELEC) напряже́ние

volume ['vɔljuːm] n объём; (book) том; (sound level) гро́мкость f

voluntarily ['vɔləntrɪlɪ] adv доброво́льно

voluntary ['vɔləntərɪ] adj (willing) доброво́льный; (unpaid) обще́ственный

volunteer [vɔlən'tɪə] n (unpaid helper) доброво́льный помо́щник(ица), волонтёр; (to army etc) доброво́лец ♦ vi (for army etc) идти́ (пойти́ pf) доброво́льцем; **to ~ to do** вызыва́ться (вы́зваться pf) +infin

vomit ['vɔmɪt] n рво́та ♦ vi: **he ~ed** его́ вы́рвало

vote [vəut] n (indication of opinion) голосова́ние; (votes cast) число́ по́данных голосо́в; (right to vote) пра́во го́лоса ♦ vi голосова́ть (проголосова́ть pf) ♦ vt (Labour etc) голосова́ть (проголосова́ть pf) за +acc; (elect): **he was ~d chairman** он был и́збран председа́телем; (propose): **to ~ that** предлага́ть (предложи́ть pf), что́бы; **to put sth to the~, take a ~ on sth** ста́вить (поста́вить pf) что-н на голосова́ние; **~ of thanks** благода́рственная речь f; **to pass a ~ of confidence/no confidence** выража́ть (вы́разить *pf*) вóтум довéрия/недовéрия; **to ~ for** или **in favour of/against** голосовáть (проголосовáть *pf*) за +*acc*/прóтив +*gen*; **~r** *n* избирáтель(ница) *m(f)*

voting ['vəʊtɪŋ] *n* голосовáние

voucher ['vaʊtʃə^r] *n* (with petrol, cigarettes etc) вáучер

vow [vaʊ] *n* клятва ♦ *vt*: **to ~ to do/that** клясться (поклясться *pf*) +infin/, что; **~s** *npl* (REL) обéт *msg*

vowel ['vaʊəl] *n* глáсный *m adj*

voyage ['vɔɪɪdʒ] *n* (by ship) плáвание; (by spacecraft) полёт

vulgar ['vʌlgə^r] *adj* (rude) вульгáрный; (tasteless) пóшлый

vulnerable ['vʌlnərəbl] *adj* (position) уязвимый; (person) ранимый; **he is ~ to ...** он подвéржен +*dat* ...

vulture ['vʌltʃə^r] *n* (ZOOL) гриф

W, w

wad [wɔd] *n* (of cotton wool) тампóн; (of banknotes, paper) пáчка

wade [weɪd] *vi*: **to ~ through** (water) пробирáться (пробрáться *pf*) чéрез +*acc*

waft [wɔft] *vi* доноситься (донестись *pf*)

wage [weɪdʒ] *n* (also: **~s**) зарплáта ♦ *vt*: **to ~ war** вести (*impf*) войнý

wail [weɪl] *n* (of person) вопль *m* ♦ *vi* (person) вопить (*impf*); (siren) выть (*impf*)

waist [weɪst] *n* тáлия; **~coat** *n* (BRIT) жилéт

wait [weɪt] *vi* ждать (*impf*) ♦ *n* ожидáние; **to keep sb ~ing** заставлять (застáвить *pf*) когó-н ждать; **I can't ~ to go home** мне не тéрпится пойти домóй; **to ~ for sb/sth** ждать (*impf*) когó-н/ чегó-н; **we had a long ~ for the**

bus мы дóлго ждáли автóбуса; **~ on** *vt fus* (serve) обслýживать (обслужить *pf*); **~er** *n* официáнт; **~ing list** *n* óчередь *f*, спúсок очередникóв; **~ing room** *n* (in surgery) приёмная *f adj*; (in station) зал ожидáния *m*; **~ress** *n* официáнтка

wake [weɪk] (*pt* **woke** или **~d**, *pp* **woken** или **~d**) *vt* (also: **~ up**) будить (разбудить *pf*) ♦ *vi* (also: **~ up**) просыпáться (проснýться *pf*) ♦ *n* бдéние (у грóба); (NAUT) кильвáтер; **in the ~ of** (fig) вслéдствие +*gen*; **~n** *vti* = **wake**

Wales [weɪlz] *n* Уэльс

walk [wɔːk] *n* (hike) похóд; (shorter) прогýлка; (gait) похóдка; (path) тропá ♦ *vi* (go on foot) ходить/идти (*impf*) (пешкóм); (for pleasure, exercise) гулять (*impf*) ♦ *vt* (distance) проходить (пройти *pf*); (dog) выгýливать (выгулять *pf*); **10 minutes' ~ from here** в 10-ти минýтах ходьбы отсюда; **~ out** *vi* (audience) демонстративно покидáть (покинуть *pf*) зал; (workers) забастовáть (*pf*); **~er** *n* (hiker) турист(ка); **~ing stick** *n* трость *f*

wall [wɔːl] *n* стенá; **~ed** *adj* обнесённый стенóй

wallet ['wɔlɪt] *n* бумáжник

wallpaper ['wɔːlpeɪpə^r] *n* обóи *pl* ♦ *vt* оклéивать (оклéить *pf*) обóями

walnut ['wɔːlnʌt] *n* (nut) грéцкий орéх; (wood) орéх

walrus ['wɔːlrəs] (*pl* **~** или **~es**) *n* морж

waltz [wɔːlts] *n* вальс

wander ['wɔndə^r] *vi* (person) бродить (*impf*); (mind, thoughts) блуждáть (*impf*) ♦ *vt* бродить (*impf*) по +*dat*

vane [veɪn] *vi* (*enthusiasm, influence*) ослабевать (ослабеть *pf*)

vant [wɒnt] *vt* (*wish for*) хотеть (*impf*) +*acc or* +*gen*; (*need*) нуждаться в +*prp* ♦ *n*: **for ~ of** за недостатком +*gen*; **to ~ to do** хотеть (*impf*) +*infin*; **I ~ you to apologize** я хочу, чтобы Вы извинились; **~ed** *adj* (*criminal etc*) разыскиваемый; **~ing** *adj*: **he was found ~ing** он оказался не на высоте положения

wanton [wɒntn] *adj* (*gratuitous*) беспричинный

var [wɔ:ᵊ] *n* война; **to declare ~ (on)** объявлять (объявить *pf*) войну (+*dat*)

ward [wɔ:d] *n* (*MED*) палата; (*BRIT: POL*) округ; (*LAW*) ребёнок, под опёкой; **~ off** *vt* (*attack, enemy*) отражать (отразить *pf*); (*danger, illness*) отвращать (отвратить *pf*)

warden [wɔ:dn] *n* (*of park, reserve*) смотритель(ница) *m(f)*; (*of prison*) начальник; (*of youth hostel*) комендант

wardrobe [wɔ:drəub] *n* шифоньер, платяной шкаф; (*clothes*) гардероб; (*THEAT*) костюмерная *f adj*

warehouse [wɛəhaus] *n* склад

wares [wɛəz] *npl* товары *mpl*

warfare [wɔ:fɛəᵊ] *n* военные *or* боевые действия *ntpl*

warily [wɛərɪlɪ] *adv* настороженно

warm [wɔ:m] *adj* тёплый; (*thanks, supporter*) горячий; (*heart*) добрый; **it's ~ today** сегодня тепло; **I'm ~** мне тепло; **~ up** *vi* (*person, room*) согреваться (согреться *pf*); (*water*) нагреваться (нагреться *pf*); (*athlete*) разминаться (размяться *pf*) ♦ *vt* разогревать (разогреть *pf*); **the weather ~ed up** на улице

потеплело; **~-hearted** *adj* сердечный; **~ly** *adv* (*applaud*) горячо; (*dress, welcome*) тепло; **~th** *n* тепло

warn [wɔ:n] *vt*: **to ~ sb (not) to do/that** предупреждать (предупредить *pf*) кого-н (не) +*infin*/o +*prp*/, что; **~ing** *n* предупреждение

warp [wɔ:p] *vi* (*wood*) коробиться (покоробиться *pf*) ♦ *vt* (*fig*) извращать (извратить *pf*)

warrant [wɒrənt] *n* (*also*: **search ~**) ордер на обыск; **~y** *n* гарантия

Warsaw [wɔ:sɔ:] *n* Варшава

warship [wɔ:ʃɪp] *n* военный корабль *m*

wart [wɔ:t] *n* бородавка

wartime [wɔ:taɪm] *n*: **in ~** в военное время

wary [wɛərɪ] *adj*: **to be ~ of sb/sth** относиться (*impf*) к кому-н/ чему-н с опаской

was [wɒz] *pt of* **be**

wash [wɒʃ] *n* мытьё; (*clothes*) стирка; (*washing programme*) режим стирки (*в стиральной машине*); (*of ship*) пенистый след ♦ *vt* (*hands, body*) мыть (помыть *pf*); (*clothes*) стирать (постирать *pf*); (*face*) умывать (умыть *pf*) ♦ *vi* (*person*) мыться (помыться *pf*); (*sea etc*): **to ~ over sth** перекатываться (перекатиться *pf*) через что-н; **to have a ~** помыться (*pf*); **to give sth a ~** помыть (*pf*) что-н; **~ off** *vi* отмываться (отмыться *pf*); (*stain*) отстирываться (отстираться *pf*); **~ up** *vi* (*BRIT*) мыть (вымыть *pf*) посуду; (*US*) мыться (помыться *pf*); **~er** *n* шайба; **~ing** *n* стирка; **~ing-up** *n* (*грязная*) посуда

wasn't [wɒznt] = **was not**

wasp [wɒsp] *n* оса

wastage ['weɪstɪdʒ] n (waste) трата

waste [weɪst] n (act) трата; (rubbish) отходы mpl; (also: ~ **land**: in city) пустырь m ♦ adj (rejected, damaged) бракованный; (left over) отработанный ♦ vt растрачивать (растратить pf); (opportunity) упускать (упустить pf); **~s** npl (area) пустыня fsg; **~ful** adj неэкономный; **~paper basket** n корзина для (ненужных) бумаг

watch [wɒtʃ] n (also: **wrist~**) (наручные) часы pl; (act of watching) наблюдение ♦ vt (look at) наблюдать (impf) за +instr; (match, programme) смотреть (посмотреть pf); (events, weight, language) следить (impf) за +instr; (be careful of: person) остерегаться (impf) +gen; (look after) смотреть (impf) за +instr ♦ vi (take care) смотреть (impf); (keep guard) дежурить (impf); **~ out** vi остерегаться (остеречься pf); **~ful** adj бдительный

water ['wɔ:tə] n вода ♦ vt поливать (полить pf) ♦ vi (eyes) слезиться (impf); **in British ~s** в британских водах; **~ down** vt разбавлять (разбавить pf) (водой); (fig) смягчать (смягчить pf); **~colour** (US **~color**) n (picture) акварель f; **~fall** n водопад; **~ing can** n лейка; **~logged** adj затопленный; **~melon** n арбуз; **~proof** adj непромокаемый; **~shed** n водораздел; **~tight** adj (seal, door) водонепроницаемый; **~way** n водный путь m; **~y** adj (soup etc) водянистый

watt [wɒt] n ватт

wave [weɪv] n волна; (of hand) взмах ♦ vi (signal) махать (impf); (branches) качаться (impf); (flag)

развеваться (impf) ♦ vt махать (impf) +instr; (stick, gun) размахивать (impf) +instr; **~length** n (RADIO) длина волны; **they are on the same ~length** (fig) они смотрят на вещи одинаково

wax [wæks] n (polish) воск; (: for floor) мастика; (: for skis) мазь f; (in ear) сера ♦ vt (floor) натирать (натереть pf) мастикой; (car) натирать (натереть pf) воском; (skis) мазать (смазать pf) мазью

way [weɪ] n (route) путь m, дорога; (manner, method) способ; (usu pl: habit) привычка; **which ~? - this - ~** куда? - сюда; **is it a long ~ from here?** это далеко отсюда?; **which - do we go now?** куда нам теперь идти?; **on the ~** (en route) по пути или дороге; **to be on one's ~** быть (impf) в пути; **to go out of one's ~** to do стараться (постараться pf) изо всех сил +infin; **to be in sb's ~** стоять (impf) на чьём-н пути; **to lose one's ~** заблудиться (pf); **the plan is under ~** план осуществляется; **in a ~** в известном смысле; **in some ~s** в некоторых отношениях; **no ~!** (inf) ни за что!; **by the ~** кстати ..., между прочим ...; **"~in"** (BRIT) "вход"; **"~ out"** (BRIT) "выход"; **"give ~"** (BRIT : AUT) "уступите дорогу"

WC n abbr (= water closet) туалет

we [wi:] pron мы

weak [wi:k] adj слабый; **to grow ~** слабеть (ослабеть pf); **~en** vi (person) смягчаться (смягчиться pf) ♦ vt (government, person) ослаблять (ослабить pf); **~ness** n слабость f; **to have a ~ness for** иметь (impf) слабость к +dat

wealth [welθ] n (money, resources) богатство; (of details, knowledge etc) обилие; **~y** adj богатый

vean [wi:n] vt (baby) отнима́ть (отня́ть pf) от груди́

weapon ['wɛpən] n ору́жие

wear [wɛəʳ] (pt **wore**, pp **worn**) n (use) но́ска; (damage) изно́с ♦ vi (last) носи́ться (impf); (rub through) изна́шиваться (износи́ться pf) ♦ vt (generally) носи́ть (impf); (put on) надева́ть (наде́ть pf); (damage) изна́шивать (износи́ть pf); he was ~ing his new shirt на нём была́ его́ но́вая руба́шка; ~ **down** vt (resistance) сломи́ть (pf); ~ **out** vt (shoes, clothing) изна́шивать (износи́ть pf); ~ **and tear** n изно́с

weary ['wɪərɪ] adj утомлённый ♦ vi: **to ~** утомля́ться (утоми́ться pf) от +gen

weasel ['wi:zl] n (ZOOL) ла́ска

weather ['wɛðəʳ] n пого́да ♦ vt (crisis) выде́рживать (вы́держать pf); **I am under the ~** мне нездоро́вится; **~ forecast** n прогно́з пого́ды

weave [wi:v] (pt **wove**, pp **woven**) vt (cloth) ткать (сотка́ть pf); **~r** n ткач(и́ха)

weaving ['wi:vɪŋ] n (craft) тка́чество

web [wɛb] n паути́на; (fig) сеть f; (COMPUT) = (**World Wide**) **Web**; **~ page** n электро́нная страни́ца, страни́ца на интерне́те; **~site** n сайт

wed [wɛd] (pt, pp **~ded**) vi венча́ться (обвенча́ться pf)

we'd [wi:d] = **we had**, **we would**

wedding ['wɛdɪŋ] n сва́дьба; (in church) венча́ние; **silver/golden ~** сере́бряная/золота́я сва́дьба

wedge [wɛdʒ] n клин ♦ vt закрепля́ть (закрепи́ть pf) кли́ном; (pack tightly): **to ~ in** вти́скивать (вти́снуть pf) в +acc

Wednesday ['wɛnzdɪ] n среда́

wee [wi:] adj (SCOTTISH) ма́ленький

weed [wi:d] n сорня́к ♦ vt поло́ть (вы́полоть pf)

week [wi:k] n неде́ля; **a ~ today** че́рез неде́лю; **a ~ on Friday** в сле́дующую пя́тницу; **~day** n бу́дний день m; **~end** n выходны́е pl adj (дни), суббо́та и воскресе́нье; **~ly** adv еженеде́льно ♦ adj еженеде́льный

weep [wi:p] (pt, pp **wept**) vi (person) пла́кать (impf)

weigh [weɪ] vt взве́шивать (взве́сить pf) ♦ vi ве́сить (impf); ~ **down** vt отягоща́ть (отяготи́ть pf); (fig) тяготи́ть (impf)

weight [weɪt] n вес; (for scales) ги́ря; **to lose ~** худе́ть (похуде́ть pf); **to put on ~** поправля́ться (попра́виться pf); **~y** adj (important) весо́мый

weir [wɪəʳ] n (in river) запру́да

weird [wɪəd] adj (strange) стра́нный, дико́винный

welcome ['wɛlkəm] adj жела́нный ♦ n (hospitality) приём; (greeting) приве́тствие ♦ vt (also: **bid ~**) приве́тствовать (impf); **thank you - you're ~!** спаси́бо - пожа́луйста!

weld [wɛld] vt сва́ривать (свари́ть pf)

welfare ['wɛlfɛəʳ] n (well-being) благополу́чие; (US: social aid) социа́льное посо́бие; ~ **state** n госуда́рство всео́бщего благосостоя́ния

well [wɛl] n (for water) коло́дец; (also: **oil ~**) (нефтяна́я) сква́жина ♦ adv хорошо́ ♦ excl (anyway) ну; (so) ну вот ♦ adj: **he is ~** он здоро́в; **as ~** та́кже; **I woke ~ before dawn** я проснулся задо́лго до рассве́та; **I've brought my anorak as ~ as a**

jumper кро́ме сви́тера я взял ещё и ку́ртку; ~ **done!** молоде́ц!; **get** ~ **soon!** поправля́йтесь скоре́е; **he is doing** ~ **at school** в шко́ле он успева́ет; **the business is doing** ~ би́знес процвета́ет; ~ **up** vi (tears) наверну́ться (pf)

we'll [wi:l] = **we will, we shall**

well-being ['wel'bi:ɪŋ] n благополу́чие

well-dressed ['wel'drest] adj хорошо́ оде́тый

wellies ['welɪz] npl (inf) = **wellingtons**

wellingtons ['welɪŋtənz] npl (also: **wellington boots**) рези́новые сапоги́ mpl

well-known ['wel'nəun] adj изве́стный

well-off ['wel'ɔf] adj (wealthy) обеспе́ченный

Welsh [welʃ] adj уэ́льский; **the** ~ npl (people) уэ́льсцы mpl, валли́йцы mpl; ~ **Assembly** n Ассамбле́я Уэ́льса; ~**man** (irreg) n уэ́льсец, валли́ец; ~**woman** (irreg) n валли́йка, жи́тельница Уэ́льса

went [went] pt of **go**

wept [wept] pt, pp of **weep**

were [wə:r] pt of **be**

we're [wɪər] = **we are**

weren't [wə:nt] = **were not**

west [west] n за́пад ♦ adj за́падный ♦ adv на за́пад; **the West** (POL) За́пад; ~**erly** adj за́падный; ~**ern** adj за́падный ♦ n (CINEMA) ве́стерн

wet [wet] adj (damp, rainy) вла́жный, сыро́й; (soaking) мо́крый; **to get** ~ мо́кнуть (промо́кнуть pf)

we've [wi:v] = **we have**

whale [weɪl] n кит

wharf [wɔ:f] (pl **wharves**) n при́стань f

KEYWORD

what [wɔt] adj 1 (interrogative: direct, indirect) како́й (f кака́я, nt како́е, pl каки́е); **what books do you need?** каки́е кни́ги Вам нужны́?; **what size is the dress?** како́го разме́ра э́то пла́тье?
2 (emphatic) како́й (f кака́я, nt како́е, pl каки́е); **what a lovely day!** како́й чуде́сный день!; **what a fool I am!** како́й же я дура́к!
♦ pron 1 (interrogative) что; **what are you doing?** что Вы де́лаете?; **what are you talking about?** о чём Вы говори́те?; **what is it called?** как э́то называ́ется?; **what about me?** а как же я?; **what about doing ...?** как насчёт того́, что́бы +infin ...?
2 (relative) что; **I saw what was on the table** я ви́дел, что бы́ло на столе́; **tell me what you're thinking about** скажи́те мне, о чём Вы ду́маете; **what you say is wrong** то, что Вы говори́те, неве́рно
♦ excl (disbelieving) что; **I've crashed the car - what!** я разби́л маши́ну - что!

whatever [wɔt'evər] adj (any) любо́й; ~ **book** люба́я кни́га
♦ pron (any) всё; (regardless of) что бы ни; ~ **you do ...** что бы ты ни де́лал ...; ~ **the reason** ... кака́я бы ни была́ причи́на ...; **do** ~ **is necessary/you want** де́лайте всё, что необходи́мо/хоти́те; ~ **happens** что бы ни случи́лось; **there is no reason** ~ нет никако́й причи́ны; **nothing** ~ абсолю́тно ничего́

whatsoever [wɔtsəu'evər] adj: **there is no reason** ~ нет никако́й причи́ны

wheat [wi:t] n пшени́ца

wheel [wi:l] n (of car etc) колесо́; (also: **steering ~**) руль m; **~barrow** n та́чка; **~chair** n инвали́дная коля́ска

wheeze [wi:z] vi хрипе́ть (impf)

when [wɛn] adv, conj когда́; **~ you've read the book ...** когда́ Вы прочита́ете кни́гу ...

whenever [wɛn'ɛvəʳ] adv в любо́е вре́мя ♦ conj (any time) когда́ то́лько; (every time that) ка́ждый раз, когда́

where [wɛəʳ] adv (position) где; (motion) куда́ ♦ conj где; **~ from?** отку́да ...?; **this is ~ ...** э́то там, где ...

whereabouts adv [wɛərə'bauts] n ['wɛərəbauts] n (position) где; (motion) куда́ ♦ n местонахожде́ние; **~as** conj тогда́ or в то вре́мя как; **~by** adv (formal) посре́дством чего́; **~ver** [wɛərˈɛvəʳ] conj (no matter where): **~ver he was** где бы он ни́ был; (not knowing where): **~ver that is** где бы то ни́ было ♦ adv (interrogative: position) где же; (: motion) куда́ же; **~ver he goes** куда́ бы он ни шёл

wherewithal ['wɛəwiðɔ:l] n: **the ~** (to do) сре́дства ntpl (+infin)

whether ['wɛðəʳ] conj ли; **I doubt ~ she loves me** я сомнева́юсь, лю́бит ли она́ меня́; **I don't know ~ to accept this proposal** я не зна́ю, приня́ть ли э́то предложе́ние; **~ you go or not** пойдёте Вы и́ли нет

which [wɪtʃ] adj 1 (interrogative: direct, indirect) како́й (f кака́я, nt како́е, pl каки́е); **which picture would you like?** каку́ю карти́ну

Вы хоти́те?; **which books are yours?** каки́е кни́ги Ва́ши?; **which one?** како́й? (f кака́я, nt како́е); **I've got two pens, which one do you want?** у меня́ есть две ру́чки, каку́ю Вы хоти́те?; **which one of you did it?** кто из Вас э́то сде́лал?

2: **in which case** в тако́м слу́чае; **by which time** к тому́ вре́мени ♦ pron 1 (interrogative) како́й (f кака́я, nt како́е, pl каки́е); **there are several museums, which shall we visit first?** здесь есть не́сколько музе́ев. В каку́ю мы пойдём снача́ла?; **which do you want, the apple or the banana?** что Вы хоти́те - я́блоко и́ли бана́н?; **which of you are staying?** кто из Вас остаётся?

2 (relative) кото́рый (f кото́рая, nt кото́рое, pl кото́рые); **the apple which is on the table** я́блоко, кото́рое лежи́т на столе́; **the news was bad, which is what I had feared** ве́сти бы́ли плохи́е, чего́ я и опаса́лся; **I had lunch, after which I decided to go home** я пообе́дал, по́сле чего́ я реши́л пойти́ домо́й; **I made a speech, after which nobody spoke** я вы́ступил с ре́чью, по́сле кото́рой никто́ ничего́ не сказа́л

whichever [wɪtʃ'ɛvəʳ] adj (any) любо́й; (regardless of) како́й бы ни; **take ~ book you prefer** возьми́те любу́ю кни́гу; **~ book you take** каку́ю бы кни́гу Вы ни взя́ли

whiff [wɪf] n (smell): **he caught a ~ of her perfume** на него́ пахну́ло её духа́ми

while [waɪl] n (period of time) вре́мя nt ♦ conj пока́, в то вре́мя как; (although) хотя́; **for a ~**

ненадо́лго; ~ away vt: to ~ away
the time корота́ть (скорота́ть pf)
вре́мя

whim [wɪm] n при́хоть f

whimper ['wɪmpə⁺] n хны́канье
♦ vi хны́кать (impf)

whimsical ['wɪmzɪkl] adj чудно́й

whine [waɪn] n (of person, animal)
скули́ть (impf); (engine, siren) выть
(impf)

whip [wɪp] n кнут, хлыст; (POL,
person) организа́тор
парла́ментской фра́кции ♦ vt
(person, animal) хлеста́ть (impf);
(cream, eggs) взбива́ть (взбить
pf); to ~ sth out выха́тывать
(вы́хватить pf) что-н; to ~ sth
away выры́вать (вы́рвать pf) что-н

whirl [wə:l] vt кружи́ть (impf),
враща́ться (impf) ♦ vi (dancers)
кружи́ться (impf); ~ wind n вихрь m

whirr [wə:⁺] vi треща́ть (impf)

whisk [wɪsk] n (CULIN) ве́нчик ♦ vt
(CULIN) взбива́ть (взбить pf); to ~
sb away or off увози́ть (увезти́ pf)
кого́-н

whiskers ['wɪskəz] npl (of animal)
усы́ mpl; (of man) бакенба́рды
fpl

whisky ['wɪskɪ] (US, IRELAND
whiskey) n ви́ски nt ind

whisper ['wɪspə⁺] n шёпот ♦ vi
шепта́ться (impf) ♦ vt шепта́ть
(impf)

whistle ['wɪsl] n (sound) свист;
(object) свисто́к ♦ vi свисте́ть
(сви́стнуть pf)

white [waɪt] adj бе́лый ♦ n (colour)
бе́лый цвет; (person) бе́лый(ая)
m(f) adj; (of egg, eye) бело́к; ~ lie
n безоби́дная ложь f; ~wash
n (paint) известко́вый раство́р (для
побе́лки) ♦ vt (building) бели́ть
(побели́ть pf); (fig: incident)
обеля́ть (обели́ть pf)

whiting ['waɪtɪŋ] n inv хек

whizz [wɪz] vi: to ~ past or by

проноси́ться (пронести́сь pf)
ми́мо

who [hu:] pron 1 (interrogative) кто;
who is it? кто э́то?; **who is that**
or там?; **who did you see there?**
кого́ Вы там ви́дели?
2 (relative) кото́рый (f кото́рая, nt
кото́рое, pl кото́рые); **the woman**
who spoke to me же́нщина,
кото́рая говори́ла со мной

whole [həul] adj це́лый ♦ n (entire
unit) це́лое nt adj; (all): **the ~ of**
Europe вся Евро́па; **on the~, as a**
~ в це́лом; ~meal adj (BRIT):
~meal flour мука́ гру́бого
помо́ла; ~meal bread хлеб из
муки́ гру́бого помо́ла; ~sale
(price) опто́вый; (destruction)
ма́ссовый ♦ adv (buy, sell) о́птом;
~some adj здоро́вый

wholly ['həulɪ] adv по́лностью,
целико́м

whom [hu:m] pron 1 (interrogative:
+acc, +gen) кого́; (: +dat) кому́;
(: +instr) кем; (: +prp) ком; **whom**
did you see there? кого́ Вы там
ви́дели?; **to whom did you give**
the book? кому́ Вы отда́ли
кни́гу?
2 (relative: +acc) кото́рого (f
кото́рую, pl кото́рых); (: +gen)
кото́рого (f кото́рой, pl кото́рых);
(: +dat) кото́рому (f кото́рой, pl
кото́рым); (: +instr) кото́рым (f
кото́рой, pl кото́рыми); (: +prp)
кото́ром (f кото́рой, pl кото́рых);
the man whom I saw/to whom I
spoke челове́к, кото́рого я
ви́дел/с кото́рым я говори́л

whore [hɔː⁺] n (inf: pej) шлю́ха

whose 713 **will**

KEYWORD

whose [hu:z] adj 1 (possessive: interrogative) чей (f чья, nt чьё, pl чьи); **whose book is this?, whose is this book?** чья это книга? 2 (possessive: relative) который (f которая, nt которое, pl которые); **the woman whose son you rescued** женщина, сына которой Вы спасли
♦ pron чей (f чья, nt чьё, pl чьи); **whose is this?** это чьё?; **I know whose it is** я знаю, чьё это

why [waɪ] adv, conj почему ♦ excl: **it's you!** как, это Вы?; **~ is he always late?** почему он всегда опаздывает?; **I'm not going - ~ not?** я не пойду - почему?; **~ not do it now?** почему бы не сделать это сейчас?; **I wonder ~ he said that** интересно, почему он это сказал; **that's not ~ I'm here** я здесь не по этой причине; **that's ~** вот почему; **there is a reason ~ I want to see him** у меня есть причина для встречи с ним; **~, it's obvious/ that's impossible!** но ведь это же очевидно/невозможно!

wicked ['wɪkɪd] adj злобный, злой; (mischievous: smile) лукавый

wide [waɪd] adj широкий ♦ adv: **to open ~** широко открывать (открыть pf); **to shoot ~** стрелять (impf) мимо цели; **the bridge is 3 metres ~** ширина моста - 3 метра; **~ly** adv (believed, known) широко; (travelled) много; (differing) значительно; **~n** vt расширять (расширить pf) ♦ vi расширяться (расшириться pf); **~ open** широко раскрытый; **~spread** adj (belief etc) широко распространённый

widow ['wɪdəu] n вдова; **~ed** adj вдовый; **to be ~ed** овдоветь (pf); **~er** n вдовец

width [wɪdθ] n ширина

wield [wi:ld] vt (power) обладать (impf) +instr

wife [waɪf] (pl **wives**) n жена

wig [wɪg] n парик

wiggle ['wɪgl] vt (hips) трясти (impf) +instr; (ears) шевелить (пошевелить pf)

wild [waɪld] adj (animal, plant, guess) дикий; (weather, sea) бурный; (person, behaviour) буйный; **the ~s** npl (remote area) дикие места ntpl; **in the ~s of** +gen: в дебрях +gen; **~erness** n ['wɪldənɪs] n дикая местность f; (desert) пустыня; **~life** n дикая природа; **~ly** adv (behave) буйно, дико; (applaud) бурно; (hit) неистово; (guess) наобум

wilful ['wɪlful] (US **willful**) adj (obstinate) своенравный; (deliberate) умышленный

KEYWORD

will [wɪl] aux vb 1 (forming future tense): **I will finish it tomorrow** я закончу это завтра; **I will be working all morning** я буду работать всё утро; **I will have finished it by tomorrow** я закончу это к завтрашнему дню; **I will always remember you** я буду помнить тебя всегда; **will you do it? - yes, I will/no, I won't** Вы сделаете это? - да, сделаю/ нет, не сделаю; **the car won't start** машина никак не заводится
2 (in conjectures, predictions): **he will** or **he'll be there by now** он, наверное, уже там; **mistakes will happen** ошибки неизбежны
3 (in commands, requests, offers):

will you be quiet! а ну-ка,
потише!; **will you help me?** Вы
мне не поможете?; **will you have
a cup of tea?** не хотите ли чашку
чая?
♦ *vt* (*pt,pp* **willed**): **to will o.s. to
do** заставлять (заставить *pf*)
себя +*infin*; **to will sb to do**
заклинать (impf) кого-н +*infin*
♦ *n* (*volition*) воля; (*testament*)
завещание

willful ['wɪlful] *adj* (*US*) = **wilful**
willing ['wɪlɪŋ] *adj* (*agreed*)
согласный; (*enthusiastic*)
усердный; **he's ~ to do it** он
готов сделать это; **~ly** *adv* с
готовностью, охотно; **~ness** *n*
готовность *f*
willow ['wɪləu] *n* (*tree*) ива
willpower ['wɪl'pauə'] *n* сила воли
wilt [wɪlt] *vi* никнуть (поникнуть
pf)
wily ['waɪlɪ] *adj* лукавый
win [wɪn] (*pt, pp* **won**) *n* победа
♦ *vt* выигрывать (выиграть *pf*);
(*support, popularity*) завоёвывать
(завоевать *pf*) ♦ *vi* побеждать
(победить *pf*), выигрывать
(выиграть *pf*); **~ over** *vt* (*person*)
покорять (покорить *pf*)
winch [wɪntʃ] *n* лебёдка
wind¹ [wɪnd] *n* ветер; (*MED*) газы
mpl ♦ *vt*: **the blow ~ed him** от
удара у него захватило дух
wind² [waɪnd] (*pt, pp* **wound**) *vt*
(*rope, thread*) мотать (смотать *pf*);
(*toy, clock*) заводить (завести *pf*)
♦ *vi* (*road, river*) виться (impf)
~ up *vt* (*toy, clock*) заводить
(завести *pf*); (*debate*) завершать
(завершить *pf*)
windfall ['wɪndfɔːl] *n* (*money*)
неожиданный доход
windmill ['wɪndmɪl] *n* ветряная
мельница

window ['wɪndəu] *n* окно; (*in shop*)
витрина; **~sill** *n* подоконник
windscreen ['wɪndskriːn] *n*
ветровое стекло
windswept ['wɪndswept] *adj* (*place*)
продуваемый ветрами; (*person,
hair*) растрёпанный
windy ['wɪndɪ] *adj* ветреный; **it's ~
today** сегодня ветрено
wine [waɪn] *n* вино
wing [wɪŋ] *n* (*also* AUT) крыло; **~s** *npl*
(*THEAT*) кулисы *fpl*; **~er** *n* (*SPORT*)
крайний нападающий *m adj*
wink [wɪŋk] *n* подмигивание ♦ *vi*
подмигивать (подмигнуть *pf*),
мигать (мигнуть *pf*); (*light*)
мигать (мигнуть *pf*)
winner ['wɪnə'] *n*
победитель(ница) *m(f)*
winnings ['wɪnɪŋz] *npl* выигрыш
msg
winter ['wɪntə'] *n* (*season*) зима; **in
~** зимой
wintry ['wɪntrɪ] *adj* зимний
wipe [waɪp] *n*: **to give sth a ~**
протирать (протереть *pf*) что-н
♦ *vt* (*rub*) вытирать (вытереть *pf*);
(*erase*) стирать (стереть *pf*); **~
out** *vt* (*city, population*) стирать
(стереть *pf*) с лица земли
wire ['waɪə'] *n* проволока; (*ELEC*)
провод; (*telegram*) телеграмма
♦ *vt* (*person*) телеграфировать
(impf/*pf*) +*dat*; (*ELEC*: *also*: **~ up**)
подключать (подключить *pf*); **to
~ a house** делать (сделать *pf*)
(электро)проводку в +*prp*
wireless ['waɪəlɪs] *n* (*BRIT*) радио *nt
ind*
wiring ['waɪərɪŋ] *n*
(электро)проводка
wiry ['waɪərɪ] *adj* (*person*)
жилистый; (*hair*) жёсткий
wisdom ['wɪzdəm] *n* мудрость *f*
wise [waɪz] *adj* мудрый
...wise [waɪz] *suffix*: **timewise** в

смысле времени

vish [wɪʃ] n желание ♦ vt желать
(пожелать pf); **best ~es** (for
birthday etc) всего наилучшего;
with best ~es (in letter) с
наилучшими пожеланиями; **to ~
sb goodbye** прощаться
(попрощаться pf) с кем-н; **he ~ed
me well** он пожелал мне всего
хорошего; **to ~ to do** хотеть
(impf) +infin; **I ~ him to come** я
хочу, чтобы он пришёл; **to ~ for**
желать (пожелать pf) +acc or +gen;
~ful adj: **it's ~ful thinking** это –
принятие желаемого за
действительное

vistful ['wɪstful] adj тоскливый

vit [wɪt] n (wittiness) остроумие;
(intelligence: also: **~s**) ум, разум

vitch [wɪtʃ] n ведьма; **~craft** n
колдовство

KEYWORD

with [wɪð, wɪθ] prep **1**
(accompanying, in the company of)
с +instr; **I spent the day with him**
я провёл с ним день; **we stayed
with friends** мы остановились у
друзей; **I'll be with you in a
minute** я освобожусь через
минуту; **I'm with you** (I
understand) я Вас понимаю; **she
is really with it** (inf: fashionable)
она очень стильная; (: aware)
она всё соображает
2 (descriptive) с +instr; **a girl with
blue eyes** девушка с голубыми
глазами; **a skirt with a silk lining**
юбка на шёлковой подкладке
3 (indicating manner) с +instr;
(indicating cause) от +gen;
(indicating means): **to write with a
pencil** писать (impf) карандашом;
with tears in her eyes со слезами
на глазах; **red with anger**
красный от гнева; **you can open

the door with this key Вы
можете открыть дверь этим
ключём; **to fill sth with water**
наполнять (наполнить pf) что-н
водой

---

withdraw [wɪθ'drɔ:] (irreg: like
draw) vt (object) извлекать
(извлечь pf); (remark) брать
(взять pf) назад; (offer) снимать
(снять pf) с +gen; (troops, person)
уходить (уйти pf); **to ~ money
from an account** снимать (снять
pf) деньги со счёта; **~al** n (of
offer, remark) отказ; (of troops)
вывод; (of money) снятие; **~n** pp
of **withdraw** ♦ adj замкнутый

wither ['wɪðə] vi (plant) вянуть
(завянуть pf)

withhold [wɪθ'həuld] (irreg: like
hold) vt (money) удерживать
(удержать pf); (information)
утаивать (утаить pf)

within [wɪð'ɪn] prep (place, distance,
time) внутри +gen, в пределах
+gen ♦ adv внутри; **~ reach** в
пределах досягаемости; **~ sight
(of)** в поле зрения (+gen); **the
finish is ~ sight** конец не за
горами

without [wɪð'aut] prep без +gen; **~
a hat** без шапки; **~ saying a word**
не говоря ни слова; **~ looking** не
глядя; **to go ~ sth** обходиться
(обойтись pf) без чего-н

withstand [wɪθ'stænd] (irreg: like
stand) vt выдерживать
(выдержать pf)

witness ['wɪtnɪs] n
свидетель(ница) m(f) ♦ vt (event)
быть (impf) свидетелем/льницей
+gen; (document) заверять
(заверить pf); **~ box** n
свидетельское место

witty ['wɪtɪ] adj остроумный

wives [waɪvz] npl of **wife**

wobble ['wɒbl] vi (legs) трясти́сь (impf); (chair) шата́ться (impf)

wobbly ['wɒblɪ] adj (table etc) ша́ткий

woe [wəu] n го́ре

woke [wəuk] pt of **wake**; **~n** pp of **wake**

wolf [wulf] (pl **wolves**) n волк

woman ['wumən] (pl **women**) n же́нщина

womb [wu:m] n ма́тка

women ['wɪmɪn] npl of **woman**

won [wʌn] pt, pp of **win**

wonder ['wʌndə'] n (feeling) изумле́ние ♦ vi: **I ~ whether you could tell me** ... не мо́жете ли Вы сказа́ть мне ...; **I ~ why he is late** интере́сно, почему́ он опа́здывает; **to ~ at** удивля́ться (impf) +dat; **to ~ about** разду́мывать (impf) о +prp; **it's why to ~ (that)** не удиви́тельно, что; **~ful** (excellent) чуде́сный; **~fully** adv чуде́сно

won't [wəunt] = **will not**

wood [wud] n (timber) де́рево; (forest) лес; ♦n adj (object) деревя́нный; (fig) дубо́вый; **~pecker** n дя́тел; **~work** n (skill) столя́рное де́ло; (~ worm n (larvae) личи́нка древото́чца

wool [wul] n (material, yarn) шерсть f; **to pull the ~ over sb's eyes** пуска́ть (пусть pf) пыль в глаза́ кому́-н; **~len** (US **~en**) adj шерстяно́й; **~ly** (US **~y**) adj шерстяно́й; (fig: ideas) расплы́вчатый; (: person) вя́лый

word [wə:d] n сло́во; (news) слух ♦ vt формули́ровать (сформули́ровать pf); **in other one's ~** други́ми слова́ми; **to break/keep one's ~** наруша́ть (нару́шить pf)/сде́рживать (сдержа́ть pf) сло́во; **to have ~s with sb** име́ть (impf) кру́пный разгово́р с кем-н;

~ing n формулиро́вка; **~ processor** n те́кстовый проце́ссор

wore [wɔ:'] pt of **wear**

work [wə:k] n рабо́та; (ART, LITERATURE) произведе́ние ♦ vi рабо́тать (impf); (medicine etc) де́йствовать (поде́йствовать pf) ♦ vt (clay) рабо́тать (impf) с +instr; (wood, metal) рабо́тать (impf) по +dat; (land) обраба́тывать (обрабо́тать pf); (mine) разраба́тывать (разрабо́тать pf); (machine) управля́ть (impf) +instr; (miracle) соверша́ть (соверши́ть pf); **he has been out of ~ for three months** он был без рабо́ты три ме́сяца; **to ~ loose** (part) расша́тываться (расшата́ться pf); (knot) осла́бнуть (осла́бнуть pf); **~ on** vt fus (task) рабо́тать (impf) над +instr; (person) рабо́тать (impf) с +instr; (principle) исходи́ть (impf) из +gen; **~ out** vi (plans etc) удава́ться (уда́ться pf) ♦ vt (problem) разреша́ть (разреши́ть pf); (plan) разраба́тывать (разрабо́тать pf); **it ~s out at £100** (cost) выхо́дит £100; **~er** n (in factory) рабо́чий(ая) m(f) adj; (in community etc) рабо́тник(ница) m(f); **~force** n рабо́чая си́ла; **~ing-class** adj рабо́чий; **~ing order** n: **in ~ing order** в испра́вности; **~man** (irreg) n (квалифици́рованный) рабо́чий m adj; **~s** n (BRIT: factory) фа́брика; (: steel, brick) заво́д; **~shop** n (мастерска́я f adj); (in session) семина́р; (THEAT, MUS) сту́дия

world [wə:ld] n мир ♦ adj мирово́й; **to think the ~ of sb** быть (impf) о́чень высо́кого мне́ния о ком-н; **~ champion** чемпио́н ми́ра; **~ly** adj

(*knowledgeable*) искушённый;
~wide *adj* всеми́рный; **(World Wide) Web** *n* (Всеми́рная) Паути́на

worm [wɜ:m] *n* (ZOOL) червь *m*

worn [wɔ:n] *pp of* **wear** ♦ *adj* (*carpet*) потёртый; **~-out** *adj* (*object*) изно́шенный; (*person*) изму́ченный

worried ['wʌrɪd] *adj* обеспоко́енный, встрево́женный

worry ['wʌrɪ] *n* (*anxiety*) беспоко́йство, волне́ние ♦ *vi* беспоко́иться (*impf*), волнова́ться (*impf*) ♦ *vt* (*person*) беспоко́ить (обеспоко́ить *pf*), волнова́ть (взволнова́ть *pf*); **~ing** *adj* трево́жный

worse [wɜ:s] *adj* ху́дший ♦ *adv* ху́же ♦ *n* ху́дшее *nt adj*; **a change for the ~** ухудше́ние; **~n** *vi* ухудша́ться (ухудши́ться *pf*); **~ off** (*financially*) бо́лее бе́дный

worship ['wɜ:ʃɪp] *n* поклоне́ние, преклоне́ние ♦ *vt* поклоня́ться (*impf*) +*dat*, преклоня́ться (*impf*) пе́ред +*instr*

worst [wɜ:st] *adj* наиху́дший ♦ *adv* ху́же всего́ ♦ *n* наиху́дшее *nt adj*; **at ~** в ху́дшем слу́чае

worth [wɜ:θ] *adj*: **to be ~** сто́ить (*impf*); **it's ~ it** того́ сто́ит; **~less** *adj* никчёмный; **~while** *adj* сто́ящий

worthy [wɜ:ði] *adj*: **~ (of)** досто́йный (+*gen*)

KEYWORD

would [wud] *aux vb* 1 (*conditional tense*): **I would tell you if I could** я бы сказа́л Вам, е́сли бы мог; **if you asked him he would do it** е́сли Вы его́ попро́сите, (то) он сде́лает э́то; **if you had asked him he would have done it** е́сли бы Вы попроси́ли его́, (то) он

бы сде́лал э́то

2 (*in offers, invitations, requests*): **would you like a cake?** не хоти́те (ли) пирога́?; **would you ask him to come in?** пожа́луйста, пригласи́те его́ войти́!; **would you open the window please?** откро́йте, пожа́луйста, окно́!

3 (*in indirect speech*): **I said I would do it** я сказа́л, что сде́лаю э́то; **he asked me if I would stay with him** он попроси́л меня́ оста́ться с ним; **he asked me if I would resit the exam if I failed** он спроси́л меня́, бу́ду ли я переса́давать экза́мен, е́сли я провалю́сь

4 (*emphatic*): **it WOULD have to snow today!** и́менно сего́дня до́лжен пойти́ снег!; **you WOULD say that, wouldn't you!** Вы, коне́чно, э́то ска́жете!

5 (*insistence*): **she wouldn't behave** она́ ника́к не хоте́ла хорошо́ себя́ вести́

6 (*conjecture*): **it would have been midnight** должно́ быть, была́ по́лночь; **it would seem so** должно́ быть, так; **it would seem that ...** похо́же, что ...

7 (*indicating habit*): **he would come here on Mondays** он (обы́чно) приходи́л сюда́ по понеде́льникам

would-be ['wudbɪ] *adj* (*pej*) начина́ющий

wouldn't ['wudnt] = **would not**

wound[1] [waund] *pt, pp of* **wind**[2]

wound[2] [wu:nd] *n* ра́на ♦ *vt* ра́нить (*impf/pf*)

wove [wəuv] *pt of* **weave**; **~n** *pp of* **weave**

wrangle ['ræŋgl] *n* препира́тельства *ntpl*

wrap [ræp] *vt* (*also*: **~ up**)

заворáчивать (заверну́ть *pf*); (wind): **to ~ sth round sth** (tape etc) обора́чивать (оберну́ть *pf*) что-н вокру́г чего́-н; **~per** *n* (on chocolate) обёртка

wrath [rɒθ] *n* гнев

wreath [riːθ] (*pl* **~s**) *n* (for dead) вено́к

wreck [rek] *n* (vehicle, ship) обло́мки *mpl* ♦ *vt* (car) разбива́ть (разби́ть *pf*); (stereo) лома́ть (слома́ть *pf*); (weekend) по́ртить (испо́ртить *pf*); (relationship) разруша́ть (разру́шить *pf*); (life, health) губи́ть (погуби́ть *pf*); **~age** *n* обло́мки *mpl*; (of building) разва́лины *fpl*

wren [ren] *n* крапи́вник

wrench [rentʃ] *n* (TECH) га́ечный ключ; (tug) рыво́к; (fig) тоска́ ♦ *vt* (twist) выве́ртывать (вы́вернуть *pf*); **to ~ sth from sb** вырыва́ть (вы́рвать *pf*) что-н у кого́-н

wrestle [ˈresl] *vi* (SPORT): **to ~ (with sb)** боро́ться (*impf*) (с кем-н)

wrestling [ˈreslɪŋ] *n* борьба́

wretched [ˈretʃɪd] *adj* несча́стный

wriggle [ˈrɪɡl] *vi* (also: **~ about**: worm) извива́ться (*impf*); (person) ёрзать (*impf*)

wring [rɪŋ] (*pt, pp* **wrung**) *vt* (hands) лома́ть (*impf*); (also: **~ out**: clothes) выжима́ть (вы́жать *pf*); (fig): **to ~ sth out of sb** выжима́ть (вы́жать *pf*) что-н из кого́-н

wrinkle [ˈrɪŋkl] *n* (on face) морщи́на ♦ *vt* (nose etc) мо́рщить (смо́рщить *pf*) ♦ *vi* (skin etc) мо́рщиться (смо́рщиться *pf*)

wrist [rɪst] *n* (ANAT) запя́стье

writ [rɪt] *n* (LAW) о́рдер

write [raɪt] (*pt* **wrote**, *pp* **written**) *vt* (letter, novel etc) писа́ть (написа́ть *pf*); (cheque, receipt)

выпи́сывать (вы́писать *pf*) ♦ *vi* писа́ть (*impf*); **to ~ to sb** писа́ть (написа́ть *pf*) кому́-н; **~ down** *vt* (note) запи́сывать (записа́ть *pf*); **~ off** *vt* (debt) спи́сывать (списа́ть *pf*); (plan) отменя́ть (отмени́ть *pf*); **~r** *n* писа́тель *m*

writhe [raɪð] *vi* извива́ться (*impf*)

writing [ˈraɪtɪŋ] *n* (words written) на́дпись *f*; (of letter, article) (на)писа́ние; (also: **hand~**): по́черк; **~ is his favourite occupation** бо́льше всего́ он лю́бит писа́ть; **in ~** в пи́сьменном ви́де

written [ˈrɪtn] *pp of* **write**

wrong [rɒŋ] *adj* непра́вильный; (information) неве́рный; (immoral) дурно́й ♦ *adv* непра́вильно ♦ *n* (injustice) несправедли́вость *f* ♦ *vt* нехорошо́ поступа́ть (поступи́ть *pf*) с +*instr*; **you are ~ to do it** это нехорошо́ с Ва́шей стороны́; **you are ~ about that, you've got it ~** Вы непра́вы; **who is in the ~?** чья э́то вина́?; **what's ~?** в чём де́ло?; **to go ~** (plan) не удава́ться (уда́ться *pf*); **right and ~** хоро́шее и дурно́е; **~ful** *adj* несправедли́вый

wrote [raʊt] *pt of* **write**

wrought [rɔːt] *adj*: **~ iron** сва́рочная *or* ко́вкая сталь *f*

wrung [rʌŋ] *pt, pp of* **wring**

wry [raɪ] *adj* (humour, expression, smile) лука́вый

WWW *n abbr* = **World Wide Web**

X, x

Xmas [ˈeksməs] *n abbr* = **Christmas**

X-ray [ˈeksreɪ] *n* (ray) рентге́новские лучи́ *mpl*; (photo) рентге́новский сни́мок ♦ *vt* просве́чивать (просвети́ть *pf*)

(рентге́новскими луча́ми)
ylophone ['zaɪləfəun] n ксилофо́н

Y, y

yacht [jɒt] n я́хта
yard [jɑ:d] n (of house etc) двор;
(measure) ярд

> **yard** – ярд. Ме́ра длины́ ра́вная
> 90.14 см.

yawn [jɔ:n] n зево́к ♦ vi зева́ть
(зевну́ть pf)
year [jɪəʳ] n год; **he is eight ~s old**
ему́ во́семь лет; **an eight---old
child** восьмиле́тний ребёнок; **~ly**
adj ежего́дный ♦ adv ежего́дно
yearn [jəːn] vi: **to ~ for sth**
тоскова́ть (impf) по чему́-н; **to ~
to do** жа́ждать (impf) +infin
yeast [ji:st] n дро́жжи pl
yell [jel] vi вопи́ть (impf)
yellow ['jeləu] adj жёлтый
yes [jes] particle да; (in reply to
negative) нет ♦ n
проголосова́вший(ая) m(f) adj
"за"; **to say ~** говори́ть (сказа́ть
pf) да
yesterday ['jestədɪ] adv вчера́ ♦ n
вчера́шний день m; **~ morning/
evening** вчера́ у́тром/ве́чером;
all day ~ вчера́ весь день
yet [jet] adv ещё, до сих пор ♦ conj
одна́ко, всё же; **the work is not
finished** рабо́та ещё не
око́нчена; **the best ~** са́мый
лу́чший на сего́дняшний день;
as ~ ещё, пока́
yew [ju:] n тис
yield [ji:ld] n (AGR) урожа́й m ♦ vt
(surrender) сдава́ть (сдать pf); vt
(produce) приноси́ть (принести́ pf)
♦ vi (surrender) отступа́ть
(отступи́ть pf); (US : AUT) уступа́ть

(уступи́ть pf) доро́гу
yog(h)ourt ['jɒgət] n йо́гурт
yog(h)urt ['jɒgət] n = **yog(h)ourt**
yoke [jəuk] n (also fig) ярмо́
yolk [jəuk] n желто́к

KEYWORD

you [ju:] pron 1 (subject: familiar)
ты; (: polite) Вы; (: 2nd person pl)
вы; **you English are very polite**
вы, англича́не, о́чень ве́жливы;
you and I will stay here мы
с тобо́й/Ва́ми оста́немся
здесь
2 (direct: familiar) тебя́; (: polite)
Вас; (: 2nd person pl) вас; **I love
you** я тебя́/Вас люблю́
3 (indirect: familiar) тебе́; (: polite)
Вам; (: 2nd person pl) вам; **I'll give
you a present** я тебе́/Вам что́-
нибудь подарю́
4 (after prep: +gen familiar) тебя́;
(: polite) Вас; (: 2nd person pl) вас;
(: +dat: familiar) тебе́; (: polite)
Вам; (: 2nd person pl) вам;
(: +instr: familiar) тобо́й; (: polite)
Ва́ми; (: 2nd person pl) ва́ми;
(: +prp: familiar) тебе́; (: polite)
Вас; (: 2nd person pl) вас; **they've
been talking about you** они́
говори́ли о тебе́/Вас
5 (after prep: referring to subject of
sentence: +gen) себя́; (: +dat, +prp)
себе́; (: +instr) собо́й; **will you
take the children with you?** Вы
возьмёте дете́й с собо́й?; **she's
younger than you** она́ моло́же
тебя́/Вас
6 (impersonal: one): **you never
know what can happen** никогда́
не зна́ешь, что мо́жет
случи́ться; **you can't do that!** так
нельзя́!; **fresh air does you good**
све́жий во́здух поле́зен для
здоро́вья

you'd [ju:d] = **you had**, **you would**

you'll [ju:l] = **you shall**, **you will**

young [jʌŋ] adj молодо́й; (child) ма́ленький ♦ npl (of animal) молодня́к msg; **the ~** (people) молодёжь f; **~er** adj мла́дший; **~ster** n ребёнок

your [jɔːʳ] adj (familiar) твой; (polite) Ваш; (2nd person pl) ваш; see also **my**

you're [juəʳ] = **you are**

yours [jɔːz] pron (familiar) твой; (polite) Ваш; (2nd person pl) ваш; (referring to subject of sentence) свой; **is this ~?** э́то твоё/Ва́ше?; **~ sincerely**, **~ faithfully** и́скренне Ваш; see also **mine[1]**

yourself [jɔː'sɛlf] pron (reflexive) себя́; (after prep: +gen) себя́; (: +dat, +prp) себе́; (: +instr) собо́й; (emphatic) сам (f сама́, pl са́ми); (alone) сам, один; **(all) by ~** ты сам or один; **you ~ told me** Вы са́ми сказа́ли мне; see also **myself**

yourselves [jɔː'sɛlvz] pl pron (reflexive) себя́; (after prep: +gen) себя́; (: +dat, +prp) себе́; (: +instr) собо́й; (emphatic) са́ми, одни; **(all) by ~** са́ми, одни; **talk amongst ~ for a moment** поговори́те ме́жду собо́й пока́; see also **myself**

youth [ju:θ] n (young days) ю́ность f, мо́лодость f; (young people) молодёжь f; (pl **~s**; young man) ю́ноша m; **~ful** adj ю́ношеский; (person, looks) ю́ный

you've [ju:v] = **you have**

Z, z

zany ['zeɪnɪ] adj заба́вный

zap [zæp] vt (COMPUT) стира́ть (стере́ть pf)

zeal [zi:l] n рве́ние; **~ous** ['zɛləs] adj ре́вностный

zebra ['zi:brə] n зе́бра; **~ crossing** n (BRIT) зе́бра, пешехо́дный перехо́д

zero ['zɪərəu] n ноль m, нуль m

zest [zɛst] n (for life) жа́жда; (of orange) це́дра

zigzag ['zɪgzæg] n зигза́г

zinc [zɪŋk] n цинк

zip [zɪp] n (also: **~ fastener**) мо́лния ♦ vt (also: **~ up**) застёгивать (застегну́ть pf) на мо́лнию; **~per** n (US) = **zip**

zodiac ['zəudɪæk] n зодиа́к

zombie ['zɒmbɪ] n (fig) зо́мби ind

zone [zəun] n зо́на

zoo [zu:] n зоопа́рк

zoology [zu:'ɒlədʒɪ] n зооло́гия

zoom [zu:m] vi: **to ~ past** мелька́ть (промелькну́ть pf) ми́мо; **~ lens** n объекти́в с переме́нным фо́кусным расстоя́нием

Glossary of General Business Terms

account n счёт
account number n но́мер счёта
accounting n бухга́лтерский учёт
accounting period n бюдже́тный год
accounts payable npl счета́, подлежа́щие упла́те
accounts receivable npl ожида́емые поступле́ния
acid-test ratio n отноше́ние теку́щих акти́вов к теку́щим пасси́вам
acquisition n приобрете́ние
active partner n акти́вный партнёр
advertising n рекла́ма
advertising agency n рекла́мное аге́нтство
affiliate n аффили́рованная компа́ния
after-tax adj по́сле упла́ты нало́гов
aftermarket n по́сле ры́нка
after-sales service n гаранти́йное обслу́живание
AGM n ежего́дное о́бщее собра́ние
agribusiness n агроби́знес
amortization n амортиза́ция
annual general meeting = AGM
annual percentage rate n годова́я проце́нтная ста́вка
annual report n годово́й отчёт
annuity n ре́нта
antitrust law n антитре́стовский зако́н
arbitration n арбитра́ж
arrears npl задо́лженность
asking price n запра́шиваемая цена́
assets npl акти́вы
asset-stripping n распрода́жа непри́быльных акти́вов
audit n ауди́т
audited statement n одо́бренный ауди́тором отчёт
auditor n ауди́тор
authorized capital n уставно́й капита́л

bad debt n спи́санный долг (по несостоя́тельности)
balance due n су́мма к упла́те
balance of trade n торго́вый бала́нс
balance sheet n сво́дный бала́нс, бала́нсовая ве́домость
bank draft, banker's draft n ба́нковская тра́тта
bank giro n креди́тный перево́д (жи́ро)
bankrupt adj обанкро́тившийся
bankruptcy n банкро́тство

bargaining unit n си́льный аргуме́нт
basic rate n ба́зисный курс
basis point n ба́зисный пункт
basket of currencies n валю́тная корзи́на
bear market n ры́нок "медве́дей"
benchmark n ориенти́р
bid price n цена́ покупа́теля
bidder n покупа́тель
bill of exchange n перево́дный ве́ксель
bill of lading n коносаме́нт
bill of sale n купча́я
black market n чёрный ры́нок
bond n облига́ция
bonded warehouse n тамо́женный склад
boom-bust cycle n цикл, характеризу́ющийся подъёмом и спа́дом
borrower n заёмщик
borrowing capacity n заёмная си́ла
borrowing requirement n потре́бности в за́ймах
brand n (торго́вая) ма́рка
brand awareness n зна́ние торго́вой ма́рки
brand image n и́мидж торго́вой ма́рки
brand leader n веду́щая ма́рка
brand name n торго́вая ма́рка, фи́рменная ма́рка
break-even point n то́чка "при свои́х"
bridge loan, bridging loan n промежу́точный креди́т
brokerage n бро́керская коми́ссия
budget n бюдже́т
budget deficit n дефици́т бюдже́та
budget surplus n акти́в бюдже́та
building society n ипоте́чный банк, строи́тельное о́бщество
bull market n ры́нок "бы́ков"
business n предприя́тие, фи́рма
business card n визи́тная ка́рточка
business class n би́знес-класс
business man n бизнесме́н
business plan n би́знес-план
business woman n бизнесме́нка
buyer's market n ры́нок покупа́теля
by-laws npl вну́тренние пра́вила де́ятельности корпора́ции
by-product n побо́чный проду́кт

calendar year n календа́рный год

capital n капита́л

capital account n бала́нс движе́ния капита́лов

capital assets npl основно́й капита́л

capital expenditure n расхо́ды на приобре́те́ние основно́го капита́ла

capital gains tax n нало́г на реализо́ванный приро́ст капита́ла

capital goods npl капита́льные това́ры

capital investment n капиталовложе́ние

capitalization n капитализа́ция

cartel n карте́ль

cash account n нали́чный счёт

cash cow n би́знес, даю́щий прито́к нали́чных де́нег

cash discount n ски́дка с цены́ при поку́пке за нали́чные

cash on delivery n нало́женный платёж

CEO n гла́вный администра́тор

certificate of origin n сертифика́т происхожде́ния това́ра

certified public accountant n дипломи́рованный бухга́лтер

chamber of commerce n торго́вая пала́та

charge account n креди́т по откры́тому счёту

clearing account n кли́ринговый счёт

clearing bank n кли́ринговый банк

COD n нало́женный платёж

collateral n обеспе́че́ние креди́та

collective bargaining n колле́кти́вные перегово́ры

command economy n кома́ндная эконо́мика

commercial bank n комме́рческий банк

commerical loan n краткосро́чная ссу́да

commission n комиссио́нное вознагражде́ние, комисси́я

commodities npl сырьё

commodity market n това́рный ры́нок

common stock n обыкнове́нная а́кция

conference call n конфере́нц-связь

conference room n конфере́нц-за́л

consortium n консо́рциум

consumer n потреби́тель

consumer credit n потреби́тельский креди́т

consumer durables npl долгосро́чные потреби́тельские това́ры

consumer goods npl потреби́тельские това́ры

consumer price index n = CPI

contract n контра́кт

cooperative n коопера́ти́в

corporate identity n корпорати́вное созна́ние

corporate image n корпорати́вный и́мидж

corporation n корпора́ция

cost of living n сто́имость жи́зни

cost, insurance and freight n сто́имость, страхова́ние и фрахт

cost-benefit analysis n ана́лиз изде́ржек и при́былей

cottage industry n куста́рная промы́шленность

counteroffer n встре́чное предложе́ние

cover letter, covering letter n сопроводи́тельное письмо́

CPI n и́ндекс потреби́тельских цен

credit n креди́т

credit card n креди́тная ка́рточка

credit limit n креди́тный лими́т

credit note n креди́тный биле́т

credit rating n показа́тель кредитоспосо́бности

credit risk n креди́тный риск

credit union n креди́тный сою́з

creditor n креди́тор

crisis management n разреше́ние кри́зиса

currency unit n валю́тная едини́ца

current account n теку́щий счёт

customs clearance n тамо́женная очи́стка

customs duty n тамо́женная по́шлина

data capture n сбор информа́ции

data entry n ввод информа́ции

data processing n обрабо́тка информа́ции

daybook n журна́л

debit card n де́бетовая ка́рточка

debt n долг

debtor n должни́к

deflation n дефля́ция

deposit account n депози́тный счёт

depreciation n (of assets) сниже́ние сто́имости акти́вов
(of currency) девальва́ция

derivatives market n ры́нок дерива́ти́вов

direct debit *n* прямо́е дебетова́ние

discount *n* ски́дка

distribution *n* распределе́ние

distributor *n* дистрибью́тор

down payment *n* взнос нали́чных де́нег

early retirement *n* ра́нний ухо́д на пе́нсию

earned income *n* зарабо́танный дохо́д

earnings *npl* за́работок

e-business *n* би́знес по интерне́ту

ECB *n* Европе́йский центра́льный банк

e-commerce *n* би́знес по интерне́ту

Economic and Monetary Union = **EMU**

economies of scale *npl* сниже́ние сто́имости за счёт увеличе́ния объёма произво́дства

electronic funds transfer *n* систе́ма электро́нных платеже́й

EMS *n* ЕВС

EMU *n* Экономи́ческий и валю́тный сою́з

end product *n* коне́чный проду́кт

end user *n* коне́чный по́льзователь

enterprise *n* предприя́тие

entrepreneur *n* предпринима́тель

equities market *n* фо́ндовый ры́нок

escape clause *n* пункт догово́ра, освобожда́ющий от отве́тственности

escrow account *n* контра́кт, депони́рованный у тре́тьего лица́

etailer *n* интерне́т-продаве́ц

etailing *n* интерне́т-прода́жа

euro area *n* еврозо́на

European Central Bank *n* = **ECB**

European Monetary System *n* = **EMS**

exchange rate *n* валю́тный курс

excise tax *n* акци́з

expense account *n* счёт подотчётных сумм

export duty *n* э́кспортная по́шлина

export licence *n* э́кспортная лице́нзия

feasibility study *n* те́хнико-экономи́ческое обоснова́ние

finance company *n* фина́нсовая компа́ния

financial advisor *n* фина́нсовый консульта́нт

financial services *npl* фина́нсовые услу́ги

financial statement *n* фина́нсовый отчёт

financial year *n* фина́нсовый год

fiscal policy *n* бюдже́тная и нало́говая поли́тика

fiscal year *n* фина́нсовый год

fixed assets *npl* капита́льные акти́вы

flat rate *n* единообра́зная ста́вка

floating capital *n* оборо́тный капита́л

floating currency *n* пла́вающая валю́та

foreign exchange *n* иностра́нная валю́та

foreign trade *n* вне́шняя торго́вля

forex *n* иностра́нная валю́та

franchise agreement *n* франши́зный догово́р

freehold *n* по́лное пра́во на владе́ние

fringe benefits *npl* дополни́тельные льго́ты

GDP *n* ВВП

global economy *n* глоба́льная эконо́мика

globalization *n* глобализа́ция

GNP *n* ВНП

going concern *n* де́йствующее предприя́тие

goods on consignment *npl* па́ртия това́ров к отпра́вке

goodwill *n* до́брая во́ля

grievance procedure *n* поря́док рассмотре́ния жа́лоб

gross domestic product *n* = **GDP**

gross profit *n* о́бщая при́быль

gross national product *n* =**GNP**

Group of Seven *n* Больша́я Семёрка

guaranteed loan *n* гаранти́рованный заём

hard currency *n* твёрдая валю́та

headhunting *n* прямо́й найм высококвалифици́рованных рабо́тников

hedge fund *n* хе́джевый фонд

hidden reserves *npl* скры́тые резе́рвы

holding company *n* хо́лдинговая компа́ния

hostile takeover bid *n* поглоще́ние компа́нии путём ску́пки её а́кций на ры́нке

HR *n* отде́л ка́дров

import duty *n* и́мпортная тамо́женная по́шлина

import licence *n* и́мпортная лице́нзия

income n доход

income tax n подоходный налог

indemnity n гарантия возмещения убытка

indexation n индексация

industrial action n забастовка

industrial espionage n промышленный шпионаж

inflation n инфляция

information technology n информационная технология

insider dealing, insider trading n незаконные операции с ценными бумагами лицами, располагающими конфиденциальной информацией

insolvency n неплатежеспособность

insurance n страхование

insurance company n страховая компания

insurance policy n страховой полис

intangible assets npl "неосязаемые" активы

interest payment n оплата процентов

interest-free loan n беспроцентный займ

interest rate n процентная ставка

Internet business n интернет-бизнес

Internet Service Provider n = ISP

investment n инвестирование

investment income n доход от инвестиций

invoice n счёт-фактура

ISP n провайдер сетевых услуг

issue price n цена эмиссии

job description n описание служебных обязанностей

job sharing n распределение рабочего места на двоих

job title n наименование служебного положения

joint ownership n совместное владение

joint stock company n акционерная компания

joint venture n совместное предприятие

junk bond n бросовые облигации

key account n ключевой клиент

labour market n рынок рабочей силы

labour relations npl трудовые отношения

lead time n время реализации заказа

leaseback n лиз-бэк

leasehold n арендованная собственность

legal fees npl судебные издержки

legal tender n законное средство платежа

lender n кредитор, заимодавец

lending rate n ссудный процент

letter of credit n аккредитив

letter of intent n письмо о намерении совершить сделку

leveraged buyout n покупка контрольного пакета акций

liabilities npl обязательства

limited liability company n компания с ограниченной ответственностью

limited partnership n ограниченное товарищество

liquid assets npl ликвидные активы

liquidation n ликвидация

liquidator n ликвидатор

liquidity ratio n коэффициент ликвидных активов

listed company n официально зарегистрированная компания

list price n каталожная цена

loss leader n товар, продаваемый в убыток для привлечения покупателей

lump sum n паушальная сумма

management buyout n = MBO

managing director n = MD

man management n руководство кадрами

manpower n рабочая сила

manufactured goods npl произведённые товары

manufacturing industry n производственная сфера

man-year n человеко-год

markdown n снижение цены

market n рынок

market economy n рыночная экономика

market leader n ведущий игрок на рынке

market research n анализ рынка

market share n доля на рынке or удельный вес в обороте рынка

marketing n маркетинг

marketing strategy n маркетинговая стратегия

markup n надбавка, маржа

mass market *n* ма́ссовый спрос
mass production *n* ма́ссовое произво́дство
MBO *n* вы́куп контро́льного паке́та а́кций компа́нии её управля́ющими
MD *n* дире́ктор-распоряди́тель
merger *n* слия́ние
middleman *n* посре́дник
middle management *n* сре́днее звено́ управле́ния
mission statement *n* изложе́ние це́лей
money market *n* де́нежный ры́нок
monopoly *n* монопо́лия
mortgage *n* ипоте́чный креди́т
mortgage lender *n* ипоте́чная компа́ния
mutual fund *n* паево́й фонд

natural wastage *n* есте́ственная у́быль
net income *n* чи́стый дохо́д
net profit *n* чи́стая при́быль
nominal interest rate *n* номина́льная проце́нтная ста́вка
non-cash payment *n* безнали́чная опла́та
nonprofit organization *n* некомме́рческая организа́ция

offer price *n* цена́ продавца́
offshore bank *n* оффшо́рный банк
online banking *n* веде́ние ба́нковских дел по интерне́ту
online business *n* интерне́т-би́знес
on-the-job training *n* обуче́ние без отры́ва от произво́дства
open economy *n* откры́тая эконо́мика
open market *n* откры́тый ры́нок
operating costs *npl* операцио́нные изде́ржки
operating profit *n* операцио́нная при́быль
order book *n* кни́га зака́зов
order form *n* бланк зака́за
ordinary share *n* обыкнове́нная а́кция
outgoings *npl* расхо́ды
outsourcing *n* заку́пка на стороне́
outstanding debt *n* неупла́ченный долг
overcapacity *n* изли́шний потенциа́л
overdraft *n* перерасхо́д, овердра́фт
overhead(s) *n(pl)* накладны́е расхо́ды
overproduction *n* перепроизво́дство
overstaffing *n* изли́шек ка́дров
own brand, own label *n* това́р, несу́щий торго́вую ма́рку самого́

магази́на

paper profit *n* бума́жная при́быль, при́быль на бума́ге
par value *n* номина́льная сто́имость
parent company *n* матери́нская компа́ния
partnership *n* партнёрство
patent *n* пате́нт
payment in kind *n* опла́та нату́рой
penny stock(s) *n(pl)* а́кция ценой ме́ньше до́ллара
pension fund *n* пенсио́нный фонд
pension plan, pension scheme *n* пенсио́нный план
people management *n* руково́дство ка́драми
per capita *adj* на ду́шу (населе́ния)
per diem *adj* за день
performance-related pay *n* опла́та по результа́там труда́
personal identification number *n* = PIN
petty cash *n* небольша́я нали́чность
piece rate *n* сде́льный тари́ф
piecework *n* сде́льная рабо́та
PIN *n* ПИН
planned economy *n* пла́новая эконо́мика
point of sale *n* торго́вая то́чка
policy statement *n* изложе́ние поли́тики
PR *n* связи с обще́ственностью
preference shares *npl* привилегиро́ванная а́кция
preferred stock *n* привилегиро́ванная а́кция
price fixing *n* фикси́рование цен
price freeze *n* замора́живание цен
price war *n* война́ цен
price-earnings ratio *n* отноше́ние ры́ночной цены́ а́кции к её чи́стой при́были
private company *n* ча́стная компа́ния
private investor *n* ча́стный инве́стор
private sector *n* ча́стный се́ктор
privatization *n* приватиза́ция
product development *n* разрабо́тка проду́кта/това́ра
product launch *n* за́пуск проду́кта/ това́ра
product line *n* ли́ния това́ров
product placement *n* позициони́рование проду́кта/това́ра

profit n при́быль

profit margin n маржа́ при́были

profit sharing n уча́стие в при́былях

profitmaking adj при́быльный

profitability n при́быльность

proforma invoice adj предвари́тельный счёт-факту́ра

promissory note n просто́й ве́ксель

public relations npl = PR

public sector n обще́ственный се́ктор

purchase order n зака́з на това́ры

purchasing power n покупа́тельная спосо́бность

pyramid selling n пирами́дальная прода́жа

quality control n контро́ль ка́чества

quota n кво́та

rebranding n присвое́ние но́вой торго́вой ма́рки

recommended retail price n = RRP

redundancy n увольне́ние

redundancy package n вы́плата при увольне́нии

relaunch n но́вый за́пуск проду́кта/ това́ра

relocation expenses npl расхо́ды по перее́зду

remuneration n вознагражде́ние

replacement value n сто́имость замеще́ния

research and development n нау́чно-иссле́довательские и о́пытно-констру́кторские рабо́ты

reserve price n резе́рвная цена́

retail n ро́зничная торго́вля, ро́зница

retail price index n и́ндекс ро́зничных цен

retailer n ро́зничный торго́вец

retirement plan n пенсио́нный план

return (on investment) n дохо́д (от инвести́ции)

risk management n управле́ние ри́ском

royalty n гонора́р

RRP n рекоменду́емая ро́зничная цена́

salary n окла́д, зарабо́тная пла́та

salary scale n шкала́ окла́дов

sales npl прода́жи

sales force n сбытовики́

sales tax n нало́г с прода́ж

savings account n сберега́тельный счёт

savings bank n сберега́тельный банк

second mortgage n дополни́тельный ипоте́чный креди́т

secondary market n втори́чный ры́нок

securities npl це́нные облига́ции

self-financing adj самофинанси́рующий

seller's market n ры́нок продавца́

selling point n наибо́лее привлека́тельный аспе́кт това́ра

selling price n реализацио́нная цена́

service charge n ба́нковская коми́ссия

service industry n индустри́я се́рвиса

settlement of accounts n погаше́ние счето́в

severance pay n вы́плата при увольне́нии

share capital n акционе́рный капита́л

share index n фо́ндовый и́ндекс

share option n предоставле́ние слу́жащим компа́нии пра́ва на поку́пку а́кции да́нной компа́нии

shell company n зарегистри́рованная компа́ния с небольши́ми акти́вами

sick pay n больни́чные

silent partner n пасси́вный член това́рищества

single currency n еди́ная валю́та

Single Market n О́бщий ры́нок

sinking fund n фонд погаше́ния

sleeping partner n пасси́вный член това́рищества

soft currency n сла́бая валю́та

spot price n нали́чная цена́

spreadsheet n электро́нная табли́ца

stagflation n стагфля́ция

stakeholder pension n пе́нсия, получа́емая при уча́стии в капита́ле акционе́рной компа́нии

stamp duty n ге́рбовый сбор

standing order n постоя́нное поруче́ние

start-up capital n нача́льный капита́л

start-up cost n сто́имость первонача́льного вложе́ния

statement of account n вы́писка с ба́нковского счёта

state-owned enterprise n госуда́рственное предприя́тие

stock certificate n сертифика́т депони́рования а́кции

stock company n акционе́рная компа́ния

stock exchange n фо́ндовая би́ржа

stock market n фо́ндовый ры́нок

stock market index n и́ндекс фо́ндового ры́нка

stock option n фо́ндовый опцио́н

subcontractor n субподря́дчик

subcontracting n субконтра́кт

sublease n субаре́нда

subletting n субаре́нда

subsidiary n доче́рняя компа́ния

subsidy n субси́дия

sunrise industry n но́вая о́трасль эконо́мики

superannuation fund n пенсио́нный фонд (предприя́тия)

supplier n поставщи́к

supply and demand n спрос и предложе́ние

suspense account n промежу́точный счёт

takeover n поглоще́ние

takeover bid n попы́тка поглоще́ния

tangible assets, tangibles npl реа́льные акти́вы

tariff n тари́ф

tariff barrier n тари́фный барье́р

tax n нало́г

taxable income n дохо́д, подлежа́щий налогообложе́нию

taxation n налогообложе́ние

tax bracket n ме́сто в нало́говой шкале́

tax evasion n уклоне́ние от нало́гов

tax incentive n нало́говое стимули́рование

tax loophole n нало́говая лазе́йка

tax shelter n нало́говая защи́та

technology transfer n переда́ча техноло́гии

telecommuting n рабо́та на дому́ через компью́терную связь

teleconferencing n телеконфере́нция

telemarketing n телефо́нный ма́ркетинг

teleworking n рабо́та на дому́ через компью́терную связь

tender n те́ндер

terms and conditions npl постановле́ния и усло́вия

time management n рациона́льное испо́льзование вре́мени

trade n торго́вля

trade agreement n торго́вое соглаше́ние

trade discount n торго́вая ски́дка

trade relations npl торго́вые отноше́ния

trade secret n торго́вый секре́т

trade surplus n акти́вное са́льдо

trade war n торго́вая война́

trademark n торго́вый знак

trading partner n торго́вый партнёр

treasury bill n казначе́йский ве́ксель

treasury bond n казначе́йская облига́ция

turnover n оборо́т

underinvestment n недоинвести́рование

underwriter n гара́нт (размеще́ния це́нных бума́г)

unique selling point n = USP

unit cost n сто́имость едини́цы проду́кции

unit price n сто́имость едини́цы проду́кции

unit sales npl объём прода́ж едини́цы проду́кции

unsecured loan n необеспе́ченный заём

upset price n резерви́рованная цена́

USP n УСП

usury n ростовщи́чество

value-added tax n = VAT

VAT n НДС

venture capital n ри́сковый капита́л

venture capitalist n ри́сковый капитали́ст

videoconferencing n телеконфере́нция

wage freeze n замора́живание зарпла́ты

waybill n коносаме́нт

wholesale price n опто́вая цена́

wholesale price index n и́ндекс опто́вых цен

wholesaler n опто́вик

wholly-owned subsidiary n доче́рняя компа́ния, находя́щаяся в индивидуа́льном владе́нии

windfall profit n неожи́данный дохо́д

withholding tax n налогообложе́ние путём вы́четов

working capital n рабо́чий капита́л

World Bank n Мирово́й банк

World Trade Organization n = WTO

WTO n ВТО

zero growth n нулево́й рост

Деловая терминология

ава́нс м advance
ави́зо ср advice
авуа́ры мн assets
аккредити́в м letter of credit
акти́в бюдже́та м budget surplus
акти́вное са́льдо ср surplus account, trade surplus
акти́вы мн assets
акци́з м excise tax
акционе́рная компа́ния ж joint stock company, stock company
акционе́рный капита́л м share capital
аммортиза́ция ж amortization
ана́лиз ры́нка м market research
арбитра́ж м arbitration
арендо́ванная со́бственность ж leasehold
ассортиме́нт това́ров м product range
ауди́т м audit
ауди́тор м auditor
аукцио́н м auction

ба́зисный курс м basic rate
бала́нс м balance
бала́нс нали́чности м cash balance
бала́нсовая ве́домость ж balance sheet
ба́нковская коми́ссия ж service charge
ба́нковская тра́тта ж bank draft, banker's draft
банкома́т м ATM
банкома́тная ка́рточка ж ATM card
ба́ртер м barter
безнали́чная опла́та ж non-cash payment
беспроце́нтный займ м interest-free loan
би́знес в Сети́ м Internet business
бизнесме́н м business man
бизнесме́нка ж business woman
би́знес-класс м business class
би́знес-план м business plan
би́ржа ж exchange
бланк зака́за м order form
больни́чные мн sick pay
Больша́я Семёрка ж Group of Seven
бро́керская коми́ссия ж brokerage
бухга́лтерский учёт м accounting
бюдже́т м budget
бюдже́тная и нало́говая поли́тика ж fiscal policy

валово́й вну́тренний проду́кт м gross domestic product
валово́й национа́льный проду́кт м gross national product
валю́тная едини́ца ж currency unit
валю́тная корзи́на ж basket of currencies
валю́тный курс м exchange rate
ввод информа́ции м data entry
ВВП м GDP
визи́тная ка́рточка ж business card
вне́шняя торго́вля ж foreign trade
ВНП м GNP
Всеми́рная торго́вая организа́ция ж World Trade Organization
встре́чное предложе́ние ср counteroffer
ВТО ж WTO
втори́чный ры́нок м secondary market
вы́писка с ба́нковского счёта ж statement of account

гара́нт м guarantor
гаранти́йный срок м guarantee period
гаранти́йное обслу́живание ср after-sales service
гара́нтия ж guarantee
гара́нтия возмеще́ния убы́тка ж indemnity
ГАТТ, Генера́льное соглаше́ние по тари́фам и торго́вле ср GATT
ге́рбовый сбор м stamp duty
гла́вный исполни́тельный дире́ктор м chief executive
глобализа́ция ж globalization
годова́я проце́нтная ста́вка ж annual percentage rate
годово́й отчёт м annual report
головно́й о́фис м headquarters
гонора́р м royalty
госуда́рственное предприя́тие ср state-owned enterprise

де́бетовая за́пись ж debit entry
де́бетовая ка́рточка ж debit card
девальва́ция ж depreciation (of currency)
де́йствующее предприя́тие ср going concern
де́нежный ры́нок м money market
депози́тный счёт м deposit account
дефици́т бюдже́та м budget deficit

дефляция ж deflation
дефолт м default
дивиденд м dividend
директор-распорядитель м managing director, MD
дисконт м discount
дисконтная карта ж discount card
дистрибьютор м distributor
долг м debt
долгосрочный контракт м long-term contract
должник м debtor
доход м income
доход от инвестиций м investment income
дочерняя компания ж subsidiary

Европейский валютный союз м European Monetary System
Европейский центральный банк м ECB, European Central Bank
ЕВС м EMS
единая валюта ж single currency
однообразная ставка ж flat rate
ежегодное общее собрание ср annual general meeting

жирорасчёт м giro
жирочёк м giro (cheque)

забастовка ж industrial action
задолженность ж arrears
заёмщик м borrower, mortgagor
займ м loan
займ с фиксированной ставкой м fixed-rate loan
заказ на товары м purchase order
законное средство платежа ср legal tender
замораживание цен ср price freeze
запись в приходной части ж credit entry
запрашиваемая цена ж asking price
запуск товара м product launch
заработанный доход м earned income
заработная плата ж salary
заработок м earnings
застройщик м developer (of property)
защита потребителя ж consumer protection
зона свободного предпринимательства ж free enterprise zone

избежание налогов ср tax avoidance
избыток м surplus
импортная лицензия ж import licence
импортная таможенная пошлина ж import duty
инвестирование ср investment
индекс оптовых цен м wholesale price index
индекс потребительских цен м consumer price index, CPI
индекс розничных цен м retail price index
индекс фондового рынка м stock market index
индексация ж indexation
индоссамент м endorsement
иностранная валюта ж foreign exchange, forex
интеллектуальная собственность ж intellectual property
интернет-бизнес м Internet business
интернет-шопинг м Internet shopping
инфляция ж inflation
информационная технология ж information technology
ипотечная компания ж mortgage lender
ипотечный банк м building society n
ипотечный кредит м mortgage
ипотека ж mortgage

казначейская облигация ж treasury bond
казначейский вексель м treasury bill
календарный год м calendar year
капитал м capital
капитализация ж capitalization
капиталовложение ср capital investment
капитальные активы мн fixed assets
картель м cartel
католожная цена ж list price
квота ж quota
клиент м client
клиринговый банк м clearing bank
клиринговый счёт м clearing account
ключевой клиент м key account
книга заказов ж order book
коллективные переговоры мн collective bargaining
командная экономика ж command economy
комиссионное вознаграждение ср commission

коми́ссия ж commission

комите́нт м consigner

комме́рческий банк м commercial bank

компа́ния с ограни́ченной отве́тственностью ж limited liability company

конве́рсия ж conversion

коне́чный по́льзователь м end user

коне́чный потреби́тель м end consumer

коне́чный проду́кт м end product

конса́лтинг м consultation

коносаме́нт м bill of lading, waybill

консо́рциум м consortium

контра́кт м contract

контра́кт без оговорённого сро́ка де́йствия м open-ended contract

кооперати́в м cooperative

копира́йт м copyright

корпорати́вная организа́ция ж corporate body

корпорати́вное созна́ние ср corporate identity

корпорати́вный и́мидж м corporate image

корпора́ция ж corporation

корреспонде́нт м correspondent

краткосро́чная ссу́да ж commerical loan

креди́т м credit

креди́т по откры́тому счёту м charge account

креди́тная ка́рточка ж credit card

креди́тный биле́т м credit note

креди́тный лими́т м credit limit

креди́тный перево́д (жи́ро) м bank giro

креди́тный риск м credit risk

кредито́р м creditor, lender

ку́пчая ж bill of sale

лиз-бэк м leaseback

ли́зинг м leasing

ликвида́тор м liquidator

ликвида́ция ж liquidation

ликви́дные акти́вы мн liquid assets

ли́ния това́ров ж product line

логоти́п м logo

лот м lot

маржа́ ж premium, markup

маржа́ при́были ж profit margin

ма́ркетинг м marketing

ма́ссовое потребле́ние ср mass consumption

ма́ссовое произво́дство ср mass production

ма́ссовый спрос м mass market

Мирово́й банк м World Bank

монопо́лия ж monopoly

на ду́шу (населе́ния) прил per capita

надба́вка ж markup

накладны́е расхо́ды мн overhead(s)

нали́чная цена́ ж spot price

нали́чный счёт м cash account

нало́г м tax

нало́г на доба́вленную сто́имость м value-added tax

нало́г на реализо́ванный приро́ст капита́ла м capital gains tax

нало́г с прода́ж м sales tax

нало́говая деклара́ция ж tax declaration

нало́говая защи́та ж tax shelter

нало́говая лазе́йка ж tax loophole

нало́говое стимули́рование ср tax incentive

нало́говое убе́жище ср tax haven

налогообложе́ние ср taxation

нало́женный платёж м cash on delivery, COD

нау́чно-иссле́довательские и о́пытно-констру́кторские рабо́ты ж tax research and development

нача́льный капита́л м start-up capital

НДС м VAT

недоинвести́рование ср underinvestment

недоста́ча ж shortfall

некомме́рческая организа́ция ж nonprofit organization

необеспе́ченный заём м unsecured loan

неплатежеспосо́бность ж insolvency

неупла́ченный долг м outstanding debt

неусто́йка ж forfeit

но́вый за́пуск (проду́кта) м relaunch

но́мер счёта м account number

номина́л м par value

номина́льная сто́имость ж par value

обанкро́титься сов to go bankrupt

обеспе́чение креди́та ср collateral

облига́ция ж bond

оборо́т м turnover

оборо́тные докуме́нты мн negotiable instruments

оборо́тный капита́л м floating capital

обрабо́тка информа́ции ж data processing

обуче́ние без отры́ва от произво́дства ср on-the-job training

о́бщая при́быль ж gross profit

обще́ственный пра́здник м public holiday

обще́ственный се́ктор м public sector

О́бщий ры́нок м Single Market

обыкнове́нная а́кция ж ordinary share

обяза́тельства мн liabilities

овердра́фт м overdraft

окла́д м salary

операцио́нная при́быль ж operating profit

операцио́нные изде́ржки мн operating costs

опера́ция ж transaction

опла́та в рассро́чку ж instalment payment

опла́та нату́рой ж payment in kind

опла́та проце́нтов ж interest payment

о́птовая цена́ ж wholesale price

опто́вик м wholesaler

основно́й капита́л м capital assets

отгру́зка ж shipment

отде́л ка́дров м HR, human resources

откры́тая эконо́мика ж open economy

откры́тый ры́нок м open market

официа́льно зарегистри́рованная компа́ния ж listed company

офф-шо́р м offshore

оффшо́рный банк м offshore bank

оце́нка ж appraisal

паево́й фонд м mutual fund

па́ртия това́ров к отпра́вке ж goods on consignment

партнёрство ср partnership

пате́нт м patent

паушá́льная су́мма ж lump sum

пенсио́нный план м pension plan, pension scheme, retirement plan

пенсио́нный фонд м pension fund

перево́дный ве́ксель м bill of exchange

перегово́ры мн negotiations

переда́ча техноло́гии ж technology transfer

перепроизво́дство ср overproduction

перерасхо́д м overdraft

персона́льный идентификацио́нный но́мер м personal identification number

ПИН м PIN

пла́вающая валю́та ж floating currency

пла́новая эконо́мика ж planned economy

платёжеспосо́бность ж creditworthiness

платёжный бала́нс м balance of payments

побо́чный проду́кт м by-product

погаше́ние счето́в ср settlement of accounts

погло́щение ср takeover

подохо́дный нало́г м income tax

подря́дчик м contractor

покупа́тельная спосо́бность ж purchasing power

попы́тка поглоще́ния ж takeover bid

поря́док рассмотре́ния жа́лоб м grievance procedure

посре́дник м middleman

посре́дничество ср mediation

поставщи́к м supplier

постановле́ния и усло́вия мн terms and conditions

постоя́нное поруче́ние ср standing order

поступле́ния мн proceeds

потреби́тель м consumer

потреби́тельские това́ры мн consumer goods

потреби́тельский креди́т м consumer credit

прави́тельственная це́нная бума́га ж government security

предвари́тельный счёт-факту́ра м proforma invoice

предопла́та ж prepayment

предпринима́тель м entrepreneur

предприя́тие ср enterprise, business

прейскура́нт м price list

при́быль ж profit

при́быльность ж profitability

при́быльный прил profitmaking

приватиза́ция ж privatization

привилегиро́ванная а́кция ж preference shares, preferred stock

прова́йдер сетевы́х услу́г м Internet service provider, ISP

произво́дственная сфе́ра ж manufacturing industry

промежу́точный креди́т м bridge loan, bridging loan

промы́шленный шпиона́ж м industrial espionage

просто́й ве́ксель м promissory note

проце́нтная ста́вка ж interest rate

прямо́е дебетова́ние ср direct debit

рабо́тник м employee

работода́тель м employer

рабо́чая си́ла ж labour force, manpower

рабо́чее ме́сто ср workplace

рабо́чий капита́л м working capital

разреше́ние на рабо́ту ср work permit

распределе́ние ср distribution

расхо́ды мн outgoings

реа́льные акти́вы мн tangible assets, tangibles

резе́рвная цена́ ж reserve price

рекоменду́емая ро́зничная цена́ ж recommended retail price, RRP

ре́нта ж annuity

рента́бельность ж cost-effectiveness

рента́бельный прил cost-effective

ри́сковый капита́л м venture capital

ро́зница ж retailing

ро́зничная торго́вля ж retail

ро́зничный торго́вец м retailer

ростовщи́чество ср usury

руково́дство ка́драми ср man management, people management

ры́нок м market

ры́нок деривати́вов м derivatives market

ры́нок недви́жимости м property market

ры́нок облига́ций м bond market

ры́нок покупа́теля м buyer's market

ры́нок рабо́чей си́лы м labour market

ры́нок "бы́ков" м bull market

ры́нок "медве́дей" м bear market

ры́ночная цена́ ж market price

ры́ночная эконо́мика ж market economy

рэ́кет м racketeering

самофинанси́рующий прил self-financing

сберега́тельный банк м savings bank

сберега́тельный счёт м savings account

сбереже́ния мн savings

сбо́рочная ли́ния ж assembly line

сво́дный бала́нс м balance sheet

свя́зи с обще́ственностью мн PR

сде́льная рабо́та ж piecework

сде́льный тари́ф м piece rate

сертифика́т происхожде́ния това́ра м certificate of origin

систе́ма электро́нных платеже́й ж electronic funds transfer

ски́дка ж discount

сла́бая валю́та ж soft currency

слия́ние ср merger

сниже́ние сто́имости акти́вов ср depreciation (of assets)

совме́стное владе́ние ср joint ownership

совме́стное предприя́тие ср joint venture

сопроводи́тельное письмо́ ср cover letter, covering letter

социа́льная защи́та ж social security

со-дире́ктор м co-manager

спад м recession

спрос и предложе́ние м supply and demand

срок го́дности м shelflife

ссу́дный проце́нт м lending rate

стагфля́ция ж stagflation

сто́имость едини́цы проду́кции ж unit cost

сто́имость жи́зни ж cost of living

сто́имость, страхова́ние и фрахт ср cost, insurance and freight

страхова́ние ср insurance

страхова́я компа́ния ж insurance company

страхово́й аге́нт м insurance agent

страхово́й по́лис м insurance policy

строи́тельное о́бщество ср building society

субаре́нда ж sublease, subletting

субконтра́кт м subcontracting

субподря́дчик м subcontractor

субси́дия ж subsidy

суде́бные изде́ржки мн legal fees

су́мма к упла́те ж balance due

сумма́рная вы́писка с ба́нковского счёта ж summary statement

счёт м account

счёт подотчётных сумм м expense account

счёт-факту́ра ж invoice

тамо́женная очи́стка ж customs clearance

тамо́женная по́шлина ж customs duty

тари́ф м tariff

тари́фный барье́р м tariff barrier

твёрдая валю́та ж hard currency

теку́щий счёт м current account

телеконфере́нция ж teleconferencing

телефо́нный марке́тинг м telemarketing

те́ндер м tender

теневая эконо́мика ж underground economy

те́хника безопа́сности на произво́дстве ж occupational health and safety

те́хнико-экономи́ческое обоснова́ние ср feasibility study

това́рные запа́сы мн inventory

това́рный ры́нок м commodity market

торго́вая война́ ж trade war

торго́вая ма́рка ж brand name

торго́вая пала́та ж chamber of commerce

торго́вая ски́дка ж trade discount

торго́вая то́чка ж point of sale

торго́вая я́рмарка ж trade show

торго́вля ж trade

торго́вое соглаше́ние ср trade agreement

торго́вое эмба́рго ср trade embargo

торго́вые отноше́ния мн trade relations

торго́вые са́нкции мн trade sanctions

торго́вый бала́нс м balance of trade

торго́вый знак м trademark

торго́вый партнёр м trading partner

торго́вый секре́т м trade secret

тра́тта ж draft

трудовы́е отноше́ния мн labour relations

увольне́ние ср redundancy

уде́льный вес в оборо́те ры́нка м market share

уклоне́ние от нало́гов ср tax evasion

уника́льная характери́стика това́ра ж unique selling point

усло́вия труда́ мн working conditions

уставно́й капита́л м authorized capital

уча́стие в при́былях ср profit sharing

уча́стник перегово́ров м negotiator

ФАС FAS, free alongside ship

фина́нсовая компа́ния ж finance company

фина́нсовые услу́ги мн financial

services

фина́нсовый год м financial year, fiscal year

фина́нсовый консульта́нт м financial advisor

фина́нсовый отчёт м financial statement

фи́рма ж business, firm

фи́рменная ма́рка ж brand name

фи́рменное наименова́ние ср proprietary name

ФОБ FOB, free on board

фо́ндовая би́ржа ж stock exchange

фо́ндовый и́ндекс м share index

фо́ндовый ры́нок м equities market, stock market

ФОР FOR, free on rail

фра́нко прил free

франши́зный догово́р м franchise agreement

хе́джевый фонд м hedge fund

хо́лдинговая компа́ния ж holding company

цена́ покупа́теля ж bid price

цена́ продавца́ ж offer price

це́нник м price tag

це́нные облига́ции мн securities

це́новый контро́ль ж price control

ча́ртер м charter

ча́стная компа́ния ж private company

ча́стный инве́стор м private investor

ча́стный се́ктор м private sector

челове́ко-год м man-year

челове́ко-час м man-hour

чёрный ры́нок м black market

чи́стая при́быль ж net profit

чи́стый дохо́д м net income

шкала́ окла́дов ж salary scale

шта́тное расписа́ние ср payroll

Экономи́ческий и валю́тный сою́з м Economic and Monetary Union, EMU

экспортная по́шлина ж export duty

экспортная лице́нзия ж export licence

электро́нная связь для соверше́ния платёжей ж wire transfer

электро́нная табли́ца ж spreadsheet

ярлы́к м price tag

APPENDICES

АНГЛИЙСКИЕ НЕПРАВИЛЬНЫЕ ГЛАГОЛЫ

present	pt	pp	present	pt	pp
arise	arose	arisen	dwell	dwelt	dwelt
awake	awoke	awaked	eat	ate	eaten
be (am, is, are; being)	was, were	been	fall	fell	fallen
			feed	fed	fed
bear	bore	born(e)	feel	felt	felt
beat	beat	beaten	fight	fought	fought
become	became	become	find	found	found
begin	began	begun	flee	fled	fled
behold	beheld	beheld	fling	flung	flung
bend	bent	bent	fly (flies)	flew	flown
beseech	besought	besought	forbid	forbade	forbidden
beset	beset	beset	forecast	forecast	forecast
bet	bet, betted	bet, betted	forget	forgot	forgotten
bid	bid, bade	bid, bidden	forgive	forgave	forgiven
bind	bound	bound	forsake	forsook	forsaken
bite	bit	bitten	freeze	froze	frozen
bleed	bled	bled	get	got	got, (US) gotten
blow	blew	blown			
break	broke	broken	give	gave	given
breed	bred	bred	go (goes)	went	gone
bring	brought	brought	grind	ground	ground
build	built	built	grow	grew	grown
burn	burnt, burned	burnt, burned	hang	hung, hanged	hung, hanged
burst	burst	burst	have (has; having)	had	had
buy	bought	bought			
can	could	(been able)	hear	heard	heard
cast	cast	cast	hide	hid	hidden
catch	caught	caught	hit	hit	hit
choose	chose	chosen	hold	held	held
cling	clung	clung	hurt	hurt	hurt
come	came	come	keep	kept	kept
cost	cost	cost	kneel	knelt, kneeled	knelt, kneeled
creep	crept	crept			
cut	cut	cut	know	knew	known
deal	dealt	dealt	lay	laid	laid
dig	dug	dug	lead	led	led
do (3rd person: he/she/it does)	did	done	lean	leant, leaned	leant, leaned
			leap	leapt, leaped	leapt, leaped
			learn	learnt, learned	learnt, learned
draw	drew	drawn			
dream	dreamed, dreamt	dreamed, dreamt	leave	left	left
			lend	lent	lent
drink	drank	drunk	let	let	let
drive	drove	driven	lie (lying)	lay	lain

АНГЛИЙСКИЕ ГЛАГОЛЫ / 2

present	pt	pp	present	pt	pp
light	lit, lighted	lit, lighted	spell	spelt, spelled	spelt, spelled
lose	lost	lost	spend	spent	spent
make	made	made	spill	spilt, spilled	spilt, spilled
may	might	—	spin	spun	spun
mean	meant	meant	spit	spat	spat
meet	met	met	split	split	split
mistake	mistook	mistaken	spoil	spoiled, spoilt	spoiled, spoilt
mow	mowed	mown, mowed	spread	spread	spread
must	(had to)	(had to)	spring	sprang	sprung
pay	paid	paid	stand	stood	stood
put	put	put	steal	stole	stolen
quit	quit, quitted	quit, quitted	stick	stuck	stuck
read	read	read	sting	stung	stung
rid	rid	rid	stink	stank	stunk
ride	rode	ridden	stride	strode	stridden
ring	rang	rung	strike	struck	struck, stricken
rise	rose	risen	strive	strove	striven
run	ran	run	swear	swore	sworn
saw	sawed	sawn	sweep	swept	swept
say	said	said	swell	swelled	swollen, swelled
see	saw	seen			
seek	sought	sought	swim	swam	swum
sell	sold	sold	swing	swung	swung
send	sent	sent	take	took	taken
set	set	set	teach	taught	taught
shake	shook	shaken	tear	tore	torn
shall	should	—	tell	told	told
shear	sheared	shorn, sheared	think	thought	thought
shed	shed	shed	throw	threw	thrown
shine	shone	shone	thrust	thrust	thrust
shoot	shot	shot	tread	trod	trodden
show	showed	shown	wake	woke, waked	woken, waked
shrink	shrank	shrunk			
shut	shut	shut	wear	wore	worn
sing	sang	sung	weave	wove, weaved	woven, weaved
sink	sank	sunk			
sit	sat	sat	wed	wedded, wed	wedded, wed
slay	slew	slain			
sleep	slept	slept	weep	wept	wept
slide	slid	slid	win	won	won
sling	slung	slung	wind	wound	wound
slit	slit	slit	wring	wrung	wrung
smell	smelt, smelled	smelt, smelled	write	wrote	written
sow	sowed	sown, sowed			
speak	spoke	spoken			
speed	sped, speeded	sped, speeded			

TABLES OF RUSSIAN IRREGULAR FORMS

For all tables, where there are alternatives given under the accusative, these are animate forms which are identical with the genitive.

Nouns

Table 1	мать	
	Singular	*Plural*
Nom	мать	ма́тери
Acc	мать	матере́й
Gen	ма́тери	матере́й
Dat	ма́тери	матеря́м
Instr	ма́терью	матеря́ми
Prp	о ма́тери	о матеря́х

Table 2	дочь	
	Singular	*Plural*
Nom	дочь	до́чери
Acc	дочь	дочере́й
Gen	до́чери	дочере́й
Dat	до́чери	дочеря́м
Instr	до́черью	дочерьми́
Prp	о до́чери	о дочеря́х

Table 3	путь	
	Singular	*Plural*
Nom	путь	пути́
Acc	путь	пути́
Gen	пути́	путе́й
Dat	пути́	путя́м
Instr	путём	путя́ми
Prp	о пути́	о путя́х

Table 4	время	
	Singular	*Plural*
Nom	вре́мя	времена́
Acc	вре́мя	времена́
Gen	вре́мени	времён
Dat	вре́мени	времена́м
Instr	вре́менем	времена́ми
Prp	о вре́мени	о времена́х

(Similarly with nouns like и́мя, пле́мя etc)

Pronouns

Table 5	*m*	*f*	*nt*	*pl*
Nom	чей	чья	чьё	чьи
Acc	чей/чьего́	чью	чьё	чьи/чьих
Gen	чьего́	чьей	чьего́	чьих
Dat	чьему́	чьей	чьему́	чьим
Instr	чьим	чьей	чьим	чьи́ми
Prp	о чьём	о чьей	о чьём	о чьих

(The instrumental form чьей has the alternative чье́ю)

Table 6a

Nom	я	ты	он	она́	оно́
Acc/Gen	меня́	тебя́	его́	её	его́
Dat	мне	тебе́	ему́	ей	ему́
Instr	мной	тобо́й	им	ей	им
Prp	обо мне	о тебе́	о нём	о ней	о нём

(The instrumental forms мно́й, тобо́й, ей have alternatives мно́ю, тобо́ю and е́ю respectively. The reflexive personal pronoun себя́ declines like тебя́)

Table 6b

Nom	мы	вы	они́
Acc/Gen	нас	вас	их
Dat	нам	вам	им
Instr	на́ми	ва́ми	и́ми
Prp	о нас	о вас	о них

Table 7

Nom	кто	что
Acc	кого́	что
Gen	кого́	чего́
Dat	кому́	чему́
Instr	кем	чем
Prp	о ком	о чём

Table 8

	m	f	nt	pl
Nom	мой	моя́	моё	мои́
Acc	мой/моего́	мою́	моё	мои́/мои́х
Gen	моего́	мое́й	моего́	мои́х
Dat	моему́	мое́й	моему́	мои́м
Instr	мои́м	мое́й	мои́м	мои́ми
Prp	о моём	о мое́й	о моём	о мои́х

(твой declines like мой, as does the reflexive possessive pronoun свой. The instrumental form мое́й has the alternative мое́ю)

Table 9	m	f	nt	pl
Nom	наш	на́ша	на́ше	на́ши
Acc	наш/на́шего	на́шу	на́ше	на́ши/на́ших
Gen	на́шего	на́шей	на́шего	на́ших
Dat	на́шему	на́шей	на́шему	на́шим
Instr	на́шим	на́шей	на́шим	на́шими
Prp	о на́шем	о на́шей	о на́шем	о на́ших

(ваш declines like наш. The instrumental form на́шей has the alternative на́шею. The possessive pronouns его́, её and их are invariable)

Table 10	m	f	nt	pl
Nom	э́тот	э́та	э́то	э́ти
Acc	э́тот/э́того	э́ту	э́то	э́ти/э́тих
Gen	э́того	э́той	э́того	э́тих
Dat	э́тому	э́той	э́тому	э́тим
Instr	э́тим	э́той	э́тим	э́тими
Prp	об э́том	об э́той	об э́том	об э́тих

(The instrumental form э́той has the alternative э́тою)

Table 11	m	f	nt	pl
Nom	тот	та	то	те
Acc	тот/того́	ту	то	те/тех
Gen	того́	той	того́	тех
Dat	тому́	той	тому́	тем
Instr	тем	той	тем	те́ми
Prp	о том	о той	о том	о тех

(The instrumental form той has the alternative тою)

Table 12	m	f	nt	pl
Nom	сей	сия́	сие́	сий
Acc	сей/сего́	сию́	сие́	сий/сих
Gen	сего́	сей	сего́	сих
Dat	сему́	сей	сему́	сим
Instr	сим	сей	сим	си́ми
Prp	о сём	о сей	о сём	о сих

(The instrumental form сей has the alternative се́ю)

Table 13	m	f	nt	pl
Nom	весь	вся	всё	все
Acc	весь/всего́	всю	всё	все/всех
Gen	всего́	всей	всего́	всех
Dat	всему́	всей	всему́	всем
Instr	всем	всей	всем	все́ми
Prp	обо всём	обо всей	обо всём	обо всех

(The instrumental form всей has the alternative все́ю)

Verbs

Table 14	хоте́ть
я	хочу́
ты	хо́чешь
он/она́	хо́чет
мы	хоти́м
вы	хоти́те
они́	хотя́т
Past tense:	хоте́л, хоте́ла, хоте́ло, хоте́ли

(Similarly with verbs such as расхоте́ть, захоте́ть etc)

Table 15	есть
я	ем
ты	ешь
он/она́	ест
мы	еди́м
вы	еди́те
они́	едя́т
Past tense:	ел, е́ла, е́ло, е́ли
Imperative:	е́шь(те)!

(Similarly with verbs such as съесть, пое́сть, перее́сть etc)

Table 16	дать
я	дам
ты	дашь
он/она́	даст
мы	дади́м
вы	дади́те
они́	даду́т
Past tense:	дал, дала́, дало́, да́ли
Imperative:	да́й(те)!
(Similarly with verbs such as переда́ть, изда́ть, отда́ть, разда́ть etc)	

Table 17	чтить
я	чту
ты	чтишь
он/она́	чтит
мы	чтим
вы	чти́те
они́	чтут/чтят
Past tense:	чтил, чти́ла, чти́ло, чти́ли
Imperative:	чти́(те)!
(Similarly with verbs such as почти́ть etc)	

Table 18	идти́
я	иду́
ты	идёшь
он/она́	идёт
мы	идём
вы	идёте
они́	иду́т
Past tense:	шёл, шла, шло, шли
Imperative:	иди́(те)!
(Similarly with verbs such as прийти́, уйти́, отойти́, зайти́ etc)	

Table 19	éхать
я	éду
ты	éдешь
он/она́	éдет
мы	éдем
вы	éдете
они́	éдут
Past tense:	éхал, éхала, éхало, éхали
Imperative:	поезжа́й(те)!
(Similarly with verbs such as приéхать, переéхать, уéхать, въéхать etc)	

Table 20	бежа́ть
я	бегу́
ты	бежи́шь
он/она́	бежи́т
мы	бежи́м
вы	бежи́те
они́	бегу́т
Past tense:	бежа́л, бежа́ла, бежа́ло, бежа́ли
Imperative:	беги́(те)!

(Similarly with verbs such as побежа́ть, убежа́ть, прибежа́ть etc)

Table 21	быть
я	бу́ду
ты	бу́дешь
он/она́	бу́дет
мы	бу́дем
вы	бу́дете
они́	бу́дут
Past tense:	был, была́, бы́ло, бы́ли
Imperative:	бу́дь(те)!

(Not used in present tense, except есть in certain cases)

Numerals

Table 22	m	f	nt	pl
Nom	оди́н	одна́	одно́	одни́
Acc	оди́н/одного́	одну́	одно́	одни́/одни́х
Gen	одного́	одно́й	одного́	одни́х
Dat	одному́	одно́й	одному́	одни́м
Instr	одни́м	одно́й	одни́м	одни́ми
Prp	об одно́м	об одно́й	об одно́м	об одни́х

(The instrumental form одно́й has the alternative одно́ю)

Table 23	m	f	nt
Nom	два	две	два
Acc	два/двух	две/двух	два/двух
Gen	двух	двух	двух
Dat	двум	двум	двум
Instr	двумя́	двумя́	двумя́
Prp	о двух	о двух	о двух

Table 24		
Nom	три	четы́ре
Acc	три/трёх	четы́ре/четырёх
Gen	трёх	четырёх
Dat	трём	четырём
Instr	тремя́	четырьмя́
Prp	о трёх	о четырёх

Table 25	m/nt	f
Nom	о́ба	о́бе
Acc	о́ба/обо́их	о́бе/обе́их
Gen	обо́их	обе́их
Dat	обо́им	обе́им
Instr	обо́ими	обе́ими
Prp	об обо́их	об обе́их

Table 26		
Nom/Acc	пять	пятьдеся́т
Gen/Dat	пяти́	пяти́десяти
Instr	пятью́	пятью́десятью
Prp	о пяти́	о пяти́десяти

(шесть to два́дцать and три́дцать decline like пять; шестьдеся́т, во́семьдесят and се́мьдесят decline like пятьдеся́т)

Table 27		
Nom/Acc	со́рок	сто
Gen/Dat/Instr	сорока́	ста
Prp	о сорока́	о ста

(девяно́сто declines like сто. After мно́го and не́сколько the genitive plural is сот, the dative plural is стам, the instrumental plural is ста́ми and the prepositional plural is стах.)

Table 28				
Nom/Acc	две́сти	три́ста	четы́реста	пятьсо́т
Gen	двухсо́т	трёхсо́т	четырёхсо́т	пятисо́т
Dat	двумста́м	трёмста́м	четырёмста́м	пятиста́м
Instr	двумяста́ми	тремяста́ми	четырьмяста́ми	пятьюста́ми
Prp	о двухста́х	о трёхста́х	о четырёхста́х	о пятиста́х

(шестьсо́т, семьсо́т, восемьсо́т and девятьсо́т decline like пятьсо́т)

Table 29	Singular	Plural
Nom	ты́сяча	ты́сячи
Acc	ты́сячу	ты́сячи
Gen	ты́сячи	ты́сяч
Dat	ты́сяче	ты́сячам
Instr	ты́сячей	ты́сячами
Prp	о ты́сяче	о ты́сячах

(The instrumental singular form ты́сячью also exists)

Table 30a			
Nom	дво́е	тро́е	че́тверо
Acc	дво́е/двои́х	тро́е/трои́х	че́тверо/четверы́х
Gen	двои́х	трои́х	четверы́х
Dat	двои́м	трои́м	четверы́м
Instr	двои́ми	трои́ми	четверы́ми
Prp	о двои́х	о трои́х	о четверы́х

Table 30b			
Nom	пя́теро	ше́стеро	се́меро
Acc	пя́теро/пятеры́х	ше́стеро/шестеры́х	се́меро/семеры́х
Gen	пятеры́х	шестеры́х	семеры́х
Dat	пятеры́м	шестеры́м	семеры́м
Instr	пятеры́ми	шестеры́ми	семеры́ми
Prp	о пятеры́х	о шестеры́х	о семеры́х

КОЛИЧЕСТВЕННЫЕ ЧИСЛИТЕЛЬНЫЕ

CARDINAL NUMBERS

оди́н (одна́, одно́, одни́)	1	one
два (две)	2	two
три	3	three
четы́ре	4	four
пять	5	five
шесть	6	six
семь	7	seven
во́семь	8	eight
де́вять	9	nine
де́сять	10	ten
оди́ннадцать	11	eleven
двена́дцать	12	twelve
трина́дцать	13	thirteen
четы́рнадцать	14	fourteen
пятна́дцать	15	fifteen
шестна́дцать	16	sixteen
семна́дцать	17	seventeen
восемна́дцать	18	eighteen
девятна́дцать	19	nineteen
два́дцать	20	twenty
два́дцать оди́н (одна́, одно́ одни́)	21	twenty-one
два́дцать два (две)	22	twenty-two
три́дцать	30	thirty
со́рок	40	forty
пятьдеся́т	50	fifty
шестьдеся́т	60	sixty
се́мьдесят	70	seventy
во́семьдесят	80	eighty
девяно́сто	90	ninety
сто	100	a hundred
сто оди́н (одна́, одно́, одни́)	101	a hundred and one
две́сти	200	two hundred
две́сти оди́н (одна́, одно́, одни́)	201	two hundred and one
три́ста	300	three hundred
четы́реста	400	four hundred
пятьсо́т	500	five hundred
ты́сяча	1 000	a thousand
миллио́н	1 000 000	a million

COLLECTIVE NUMERALS

дво́е
тро́е
че́тверо
пя́теро
ше́стеро
се́меро

ПОРЯДКОВЫЕ
ЧИСЛИТЕЛЬНЫЕ

ORDINAL NUMBERS

пе́рвый	1-ый	first	1st
второ́й	2-о́й	second	2nd
тре́тий	3-ий	third	3rd
четвёртый	4-ый	fourth	4th
пя́тый	5-ый	fifth	5th
шесто́й	6-о́й	sixth	6th
седьмо́й	7-о́й	seventh	7th
восьмо́й	8-о́й	eighth	8th
девя́тый	9-ый	ninth	9th
деся́тый	10-ый	tenth	10th
оди́ннадцатый		eleventh	
двена́дцатый		twelfth	
трина́дцатый		thirteenth	
четы́рнадцатый		fourteenth	
пятна́дцатый		fifteenth	
шестна́дцатый		sixteenth	
семна́дцатый		seventeenth	
восемна́дцатый		eighteenth	
девятна́дцатый		nineteenth	
двадца́тый		twentieth	
два́дцать пе́рвый		twenty-first	
два́дцать второ́й		twenty-second	
тридца́тый		thirtieth	
сороково́й		fortieth	
пятидеся́тый		fiftieth	
восьмидеся́тый		eightieth	
девяно́стый		ninetieth	
со́тый		hundredth	
сто пе́рвый		hundred-and-first	
ты́сячный		thousandth	
миллио́нный		millionth	

ДРОБИ

FRACTIONS

однá вторáя	½	a half
однá трéтья	⅓	a third
однá четвёртая	¼	a quarter
однá пя́тая	⅕	a fifth
три чéтверти	¾	three quarters
две трéти	⅔	two thirds
полторá (полторы́)	1½	one and a half
ноль цéлых (и) пять деся́тых	**0.5**	(nought) point five
три цéлых (и) четы́ре деся́тых	**3.4**	three point four
шесть цéлых (и) вóсемьдесят дéвять сóтых	**6.89**	six point eight nine
дéсять процéнтов	**10%**	ten per cent
сто процéнтов	**100%**	a hundred per cent

ДАТЫ И ВРЕМЯ

DATE AND TIME

котóрый час?	what time is it?
сейчáс 5 часóв	it is *or* it's 5 o'clock
в какóе врéмя?	at what time?
в *+acc* ...	at ...
в час дня	at one p.m.
пóлночь (*f*)	00.00, midnight
двáдцать четы́ре (часá) дéсять (минут), дéсять минýт пéрвого	00.10, ten past midnight, ten past twelve
дéсять минýт вторóго, час дéсять	01.10, ten past one, one ten
чéтверть вторóго, час пятнáдцать	01.15, (a) quarter past one, one fifteen
половúна вторóго, час трúдцать	01.30, half past one, one thirty
без чéтверти два, час сóрок пять	01.45, (a) quarter to two, one forty-five
без десятú два, час пятьдеся́т	01.50, ten to two, one fifty
двенáдцать часóв дня, пóлдень (*m*)	12.00, midday
половúна пéрвого, двенáдцать трúдцать дня	12.30, half past twelve, twelve thirty p.m.
тринáдцать часóв, час дня	13.00, one (o'clock) (in the afternoon), one p.m.
девятнáдцать часóв, семь часóв вéчера	19.00, seven (o'clock) (in the evening), seven p.m.
двáдцать одúн (час) трúдцать (минýт), дéвять трúдцать вéчера	21.30, nine thirty (p.m. or at night)
двáдцать три (часá) сóрок пять (минýт), без чéтверти двенáдцать, одúннадцать сóрок пять	23.45, (a) quarter to twelve, eleven forty-five p.m.

...рез два́дцать мину́т	in twenty minutes
...а́дцать мину́т наза́д	twenty minutes ago
...ближа́йшие два́дцать мину́т	in the next twenty minutes
...два́дцать мину́т	within twenty minutes
...усти́ два́дцать мину́т	after twenty minutes
...йча́с два́дцать мину́т	it's twenty after three (US)
...четвёртого	
...олчаса́	half an hour
...тверть часа́	quarter of an hour
...олтора́ часа́	an hour and a half
...ас с че́твертью	an hour and a quarter
...ерез час	in an hour's time
...а́ждый час	every hour, on the hour
...е́рез час, ка́ждый час	hourly
...е́рез час	in an hour from now
...азбуди́те меня́ в семь часо́в	wake me up at seven
...девяти́ до пяти́	from nine to five
...двух до трёх (часо́в)	between two and three (o'clock)
...его́дня с девяти́ утра́	since nine o'clock this morning
...о десяти́ часо́в ве́чера	till ten o'clock tonight
...коло трёх часо́в дня	at about three o'clock in the afternoon
...ри часа́ по Гри́нвичу	three o'clock GMT
...ейча́с то́лько нача́ло пя́того	it's just gone four
...о́сле четырёх	at the back of four
...его́дня	today
...а́ждый день/вто́рник	every day/Tuesday
...чера́	yesterday
...его́дня у́тром	this morning
...а́втра днём/ве́чером	tomorrow afternoon/night
...озавчера́ ве́чером, позапро́шлой но́чью	the night before last
...озавчера́	the day before yesterday
...чера́ ве́чером, про́шлой но́чью	last night
...ва дня/шесть лет наза́д	two days/six years ago
...послеза́втра	the day after tomorrow
...в сре́ду	on Wednesday
...он хо́дит туда́ по сре́дам	he goes there on Wednesdays
..."закры́то по пя́тницам"	"closed on Fridays"
...с понеде́льника до пя́тницы	from Monday to Friday
...к четвергу́	by Thursday
...в одну́ из суббо́т в ма́рте	one Saturday in March
...че́рез неде́лю	in a week's time
...во вто́рник на сле́дующей неде́ле	a week on or next Tuesday
...в воскресе́нье на про́шлой неде́ле	a week last Sunday
...че́рез понеде́льник	Monday week
...на э́той/сле́дующей/про́шлой неде́ле	this/next/last week
...че́рез две неде́ли	in two weeks or a fortnight
...в понеде́льник че́рез две неде́ли	two weeks on Monday

в э́тот день шесть лет наза́д	six years to the day
пе́рвая/после́дняя пя́тница ме́сяца	the first/last Friday of the month
сле́дующий ме́сяц	next month
про́шлый год	last year
в конце́ ме́сяца	at the end of the month
два ра́за в неде́лю/ме́сяц/год	twice a week/month/year
како́е сего́дня число́?	what's the date?, what date is it today?
сего́дня 28-ое	today's date is the 28th, today is the 28th
пе́рвое января́	the first of January, January the first
ты́сяча девятьсо́т шестьдеся́т пя́тый год	1965, nineteen (hundred and) sixty-five
я роди́лся в 1967-ом году́	I was born in 1967
у него́ день рожде́ния 5-го ию́ня	his birthday is on June 5th (*BRIT*) or 5th June (*US*)
18-го а́вгуста 1992	on 18th August (*BRIT*) or August 18th 1992
с 19-го до 3-го	from the 19th to the 3rd
в 89-ом году́	in '89
весна́ 87-го го́да	the Spring of '87
в 1930-ых года́х	in (*or* during) the 1930s
в 1940-ы́х года́х	in 1940 something
в 2006-ом году́	in the year 2006
в 13-ом ве́ке	in the 13th century
4-ый год до н.э.	4 B.C.
70-ый год н.э.	70 A.D.